The Edward G. Robinson Encyclopedia

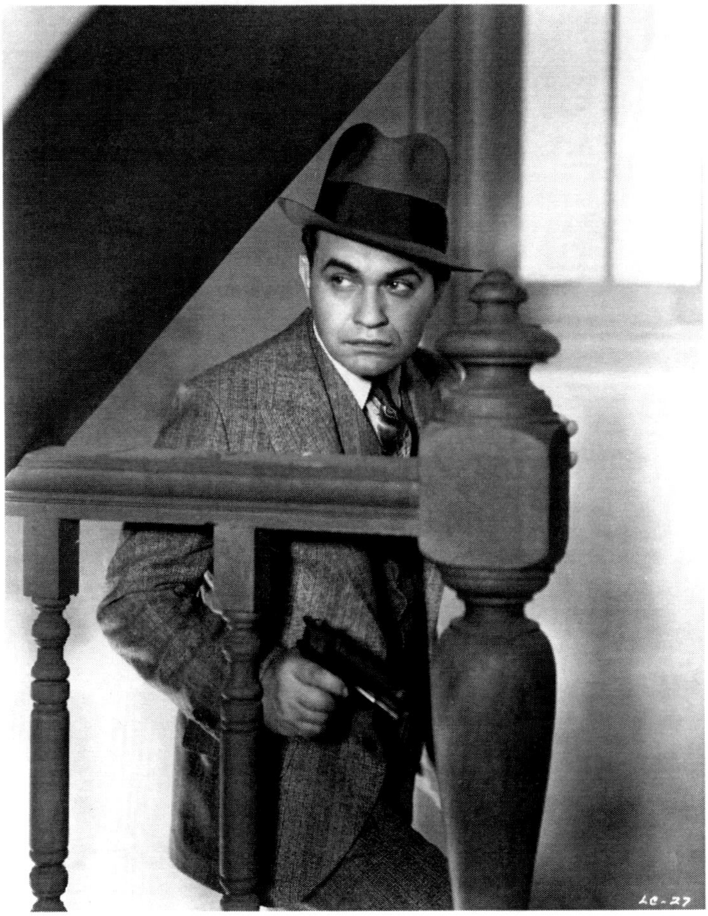
LC-27

The Edward G. Robinson Encyclopedia

by Robert Beck

McFarland & Company, Inc., Publishers
Jefferson, North Carolina, and London

The present work is a reprint of the library bound edition of The Edward G. Robinson Encyclopedia, *first published in 2002 by McFarland.*

Frontispiece: Robinson as "Little Caesar," 1931.

LIBRARY OF CONGRESS CATALOGUING-IN-PUBLICATION DATA

Beck, Robert, 1947–
The Edward G. Robinson encyclopedia / by Robert Beck.
p.   cm.
Includes bibliographical references and index.

ISBN 978-0-7864-3864-8
softcover : 50# alkaline paper ∞

1. Robinson, Edward G., 1893–1973 — Encyclopedias.   I. Title.
PN2287.R67B43   2008   791.43′028′092 — dc21   2002004271

British Library cataloguing data are available

©2002 Robert Beck. All rights reserved

No part of this book may be reproduced or transmitted in any form or by any means, electronic or mechanical, including photocopying or recording, or by any information storage and retrieval system, without permission in writing from the publisher.

On the cover: Edward G. Robinson as "Rico" Bandello
in *Little Caesar*, 1931 (Warner Bros./Photofest);
cigar and smoke background ©2008 Shutterstock.

Manufactured in the United States of America

*McFarland & Company, Inc., Publishers
Box 611, Jefferson, North Carolina 28640
www.mcfarlandpub.com*

To my family, especially Grace Elizabeth Pekny,
and the fine people of DeSoto, Missouri

Acknowledgments

This book would not have been possible without the love, patience, support, and encouragement of a number of people. First, the immediate members of my family, all of whom had a hand in the editing, computerizing, or just plain paper sorting: my deepest appreciation to Joe and Tina, Jenny and Marc Pekny, Emily, Toby, Molly, Mandy, and my wife, Suzie.

The following individuals also gave me invaluable assistance: Marvin and Olive Beck, Father Larry Gerst, Alan Hanson, Cathy and Thomas Hischak, Edna Kelpe, John Lesser, Harvey MacNaughton, Marie Montgomery, Dodie Nelke, Pru Perkins, Audrey Reilly, Jim and Diane Relleke, Ernest Seward, Zelda Sparks, Patrick Spillman, and James Weber.

A special note of gratitude goes to the following members of Edward G. Robinson's family: Francesca Robinson-Sanchez, Adam Sanchez, Martha Geiger, Beulah Robinson, and Jane Robinson Sidney.

Contents

Acknowledgments vi
Preface 1
Introduction 3
The Encyclopedia 17
Bibliography 351
Index 357

Preface

When I was ten years old, my grandfather took me to see Cecil B. DeMille's remake of his silent epic *The Ten Commandments*. A Methodist deacon nearing eighty, he saw in that three-hour extravaganza a certain religious value. He had no idea that the film's most significant impact on me would be to initiate a lifelong admiration for one remarkable actor, Edward G. Robinson.

Robinson in that biblical epic was followed by another Robinson performance, as a mean gangster in *Black Tuesday*. The two performances were separated by only a day or so, and to see the same dynamic actor in such differing roles made an indelible impression on me.

And so I began a collection: a cigar box of clippings and photographs that evolved into an Edward G. Robinson scrapbook. A fan letter to the actor brought me a warm and immediate personal response, which motivated me toward genuine research in my collecting. Library stacks provided reviews, interviews, biographical information. I placed ads seeking more material, and the raw data accumulated over the years, until at last it became this book.

The Edward G. Robinson Encyclopedia is an alphabetical reference to Robinson's life and career. There are entries on his every known public performance or appearance, including feature films, documentaries, short subjects, cartoons, television and radio programs, recordings, live theatre, narrations, and pageants. Commentary on co-workers, source material, and criticism also are included, as well as background on Robinson's personal life, from his art collection to his family members, his marriages, and his political difficulties.

The book began as a simple chronological listing of performances, but adding information on personalities and topics related to Robinson's career prompted the change to an alphabetical format. In addition to looking up performances by name, the reader can use this format to discover, say, the *accidents*, or the *babies*, or the *courtrooms* in Robinson's life — both fictional and real. A reader curious about Robinson's dealings with anti–Communist crusaders of the 1950s can look under *Communism* to find a discussion both of the suspicions about Robinson and of his films and plays dealing with Communism.

To be sure, there are earlier works on Robinson's life and career — excellent volumes by James Robert Parish, Alvin H. Marill, and Foster Hirsch among them, plus Robinson's own autobiography, *All My Yesterdays*, and *My Father — My Son*, written by Edward G. Robinson, Jr. The difference between those works and *The Edward G. Robinson Encyclopedia* — and the reason this volume was put together — is that this encyclopedia is the only volume in which the actor's life and career are referenced in their entirety.

Introduction

"Awright, you guys," barks the sharp nasal voice through the smoke of a long, foul cigar. "This operation's gonna be smooth, see!" A short, swarthy, bulldog-faced man in a pin-striped suit — wearing a derby, spats, and machine gun — is surrounded by an entourage of mobsters in a dingy, shadowed room. As he speaks again, we recognize a classic image from the silver screen: Edward G. Robinson in the role of Little Caesar. "You can dish it out, Sam," the voice continues, "but yer gettin' so's ya can't take it no more." And finally: "Boys, take him for a ride."

In 1997 *Entertainment Weekly* published a special edition of its magazine called "The 100 Greatest Stars of All Time" in which Edward G. Robinson was ranked Number 66, attesting to the staying power of a top character star, dead now for more than a quarter of a century. Similarly, the American Film Institute's television special in June 1999, "100 Years, 100 Stars," ranked Robinson 24th among male stars prior to 1950.

And, most recently, in October 2000 the United States Post Office issued a commemorative stamp bearing Edward G. Robinson's likeness, making him the sixth among "the Legends of Hollywood" so honored. The other five are Marilyn Monroe, James Dean, Alfred Hitchcock, Humphrey Bogart, and James Cagney.

Robinson, a 1930s cinema icon, continues to gain familiarity long after his six-decade performing career came to a close. In truth, Robinson personified the American movie gangster. But while his fame rests squarely on the gangster image, it is only the tip of an iceberg; he was acting that way for only a relatively small portion of his moments on the stage, radio, and movie and television screens.

The complete picture of Edward G. Robinson is that of a classically trained performer whose imagination, distinctive voice, and even runtish looks made him a magnetic character star for more than four decades. His versatility afforded him roles ranging from these serious (and sometimes comic) gangsters to dedicated doctors, teachers, dogged investigators, savvy businessmen, and even lovable uncles and patriarchs.

His family roots were in Rumania, going back several generations. Born in Bucharest in 1893, he was the fifth of Morris and Sarah Goldenberg's six sons. They named him Emanuel. The family was Jewish, and they had experienced enough stifled freedoms of anti–Semitism to yearn for a better life in America at the turn of the century. In 1902 the Goldenberg family, which also included Emanuel's maternal grandmother, emigrated to New York.

Young Emanuel attended the New York public schools with American-born children, and the fortunate result was that his English — as he learned to speak it — was without European accent. English (and ultimately the study of as many as eleven different languages) came

Introduction

easily to the young immigrant. Unathletic, Emanuel discovered the competitive power of words. He thrilled at captivating his audience with a bilingual English and Yiddish bar mitzvah speech; he briefly considered becoming a rabbi or a teacher.

At an early age, one of his heroes was William Randolph Hearst, whose crusading nature impressed the idealistic student, despite rampant accusations of yellow journalism. Emanuel stumped for Hearst in his bid for the New York mayoral race of 1909.

Despite stimulating and rewarding challenges offered in championing the causes of justice, Emanuel rejected the study of law, and instead auditioned for the Elizabethan Society while a student at the College of the City of New York. His brothers went into upholstery, lithography, dentistry, luggage sales. These choices allowed them independence as their own bosses, and they also pleased Morris and Sarah Goldenberg because they were respectably stable. Emanuel's choice frightened them. But his brothers helped him plead his case. Thus encouraged, he read biographies of the great actors, and the classic plays from Shaw to Shakespeare. He saw all the productions he could afford in the Bronx and across town on Broadway.

The young actor-to-be soon was awarded a scholarship to the American Academy of Dramatic Arts, appearing in a production of Ibsen's *Pillars of Society*. He adapted Henry James' story of hypnotism and murder, *The Bells*, into a short play called *The Bells of Conscience*, and auditioned for the Loew's Circuit professional tryouts. He earned a four-week booking, which was followed by a stint with Rudolph Schildkraut in the Yiddish play *Number 37*. Robinson played a character nearly three times his nineteen years.

Meanwhile, at the Academy it had been strongly suggested to him that he change his name to something that sounded more Anglo-Saxon. Thus, Emanuel became Edward, who was then king of England; the G stood for Goldenberg; and Robinson was the elegant sounding name of an unseen character in a play he had recently watched, *The Passerby*.

He graduated from the Academy in 1913 and sought steady theater work. He was soon off to Albany, New York, and the S. M. Stainach Stock Company, where he made his first professional appearance on stage. The play was Eugene Walter's *Paid in Full*, and he played the role of Sato. During that time he also appeared in two roles in *The Gamblers*.

Self-conscious about his looks, when he was seeking acting work he came up with the credo "Not much face value, but when it comes to stage value, I'll deliver." He was off to Cincinnati for twenty-two weeks with the Orpheum Players, amassing more acting credentials, including a role as Dick the Rat in *Alias Jimmy Valentine*. On the road again in Ottawa and Montreal playing Wazir Mansur in *Kismet*, Robinson was obliged to return to New York in November 1914 when World War I cut the play's tour short.

Except for *Electrocution*, a failed vaudeville sketch, there was no acting work for him until the following spring, but then he won four roles in one play. His facility with languages was responsible. In Roi Cooper Megrue's pro–Ally, anti-war play *Under Fire*, he played a Frenchman, a German, a Belgian, and a Cockney. After an initial tour, it opened in New York on August 11, 1915, ran six months, and became a hit. It was the first of Edward G. Robinson's thirty-two Broadway productions over the next fifteen years. A second Megrue play, about prison reform, written in collaboration with Irvin S. Cobb, was next. Called *Under Sentence*, it opened in New York in October 1916.

Between these assignments Edward G. Robinson appeared as an extra in a film, *Arms and the Woman*. He did not recall the experience, and the film is now lost, but his face is unmistakable in a still picture from the five-reel silent movie, which was directed by George Fitzmaurice.

His next role was in *The Pawn*—twice, apparently—in one production with Frank Keenan that lasted two weeks in the spring of 1917, and a later version with Walker Whiteside in September. In between, Robinson worked for producer Arthur Hopkins for the first time in *The Deluge*, which featured Pauline Lord, in August. *Drafted* followed in October and again featured Miss Lord, but it closed out of town.

For George M. Cohan and Sam Harris, Robinson was Batiste, a French Canadian, in *The Little Teacher*, a comedy, in February 1918. However, enlistment in the Navy interrupted his engagement. After his discharge he joined the Garrick Players of Washington, D.C., appearing in *Polly with a Past*.

Returning to New York, he acted in *First Is Last*, which in 1919 made a star of Richard Dix. That was followed by another Arthur Hopkins production, Maxim Gorky's *Night Lodging*, in 1920, in which Robinson played the part of Satan. (The play is otherwise known as *The Lower Depths*.) Booth Tarkington's *Poldekin*, an anti–Bolshevik comedy starring George Arliss, was next, and then for Hopkins again came an appearance with Jacob Ben-Ami, Pauline Lord, and Robinson's lifelong friend, Sam Jaffe, as the Stage Director in *Samson and Delilah*. During that run he also played matinees of *Eyvind of the Hills*, in February 1921.

Robinson then accepted an offer from the Goldwyn Company to make a film called *Fields of Glory* at Fort Lee, New Jersey, but he was not happy with the project and asked to be let out of his contract. He went to Denver to perform in the first of his two summer seasons of five plays at Elitch's Gardens. One season he acted with Helen Menken in *Enter Madame*.

In December Robinson was reunited with Ben-Ami and Jaffe, while continuing his association with Arthur Hopkins, in the translation of a Yiddish script, *The Idle Inn*. This was followed immediately by Hopkins' revival of *The Deluge*, which originally had been produced four years earlier. In September 1922 Edward G. Robinson worked for the first time with Alfred Lunt, in *Banco*.

Film director John S. Robertson convinced Robinson to go to Havana to appear in the silent film *The Bright Shawl* late in 1922. He played Mary Astor's father. Richard Barthelmess, Dorothy Gish, William Powell, and Jetta Goudal also were featured.

Back in New York, Robinson distinguished himself as The Button Moulder in Ibsen's *Peer Gynt*, with Joseph Schildkraut in the title role, marking the first of his ten productions in the next four years with the Theatre Guild. In addition to Schildkraut, the company of players included Lunt, his wife, Lynn Fontanne, Dudley Digges, Helen Westley, Margaret Wycherly, Tom Powers, Clare Eames, Morris Carnovsky, Henry Travers, Earle Larimore, Sanford Meisner, Erskine Sanford, Elisabeth Risdon, Laura Hope Crewes, and two men destined to become legends of the modern New York theater, Harold Clurman and Lee Strasberg.

For the Guild Robinson next created the role of Shrdlu in Elmer Rice's *The Adding Machine*. The play's expressionism fascinated Robinson. He was in Chicago in May 1923, appearing in *The Voice*, then reteamed twice more with producer Arthur Hopkins—for *Launzi* in October, featuring Pauline Lord, and with Spencer Tracy in support of Ethel Barrymore in *A Royal Fandango* in November. Neither play was successful.

He played the role of Ed Munn opposite Mrs. Leslie Carter's *Stella Dallas* in early 1924; and then, again appearing with Joseph Schildkraut, Robinson was Ottaviano in *The Firebrand*, an historical comedy that also featured Frank Morgan. November 1925 saw Robinson in the Theatre Guild's version of Shaw's double bill, *Androcles and the Lion*, as the emperor Caesar, and *The Man of Destiny*. An avowed Shaw enthusiast, Robinson was delighted, regretting only that he had missed a chance to play Napoleon. In 1926 came the Guild production of *The Goat Song* with the Lunts, a sweeping allegorical folk tale by Franz Werfel, and *The Chief Thing*, a highly theatrical Russian work that featured Henry Travers.

That summer he played in *We Americans* in Atlantic City, *The Stolen Lady*, and *Henry, Behave*. *We Americans* was destined to be a big hit, but Robinson's contract with the Guild forced him to withdraw, affording Paul Muni (Muni Weisenfreund) a break as his replacement. *The Stolen Lady* featured Leo Carillo but failed. The last play featured Pat O'Brien, Elisha Cook, Jr., and an actress named Gladys Lloyd, who on January 21, 1927, became Mrs. Edward G. Robinson.

The Guild's new season saw Robinson in Franz Werfel's *Juarez and Maximilian* (as Porfirio Diaz), Sidney Howard's *Ned McCobb's Daughter* (as Lawyer Grover), Feodor Dostoevsky's *The Brother's Karamazov* (as Smerdiakov), and Luigi Pirandello's *Right You Are If You Think You Are* (as Ponza). Then in Atlantic City he starred in *The Kibitzer*, a Jo Swerling comedy about the owner of a cigar store. Robinson loved the play and, with Swerling, acted out possible changes, hoping the author would rewrite. Despite a clever premise, it failed.

The Racket, which opened in New York in November 1927, did not fail. It was an exciting melodrama written by Bartlett Cormack, a newspaperman, and in it Robinson played Nick Scarsi, a literary but thinly-disguised version of Al Capone. Although it was a big hit in New York, the play's tour to Chicago (Al Capone territory) was cancelled by a fearful mayor. So engagements were substituted in Los Angeles and San Francisco, with the result that film executives saw Edward G. Robinson for the first time and offered immediate contracts. He turned them down and went back to star on Broadway in the Hugh Walpole suspense thriller *A Man with Red Hair*. During its run he was persuaded to appear as a gangster in a talking picture with Claudette Colbert, *The Hole in the Wall*, which was filmed at the Astoria Studios in New York.

Jo Swerling now surprised Edward G. Robinson by giving him a joint authorship credit on the rewrite of *The Kibitzer*. It reopened in February 1929 to very favorable reviews. But for the imminent Wall Street crash, it might have become a much greater milestone in Robinson's career.

MGM, in the person of studio executive Irving Thalberg, offered Robinson the lead opposite Vilma Banky in the film *A Lady to Love*, and Robinson accepted because of the quality of Sidney Howard's screenplay, which had been based on his own play *They Knew What They Wanted*. It was followed by *The Night Ride*, *Outside the Law,* and *East Is West*, in quick succession. For the last, Robinson refilmed scenes originally made with Jean Hersholt as an Oriental. *The Night Ride* featured Joseph Schildkraut, and *Outside the Law* was a remake by Tod Browning of his silent film; all had Robinson playing gangster roles.

Filmmaking was not popular with Robinson. He was pleased neither with the shooting experience nor the outcome of these few pictures. The story of his rejection of a three-year, six-picture, one-million-dollar contract offered by Thalberg because it didn't allow him time to do a Broadway play is Hollywood legend: He left Thalberg's office and threw up.

Robinson thought of himself as a stage actor, and he went back to New York with confidence to appear in *Mr. Samuel*. Despite his star name and acceptable notices, the play failed. As he told a *New York Post* interviewer, "That disaster decided me. I thought, 'What's the good of being true to the theatre when in eighteen years, one hasn't built up a following...?'" He then signed a film contract with Warner Brothers.

If the first film under his new contract, another gangster story called *The Widow from Chicago*, echoed his earlier unpleasant experiences with the movies, the next made a world of difference.

True, it was his fifth gangster role in nine pictures, but *Little Caesar* irrevocably changed

Edward G. Robinson. He was at the center of an event caused by several conditions occurring at once — he was at the right place at the right time. Warners' films were "grabbed from headlines" and put before Depression audiences in a new and revolutionary form — "talkies." The audiences, in turn, devoured them while forgetting their troubles. But they also identified with and glorified the ordinary and often lowlife film characters they saw projected on the silver screen. And so it was perhaps natural they would idolize the impersonator of Capone, because he wasn't really a villain, just a good actor.

With *Little Caesar*, Edward G. Robinson became a major film star and an overnight celebrity. For the next four decades Robinson *was* Little Caesar. In virtually everything he did thereafter, there were inevitable comparisons. His skill as an actor fortunately helped him surmount the image while at the same time reaping its benefits. *Little Caesar* was directed by Mervyn LeRoy and co-starred Douglas Fairbanks, Jr., and Glenda Farrell.

Warners immediately teamed Robinson with another tough guy on the rise — from *The Public Enemy*— James Cagney. The film was *Smart Money*, and it was about gamblers instead of gangsters, but the similarity was noticeable. *Smart Money* was followed by *Five Star Final*, a newspaper story with Robinson playing a city editor. Boris Karloff had small roles in both these films just prior to finding his own gold mine, *Frankenstein*.

Robinson appeared in four films in 1932: *The Hatchet Man*, opposite Loretta Young, with both of them playing Chinese; *Two Seconds*, a third project for director Mervyn LeRoy; *Tiger Shark*, a love triangle story with a tuna fishing setting, for Howard Hawks; and a biographical drama, *Silver Dollar*, about Denver's Horace Tabor. Only the last two films were apart from the urban milieu of the tough guy.

He was reunited with Mary Astor as her love interest in the gangster comedy *The Little Giant* the following year. His beer baron character was trying to go straight by busting into high society. The film was made during a California earthquake, the effects of which are visible in the completed print.

In New York Edward G. Robinson, Jr., was born in March, and the Robinsons bought their Tudor-style mansion on Rexford Drive in Beverly Hills later in 1933.

In *I Loved a Woman*, the story of a meat packer who sold tainted beef to the Army during the Spanish-American War, Robinson starred with Kay Francis and Genevieve Tobin. Tobin played Robinson's wife; they were married again in *Dark Hazard*, the story of a compulsive gambler, and Glenda Farrell played the other woman. He was Mary Astor's brother in their third film together, *The Man with Two Faces*. They played stage actors involved in murder.

Robinson's work got even better when he was loaned out from Warners for two pictures in 1935. Columbia's *The Whole Town's Talking* had him opposite Jean Arthur in a dual role as a meek clerk who is mistaken for his sinister gangster double; and for United Artists he was a turn-of-the-century gangster running San Francisco's gambling and gold enterprises in *Barbary Coast*. John Ford directed the first film, which was written by Jo Swerling from a novel by *Little Caesar*'s W. R. Burnett. Howard Hawks directed the second from a script by Charles MacArthur and Ben Hecht.

Warners teamed Robinson with Joan Blondell and Humphrey Bogart in *Bullets or Ballots*, a gangster story, but he was cast as a tough cop who infiltrates the rackets. He went to England to make a comedy called *Thunder in the City* about a high-styled promoter. Co-stars were Nigel Bruce, Constance Collier, and Ralph Richardson.

While he was in London, Robinson stopped by Reed and LeFevre, art dealers, and bought Renoir's *The Girl with the Red Plume*. At the Wildenstein Gallery he purchased Berthe Morisot's *Avant le Theatre* and was told that the collection it came from was in Paris. He went to Wildenstein in Paris and bought Paul Gauguin's *Fleurs de Tahiti* and several other works, and returned to London. There he exchanged a Cezanne landscape acquired in Paris for the artist's *Black Clock*, which Robinson "wanted more than any other in the world." Gladys Robinson was as susceptible as her husband to the fever of collecting art. Their paintings and sculptures by Monet, Degas, Pissarro, Corot, Rouault, Bonnard, Utrillo, Vuillard, Picasso, and others became in the next twenty years one of the greatest collections of French Impressionist art ever assembled in America.

Edward G. Robinson was thus compelled to be a success in order to support his art collecting. Returning to Warner Brothers, he and Bogart teamed with Bette Davis in *Kid Galahad* for director Michael Curtiz. The film is one of the best ever made about prizefighting. In his last role in 1937 Robinson played the part of *The Last Gangster*, co-starring James Stewart, at MGM.

Beginning in the early thirties, Robinson was heard regularly on the radio, often in adaptations of his films, on such programs as *Lux Radio Theatre* and *Hollywood Hotel*. There were also many original stories, often patriotic and documentary in nature. But easily his greatest impact on the air was as Steve Wilson, the crusading newspaper editor of *Big Town*, in which he gave over 200 performances from 1937 to 1942. The weekly programs ran one hour. Claire Trevor co-starred. She was succeeded by Ona Munson.

In 1938 there was another popular gangster comedy, *A Slight Case of Murder*. The gimmick was four corpses that seemed to turn up everywhere; and he teamed for the third time with Bogart in *The Amazing Dr. Clitterhouse*, directed by Anatole Litvak, with Claire Trevor as the female lead. Robinson played a society doctor who stole jewels as he conducted scientific research into crime. He was then loaned to Columbia, where he played a law professor on sabbatical cleaning up the rackets in *I Am the Law*.

Confessions of a Nazi Spy in 1939, directed by Litvak, was a timely semi-documentary. Its production brought death threats to Robinson and Jack L. Warner from U.S.-based factions of the Third Reich. *Blackmail* at MGM was politically tame but an entertaining story of oil fires and chain gangs.

1940 brought Edward G. Robinson his second major career highlight. Having played in two biographies in the early thirties, there now came an opportunity to play the role of the Nobel Prize–winning scientist who discovered a cure for syphilis in *Dr. Ehrlich's Magic Bullet*. Paul Muni had won an Academy Award for his biographical portrait in *The Story of Louis Pasteur*, and Warners was now having great success with the biography genre. Robinson was anxious to break out of the gangster mold. That he managed it so effectively with this film came as a surprise to some who were not yet aware of his versatility. Ruth Gordon and Otto Kruger were in the film, too, directed by William Dieterle. John Huston was one of the screenwriters.

The privilege of filming *Dr. Ehrlich* apparently was at the cost of doing another comic gangster film. Teamed for the fourth time with Humphrey Bogart, in *Brother Orchid* Robinson was also appearing with Ann Sothern, Ralph Bellamy, and Donald Crisp. In the film Robinson escaped mob assassination by hiding out in a monastery, and then realized the life was pretty good and joined the brothers. *A Dispatch from Reuter's*, which featured much of the cast of *Dr. Ehrlich* and direction by Dieterle, followed. It was the story of Baron Julius Reuter, who founded the first newsgathering service in Europe in the 1800s.

In 1941 there were three more tough-guy films, but at least the two at Warners were not explicitly about gangsters. *The Sea Wolf*, which featured John Garfield, Ida Lupino, Alexander Knox, Barry Fitzgerald, and Gene Lockhart, had Robinson as the sadistic sea captain of Jack London's famous novel. *Manpower* reworked a familiar love triangle plot (used, for example, in

Tiger Shark) of a man's wife falling for his best friend, only to conclude with the man dying to accommodate their relationship. Robinson was joined by George Raft as the friend and Marlene Dietrich as the wife, under the direction of Raoul Walsh. MGM's *Unholy Partners*, directed by Mervyn LeRoy, was a newspaper-gangster story with, for a change, Edward Arnold as the gangster. Laraine Day played editor Robinson's secretary.

Larceny, Inc., in 1942, was the last film on Edward G. Robinson's Warner Bros. contract. It was yet another gangster comedy, and it featured Jane Wyman, Broderick Crawford, Jack Carson, and Anthony Quinn. As a freelance actor, Robinson appeared in the fourth episode of five *Tales of Manhattan* at Twentieth Century–Fox, directed by Julien Duvivier. His story was about a bowery bum challenged to make a showing at his law school reunion.

Flesh and Fantasy was divided into three parts, of which Robinson's was the second, about a lawyer who is told by a palm reader that he will commit murder. He becomes obsessed with the prophecy until he carries it out. Duvivier directed, and Thomas Mitchell played the palmist — and victim.

Other than *Confessions of a Nazi Spy,* Robinson's movies had little to do with the current troubles of World War II. However, three of his next four films had war settings, despite the irony that Robinson, at age 48, was a bit past the prime age of active duty. *Destroyer* saw him as a retired Navy man who at first teaches new recruits and then spars with younger officer Glenn Ford aboard ship. The other two were *Tampico,* about a ship's captain whose new bride (Lynn Bari) might be an Axis spy, and *Mr. Winkle Goes to War,* in which he played an overage draftee who becomes a hero fighting the Japanese.

Robinson's real life wartime efforts were more significant. In New York in March 1943 he narrated, with Paul Muni, a two-performance stage pageant called *We Will Never Die,* commemorating the loss of six million Jews in the Holocaust. He traveled to Europe to broadcast messages of hope on the radio and was the first Hollywood figure to entertain the troops following D-Day.

Edward G. Robinson's film career took a major turn in the 1940s. While his physical appearance suited him for the hard-boiled, often semi-literate types either at the center or on the fringe of crime, and he had spent a dozen years at Warners in these kinds of films, there was now developing a darker, more psychological kind of film drama called *film noir*. Robinson was an ideal choice to play some of its characters. If in the thirties Robinson was the personification of the gangster, the forties saw him still embroiled in crime, but, more often than not, as an unwitting victim or a probing, thinking investigator.

His first film typefying *noir* was Billy Wilder's *Double Indemnity*, made at Paramount in 1944. The screenplay was by Wilder and Raymond Chandler, writer of detective novels. It was based on a *Liberty* magazine story of the real murder of a man by his wife and her lover to collect his life insurance. With Fred MacMurray and Barbara Stanwyck in the leads as the murderous couple, and Robinson in careful pursuit as the insurance investigator, *Double Indemnity* became a time-honored masterpiece of the *film noir* genre.

Three months later *The Woman in the Window* appeared, with Edward G. Robinson and Joan Bennett trying to cover up an act of self defense that looks like murder. The director was Fritz Lang, and co-players were Raymond Massey as the district attorney and Dan Duryea as a blackmailer.

Our Vines Have Tender Grapes in 1945 featured eight-year-old Margaret O'Brien as Robinson's daughter in a tender MGM story of farm life in Wisconsin. Both Agnes Moorehead as the mother and Robinson were effective playing against type. Robinson was an American flight instructor in *Journey Together*, which featured a young Richard Attenborough in a story about the English pilots in the RAF.

Robinson went immediately back to *noir*, joining Lang, Bennett, Duryea, and some of the supporting players from *The Woman in the Window* in a similar but sleazier story called *Scarlet Street*. In it Robinson's character progresses from henpecked husband to ice-pick murderer to bowery bum.

For marquee value, Robinson replaced Agnes Moorehead as the war crimes investigator in Orson Welles' *The Stranger* in 1946. Welles played a Nazi tracked by Robinson, and Loretta Young, who had played Robinson's Chinese wife fourteen years earlier in *The Hatchet Man*, was married to Welles. Edward G. Robinson's only film in 1947 was a chiller he helped to produce called *The Red House*, about a farmer and his sister (Judith Anderson) who are keeping a dark secret in the woods.

His three 1948 ventures had him dead by gunshot at the finale. The melodrama, however, was strong in all of them. First, he played the father whose lies are discovered by son Burt Lancaster in an adaptation of Arthur Miller's Pulitzer Prize–winning play *All My Sons*. Robinson's character commits suicide when his guilt is too much for him to bear.

In a fifth and final confrontation with Humphrey Bogart, Robinson returned to Warner Bros. to make *Key Largo*. The film reunited them with Claire Trevor, who won an Oscar for her performance, and also starred Lauren Bacall and Lionel Barrymore. John Huston directed, based on Maxwell Anderson's play. Robinson renewed his gangster character with great effect, terrorizing the others at a run-down Florida hotel in a last ditch effort to keep his power. Finally, in *Night Has a Thousand Eyes* for Paramount, Robinson tries to save Gail Russell from "death at the feet of a lion," as foreseen by his character, a clairvoyant.

House of Strangers, which came next in 1949, was directed by Joseph L. Mankiewicz and featured Susan Hayward, Richard Conte, and Luther Adler. It was about an immigrant barber-turned-banker unable to communicate with his four sons. For his performance, Edward G. Robinson received his only major performing award, as Best Actor at the Cannes, France, Film Festival. He closed out the decade by appearing as himself, spoofing his gangster image in the Warners musical *It's a Great Feeling*.

Robinson's generous contributions to charity brought him under investigation by the House Un-American Activities Committee in the late 1940s as an alleged supporter of Communist fronts. He voluntarily testified in Washington on three occasions over a four-year period and finally managed to convince the Committee of what he later grudgingly came to accept about himself: that he had been a dupe, but he was no Communist. Although many Hollywood careers were ruined by the aftermath of the Committee's attacks, Robinson hung on and managed to work. It took ten or more years, however, before what he was offered in films was up to standard.

Domestically, things were not good either. Gladys Robinson, he gradually came to learn, was a manic-depressive. Private clinics, shock treatments, and threats of divorce alternated with moments of peace. Robinson, Jr., now a teenager, was headed for troubles of his own — drinking and brushes with the law.

Robinson tried to escape his difficulties by going to Europe. But he could not escape the disaster of a film he made there in 1950 called *Operation X*, about a megalomaniac with a strange attachment to his daughter, played by Peggy Cummins.

He was offered the lead on Broadway in Sidney Kingsley's play about an imprisoned Bolshevik leader, *Darkness at Noon*. Claude Rains took the role instead, but several months later was too exhausted to do the national tour. So, for the first time in more than twenty years, Edward G. Robinson returned to the stage. The play's anti–Communist message could only help him.

His Hollywood films for the next four years were generally second rate, but Robinson did what he could with them. "Actor's Blood" was the gloomy first half of a double bill called

Actors and Sin. It was about a faded Shakespearean actor and the death of his self-centered actress daughter, played by Marsha Hunt. *Big Leaguer* featured dancer Vera-Ellen in a non-dancing role as his niece; the film was about baseball training camp. *Vice Squad* had him playing a police captain on a routine day of murder, bank robbery, car theft, and marriage bunco. *The Glass Web*, co-starring John Forsythe, was about murder via television, but at least it was filmed in 3–D.

Television offered Edward G. Robinson opportunities that films denied him. In 1954 he was in a pilot film for a series, *For the Defense*. An hour-long episode called "The Case of Kenny Jason" was produced, but the series never materialized. He appeared on *Climax!* the same year in a tense melodrama, "Epitaph for a Spy."

A good film role came his way in *Black Tuesday*, even if it was an obvious throwback to his glory days as a gangster. He was a killer who escapes the electric chair and takes hostages in a warehouse. Threatening to kill one of them, a priest, Robinson causes his partner, played by Peter Graves, to shoot him. In *The Violent Men* Robinson was reteamed with Barbara Stanwyck and Glenn Ford in his first western. He played Stanwyck's crippled, cuckolded husband, and nearly died at her hands in a Technicolor fire.

Brian Keith, who had also played in *The Violent Men*, joined Ginger Rogers, Lorne Greene, and Robinson in *Tight Spot*, about a D.A.'s attempt to protect a state's witness (Ginger) from a mobster (Greene). Robinson was the district attorney and Keith a cop on the take. In *A Bullet for Joey* George Raft again starred with Edward G. Robinson as a gangster tracked by Robinson's Canadian police inspector on his trail.

In 1955 television audiences saw Robinson in two *Ford Theatre* programs: "...And Son," and "A Set of Values." He was also on CBS for six weeks challenging Vincent Price in the category of art on *The $64,000 Challenge*.

Robinson returned to Warner Brothers as a sometimes-crooked lawyer in *Illegal*, notable as the film debut of Jayne Mansfield. *Hell on Frisco Bay* starred Alan Ladd as a cop framed by Robinson as the boss of the San Francisco docks. And *Nightmare* had Robinson on the right side of the law to save his brother-in-law, played by Kevin McCarthy, from murder charges.

Cecil B. DeMille chose him to play the Hebrew overseer in his mammoth *The Ten Commandments* and thus rescued the actor from his B-picture career. There are still jokes nearly forty years later about the film's grandiose spectacle, its stilted dialogue, and about Robinson's appearance in it—wasn't there a tommy gun hidden under his robes? But both the film and the actor stand the test of time. *The Ten Commandments* is still impressive in the scope of its storytelling and its special effects. And Robinson is watchable, along with the rest of the cast—Vincent Price, Judith Anderson, Nina Foch, John Carradine, and Sir Cedric Hardwicke in fine support of Yul Brynner, Anne Baxter, and Charlton Heston.

Before the release of *The Ten Commandments*, Edward G. Robinson returned to Broadway to play a middle-aged manufacturer who falls in love with a girl half his age in Paddy Chayefsky's tender *Middle of the Night*. The play opened to generally favorable reviews and ran well over a year. In the cast were Gena Rowlands, Martin Balsam, and Anne Jackson. It was directed by Joshua Logan.

Although his political difficulties had subsided and he was in demand again as an actor, his marriage to Gladys was still plagued. She again sued for divorce, and this time he did not resist. A major consequence was the dissolution of their fabulous collection of art in order to comply with community property laws in California. Robinson wanted to buy her share, but ultimately the collection was purchased by the highest bidder, Greek shipping tycoon Stavros Niarchos, for $3,250,000. The sale made the front page of *The New York Times*.

Middle of the Night began its national tour in October of 1957. Three months later, on January 16, in Washington, D.C., Edward G. Robinson married Jane Adler, who, as a couturiere, had been associated with the play. *Middle of the Night* closed in San Francisco in March.

In 1958 the actor's son, Edward G. Robinson, Jr., published *My Father—My Son*, an autobiography detailing the troubles of growing up and living in the shadow of famous parents. He played occasional film roles, including parts in two Marilyn Monroe films, *Bus Stop* and *Some Like It Hot*.

Robinson, Jr., and his first wife, actress-model Frances Chisholm, had a daughter, Francesca, born in 1954. They were divorced in 1956. A suicide attempt and a conviction on drunk driving charges followed before Manny, as the younger Robinson was called, appeared on television with his father. The April 1959 *Zane Grey Theatre* episode was called "Heritage." Robinson, Sr., had appeared on a *Goodyear Theatre* presentation, "A Good Name," one month earlier.

Edward G. Robinson began to receive quality film offers again, the first being a co-starring role as Frank Sinatra's older brother in *A Hole in the Head,* a comedy directed by Frank Capra. Thelma Ritter played his wife, and Eleanor Parker, Carolyn Jones, and Keenan Wynn were also in the cast.

In February 1960 Robinson appeared on a partially live television special, "The Devil and Daniel Webster," which co-starred David Wayne as Mr. Scratch. Another special in October, called *The Right Man,* about famous presidential campaigns, had him playing Theodore Roosevelt in a cast that included Thomas Mitchell, Art Carney, Richard Boone, Celeste Holm, Paul Ford, and Tom Bosley.

Seven Thieves, a crime caper film set in France, was Robinson's next feature film, directed by Henry Hathaway and featuring Rod Steiger, Eli Wallach, and Joan Collins. In it his character, an elderly professor of crime, plans to rob the casino at Monte Carlo of $4,000,000 in francs and thereby finally "put the cork on the bottle" of his career.

George Sidney directed Robinson and 25 others playing themselves in the musical *Pepe*, which starred Cantinflas in the title role as a Mexican ranch hand who, in his efforts to keep his favorite white stallion, Don Juan, wanders through Hollywood and Las Vegas.

In 1961 Robinson was on *General Electric Theatre* with Billy Gray in "The Drop-Out," and on *Robert Taylor's Detectives* as an old-time gangster in "The Legend of Jim Riva." He narrated a special for *Project 20* called "Cops and Robbers" in 1962.

His next film roles took him out of the country for several months. *My Geisha*, starring Shirley MacLaine as a film star who tries to convince her husband (Yves Montand) that she is a geisha, was filmed on location in Japan. *Two Weeks in Another Town* was filmed in Rome with Kirk Douglas, Cyd Charisse, George Hamilton, and Claire Trevor (together once more after a dozen years) as Robinson's wife. The picture, directed by Vincente Minelli and produced by John Houseman, was based on an Irwin Shaw novel about filmmaking.

While filming *A Boy Ten Feet Tall* in Africa in June 1962, the actor suffered a heart attack. He was treated and flown to London, where he recuperated in the same hospital in which Winston Churchill was a patient. The two traded cigars. Robinson later completed the film, which had a London premiere attended by royalty. After a two-year delay it was released in the United States. Robinson played the part of a warm-hearted diamond smuggler who befriends a ten-year-old boy traveling to Durban, South Africa, on foot from the Suez.

In 1963–64 Robinson was busier than ever. He was on television in April as a presenter at the *36th Annual Motion Picture Academy of Arts and Sciences Awards*, handing out screenplay Oscars for *Tom Jones* and *How the West Was Won*. He had grown a beard and moustache for *A Boy Ten Feet Tall* and was now nearly seventy years old. The parts he was now offered were often not as large as in times past, but the billing was always prominent and the role key. He played dual roles in *The Prize*, as a Nobel Prize–winning German physicist and as an actor-impersonator when the physicist is kidnapped. The film was a star vehicle for Paul Newman (as a Nobel Prize-winning author) and featured Elke Sommer, Diane Baker, Leo G. Carroll, and Kevin McCarthy.

Cast purposefully against type, Robinson was a pristine Bible-spouting dairy client of Jack Lemmon's ad agency in *Good Neighbor Sam*. Co-stars were Romy Schneider and Dorothy Provine. Back at Warners for a two-minute bit at the beginning of Frank Sinatra's *Robin and the 7 Hoods*, he spoofed Little Caesar, and no billing was necessary; his presence spoke for itself. Sammy Davis, Jr., and Dean Martin of "the Clan" were joined by Peter Falk, Bing Crosby, and Barbara Rush. The story had rival twenties gangs vying for power (with musical numbers) after Robinson is bumped off.

For those last-named films Robinson shaved his whiskers, but they were back to stay when he worked with Paul Newman again in *The Outrage*. He played a seedy con man who listens to four different versions of a rape and murder in the old Southwest in a remake of Akiro Kurosawa's *Rashomon*. The director was Martin Ritt. Newman played the bandit who attacked the wife (Claire Bloom) and killed the husband (Laurence Harvey). William Shatner and Howard DaSilva were also featured.

Staying out West and working for the second time with John Ford, Edward G. Robinson replaced an ailing Spencer Tracy in *Cheyenne Autumn*. He played Secretary of the Interior Carl Schurz, who intervenes on behalf of the Cheyenne Indians as they make a 1,500–mile trek from Oklahoma to Yellowstone, Wyoming. The all-star cast was headed by Richard Widmark, Carroll Baker, Sal Mineo, Karl Malden, Dolores Del Rio, Ricardo Montalban, Gilbert Roland, and James Stewart.

Robinson did a dramatic reading by Milton Geiger, "This Is It," on *Hollywood Palace* in January 1965. Working with George Sidney again, he was in a *Xerox Special* on television, "Who Has Seen the Wind?" about displaced persons living on a freighter. Robinson played the ship's captain. Other key roles were played by Theodore Bikel, Maria Schell, and Gypsy Rose Lee.

In 1965 Robinson again replaced Spencer Tracy, this time in a more or less contemporary gambling story, *The Cincinnati Kid*. The star was Steve McQueen, and support came from Karl Malden, Rip Torn, Cab Calloway, and Jack Weston. The ladies were Ann-Margret, Tuesday Weld, and, working with Robinson for the first time since 1936, Joan Blondell. The film had McQueen's character challenging Robinson's as reigning stud poker champion. Norman Jewison directed a script based on the novel by Richard Jessup.

The heart attack Robinson suffered in Africa was only the first among many problematic health factors. In 1966 he was in a serious car accident in Beverly Hills, having to undergo considerable abdominal and facial surgery. And he was plagued by recurring cancer. These factors, in addition to the fact that he was more than a little hard of hearing, limited his performing, but he continued, nonetheless, often traveling to do inferior foreign pictures — as much to see the art treasures of the world, he claimed.

There were several such films in the late sixties, usually with the actor as the brains behind some sort of crime caper. *Peking Blonde* had him tracking Chinese spies from France to Hong Kong. A comedy, *The Biggest Bundle of Them All*, returned him to old times as a surviving contemporary of Dillinger and Capone, now masterminding a platinum robbery — via Madison Avenue advertising techniques. Robert Wagner, Raquel Welch, and

Vittorio DeSica starred. In *Grand Slam* he was a teacher about to retire from a convent in Rio de Janeiro that just happens to be across the street from a diamond company. His partner in crime turned out to be the company president's secretary, played by Janet Leigh.

In *Mad Checkmate* Robinson found four lookalikes to impersonate bank employees in order to stage a heist. Michelangelo's *Pietà* is stolen and then fenced by retired crook Robinson in *Operation San Pietro*; and finally, the actor worked for Walt Disney in a movie about a plot to steal a mural from the Los Angeles County Museum. His character's name was Leo Joseph Smooth, and he was, naturally enough, a retired gangster. The picture was called *Never a Dull Moment*, and it starred Dick Van Dyke and Dorothy Provine.

On television Robinson played an aging surgeon in need of a heart transplant in *U.M.C.*, the pilot for the *Medical Center* series. An impressive cast included James Daly, Kim Stanley, Maurice Evans, Kevin McCarthy, and William Windom. He also did two episodes of *Laugh-In* and one of *Batman*.

Robinson's stature as a veteran film star is evident in *Mackenna's Gold*, a large-scale western embarrassingly full of cliches and poor filming techniques. His role as Old Adams affords him a splendid five-minute monologue about gold fever. Lee J. Cobb, Burgess Meredith, Anthony Quayle, Raymond Massey, Eduardo Cianelli, Keenan Wynn, and Eli Wallach all had roles in the film, but none of them had such scope. The leads were Gregory Peck, Omar Sharif, and Telly Savalas.

In October 1970 Edward G. Robinson made three television appearances. He was *The Old Man Who Cried Wolf* on ABC in a touching story about an old man who sees his best friend murdered but can get no one to believe him. In support were Martin Balsam as Robinson's son, Diane Baker, Ruth Roman, Ed Asner, and Sam Jaffe as his friend. Ten days later, at the same time but on different stations, he did dramatic readings by Milton Geiger and Rudyard Kipling on *This Is Tom Jones* (ABC) and was guest star on *Bracken's World* in the episode "The Mary Tree" (NBC). The latter featured Diana Hyland as his daughter and Leslie Nielson as John Bracken.

Andrew Stone's film version of the musical *Song of Norway* featured Robinson in a small role as a piano seller. Florence Henderson and Norwegian actor Toralv Maurstad starred as Mr. and Mrs. Edvard Grieg. Robinson played himself in *Mooch* in 1971 and another small role in the Israeli film *Neither by Day Nor Night* in 1972, as the father of a young man facing blindness.

Television in 1971–72 had Robinson interviewed, along with old-guard Warner colleagues Joan Blondell, Bette Davis, Pat O'Brien, and Busby Berkeley, in *The Movie Crazy Years*, and briefly as narrator of *U.S.A.*, a John Dos Passos play, both on PBS. His last dramatic acting role on television was as an impoverished old man waiting for "The Messiah on Mott Street" on Rod Serling's *Night Gallery*.

Gladys Lloyd Robinson, who had been divorced from the actor for fifteen years, died in June 1971 of a heart attack suffered at her granddaughter's high school commencement exercises. She had continued to collect fine art and was herself an accomplished artist. Edward G. Robinson and his second wife, Jane, rebuilt a private collection. In 1972 she published a book of color prints of the works, "a gift to my husband," called *Edward G. Robinson's World of Art*.

His last feature film was made at MGM. It took him fifty years into the future as a crime researcher, known as a "book," in the science fiction thriller *Soylent Green*. The story follows a cop (Charlton Heston) investigating the assassination of a wealthy executive (Joseph Cotten) and ultimately leads to uncovering the grisly truth about futuristic food processing. The movie contains a poignant suicide scene for Robinson, and the fact that he died of cancer only a few months before the film premiered had a major effect on the film's publicity.

Filming of *Soylent Green* was completed in October of 1972. By the end of the year, Robinson's cancer required hospitalization. In January it was announced that he would receive an honorary award from the Academy of Motion Picture Arts and Sciences for his contribution to films. An Oscar statuette was inscribed, "To Edward G. Robinson, who achieved greatness as a player, a patron of the arts and a dedicated citizen ... in sum, a Renaissance man. From his friends in the industry he loved."

Leonard Spigelgass, a playwright and screenwriter friend who had been working with Robinson on his autobiography *All My Yesterdays*, told him in the hospital about the Oscar when it became apparent the actor might not live to receive it in the spring. In fact, Edward G. Robinson died two weeks later, on January 26, 1973. Following ceremonies at Temple Israel in Los Angeles, he was entombed in the family mausoleum at Beth El Cemetery in Brooklyn.

His widow accepted Robinson's honorary Oscar on the televised broadcast of the *45th Academy of Motion Picture Arts and Sciences Awards* on March 27.

Robinson's will named Jane to receive fifty percent of his estate and Edward, Jr., and Francesca twenty-five percent each, in trusts. His papers, scripts, photos, and mementos, including the Oscar, were also left to Jane, who later turned them over to the University of Southern California. The Robinson art collection was purchased by corporate executive Armand Hammer for $5,125,000.

All My Yesterdays, Robinson's autobiography, was completed by Leonard Spigelgass and published by Hawthorn Books in the fall of 1973.

On February 26, 1974 — thirteen months to the day after the actor's death — his son, Edward G. Robinson, Jr., died of a drug overdose.

Two biographical works on Edward G. Robinson were completed in the late 1970s. *Manny*, by Raymond Serra, was an unsuccessful play on Broadway. The British Broadcasting Corporation (BBC) produced a comprehensive television account of his life and career — *The Hollywood Greats: Edward G. Robinson* — which used clips from several films and had appearances by George Raft, Vincent Price, Sam Jaffe, Frank Capra, John Huston, Hal Wallis, the actor's widow, Jane, and his granddaughter, Francesca.

Jane Robinson suffered from lupus disease for several years following her husband's death. It forced her confinement in bed for several months at a time. In July 1977 she attended an auction of much of the actor's personal effects, paintings, jewelry, home furnishings, and memorabilia. In March 1978 she married director George Sidney. They continued to live in the Robinson's Beverly Hills mansion until her death on July 21, 1991.

The *A&E Biography* series produced "Little Big Man" about Edward G. Robinson in 1996.

Francesca Robinson married Richard Sanchez, a real estate broker, in 1977. Adam Edward, born in 1983 and named for the actor, became Edward G. Robinson's great grandson.

The Encyclopedia

A&E Biography see "Little Big Man"; Biographies

ABC Movie of the Week see "The Old Man Who Cried Wolf"

Academy of Motion Picture Arts and Sciences Awards Edward G. Robinson was named to receive an honorary Oscar in 1973, recognizing contributions and achievements during a fifty-seven-year film career. His death in January necessitated a posthumous presentation to his widow, Jane, at ceremonies on March 27. Robinson had appeared in nineteen films that received mention in one or more Oscar categories, earning a total of 38 nominations. In the list that follows, winners are indicated in **bold** type.

1930–31: *Little Caesar*, SCREENPLAY, Francis Faragoh and Robert N. Lee; *Smart Money*, ORIGINAL STORY, Lucien Hubbard and Joseph Jackson

1931–32: *Five Star Final*, PICTURE, Hal B. Wallis, producer

1935: *Barbary Coast*, CINEMATOGRAPHY, Ray June

1940: *Dr. Ehrlich's Magic Bullet*, ORIGINAL SCREENPLAY, Norman Burnside, Heinz Herald, and John Huston

1941: *The Sea Wolf*, SPECIAL EFFECTS, Byron Haskin and Nathan Levinson

1942: *Moscow Strikes Back* DOCUMENTARY, Artkino, Russia

1944: *Double Indemnity*, PICTURE, Joseph Sistrom, producer; ACTRESS, Barbara Stanwyck; DIRECTOR, Billy Wilder; SCREENPLAY, Raymond Chandler and Billy Wilder; MUSIC, Miklos Rozsa; SOUND RECORDING, Loren Ryder; CINEMATOGRAPHY, John Seitz

1945: *The Woman in the Window*, MUSIC, Hugo Friedhofer and Arthur Lange

1946: *The Stranger*, ORIGINAL STORY, Victor Trivas

1948: *Key Largo*, SUPPORTING ACTRESS, Claire Trevor

1949: *It's a Great Feeling*, SONG (of the same name), music by Jule Styne, lyrics by Sammy Cahn

1956: *The Ten Commandments*, PICTURE, Cecil B. DeMille, producer; ART / SET DIRECTION, Hal Pereira, Walter H. Tyler, Albert Nozaki, Sam M. Comer, and Ray Moyer; CINEMATOGRAPHY, Loyal Griggs; COSTUME DESIGN, Edith Head, Ralph Jester, John Jensen, Dorothy Jeakins, and Arnold Friberg; FILM EDITING, Anne Bauchens; SOUND RECORDING, Loren Ryder; SPECIAL EFFECTS, John Fulton

1959: *A Hole in the Head*, SONG *High Hopes*, music by James Van Heusen, lyrics by Sammy Cahn

1960: *Seven Thieves*, COSTUME DESIGN, Bill Thomas; *Pepe*, ART DIRECTION / SET DECORATION, Ted Haworth / William Kiernan; COSTUME DESIGN, Edith Head; SOUND, Charles Rice; FILM EDITING, Viola Lawrence and Al Clark; MUSIC, Johnny Green; SONG "Faraway Part of Town," music, by Andre Previn, lyrics by Dory Langdon; CINEMATOGRAPHY, Joe McDonald

1962: *My Geisha*, COSTUME DESIGN, Edith Head

1964: *Robin and the 7 Hoods*, MUSIC, Nelson Riddle; SONG "My Kind of Town," music by James Van Heusen, lyrics by Sammy Cahn; *Cheyenne Autumn*, CINEMATOGRAPHY, William H. Clothier

1972: HONORARY **award to Edward G. Robinson** in recognition of lifetime achievement in films. For commentary on the presentation see *Academy of Motion Picture Arts and Sciences Awards (45th Annual)*.

The honorary Oscar was, of course, Robinson's only Academy Award. One can only speculate why films such as *My Geisha, Pepe,* and *Cheyenne Autumn* in the latter part of Robinson's career received any nominations when such worthy films as, for example, *The Whole Town's Talking, Bullets or Ballots, Kid Galahad, Confessions of a Nazi Spy, Scarlet Street, All My Sons,* and *The Cincinnati Kid* were overlooked. *Little Caesar, Smart Money, Barbary Coast, Dr. Ehrlich's Magic Bullet, The Woman in the Window, Key Largo,* and *A Hole in the Head,* among others, surely merited greater consideration than the sometimes minor nominations they received. The sad fact is that Robinson's acting was never nominated by the Academy of Motion Picture Arts and Sciences during his six-decade career. Charles Matthews, in his book *The Oscar A to Z*, notes that for *Double Indemnity* in particular, "the absence from the supporting actor nominees of Robinson ... is one of the Academy's worst sins of omission." Matthews maintains that Robinson was "infinitely preferable to cuddly old Monty Woolley, nominated for *Since You Went Away,* or for that matter, Barry Fitzgerald's lovable priest in *Going My Way*." Fitzgerald's win in 1944 for best supporting actor doubtless was helped by losing to Bing Crosby as best actor for the same film; Fitzgerald's was the only performance ever nominated in *both* acting categories; thereafter the Academy rules were changed.

The Oscar statuette was used as a prop in *Two Weeks in Another Town* in 1962.

See also **National Board of Review**; **Cannes Film Festival**; **Antoinette Perry (Tony) Award**.

Academy of Motion Picture Arts and Sciences Awards (36th Annual)

(Television, 1964) At the ceremonies recognizing 1963 achievements, Edward G. Robinson was the presenter of Oscars for writing to James R. Webb, for the best original screenplay for *How the West Was Won*, and to John Osborne for the best screenplay based on material from another medium, for *Tom Jones*.

Producer, George Sidney; director, Richard Dunlap; writers, George Axelrod, Richard Breen, Mort Lachman, Stanley Roberts, Melville Shavelson; music, John Green; participants: Julie Andrews, Annabella, Anne Bancroft, Anne Baxter, Ed Begley, James Darren, Sammy Davis Jr., Brandon DeWilde, Angie Dickinson, Patty Duke, Dame Edith Evans, Federico Fellini, Arthur Freed, Rita Hayworth, Rock Hudson, Shirley Jones, Jack Lemmon, Jack Lord, Shirley MacLaine, Fred MacMurray, Steve McQueen, Gregory Peck, David V. Picker, Sidney Poitier, Harve Presnell, Katina Ranieri, Donna Reed, Debbie Reynolds, Edward G. Robinson, Frank Sinatra, Sam Spiegel, James Stewart, Peter Ustinov, Tuesday Weld, Andy Williams; Santa Monica (California) Civic Auditorium; ABC-TV, April 13, 1964

Academy of Motion Picture Arts and Sciences Awards (45th Annual)

(Television, 1973) Edward G. Robinson's honorary Academy Award was presented posthumously at the Oscar ceremonies for 1972 films. Ironically, the best actor award to Marlon Brando as Don Corleone in *The Godfather* was for a role for which Robinson had been considered; moreover, the film was significant in the gangster genre, which had started with Robinson's *Little Caesar* forty years earlier. In his autobiography, Robinson referred to *The Godfather* as "my grandchild."

The award was presented on March 27, two months after the actor's death from cancer on January 26, 1973. Two elements outside his career were recognized in the citation — his long standing as a collector of fine art, and, perhaps more meaningfully, his patriotism, which had been subjected to stressful scrutiny during the Red scare in the 1950s. The inscription read, "To Edward G. Robinson, who achieved greatness as a player, a patron of the arts and a dedicated citizen ... in sum, a Renaissance man. From his friends in the industry he loves."

Jane Robinson accepted the Academy Award for her late husband; the acceptance speech was brief: "Thank you. My husband knew he was to be honored tonight. May I read what he wrote: 'It couldn't have come at a better time in a man's life. Had it come earlier, it would have aroused deep feelings in me. Still, not so deep as now. I am so very grateful to my rich, warm, creative, talented, intimate colleagues who have been my life's associates. How much richer can you be?' Thank you for Eddie."

The *St. Louis Post-Dispatch* called the presentation "the evening's most sentimental moment ... [Robinson] received the Oscar in the hospital just before his death early this year."

A story was widely circulated at the time that Robinson's Academy Award would be presented at the ceremonies by Sir Laurence Olivier. Leonard Spigelgass, who, after Robinson's death, had finished writing *All My Yesterdays,* the actor's autobiography, claimed he *invented* the story about Olivier as a white lie to Robinson who had asked — from his hospital bed — who the presenter would be.

The Oscar was presented by Charlton Heston. He was scheduled as one of the co-hosts for the telecast but had a flat tire on the way and arrived almost forty-five minutes late. Clint Eastwood substituted until his arrival, stumbling nervously over Heston's cue cards.

The presentation of Robinson's posthumous Oscar was preceded by film clips that were introduced with a voiceover by James Cagney. Included were brief segments from the silent picture *The Bright Shawl*, and the as-yet-unreleased *Soylent Green*. Filming on the latter, in which Heston co-starred, had been completed only two months prior to Robinson's hospitalization over New Year's, 1973.

Producer, Howard W. Koch; director, Marty Pasetta; writers, William Ludwig, Leonard Spigelgass; music, John Williams; participants: Eddie Albert, Edward Albert, Julie Andrews, Beatrice Arthur, Marisa Berenson, Candice Bergen, Cher, Sonny Bono, Charles A. Boren (honorary award for 38 years in the film industry's labor relations), Peter Boyle, Carol Burnett, James Cagney (recorded voice), Michael Caine, Glen Campbell, Dyan Cannon, Macdonald Carey, Dihann Carroll, Maria Cruz (an American Indian actress, a.k.a. Sacheen Littlefeather, rejecting Marlon Brando's best actor award as a protest against the film industry's treatment of Indians in films), Mike Curb Congregation, Robert Duvall, Clint Eastwood, Bob Fosse, Greer Garson, John Gavin, Joel Grey (best performance by a supporting actor, for *Cabaret*), Gene Hackman, Laurence Harvey, Eileen Heckart (best performance by a supporting actress, for *Butterflies Are Free*), Charlton Heston (host), Rock Hudson, Michael Jackson, Angela Lansbury, Cloris Leachman, Jack Lemmon, Liza Minelli (best performance by an actress, for *Cabaret*), Roger Moore, Merle Oberon, Burt Reynolds, Jane (Mrs. Edward G.) Robinson, Katharine Ross, Albert Ruddy, Rosalind Russell (Jean Hersholt Humanitarian Award), Frank Sinatra, Elke Sommer, Springfield Revival, Connie Stevens, George Stevens, Daniel Taradash, Liv Ullman, Jack Valenti, Robert Wagner, Richard Walsh, Raquel Welch, Billy Dee Williams, Natalie Wood; Dorothy Chandler Pavilion, Los Angeles; NBC-TV, March 27, 1973

Accidents Dramatic plot development often relies on the unexpected, so the definition of "accident" could cover many events in Edward G. Robinson's films and plays. A number of specific accidents do occur, however.

In *A Lady to Love* Robinson is crippled in an accident on his way to pick up his bride at the train station, but fatal accidents are not uncommon in the Robinson canon. The crash of an elevated train kills Madame Mystera, a member of Robinson's gang, in *The Hole in the Wall*. James Cagney's character is accidentally killed in a fistfight with Robinson in *Smart Money*; it is treated as manslaughter. Preston Foster argues with Robinson while they are working high up on a skyscraper, then falls to his death in *Two Seconds*. Robinson first loses a hand, and then his life, to a *Tiger Shark*. In *Manpower*, a film with a very similar plotline, he is first crippled in an accident involving a power line, then falls to his death at the film's conclusion.

In *The Stranger* Robinson's character is distinctly accident prone, as he first breaks his pipe while making an emphatic gesture, then tumbles down a flight of stairs and, later still, nearly falls from a ladder whose rung has been sawed through (to make any injury *look* like an accident). The murderers in *Double Indemnity* try to make their victim's death look like an accident.

Fortuitously, accidentally cutting his hand on the wire of a champagne bottle affords Robinson availability of a weapon (scissors) to defend himself against the man who would, in turn, kill him in *The Woman in the Window*. More happily, Frau Ehrlich lights a stove in her husband's lab and by accident adds heat — a needed element — for an experiment in *Dr. Ehrlich's Magic Bullet*. In *Larceny, Inc.* Robinson and his henchmen use the scam of allowing themselves to be "accidentally" hit by a car, then collecting from the driver.

A real-life auto accident in June 1966 nearly claimed Robinson's life. He was driving near his home in Beverly Hills when, perhaps having fallen asleep, he hit a tree. Extensive facial and abdominal surgery was required, but three weeks later, at the age of 73, Robinson walked out of the hospital on his own, carrying under his arm a get-well gift from Frank Sinatra — a skateboard!

See also **Illnesses**.

Acting and Actors   Edward G. Robinson's interest in acting began when he joined the Elizabethan Society while studying at the College of the City of New York. His audition was a reading of Marc Antony's soliloquy from *Julius Caesar*. In his junior year he left to attend the American Academy of Dramatic Arts, graduating in 1913. George Arliss was the commencement speaker. Rosalind Russell has noted that Robinson returned to the Academy in 1929 to speak at her commencement exercises.

Robinson played actors onscreen in *The Man with Two Faces, Actors and Sin,* and *The Prize*, and when he appeared as himself in *It's a Great Feeling, Pepe* and *Mooch*.

Several actors have discussed Robinson as a performer, often linking him with others of his generation.

George C. Scott: "The actors I admired were all character actors — Muni, Tracy, Cagney, Robinson ... I was brought up on the movies; they kept me off the streets and out of poolrooms. I found myself walking down the street like Cagney and doing his famous spring-heeled glide; or even adopting the explosion technique of Robinson. He would blow up certain words in a sentence, adjectives particularly...."

Scott's appreciation is revealed further in William Goldman's book about Broadway, *The Season*. Scott was directing Burl Ives in *Dr. Cook's Garden*: "He [Ives] looks great, speaks well, he's warm, easy to love, etc. What's working against him is this incredible lack of acting ability. He's a personality, and nothing I did seemed to help ... I said to Saint [Subber, the producer], 'Let me try for Eddie Robinson, Charles Boyer; let me get an actor so I can *talk* to him.'"

Richard Burton: "The main thing about acting is luck, to be born with the proper set of shoulders; to be as enormous as John Wayne, to be beautifully ugly as Humphrey Bogart was; as short, squat and vital as James Cagney; as solid as Eddie Robinson. Most importantly, you must have that particular compulsion for an audience, and it is productive if you can tell the imagination of that audience."

Donald Pleasence: "The American movies of the early thirties in particular had a very strong effect on me. I used to devour the gangster ones and the prison ones ... I was very much impressed by Hollywood actors Edward G. Robinson and Thomas Mitchell, but I really didn't appreciate them until later."

Helen Hayes (in a telegram when Robinson received the Screen Actors Guild award in 1969): "I hold in special high esteem those actors, like Eddie, who have always been good stewards of their God-given talents. Tell him I love him."

Ben Gazzara: "...Going to the movies to see the actors who had become my favorites —

Spencer Tracy, Clark Gable, James Cagney, and Edward G. Robinson ... John Garfield."

See also individual actors who appeared with Robinson.

Actors and Sin (Film, 1952) Edward G. Robinson was absent from American movie screens for nearly three years from 1949 to 1952, discounting the British *Operation X* and a cameo role in *It's a Great Feeling*. Part of the time he was on tour with the national company of the play *Darkness at Noon*, but it was doubtless the best film work Robinson could get in Hollywood at the time because of his problems with the House Un-American Activities Committee. *Actors and Sin* was his second picture with Marsha Hunt, a decade after *Unholy Partners*. She plays his daughter, both of them stage actors, in the first half of the picture, entitled "Actors' Blood."

"Actor's Blood" is a look at Broadway. Marcia Tillayou, a temperamental and fading stage star, is found dead in her New York apartment. Her story is narrated in flashback by her former husband, Alfred O'Shea, a writer. She has alienated herself from everyone but her doting father, a hammy Shakespearean, Maurice Tillayou. He plans to name her killer at a dinner party, but instead, in a grand gesture, he stabs himself as the lights go out. Sadly, the mystery is that Maurice, unable to admit Marcia's failure, wanted to make his daughter's suicide look like murder. "Woman of Sin," the second part of the film, is a satire on Hollywood. Fast-talking agent Orlando Higgens sells a screenplay about a seamy romance to a big studio. After the film is completed, Higgens blackmails the studio head, J. B. Cobb, into offering a five-year contract to its author, Daisy Marcher, a nine-year-old girl!

Benjamin B. Smith presents a Sid Kuller production; producer, director, screenplay, Ben Hecht; executive producer, Sid Kuller; co-director, Lee Garmes; set decorator, Howard Bristol; music, George Antheil; editors, Otto Ludwig, Jack Gleason; production supervisor, Ben Hersh; sound, Victor Appel, Mac Dalgleish; production design, Ernst Fegte; makeup, Gus Norin; assistant directors, Richard McWhorter, Ralph Hoge; assistant producer, Robert Justman; electrician, Victor V. Jones; cast "Actor's Blood": Edward G. Robinson (Maurice Tillayou), Marsha Hunt (Marcia Tillayou), Dan O'Herlihy (Alfred O'Shea), Rudolph Anders (Otto Lachsley), Alice Key (Tommy), Rick Roman (Clyde Veerling), Peter Brocco (Mr. Herbert), Elizabeth Root (Mrs. Herbert), Joe Mell (George Massy), Irene Martin (Mrs. Massy), Herb Bernard (Emile), Robert Carson (Thomas Hayne); "Woman of Sin": Eddie Albert (Orlando Higgens), Alan Reed (J. B. Cobb), Tracey Roberts (Miss Flannigan), Jenny Hecht (Daisy Marcher), Paul Guilfoyle (Mr. Blue), Doug Evans (Mr. Devlin), Jody Gilbert (Mrs. Egelhofer), John Crawford (Movie Hero), George Baxter (Mr. Brown), George Keymas (Producer), Toni Carroll (Movie Star), Alan Mendez (Moriarty), Kathleen Mulqueen (Miss Wright), Sam Rosen (Joseph Danello); United Artists, 85 minutes; May, 1952

In Doug McClelland's *Hollywood Talks Turkey,* Marsha Hunt charitably refers to *Actors and Sin* as "one of the most unusual films I ever did, and an interesting one ... a drama about the theatre with Edward G. Robinson (an irreplaceable man and artist) ... shot in five days!" Hunt continues: "Why didn't *Actors and Sin* do better? Several of us on the production were known to be liberals, an extremely unpopular belief at that time. Also, the picture was produced on such a shoestring that there was no money for promotion."

In addition, *Actors and Sin* seemed to insult Hollywood, at least in its second half about moviemaking. An article in *The New York Times* in July 1952 tells of a legal battle between United Artists / Sid Kuller Productions and the A.B.C. Theatres Company over alleged refusal to play the picture "on the ground that it lampooned Hollywood and its moviemakers." One of the defendants in the suit was quoted, "Mr. Hecht went too far with his satire."

The reviews generally were negative. *The New York Times* called *Actors and Sin* "a stiff, glum, and narcissistic tale," adding that, "Robinson and Marsha Hunt ... bleakly intone Mr. Hecht's sonorous dialogue." James

Robert Parish in *The Tough Guys* called it "middling screen fare," and Lindsay Anderson referred to the film as "a depressing double bill."

Ad Ogni Costo see ***Grand Slam***

Adam, Ronald (1896–1979) a British writer and character actor, made three films with Edward G. Robinson—*Journey Together, Operation X,* and *Song of Norway.* His other films include *Escape to Danger, Cleopatra, The Tomb of Ligeia,* and *Zeppelin.*

Adams, Stanley (1915–77) appeared in more than 35 films and played the gangster Hammy in *Hell on Frisco Bay* with Edward G. Robinson. His other pictures include *Breakfast at Tiffany's, Requiem for a Heavyweight,* and *Thunder Alley.*

The Adding Machine (Theater, 1923) Edward G. Robinson commented, "Playing in the original production of *The Adding Machine* was a most memorable event in my career. It was very much avant garde in its day and contained any number of innovations by Elmer Rice, who was an extraordinary playwright." Robinson was particularly impressed by the play's symbolism and its enduring topicality. The play was one of his earliest critical successes, his fourteenth professional stage appearance in ten years, and only his second venture with the Theatre Guild.

Ludwig Lewisohn, in *The Nation,* qualified the play's success: "Mr. Rice's vision of the world may infuriate you. There were people behind me at the Garrick Theatre who first grumbled and then cursed politely. You cannot miss it; you cannot withdraw yourself from its coherence and completeness. Examine his play scene by scene, symbol by symbol. The structure stands.... It gives you the pleasure of both poetry and science, the warm beauty of life and love, the icy delight of mathematics ... here is an American drama with no loose ends or silly last-act compromises, retractions, reconciliations. The work, on its own ground, in its own mood, is honest, finished, sound." Lewisohn continued, "Mr. Edgar [sic] G. Robinson ... contributes to the strange eloquence of this play and production, which constitute without question one of the major achievements in the entire field of the American arts."

"The acting was excellent throughout," said *The New York Times.* "Excellent ... it need hardly be said, is Robinson." Further, the *Times* called *The Adding Machine* "the best and fairest example yet of the newer expressionism in the theatre." *The Oxford Companion to the American Theatre* calls it "perhaps the most famous and completely successful expressionistic play in our literature."

When Mr. Zero is told that he is to be fired from his accounting job (to be replaced by a modern adding machine), he murders the boss. He is tried and executed and progresses through the hereafter via the grave and the Elysian Fields. In the course of Mr. Zero's journey he encounters a complex soul named Shrdlu, who cannot comprehend having murdered his own mother with a carving knife instead of slicing the Thanksgiving turkey. Mr. Zero works briefly at a giant adding machine, but he is subsequently returned to earth. His soul has been recycled.

A tragedy in seven scenes, produced by the Theatre Guild; playwright, producer, Elmer Rice; director, Philip Moeller; settings and costumes, Lee Simonson; incidental music, Deems Taylor; cast: Dudley Digges (Mr. Zero), Helen Westley (Mrs. Zero), Margaret Wycherly (Daisy Diana Dorothea Devore), Edward G. Robinson (Shrdlu), Elise Bartlett (Judy O'Grady), Louis Calvert (Lt. Charles), Irving Dillon (The Boss, Policeman), Gerald Lundegard (Young Man, Mr. Three), William W. Griffith (Joe, Mr. Five), Daniel Hamilton (A Head, Mr. Six), Harry McKenna (Mr. One), Marcia Harris (Mrs. One), Paul Hayes (Mr. Two), Therese Stewart (Mrs. Two), Georgiana Wilson (Mrs. Three), George Stehli (Mr. Four), Edith Burnett (Mrs. Four), Ruby Craven (Mrs. Five), Louise Sydmeth (Mrs. Six), Lewis Barrington; opened at the Garrick Theatre, New York; March 19, 1923 (72 performances)

Adler, Jay (1896–1978) appeared in Yiddish and English stage productions before coming to films in 1938. He is in *The Juggler, Sweet Smell of Success, The Brothers Karamazov*, and two with Edward G. Robinson — *Vice Squad,* as Frankie Pierce, an informer, and *Illegal*, in which he plays Carter, a jailed defendant.

Adler, Luther (1903–84) played Joe, eldest of Edward G. Robinson's four sons, in *House of Strangers,* and he and his wife, Sylvia Sidney, were in the tribute *We Will Never Die.* The son of Yiddish-American actor Jacob Adler, he is the brother of actors Stella and Jay. Films include *The Desert Fox, The Last Angry Man,* and *The Man in the Glass Booth.*

Advertising Robinson and his wife, Gladys Lloyd, were photographed for a full-page color magazine ad for Pabst Blue Ribbon beer in the 1940s. In another black and white magazine ad, in a tie-in with the film *The Stranger,* Stratford pens and pencils were touted, along with Robinson, as "reliable performers."

Claudette Colbert, Barbara Stanwyck, and Edward G. Robinson sold Maxwell House Coffee via television commercials in 1964. He spoofed his gangster image by snarling at the camera to potential coffee buyers, "Now do it my way, see," then adding with a smile, "You'll enjoy it." Robinson also did in-house commercials for Anheuser-Busch and Wilkinson Sword Blades.

Some years after suffering a heart attack on location in Africa in 1962, Robinson agreed to do a print ad for the American Stair-Glide Corporation, makers of staircase elevators. The ad copy read, "Save Your Heart," and showed Robinson riding the elevator in his home. Unfortunately, the advertisements were published in magazines several months after he had died.

Some of the poster advertisements for Robinson's early films were misleading, doubtless to sensationalize their stories for the public. *A Slight Case of Murder* was called "the story of the mobster who killed and laughed," although Robinson's character did not commit the murder of the title. *Thunder in the City,* an airy British comedy about sales and industry (with a send-up of advertising as well), had a poster with the strangely dramatic legend, "Lashing your emotions with the fury of a thunderbolt!"

Advertising was key to the plot of two of Robinson's 1960s comedies. Jack Lemmon comes up with a billboard campaign to sell the wholesome image of Robinson's dairy products in *Good Neighbor Sam;* and in *The Biggest Bundle of Them All,* Robinson demonstrates the Madison Avenue approach to pulling off a heist, using an easel and placards as visual aids.

Airplanes According to Gene Brown's *Movie Time,* on Valentine's Day 1946, Edward G. Robinson was aboard the first TWA Constellation flight from Los Angeles to New York. Also aboard were Paulette Goddard, Cary Grant, Alfred Hitchcock, Bugsy Siegel, Lana Turner, and Howard Hughes, who was the pilot.

Air travel is not common in Edward G. Robinson's films. Advertising is done by airplane in *Thunder in the City.* Bugs Ahearn's mob is transported from Chicago to the west coast by plane in *The Little Giant.* Robinson's character takes a trans–Atlantic flight that goes down at sea at the end of *Unholy Partners.* More significantly, Robinson played a U.S. Air Force flying instructor in *Journey Together.*

Robinson sees the New York skyline during a flight from Rio de Janiero in *Grand Slam.* The end of *The Biggest Bundle of Them All* takes place aboard a rickety plane carrying stolen platinum. In an effort to lower the landing gear, the pilot mistakenly opens the cargo hold and the platinum falls out of the plane.

Finally, in *Tales of Manhattan* the tailcoat that is the link between the five stories of the title is stolen from a pawnshop and used in a casino robbery. J. Carroll Naish, as the thief, flies to Mexico in a biplane. Lightning strikes, and the coat, with the money, catches fire and is discarded; it lands in a rocky field, which is the setting for the last episode.

Alberni, Luis (1887–1962) a Spanish character actor, is in two films with Edward G. Robinson — *The Bright Shawl* (as Vincente Escobar) and *The Ten Commandments* (as an old Hebrew). He is also in *Roberta, Anthony Adverse,* and *That Hamilton Woman.*

Albert, Eddie (1908–) a circus performer, and radio and stage actor, appeared with Edward G. Robinson in *A Dispatch from Reuter's* and *Actors and Sin*, and was also on the *45th Academy Awards*. He was nominated for Oscars for *Roman Holiday* and *The Heartbreak Kid*. His wife was the actress Margo, and their son is actor Edward Albert.

Aldrich, Robert (1918–83) worked as a script clerk, assistant director, production manager, and associate producer before directing the baseball film *Big Leaguer,* starring Edward G. Robinson. He produced and directed such features as *The Big Knife, Whatever Happened to Baby Jane?, Hush ... Hush Sweet Charlotte,* and *Flight of the Phoenix.*

Alexander, John (1897–1982) was the "Teddy" Roosevelt on Broadway and in the film version of *Arsenic and Old Lace*. On TV in *The Right Man* Edward G. Robinson is Roosevelt while Alexander plays Wendell Willkie. He appears with Robinson as a murder suspect in *Night Has a Thousand Eyes*. Other films include *The Petrified Forest* and *A Tree Grows in Brooklyn.*

Alias Jimmy Valentine (Theater, 1913) Following his professional theater debut in Albany, New York, in 1913, Edward G. Robinson went to Cincinnati to appear in stock. In the four-act melodrama *Alias Jimmy Valentine*, by Paul Armstrong, he doubled in two roles — as a sneak thief and a bank clerk. He was billed as E. Gould Robinson and Edward Gould Robinson, respectively, arbitrary name changes made by the theater manager. The play, originally presented in New York in January 1910, is based on an O. Henry short story. It tells of a trusted bank employee who tries to hide his past as a safecracker. *The Oxford Companion to the American Theatre* calls *Alias Jimmy Valentine* "a fast-moving, if transparent melodrama."

According to a plot summary in Burns Mantle's *Best Plays of 1921–22,* "Lee Randall, a gentleman safe breaker, is released from Sing Sing through the influence of the lieutenant-governor's daughter, Rose Lane, whom he had befriended. Determined to go straight, Randall (alias Jimmy Valentine) fights off his tempting crook friends and eludes the police, who are unable to break down his perfect alibi — until the little daughter of his employer gets herself locked in the bank vault. Then Jimmy risks re-arrest by opening the vault. The detective sees him, but turns his back. And Jimmy marries Rose."

Produced by the Orpheum Players; playwright, Paul Armstrong; based on a short story, "A Retrieved Reformation," by O. Henry; cast: Edward G. Robinson (Dick the Rat; Williams); Cincinnati, Ohio; 1913 (22 weeks)

All About People (Short film, 1967) This film was about the Jewish Foundation Council and the United Jewish Welfare Fund.

Producer, Saul Rubin; associate producer, Louis Rudolph; Lucille Ball, Jack Benny, George Burns, Carol Channing, Henry Fonda, Eydie Gorme, Charlton Heston, Eartha Kitt, Burt Lancaster, Edward G. Robinson (narrators); United Jewish Welfare Fund; 30 minutes; 1967

All My Sons (Film, 1948) Arthur Miller's first Broadway play, *All My Sons*, was a triumph, winning for him the Pulitzer Prize for literature. Concerned with a man who is confronted by his son for war profiteering, the play seems to have become more timely with the passing years as it balances questions of moral guilt with corporate power. Edward G. Robinson played the lead role of the father, Joe Keller, in the 1948 film version of the play, with Burt Lancaster as his son, Chris. The screenplay was adapted by producer Chester Erskine. In 1986 the play's script was filmed for television with James Whitmore and Aidan Quinn.

This "may well be Robinson's finest performance," wrote Foster Hirsch in his study on the actor for *The Pyramid Illustrated History of the Movies*. "As he gets underneath the mask of confidence and good cheer ... Robinson is immense. He approaches the character sympathetically. His character is not a villain ... but a decent man corrupted by superficial values.... A stubborn fighter who celebrates the Protestant ethic of hard work, he doesn't yield until he's forced to face his responsibility for his son's death. That moment of recognition when he sees, perhaps for the first time, exactly what his values have made him, is Robinson's finest movie moment. As he climbs the stairs, the lifeblood drained from him, Robinson is moving and human in a way that movies had never let him be before."

Robinson was proud of his work in the film. Burt Lancaster campaigned to land the role of Chris because he wanted the chance to break away from crime films. Shot in 43 days, the location work was done at Santa Rosa, California, north of San Francisco.

All My Sons was Louisa Horton's first film; she played the role of Ann Deever. Interviewed by Harry Haun in the *New York Daily News* in 1989, she commented on the filming. She felt strongly that her character wouldn't step aside for anything, she said, when the director asked her to move away so he could get the camera in for a close-up. "That's when Robinson took me aside and gave me a wonderful talk," she said, "without hurting my feelings. He said, 'I can see you're serious about your work, but this is film, and if the director wants you to say 'I love you more than life itself' standing on the mantelpiece, you ought to be able to deliver that and mean it. He needs to get that camera in for certain shots.'

"He told me this story about visiting Matisse's studio once when the artist was doing a line drawing of a mother and child:

"Looking through the drawings, he came to one, and he said, 'This is it. Why did you even bother to go further?' And Matisse said, 'Oh, but that's only the seventeenth.'

"Robinson then said to me, 'I want you to go home, and I want you to do this scene seventeen different ways, and you'll find you can move anywhere and still say the line and be the character.'"

Producer, screenplay, Chester Erskine; director, Irving Reis; based on the play by Arthur Miller; art directors, Bernard Herzbrun, Hilyard Brown; camera, Russell Metty; set, Russell A. Gausman, Al Fields; sound, Leslie I. Carey, Corson Jowett; editor, Ralph Dawson; music, Leith Stevens; orchestra, David Tamkin; costumes, Grace Houston; makeup, David S. Horsley; hairstyles, Carmen Dirigo; assistant director, Frank Shaw; cast: Edward G. Robinson (Joe Keller), Burt Lancaster (Chris Keller), Mady Christians (Kate Keller), Louisa Horton (Ann Deever), Howard Duff (George Deever), Frank Conroy (Herb Deever), Lloyd Gough (Jim Bayliss), Arlene Francis (Sue Bayliss), Harry Morgan (Frank Lubey), Elisabeth Fraser (Lydia Lubey), Helen Brown (Mrs. Hamilton), Pat Flaherty (Bartender), William Johnstone (Attorney), Jerry Hausner (Halliday), Charles Meredith (Ellsworth), Walter Soderling (Charley), George Sorel (Headwaiter), Herb Vigran (Wertheimer), Therese Lyons (Minnie), Harry Harvey (Judge), Joseph Kerr (Norton), Frank Krieg (Foreman), William Ruhl (Ed), Al Murphy (Tom), Walter Bonn (Jorgenson), Jack Gargan (Workman), Victor Zimmerman, George Slocum (Attendants), Richard LaMarr [Robinson's stand-in] (Bill); Universal-International; 94 minutes; March, 1948

Joe Keller, an appliance manufacturer, has been exonerated during a trial on the allegation his company built and shipped defective airplane cylinders to the Army Air Force during World War II. The faulty aircraft resulted in twenty-one pilot deaths. Joe's partner, Herb Deever, was convicted and is serving time in prison. Suspicions are renewed about Joe's involvement when Chris, his son, now plans to marry Deever's daughter, Ann. The Kellers and Deevers had been neighbors, and their children grew up together. Ann had been engaged to Larry Keller, Joe's elder son, but Larry has been missing in action for three years following the war; and Kate, Joe's wife, says that if Chris and Ann marry, it will be a pronouncement of Larry's death. Ann's brother, George, demands that she leave town with him, declaring that "everything they [the Kellers] have is touched with blood." After Chris visits Herb Deever in jail, his doubts about his father increase. Joe finally admits guilt when he is confronted, justifying that what he did was to save his business and family. Ann shows Kate a letter from Larry saying he will not return from an upcoming flying mission because of his shame at reading in the newspaper about his father's actions. Chris now shows Larry's letter to Joe. The letter not only confirms Larry's death, but it makes Joe see that some things — such as commitment to country — can be bigger than the family. Instead of turning himself in, Joe commits suicide. Chris and Ann go off to be married, with Kate's blessing.

Reviews of the film were good to mixed. According to *The New York Herald-Tribune*, "While there are scenes of fine indignation ... realized to the full by Edward G. Robinson, Burt Lancaster, Mady Christians and Frank Conroy, they do not offset fabricated situations and blurred characterizations."

A reaction from Arthur Miller was glum: "The director ... tells you that this is sinister or that this is good news or this is whatever. The picture tells you after fifteen minutes that Joe is guilty, and so what is there to wait for?" Neither Robinson nor Miller needed unfavorable notices at the time, since in the real world both were caught up in the House Un-American Activities Committee's witch hunt for Communists in the arts.

The New York Times commentary glowed: "...A fine performance by Edward G. Robinson.... [He] does a superior job of showing the shades of personality in a little tough guy who has a softer side.... Clearly he reveals the blank bewilderment of a man who can't conceive in the abstract the basic moral obligation of the individual to society."

And *Variety* praised the actor: "It's a humanized study that rates among [Robinson's] best and lends the thought behind the film much strength."

"All My Sons"   (Radio, 1948, 1949) Edward G. Robinson performed in two radio adaptations of the Arthur Miller play.

Cast: Edward G. Robinson (Joe Keller), Burt Lancaster (Chris Keller); *Camel's Screen Guild Players*; NBC; November 11, 1948

Cast: Edward G. Robinson (Joe Keller); Jeff Chandler (Chris Keller), Irene Tedrow, Jack Edwards, Jimmy Wallington (announcer); 30 minutes; *Screen Director's Playhouse*; NBC; December 2, 1949

All My Yesterdays   Edward G. Robinson's autobiography, *All My Yesterdays*, written with Leonard Spigelgass, was published by Hawthorn Books in 1973. Spigelgass was collaborating with Robinson on the writing, but with the actor's untimely death, he finished from notes.

The work was well received, with such comments as TV *Radio Mirror*'s "a beautiful book written with great sensitivity by a great man" and by *Daily Variety*, "It reveals Robinson as the kind of human being he was at heart — very different from the gangster roles that brought him fame. The autobiography also is an authoritative contribution to Hollywood history. It is an unusually frank story, told without glamorization or dramatization, letting the facts speak for themselves." *The Philadelphia Bulletin* called the book "a front row look at sixty years of the movies and theater by one of its great stars"; and *Publishers Weekly* found it "an engrossing personal document reflecting its author's deep love for, and knowledge of, the art of acting."

Finally, *Variety* said, "The most riveting sections ... concern the actor's long and ultimately victorious battle with the House Un-American Activities Committee during a period in Hollywood history that even today is rarely discussed openly."

See also **Biographies**.

Allen, Lewis   (1905–86) A former stage actor in England, he directed American films beginning with *The Uninvited* in 1943. Others include *Our Hearts Were Young and Gay*, *Desert Fury*, *Valentino*, *Suddenly*, and two with Edward G. Robinson — *A Bullet for Joey* and *Illegal*.

Alternate Titles   Great Britain often substituted different titles for American films: *Port of Wickedness* (*Barbary Coast*), *The Girl in Room 17* (*Vice Squad*), *Rough Company* (*The Violent Men*), *That Man Reuter* (*A Dispatch from Reuter's*), *My Daughter Joy* (*Operation X*). *Kid Galahad* became *The Battling Bellhop* when the original title was used for an Elvis Presley remake in 1962. *Operazione San Pietro*, *Uno Scacco Tutto Matto*, *It's Your Move*, *Une Blonde de Pekin*, and *Ad Ogni Costo* are variations of titles of Italian, Spanish, and/or French films Robinson made in the late 1960s. *Judgment in the Sun* was the original working title for *The Outrage*, which, of course, is based on the Japanese film *Rashomon*; and *Cheyenne Autumn* had the working title *The Lost Flight*.

Others alternative titles include *The Mouthpiece* (*Illegal*); *Arms and the Woman* (the title of Robinson's first silent film in 1916, somehow substituted for *Mr. Winkle Goes to War*); *The Honorable Mr. Wong* (*The Hatchet Man*); *Thorn: 2022* (*Soylent Green*); plus these books and plays as the basis for retitled screenplays: *Tuna* (*Tiger Shark*); *Sammy Going South* (*A Boy Ten Feet Tall*); *Make Room, Make Room!* (*Soylent Green*); *Lions at the Kill* (*Seven Thieves*); *The Night Before Christmas* (*Larceny, Inc.*); *The Dark Tower* (*The Man with Two Faces*); *I'll Never Go There Again* (*House of Strangers*); *The Nazi Spy Conspiracy in America* (*Confessions of a Nazi Spy*); *Once Off Guard* (*The Woman in the Window*); *La Chienne* (*Scarlet Street*); *For Our Vines Have Tender Grapes* (*Our Vines Have Tender Grapes*); and *Red Meat* (*I Loved a Woman*).

The Amazing Dr. Clitterhouse (Film, 1938) This 1938 film featured Claire Trevor as Robinson's onscreen leading lady for the first time, fresh from their first year co-starring in the *Big Town* series on radio. Humphrey Bogart was pitted against Robinson for the third time; and John Huston began his four-picture association with Robinson, as screenwriter. At one point William Faulkner worked on a treatment of the film's script, entitled *Fog Over London*, but his writing was deemed too somber and went unused. The film was based on a play that came from the London stage via New York and starred Sir Cedric Hardwicke. Perhaps because critics were not yet recognizing Edward G. Robinson's versatility as an actor, there were silly reviews of the film comparing him with Hardwicke, insisting that the gangster image got in the way. However, Robert Bookbinder, in *Classics of the Gangster Film*, called *The Amazing Dr. Clitterhouse* "memorable for Robinson's excellent performance in the title role." He also noted that the film was "blessed with a title that no one could forget." Bogart, playing his usual nasty thug and still three years away from stardom, referred to the film as *The Amazing Dr. Clitoris*.

Associate producer, Robert Lord; director, Anatole Litrak; screenplay, John Wexley, John Huston; based on the play by Barre Lyndon; art director, Carl Jules Weyl; music, Max Steiner; sound, C. A. Riggs; camera, Tony Gaudio; costumes, Milo Anderson; editor, Warren Low; assistant director, Jack Sullivan; cast: Edward G. Robinson (Dr. Clitterhouse), Claire Trevor (Jo Keller), Humphrey Bogart (Rocks Valentine), Donald Crisp (Inspector Lane), Gale Page (Nurse Randolph), Allen Jenkins (Okay), Thurston Hall (Grant), Maxie Rosenbloom (Butch), John Litel (Prosecutor), Henry O'Neill (Judge), Curt Bois (Rabbit), Bert Hanlon (Pal), Ward Bond (Tug), Vladimir Sokoloff (Popus), Billy Wayne (Candy), Irving Bacon (Jury Foreman), William Haade (Watchman), Thomas Jackson (Connors), Edward Gargan (Sergeant), Robert Homans (Lt. Johnson), Romaine Callender (Roberts, the butler), Georgia Caine (Mrs. Updike), Mary Field (Maid), Winifred Harris (Mrs. Ganswoort), Eric Stanley (Dr. Ames), Lois Cheaney (Nurse), Wade Boteler (Captain MacLevy), Libby Taylor (Mrs. Jefferson), Sidney Bracey (Chemist), Vera Lewis (Juror), Edgar Dearing (Patrolman), Ray Dawe, Bob Reeves (Policemen), Ed Mortimer, Larry Steers, William Worthington (Guests), Bruce Mitchell (Bailiff); Ronald Reagan (Announcer), Susan Hayward (Patient), Frank Anthony, Earl Devine, Frank Fanning, John Harron, Mike Lally, Al Lloyd, Monte Vandergrift, Ky Robinson, Joyce Williams; Warner Bros.; 87 minutes; July, 1938

Dr. Clitterhouse, a prominent physician, burglarizes the homes of his society acquaintances and later "fences" the loot through a local gang solely as criminology research for a forthcoming book. He teams up with Jo Keller and studies the physical reactions of members of her mob during robberies. Jealous of the attention Jo gives the doctor, gang member Rocks Valentine tries to kill Clitterhouse by locking him in a cold storage vault during a fur robbery. Later, his work finished, the doctor quits the gang. When Rocks attempts to blackmail him, Dr. Clitterhouse does unanticipated further research by committing the ultimate crime. In his trial for murdering Rocks, the jury acquits him, reasoning Clitterhouse must be insane to be proclaiming his sanity (in authoring his book) when only a plea of insanity could save his life.

According to *The New York Herald-Tribune*, Robinson "performs the assignment capably. Perhaps it is because he has been so clearly identified with gangster roles that he has trouble in underlining the Jekyll and Hyde quality.... In any case, he never fails to give the picture dramatic punch." Less praise came from the *New York Times*: "He never quite succeeds in shaking the role free from the shadowy Public Enemies, Nos. 1 to 10 which have been the larger part of his past." Carlos Clarens, however, in *Crime Movies*, notes that the "indispensable Edward G. Robinson, now eons away from Rico Bandello, is a Manhattan doctor...."

"From the first sequence, a fancy party attending to a florid soprano singing "Una voce poco fa" from *The Barber of Seville* (but note the filleted version—Warners is still moving quickly, can't waste a moment), we ... see the world through leadership-class eyes. Like Robinson's Dr. Clitterhouse, we are not partakers but witnesses."—Ethan Mordden, *The Hollywood Studios*

"The Amazing Dr. Clitterhouse"

(Radio, 1941, 1944) The film was twice adapted for radio, with Robinson and Bogart recreating their roles in one version, and Robinson and Trevor repeating their roles in the other.

Cast: Edward G. Robinson (Dr. Clitterhouse), Humphrey Bogart (Rocks Valentine), Marsha Hunt (Jo Keller); *Gulf Screen Guild Theatre*; CBS-radio; November 2, 1941

Cast: Edward G. Robinson (Dr. Clitterhouse), Claire Trevor (Jo Keller), Lloyd Nolan (Rocks Valentine); *Lady Esther's Screen Guild Theatre*; NBC-radio; June 5, 1944; 30 min.

American Academy of Dramatic Arts (AADA)

Founded in 1884 in New York, it is the oldest school of acting in the United States. Edward G. Robinson was a 1913 graduate of its two-year program, having attended on scholarship. The commencement address was delivered by George Arliss.

Gena Rowlands, who had co-starred opposite Edward G. Robinson in *Middle of the Night*, and her husband, John Cassavetes, were also Academy graduates. At a 1996 seminar at the Academy, the following story surfaced about the couple's arrival in Hollywood and one of their first party invitations — to the Robinsons. "Too new in town to understand that no one in Hollywood is expected at the specified hour, the Cassavetes were the first guests to arrive. Edward G. didn't mind a bit. It gave him a chance to show off his modern art collection — and in particular his pride and joy, one of Monet's waterlilies scenes. 'It was staggeringly lovely,' Gena Rowlands recollected. Robinson asked his guest what he thought of it. 'It's nice,' said John, deadpan. Edward G. was puzzled: 'What do you mean, nice?' 'Do you know who painted this?' Mrs. Edward G. wanted to know. 'Well, yes I do,' John said. 'But there's something missing.' Edward G. said, 'What? What do you think is missing?' 'A little dog,' said John. 'It would be nice to see a little dog running around with the stream and all. It would be nice.' Mrs. Edward G. turned purple, but her husband considered for a minute. 'You're absolutely right,' he chuckled. 'I've been wondering what was missing in this thing!'"

Others who attended the Academy include Lauren Bacall, Anne Bancroft, Hume Cronyn, Cecil B. DeMille, Danny DeVito, Kirk Douglas, Clare Eames, Betty Field, Nina Foch, Martin Gabel, Ruth Gordon, Agnes Moorehead, Pat O'Brien, William Powell, Robert Redford, Jason Robards Jr., Rosalind Russell, Joseph Schildkraut, Annabelle Sciorra, French Stewart, Renee Taylor, Spencer Tracy, Claire Trevor, and Margaret Wycherly.

America Calling see "Ship Forever Sailing"

The American Creed

(Short film, 1946) Robinson joined other stars in a short film for Brotherhood Week in 1946.

Producer, David O. Selznick; director, Robert Stevenson; Ingrid Bergman, Eddie Cantor, Katharine Hepburn, Van Johnson,

Jennifer Jones, Walter Pidgeon, Edward G. Robinson, James Stewart, Shirley Temple; 1946

The American Idea: The Land (Television, 1973) Edward G. Robinson narrated a segment about Peacham, Vermont, in this television documentary, which was telecast almost two months after his death.

Producer, director, William Cart-wright; producer, Alan Landsburg; writer, Jeff Myrow; music, Richard Rodgers; Dick Van Dyke, Henry Fonda, Cloris Leachman, Edward G. Robinson (narrators), Roger Wagner Chorale; ABC-TV; 60 minutes; March 18, 1973

American-International Pictures This independent production company was founded in the 1950s by Samuel Z. Arkoff and James H. Nicholson. It filmed Roger Corman horror pictures of the 1960s and one with Edward G. Robinson, *Mad Checkmate*, a.k.a. *Uno Scacco Tutto Matto* or *It's Your Move*.

Ames, Robert (1889–1931) appeared in *A Lady to Love* with Edward G. Robinson. He was replaced by Joseph Schildkraut in a German-language version. Silent and sound feature films include *Three Faces East*, *Rebound*, and *Holiday*.

Amos 'n' Andy (Radio, 1943) Edward G. Robinson was a guest on the popular wartime radio program *Amos 'n' Andy*. Andy dreams about meeting a gangster with only a few hours to live — actually a personification of the year 1943. *Radio Yesteryear* called the New Year's Eve show "a moving and unusual script, with possibly the only suicide on-mike heard on a network comedy show."

Charles Correll (Andy), Freeman Gosden (Amos), Edward G. Robinson (Guest star, as 1943), Harlow Wilcox (announcer); NBC-radio, December 31, 1943

"...And Son" (Television, 1955) This was the first of Edward G. Robinson's two appearances on television's *Ford Theatre*.

Producers, Joseph Hoffman, Fletcher Markle, Garth Montgomery, Winston O'Keefe, Irving Starr; writers, Robert Bassing, Peter Packer; story, I. A. R. Wylie; cast: Edward G. Robinson (John Derwent), John Baer (Larry Derwent), Willis Bouchey (Charlie Crichton), Erin O'Brien-Moore (Else Derwent), J. P. O'Donnell (receptionist); *Ford Theatre*, NBC-TV; January 13, 1955; 30 minutes

Anders, Rudolph (1902–87) with his pronounced German accent, acted under the name Robert Davis as Nazi military advisor Straubel in *Confessions of a Nazi Spy*, but shared no scenes with Edward G. Robinson. He also is in *Actors and Sin* as theater critic Otto Lachsley, and in *The Prize* as Mr. Bergh of the Swedish foreign office. His other films include *She Demons* and *On the Double*.

Anderson, Eddie "Rochester" (1905–77) was known chiefly as Jack Benny's comic sidekick on the radio and tv. He appears in the final episode of *Tales of Manhattan*. His other films include *The Green Pastures*, *Gone with the Wind*, *Buck Benny Rides Again*, and *It's a Mad, Mad, Mad, Mad World*.

Anderson, Dame Judith (1898–1992) born in Australia and named a Dame Commander of the British Empire in 1960, played the title role in *Medea* and was Mrs. Danvers in *Rebecca* (Oscar nomination). With Edward G. Robinson she appears in *The Red House* as his sister, Ellen, and in *The Ten Commandments* as the servant Memnet.

Anderson, Warner (1911–76) was perhaps best known to television audiences as one of the two police detectives on *The Line-Up*. He is featured in *The Violent Men* with Edward G. Robinson and appears also in *Command Decision*, *Detective Story*, and *The Caine Mutiny*.

Andrews, Edward (1914–85) He played the ad agency boss Mr. Burke in *Good Neighbor Sam*, with Edward G. Robinson, and also had roles in *The Harder They Fall*, *Tea and Sympathy*, *Elmer Gantry*, *Advise and Consent*, and *Send Me No Flowers*.

Androcles and the Lion (Theater, 1925) Edward G. Robinson played the emperor Caesar in this George Bernard Shaw comedy, presented by the Theatre Guild as a double bill with Shaw's *The Man of Destiny* as the curtain raiser. He willingly accepted these roles because the Guild was producing Shaw; they were his seventeenth Broadway appearance. Although his acting was praised in both productions, *Androcles* received the better reviews. Based loosely on the fable of the mouse befriended by a lion for removing a thorn from its paw, Shaw transformed the mouse into a wife-dominated Christian fighting the lion in a Roman arena.

The play's climax has Caesar proclaiming Christianity as Rome's state religion following the "miracle" of the lion sparing Androcles' life in the arena. Shaw's Caesar was a fictitious conglomerate of Caesars, since, historically, Androcles lived in the first century, and it was Constantine I, known to his troops as "Caesar," who converted Rome three centuries later.

Both *The Nation* and *The New York Times* liked *Androcles and the Lion*. The former said, "On the whole, the present production is the most thoroughly satisfactory of the three presentations of Shaw plays made recently by the Theatre Guild ... the whole performance is carried off with the sprightliness which the piece demands." The *Times* called *Androcles* "a rattling good performance ... passed with gaiety and the healthy humor of this perverse dramatist.... As the emperor Caesar, mighty and omnipotent, Mr. Robinson ... gave an enjoyable performance running to low comedy."

Produced by the Theatre Guild; playwright, George Bernard Shaw; director, Philip Moeller; designer, Manuel Covarrubias; cast, *Androcles and the Lion*: Henry Travers (Androcles), Tom Powers (The Captain), Clare Eames (Lavinia), Edward Robinson (Caesar), Edward Reese (The Editor), Romney Brent (The Lion; Lentullus), Orville Caldwell (Ferrovius), Frederick Chilton (Secutor), Alice Belmore Cliffe (Magaira), William W. Griffith (Ox Driver; Retiarius), Galwey Herbert (Centurion; Menagerie Keeper), Philip Leigh (Spintho), Alfred Little (The Call Boy), Richard Nye (Beggar), Allan Ward (Metellus); opened at the Klaw Theatre, New York; November 23, 1925; 68 performances

Burns Mantle's *Best Plays of 1925–26* described *Androcles and the Lion* as "the fable play based on the legend of the Greek tailor who, being kind to the dumb, picks a thorn from the paw of a lion in the forest. Later when he enters the arena at Rome as a Christian martyr, the lion meets him and kisses in place of killing him."

Animals The personification of animals is obvious in two Robinson titles: In the George Bernard Shaw play *Androcles and the Lion* the role of the actual lion of the title was played by Romney Brent. And Edward G. Robinson played the title role of *The Sea Wolf* in 1941. Personification was heightened with Robinson's six-minute screen test as the simian Dr. Zaius of *Planet of the Apes*, although ultimately he did not appear in the film.

A few of Robinson's films have animal co-stars, or they figure prominently in the plots. Probably the most famous animal performer is the canine personality Asta, who had appeared with William Powell and Myrna Loy in the *Thin Man* films. Asta lent humor to scenes in *I Am the Law* as the pet, named Habeas, of law professor Robinson and his wife, Barbara O'Neil. More importantly, however, the dog saves Robinson's life in one scene by alerting his master about an intruder wielding a gun.

Gunfire saves Robinson's life in the African jungle in *A Boy Ten Feet Tall*. His character, Cocky Wainwright, has taught young Sammy, the boy of the title, how to shoot a small rifle. Just as a leopard leaps to attack Robinson, the boy kills it with one shot. Cocky's grateful response: "Jumpin' Jehosephat!"

Deadly sharks figure in the plots of both *Tiger Shark* and *The Sea Wolf*. Robinson first loses a hand, and finally is mauled to death at the climax of the former film. In the latter, Barry Fitzgerald is keel-hauled from the schooner ship *The Ghost*, attacked by a shark, and then pulled from the water — but too late to save his leg.

Taken out of context, Robinson's dialogue in one film is curiously contradicted by his dialogue in another. It all has to do with monkeys. In 1965 in *The Cincinnati Kid*, his character, Lancey Howard, makes his first entrance stepping off a train in New Orleans. He walks through the station, stopping to talk to an organ grinder, who tells Robinson that his monkey's name is Tricky Bob. Robinson then obliges the monkey with a dollar, saying, "Here you are, Tricky." Consider now the plot of *A Bullet for Joey,* made ten years earlier, in which an organ grinder has been murdered. George Dolenz, playing a scientist, wonders why anyone would kill an organ grinder. Robinson, as a bemused police inspector, counters the question with one of his own: "Why would a man talk to a monkey?"

In *Our Vines Have Tender Grapes* Edward G. Robinson, as farmer Martinius Jacobson, takes his young daughter Margaret O'Brien to see a circus passing through town, and she is given a ride on an elephant. There are also several scenes with milk cows and O'Brien tending to a new calf. In the most dramatic scenes of the film Robinson must shoot cattle in a burning barn, managing to save a horse. A prop animal is the golden calf shown in several scenes at the climax of *The Ten Commandments,* with Robinson reveling with other worshipers.

Robinson is shown on horseback (though a double is used for scenes of actual riding) in *Mackenna's Gold, The Violent Men, Cheyenne Autumn,* and *The Little Giant.* He buys horses in the latter film and in *Brother Orchid.* Don Juan, a white stallion, is a key character in *Pepe.* For that film Edward G. Robinson also appears with his pet Chihuahua in the preview trailer, commenting to the theater audience through the dog's continual barking, "I guess he wants to tell you about it [the film] himself." In *Dark Hazard* Robinson's Jim Turner buys a greyhound, the film's title character, for $25 after the dog goes lame and can no longer race. There were also dog racing scenes in *A Hole in the Head.* In *The Whole Town's Talking* one of the two characters that Robinson plays has pets named Abelard, a cat, and Edouard, a canary. *Good Neighbor Sam* features a pet duck.

Carrier pigeons are key to the beginning of the story of *A Dispatch from Reuter's,* as Robinson, appearing as Julius Reuter, founder of the news service, gets his start with a long-distance message service. Finally, the record for the variety of animals in a Robinson film probably is held by *Dr. Ehrlich's Magic Bullet,* in which he has a pet dachshund named Pretzel and several lab animals — a racehorse, a chimpanzee, mice, snakes, worms, and rabbits.

Ankrum, Morris   (1896–1964) worked in three media with Edward G. Robinson — in the radio cast of "The Taming of the Shrew," in *Tales of Manhattan* (as the classmate at the 25-year college reunion who became a judge), and finally as the prosecuting attorney in TV's *The Case of Kenny Jason.* His other films include *Roxie Hart, Apache,* and *The Harvey Girls.*

Ann-Margret   (1941–   ) is one of the stars of *The Cincinnati Kid*, but she appears only briefly onscreen with Edward G. Robinson; most of her scenes are with Steve McQueen and Karl Malden. She is married to actor Roger Smith and also appears in *Carnal Knowledge* and *Tommy* (Oscar nominations), *Bye Bye Birdie,* and *Grumpy Old Men.*

Anthologies   This classification covers film and television presentations that contained multiple stories. Edward G. Robinson was in the fourth of five episodes (originally six) in *Tales of Manhattan,* the second of three in *Flesh and Fantasy,* and the first of two, in both *Actors and Sin* (entitled "Actor's Blood") and TV's *The Night Gallery* (called "The Messiah on Mott Street").

Antoinette Perry (Tony) Awards   In 1956, for his Broadway role of the Manufacturer in Paddy Chayefsky's romantic drama *Middle of the Night,* Edward G. Robinson received a nomination for the Antoinette Perry (Tony) Award for best actor in a dramatic role, along with Boris Karloff in *The Lark*, Ben Gazzara in *A Hatful of Rain*, Michael Redgrave in *Tiger at the Gates*, and Paul Muni in *Inherit the Wind*. Muni, Robinson's longtime

Warner Brothers rival, won. Harry Green, who was electrician and sound technician for *Middle of the Night* and *Damn Yankees*, won a Tony award for his work.

Apfel, Oscar (1880–1938) played the unscrupulous editor, Hinchecliffe, in *Five Star Final*, with Edward G. Robinson. He was a director of many silent films from 1911, and appeared in *Abraham Lincoln, I Am a Fugitive from a Chain Gang,* and *The House of Rothschild.*

Arden, Eve (1912–90) made a career out of playing wise-cracking best friends in comedies and dramas. With Edward G. Robinson she appears in *Manpower.* Her other films include *Stage Door, Cover Girl, Mildred Pierce, The Voice of the Turtle, Anatomy of a Murder,* and *Grease,* as well as *Our Miss Brooks,* based on her long-running television show.

Arlen, Richard (1899–1976) played in *Tiger Shark* with Edward G. Robinson, as his buddy, Pipes Boley, and also in *The Stolen Jools.* He began as an extra in silent films in 1920 and also appeared in *Wings, Island of Lost Souls, Artists and Models,* and *The Best Man.*

Arliss, George (1868–1946) played in *Poldekin,* featuring Edward G. Robinson, and he gave the commencement address for Robinson's graduation from the American Academy of Dramatic Arts in 1913. An English star, he was in *The Man Who Played God, Disraeli* (Oscar, 1929–30), *The Green Goddess, Old English,* and *The House of Rothschild.*

Armour, J. Ogden (1863–1927) built Armour and Company, founded in 1867 by his father Philip Danforth Armour (1832–1901), into one of the world's largest meat-packing firms. His life was the subject of David Karsner's book *Red Meat,* which evolved into *I Loved a Woman,* with Edward G. Robinson playing Armour (renamed John Hayden). The company, along with other packers, was charged with selling chemically treated inferior meat to the armed forces during the Spanish-American war.

Arms and the Woman (Film, 1916) This silent picture was Edward G. Robinson's first film, a fact revealed in 1978, five years after the actor's death. His appearance in a bit role in the film came to light when Kevin Brownlow, researching his book *The War, the West, and the Wilderness*, discovered a still picture from *Arms and the Woman* that shows Robinson among the players. Robinson did not remember the film when Brownlow asked about it. The still is proof enough, however. His face is unmistakable, even at age 22; and its publication corrects all references, which heretofore have listed 1923's *The Bright Shawl* as Robinson's first (and only other silent) film. *Arms and the Woman* was filmed in New York around the time Robinson was appearing on the stage in *Under Fire* in 1915.

Produced by Astra Films Corporation; director, George Fitzmaurice; scenario, Ouida Bergere; camera, A. C. Miller; art director, Anton Grot; cast: Mary Nash (Rozika), Lumsden Hare (David Fravoe), Robert Broderick (Marcus), Rosalind Ivan (Mrs. Marcus), H. Cooper Cliffe (Captain Halliday), Carl Harbaugh, Irene Castle, Susanne Willa, Edward G. Robinson; Pathe Exchange, Inc.-Gold Rooster Plays; 5 reels; 1916

Rozika, a Hungarian singer, emigrates with her brother to the United States. He goes into hiding after killing a man in a brawl. She attracts the attention of a wealthy steel manufacturer, marries him, and becomes an opera singer. Her brother gets involved in a plot to burn her husband's factory, which supplies munitions to the Allies in World War I. After wounding the husband, the brother is killed and the factory is destroyed by fire.

"*Arms and the Woman* included several documentary sequences which would be fascinating today if only the film had been preserved," lamented Brownlow. *Variety* reviewed the picture as "uncommonly interesting," and *Motion Picture World* agreed: "The production demands a special paragraph of praise. Starting with the opening scenes on shipboard and embracing the views of the steel works, the European battlefields, and the flashes of life at the two extremes of the social ladder, the settings are always impressive."

See also ***Mr. Winkle Goes to War.***

Armstrong, Robert (1890–1973) is probably best known for his role of the white hunter in *King Kong*. He also was in *The Lost Squadron, The Son of Kong, G-Men, The Sea of Grass, Mighty Joe Young*, and, with Edward G. Robinson, *Mr. Winkle Goes to War* (as Joe Tinker).

Arnold, Edward (1890–1956) His films include *Diamond Jim, You Can't Take It with You, Mr. Smith Goes to Washington, Johnny Apollo, Meet John Doe, Dear Ruth, Annie Get Your Gun,* and, with Edward G. Robinson, *Unholy Partners*. They also appeared together in the radio dramas "Ship Forever Sailing" and *We Hold These Truths*. He got his start on Broadway.

Art Edward G. Robinson, with his first wife, Gladys Lloyd, amassed one of the most distinguished private collections of French Impressionist art in America, including the works of dozens of masters. The paintings and sculptures were maintained at the Robinson mansion on North Rexford Drive in Beverly Hills throughout their marriage until 1956, when, to comply with California's community property laws in their divorce settlement, the collection was sold for $3,125,000 and the proceeds split between the litigants. The buyer was Greek shipping magnate Stavros Niarchos, whom Robinson pursued all over the world in an attempt to buy back some paintings. The actor never even met Niarchos. He lamented the possible damage to oil paintings being kept aboard Niarchos' yacht in the Mediterranean.

After marrying his second wife, Jane Adler, in 1958, Robinson began acquiring art once again, rebuilding his collection. She compiled the book *Edward G. Robinson's World of Art* as "a gift to my husband." It featured color reproductions of many of the paintings.

There were three major exhibitions of Robinson's art collection. The Los Angeles County Museum showed it twice: It was *The Edward G. Robinson Collection* in 1941; and in 1956–57 it was called *The Gladys Lloyd Robinson and Edward G. Robinson Collection*. The latter exhibition was at the time of the Robinsons' divorce proceedings; it also traveled to San Francisco, California, at the Palace of the Legion of Honor. In 1953 the Museum of Modern Art in New York exhibited *Forty Paintings from the Edward G. Robinson Collection*.

Individual paintings from the collection have been featured in exhibitions all over the world. In some instances the paintings were on exhibition prior to being acquired by Robinson; and at later exhibitions, such as those at Knoedler & Co. and the National Gallery of Ottawa, works had been sold already to Stavros Niarchos. Among galleries that showed paintings from the collection over the years are Thos. Agnew & Sons, Alex Reid and Levevre Gallery, O'Hana Gallery, Tate Gallery, Tooth Gallery (London); the Galerie Bernheim-Jeune, Galerie Bing, the Galerie Charpentier, and Galerie Georges Petit (Paris); Bern Kunsthalle, Switzerland; Liljevachs Konsthalle and the Museum of Stockholm; Durand-Ruel Galleries, Paul Rosenberg Galleries, Marlborough Galleries, Jacques Seligman & Co., and Wildenstein & Co. (New York); UCLA Galleries, Los Angeles; Musee de Batavia, Djakarta; National Gallery of Art, Washington, D.C.; National Gallery of Scotland, Edinburgh; Stedelijk Van Abbe Museum, Eindhoven; Gemeentemuseum, The Hague; and the Chicago Art Institute.

Two months following Robinson's death in 1973, American industrialist Armand Hammer, chairman of the Occidental Petroleum Company, paid over $5 million for the second amassed collection. Omitted from that sale was Camille Pissarro's *L'Arbre Mort* (*The Dead Tree*), one of Robinson's favorites. According to Jane Robinson, the painting was suspected to be a forgery.

In addition to Pissarro, Edward G. Robinson's collections over the years also included one or more works by Ralph Blakelock, Pierre Bonnard, Peter Brook, Eugene Boudin, Robert Brotherton, Georges Braque, Paul Cezanne, Marc Chagall, Gustave Courbet, Jean-Baptiste Camille Corot, Honore Daumier, John Decker, Edgar Degas, Eugene Delacroix, Andre Derain, Charles Dufresne, Raoul Dufy, Jean Louis Forain, Paul Gauguin,

Jean-Louis Gericault, El Greco, Edward Hopper, Robert Hosea, Yasuo Kunioshi, Henri Matisse, Amadeo Modigliani, Claude Monet, Berthe Morisot, Jules Pascin, Pablo Picasso, Horace Pippin, Maurice Prendergast, Odilon Redon, Diego Rivera, Pierre Seurat, Walter Sickert, Alfred Sisley, Chaim Soutine, Eugene Speicher, Henri de Toulouse-Lautrec, John Henry Twachtman, John Ulbricht, Maurice Utrillo, Vincent Van Gogh, Maurice Vlaminck, Jean Edouard Vuillard, and Grant Wood, plus sculptures from the Ivory Coast, the Belgian Congo, and Admiralty Island.

When he was gray-listed by the House Un-American Activities Committee in the 1950s and found it difficult to get acting work, Robinson took up painting. He did several self-portraits, since while working late at night it was not easy to find other models. He did a portrait of his friend, actor Sam Jaffe, and copied several favorite paintings in his collection, including Cezanne's *The Black Clock.*

Art and painting figure prominently in Robinson's films. In more than forty years of playing in crime films, beginning with *Little Caesar* in 1931, his characters undergo an education of a kind. In *Little Caesar* Rico is impressed with the five-figure cost of crime boss Sidney Blackmer's new painting, commenting, "Boy, those gold frames sure cost a bunch." By 1933, in the comedy *The Little Giant,* Robinson is taking art lessons and has purchased an abstract masterpiece, "a genuine Kaputzovich!" And he advises Mary Astor, his co-star, that since the owner of a copy of the Venus de Milo is so wealthy, she might think about having the statue's arms glued back on. By 1955 Robinson's underworld character was much more serious about art. In *Illegal,* as a crooked lawyer he has an eye educated enough to spot racketeer Albert Dekker's Gauguin (a real prop Robinson had lent to the film's set decorators). And in 1968 Robinson's gangster fences Michelangelo's *Pietà* after a heist from the Vatican in *Operation San Pietro.* And he masterminded the theft of a triptych mural of sunflowers from a Los Angeles gallery (while taking painting classes from Dorothy Provine) in *Never a Dull Moment.*

In both *The Woman in the Window* and *Scarlet Street,* portraits of Joan Bennett are key to the plot. In the first film Robinson meets Bennett, the model who had posed for a painting in a gallery window, and becomes involved in a killing after going to her apartment to see other works by the artist. In *Scarlet Street* Robinson is himself a Sunday painter. He paints her portrait; but as the plot eventually has Bennett signing *her* name to the works, the painting of her becomes a "self-portrait." It was in reality the work of California artist John Decker, a drinking buddy of John Barrymore's. Portraits of Edward G. Robinson are prominent in several films: *East Is West, House of Strangers, Never a Dull Moment,* and two different poses in *Robin and the 7 Hoods.*

Fine art also is evident in *The Stranger,* as Robinson's character admires pewter and antique clocks. In *Brother Orchid* he goes to Europe to seek class in the form of art and culture. Finally, he and Vincent Price parody themselves as real-life art collectors when they adorn love slave Debra Paget with flowers in *The Ten Commandments* in 1956, the same year that for six weeks the two competed on the subject of art on the television quiz show *The $64,000 Challenge.* They split the top prize when neither answered the final questions correctly.

Arthur, Jean (1905–91) was with Edward G. Robinson in *The Whole Town's Talking* and its radio adaptation. Also in *Mr. Deeds Goes to Town, You Can't Take It with You, Mr. Smith Goes to Washington, The Plainsman, Only Angels Have Wings, The More the Merrier* (Oscar nomination), and *Shane,* she played *Peter Pan* on Broadway and had her own TV show.

Asheroff, Mischa (1924–) a Russian-born actor in the theater in Israel, was in several films — *Impossible on Saturday, Three Days and a Child,* and, with Edward G. Robinson, *Neither by Day Nor by Night,* in the role of the doctor.

Asner, Edward (1929–) known to TV audiences as *Lou Grant,* played a psychiatrist in *The Old Man Who Cried Wolf,* with Edward G. Robinson. He also appeared in the miniseries *Rich Man Poor Man* and *Roots,* as well as TV's *The Life and Assassination of the Kingfish* and *The Gathering.* On the big screen, he was in *The Slender Thread, The Venetian Affair, Fort Apache the Bronx,* and *JFK.*

Astor, Mary (1906–87) Her films with Edward G. Robinson are *The Bright Shawl* (as his daughter), *The Little Giant* (as his fiancée), and *The Man with Two Faces* (as his sister). They were together in "The Checker Player" and an adaptation of *Bullets or Ballots* on radio, and *The Ed Sullivan Show* on TV. She won an Oscar for *The Great Lie,* and also was in *The Hurricane, The Maltese Falcon, Meet Me in St. Louis, Little Women,* and *Hush Hush Sweet Charlotte.* In her memoir, *A Life on Film,* she called Robinson "that little giant of an actor ... the two of us rather sadly doing a bad picture together, knowing it, telling each other, 'It might be funny.' It was. Sort of. But there was something wrong about Edward G. Robinson taking pratfalls from a polo pony."

At This Very Moment (Television, 1962) This variety program was a benefit for the American Cancer Society/Eleanor Roosevelt Cancer Fund.

Producer, Michael Abbott; writers, Arnold and Lois Peyser; director, Richard Schneider; host, Burt Lancaster; Harry Belafonte, Richard Chamberlain, Jimmy Durante, Connie Francis, Greer Garson, Charlton Heston, Bob Hope, Lena Horne, Rock Hudson, Paul Newman, Jack Paar, Edward G. Robinson, Dinah Shore, Danny Thomas, Joanne Woodward (guests); 60 minutes; ABC-TV, April 1, 1962

Attenborough, Sir Richard (1923–) won an Academy Award for directing *Gandhi.* His other films as director include *Oh! What a Lovely War!, Cry Freedom, A Chorus Line* and *A Bridge Too Far,* and as actor, *In Which We Serve, Journey Together* (with Edward G. Robinson), *Dr. Dolittle, Seance on a Wet Afternoon, The Sand Pebbles,* and *Jurassic Park.* Of Robinson he said, "I saw a great deal of this man during the months that we were filming. I toured the American Fighter Stations with him in the South of England and saw his relationship with his countrymen. For me he is a great liberal and a really exciting human being to be with. As an actor, of course, he is supreme. His film technique should surely be scarcely surpassed by anyone, and he is kindness itself.... I remember he gave me two pieces of advice; one he admitted was not exactly lacking in self interest, but he said, 'Always be kind to people when you are on the way up, because you will meet them all when you are on the way down,' and secondly, one of the soundest pieces of advice that I have ever had: 'Never believe your own publicity.' We shared many interests, in particular our mutual love of painting ... He is still a hero to me...."

Autographs If he had it all to do over again, he said he would choose a shorter name. "You have no idea how long it takes to write 'Edward G. Robinson' for a flock of autograph hunters."

The Steinway baby grand piano in his home was autographed by many great musicians, such as Arturo Toscanini, Schnabel, Igor Stravinsky, Serge Prokofiev, Mischa Elman, Godowsky, Molinari, Jose Iturbi, Jascha Heifetz, Vladimir Horowitz, and Serge Koussevitsky.

Automobiles By the time of *Soylent Green* in the year 2022, the automobile has ceased to be of much value. With overpopulation, the masses have become a nuisance to contend with, and trucks are used to transport waste and are rigged with "people scoops." The only car seen in the film is in a junkyard; its interior becomes the scene for planning a murder. In many of Edward G. Robinson's earlier films and television shows, however, automobiles are commonplace.

Car chases are highlights in some of his films. In a scene that now seems a cliché, a dozen police cars careen around the corner out of the station, headlights glaring, sirens wailing, to confront Rico in *Little Caesar.* A similar scene occurs with comic effect in *The Whole Town's Talking* (there might be a hundred cars!) as they arrest an innocent Robinson at the Blue Bird Cafe at lunch time.

Later a second Robinson (a twin, *Public Enemy Number One*) overtakes a guard's car and kidnaps the boss. In *Tight Spot* the police speed through the night to bring Ginger Rogers from jail to a hotel as a state's witness; and in *Illegal*, sweet-looking Ellen Corby (as Robinson's secretary) does some nifty driving with him as passenger to escape the mob.

In *The Prize* Edward G. Robinson and Elke Sommer, kidnapped and held aboard a Russian steamer, are rescued by Paul Newman. In the ship's cargo hold, new cars are about to be hoisted out onto the dock, and the three of them hop into one, then speed away from the scene. Earlier in the same film Newman is chased by a car on a high bridge, escaping by jumping onto the side of a truck going the other way. The climax of *Operation San Pietro* has virtually everyone from the Vatican chasing crooks to retrieve the statue of Michelangelo's *Pietà*. One cardinal drives his car off the dock onto the deck of the ship where the statue has been stashed.

Among more dramatic car chases is one in *Blackmail*, where, after an escape on foot from the chain gang, Robinson speeds by the authorities in a green sedan he's had stashed by the side of the road. Later, forced to abandon the car, he hangs on the underside of a truck, escaping authorities once again, until he drops to the ground, exhausted. The opening of *Double Indemnity* has Fred MacMurray speeding down the boulevard in the wee hours of the morning, ignoring signals and other traffic, in order to get to his office to relate his story into his dictaphone.

Seven Thieves features two vehicles, a Citroen and a war surplus ambulance, as getaway cars. Robinson, as a captain, rides around in a police car in the second half of *Vice Squad*. In *The Woman in the Window* Robinson's car — a 1940s Cadillac — is used to transport the body of the man he has killed in self defense in Joan Bennett's apartment. Complications include his forgetting to turn the car's lights on, attempting to speed unseen through a toll booth, faulty brakes, and encountering a cop on a motorcycle at a signal. When he gets to the spot to dispose of the body, it is a rainy night, and the car leaves tire tracks in the mud.

Awards Edward G. Robinson's acting was highlighted by honors from the Cannes Film Festival and the National Board of Review: In 1949 he was named best actor for *House of Strangers* at Cannes, France. The latter citation recognized him, among performers in several other films, for his performance in *Tales of Manhattan* in 1942.

Despite a distinguished career of ninety films over several decades, he was never nominated by the Academy of Motion Picture Arts and Sciences for an acting award. He received a posthumous honorary Oscar in 1972, recognizing a lifetime of achievement. He was honored by the Masquers in 1968 and the Screen Actors Guild in 1969.

Robinson was nominated for a Tony Award for his Broadway performance in *Middle of the Night* in 1956.

There were non-performing honors. He received the Townshend Harris Medal in 1936, awarded by the Alumni Association of the College of the City of New York; the Chevalier de la Legion d'Honneur, presented by the Officer de l'Instruction Publique in 1952; the Eleanor Roosevelt Humanitarian Award in 1963; and a State of Israel Bonds Organization award in 1968.

See **Academy of Motion Picture Arts and Sciences Awards, Antoinette Perry (Tony) Awards; Cannes Film Festival, Masquers, National Board of Review,** and **Screen Actors Guild.**

Ayres, Lew (1908–96) was in *East Is West* with Edward G. Robinson. A conscientious objector during World War II, he served with distinction in the medical service. Films include *The Kiss* (with Garbo), the anti-war classic *All Quiet on the Western Front, State Fair, Johnny Belinda, Advise and Consent,* and ten as Dr. Kildare.

'B' Pictures These were feature films produced on a small budget and often paired in theaters with a bigger film as a double feature. Often the 'B' picture had writing, acting, and overall production values that impressed audiences and critics. Robinson's name was always prominent, so when his political difficulties in the 1950s made it difficult for him to obtain prime roles, his name distinguished several 'B' pictures, which often capitalized on his tough guy image: *Vice Squad, Black Tuesday, The Violent Men, Tight Spot, A Bullet for Joey, Illegal,* and *Hell on Frisco Bay.* It was with the making of *Actors and Sin* in 1952 that Robinson commented, "I entered the B-phase of my picture career." Other 'B' films include *Big Leaguer, The Glass Web,* and *Nightmare.*

Babies In *Illegal* Edward G. Robinson's character, a district attorney who has plans to run for governor, tells a reporter, "Now, I'm not going to start kissing babies [to get elected]." His association with babies in his career generally has been as slight as this. Exceptions include *The Hatchet Man*, in which Robinson, a Chinese assassin, is obliged to kill his best friend and becomes guardian of his baby. She grows up to be Loretta Young and marries Robinson! In *The Last Gangster* his obsession with the birth of his son alienates his foreign-born wife; wife and baby visit prisoner Robinson at Alcatraz.

In both *A Dispatch from Reuter's* and *Nightmare,* Robinson lovingly enacts the role of expectant father, perhaps straining credibility at the respective ages of 47 and 62. In *Dark Hazard* (when he was 41) his wife left him before the baby was born. An abandoned baby discovered at the denouement of *The Outrage* gives hope to a disillusioned preacher and prospector.

In *Middle of the Night* on Broadway, Robinson is already a sympathetic character as a middle-aged widower who falls in love with a girl half his age. He is further domesticated in a scene in which he plays with his blanketed grandson. Walter Kerr said, "On him, the baby looks great!"

Edward G. Robinson received fan mail from new mothers, sometimes enclosing pictures of their babies, claiming the infants looked just like the actor. He wrote back that they should not worry, that the baby would outgrow it.

In 1933 Edward G. Robinson's only son, Emanuel Goldenberg, Jr. (Manny), was born. Robinson's wife returned to New York to spend her pregnancy in bed; delivery was Caesarean. Dozens of photographs showing Manny with his parents made the newspapers and magazines.

Bacall, Lauren (1925–) began in films opposite Humphrey Bogart in *To Have and Have Not,* marrying him in 1945. Onscreen with him and Edward G. Robinson in *Key Largo,* the three also appeared on TV's *The Ed Sullivan Show* and on the radio in *Hollywood Fights Back.* She said in her autobiography *Lauren Bacall By Myself,* "The cast [of *Key Largo*] was fabulous — Eddie Robinson, Lionel Barrymore, Claire Trevor ... Eddie Robinson was a marvelous actor and a lovely, funny man ... [He] did 'Molly Malone' with a Yiddish accent which was wildly funny." Her other films include *The Big Sleep, How to Marry a Millionaire, Murder on the Orient Express,* and *The Mirror Has Two Faces* (Oscar nomination), and she won a Tony award for *Applause.* She married and divorced Jason Robards, Jr.

Bacon, Irving (1893–1965) His more than 200 films include *It Happened One Night, Gone with the Wind, The Grapes of Wrath, Tobacco Road, Shadow of a Doubt, A Star is Born,* and, with Edward G. Robinson, *The Amazing Dr. Clitterhouse* (jury foreman), *Dr. Ehrlich's Magic Bullet* (Dr. Becker), and *It's a Great Feeling* (a railway clerk).

Bacon, Lloyd (1890–1955) directed Edward G. Robinson's comedies *A Slight Case of Murder, Brother Orchid,* and *Larceny Inc.,* and was with him on an early *Warner Brothers Radio Broadcast.* Bacon appeared with Charlie Chaplin in silent films and directed *42nd Street, Marked Woman, San Quentin, The Oklahoma Kid,* and *Knute Rockne—All American.*

Baker, Diane (1938–) made two films with Edward G. Robinson — *The Prize* (as his niece) and *The Old Man Who Cried Wolf* (as his daughter-in-law). Her first film was *The Diary of Anne Frank,* and she also was in *Journey to the Center of the Earth, Strait-Jacket, Mirage,* and more recently, as the senator, *The Silence of the Lambs.*

Baker, Elsie (1893–1971) played Mrs. Nurdlinger, Edward G. Robinson's puritanical wife, in *Good Neighbor Sam*. She was in *No Room for the Groom*. She made her stage debut as an infant.

Baker, Sir Stanley (1927–76), knighted one month prior to his death, was onscreen from 1943 in *Captain Horatio Hornblower, Alexander the Great, The Guns of Navarone, Zulu,* and *Accident*. With Edward G. Robinson he plays Janos in *Who Has Seen the Wind?*

Baldwin, Walter (1887–1977) appeared with Edward G. Robinson in *Mr. Winkle Goes to War, Cheyenne Autumn* (as Carroll Baker's Quaker uncle), and, on TV, *The Devil and Daniel Webster* and "The Drop-Out." Other films include *The Lost Weekend, The Best Years of Our Lives,* and *Rosemary's Baby*.

Ball, Lucille (1911–89) had a bit role in *The Whole Town's Talking*, with Edward G. Robinson. She starred in *DuBarry Was a Lady* and *Mame*, but she was the First Lady of Television in *I Love Lucy*. He appeared on *The Lucy Show*, a later series, and they were together in *Twelve Star Salute, All About People*, and, on radio, *Hollywood Fights Back* and *The Roosevelt Special*.

Ballantine, E.J. (1888–1968) was on Broadway in *Redemption* and also with Edward G. Robinson in *The Night Lodging*. They were onscreen together 25 years later in *Tampico*. His other films include *The Moon Is Down* and *Magic Town*.

Balsam, Martin (1919–96) played Edward G. Robinson's son-in-law in *Middle of the Night*. By the time they appeared as father and son in *The Old Man Who Cried Wolf*, Balsam had adjusted to Robinson's scene stealing: "Watch him, watch him," he'd say to director Walter Grauman. He was in *On the Waterfront, Twelve Angry Men, Al Capone, A Thousand Clowns* (Oscar), *Psycho,* and *All the President's Men*. He won a Tony Award for *You Know I Can't Hear You When the Water's Running*.

Banco (Theater, 1922) This comedy in three acts was the first of Edward G. Robinson's five stage appearances with Alfred Lunt, and his eleventh Broadway play. *The New York Times* said, "The piece is delightfully acted with only Edward G. Robinson rather at a loss."

Producer, William Harris, Jr.; playwright, Alfred Savoir; adaptation, Claire Kummer; director, Robert Milton; cast: Alfred Lunt (Count Alexandre de Lussac [Banco]), Lola Fisher (Charlotte), Edward G. Robinson (Louis), Francis Byrne (Baron Henri Delignieres), J. Malcolm Dunn (Feydal), Charlotte Granville (Baroness Delignieres), Hall Higley (Porter), Robert Strange (George Dalou), Alice John (Julie); opened at the Ritz Theatre, New York; September 20, 1922

Banco (the nickname for Count Alexander de Lussac) and his wife, Charlotte, have an 84–hour standoff at the casino. She wants him to quit gambling; he wants to be left alone. Charlotte leaves and sues for divorce. A year later, on the night of Charlotte's wedding to a country squire, Banco breaks into her room. To keep her respectability, Charlotte plays cards with him till dawn. Becoming convinced that she and Banco are still in love, she applies for an annulment of her second marriage, probably on grounds that it was never consummated.

Banky, Vilma (1902–91), a Hungarian actress discovered by Samuel Goldwyn, was a romantic silent star opposite Ronald Colman and Rudolph Valentino. Films include *The Dark Angel, The Son of the Shiek,* and *The Winning of Barbara Worth*. One of her few sound features before retiring in 1932 was *A Lady to Love*, with Edward G. Robinson.

Barbary Coast (Film, 1935) Edward G. Robinson's two films in 1935 were the first he made away from Warner Bros. since being contracted by the studio. The first was Columbia's *The Whole Town's Talking*. The second was *Barbary Coast* for United Artists, his only picture for Samuel Goldwyn. It was a turn-of-the-century Gold Rush melodrama written by Ben Hecht and Charles Mac-

Arthur, but Robinson's gang boss character fit right in; this time he owned San Francisco! Howard Hawks, who had earlier done *Tiger Shark* with Robinson, was the director.

Film historians have chronicled *Barbary Coast* as a starring vehicle originally designed for Gary Cooper and Anna Sten, with William Wyler directing. Apparently Goldwyn soon halted production and later replaced the three with Joel McCrea, Miriam Hopkins, and Hawks. Unclear is whether Robinson was acting in the earlier version or was hired later with the replacements. Adding to the confusion is William Wyler's statement in a 1978 letter, "I had absolutely nothing to do with *Barbary Coast*!"

By nearly all accounts the final film was a hit. *The New York American* called it "a gaudy, gripping melodrama of guns and gold ... made colorful by the histrionics of Edward G. Robinson ... thoroughly satisfying entertainment.... [He] dominates every instant of the drama with a superlative conception of the sinister spoilsman ... and he manages, with ineffable artistry, to be so appealing a rogue that one regrets to see his final justice.... The film blazes with action and romance through every sequence, is studded with color and bespangled with scintillance of a half dozen stirring performances. Howard Hawks has directed with brilliance."

James Robert Parish in *The Tough Guys* agreed: "Robinson gave a zesty account of the corrupt big boss." *The New York Sun* also agreed, saying, "Not since his remarkable performance in *Little Caesar* has Mr. Robinson been as convincingly tough." And *The New York Daily News* joined the praise, saying, "Robinson has again found a character that suits him from the top of his black thatch to his lacquered toes." Finally, *The New York Herald-Tribune* noted that *Barbary Coast* was "a thumping melodrama of the Gold Rush days filled with gusto and gaudy colorfulness ... a typically excellent Goldwyn product."

Robinson liked the finished film, but he found the atmosphere on the set tense, for two reasons. One was the political climate in which he allied himself with liberal writers Ben Hecht and Charles MacArthur against conservative director Howard Hawks and co-players Joel McCrea, Miriam Hopkins, Walter Brennan, and Harry Carey. But worse was Hopkins' temperament. Her complaining and upstaging tactics drove Robinson to the point of telling her off in front of the entire company.

Despite Robinson's assessment of the political atmosphere, Joel McCrea remembered Robinson fondly. "[He] was what we call an actor's actor! He'd rather act than eat. He was serious, and he loved acting. We got along fine. He would ask me, 'How in the world do you get along in the scenes with her [Hopkins]?' I said, 'I'm not as good an actor as you, maybe she isn't scared of me.'"—Quoted in *Ray's Way*, a column by Ray Nielsen

Any difficulties did not prevent Robinson from giving a fine performance. Foster Hirsch comments, "There is often a scene in a Robinson film when his character cracks, revealing the demons that lurk beneath the authoritative mask... Chamalis begs Swan to love him. When she refuses he rages at her, [revealing] the depth of his pathetic maladjustment.... The grasping for power seems to compensate for the inability to give and receive love."—*Edward G. Robinson, A Pyramid Illustrated History of the Movies*

Mary Rutledge sails to San Francisco during the Gold Rush only to learn that her fiancé has lost his stake and been killed. She meets Louis Chamalis, owner of both the Bella Donna saloon and the town. Deciding to stay, she accepts his offer to run a crooked roulette wheel and his nickname for her, Swan, but she struggles against his attempts to own her. Out riding one day, she takes refuge in an abandoned shack during a rainstorm and meets Jim Carmichael, a handsome miner and poet on his way back East with his gold. She falls in love with him and tells him only that she is visiting from New York. Unfortunately, Jim is tempted to stop at the Bella Donna before boarding ship. He sees Swan there and becomes disillusioned, loses his money at the crooked wheel, and is forced to take a lackey's job. The citizens of San Francisco rally to form the Vigilantes and begin to clean up the town following several murders (including that of

Col. Cobb, the editor of the newspaper *The Clarion*) by Chamalis' henchman, Knuckles Jacoby. Vigilantes hang Knuckles in the town square after a makeshift trial. Then they begin looking for Chamalis. Mary arranges for Jim to win back his money at the wheel, and the two try to escape. Chamalis and his men follow them, and Jim is shot. Chamalis, however, realizes that Mary/Swan will never love him and surrenders to the Vigilantes. Mary boards the ship for home to New York with Jim.

Producer, Samuel Goldwyn; director, Howard Hawks; screenplay, Ben Hecht, Charles MacArthur; based on a book by Herbert Asbury; camera, Ray June (Oscar nomination); art director, Richard Day; costumes, Omar Kiam; music, Alfred Newman; sound, Frank Maher; editor, Ray Curtiss; assistant director, Walter Mayo; cast: Miriam Hopkins (Mary Rutledge/Swan), Edward G. Robinson (Louis Chamalis), Joel McCrea (Jim Carmichael), Walter Brennan (Old Atrocity), Brian Donlevy (Knuckles Jacoby), Frank Craven (Col. Marcus Aurelius Cobb), Harry Carey (Jed Slocum), Donald Meek (Sawbuck McTavish), Otto Hoffman (Peebles), Rollo Lloyd (Wigham), Roger Gray (Sandy Ferguson), Clyde Cook (Oakie), J. M. Kerrigan (Judge Harper), Matt McHugh (Bronco), Wong Chung (Ah Wing), David Niven (Sailor thrown out of saloon), Harry Holman (Mayor), Edward Gargan (Bill), Russ Powell (Sheriff), Frederick Vogeding (Ship Captain), Dave Wengren (First Mate), Anders Van Haden (Second Mate), Jules Cowles (Pilot), Cyril Thornton (Steward), Clarence Wertz (Drunk), Harry Semels (Lookout), Theodore Lorch (Helmsman), Olin Francis, Larry Fisher, George Simpson (Sailors), Bert Sprotte, Claude Payton, Bob Stevenson, Frank Benson (Passengers), Herman Bing (Fish Peddler), Tom London (Ringsider), Heine Conklin, Charles West, Constantine Romanoff, Art Miles, Sammy Finn (Gamblers), Jimmie Dime (Henchman), Victor Potel (Wilkins), Sidney D'Albrook, Edward Piel Sr. (Vigilantes), Harry Depp (Jewelry), Ben Hall (Printer), John Ince, Nina Campana, Patricia Farley, Kit Guard, Robert Homans, George Lloyd, Hank Mann, Monte Montague, George Magrill, Jack Pennick, Frank Rice, Harry Tenbrook, Ethel Wales, Jim Thorpe, Blackie Whiteford, Bob Wilbur, Leo Willis; United Artists; 91 minutes; October, 1935

Some of the other reviews were mixed, but few were unfavorable. *The New York Times* called *Barbary Coast* "a bounding melodrama ... a merry, vigorous and delectably phrased tale ... Robinson is an effective Chamalis, although the gangster pictures have made his snarl overly familiar." While *The New York Post* referred to "the footlight savagery of Edward G. Robinson," John Baxter, in his book *Hollywood in the Thirties,* noted that, "Edward G. Robinson in ringlets, gold earring, cheroot, and ruffled shirt as the elegant Chamalis is visually if not intellectually arresting."

Bari, Lynn (1913–89) was Edward G. Robinson's leading lady in *Tampico*. Generally hers were B films, including several Charlie Chan and Mr. Moto mysteries. Among her other features were *The Magnificent Dope, Orchestra Wives, The Bridge of San Luis Rey, Captain Eddie,* and *Margie*. She was on television in the series *Boss Lady*.

Barker, Jess (1912–2000) appeared in *Scarlet Street* with Edward G. Robinson, as Elliott Janeway, the art critic. His other films include *Cover Girl, Keep Your Powder Dry, The Ghost Steps Out, Shack Out on 101,* and *The Night Walker*. He was married to Susan Hayward.

Barnett, Vince (1902–1977) played the comic character Engineer in *Tiger Shark*, with Edward G. Robinson. He had roles in *All Quiet on the Western Front, Scarface, A Star Is Born, Springfield Rifle,* and *Knock on Any Door*. He was known as a show business practical joker.

Barr, Byron (1917–1966) played Nino Zachette in *Double Indemnity*, with Edward G. Robinson, and was also in *The Man Who Came to Dinner* and *The File on Thelma Jordan*. He should not be confused with actor Gig Young, whose real name also was Byron Barr.

Barrat, Robert (1891–1970) came from Broadway to Hollywood to appear in over 150 films, including two with Edward G. Robinson — as his father-in-law, Charles Lane, in *I Loved a Woman,* and as Tex in *Dark Hazard.* Barrat also appeared in *Mayor of Hell, Dames, Mary of Scotland, The Life of Emile Zola, Road to Utopia, Sea of Grass,* and *Joan of Arc.*

Barrymore, Ethel (1879–1959) starred in *A Royal Fandango* on Broadway, featuring Edward G. Robinson and Spencer Tracy in minor roles. Her career as First Lady of the American Theater spanned fifty years, beginning in 1894, and included *The Rivals, The Second Mrs. Tanqueray,* and *The Corn Is Green.* Apart from a few silent films and an isolated talkie (*Rasputin and the Empress*), her films generally followed her stage career. She won a supporting Oscar for *None But the Lonely Heart.*

Barrymore, Lionel (1878–1954), elder brother of Ethel and John, and son of stage actors Maurice and Georgiana Drew Barrymore, was on Broadway before moving to Hollywood, where he won an Oscar for *A Free Soul* and was seen in *Grand Hotel, Rasputin and the Empress, Dinner at Eight, Ah Wilderness!,* the *Dr. Kildare* films (as Dr. Gillespie), *It's a Wonderful Life,* and, with Edward G. Robinson, *Key Largo.* On the radio he appeared with Robinson in *Ship Forever Sailing, We Hold These Truths, The Victory Chest Program, Command Performance* ("Victory Extra"), and a Savings Bond Show.

Barthelmess, Richard (1895–1963) was the star of the silent film *The Bright Shawl,* with Edward G. Robinson. His films, from 1916, include *Broken Blossoms, Way Down East, Tol'able David, The Noose, The Patent Leather Kid* (Oscar nominations for the latter two, 1927–28), *The Dawn Patrol, Cabin in the Cotton, Only Angels Have Wings,* and *The Spoilers.*

Bartlett, Elise (1900?–44), once married to Joseph Schildkraut, acted on the New York stage with him and Edward G. Robinson in *Peer Gynt,* and appeared with Robinson in *First Is Last* and *The Adding Machine.* Her films include *Angels Over Broadway* and *Show Boat.*

Basserman, Albert (1867–1952), a German character actor, fled the Nazis in 1933 to the United States. His American films include *Foreign Correspondent* (Oscar nomination), *The Moon and Sixpence, Reunion in France, Madame Curie, Rhapsody in Blue,* and the Robinson biographies *Dr. Ehrlich's Magic Bullet* (as Dr. Robert Koch) and *A Dispatch from Reuter's* (as Herr Geller).

Baths In *House of Strangers* Edward G. Robinson's son, played by Luther Adler, scrubs his back while he takes a bath; later in the same film Robinson "sweats it out" in a Turkish bath with son Richard Conte when bank examiners want to look over his books. Ten years later, in *A Hole in the Head,* Robinson's character refers to such baths fondly: "You go in, take off your clothes, and meet people!"

Robinson's character in *Our Vines Have Tender Grapes,* farmer Martinius Jacobson, decides to go to the barn to take a bath after having had to shoot livestock during a fire. Later in the film his daughter and nephew (played by Margaret O'Brien and Jackie "Butch" Jenkins) are rescued after playing with the bathtub as a boat, and the river's current drags them downstream. One of the visual gags in *The Whole Town's Talking* has the bathtub overflowing as Robinson's character rushes out of his apartment, late for work. Vilma Banky, as his mail-order bride in *A Lady to Love,* gives Robinson a bath!

Edward G. Robinson's most famous bathtub scene is in *Key Largo.* Gangster Johnny Rocco is seen sweltering in the tub, a moment critic James Agee called "one of the most effective first entrances in movies." Director John Huston claimed only that he "wanted to get a look at the monster with its shell off."

"Batman's Satisfaction" (Television, 1967) In this early episode of *Batman* on television, Robinson appears unbilled as himself, leaning out a window to discuss art with

Robin and "the Caped Crusader" as they climb the side of a building. Adam West called Robinson's appearance "our classiest cameo."

A Greenway Production; executive producer, William Dozier; William Self in charge of production; assistant, Charles B. Fitzsimmons; associate producer, William P. D'Angelo; producer, Howie Horwitz; director, Oscar Rudolph; assistant director, David Whorf; writer/editor, Charles Hoffman; based on characters created by Bob Kane appearing in *Batman* Comics; script consultant, Lorenzo Semple, Jr.; film editor, Homer Powell; music, Nelson Riddle; supervisor, Lionel Newman; theme, Neal Hefti; editors, Leonard A. Engel, Sam Horta; production supervisor, Jack Sonntag; sound effects, Ralph B. Hickey, Harold Wooley; special photographic effects, L. B. Abbott, Margaret Donovan; color by DeLuxe; men's wardrobe, Andrew Pallack; makeup, Ben Nye; camera, Meredith P. Nicholson; unit production manager, Sam Strangis; post production supervisor, James Blakeley; post production coordinator, Robert Mintz; set, Walter M. Scott, Chester Bayhi; art directors, Jack Martin Smith, Serge Krizman; cast: Adam West (Batman), Burt Ward (Robin), Roger C. Carmel (Colonel Gumm), Diane McBain (Pinky Pinkston), Van Williams (Green Hornet), Bruce Lee (Kato), Alan Napier (Alfred), Neil Hamilton (Commissioner Gordon), Stafford Repp (Chief O'Hara), Rico Cattani (Reprint), Alex Rocco (Block), Seymour Cassel (Cancelled), James O'Hara (Police sergeant), Harry Frazier (Mr. Stample), Angelique Pettyjohn, Dusty Cadis, and Edward G. Robinson (himself); March 2, 1967, 30 minutes

Baxter, Anne (1923–85) won an Academy Award for her role in *The Razor's Edge*. She was nominated also for the title role in *All About Eve*. She plays Nefretiri in *The Ten Commandments* with Edward G. Robinson, and they were also on the *36th Academy Awards*. She is in *The Magnificent Ambersons, Five Graves to Cairo,* and *Chase a Crooked Shadow*.

Beal, John (1909–97) was in dramas by Eugene O'Neill and on radio and TV (daytime's *Another World*). He is with Edward G. Robinson in *I Am the Law,* and also on the radio programs *Hollywood Fights Back* and "Cancer in Men." He is in *The Little Minister, Les Miserables, Madame X, The Cat and the Canary,* and *The Sound and the Fury.*

Beavers, Louise (1902–62), remembered for her role as the black mother in *Imitation of Life,* also appeared in *Coquette, Mr. Blandings Builds His Dream House,* and three films with Edward G. Robinson — *Outside the Law, The Last Gangster,* and *Bullets or Ballots.* She played the title role of *Beulah* on television.

Beecher, Janet (1884–1955) was onstage with Edward G. Robinson in *Under Sentence* and on the radio in *Children's Crusade for Children.* She played in New York in *A Bill of Divorcement* and *The Late George Apley,* and onscreen in *All This and Heaven Too, The Mark of Zorro,* and *The Lady Eve,* among others.

Begley, Ed (1901–70) won an Oscar for *Sweet Bird of Youth.* He and Edward G. Robinson appeared together three times: in *Eyvind of the Hills* on Broadway; the "What Are We Fighting," segment of the radio medical series *For the Living*; and on the *36th Academy Awards* telecast. He created the role of Joe Keller in *All My Sons* in New York and played both leads in *Inherit the Wind.* He is the father of actor Ed Begley, Jr.

Bellamy, Ralph (1904–91) played the "other man" in films, but won Ann Sothern away from Edward G. Robinson in *Brother Orchid.* He received an Oscar nomination for *The Awful Truth,* and was in *The Wolf Man, Sunrise at Campobello* (as FDR), *The Professionals, Rosemary's Baby, Oh God!, Trading Places,* and *Pretty Woman.* He was on Broadway in *State of the Union, Detective Story,* and *Sunrise at Campobello* (Tony Award), and with Robinson in the tribute *We Will Never Die* and one of many *Chanukah Festivals for Israel.*

The Bells of Conscience (Theater, 1913) At the age of nineteen, Edward G. Robinson dramatized *The Bells*, a story by Henry James, into a short play and called it *The Bells of Conscience*. He undertook the lead role, booked it on the Loew's circuit, and thus made his first appearance as a professional actor under the name Edward G. Robinson. The play was about a burgomaster who, under hypnosis, revealed that earlier, as an innkeeper, he had committed a murder and theft and kept it a dark secret for many years.

Cast: Edward G. Robinson (The Burgomaster); opened at the Plaza Theatre, New York; 1913

Ben-Ami, Jacob (1890–1977), emigrating from Russia in 1912, was in *Samson and Delilah* and *The Idle Inn*, with Edward G. Robinson, and the tribute *We Will Never Die*. He staged *The Goat Song* for The Theatre Guild. Alternating between American and Yiddish Theater, he appeared with Eva Le Gallienne in *The Sea Gull* and *The Cherry Orchard*.

Benchley, Robert (1889–1945), an actor and humorist, appeared with Edward G. Robinson in *Flesh and Fantasy* as Doakes, a skeptic whose talk about his bad dreams links the film's episodes. *How to Sleep*, his short film, won an Oscar. Other films include *The Major and the Minor, Foreign Correspondent, I Married a Witch, Road to Utopia*, and *Duffy's Tavern*. His son, Peter, is a screenwriter (*Jaws*).

Bennett, Joan (1910–90), Edward G. Robinson's leading lady in *The Woman in the Window* and *Scarlet Street*, was on the radio in adaptations of the former and *Kid Galahad*, and also *The Roosevelt Special*. Daughter of actor Richard Bennett, and sister of actresses Barbara and Constance, her other films include *Little Women* (as Amy), *The Man in the Iron Mask, Man Hunt, The Macomber Affair, Father of the Bride, We're No Angels,* and *House of Dark Shadows*. Her husbands were Gene Markey and Walter Wanger (producer of *The Hole in the Wall* and *The Woman in the Window*). She commented in *Films in Review* that at the time of their filming together, Robinson "was going through a terrible time with his wife, Gladys. She was being given shock treatments, and despite his personal problems, he was always a sweet, kind man."

Benny, Jack (1894–1974), legendary comedian, was a Hillcrest Country Club pal of Edward G. Robinson's, helping him write material when he entertained the troops overseas during the war. He was also an honorary pallbearer at Robinson's funeral. They appeared together in the short film *All About People,* on the TV special *Here Come the Stars,* and on the radio in *The Chevrolet Program*. Beginning his career as a violinist, Benny moved to vaudeville and movies, but was most successful on radio and TV with *The Jack Benny Show*.

Berardino, John (1922–96) was the chief of detectives in *Seven Thieves*, with Edward G. Robinson. He also had roles in *North by Northwest* and the TV soap opera *General Hospital*.

Beregi, Oscar (1918–76), a Hungarian character actor, played in "The Legend of Jim Riva," with Edward G. Robinson, as Arnie. His films include *The Fiercest Heart, 36 Hours, Ship of Fools, The Great White Hope,* and *Young Frankenstein*. His father, Oscar Beregi, Sr., was a Shakespearean actor.

Best, Edna (1900–74) played Ida Magnus, who fell in love with and married Julius Reuter (Edward G. Robinson) in *A Dispatch from Reuter's*. She appeared in *The Man Who Knew Too Much* and, moving from London to Hollywood in 1939, was in *Intermezzo, The Swiss Family Robinson, The Ghost and Mrs. Muir,* and *The Late George Apley*.

"The Betrothed"   see   ***This Is Tom Jones***

Big Leaguer (Film, 1953) This was a first directing assignment for Robert Aldrich. In the November 1978 issue of *American Film*, he commented, "I was invited to do a picture, a nineteen-day marvel called *Big Leaguer*, with

Edward G. Robinson as a baseball manager. Eddie Robinson was a marvelous actor and a brilliant man, but he was not physically coordinated. He would walk to first base and trip over home plate."

Robinson was a baseball fan, but casting him in this film made sense only in that he was enacting the biography of Hans Lobert, former New York Giants third baseman and training coach.

Reviews of the *Big Leaguer* were mixed. "The presence of Edward G. Robinson helps bolster the presentation," noted *Variety*, saying that he "is good as the camp founder and believable in the hokum that has been mixed in with fact." According to the *Monthly Film Bulletin*, "The surprise is that such routine studio material should be so confidently and cleverly wrought.... The film treats its subject with an almost hushed reverence and its appeal is restricted almost entirely to baseball enthusiasts.... Edward G. Robinson's reliable performance and some effectively shot match scenes barely compensate for the trite story and conventional characterization."

James Robert Parish in *The Tough Guys* referred to *Big Leaguer* as "nothing more than a double bill entry." Parish also noted in *The Cinema of Edward G. Robinson* that the MGM film, despite being about a genuine New York baseball team, was the first among Robinson's feature films that did not have a regular Manhattan first-run engagement.

Producer, Matthew Rapf; director, Robert Aldrich; screenplay, Herbert Baker; based on a story by John McNulty and Louis Morheim; camera, William Mellor; art directors, Cedric Gibbons, Eddie Imazu; set, Edwin B. Willis; music, Alberto Colombo; editor, Ben Lewis; sound, Douglas Shearer; assistant director, Sid Sidman; technical adviser, Hans Lobert; cast: Edward G. Robinson (John B. "Hans" Lobert), Vera-Ellen (Christy), Jeff Richards (Adam Polachuk), Richard Jaeckel (Bobby Bronson), William Campbell (Julie Davis), Paul Langton (Brian McLennan), Lalo Rios (Chuy Aguilar), Bill Crandall (Tippy Mitchell), Frank Ferguson (Wally Mitchell), John McKee (Dale Alexander), Mario Siletti (Mr. Polachuk), Robert Caldwell (Pomfret), Donald "Chippie" Hastings (Little Joe), Carl Hubbell, Al Campanis, Bob Trocolor, Tony Ravish (Themselves), Bing Russell; MGM; 73 minutes; July, 1953

It is spring training in Florida for the New York Giants. Promising ballplayers are given the chance to be looked over by coach Hans Lobert and his camp training staff. Among the hopefuls are Adam Polachuk, Bobby Bronson, and Tippy Mitchell. Polachuk falls in love with Lobert's niece, Christy. He has not told his immigrant father that he isn't studying law. Mitchell, the son of a famous retired first baseman, is anxious to please Dad, but he would really like to be an architect. Bronson is rejected by the Giants but is picked up as a pitcher by the rival Brooklyn Dodgers. Lobert is concerned, meanwhile, that the Giants' front office wants to replace him in the recruiting program. Weeks of practice culminate in an exhibition game between the Giants and the Dodgers. During the game the senior Polachuk and Mitchell come to accept their respective sons' abilities on the field, and Bronson almost wins for Brooklyn. Lobert is relieved when the ball club decides to continue the recruiting program under his leadership.

Big Town (Radio, 1937–1942) Edward G. Robinson became a major radio personality when he originated the role of *Illustrated Press* crusading editor Steve Wilson on *Big Town* in 1937. He stayed with the show for nearly five years; its run continued well into the 1940s with Edward Pawley and Walter Greaza as replacements. *Big Town* was the first of Robinson's many projects with Claire Trevor, who co-starred as Lorelei Kilbourne.

"The *Illustrated Press* was a rugged training ground for aspiring newspapermen," said Jim Harmon in *The Great Radio Heroes*, suggesting that the likes of *Superman*'s Clark Kent could have started there, "dodging bullets, catching crooks, and writing a feature story on the back of a matchbook while hanging to the rear bumper of a black sedan. Surely, if any newspaperman wanted to learn how to be a superman, he could do far worse than follow the example of Editor Steve Wilson." Harmon was impressed with the star of *Big Town*: "Edward G. Robinson, in a change of pace from his movie gangster roles, was a reformed man as the *Illustrated Press* editor. It was not quite enough of a change. According to published interviews, Robinson wanted less violence and hokum on the radio series, more stories with better acting parts for him and his co-star, Claire Trevor…. One of the stories that offered Robinson a greater range for his talents I remember vividly. Steve Wilson was blinded by racketeers, forced to quit the newspaper, and gave up to despair, winding up on skid row. Then he heard a call for help from a burning building, and even though blind, he went into the inferno and led a child to safety. His eyes were damaged again in the fire, and a dangerous thousand-to-one-chance operation was performed. The scene where Wilson's sight, hope, and job were restored offered an acting tour de force, to say the least!"

Producers, Jerry McGill, Phil Cohn, Clark Andrews, Crane Wilbur; assistant producer, Thomas Freebairn-Smith; music conductors/composers, Leith Stevens, Fran Frey; writers, Crane Wilbur, Jerry McGill; directors, Richard Uhl, William N. Robson, Wilbur, McGill; announcers, Carlton KaDell, Ken Niles; sound effects, John Powers; organist, John Gart; casts included: Edward G. Robinson (Steve Wilson), Claire Trevor (Lorelei), Ona Munson*, Bill Adams, Mason Adams, Casey Allen, Helen Brown, Fran Carlon**, Helen Chalmers, Ted DeCorsia, Robert Dryden, Howard Duff, Gale Gordon, Larry Haines, Jerry Hausner, Cy Kendall, Donald MacDonald, Ed McDaniel, Gloria McMillan, Lou Merrill, Michael O'Day, George Petrie, Zasu Pitts, Thelma Ritter, Jack Smart, Hanley Stafford, Dwight Weist, Crane Wilbur, Bobbie Winkler, Paula Winslowe, Frances Woodward, Lawson Zerbe; CBS; 60–minute episodes, October 19, 1937 through June 2, 1942; *replacing Claire Trevor; **replacing Ona Munson

The following is a sampling of storylines for a variety of episodes, several without titles. In February 1938 Steve and Lorelei protected Eddie, Dutch Marco's son, when his cop-killing father was sentenced to death and escaped. In May Steve broke up a protection racket in "The Case of the Missing Milk." The following month he was on the trail of graver-obbers who took the jewelry left on corpses at burial; another show focused on Red Bennett, a poor boy from Big Town. In October Steve broke up a poultry racket and was involved in exposing the gamblers forcing Chuck Gordon, Big Town's university football star, to throw a big game. December saw Steve defending himself against libel charges after he accused a politician of building a dam with defective materials; he then brought to justice an orphanage superintendent who beat and underfed the children. In the Christmas show Steve and Lorelei aided a crippled newsboy in finding his missing father (during the show's intermission interview Claire Trevor commented on her six-month marriage to producer Clark Andrews). The final show of the year dealt with the deaths of firemen and cheating on civil service exams.

Episodes in 1939 included one on hit-and-run drivers called "Every Eighteen Hours." In January Steve tackled a women's court mob, and in February a crooked doctor and lawyers involved in traffic accident scams. Two teenagers were killed at a railway crossing in a March episode; and in June young Bobby Warner went to reform school when his mother was sentenced to jail. 1940 had a story entitled "Death Rides the Highway." By September 1942 Steve and Lorelei were part of the war effort, fighting Nazis in occupied France.

See **"The Case of the Missing Milk"**; **"Every Eighteen Hours"**; **"Death Rides the Highway"**; **"The Million Dollar Dog Stealing Racket"**

The Biggest Bundle of Them All (Film, 1968) "It begins like one of those really bad movies that are unintentionally funny," said *The New York Times*. "Then it becomes clear that it intends to be funny and isn't…. By the time Edward G. Robinson appears, his wrinkled countenance, flat eyes and generally turtlish appearance make it seem everyone might be on location for *The Wind in the Willows*." One reviewer underscored the silliness of *The Biggest Bundle of Them All* by quoting a line by Vittorio DeSica, delivered in thick, Italian-accented English: "He was taken by a mustard [master]!"

The Biggest Bundle of them All was hardly a good movie. It presented Robinson in a by-now familiar role, that of an aging professor of crime on hand briefly to mastermind one more big heist. In a new vein, however, the script has him imparting his elaborate plan to the gang with visual aids, pointer, and an easel. "We've gone Madison Avenue," says Robinson. Late in the film he dances the frug in a nightclub with Raquel Welch; and so the assembled talent, which also includes Robert Wagner and Godfrey Cambridge, does seem to be having some fun.

A gang of five — Harry Price, Benjamin Brownstead, Davy Collins, Antonio Tozzi, and Harry's girl, Juliana — kidnap Cesare Celli, a legendary Italian gangster, now retired. Various attempts to collect a ransom fail because no one is willing to pay. As a matter of pride, Don Cesare joins the gang to pull off a robbery. Professor Samuels, an old friend of the Don from Chicago, is brought in to help plot the heist of a platinum shipment worth $5 million. The gang members rehearse elaborate schemes but bungle their work repeatedly in an effort to raise funds to pull off the caper. Their eventual success is short-lived when they lose the stolen platinum as it drops out the hatch of a rented plane.

Leslie Halliwell, in his *Film Guide*, called it all "moderately amusing," but *The New York Post* objected to the acting, noting that "Cambridge and ... Robinson go through their criminal paces without the distinction that marks their work in other lines." Still other reviews favored Robinson. According to *Variety*, he "contributes one of his usual smooth performances," and *Monthly Film Bulletin* agreed: "Robinson is in fine form as a smooth-talking, impeccably dressed master crook."

A Shaftel-Stewart production; producer, Josef Shaftel; associate producer, Sy Stewart; director, Ken Annakin; screenplay, Shaftel, Sy Salkowitz, Riccardo Aragno; based on a story by Shaftel; camera, Piero Portalupi; camera operator, Dudley Lovell; special effects, Robert MacDonald; art director, Arrigo Equini; music, Riz Ortolani; songs, Sal Trimachi, Richie Cordell, Norman Newell, The Counts, Ortolani; sung by Johnny Mathis, The Animals; sound, Kurt Doubravsky, David Hawkins; continuity, Joy Mercer; costumes, Itala Scandanato; dubbing mixer, J. B. Smith; production manager, Fred S. Wallach; production supervisor, Basil Keys; unit manager, Mario Pisari; editor, Ralph Sheldon; assistant director, Victor Merenda; cast: Robert Wagner (Harry Price), Raquel Welch (Juliana), Godfrey Cambridge (Benjamin Brownstead), Vittorio DeSica (Cesare Celli), Edward G. Robinson (Professor Samuels), Davy Kaye (Davy Collins), Francesco Mule (Antonio Tozzi), Victor Spinetti (Capt. Giglio), Yvonne Sanson (Teresa), Mickey Knox (Joe Ware), Femi Benussi (Carlo's Bride), Paola Borboni (Signora Rosa), Andrea Aureli (Carabiniere), Aldo Bufi Landi (Capitano del Signore), Carlo Croccolo (Franco), Roberto DeSimone (Uncle Carlo), Piero Gerlini (Capt. Capuano), Giulio Marchetti (Lt. Naldi), Ermelinda DeFelice (Emma), Gianna Dauro (Signora Clara), Carlo Rizzo (Maitre d'Hotel) Nino Musco (Chef), Calisto Calisti (Inspector Bordoni), Milena Vukotic (Angelini), Clara Bindi (Davy's Wife), Lex Monson, Massimo Sarchielli, The Counts; Panavision/Metro-Color; MGM; 106 minutes; January 1968

Bikel, Theodore (1924–), known for his stage roles as Captain von Trapp in *The Sound of Music* and Tevye in *Fiddler on the Roof*, was in the films *The African Queen*, *The Defiant Ones* (Oscar nomination), *My Fair Lady*, and *The Russians Are Coming, the Russians Are Coming*. With Edward G. Robinson he was in the TV drama *Who Has Seen the Wind?* and also the special *Stars Salute '64*, and in three *Chanukah Festivals for Israel* at Madison Square Garden.

Billing After *Little Caesar* made him a star, Edward G. Robinson was offered billing above the title. He resisted initially on the theory that sudden failure could easily reduce him to has-been status. When he did agree to being starred, it was in his contract from that point on. In his career of nearly one hundred films there are only 34 instances when Robinson was not billed first; eight prior to *Little Caesar*: *Arms and the Woman, The Bright Shawl, The Hole in the Wall, The Night Ride, A Lady to Love, Outside the Law, East Is West,* and *The Widow from Chicago.*

He received less than top billing in six films in the 1930s and 1940s. In *Barbary Coast* he took second billing to Miriam Hopkins. In *Tales of Manhattan* billing was in order of the appearance, but he was the star of the fourth episode. *Double Indemnity* gave him the third lead. In *Journey Together* the role was small, amounting to a cameo. For *Key Largo*, in both the ads and on the screen Robinson's name was listed higher but to the right of Humphrey Bogart's; technically, he had the second lead. Finally, he plays himself in cameo as a guest star in *It's a Great Feeling.*

The Violent Men in 1954 billed him third. With this film, Robinson, now age sixty, had become a character star. Thereafter his name was often listed second, or he was given special guest star billing.

Robinson received second billing in *Tight Spot, Hell on Frisco Bay, A Hole in the Head, Two Weeks in Another Town, The Prize, The Cincinnati Kid,* and *Never a Dull Moment*; third billing in *My Geisha, Peking Blonde,* and *Neither by Day Nor by Night;* and fourth billing in *The Ten Commandments* and *The Outrage.*

He was a guest star in *Pepe, Good Neighbor Sam, Cheyenne Autumn, The Biggest Bundle of them All, Mackenna's Gold, Song of Norway,* and *Soylent Green.* In *Robin and the 7 Hoods* Robinson received no billing at all, recognizing his well established image as a screen gangster. It was a cameo guest star role.

Robinson did command star billing in seven films after 1955: *A Bullet for Joey, Illegal, Nightmare, Seven Thieves, A Boy Ten Feet Tall, Grand Slam, Mad Checkmate,* and *Operation San Pietro.*

See Bit parts; Guest Stars; Dual roles; *Key Largo*; Uncredited; Special appearances.

Binns, Edward (1916–90) was in *Twelve Angry Men, Compulsion, Fail Safe, North by Northwest,* and *Patton.* He was Al Barkis, one of the bank robbers, in *Vice Squad,* with Edward G. Robinson. In later years his voice was heard in commercials for Anheuser-Busch, among others.

Biographies Although short biographies of Edward G. Robinson appeared in many film encyclopedias and other reference books, it was not until after his death that there appeared books devoted to him alone. The exceptions are his son's book, listed first here, and his wife's book about his art collection.

*My Father — My Son, the autobiography of Edward G. Robinson, Jr., with William Dufty, was published in 1957 when Robinson, Jr., was only 23 years old. It was the first book with any substantial biographical content about Edward G. Robinson, and it chronicles the boy's difficult adjustment as the son of famous people — and of Little Caesar in particular.

*Edward G. Robinson's World of Art, by Jane Robinson, was published in 1971 as "a gift to my husband" and includes color prints of 39 Impressionist paintings and other works of art, along with commentary from Leonard Spigelgass, Robinson, and his wife.

*All My Yesterdays, the senior Robinson's autobiography, was started in collaboration with Leonard Spigelgass in 1972. The two met daily to discuss Robinson's life, and then Spigelgass put notes together for Robinson to review and edit. Robinson considered his editing skills stronger than his writing ability. Reviewers praised the work when it was published in 1973, allowing for inconsistencies when it was necessary for Spigelgass to complete the book following Robinson's death. Robinson's contribution ends chronologically after his ordeal with the House Un-American Activities Committee and his return to "A" films in *The Ten Commandments.* During earlier discussions about MGM, Robinson digressed about his experiences making both *The Cincinnati Kid* and *Soylent Green;* otherwise these impressions would have been unrecorded, as were his comments about the other twenty or so pictures he made in his last

seventeen years. The 1960 feature *Seven Thieves* is not even mentioned in the book's filmography. Also missing is Robinson's version of the struggles between him, playwright Paddy Chayefsky, and director Joshua Logan during the rehearsals and run of *Middle of the Night* on Broadway.

***The Cinema of Edward G. Robinson*, by James Robert Parish and Alvin H. Marill, appeared in 1973, shortly after the actor had died. A last-minute addition to the biographical essay mentions the date of death. The book was in production in 1972, and Robinson was at the time still acting in films. Consequently, both *Soylent Green* and the Israeli film *Neither by Day Nor by Night* were not included.

***Edward G. Robinson: A Pyramid Illustrated History of the Movies*, by Foster Hirsch (1975), provides an excellent biography and analysis of the actor's career.

**The Tough Guys (1976), by James Robert Parish, included a biography and filmography of Edward G. Robinson and six other actors.

***Little Caesar, a Biography of Edward G. Robinson*, by Alan Gansberg, was published in England in 1983. It is a full length chronicle of the actor's life, with particular emphasis on the political difficulties of the HUAC period. Unfortunately, Gansberg's work, in focusing on the House Un-American Activities Committee episode, unsuccessfully names Ronald Reagan as a villain responsible for Robinson's fate.

***The Complete Films of Edward G. Robinson*, by Alvin H. Marill, is a reworking of the earlier *Cinema of Edward G. Robinson* by Parish and Marill, but published by Citadel in 1991 and included in their "Films of" series. More photographs were added.

***The Hollywood Greats: Edward G. Robinson*. The British Broadcasting Company (BBC) produced this television documentary in 1977. His widow, Jane, and his granddaughter, Francesca, contributed videotaped observations, along with Frank Capra, John Huston, Sam Jaffe, Vincent Price, George Raft, and Hal Wallis. It also contained filmed interviews of the late actor and clips from several of his pictures.

*Manny. In 1978 actor-author Raymond Serra presented this play on Broadway and played the title role. (Manny was a nickname evolving from his real name, Emanuel, and was what Robinson's close friends called him.) Reviews were poor. Robinson's widow, Jane, who was not represented as a character in the play, was not consulted about the project. She commented that she "thought the whole thing was ridiculous." Receiving acknowledgment in the playbill was actress Bettye Ackerman Jaffe, wife of Sam Jaffe, Robinson's lifelong friend.

*Little Big Man was a long overdue *A&E Biography* television treatment of Edward G. Robinson's life. (The BBC program from two decades earlier is not available for TV viewing in the United States.) Featuring luminaries Peter Graves (host), Charlton Heston, Bettye Ackerman Jaffe, Norman Lloyd, Gena Rowlands, Claire Trevor, and Billy Wilder, as well as Robinson's granddaughter, Francesca Robinson-Sanchez, and his niece, Beulah Robinson, it was narrated and produced by Peter Jones in 1996.

Edward G. Robinson appeared in several films about real characters. Most obvious were the two gangster films *Little Caesar* and *Key Largo*, thinly disguising the lives of Al Capone and Lucky Luciano, respectively.

Silver Dollar told the story of Horace Tabor, a simple miner who prospered to become benefactor of the city of Denver; and *I Loved a Woman* was based on David Karsner's *Red Meat*, about packing tycoon J. Ogden Armour. In *Bullets or Ballots* Robinson's character was based on the work of New York detective Johnny Broderick.

Confessions of a Nazi Spy was more documentary than biography, but the film and Robinson's character, G-man Ed Renard, were based on events in the life of author Leon G. Turrou, as chronicled in his book *The Nazi Spy Conspiracy in America*.

Dr. Ehrlich's Magic Bullet was about physician Paul Ehrlich, a German Jew who won the Nobel Prize for Medicine in 1908 for his discovery of Salvarsan, the cure for syphilis. *A Dispatch from Reuter's* also had a German protagonist, Paul Julius Baron von Reuter, whose name continues to this day to identify the European news service.

Big Leaguer, a baseball training story, had Robinson impersonating former New York Giants third baseman John B. "Hans" Lobert.

In *The Ten Commandments* Robinson played Dathan, a Biblical character who rebelled against Moses. He was swallowed up by the earth.

Cheyenne Autumn featured Robinson in a guest star role impersonating Secretary of the Interior Carl Schurz. *Song of Norway*, a biography of composer Edvard Grieg, featured Robinson in a fictional role.

On the stage Robinson played General Porfirio Diaz in the Theatre Guild's production of *Juarez and Maximilian*, and he played Caesar in *Androcles and the Lion*. He regretted never playing Napoleon in the curtain-raiser for *Androcles, The Man of Destiny*. Several projects to film a life of Napoleon with Robinson playing him never materialized.

On television he was Theodore Roosevelt in *The Right Man*, and he narrated *Cops and Robbers*, which told about celebrated criminals in America, past and present. Robinson also was seen on television paying tribute to Hollywood directors — *This Is Your Life* (Frank Capra and Mervyn LeRoy), a special called *The World's Greatest Showman* (Cecil B. DeMille), and *The Ed Sullivan Show* (John Huston).

In 1952 Robinson was on the radio in *Trial and Error*, portraying Chaim Weizmann.

Birthday Edward G. Robinson was born on December 12, 1893, in Bucharest, Rumania. (The date was originally recorded as November 28, but it was adjusted with the Soviet calendar reform — a change from the Julian to the Gregorian calendar — in 1918.) Robinson shared his birthday with such notables as John Jay (1745), Gustave Flaubert (1821), Joseph B. Ismay (1862), Arthur Brisbane (1864), Laura Hope Crewes (1879), Harry Warner (1881), Helen Menken (1901), Jules Dassin (1911), Curt Jurgens and Frank Sinatra (1915), Alan Schneider (1917), Ferdinand Waldo Demara, Jr., "The Great Impostor" (1921), Bob Barker (1923), New York mayor Ed Koch (1924), Edward M. (Ted) Kennedy (1925), Dan Blocker (1927), Connie Francis (1938), Dionne Warwick (1940), Emerson Fittipaldi (1946), Cathy Rigby (1952), and Tracy Austin (1962).

In 1968, for his 75th birthday, Edward G. Robinson was at Madison Square Garden to see a ballet, *Scenes from the Yiddish Theatre*, by the Sophie Maslow Dancers, dedicated to him as part of that year's *Chanukah Festival for Israel*. Congratulatory telegrams were read from President Lyndon B. Johnson and Israeli Premier Levi Eshkol.

Frank Sinatra and Robinson worked together a number of times and had a joint birthday party on the set of *A Hole in the Head*. The two exchanged elaborate gifts for many years thereafter, including Sinatra's exchange of a framed Constantin Guys drawing for one of Robinson's self portraits.

Bissell, Whit (1919–96) played the role of Governor Santini in *Soylent Green*, with Edward G. Robinson. He also appeared in *Destination Tokyo, A Double Life, The Caine Mutiny, Riot in Cell Block 11, The Manchurian Candidate, Seven Days in May,* and *Airport*.

Bit Roles Robinson played his only bit part in his first film, the silent *Arms and the Woman*. David Niven in *Barbary Coast*, Lucille Ball in *The Whole Town's Talking*, Susan Hayward and Ronald Reagan in *The Amazing Dr. Clitterhouse*; Lloyd Bridges in *Destroyer*, Peter Lawford in *Flesh and Fantasy*, Robert Mitchum in *Mr. Winkle Goes to War*, Robert Blake in *The Woman in the Window*, Kathryn Grant in *Tight Spot*, Jayne Mansfield in *Hell on Frisco Bay*, and Michael Ansara, Michael Connors, Robert Vaughn, Clint Walker, Herb Alpert, and Carl "Alfalfa" Switzer in *The Ten Commandments* all play bits, many of them uncredited.

See Billing; Guest Stars; Dual roles; Uncredited; Special appearances.

Black, Maurice (1891–1938) appeared in two films with Edward G. Robinson — *Little Caesar*, as rival gang leader Little Arnie

Lorch, and *Smart Money*, as a Greek barber. His other pictures include *I Cover the Waterfront, The Crusades,* and *The Front Page.*

Black Tuesday   (Film, 1955) Edward G. Robinson once claimed that the meanest character he ever played among all his screen villains was Johnny Rocco in *Key Largo*. "And I even tried to soften him," he said. Robinson may have forgotten about playing Vince Canelli in *Black Tuesday*, which possibly is the actor at his most vicious. Screenwriter Sidney Boehm specialized in crime films, writing three for Robinson — *Black Tuesday, Hell on Frisco Bay,* and *Seven Thieves.*

Black Tuesday is a product of the B-period of Robinson's career during the 1950s and was not particularly original. But as noted in Peter Cowie's *Seventy Years of Cinema,* it was anything but B-grade. Cowie called it "a superbly shot melodrama with Edward G. Robinson."

"Robinson makes a return to gang czar roles in this story and has lost none of his menacing qualities," exclaimed *Variety*. "His performance is remarkable," added the *Monthly Film Bulletin*. "In a role that he has played to exhaustion he is still able to expand, and to fascinate." And finally, championing his work, *The New York Herald-Tribune* said he was "still the old pro in this kind of thing and at no point in this film imitates his own past portrayals, but gives a fresh and convincing portrait of an egomaniacal killer."

Other reviews praised Robinson but found the film wanting. "Edward G. Robinson plays his old snarling, savage self ... slips back into evil gear," *The New York Times* said. "It's a pleasure to see Mr. Robinson shedding his good citizenship in such a colorful, lively show. But the picture needs a good stool pigeon to tell us what makes Eddie run." Leslie Halliwell's *Film Guide*: "The star up to his old tricks. Good tension, but generally rather unpleasant."

Vince Canelli, who is scheduled to die in the electric chair on "black" Tuesday, the traditional day of execution, instead breaks out of prison. His escape has been aided by his girlfriend, Hatti Combest, who has kidnaped Ellen Norris, daughter of one of the prison guards. Also escaping with Canelli is Peter Manning, who has $200,000 from a bank robbery stashed in a safety deposit box. Wounded during the escape, Manning drips blood at the bank after retrieving the money, and the police trail him to a warehouse where Canelli is holding several hostages. Canelli is prepared to sacrifice all the hostages, one at a time, until he gets his freedom, but Manning kills Canelli when he threatens to shoot a priest and is himself gunned down by the police.

Hollywood columnist James Bacon provides an entertaining insight: "This particular movie called for Robinson to walk up to the electric chair and be executed. Since I covered a few executions in my legitimate days as an AP man, producer Leonard Goldstein asked me to be technical adviser. I'll never forget the first time the screen's alltime tough guy saw that deathroom set. He trembled. That's because Eddie was the most gentle and sensitive of men. Anyhow, came time to shoot the execution scene, and Eddie, the consummate actor, forgot his trembling and walked up to the chair like the cocky Little Caesar so familiar to movie audiences. I shook my head. Goldstein called a halt and asked what was wrong. 'Leonard,' I said, 'at every execution I ever witnessed — and I know reporters who have seen dozens more than I — no one walks cockily to the electric chair. It always takes about eight to ten cops to drag them there. Would you walk under your own power to the electric chair?' Leonard conferred with the director. Then he returned to mc and said, 'How would you like to be an actor? We'll pay you $200 and buy your SAG card.' I became one of the reporters covering the execution. I was out as technical adviser and I didn't really give a damn. Eddie was once more the cocky Little Caesar that movie audiences loved. As I recall, the picture didn't have the black guy on Death Row singing *Swing Low, Sweet Chariot*. That was a minor victory." — *Made in Hollywood*

A Leonard Goldstein production; producers, Leonard and Robert Goldstein; director, Hugo Fregonese; story, screenplay, Sydney Boehm; camera, Stanley Cortez; art director,

Hilyard Brown; set, Al Spencer; music, Paul Dunlap; lyrics, Robert Parrish; sound, Tom Lambert; editor, Robert Golden; assistant director, Sam Wurtzel; cast: Edward G. Robinson (Vincent Canelli), Peter Graves (Peter Manning), Jean Parker (Hatti Combest), Milburn Stone (Father Slocum), Warren Stevens (Joey Stewart), Jack Kelly (Frank Carson), Sylvia Findley (Ellen Norris), James Bell (John Norris), Victor Perrin (Dr. Hart), Hal Baylor (Lou Mehrtens), Harry Bartell (Boland), Simon Scott (Parker), Russell Johnson (Howard Sloane), Philip Pine (Fiaschetti), Paul Maxey (Donaldson), William Schallert (Collins), Don Blackman (Selwyn), Dick Rich (Benny), James Bacon (Reporter), Ken Christy (Norris); United Artists; 80 minutes; December 1954

Blackmail (Film, 1939) More than one retrospective essay on Hollywood has declared 1939 as the greatest year of the movies. A score of truly grand movies emerged: *Beau Geste, Destry Rides Again, Dark Victory, Gunga Din, The Hunchback of Notre Dame, Mr. Smith Goes to Washington, Ninotchka, Of Mice and Men, The Private Lives of Elizabeth and Essex, Stagecoach, The Wizard of Oz, The Women, Wuthering Heights, Young Mr. Lincoln,* and, of course, *Gone with the Wind.* Edward G. Robinson was in two films in 1939—*Confessions of a Nazi Spy*, which did appear on a few "ten best" lists as a documentary precursor to the threat of war, and *Blackmail*.

Possibly in any other year *Blackmail* might not be so low on a list of good films. In fact, it is a very entertaining melodrama, somewhat similar to the modern day *The Fugitive*, complete with an innocently accused hero, villain, rugged storyline, visual excitement, and a denouement with a sense of justice to satisfy an audience. That Robinson played the hero and not the villain should not have been cause for concern. Unfortunately though, the specter of Little Caesar was ever-present, and the film's reviews reflected this. As Foster Hirsch put it in *Edward G. Robinson: A Pyramid Illustrated History of the Movies,* "His character here isn't entitled to middle-class contentment until he's proved himself…. It's as if the character, like Robinson himself, must exorcise the shadow of the criminal that hangs over him."

The New York Herald-Tribune said, "The greater part of the film paints the villainy and inhuman treatment that exists in chain gangs. It is not a pretty picture; it becomes a fairly real one, though, as Mr. Robinson and his unfortunate comrades conduct it, but even with an exciting escape and the ultimate atonement of justice, *Blackmail* proves little more than the fact that Mr. Robinson is a sturdy villain." *The New York Times* was even less impressed, lamenting that, "in his day, Edward G. Robinson has been one of the screen's greatest criminals. There was a time in fact … when he was said to be widely imitated in the underworld. What a sad thing it is, then, to see this distinguished inhabitant of the Rogues' Gallery, this Napoleon of crime, this indomitably amoral spirit who belongs with the Borgias, feebly trying to go straight…." Leslie Halliwell's *Film Guide* said that *Blackmail* was "not bad in its way," but Robinson was just a "star marking time."

John Ingram puts out oil fires and has earned enough to buy his own well. William Ramey appears from John's past, having recognized him in a newsreel. Ramey, who is down on his luck, is given a job at the well. Eventually he tells John that it was he who robbed a ship's purser nine years earlier, when they were stationed together in the Navy. John went to prison for the crime, later escaped, changed his name and married. He and his wife, Helen, now have a son, Hank. Ramey now writes a confession to the theft in exchange for $25,000, part in cash, the rest as a note, with John's oil well as security. Ramey is able to retrieve the confession, however, and John, still a wanted man, is arrested and sent back to the chain gang to serve out his sentence. Ramey takes over the well and moves East. Learning that Helen and Hank have become poor because of payments on the note to Ramey, John escapes a second time with the help of his friend, Moose McCarthy. To lure Ramey back, he sets fire to the well. Then John confronts him and drags him close to the fire. Moose prevents John from killing Ramey, who hysterically screams a full confession.

Cleared finally of all wrongdoing, John saves his well from the fire.

Producer, John Considine, Jr.; director, H. C. Potter; screenplay, David Hertz, William Ludwig; based on a story by Endre Bohem, Dorothy Yost; associate producer, Albert E. Levy; camera, Clyde DeVinna; sound, Douglas Shearer; music, David Snell, Edward Ward; art director, Cedric Gibbons; set, Edwin B. Willis; second unit, Charles Dorian; editor, Howard O'Neill; associate art director, Howard Campbell; wardrobe, Dolly Tree; cast: Edward G. Robinson (John Ingram / John Harrington), Ruth Hussey (Helen Ingram), Gene Lockhart (William Ramey), Bobs Watson (Hank Ingram), Guinn "Big Boy" Williams (Moose McCarthy), John Wray (Diggs), Arthur Hohl (Rawlins), Esther Dale (Sarah), Joe Whitehead (Anderson), Joseph Crehan (Blaine), Victor Kilian (Boss Miller), Gil Perkins (Kearney), Mitchell Lewis (First Workman), Ted Oliver (Second Workman), Lew Harvey (Third Workman), Willie Best (Sunny), Art Miles (Driver), Robert Middlemass (Desk Sergeant), Ivan Miller (Weber), Hal K. Dawson (Desk Clerk), Philip Morris (Trooper), Charles Middleton, Trevor Bardette (Deputies), Everett Brown (Prisoner), Ed Montoya (Juan), Joe Dominguez (Pedro), Eddy Chandler (Boss Brown), Lee Phelps (Guard); Cy Kendall (Sheriff), Wade Boteler (Sergeant), Harry Fleischmann (Oil Worker), Robert Homans, James C. Morton, Harry Strang (Cops), Blackie Whiteford (Convict), Ed Brady; MGM; 81 minutes; September 1939

Blackmer, Sidney   (1895–1973) appeared in silent films and on Broadway, winning a Tony award for *Come Back, Little Sheba*. His two films with Edward G. Robinson are *Little Caesar* (as The Big Boy) and *The Last Gangster*. Others include *In Old Chicago, Duel in the Sun, The High and the Mighty, High Society,* and *Rosemary's Baby*.

Blake, Robert (Bobby)   (1933–) played Edward G. Robinson's son two times — as a youngster in *The Woman in the Window,* and fifteen years later as a Confederate deserter in "Heritage" on *Zane Grey Theatre*. He was in the Our Gang comedies and also the TV series *Baretta*, and the films *Treasure of the Sierra Madre, In Cold Blood* and *Tell Them Willie Boy Is Here*.

Blane, Sally   (1910–97) was Loretta Young's elder sister. She appeared briefly in *A Bullet for Joey* with Edward G. Robinson. Earlier films include *I Am a Fugitive from a Chain Gang, Way Down South,* and *The Story of Alexander Graham Bell*.

"Blind Alley"   (Radio, 1940, 1946) Edward G. Robinson appeared in two radio dramatizations of this 1939 Columbia gangster film about a mad killer who holds a psychiatrist prisoner.

Cast: Edward G. Robinson, Joseph Calleia, Isabel Jewell, Leatrice Joy, Roger Pryor (host); *Gulf Screen Guild Theatre*; CBS-radio; February 25, 1940; 30 minutes

Cast: Edward G. Robinson, Broderick Crawford, Isabel Jewell, Frank Albertson; *Lady Esther's Screen Guild Players*; CBS-radio; November 18, 1946; 30 minutes

Blindness   In a rather melodramatic episode of *Big Town* on the radio, Edward G. Robinson's character, crusading editor Steve Wilson, is blinded by racketeers. Later he rescues a child from a burning building, doing further damage to his eyes. The conclusion had him operated on, with a hundred-to-one chance of recovery.

In *The Sea Wolf* his character, Wolf Larsen, suffers headaches before he goes blind. When this is discovered by the crew of his ship, *The Ghost,* Larsen must fight off their attack.

Finally, Robinson plays Old Adams in *Mackenna's Gold*. In his youth he was the only person to survive a massacre after seeing a lost Apache canyon of gold; instead of killing him, the Indians gouged out his eyes.

See also **Disabilities**.

Une Blonde de Pekin   see   *Peking Blonde*

The Blonde from Peking   see   *Peking Blonde*

Blondell, Joan (1909–79) acted with Edward G. Robinson in *Bullets or Ballots* and in *The Cincinnati Kid*, for which she was named best supporting actress by the National Board of Review. She also appears in cameo roles as herself in *Dark Hazard* and *An Intimate Dinner in Celebration of Warner Bros. Silver Jubilee.* Coming from vaudeville and Broadway, her other films include *The Public Enemy, Cry Havoc, A Tree Grows in Brooklyn, The Blue Veil* (Oscar nomination), *Desk Set, Opening Night,* and *Grease.* She was married to cameraman George Barnes, actor Dick Powell, and producer Mike Todd.

Bloom, Claire (1931–) was in *The Outrage*, with Edward G. Robinson, and the stage production of *Rashomon,* on which it was based. She performed at Oxford, Stratford-on-Avon, and the Old Vic, and is in Chaplin's *Limelight, Richard III, Look Back in Anger, The Haunting, Charly,* and *A Doll's House.* She was married to Rod Steiger.

Blue, Monte (1890–1963) was with Edward G. Robinson as Sheriff Ben Wade in *Key Largo.* He began with D. W. Griffith on such silents as *The Birth of a Nation* and *Intolerance,* appearing in both, and in *The Marriage Circle, Dodge City, Juarez, Life with Father,* and *Johnny Belinda.*

"The Blue Albatross" (Radio, 1945) Syndication by the Department of the Treasury; director, Louis Graf; cast: Edward G. Robinson, Shepard Menken, Ted deCorsia, Byron Kane, John Conte (announcer), Harry Sosnik and the Savings Bonds Orchestra; *Guest Star*; December 26, 1954; radio, 15 minutes

Boats and the Sea Among Edward G. Robinson's films, these stories had ocean locales: the TV movie *Who Has Seen the Wind?,* about refugees living aboard steamer after their country was voted out of existence; *The Sea Wolf* and *Barbary Coast,* both with turn-of-the-century San Francisco locales; *Key Largo,* with a climax aboard a boat bound from Miami to Cuba; *The Little Giant; Confessions of a Nazi Spy; Tiger Shark* (tuna fishing); *The Ten Commandments* (Moses parts the Red Sea, and the children of Israel cross over on dry land); and *Destroyer* and *Tampico* (World War II Naval battles). *Hell on Frisco Bay* has its climax aboard a speedboat racing out of control as antagonists Robinson and Alan Ladd engage in a fist fight. The climax of *A Bullet for Joey* occurs aboard a freighter. Robinson's character's hobby in *Nightmare* is refinishing his new acquisition, a cabin cruiser. Plots of these stories often had Edward G. Robinson in the water, but, as he observed, it was usually a double or a shallow studio tank, because he couldn't swim!

Boehm, Sidney (1908–90), a gin rummy–playing buddy of Edward G. Robinson's, was an honorary pallbearer at his funeral. He wrote three screenplays for the star: *Black Tuesday, Hell on Frisco Bay,* and *Seven Thieves,* also producing the latter. Other films, from 1947, include *High Wall, The Big Heat, Violent Saturday,* and *Shock Treatment.*

Bogart, Humphrey (1899–1957) ranked Number One in the American Film Institute's 1996 poll as the ultimate movie star. He began his career on the stage in 1920 and went to Hollywood ten years later. He returned to Broadway in 1935 to play gangster Duke Mantee in *The Petrified Forest.* When Warner Bros. made the film version the following year, they planned to cast Edward G. Robinson, but Leslie Howard, who was recreating his lead role from the play, threatened to quit the film without Bogart. Bogart and Robinson appeared together on the screen for the first of five confrontations in *Bullets or Ballots,* then in *Kid Galahad, The Amazing Dr. Clitterhouse, Brother Orchid,* and, finally, *Key Largo.* Bogart survives Robinson in the latter film, shooting him on board a boat bound for Cuba; however, the score is even between them, as Robinson had poisoned Bogart ten years earlier as Dr. Clitterhouse. In both *Bullets or Ballots* and *Kid Galahad,* the two kill each other in a shoot-out, while in *Brother Orchid* both survive a brutal fistfight. It was all an act; they were friendly offscreen. Commented Robinson in *All My Yesterdays*, "Between takes we would discuss the world and war as friends. We were never close friends, but we respected each other." They were also political liberals, appearing together several times on the radio — as part of a fourth-term presidential campaign in *The Roosevelt Special;* reacting to the House Un-American Activities Committee's infamous search for Communists in the film industry in *Hollywood Fights Back*; plus in adaptations of *Bullets or Ballots* and *The Amazing Dr. Clitterhouse*. They were also in a segment of *Screen Snapshots* and a TV tribute to John Huston on *The Ed Sullivan Show*. Bogart made a remarkable number of films of classic quality: *The Maltese Falcon, Casablanca* (Oscar nomination and winner, best picture), *To Have and Have Not, The Big Sleep, The Treasure of the Sierra Madre, The African Queen* (1951 best actor Oscar), *The Caine Mutiny* (Oscar nomination), *Sabrina, The Barefoot Contessa,* and *The Desperate Hours*. Humphrey Bogart's fourth wife was actress Lauren Bacall. He was married previously to Helen Menken, Mary Phillips, and Mayo Methot.

Bohnen, Roman (1894–1949) appeared onscreen with Edward G. Robinson in *Night Has a Thousand Eyes*. He also appeared in *Of Mice and Men, The Song of Bernadette, The Hitler Gang, Mission to Moscow, None but the Lonely Heart, The Best Years of Our Lives,* and *Song of Love*.

Bois, Curt (1900–91) was in *The Amazing Dr. Clitterhouse* and *Destroyer* with Edward G. Robinson. The time span between his first film, *Der Fidele Bauer*, at age eight in his native Germany, and 1988's *Wings of Desire* has him in the *Guinness Book of World Records* for the longest screen acting career. Other films: *Tovarich, The Great Waltz, Boom Town, Casablanca,* and *The Desert Song*.

Bonanova, Fortunio (1893–1969) plays Sam Gorlopis, who files a false claim on his burnt-out truck in *Double Indemnity*, with Edward G. Robinson; and in *Larceny, Inc.* he is a barber. Born in Spain, he studied music and law. He was on Broadway and in the films *Citizen Kane, Five Graves to Cairo, Going My Way, The Moon Is Blue,* and *The Running Man*.

Bond, Ward (1903–60) appeared in a number of impressive films: *It Happened One Night, Young Mr. Lincoln, Gone with the Wind, The Quiet Man, The Searchers, The Grapes of Wrath, Sergeant York, The Maltese Falcon, A Guy Named Joe, It's a Wonderful Life, Fort Apache, Mister Roberts,* and *Rio Bravo*. His three with Edward G. Robinson were *The Amazing Dr. Clitterhouse, Confessions of a Nazi Spy,* and *Manpower*. He became a TV star on *Wagon Train*. A Hollywood conservative, he helped fight Communism in the film industry. In 1950 he campaigned unsuccessfully in *Daily Variety* against Oscar nominations for liberals Judy Holliday, Jose Ferrer, and Sam Jaffe, saying also that if Ferrer and Robinson claimed they were not sympathetic to Communists, it was "outright perjury."

Boros, Ferike (1880–1951) played the mother of Tony Passa in *Little Caesar*, with Edward G. Robinson. She had roles also in *Svengali, Bachelor Mother,* and *Make Way for Tomorrow*.

Bosley, Tom (1927–) was on TV with Edward G. Robinson as Throttlebottom in *The Right Man*, and he is perhaps best known as the father on TV's *Happy Days*. He was on Broadway as New York Mayor LaGuardia in *Fiorello!*, and his films include *Call Northside 777, The World of Henry Orient,* and *Love with the Proper Stranger*.

"The Boss" (Radio, 1936) This was the first of eleven appearances by Edward G. Robinson on *Lux Radio Theatre*.

Based on the play by Edward Sheldon; cast: Edward G. Robinson (Michael Regan), Lillian Emerson, John Milton, Howard Phillips, John Wheeler, Donald Cameron, Walter Kinsella, William Ponstance, Clyde Franklin, Billy Murray, Frank McCullough, J. Francis Kirk; Frances Woodbury, Alfred Cora (Commercials); *Lux Radio Theatre*; CBS-radio; January 13, 1936

Boteler, Wade (1891–1943) was in six films with Edward G. Robinson—*Silver Dollar* (as a miner), *The Man with Two Faces* (detective), *The Last Gangster* (jailer), *A Slight Case of Murder* (cop), *The Amazing Dr. Clitterhouse* (police captain), and *Blackmail* (police sergeant). Films, from 1919, include *Seven Keys to Baldpate, In Old Chicago, The Oklahoma Kid,* and *My Little Chickadee.*

Bouchey, Willis (1895–1977) appears with Edward G. Robinson in three films—*The Violent Men* (as Sheriff Kenner), *Hell on Frisco Bay* (as Lt. Neville), and *Cheyenne Autumn* (an Army colonel)—and also in the *Ford Theatre* television episode "…And Son." He appeared onscreen also in *Suddenly, The Last Hurrah,* and *Support Your Local Sheriff.*

Boulting, John (1913–1985) wrote and directed *Journey Together*. After several successful British films, he and his twin brother, Roy, as a producing-directing-writing team, were responsible for such comedies as *I'm All Right, Jack* and *There's a Girl in My Soup.*

A Boy Ten Feet Tall (Film, 1965) World travel held a lifelong fascination for Edward G. Robinson (except when he immigrated to the United States from Rumania in steerage in 1903 — the voyage made him sick). From the 1960s his film roles took him on location to such places as Rome, Japan, Scandinavia, and Israel; and he enjoyed the chance to travel "on the company" and see the art treasures of the world. In 1962 he reported to Kenya to work on *A Boy Ten Feet Tall*. The role was well-written and colorful, but a heart attack he suffered on location nearly killed him. Following a three-month recovery period, Robinson was able to complete the film "on location" in England.

Compared to a heart attack, difficulty with Robinson's makeup for the film perhaps would seem trivial. But Phil Leakey, a freelance makeup artist assigned to *A Boy Ten Feet Tall*, faced an unusual challenge, as noted in *Making a Monster,* by Al Taylor and Sue Roy: "Robinson … was unavailable for the first three weeks of shooting, so a standby painter, who happened to be about the same size … was commandeered to double for him until his arrival. An artist's impressions of the beard Robinson was in the process of growing were forwarded…. When Robinson finally arrived, Leakey 'nearly had a fit' [since] the artist's impressions of Robinson's beard were far from accurate…. For the remaining week to ten days, Leakey had to make up Edward G. Robinson to look like his double! … by adding fake hair to his beard."

In 1964, two years after production had begun, *A Boy Ten Feet Tall* was selected as the Royal Film Performance, an annual British charity function. The Queen Mother and Princess Margaret attended, along with Robinson and other members of the film company. Showing was delayed to most American audiences until 1965.

An early review of *A Boy Ten Feet Tall* in *Variety*, in March 1963, said that, "with the exception of Robinson, looking like a slightly junior Ernest Hemingway, and Paul Stassino, as a glib crook of a guide, the others are cardboard." In showings two years later, cut by forty minutes, the film's high spot still seemed to be Robinson. *The New York Herald-Tribune* proclaimed him "nothing short of brilliant."

A Michael Balcon production; producer, Hal Mason; director, Alexander Mackendrick; screenplay, Denis Cannan; based on the novel *Sammy Going South* by W. H. Canaway; camera, Erwin Hillier; art director, Edward Tester; music, Tristram Carey, Les Baxter; conductor, Muir Matheson; casting, Robert Leonard; second unit, Norman Warwick; sound, H. L. Bird; set, Scott Slimon; editor, Jack Harris; makeup, Phil Leakey; cast: Edward G. Robinson (Cocky Wainwright), Fergus McClelland (Sammy Hartland), Constance Cummings (Gloria van Imhoff), Harry H. Corbett (Lem), Paul Stassino (Spyros Dracondopolous), Zia Mohyeddin (Syrian), Orlando Martins (Aba Lubaba), John Turner (Heneker), Zena Walker (Aunt Jane), Jack Gwillim (Commissioner), Patricia Donahue (Cathy), Jared Allen (Bob), Guy Deghy (Doctor), Steven Scott (Egyptian policeman), Marnie Maitland (Hassan), Frederick Schiller (Porter); Paramount; British Lion/Bryanston–Seven Arts; CinemaScope / Eastman Color; 88 minutes; May 1965

When his parents are killed in an air raid in Port Said, Egypt, in 1956, ten-year-old Sammy Hartland runs away. Remembering that his Aunt Jane lives in Durban, South Africa, he starts a trek toward the desert, not realizing the journey will be almost 5,000 miles. He travels with a Syrian peddler for several days, but the man wants to ransom the boy. The peddler is blinded by an explosion at their campfire and later dies. Sammy is befriended by a wealthy woman, Gloria van Imhoff, when he is taken ill. When she decides to take him home with her, Sammy runs away again. The police are now searching for him. Cocky Wainwright, an old diamond smuggler, meets Sammy in the wild and regales him with stories of hunting and sailing. Cocky teaches Sammy to shoot, and one day while hunting, the party encounters a leopard. Sammy becomes a hero by shooting the leopard, saving Cocky's life. Sammy decides he would like to stay with Cocky at his camp. But the old man is wanted by the police, and it is not long before they close in on him and destroy the camp. Cocky tells Sammy that he was only interested in the reward. In jail, Cocky convinces Aunt Jane to allow Sammy to complete his journey. Months later Sammy turns up at the hotel she runs in Durban, and he discovers his leopard skin. He realizes that Cocky had to lie so he could escape and complete his trek on his own.

The first hour of the film has Sammy meeting a variety of strangers, both kindhearted and opportunistic. "Most fortunately, indeed, at about mid-point," said the *New York Times*, "that wonderful old actor, Edward G. Robinson, saunters into view as a grizzled, warmhearted diamond smuggler and gives the picture its real substance."

Time said the picture contained Robinson's "strongest performance in years," and *Life* called the film "a simple, charming, totally unpretentious little movie," observing that "Robinson plays ... with a perfect blend of toughness and manly sentiment." Judith Crist raved about "Alexander Mackendrick's beautiful 1963 film [featuring] Edward G. Robinson at his best [as] a hoary old diamond smuggler [in a story] to enthrall and delight you."

Edward G. Robinson was highly regarded by his co-workers. Harry H. Corbett, the English actor who played Lem in the film: "What can one say about such a man ... that hasn't been said? As a child he acted me off the stage when I watched mouth agog.... He is a stimulating, exciting, and vital person, and I am sure this is part of the magic that comes across from him on the screen."

Boyer, Charles (1897–1978) was in separate episodes of *Tales of Manhattan* and *Flesh and Fantasy*, with Edward G. Robinson, producing the latter, in which they were onscreen briefly in a transitional scene. On the radio both were in *The Roosevelt Special, Hollywood Fights Back*, and *Document A/777*. Boyer was also in *All This and Heaven Too, Back Street, The Happy Time, Barefoot in the Park*, and four for which he was Oscar-nominated: *Conquest, Algiers, Gaslight*, and *Fanny*. He received a special Oscar for establishing the French Research Foundation.

Bracken's World see "The Mary Tree"; "Panic"

Bradford, Richard (1397–) With Edward G. Robinson he played Dr. Joseph Gannon in *U.M.C.*, on which the long-running *Medical Center* series was based. His character was played in the series by Chad Everett. Films include *The Chase, Goin' South, The Untouchables, The Trip to Bountiful, The Milagro Beanfield War*, and *More American Graffiti*.

Brecher, Egon (1885–1946), a German-Austrian character actor, appeared in four films with Edward G. Robinson, most notably *Manpower,* in which he played Marlene Dietrich's father. He was also in *Confessions of a Nazi Spy, Dr. Ehrlich's Magic Bullet*, and *A Dispatch from Reuter's*. Other films include *Juarez, Heidi*, and *The Hairy Ape*.

Breck Golden Showcase see "The Devil and Daniel Webster"

Breese, Edmund (1871–1936) played a Chinese in *The Hatchet Man*, with Edward G.

Robinson. He was in silents from 1914 (*Wildfire, The Brown Derby*), plus *All Quiet on the Western Front, Mata Hari,* and *Platinum Blonde.*

Brennan, Walter (1894–1974) was with Edward G. Robinson in *Barbary Coast* and on the radio in *We Hold These Truths.* He won Oscars for *Come and Get It, Kentucky,* and *The Westerner.* Nominated also for *Sergeant York,* he was also in *Meet John Doe, To Have and Have Not, Red River, Tammy and the Bachelor, Rio Bravo,* and TV's *The Real McCoys.*

Brent, Romney (1902–76) appeared in three Theatre Guild productions with Edward G. Robinson — *Peer Gynt,* as the Thief; *Androcles and the Lion,* as the Lion; and *The Chief Thing,* as Petronius. He was in the films *Dinner at the Ritz, The Adventures of Don Juan, Cradle Snatchers, Don't Go Near the Water,* and *The Virgin Queen.*

Breon, Edmond (1889–1951) played Dr. Barksdale, one of the members of Edward G. Robinson's club in *The Woman in the Window.* He appeared also in *The Dawn Patrol, Goodbye Mr. Chips, Gaslight,* and *Forever Amber.*

Brialy, Jean-Claude (1933–), a French leading man in films from the 1950s, appeared in the role of Cajella in *Operation San Pietro,* with Edward G. Robinson. He also directed films. He acted in *The Four Hundred Blows, King of Hearts, La Ronde* and *Claire's Knee.* Brialy was quoted in *The Great Movie Stars:* "Robinson is marvelous. I can't believe he's 74 — he doesn't seem like an elderly man but a young man disguised as one. His eyes glint, his mouth is mocking and tender. But what really catches you looking into the famous face, makes you draw up short, is his goodness. He knows the world and people — his experience of humanity is immense. And, he has almost fifty years of career behind him, but there's one thing he has never lost from view — that is to act. To act, for any actor worthy of the name is *essential*… that's why he remains so curious, so warm, and so understanding."

Bridges, Lloyd (1913–98), leading man (and father of actors Jeff and Beau Bridges), is known for his role as Mike Nelson in the TV series *Sea Hunt.* He had a small role as a sailor in *Destroyer,* with Edward G. Robinson. His other films include *Home of the Brave, High Noon, The Rainmaker,* and *Airplane.*

The Bright Shawl (Film, 1923) This was Edward G. Robinson's second film and one of only two silent features he made, following the first after a seven-year interval. Just as Robinson had been in New York at the time of filming *Arms and the Woman* in 1916, the offer to appear in *The Bright Shawl* also came while he was on Broadway appearing with Alfred Lunt in *Banco* in the fall of 1922. He was invited by John S. Robertson to be in the film because of his resemblance to Oscar Hammerstein. The picture, which was to be shot on location in Cuba, meant two things to Robinson — travel, to exotic pre–Castro Havana, and the world's finest cigars! The players in the film were stellar, even if some, like Robinson, were not yet established. He joined Richard Barthelmess, Dorothy Gish, Mary Astor (in the role of her father in the first of their three films together), and William Powell, a fellow graduate of the American Academy of Dramatic Arts.

Producer, Charles H. Duell; director, John S. Robertson; screenplay, Edmund Goulding; based on the novel by Joseph Hergesheimer; camera, George Folsey; art director, Everett Shinn; editor, William Hamilton; cast: Richard Barthelmess (Charles Abbott), Dorothy Gish (La Clavel), Mary Astor (Narcissa Escobar), William Powell (Captain Caspar de Vaca), Edward G. Robinson (Domingo Escobar), Jetta Goudal (La Pilar), Anders Randolf (Captain Cesar y Santacilla), Andre De Beranger (Andres Escobar), Margaret Seddon (Carmenita Escobar), Luis Alberni (Vincente Escobar), George Humbert (Jaime Quintara); Inspiration Pictures-First National; 8 reels (80 minutes); 1923

Charles Abbott is an American visiting his college friend, Andres Escobar, in Spanish-oppressed Cuba in 1850. He falls in love with Narcissa, his friend's sister. Andres also introduces him to La Clavel, an Andalusian dancer, who is being courted by Captain deVaca. She obtains military information from deVaca and passes it on to Abbott, who, in turn, gives it to Andres. La Pilar, a spy for the Spaniards, sets a trap, and Andres is captured, tortured, and killed; his body is returned to his father, Don Domingo Escobar. The Don, realizing his aristocratic family is in danger, sees to it that the body of his son is missing when the house is searched for evidence. Further, his son's body has been discarded and its face shattered with a pistol by the Don to prevent recognition. La Clavel and La Pilar tangle, and La Clavel is stabbed. Dying, she gives Abbott her bloodstained shawl. Abbott duels with Captain de Vaca to avenge his friend's death and is badly wounded. He is sent home to America under the care of Narcissa and her mother.

Not remembering his bit as an extra in *Arms and the Woman,* Robinson claimed that *The Bright Shawl* was his only silent film role. His disdain for film acting was clear, based on his withdrawal from a project called *Fields of Glory* in 1922. Robinson said in *All My Yesterdays,* "I hated the movies, but I was unemployed, and the money ... was equivalent to twenty weeks' salary in a play. To top everything, the film was to be shot in Havana...."

The New York Times praised the film: "There is plenty of interesting local color in the production, as the exterior scenes were all made in Havana. The picture is an elaborate one, with fascinating costumes. There is good acting by the members of the well-chosen cast." *Photoplay* agreed, calling it "a pretty play of distinct atmospheric charm, the tale of Havana intrigue with Cuban strugglers of liberty on one side and soldiers of Spanish oppression on the other. Well acted."

Broderick, Johnny   He was a real-life New York detective whose efforts to rout crime in the city became the basis for Edward G. Robinson's character, called Johnny Blake, in *Bullets or Ballots.* One of Broderick's methods, which was used in the film, was to infiltrate by impersonating a member of the mob.

Brodie, Don   (1899–2001) made six films with Edward G. Robinson—*The Whole Town's Talking, Kid Galahad, Tales of Manhattan, The Woman in the Window, Scarlet Street,* and *Larceny, Inc.* Credited as dialogue director for *Flesh and Fantasy,* he was also in *Island of Lost Souls* and *Lady in the Dark.*

Brophy, Ed   (1895-1959) was in five films with Edward G. Robinson: *The Whole Town's Talking* (Slugs Martin); *The Last Gangster* (Fats Garvey); *A Slight Case of Murder* (Lefty); *Larceny, Inc.* (Weepy Davis); and *Destroyer* (Casey). Short, rotund, and comic, he was first in the silent *Yes or No,* with Norma Talmadge. Others include *The Champ, You Can't Cheat an Honest Man, Air Force,* several in the *Falcon* series, *Dumbo* (voice of the circus mouse), and *The Last Hurrah.*

Brother Orchid   (Film, 1940) The fourth of the five gangster films Edward G. Robinson made with Humphrey Bogart was this popular comedy. For a change, neither of them was dead at the fadeout, despite a tough and rousing fistfight at the climax. The leading lady was Ann Sothern, playing in the mold of her current success as the popular, scatterbrained blonde of the *Maisie* films. Ralph Bellamy played the "other man," as usual, almost losing Sothern to Robinson, and Allen Jenkins and Donald Crisp were also in the cast. Robinson's appearance in *Brother Orchid* was a concession he made to Warner Bros. for the studio giving him the role of *Dr. Ehrlich* earlier in the year.

Robinson had made a few gangster comedies in the 1930s—*The Little Giant, The Whole Town's Talking,* and *A Slight Case of Murder. Brother Orchid* had a plotline similar to *The Little Giant,* with Robinson's hero earnestly trying to quit as a racket boss in search of class.

The New York Times called the film "a spanking farce melodrama.... A funnier piece of hard-boiled impudence hasn't been enjoyed hereabouts since Mr. Robinson's ... *A Slight Case of Murder.*" Citing Robinson's enjoyable star presence, the *Times* continued, "The thing about Mr. Robinson's comic gangsters is that they are cultural snobs, superior to the sloppy muggs around them.... Obviously, this is a story which was destined for no one but Mr. Robinson, and he plays it with all the egotistical but vaguely cautious push that one would expect.... [He] can't help but swagger ... but he is also awkwardly aware of a feeling of humbleness. Fra Eddie makes a strange but earnest convert."

The New York Herald-Tribune said *Brother Orchid* was "the gayest variation of the gangster film since *A Slight Case of Murder* ... midway between straight melodrama and outright burlesque ... funnier than the treatment given it ... but ... [it] keeps to a high level of entertaining nonsense and is frequently hilarious." Comparison to the earlier film was inevitable, since the director was Lloyd Bacon. In particular, Robinson was cited for playing "with vigor and humor."

In his autobiography Edward G. Robinson made a critical assessment of *Brother Orchid* after seeing it on television some thirty years later: "I thought both Bogart and Robinson overacted, shouted a little too much, and occasionally were very good indeed. Robinson would have played the character quite differently today; I suspect Bogie would have too." Robinson also praised co-star Ralph Bellamy. He didn't comment about fellow actor Donald Crisp, but a reviewer did, calling his performance as Brother Superior "painfully holy."

Little John Sarto is discouraged with the life of a gang leader and goes off to Europe in search of class. After five years he returns to find that his mob prefers Jack Buck as their new boss. John's girlfriend, Flo Addams, has bought the ritzy Crescent Club, with the help of a wealthy rancher, Clarence Fletcher. Willie the Knife, who had been hiding out in a sanitarium, helps John organize a new gang to take back some of his old rackets. Flo goes to Jack Buck to see if he and John can patch up their differences. Jack, however, has hired a gunman to kill John. John is shot but escapes, and collapses outside the monastery of the Little Brothers of the Flowers, who nurse him back to health. Thinking he has found a great hideout, John, asks to "sign up" and, as a novice, takes the name "Brother Orchid." He works hard milking and raising flowers but is chastised by Brother Superior when he promises a boy money to do his work and then fails to pay him. Reading an old newspaper announcement that Flo will marry Clarence, he hitches a ride with Brother Superior, who is on his way to town to sell the flowers. He convinces Flo that he wasn't killed by Jack Buck and that he, not Clarence, will marry her. Learning that the brothers are unable to sell their flowers because they do not belong to Buck's protective association, John goes after Jack, enlisting the help of Clarence and his cowboy buddies, who are in town for the wedding. In the melee Jack Buck is turned over to the police. John tells Clarence to go back to Flo. He returns to the monastery, where he tells the brothers, "This is the real class."

Executive producer, Hal B. Wallis; associate producer, Mark Hellinger; director, Lloyd Bacon; story, Richard Connell; screenplay, Earl Baldwin, Richard Macaulay; assistant director, Dick Mayberry; dialogue director, Hugh Cummings; art director, Max Parker; montages, Robert Burks, Don Siegel; sound, C. A. Riggs; special effects, Byron Haskin, Willard Van Enger, Edwin B. DuPar; music, Heinz Roemheld; orchestra, Ray Heindorf; musical director, Leo F. Forbstein; camera, Tony Gaudio; makeup, Perc Westmore; editor, William Holmes; cast: Edward G. Robinson (Little John Sarto), Ann Sothern (Flo Addams), Humphrey Bogart (Jack Buck), Ralph Bellamy (Clarence Fletcher), Donald Crisp (Brother Superior), Allen Jenkins (Willie the Knife Corson), Charles D. Brown (Brother Wren), Cecil Kellaway (Brother Goodwin), Joseph Crehan (Brother MacEwen), Wilfred Lucas (Brother MacDonald), Edward McWade (Brother Sebastian), Morgan Conway (Philadelphia Powell), Richard Lane (Mugsy O'Day), John Ridgely (Texas Pearson), Dick Wessel (Buffalo Burns), Tom Tyler (Curly Matthews), Paul Phillips (French Frank), Don Rowan (Al Muller), Granville Bates (Pattonsville superintendent), Nanette Vallon (Fifi), Paul Guilfoyle (Red Martin), Tim Ryan (Turkey Malone), Joe

Caites (Handsome Harry Edwards), Pat Gleason (Dopey Perkins), Tommy Baker (Joseph), G. Pat Collins (Tim O'Hara), John Qualen (Mr. Pigeon), Leonard Mudie, Charles Coleman (Englishmen), Edgar Norton (Meadows), Jean Del Val, Armand Kaliz (Frenchmen), Charles De Ravenne (Stable boy), Gino Corrado (Artist), Paul Porcasi (Warehouse manager), George Sorel (Casino attendant), Georges Renavent (Cable clerk), DeWolfe Hopper, George Haywood, Creighton Hale (Reporters), Mary Gordon (Mrs. Sweeney), Frank Faylen (Hotel supervisor), Lee Phelps (Policeman), Sam McDaniel (Janitor), James Flavin (Parking attendant); Warner Bros., 91 minutes; June, 1940

The Brothers Karamazov (Theater, 1927) Fyodor Dostoevsky's nineteenth-century novel of Russian family life was adapted by a French writer, Jean Croue, and translated by Rosalind Ivan for its English-speaking premiere by the Theatre Guild. It is the story of four brothers—the passionate Dmitri, the intellectual Ivan, the mystical Aliocha, and the misanthrope Smerdiakov. Edward G. Robinson played the latter role, an epileptic who murders their father. According to literary scholar Edward Wasiolek, Dostoevsky dramatized the brothers' fate, their relationships with their father, and the guilt they suffer because of his murder. "The novel concerns itself with everything Dostoevsky struggled with during his lifetime: faith and doubt, love of authority and hatred of it, sensuality and abstinence, hatred of the human race and love of it.... The central theme explores the possibility of the child raising his hand against his father and, by extension, the right of a human being to raise his hand against God."

The production presented Robinson with several challenges, not all of them theatrical. At first "dazzled" by the prospect of playing Smerdiakov, he became disheartened when the director, Jacques Copeau, demanded from the actors rigid performances along the lines of earlier productions he had done in France. By opening night, with rebellion in the air, Robinson had also become ill; however, he ignored a doctor's warning to take to his bed. Two weeks later the actor was summoned to the deathbed of his father and did miss performances due to the Jewish funeral ritual of sitting *shivah*. Before the run of the play was over, Robinson developed a case of bursitis following an injury during a performance. A dramatic moment near the end of the play had Robinson's character, in defeat, slowly climbing a long flight of stairs on the set. While clinging to the railing, he cut his hand on an exposed nail. After playing a week of performances with his arm in a sling, the pain eventually necessitated hospitalization.

Theresa Helburn, executive director of the Theatre Guild at the time, recounted in her book *A Wayward Quest* that Robinson's stage business, ironically, was the highlight of the production. "We did a play that was saved by a detail. That was *The Brothers Karamazov*, a difficult play whose material was not popular, but with a magnificent cast. The Lunts and Edward G. Robinson appeared in it. The audience was pretty weighted down by the material until there was an electric moment in which Eddie Robinson went up a staircase. He endowed that piece of business with such a terrific quality of tension, suspense, and horror that its single thrilling moment lifted the whole play."

Produced by the Theatre Guild; playwright, Jean Croue; based on the novel by Feodor Dostoevsky; translated by Rosalind Ivan; directors, Jacques Copeau, Philip Moeller; set design, Raymond Sovey; cast: Alfred Lunt (Dmitri), Lynn Fontanne (Groushenka), Dudley Digges (The Father), Edward G. Robinson (Smerdiakov), Morris Carnovsky (Aliocha), George Gaul (Ivan), Clare Eames, Herbert Ashton, Charles Carden, Phyllis Connard, Charles Courtneidge, Dorothy Fletcher, Philip Leigh, Philip Loeb, Thomas Meegan, Bernard Savage; opened at the Guild Theatre; January 3, 1927

Robinson's notices were good. Although the play was "a cloudy, snarling melodrama with a broody Russian spirit," in the view of *The New York Times,* "in the part of the insidious, treacherous epileptic, Mr. Robinson is excellent." And *The New Republic* allowed that "Mr. Edward G. Robinson as the epileptic gets farther into his part than anyone else."

Brown, Charles D. (1887–1948) plays Brother Wren in *Brother Orchid*, with Edward G. Robinson, and is also a Navy doctor in *Destroyer*. His other films include *It Happened One Night, The Grapes of Wrath, The Killers, Notorious, Algiers,* and *Merton of the Movies.*

Brown, Helen (1915–74) appeared on the radio with Edward G. Robinson in *Big Town* and had key roles in *Tampico*, as Mrs. Kelly, who learns her husband has died a hero, and as Mrs. Hammond, a drunken woman who publicly accuses Robinson's character, Joe Keller, of murder in *All My Sons*. She also appears in *Magnificent Obsession, When Tomorrow Comes,* and *Shane.*

Browning, Tod (1882–1962), director of horror pictures, remade his silent gangster film *Outside the Law* with Edward G. Robinson replacing Lon Chaney. His films, beginning in 1916, include *The Unholy Three* and *Freaks*, plus talking films *Dracula, The Iron Man, Mark of the Vampire, The Devil-Doll,* and *Miracles for Sale.*

Bruce, Nigel (1895–1953), known as Dr. Watson in the Sherlock Holmes films, was in *Becky Sharp, Kidnapped, Suez, Rebecca, Suspicion, Roxie Hart, Son of Lassie, The Corn Is Green, The Two Mrs. Carrolls,* and *Limelight*, as well as *Thunder in the City* and *A Dispatch from Reuter's*, with Edward G. Robinson.

Bruce, Virginia (1910–1982) and Edward G. Robinson were in love but destined not to wed in *Night Has a Thousand Eyes*. She appeared with him on the radio in *The Roosevelt Special* and also was in the films *The Love Parade, Jane Eyre* (for Monogram Pictures — title role), *The Great Ziegfeld, Pardon My Sarong,* and *Strangers When We Meet*. She was married to actor John Gilbert.

Bryan, Jane (1918–) played Edward G. Robinson's sister in *Kid Galahad* and his daughter in *A Slight Case of Murder*. In the former she and Bette Davis caused Robinson to complain to director Michael Curtiz during his death scene, "Don't you think the girls are crying too much?" She retired after making eighteen films in three years to marry Justin Dart, who became president of Rexall Drugs.

Bryant, Nana (1888–1955) was in *The Firebrand*, with Edward G. Robinson, in the role of the Duchess. She was also in the films *Theodora Goes Wild, Calling Dr. Gillespie, The Song of Bernadette, The Unsuspected, Harvey,* and *The Private War of Major Benson.*

Brynner, Yul (1915–85) came from Broadway in *The King and I* to recreate his role and win an Academy Award in 1956, the same year he played Rameses II in *The Ten Commandments*, with Edward G. Robinson. They were on TV in *The World's Greatest Showman*. His other films include *Anastasia, The Buccaneer, The Magnificent Seven,* and *Westworld.*

Buchanan, Edgar (1903–79) was Edward G. Robinson's comic sidekick in *Destroyer*. Perhaps best known for his role on TV's *Petticoat Junction*, he appeared in many film westerns — *When the Daltons Rode, Buffalo Bill, The Sea of Grass, The Big Trees,* and *Shane* among them.

The Buick–Berle Show (Radio, 1953) Cast: Milton Berle, Edward G. Robinson, Eddie Fisher; NBC-radio; October 6, 1953

A Bullet for Joey (Film, 1955) Fourteen years after making headlines with their offscreen fighting in *Manpower*, Edward G. Robinson and George Raft reunited to appear in *A Bullet for Joey*. There is no record of further animosity between them. Both actors were aging, but more telling was the fact that their careers were in a slump. Raft was known for his poor judgment of scripts. Robinson, though, was in the position of accepting virtually any film role offered to an actor "graylisted" for alleged political errors. It was ironic and possibly of help to Robinson's situation, then, that the villains of *A Bullet for Joey* were the Communists; his Canadian police inspector doggedly tracks the gangsters who have kidnaped an important scientist to work for the other side. Yet Robinson knew how bad the film was. In response to a question from interviewer D. Overbey in *Take One* magazine, about the surprising quality of some of his "B" films in the 1950s, Robinson responded, "You aren't about to tell me you respect a picture like *A Bullet for Joey*, are you?" On a positive note, the supporting cast was pretty good, featuring George Dolenz, Audrey Totter, Peter Van Eyck, Kaaren Verne, and, briefly, Sally Blane (Loretta Young's sister).

Producers, Samuel Bischoff, David Diamond; director, Lewis Allen; story, James Benson Nablo; screenplay, Geoffrey Homes, A. I. Bezzerides; art director, Jack Okey; assistant director, Bert Glazer; music, Harry Sukman; camera, Harry Neumann; editor, Leon Barsha; cast: Edward G. Robinson (Inspector Raoul Leduc), George Raft (Joe Victor), Audrey Totter (Joyce Geary), George Dolenz (Carl Macklin), Peter Hanson (Fred), Peter Van Eyck (Eric Hartman), Kaaren Verne (Mrs. Hartman), Ralph Smiley (Paola), Henri Letondal (DuBois), John Cliff (Morrie), Joseph Vitale (Nick), Bill Bryant (Jack Allen), Stan Malotte (Paul), Toni Gerry (Yvonne Temblay), Sally Blane (Marie), Steven Geray (Garcia), John Alvin, (Percy), Bill Henry (Artist), Tina Carver (Girl), Frank Hagney (Bartender), Barry Regan (Chemist), Mal Alberts, Roy Engel, John Frederick, Carmelita Gibbs, John Goddard, Fred Libby, Rory Mallinson, Peter Mamakos, Paul Marion, John Merrick, Carlyle Mitchell, Bill Neff, Frank Richards, Carlos Rivera, Sandy Sanders, Joel Smith, Sandra Stone, Paul Toffel, Alan Welles; United Artists; 85 minutes; April 1955

A Communist spy ring led by Eric Hartman wants the scientific research of Dr. Carl Macklin. Hartman hires Joe Victor and his gang to set up Macklin for a kidnaping. Joe's mob includes Jack, who courts Yvonne, Macklin's secretary, and Joyce, who goes after the doctor. Joyce and Macklin develop a genuine attachment for each other, but things go awry when Jack kills Yvonne. Canadian inspector Raoul Leduc is investigating this and another recent murder, of which a connection seems to be Macklin. Leduc and his men track the kidnaping in a truck but are hijacked onto a steamer, truck and all. Joe wants payment for his job, but Hartman stalls. Meanwhile, Leduc pressures Joe about turning against his country. The Communists are foiled when Joe kills Hartman. Joe is also killed, but he will doubtless be considered a hero for the nobility of his last-minute efforts.

The reviews reflected the tiredness of the proceedings. "Age cannot wither nor custom stale the infinite uniformity of Edward G. Robinson and George Raft," said *The New York Times*. "We need only scan the details of Mr. Raft's laying out the job and Mr. Robinson's patient checking on him every step of the way. These are the things Mr. Raft and Mr. Robinson can act with their eyes shut—and sometimes do."

The New York Herald-Tribune simply and uncritically called Raft and Robinson "veterans of make-believe mayhem," and *Variety* talked about "performances [that] follow generally acceptable patterns, but are not outstanding."

The movie's anti–Communist storyline was noted in two retrospective works. "The cycle of anti–Communist films almost exactly coincided with the period immediately following the first HUAC Hollywood hearings in 1947 and the Senate rebukes of McCarthy," commented Andrew Dowdy in *Films of the Fifties*. "*A Bullet for Joey* ... [had] Edward G. Robinson erasing any lingering doubts about his patriotic contempt for Communism." And in *The Bad Guys*, William K. Everson cited the film's Americanism: "In the post-war years, when the Communists supplanted the Nazis as the principal villains, one memorable moment had G-man Edward G. Robinson appealing to the latent patriotism of George Raft by listing his mistakes: 'Murder ... arson ... blackmail ... theft ... those were all petty crimes compared to what these people are planning.'"

Bullets or Ballots (Film, 1936) Based loosely on events in the life of famed New York police detective Johnny Broderick, *Bullets or Ballots* was Edward G. Robinson's only film in 1936. His character, a racket-buster, was on the right side of the law, uncharacteristically. "It was a hard part," said Robinson in a June

16, 1936, interview in *The New York Sun*. "I had to play it differently from those gangster roles, play it down, make it quieter." Despite the acting challenge, Robinson's expectations were higher than the standard of *Bullets or Ballots*. "Detective Broderick was furious about the script, and so was I," he complained in *All My Yesterdays*, but it didn't matter. "It was an eighteen-karat, walloping wowsie of a hit."

Joan Blondell was Robinson's leading lady for the first time, which didn't happen again for 29 years. Humphrey Bogart was also featured with Robinson in the first of five films. At the climax the two tough guys had a shootout on a staircase, which proved fatal to both.

Associate producer, Louis F. Edelman; director, William Keighley; story, Martin Mooney, Seton I. Miller; screenplay, Miller; assistant director, Chuck Hansen; art director, Carl Jules Weyl; special effects, Fred Jackman, Jr., Warren E. Lynch; sound, Oliver S. Garretson; music, Heinz Roemheld; camera, Hal Mohr; editor, Jack Killifer; cast: Edward G. Robinson (Johnny Blake), Joan Blondell (Lee Morgan), Barton MacLane (Al Kruger), Humphrey Bogart (Nick "Bugs" Fenner), Frank McHugh (Herman), Joseph King (Captain Dan McLaren), Richard Purcell (Ed Driscoll), George E. Stone (Wires), Louise Beavers (Nellie LaFleur), Joseph Crehan (Grand Jury spokesman), Henry O'Neill (Bryant), Gilbert Emery (Thorndyke), Henry Kolker (Hollister), Herbert Rawlinson (Caldwell), Rosalind Marquis (Specialty), Norman Willis (Vinci), Frank Faylen (Gatley), Alice Lyndon (Old lady), Victoria Vinton (Ticket seller), Addison Richards (Announcer), Harry Watson, Jerry Madden (Kids), Ray Brown (Proprietor), Eddie Shubert (Truck driver), Max Wagner (Actor as Kruger), Ed Stanley (Judge), Milton Kibbee (Jury foreman), William Pawley (Crail), Jack Goodrich (Cigar clerk), Alma Lloyd (Beautician), Ralph M. Remley (Kelly), Anne Nagel, Gordon [Bill] Elliott (Bank secretaries), Carlyle Mitchell, Jr. (Kruger's secretary), Virginia Dabney (Mary), Benny the Gouge, Tom Brown, Roy Brown, Chick Bruno, Ed Butler, Eddy Chandler, Joe Connors, Hal Craig, Ralph Dunn, Jack Gardner, Saul Gorss, Harrison Green, Wallace Gregory, Edna Mae Harris, Ben Hendricks, Al Hill, John Lester Johnson, Guy Kingsford, George Lloyd, Herman Marks, Frank Marlowe, Howard Mitchell, Frances Morris, Garry Owen, Dutch Schlickenmeyer, Henry Watson, Tom Willis; Warner Bros.-First National, 81 minutes; May 1936

Johnny Blake, a New York detective who believes in keeping mugs in line, is discouraged by an apparent lax attitude on the force and increasing racketeering. He is demoted to patrolman and later fired. He assaults chief Dan McLaren in public. Based on this turn of events, Al Kruger, boss of the racketeers, offers Blake the opportunity to join in with him. Blake accepts and is given a thorough orientation on the workings of organized crime. Kruger answers to unknown big bosses. When he is killed by Bugs Fenner, Blake and Fenner vie for control of the rackets. The big bosses, pleased with Blake's progress, name him to succeed Kruger. Blake is forced to betray his friend, Lee Morgan, by turning over her independently run numbers game to the gang as an appeasement when they suspect him of being an informant for the police. Of course, it all has been a ploy, and Blake finally organizes a police raid on the racketeering headquarters. He plans to catch the big bosses when he makes a delivery of cash to them. Fenner learns the truth but cannot warn the bosses because he doesn't know who they are. Lee inadvertently tells Fenner where he can find Blake. There is a shootout, Fenner is killed, and Blake is mortally wounded also, but he survives long enough to make the crucial delivery and expose the bosses.

The reviews were generally favorable. *Variety* said that the work "tops all of Robinson's previous gangster performances." Foster Hirsch's assessment in *Edward G. Robinson: A Pyramid Illustrated History of the Movies* focused on the picture's final moments: "Robinson's career is littered with death scenes, but his expiration here is one of his grandest." Still, Hirsch called the performance "convincing."

In his autobiography, *Starmaker*, Warner Bros. producer Hal Wallis said *Bullets or*

Ballots was "one of our best pictures with Eddie Robinson." Robert Bookbinder's *Classics of the Gangster Film* affirmed Wallis' opinion: "Robinson was excellent in this mini tour de force, and he made Johnny Blake a ... complex character ... a finely shaded performance!"

The New York Times said, "The Brothers Warner, who have been making crime pay (cinematically, of course) ever since they produced *Little Caesar,* have turned out another crackling underworld melodrama in *Bullets or Ballots* ... [with] a crisp, cohesive and fast-moving script." The *Times* reviewer also cited Robinson's acting as "a top-notch performance."

Most other New York critics were in agreement. "With Edward G. Robinson in an engagingly tough and slugging role, a proficient supporting cast and crafty direction, it is a taut and compelling melodrama," said the *New York Herald-Tribune*, adding that Robinson "gives a powerful and persuasive performance that dominates the show. As a demoted detective who is asked by a crusading commissioner to join the gangsters and then double-cross them, he has ample opportunities to be menacing." The *New York American* said, "He dominates the drama with the sheer strength of his characterization. Never for an instant does he lose control. He knows his man and limns him in clear incisive colors. The character has its shades and moods and vagaries. Mr. Robinson registers each with keen, accurate artistry of a super craftsman in the theatre." Finally, the *New York World Telegram* noted that "the role of Johnny Blake ... is a natural for Edward G. Robinson." Attached to the commentary was what was to become a standard comparison by reviewers: "unequalled since his *Little Caesar*."

"Bullets or Ballots" (Radio, 1936) Twice the film script was adapted for radio on CBS, with Robinson repeating his role as Johnny Blake — on *Lux Radio Theatre* and on *Hollywood Hotel.* On the former, Humphrey Bogart repeated his role, but the character was renamed "Brenner." On the latter, Joan Blondell reappeared as Lee Morgan.

Director, Frank Woodruff; adaptation, George Wells; sound, Charlie Forsyth; cast: Edward G. Robinson (Johnny Blake), Mary Astor (Lee Morgan), Humphrey Bogart (Bugs Brenner), Otto Kruger (Al Kruger), Chester Clute, Edward Marr, Wallis Clark, Wally Maher, Galan Galt, Lindsay MacHarrie, Lou Merrill, Earle Ross, Ross Forrester, Frank Nelson, Frank Gomphert (intermission guest), Melville Ruick (announcer), Cecil B. DeMille (host); *Lux Radio Theatre*; CBS-radio; April 17, 1936

Cast: Edward G. Robinson (Johnny Blake), Joan Blondell (Lee Morgan), Kay Kenney, James Melton; *Hollywood Hotel*, CBS-radio; May 8, 1936

Buono, Victor (1938–82) was an overnight success in *Whatever Happened to Baby Jane?* Large and comic, he also could be sinister. With Edward G. Robinson, he is Deputy Sheriff Glick in *Robin and the 7 Hoods.* Other films include *Four for Texas, The Strangler, Hush Hush Sweet Charlotte,* and *Young Dillinger.*

Burnett, W. R. (1899–1982) wrote the novels *Little Caesar* and *Dark Hazard,* which Edward G. Robinson made into films; and *The Whole Town's Talking* was also based on one of his books. He also co-wrote the screenplay for *Illegal.* Other major films based on his stories include *Scarface, High Sierra,* and *The Asphalt Jungle.*

Burns, George (1896–1996), a Hillcrest Country Club pal of Edward G. Robinson's and an honorary pallbearer at his funeral, appeared with him in the short film *All About People,* on TV in *Here Come the Stars* and *The Tonight Show,* and on a Red Cross radio show. Burns and his wife, Gracie Allen, had a hit TV show and made several films. He won an Oscar for *The Sunshine Boys* and was in *Oh, God* and *Going in Style.*

Burton, Frederick (1871–1957), a distinguished character actor who often played governors or judges, he appeared with Edward G. Robinson in *Two Seconds, Silver Dollar, The*

Last Gangster, I am the Law, and *Confessions of a Nazi Spy.*

"By-products of the Atom" (Radio, 1950) Syndicated by the American Cancer Society; cast: Edward G. Robinson, Sam Jaffe; *For the Living* (segment M); radio; 1950; 15 minutes

Byron, Arthur (1872–1943) appeared with Edward G. Robinson in *The Man with Two Faces* (Dr. Kendall) and *The Whole Town's Talking* (District Attorney Spencer). On Broadway he acted with Maxine Elliott, Maude Adams, and Mrs. Fiske, and also was Polonius to John Gielgud's *Hamlet.* Films include *The Mummy* and *Fog Over Frisco.*

Cabot, Sebastian (1918–77), heavy set, bearded, and British, plays the casino director (with a French accent) in *Seven Thieves,* with Edward G. Robinson. He is known for his work on the television shows *Checkmate* and *A Family Affair,* but other films include *Secret Agent, Romeo and Juliet, Kismet, The Jungle Book,* and *The Time Machine.*

Caesar Edward G. Robinson enacted the emperor Caesar in *Androcles and the Lion.* It is doubtful, though, that George Bernard Shaw intended his character in the play to be one ruler in particular from ancient Rome, but rather he is a "conglomerate" of Caesars. The plot of the play had him proclaiming Christianity as Rome's state religion following a "miracle": Androcles, a Christian slave, is tossed to the lions in the Roman arena; but instead of eating Androcles, a lion caresses him out of gratitude, remembering him as the gentle soul who had earlier removed a thorn from its paw. For dramatic purposes, Shaw condensed three hundred years into one act, since the historical Androcles lived during the first century, and persecution of the Christians existed in Rome as late as the conversion of Constantine I in the fourth century. Nevertheless, the stage role was Edward G. Robinson's first Caesar, preceding *Little Caesar* by five years.

Cagney, James (1899–1986) Hollywood's other great gangster star of the 1930s was in one film with Edward G. Robinson — *Smart Money* — immediately following their respective successes in *Little Caesar* and *The Public Enemy.* They were on the radio together in *Ship Forever Sailing,* and Cagney did the voice-over introduction to the tribute to Robinson on the *45th Annual Academy Awards.* Cagney won an Oscar for *Yankee Doodle Dandy,* and also starred in *Footlight Parade, Angels with Dirty Faces, The Roaring Twenties, White Heat, Mister Roberts, Man of a Thousand Faces, One Two Three,* and *Ragtime.*

Cahn, Sammy (1913–93) was a lyricist who, in collaboration (with variously Nicholas Brodsky, Victor Young, Jule Styne, and James Van Heusen), received a total of twenty-five Oscar nominations. With Van Heusen, he wrote the Oscar-winning "High Hopes" for *A Hole in the Head.* Nominations for songs in other films in which Edward G. Robinson appeared were "My Kind of Town" (*Robin and the 7 Hoods,* music by Van Heusen) and the title song for *It's a Great Feeling* (music by Styne). Cahn and Van Heusen also won Oscars for "Three Coins in the Fountain," "All the Way," and "Call Me Irresponsible."

See **James Van Heusen**.

Calhern, Louis (1895–1956) was on Broadway in *Hedda Gabler, Life with Father, The Magnificent Yankee* (also onscreen), and *King Lear.* In films he was in *The Life of Emile Zola, The Bridge of San Luis Rey, Notorious, Annie Get Your Gun* (as Buffalo Bill), *The Asphalt Jungle, Julius Caesar* (title role), *High Society,* and, with Edward G. Robinson, *The Man with Two Faces* and *Dr. Ehrlich's Magic Bullet.*

Calhoun, Rory (1922–99), appeared with Edward G. Robinson, in *The Red House,* his second film. Others include *Rogue River, With a Song in My Heart, How to Marry a Millionaire, River of No Return,* and, more recently, the horror film *Motel Hell.*

California Melodies (Radio, 1933) Edward G. Robinson; CBS-radio; November 7, 1933

Callender, Romaine   played the butler, Roberts, in *The Amazing Dr. Clitterhouse*, with Edward G. Robinson. Ten years earlier he had played State's Attorney Welch onstage in *The Racket*.

Calloway, Cab   (1907–94), legendary black bandleader and singer, appeared with Edward G. Robinson as one of the gamblers in *The Cincinnati Kid*. His other films include *The Big Broadcast, International House, Stormy Weather,* and *The Blues Brothers*.

Cambridge, Godfrey   (1929–76), a heavyset black comic, was with Edward G. Robinson as one of the gang members in *The Biggest Bundle of them All*. He is also in *The Last Angry Man, The President's Analyst, Watermelon Man, Cotton Comes to Harlem,* and *Come Back Charleston Blue*.

Camel's Screen Guild Players see "All My Sons"

Cameramen   Cameramen are cinematographers or directors of photography on motion pictures and television shows. According to Ephraim Katz in *The Film Encyclopedia*, the cameraman is "the person in charge of lighting a set and photographing a film ... [and] is responsible for transforming the screenwriter's and director's concepts into real visual images."

Italian émigrés (Gaetano) Tony Gaudio and Sol Polito served as cinematographer on thirteen Robinson films between them. William Daniels and Milton Krasner each filmed four, while Burnett Guffey, Sid Hickox, James Wong Howe, John Seitz,* and James Van Trees** were head cameramen on three films each. *Oscar Nominated for *Double Indemnity* **two films, plus the TV program *The Case of Kenny Jason*

Eight cameramen made two films each with Robinson—Joseph Biroc (*Nightmare, Vice Squad*), Stanley Cortez (*Black Tuesday, Flesh and Fantasy*), Antonio Macasoli (*Grand Slam, Mad Checkmate*), J. Peverell Marley (*Illegal, The Ten Commandments*), Joseph MacDonald (*Mackenna's Gold, Pepe*—Oscar nomination), Russell Metty (*The Stranger, All My Sons*), and Joseph Walker (*Mr. Winkle Goes to War, Tales of Manhattan*). Other cinematographers who worked on Robinson films include Loyal Griggs, Ray June, and William Clothier, who received Academy Award nominations for *The Ten Commandments, Barbary Coast,* and *Cheyenne Autumn*, respectively; Jack Cardiff, who, having won an Oscar for his camerawork for *Black Narcissus*, subsequently directed *My Geisha*; and Rudolph Maté, director of *The Violent Men*, who received five cinematography Oscar nominations in the 1940s.

Campbell, William   (1926–   ), handsome character actor of the 1950s, appeared as a baseball rookie with Edward G. Robinson in *Big Leaguer*. He also had roles in *The People Against O'Hara, The High and the Mighty,* and *Hush Hush Sweet Charlotte*.

"Cancer, Cause for Hope"   (Radio, 1950) Syndicated by the American Cancer Society; cast: Edward G. Robinson, Michael O'Shea, Lyn Murray and His Orchestra; *For the Living* (segment D); 15 minutes; 1950

"Cancer in Men"   (Radio, 1950) Syndicated by the American Cancer Society; cast: Edward G. Robinson, John Beal, Gerald Mohr, Lyn Murray and His Orchestra; *For the Living* (segment A); 15 minutes; 1950

"Cancer in Women"   (Radio, 1950) Syndicated by the American Cancer Society; cast: Edward G. Robinson, Lurene Tuttle, Lyn Murray and His Orchestra; *For the Living* (segment L); 15 minutes; 1950

Cannes Film Festival   The Cannes Film Festival is, according to Roy Pickard in his book *The Award Movies*, "the most illustrious of all European festivals." The prize he received for his performance as Gino Monetti in *House of Strangers* in 1949 was the only exclusive acting award of Edward G. Robinson's career. He was the second "best actor" to be named in the history of the festival. In 1946 Ray Milland was named for *The Lost Weekend*; no actors were selected in 1947 and 1948.

Michael Redgrave, Marlon Brando, Paul Newman, Jean Louis Trintignant, and Marcello Mastroianni have been later winners.

Cantinflas (1912–93), real name Mario Moreno, a popular Mexican comedian, made only two American films, both loaded with Hollywood guest stars—*Around the World in Eighty Days* and *Pepe*, the latter featuring Edward G. Robinson as himself. Cantinflas starred in many films in his native country.

Caper Films Gangsters from the days of *Little Caesar* and *Key Largo* were serious-minded men. Even in comedies like *A Slight Case of Murder* and *Brother Orchid*, emphasis was placed on the plight of the characters, usually with them proving yet again how crime did not pay. In more recent times, and surely after Edward G. Robinson had aged gracefully into a wise and avuncular character on the screen, crime films developed a new style with a lighter tone.

The focus of a caper film is generally on an elaborate plan for a robbery, and Robinson was an ideal choice as a masterminding leader. *Seven Thieves,* his first caper venture, was anything but comic. Robinson's character had a lot at stake and eventually died of a heart attack, relieved to have pulled off one last job in the robbery of the Monte Carlo casino, or, as he phrased it in the film, "to finally put the cork in the bottle."

His other caper films are *Grand Slam* and the comedies *The Biggest Bundle of Them All*, *Operation San Pietro*, *Mad Checkmate*, and *Never a Dull Moment*.

Capital Punishment Early in his stage career Edward G. Robinson appeared in a vaudeville sketch entitled *Electrocution*. He often claimed in interviews that he made crime pay when he experienced a series of sizzling electric chairs during his career as a Hollywood tough guy. In fact, the electric chair was referred to in only four of his films, and he was to sit in only two. The premise of *Two Seconds* was that it took that much time for a man to die in the electric chair once the switch was thrown. In that short duration, Robinson's character relives the events leading up to his execution. In *Black Tuesday*, as a condemned killer making his final walk to the chair, he and other inmates stage a dramatic escape; at the film's fade-out they face death in a shoot-out with police.

In *Illegal* Robinson plays a district attorney who discovers he has wrongfully sent a man to the chair, and when he cannot stop the execution, his guilt overwhelms him and forces him to leave office for private practice. Dan Duryea's character in *Scarlet Street* is innocent of murdering Joan Bennett, but he is sent to the chair. A scene in the film was deleted showing Robinson, the real killer, climbing a telephone pole to get a look inside the prison when the switch is thrown.

Another form of capital punishment referred to but not shown in a Robinson film is the gas chamber. A scene was shot for the conclusion of *Double Indemnity* in which Fred MacMurray was executed. A replica of the gas chamber at Folsom Prison was constructed for the scene, but seeing it with the finished film, director Billy Wilder opted to delete it in favor of the ending showing MacMurray collapsed on the floor with Robinson lighting a cigarette for him.

Capone, Al (1899–1947), notorious Italian-born American gangster, was portrayed onscreen by Rod Steiger, Paul Muni, Neville Brand, Robert DeNiro, Ben Gazzara, Jason Robards, Jr., Louis Wolheim, and, of course, Edward G. Robinson, as *Little Caesar*. Robinson's character on the stage in *The Racket* was clearly modeled after Capone also, as were Joe Krozac in *The Last Gangster* and his Big Jim in *Robin and the 7 Hoods*. The ads for *Seven Thieves*, starring Robinson and Steiger, read, "Little Caesar and Al Capone together in Monte Carlo's greatest heist!"

The Prohibition era afforded Capone's gang control over illegal liquor operations, gambling, and vice, and he was responsible for numerous murders, including the infamous St. Valentine's day massacre of 1929. His reign over Chicago crime lasted roughly ten years, from 1921 to 1931, when he was convicted of income tax evasion. Released from prison after a mental breakdown, he spent his last eight years in seclusion before dying of syphilis.

Capra, Frank (1898–1991) won Oscars for *It Happened One Night, Mr. Deeds Goes to Town,* and *You Can't Take It with You,* with nominations also for *Lady for a Day, Mr. Smith Goes to Washington,* and *It's a Wonderful Life.* With Edward G. Robinson he directed the radio program *Ship Forever Sailing.* One of his last films was *A Hole in the Head,* with Robinson and Frank Sinatra, which he produced and directed. Capra referred to Robinson as "kind, good-natured" during the difficulties during shooting, in which "Sinatra plays his best scenes *without* rehearsing, and Robinson plays his best scenes after an *hour* of rehearsing." Capra claimed, "He's great in the picture ... The heart and maleness of this sentimental man were something to experience."

See ***A Hole in the Head.***

Car Chases see **Automobiles**

Card games see **Games and Gambling**

Carey, Harry (1878–1947) began in films in 1909 with D. W. Griffith and John Ford. His features include *Barbary Coast* and *Kid Galahad,* both with Edward G. Robinson, *Mr. Smith Goes to Washington* (Oscar-nominated as the Vice President of the United States), *The Shepherd of the Hills, The Spoilers,* and *Red River.* He is the father of **Harry Carey, Jr.** (1921–), who appears as one of the soldiers in *Cheyenne Autumn.*

Carillo, Leo (1880–1961) appeared with Edward G. Robinson on stage in the failed play *The Stolen Lady.* He played Pancho, sidekick to *The Cisco Kid,* on TV. In between, his many films include *Viva Villa!, Too Hot to Handle, The Gay Desperado,* and *History Is Made at Night.*

Carney, Art (1918–) was on television with Edward G. Robinson in an episode of *The Honeymooners,* in which Carney was a fixture as Jackie Gleason's upstairs neighbor, Ed Norton, and also in *The Right Man,* as Franklin D. Roosevelt. He won an Oscar for *Harry and Tonto,* and was in *The Yellow Rolls Royce, The Late Show,* and *Movie Movie.* On Broadway he was the original Felix in *The Odd Couple.*

Carnovsky, Morris (1898–1992) was in the film *Our Vines Have Tender Grapes* with Edward G. Robinson and four plays for the Theatre Guild — *The Brothers Karamazov, Juarez and Maximilian, Ned McCobb's Daughter,* and *Right You Are If You Think You Are.* With the Group Theatre he was in *Men in White, Awake and Sing!* and *Golden Boy,* and later he specialized in the Shakespearean roles Shylock and Lear. Films include *The Life of Emile Zola, Dead Reckoning, A View from the Bridge, Cyrano de Bergerac,* and *The Gambler.*

Carradine, John (1906–88), was in over 200 films, including *Tol'able David, The Sign of the Cross, The Black Cat, Clive of India, Les Miserables, Bride of Frankenstein, The Prisoner of Shark Island, Winterset, Captains Courageous, The Hurricane, Stagecoach, Drums Along the Mohawk, The Grapes of Wrath, Man Hunt, Hitler's Madman, Bluebeard, House of Dracula, The Kentuckian, The Last Hurrah,* and *The Shootist.* With Edward G. Robinson he is in *The Last Gangster, Cheyenne Autumn,* and *The Ten Commandments* (as Aaron). His sons are actors David, Keith, and Robert.

Carroll, Leo G. (1892–1972) His career began in England in 1911. He is known for his TV characters — the title role in *Topper,* and Mr. Waverly in *The Man from U.N.C.L.E.* With Edward G. Robinson he appears in *The Prize* as Count Bertil Jacobbson. He is in several Hitchcock films: *North by Northwest, Spellbound, Suspicion, The Paradine Case.*

Carson, Jack (1910–63) appears with Edward G. Robinson in *Larceny, Inc.,* supplying the comedic love interest for Jane Wyman. Robinson plays himself in *It's a Great Feeling,* in which Carson starred. The two also worked on TV in *Operation Entertainment.* Other films include

Stage Door, The Strawberry Blonde, Mildred Pierce, and *A Star Is Born.*

Carter, Mrs. Leslie (1862–1937) began onstage in 1890 for David Belasco in *The Ugly Duckling.* A popular star in New York and on tour for over thirty years, she undertook, at age 62, the title role in a tour of *Stella Dallas,* in which Edward G. Robinson played the role of Ed Munn. Her other plays include *Zaza, DuBarry,* and *The Circle.*

Cartoons Edward G. Robinson's face was a natural for caricature, and animators lost no time in parodying him, among other Hollywood personalities, in their cartoons: *The Coo Coo Nut Grove, Hollywood Steps Out, Hollywood Canine Canteen, Hush My Mouse, Porky's Double Trouble, Porky's Tire Trouble, Racketeer Rabbit, Thugs with Dirty Mugs,* and *What's Cookin' Doc?* produced by Merrie Melodies and Looney Tunes.

Al Hirschfeld did caricatures of Robinson on several occasions in groups of celebrities. When Robinson appeared in *Middle of the Night* on Broadway, his likeness was drawn individually.

See individual titles.

"A Case for the F.B.I." (Radio, 1943) According to *Radio Yesteryear*, this program was a dramatization of the capturing of a kidnaper. A message from F.B.I. director J. Edgar Hoover on juvenile delinquency was read.

DuPont Cavalcade of America; NBC; cast: Edward G. Robinson, Bud Collyer; composer/conductor, Donald Voorhees; March 15, 1943

"The Case of Kenny Jason" (Television, 1954) This hour-long drama was to have been the pilot for a series; however, it is not known if the program actually aired.

Producer, Samuel Bischoff; director, James Nielson; writer, Don Mullally; art director, Walter Keller; camera, James Van Trees; set, Claude Carpenter; assistant director, Ira Webb; editor, George White; casting, Arthur Landau; cast: Edward G. Robinson (Matthew Considine), John Hoyt (Captain Hardy), Ann Doran (Mrs. Jason), Glenn Vernon (Kenny Jason), Morris Ankrum (District Attorney), Vic Perrin (Barney), Robert Osterloh (Duke), Tom Dugan (Desk sergeant), Herbert Heyes (Judge); *For the Defense*; 60 minutes; October 9, 1954

"A Case of Nerves" (Radio, 1950) According to *Radio Yesteryear*, this story was about "an evil little man, an invalid wife, and temptation."

Producer/editor, William Spier; director, Norman Macdonnell; writer, Lawrence Goldman; composer, Lucien Moraweck; conductor, Lud Gluskin; Harlow Wilcox (announcer); cast: Edward G. Robinson; *Suspense*; CBS-radio; June 1, 1950

Castle, Irene (1894–1969), half the dance team of Vernon and Irene Castle, was in Edward G. Robinson's first film, the silent *Arms and the Woman.* Vernon died in 1918 at age 32. Fred Astaire and Ginger Rogers portrayed the Castles in *The Story of Vernon and Irene Castle.*

Catlett, Walter (1889–1960), a comic staple, was laid up in traction in two hospital scenes in *Manpower,* with Edward G. Robinson. He is also in *Bringing Up Baby* as the sheriff, *Mr. Deeds Goes to Town, Look for the Silver Lining,* and *Friendly Persuasion.*

Cavalcade of America see ***DuPont Cavalcade of America***; **"A Case for the F.B.I."; "The Man with Hope in His Hands"** (**"The Doctor with Hope in His Hands"**); **"The Philippines Never Surrendered"; "The Voice on the Stairs**

Ceiling Unlimited was created by Orson Welles in November 1942, and he served as producer/director/writer through June 1943. Edward G. Robinson guest-starred later that year in his role as *Big Town* editor Steve Wilson in an episode called "World of Tomorrow." *Ceiling Unlimited* was on the air through 1944.

See **"World of Tomorrow."**

Celi, Adolfo (1922–86), an Italian character actor, appeared with Edward G. Robinson in *Grand Slam* and *It's Your Move*, both 1968 crime caper movies with international settings and casts. He is also in *That Man from Rio, Thunderball,* and *Grand Prix*.

Chandler, Raymond (1888–1959) co-authored the screenplay of *Double Indemnity* with director Billy Wilder in a fitful and humorous collaboration. He also worked on screenplays for *The Unseen, The Blue Dahlia,* and *Strangers on a Train*. His novels *Farewell My Lovely* and *The Big Sleep* feature detective Philip Marlowe.

Chanukah Festivals for Israel (Theater, 1956–1968) Edward G. Robinson was a regular headliner beginning in 1956 with the annual Jewish festivals held at Madison Square Garden. He appeared consecutively from 1962 to 1968.

Sixth year. The festival celebrated the 75th birthday of David Ben-Gurion. Producer-director, Himan Brown; written by Allan Sloane; music, Symphony of the Air; conductor, Robert Zeller; choreography, Sophie Maslow; set, lighting, Sam Leve; costumes, Paul DuPont; participants: Ralph Bellamy, Alexander Brailowsky, Leon Janney, Elaine Malbin, Daniel Nigrin, Orna Porat, Edward G. Robinson, Richard Tucker; Madison Square Garden, New York; December 6, 1956.

Tenth year. Producer-director, Himan Brown; written by Sam Dann; choreography, Sophie Maslow; stage design, lighting, Sam Leve; costumes, Mostoller; New York Philharmonic conducted by Maurice Levine; participants: Marlene Dietrich, Edward G. Robinson, Mike Wallace, Sylvia Sidney, Isaac Stern, Nathan Milstein, Risë Stevens, Norma Atkins, David Bar-Illan; Madison Square Garden, New York; December 19, 1960, January 1961

Twelfth year. Producer-director, Himan Brown; written by Jerome Weidman; New York Philharmonic conducted by Maurice Levine; choreography, Sophie Maslow; design, Sam Leve; costumes, Mostoller; chairman, Ira Guilden; participants: Edward G. Robinson, Theodore Bikel, Mike Wallace, Eartha Kitt, Shelley Winters, Roberta Peters, Judith Raskin, Shalom Ronly-Riklis, Rivat Choir of Israel; Madison Square Garden, New York; December 17, 1962, January 1, 1963

Thirteenth year. Producer, Himan Brown; written by Jerome Weidman; lighting design, Sam Leve; costumes, Mostoller; participants: Steve Lawrence, Edward G. Robinson, Robert Ryan, Roberta Peters, Jan Peerce, Judith Raskin, Alexander Brailowsky, Shmuel Ashkenasi, David Bar-Illan, Sidor Belarsky, Geula Gill, Sophie Maslow Dance Company, Carmen deLavallade, Bert Ross; Madison Square Garden, New York, December 9 and 23, 1963, January 2, 1964

Fourteenth year. Producer-director, Himan Brown; written by Henry Denker; choreography, Sophie Maslow; lighting, Sam Leve; costumes, Mostoller; Festival Philharmonic conducted by Maurice Levine; chairman, Charles H. Silver; participants: Ed Sullivan, Jan Peerce, Roberta Peters, Ivry Gitlis, Edward G. Robinson, Bess Myerson, Martha Schlamme, Ethel Winter, Eli Wallach, Eartha Kitt, Eugene Istomin, Bertram Ross; Madison Square Garden, New York; December 17, 1964, January 4, 1965

Fifteenth year. Producer-director, Himan Brown; written by Henry Denker; stage design, Sam Leve; costumes, Mostoller; music, Festival Harmonic; conductor, Maurice Levine; participants: Theodore Bikel, Natania Davrath, Joan Fontaine, Ivry Gitlis, Gary Graffman, Sophie Maslow Dance Company, Bess Myerson, Jan Peerce, Itzhak Perlman, Anthony Quinn, Judith Raskin, Rivka Raz, Edward G. Robinson; Madison Square Garden, New York; December 6 and 26, 1965, January 3, 1966

Sixteenth year. Producer-director, Himan Brown; written by Henry Denker; ballet based on *The Gentleman from Cracow* by Isaac Bashevis Singer; stage design, Sam Leve; costumes, Mostoller; music, Festival Harmonic; conductor, Maurice Levine; participants: Samuel Ashkenasi, David Bar-Illan, Ralph Bellamy, Theodore Bikel, Sophie Maslow Dance Company, Eartha Kitt, Burgess Meredith, Bess Myerson, Jan Peerce, Itzhak Perlman,

Judith Raskin, Regina Resnik, Edward G. Robinson; Madison Square Garden, New York; December 5 and 22, 1966, January 2, 1967

Seventeenth year. Producer-director, Himan Brown; written by Henry Denker; stage design, Sam Leve; costumes, Mostoller, Jerry Boxhorn; music, Festival Harmonic; conductor, Maurice Levine; original music, Sol Kaplan, Arthur Harris, Jacques Press; participants: David Bar-Illan, Theodore Bikel, Natania Davrath, Carmen deLavallade, Ivry Gitlis, Sophie Maslow Dance Company, Burgess Meredith, Bess Myerson, Itzhak Perlman, Roberta Peters, Judith Raskin, Edward G. Robinson, Eli Wallach; Madison Square Garden, New York; December 4 and 18, 1967, January 1, 1968

Eighteenth year. Participants: Sophie Maslow Dance Company, Edward G. Robinson; December 16, 1968

"A sold-out performance of the Chanukah Festival for Israel Bonds last night enabled Edward G. Robinson to celebrate his 75th birthday with close to 20,000 people. Congratulatory telegrams from President Johnson and Premier Levi Eshkol of Israel were read as part of the festival birthday salute which was a tribute to the actor's prominent part in the bond drive. As a special gesture, one of the four new ballets presented by the Sophie Maslow Dance Company was dedicated to Mr. Robinson."—Anna Kisselgoff, *The New York Times*

The telegram from President Johnson read:

> Your career has combined an enviable stage talent with a selfless concern for public service. You have enriched the cultural heritage of America. You have participated in the effort to enhance the beauty of our countryside and you have advanced rightful aspiration of men of good will everywhere to live in freedom and dignity. Please accept my warm congratulations on this happy milestone.— Lyndon B. Johnson, President of the United States

Chapman, Marguerite (1920–99) appears in *Destroyer* as Edward G. Robinson's daughter and in the *Lux Radio Theatre* adaptation of the film. Her other pictures include *Charlie Chan at the Wax Museum, Navy Blues, Appointment in Berlin, Counter-Attack, Pardon My Past,* and *The Seven Year Itch.*

Character names In his lengthy career in film, the theater, and on television, Edward G. Robinson played a character named "John" or a variation of that name more often than any other—eleven times: John Allen (*Two Seconds*), Johnny Blake (*Bullets or Ballots*), John Harrington/John Ingram (*Blackmail*), John Lindsay (*I Am the Law*), Johnny Rocco (*Key Largo*), Little John Sarto (*Brother Orchid*), John Triton (*Night Has a Thousand Eyes*), John B. [Hans] Lobert (*Big Leaguer*), John Hayden (*I Loved a Woman*), and John Derwent ("…And Son").

His seven "Joseph" characters were Joe Krozac (*The Last Gangster*), Joseph Randall (*Five Star Final*), Joe Keller (*All My Sons* [the name is almost an eponym: "G. I. Joe Killer"), Joe Ventura (*Operation San Pietro*), Leo Joseph Smooth (*Never a Dull Moment*), Giuseppe (*The Man of Destiny*), and Josef Vadassy ("Epitaph for a Spy"). He was Jim or James five times: James Francis "Bugs" Ahearn (*The Little Giant*), Prof. James Anders (*Grand Slam*), Jim "Buck" Turner (*Dark Hazard*), Big Jim (*Robin and the 7 Hoods*), and in the title role in "The Legend of Jim Riva."

Robinson played Victor Scott in *Illegal*, Victor Amato in *Hell on Frisco Bay*, and Victor Bers in "Heritage." He was Louis Chamalis in *Barbary Coast*, Lew Wilkison in *The Violent Men*, and simply Louis in the stage plays *Banco* and *Launzi*. His character was named Steve in *First Is Last, Destroyer,* and the radio series *Big Town* (Steve Wilson). He was named Nick in *Kid Galahad, Smart Money,* and *The Racket*. Twice each he played a character named Tony (*A Lady to Love, The Night Ride*), George (*Operation X, Mad Checkmate*), Bart (*Tampico, Double Indemnity*), Dan (*Thunder in the City, The Devil and Daniel Webster*), and Wilson (*The Stranger, Big Town*).

He also played characters with such names or titles as Old Adams, Cesare Enrico Bandello—Rico, Captain Barnaby, Batiste,

Westcott P. Bennett, Rene Bressard, Samuel Brisach, Avery L(arry) Browne, The Button Moulder, Caesar, Chautard, Cobra Collins, The Con Man, Mr. Crispin, Christopher Cross, Dathan, Porfirio Diaz, Dominic, Douglas, Domingo Escobar, Fagan, The Father, Reb Feiwal, The Fox, Lawyer Grover, Henry Hayes, Hicks, Lancey Howard, Martinius Jacobson, Arthur Ferguson Jones, Jerry Kingsley (the Manufacturer), Hushmaru, Krogstad, Edward Kuder, Lazarus, Inspector Raoul Leduc, Andre LeMaire, Mario Manetta, Killer Mannion, Remy Marco, Yates Martin, Mike Mascarena, J. Chalmers (Pressure) Maxwell, Hank McHenry, Dean McWilliams, Mendel, Gino Monetti, Pete Morgan, Nordling, Simon Nurdlinger, Ottaviano, Pascual, Pinsky, Ponza, Ed Renard, Theodore Roosevelt, Sol Roth, Rubashov, Professor Samuels, Satin, Sato, Carl Schurz, Shrdlu, Smerdiakov, the Stage Director, Thomas (a butler), Maurice Tillayou, an Unidentified Man, Von Eberkopf, Professor Richard Wanley, Chaim Weizmann, Damon Wells, Theo Wilkins, Wong Low Get, and Charlie Yong, the Chop Suey King.

Robinson played the title roles in *The Amazing Dr. Clitterhouse, Mr. Winkle Goes to War* (Wilbert), *The Sea Wolf* (Wolf Larsen), *Dr. Ehrlich's Magic Bullet*, and *A Dispatch from Reuter's*. In the last two his given name was Paul.

Charisse, Cyd (1921–), an MGM dancing star (partnered with Fred Astaire, Gene Kelly, etc.), played a dramatic role as Carlotta, voluptuous ex-wife of Kirk Douglas, in *Two Weeks in Another Town*. She commented in her book *The Two of Us*, "Dear, brilliant Edward G. Robinson was in the movie, and he was always taking off, when he had even an hour free, rushing to one art gallery after another...." Her other films include *As Thousands Cheer, Fiesta, The Unfinished Dance, Singin' in the Rain, The Band Wagon*, and *It's Always Fair Weather*.

Chayefsky, Paddy (1923–81) wrote a number of successful television dramas that evolved into plays or films. *Middle of the Night*, which brought Edward G. Robinson back to Broadway after 25 years, is one example; his Oscar-winning screenplay for *Marty* is another. Writing directly for the screen, he was nominated for *The Goddess, The Hospital*, and *Network*, winning for the latter two.

While Edward G. Robinson received generally favorable reviews for *Middle of the Night*, Chayefsky became irritated by Robinson's ability to get what he felt were unwarranted laughs in the script. Director Joshua Logan argued that "Robinson was created by God for the part." Chayefsky countered Logan's comment: "Well, he ain't going to be in the film," in which Fredric March played Robinson's role.

See **Middle of the Night**.

"The Checker Player" (Radio) This was one of three appearances that Edward G. Robinson made on *Treasury Star Parade*, which aired on the radio between 1942 and 1944. According to *Radio Yesteryear*, this episode was "a suspenseful story about a gas tank filled with blood."

Cast: Edward G. Robinson, Mary Astor, Paul Douglas (announcer), David Broekman and His Orchestra; *Treasury Star Parade;* (date unknown); 15 minutes

See **Treasury Star Parade**.

Checkmate for MacDowell see ***Mad Checkmate***

Chevalier, Maurice (1888–1972), celebrated French singer-actor, appeared as himself in both *The Slippery Pearls* and *Pepe*. His forty-year screen career includes performances in *Love Me Tonight, One Hour with You, Le Silence Est d'Or, Gigi, Fanny,* and *Can-Can*. He was nominated for an Oscar for *The Love Parade* and *The Big Pond*, and was awarded an honorary statuette in 1958.

The Chevrolet Program (Radio, 1933) Cast: Jack Benny, Edward. G. Robinson, Mary Livingstone, James Melton, Frank Black & his Orchestra, Howard Claney (announcer); NBC-radio; April 21, 1933

Cheyenne Autumn (Film, 1964) John Ford's final western film in his fifty-year directing career was *Cheyenne Autumn*. His intent was to make the American Indians the good guys at long last after decades of films in which they had repeatedly villainized cowboys, settlers, and the U. S. Cavalry. The epic sweep of the film, running two hours and 36 minutes plus intermission, was to have been enhanced by its big cast. Spencer Tracy was to have played the role of Carl Schurz, Secretary of the Interior, but due to illness, he was replaced by Edward G. Robinson. Another story is that Tracy did not like the script. James Stewart's presence as Wyatt Earp, and the casting of such western regulars as Richard Widmark, John Carradine, Harry Carey, Jr., Ben Johnson, George O'Brien, Mike Mazurki, and Patrick Wayne gave the film some authenticity, but it was an error to cast so many Latin stars (Sal Mineo, Ricardo Montalban, Gilbert Roland, Dolores Del Rio) in the key Indian roles when the plight of their characters was so central to the film. Critics complained also about the performances, the writing, and historical inaccuracies.

Andrew Sinclair, in his biography *John Ford*, sums up the major problems with the film: "[The Dodge City] interlude was meant to break up the film, and did it only too well, interfering with the drive and purpose of the whole for box-office reasons. The other failure in the final version of *Cheyenne Autumn* was the commercial decision to cast the chief Indian roles with non-Indian actors like Sal Mineo and Ricardo Montalban...." Quoting John Ford, Sinclair continued, "'I wanted to show their [Indian] point of view for a change. Let's face it, we've treated them very badly — it's a blot on our shield; we've cheated and robbed, killed, murdered, massacred and everything else, but they kill one white man and, God, out come the troops.' Yet expiation was not enough to save *Cheyenne Autumn*.... Visually gorgeous and sympathetic to its subject, the film could not survive the miscasting and an unlikely love affair between a Quaker schoolteacher, played by Carroll Baker, and a cavalry officer, played by Richard Widmark. None of the actors distinguished themselves except for Edward G. Robinson.... He gave nobility to the part of the peacemaker and binder of wounds."

Newsweek disagreed: "Performances by Edward G. Robinson, Carroll Baker, Karl Malden and the rest are [uniformly] terrible.... Sal Mineo, the worst of all, walks with a pelvic lead, as if he were playing the first Cheyenne female impersonator."

Robinson's acting received less criticism than some of the others, but reviews were somewhat vague about him, if lacking in praise. "The secretary [of the Interior] herein is Carl Schurz, as park loving New Yorkers may guess, and it's Edward G. Robinson in cameo," said *The New York Herald-Tribune*. *The New York Post* noted that, "Edward G. Robinson ... seems extremely earnest, too earnest to shave all the time." *Life* was no more generous: "Edward G. Robinson plays Carl Schurz ... who complains of his lumbago and eventually solves the problems of the Cheyenne in a confrontation scene that is just as hilarious [as the James Stewart-Arthur Kennedy interlude] but unintentionally."

"In *Cheyenne Autumn*, John Ford, that old master of the Western, has come up with an epic frontier film," according to *The New York Times*. "[But] the climax with Carl Schurz [Robinson] interceding on behalf of the Indians after a hurried trip to Washington is neither effective and convincing drama nor is it faithful to the novel of Mari Sandoz on which the script is based." Nor was there any relief from Stanley Kauffmann: "Edward G. Robinson ... has a few scenes in which he stubs out long, nice-looking cigars soon after lighting them. In these days of shortage of good cigars, I was more disturbed by the reality of this waste than by the much less real plight of the Cheyenne ... the acting is bad, the dialogue trite and predictable, the pace funereal, the structure fragmented, and the climaxes puny."

"The biggest absurdity in the picture is to have Edward G. Robinson as Secretary of the Interior Schurz, after talking to Lincoln's portrait, decide to come out to the Black Hills, meet with the Cheyenne, and magnanimously give them their reservation on the spot. What he did in history — in U. S. Congress, 46th,

2nd Session, Senate Report 708 — was to say 'the Indians should be taken back to their reservation,' by which he meant they should be taken back to Indian Territory from whence they had fled." — Jon Tuska, *The American West on Film*

Leslie Halliwell mixed praise with dismay, calling *Cheyenne Autumn* a "dispirited, shapeless John Ford western with little of the master's touch. Good to look at, however, with effective cameos." Praise came from *Variety*: "Edward G. Robinson does well by the Interior Secretary part." And David Shipman, in *The Great Movie Stars,* said, "the best thing about *Cheyenne Autumn* was Edward G. Robinson's cameo."

"He plays with a serenity that comes from forty years on the job," wrote Foster Hirsch. "In a memorable scene ... the character looks at a picture of Abraham Lincoln and asks, 'What would you do, friend?.... Ford is clearly trying to link his character to Lincoln, and Robinson makes the man grand enough to sustain the comparison." — *Edward G. Robinson: A Pyramid Illustrated History of the Movies*

A John Ford-Bernard Smith production; producer, Bernard Smith; director, John Ford; suggested by the novel of Mari Sandoz; screenplay, James R. Webb; associate director, Ray Kellogg; assistant directors, Wingate Smith, Russ Saunders; art director, Richard Day; set, Darrell Silvera; sound, Francis E. Stahl, Jack Solomon; music, Alex North; camera, William Clothier; editor, Otho Lovering; makeup, Norman Pringle; costumes, Ann B. Peck, Frank Beetson; technical adviser, David H. Miller; cast: Richard Widmark (Captain Thomas Archer), Carroll Baker (Deborah Wright), Karl Malden (Captain Oscar Wessels), James Stewart (Wyatt Earp), Edward G. Robinson (Carl Schurz), Sal Mineo (Red Shirt), Dolores Del Rio (Spanish Woman), Ricardo Montalban (Little Wolf), Gilbert Roland (Dull Knife), Arthur Kennedy (Doc Holliday), Patrick Wayne (Lt. Scott), Elizabeth Allen (Miss Plantaganet), John Carradine (Major Jeff Blair), Victor Jory (Tall Tree), Judson Pratt (Mayor Dog Kelly), Mike Mazurki (Sgt. Stanislaus Wichowsky), Ken Curtis (Homer), George O'Brien (Major Braden), Shug Fisher (Trail boss), Carmen D'Antonio (Pawnee Woman), Walter Baldwin (Deborah's uncle), Nancy Hseuh (Little Bird), Chuck Roberson (Trail hand), Nanomba "Moonbeam" Martin (Running Deer), Many Muleson (Medicine man), John Qualen (Svenson), Sean McClory (Dr. O'Carberry), Walter Reed (Lt. Peterson), James Flavin (Sergeant of the Guard), Jean Epper, Stephanie Epper, Donna Hall, Mary Statler (Entertainers), Ben Johnson (Plumtree), Harry Carey, Jr. (Smith), Bing Russell (Telegrapher), Major Sam Harris (Townsman), Denver Pyle (Senator Harris), Carleton Young (Schurz's secretary), William Henry (Captain), Willis Bouchey (Colonel), Louise Montana, Dan Borzage, Frank Bradley, Lee Bradley, Dan Carr, Chuck Hamilton, Chuck Hayward, Ted Mapes, Philo McCullough, John McKee, Zon Murray, Kevin O'Neal, Charles Seel, Dean Smith, Syd Saylor, Dan M. White, Jack Williams, James O'Hara, David Miller; Warner Bros.; Super Panavision 70, Technicolor; 156 minutes; December 1964; working title: *The Long Flight*

In 1878 the Cheyenne Indians, chafing under the authority of the United States Army, begin a trek from their Oklahoma reservation toward their homeland 1,500 miles to the north. They are trailed peacefully by Captain Thomas Archer. Deborah Wright, a Quaker schoolteacher with whom Archer is in love, travels with the Indians. To Archer's frustration, the Army attacks the Indians for crossing the river out of military jurisdiction. When the Indians fight back, rumors abound that they have turned savage. A group of Indians is imprisoned in a freezing barracks at Fort Robinson, run by Captain Wessels. When they revolt and break free, there is a massacre. Archer goes to Washington, where Secretary of the Interior Carl Schurz promises help. Schurz arrives at the western camp before an Army attack and agrees that the Indians should be returned to their homeland in Yellowstone, Wyoming. Within the Indian group, Little Wolf now kills Red Shirt, who had taken the former's wife. Red Shirt's father, Dull Knife, and his squaw, Spanish Woman, are grief-stricken, but Dull Knife is named chief and Little Wolf goes into exile. Archer and Deborah are reunited.

The Chief Thing (Theater, 1926) Edward G. Robinson's fifth venture for the Theatre Guild was perhaps most notable for the presence of future big names in its cast — Lee Strasberg and Harold Clurman, who five years later formed the Group Theatre with Cheryl Crawford. Strasberg was destined to become a major influence on the Actors Studio as the leading proponent of the "method" school, while Clurman's reputation was forming as a leading producer and director.

The Chief Thing, by the Russian writer Nicholas Evreinoff, was a comedy, which Robinson admired for its theatricality, charm, and clarity, but it was not a big hit. "A performance colorful, but seldom crisp," is how *The New York Times* described it, but added that, "for such loose comedy the actors seem far too stiff and cautious." *The Nation,* however, called *The Chief Thing* "one of the smoothest, most consistent, and best of Guild performances."

A Theatre Guild production; playwright, Nicholas Evreinoff; translation, Herman Bernstein, Leo Randole; director, Philip Moeller; set design, costumes, Sergei Soudiekinem; cast: Henry Travers (Retired Government Clerk), Helen Westley (A School Teacher), Edward G. Robinson (A Stage Director), Lee Strasberg (A Prompter), Harold Clurman (Nero), McKay Morris (Paraklete), Estelle Winwood (A Dancer), Donald Angus (Tigclin), Patricia Barron (A Fallen Woman), Romney Brent (Petronius), Alice Belmore Cliffe (Landlady in a Rooming House), Peggy Conway (Popea Sabina), Ernest Cossart (A Comedian), C. Stafford Dickens (An Actor), Dwight Frye (A Student), William Griffith (Electrician), Hildegarde Holliday (Nigidia; Deaf Mute), House Baker Jameson (Lucian), Kate Lawson (Ligia), Edith Meiser (Lady with the Dog), Esther Mitchell (Landlady's Daughter), Willard Tobias (A Slave), Stanley G. Wood (Manager of a Provincial Theatre), Mary True (Calvia Crispinilla); opened at the Guild Theatre, New York; March 22, 1926; 40 performances

According to *Best Plays, 1925–26:* "Paraklete (the Comforter whose coming is heralded by John the Baptist) appears in the guise of a fortune teller. Listening to the woes and miseries of a boarding house group, he engages three provincial actors to appear at the boarding house as messengers of mercy. One brings love and romance into the life of the landlady's daughter. Another comforts and inspires an aging government clerk. A third restores the faith and zest for life of a student who had tried to kill himself. Thus, though they all realize when the trick is exposed that they have known only the illusion of happiness, their mental outlook is brightened."

Children Emanuel Goldenberg, Jr., was Edward G. Robinson's only child, born in New York in March 1933. He was called Manny. He died on February 26, 1974, thirteen months to the day (January 26, 1973) after his father. His 1958 autobiography, entitled *My Father—My Son,* told the story of a tormented child trying to grow up and live in the shadow of famous parents. Edward G. Robinson, Jr., was the father of the senior Robinson's only grandchild, Francesca. She, in turn, married and had a son, Adam Edward, the actor's only great-grandchild.

Gladys Lloyd, Edward G. Robinson's first wife, had a daughter, Jeanne, by a former marriage.

Onscreen in the roles of Robinson's young children were Douglass Scott and Larry Simms (*The Last Gangster*), Bobs Watson (*Blackmail*), Ann Todd and Polly Stewart (*Dr. Ehrlich's Magic Bullet*), Richard Nichols (*A Dispatch from Reuter's*), Bobby Blake and Carol Cameron (*The Woman in the Window*), and, perhaps the best-known, Margaret O'Brien (*Our Vines Have Tender Grapes*).

Other child actors appearing in Robinson films include Marcia Kagno in *The Hole in the Wall,* Delmar Watson in *Outside the Law,* David Durand and Bonita Granville in *Silver Dollar,* Bobby Jordan in *A Slight Case of Murder,* Dickie Moore (as Robinson as a boy) and Billy Dawson in *A Dispatch from Reuter's,* Ted Donaldson in *Mr. Winkle Goes to War,* Spanky McFarland in *The Woman in the Window,* Jackie "Butch" Jenkins in *Our Vines Have Tender Grapes,* Jenny Hecht in *Actors and Sin,* Peter Votrian in *Hell on Frisco Bay,* Eddie

Hodges in *A Hole in the Head,* Duncan Richardson and Jeri Lou James in *The Glass Web,* Larry and Robin Adare in *The Prize,* Ida Augustian and Luis Mata, Jr., in *Seven Thieves,* Jay North in *Pepe,* Fergus McClelland in *A Boy Ten Feet Tall,* Vickie Cos and Kym Karath in *Good Neighbor Sam,* Jerry Davis, Manuel Padilla, and Mark Sherwood in *Robin and the 7 Hoods,* and, on television, James A. Watson in *The Old Man Who Cried Wolf,* Butch Patrick in "The Legend of Jim Riva," Veronica Cartwright in "Who Has Seen the Wind?" and Ricky Powell in "The Messiah on Mott Street."

Onscreen, a number of actors played Robinson's adult sons and daughters: Burt Lancaster (*All My Sons*), Rod Steiger (*Seven Thieves*), Luther Adler, Richard Conte, Paul Valentine, and Efrem Zimbalist, Jr. (*House of Strangers*), James Komack (*A Hole in the Head*), Zalman King (*Neither by Day Nor by Night*), Robert Blake ("Heritage"), Billy Gray ("The Drop-Out"), Rudy Solari ("The Legend of Jim Riva"), Martin Balsam (*The Old Man Who Cried Wolf*), Mary Astor (*The Bright Shawl*), Dianne Foster (*The Violent Men*), Jane Bryan (*A Slight Case of Murder*), Peggy Cummins (*Operation X*), Marguerite Chapman (*Destroyer*), Marsha Hunt (*Actors and Sin*), Anne Jackson (*Middle of the Night*), and Diana Hyland ("The Mary Tree").

Children's Crusade for Children

(Radio, 1940) Edward G. Robinson was one of the few adult actors appearing on this coast-to-coast radio broadcast that raised pennies to help the children of war-stricken Europe. Janet Beecher, Bonita Granville, Cordell Hickman, Billy Lee, Leni Lynn, Gene Reynolds, Edward G. Robinson, Virginia Weidler (Participants); April 30, 1940.

Chisholm, Frances Lundie

(1923–83), model and actress, married Edward G. Robinson, Jr., in 1952. They were divorced in 1955. Having studied at the University of North Carolina at Chapel Hill, she understudied Faye Emerson on Broadway prior to a very successful modeling career for Conover, Huntington Hartford, and John Robert Powers. She was featured in print ads in such publications as *Esquire.* She was the mother of Francesca Robinson Sanchez, Edward G. Robinson's granddaughter.

Christians, Mady

(1900–51), Austrian-born character actress, played Edward G. Robinson's wife, Kate, in *All My Sons.* Other films include *Seventh Heaven, Heidi,* and *Letter from an Unknown Woman.* On Broadway she was in *Hamlet,* with Maurice Evans, and in *I Remember Mama.* She suffered under the Hollywood witch hunt of the late 1940s.

Christine, Virginia

(1920–96) was Mrs. Olson in the Folger coffee commercials. She is Edward G. Robinson's wife in *Nightmare,* was a member of the Swedish foreign service in *The Prize,* and played a tough-minded nurse in *The Old Man Who Cried Wolf.* Her other films include *The Killers, Guess Who's Coming to Dinner,* and *Judgment at Nuremberg.*

Churchill, Berton

(1876–1940) was in two films with Edward G. Robinson — *Two Seconds,* as the prison warden, and *The Little Giant,* as Donald Hadley Cass. He also had roles in *The Mouthpiece, I Am a Fugitive from a Chain Gang, In Old Chicago,* and *Stagecoach.*

The Cincinnati Kid

(Film, 1965) For the second time in two years, Edward G. Robinson replaced Spencer Tracy on the screen. As he had been slated to play in John Ford's *Cheyenne Autumn,* Tracy also was scheduled to appear opposite Steve McQueen in *The Cincinnati Kid.* The picture afforded Robinson perhaps his best role in the latter part of his career.

Robinson wasn't the only replacement. The original director, Sam Peckinpah, was replaced by Norman Jewison. There were several heated disagreements between Peckinpah and producer Martin Ransohoff. Among other disputes, Peckinpah had wanted to shoot the film in black and white. Ransohoff had wanted Sharon Tate in the part ultimately played by Tuesday Weld. Peckinpah felt that Ann-Margret in the other role was too similar to Weld.

Peckinpah wanted to film in California instead of on location in Louisiana. The first scene Peckinpah shot was of Edward G. Robinson checking into a hotel, carrying his own bags up a staircase. Associate producer John Calley wondered why his character wouldn't logically have taken an elevator or used a bellboy. Peckinpah's argument was that the shot allowed the set to be seen. Jim Silke, a collaborator of Peckinpah's, wrote a telephone conversation between Robinson and Rip Torn to help establish their characters. It was rewritten by Terry Southern. Ring Lardner, Jr., then completed the entire script to give it more humor. Peckinpah spent three days shooting the phone conversation, including nude scenes of a prostitute in bed with Torn. Ultimately, the decision was made to fire Sam Peckinpah as director, and production was shut down for two weeks.

Prior to the treatments by Southern and Lardner, the screenplay had been worked on by Paddy Chayefsky, who, with Ransohoff, elected to change the novel's present day St. Louis setting to 1930s New Orleans. This decision apparently pleased director Norman Jewison, who explained, "The book *The Cincinnati Kid*, on which the screenplay is based, was set in St. Louis and played against the contemporary scene. To me, the big gamblers today are businessmen dealing in vast financial empires. They are not the colorful gamblers of three decades ago. The characters in the book were too Runyonesque to be contemporary, so we moved back in time and south from St. Louis to colorful New Orleans, the fountainhead of modern jazz."

Robinson knew he had undertaken a good role, and a challenging one. "I could hardly say I identified with Lancey," he said in his autobiography. "I *was* Lancey. That man on the screen, more than in any other picture I ever made, was Edward G. Robinson with great patches of Emanuel Goldenberg showing through. He was all cold and discerning and unflappable on the exterior; he was aging and full of doubt on the inside.... It was one of the best performances I ever gave on stage or screen or radio or TV, and the reason for it is that it wasn't a performance at all; it was symbolically the playing out of my whole gamble with life."—*All My Yesterdays*

Virtually all reviews praised Robinson's work. Malachy McCoy, in his biography *Steve McQueen*, said, "The acting throughout is extraordinarily good, with Edward G. Robinson outperforming everyone in sight." Brendan Gill in *The New Yorker* apparently liked Robinson more than the film: "I had a pretty good time watching Mr. Robinson have a very good time portraying an old-time card player and aphorist, but nearly everything else in the picture proved radically irritating."

The New York Times called Robinson "one of the film's two genuine bright spots. The other is Joan Blondell, bless her.... Appearing briefly as a wily card king, Mr. Robinson is quiet, precise and deadly — all with his eyes. And, fortunately, for spectators bored by cards, into that interminable climax there breezes Joan Blondell, like a blowsy, good-natured gale."

The New York Herald-Tribune said, "Mr. Robinson proves himself The Man both as an actor and as Lancey Howard, suave, weary and unyielding in his tenure as the shrewdest gentleman gambler of all." *Variety* said, "Robinson is at his best in some years as the aging, ruthless Lancey Howard, champ of the poker tables for more than thirty years and determined now to defend his title against a cock-sure but dangerous opponent who believes he is ready for the big moment ... may well be the most suspenseful account of a poker game in film record." *Life* continued in a similar vein: "A game rich in atmosphere, traditions, rituals, lore and language, all of which are caught, with striking rightness, in the soft-colored, smoky haze of *The Cincinnati Kid* ... Robinson is a marvelous blend of the tough and the courtly as The Man."

"McQueen v. Robinson put on a bristling good show whenever they interrupt their marathon long enough for a few words of subtly guarded small talk — about health, luck, women trouble, anything that might make an opponent's mind wander," said *Time*. And finally, *The Saturday Review* noted simply that, "the elderly card shark is played consummately by Edward G. Robinson."

A Filmways Solar/Martin Ransohoff production; producer, Martin Ransohoff; associate producer, John Calley; director, Norman Jewison; based on the novel by Richard Jessup;

Cincinnati

screenplay, Ring Lardner, Jr., Terry Southern; art directors, George W. Davis, Edward Carfagno; assistant director, Kurt Neumann; set, Henry Grace, Hugh Hunt; music, Lalo Schifrin; orchestra, Robert Armbruster; song, Dorcas Cochran; sung by Ray Charles; costumes, Donfeld; hairstyles, Sydney Guillaroff; unit production manager, Austin Jewell; makeup, William Tuttle; sound, Franklin Milton; camera, Philip H. Lathrop; editor, Hal Ashby; cast: Steve McQueen (Eric Stoner/The Cincinnati Kid), Edward G. Robinson (Lancey Howard/The Man), Ann-Margret (Melba), Karl Malden (Shooter), Tuesday Weld (Christian), Joan Blondell (Lady Fingers), Rip Torn (Slade), Jack Weston (Pig), Cab Calloway (Yeller), Jeff Corey (Hoban), Theo Marcuse (Felix), Milton Selzer (Doc Sokal), Karl Swenson (Mr. Rudd), Emile Genest (Cajun), Ron Soble (Danny), Irene Tedrow (Mrs. Rudd), Midge Ware (Mrs. Slade), Dub Taylor (Dealer), Joyce Perry (Hoban's wife), Claude Hall (Gambler), Olan Soule (Desk clerk), Barry O'Hara (Eddie), Howard Wendell (Charlie), Pat McCaffrie, Bill Zuckert, Sandy Kevin (Players), Andy Albin (Referee), Hal Taggart (Bettor), Robert DoQui (Philly), Sweet Emma Barrett (Pianist / singer), William Challee, Mimi Dillard, Virginia Harrison, Harry Hines, Breena Howard, Greg Martel, Burt Mustin, Charles Wagenheim, Donald Elson, Dorcas Cochran; MGM; MetroColor; 113 minutes; October 1965

Eric Stoner, known as the Cincinnati Kid, is the best stud poker player in New Orleans in the 1930s. He is ready to challenge Lancey Howard, the Man, reigning poker king in the country. Eric has a relationship with Christian, but she feels she is in his way and goes home to the country. Melba, the vixenish wife of Shooter, Eric's friend and mentor, makes a play for the Kid, but his interest is only in the game. Slade, a wealthy local kingpin who has lost to Lancey, blackmails Shooter into dealing from the bottom to help the Kid. Tense, the Kid visits Christian and impresses her farmer parents with card tricks. He returns for the big game. Joining in marathon rounds of poker are Yeller, Pig, Doc Sokal, and Lady Fingers, a faded woman dealer. Lancey and the Kid best the other players and finally are alone. The Kid discovers that Shooter has been cheating to help him and prevents his further dealing. During a break the Kid gives in to Melba's advances, only to face Christian, who realizes she has appeared at the wrong time. Back at the game, Lancey is losing steadily until a fateful hand in which he holds four cards to a straight flush against the Kid's two pairs — aces and tens. The Kid offers his marker for $5,000 to call Lancey's hand, sure that the older man is bluffing and that his third ace, making a full house, will win. But Lancey reveals the high card to his straight flush. The Kid retreats to the alley outside the hotel, feeling gutted.

Karl Malden remembers *The Cincinnati Kid* in his autobiography *When Do I Start?*: "To New Orleans for the grand opening of the picture. It was one of those great big, old-fashioned premiers, but New Orleans style. Parade cars, a Dixieland band, huge crowds ... I remember that one night Eddie asked me to go with him to a special place he had heard of for dinner. We drove about an hour out of town before we turned up a long driveway surrounded by lush greenery that led up to what looked like a grand old colonial estate, columns and all. When we stepped inside, all the restaurant personnel (black men wearing tuxedos) snapped to attention around Eddie. They led us to this tremendous dining room and sat us — just the two of us — at a table for ten. Eddie said, 'Let me order.' And I spent the next few hours eating one of the best meals I have ever eaten in my life. Oysters, shrimp, real Southern fried chicken, the works. At the end of the meal when Eddie asked for the check, the chef, a very young man, emerged from the kitchen. He wouldn't hear of Eddie paying. Eddie insisted, but the young chef simply refused to let Eddie pay. 'My father would kill me if you paid for this meal, Mr. Robinson, you of all people.' Eddie asked, 'Who's your father?' The young man answered; it was an Italian name, and he said he was from Chicago. Eddie sent his regards to the chef's father; we thanked him profusely, and said goodbye. On the way back in the car I asked Eddie what that was all about. 'It happens all the time,' he said. 'They think I'm one of the boys. I know who the father is. He set the kid up in the restaurant business.' I got the picture. I had just eaten a four-star New Orleans meal courtesy of the Chicago mob ... and of course, courtesy of the fact that everyone, including the mob, loved Edward G. Robinson."

Clarke, Gage   (1900–64) played the hypnotist-murderer in *Nightmare*, with Edward G. Robinson. He appeared onscreen also in *The Bad Seed, I Want to Live!, Midnight Lace,* and *The Brothers Karamazov*.

Clarke, Mae   (1907–92) took a grapefruit in the face from James Cagney in *Public Enemy*. Her other films include *The Front Page, Frankenstein, Annie Get Your Gun, Singin' in the Rain, Pat and Mike, Thoroughly Modern Millie*, and, with Edward G. Robinson, *The Man with Two Faces*.

Climax! see **"Epitaph for a Spy"**

Clurman, Harold   (1901–80), New York producer-director, began his career with the Theatre Guild as an actor, appearing in three plays with Edward G. Robinson—*The Chief Thing, The Goat Song,* and *Juarez and Maximilian*. He helped found the Group Theatre. His Broadway credits include *Golden Boy, The Member of the Wedding, All My Sons, Bus Stop, Time of the Cuckoo,* and *Incident at Vichy*.

Of Edward G. Robinson, Clurman said, "I knew him fairly well. He was a very sweet man, really very sincere in his work, very devoted. He was a real craftsman in the sense that he played any kind of part. Before the Guild I saw him in a play called *The Deluge* by Hjalmar Bergman, which was a Danish play which took place along the Mississippi. Arthur Hopkins produced it. Robinson also played Japanese roles, Filipinos, Norwegians. He was always playing some foreign character, and he always did it with a great deal of feeling that it didn't matter what he played—he was an actor and he was acting. He had a kind of openness toward the acting profession. In other words, that was his job and he did it, and he always did it with a great deal of skill, aplomb. He was not an actor you needed to direct much. He seemed always to know what to do without much guidance. He had a certain natural flair. He was very honest in his acting ... I remember he invested a lot of money on Wall St. in later years, in the '20s boom period, when we were in a play together called *Juarez and Maximilian*—that was around 1927. He was losing a lot of money at that time, and was very worried about it. I think that's one of the things that precipitated his move to Hollywood. He would have gone anyhow because for a character actor of that kind at that time, the amount of money you could make on the stage was not very great. It was not as if he was a leading man like Lunt. So it was natural for Robinson, especially after 1929, when the theatre began to shrink, to go to Hollywood."—*The Collected Works of Harold Clurman*, edited by Marjorie Loggia and Glenn Young

Clute, Chester   (1891–1956) was on *Lux Radio Theatre* with Edward G. Robinson in adaptations of *Bullets or Ballots* and *Kid Galahad*. He also had roles in the films *Manpower* and *Larceny, Inc*. Among his other pictures are *The Man Who Came to Dinner, Yankee Doodle Dandy, Anchors Aweigh,* and *My Favorite Spy*.

Cobb, Irvin S.   (1876–1944), a novelist, playwright, and screenwriter, was, with Roi Cooper Megrue, the author of *Under Sentence*, Edward G. Robinson's second Broadway play. His *Judge Priest* stories were filmed by John Ford. Also an actor, Cobb appeared in *Steamboat Round the Bend, The Young in Heart,* and *The Arkansas Traveler*, among others.

Cobb, Lee J.   (1911–76) played Willy Loman in *Death of a Salesman* on Broadway, and on film was in *On the Waterfront, The Brothers Karamazov* (Oscar nominations), *Golden Boy, The Three Faces of Eve, Exodus, Come Blow Your Horn,* and *Twelve Angry Men*. With Edward G. Robinson he is one of the "Gentlemen from Hadleyburg" in *Mackenna's Gold*, and was on the radio in *Document A777*.

Cohan, George M.   (1878–1942), songwriter, performer, and playwright, produced

The Little Teacher, in which Edward G. Robinson was featured on Broadway. His songs include "Give My Regards to Broadway," "Over There," and "Yankee Doodle Dandy." His life is the subject of the film *Yankee Doodle Dandy* and the Broadway musical *George M.*

Colbert, Claudette (1905–96) and Edward G. Robinson made their first talking film together, *The Hole in the Wall*, at a New York studio in 1928. They were also in *The Stolen Jools* and on the radio in *The Roosevelt Special*. She starred in *Imitation of Life, Cleopatra, Tovarich, The Palm Beach Story*, and *The Egg and I*, and won an Oscar for *It Happened One Night*. She was nominated also for *Private Worlds* and *Since You Went Away*.

Coleman, Charles (1885–1951) was onscreen from 1923, often playing butlers, as in *Captains Courageous*. He was also in *Becky Sharp, DuBarry Was a Lady, Jane Eyre, My Friend Irma*, and four with Edward G. Robinson —*Silver Dollar, I Loved a Woman, The Little Giant*, and *Brother Orchid*.

Colgate Theatre of Romance see "The Woman in the Window"

Collier, Constance (1878–1955) appears with Edward G. Robinson in *Thunder in the City* as the Duchess of Glenavon. Her other films include D. W. Griffith's *Intolerance* (debut, 1916), *Stage Door, An Ideal Husband, Rope*, and *Whirlpool*. She also wrote several plays.

Collier, William, Jr. (1902–87), also known as "Buster," played Tony Passa, the gang member in *Little Caesar* who was "taken for a ride" because he stalled during the getaway of a robbery. He also appeared in *Cimarron, Street Scene, All of Me*, and *The Fighting Gentleman*.

Collins, Joan (1933–) was Melanie, the sultry striptease dancer among Edward G. Robinson's *Seven Thieves*. Her other films include *The Virgin Queen, The Girl in the Red Velvet Swing, Rally 'Round the Flag Boys*, and *Esther and the King*, plus several movies made for television. She starred on the TV series *Dynasty* for eight years.

Color Although color was used in films as early as the silents and perfected in the 1930s, Edward G. Robinson was not in a color film until 1949's *It's a Great Feeling*, in which he had only a cameo role as himself. His first major picture in color was *The Violent Men*. Twenty-one others followed: *Hell on Frisco Bay, The Ten Commandments, A Hole in the Head, Pepe, My Geisha, Two Weeks in Another Town, A Boy Ten Feet Tall, The Prize, Good Neighbor Sam, Robin and the 7 Hoods, Cheyenne Autumn, The Cincinnati Kid, Peking Blonde, Grand Slam, The Biggest Bundle of Them All, Mad Checkmate, Operation San Pietro, Never a Dull Moment, Mackenna's Gold, Neither by Day Nor by Night*, and *Soylent Green*. His last film shot in black and white was *The Outrage* in 1964.

Colors in the titles of his performances include *A Man with Red Hair, Silver Dollar, Blackmail, Brother Orchid, Scarlet Street, The Red House, Black Tuesday,* "The Blue Albatross," *Mackenna's Gold*, and *Soylent Green*. The most dramatic use of color in a Robinson film was the special effect in *The Ten Commandments* of turning the Nile red as one of the plagues on Egypt.

Columbia Pictures The studio began in 1924, growing out of C.B.C. / Film Sales Company, which had been founded by Harry Cohn, his brother, Jack, and Joe Brandt. Columbia became a major production and distribution company through its success with Frank Capra's films and such 1940s titles as *Gilda, The Jolson Story*, and *All the King's Men*, and also by embracing television as part of its product.

Edward G. Robinson made several films for Columbia Pictures, although they did not represent his best work. *The Whole Town's Talking*, the first, was an exception, and *Good Neighbor Sam* thirty years later was certainly popular. The others were *Thunder in the City, I Am the Law, Destroyer, Mr. Winkle Goes to War, Operation X, The Violent Men, Tight Spot, Pepe*, and *Mackenna's Gold*.

Columbia's Shakespeare (Radio, 1937) Also known as *The Shakespeare Cycle*, this radio program was developed by CBS as competition for a 45-minute program on the Blue Network, hosted by John Barrymore, called

Streamlined Shakespeare. Edward G. Robinson was featured in *The Taming of the Shrew*. Others participating in the eight-week series were Burgess Meredith (*Hamlet*), Claude Rains and Raymond Massey (*Julius Caesar*), Humphrey Bogart (*Henry IV, Part I*), Rosalind Russell and Leslie Howard (*Much Ado About Nothing*), Thomas Mitchell (*King Lear*), Walter Huston, and Elissa Landi.

See **"The Taming of the Shrew."**

Comedy Perhaps Edward G. Robinson's flair for playing comedy was first apparent on the screen in *Smart Money*, an immediate but much lighter follow-up to *Little Caesar*. The story, about a gambler's rise and fall in the big city, although not predominantly humorous, had several amusing moments. Scenes of flirtation between Robinson and several ladies in the film are delightful, one scene culminating in a kick down the stairs when it becomes obvious that the lady is a stooge for the district attorney. Most entertaining, however, is a brief pantomime between Robinson and co-star James Cagney describing a woman who is about to enter the scene.

The Little Giant gave the Little Caesar gangster a chance to redeem himself by falling in love. He was given two choices — sweet Mary Astor or hollow Helen Vinson. The comedy derived from gangster Robinson's inept social behavior and a polo match.

The Whole Town's Talking offered two comic Robinsons, one a meek clerk who is mistaken for the other, Public Enemy Number One. Jean Arthur and a host of comic actors — Ed Brophy, Paul Harvey, Wallace Ford, Etienne Girardot, Donald Meek, Arthur Hohl, and James Donlan — provided laughs, but a highlight is Robinson as a first-time drunk.

A Slight Case of Murder, about a gangster who discovers four corpses at his summer home, was one of the funniest movies of 1938, and it, too, benefited from sterling players — Ruth Donnelly, Allen Jenkins, Ed Brophy, Paul Harvey, Harold Huber, Bobby Jordan, and even a pre–Wicked Witch Margaret Hamilton. Its success was assured by Damon Runyon and Howard Lindsay, who had written the original play.

Brother Orchid reprised the social-climbing gangster of *The Little Giant* but with redemption in the form of a monastic life and flower-growing. Robinson lost the girl, Ann Sothern, to Ralph Bellamy, who was long known in Hollywood, ironically, for playing "the other man" in romantic films.

The problem with *Larceny, Inc.* may have been that it was too droll, if not top heavy. It is crammed with wonderful character players who make the episodic adventures of a trio of crooks nearly endless as they burrow into a bank from a luggage store next door.

The laughs were toned down in *Our Vines Have Tender Grapes* in favor of gentle family reflection. Serious portions included a near drowning during a scene of raging flood waters and Robinson having to shoot cattle in a burning barn. Young Margaret O'Brien, as Robinson's daughter, has several seasonal experiences in a year of growing up in the film's lighter moments.

In *It's a Great Feeling* Edward G. Robinson is among a dozen Warner Brothers stars who have a couple of minutes of footage. He spoofs his gangster image in a scene with Jack Carson and Doris Day on the studio lot.

In 1959, returning to films after a three-year absence, Robinson had one of his best comic roles as Frank Sinatra's stodgy brother in *A Hole in the Head*. He is genuinely funny as he tries to reason with his swinging younger sibling and gets a great deal of mileage out of physical business with a troublesome chair.

About all Robinson could do in both *Pepe* and *My Geisha*, in which he played Hollywood film executives, is be congenial. In the former, ostensibly as himself among thirty other guest stars, he cannot save the film from its own weight. In the latter comedy, wherein Shirley MacLaine plays a movie star masquerading as a Japanese geisha, he keeps a flimsy and lengthy plot moving along.

Paul Newman had the most to do comically in *The Prize*, a story about Nobel winners in Stockholm. Robinson, however, again played twins, as in *The Whole Town's Talking*. In one scene, exhausted from the physical demands of being rescued from kidnapers, he elicits a laugh with a reading (in German) of "Kaput bin Ich."

Like Newman, Jack Lemmon was the star in a Robinson comedy, *Good Neighbor Sam*. Humorous due to irony is the casting of long-time gangster Robinson as a pristine dairy farmer spouting Biblical passages, a client of the advertising firm where Lemmon works.

Four later films of varying quality traded on Robinson's persona as a wise and respected crime czar. His funny moments in the otherwise dull *The Biggest Bundle of Them All* have him outlining an upcoming heist via Madison Avenue, complete with placards and easel. *Mad Checkmate* and *Operation San Pietro* were even less distinguished, the former involving an elaborate impersonation of bank employees for a robbery, and the latter the tastelessness of the theft of Michelangelo's *Pieta`* from the Vatican. *Never a Dull Moment*, for Disney, was entertaining and featured a lot of physical clowning by Dick Van Dyke, and Robinson was given the opportunity to spoof himself as both a painter and collector of modern artworks.

Comedies Edward G. Robinson appeared in on the stage include *The Little Teacher, Polly with a Past, First Is Last, Banco* (with Alfred Lunt), *A Royal Fandango* (with Ethel Barrymore and Spencer Tracy), *The Firebrand, Androcles and the Lion, The Man of Destiny, The Chief Thing, The Stolen Lady, Henry Behave* (with Pat O'Brien), *The Kibitzer,* and *Mr. Samuel.*

On television he appeared in episodes of *The Honeymooners, The Lucy Show, Batman, Laugh-In,* and *Happy Days* (not the series featuring Henry Winkler and Ron Howard).

Command Performance (Radio, 1945) Edward G. Robinson appeared on *Command Performance* twice. The first episode was entitled "Victory Extra." The title of the second, with credits below, is unknown.

Participants: Kay Kyser, Pat Friday, Gary Cooper, Jerry Colonna, Edward G. Robinson; AFRS; August 19, 1945; 30 minutes

See **"Victory Extra."**

Communism The doctrine of Communism interprets history as a relentless class war that will eventually result in the victory and/or dictatorship of the proletariat (wage-earning class). The regulation of all social, economic, and cultural activities follows, leading ultimately toward a classless society. In 1845 Karl Marx penned this theory in the *Communist Manifesto*, which, with other writings, provided a basis for the government of Soviet Russia. Through several decades, which encompassed two world wars, modern-day Communist leaders systematically began revolutionary takeovers of non–Communist countries. This became particularly daunting to freedom-loving twentieth-century America.

In an attempt to determine "the extent of Communist infiltration in the Hollywood motion picture industry," the House Un-American Activities Committee of the United States Congress held hearings to investigate alleged party membership in Hollywood. Within three years, over 300 personalities, some of whom cooperated with the committee and admitted membership, and many who would not do so, were identified as Communists. Many were blacklisted. A small group of producers, writers, and directors who refused to cooperate with the Committee was cited for contempt of Congress, convicted, fined, and sentenced to a year in jail. The group became known as "The Hollywood Ten." Careers were in chaos.

The case against Edward G. Robinson was little more than innuendo, but it was amazingly troublesome. Although he was not officially blacklisted, his career suffered long-lasting ill effects when a pamphlet called *Red Channels* named him as a contributor to a number of Communist-front organizations. In his autobiography he maintained that the support was for causes of the discriminated and underprivileged: migrant workers, blacks, victims of Nazism. His commentary is about frustration in trying to fight back, and loss of livelihood and self respect. In addition to *Red Channels*, attacks came from Gerald L. K. Smith, the American Legion, and *The Hollywood Reporter* (Hedda Hopper's column). Robinson was among dozens of signers of the Committee for the First Amendment, which questioned the constitutionality of the House

Committee's investigations. He was disconcerted about the behaviors of both the Hollywood Ten *and* the right-wing witnesses who saw Hollywood as a haven of Communism. But he never received a subpoena and was never asked the HUAC's searing question, "Are you now or have you ever been a member of the Communist Party?" Finally, he was allowed to testify before Congress, returning for two more sessions over as many years. The investigators eventually labeled Robinson a "very choice sucker," a dupe. And it was admitting this publicly, with humiliation, that finally enabled him to clear his name.

He made a dozen films from 1950 to 1956, usually playing leads, but none with the distinction that marked his best work. Late in 1951 he elected to do a seven-month tour of a Broadway play. Inevitably, during his career Robinson's work dealt with Communism at some level, so for him the topic ultimately became a source of drama both onstage and off. The following performances, listed chronologically, are noted for their connection to the issue.

1920: *Poldekin* was an anti–Bolshevik comedy starring George Arliss. The Bolsheviks, under the leadership of Lenin, stressed a more extremist revolutionary Marxism than the minority wing. In 1919 the Bolshevik party had been renamed the Communist party. The play was not critically acclaimed.

1935: *Barbary Coast*. In *All My Yesterdays* Robinson refers to the polarized political atmosphere on the set of this film. A liberal, he found himself allied with writers Ben Hecht and Charles MacArthur against a contingent of vocal conservatives, including Howard Hawks, Joel McCrea, Miriam Hopkins, Walter Brennan, and Harry Carey.

1941: *Moscow Strikes Back* was the winner of the Academy Award as the best documentary film. Edward G. Robinson provided the English narration.

1945: *Our Vines Have Tender Grapes* had a screenplay by Dalton Trumbo, who was indicted as one of the Hollywood Ten; in commentaries the film is listed among several from the 1940s whose dialogue allegedly is thinly disguised Communist ideology.

1948: *All My Sons*, based on the Pulitzer Prize–winning Arthur Miller play, also was cited for its liberal views, possibly because its morally misguided protagonist was successful in the American free enterprise system, and his enlightenment and punishment came only at the story's denouement. The Arthur Miller name was also a factor, though, since the playwright had admitted past party membership.

1948: *Key Largo*, like *All My Sons,* was based on a Broadway play, Maxwell Anderson's 1939 work in verse. Robinson's character, a notorious gangster named Johnny Rocco, is another twisted opportunist, attempting to make a big comeback after having been kicked out of the country. His memorable line about being deported was, "Yeah. Like I was a dirty Red or somethin'."

1951: *Darkness at Noon,* a hit play by Sidney Kingsley (from the novel by Arthur Koestler), starred Claude Rains in New York. Robinson undertook the national tour in an exhausting role, with his character onstage throughout. It was a good part, that of a deposed Communist official facing execution. Robinson's decision to perform it, however, was at least as motivated by a lack of quality film offers due to his being "graylisted." He also hoped the play's anti–Communist message might help his situation.

1955: *A Bullet for Joey*. The plot of this picture had Communist agents plotting to kidnap an atomic scientist, enlisting the aid of gangsters. A typical B-film of the period, this bland thriller took for granted America's concern about the cold war; but, like *Darkness at Noon*, it may have helped Robinson, in the role of the police inspector, in improving his public image.

1956: *Hell on Frisco Bay* provided Robinson with one of his better roles during the 1950s, when he was obliged to take whatever film assignments he could. One can only speculate about his relationship with the director, Frank Tuttle, who had admitted past party membership and named names as a star witness for the HUAC five years before.

1956: *The Ten Commandments* marked Robinson's return to A-quality pictures after producer-director Cecil B. DeMille investigated the actor's politics, found no stigma, and offered him the role of Dathan.

1962: *My Geisha* had Robinson speaking a line of dialogue that surely was gallows humor in reality when he responded to a question from Shirley MacLaine about his surprising deviousness of character. As movie star Lucy Dell, she asks him, "Are producers born that way or do they teach you those things when you join the studio?" Robinson jokes an answer: "Well, like the man said who was asked if he was a Communist, 'We're not allowed to tell.'"

1965: *The Cincinnati Kid* had a screenplay by Ring Lardner, Jr. (with Terry Southern), seventeen years following his conviction as one of the Hollywood Ten. Edward G. Robinson made it a point in his autobiography to praise Lardner, noting that an embarrassed film community was now finally giving him public credit again as a writer.

Over the years Edward G. Robinson worked with many personalities on both sides of the Communism issue. Some were liberals, others conservatives, some were friendly and others hostile witnesses. As in the instance above with *Hell on Frisco Bay* and director Frank Tuttle, Robinson's actual relationship with accusers and victims remains a matter of conjecture. Listed alphabetically here, however, are some of the individuals involved either before, during, or after: Ward Bond, Lloyd Bridges, Morris Carnovsky, Mady Christians, Lee J. Cobb, Jeff Corey, Howard DaSilva, Walt Disney, Jose Ferrer, John Garfield, Lloyd Gough, Paul Henreid, Katharine Hepburn, John Huston, Alexander Knox, Ring Lardner, Jr., Marc Lawrence, Richard Macaulay, Fred Niblo, Jr., Larry Parks, Ronald Reagan, Robert Rossen, Lionel Stander, Robert Taylor, Dorothy Tree, Dalton Trumbo, Frank Tuttle, and Jack L. Warner.

Confessions of a Nazi Spy (Film, 1939)

"In 1938," wrote Hal Wallis in his autobiography, *Starmaker*, "Leon Turrou ... was working for J. Edgar Hoover, exposing espionage in our cities. He contacted me, suggesting that we do a picture.... President Roosevelt was extremely enthusiastic about the project, and he and Hoover promised extraordinary cooperation." This was the beginning of *Confessions of a Nazi Spy,* Edward G. Robinson's thirtieth motion picture. Wallis continued: "In August of 1938, I instructed [writer Milton] Krims to go to New York, disguise himself as a Nazi, and attend meetings of the ... German-American Bund.... Edward G. Robinson was obviously the best man to play Turrou."

Robinson was anxious to do the picture; however, he "was compelled by anonymous threats to place his family and himself under surveillance for a time," according to *Crime Movies, an Illustrated History,* by Carlos Clarens. "The relative boldness of the [production] must have been greatly relished by Jack L. Warner, who, in his memoirs, claimed that making *Confessions of a Nazi Spy* placed him on Hitler's personal death list." According to Wallis, "the Nazi government lodged complaints with the State Department in Washington, [but] we stood firm."— Hal Wallis, with Charles Higham, *Starmaker*

"Turrou's book ... told of German subversion in the United States, including the arrest and conviction of four agents who received prison sentences ranging from two to eight years in December, 1938," noted Clarens. "Our art director began to build eighty-three sets," noted Wallis. "In January, 1939, we went into production ... under the working title *Storm Over America*.... The German ambassador, Hans Thomsen, delivered a message to Secretary of State Cordell Hull denouncing the picture as an example of 'pernicious propaganda poisoning German-American relations.' Fortunately, the critics took no notice." The National Board of Review, in fact, named it best among the top ten films of the year, ahead of *Wuthering Heights, Stagecoach, Ninotchka, Goodbye Mr. Chips,* and *Mr. Smith Goes to Washington.* (Surprisingly, *not* on that list were *Gone with the Wind* and *The Wizard of Oz.*)

"Robinson supplied a calm omniscience to his role that further ingrained the image of the G-man as the man who knew best, assuring the viewer that the nation was in good hands," said Clarens in *Crime Movies.* "Robinson carries a pipe instead of a pistol." Several reviewers of the day agreed. "Edward G. Robinson is eloquently persuasive as the investigator of spy ring doings," wrote *The New York Herald-Tribune*. *The New York Journal-American* felt, "it is one of Robinson's finest roles, one which he plays with neither bluster nor ranting heroics, but with a quiet and authoritative conviction." A memorable moment had him explaining jurisdiction to an alleged spy played by Dorothy Tree: "New York harbor is still very much a part of the United States." Paul Lukas, by contrast, evokes the madman Hitler himself in a ranting and raving declamation before a German-American Bund meeting. *The New York Times* was pleased: "As Edward (G-man) Robinson remarks, the Nazis must be mad to think they can get away with it. As melodrama, the film isn't bad at all. Anatole Litvak has paced it well, and key performances of ... [Mr.] Robinson as the Federal Man, Mr. Lederer as the weak link in the Nazi spy network, and Mr. Lukas as the propaganda agent are thoroughly satisfactory."

While some argue today that the film is dated, its impact is still strong. Leonard Maltin calls *Confessions of a Nazi Spy* "bristling drama," and its "patriotic zest [is] forgivable." William R. Meyer, in *Warner Brothers Directors*, allowed that, "while its dated message has tarnished the film's impact somewhat, the work still serves as a symbol of the studio's courage in producing stories which attacked bigotry, oppression, and poverty." Adam Garbicz and Jacek Klinowski, in their book *Cinema, the Magic Vehicle: A Guide to Its Achievement*, said, "the aim was to draw attention to the strength and influence of Nazi intelligence all over the world, but especially in the U.S.A. A middle-aged Scotswoman acts as a link between the U.S. network and Berlin. Nazi agents are everywhere.... Litvak dispensed with a fictional plot and chose the style of the semi-documentary 'March of Time' newsreel.... A spoken commentary and a number of maps and diagrams were also included.... *Confessions of a Nazi Spy* was not only a suspenseful and gripping thriller, surrounded by a ring of truth and urgency, but a warning of a threat which still seemed remote but was soon to develop into a nightmare."

Schneider, a German-American living in New York, dreams of being an important man, but he is out of work and has a wife and child to support. His sense of nationalism is spurred on by American Nazi Bund meetings and, in particular, by the fervor of Dr. Kassel's speechmaking. He offers his services to the Third Reich as a spy. Schlager, a German agent, sails to New York from Europe and, with Hilda Keinauer, visits Schneider and assigns him the mission of getting information on U.S. troops stationed in the area. Eventually, Schneider, Hilda, and Dr. Kassel are arrested as spies. Each confesses to Ed Renard, an FBI investigator. Kassel's lawyer arranges to have him return to Germany, but the others, now including Schneider's friend, Werner Renz, and a man named Helldorf, are tried and convicted of espionage.

Director, Anatole Litvak; associate producer, Robert Lord; based on the book *The Nazi Spy Conspiracy in America* by Leon G. Turrou; screenplay, Milton Krims, John Wexley; camera, Sol Polito; sound, C. A. Riggs; art director, Carl Jules Weyl; music, Leo F. Forbstein; editor, Owen Marks; cast: Edward G. Robinson (Ed Renard), Francis Lederer (Schneider), George Sanders (Schlager), Paul Lukas (Dr. Kassel), Lya Lys (Erika Wolff), Henry O'Neill (District Attorney Kellogg), Sig Rumann (Krogman), Joe Sawyer (Werner Renz), Celia Sibelius (Mrs. Kassel), Grace Stafford (Mrs. Schneider), James Stephenson (Scotland Yard man), Dorothy Tree (Hilda Keinauer), Ward Bond (Legionnaire), Egon Brecher (Nazi agent), Frederick Burton (District Judge), Alec Craig (Postman), Robert Davis [Rudolph Anders] (Straubel), John Deering (Narrator), John Hamilton (Judge), Selmer Jackson (Customs official), Martin Kosleck (Goebbels), Eily Malyon (Mrs. MacLaughlin), Charles Trowbridge (Intelligence officer), Emmett Vogan (Hotel clerk), Frederick Vogeding (Captain Richter), Jon Voigt [Paul Andor / Wolfgang Zilzer] (Westphal), Lisa Golm (Mrs. Westphal), Jean Brooks [Lotte Palfi] (Kassel's nurse), Willy Kaufman (Gruetzwald), Edward Keane (FBI man), Robert Emmett Keane (Harrison), Frank

Mayo (Staunton), Jack Mower (McDonald), Lucien Prival (Kranz), John Ridgely (Hospital clerk), George Rosener (Klauber), Lionel Royce (Hintze), Fred Tozere (Phillips), William Vaughn [von Brinken] (Captain Von Eichen), Henry Victor (Helldorf), Hans von Twardowsky (Wildebrandt), Tommy Bupp, Creighton Hale, William Gould, Max Hoffman, Jr., Lon McCallister, George Offerman, Gaylord [Steve] Pendleton, Bodil Rosing, Charles Sherlock, Hans Schumm, Edwin Stanley, Regis Toomey, Niccolai Yoshkin, Louis Aldon, Sherwood Bailey, Glen Cavender, John Conte, John Harron, Tempe Pigott, Lester Sharpe, Rudolph Steinbeck, Dave Wengren; Warner Bros.; 102 minutes; April 1939

Conroy, Frank (1890–1964) With Edward G. Robinson, he is in *The Last Gangster, All My Sons* and "Shadows Tremble" on TV's *Playhouse 90*. His other films include *Grand Hotel, Call of the Wild, The Gorgeous Hussey, The Ox-Bow Incident, The Naked City,* and *Compulsion*.

Conte, Richard (1914–75), a rugged-looking Italian, plays himself, as did Edward G. Robinson, in *Pepe*; and they were son and father in *House of Strangers*. Conte was also in *Guadalcanal Diary, A Bell for Adano, Captain Eddie, Call Northside 777, New York Confidential, I'll Cry Tomorrow, Ocean's 11,* and *The Godfather*.

The Coo Coo Nut Grove This was the first cartoon to caricature Hollywood celebrities as animals; featured are likenesses of Katharine Hepburn, Laurel and Hardy, Harpo Marx, and Edward G. Robinson.

Supervisor, Friz Freleng; animation, Bob McKimson, Sandy Walker; musical direction, Carl W. Stalling; Merrie Melodies, 1936; 7 minutes

Cook, Elisha, Jr. (1906–95) He appeared on the Broadway stage with Edward G. Robinson in *Henry, Behave,* and was in films from the 1930s, memorably in *The Maltese Falcon, Phantom Lady, The Big Sleep, Shane,* and *The Great Bank Robbery*.

Coolidge, Philip (1909–67) was "Fingers" Felton, a member of Edward G. Robinson's gang, in the Disney comedy *Never a Dull Moment*. He appeared in the Broadway production of *Darkness at Noon* and in such films as *North by Northwest, Inherit the Wind,* and *I Want to Live!*

"Cops and Robbers" (Television, 1962) It seemed a natural choice to have Edward G. Robinson narrate a program like "Cops and Robbers," a television documentary that presented an overview of crime in the United States. However, there was criticism at the time that his image, being that of a gangster — a celluloid one, at that — somehow made his appearance inappropriate. Or was it due to lingering impressions from the Congressional investigations of the 1950s?

Director, producer, Don Hyatt; writer, Phil Reisman, Jr.; narrator, Edward G. Robinson; *Project 20: DuPont Show of the Week*; NBC; March 18, 1962

Corby, Ellen (1913–97), beloved for her latter-day television role as the grandmother on *The Waltons*, played Miss Hinkle, Edward G. Robinson's trusty secretary, in *Illegal*. She was also seen onscreen in *It's a Wonderful Life, The Spiral Staircase, I Remember Mama* (Oscar nomination), *A Pocketful of Miracles,* and *Vertigo,* among others.

Cormack, Bartlett (1898–1942) wrote the Broadway hit drama *The Racket*, which featured Edward G. Robinson in his first gangster role. He also collaborated on the screenplay of *Unholy Partners*. Cormack studied at the University of Chicago and worked on a newspaper, in little theater, and as a press agent.

Cortez, Ricardo (1899–1977) was Mary Astor's romantic interest (she played Edward G. Robinson's sister) in *The Man with Two Faces*. He began in silents and played Sam Spade in the original *The Maltese Falcon*. He directed films and was also seen in *Mandalay, The Case of the Black Cat, The Locket,* and *The Last Hurrah*. His brother, **Stanley Cortez** (1908–92), was cinematographer for Robinson's *Flesh and Fantasy* and *Black Tuesday*.

Costumes In the majority of his film and television roles, Edward G. Robinson's manner of dress was the business suit. Even as vicious and unenlightened tough guys, he was nattily dressed. He wore tuxedoes in *The Hole in the Wall, Little Caesar, Smart Money, The Little Giant, Kid Galahad, Thunder in the City, A Slight Case of Murder, The Amazing Dr. Clitterhouse, Blackmail, Tales of Manhattan, Scarlet Street, Night Has a Thousand Eyes, Seven Thieves, Two Weeks in Another Town, The Prize, Good Neighbor Sam,* and *Robin and the 7 Hoods*. He was in prison stripes in *Two Seconds, Blackmail, Under Sentence* (on the stage), *Black Tuesday,* and *The Last Gangster*.

His look included military uniforms *(Confessions of a Nazi Spy, Mr. Winkle Goes to War, Tampico, Destroyer, Journey Together, Cheyenne Autumn)*, but Robinson also played roles in such atypical costumes as baseball uniforms *(Larceny, Inc., Big Leaguer)* and the garb of a farmer, rancher, or prospector *(Silver Dollar, Mackenna's Gold, The Red House, Our Vines Have Tender Grapes, The Outrage)*. In *The Violent Men* he was reviewed as "Little Caesar in buckskin."

He was dressed in Biblical robes in *The Ten Commandments*, Chinese robes in *The Hatchet Man*, and, on Broadway, robes of state in *Androcles and the Lion*. He wore period costumes in several films, such as *The Bright Shawl, Barbary Coast,* and *Dr. Ehrlich's Magic Bullet*; but on the stage he had an even more dramatic look—wearing expressionistic clothing in *Peer Gynt* and red tights in *The Firebrand*.

See also **Disguises**.

Cotten, Joseph (1905–94) came to films via Orson Welles' Mercury Theatre in *Citizen Kane, The Magnificent Ambersons, Journey Into Fear, The Third Man,* and *Touch of Evil*. He played also in *Shadow of a Doubt, Gaslight, Hush Hush Sweet Charlotte, The Abominable Dr. Phibes,* and, with Edward G. Robinson, *Soylent Green*. They appear together also on the radio in *Hollywood Fights Back* and *The Roosevelt Special*.

Courtenay, William (1875–1933), a Broadway matinee idol for twenty-five years, was the lead in and also directed, *Under Fire*, Edward G. Robinson's first Broadway play. They acted together also in *The Voice*. Courtenay's other successes include *Camille, Mrs. Leffingwell's Boots, Arsene Lupin, Under Cover,* and the United States premiere of Shaw's *The Devil's Disciple*.

Courtrooms In several of Edward G. Robinson's films courtrooms have provided major dramatic moments, often at the climax of the story. In *A Dispatch from Reuter's* protagonist Reuter proves his reliability as a source for news gathering when evidence is presented in a London court that President Lincoln really has been assassinated. In *Dr. Ehrlich's Magic Bullet* the doctor is similarly vindicated by testimony that his compound to cure syphilis actually does work.

Robinson's courtroom victory prior to the opening of *All My Sons*—exoneration from charges of shipping defective airplane cylinders to the Army Air Force—is short lived, because he is actually guilty. In *Two Seconds* Robinson is condemned to death for murder; but he is found innocent by reason of insanity in *The Amazing Dr. Clitterhouse*. In *House of Strangers* he is on trial for illegal bank practices. The *Confessions of a Nazi Spy* result in four convictions; while a judge and jury in *Robin and the 7 Hoods* find Frank Sinatra (Robbo/Robin) innocent of murdering the sheriff.

Robinson plays attorneys in *Tight Spot*, where, with Ginger Rogers as his star witness, he is attempting to deport gangster Lorne Greene; in *Illegal*, where he collapses in the courtroom (he has been shot) after proving Nina Foch innocent of murdering her husband; and in "The Case of Kenny Jason," a pilot film for a dramatic TV series that never materialized. He plays a law professor turned racket buster in *I Am the Law*.

Unusual examples of courtroom scenes include one where prudish dairy man Robinson turns up in a barrister's white wig during Jack Lemmon's nightmare to judge his philandering, in a scene cut from *Good Neighbor Sam*. In *The Outrage* outlaw Paul Newman has burned the courtroom and jail to the ground, so proceedings are held outside the ruins. Robinson owns the town in *Barbary Coast* and is thus able to order the judge to set up court in his saloon. And, finally, in *Tales of Manhattan* lawyers at their 25-year college reunion set up a mock trial to determine Robinson's guilt of theft.

Cowan, Jerome (1897–1972) played Edward G. Robinson's vaudeville partner, Whitney Courtland, in *Night Has a Thousand Eyes*. He was also Miles Archer, Sam Spade's law partner, in *The Maltese Falcon*, and appeared in *The Hurricane, High Sierra, The Great Lie, Claudia and David, Miracle on 34th Street, June Bride, Pocketful of Miracles*, and *Critic's Choice*.

Craig, Alec (1885–1945), a Scotsman, appeared with Edward G. Robinson in three films—*Confessions of a Nazi Spy, A Dispatch from Reuter's*, and *The Woman in the Window*. Craig was also seen in *Mutiny on the Bounty, Abe Lincoln in Illinois, The Sea Hawk*, and *Mrs. Miniver*.

Craig, James (1912–85) played editor Nels Halverson in *Our Vines Have Tender Grapes*, with Edward G. Robinson. He had roles also in *The Buccaneer, Zanzibar, Kitty Foyle, All That Money Can Buy, The Human Comedy, Kismet, Hurricane Smith*, and *While the City Sleeps*.

Craven, Frank (1875–1945) was on Broadway for 35 years, appearing with Edward G. Robinson in *Under Fire*. He wrote and starred in *The First Year*, and was the original Stage Manager in *Our Town*. In films he was Colonel Cobb, the newspaper editor, in *Barbary Coast*, with Robinson; and he appeared in *We Americans, Our Town, The Human Comedy*, and *Keeper of the Flame*.

Crawford, Broderick (1911–86) starred on TV (*Highway Patrol*), Broadway (*George in Of Mice and Men*), and films (Best Actor Oscar for *All the King's Men*). Other films include *Beau Geste, Larceny, Inc.* (with Edward G. Robinson), *Born Yesterday, Stop You're Killing Me, The Private Files of J. Edgar Hoover*, and *A Little Romance*. On radio he and Robinson were in an adaptation of "Blind Alley."

Crawford, Joan (1908–77) played herself in *The Stolen Jools* and *It's a Great Feeling*, but she and Edward G. Robinson shared no scenes. She appeared with him on the radio in *Document A/777*. She won an Oscar for *Mildred Pierce*, and was nominated also for *Possessed* and *Sudden Fear*. Other films include *Grand Hotel, The Gorgeous Hussy, The Women, Queen Bee, Whatever Happened to Baby Jane*, and *Trog*.

Crehan, Joseph (1886–1966) was in eight films with Edward G. Robinson—as newspaper editors in *The Man with Two Faces* and *Kid Galahad*; a grand jury spokesman in *Bullets or Ballots*; an oil well owner in *Blackmail*; a line foreman in *Manpower*; a detective in *Flesh and Fantasy*; a warden in *Larceny Inc*; and Brother MacEwan in *Brother Orchid*. He was in over 200 films altogether, including *Black Fury, Alexander's Ragtime Band, Mission to Moscow*, and *Deadline U.S.A.*

"The Criminal Code" (Radio, 1937) Director, Frank Woodruff; based on the play by Martin Flavin; adaptation, George Wells; sound, Charlie Forsyth; music director, Louis Silvers; cast: Edward G. Robinson (Martin Brady), Beverly Roberts, Noel Madison, Paul Guilfoyle, Walter Kingsford, Ernie Adams, Frank Nelson, Lou Merrill, Earle Ross, William Williams, Richard Abbott, Justina Wayne, Joe Franz, Hilda Haywood, Margaret Brayton, Ross Forrester, David Kerman, Charles Emerson; intermission guests: Gladys Lloyd, James B. Holohan (former warden of San Quentin); Cecil B. DeMille (host); Melville Ruick; *Lux Radio Theatre*; CBS; January 18, 1937

The Criminal Code, presented on Broadway in 1929, was "quite possibly the best of all American prison dramas," according to *The Oxford Companion to American Theatre*. After a clerk is sent to prison on a murder charge by the state's attorney, he becomes involved with the attorney's daughter, who works at the prison. Ultimately he loses his chance for parole when he kills a guard. In 1931 Howard Hawks filmed *The Criminal Code*, with Walter Huston, Constance Cummings, and Boris Karloff.

Crisp, Donald (1880–1974) appeared with Edward G. Robinson as Inspector Lane in *The Amazing Dr. Clitterhouse*; as Dr. Althoff in *Dr. Ehrlich's Magic Bullet*; and Brother Superior in *Brother Orchid*. They also appeared together on the radio in "Ship Forever Sailing." Beginning in silent films, assisting D. W. Griffith on *Birth of a Nation*, Crisp won the supporting actor Oscar for *How Green Was My Valley*.

Crosby, Bing (1904–77) plays Allan A. Dale in *Robin and the 7 Hoods*, and he and Edward G. Robinson play themselves in *Pepe*. They are also narrators for *The Heart of Show Business* and were on an early *U.S. Olympic Committee Telethon*. On the radio both appeared on *Command Performance* ("Victory Extra") and on an ABC Savings Bond show. Crosby was the most popular singer of the 1930s. His second wife and widow, **Kathryn Grant** (1933–), played a small role as a newlywed in Robinson's *Tight Spot*.

Crying   A story about the filming of *Kid Galahad* concerns Edward G. Robinson's death scene in the picture. He and Humphrey Bogart have exchanged fatal gunshots. Bette Davis, playing Robinson's girlfriend, remembers that she was standing by, weeping. Jane Bryan, playing his kid sister, was standing next to her, also weeping. At one point during the scene, Robinson turned to director Michael Curtiz and complained, "Don't you think the girls are crying too much?"

An entertaining crying moment occurs in *The Stranger*, as Martha Wentworth, playing the household maid, weeps, wails, and even stages a fake attack and collapses on the floor in order to prevent Loretta Young from leaving the house. Other characters in Robinson films do their share of crying. Rod Steiger sheds tears when he admits to Joan Collins in *Seven Thieves* that Robinson was his father. Years earlier, Bobs Watson, as Robinson's son in *Blackmail*, was a master at weeping on camera. Bobby Jordan is effective as a homesick sailor in *Destroyer*, crying after "lights out" in the barracks.

Robinson quite often was able to punctuate his film acting with moving scenes of tears. Usually the characters are left with no recourse; the fight is all but gone from them. After eating a real meal of beef and vegetables for the first time in years in the futuristic *Soylent Green*, his character becomes painfully aware of loss, crying, "Have we come to this?" In *Scarlet Street* Robinson, riddled with guilt and memories, has pathetically tried and failed to commit suicide. Rescued from hanging himself, he laughs bitterly at the irony of his failure, and the laughter turns to weeping. Finally, in *All My Sons*, before being forced to admit his guilt to his son who had believed him innocent, he has a scene with his wife, who knows the truth, and he has no comment; he just breaks down, piteously.

He also sheds tears of joy in *Our Vines Have Tender Grapes*, at his daughter Margaret O'Brien's Christmas recital; and in *A Hole in the Head*, at the thought that his brother, Frank Sinatra, might have found a wife.

Cummings, Constance (1910–) was in *A Boy Ten Feet Tall*, with Edward G. Robinson, but they shared no scenes. Other films include *The Criminal Code, Seven Sinners,* and *Blithe Spirit*. She was married to playwright Benn W. Levy, author of *A Man with Red Hair*, which starred Robinson.

Cummings, Robert (Bob) (1908–87) was in the first episode of *Flesh and Fantasy*, and also in *My Geisha*, with Edward G. Robinson; they share scenes only in the latter. He was also onscreen in *King's Row*, Hitchcock's *Saboteur* and *Dial M for Murder,* and on TV in *The Bob Cummings Show*. His father, Robert Cummings, Sr., has a small role in *I Am the Law*.

Cummins, Peggy (1925–) played *My Daughter Joy* (the English title of *Operation X*), with Edward G. Robinson as her father. After such American films as *The Late George*

Apley and *Moss Rose*, she was mainly in British features, such as *Carry On Admiral* and *In the Doghouse*.

Curtiz, Michael (1888–1962) was a stage and film actor and director in his native Budapest, expanded his work to other European countries, then came to Hollywood and Warner Bros. in 1926. His more than 100 features include *Kid Galahad* and *The Sea Wolf* with Edward G. Robinson, *20,000 Years in Sing Sing*, *The Mystery of the Wax Museum*, *Captain Blood*, *The Adventures of Robin Hood*, *Four Daughters*, *The Sea Hawk*, *Mildred Pierce*, *Life With Father,* and *White Christmas*. He had Oscar nominations for *Angels With Dirty Faces* and *Yankee Doodle Dandy*, and won for *Casablanca*.

Dailey, Dan (1914–78) plays movie director Ted Holt in *Pepe*. He was a singer-dancer in vaudeville prior to appearing on Broadway in *Babes in Arms*. His films include *Ziegfeld Girl*, *Mother Wore Tights*, *Give My Regards to Broadway*, *The Pride of St. Louis*, and *There's No Business Like Show Business*.

Dale, Esther (1885–61) played Sarah, the maid, in *Blackmail*, with Edward G. Robinson. She also appears in *Fury*, *Dead End*, *The Mortal Storm*, *The Awful Truth* and *The Egg and I*, and several of the *Ma and Pa Kettle* series.

Dancing Edward G. Robinson dances "The Big Apple" with Wendy Barrie in *I Am the Law*, the merengue with Peggy Cummins in *Operation X*, and years later he dances with Rossanna Schiaffino in *Two Weeks in Another Town*, and with Raquel Welch in *The Biggest Bundle of them All* ("the frug"). He does an impromptu solo dance to a blaring juke box in *Big Leaguer*, in which Vera-Ellen co-stars but does *not* dance. Dancing is the occupation of Douglas Fairbanks, Jr., and Glenda Farrell in *Little Caesar*, and Robinson, as Rico, is scornful: "Dancin'? Women? That's for sissies. I aim on makin' other people dance." In *Two Seconds* his character meets his wife at a dance hall. Leroy Prinz choreographed several dances for *The Ten Commandments*. The Mazzone-Abbott dancers are featured in *It's a Great Feeling*, and the Gamby-Hall Girls in *The Hole in the Wall*. Cantinflas, Dan Dailey, Shirley Jones, Michael Callan, Matt Mattox, Debbie Reynolds, and Maurice Chevalier do dance routines in *Pepe*; Frank Sinatra, Sammy Davis, Jr., Dean Martin, and Bing Crosby dance in *Robin and the 7 Hoods*; and Florence Henderson and the cast of *Song of Norway* perform several dance numbers.

See **Music / Singing**

Daniels, Bebe (1901–71) was a popular star of the silent screen in Hal Roach comedies. She and her husband Ben Lyons and Edward G. Robinson appeared in the short *The Stolen Jools,* and she was Robinson's leading lady in *Silver Dollar*. They were together also on a Warner Brothers radio broadcast. Her other pictures include *Rio Rita*, *42nd Street*, and *Counsellor at Law*.

Daniels, William H. (1895–1970) was cinematographer for four of Edward G. Robinson's films — *The Last Gangster*, *A Hole in the Head*, *The Prize*, and *Robin and the 7 Hoods* (which he also co-produced). He won an Oscar for *The Naked City* and was nominated for *Anna Christie*, *Cat on a Hot Tin Roof,* and *How the West Was Won*. He became known as Greta Garbo's cameraman, having worked on many of her films.

Dante, Michael (1931–) appeared with Edward G. Robinson in *Seven Thieves* as Louis, the safecracker. He was in the Elvis Presley remake of *Kid Galahad*, and also had roles in *Operation Bikini*, *Harlow*, *Willard*, and *Crazy Horse and Custer — the Untold Story*.

Darc, Mireille (1938–) played the title role in *Peking Blonde*, with Edward G. Robinson. Onscreen in her native France from 1960, her other films include *Les Distractions*, *Galia*, *Weekend*, *The Tall Blond Man with One Black Shoe,* and *Les Ringards*.

Darien, Frank (1878–1955) appeared onscreen with Edward G. Robinson in *Five*

Star Final, The Man with Two Faces, and *Tales of Manhattan.* He appeared also in *The Grapes of Wrath, Magic Town, Merton of the Movies,* and *Hello, Frisco, Hello.*

Dark Hazard (Film, 1934) W. R. Burnett, author of *Little Caesar*, also wrote *Dark Hazard*, the story of a compulsive gambler. It was filmed by Warner Bros., with Edward G. Robinson; his two leading ladies were Genevieve Tobin from *I Loved a Woman*, again playing his wife, and Glenda Farrell, who had been in *Little Caesar*.

"Again the combination of Edward G. Robinson and W. R. Burnett results in that singular emotional quality which was the touchstone of *Little Caesar*," wrote *The New York Herald-Tribune*. "While the latter was a far more sensational and melodramatic piece, the star's performance in *Dark Hazard* is just as true to type and poignantly drawn.... It is the contrast in Mr. Robinson's characters which gives them much of their fascination. His heroes are never completely heroic and his villains are never altogether unsympathetic." Nevertheless, Robinson disliked the film.

"Jim Turner, the hunch gambler, spills himself noisily on the screen in Edward G. Robinson's familiar style of alternately shy and snarling moods," said *The New York Times*. "Mr. Robinson provides a hearty cartoon character which is admirably suited to the unexpected guffaw and the well-timed hook to the chin." *The New York Sun* agreed, saying that, "Robinson adds one more portrait to his gallery of quaint likable misfits."

Variety noted a difference. "It's an unusual portrayal for Robinson, despite the fact that he's cast as a gambler. A big shot for a few moments, a bum most of the time, he's always dominated by those around him and near him, instead of, as in his past pictures, being the head man."

Director, Alfred E. Green; based on the novel by W(illiam). R. Burnett; screenplay, Ralph Block, Brown Holmes; camera, Sol Polito; art director, Robert Haas; gowns, Orry-Kelly; editor, Herbert Levy; music, Leo F. Forbstein; cast: Edward G. Robinson (Jim "Buck" Turner), Genevieve Tobin (Marge Mayhew), Glenda Farrell (Valerie), Robert Barrat (Tex), Gordon Westcott (Joe), Hobart Cavanaugh (George Mayhew), George Meeker (Pres Barrow), Henry B. Walthall (Schultz), Sidney Toler (Bright), Emma Dunn (Mrs. Mayhew), Willard Robertson (Fallon), Barbara Rogers (Miss Dolby), William V. Mong (Plummer), George Chandler (Soapy Sam Lambert), James Donlan (Man at dog track), Sam McDaniel (George, the Porter), Joe E. Brown, Joan Blondell, Johnny Mack Brown, Warren William, Frank McHugh, Guy Kibbee, Sheila Terry, Patricia Ellis, Theodore Newton, George Blackwood, Phillip Reed, Phillip Faversham, Marjorie Lytell, Gordon Westcott (Guest stars at racetrack); First-National; 72 minutes; February 1934

Gambler Jim Turner wins and loses big at horse races and dice. Down on his luck, he moves into Marge Mayhew's rooming house in Barrowsville, Ohio. They fall in love and move to Chicago, Jim vowing to stop gambling. His job as a hotel desk clerk pays little, and he endures insults from a man named Bright until one day he is fired. Bright, however, had been teasing Jim and now wants him to oversee his dog-racing enterprise in California. Jim and Marge move west, but he cannot refrain from gambling. She dislikes his friends, among them an old flame named Val. Jim spots a black greyhound named Dark Hazard and wants to buy him, but the owner, Tex, wants $5,000 for him and Marge detests the idea. When Marge learns she is expecting a child, she takes most of Jim's recent $20,000 in winnings and moves back to Ohio. Jim tries to go on without her, but, ultimately, again down on his luck, he follows her. Pres Barrow is set to marry Marge as soon as she divorces Jim. She decides, though, to try again with Jim for the sake of the baby, now two. Pres sets Jim up in a cashier's job at a barber shop, and Jim is able to buy Dark Hazard, who has been injured, for only $25. Jim confronts Marge about the deterioration in their relationship, but he comes to realize they are not right for one another and leaves town with the dog. He goes back to the rounds of gambling and is last seen in the money once again, Val on his arm, enjoying the company of Dark Hazard.

The Dark Tower see ***The Man with Two Faces***

Darkness at Noon (Theater, 1951) Prior to the national tour of *Darkness at Noon*, Edward G. Robinson's last appearance in a play had been in New York late in 1930, two months prior to the release of *Little Caesar*. Now, after twenty years of stardom on the silver screen, Robinson's career was in a decided slump due to the Communist witch hunt in the film industry. According to his autobiography *All My Yesterdays*, he was approached to appear in the original production. He declined because he felt it would seem too obvious an attempt to disassociate himself from the investigations. The role went to Claude Rains. Four months later, after the play had won the Pulitzer Prize, Robinson was again approached when Rains was too tired to do the national tour. This time he accepted. The demanding role was also a great one, and the anti–Communist excuse seemed sensible. The director was Sidney Kingsley, the play's author. Kingsley and Robinson were constantly embattled over interpretation. Robinson's arguments had to do with seeing the role differently from Claude Rains, but in retrospect he acknowledged that the cast might have viewed him as a temperamental film actor.

Potential disaster was avoided when the play opened in Princeton. Robinson had been nervous about returning to the stage all along, and described the culmination of those worries on opening night as "psychological laryngitis," in which he had "a croak for a voice." After several minutes of terror, he commanded his star power, walked forward to the audience, and apologized. He announced that he would like to start the play anew. The curtain was lowered, and the performance was begun once again, this time finishing to bravos.

A theatrical journal at the time quoted Edward G. Robinson almost prophetically: "I never thought I would get stage fright. I didn't in my younger days.... But I am so anxious about this play because, aside from entertainment value, it concerns a major problem of our time, the individual versus the totalitarian state. I believe in what it has to say so much, I know that when I give the first performance before an audience I will get over being nervous about returning to the theatre."

Cities on the seven-month tour included Wilmington, Baltimore, Boston, Dallas, Chicago, and Cincinnati. His audiences afforded Robinson the treatment and respect due a major film star, and he gratefully acknowledged their support. Four days after *Darkness at Noon* closed, Robinson testified before the House Un-American Activities Committee for the third time. (He had testified voluntarily on October 27, 1947, and again on December 21, 1951, during the play's tour.) He now "explained that his voice was hoarse due to having just completed 250 performances of *Darkness at Noon*. 'It is, perhaps,' said Robinson, certifying his Americanism, 'the strongest indictment of Communism ever presented.'"—quoted in *Only Victims*, by Robert Vaughn

Playwright, Sidney Kingsley; director, Kingsley; based on the novel by Arthur Koestler; associate producer, May Kirshner; song, Dan and Dmitri Pokras; lyrics, Olga Paul; general manager, Warren P. Munsell; company manager, Harry Shapiro; set, lights, Frederick Fox; assistant, Margery Quitzau; stage managers, Allan Rich, William McFadden, Ralph Simone; scenery, Triangle Studios, Nolan Bros.; carpenter, Ralph Guy; electric, William Froehlich; curtains, J. Weiss & Sons, Inc.; sound, Sound Associates; props, Harry Thompson; costumes, Eaves Costumes, Elena, Ken Barr, Jessie Zimmer (hosiery), A. S. Beck (shoes); wigs, Eddie Senz; wardrobe, Phoebe Lee; jewelry, Gale Grant; furnishings, Newel Art Galleries; fabrics, Dazians; press representative, John Montague; Benson & Hedges and Park C. Tilford products used; Artur Rubinstein recording used; cast: Edward G. Robinson (Rubashov), Lois Nettleton (Luba), Leo Gordon (Gletkin), Tony Ancona, Guy Arbury, Archie Benson, Maurice Brenner, Allen Derrick, Louis Edmonds, Johnson Hayes, Virginia Howard, Norman Keats, Anne Kevin, Adams McDonald, John Morny, Daniel Polis, Jon Quigg, Allan Rich, Richard Seff, David Sheiner, Ralph Simone; toured from September 28, 1951 (McCarter Theatre,

Princeton, New Jersey), to April 26, 1952 (Cox Theatre, Cincinnati)

DaSilva, Howard (1909–86) played on Broadway in the musicals *Oklahoma!* (Jud Fry) and *1776* (Ben Franklin). Films include *Abe Lincoln in Illinois, Sergeant York, The Lost Weekend, The Blue Dahlia, David and Lisa, The Great Gatsby* (in 1949 and 1974), and *1776*. With Edward G. Robinson he is in *The Sea Wolf* and *The Outrage*. He was blacklisted in 1951 for refusing to affirm or deny Communist party membership.

Dathan He is described in *The Abingdon Bible Commentary* as one who, with Abiram, challenged the authority of Moses. Chapter XVI of the book of Numbers has sections dealing with Dathan and Abiram separate from Korah. It is the former two who are miraculously destroyed by being swallowed up by the earth (Korah is burned by fire from Jehovah). The screenplay of *The Ten Commandments* makes Dathan the chief critic of Moses for failing to bring the people to the promised land. He is also the catalyst for whipping the Israelites into a frenzy to create the Golden Calf, and for convincing them that they should return to Egypt. Logical extrapolation from Biblical references has the screen Dathan, played by Edward G. Robinson, as a faithless Hebrew loyal to the Egyptian prince, a spy rewarded for naming "the Deliverer" by being made governor of Goshen. He also lusts after, and coerces into his household, Joshua's girlfriend.

Davenport, Harry (1866–49) is in *The Life of Emile Zola, The Sisters, Gone with the Wind, The Hunchback of Notre Dame, Foreign Correspondent, The Ox-Bow Incident, Meet Me in St. Louis, Courage of Lassie,* and, with Edward G. Robinson, *Dr. Ehrlich's Magic Bullet,* as the judge; *Tales of Manhattan,* as Professor Lyons; and *Larceny, Inc.,* as Mr. Bigelow.

Daves, Delmer (1904–77) was a writer-producer-director whose career began in 1943 with *Destination Tokyo*. His other films include *Dark Passage, 3:10 to Yuma, The Hanging Tree, Spencer's Mountain,* and, with Edward G. Robinson, *The Red House*.

Davis, Bette (1908–89) made one film with Edward G. Robinson—*Kid Galahad*—playing his mistress, Fluff Phillips. She felt the film was valuable to her career for its storyline dealing with prizefighting. Davis respected Robinson's acting ability, but they did not get along well. She thought him self-impressed, and several biographies made no secret of her petty revulsion at his physical appearance. In his autobiography Robinson allowed little appreciation for her acting ability when they worked together, but later he conceded her improvement and his admiration. Given Davis' volatile nature, the situation undoubtedly was a simple clash of personality. Producer Hal Wallis understood, saying in his autobiography, "He did not warm to her, nor she to him. Neither recognized the other's talent." Wallis appeared with both of them in the PBS documentary *The Movie Crazy Years,* and Davis and Robinson were in the short *A Day at Santa Anita*. Her films include *Of Human Bondage, Dark Victory, The Letter, The Little Foxes, Now Voyager, The Corn Is Green, All About Eve,* and *Whatever Happened to Baby Jane?* Nominated ten times for the Academy Award, she won for *Dangerous* and *Jezebel,* and received the American Film Institute's life achievement award in 1977.

Davis, Sammy, Jr. (1925–90), a versatile black entertainer, appears in two Robinson films, though they have no scenes together—*Pepe* (as himself) and *Robin and the 7 Hoods*. He was also on the *36th Annual Academy Awards,* and in the films *Anna Lucasta, Porgy and Bess, Threepenny Opera, Sweet Charity,* and *Tap,* his last.

A Day at Santa Anita (Short film, 1935) This title appears in several lists of Edward G. Robinson's films. It is a short subject about the California racetrack.

Director, Crane Wilbur; cast: Edward G. Robinson, Bette Davis, Olivia deHavilland (as themselves); 1935

Day, Doris (1924–) became a musical star with her first film, *Romance on the High Seas*. Her third film, *It's a Great Feeling*, featured Edward G. Robinson in a cameo role as himself. Her other pictures include *Storm Warning, Calamity Jane, Young at Heart, Love Me or Leave Me, The Pajama Game, Pillow Talk,* and *That Touch of Mink*.

Day, Laraine (1917–) played opposite Edward G. Robinson in *Unholy Partners*. She was also in *Stella Dallas, Mr. Lucky, Journey for Margaret, My Dear Secretary, The Locket, The High and the Mighty, The Third Voice,* and several films in the *Dr. Kildare* series.

Deafness Carolyn Jones, co-starring with Edward G. Robinson in *A Hole in the Head*, notes in Victor Scherle and William Turner Levy's *The Films of Frank Capra* that during the filming, "We all worked a little harder for his [Capra's] quiet chuckle in the comedy scenes or his long, tender sigh in the dramatic ones. Even Eddie Robinson, who was hard of hearing, played to Mr. Capra." Thus it is apparent that Robinson was growing deaf for at least fifteen years before he died. He commented in 1972, during the filming of his last picture, *Soylent Green*, that increasing deafness was not the problem it might have been: "If the directions are given from a distance, I ask the other actors what the director is saying...."

Dean, Julia (1880–1952), a Broadway actress beginning in 1902, was in a touring production of *Paid in Full* in 1908, and later appeared with George Arliss and Edward G. Robinson in *Poldekin*. Her films include silents and *The Curse of the Cat People, Magic Town,* and *The Emperor Waltz*.

Dearing, Edgar (1893–1974) appeared with Edward G. Robinson as a policeman in three films — *The Amazing Dr. Clitterhouse, Scarlet Street,* and *Vice Squad*. He also had roles in *Swing Time* and *Miss Annie Rooney*.

Death see **Funeral**

Death scenes A number of Edward G. Robinson's films are heightened by effective death scenes. His climactic suicide in *Soylent Green*, in fact, was the last scene he ever filmed. Early in his career Robinson played a man who was already dead, in *The Adding Machine*, for the Theatre Guild. The character, named Shrdlu, existed in limbo in the Elysian Fields, having committed the act of free will in murdering his mother, been tried, and executed.

In *The Racket* on the stage and *Little Caesar* on the screen (as well as *Key Largo, Outside the Law, Black Tuesday, The Whole Town's Talking,* and *The Last Gangster)*, shots fired near the end of the story got rid of Robinson as the principal villain. Gunfire ends his life also in *The Night Has a Thousand Eyes, Illegal, Bullets or Ballots, Kid Galahad, All My Sons* (suicide), *The Glass Web, Robin and the 7 Hoods,* and *The Old Man Who Cried Wolf*.

He played suicidal characters in *The Woman in the Window* (poison), *The Red House* (driving his truck into a swamp), and *Actors and Sin* (stabbing). Similarly, he goes down with his ship at the conclusion of *The Sea Wolf*, and he does not save himself from drowning in *Unholy Partners*. Robinson's character dies of natural causes in *Silver Dollar, Dr. Ehrlich's Magic Bullet, House of Strangers,* and *Seven Thieves*.

He is executed in the electric chair in *Two Seconds;* is the victim of an attack by the title character of *Tiger Shark;* and one of his two characters in *The Prize* is stabbed to death. In *Mackenna's Gold* he is among the group massacred in an Indian attack. He falls to his death from an electrical pole in *Manpower*. His most bizarre death scene is in *The Ten Commandments*, as, according to scriptures, "the ground clave asunder that was under [him]: and the earth opened her mouth, and swallowed [him] up." He thanked screenwriter Jesse Lasky for that, for giving him "the best exit an actor ever had."

Robinson survived a gunshot wound in *Brother Orchid*, arson in *The Violent Men*, and a heart attack in *Two Weeks in Another Town*.

DeCarlo, Yvonne (1922–) was Moses' wife, Sephora, in *The Ten Commandments*, and she also starred in *The Munsters* on television. Her other films, from 1942, include *Brute Force, Song of Scheherazade, Casbah, Criss Cross, The Captain's Paradise, Death of a Scoundrel,* and *Munster Go Home*.

Dekker, Albert (1904–68) had a lengthy career on Broadway and on the big screen. His films include *The Great Garrick, Dr. Cyclops, Honky Tonk, The Killers, East of Eden, Illegal* (with Edward G. Robinson), *Middle of the Night, The Wonderful Country, Suddenly Last Summer,* and *The Wild Bunch*.

DeKova, Frank (1910–81) is onscreen in *Viva Zapata!, The Big Sky, The Brothers Karamazov, The Rise and Fall of Legs Diamond, The Desert Song,* and *The Greatest Story Ever Told*. In *The Ten Commandments* he and Edward G. Robinson play Abiram and Dathan, respectively, Hebrews (brothers in the film) who rebel against Moses.

Del Rio, Dolores (1905–83) was an exotic star from 1925 (*Joanna*) through the 1940s: *The Loves of Carmen, Flying Down to Rio, Journey Into Fear*. She appeared with Edward G. Robinson in *Cheyenne Autumn* as an Indian matriarch named Spanish Woman.

Deleted Scenes *Tales of Manhattan*: A sixth episode was deleted from the finished film following the Robinson episode because the film was too long. It starred W. C. Fields and Margaret Dumont. More recently, the final episode with Paul Robeson and Ethel Waters has been cut from showings because of its "Uncle Tom" treatment of blacks, but the segment was in the release version.

East Is West: All of Edward G. Robinson's scenes in the film were reshot; he replaced Jean Hersholt in the role of Charlie Yong, the Chop Suey King, when preview audiences laughed at the Danish actor's performance as a Chinaman.

Double Indemnity: The film originally ended with Walter Neff's execution at Folsom Prison, but director Billy Wilder felt that ending was too harsh, and he substituted the ending in the release print of Keyes lighting Neff's cigarette after he collapses trying to make a getaway.

Flesh and Fantasy: There was a fourth episode, which was deleted from the finished film. It was later developed into the film *Destiny*.

Good Neighbor Sam: A dream sequence that turns into a nightmare was shortened. A scene is missing which shows Robinson in barrister's white wig in court presiding over Jack Lemmon's debauchery.

The Whole Town's Talking: Aunt Agatha is reduced to a bit role. Lucille Ball is credited with a bit role, but it is impossible to find her in the film.

The Sea Wolf: Barry Fitzgerald's role as Cooky was extensively cut by the editors, as was David Bruce's role altogether as a young sailor. John Garfield delivers a line to Ida Lupino regarding the sound of a harmonica: "That's the kid." Who?

Kid Galahad: A still shows Robinson and Bette Davis in an ambulance, probably the end of the film, which was edited to have Robinson die in the locker room.

The Stranger: Several scenes in an opening episode in Latin America were deleted. Konrad Meineke is being followed by a woman government agent. In the deleted sequence she is murdered.

Barbary Coast: Robinson mentions filming a scene in which he slaps Miriam Hopkins. Although he has several verbal fights with her in the film, he never hits her.

Scarlet Street: A sequence where Robinson climbs a telephone pole to get a view of Dan Duryea's death house execution was deleted from the finished film.

The Deluge (Theater, 1917, 1922) In his tenth Broadway appearance Robinson played the role of Nordling in *The Deluge*. He was excited about auditioning for Arthur Hopkins, although they both knew the play would not be successful, despite its being a labor of love. It did reopen in 1922.

Adapted by Frank Allen from the original Scandinavian *Syndafloden* by Henning Berger*; producer, director, Arthur Hopkins; cast: Pauline Lord (Sadie), (Nordling), William Dick, Henry E. Dixey, William Riley Hatch, Robert McWade, Guy Nichols, Clyde North, Frederick Perry, William J. Phinney; opened at the Hudson Theatre, New York; August 20, 1917; *Hjalmar Bergman, according to Harold Clurman

In the 1922 revival cast were Edward G. Robinson (Nordling, an Immigrant), William Dick (Higgins, an Actor), and Robert McWade (Fraser, a Promoter) from the earlier production, and Charles Ellis (Adams, a Broker), Arthur Hurley (First Customer), James Spottswood (Charlie, a Waiter), Kathleen McDonald (Sadie), Lester Lonergan (O'Neill, a Lawyer), John Ravold (Second Customer), and Robert E. O'Connor (Stratton, a Saloonkeeper); opened at the Plymouth Theatre, January 27, 1922

Best Plays of 1921–22 said, "Seven men and a girl are caught in the barroom of a basement saloon during a cloudburst in a city located on the banks of the Mississippi River. The storm continues, the river overflows, and finally, with the steel shutters up and all the doors barred, the trapped customers find themselves shut off from all communication with the outside world and facing probable death by suffocation. In their extremity the natures of all eight undergo definite reactions. Alcoholically stimulated, a cheating broker becomes fanatically inspired by the thought of forming a great human chain of brotherhood; a philosophical "shyster" lawyer preaches eloquently the claims of the soul; a self-seeking and inordinately ambitious broker admits to the girl of the streets imprisoned with them whom he had known in his clerkship days, that she is the only woman he ever loved, and that he left her to marry a rich girl to give him power in the business world. With their respective souls shriven the storm ceases and release follows. Within a half hour they have reverted to type and are as tricky as they were before — selfish, human, honest or tricky, according to their kind."

It was "an excellent performance of a searching and sardonic comedy," according to *The New Yorker*. "The play called *The Deluge* rose from the dead ... Arthur Hopkins first produced it here in the oppressive heat of that nervous August of 1917.... The play's career then was so brief that it is a mere technicality to call its present production a revival.... The present company of actors is a good one, particularly in lesser roles.... Edward G. Robinson, James Spottswood, Robert E. O'Connor, and Charles Ellis are sources of especial strength."

The New Republic singled out Robinson's performance: "Mr. Edward Robinson in the character of the Swedish immigrant has soaked himself all through with the part. His performance is always beautiful and shyly right. That Nordling of his is ... a creature whose ... minute and pathetic continuity supplies the one really poignant note that manages to run throughout the play."

Demarest, William   (1892–1983), best known as Uncle Charley on TV's *My Three Sons*, made three films with Edward G. Robinson, playing policemen in both *Night Has a Thousand Eyes* and *Hell on Frisco Bay,* and a studio guard in *Pepe*. Other films: *The Jazz Singer, Rebecca of Sunnybrook Farm, Mr. Smith Goes to Washington,* and *The Lady Eve*.

DeMille, Cecil B.   (1881–1959), pioneer film director-producer, won the best picture Oscar for *The Greatest Show on Earth* and received a special award in 1949. He filmed *The Ten Commandments* twice, first as a silent, and the second thirty years later. The HUAC situation had made Robinson "unacceptable," but DeMille instead had him investigated and found no reason not to hire him to play the Hebrew overseer, Dathan, thus helping restore Robinson's status in Hollywood. DeMille hosted *Lux Radio Theatre* on CBS, with Robinson appearing in as many as nine adaptations of his and other films. They were in

The Heart of Show Business, and Robinson was among stars saluting the director in the TV and radio special *The World's Greatest Showman: The Legend of Cecil B. DeMille.* Other films include *The Squaw Man, The King of Kings, Cleopatra, The Crusades, Union Pacific,* and *Samson and Delilah.*

Democratic National Committee radio program see ***The Roosevelt Special***

Denning, Richard (1914–97) was in two TV series — *Mr. and Mrs. North* and *Hawaii Five-O* (as the governor). With Edward G. Robinson he was onscreen in *The Glass Web,* and Denning also appeared in *Hold 'Em Navy, Union Pacific, Adam Had Four Sons, Black Beauty,* and *The Creature from the Black Lagoon.*

Derek, John (1926–98) appeared with Edward G. Robinson as Joshua in *The Ten Commandments.* His other films include *All the King's Men, Knock on Any Door,* and *Exodus.* At the end of his career he directed his wife, Bo Derek, in films such as *Bolero* and *Tarzan the Ape Man.*

Desert Battalion During World War II Gladys Lloyd, Edward G. Robinson's wife, helped form this group of women who, allied with the USO, toured military bases around the country, helping to boost morale.

DeSica, Vittorio (1902–74), Italian director-actor, won best foreign film Oscars for *Shoeshine, The Bicycle Thief, Yesterday Today and Tomorrow,* and *The Garden of the Finzi-Continis.* Other films include *Marriage Italian Style, Two Women,* and, as actor, *A Farewell to Arms* (Oscar nomination), *General Della Rovere, The Shoes of the Fisherman,* and, with Edward G. Robinson, *The Biggest Bundle of them All.*

Destroyer (Film, 1943) While many big name leading men of Hollywood were actually away fighting during the war (Clark Gable and James Stewart, to name two), Edward G. Robinson, in middle age, was recruited for pictures like *Destroyer.* Routine to be sure, it is perhaps the best of the three action wartime adventures he made.

"Another ripe old-timer in the Hollywood actor ranks has been mustered into service for the movies' own particular brand of war," said *The New York Times.* "This time it is Edward G. Robinson, complete with haunch, paunch and scowl.... As this indestructible hero, Mr. Robinson utilizes the same tough snarl, the same withering looks and mute sarcasm that made him the scourge of muggs in days gone by. He also possesses a humility and a rare streak of tenderness.... [However,] the quality of warfare here depicted is peculiarly theatrical.... It is a leaky and top-heavy vessel on which [he] serves."

The New York Sun was a bit more generous: "Edward G. Robinson plays Boley with a skillful mixture of comedy and sentiment. This is the kind of role that might have had Wallace Beery afloat with tears. Mr. Robinson keeps his Boley within the bounds of reason, a likable and believable fellow."

And finally, *The New York Herald-Tribune* pointed out a quality moment in what was otherwise average: "The film catches the spirit of naval camaraderie in one scene in which Mr. Robinson relates the story of the *Bonhommie Richard*'s last fight, but on the whole, the film contains none of the incisive character lines and sharp technique [of] *In Which We Serve.*"

Producer, Louis F. Edelman; director, William A. Seiter; based on a story by Frank Wead; screenplay, Wead, Lewis Melzer, Borden Chase; art directors, Lionel Banks, Cary Odell; music, Anthony Collins; music director, M. W. Stoloff; camera, Franz F. Planer; montage effects, Aaron Nibley; editor, Gene Havlick; makeup, William Tuttle; assistant director, Milton Carter; technical adviser, Lt. Commander H. D. Smith, USN; cast: Edward G. Robinson (Steve Boleslavski), Glenn Ford (Mickey Donohue), Marguerite Chapman (Mary Boleslavski), Edgar Buchanan (Kansas Jackson), Leo Gorcey (Sarecky), Regis Toomey (Commander Clark), Ed Brophy (Casey), Warren Ashe (Lt. Morton), Charles D. Brown (Doctor), Craig

Woods (Bigbee), Curt Bois (Yasha), Pierre Watkin (Admiral), Al Hill (Sailor in mess hall), Bobby Jordan (Sailor crying), Roger Clark (Chief engineer), Charles McGraw (Assistant), Dean Benton (Moore), David Alison (Thomas), Paul Perry, Tristram Coffin (Doctors), John Merton (Quartermaster), Don Peters (Helmsman), Virginia Sale (Spinster), Eleanor Counts (Sarecky's girl), Dale Van Sickel (Sailor), Addison Richards (Ferguson), Lester Dorr, Bud Geary (Ship fitters), Eddie Dew (Survivor), Larry Parks (Ensign Johnson), Eddie Chandler (Gunner's mate), Lloyd Bridges (Fireman), Dennis Moore (Communications officer), Edmund Cobb (Workman), Eddy Waller (Riveter), Pat O'Malley, Shirley Patterson, Billy Bletcher, Kenneth MacDonald; Columbia; 99 minutes; September 1943

Steve Boleslavski (Boley), a Navy retiree, is now a ship welder building the destroyer *John Paul Jones*. He is eager to return to active duty, and, following a stint as a camp training officer, he is assigned to the *Jones* as a chief bosun's mate, serving under Commander Clark, an old friend. His assignment reduces Mickey Donohue, a young officer, to a lower rank. The ship does poorly on its shakedown missions, and several discouraged crew members, also resenting old-timer Boley's constant badgering, put in for a transfer. Boley, however, has faith in the ship and regales the men with the heroic story of the *Bonhomie Richard*, commanded by John Paul Jones during the Revolutionary War in battle with the British. The *Jones* is seriously damaged by a Japanese submarine. Boley and Mickey choose a select few to make repairs while the rest of the crew abandons ship. The destroyer is repaired in time to sink the Japanese vessel, and Boley, now regarded as a hero, relinquishes his duties to Mickey, who, meanwhile, has fallen in love with Boley's daughter, Mary.

"Destroyer" (Radio, 1944) Director, Fred MacKaye; adaptation, Sanford Barnett; sound, Charlie Forsyth; music director, Louis Silvers; cast: Edward G. Robinson (Boley), Marguerite Chapman (Mary), Dennis O'Keefe (Mickey), Bob Young, Charles Seel, Ed Emerson, Edward Marr, Frank Barton, John McIntire, Leo Cleary, Kay Dibbs, Norman Field, Tom Holland, Tyler McVey; John Milton Kennedy (announcer); Cecil B. DeMille (host); *Lux Radio Theatre;* CBS; April 3, 1944

Detectives / Investigators Once it became established that a key screen persona for Edward G. Robinson was a tough guy on the wrong side of the law, it was inevitable, perhaps, that he would play roles in the opposition camp as well — that is, tough guys, still, but on the *right* side of the law.

Discounting his having played a small role as a plainclothes detective in *The Gambler* — one of his initial stage characters — Robinson did not play a major role as a policeman until 1936. The film, *Bullets or Ballots*, had his character, Detective Johnny Blake, go undercover, joining the mob to infiltrate and clean up the rackets. Thus, he played the good guy *impersonating* the criminal.

Two years later, as a law professor on sabbatical, he cleaned up the rackets again in *I Am the Law*. Perhaps because he was still so effective as a tough guy, and because the gangster genre was on the wane, no similar stories followed. He did play a lawyer and a law professor again, in later performances — *Flesh and Fantasy* and *The Woman in the Window*, respectively — but they were films about the criminal activities of the characters, and not about how he enforced the law.

Robinson became an impressive investigator routing American Nazis in both *Confessions of a Nazi Spy* and *The Stranger*. And for the insurance business, he skillfully investigated murder in *Double Indemnity*.

The 1950s saw him as staunch police investigators in *Vice Squad, A Bullet for Joey,* and *Nightmare,* and as district attorneys in *Tight Spot* and *Illegal*. In the latter, if his character veered to the wrong side of the law, at least his intentions were good. On television, too, Robinson played a former policeman turned lawyer, defending a wrongly accused youth in "The Case of Kenny Jason," a prospective TV pilot for a series called *For the Defense*. In *Peking Blonde* he was a federal agent investigating on an international level.

In his last film, *Soylent Green*, Edward G. Robinson was a retired professor, now called a "book," a twenty-first century invented term for police researcher.

The Devil and Daniel Webster (Television, 1960) Stephen Vincent Benet had dramatized his own short story, *The Devil and Daniel Webster*, as a musical folk play in 1939. It was also a film, *All That Money Can Buy,* in 1941, and had a second musical treatment on Broadway, *Scratch,* in the 1970s. The Edward G. Robinson version, with him starring as Webster and David Wayne as Mr. Scratch, was a television special aired in 1960. The third act was on videotape because of the elaborate special effects used at the story's conclusion, but the first two acts were performed live. Robinson's reviews, like the teleplay itself, were generally positive.

"A brilliant cast, headed by Edward G. Robinson, served Stephen Vincent Benet's classic folk tale," said the *New York Daily News.* "Robinson may not have been bombastic or fiery as the great orator he portrayed," commented *Variety,* "but nonetheless did a highly effective job...."

The New York World Telegram and Sun said that, "as Daniel Webster, Robinson was eloquent but restrained. It would have been easy for him to disfigure the image of Webster we all carry in our minds. Instead, he played him with blunt Yankee honesty. If he lacked the dry intellectual air we'd expect to encounter ... he had the gift of tongues.... Webster's defense of Jabez is moving and poetic." And finally, *The New York Times* noted that, "Edward G. Robinson as Webster had some effective moments, particularly in his closing address about freedom and its symbols."

Producer, Davis Susskind; director, Tom Donovan; teleplay, Phil Reisman, Jr.; based on the story by Stephen Vincent Benet; cast: Edward G. Robinson (Daniel Webster), David Wayne (Mr. Scratch), Tim O'Connor (Jabez Stone), Betty Lou Holland (Dorcas Stone), Walter Baldwin, Byron Foulger (Selectmen), John Hoyt (Frank Post), Howard Freeman (Pinkham), Stuart Germain (Stevens), Royal Beal (Justice Hawthorne), Lori March (Felicia Field); Edgar Bergen (host); *Breck Golden Showcase*; NBC-tv; 60 minutes; February 14, 1960

Devlin, Joe (1903–73) was in four films with Edward G. Robinson, as a baseball umpire in *Larceny, Inc.,* a bartender in *Manpower,* a crime reporter in *Scarlet Street,* and a tollbooth attendant in *The Woman in the Window.* He was Singapore Smith in the *Phantom* series, *Body and Soul,* and *They Got Me Covered.*

Diaz, Porfirio (1830–1915) helped rid Mexico of its French ruler, the Emperor Maximilian, and later opposed Benito Juarez for the presidency. He succeeded to the dictatorship from 1876 to 1910. He aided Mexico economically, but he was not popular. Edward G. Robinson portrayed him in the Theatre Guild's production of *Juarez and Maximilian.*

Dieterle, William (1893–1972) directed two of Edward G. Robinson's biographical films — *Dr. Ehrlich's Magic Bullet* and *A Dispatch from Reuter's.* He acted in and directed silent films in Germany, coming to Hollywood in 1930. His other pictures include *A Midsummer Night's Dream, The Story of Louis Pasteur, The Life of Emile Zola* (Academy Award nomination), *The Hunchback of Notre Dame, All That Money Can Buy, Love Letters, Elephant Walk,* and *Omar Khayyam.*

Dietrich, Marlene (1901–92), one of the screen's most glamorous actresses, appeared opposite Edward G. Robinson in *Manpower,* with a love triangle plot involving them and George Raft. They also were in its adaptation on *Lux Radio Theatre.* If offscreen Raft and Dietrich were lovers, more than one account had Robinson enamored of her as well. The two respected each other, sharing a passion for work and fine art. Dietrich once voiced dissatisfaction with Brando as *The Godfather,* saying he was too slow for it: "I don't know why they didn't get Eddie Robinson." In 1961 Robinson and Dietrich appeared at Madison Square Garden in the annual *Chanukah Festival for Israel. The Blue Angel* established her as an international star. Other films include *Morocco, Shanghai Express, Blonde Venus, Destry Rides Again, Golden Earrings, A Foreign Affair, Stage Fright, No Highway in the Sky, Rancho Notorious, Witness for the Prosecution, Touch of Evil,* and *Judgment at Nuremberg*. She entertained U.S. troops, sold war bonds, broadcast anti–Nazi propaganda (earning the Medal of Freedom), and was a cabaret performer.

Difficult Co-Workers By virtually all accounts, Edward G. Robinson was a warmhearted and scholarly professional on the set of his films and in the theater. Those few with whom he had difficulty form a roster of personalities well known for their touchiness or disagreeability, not to mention their talent. And to the credit of all, most of the difficulties were patched up over time.

Paul Muni and Edward G. Robinson came from New York to Hollywood at about the same time. Though they worked together only once, as narrators for the 1943 Holocaust pageant *We Will Never Die*, theirs was an understandable rivalry. In 1926 Robinson was in the Yiddish comedy *We Americans* in Atlantic City, and due to a commitment to the Theatre Guild, he could not stay with the production. Muni Weisenfreund, later to become Paul Muni, replaced him, and the show went to Broadway. Within a few years Muni had established himself and, like Robinson, made an impact in crime films (*I Am a Fugitive from a Chain Gang* and *Scarface*) and prestigious biographies (*The Story of Louis Pasteur* and *The Life of Emile Zola*). Robinson disliked being offered projects that Muni rejected. Muni was difficult, pompous, and highly mannered. Robinson allowed in *All My Yesterdays*, "I disliked Muni, and Muni detested me." In 1956, when both had returned to Broadway — Muni was starring in *Inherit the Wind*, Robinson in *Middle of the Night* — Robinson's intent to "bury the hatchet" backfired when he invited Muni to his dressing room at the ANTA Theater. Seeing the luxury of Robinson's accommodations, Muni left, howling, "I knew Robinson when he was a spear carrier!"

Miriam Hopkins also came to films from the New York stage. She had top billing in *Barbary Coast* and was a temperamental and demanding leading lady. Problematic was a set polarized by politics, with Robinson allying himself with liberal writers Ben Hecht and Charles MacArthur against most of the actors on the film, including Hopkins. But the bigger challenge was Hopkins' lack of professionalism. According to Robinson, she would not stand on her marks, would not read off-scene lines for closeups, failed to read lines as written, was repeatedly late, and complained and delayed proceedings merely to prove her star status. He recounts doing a scene for *Barbary Coast* where he had to slap her (it does not appear in the finished film). When encouraged by her to get it right the first time by slapping her hard, he says he willingly obliged.

Hopkins was disliked also by Bette Davis, the two having appeared together in both *The Old Maid* and *Old Acquaintance*. (Did the word "old" in the titles hurt their situation?) Robinson's troubles with Davis, who co-starred as his mistress in *Kid Galahad*, had more to do with his assessment of her talent. Davis, in a recent publication, sophomorically laments having had to kiss Robinson's ugly purple lips. But she also thought him a powerful actor, if egotistical.

As a youngster growing up in Hoboken, New Jersey, Frank Sinatra idolized film tough guy Edward G. Robinson. Many years later, as an established star in his own right, Sinatra chose Robinson to co-star with him in *A Hole in the Head*. On the set, a conflict evolved concerning Robinson's rehearsing, which improved his performance, and Sinatra's spontaneity. The two were not embattled, because Sinatra was seldom around. But Robinson complained to director Frank Capra and threatened to walk off the picture unless Sinatra rehearsed with him. Through agents, a threatened lawsuit from Capra was averted, and Robinson, Sinatra, Capra, and the picture were a success. Thereafter the two were close, regularly exchanging gifts on their common December 12 birthday, and sharing the same liberal politics — at least during the Kennedy years.

The most publicized trouble between Robinson and a co-player occurred on the set of *Manpower*. George Raft tended to play himself—or at least his idealized version of a romantic tough guy—in his films. The situation was one of actor versus personality. Possibly Raft resented Robinson's acting ability, and there was either a real or imagined rivalry between them over the attentions of Marlene Dietrich. *Life* magazine was on hand to capture amazing publicity shots of when Raft and Robinson came to blows. Filming was halted and arbitrators were called in before *Manpower* was completed. More than a decade later the two tough guys appeared together again in *A Bullet for Joey*, but without apparent incident.

In his early days in the theater Robinson and his fellow actors found international star-director Jacob Ben-Ami intolerable, and his directing forced and wooden. To make matters worse, Ben-Ami got the best reviews from the critics.

Sidney Kingsley directed Robinson in the touring company of his adaptation of Arthur Koestler's *Darkness at Noon*. Robinson had replaced Claude Rains, who won a Tony Award for his performance. Robinson saw his role as a deposed Communist military leader differently from Rains, but Kingsley seemed to want a carbon copy of Rains' performance from Robinson, who felt he was "fighting for the play." The tour's success helped outweigh the troubles.

In *Middle of the Night*, troubles began with author Paddy Chayefsky's insistence that Robinson was wrong for his play, despite director Joshua Logan's assertion that he "was created by God for the part" of the Jewish manufacturer who experiences the sweetness of a May-December romance with Gena Rowlands. Chayefsky was very serious-minded about the script, and he didn't like the humor Robinson found in the dialogue. "He's cuing the audience when to laugh!" Chayefsky argued with Logan. Despite the play's success in New York and on tour, Robinson ultimately lost the role in the film version to Fredric March because Chayefsky had control of the casting and had already warned Logan that Robinson "sure ain't gonna be in the movie." *Middle of the Night* nevertheless proved to be a major milestone for both artists.

Digges, Dudley (1879–1947) came to Broadway from the Irish National Players. With Edward G. Robinson he was in the Theatre Guild's *The Adding Machine* (as Mr. Zero), as father to *The Brothers Karamazov*, and also *Juarez and Maximilian* and *Ned McCobb's Daughter*. They were onscreen in *The Hatchet Man*. Other plays include *Major Barbara, On Borrowed Time, George Washington Slept Here*, and *The Iceman Cometh*; and films: *Mutiny on the Bounty* and *The General Died at Dawn*.

Directors Directors are those artists who interpret and stage the action of the writers' words as a scene goes into production, either in film and television or the live theater. Sometimes they function also as producers or writers, and thus have a greater investment in the success of the final product.

Edward G. Robinson worked frequently with Arthur Hopkins, a producer-director in the New York theater (six plays), and with Philip Moeller, while he was associated with the Theatre Guild (eight plays). He worked also with Sam Forrest and Joshua Logan on Broadway.

Robinson was in four films directed by Mervyn LeRoy, beginning with *Little Caesar*; five by Alfred E. Green, and three by Lloyd Bacon. He worked on two films each with John Ford, Howard Hawks, Anatole Litvak, Michael Curtiz, George Sidney, Lewis Allen, Julien Duvivier, William Dieterle, and John S. Robertson, and once with William Keighley, Billy Wilder, Orson Welles, Joseph L. Mankiewicz, Cecil B. DeMille, Frank Capra, Vincente Minelli, Henry Hathaway, Martin Ritt, and Norman Jewison, among others. Although John Huston directed *Key Largo*, his other work with Robinson was as a writer.

Robinson's television directors included such former actors as Paul Henreid, Don Taylor, and Richard Carlson.

Disabilities   Edward G. Robinson played a number of emotionally warped and misguided characters. To underscore their abnormality, several suffered physical disabilities, all of them the result of situation rather than birth. He is blind in *Mackenna's Gold* and *The Sea Wolf*. Crippling accidents occur during *A Lady to Love, Tiger Shark,* and *Manpower*; and they preexist *The Red House, The Violent Men,* and "Heritage." All have him using crutches or a cane, except *Tiger Shark*, in which he uses a hook for a lost hand.

The most memorable use of crutches in a Robinson film, however, is in *Double Indemnity*. The murdered man is even shown in the opening credits walking away from the camera.

See **Blindness**.

Disguises   An actor named as Sid Raymond has a brief role in *The Prize*, playing the actor made up to look like Edward G. Robinson's double. For most of the film the double is played by Robinson himself, but in the scene where he dies in the arms of Elke Sommer and Diane Baker, Raymond takes over, confessing he is only an actor made up to look like Baker's uncle, pulling off his latex beard, moustache, and hairpiece. In the other film where Robinson plays a dual role — *The Whole Town's Talking* — bad guy Robinson convinces good guy Robinson to wear a moustache to disguise himself from the police.

Robinson impersonated a Frenchman, complete with moustache, goatee, and monocle, in *The Man with Two Faces*. Not necessarily disguises, Robinson wore moustaches also in *Silver Dollar, A Dispatch from Reuter's, Dr. Ehrlich's Magic Bullet* (plus beard), *Our Vines Have Tender Grapes, House of Strangers, Operation X, The Violent Men,* and on TV's "Heritage." From 1964, with his appearance in *The Outrage*, Edward G. Robinson sported a moustache and beard offscreen as well.

A Dispatch from Reuter's   (Film, 1941) Depicting the lives of historical European figures had become a popular formula in filmmaking (Disraeli, Richelieu, Voltaire, Zola, Pasteur, Ehrlich), especially at Warner Bros. *A Dispatch from Reuter's* was the story of a man with an obsession for news. Paul Julius Baron de Reuter (1816–1899) founded a news service that bears his name to this day. With the success of *Dr. Ehrlich's Magic Bullet* the year before, Edward G. Robinson had graduated to biographical pictures, the specialty of George Arliss and Paul Muni over the past decade. Several participants from *Dr. Ehrlich* also worked on *Reuter's,* notably director William Dieterle, cameraman James Wong Howe, and actors Albert Basserman, Otto Kruger, Montagu Love, and, in lesser roles, Jon Voigt, Ernst Hausman, and Theodore von Eltz. "The film missed the high intensity, crisis-ridden situations of Dieterle's other cinema biographies," noted William R. Meyer in *Warner Brothers Directors*. "Despite the lack, or perhaps because of it, *A Dispatch from Reuter's* has a lighter overall mood; Robinson is a bit more flighty in the lead, and he is even allowed to fall in love." The picture was intelligent, entertaining, and, after *Dr. Ehrlich,* it was Robinson's personal favorite.

"Generally interesting ... [but] only occasionally stimulating," said *The New York Times*. "The production is handsomely mounted and the story flows smoothly. Edward G. Robinson gives a sincere though not always convincing performance in the leading role."

"The Warners have given Edward G. Robinson a fat and rewarding role in Reuter," noted *The New York Herald-Tribune,* "and his performance justifies their good judgment.... Robinson, with the aid of William Dieterle's thoughtful direction, makes Reuter a compelling figure, one that the Fourth Estate should be happy to extol.... [It] isn't a great picture by any means, but it shows that screen biography has its own proper role to play in motion picture education."

Stronger praise came from the *New York Daily News*: "Robinson, in an immaculate performance, reflects his admiration and reverence for the man who fought against ridicule, prejudice and competition to revolutionize the newspaper business.... The film ... gives evidence of all the pains and care put into the making of it. The acting is first rate, the settings are effective, and William Dieterle's direction is adequate." Archer Winsten in *The New York Post* added that the film was "a decidedly interesting tale."

And finally, *Variety* said, "Robinson provides an excellent characterization of the resourceful Reuter, who time after time, stakes everything on his aim to 'make the world smaller by quicker transmission of the news.'"

Producer, Hal B. Wallis; associate producer, Henry Blanke; director, William Dieterle; story, Valentine Williams, Wolfgang Wilhelm; screenplay, Milton Krims; music director, Leo F. Forbstein; sound, C. A. Riggs; art director, Anton Grot; special effects, Byron Haskin; camera, James Wong Howe; editor, Warren Low; cast: Edward G. Robinson (Julius Reuter), Edna Best (Ida Magnus Reuter), Eddie Albert (Max Stargardt), Albert Basserman (Franz Geller), Nigel Bruce (Sir Randolph Persham), Gene Lockhart (Herr Bauer), Otto Kruger (Dr. Magnus), Montagu Love (Delane), James Stephenson (Carew), Walter Kingsford (Napoleon III), David Bruce (Bruce), Alec Craig (Geant), Dickie Moore (Young Julius), Billy Dawson (Young Max), Richard Nichols (Herbert), Lumsden Hare (Anglo-Irish chairman), Egon Brecher (Reingold), Frank Jacquet (Stein), Hugh Sothern (American ambassador), Walter O. Stahl (Von Danstadt), Paul Irving (Josephat Benfey), Edward McWade (Chemist), Gilbert Emery (Lord Palmerston), Robert Warwick, Ellis Irving (Speakers), Henry Roquemore (Otto), Paul Weigel (Gauss), Joseph Stefani (Assistant), Mary Anderson, Grace Stafford (Girls), Jon Voigt (Post office clerk), Stuart Holmes (Attendant), Sunny Boyne (Companion), Ernst Hausman (Heinrich), Theodore Von Eltz (Actor), Kenneth Hunter, Holmes Herbert, Leonard Mudie, Lawrence Grant (Members of Parliament), Pat O'Malley (Workman), Cyril Delevanti, Norman Ainsley, Bobby Hale (News vendors), Frederic Mellinger; Warner Bros.; 89 minutes, December 1940

Julius Reuter is a boy in Germany when it is discovered that the telegraph can revolutionize world communications. But the efficiency of the telegraph takes several years to develop. As an adult Julius promotes a carrier pigeon service. Ridiculed for his efforts as the "pigeon fool," he is finally successful when a message sent by pigeon prevents a poisoning disaster at a hospital in Aachen. The telegraph eventually renders the pigeon service obsolete. Julius makes a further advance by telegraphing a vital speech by Napoleon III, and thus begins Reuter's news service. Competition threatens, but Julius enlists investors to help him develop more efficient transmission of news from across the ocean in America. A scandal in London is averted when Abraham Lincoln's assassination is confirmed by the American ambassador several hours after an announcement from Reuters. The integrity of the Reuters news service is assured.

Dixey, Henry E. (1859–1943) was a Broadway comic, known for his role in the musical *Adonis* (1884) as a statue who comes to life. His other plays include *Under the Gaslight, Evangeline, Rip, Mrs. Bumpstead Leigh,* and *The Deluge*, which featured Edward G. Robinson.

Dobkin, Lawrence (1919–) was gangster Al Carol in *Illegal* and Hur Ben Caleb in *The Ten Commandments* with Edward G. Robinson, and he was in the cast of "Man on a Tightrope" on the radio. He is also in *Twelve O'Clock High, Sweet Smell of Success, North by Northwest, The Defiant Ones,* and *Patton*.

Dr. Ehrlich's Magic Bullet (Film, 1940) If there had never been a *Little Caesar* to make Edward G. Robinson's name a household word, it is possible the actor would have been remembered for his role as the Nobel Prize–winning Dr. Paul Ehrlich in *Dr. Ehrlich's Magic Bullet* ten years later. But the film's quiet intensity probably would have allowed Robinson only distinguished character actor status and not the superstardom that went with his gangster image. Nevertheless, this film and character were Robinson's personal favorite.

"Robinson fought his studio for the part," noted Foster Hirsch in *Edward G. Robinson, A Pyramid Illustrated History of the Movies*. "The voice is studiously subdued, the usually staccato delivery muted and slowed down to a hum ... his performance is excellent...." Walter Winchell touted Robinson's performance as Oscar-worthy, but the film received only one nomination, for its original screenplay.

"John [Huston, one of the writers] wanted to do something daring: he wanted to eliminate any love story.... The drama, for Huston, was in the experiments themselves, not in Ehrlich's life.... Huston wasn't happy with what Dieterle did with *Dr. Ehrlich's Magic Bullet*.... [He] tried to dramatize things that didn't need to be dramatized in a heavy-handed way.... Huston agreed that Robinson did 'the best acting of his career.' Eddie Robinson was always longing to be respectable and to play men with great minds and high ideals and souls." — *The Hustons* by Lawrence Grobel.

Producer Hal Wallis comments on the filming in his autobiography *Starmaker*: "It was a forbidden subject: the story of the scientist who found the cure for syphilis. Only Edward G. Robinson could play the part. He had Ehrlich's rugged honesty, compassion, and strength.... We had difficulty in obtaining research material.... No biography of Ehrlich could be found.... We were angered by Hitler's widely quoted statement in 1938 that 'a scientific discovery by a Jew is worthless.' When Jewish organizations asked us to prove that statement wrong with another picture, we were happy to do so.... It became necessary to contact members of the Ehrlich family.... [His] daughter, Mrs. Schwerin, was in town that Christmas, so I took her to lunch, and she talked charmingly of her father.... George Schwerin, Ehrlich's grandson, proved to be extremely difficult ... proceeded to insist that a very large sum of money be paid to the family for the right to use Mrs. Ehrlich's name.... One bright note in this period of struggle was Edward G. Robinson's approval of the screenplay.... Jack [Warner] wanted Gale Page to play Mrs. Ehrlich, but I felt Ruth Gordon was far more suitable. Dieterle directed, and the box office was good." — Hal Wallis, with Charles Higham, *Starmaker*

Ruth Gordon, making an early and rare film appearance as Robinson's wife, recalled in her memoir *An Open Book* that she and Robinson quickly became friends. He invited her to his house for dinner, and afterwards they drove back to the studio. "We ran about half, maybe a little more of *Dr. Ehrlich*, it held us riveted," wrote Gordon. "No background music, just what is called 'the rough cut,' but Dieterle's direction, Eddie's performance of the doctor and the great Basserman playing the great scientist.... In the projection room, Eddie and I sat awed.... Next morning on the set, I waited to speak to Mr. Dieterle. 'It is just great.' 'What is?' 'The film.' 'The film?' 'What we're doing.' 'You saw it?' 'Oh, yes, Eddie invited me to see it last night.' 'Where did you see it?' 'In a projection room.' Eddie hadn't told me not to tell. All hell broke loose, Dieterle thought it was the most highhanded behavior he'd met with. I told Eddie I was sorry. 'Don't be,' he said. A reigning movie star reigns."

Producers, Jack L. Warner, Hal B. Wallis; associate producer, Wolfgang Reinhardt; director, William Dieterle; screenplay, John Huston, Norman Burnside, Heinz Herald; story, Burnside; music, Max Steiner; orchestra, Hugo Friedhofer; music director, Leo F. Forbstein; dialogue director, Irving Rapper; art director, Carl Jules Weyl; sound, Robert E. Lee; camera, James Wong Howe; costumes, Howard Shoup; makeup, Perc Westmore; editor, Warren Low; special microscopic effects, Robert Burks; cast: Edward G. Robinson (Dr. Paul Ehrlich), Ruth Gordon (Hedi Ehrlich), Otto Kruger (Dr. Emil Von Behring), Donald Crisp (Althoff), Albert Basserman (Dr. Robert Koch), Sig Rumann (Dr. Hans Wolfert), Maria Ouspenskaya (Franziska Speyer), Henry O'Neill (Dr. Lentz), Edward Norris (Dr. Morgenroth), Harry Davenport (Judge), Montagu Love (Dr. Hartmann), Louis Jean Heydt (Dr. Kunze), Donald Meek (Mittelmeyer), Douglass Wood (Speidler), Irving Bacon (Becker), Charles Halton (Sensenbrenner), Hermine Sterler (Miss Marquardt), Louis Calhern (Dr. Brockdorf), John Hamilton (Hirsch), Paul Harvey (Defense Attorney), Frank Reicher (Old Doctor), Torben Meyer (Kadereit), Theodore Von Eltz (Dr. Kraus), Louis Arco (Dr. Bertheim), Wilfred Hari (Dr. Hata), John Henrick (Dr.

Bucher), Ann Todd (Marianne), Polly Stewart (Steffi), Ernst Hausman (Hans Weisgart), Stuart Holmes (Male Nurse), Frank Lackteen (Arab), Elaine Renshaw (Arab woman), Herbert Anderson (Assistant), Egon Brecher (Martl), Robert Strange (Koerner), Cliff Clark (Haupt), Jon Voigt (Kellner); Warner Bros., 103 minutes; February 1940

Paul Ehrlich, a German doctor, treats syphilis cases without a successful cure in the late 1800s. His work with dyes and specific staining experiments bring him in contact with Dr. Robert Koch, an eminent researcher, and his associate, Dr. Emil von Behring. A bout with tuberculosis contracted during experimentation sends Ehrlich to Egypt for a rest cure. He attends a boy and his father there for snake bites, and begins research on antibodies. With Behring he develops a successful serum for diphtheria. The government supports his research studies for several years but stops funding, partly through the influence of Behring, who opposes the use of chemicals in treating disease. Ehrlich is helped by the philanthropy of Franziska Speyer. He and his staff spend years working on a cure for syphilis, and after hundreds of tries, number 606 proves successful. When there are deaths attributed to the drug due to premature marketing and demand, Ehrlich must defend himself in a libel suit against his accusers. Von Behring comes forward to attest to 606's benefits, and Ehrlich is vindicated. On his deathbed, as his wife, Hedi, plays a waltz, Ehrlich urges his colleagues not to stop fighting the diseases that afflict mankind.

Reviews for the film were good to excellent, and nearly all focused on Robinson's superior performance as the high spot. *The New York Times* said, "We have to go ... [to] *The Story of Louis Pasteur* to match it in its line, combing out new synonyms for 'great' to classify Edward G. Robinson's performance.... There is a perfect delineation of the man by Mr. Robinson. It is a rounded gem of portraiture, completely free from the devastating self-consciousness that plagues so many actors when they are forced to wear a beard, almost electric in its attractiveness, astonishingly apart from the manneristic screen behavior of *Little Caesar*."

"As the stubborn, cigar-smoking, bearded little man with a bad lung, Robinson avoids every one of his facile tricks. He does not gesture, or rant, or resort to his rasping voice, or freeze into a posture; on the contrary, he presents as simple and charming and honest a portrait as I've ever seen.... A superb motion picture!"—Pare Lorentz, *Lorentz on Film: Movies 1927 to 1941*.

"The most dramatic and moving medical film I have ever seen ... due in no small degree to the brilliant portrayal of Dr. Ehrlich by Edward G. Robinson. Aided by superb makeup, the erstwhile player of gangster roles gives a modulated and understanding performance which is in the first rank of biographical portraits."—*The New York Herald-Tribune*

The film is "one of [his] most distinguished performances," said *Variety,* and *Newsweek* called the film "an absorbing biography ... honest, unmannered characterization that ranks with [his] best."

"Edward G. Robinson as Dr. Ehrlich is not only better than he has ever been before, but he gives one of the greatest performances ever seen on the screen," exclaimed *The Nation*. "His simplicity in portraying a great man without putting his words in quotes should be an example for other actors called to similar tasks. There is not one false touch in his moving characterization." *The Nation* stated further that, "with *Dr. Ehrlich's Magic Bullet* ... Hollywood takes a giant step forward. The picture is in theme and presentation so mature that it provides a deep and exciting experience. It surpasses the films of the biographical genre that we have seen before in every respect...."

And finally, Otis Ferguson, in *The New Republic,* said what might have needed saying all along: "Although Edward G. Robinson has been typed unmercifully, I have always found him an arresting personality and so cannot take part in the surprise currently shown over his being an 'actor,' too. The part calls for a quiet and steady intensity, and Robinson has it."

See **Ruth Gordon**.

"The Doctor with Hope in His Hands" see **"The Man with Hope in His Hands"**

Doctors Edward G. Robinson's roles include the title characters in *The Amazing Dr. Clitterhouse* and *Dr. Ehrlich's Magic Bullet*. He is called "Professor" in *Seven Thieves, The Biggest Bundle of Them All, Grand Slam, The Woman in the Window, The Prize,* and *Soylent Green*. The scheme of *Seven Thieves* is nearly foiled by a doctor suspicious of Eli Wallach's "seizure." Robinson's characters receive medical treatment by doctors in *The Prize, Dr. Ehrlich's Magic Bullet, Two Weeks in Another Town, Manpower, Two Seconds,* and *A Lady to Love*.

Document A/777 (Radio, 1950) Radio offered Edward G. Robinson little relief from a dearth of performing opportunities during the period of the House Committee witch hunt. One of the better programs was *Document A/777*, written and produced by Norman Corwin in the spring of 1950.

According to R. LeRoy Bannerman in his book *On a Note of Triumph*, "It was a strange, unpredictable time. On one hand, Corwin was commended for touting the prerogatives of peace and unanimity among nations; on the other, he was distrusted and looked upon with suspicion for his liberal views. With the arrival of the new decade, the same disquieting concerns clouded the field of communications and the arts. New lists involved new people daily. Most broadcast executives despised the witch hunt, then accepted it, and later participated.... The Mutual Broadcasting System, however, consented to collaborate with UN Radio for the broadcast of six special documentaries in the spring of 1950. Corwin was to supervise the programs, which were presented under the series title *The Pursuit of Peace*.... Corwin set about to prepare the first broadcast, an hour-long documentary depicting the significance of the Universal Declaration of Human Rights.... The voting which marked the adoption of the Human Rights Bill had been fully recorded at the UN General Assembly in Paris in December 1948. Corwin therefore listened to the tapes of the conference, heard the discussion — the delegates voicing their approval or disapproval — and the final decision. He hit upon the idea of using the actual roll call as the unifying thread.... The roll call was interrupted at particular countries as Corwin dramatized incidents peculiar to each, illustrating the basis of the various articles accepted by the United Nations Commission on Human Rights.... By the facility of audio tape, Corwin recorded separate scenes to be inserted among the actuality. In this way, no more than several actors had to be present at a time. Sir Laurence Olivier was added when Corwin decided to use recordings of the actor reading the preamble and articles as originally performed four months before at Carnegie Hall.... Following introductory credits, the setting of mystery is enhanced by the suggestion of 'a rendezvous near a huge plant next to a bombsight factory'.... By its scope, its skill, its poetry of sound and movement, its purpose, *Document A/777* approached a pinnacle achieved in Corwin's established classics." The program was the winner of a Peabody Award.

Writer, Norman Corwin; music, Lyn Murray; cast: Richard Basehart, Charles Boyer, Lee J. Cobb, Ronald Colman, Joan Crawford, Maurice Evans, Jose Ferrer, Reginald Gardner, Van Heflin (Narrator), Jean Hersholt, Lena Horne, Marsha Hunt, Alexander Knox, Charles Laughton, Laurence Olivier, Vincent Price, Edward G. Robinson, Robert Ryan, Hilda Vaughn, Emlyn Williams, Robert Young; premiere episode of a six-program series, *The Pursuit of Peace*; Mutual Network, March 26, 1950; 60 minutes

The following reviews also are from Bannerman's book, *On a Note of Triumph: Norman Corwin and the Golden Years of Radio*. "*Variety* pointed out that (*Document A/777*) possessed 'almost epic quality.' Critic Jack Gould of *The New York Times* [said], 'The radio documentary was restored to its place of honor last week by Norma Corwin and the United Nations radio staff.' *Billboard* called the program 'outstanding ... a potent expression of the needs and aspirations of the world's population.' In her column, Harriet Van Horne wrote: 'It was a beautiful program. Yes, beautiful — in concept, in production, in the force and clarity of its message. The cast was worthy of the noble spirit implicit in the program.' *The London Evening Express*: 'A magnificent presentation.' *The Glasgow Herald*: 'Another of [Corwin's] triumphs....'"

Documentaries see **Short Films**

Dolenz, George (1908–63) appeared in *Enter Arsene Lupin, My Cousin Rachel, The Last Time I Saw Paris, The Four Horsemen of the Apocalypse*, and, with Edward G. Robinson, *A Bullet for Joey* (as Professor Macklin). He was in two TV series, *The Count of Monte Cristo* and *Four Just Men*, and is the father of Mickey Dolenz of the Monkees.

Donlevy, Brian (1899–1972) played Knuckles Jacoby, Edward G. Robinson's henchman, in *Barbary Coast*. He received an Oscar nomination for *Beau Geste* and also appeared in *Union Pacific, Destry Rides Again, The Great McGinty, The Glass Key, The Miracle of Morgan's Creek, Command Decision,* and *Never So Few,* among others.

Donnelly, Ruth (1896–1982) played Nora, wife of Remy Marco (Edward G. Robinson), in *A Slight Case of Murder*. A versatile comedienne, she had roles also in *Footlight Parade, Mr. Deeds Goes to Town, Holiday, Mr. Smith Goes to Washington, My Little Chickadee, The Snake Pit,* and *The Spoilers* in a career that began on Broadway in 1913.

Dorr, Lester (1893–1980) appeared in a variety of roles in four films with Edward G. Robinson—*The Little Giant, Unholy Partners, Destroyer,* and *Night Has a Thousand Eyes*. He was also in *Riders of the Purple Sage* and *The Main Event*.

Double Indemnity On June 16, 1998, *Double Indemnity* was named one of the 100 greatest movies of all time by the American Film Institute. The only Robinson film on the list, its ranking was 38.

Having left Warner Bros. and its roster of contract players to become a freelance actor in 1942, Edward G. Robinson appeared in multi-part films for director Julien Duvivier and routine World War II dramas before Billy Wilder offered him the role of the insurance investigator in *Double Indemnity* at Paramount. Robinson had to weigh the part's quality against the step down to third billing following Fred MacMurray and Barbara Stanwyck. Fortuitously, he decided to accept the role and began a phase of his career which was to become almost as important as his gangster image—*film noir*.

Based on the quality of *Double Indemnity* as a finished film and his superb contribution of character to it, Edward G. Robinson might well have agreed with this comment from Fred MacMurray: "I never dreamed it would be the best picture I ever made." Director Billy Wilder had talked MacMurray into playing the lead role of Walter Neff after it had been turned down by both George Raft and Alan Ladd. He also had to convince Barbara Stanwyck to play the villainous wife, and to do so in an unflattering blonde wig. Paramount executive Buddy DeSylva complained after seeing tests of her, "We hire Barbara Stanwyck, and we get George Washington!"

Despite the casting negotiations, the three stars never performed better. Stanwyck received a best actress Oscar nomination (her third of four). The picture was also nominated, as were its director, writers, sound, cinematography, and musical score. MacMurray and Robinson, good as they were, were not nominated. "The absence from the supporting actor nominees of Robinson—who never received an Oscar nomination—is one of the Academy's worst sins of omission," noted Charles Matthews in his book *Oscar A to Z*.

Double Indemnity was a classic from the outset. Billy Wilder's adaptation of James M. Cain's story into a witty screenplay was done in collaboration with another leading mystery writer of the day, Raymond Chandler, when Cain was unavailable. The relationship between Wilder and Chandler was bizarre and testy, but the resulting dialogue was superb. "Chandler ... was on the set each day," noted Maurice Zolotow in *Billy Wilder in Hollywood*. "He once expressed his delight at how Robinson memorized long speeches—and did them freshly at every take."

Cain had based his novel on a sensational 1928 murder case. The story was serialized in *Liberty* magazine in 1936. Ruth Snyder, with the help of her lover, Judd Gray, murdered her husband, Albert, for his insurance. Apprehended and brought to trial, the defendants gained notoriety through press accounts of the crime. Even more publicity came from the circulation of a photograph of Ruth Snyder being electrocuted in the death house; the picture was surreptitiously taken by a reporter with a trick camera device attached to his leg.

The film is full of memorable scenes. The suspense is heightened when, after leaving the husband's body on the train tracks, the murderous couple's getaway car will not start. Robinson is delightful and impressive as he tells off his boss with a recitation on the multiple methods of committing suicide. And finally, the end of the picture substitutes a powerful new scene for one originally shot, an execution, which was filmed in five days on a $150,000 replica set of the gas chamber at Folsom prison. Wilder decided the execution segment was too strong. Bernard F. Dick comments in *Billy Wilder*: "Wilder disliked the ending; it was exactly what the self-righteous would expect. Despite Chandler's objections, Wilder replaced the gas chamber with one of the most powerful images of male love ever portrayed on the screen: a *pieta`* in the form of a surrogate father's lighting the cigarette of his dying surrogate son."

In an article entitled "Making and Remaking *Double Indemnity*" in the January-February 1996 issue of *Film Comment* magazine, James Naremore disputes reasons for changing the ending. "Actually, there were three possible conclusions," he wrote. "According to the final drafts of the screenplay ... the released print is simply a bit shorter ... omitting not only the execution sequence but also a line spoken by Walter just after he said 'I love you.' In the intermediate version ... Walter makes a final request: 'At the end of that trolley line, just as I get off, you be there to say goodbye. Will you, Keyes?' The longest of the three versions went on to show Keyes at the penitentiary, honoring his friend's wishes." Naremore makes the point also that the deleted execution scene "provides a tragic recognition scene for Keyes, who is shaken out of his moral complacency.... One of the many virtues of Wilder's original ending is that this complex, brilliantly acted character would have been made to confront his inner demon...." And finally, asserts Naremore, "Keyes' lonely walk out of the prison would have thrown a shadow over everything that preceded it."

"Wilder's ending was much better than my ending," said James M. Cain. "Billy Wilder did a terrific job. It's the only picture I ever saw made from my books that had things in it I wish I had thought of.... There are situations in the movie that can make your hands get wet, you get so nervous, like the place where Eddie Robinson comes in to talk to Fred MacMurray.... And *she* [Stanwyck] comes and is about to rap on MacMurray's door when she hears something and pulls back and the door opens and Eddie Robinson comes out ... and she's hiding behind the door. I tell you, there for a minute, it is just beautiful. I wish I had thought of something like it."

Executive producer, Buddy DeSylva; producer, Joseph Sistrom; director, Billy Wilder; screenplay, Wilder, Raymond Chandler; based on the novel by James M. Cain (based on the 1928 murder of Albert Snyder by his wife Ruth and her lover, Judd Gray); art directors, Hans Dreier, Hal Pereira; set, Bertram Granger; sound, Loren Ryder, Stanley Cooley, Walter Oberst; assistant director, C. C. Coleman, Jr.; music, Miklos Rozsa; camera, John Seitz; editor, Doane Harrison; process photography, Farciot Edouart; dialogue director, Jack Gage; costumes, Edith Head; makeup, Wally Westmore; cast: Fred MacMurray (Walter Neff), Barbara Stanwyck (Phyllis Dietrichson), Edward G. Robinson (Barton Keyes), Porter Hall (Jackson), Jean Heather (Lola Dietrichson), Tom Powers (Mr. Dietrichson), Byron Barr (Nino Zachette), Richard Gaines (Mr. Norton), Fortunio Bonanova (Sam Gorlopis), John Philliber (Joe Pete), Bess Flowers (Norton's secretary), Kernan Cripps (Conductor), Harold Garrison (Redcap), Oscar Smith, Frank Billy Mitchell, Floyd Shackelford, James Adamson (Pullman porters), Betty Farrington (Nettie), Constance Purdy (Shopper), Dick Rush (Pullman conductor), Edmund Cobb (Train conductor), Sam McDaniel (Garage attendant), Judith Gibson (Operator), Miriam

Franklin (Keyes' secretary), Lee Shumway, Edward Hearn (Men at gas chamber*), Douglas Spencer (Lou), Mona Freeman, George Magrill, Clarence Muse, George Anderson, Alan Bridge, Boyd Irwin, George Melford, William O'Leary; Paramount; 106 minutes; September 1944. *Scene cut from the picture

Insurance salesman Walter Neff falls for Phyllis Dietrichson after a series of encounters that began with his attempts to renew her husband's auto insurance. Together they plot to kill Phyllis' husband and collect the death benefit. On the way to the station to board a train, Neff kills the husband and then, impersonating the dead man, boards the train and leaps off the observation car at the rear. He and Phyllis put Dietrichson's body on the tracks, now expecting to collect double because the "accidental" death was on a train. Claims adjuster Barton Keyes, Walter's superior, doubts that the death was an accident; he also doubts that a man could expect to kill himself by jumping off the back of a slow-moving train, and thus rules out suicide. He suspects beneficiary Phyllis, and a "somebody else," of murder. His close friendship with Neff helps avert suspicion from his colleague. The curiosity of Phyllis' stepdaughter, Lola, complicates things; Neff begins seeing her to keep her quiet. Keyes brings in a witness, Jackson, who was aboard the train and now almost recognizes Neff. Neff decides to kill Phyllis when he discovers she has been seeing Nino Zachette, Lola's boyfriend. She shoots him first, however; he then turns the gun on her. Now making a confession into his office dictaphone, Neff is discovered by Keyes. It is dawn, and Neff is too weak to escape.

Barbara Stanwyck was quoted in *American Film* magazine: "The very best screenplay I was ever sent was *Double Indemnity*. It's brilliant, of course, but what's amazing is that not one word was changed while we were shooting. Billy had it all there, and I mean all—everything you see on the screen was in the script. The moves, the business, the atmosphere, all written. When I mention atmosphere in *Double Indemnity*—that gloomy, horrible house the Dietrichsons lived in, the slit of sunlight slicing through those heavy drapes—you could smell that death was in the air, you understood why she wanted to get out of there, away, no matter how. Can you imagine that picture being 'colorized'? My God! And for an actress, let me say that the way those sets were lit, the house, Walter's apartment, those dark shadows, those slices of harsh light at strange angles—all that helped my performance. The way Billy staged it and John Seitz lit it, it was all one sensational mood. Color? How dare they?"

The reviews of *Double Indemnity* were virtually all positive, both in the periodicals of the day and in retrospective accounts. Calling the film a "sophisticated observation of greed ... one of the highest summits of *film noir* ... [and] a film without a single trace of pity or love," Charles Higham and Joel Greenberg, in *Hollywood in the Forties,* also commented on the film's atmosphere: "The couple ... finally shoot each other in a shuttered room, with *Tangerine,* most haunting of numbers, floating through the windows. The Californian ambience is all important: winding roads through the hills leading to tall stuccoed villas in a Spanish style thirty years out of date, cold tea drunk out of tall glasses on hot afternoons ... Chinese Checkers played on long pre-television evenings by people who hate each other's guts. The film reverberates with the forlorn poetry of late sunny afternoons; the script is as tart as a lemon; and Stanwyck's white rat-like smoothness, MacMurray's bluff duplicity, are beautifully contrasted. A notable scene is when the car stalls after the husband's murder, the killing conveyed in a single close-up of the wife's face, underlined by the menacing strings of Miklos Rozsa's score."

In their book *Cinema, the Magic Vehicle: A Guide to Its Achievements,* Adam Garbicz and Jacek Klinowski refer to *Double Indemnity* as "an intelligent, gripping thriller ... wry; without a trace of compassion for anybody—a clinical record of a case of greed and ruthlessness."

It is "really quite a gratifying and even a good movie, essentially cheap ... but smart and crisp and cruel," said James Agee in *The Nation*. And *Time* called the picture "the season's nattiest, nastiest, most satisfying melodrama."

Continuing in this sharp vein, Ted Sennett commented that, "little humor, except of the harsh and mordant kind, graced [Wilder's] *film noir* masterpiece, *Double Indemnity* ... the film is a model of its kind, a hard-edged melodrama of sleazy passion and cold-blooded murder, played to perfection."—*Great Movie Directors*

Ethan Mordden, in *The Hollywood Studios*, said that *Double Indemnity* "may be the exemplary *noir* masterpiece.... The film is not only brilliantly but infuriatingly suspenseful for, by giving us two of Hollywood's most likable actors as the two murderers, Wilder throws us on their side, making Robinson and justice not the forces we root for but the things we fear."

Double Indemnity is "a typically black thriller ... that is redeemed by some really crackling dialogue ... interpreted with bravura wit by Edward G. Robinson and Fred MacMurray," said Peter Cowie in *Seventy Years of Cinema*.

Also noting "perfectly coordinated acting by Fred MacMurray, Barbara Stanwyck, and Edward G. Robinson," *The New York Herald-Tribune* said, "it hits clean and hard right between the eyes.... Robinson plays an insurance company sleuth with splendid authority."

And *The Oxford Companion to Film* praises *Double Indemnity*'s "sharply witty script, tremendous suspense and unsparing realism," noting further that "the superb performances of Robinson and Fred MacMurray combined to give Wilder his first box-office success."

Robinson considered *Double Indemnity* a favorite among his films, more than justifying his decision to take on its third lead. Foster Hirsch observes that, "Robinson almost walks away with the movie. He hadn't snapped out his lines so authoritatively or curled his lip so threateningly or used his hands so expressively since his heyday in the early thirties. He makes the investigator a genuine original — an eccentric, dyspeptic office joke who's the toughest, sharpest guy in the business, a claims man with remarkable insights into the criminal mind." — *The Pyramid Illustrated History of the Movies: Edward G. Robinson*

"It's a movie designed plainly to freeze the marrow in an audience's bones," said *The New York Times*. "...It's hard and inflexible as steel.... The performance of Mr. Robinson ... as a smart adjustor of insurance claims is a fine bit of characterization within its allotment of space. With a bitter brand of humor and irritability, he creates a formidable guy. As a matter of fact, [he] is the only one you care two hoots for in the film. The rest are just neatly carved pieces in a variably intriguing crime game."

The New Yorker agreed, saying that the film "shows insurance as a deadly war.... The true giant of the battle, and therefore of the film, is Edward G. Robinson, the company's claims inspector, a gentleman tortured by the thought that a client may get away with something, but practically infallible in forestalling such a calamity. When Mr. Robinson, told that the police are giving up their investigation of a policyholder, says scornfully, 'Sure, it's not their money,' he sounds the keynote of the struggle. He is very entertaining, I should add, and not a little convincing."

"An absorbing melodrama" is what *Variety* called the film, noting that, "Robinson, as the infallible insurance executive quick to determine phony claims, gives a strong performance.... It is a typically brash Robinson role."

Douglas, Kirk (1916–) starred with Edward G. Robinson in *Two Weeks in Another Town*, and they appeared as themselves with their wives in an episode of *The Lucy Show*. He notes in his autobiography, *Ragman's Son*, "Eddie was in his sixties now, still bruised from being caught in the meat grinder of the blacklist.... Nobody had formally accused Eddie of anything; innuendoes ruined him. Among Eddie's 'crimes' was his membership in a group called 'American Youth for Democracy....'" Other films include *Out of the Past, Champion, Young Man with a Horn, Detective Story, The Bad and the Beautiful, 20,000 Leagues Under the Sea, Lust for Life, Gunfight at the O.K. Corral, Spartacus, Seven Days in May,* and *The Tough Guys*. Douglas, Diana (1923–) his first wife, and mother of actor

Michael Douglas, played Robinson's daughter-in-law in *House of Strangers*. In her book, *In the Wings,* she comments, "It was part of the lore of the American Academy (of Dramatic Arts) that a nameless student had once thrown a table at (director Charles Jehlinger), who ... never missed a beat of his critique ... while the student fled...." She quotes Robinson, "That sadistic s.o.b. ... I couldn't take his riding me anymore ... Wish I'd killed the bastard!"

Downing, Joseph (1903–75) often played gangster roles, as in *A Slight Case of Murder, I Am the Law, Unholy Partners,* and *Larceny, Inc.*, with Edward G. Robinson. They are together also in the *Ford Theatre* television program "A Set of Values." Other films include *Angels with Dirty Faces, You Can't Get Away with Murder,* and *Each Dawn I Die.*

Drafted (Theater, 1917) This play never made it to Broadway. In his memoirs Edward G. Robinson called *Drafted* "an October turkey." Cast: Pauline Lord, Edward G. Robinson (Lt. Haenkel); October 1917.

Drake, Charles (1914–44) appeared in *The Man Who Came to Dinner, Yankee Doodle Dandy, The Glenn Miller Story, Harvey, Valley of the Dolls,* and, with Edward G. Robinson, *Larceny, Inc.*, as the victim who pays off in the gang's scam to get hit by big cars with wealthy drivers.

Drew, Roland (1900–88) appears in three films with Edward G. Robinson — *Thunder in the City* (as Frank), *Manpower,* and *Larceny, Inc.* He also is in *Evangeline.*

Drinking Edward G. Robinson's gangsters were usually non-drinkers, at least until their downfall. Rico in *Little Caesar* loses everything, is reduced to living in a flophouse, and takes to drink. Prohibition and bootlegging are key to *A Slight Case of Murder, Little Giant,* and *Robin and the 7 Hoods,* but Robinson's characters do not drink in any of them. Nor in *Key Largo* does Johnny Rocco drink, but he offers his mistress, Gay (Claire Trevor), a reward if she will sing an old song, then refuses to give her the drink because her performance is so bad. In *Hell on Frisco Bay* he comments, "We don't keep anything stronger than coffee in the house."

On the right side of the law, Robinson is a Bible-spouting teetotaling dairy farmer in *Good Neighbor Sam,* favoring milk over booze. He plays a Bowery alcoholic in *Tales of Manhattan*. At the fadeout of *Scarlet Street* he has been driven to drink by guilt. He probably would not have married Vivienne Osborne in *Two Seconds* had he not been drunk at the time. In *Illegal* Robinson polishes off a fifth of Scotch after he learns that, as district attorney, he sent an innocent man to the electric chair.

Perhaps there is no funnier drinking scene than Robinson with his boss and a newspaper reporter celebrating in *The Whole Town's Talking.* He gets drunk on his wedding night in *Manpower;* he also plays drunk scenes in *A Hole in the Head, Two Weeks in Another Town,* and *Silver Dollar.* In *All My Sons* a drunken widow confronts him about his past at a nightclub, calling him "murderer."

One reviewer, praising his acting, noted Edward G. Robinson's scene of "drink befuddled oratory" onstage in *The Night Lodging.*

See **Prohibition**.

"The Drop-Out" (Television, 1961) In this half-hour television drama, Robinson plays the father of Billy Gray (of *Father Knows Best*). In the story the son makes the rounds with his father, a salesman, and then reconsiders his decision to drop out of high school.

Producer, Stanley Rubin; director, Richard Irving; teleplay, Roger O. Hirson; photography: Benjamin H. Kline; music, Jerry Goldsmith; art director, John Meehan; editing, David J. O'Connell, Edward Haire; music supervisor, Stanley Wilson; sound, Clarence E. Self; assistant director, Carter deHaven III; set decoration, John McCarthy, James M. Walters; costumes, Vincent Dee; makeup, Jack Barron; hairstyles, Florence Bush; cast: Edward G. Robinson (Bert Alquist), Billy Gray (Jerry Alquist), Carmen Mathews (Mrs. Alquist), Ray Montgomery (Cooper); Russ Conway (Mr. Crane); Walter Baldwin (Rudy Johnson);

Howard Wendell; Stuffy Singer; Linda Lee; host, Ronald Reagan; *General Electric Theatre;* CBS-TV; 30 minutes; January 29, 1961

Dru, Joanne (1923–96) played in *Hell on Frisco Bay,* with Edward G. Robinson. She also appeared in *Red River, All the King's Men, She Wore a Yellow Ribbon,* and *The Light in the Forest.* She was married to John Ireland and Dick Haymes; her brother is TV host Peter Marshall.

Dual roles Twice in his film career Edward G. Robinson played dual roles, in which the special effects required two Robinsons on the screen. The first was in *The Whole Town's Talking,* when he played meek clerk Arthur Ferguson Jones, who is mistaken for Public Enemy Number One, Killer Mannion. Nearly thirty years later Robinson played Nobel Prize–winning physicist Dr. Max Stratman in *The Prize* and also the actor made up to look like his double when the doctor was kidnaped.

Anton Stengel is listed in the screen credits as Chautard in *The Man with Two Faces,* but Robinson's character, a stage actor, actually puts on makeup and crepe hair to impersonate him as another identity. On the radio Robinson played dual roles in both "The Man Who Thought He Was Edward G. Robinson" and "The Man Who Wanted to Be Edward G. Robinson."

John Rodney plays two roles in *Key Largo,* but they are not onscreen together; he is the deputy sheriff that Robinson murders, and then he reappears, or rather his voice does, on the other end of the radio answering Humphrey Bogart's "mayday" at the end of the film. Woody Strode plays two different roles in *The Ten Commandments*— briefly, as the King of Ethiopia in a scene at the Egyptian court, and later, during the Passover, as one of Bithia's bearers.

See **Billing; Bit parts; Guest Stars; Uncredited; Special appearances.**

Duff, Howard (1917–90) appeared on-screen with Edward G. Robinson as George in *All My Sons* and on the radio in "Every Eighteen Hours" on *Big Town.* Other films include *Naked City, While the City Sleeps, The Late Show, A Wedding,* and *Kramer vs. Kramer.* He was married to Ida Lupino.

Dumbrille, Douglass (1890–74) appeared with Edward G. Robinson as a bank auditor in *I Loved a Woman* and (sharing no scenes) as Jannes, a high priest, in *The Ten Commandments.* Other films include *Mr. Deeds Goes to Town, A Day at the Races, Road to Utopia, Riding High,* and *Son of Paleface.*

Dunn, Emma (1875–1966) was Edward G. Robinson's mother-in-law in *Dark Hazard.* He remembered her in his autobiography as a Broadway star in *The Easiest Way.* She played Dr. Kildare's mother in films and was also seen in *Seven Keys to Baldpate, Life with Father,* and *The Great Dictator.*

Dunn, Ralph (1902–68) was in six films with Edward G. Robinson—*Bullets or Ballots* and *Kid Galahad* (as reporters), *A Slight Case of Murder* and *Scarlet Street* (policemen), *Manpower* (man at the phone), and *The Woman in the Window* (traffic cop). He is also in *Tenth Avenue Girl, Return of the Cisco Kid,* and *Laura.*

DuPont Cavalcade of America see "A Case for the F.B.I."; "The Man with Hope in His Hands" ("The Doctor with Hope in His Hands"); "The Philippines Never Surrendered"

DuPont Show of the Week see "Cops and Robbers"

Durante, Jimmy (1893–1980) The veteran large-nosed comedian appeared as himself, as did Edward G. Robinson, in *Pepe,* and in an episode of *The Lucy Show.* He is also in *The Man Who Came to Dinner, Jumbo,* and *It's a Mad, Mad, Mad, Mad World.*

Duryea, Dan (1907–68) recreated his Broadway role of Leo on film in *The Little Foxes.* He was the blackmailer Heidt in *The Woman in the Window* (repeated on *Lux Radio Theatre*), and the gigolo Johnny in *Scarlet Street,* both with Edward G. Robinson. They also appeared together in a *Screen Snapshots* segment about the Ice Capades. Duryea is in *Ball of Fire, Sahara, Winchester '73,* and *The Flight of the Phoenix.*

Duvivier, Julien (1896–1967) directed two multiple-episode films with Edward G. Robinson — *Tales of Manhattan* and *Flesh and Fantasy*. Directing French films from 1919, he came to America twenty years later, staying only through World War II. His other films include *David Golder*, *Pepe le Moko*, *The Great Waltz*, and *Deadlier Than the Male*.

Eames, Clare (1896–1930) worked with Edward G. Robinson at the Theatre Guild in *Androcles and the Lion*, *The Man of Destiny*, *Juarez and Maximilian*, *The Brothers Karamazov*, and *Ned McCobb's Daughter*, which was written by her husband, playwright Sidney Howard. She also played Lady Macbeth, *Hedda Gabler*, and *Mary Stuart*.

East Is West (Film, 1930) Edward G. Robinson played the first of his three Oriental screen roles in *East Is West*, his seventh film. It was based on a 1918 comedy that had starred Fay Bainter on Broadway and was adapted into a 1922 silent with Constance Talmadge and Warner Oland. Robinson became involved in the talking version when preview audiences laughed at Danish actor Jean Hersholt's interpretation of Chinaman Charlie Yong, the "chop suey king" of San Francisco; Robinson refilmed Hersholt's scenes. Robinson respected Lew Ayres, appearing as the romantic lead opposite Lupe Velez. He found Velez remarkable for her sexual energies.

Producer, Carl Laemmle; associate producer, H. M. Asher; director, Monta Bell; based on the play by Samuel Shipman and John B. Hymer; screenplay, Winifred Eaton Reeve, Tom Reed; sound, C. Roy Hunter; music, Heinz Roemheld; editors, Harry Marker, Fred Allen, Maurice Pivar; special effects, Frank M. Booth; camera, Jerry Ash; cast: Lupe Velez (Ming Toy), Lew Ayres (Billy Benson), Edward G. Robinson (Charlie Yong), E. Allyn Warren (Lo Sang Kee), Tetsu Komai (Hop Toy), Henry Kolker (Mr. Benson), Mary Forbes (Mrs. Benson), Edgar Norton (Thomas), Charles Middleton (Dr. Fredericks); Universal; 75 minutes; November 1930

In China, American Billy Benson saves Ming Toy from being sold at auction by her father. With a patriarch, Lo Sang Kee, she goes to San Francisco, but soon her differences with society put her in danger of deportation. She is sold to Charlie Yong, who is known as the chop suey king. Billy now kidnaps Ming Toy. He wants to marry her. Because he is heir to a family fortune, however, their marriage is discouraged socially. When Ming Toy discovers that she is really the daughter of a murdered missionary and is not Chinese, Charlie allows the wedding to take place.

"Edward G. Robinson appears in his first talker [sic] as Charlie Yong, the chop suey 'king' of San Francisco's Chinatown, and provides most of the entertainment with his amusing characterization of an egocentric half caste," wrote the *New York Times* critic. "Both Mr. Robinson and Miss Velez liven the rambling narrative with many amusing moments, but their task is a heavy and thankless one." *Variety* simply claimed that, "Robinson, as the suey king, is allowed too much footage for mugging and repetitious action."

The Ed Sullivan Show (Television, 1956) Edward G. Robinson was among more than a dozen stars who appeared on television in a tribute to director John Huston on *The Ed Sullivan Show* in the summer of 1956. Earlier the same year he was on the show performing a scene from his Broadway hit *Middle of the Night*.

Participants (*Middle of the Night*): Edward G. Robinson, Gena Rowlands; Ed Sullivan (host); CBS-TV; 60 minutes; date unknown, 1956

Participants (Huston): Mary Astor, Lauren Bacall, Humphrey Bogart, Jose Ferrer, Sydney Greenstreet, Katharine Hepburn, John Huston, Walter Huston, Burl Ives, Peter Lorre, Billy Pearson, Gregory Peck, Vincent Price, Edward G. Robinson, Claire Trevor, Orson Welles; Ed Sullivan (host); CBS-TV; 60 minutes; July 1, 1956

Eddie Cantor's March of Dimes Special (Radio, 1944) Cast: Eddie Cantor, Harry Von Zell, Jack Haley, Nora Martin, Ida Lupino, Monty Woolley, Dick Powell, Edward G. Robinson, Bob Burns, Ginny

Simms, Chester Lauck (Lum) & Norris Goff (Abner), Cass Daley, Georgie Price, Cookie Fairchild & Orchestra; Mutual Network; January 23, 1944; Los Angeles; 60 min.

Education In his native Rumania, young Emanuel Goldenberg attended Hebrew school. When he came to the United States in 1903 at the age of nine, he enrolled at Public School 137 in New York City, and later, P.S. 20, "the Anna Silver School." Robinson, unlike his brothers who spoke with a thick accent, quickly lost the Rumanian edge to his voice when he was placed with American students and not in a class for the foreign born. He was a student at Townshend Harris High School for four years and attended the College of the City of New York. Auditioning there with a reading of Marc Antony's soliloquy from *Julius Caesar,* he was admitted to the Elizabethan Society. The same material gained him entry to the American Academy of Dramatic Arts in 1911, where he studied acting for two years.

Edward G. Robinson's World of Art

Jane Robinson, who was married to the actor from 1958 until his death in 1973, wrote *Edward G. Robinson's World of Art* in 1971. Its dedication page reads, "A Gift to My Husband." Published by Harper & Row, and with an introduction by Leonard Spigelgass and epilogue by Edward G. Robinson, the 117–page book contains 46 color plates of paintings in the actor's collection, six by Robinson himself among an impressive group of French Impressionist works.

Mrs. Robinson said, "It seemed to me that Eddie ought to have a catalogue of his collection and that it should include some of his own paintings." Robinson's initial reaction was negative; he believed he had only the remains of a collection. Later, approached by Harper & Row, he turned the project over to her. She had the paintings photographed while Robinson was out of town and even had a surprise for him, writing in the book, "I take pride in including him among first-class contemporary painters; Eddie, most certainly, would not include himself, and when he reads this, it will be the first knowledge that his work is included."

Ehrlich, Dr. Paul (1854–1912) was a German-born physician who won the Nobel Prize for Medicine in 1908. Edward G. Robinson notes in his autobiography that Ehrlich's work was principally in three areas — the staining of cells, studies in immunity, and chemotherapeutic discoveries. Robinson portrayed the doctor in *Dr. Ehrlich's Magic Bullet,* in which his scientific work was incorporated in the plot. Ehrlich's development of salvarsan, an arsenical compound, as a cure for syphilis was his major contribution.

Elam, Jack (1916–) appears as the real Ace Williams in *Never a Dull Moment,* with Edward G. Robinson. His other films include *Gunfight at the OK Corral, Baby Face Nelson, Firecreek, Once Upon a Time in the West, Rio Lobo,* and *The Cannonball Run.*

Electrocution (Theater, 1914) After early theatrical engagements in Albany, Cincinnati, and Canada, and prior to his debut on Broadway, Edward G. Robinson was booked in a vaudeville sketch, and received credit as both director and performer in *Electrocution,* which opened at the Hammerstein Victoria Theatre in New York in 1914.

See **Capital Punishment**.

Eliscu, Edward (1902–98) played Edward G. Robinson's younger brother, Joe Scarsi, on Broadway in *The Racket.* In Hollywood he was a lyricist (*Flying Down to Rio*) and composer (*Whoopee*).

Elitch Gardens In operation in Denver since 1890, Elitch's Gardens is the oldest regional summer theater in the United States. Begun as a vaudeville venue, it housed a stock company as early as 1897. Edward G. Robinson spent two seasons there, in 1921 and 1922, playing opposite Helen Menken in *Enter Madame,* and he was also in productions of *The Deluge* and *The Idle Inn.* Known also for its gardens and greenhouse where Colorado's carnations were grown, the site is today used for concerts, special engagements, and as an amusement park.

Emerson, Hope (1897–1960), a matronly character actress, played Debra Paget's mother in *House of Strangers,* with Edward G. Robinson. She was also seen in *Adam's Rib, Caged, Rock a Bye Baby,* and the TV series *Peter Gunn.*

Emery, Gilbert (1875–1945) appeared with Edward G. Robinson in *Bullets or Ballots* and *A Dispatch from Reuter's.* A distinguished English character actor, he was also in *A Farewell to Arms, Clive of India, Nurse Edith Cavell, Raffles, That Hamilton Woman,* and *Between Two Worlds.*

Enter Madame (Theater, 1920) This comedy was first produced in August 1920. It was based loosely on author Gilda Varesi's mother, who had been a famous European prima donna. Edward G. Robinson appeared as Gerald in a summer production at Elitch Gardens, Denver.

Authors, Gilda Varesi, Dolly Byrne; cast: Helen Menken (Lisa Delle Robbia), Edward G. Robinson (Gerald Fitzgerald); Elitch Gardens, Denver, Colorado; summer 1920.

Gerald Fitzgerald, married twenty years to prima donna Lisa Delle Robbia, has tired of trailing after her. He has fallen in love with widow Flora Preston, but Lisa laughs at the thought and an angry Gerald tells her off. Lisa invites both Gerald and Mrs. Preston to dinner and wins her husband back.

"Epitaph for a Spy" (Television, 1954) Edward G. Robinson's earliest dramatic role on television (other than a pilot episode of *For the Defense,* an unrealized series) was "Epitaph for a Spy," a dramatization of an Eric Ambler novel presented on *Climax!* Robinson played a refugee from behind the Iron Curtain unwittingly involved with French traitors. There was at least one review indicative of the quality that was missing from some of the films Robinson had been making: "A slightly involved but on the whole suspenseful story gave Edward G. Robinson a good vehicle for his talents," commented *Variety.* "Casting of Robinson ... was one of those happy instances of finding exactly the right actor for a part. Frightened, bumbling, and yet full of a sort of desperate courage, Robinson brought some fine touches to his performance. He's an expert in implying a great deal with little things."

Producer, Bretaigne Windust; associate producer, Tony Barr; director, Alan Reisner; teleplay, Donald S. Sanford; based on a novel by Eric Ambler; cast: Edward G. Robinson (Josef Vadassy), Melville Cooper, Ivan Triesault, Marjorie Lord, Norma Varden, Nicholas Joy, Maurice Marsac, Robert F. Simon, David O'Brien; William Lundigan (host); *Climax!*; 60 minutes; CBS-tv; December 9, 1954

Tony Barr, associate producer for "Epitaph for a Spy," tells this story in his book *Acting for the Camera*: "Robinson came to me at one point and asked me about a balcony ledge that he was supposed to walk on as he went from one balcony to another. I said, 'It will be about a foot and a half wide.' He said, 'I'm not worried about that, how high is it off the stage floor?' I said, 'Well, according to the plans, it will only be about six inches, so there's nothing to worry about.' His answer was, 'There's plenty to worry about. One of the worst accidents I ever had was when I fell off a carpet.'"

Erskine, Chester (1905–86) came to Hollywood via the stage in Vienna and Broadway. He produced and adapted the screenplay for Arthur Miller's *All My Sons.* Other films include *A Girl in Every Port, The Egg and I,* and *Androcles and the Lion,* which he also directed.

The Eternal Light see "Face to Face with Gabriel"; "Island in the Wilderness"; "Trial and Error"

Evans, Maurice (1901–89), a distinguished Shakespearean actor, worked twice with Edward G. Robinson — on the radio in *Document A/777,* and in the TV film *U.M.C.* When Robinson was forced to withdraw from the role of ape professor Dr. Zaius in *Planet of the Apes,* Evans replaced him. Evans' plays include *Richard II, Hamlet, Macbeth,* several by Shaw, and *Dial M for Murder.* Onscreen he was in *Kind Lady, Androcles and the Lion,* and *Rosemary's Baby.*

"Every Eighteen Hours" (Radio, 1939); Steve Wilson and the *Illustrated Press* led a crusade against hit and run drivers.

Big Town; cast: Edward G. Robinson (Steve Wilson), Ona Munson (Lorelei Kilburn), Howard Duff; music, Leith Stevens; CBS-radio; 1939

Eye on Art (Television, 1965) Edward G. Robinson narrated two of six segments — in Chicago and Los Angeles — of a television series that toured art galleries, museums, and studios. Edward G. Robinson (host); CBS-TV; 30 minutes; June 17 and 24, 1965

Eyvind of the Hills (Theater, 1921) While appearing in a relatively small role in *Samson and Delilah* on Broadway in 1921, Edward G. Robinson also did matinee performances of *Eyvind of the Hills*. He loved working with his co-star, Margaret Wycherly.

Produced by Conroy and Meltzer; playwright, Johann Sigurjonsson; cast: Margaret Wycherly (Halla), Edward G. Robinson (Arnes*), Edward Begley (Jon), Arthur Hohl (Kari), Charles P. Bates (District Judge), Byron Beasly (Bjorn), Gus Beuerman (First peasant), Hallem Bosworth (Second peasant), Elfin Finn (Tota), Raymond Guion (A Shepherd boy), Roy LaRue (Magnus), Beatrice Moreland (Gudfinna), Lloyd Neal (Arngrim), Helen Olcott, Eleanor Johnson (Jon's children), Edmond J. Pardy (A Farm hand), Gwendolyn Piers (Oddny), Helene Russell (Jon's wife), Marguerite Tebeau (Sigrid); opened at the Greenwich Village Theatre, New York; February 2, 1921; *replacing Henry Herbert

A youth steals a sheep and runs from the law in eighteenth-century Iceland. He is taken in by a widow who owns a farm. She falls in love with him and follows him into the hills. They live together in hiding for several years, but ultimately, conscience-stricken and having lost faith in one another, they are killed in a blizzard.

"Face to Face with Gabriel" (Radio, 1953) This program was one of Robinson's last radio appearances.

The Eternal Light; NBC-radio; December 20, 1953; cast: Edward G. Robinson

Fairbanks, Douglas, Jr. (1909–2000) The son of the silent swashbuckling star, he became adept at both debonair and action roles. He plays Joe Massara, Rico's pal, in *Little Caesar,* and he and Edward G. Robinson also were in the short films *The Stolen Jools* and *An Intimate Dinner in Celebration of Warner Bros. Silver Jubilee.* Other films include *The Dawn Patrol, Morning Glory, The Prisoner of Zenda, Gunga Din, Sinbad the Sailor,* and *Ghost Story.*

Falk, Peter (1927–) became a 1960s successor to Cagney and Robinson with *Murder, Inc.* and *A Pocketful of Miracles,* for which he won Oscar nominations. Joining Robinson onscreen in *Robin and the 7 Hoods,* he was also in *The Great Race, Luv, A Woman Under the Influence, Husbands, The Princess Bride,* and, on TV, the long-running *Columbo.*

Family The Edward G. Robinson family tree is traceable for several generations, from his maternal grandmother and his beginnings in Bucharest, Rumania, to the present day and his great-grandson, a college student in Malibu, California.

His grandmother, Anna Guttman, had ten children but was widowed at age 28. Illnesses took the lives of many of her children, and she moved in with her daughter, Sarah, who had married Morris Goldenberg. Anna Guttman could read and write; her daughter could not. The family was Jewish, and early in Robinson's life the decision was made to leave Europe for America to escape persecution. Three brothers, Jack, Zach, and Oscar, emigrated to the United States first, followed by their father; then the others made the journey in steerage, arriving at Ellis Island, New York, in February 1902.

Robinson was the fifth of six brothers. Zach, the eldest, became an upholsterer. He took the surname Garver and married a lady named Florence; they had three children, Annette, Felix, and Irving. Jack Goldenberg was a metal worker who had the artistic talent for making candlesticks and tableware. In Rumania he suffered a head injury during an anti–Semitic pogrom, later experienced blackouts and forgetfulness, and was institutionalized. He never married. Oscar Goldenberg was also a bachelor. His talent for wood carving and cabinetmaking eventually yielded to photo engraving as his chosen profession.

William Goldberg, who shortened the family surname, opened a luggage store on Sixth Avenue in New York. He married Rebecca (Rea) Essner, and they had two daughters. Beulah took the Robinson name, and Marion married Sheldon Parker and also had two daughters — Michelle, who married Jo Scatchard (producing a daughter, Willary), and Martha, who married Ronald Geiger (sons Warren and Jason). Max, the sixth son, became a dentist. He and his wife Jenny had a son, who became Dr. Marvin Robinson. He and his wife Eleanor had children named Peter and June.

Sarah Goldenberg died in 1947 at the age of 85; her husband had died twenty years earlier, while Robinson was appearing in *The Brothers Karamazov* for the Theatre Guild. Edward G. Robinson married Gladys Lloyd Cassell only months before his father's death; they remained together for 29 years until their divorce in 1956.

Gladys was the daughter of a prominent sculptor, Clement Comley Cassell, and his wife Eugenia Lloyd. She had two brothers, Lloyd and Charles Cassell, and a sister, Hortense. Lloyd Cassell's daughter, Charlotte Davidson, had three children. His son Clement, a Naval officer, died during the sinking of his ship during World War II. Charles and his wife Frances had a daughter, Anne Frances Hortense married Jack Jenson, but they had no children.

Gladys' first husband was Ralph Westervelt. Their daughter, Jeanne Lansing, married Manuel Kroman, and their children were Lisa and Carla. Lisa married Dr. Marshall Zaslove; they have a daughter, Natasha. Carla did not marry.

Edward G. Robinson, Jr., was born in 1933. Called Manny all his life, he married Frances Lundie Chisholm in 1952, and their daughter, Francesca Gladys Robinson, was born the following year. He and his wife were divorced in 1955. Manny was later married to Elaine Conte and to Nan Morris.

Francesca Robinson married Ricardo Adan Sanchez in 1977, and they had a son in 1983. Named for his great-grandfather, Adam Edward Sanchez is the only direct descendent of his generation in the Edward G. Robinson family tree.

Jane Bodenheimer was Edward G. Robinson's second wife. She had been married to David Adler previously. Five years after Robinson's death she married George Sidney. There were no children from any of the marriages.

Family Theatre This thirty-minute program aired on the Mutual Radio Network from February 1947 through July 1956. On an early broadcast, Edward G. Robinson introduced a segment featuring Pat O'Brien.

Creator, producer, host, Fr. Patrick Peyton; announcer, Tony LeFrano; producer, Bob Longenecker; directors, Richard Sanville, Mel Williamson, Fred MacKaye, Jaime del Valle, Joseph Mansfield, Robert O'Sullivan, John Kelley, Dave Young; writer, Truman Boardman; cast: Edward G. Robinson, Pat O'Brien; Mutual Network; date unknown

Farrell, Glenda (1904–71) With Edward G. Robinson, she played Olga Stassoff in *Little Caesar* and Valerie in *Dark Hazard*, both typical of her brassy, streetwise roles. She was also wisecracking reporter Torchy Blane in a series beginning in 1939. Other films include *The Talk of the Town, I Love Trouble,* and *Middle of the Night.*

Farrow, John (1904–63) came to Hollywood via the Australian Navy as a technical advisor on sea films. He directed *Men in Exile* in 1937 and also *Wake Island, The Big Clock, Alias Nick Beal, Night Has a Thousand Eyes* (with Edward G. Robinson), *Hondo,* and *John Paul Jones.* He was married to Maureen O'Sullivan; their daughter is Mia Farrow.

Faylen, Frank (1907–85) was known to television audiences as the father on *Dobie Gillis,* and to film audiences as Ernie the cabdriver in *It's a Wonderful Life*. His four films with Edward G. Robinson were *Bullets or Ballots*, *Kid Galahad*, *Brother Orchid*, and *Unholy Partners*. He is also in *They Won't Forget*, *The Blue Dahlia*, and *Riot in Cell Block 11*.

Fenton, Leslie (1902–78) became a director in 1939 after fifteen years as an actor, including roles in *The Public Enemy*, *The Hatchet Man* (with Edward G. Robinson), and *Boys Town*. He directed *The Man from Dakota*, *Pardon My Past*, *Saigon*, and *The Redhead and the Cowboy*.

Ferguson, Frank (1899–1978) was with Edward G. Robinson in *Big Leaguer* (as Wally Mitchell) and *The Violent Men* (as Mahoney), and also appeared in *This Gun for Hire*, *The Miracle of the Bells*, *Fort Apache*, *Rhapsody in Blue*, *Johnny Guitar*, *Million Dollar Mermaid*, and *Hush Hush Sweet Charlotte*.

Ferrer, Jose (1912–92) was on the radio with Edward G. Robinson in *Document A/777* and on TV's *Ed Sullivan Show*. Damage to his career notwithstanding, he, along with Robinson and John Garfield, "were the only three called [to testify] where the House Un-American Activities Committee had no proof of party membership, past or present," according to John Cogley's report, *Blacklisting: Movies*. Films include *Cyrano de Bergerac* (Oscar as best actor), *Moulin Rouge*, *The Caine Mutiny*, *I Accuse*, *Lawrence of Arabia*, *Ship of Fools*, *Joan of Arc*, *Enter Laughing*, and *A Midsummer Night's Sex Comedy*.

Field, Betty (1918–73) is in *Flesh and Fantasy* but shares no scenes with Edward G. Robinson. Her other films include *Of Mice and Men*, *King's Row*, *Picnic*, and *Bus Stop*. She was married to playwright Elmer Rice (*The Adding Machine*, *Street Scene*) and had her start on Broadway.

Fields, Stanley (1880–1941) appeared in dozens of supporting roles in talking films, including *Show Boat*, *Mutiny on the Bounty*, *Kid Millions*, *The Adventures of Marco Polo*, and *Algiers*. He was gang boss Sam Vettori in *Little Caesar*, with Edward G. Robinson.

Fights It wasn't really a fistfight that George Raft and Edward G. Robinson had on the set of *Manpower*, but the *Life* photographer got a good still of the two actors "disagreeing," and the tussle made good press for the film. The ad copy read: "Edward G. Robinson—He's mad about Dietrich; Marlene Dietrich—She's mad about Raft; George Raft—He's mad about the whole thing!"

Prizefighting was the milieu of *Kid Galahad*, and the picture had a number of excellent ringside episodes in which real fighters Bob Evans, Hank Hankinson, Bob Nestell, and Jack Kranz sparred with Wayne Morris (in the title role) and others. Referees George Blake and Mushy Callahan were also on hand; Callahan also appeared in similar but shorter scenes in *House of Strangers*.

A fistfight concludes *Smart Money*, and afterwards, Robinson's character is held responsible for the manslaughter death of his pal, played by James Cagney. There is a concluding fistfight between Robinson and Alan Ladd, which literally becomes *Hell on Frisco Bay*, aboard a runaway speedboat that crashes and explodes in flames. There are fisticuffs in both *Bullets or Ballots* and *The Sea Wolf*.

The two most impressive fistfights in Robinson's films, however, occur in *I Am the Law* and *Brother Orchid*. In the former, as the good guy, he energetically takes on three gangsters one at a time in his living room, while the press shoots before and after photographs of them. In the latter film he hunts down Humphrey Bogart for an exciting three-minute altercation in lieu of their usual shootout.

Film noir *Film noir*, according to Ephraim Katz's *The Film Encyclopedia*, is "characterized by its dark, somber tone and cynical, pessimistic mood…. [It] abounds with night scenes, both interior and exterior, with sets that suggest dingy realism, and with lighting that emphasizes deep shadows and accents the mood of fatalism … the dark and gloomy underworld of crime and corruption, films whose heroes as well as villains are cynical, disillusioned, and often insecure loners…. [The films were] influenced by … an influx of immigrant directors from central Europe and the sobering effects of World War II and its aftermath."

Fine examples of *film noir* in Edward G. Robinson's filmography are the classics *Double Indemnity, The Woman in the Window,* and *Scarlet Street.* Billy Wilder's *Double Indemnity,* which has been called the quintessential *film noir,* qualifies in virtually every aspect of the genre — mood, characters, settings. The same criteria also is true of the two Fritz Lang melodramas *The Woman in the Window* and *Scarlet Street.* Both directors were émigrés from Nazi Germany in the early 1930s.

The elements of mystery and the supernatural in *Flesh and Fantasy, Night Has a Thousand Eyes,* and *Nightmare* prompt their inclusion. The theme of *Flesh and Fantasy,* directed by Julien Duvivier (another emigrant, at least temporarily), deals with the question of fatalism and whether the occult (magic, fortune telling, dreams / nightmares) has any bearing on reality. *Night Has a Thousand Eyes* and *Nightmare* (both based on Cornell Woolrich novels) are about a clairvoyant and a hypnotic killer, respectively, and their gloomy worlds, as depicted in the films, are decidedly *noir*.

Sequences in *House of Strangers, Key Largo,* and *The Stranger* can be considered *noir*. The pervading mood of *House of Strangers* is one of cynicism, as observed through its protagonists. Also, the film contains several moody night scenes, and crime and corruption are present. *Key Largo,* similarly, has criminal Robinson central to its story, and the Bogart hero is nothing if not disillusioned. Orson Welles' *The Stranger* is worth noting for its dramatic lighting, together with villain (Welles, a deadly Nazi war criminal) and hero (Robinson, a determined war crimes investigator) as equally cynical loners.

Finally, a look at Edward G. Robinson's last film, *Soylent Green,* might justify it as a latter-day *film noir.* The future as depicted in the film looks very bleak, and the cynicism of its leading characters, a police detective (Charlton Heston) and his researcher, here called a "book" (Robinson), seem necessary as a result. There is a dark, dingy realism evident in many scenes, and the crime and corruption are key.

Film Within a Film Three of Robinson's pictures, *Two Weeks in Another Town, My Geisha,* and *Pepe,* were all partially filmed outside the United States within a two-year period. They are concerned with filmmaking and contain footage that is ostensibly another film being created. In the first, the film within a film is an unnamed Italian melodrama to be dubbed in English, as directed by Robinson's character. In the second, an American crew is filming *Madame Butterfly* on location in Japan, and Robinson is the producer. The third is a musical extravaganza being filmed in Mexico, and while Robinson plays himself, his fictionalized character might easily have been the same fellow as in *My Geisha. Two Weeks in Another Town* uses clips from *The Bad and the Beautiful. It's a Great Feeling,* a musical about Hollywood and filmmaking, does not have scenes of the film being made.

A motion picture camera is set up in an adjacent apartment in order to capture Wendy Barrie committing murder in *I Am the Law.* The footage is later shown to her when she denies her guilt. Earlier in the same film Robinson goes to the movies to see *Snow White.* In *Blackmail* a newsreel camera briefly catches Robinson's character following his heroics in putting out an oil fire. Newsreels of concentration camps (the first to be shown to American audiences) were used in *The Stranger,* and documentary film in the style of "The March of Time" figured in the plots of *Confessions of a Nazi Spy, Bullets or Ballots,* and *The Woman in the Window.* In *Grand Slam* mastermind Robinson has home movies of the school in Rio de Janiero where he taught for thirty years. It happens to be across the street from a diamond company — just perfect for a robbery!

Woody Allen used a segment from *The Last Gangster* to depict drudgery and the passage of time (Robinson's character works in the prison laundry) in *Crimes and Misdemeanors,* and a segment from *Tales of Manhattan* appears in *Myra Breckenridge.*

Films Edward G. Robinson appeared in 89 feature films between the years 1916 and 1973. The first two were silent pictures, and number nine, filmed in 1930 and released the following year, was *Little Caesar*, which established him as a Hollywood icon.

Through 1942 he was under contract at Warner Bros. Films he made there until 1934 bore the label First National–Vitaphone. Leaving the studio in 1942, Robinson continued to do freelance films at Warners through 1964. Following is a chronological listing.

Year	#	Title	Studio
1916	1.	*Arms and the Woman*	(Pathé–Gold Rooster Plays)
1923	2.	*The Bright Shawl*	(Inspiration Pictures / Associated First–National)
1929	3.	*The Hole in the Wall*	(Paramount)
1930	4.	*The Night Ride*	(Universal)
	5.	*A Lady to Love*	(MGM)
	6.	*Outside the Law*	(Universal)
	7.	*East Is West*	(Universal)
	8.	*The Widow from Chicago*	(First National–Vitaphone)
1931	9.	*Little Caesar*	(First National–Vitaphone)
	10.	*Smart Money*	(First National–Vitaphone)
	11.	*Five Star Final*	(First National–Vitaphone)
1932	12.	*The Hatchet Man*	(First National–Vitaphone)
	13.	*Two Seconds*	(First National–Vitaphone)
	14.	*Tiger Shark*	(First National–Vitaphone)
	15.	*Silver Dollar*	(First National–Vitaphone)
1933	16.	*The Little Giant*	(First National–Vitaphone)
	17.	*I Loved a Woman*	(First National–Vitaphone)
1934	18.	*Dark Hazard*	(First National–Vitaphone)
	19.	*The Man with Two Faces*	(First National–Vitaphone)
1935	20.	*The Whole Town's Talking*	(Columbia)
	21.	*Barbary Coast*	(United Artists)
1936	22.	*Bullets or Ballots*	(Warner Bros.)
1937	23.	*Thunder in the City*	(Columbia–Atlantic Films)
	24.	*Kid Galahad*	(Warner Bros.)
	25.	*The Last Gangster*	(MGM)
1938	26.	*A Slight Case of Murder*	(Warner Bros.)
	27.	*The Amazing Dr. Clitterhouse*	(Warner Bros.)
	28.	*I Am the Law*	(Columbia)
1939	29.	*Confessions of a Nazi Spy*	(Warner Bros.)
	30.	*Blackmail*	(MGM)
1940	31.	*Dr. Ehrlich's Magic Bullet*	(Warner Bros.)
	32.	*Brother Orchid*	(Warner Bros.)
	33.	*A Dispatch from Reuter's*	(Warner Bros.)
1941	34.	*The Sea Wolf*	(Warner Bros.)
	35.	*Manpower*	(Warner Bros.)
	36.	*Unholy Partners*	(MGM)
1942	37.	*Larceny, Inc.*	(Warner Bros.)
	38.	*Tales of Manhattan*	(20th Century–Fox)
1943	39.	*Destroyer*	(Columbia)
	40.	*Flesh and Fantasy*	(Universal)
1944	41.	*Tampico*	(20th Century–Fox)
	42.	*Mr. Winkle Goes to War*	(Columbia)
	43.	*Double Indemnity*	(Paramount)
	44.	*The Woman in the Window*	(RKO)
1945	45.	*Our Vines Have Tender Grapes*	(MGM)
	46.	*Journey Together*	(RAF Film Unit/RKO British)
	47.	*Scarlet Street*	(Universal)

1946	48. *The Stranger*	(RKO)
1947	49. *The Red House*	(United Artists)
1948	50. *All My Sons*	(Universal-International)
	51. *Key Largo*	(Warner Bros.)
	52. *Night Has a Thousand Eyes*	(Paramount)
1949	53. *House of Strangers*	(20th Century–Fox)
	54. *It's a Great Feeling*	(Warner Bros.)
1950	55. *Operation X*	(Columbia)
1952	56. *Actors and Sin*	(United Artists)
1953	57. *Big Leaguer*	(MGM)
	58. *Vice Squad*	(United Artists)
	59. *The Glass Web*	(Universal-International)
1954	60. *Black Tuesday*	(United Artists)
1955	61. *The Violent Men*	(Columbia)
	62. *Tight Spot*	(Columbia)
	63. *A Bullet for Joey*	(United Artists)
	64. *Illegal*	(Warner Bros.)
1956	65. *Hell on Frisco Bay*	(Warner Bros.)
	66. *Nightmare*	(United Artists)
	67. *The Ten Commandments*	(Paramount)
1959	68. *A Hole in the Head*	(United Artists)
1960	69. *Seven Thieves*	(20th Century–Fox)
	70. *Pepe*	(Columbia)
1962	71. *My Geisha*	(Paramount)
	72. *Two Weeks in Another Town*	(MGM)
1964	73. *The Prize*	(MGM)
	74. *Good Neighbor Sam*	(Columbia)
	75. *Robin and the 7 Hoods*	(Warner Bros.)
	76. *The Outrage*	(MGM)
	77. *Cheyenne Autumn*	(Warner Bros.)
1965	78. *A Boy Ten Feet Tall*	(Paramount)
	79. *The Cincinnati Kid*	(MGM)
1967	80. *Peking Blonde*	(Paramount)
1968	81. *Grand Slam*	(Paramount)
	82. *The Biggest Bundle of Them All*	(MGM)
	83. *Mad Checkmate*	(American-International)
	84. *Operation San Pietro*	(Paramount)
	85. *Never a Dull Moment*	(Buena Vista)
1969	86. *Mackenna's Gold*	(Columbia)
1970	87. *Song of Norway*	(ABC Pictures/Cinerama)
1972	88. *Neither by Day Nor by Night*	(Motion Pictures International)
1973	89. *Soylent Green*	(MGM)

See also **Documentary films**; **Short films**; **Television**; **Specific film titles and studios**.

Fire A film with fire as its subject is *Blackmail*. Its opening and closing sequences are both dramatic and exciting, showing Oklahoma oil wells burning out of control. Robinson and his men have the job of putting out the blaze, and their methods, wearing fire suits and using winches, hoses, and other modern equipment, together with a mix of nitroglycerine, is fascinating to watch.

A pillar of fire is shown by means of fairly realistic animation in two segments of *The Ten Commandments*—first, blocking Pharaoh's chariots as the Israelites cross the parted Red Sea, and second, as the source of the finger of God to carve the famous granite tablets out of the mountainside. In the same film we also see the burning bush, and hail that turns to fire as one of the plagues on Egypt.

Robinson's magnificent ranch house is set ablaze as the climax of the range war he has waged with Glenn Ford in *The Violent Men*. Crippled and on the second floor of the house, he begs his wife, played by Barbara Stanwyck, for his crutches, but instead she calculatingly throws them over the balcony into the blaze, hoping he will die. He survives.

Our Vines Have Tender Grapes has moving and powerful scenes in which a new barn catches fire in a rainstorm. Robinson is unable to rescue the livestock and so must use a pistol to shoot them. The fire costs the elderly farmer, played by Morris Carnovsky, his life savings, since he stubbornly had refused insurance on the barn.

The Firebrand

(Theater, 1924) Benvenuto Cellini's autobiography provided the basis for *The Firebrand*, a three-act comedy by Edwin Justus Mayer. This was Edward G. Robinson's only stage work in 1924, in the role of the Duke's evil brother, Ottaviano. The play ran 287 performances, well into the following year. According to *The Oxford Companion to the American Theatre*, the plot has Cellini buying his model from her mother, then losing her to the romantic attentions of the Duke of Florence. Cellini doesn't protest because the Duke has pardoned him on a murder charge; also, he has been having an affair with the Duke's wife.

"Though it is not always on the same spirited and inventive level," wrote *The New York Times*, "it is good enough in situation and in writing to do [the playwright] credit." Burns Mantle, in *The Best Plays of 1924–25*, said, "*The Firebrand* is an amusing satire done in the continental manner, and brilliantly done, I think...."

Robinson had a wonderful time doing the play. Dressed in the costume of a sixteenth-century nobleman, he reveled in a rare moment of vanity. "We all wore tights," he said in *All My Yesterdays*. "Mine were red.... One of the critics said I had 'the best set of legs in the cast.'" Apparently, the production was as amusing offstage as on. His friend from the American Academy of Dramatic Arts, Joseph Schildkraut, had the lead role. Frank Morgan was in the company also, as the Duke of Florence. There was a potential problem with his fondness for spirits — yet, according to Robinson, once he was made up and pushed before the audience, Morgan invariably gave a fine performance. The problem was that as hard as they tried, Morgan, Robinson, Schildkraut, and the other actors simply could not stop laughing.

Producers, Laurence Schwab, Horace Liveright and Frank Mandel; director, Arthur Hurley; playwright, Edwin Justus Mayer; stage manager, Wallace Fortune; set, Woodman Thompson, Robert W. Bergman Studios, Vail Construction Co.; manager, Laurence Wood; incidental music, Russell Bennett, Maurice Nitke; costumes, Fishbein Gowns, Inc.; press representative, Ben Hecht; cast: Joseph Schildkraut (Benvenuto Cellini), Frank Morgan (Allesandro, Duke of Florence), E. G. Robinson (Ottaviano), Nana Bryant (Duchess), Florence Mason (Angela), Allyn Joslyn (Polverino), Hortense Alden (Emilia), Marie Haynes (Beatrice), Charles McCarthy (Ascanio), George Drury Hart (Pier Landi), Wallace Fortune (Soldier), Edward Quinn (A Page), Dorothy Bicknell, Eleanor Ewing, Eden Gray, Lillian Kingsbury, J. Ellis Kirkham, Kenneth Dana, Wilbert Shields, Scott Hirschberg, Roland Winters, Philip Niblette (Ladies and Gentlemen of the Court, Soldiers); opened at the Morosco Theatre, New York; October 15, 1924

In the summer of 1535, in Benvenuto Cellini's workshop, a beautiful model, Angela, captures the heart of the sculptor. Benvenuto has just escaped arrest, having killed Maffio in self-defense in a street brawl, and he now barters to purchase Angela from her mother for forty ducats. The Duke of Allesandro, of the Medicis, arrives to condemn Cellini, but he is diverted by Angela's beauty and only restricts Benvenuto to his house. Ottaviano conspires to gain the throne with a plot to kill his brother, the Duke, but he is thwarted by Benvenuto. The Duchess arrives; she is enamored of Benvenuto and, interceding in his behalf, invites him to their summer palace.

In the second act, Benvenuto meets Angela in the garden of the palace, where she is awaiting the Duke. Ottaviano tells the Duke that Benvenuto has escaped, and influences him to decree that Benvenuto be hanged when caught. The Duke and Duchess, expecting separate romantic liaisons, are left on the balcony to hide their secrets from one another as Benvenuto runs off with Angela. The following morning, Benvenuto is disillusioned with Angela, who expects to be accorded greater status than his art. Captured by Ottaviano and his soldiers, Benvenuto reveals the plot to kill the Duke, and his life is spared. In gratitude he insists that the Duke have Angela.

First Is Last (Theater, 1919) In the late summer of 1919 Edward G. Robinson was rehearsing a play originally called *Dark Horses*, which was later changed to *First Is Last*. He remembered it in his autobiography chiefly because, for once, he played an Anglo-Saxon instead of a character with a foreign dialect. Other than that he found it neither important nor dull.

The *New York Times* commentary agreed with Robinson's assessment, saying the play "unfolds a pattern that becomes quite hopelessly familiar long before the first act has come to a close."

Producer, William Harris, Jr.; playwrights, Samuel Shipman, Percival Wilde; cast: Richard Dix (Phil), Edward Robinson (Steve), Franklyn Ardell (Lowell), Elise Bartlett (Helen), Kathleen Comegys (Ethel), Phoebe Foster (Madge), James Kearney (Selby, the butler), Mary Newcombe (Annabelle), Hassard Short (Doug), Robert Strange (Harvey); opened at the Maxine Elliott's Theatre, New York; September 17, 1919

A group of Columbia University graduates meet after three years to divide their profits, having elected to pool their future earnings. But they are all failures except the class poet who has become a garbage magnate. Two years later they meet again. The poet is now a rich toy manufacturer. He marries the girl who had believed in him, while the others go their separate ways.

First National Pictures Edward G. Robinson said he never was sure which of his films were made by Warner Bros. and which were First National in the fiscal arrangement at the studio. From 1930 to 1934, however, most of his films carried the name First National, along with Vitaphone (an early sound system). *The Bright Shawl* in 1923 was produced by Associated First National. A group of exhibitors founded First National in 1917 with the intent of making their own films as retaliation against the practice of blockbooking, wherein they were obligated to purchase a group of lesser films in a package that included perhaps only one major picture with a star. First National was acquired by Warner Bros. in the late 1920s. Robinson's other films for First National were *The Widow from Chicago, Little Caesar, Smart Money, Five Star Final, The Hatchet Man, Two Seconds, Tiger Shark, Silver Dollar, The Little Giant, I Loved a Woman, Dark Hazard,* and *The Man with Two Faces.*

Fitzgerald, Barry (1888–1961), nominated for best actor *and* best supporting actor Oscars as Father Fitzgibbon in *Going My Way*, he perhaps nudged Edward G. Robinson out of recognition for *Double Indemnity* in 1944, winning in the latter category. He came to the U.S. from Dublin's Abbey Theatre. Other films include *Juno and the Paycock, Bringing Up Baby, The Long Voyage Home, The Sea Wolf* (with Robinson), *And Then There Were None, The Naked City,* and *The Quiet Man.*

Five Star Final (Film, 1931) The third film Edward G. Robinson had in release in 1931 followed the enormous success of *Little Caesar* in January by nine months and *Smart Money* by three. *Five Star Final* was a newspaper drama based on the play of the same name by Louis Weitzenkorn. Its successful run on Broadway had also just concluded in the spring. The film was equally impressive, one of eight nominated by the Academy of Motion Picture Arts and Sciences as best picture, but losing to *Grand Hotel*.

Producer Hal Wallis commented in his autobiography, "One concern I had in *Five*

Star Final was to make sure that the newspaper office was authentic. Members of our staff in New York had sketches made of the interiors of two newspaper offices so that our dimensions were exactly correct. We even duplicated the neon lighting in the ceilings by having exceptionally bright arc lights blazing down from the top of the studio sound stage...." Wallis continued about Edward G. Robinson: "With his strong sense of justice, Eddie told me he regarded the part as one of the most important of his career. The whole picture revolved around him, and when he had a part he believed in there was nobody quite like him.... Eddie's attack, his vigor, his electric energy, made you forget he was a small and ugly man. He was a towering figure in pictures — a great star." — Hal Wallis, with Charles Higham, *Starmaker*

Robinson said of the character, "I loved Randall because he wasn't a gangster.... I enjoyed doing him. He made sense.... *Five Star Final* is one of my favorite films." —*All My Yesterdays*

The New York Sun called the picture the "first real smash of the season, searing, stirring, melodramatic expose ... an extremely important film. Sensationalism is in its topic; sensationalism is in its method. A really rousing rushing and wholly affecting talkie." Robinson was "magnificent.... Refreshing, spontaneous applause, studded with bravos, followed the final closeup."

The New York World-Telegram reviewer agreed, saying the picture was "smooth, fast-moving, stirring and genuinely interesting. Edward G. Robinson plays to perfection. Brilliant direction and excellent acting.... Mr. Robinson gives a vigorous, brusque and altogether fine performance. The direction of Mervyn LeRoy is of the finest."

The London Times noted that, "as Randall, Mr. Edward G. Robinson succeeds in the best way an actor can — he succeeds, that is, in endowing the character he is playing with a definite personality. Randall is a far finer man than the people for whom he works...."

"Robinson ... gives another strong performances as the editor of a muck-raking tabloid," wrote *The New York Times* ... "With a big cigar in the corner of his mouth most of the time, [he] makes the most of every line."

The film holds up decades later. James Robert Parish, in *The Tough Guys*, said that it "still packs a wallop, due mainly to its crackling dialogue and wonderful rogues gallery of performers.... It is Edward G. Robinson who makes the film sparkle.... Washing his hands throughout ... he is especially effective in the climax." Foster Hirsch noted, "Robinson's editor is a dashing figure. [He] never seemed more zestful and youthful."

"The playing of Robinson as Randall ... was magnificent, brilliantly right for the new camera techniques of the period, laying down the whole foundation of movie acting technique in the talkies for forty years to come," said Charles Higham in *Warner Brothers*.

Because circulation is down at *The New York Gazette,* publisher Hinchcliffe wants to revive and exploit a twenty-year-old scandal in which Nancy Vorhees had shot her boyfriend, Bill Matthews. Randall, the newspaper's editor, sends reporters T. Vernon Isopod and Kitty Carmody to get a new angle on the old story. Isopod, posing as a minister, discovers that Vorhees, who was cleared, is now married to Michael Townsend. They have a daughter, Jenny, who is about to marry Phillip Weeks, the son of a prominent manufacturer. Nancy and Michael try unsuccessfully to get the stories dropped. As daily segments begin to appear in *The Gazette,* however, the Townsends, unable to cope, commit suicide. Learning the horrible impact of the campaign, Randall denounces Hinchcliffe and the newspaper and quits, but not before Jenny appears in the editorial offices hysterically waving a gun and demanding to know why the paper killed her parents. Warning everyone now to leave them alone, Phillip leads Jenny away.

Producer, Hal B. Wallis; director, Mervyn LeRoy; screenplay, Byron Morgan, Robert Lord; based on the play by Louis Weitzenkorn; camera, Sol Polito; art director, Jack Okey; editor, Frank Ware; gowns, Earl Luick; music, Leo F. Forbstein, Vitaphone Orchestra; cast: Edward G. Robinson (Joseph Randall), H. B. Warner (Michael Townsend), Marion Marsh (Jenny Townsend), Frances

Starr (Nancy Vorhees Townsend), Ona Munson (Kitty Carmody), Aline MacMahon (Miss Taylor), Boris Karloff (T. Vernon Isopod), George E. Stone (Ziggie Feinstein), Anthony Bushell (Phillip Weeks), Oscar Apfel (Hinchecliffe), Purnell Pratt (French), Robert Elliott (Brannegan), Gladys Lloyd (Miss Edwards), Harold Waldridge (Goldberg), Evelyn Hall (Mrs. Weeks), David Torrence (Mr. Weeks), Polly Walters (Operator), James Donlan (Reporter), Frank Darien (Schwartz), Franklin Parker, Jack Wise, James Burtis; First National; 89 minutes; September 1931

Flaherty, Pat (1903–70) was in *The Red House, All My Sons, Key Largo,* and *It's a Great Feeling,* all with Edward G. Robinson. He also appeared in *Only Angels Have Wings, Sergeant York, Twentieth Century, Meet John Doe,* and *Gentleman Jim.*

Flashbacks An event shown in a film's story that happened earlier than the start of the film is called a flashback. It "is a useful narrative device that allows a screenwriter ... flexibility in the temporal structure of his plot," according to Ephraim Katz in *The Film Encyclopedia.* Edward G. Robinson's entire performance in *House of Strangers* is in a flashback, as remembered by Richard Conte. Similarly, *Two Seconds* tells Robinson's story in flashback — his thoughts during the time it takes to die in the electric chair. *All My Sons* contains a flashback to show Joe Keller (Robinson) hesitating to ship defective cylinders to the Army Air Force during wartime. *The Outrage* features three flashbacks, each one a different version of the story told by its characters. The first half of *Night Has a Thousand Eyes* tells Robinson's story, in flashback, of how he realized he had the "terrible gift" of clairvoyance. Finally, in *Double Indemnity* Fred MacMurray's character, Walter Neff, narrates the story of murder into a dictaphone in a flashback, saying to Keyes, his boss (Robinson), "I guess you'll call this a confession when you hear it."

Flavin, James (1906–76), an Irish character actor, typically played cops. He appears in six films with Edward G. Robinson: *Brother Orchid, Cheyenne Autumn, I Am the Law, Manpower, Mr. Winkle Goes to War,* and *Larceny, Inc.* He was also in *King Kong, The Grapes of Wrath, Mister Roberts,* and *It's a Mad, Mad, Mad, Mad World.*

Fleischer, Richard (1916–) directed *Soylent Green.* The son of cartoonist Max Fleischer (*Popeye, Betty Boop*), he made documentaries at RKO, including the *This Is America* series, and directed such features as *20,000 Leagues Under the Sea, The Girl in the Red Velvet Swing, The Vikings, Dr. Dolittle,* and a remake of *The Jazz Singer.* In his memoir, *Just Tell Me When to Cry,* he comments, "Think of Edward G. Robinson as you think of a short, tough-as-nails gangster ... Think like that and you think wrong. That wasn't Eddie at all, see? That was the actor, not the real guy. The real guy was ... like ... loveable, you know what I mean? And I gotta tell ya, I loved Eddie Robinson."

Flesh and Fantasy (Film, 1943) In the second of two episode films he made with French director Julien Duvivier, Edward G. Robinson "had an interesting brush with the occult in [this] solemn version of Oscar Wilde's black joke ['Lord Arthur Savile's Crime']," according to *Suspense in the Cinema,* by Gordon Gow. "Lord Arthur was rethought as an American solicitor working in London, and renamed Marshall Tyler [Robinson]. The plot was virtually the same as Wilde's but straight-faced instead of satirical. What might have been high comedy became elevated melodrama."

Gow's assessment about the melodrama is accurate enough; however, Robinson's segment also has quite a bit of humor. "Seldom has murder been contemplated on the screen with more diabolical delight (for the audience) than when Mr. Robinson of the flesh argues with Mr. Robinson of the fantasy ... about who the victim should be or how the crime would be committed," enthused *The New York Times.* "Julien Duvivier, the director, has underscored this sequence with mounting suspense ... the best part of the picture."

Charles Higham and Joel Greenberg, in *Hollywood in the Forties,* agreed: "Easily the film's best episode was its second, a superb adaptation.... From its beautiful opening shot of two hands—the palmist's (Thomas Mitchell) and his subject's (Edward G. Robinson)—it provided a succession of stylized pseudo-London images, strongly recalling Pabst's *Dreigroshenoper,* and a gallery of memorable performances."

The New York Herald-Tribune, referring to the film as "an example of one-act play techniques adapted for motion pictures," applauded the Robinson-Mitchell episode also: "Things pick up in this sequence as the fantasy becomes mixed with excitement and good performances by the two above-mentioned actors. But ... the one-act form is marred by repetition of the same effect and long conversational pauses."

Producers, Charles Boyer, Julien Duvivier; director, Duvivier; based on *Lord Arthur Savile's Crime* by Oscar Wilde, and stories by Laslo Vadnay and Ellis St. Joseph; screenplay, Ernest Pascal, Samuel Hoffenstein, St. Joseph; art directors, John B. Goodman, Richard Riedel, Robert Boyle; set, R. A. Gausman, E. R. Robinson; music, Alexander Tansman; music director, Charles Previn; camera, Paul Ivano, Stanley Cortez; editor, Arthur Hilton; dialogue director, Don Brodie; sound, Edwin Wetzel, Bernard B. Brown; technician, Joe Lapis; costumes, Edith Head, Vera West; assistant directors, Seward Webb, Joseph A. McDonough; special effects, Tim Barr; makeup, Jack Pierce; cast: Edward G. Robinson (Marshall Tyler), Charles Boyer (Paul Gaspar), Barbara Stanwyck (Joan Stanley), Betty Field (Henrietta), Robert Cummings (Michael), Thomas Mitchell (Septimus Podgers), Charles Winninger (King LaMar), Anna Lee (Rowena), Dame May Whitty (Lady Pamela Hardwick), C. Aubrey Smith (Dean of Norwalk), Robert Benchley (Doakes), Edgar Barrier (Stranger), David Hoffman (Davis), Mary Forbes (Lady Thomas), Clarence Muse (Jet), Doris Lloyd (Mrs. Claxton), Marjorie Lord (Justine), Peter Lawford (Pierrot), Clinton Rosemond (Old Negro), Charles Halton (Proprietor), Joseph Crehan, Arthur Loft, Lee Phelps (Detectives), Ian Wolfe (Librarian), Eddie Acuff (Policeman), James Craven (Announcer), June Lang, Jacqueline Dalya (Angels), Grace McDonald (Equestrienne), Lane Chandler (Satan), Gil Patrick (Death), Paul Bryar, George Lewis (Harlequins), Heather Thatcher, Edward Fielding (Guests), Frank Arnold, Beatrice Barrett, Anita Bolster, Jack Gardner, Leland Hodgson, Mary Ann Hyde, Frank Mitchell, Sandra Morgan, Neara Sanders, Carl Vernell, Phil Warren, Con Colleano, Marcel Dalio, Harold DeBecker, Fern Formica, Olaf Hytton, Eddie Kane, Bruce Lester, Jerry Maren, Ferdinand Munier, Harry Stubbs; Universal; 93 minutes; November 1943

Doakes meets Davis at his club and discusses a recent dream. Davis gives him a book in which there are three stories on the supernatural. In story one Henrietta, a selfish, homely dressmaker, is given the chance to attend Mardi Gras wearing a beautiful mask. She is noticed by Michael, a disillusioned student. They fall in love, and when he unmasks her at midnight, she is surprised and thrilled that her face has retained the beauty of the mask because for once she has thought of someone besides herself. Story two takes place in London. Podgers, a palm reader, is a guest at Lady Pamela Hardwick's party and makes several predictions that amazingly come to pass. Reading Marshall Tyler's palm, he predicts he will marry Rowena, but he will not reveal what else he sees. Tyler insists, however, and the next day meets Podgers, who tells him that he will commit a murder. Unnerved, Tyler becomes preoccupied by the prediction and decides to kill somebody to get the dilemma behind him. Lady Pamela dies of natural causes before he can poison her. The Dean of Norwalk, his next choice, counsels him, and Tyler cannot go through with his attack on the elderly man. He encounters Podgers walking in the fog. When the palmist rereads Tyler's hand, he lies, saying he had been mistaken about the murder. Tyler strangles Podgers and throws him into the river, In trying to escape he is run down by a truck from a nearby circus (the setting of story three). Paul Gaspar, a "drunken" tightrope walker, has a nightmare in which he falls from the high wire after focusing on the earrings of a woman in the crowd. On board ship to America from his European tour he encounters Joan Stanley, the lady in the dream. They fall in love, but their relationship is doomed because she is wanted by the police.

The short story by Oscar Wilde called *Lord Arthur Savile's Crime,* the basis for the second episode of *Flesh and Fantasy,* was first published in the magazine *Court and Society Review* in 1887. According to Isobel Murray's introduction to the *Complete Shorter Fiction of Oscar Wilde,* "the success of *Lord Arthur Savile's Crime* is entirely dependent on tone, and on the kind of inspired through-the-looking-glass logic [which], while light, is always apparently grave."

The humor of the screenplay is augmented by visions Tyler has of himself in various mirror images gleefully counseling him and reminding, "you've got to kill someone." But the comedy shifts to melodrama when a first attempt at murder fails. The story's farfetched but funny notion of a second murder attempt via a miniature exploding clock is replaced by Tyler's mounting desperation when, unable to kill the Dean of Norwalk in cold blood, he runs from the scene, only to encounter Podgers.

The film has two major deviations from Wilde's ending. In the story, on seeing Podgers, Lord Arthur merely surprises him and tosses him off the bridge into the river — without saying a word! On the screen the two meet on the bridge and argue:

PODGERS: Mr. Tyler. How are you?
TYLER: How am I? How could anyone be after what you told me?
PODGERS: But ... I didn't put it there.
TYLER: No [points to his head], but you put it there.
PODGERS: But you wanted to know. You insisted.
TYLER: Look again, perhaps you made a mistake.
PODGERS: Mr. Tyler, you better go home. Get some sleep.
TYLER: Perhaps you made a mistake.
PODGERS: Perhaps I did. Come around tomorrow and see me.
TYLER: No! No ... now.
PODGERS: [Examines his hand] How extraordinary. Afraid I owe you an apology, Mr. Tyler.
TYLER: Apology?
PODGERS: Doesn't seem to be there.
TYLER: Yes it is. It is!
PODGERS: No, no I swear!
TYLER: Liar!
PODGERS: No, I tell you...
TYLER: Liar! Liar! [Tyler strangles Podgers, and then dumps his lifeless body off the bridge]

A policeman chases Tyler; he is run down by a truck, ending the filmed episode in an appropriately melodramatic manner. Oscar Wilde, however, maintained the fun by having Lord Arthur escape the scene and, days later, calmly rejoice upon reading the news that Podgers "committed suicide." He marries and lives happily ever after with Sybil (Rowena in the film) and their children.

"Flesh and Fantasy" (Radio, 1945) The film was adapted for presentation on the radio two years later.

Cast: Edward G. Robinson (Marshall Tyler), Dame May Whitty (Lady Pamela), Vincent Price (Podgers); *Lady Esther's Screen Guild Players*; CBS; June 16 or October 13, 1945

Flowers There are moments in some of Edward G. Robinson's films in which flowers become important. One sweet moment occurs in *Tales of Manhattan* when, after helping to transform Bowery Bum Robinson into an elegant gentleman in tails, Barbara Lynn adds a carnation to his lapel. In *The Ten Commandments* Robinson spoofs his knowledge of fine art in the meticulous placement of a flower to adorn Debra Paget's hair.

He cultivates zinnia beds as a member of the Little Brothers of the Flowers in *Brother Orchid.* And in *Never a Dull Moment* (once again, back to art) he masterminds a plot to steal the painting "Field of Sunflowers," a huge mural, from a Los Angeles gallery.

Flowers, Bess (1900–84) She was known as "Queen of the Hollywood Extras" and appeared in hundreds of films over a forty-year career. With Edward G. Robinson she appears in *The Whole Town's Talking, I Am the Law, Double Indemnity* (Mr. Norton's Secretary), *The Woman in the Window, Kid Galahad, Seven Thieves,* and *Good Neighbor Sam* (Mrs. Burke).

Foch, Nina (1924–) She played in two films with Edward G. Robinson — as the female lead, Ellen Miles Borden, in *Illegal,* and, sharing brief scenes with him toward the end of the film, as Bithia, Moses' adoptive mother, in *The Ten Commandments.* She is also seen in *My Name is Julia Ross, Executive Suite, An American in Paris,* and *Spartacus.*

Fonda, Henry (1905–82) was in *Tales of Manhattan* with Edward G. Robinson, but in different episodes. They narrated segments of *All About People* and TV's *The American Idea: The Land.* Onstage at the Hollywood Bowl, they were in a program benefiting the United China Relief Fund. Fonda was Oscar-nominated for *The Grapes of Wrath* and won for *On Golden Pond.* Coming to Hollywood from the stage to recreate his role in *The Farmer Takes a Wife,* he was in *Young Mr. Lincoln, The Lady Eve, The Male Animal, The Ox-Bow Incident, Mister Roberts* (from another Broadway role), *Twelve Angry Men, Advise and Consent,* and *Once Upon a Time in the West.*

Fontanne, Lynn (1887–1983) and her husband, Alfred Lunt, were, for over thirty years, the foremost acting couple in America. Performing in her native England from 1905, she played the title roles in *Anna Christie* and *Dulcy* prior to her marriage. Thereafter the couple performed together almost exclusively — in *The Guardsman* (also one of their rare films) and for the Theatre Guild in *The Goat Song, The Brothers Karamazov* (both with Edward G. Robinson), *Arms and the Man, Pygmalion, Elizabeth the Queen, Design for Living, Idiot's Delight,* and *There Shall Be No Night.* Their later successes included *The Great Sebastians* and *The Visit.*

See **Alfred Lunt.**

Food Food — in particular food production — is a plot element in many of Edward G. Robinson's films. He is a potato farmer in *Our Vines Have Tender Grapes;* in *Good Neighbor Sam* he owns a dairy, and in *A Slight Case of Murder* a brewery. The beer is undrinkable in the latter film. Called Gold Velvet, "it tastes like shellac." There is poor quality of food in other films, as that depicted in *I Loved a Woman* (tainted beef during the Spanish American War), and the food of the future in *Soylent Green* (the reconstituted dead). Also in that film is a scene where Robinson, amazed to acquire actual beef in the year 2022, prepares an old-fashioned (and unheard of) meal for himself and Charlton Heston.

In both *Brother Orchid* and *Our Vines Have Tender Grapes* Robinson is seen milking a cow. In *Dr. Ehrlich's Magic Bullet* he watches his young daughters drink milk, and later in the same film he must drink it himself, the victim of tuberculosis. Dick Van Dyke is offered a glass of milk to wash down the dog biscuits he is eating in *Never a Dull Moment.*

Dinners, banquets, buffets, and lunches are depicted in *Good Neighbor Sam, House of Strangers* (spaghetti on Wednesday nights with the family), *Little Caesar, Dr. Ehrlich's Magic Bullet, All My Sons, The Stranger, Two Weeks in Another Town, Scarlet Street, The Prize, The Red House, The Whole Town's Talking,* and *Our Vines Have Tender Grapes.* The funniest of these is in *The Biggest Bundle of Them All,* as Francesco Mule eats his way through his favorite Italian restaurant.

Food served in Robinson's films include Marlene Dietrich's homemade biscuits in *Manpower;* Army coffee in *Cheyenne Autumn;* layer cake and hot dogs in *A Hole in the Head;* lobster in *All My Sons;* hors d'ouevres in *Never a Dull Moment* and *Larceny, Inc.;* jambalaya, fried chicken, and roast duck in *Nightmare;* steak and a piece of pie in *Barbary Coast;* post-theater sandwiches in *The Man with Two Faces;* and tomato soup, bread, and butter in "The Messiah on Mott Street." Robinson makes the eating of oysters on the half shell look exquisite in *The Cincinnati Kid.*

The cleverest use of food in a Robinson film is in *Blackmail,* in which, as a fighter of oil fires, his character puts an egg and slices of bread in the pockets of his suit, marches into the inferno, puts out the blaze, and comes back to serve his wife breakfast — a soft-boiled egg and toast!

Ginger Rogers in *Tight Spot* takes advantage of hotel room service to order an elaborate dinner, changing her mind several times before it is delivered. Robinson's Johnny Rocco savors the memory of champagne and pompano in *Key Largo*. A cop in *The Amazing Dr. Clitterhouse* nibbles away at pretzels, not realizing that stolen jewels are lying at the bottom of the bowl. A wedding cake comes to a bad end in *Manpower* because the characters have been drinking a lot of beer.

In *Destroyer* an overturned beer can on a shelf has leaked down the wall of the ship and is mistaken for a wet seam. In *Bullets or Ballots* Robinson's character dies before he can celebrate rubbing out the rackets by sharing a glass of beer with the good guys. The drinking of grape juice has an obvious ritualistic reference in *All My Sons*.

In real life Edward G. Robinson had a fondness for eggplant from an old-world recipe of his mother's, and fish prepared with tomato. In 1937 he was featured in a *Collier's* magazine story, along with Dwight Fiske, on proper ways to dress a salad. He was quoted in a *Washington Post* article in 1970 that, "he does not dabble in the kitchen. 'But give me good food.'"

For the Living (Radio, 1950) In 1950 Edward G. Robinson participated in thirteen episodes of this radio program, sponsored by the American Cancer Society. The programs were fifteen minutes long.

Episode H (untitled) was about the need for early checkups; cast: Edward G. Robinson (narrator), Herbert Rawlinson, Lurene Tuttle, Gerald Mohr, Jeff Alexander and His Orchestra; Lyn Murray, conductor

Episode I (untitled) was about current cancer research; cast: Edward G. Robinson, Hans Conried, Ray Collins (narrator)

See **"By-products of the Atom"**; **"Cancer, Cause for Hope"**; **"Cancer in Men"**; **"Cancer in Women"**; **"Frauds and Superstitions"**; **"The Power of the X-Ray"**; **"Radium Against Cancer"**; **"The Seven Symptoms"**; **"The Weapon of Surgery"**; **"What Are We Fighting?"**; **"The Why of Cancer."**

Ford, Glenn (1916–), Columbia Pictures leading man, wins Edward G. Robinson's daughter in two films—*Destroyer* and *The Violent Men*. His others include *Heaven with a Barbed Wire Fence, Gilda, The Big Heat, The Blackboard Jungle, The Teahouse of the August Moon, 3:10 to Yuma, Fate Is the Hunter, Dear Heart, Superman,* and *JFK*.

Ford, John (1895–1973) directed Edward G. Robinson in *The Whole Town's Talking* and *Cheyenne Autumn*. He won Oscars for such classics as *The Informer, The Grapes of Wrath, How Green Was My Valley,* and *The Quiet Man*. He also is known for his westerns, including *Stagecoach*, a fifth directing nomination. His career started in silent films in 1917.

Ford Theatre (Radio, 1949, and Television, 1955) The radio program aired on CBS from October 1948 to July 1949. Edward G. Robinson appeared in a sixty-minute adaptation of *The Woman in the Window*. When the program moved to television, Robinson appeared in two 1955 half-hour presentations, "…And Son," and "A Set of Values."

See **"…And Son"**; **"A Set of Values"**; **"The Woman in the Window."**

Forrest, Sam (1870–1944) was a Broadway director for three decades, often staging the works of George M. Cohan (*Seven Keys to Baldpate*). He directed Edward G. Robinson in *We Americans* and Cohan's *The Little Teacher*. Other successes include *Six-Cylinder Love, Three Faces East,* and *Cradle Snatchers*.

Forsythe, John (1918–) was on TV in *Bachelor Father, Charlie's Angels,* and *Dynasty*. His film with Edward G. Robinson, *The Glass Web*, involved writing, researching, and solving a "Crime of the Week" on TV. On Broadway Forsyth was in *Mister Roberts* and *The Teahouse of the August Moon*. Other films include *The Trouble with Harry, In Cold Blood,* and *Topaz*.

Foster, Dianne (1928–) played Edward G. Robinson's daughter, Judith, in *The Violent Men*. Canadian-born, she came via the London stage to the screen. She also had roles in *The Kentuckian, The Last Hurrah*, and *Who's Been Sleeping in My Bed?*

Foster, Eddie (1906–89) had roles in four films with Edward G. Robinson—*I Am the Law, The Last Gangster, Kid Galahad* (as a piano player), and *Larceny, Inc.* (as a ballplayer). He also appeared in *Ball of Fire, White Heat*, and *Kansas City Confidential*.

Foster, Phoebe (1910–) was in the cast of two plays with Edward G. Robinson—his first Broadway show, *Under Fire*, and, four years later, *First Is Last*. She was also in films, including *Our Betters, The Night Angel*, and *Anna Karenina*.

Foster, Preston (1902–70), a wrestler and an opera singer before coming to films from the Broadway stage, played Edward G. Robinson's pal, Bud, who falls to his death from the skyscraper they are working on in *Two Seconds*. He is in *The Last Mile, I Am a Fugitive from a Chain Gang, The Informer*, and *Annie Oakley*.

Foulger, Byron (1900–70) appeared with Edward G. Robinson in *I Am the Law* and *Scarlet Street*, and on TV in *The Devil and Daniel Webster*. His other films include *The Human Comedy, Edison the Man, Sullivan's Travels, The Long Hot Summer*, and *The Gnome-Mobile*.

Francis, Arlene (1912–2001) was a regular panelist on TV's *What's My Line?* on which Edward G. Robinson appeared twice as "mystery guest." She also worked with him in the film *All My Sons* and considered him a *bon vivant*. Her other films include *The Thrill of It All* and *One Two Three*.

Francis, Kay (1903–68) played opposite Edward G. Robinson as opera singer Laura McDonald in *I Loved a Woman*. Her other pictures include *The Cocoanuts, Raffles, Trouble in Paradise, The White Angel* (as Florence Nightingale), *In Name Only, Charley's Aunt*, and *Four Jills in a Jeep*.

"Frauds and Superstitions" (Radio, 1950) Sponsored by the American Cancer Society; cast: Edward G. Robinson, Gerald Mohr, Hans Conried; *For the Living* (Episode B); 1950

Freeman, Kathleen (1919–2001), a familiar face in television comedy (notably as Katie, the maid in the *Topper* series), plays a maid also in *The Glass Web*, with Edward G. Robinson. Other films include *The Naked City, The Fly, The Nutty Professor*, and *Support Your Local Gunfighter*. On Broadway she was in *Deathtrap* and received a 2001 Tony Award nomination for her role in the musical, *The Full Monty*.

Freeman, Mona (1926–) worked with Edward G. Robinson in a small part in *Double Indemnity*, and fourteen years later toured with him onstage as The Girl in *Middle of the Night*. A model signed to a film contract by Howard Hughes, she played teenagers, ingenues, and, later, leading ladies (*National Velvet, Junior Miss, Dear Ruth, Battle Cry*).

Fregonese, Hugo (1908–87) directed *Black Tuesday*, with Edward G. Robinson. Coming to the United States from Argentina as a technical adviser on Latin-American films, he directed his first feature in 1943. His other films include *Apache Drums, My Six Convicts*, and *Decameron Nights*.

Funeral Edward G. Robinson died on Friday, January 26, 1973, at Mount Sinai Hospital in Los Angeles, after having been admitted in late December in the final throes of cancer of the liver. A funeral service was held on Sunday, January 28. Dr. Max Nussbaum officiated. Accounts vary on the numbers (in the hundreds) in attendance, but there were mourners inside and outside Temple Israel. Charlton Heston delivered the eulogy, which included this line from the final act of Shakespeare's *Julius Caesar* (spoken by Mark Antony about Brutus, not Caesar):

"His life was gentle, and the elements / So mix'd in him that nature might stand up / And say to all the world, 'This was a man.'"

Honorary pallbearers included Jack Benny, Sidney Boehm, George Burns, Arthur Groman, Sam Jaffe, Jack Karp, Mervyn LeRoy, Sol Schwartz, Alan Simpson, Frank Sinatra, Hal Wallis, and Jack Warner. Among those present were Steve Allen, Milton Berle, Frederick Brisson and Rosalind Russell, Henry Fonda, Martha Hyer, Danny Kaye, Milton Krims, Karl Malden, Ross Martin, Tony Martin, Groucho Marx, Raymond Massey, Zero Mostel, Gregory Peck, Nehemiah Persoff, Madlyn Rhue, Cesar Romero, Danny Thomas, and, of course, his widow, Jane, his son, Edward G. Robinson, Jr., and his granddaughter, Francesca. The body was flown to Brooklyn for entombment in the family mausoleum at Beth El Cemetery on Monday, January 29.

Funerals In *Little Caesar* Rico orders the death of Tony, a driver who panicked during a New Year's Eve robbery and therefore had become unreliable. Shots of real-life gangster Dion O'Bannion's funeral procession were used for the film. Twenty-five years later, as gangster Victor Amato in *Hell on Frisco Bay*, Robinson has another unreliable henchman dispatched — this time his nephew — and the funeral parlor provides a tense but neutral spot for a meeting with the cops.

Opening scenes of *The Cincinnati Kid* show a colorful New Orleans funeral procession. It begins with a somber march, as the entourage of black mourners move off the street into the cemetery for the service. The brass and drum music then turns upbeat, and the mourners begin a joyous march, even dancing in the streets, providing the background for the opening credits of the film.

There are scenes of funerals for Robinson characters in three films. A traditional farewell at a cemetery is the conclusion of *Silver Dollar*, to the strains of Wagner. In *House of Strangers* the family mansion is the site of his wake, but we are spared a look in the open casket. This scene is where Richard Conte, as the loyal son, swears a vendetta against his three brothers.

Finally, in *Robin and the 7 Hoods*, after a very funny opening in which Robinson's character, Big Jim, is gunned down at his birthday party, there is a shift to the cemetery where, comically, the bugler plays — not "Taps," but the race track's familiar "Last Call." This scene was filmed in the fall of 1963, and the mood turned ominous. At the location a grave marker was noticed for a family named Kennedy, and shortly thereafter events in Dallas chilled any humor of the moment.

Gaines, Richard (1904–71) was Mr. Norton, Edward G. Robinson's pompous boss, in *Double Indemnity* and the same year played his equally stuffy brother-in-law, Ralph Westcott, in *Mr. Winkle Goes to War.* He also appears in *The More the Merrier, The Howards of Virginia, A Night to Remember, Humoresque, The Hucksters, Ace in the Hole,* and *Jeanne Eagles.*

The Gamblers (Theater, 1913) When Edward G. Robinson made his professional debut in *Paid in Full* in Albany, New York, he also appeared in two roles in another play, *The Gamblers*. First produced on Broadway in October 1910, it was a melodrama about high finance.

Producer, S. M. Stainach Stock Company; playwright, Charles Klein; cast included Edward G. Robinson (Thomas, the butler, and Hicks, a plainclothesman); Albany, New York; April 1913

Gambling and Games Edward G. Robinson played gamblers in three films, but it wasn't until the last — *The Cincinnati Kid* — that he came out on top, besting Steve McQueen's full house of aces and tens with a diamond flush during their climactic poker match. He was successful in *Smart Money*, complete with his own gambling joint, but at the film's fadeout he was about to begin serving ten years in prison for manslaughter. *Dark Hazard* saw him betting on dogs but never keeping his winnings for long.

Dog races were featured also in scenes in *A Hole in the Head*, but Frank Sinatra did the betting. Poker games were played also in *Big*

Leaguer and *Cheyenne Autumn,* and Robinson was a card player on the stage in *The Kibitzer*. Gambling casinos provided backdrops for *Seven Thieves* (Monte Carlo), *Barbary Coast* (San Francisco), *Robin and the 7 Hoods* (Chicago), and *Pepe* (Las Vegas). There are secret dice games in *Unholy Partners* and *The Amazing Dr. Clitterhouse*. Robinson plays checkers in *Our Vines Have Tender Grapes* and *The Stranger*. Finally, he acted in *The Gamblers* (his second stage play), and he was a celebrity contestant on the TV game show *The $64,000 Challenge.*

Gangster films More than a third of Edward G. Robinson's feature films (34 of 89) could be classified as falling within the gangster genre. An additional nine films should be considered also, because they contain elements of the genre, which raises the total to nearly half. Gangster films, typified generally by contemporary urban settings, have characters who are members of a gang involved in organized crime. There were, of course, variations, both in the story lines of several of Robinson's films and in the degree to which the elements are specific to the genre. Also, interestingly, while Robinson often was the leader of a gang, many times in the gangster films he was the opposing force on the side of the law.

First and foremost among Robinson's gangster films is *Little Caesar,* based on W. R. Burnett's novel. The film, which shares prominence with James Cagney's *The Public Enemy* and Paul Muni's *Scarface,* is a prototype, an indelible influence on every gangster film that followed in the next seven decades.

Ranking high in second place among the actor's gangster film portrayals is his Johnny Rocco in *Key Largo*. It came toward the end of his tenure as a major Hollywood star. *Key Largo* also brings Robinson's gangland portraiture full circle in that Johnny Rocco is less naive than Rico by virtue of being almost twenty years older.

Robinson's gallery of gangsters contains several other serious studies: Tony Garotta in *The Night Ride,* The Fox in *The Hole in the Wall,* Cobra Collins in *Outside the Law,* and Dominic in *The Widow from Chicago,* all in the year preceding *Little Caesar.* Joe Krozac in *The Last Gangster,* Vince Canelli in *Black Tuesday,* and Victor Amato in *Hell on Frisco Bay* are his only other purely melodramatic gang characters; however, many others, with qualification, come close.

In *Smart Money,* for instance, the gang influence becomes dominant after barber Nick Venezelos begins his climb to success. James Cagney's co-starring presence in the film, fresh from his role in *The Public Enemy,* and paired with Robinson immediately after *Little Caesar,* helps underscore the gang connection. *Dark Hazard,* two years later, and *The Cincinnati Kid* three decades later both deal with gamblers, but they have only fringe connections to the mob.

The Hatchet Man, with an Americanized Chinese setting, complete with Tong wars, became a curious gangster story. Similarly, *East Is West* had Robinson as the Oriental Charlie Yong, chop suey king, on the fringe of organized crime. The 1968 foreign feature *Peking Blonde* begins and ends with Oriental intrigue; however, Robinson's role is that of an American government agent.

Each of the following gangster films has qualifying twists, either in connection with the gang or with Robinson's character. *Barbary Coast* has all the requisite elements of the genre, except that it takes place in the nineteenth century at the time of the Gold Rush, thus also giving it a western quality. In *Bullets or Ballots* Robinson plays a detective who poses as a gangster to infiltrate and destroy the rackets. *Kid Galahad* is basically a story about prizefighting, but its crooked managers lead opposing gangs.

Robinson has the title role as *The Amazing Dr. Clitterhouse,* as a high society physician who mixes with a gang to research the physiology of criminals. In *I Am the Law* Robinson is a law professor who spends his sabbatical ridding the town of organized crime. *Unholy Partners* has him as an editor exposing the activities of a gangster who finances his newspaper.

It could be argued that gangster elements are evident in *The Sea Wolf* (a sadistic captain and crew), *Confessions of a Nazi Spy* and *Tampico* (Nazis), and *House of Strangers* (vendetta-minded Italian brothers).

In the 1950s Edward G. Robinson played

the lead in a few gangster films, but except for the aforementioned *Black Tuesday* and *Hell on Frisco Bay,* he was on the right side of the law — as police detectives in *Vice Squad* and *A Bullet for Joey*, and lawyers in *Tight Spot* and *Illegal*. One other odd exception is *The Violent Men*, in which, as in *Barbary Coast*, Robinson is a gang leader in a western — this time in a ranchers' range war against farmers. As one reviewer remarked, "Robinson plays Little Caesar in buckskin."

A gang in *The Prize* is Russian Communists who kidnap a physicist, portrayed by Edward G. Robinson. He had a dual role as the physicist and as an actor in the gang made up to be his double.

In *Seven Thieves* and *Grand Slam* Robinson's character, an elderly educator who has turned to crime, masterminds a heist pulled off by a gang. In both films there is a twist ending. In the former picture, his character dies of a heart attack during the getaway; in the latter the loot ends up in the hands of a purse-snatcher at the fade-out. These two movies, and several from the 1960s in the group that follows, can also be labeled "caper" films.

Late in his career Edward G. Robinson played in these comedy caper films (also involving gangs): *The Biggest Bundle of Them All, Mad Checkmate, Never a Dull Moment,* and *Operation St. Peter*. Several were foreign efforts, but the one clearly American movie, *Never a Dull Moment*, was made for Disney. Its "urban American settings" were a Los Angeles mansion and art gallery.

If gangster films are perceived only as serious dramas, it should be noted that a number of Edward G. Robinson's contributions to the genre were comedies. One of the reasons is that the studios (chiefly Warner Bros.) soon saw the value of parody as they continued production. Robinson, who was under contract, had become synonymous with the portrayals and thus seemed destined to continue performing in them.

The Little Giant in 1933 was his first gangland comedy. The story line was about a bored Chicago beer baron, "Bugs" Ahearn, who, after the repeal of Prohibition, tries to go straight by crashing California society.

A Slight Case of Murder also dealt with a post–Prohibition dilemma. Robinson's Remy Marco and his gang try to go straight by marketing a virtually undrinkable beer (which seemed to sell well enough when it was illegal).

Brother Orchid bore the influence of *The Little Giant*, with gangster John Sarto, weary of the stigma of crime, looking for class in all the wrong places and finally finding it in a monastery.

Robinson's humorous slants on the gangster came at the rate of one every two or three years, through *Larceny, Inc.* in 1942. In it, a gang that might go straight after being released from prison finds the temptation to steal too great after setting up business in a luggage store — next to a bank.

The finest of Robinson's gang farces was *The Whole Town's Talking*. The film presented him in two roles — one a meek clerk named Arthur Ferguson Jones, and the other as his double, a vicious gang leader called Killer Mannion. One of the two displaces the other to reach the happy ending.

In the musical comedy *Robin and the 7 Hoods*, Robinson made an unbilled cameo appearance at the beginning, parodying himself. His self-parody was even broader in an earlier musical, *It's a Great Feeling*, in which he appeared as himself, worrying about his tough-guy image.

Robinson's first gangster role was on the Broadway stage, as An Unidentified Man (later identified as gang leader Nick Scarsi) in Bartlett Cormack's *The Racket*. According to Robinson's autobiography *All My Yesterdays*, when the play went on tour, the political climate in Chicago, with Al Capone in residence, prompted the mayor to cancel the play's booking, and so it went to the West Coast. There film producers got their first taste of Edward G. Robinson in what was to become his best-known character type.

On television Robinson was a gangster in the *Ford Theatre* drama "A Set of Values," and a few years later guest-starred on *Robert Taylor's Detectives* in an episode entitled "The Legend of Jim Riva." The following year Robinson narrated a documentary called

"Cops and Robbers," which chronicled, among other things, events in the life of real-life gangster John Dillinger.

On the radio Robinson acted in adaptations of *The Whole Town's Talking*, *The Boss*, *Bullets or Ballots*, *The Criminal Code*, *Kid Galahad*, *Key Largo*, *Blind Alley*, *The Amazing Dr. Clitterhouse*, *The Maltese Falcon*, and original scripts called "The Man Who Thought He Was Edward G. Robinson" and "The Man Who Wanted to Be Edward G. Robinson," in both of which he played dual roles. All involved gangsters. Additionally, the long-running series *Big Town* often dealt with racket-busting and other crime-related stories.

Robinson actually *played* gangsters only about twenty times, less often than he appeared in stories about them.

Films: *The Hole in the Wall*, *The Night Ride*, *Outside the Law*, *The Widow from Chicago*, *Little Caesar*, *Smart Money*, *The Hatchet Man*, *The Little Giant*, *The Whole Town's Talking*, *Barbary Coast*, *Bullets or Ballots*, *Kid Galahad*, *The Last Gangster*, *A Slight Case of Murder*, *The Amazing Dr. Clitterhouse*, *I Am the Law*, *Brother Orchid*, *Unholy Partners*, *Larceny, Inc.*, *Key Largo*, *Vice Squad*, *Black Tuesday*, *The Violent Men*, *Tight Spot*, *A Bullet for Joey*, *Illegal*, *Hell on Frisco Bay*, *Seven Thieves*, *Robin and the 7 Hoods*, *Peking Blonde*, *The Biggest Bundle of Them All*, *Grand Slam*, *Mad Checkmate*, *Operation St. Peter's*, *Never a Dull Moment*. Additional films with gang elements: *East Is West*, *Dark Hazard*, *Confessions of a Nazi Spy*, *The Sea Wolf*, *Tampico*, *House of Strangers*, *It's a Great Feeling*, *The Prize*, *The Cincinnati Kid*. Television: "The Legend of Jim Riva" on *Robert Taylor's Detectives*, "A Set of Values" on *Ford Theatre*, "Cops and Robbers" on *Project Twenty*. Stage: *The Racket*.

Gardner, Jack (1915–55) appears in three films with Edward G. Robinson — *Bullets or Ballots*, *Flesh and Fantasy*, and *The Woman in the Window*. He had roles also in *The Pride of the Yankees* and *The Glass Key*.

Garfield, John (1913–52) stars in *The Sea Wolf* with Edward G. Robinson, and also was on stage with him in *We Will Never Die*, and on the radio in *Hollywood Fights Back* and *The Roosevelt Special*. Among his films are *Four Daughters*, *Out of the Fog*, *Air Force*, *The Postman Always Rings Twice*, *Body and Soul*, and *He Ran All the Way*. He died of a heart attack prompted by the intensity of his battles with the House Un-American Activities Committee. His son, **John Garfield, Jr.**, (1943–94) appears in *Mackenna's Gold*.

Gargan, Edward (1902–1964), character actor brother of William Gargan, appeared with Edward G. Robinson in *The Amazing Dr. Clitterhouse* and *Barbary Coast*. His other films include *Anything Goes*, the *Falcon* series, and *The Princess O'Rourke*.

Garson, Greer (1908–96) was in *Pepe* with Edward G. Robinson, and also appeared on the *45th Academy Awards* broadcast. She won an Oscar for *Mrs. Miniver* and was also nominated for *Goodbye Mr. Chips*, *Blossoms in the Dust*, *Madame Curie*, *Mrs. Parkington*, *The Valley of Decision*, and *Sunrise at Campobello*. Other films include *Pride and Prejudice*, *Random Harvest*, and *Julius Caesar*.

Gaudio, Tony (1885–1951), a cinematographer, came to New York from Rome to head the film labs at Vitagraph studios. He received Oscar nominations for *Hell's Angels*, *The Letter*, *Corvette K-225*, and *A Song to Remember*, and won for *Anthony Adverse* in 1936. Other films: *The Racket*, *The Story of Louis Pasteur*, *The Red Pony*, and seven with Edward G. Robinson — *Little Caesar*, *Tiger Shark*, *The Man with Two Faces*, *Kid Galahad*, *The Amazing Dr. Clitterhouse*, *Brother Orchid*, and *Larceny, Inc.*

Geiger, Milton wrote such dramatic pieces as "This Is It" and "I Will Not Go Back," which Edward G. Robinson performed on television (*Hollywood Palace*, *This Is Tom Jones*) and publicly, as with the United States Air Force Band. He also wrote for the *Screen Directors Playhouse* on radio, adapting *Night Has a Thousand Eyes*, and *Sealtest Variety Theatre*, with a drama called "Sleight of Hand."

General Electric Theatre see "The Drop-Out"

Gering, Marion (1901–77) emigrated from Russia in 1924 to produce, direct, and write for the theater. In Hollywood he directed fourteen films between 1931 and 1938, including *The Devil and the Deep* and *Madame Butterfly.* In England he directed *Thunder in the City*, with Edward G. Robinson.

Getaways Dramatic escapes are staged in several Robinson films—*Little Caesar, Blackmail, Black Tuesday, Vice Squad,* and *Seven Thieves.* In *Key Largo* the gangsters try to escape via cabin cruiser to Cuba.

See **Automobiles**; **Boats and the Sea**.

Gibbons, Cedric (1893–1960) won eleven Oscars in 39 nominations for art direction, for *The Bridge of San Luis Rey, The Merry Widow, Pride and Prejudice, Blossoms in the Dust, Gaslight, The Yearling, Little Women, An American in Paris, The Bad and the Beautiful, Julius Caesar,* and *Somebody Up There Likes Me*. His six films with Edward G. Robinson, all at MGM, were *A Lady to Love, The Last Gangster, Blackmail, Unholy Partners, Our Vines Have Tender Grapes,* and *Big Leaguer.*

Gifford, Frances (1920–94) appeared with Edward G. Robinson in *Our Vines Have Tender Grapes,* as schoolteacher Viola Johnson. She made her first film in 1937, fresh out of high school. Four years later she was the heroine of the *Jungle Girl* serial. She retired from the screen in 1953.

Girardot, Etienne (1856–1939) played Edward G. Robinson's diminutive and lovable boss, Mr. Seaver, in *The Whole Town's Talking.* Making his debut on the London stage in 1883, he came to this country ten years later. His first film was *The Violin of M'sieur* in 1912, and he was subsequently in *The Hunchback of Notre Dame, Clive of India,* and *In Old Kentucky.*

Gish, Dorothy (1898–1968) made her silent film debut in 1912 with her elder sister, Lillian, in D. W. Griffith's *An Uneasy Enemy,* but both already had ten years experience on the stage. Among her films was *The Bright Shawl,* the second of Edward G. Robinson's two silents. She was also in the cast of Samuel Goldwyn's *Fields of Glory* with Robinson, from which he withdrew.

The Glass Web (Film, 1953) Filmed in 3-D, this film's title referred to the new medium of television as a setting for murder and intrigue. Television was fast gaining prominence in America, which threatened movie attendance. A counter-effort by the film industry was to develop wide screen processes such as CinemaScope and to present blockbuster entertainments. Also for a year or two, 3-D (three dimensional), or stereoscopic, cinema was in vogue. *The Glass Web* did double duty in the effort to attract audiences back to theaters, because it was filmed in 3-D, and its story indicted television.

Unfortunately, neither 3-D nor *The Glass Web* was a big success. *The New York Times* called the film "a minor criminal excursion." James Robert Parish, in *The Tough Guys*, called it "a crime story with such an involved plotline that the histrionics were nearly sidetracked." In his *Film Guide* Leslie Halliwell said it was a "boring thriller."

The New York Herald-Tribune said of Robinson's performance that he "meanders through the part of a studio technician...." Nearing age sixty, he strained credibility as a would-be lover of starlet Kathleen Hughes. That he played the villain was a minor consolation.

Producer, Albert J. Cohen; director, Jack Arnold; screenplay, Robert Blees, Leonard Lee; based on the novel by Max S. Ehrlich; art directors, Bernard Herzbrun, Eric Orbom; set, Russell A. Gausman, Ruby R. Levitt; camera, Maury Gertsman; special photography, David S. Horsley; sound, Leslie I. Carey, Robert Pritchard; hairstyles, Joan St. Oegger; gowns, Bill Thomas; makeup, Bud Westmore; editor, Ted J. Kent; music director, Joseph Gershenson; assistant director, Joseph E. Kenny; cast: Edward G. Robinson (Henry Hayes), John Forsythe (Don Newell), Marcia Henderson (Louise Newell), Kathleen Hughes (Paula Ranier), Richard Denning (Dave Markson),

Hugh Sanders (Lt. Stevens), Jean Willes (Sonia), Harry O. Tyler (Jake), Clark Howat (Bob Warren), Paul Dubov (Other man), John Hiestand (Announcer), Bob Nelson (Plainclothesman), Dick Stewart (Everett), Jeri Lou James, Duncan Richardson (Newell children), Jack Kelly (Engineer), Alice Kelley (Waitress), Lance Fuller (Ad lib), Brett Halsey (Lew), Kathleen Freeman (Mrs. O'Halloran), Eve McVeagh (Viv), Beverly Garland (Sally), Jack Lomas (Cliffie), Helen Wallace (Mrs. Doyle), Howard Wright (Weaver), Herbert C. Lytton (Gilbert), James Stone (Weatherby), John Verros (Fred Abbott), Benny Rubin (Tramp comic), Eddie Parker (Tourist), Donald Kerr (Paper man), Tom Greenway (District attorney); Universal-International; 81 minutes; 3-D; November 1953

Henry Hayes, a researcher for the TV show *Crime of the Week*, is jealous of writer Don Newell's success. Both are involved with Paula Ranier, a ruthless starlet who uses them to advance her career. Don had a brief affair with her, and she is blackmailing him. When Paula is murdered, the crime is given a reenactment on the show, despite the fact that the killer is still unknown. Circumstantial evidence seems to implicate Don, but he discovers that the killer is Henry, whose meticulous research for the show includes the actual music, *Temptation*, playing on her apartment phonograph the night she was killed—information only the killer would know. Henry traps Don and his wife, Marcia, in an empty studio and intends to shoot them. Don, however, is able to turn on a camera to show the confrontation on a monitor, which the police see. They move in and Henry is killed.

Gleason, Jackie (1916–87) made his mark as a comedian in *The Honeymooners* on television beginning in 1954. Edward G. Robinson made a guest appearance on the program in 1956. Gleason had an early comic role with Robinson in *Larceny, Inc.* as a soda jerk. He was nominated for a best supporting actor Oscar for a dramatic role in *The Hustler*.

Gleason, James (1886–1959) An actor and writer, his plays *Is Zat So?*, *Mammy*, and *Rain or Shine* later became films. He appeared in *A Free Soul*, *Meet John Doe*, *Tales of Manhattan* (with Edward G. Robinson), *A Guy Named Joe*, *Arsenic and Old Lace*, *A Tree Grows in Brooklyn*, *Suddenly*, and *The Last Hurrah*. He was with Robinson on the radio in *The Roosevelt Special*.

The Goat Song (Theater, 1926) In his third year with the Theatre Guild, Edward G. Robinson appeared in *The Goat Song*, the story of a monster born to a noble household of Europe and kept hidden for years. The monster finally escapes, and the country is quickly overrun in a nightmare of revolt. Robinson considered whether Franz Werfel's sometimes confusing play was meant as a message of Communism or of Christianity, or if, in fact, it might be a prophetic symbol of the rise of Nazism. Public concern resulted in meetings held by the Theatre Guild to clarify the play, but little was resolved.

The New York Times found that, "in spite of excellent exhibitions of acting and a richness of color in the general performance, [it] ... leaves no single purposeful impression on the audience," but added that, "Mr. Robinson is refreshingly amusing as the peddler Jew."

The New Republic concurred, saying, "Robinson does his poignant and grotesque Jewish part uncannily well." *The Nation* said, "The Guild has given the piece a gorgeously beautiful series of settings ... and has entrusted the leading parts to a group of unusually capable actors."

Actress Blanche Yurka, who was a member of the cast, discusses the play and Robinson in her autobiography *Bohemian Girl*, saying *The Goat Song* was "an exciting and deeply moving experience. Appearing briefly as the peddler in the last act, Edward G. Robinson gave one of those richly colored performances which made him, at that time, a real asset to the Guild. Losing him for so many years to the screen was one of the theatre's calamities."

Produced by the Theatre Guild; playwright, Franz Werfel; translation, Ruth Langner; director, Jacob Ben-Ami; cast: Alfred Lunt (Juvan), Lynn Fontanne (Stanja), Edward G. Robinson (Reb Feiwall), Helen Westley (Babka), Zita Johann (Kruna), Harold Clurman (Clerk), Blanche Yurka (Mirko's Mother), Erskine Sanford (Starsina; Priest), Anthony Andre (Elder of Medegya; An Old Man), Bela Blau (Messenger), Edward Fielding (The American), Dwight Frye (Mirko), George Gaul (Gospodar Stevan Milic), William Ingersoll (Gospodar Jevrem Vesilic; Scavenger), House Baker Jameson (Bashi Bazook), Philip Loeb (Elder of Modrygor; Young Servant), Judith Lowry (Stanja's Mother), Albert Bruning (Physician), Lorna McLean (Maid), Frank Reicher (Bogoboj), Martin Wolfson (Innkeeper), Stanley G. Wood (Elder of Krasnokraj), Herbert Yost (Teiterlik); opened at the Guild Theatre, New York; January 25, 1926

In the mid-eighteenth century a deformed infant, half man, half beast, is born to the aristocratic Milic family of rural Serbia. Kept hidden for twenty years, the man-beast escapes, only to be imprisoned by peasants on the verge of revolt. Led by Juvan, the peasants burn and pillage. Naming the man-beast a messenger from the gods, they demand the bride of Milic's youngest son as a sacrifice. The man-beast is killed, but the bride announces that through her the curse will live on for another generation.

Goddard, Paulette (1911–90), Ziegfeld girl and Goldwyn Girl, married Charlie Chaplin and was in his *Modern Times* and *The Great Dictator*. Other roles were in *The Women, Second Chorus, Reap the Wild Wind,* and, with Edward G. Robinson, *Vice Squad*. She was also on the radio with him in *Hollywood Fights Back* and *The Roosevelt Special*. Her other husbands were Burgess Meredith and novelist Erich Maria Remarque.

Goldwyn, Samuel (1882–1974), a legendary film producer, formed a partnership with Jesse L. Lasky and Cecil B. DeMille to produce *The Squaw Man* in 1913 and, later, the Goldwyn company, which eventually became MGM. Separately, Samuel Goldwyn Productions was established in 1923, producing eighty feature films over four decades, including *Street Scene, Dodsworth, Arrowsmith, Barbary Coast* (with Edward G. Robinson), *Dead End, Stella Dallas, The Hurricane, Wuthering Heights, The Little Foxes, Ball of Fire, Pride of the Yankees, The Best Years of Our Lives, A Song Is Born, Guys and Dolls,* and *Porgy and Bess*. Goldwyn also appeared on television with Robinson in *The World's Greatest Showman*, a tribute to DeMille. Robinson worked briefly in Goldwyn's 1921 silent *Fields of Glory* but became dissatisfied and asked out of his contract.

Gomez, Thomas (1905–71) played Curly Hoff, Johnny Rocco's chief henchman in *Key Largo*. He was on the stage before coming to films, which include *Pittsburgh, Ride a Pink Horse* (Oscar nomination), *The Dark Mirror, Trapeze, But Nor for Me,* and *Summer and Smoke*.

"A Good Name" (Television, 1959) Lee Philips plays Edward G. Robinson's son in "A Good Name." He had originated the role of Gena Rowlands' jazz-playing husband in *Middle of the Night* on Broadway three years earlier. As in the play, Robinson is a clothing manufacturer in "A Good Name," but there the similarities end.

When a woman is killed while wearing a dress made of a flammable synthetic fabric, the manufacturers must decide on a course of action. Vincent Harper, as president of the company, decides to track down the dangerous materials. His father, Harry, who founded the firm, wants an immediate recall to prevent further deadly accidents. The matter is settled following confrontation between father and son, and the Harper firm keeps its good name by accepting responsibility.

Producer, Winston O'Keefe; executive producer, William Sackheim; director, Eliot Silverstein; teleplay, Richard Alan Simmons; based on a story by Julian Claman; camera, Fred Jackman; editor, Robert Peterson; set, Milton Stumpf; makeup, Clay Campbell; production assistant, Seymour Friedman; hairstyles, Helen Hunt; assistant director, Donald Gold; cast: Edward G. Robinson (Harry Harper), Lee Philips (Vincent Harper), Parley Baer (Walter Brodsky), Jacqueline Scott (Ann Harper), Carleton Young (Gene Morley), Olan Soule, Glenn Taylor (Board members); *Goodyear Theatre*; NBC-TV; 30 minutes; March 2, 1959

Good Neighbor Sam (Film, 1964) For the first time since the early thirties, Edward G. Robinson was featured in no less than four films in a year. In *Good Neighbor Sam* he teamed with a group of comics in support of Jack Lemmon. Lemmon regretted the commercial simplicity of the film, but it was a hit, ranking ninth among the moneymakers of the year. Robinson's funny performance benefited from being the antithesis of his gangster image. As a modern-day dairy farmer, he discusses raising ducks and quotes from the scriptures, espousing the need for wholesomeness in daily living.

The New York Times called *Good Neighbor Sam* a "swiftly-paced, pleasingly wacky, but loosely assembled farce," and that "aiding in these manufactured frolics [was] Edward G. Robinson, as the rich, Bible-spouting client." *The New Yorker* praised Robinson among "the supporting cast ... of accomplished clowns ... as the fussy client."

A David Swift production; producer-director, David Swift; associate producer, Marvin Miller; screenplay, James Fritzell, Everett Greenbaum, Swift; based on the novel by Jack Finney; production design, Dale Hennesy; assistant director, R. Robert Rosenbaum; set, Ray Moyer; music, Frank DeVol; camera, Burnett Guffey; sound, James Z. Flaster; costumes, Micheline & Jacqueline; makeup, Ben Lane; choreography, Miriam Nelson; script supervisor, Charles J. Rice; editor, Charles Nelson; cast: Jack Lemmon (Sam Bissell), Romy Schneider (Janet Lagerlof), Dorothy Provine (Min Bissell), Edward G. Robinson (Simon Nurdlinger), Michael Connors (Howard Ebbets), Edward Andrews (Mr. Burke), Louis Nye (Reinhold Schiffner), Robert Q. Lewis (Earl), Joyce Jameson (Girl at hotel), Anne Seymour (Irene), Charles Lane (Jack Bailey), Linda Watkins (Edna), Peter Hobbs (Phil Reisner), Tris Coffin (Sonny Blatchford), Neil Hamilton (Larry Boling), Riza Royce (Miss Halverson), William Forrest (Mellner), Bernie Kopell (Taragon), The Hi-Lo's (Themselves), Patrick Waltz (Wyeth), William Bryant (Hausner), Vickie Cos (Jenna), Kym Karath (Ardis), Quinn O'Hara (Marsha), Jan Brooks (Gloria), Peter Camlin (French waiter), Tom Anthony (Assistant director), Bess Flowers (Mrs. Burke), Dave Ketchum (Hertz actor), David Swift (Commercial director), Elsie Baker (Mrs. Nurdlinger), Richard Hale (Mr. Bernier), Gil Lamb (Drunk), Joe Palma (Postman), Harry Ray (Milkman), Zanouba (Belly dancer), Jim Bannon, Barbara Bouchet, Aneta Corsaut, George Savalas, Hal Taggart; Columbia; 130 minutes; Eastman color by Pathe; July 1964

Sam Bissell, an artist for an advertising firm, lives in the San Francisco suburbs with his wife, two small daughters, and their pet duck. He impresses dairy farmer Simon Nurdlinger, an important client of the firm, with his wholesome lifestyle. Nearly all the company executives, including Mr. Burke, its chairman, are exposed by Nurdlinger as slightly less than respectable. Janet Lagerlof, the best friend of Sam's wife, Min, moves in next door to the Bissells. She is immediately visited by lawyers who advise her that she will inherit $15,000,000—provided she is happily married; but Janet is in the process of divorcing her husband. Reluctantly, Sam agrees to pose as her husband in order to fool her snooping relatives. This also fools Nurdlinger, who orders billboards all over town of Sam and Janet as "Mr. and Mrs." to sell his milk and eggs. Janet's real husband shows up, a private eye takes night photos of Sam sneaking across the lawn to Janet's house, and the couple spends a night defacing a dozen billboards with paint before all ends happily.

Goodyear Theatre see **"A Good Name"**

Gorcey, Leo (1915–69) was one of the Dead End kids who came to films when recreating their original stage roles in Samuel Goldwyn's version of the play *Dead End*. With Edward G. Robinson, he plays Sarecky in the Navy drama *Destroyer*. He is also in *Angels with Dirty Faces*.

Gordon, Ruth (1896–1985) was a Broadway star (*A Doll's House, The Matchmaker*) following studies at the American Academy of Dramatic Arts. Screenplays for *A Double Life, Pat and Mike,* and *Adam's Rib,* which she wrote with her husband, Garson Kanin, were nominated for Oscars. Acting in films from the silent era, she was nominated for *Inside Daisy Clover*, then won the supporting actress award for *Rosemary's Baby*. She played Frau Ehrlich to Edward G. Robinson's title role in *Dr. Ehrlich's Magic Bull*et. In her memoir *An Open Book,* she said, "Eddie had seen me in plays, I'd seen him, but we'd never met, we liked each other right away. We had to, I'm apt to speak out…. Rehearsing a scene, Eddie got some words mixed up. 'You're such a big star, why can't you say your line straight?' I asked. The surrounding group tensed, then Eddie laughed, then they laughed, then we all laughed, then we were friends.'"

Grand Slam (Film, 1968) The title refers to a state-of-the-art computer protecting a diamond vault targeted by a gang hand-selected by Edward G. Robinson. In *Grand Slam,* as in the earlier *Seven Thieves* and *The Biggest Bundle of Them All*, he provides a concise, if brief, characterization as the mastermind behind a heist. "As a retired teacher who engineers the caper, [he] smoothly ambles in early and returns for the fadeout," said *The New York Times*. *The New York Daily News* concurred: "Edward G. Robinson … returns as a real mastermind in *Grand Slam* … portraying a mild school teacher."

"A fine, tight script is proof—in this instance at any rate—that five heads are better than one," said *Film Facts* of the picture's multiple screenwriters. "The yarn is synched like a Swiss watch with suspense action rigged to a safe-cracking jewel robbery climaxed by an ingenious ironic twist in the final sequence." And of the fine international cast: "Performances by Robinson, Janet Leigh, Robert Hoffman, Klaus Kinski, Riccardo Cucciolla, and Adolfo Celi are all standout … under [Giuliano] Montaldo's shrewd helming."

A co-production of Jolly Films (Rome) / Coral Productions (Madrid) / Constantine Films (Munich); producers, Harry Colombo, George Papi; director, Giuliano Montaldo; screenplay, Mino Roli, Caminito, Marcello Fondato, Antonio De La Loma, Marcello Coscia; art director, Alberto Boccianti; camera, Antonio Macasoli; set decoration, Juan Albert Soler; music, Ennio Morricone; conductor, Bruno Nicolai; sound, Umberto Picistrelli; editor, Nino Baragli; assistant directors, Mauro Sacripanti, Carlos Luiz Corito, Federico Canudas; cast: Edward G. Robinson (Prof. James Anders), Janet Leigh (Mary Ann), Robert Hoffman (Jean-Paul Audry), Adolfo Celi (Mark Milford), Klaus Kinski (Erich Weiss), George Rigaud (Gregg), Riccardo Cucciolla (Agostino Rossi), Jussara (Stetuaka), Miguel Del Castillo (Manager), Luciana Angiolillo, Valentino Macchi, Aldo Bonamano, Anny Degli Uberti; Paramount; a.k.a. *Ad Ogni Costo;* 120 minutes; Techniscope/Technicolor; February 1968

Professor James Anders has taught at a convent school in Rio de Janeiro for thirty years. He is given a retirement party and, with emotion, leaves the sisters and pupils for New York. He seeks Mark Milford and shows him film of the bank across the street from the convent, where one day a year, like clockwork, a shipment of diamonds is made. He uses Milford's extensive resources to recruit a team of experts. They include a safecracker, a driver, and, most importantly, a gigolo, whose job it is to seduce Mary Ann, the bank president's secretary, in order to get her key to the vault. It is carnival time in Rio. The team works intensely, dismantling the elaborately triggered "Grand Slam 70" computer on the vault. In the course of their escape, the team members are ambushed one by one and killed by the double-crossing Milford, but when he examines the briefcase for the gems, it is empty. Mary Ann meets Anders in Rome with the real briefcase of diamonds. While toasting their success, a thief rides by on a motorcycle and steals the briefcase.

Playboy's review hinted at an adult treatment already prevalent in movies the very year the MPAA ratings were developed (1968): "How to get Janet Leigh out of her stern secretarial eyeglasses and into a warm bed is the mission undertaken by a smooth gigolo (Robert Hoffman) in *Grand Slam*. Seducing Janet, who carries the keys to a vault loaded with ten million dollars worth of diamonds, becomes the trickiest part of a plan devised by a Machiavellian retired history professor (Edward G. Robinson) who has spent thirty dedicated years in a Rio de Janeiro convent casing the diamond company across the street. Several unnerving new faces loom on the horizon among the supporting cast of heavies;

the robbery itself—performed with the very latest gadgets—is as meticulously detailed as a brain operation. Treacherous surprises start popping like firecrackers during the closing scenes, and Rio at carnival time provides a voluptuously scenic background."

Leonard Maltin, in *TV Movies,* commented that *Grand Slam* had "all the trappings. Nothing new, but smoothly done, most enjoyable." And Judith Crist, in *TV Guide,* praised the movie: "With Rio at carnival time in color, Edward G. Robinson superb as a mastermind and Janet Leigh his match and partner … *Grand Slam*, a $10,000,000 heist caper, turns out, if not grand, at least good fun."

Graves, Peter (1925–) made his biggest impact on television in two series, *Fury* and *Mission Impossible.* His films include *Stalag 17, The Court Martial of Billy Mitchell,* and, with Edward G. Robinson, *Black Tuesday* (as a fellow gangster on the lam). He narrates "Little Big Man," the *A&E Biography*, in which he comments, "Edward G. Robinson was an actor whose mannerisms were often imitated but never equaled…. What he did have was superior acting skill. Robinson gave his characters believability and depth…. I enjoyed working with him and learned a great deal. All the time he was on the set I felt that I was kind of learning at the feet of the master. He was superb."

Gray, Billy (1938–) is best known to television audiences as Bud Anderson, the son in *Father Knows Best* (1954–60). He played Edward G. Robinson's son on television in *The Drop-Out* and also had a small role in *U.M.C.* as a student. Other films include *Fighting Father Dunne* and *The Day the Earth Stood Still.*

"The Great Man Votes" On radio Edward G. Robinson appeared in a role originated on film by John Barrymore in 1939, as an alcoholic ex-professor fighting for custody of his children.

Cast: Edward G. Robinson, Edmund Gwenn, Frank McHugh; *Camel's Screen Guild Players*; CBS-radio; April 12, 1948

Green, Alfred E. (1889–1960) directed Edward G. Robinson in five pictures—*Smart Money, Silver Dollar, I Loved a Woman, Dark Hazard,* and *Mr. Winkle Goes to War.* He began as an actor in silent films, directing his first feature in 1917. Other films include *Little Lord Fauntleroy, The Green Goddess, Dangerous, The Gracie Allen Murder Case, The Jolson Story, The Jackie Robinson Story,* and *The Eddie Cantor Story.*

Greene, Jeanne was Edward G. Robinson's leading lady in *The Kibitzer*, playing the part of his daughter, Josie.

Greene, Lorne (1915–87) had a successful thirteen-year run as Ben Cartwright, the father on the *Bonanza* television series, beginning in 1959, and later the outer space series *Battlestar Galactica.* He was the gangster Benjamin Costain in *Tight Spot*, with Edward G. Robinson, and also appears with him on a TV special, *I Am an American.* Other films include *Peyton Place, The Trap,* and *Earthquake.*

Greene, Richard (1918–85) came to Hollywood from England in 1938. He appears in *Operation X* with Edward G. Robinson but is probably best remembered as *Robin Hood* on television from 1955 to 1959. Other films include *Four Men and a Prayer, Kentucky,* and *Forever Amber.*

Grieg, Edvard (1843–1907), a Norwegian composer influenced by Mendelssohn and Schumann, wrote music for Ibsen's play *Peer Gynt.* The film *Song of Norway* (in which Edward G. Robinson plays the fictitious role of a piano seller) is based on Grieg's life (from a long-running Broadway operetta produced in 1944). Grieg's music was used also in the euthanasia scene in *Soylent Green.*

Griffith, William W. (1897–1960) was in four Theatre Guild plays with Edward G. Robinson—as Mr. Five in *The Adding Machine,* Solvieg's father in *Peer Gynt,* an electrician in *The Chief Thing,* and as an Ox driver in *Androcles and the Lion.* He is in the films *Time Out for Romance, Everybody Does It,* and *Devil Goddess.*

Grot, Anton (1884–1974) was art director for eight of Edward G. Robinson's films: *Arms and the Woman, The Widow from Chicago, Little Caesar, Two Seconds, The Hatchet Man, Silver Dollar, A Dispatch from Reuter's,* and *The Sea Wolf*. He received Oscar nominations for *Svengali, Anthony Adverse, The Sea Hawk, The Life of Emile Zola,* and *The Private Lives of Elizabeth and Essex*.

Guest Star see **"The Blue Albatross"**

Guest Stars Edward G. Robinson was a frequent guest star on television. In virtually all of his dramatic appearances he is so credited, with an occasional "and special guest star," as in *U.M.C.* (Guest star billing went to Kim Hunter) and *Robert Taylor's Detectives*.

In films he was billed as a guest star playing himself in *The Stolen Jools, It's a Great Feeling,* and *Pepe,* as did nearly everyone else except Ernie Kovacs, William Demarest, and Jay North (whose characters had other names in *Pepe*), and Errol Flynn (who played Jeffry Bushdinkel in *It's a Great Feeling*). *Good Neighbor Sam, Cheyenne Autumn, Grand Slam,* and *Song of Norway* are other films in which Robinson was billed as a guest star.

See also **Billing**; **Bit parts**; **Dual roles**; **Uncredited appearances**; **Special appearances**.

Guffey, Burnett (1905–83) won cinematography Oscars for *From Here to Eternity* and *Bonnie and Clyde,* with nominations for *The Harder They Fall, Birdman of Alcatraz,* and *King Rat*. Other films include: *All the King's Men, Foreign Correspondent, The Informer,* and, with Edward G. Robinson, *The Violent Men, Tight Spot,* and *Good Neighbor Sam*.

Guilt As one who portrayed so many underworld figures, Edward G. Robinson always seemed guilty of something. But in particular his guilt was a main focus of several of his films. *All My Sons* progresses nearly to its conclusion before he recognizes his culpability, not only in the death of twenty-one Air Force pilots, but even in his son's suicide. In *Scarlet Street* he is hounded by the voices of Joan Bennett and Dan Duryea (he had stabbed her to death and allowed him to go to the chair innocent of her murder). Robinson and Bennett try to cover up the death of her lover for much of *The Woman in the Window*.

Robinson's character experiences mental collapse because of his guilt in *Two Seconds* and *The Red House*. The cause is the death of his buddy, Preston Foster, in the former, and his murder of his ward's parents years earlier in the latter. Onstage in *The Adding Machine,* his character, Shrdlu, was obsessed with guilt over murdering his mother, unable to comprehend his existence in the hereafter.

Other films where Robinson's character is guilt-ridden include *Smart Money* (the manslaughter death of James Cagney); *Five Star Final* (raking up a twenty-year-old crime that results in two suicides); and *Soylent Green,* wherein he laments not having done enough to save the world against ecological problems of the future. He was innocent of a robbery, attempting to clear his name, in *Blackmail,* and was the good guy on the trail of the guilty in *Nightmare, Illegal, A Bullet for Joey, The Stranger, Double Indemnity, Tampico, Confessions of a Nazi Spy, I Am the Law, Bullets or Ballots, The Man with Two Faces,* and *The Hatchet Man*.

Gulf Screen Guild Theatre see **"The Amazing Dr. Clitterhouse"**; **"Blind Alley"**

Gulf's We the People (Radio, 1947) Cast: Edward G. Robinson; NBC-radio; November 25, 1947

Haade, William (1903–66) appeared in three films with Edward G. Robinson and Humphrey Bogart — as the boxer Chuck McGraw in *Kid Galahad,* gangster Ralph Feeney in *Key Largo,* and a cop in *The Amazing Dr. Clitterhouse*. He also appeared with Robinson as a cop in *Night Has a Thousand Eyes*. Other films include *Pittsburgh* and *Union Pacific*.

Haas, Robert M. (1889–1962), art director for five of Edward G. Robinson's films (*Smart Money, Silver Dollar, Dark Hazard, I Loved a Woman,* and *The Little Giant*), was an Oscar nominee for *Life with Father* and *Johnny Belinda*. His other films include *The Story of Louis Pasteur, Jezebel, Dark Victory,* and *The Man Who Came to Dinner.*

Hale, Alan (1892–1950), a big Irishman who appeared in Errol Flynn films (*The Adventures of Robin Hood,* as Little John, *Gentleman Jim, Dodge City, The Sea Hawk*), was with Edward G. Robinson in *Manpower,* playing the role of Jumbo. He is also in *Desperate Journey* and *Stella Dallas*. His lookalike son, Alan Hale, Jr., was the Skipper on *Gilligan's Island*.

Hale, Louise Closser (1872–1933) made her Broadway debut in 1903, appearing in *Candida* and, later, *The Blue Bird*; with Edward G. Robinson, she acted in *Peer Gynt* for the Theatre Guild. They were reunited in *The Hole in the Wall*. She went on to play in *Platinum Blonde, Rasputin and the Empress,* and *Dinner at Eight,* among others.

Hall, Porter (1883–1953) came to Hollywood via Broadway, having appeared in *Peer Gynt* with Edward G. Robinson. He was in *Double Indemnity* as Mr. Jackson and *Vice Squad* as Mr. Hartrampf, also with Robinson, and *The Story of Louis Pasteur, Mr. Smith Goes to Washington, The Plainsman,* and *Ace in the Hole*. He was a Presbyterian deacon.

Hall, Thurston (1883–1958) played Grant, an attorney patient of *The Amazing Dr. Clitterhouse* (Edward G. Robinson) who defends him on murder charges. He went from the New York stage to silent films (Antony in *Cleopatra*), and was also in *The Great McGinty, Brewster's Millions, The Hard Way,* and *The Farmer's Daughter,* and played an ongoing role on TV's *Topper*.

Halton, Charles (1876–1959) was a character actor who specialized in playing fussy little men. He appeared with Edward G. Robinson five times—in the films *I Am the Law, Dr. Ehrlich's Magic Bullet, Unholy Partners,* and *Flesh and Fantasy,* and on the Broadway stage in *Peer Gynt.*

Hamilton, George (1939–) played a juvenile in his early films, including Davie Drew, a young actor in *Two Weeks in Another Town,* with Edward G. Robinson. Other films include *Crime and Punishment USA, By Love Possessed, Act One, The Power, Zorro the Gay Blade,* and *The Godfather Part III.*

Hamilton, John (1886–1958), familiar as Perry White, editor of *The Daily Planet* on TV's *Superman,* appeared with Edward G. Robinson in *Dr. Ehrlich's Magic Bullet* (as his attorney) and *Confessions of a Nazi Spy* (as the judge). Other films include *The Maltese Falcon* and *On the Waterfront.*

Hamilton, Margaret (1902–85) was the Wicked Witch of the West in *The Wizard of Oz,* a role she repeated in several stage productions. With Edward G. Robinson, she is Mrs. Cagle in *A Slight Case of Murder.* Other films include *My Little Chickadee, State of the Union,* and *Brewster McCloud.*

Hamilton, Neil (1899–1984) was Commissioner Gordon on TV's *Batman,* a show on which Edward G. Robinson made a cameo appearance as himself. Among Hamilton's films are *The Kibitzer,* based on the play by Robinson and Jo Swerling, *The Widow from Chicago, Good Neighbor Sam,* the silents *Beau Geste* and *The Great Gatsby,* and *The Dawn Patrol* and *Madame X.*

Hammer, Armand (1898–1991), industrialist, philanthropist, and art collector, purchased Edward G. Robinson's art collection in April, 1973, for more than $5 million through the Knoedler Gallery in New York. During that time he also signed a multi-billion-dollar barter agreement with the Soviet Union. A pioneer in American-Soviet relations, he deployed a mobile hospital to fight that country's typhus epidemic and famine in 1921 and initiated the trade of American wheat for

Russian furs and caviar. He bought art, including a Faberge Easter Egg of Czar Nicholas II. Pencils, pharmaceuticals, cattle, whiskey, broadcasting, and oil (he was board chairman of the Occidental Petroleum Company) were among his empires. He held a degree from Columbia medical school.

Hanlon, Bert (1895–1972) plays comic underworld roles in two films with Edward G. Robinson — *The Amazing Dr. Clitterhouse* (as Pal) and *A Slight Case of Murder* (as Sad Sam). He is also in *Boy Meets Girl, Society Girl,* and *The Roaring Twenties.*

Hanson, Peter (1922–) is in several 1950s films with Edward G. Robinson, as policemen in *Hell on Frisco Bay* and *A Bullet for Joey,* a drunken suitor in *The Violent Men,* and in *The Ten Commandments.* He also appears in *When Worlds Collide, Three Violent People,* and *Harlow.*

Happy Days (Television, 1970) This musical variety show was a summer replacement series during the 1970 television season. Participants: Alan Copeland, Bob Elliott, Ray Goulding, Chuck McCann, Julie McWherter, Louis Nye, Edward G. Robinson (Guest); June– August 1970

Hardwicke, Sir Cedric (1883–1964) was the Broadway stage's *The Amazing Dr. Clitterhouse* (later filmed by Edward G. Robinson); the two shared no scenes in *The Ten Commandments.* Knighted in 1934, Hardwicke was also in *On Borrowed Time, The Hunchback of Notre Dame, The Lodger, I Remember Mama, A Connecticut Yankee in King Arthur's Court,* and *Richard III.*

Hare, Lumsden (1875–1964), an Irishman, was in *Arms and the Woman* and *A Dispatch from Reuter's* (both with Edward G. Robinson), *The Lives of a Bengal Lancer, The Little Minister, Rebecca, Suspicion, The Charge of the Light Brigade, The White Cliffs of Dover,* and *Count Your Blessings.*

Harolde, Ralf (1899–1974) appeared with Edward G. Robinson in *Smart Money* as gambler Sleepy Sam, and in *The Sea Wolf* as a crooked agent getting sailors to ship on *The Ghost.* His other films include *A Tale of Two Cities, Farewell My Lovely,* and *Alaska Patrol.*

Harris, Sam (1872–1941) was the producer, with George M. Cohan, of *The Little Teacher,* with Edward G. Robinson. His other credits include *Animal Crackers, Of Thee I Sing, Dinner at Eight, Stage Door, You Can't Take It with You, Of Mice and Men, The Man Who Came to Dinner, George Washington Slept Here,* and *Lady in the Dark.* He should not be confused with actor **Major Sam Harris** (1877–1969), who is onscreen with Robinson in *Night Has a Thousand Eyes* and *Cheyenne Autumn* and is also in *Meet Me in St. Louis* and *Hatari.*

Harvey, Laurence (1928–1973) They shared no scenes in *The Outrage,* but Harvey appeared on the 1973 telecast during which the posthumous Oscar went to Edward G. Robinson — and died of cancer eight months later. Nominated for *Room at the Top,* Harvey's other films include *The Alamo, The Manchurian Candidate,* and *The Magic Christian.*

Harvey, Paul (1884–1955) Blustery, often comic, he was with Edward G. Robinson in *The Whole Town's Talking* as J. J. Carpenter, and as Mr. Whitewood, future in-law, in *A Slight Case of Murder.* There were also serious roles in *The Ten Commandments* and *Dr. Ehrlich's Magic Bullet.* He should not to be confused with the radio commentator of the same name.

The Hatchet Man (Film, 1932) Edward G. Robinson called his twelfth film, *The Hatchet Man,* "horrible" in his memoirs. It was his third time in two years appearing in Oriental makeup, and his first of two films opposite Loretta Young. Robinson's wife, Gladys Lloyd, had a small role.

Reviews seconded Robinson's assessment of the film. *The New York Times* said he was "a better barber, gambler, gangster and tabloid writer than he is a Chinese hatchet man." A follow-up commentary in *The Sunday New*

York Times was kinder: "Mr. Robinson's acting is of high order, but his intonation and general manner of talking seem rather far from the Oriental."

James Robert Parish, in *The Tough Guys,* called the film "a heavy tale of Chinatown tong wars in San Francisco.... Rumanian Jew Robinson as Oriental Wong Low Get is an entertaining sight, though he carries off the masquerade far better than a still unpolished Loretta Young."

Wong Low Get is the honorable hatchet man, or paid assassin, for the Lem Sing Tong. He is obliged to follow an order to kill his best friend, Sun Yat Ming, because the latter has murdered a Tong member. Wong is given custody of Sun's daughter, Toya, and promises to marry her. Several years pass, and the Tong's ancient ways modify to twentieth-century San Francisco. Toya, now grown, marries Wong. The Tong regroups to fight racketeering and wants to declare war. Wong convinces the members that negotiations might be more effective, but young bodyguards are brought in to protect all the members. Harry En Hai, who is acquainted with Toya, becomes Wong's bodyguard. While Wong is away on Tong business, Harry and Toya fall in love. Returning and discovering the two, Wong banishes them. He is shunned for not killing his wife's lover. He gives up his business interests and becomes a farmer. Learning that Harry has been deported and Toya is now enslaved at a teahouse in China, Wong goes to find them. He takes Toya away after Harry is killed by his hatchet.

Producer, Hal B. Wallis; director, William A. Wellman; screenplay, J. Grubb Alexander; based on the play *The Honorable Mr. Wong* by Achmed Abdullah and David Belasco; camera, Sid Hickox; art director, Anton Grot; gowns, Earl Luick; editor, Owen Marks; music, Leo F. Forbstein; cast: Edward G. Robinson (Wong Low Get), Loretta Young (Toya San), Leslie Fenton (Harry En Hai), Dudley Digges (Nag Hong Fa), Edmund Breese (Yu Chang), Tully Marshall (Long Sen Yat), Noel Madison (Charley Kee), Blanche Frederici (Madame Si-Si), J. Carroll Naish (Sun Yat Ming), Toshia Mori (Miss Ling), Charles Middleton (Li Hop Fat), Ralph Ince (Malone), Otto Yamaoka (Chung Ho), Evelyn Selbie (Wah Li), E. Allyn Warren (Soo Lat), Eddie Piel (Foo Ming), Willie Fung (Fung Loo), Gladys Lloyd (Fan Yi), Anna Chang (Sing girl), James Leong (Tong member), Mike Morita; First National–Vitaphone; 74 minutes; February 1932

Hathaway, Henry (1898–1985) acted in silents prior to directing his first film, a western. Others include *The Trail of the Lonesome Pine, Johnny Apollo, The Shepherd of the Hills, Niagara,* and *Kiss of Death,* plus such numbered titles as *The House on 92nd Street, 13 Rue Madeleine, Call Northside 777, Fourteen Hours, 23 Paces to Baker Street, Seven Thieves* (with Edward G. Robinson), and *Five Card Stud.*

Havoc, June (1916–) was on the radio with Edward G. Robinson in *Hollywood Fights Back* and in an adaptation of *House of Strangers* on *Screen Directors Playhouse.* She is Baby June of the *Gypsy* legend, sister of Gypsy Rose Lee. She appears in *My Sister Eileen* and *Gentleman's Agreement.*

Hawks, Howard (1896–1977) directed Edward G. Robinson in *Tiger Shark* and *Barbary Coast.* He wrote and directed comedy shorts in 1922 and continued his career through 1970. Among his classics are *Scarface, Twentieth Century, Only Angels Have Wings, His Girl Friday, Bringing Up Baby, Ball of Fire, Air Force, To Have and Have Not, The Big Sleep, Gentlemen Prefer Blondes, Monkey Business, Red River,* and *Rio Bravo.*

Hayden, Harry (1882–1955) appeared in three films with Edward G. Robinson — *Larceny, Inc.* (as a member of the Salvation Army), *Tales of Manhattan* (as lawyer Soupy Davis), and *The Woman in the Window* (as a druggist). Other films include *Hail the Conquering Hero* and *The Killers.* He was married to actress **Lela Bliss** (1896–1980), who appears in *Pepe,* among many other films.

Hayward, Susan (1918–75) starred with Edward G. Robinson in *House of Strangers* and had a bit role in *The Amazing Dr. Clitterhouse*. They appeared together also on radio on *The Roosevelt Special*. Oscar nominated for *Smash Up — The Story of a Woman*, *My Foolish Heart*, *With a Song in My Heart*, and *I'll Cry Tomorrow*, she won for *I Want to Live!* She was married to Jess Barker (*Scarlet Street*).

Hayworth, Rita (1918–87) and Edward G. Robinson were in separate episodes of *Tales of Manhattan*. She was on CBS-radio's *Network of the Americas* and *The Roosevelt Special* with him, and also on the *45th Academy Awards* telecast. Her films include *Only Angels Have Wings*, *The Strawberry Blonde*, *Gilda*, *The Lady from Shanghai*, *Pal Joey*, and *Separate Tables*. She was married to Orson Welles.

Hearst, William Randolph (1863–1951), American journalist and publisher, founded and/or owned a chain of newspapers and magazines that included the *Boston American*, *Chicago Herald*, *New York American*, *Washington Times*, *Good Housekeeping*, and *Harper's Bazaar*. His sensational treatments of crime and scare headlines sold papers but unfavorably linked him to "yellow journalism." His personal fortunes were reflected in his massive estate at San Simeon. As a motion picture producer in the 1920s and 1930s, he promoted Marion Davies (1897–1961) to stardom. Their life together was thinly disguised in Orson Welles' *Citizen Kane*.

It was Hearst's second New York mayoral race in 1909 that connected him to Edward G. Robinson. His attacks against the political establishment made the publisher a hero to an eleven-year-old elocutionist and future actor. By age sixteen Robinson was stumping publicly against machine politics, with the result that the Committee to Elect William Randolph Hearst invited him to do so officially on Eighth Avenue.

In 1947, during difficulties with the House Un-American Activities Committee and its investigations into alleged Communist ties, Robinson was invited to speak at Chicago Stadium at "I Am an American Day," a program sponsored by the *Chicago Herald-American*, a Hearst paper. He received a telegram canceling the invitation, saying he was unacceptable. A letter from Robinson to Hearst that recalled their relationship from forty years earlier resulted in Robinson's being invited once again to speak at the function — to a rave review from the paper: "Your message touched the hearts of everyone...."

Heart Attack Edward G. Robinson suffered a heart attack in Africa during the filming of *A Boy Ten Feet Tall*. A Reuters news story from Nairobi in June 1962 reported that the attack occurred during the night, following location shooting in the foothills of Mt. Kilimanjaro near the Kenya-Tanganyika border. "He was driven to a nursing home at Arusha, Tanganyika, thirty miles away, and examined by a specialist [who] recommended his removal to [Princess Elizabeth Hospital]." The danger of the 9,000–foot altitude of Nairobi prompted doctors to have the ailing Robinson flown to London for treatment and recuperation. Sir Winston Churchill was hospitalized there at the same time, and the two celebrities exchanged cigars!

Coincidentally, Robinson's appearance onscreen in *Two Weeks in Another Town* was playing in theaters shortly afterwards. In it his character suffers a heart attack. His characters in both *Silver Dollar* and *Seven Thieves* die of a heart attack. In *U.M.C.* his character, a heart surgeon, receives a transplant after suffering a heart attack.

As a warning to actors, particularly on the stage, always to check their props, Edward G. Robinson tells of a performance of *The Racket* when his character, notorious gangster Nick Scarsi, was to be gunned down at the play's climax. The actor playing the cop who was to shoot him had failed to check for blanks in the gun; it wouldn't fire. Robinson improvised by having Scarsi drop dead of heart failure!

Edward G. Robinson posed for a magazine ad for Stair-Glide, with the selling phrase, "Save Your Heart." Unfortunately, the ad was published several months after his death.

The Heart of Show Business (Short film, 1957) This short film was produced by Variety Clubs International. Director, Ralph

Staub; Harry Belafonte, Edgar Bergen & Charlie McCarthy, Victor Borge, Cantinflas, Maurice Chevalier, Jimmy Durante, Lena Horne, Art Linkletter, Sophie Tucker (participants); Bing Crosby, Burt Lancaster, Cecil B. DeMille, Bob Hope, Edward G. Robinson, and James Stewart (narrators); 1957

Hecht, Ben (1893–1964) His play *The Front Page* was filmed several times. Film credits include *Underworld* and *The Scoundrel* (writing Oscars); *Viva Villa, Wuthering Heights, Angels Over Broadway,* and *Notorious* (nominations); *Gunga Din, Spellbound,* and *Miracle in the Rain* (from his novel). He had been press agent for *The Firebrand,* and again worked with Edward G. Robinson writing *Barbary Coast* (with Charles MacArthur), an episode of *Tales of Manhattan, Actors and Sin* (which he also produced and directed), and the stage pageant *We Will Never Die.* For the opening of the United Nations in April 1944 he wrote a radio play in which Robinson appeared on the Mutual Network.

Heflin, Van (1910–71), an Oscar winner for *Johnny Eager,* was on the radio with Edward G. Robinson in *Hollywood Fights Back* and *Document A/777.* Onstage he was in *The Philadelphia Story* and *A View from the Bridge.* Films include *The Strange Love of Martha Ivers, Shane, Patterns, 3:10 to Yuma,* and *Airport.*

Hell on Frisco Bay (Film, 1956) "The Robinson of the prime years surfaced ... the Robinson of *Little Caesar,* older by 25 years, but excitingly alive in a meaty, incisive role, spiced with sharp dialogue, sardonic wit, and the perfect opportunity—with one snarl wrapped behind him—to act rings around the entire cast. And Edward G. Robinson was never one to let a good role slip by unmolded." This was an assessment of *Hell on Frisco Bay* by James Robert Parish and Alvin H. Marill in their book *The Cinema of Edward G. Robinson.* Robinson had made "B" films for five years or more during the aftermath of the House Un-American Activities Committee investigations, and *Hell on Frisco Bay* came at the end of this period. Virtually all the reviews of Robinson's performance were as good as the foregoing, even if those of the film itself were mixed. "[He] is tops as a ruthless gangster," said the *New York Post.*

The New York Times praised him: "Thanks to Edward G. Robinson, who wears his role as snugly as he wears his shoes, and to some sardonic dialogue written for him by Martin Rackin and Sydney Boehm ... *Hell on Frisco Bay* is two or three cuts above the quality of the run of pictures in this hackneyed genre.... Cut to Mr. Robinson (in his role as Mr. Big), the ruthless killer of the San Francisco wharfs, and slowly this routine, senseless fable takes on a little flash and style.... Every time Mr. Robinson slouches upon the scene, gnawing cigars and slobbering cynicisms, it is amusing, interesting—and good."

In reviewing Robinson's career for the *Pyramid Illustrated History of the Movies,* Foster Hirsch found him "as surly and ornery as ever ... [in] a role that was as meaty as some of his best parts.... He has some wonderfully nasty dialogue.... 'You're nothing but a broken-down has-been broad,' he snarls at [Fay Wray]. 'Get out of here, you filthy peasant,' the woman rejoins. 'A slob like you, calling me names,' Robinson spits out at her, 'a washed up dame in love with a guy with a twisted face!' Alan Ladd was the hero, but it was Robinson's movie."

"[In it,] it is Robinson who reigns supreme," wrote *The New York Herald-Tribune.* "Even after all these years he is a fascinating boss, in his pearl gray homburg and gray silk vest, glaring out of settled eyes at a man he is soon to kill, flicking the ashes of an expensive cigar nonchalantly on the rug. His commands are edged with a sardonic wit, and he is quick to give a girl the back of his hand if she spurns his silky advance. This is the old meanie at the top of his form, relishing every black minute of his role."

Steve Rollins, a former cop, is released after serving five years in prison. Framed for murder by Victor Amato, a gang lord who runs the San Francisco docks, Rollins is intent on clearing himself. He rejects help from his former partner, Dan Bianco, and from his wife,

Marcia, who has been unfaithful to him. Pawns in the game of survival as Rollins closes in on Amato include Lou Fiaschetti, an aging gang lord who is found murdered; Hammy, a muscleman who is no match for Rollins; Mario, Amato's nephew, who proves unreliable and must be eliminated; and Joe Lye, Amato's lieutenant, who had been saved from the deathhouse. Kay Stanley, a former film actress who is now dating Joe, overhears Amato's order that Mario be killed and thus becomes a key witness to help Rollins. Amato briefly holds Marcia hostage and then tries to escape in a speedboat. Rollins dives into the bay and climbs aboard the boat, and during the fight that ensues, both men are pitched overboard as the boat crashes into the dock in flames. Amato is arrested and Rollins is reunited with Marcia.

"The resident devil is Edward G. Robinson, a sort of menace emeritus who is invited by Alan Ladd, a cop he once framed, to retire from the daily grind to a peaceful chair at San Quentin. Eddie replies at some length: 'Oh ya-a-a-a-a?'"— *Time*

A Jaguar Production; associate producer, George Bertholon; director, Frank Tuttle; screenplay, Sydney Boehm, Martin Rackin; based on a novel by William P. McGivern; art director, John Beckman; set decoration, William L. Kuehl; music, Max Steiner; orchestra, Murray Cutter; sound, Charles B. Lang; camera, John Seitz; makeup, Gordon Bau; costumes, Moss Mabry; editor, Folmar Blangsted; assistant director, William Kissel; cast: Alan Ladd (Steve Rollins), Edward G. Robinson (Victor Amato), Joanne Dru (Marcia Rollins), William Demarest (Dan Bianco), Paul Stewart (Joe Lye), Fay Wray (Kay Stanley), Perry Lopez (Mario Amato), Renata Vanni (Anna Amato), Nestor Paiva (Lou Fiaschetti), Stanley Adams (Hammy), Willis Bouchey (Lt. Neville), Peter Hanson (Connors), Jayne Mansfield (Blonde), Tina Carver (Bessie), Rodney Taylor (Brody Evans), Anthony Caruso (Sebastian Pasmonik), Peter Votrian (George Pasmonik), George J. Lewis (Father LaRocca), Herb Vigran (Waiter), Mae Marsh (Landlady), Frank Hagney; Warner Bros.; CinemaScope, WarnerColor; 98 minutes; February 1956

Helton, Percy (1894–1971), equally humorous or sinister, was in *Vice Squad*, with Edward G. Robinson, as Mr. Jenner. His other films include *Miracle on 34th Street, The Robe, The Set Up, Call Me Madam, Butch Cassidy and the Sundance Kid,* and *Hush Hush Sweet Charlotte.*

Henreid, Paul (1908–92) was with Edward G. Robinson on the radio in *Hollywood Fights Back;* and for television he directed *The Mary Tree.* An Austrian émigré, his films include *Now Voyager, Casablanca* and *Song of Love* as actor, and *A Woman's Devotion* and *Dead Ringer* as director.

Henry, Behave (Theater, 1926) Of the five Broadway plays in which Edward G. Robinson appeared in 1926, the only one not produced by the Theatre Guild was the comedy *Henry, Behave*. However, it was written by Lawrence Langner, one of the Guild founders. Robinson did the play between Guild engagements, but he was unimpressed with it. His wife-to-be, Gladys Lloyd, appeared in it with him, which Robinson considered a redeeming factor.

Calling it "a farce comedy which is based on an intrinsically funny idea," the review in *The New York Times* was positive. "The honors of the play go to ... Robinson, who ... donate[s] a flawless portrayal of the smug, oleaginous vice president of the realty company."

Producer-director, Gustav Blum; playwright, Lawrence Langner; cast: John Cumberland (Henry Wilton), Edward G. Robinson (Westcott P. Bennett), Pat O'Brien (Anthony Alexander), Elisha Cook, Jr. (Dick Wilton), Gladys Lloyd (Evelyn Hollis), Walton Butterfield (Clement Courtney), Charlyne Courtland (Lavinia Courtney), Charles DeBevoise (Archibald Musgrove), Gail DeHart (Blanche Wilton), Waldo Edwards (Arthur Courtney), Violet Hill (Susan), Lorraine Lally (Beatrice Beamish), Beresford Lovett (Alton B. Stevens), James Newcombe (Frank Adair), Darrel Starnes (Policeman), Mary Walsh (Geraldine Tussant), Justine Wayne (Kate Wilton), Carrie Weller (Mrs. Huxley), Irene Young (Adelaide Musgrove), Jacob Zollinger (George);

opened at the Nora Bayes Theatre, New York; August 23, 1926

When Henry Wilton, a Long Island realtor, is hit by a taxi, he loses his memory. He plays around with the girls and gets drunk with the boys. No longer strict with his grown children or intolerant about free living, his life has changed. He even runs for Congress.

Hepburn, Katharine (1909–) appeared with Edward G. Robinson in *The American Creed*, and they also were on the *Ed Sullivan Show* together. Serving on the Committee for the First Amendment, she was one of the signers of a document drafted by Hollywood stars in reaction to the House Committee on Un-American Activities witch hunt. "Secure in her Yankee roots, [she] told more vulnerable colleagues like Edward G. Robinson who were of immigrant stock to let her handle the tough assignments. 'I said to Eddie: 'Don't! You let *me* do it because — God! I'm practically the American flag! They can't say *anything*!'" — quoted in *Bogart*, by A. M. Sperber and Eric Lax. Her unprecedented four best actress Oscars are for *Morning Glory, Guess Who's Coming to Dinner, The Lion in Winter,* and *On Golden Pond*. She received eight other nominations: *Alice Adams, The Philadelphia Story, The African Queen, Summertime, The Rainmaker, Suddenly Last Summer,* and *Long Day's Journey Into Night*. She was also in *A Bill of Divorcement, Little Women, Bringing Up Baby,* and, with Spencer Tracy, *Adam's Rib, Pat and Mike,* and *The Desk Set*.

Here Come the Stars (Television, 1968) Robinson was a guest on this television variety show. Participants: Jack Benny, Pat Boone, George Burns, George Jessel, Della Reese, Edward G. Robinson, Roberta Sherwood; September 15, l968

Here's Hollywood (Television, 1961) Edward G. Robinson was interviewed at his Rexford Drive home in Beverly Hills for this program, which aired daily in the late afternoon. Helen O'Connell (Hostess); Edward G. Robinson; NBC-TV, 1961

"Heritage" (Television, 1959) Within one month's time during 1959, Edward G. Robinson made two half-hour dramatic appearances on television — on *Goodyear Theatre* in March, and *Zane Grey Theatre* in April. The title of the *Zane Grey* episode is sometimes incorrectly listed as "Loyalty," and, doubtless for publicity purposes, Edward G. Robinson, Jr., is identified as the actor playing Robinson's son. Robinson Jr. *does* appear in the episode as a rebel soldier, but it is Robert Blake who plays Robinson's son.

A Four-Star Production; producer, Hal Hudson; production executive, Frank Baur; director, David Lowell Rich; teleplay, Christopher Knopf; editor, Charles E. Burke; assistant producer, Dorothy Brogan; sound effects, Norval Crutcher, Jr.; music, Earl Dearth; assistant director, William Dalio Faralla; set, Budd S. Friend; wardrobe, Robert B. Harris; story editor, Nina Laemmle; sound, Donald McKay; art director, Bill Ross; makeup, Robert J. Schiffer; production manager, Jack Sonntag; cast: Edward G. Robinson (Victor Bers), Robert Blake (Michael Bers), John Hackett (Lieutenant), Edward G. Robinson, Jr. (Hunt), Dan Barton, Lew Gallo, Quentin Sondergaard, George Wallace; Dick Powell (Host); *Zane Grey Theatre*; CBS; 30 minutes; April 2, 1959.

Heston, Charlton (1923–) He won the best actor Oscar for his portrayal of *Ben-Hur* in 1959 and is known for his portrayal of Moses in DeMille's *The Ten Commandments*, the first of two films he made with Edward G. Robinson. The second, *Soylent Green,* was Robinson's final film. "Eddie Robinson's a lovely actor to work with," commented Heston in *The Actor's Life, Journals 1956–1976*. "The chemistry between us is good…. The film is very good, not least because of Eddie Robinson's performance. He knew while we were shooting, though we did not, that he was terminally ill. He never missed an hour of work, nor was late to a call. He never was less than the consummate professional he had been all his life. I'm still haunted, though, by the knowledge that the very last scene he played in the picture, which he knew was the last day's acting he would ever do, was his death scene. I know now why I was so overwhelmingly moved playing it with him." In a later autobiography, *In the Arena*, Heston commented further: "I think the central reason why people turned out in such multitudes to see the film was Eddie Robinson.... He sat in a chair on the sound stage all day, seldom going back to his trailer, talking to the other actors, the crew people.... I think he wanted to feel the banter behind the cameras once more too, not just the work." Heston reiterated his comments in October 2000, speaking at the dedication of a 33-cent stamp honoring Robinson in the U. S. Postal Service's "Legends of Hollywood" series.

An earlier project for the two actors was to have been *Planet of the Apes* (1968), for which they filmed a six-minute screen test. Heston thought Robinson "seemed a likely final casting for Zaius, the arrogant orangutan.... He endured the two-and-a-half-hour makeup the role required, and performed wonderfully in the test we shot.... Then Eddie opted out of the project. 'It's a good part, but that makeup is a bitch. My heart's just about gone to hell as it is; I couldn't stand it.'" Robinson was replaced by Maurice Evans.

At Edward G. Robinson's funeral in 1973, Heston delivered the eulogy, which included Antony's speech over the fallen body of Brutus from the last scene of Shakespeare's *Julius Caesar*: "His life was gentle; and the elements / so mix'd in him that nature might stand up / and say to all the world, *This was a man!*" On Oscar night, March 27, 1973, Charlton Heston presented Robinson's posthumous lifetime achievement statuette to his widow, Jane. Scheduled as one of the hosts for the telecast, Heston had a flat tire on the freeway, while Clint Eastwood nervously substituted for him for the first forty minutes of the live program.

Heston and Robinson also appeared as television narrators of *The World's Greatest Showman*, a special about director Cecil B. DeMille, and *All About People*, a documentary about the Jewish Federation. Heston's other films include *The Greatest Show on Earth, Touch of Evil, The Agony and the Ecstasy,* *Will Penny, The Omega Man, Earthquake, True Lies,* and *Any Given Sunday.*

Heydt, Louis Jean (1905–60) played a murder victim, Butler, in *I Am the Law*. Dr. Kunze in *Dr. Ehrlich's Magic Bullet,* and Mr. Hanson in *Our Vines Have Tender Grapes* all with Edward G. Robinson. He is also in *Make Way for Tomorrow, Test Pilot, Each Dawn I Die, Gone with the Wind, Thirty Seconds Over Tokyo, The Big Sleep,* and *The Furies.*

Hickox, Sid (1895–1982) was a cinematographer at Warner Bros. from the silent era, and later for television. His films with Edward G. Robinson were *The Hatchet Man, The Little Giant,* and *A Slight Case of Murder.* Others include *A Bill of Divorcement, Gentleman Jim, The Horn Blows at Midnight, To Have and Have Not, The Big Sleep, White Heat,* and *Them.*

Hicks, Russell (1895–1957) played J. J. Hogarth, Edward G. Robinson's boss, in *Scarlet Street*. He is also onscreen in *Follow the Fleet, Kentucky, The Story of Alexander Graham Bell, Virginia City, The Bank Dick, The Great Lie, The Sea of Grass,* and *Samson and Delilah.*

The High Holy Days (Television, 1970) Edward G. Robinson narrated a television program that discussed the meaning of such Jewish holidays as Yom Kippur and Rosh Hashonah, and the commitment of Jews and their community.

Sponsored by the Jewish Federation-Council of Los Angeles, Brian Goldsmith, president; script, Baruch J. Cohon and Sheldon I. Altfield; director, Altfield; Edward G. Robinson (Narrator); Dr. Will Kramer, Cantor Baruch J. Cohon (Participants); NBC-TV, October 3, 1970

Hill, Al (1892–1954) is in ten films with Edward G. Robinson, usually playing dimwitted tough guys: *The Widow from Chicago, Little Caesar, The Little Giant, The Whole Town's Talking, Bullets or Ballots, The Last Gangster, A Slight Case of Murder, Kid Galahad, Unholy Partners,* and *Destroyer.* Among his other films, from 1927, are *The Last Mile, Ten Cents a Dance, San Quentin,* and *The Big Shot.*

Hinds, Samuel S. (1875–1948) He plays Edward G. Robinson's friend, Charlie, in *Scarlet Street.* He was Lew Ayres' father in the *Dr. Kildare* films and also appeared in *You Can't Take It with You, Destry Rides Again, It's a Wonderful Life* (James Stewart's father), and *The Bribe.*

Historical People and Events Ranging from Biblical times through the New York Giants of the twentieth century, several of Edward G. Robinson's characterizations were based on historical events. Korah, Abiram, and Dathan of the Old Testament were Hebrews who were a nemesis to Moses. If Korah was the best known Biblically, perhaps Robinson's character in *The Ten Commandments* was named Dathan because it sounded more sinister.

A comedy on Broadway, *The Firebrand,* dealt loosely with the life and times of Benvenuto Cellini; in it, Robinson played a character called Ottaviano. He was one of the Caesars (several years prior to *Little Caesar* on the screen) in the Theatre Guild's *Androcles and the Lion*; and in its curtain-raiser, *The Man of Destiny,* he was a servant who encountered Napoleon.

On TV he played Daniel Webster. Porfirio Diaz, Mexican dictator at the turn of the century, was played by Robinson on stage in *Juarez and Maximilian.* His other nineteenth century characters include Reuter, Dr. Ehrlich, Carl Schurz (*Cheyenne Autumn*), Horace Tabor (*Silver Dollar*), Armour (*I Loved a Woman*), and Theodore Roosevelt (*The Right Man*). He sold a piano to Mrs. Edvard Grieg, the central character in *Song of Norway.*

The story of Johnny Broderick, a New York detective, was the basis for *Bullets or Ballots.* *Confessions of a Nazi Spy* was based on actual trials, as documented by Leon G. Turrou (and played by Robinson). More infamously, *Little Caesar* disguised the rise of Al Capone; *Key Largo* chronicled Lucky Luciano, and *Double Indemnity* dealt with the famous case which saw the electrocution of Ruth Snyder, who, with her lover, Judd Gray, murdered her husband for his insurance. *Big Leaguer* featured the most recent figure, New York Giants ballplayer and coach Hans Lobert toward the end of his career, running the Florida training camp.

See also **Biographies**.

Hohl, Arthur (1889–1964) was on the New York stage with Edward G. Robinson in *Eyvind of the Hills,* and later appeared with him in three films—*The Whole Town's Talking, Blackmail,* and *Our Vines Have Tender Grapes.* Other films include *Island of Lost Souls, Cleopatra,* and *The Yearling.*

A Hole in the Head (Film, 1959) Edward G. Robinson came back to films after a successful two-year Broadway run and national tour of *Middle of the Night.* Frank Sinatra's production company (with director Frank Capra) was producing a film of Arnold Schulman's play *A Hole in the Head,* and Sinatra wanted Robinson, whom he had once idolized for his tough guy performances, to play the part of his older brother. "First rehearsal: Sinatra great, others need straightening out. Second rehearsal: Sinatra cools off, others improve. First photographic take: Sinatra cold, others fine. I took Frank aside," relates Frank Capra in his book *The Name Above the Title.* "'Something bothering you, Frank?' 'Hell, yes. All those rehearsals, repeating the same jokes to the same jerks. It'd bother *any*body.'"

There were problems, Capra notes, "...because Edward G. Robinson, a star of major magnitude, wants to rehearse all day! And the more he rehearses the better he plays the scene. Eddie may not like it if I don't rehearse him with Sinatra. He didn't like it at all. In fact, kind, good-natured Eddie Robinson blew his top before a set full of people when we got back to the Goldwyn Studios. In a voice choking with anger and tears he shouted, 'I won't stand for this degradation any longer. I was a star for twenty years at Warners and nobody, *nobody* refused to rehearse with me. You're toadying to Sinatra.

You're afraid of him. *That's* why he won't rehearse with me. But that's all. I'm finished. No more. No more. I'm out of this picture. Out. Out. I'm calling my agent—' His choking voice trailed off in sobs as he stomped toward his dressing room....

"Thelma Ritter, that best of all character actresses ... whispered in my ear: 'Told you Robinson was going to stink. And I'm gonna stink, Sinatra's gonna stink, you're gonna stink, and the picture's gonna stink!.... I entered my stage dressing room-office. The phone rang. Sinatra. 'What's the matter, Cheech? True Eddie Robinson's taking a powder?' 'No. Just butterflies; hasn't worked in some time. I'll handle this, Frank. You stay out of it....' Within twenty minutes, my longtime friend Phil Kellogg, of the William Morris Agency, burst in, very upset. 'Frank, you of all people. Robinson called me. Wants off the picture. What happened?' 'Simple, Phil. Sinatra plays his best scenes without rehearsing, and Robinson plays his best scenes after an *hour* of rehearsal. If I rehearse them together they'll wreck each other. So I rehearse Robinson with someone else playing Sinatra's lines. Robinson says 'No!' Sinatra must rehearse with him. I say *I'll* tell Sinatra what to do, not Robinson. So Eddie ups and runs and says he'll quit. If he does, he's a damn fool. He's great in the picture. But if he does quit, if he doesn't report on the set at one o'clock ready for work, you tell him I'll sue him seven ways from Sunday for every dime it'll cost to replace him—'

"Phil Kellogg wasn't with Robinson over ten minutes before he phoned. Would I please come to Eddie's dressing room. I opened the door. Eddie is sobbing like a child. He runs to me, embraces me roughly, and plants warm wet kisses all over my face. The heart and maleness of this sentimental man were something to experience. 'How could I do this to you, Frank. My old, dear friend. Me! Who's been in the theatre since before I could blow my own nose—How could I *do* this to you?' The cast and crew couldn't have been more surprised when they assembled on the set for the one o'clock call. There was Robinson on the set, clowning and laughing.... 'Bill!' I shouted to our cameraman William Daniels. 'Our first set-up is a big head close-up of the best damned actor in the world—Mr. Edward G. Robinson!' The applause was spontaneous and loud. Sinatra walked on the set—and gaped. Robinson was taking bows! Not only that—he rushed to Sinatra with a happy grin, embraced him roughly, and pinched his cheeks till they hurt. 'You squirt! With all those dames. I used to be all rooster and bones, too, when I was young—' It was a happy picture from then on, so happy that I think neither Sinatra nor Robinson—nor Thelma Ritter for that matter—ever gave warmer or better performances...."

It *was* a happy picture, because the two stars, despite different acting styles, were professionals who respected one another. According to Michael Freedland in *All the Way, a Biography of Frank Sinatra, 1915–1998*, Sinatra once told Robinson, "I don't believe in exhausting myself before the take.... On the other hand, I read the script fifty times before I ever go to work. So you can't say I'm unprepared." Regarding Robinson, on the other hand: "As he rehearses, he improves," Capra reminds us. "He finds little things to do, tries little gadgets to do, little things to do with his hands, little things to do with his eyes, things like that."

"I think the thing that impressed me most was Capra's ability to make his actors feel that they were entertaining him as well as the audience ... we all worked a little harder for his quick chuckles in the comedy scenes ... Even Eddie Robinson, who was hard of hearing, played to Capra."—Carolyn Jones, quoted in *The Films of Frank Capra,* by Victor Scherle and William Turner Levy

Robinson and Sinatra shared the same birthday, December 12, and the film company celebrated with a party on the set. They exchanged birthday gifts, a custom that continued through the next decade. Jane Robinson noted in her book *Edward G. Robinson's World of Art,* "Frank sent Eddie a Constantin Guys drawing, which he had autographed on the back of the canvas.... A week or so before, Sinatra had a party at his home and Eddie said to him that he thought it charming.... Eddie was embarrassed; he's not a 'happy receiver'; we were both at a loss.... Frank, however ... wished something personal from Eddie, something that money could not buy, he wanted one of Eddie's self-portraits. Eddie gave it to him with pleasure. It is the only painting by Edward G. Robinson that is in the hands of anybody but Edward G. Robinson."

"Acted by those two powerful performing personalities, Frank Sinatra and Edward G. Robinson, the film turns out to be genuinely entertaining," said *Newsweek*. "Robinson displays such finesse as a comedy foil ... that he almost steals the show from Sinatra."

"This is a funny picture," wrote Joseph Kostolefsky in *Film Comment*, "getting its laughs often and nearly always legitimately ... But most of the humor, even though the idiom is basically Yiddish ... gets the greatest possible mileage from insults, shrugs, groans of despair, and downright boorishness. Some of this has been done before ... but seldom as well, and never better than when delivered by Edward G. Robinson, whose performance here is a revelation. Rescued from a set of mannerisms so rigid in recent years as to cut off all feeling, Robinson — whether describing Turkish baths 'where you can take off your clothes and meet people' or arranging a marriage in front of the parties involved and wondering, 'What did I say?'—is brilliant, a *schnorrer* to the hilt."

Indeed, Robinson received his best reviews in years for *A Hole in the Head*. "Robinson competently reads some of the film's best lines," said *Films in Review*. And he "shone brightly in this flavorful comedy ... [through a] zesty performance," noted James Robert Parish in *The Tough Guys*. "As the brother, a narrow-minded dullard, Edward G. Robinson is superb; funny while being most officious and withering while saying the drollest things," said *The New York Times*.

And, commenting about him and Thelma Ritter, who played his wife, "in broad Italian accents and gestures, [they] provide the film's funniest moments," said the *Saturday Review*. And *The New Yorker* singled the couple out at the expense of the film overall: "Occasionally, thank the Lord, Edward G. Robinson and Thelma Ritter come along to relieve the general tedium."

"[It] does have two yeasty performances by Thelma Ritter and Edward G. Robinson as the brother and sister-in-law who bail Frank Sinatra out of his financial difficulties," wrote *The New York Herald-Tribune*. "...As entertainment it owes most of its success to Miss Ritter and Robinson, whose sense of timing in dialogue is fascinating to watch."

"Robinson's flair for the barbed line and the sarcastic grimace was never brushed with such an airy touch," claimed Foster Hirsch. "This is the actor's lightest and perhaps most graceful performance.... He and Ritter ... are models of comic timing, and Robinson's misfortunes with a collapsible chair provide a beautiful vaudeville turn."

A SinCap Production; producer-director, Frank Capra; co-producer, Frank Sinatra; screenplay, Arnold Schulman; based on the play by Schulman; assistant director, Arthur S. Black, Jr.; art directors, Edward Imazu, Jack R. Berne; set, Fred MacLean; music, Nelson Riddle; songs "High Hopes," "All My Tomorrows" by James Van Heusen, Sammy Cahn; orchestra, Arthur Morton; production designer, Joe Cooke; costumes, Edith Head; sound, Fred Lau; makeup, Bernard Ponedel; hairstyles, Helene Parrish; camera, William H. Daniels; editor, William Hornbeck; cast: Frank Sinatra (Tony Manetta), Edward G. Robinson (Mario Manetta), Eddie Hodges (Ally), Eleanor Parker (Mrs. Rogers), Carolyn Jones (Shirl), Thelma Ritter (Sophie Manetta), Keenan Wynn (Jerry Marks), Joi Lansing (Dorine), Connie Sawyer (Mrs. Wexler), George DeWitt (Mendy), James Komack (Julius), Dub Taylor (Fred), Benny Rubin (Diamond), Ruby Dandridge (Sally), B. S. Pully (Hood), Joyce Nizzari (Alice) Pupi Campo (Master of Ceremonies), Emory Parnell (Sheriff), Bill Walker, Robert B. Williams; United Artists; CinemaScope; Color by DeLuxe; photographic lenses by Panavision; 120 minutes; July 1959

Tony Manetta has a rundown hotel on Miami Beach and a ten-year-old son named Ally. He can't pay his rent. He asks his prosperous brother Mario, who has done so before, to help him. Instead, Mario and his wife, Sophie, fly to Miami from New York. Hoping Tony will settle down, Sophie sets up a matchmaking session between Tony and Mrs. Rogers, a lovely widow, but the meeting backfires badly when Mario embarrasses everybody with talk of money. To complicate things, Shirl, a free-spirited surfboarding friend of Tony's, is jealous. Tony soothes over the situation with Mrs. Rogers, and the two spend a quiet evening together. Tony is thrilled to learn that his old buddy, Jerry Marks, is in town; it may be the answer to his financial troubles if Jerry, now a multimillionaire promoter, becomes interested in Tony's idea for a Disneyland development in Florida. Jerry invites Tony to a party and to the dogtracks. Grandstanding, Tony wins at first, then loses everything. Jerry rejects Tony's project but offers Tony money. Tony is disillusioned about their friendship and throws the money back; Jerry's henchmen punch Tony in the stomach, and he returns to the hotel, worse off than ever. Mario and Sophie now decide to take Ally to New York to live with them. Tony agrees. But in the end, Ally runs from the taxicab to his father, and they are reunited on the beach with Mrs. Rogers, who has come to say goodbye. Mario and Sophie realize that happiness is the most important thing, and they stay, too, for a vacation.

The Hole in the Wall (Film, 1929) Together, Claudette Colbert and Edward G. Robinson made their talking film debuts in *The Hole in the Wall*. This, only Robinson's third movie, was filmed in New York at the time he was appearing on the stage in *A Man with Red Hair*. *The New York Times* found the film "a queer combination of senseless drama and excellent pictorial direction," and stated that Colbert and Robinson were "competent so far as the lines and action permit." Similarly, *Photoplay* called it a "confusing crook story acted by a good cast."

Supervisor, Monta Bell; director, Robert Florey; screenplay, Pierre Collings; based on the play by Fred Jackson; camera, George Folsey; editor, Morton Blumenstock; cast: Claudette Colbert (Jean Oliver), Edward G. Robinson (The Fox), Donald Meek (Goofy), Louise Closser Hale (Mrs. Ramsey), David Newell (Gordon Grant), Nellie Savage (Madame Mystera), Alan Brooks (Jim), Katherine Emmett (Mrs. Carslake), Marcia Kagno (Marcia), Barry Macollum (Dogface), George MacQuarrie (Inspector), Helen Crane (Mrs. Lyons), Gamby-Hall Girls (Dancers); Paramount; 73 minutes (7 reels); April 1929

When Madame Mystera, a crooked fortune teller, is killed in an accident, Jean Oliver joins her gang and takes on her identity. Jean is just out of prison, having been framed for a theft by wealthy Mrs. Ramsey, who did not approve of Jean as a future daughter-in-law. Now seeking revenge, Jean kidnaps Mrs. Ramsey's granddaughter, Marcia, and plans to teach her a life of crime. The Fox, leader of the gang, falls in love with Jean, but she falls for Gordon Grant, a reporter trying to solve the kidnapping. The Fox takes Marcia away from Jean, holding her for ransom. Realizing that Jean does not love him, he agrees to tell the police the child's whereabouts in exchange for a confession from Mrs. Ramsey to clear Jean.

The Hole in the Wall was a gangster film, Edward G. Robinson's first. Walter Wanger, an executive at Paramount, doubtless had seen the actor onstage in *The Racket* and sought him for the role of The Fox. Filming was something of a trial because it combined silent film technique with fledgling sound methods. Lawrence J. Quirk comments in *The Films of Claudette Colbert*, "Gradually, amidst retakes, mikes that picked up their voices too loudly and then again too faintly, the endless marks over which they could not tread, the director's unsureness, the limited facilities of the Astoria Studio, the stars managed to work out performances that did them credit."

Quirk interviewed Robinson: "'It was a nightmare,' he growled. It was a whole new technique, a revolutionary approach, for both Claudette and myself. We had to scale everything down.... I know she felt the strain as much as I did.... She was one grand trouper—a pro all the way....'"

Claudette Colbert added, "I do remember one annoying circumstance — some of it was shot silent, in the old way ... and there was no music score then and we came out mouthing dialogue, at times, that had no vocal accompaniment on the sound track — or what passed for a sound track!'"

It seems clear that the film was a victim of the movies' first year of learning how to talk, following decades of technique established in silent films. In his autobiography Robinson acknowledged that the script was inferior to his expectations in the theater and accepted Wanger's offer for the money. When he saw himself on the screen, he was appalled, feeling that he sounded pretentious and that his appearance was at best rather runtish. As a result, he didn't attend the preview for the film or any subsequent showing of it over the next forty years.

Hollywood Canine Canteen This cartoon was billed as a USO Canteen for the pets of Hollywood stars, who were drawn as dogs. Edward G. Robinson listens to Lionel "Hambone" and "Schnauser" Durante.

Director, Robert McKimson; story, Warren Foster; animation, Cal Dalton, Don Williams, Richard Bickenbach; backgrounds, Richard H. Thomas; musical direction, Carl W. Stalling; Merrie Melodies; 1946; 7 minutes

Hollywood Fights Back (Radio, 1947) This was the first of two broadcasts protesting the House Un-American Activities Committee investigation of the film industry.

Directors, Norman Corwin, William N. Robson; participants: Lauren Bacall, Lucille Ball, John Beal, Humphrey Bogart, Eddie Cantor, Charles Boyer, Norman Corwin, Richard Conte, Joseph Cotten, Melvyn Douglas, Florence Eldredge, Ava Gardner, John Garfield, Judy Garland, James Gleason, Paulette Goddard, June Havoc, Arthur Gardner Hays, Van Heflin, Paul Henreid, William Holden, Marsha Hunt, John Huston, Danny Kaye, Gene Kelly, Evelyn Keyes, Sen. Harry Kilbore, Burt Lancaster, Peter Lorre, Myrna Loy, Fredric March, Henry Morgan, Sen. Wayne Morse, Audie Murphy, Sen. Claude Pepper, Vincent Price, Edward G. Robinson, Robert Ryan, Dr. Harlow Shapley, Artie Shaw, Frank Sinatra, Margaret Sullavan, Deems Taylor, Sen. Glen Taylor, Sen. Albert D. Thomas, Walter Wanger, Cornel Wilde, Jane Wyatt, William Wyler, Keenan Wynn, Robert Young; *Special: Committee for the First Amendmen*t; ABC; 30 minutes; October 26, 1947

The Hollywood Greats: Edward G. Robinson (Television, 1979) The British Broadcasting Company (BBC) produced an hour-long biography of Edward G. Robinson, which included interviews with family and coworkers, and film clips from *Little Caesar, Smart Money, The Cincinnati Kid, Key Largo, A Slight Case of Murder, A Hole in the Head, Manpower, Two Weeks in Another Town,* and *Soylent Green.*

Producer, Barry Brown; director, Julie Lindsay; writer, Barry Norman; editor, Norman Carr; research, Barbara Paskin, Jill Talbot; participants: Frank Capra, John Huston, Sam Jaffe, Vincent Price, George Raft, Francesca Robinson Sanchez, Jane Robinson Sidney, Leonard Spigelgass, Hal B. Wallis; Barry Norman (Host); British Broadcasting Corporation (BBC-tv); August 3, 1979; 60 minutes

Hollywood Hotel (Radio) This radio show consisted of half-hour adaptations of current films, often featuring the original stars.

See **"Bullets or Ballots"; "Kid Galahad"; "The Whole Town's Talking."**

Hollywood Independent Citizens Committee of the Arts, Sciences and Professions This organization was formed in 1946 by a group of liberals in the film community as a response to the workings of the House Un-American Activities Committee. Members included Humphrey Bogart, Charles Boyer, George Burns, Abe Burrows, Eddie Cantor, Joseph Cotten, Olivia deHavilland, Joan Fontaine, John Garfield, Paulette Goddard, Rita Hayworth, John Houseman, Walter Huston, George Jessel, Jerome Kern, Jesse Lasky, Gregory Peck, Edward G. Robinson, Artur Rubinstein, Artie Shaw, Frank Sinatra, Walter Wanger, and Orson Welles.

Hollywood Palace (Television, 1965) Cast: Edward G. Robinson, Liberace (host); writer, Milton Geiger ("This Is It"); Hollywood Palace; ABC-TV, January 9, 1965

Hollywood Showcase (Radio, 1938) This summer replacement for *Hollywood Hotel* ran five years on CBS-radio beginning in July 1937. Performances of music, song, and drama were judged by members of the studio audience — who were selected for that purpose if they could catch one of a dozen ping pong balls tossed their way. Edward G. Robinson appeared on a Jean Hersholt anniversary program.

Producer, Charles Vanda; director, Bill Lawrence; orchestra, Lud Guskin; announcer, Bill Goodwin; vocals, Roy Scott Quintet; cast: Edward G. Robinson, Jean Hersholt, Edmund MacDonald; CBS-radio; 30 minutes; March 10, 1938

Hollywood Steps Out Edward G. Robinson meets the "Oomph Girl" at Ciro's in this cartoon.

Supervisor, Fred (Tex) Avery; musical direction, Carl W. Stalling; Merrie Melodies; 1941; 7 minutes

Hollywood Television Theatre see **U.S.A.**

Hollywood War Savings (Radio, 1943) Edward G. Robinson (Narrator, master of ceremonies); Motion Picture Committee for Hollywood War Savings Staff; NBC; June 30, 1943

Holm, Celeste (1919–), best supporting Oscar winner for *Gentleman's Agreement*, was in *Come to the Stable*, *All About Eve* (nominations), *The Snake Pit*, and *High Society*. On TV she played the first woman presidential candidate, Victoria Woodhull, in *The Right Man*, with Edward G. Robinson. On Broadway she was Ado Annie in *Oklahoma!*

Holman, Harry (1874–1947), chubby, nervous, and pompous, was with Edward G. Robinson, as Adams, in *Silver Dollar*, played the Mayor of San Francisco in *Barbary Coast*, and a Justice of the Peace in *Manpower*. He was also in the Capra films *Meet John Doe*, *It Happened One Night*, and *It's a Wonderful Life*.

Holmes, Stuart (1887–1971) was on-screen from 1911 in *The Prisoner of Zenda* and *The Scarlet Letter*, then, with Edward G. Robinson, in *Dr. Ehrlich's Magic Bullet*, *A Dispatch from Reuter's*, and *Night Has a Thousand Eyes*, plus *Stardust*, *The Rose Tattoo*, and *The Man Who Shot Liberty Valance*.

Homans, Robert (1875–1947) was in six films with Edward G. Robinson — *The Widow from Chicago*, *The Whole Town's Talking*, *The Amazing Dr. Clitterhouse*, and *Blackmail* (playing policemen in all four), plus *Unholy Partners*, and *Barbary Coast*. Other films include *Black Legion* and *Out of the Fog*.

Homosexuality Several critics noted an aspect of homosexuality in *Little Caesar*, analyzing Rico's attachment to his friend, Joe Massara (Douglas Fairbanks, Jr.). "That's what I get for likin' a guy too much," says Rico when he cannot shoot Joe. Similarly, some critics saw an unusually strong male bonding between Walter Neff (Fred MacMurray) and Barton Keyes (Robinson) in *Double Indemnity*. Robinson's stage character of Caesar in *Androcles and the Lion* was played as gay. These are rare instances among Edward G. Robinson's films and plays.

The Honeymooners (Television, 1956) Jackie Gleason (Ralph Kramden), Audrey Meadows (Alice), Art Carney (Norton), Joyce Randolph (Trixie); and Charles Laughton, Peter Lorre, Zasu Pitts, William Boyd, Edward G. Robinson (Guest stars)

"[The guest stars were] introduced for about a minute each and then excused. Seldom has the celebrity-conscious set owner been so wantonly conned."— Jack Gould, *The New York Times*, as noted in *The Great One: The Life and Legend of Jackie Gleason*, by William A. Henry

The Honorable Mr. Wong see ***The Hatchet Man***

Hope, Bob (1903–) narrated several specials with Edward G. Robinson — a U.S.

Olympic Committee Telethon, *Operation Entertainment, At This Very Moment,* and *The World's Greatest Showman* on television; the short film *The Heart of Show Business*; and on radio, *The Victory Chest Program* and a Savings Bond Show. In 1939, while sailing to Europe on the *Normandie,* Hope staged a ship's concert in which tough guys Robinson and George Raft danced in a comic routine. He was in the *Road* pictures with Bing Crosby and Dorothy Lamour, plus *Roberta, My Favorite Blonde, The Paleface, Fancy Pants,* and *The Facts of Life.*

Hopkins, Arthur (1878–1950) A Broadway producer, his shows include *Good Gracious Annabelle, The Jest, Anna Christie, What Price Glory?, Burlesque, Machinal, Holiday, The Hairy Ape, The Magnificent Yankee,* and, starring John, Lionel, and Ethel Barrymore, respectively, *Richard III, Macbeth,* and *Romeo and Juliet.* With Edward G. Robinson, he produced and directed *The Deluge* (twice), *The Idle Inn, Launzi, The Night Lodging, A Royal Fandango,* and *Samson and Delilah.*

Hopkins, Miriam (1902–72) played in several Samuel Goldwyn films, often opposite Joel McCrea. They were in *Barbary Coast,* with Edward G. Robinson, and also *These Three* and *Splendor.* Her other films include *The Story of Temple Drake, Becky Sharp* (Oscar nomination), *The Heiress, The Old Maid, Old Acquaintance,* and *The Chase.*

Hopper, William (1915–69), son of actors DeWolff and Hedda Hopper, was in films in the 1930s and 1940s (supporting Edward G. Robinson in *Larceny, Inc., Manpower,* and *Brother Orchid*), but was best known as Paul Drake, detective on TV's *Perry Mason.* His mother (1891–1966), a Hollywood gossip columnist, played herself in *The Slippery Pearls* and *Pepe.*

Hopton, Russell (1900–45) played Al, Edward G. Robinson's sidekick, in *The Little Giant.* Other pictures include *Street Scene, High Wide and Handsome, The Saint Strikes Back,* and *Zombies on Broadway.*

Horton, Louisa (1924–) played the ingénue Ann Deever in *All My Sons,* with Edward G. Robinson, but was in few other films. *Swashbuckler* was the most recent. Married to director George Roy Hill (*The Sting, The World According to Garp*), she had a role on the TV soap *All My Children* and was in the films *Walk East on Beacon* and *Communion.*
See ***All My Sons.***

Hospitals Hospitals are the settings for these films with Robinson as a patient: *Two Weeks in Another Town* (heart attack), *The Prize* (kidnaping victim), *Mr. Winkle Goes to War* (war wounds), and *Manpower* (he and George Raft are accident victims). Robinson played a physician in *U.M.C., Dr. Ehrlich's Magic Bullet,* and *The Amazing Dr. Clitterhouse.* In *A Slight Case of Murder* a crony dies while listening to his pals singing to him long distance on the telephone. District attorney Robinson is too late to save a condemned man following a scene of a deathbed confession at a hospital in *Illegal.* He visits his hospitalized son, injured during a bombing, in *Neither by Day Nor by Night.*

Hotels Hotels are the setting in several of Edward G. Robinson's films: *Two Weeks in Another Town* (Rome), *My Geisha* (Japan), *Seven Thieves* (France), *I Loved a Woman* (Athens), and *Nightmare* (New Orleans). They are key to the plot of others. His character, Louis Chamalis, runs San Francisco's Bella Donna in *Barbary Coast.* In *A Hole in the Head* Frank Sinatra's character is about to be evicted from the Miami hotel he runs, The Garden of Eden. And not far away, on the Florida Keys, the Largo Hotel is taken over during off-season by Robinson's gang in *Key Largo.*

Claire Trevor's character, Jo Keller, runs a hotel in *The Amazing Dr. Clitterhouse;* and gang members in *Smart Money, The Little Giant, Brother Orchid,* and *Kid Galahad* either reside, party, or gamble at a hotel. In *The Cincinnati Kid* a New Orleans hotel becomes the setting for a climactic, marathon stud poker game. Aunt Jane runs a hotel in Durban, South Africa, to which young Sammy of

A Boy Ten Feet Tall is making his way. In *Tales of Manhattan* the Waldorf-Astoria Hotel is where a 25-year reunion for law school graduates is being held. More melodramatically, Robinson disguises himself as a Frenchman, murders his brother-in-law, and shoves him in a hotel closet in *The Man with Two Faces*.

House In 1933 Edward G. Robinson bought a Tudor-style mansion at 910 North Rexford Drive in Beverly Hills. His dislike of physical exercise (and the fact that he didn't know how to swim) prompted him to replace the pool with an art gallery. After his divorce from Gladys, his first wife, he repurchased the house, where he lived with his second wife Jane until his death. She married director George Sidney and continued to live there, and on her death and his remarriage to Corinne Entratter it was still occupied, as late as 1998, when the Sidneys moved to Palm Springs.

House, Billy (1890–1961), a vaudeville comedian and dancer, appeared with Edward G. Robinson in *Smart Money*, as a gambler, and as Mr. Potter, the druggist, in *The Stranger*. His other pictures include *The Egg and I, Imitation of Life,* and *People Will Talk*.

House of Strangers (Film, 1949) Edward G. Robinson received his only major acting award in 1949. The Cannes Film Festival, in its fourth year, named him as best actor for his portrayal of Gino Monetti in *House of Strangers*. Wanda Hale, in *The New York Daily News,* said that, "The lusty, domineering Papa Monetti … surpasses all other roles of his twenty-year film career." Robinson's comment in his autobiography? "I loved it."

Other American critics favored Robinson and the film, but with slightly less enthusiasm. *Time* called the film "a richly detailed exploration of a family vendetta on Manhattan's Lower East Side … into its making went an intelligent screenplay … some distinguished lighting effects and camera work, and … Mankiewicz's talent for handling atmosphere and sets as effective projections of character. Meatiest character, of course, is arrogant old Monetti, a role which Robinson plays (Italian accent, organ-grinder moustache and all) with bravura and relish."

"Despite a rather weak title, *House of Strangers* is a strong picture," noted *Variety*. "…The stars, Edward G. Robinson, Susan Hayward and Richard Conte, contribute some of their finest work in this film…. Robinson is especially vivid when he realizes that the three sons have turned against him and when he seeks revenge through a fourth."

"It has solid characterizations by Edward G. Robinson, Richard Conte, Luther Adler, Susan Hayward and their assistants," said *The New York Herald-Tribune*. "Robinson gives [Monetti] ominous quality, but he lingers too fondly over reminiscences of his youth as a barber on Mulberry Street and makes far too much of an Italian accent."

"There hasn't been a picture in years as somber as *House of Strangers*," noted *The New Republic*. "It is *King Lear* in Little Italy with Edward G. Robinson … the characterizations are striking, and there is some good moody detail."

"Edward G. Robinson, as usual, does a brisk and colorful job of making Papa Monetti a brassy despot with a Sicilian accent."—*The New York Times*

"If one can accept the artificiality of Robinson's theatrical Italian accent," observed Kenneth L. Geist in *Pictures Will Talk, the Life and Films of Joseph L. Mankiewicz,* "his performance is one of his most robust and memorable."

Producer, Sol C. Siegel; director, Joseph L. Mankiewicz; screenplay, Philip Yordan; based on the novel *I'll Never Go There Again,* by Jerome Weidman; music, Daniele Amfitheatrof; orchestra, Maurice de Packh; special effects, Fred Sersen; art directors, Lyle Wheeler, George W. Davis; set, Thomas Little, Walter M. Scott; camera, Milton Krasner; editor, Harmon Jones; costumes, Charles LeMaire; production manager, Sid Bowen; assistant director, William Eckhardt; sound, W. D. Flick, Roger Heman; script supervisor, Wesley Jones; makeup, Ben Nye, Dick Smith; cast: Edward G. Robinson (Gino Monetti), Susan Hayward (Irene Bennett), Richard

Conte (Max Monetti), Luther Adler (Joe Monetti), Debra Paget (Maria Domenico), Efrem Zimbalist, Jr. (Tony Monetti), Paul Valentine (Pietro Monetti), Hope Emerson (Helena Domenico), Esther Minciotti (Theresa Monetti), Diane Douglas (Elaine Monetti), Tito Vuolo (Lucca), Alberto Morin (Victoro), Sid Tomack (Bartender), Thomas Browne Henry (Judge), David Wolfe (Prosecutor), John Kellogg (Danny), Ann Morrison (Woman juror), Dolores Parker (Nightclub singer), Mario Siletti, Maurice Samuels (Bits), Tommy Garland (Pietro's opponent), Charles J. Flynn (Prison guard), Joseph Mazzuca (Batboy), George Magrill, John Pedrini (Cops), Argentina Brunetti (Applicant), Mike Stark, Herb Vigran (Neighbors), Mushy Callahan (Referee), Bob Cantro, Eddie Saenz (Fighters), George Spaulding (Doorman), John "Red" Kullers (Taxi driver), Scott Landers, Fred Hillebrand (Detectives), Sally Yarnell, Geraldine Jordan (Dancers), Phil Tully (Guard), Lawrence Tibbett (Opera recording), Maxine Ardell, Marjorie Holliday, Frank Jaquet, Donna Latour, James Little, Charles McClelland, Howard Mitchell, Rhoda Williams, Sylvio Minciotti; 20th Century–Fox; 101 minutes; June 1949

Max Monetti, just released from prison after seven years, visits his three brothers, Joe, Pietro, and Tony, who now run their late father's bank. At their old house Max remembers his father, Gino Monetti, an immigrant barber turned banker who ruled the brothers with an iron hand. Only Max, who had a law office in the bank, was free from Gino's dominance. Engaged to the lovely Maria Domenico, Max became involved with the more worldly Irene Bennett, who was seeking his legal counsel. During a bank investigation and trial, Joe, Pietro, and Tony turned on their father. When Max realized that Gino's old-world banking methods would not stand up under the law, he attempted to bribe a juror, was caught, and sent to jail. Gino begged Max to make his brothers pay for taking the bank away. He died while Max was in prison, and at the funeral Max vowed a vendetta. Now at the house, the brothers try to kill him. But Max has changed his mind and leaves town with Irene.

"House of Strangers" (Radio, 1950) Edward G. Robinson repeated his role of Gino Monetti in a radio adaptation eighteen months later.

Cast: Edward G. Robinson, Victor Mature, June Havoc; *Screen Director's Playhouse*; ABC-radio; January 25, 1951

House Un-American Activities Committee

The United States government has long maintained programs to monitor, investigate, and regulate behavior by its citizens that constitutes a potential threat to national security. Naturally, Communist ideology and infiltration is a target because of its basic opposition to the democratic system. With the defeat of Nazi Germany in World War II (achieved through an uneasy partnership with the Russians), focus shifted back to Communism as the enemy, specifically in areas where its propaganda could be effective.

A contingent of liberals and Communists, mostly writers, existed in Hollywood in the 1930s, and their influence on films was a growing fear. A standing committee in the House of Representatives to rout subversiveness, called the House Un-American Activities Committee, began investigations in 1947, specifically seeking "to expose the 'subversive' nature of Hollywood films and film makers," according to *The Inquisition in Hollywood* by Larry Ceplair and Steven Englund. "Subpoenas (printed on pink paper) flowed out to screen artists of all categories. Four years later, a second, more extensive bombardment nearly demolished organized radicalism in the film industry."

Friendly and unfriendly witnesses testified, many naming names of Communists and "fellow travelers." A group which came to be known as The Hollywood Ten refused to testify, were found in contempt of Congress, and imprisoned. Liberal groups in the film community organized protests, but in the end careers were in chaos.

Edward G. Robinson testified before the HUAC on three occasions, finally managing to clear his name at the expense of being labeled "a choice sucker." During the war he had supported several liberal organizations that were identified later as Communist fronts.

As actor Norman Lloyd commented during the Robinson *A&E Biography* "Little Big Man," "There was an air of ... awfulness! That's the simplest way to describe it." The proceedings were an embarrassment. Freedom had been encroached by the government's interference with an individual's right to political beliefs.

In the Senate, Joseph McCarthy's zeal paralleled the craziness of the times, and the name "McCarthyism" was given to the hysterical cry of the modern-day witch hunts. The House Un-American Activities Committee was still a part of Congress in the late 1950s, but a decade later the name was changed to the House Committee on Internal Security.

See also **Communism**.

Houseman, John (1902–88), an Oscar winner for *The Paper Chase*, was a TV star in the series of the same name. A writer on *Tiger Shark*, with Edward G. Robinson, he founded the Mercury Theatre with Orson Welles and later the Acting Company. He produced *Two Weeks in Another Town*. Like Robinson, he was Rumania-born and had a love for modern art.

How I Play Golf—Trouble Shots (Short film, 1931) This was among a series of short films in which professional Bobby Jones gave golf instructions to such celebrities as Richard Barthelmess, Joe E. Brown, and Frank Craven. Edward G. Robinson was in a later segment.

Director, George Marshall; cinematographer, Frank Kesson; editor, F.Y. Smith; participants: Bobby Jones, Edward G. Robinson, O.B. Keeler (Narrator); 1931

Howard, Sidney (1891–1939) wrote *Ned McCobb's Daughter*, in which his wife, Clare Eames, and Edward G. Robinson appeared, and also *They Knew What They Wanted*, a much-adapted love story which became Robinson's *A Lady to Love* on the screen. Other works include *The Late Christopher Bean* and *The Silver Cord*. He was working on *Gone with the Wind* at the time of his death in a farming accident, and posthumously won the writing Oscar.

Howe, James Wong (1899–1976), Oscar-winning cinematographer for *The Rose Tattoo* and *Hud*, was also nominated for *Algiers, Abe Lincoln in Illinois, Kings Row, Air Force, The North Star, The Old Man and the Sea, Seconds,* and *Funny Lady*. He photographed *Dr. Ehrlich's Magic Bullet, A Dispatch from Reuter's,* and *The Outrage*, with Edward G. Robinson, as well as such features as *The Thin Man, Yankee Doodle Dandy, Picnic, The Sweet Smell of Success,* and *The Last Angry Man*.

Hughes, Kathleen (1929–) played the starlet/murder victim, Paula Ranier in *The Glass Web*, with Edward G. Robinson. She appeared also in *Mother Is a Freshman, It Came from Outer Space,* and *The President's Analyst*. She married producer-director Stanley Rubin.

Humbert, George (1880–1963) was a chubby Italian character actor who played in two films with Edward G. Robinson—*The Bright Shawl* and (as a barber) *Kid Galahad*. He was in silent films as well as *The Rose Tattoo, Lucky Jordan, Blondie, Heidi, Bringing Up Baby, Down Argentine Way,* and *Dead End*.

Hunt, Marsha (1917–) appeared in two films with Edward G. Robinson—*Unholy Partners* and *Actors and Sin,* and three radio programs—"The Amazing Dr. Clitterhouse," *Hollywood Fights Back,* and *Document A/777*. Her film credits also include *Pride and Prejudice, Blossoms in the Dust, Cry Havoc, Smash-Up, The Happy Time, Blue Denim,* and *Johnny Got His Gun*.

Hush My Mouse An animated "Edward G. Robincat" patronizes radio's *Duffy's Tavern*.

Director, Chuck Jones; story, Tedd Pierce; animation, Ken Harris, Ben Washam, Lloyd Vaughn, Basil Davidovich; layouts and backgrounds, Earl Klein, Robert Gribboek; voices, Mel Blanc; musical direction, Carl W. Stalling; Looney Tunes; 1946; 7 minutes

Hussey, Ruth (1914–) was Edward G. Robinson's wife in *Blackmail*, and also appeared with him in a radio adaptation of

The Stranger. Her other films include *Susan and God, The Women, The Philadelphia Story* (Oscar nomination), *The Uninvited, Stars and Stripes Forever,* and *The Facts of Life.*

Huston, John (1906–1987), legendary writer and director, was associated with Edward G. Robinson on four films, collaborating on the screenplays of *The Amazing Dr. Clitterhouse, Dr. Ehrlich's Magic Bullet* (Oscar nomination), *The Stranger* (uncredited), and *Key Largo,* which he also directed. A 1956 *Ed Sullivan Show* included tributes to him from Robinson and many others. Huston and Robinson were heard on radio in *The Roosevelt Special* and *Hollywood Fights Back,* and Huston spoke about Robinson in the BBC special *The Hollywood Greats: Edward G. Robinson.* Huston won writing and directing Oscars for *The Treasure of the Sierra Madre;* similar nominations for *The Asphalt Jungle* and *The African Queen;* a directing nomination for *Moulin Rouge;* writing nominations for *Sergeant York, Heaven Knows Mr. Allison,* and *The Man Who Would Be King;* and a best supporting actor nomination for *The Cardinal. The Maltese Falcon, Sergeant York,* and *Moulin Rouge* were also nominated for best picture.

Huston, Walter (1884–1950), Oscar-winner for *The Treasure of the Sierra Madre,* received nominations also for *Dodsworth, All That Money Can Buy,* and *Yankee Doodle Dandy.* With Edward G. Robinson he was on TV's *Ed Sullivan Show;* in a United China Relief Fund benefit at the Hollywood Bowl; and on the radio in *The Voice on the Stairs, We Hold These Truths,* and *The Roosevelt Special.* Other credits: *Desire Under the Elms* and *Knickerbocker Holiday* (stage), and films *Abraham Lincoln, And Then There Were None,* and *Duel in the Sun.*

Hyland, Diana (1936–77) played Edward G. Robinson's daughter in television's *Bracken's World* episode "The Mary Tree." Her other credits include *One Man's Way, The Chase,* the TV movie *The Boy in the Plastic Bubble,* and the series *Eight Is Enough.*

I Am an American (Television, 1964) Edward G. Robinson appeared on television in a documentary about the formative years of America, leading up to the John F. Kennedy assassination.

Edward G. Robinson, Lorne Greene, Johnny Mathis, Patricia Morison, Ricky Der (Narrators, participants); musical score, Jack Quigley; teleplay, Noel Wedder; NBC-TV, September 1964

I Am an American see "Musical Americana"

"I Am an American Day" Edward G. Robinson was rejected for this live appearance in Chicago shortly after he was invited. He wrote to William Randolph Hearst, owner of the *Chicago Herald-American,* professing his patriotism in the face of his troubles with the House Un-American Activities Committee. His letter to Hearst prompted his reinvitation to appear.

Sponsored by the *Chicago Herald-American;* participants, Joe E. Brown, Bebe Daniels, Dale Evans, Gov. Dwight H. Green (Illinois), Rev. Ray Freeman Jenny (Church Federation of Greater Chicago), Hon. Martin Kennelly (Mayor of Chicago), Gen. Kenney (Commander, Strategic Air Command), Ben Lyon, Marilyn Maxwell, Phil Regan, Edward G. Robinson, Rev. Samuel Stritch (Archbishop of Chicago), Dr. Shimaryahu T. Swirsky (Chicago Rabbinical Council); Chicago Stadium, May 19, 1947

I Am the Law (Film, 1938) "The liveliest melodrama in town" was how *The New York Times* assessed *I Am the Law,* Edward G. Robinson's fifteenth gangster film. He did not play a gangster. Atypically, his character was on the right side of the law, as a professor hired to clean up the rackets. Reviewers continued to have trouble separating Little Caesar from the actor who played him. "It isn't so much that we feel Mr. Robinson is limited in his screen roles since the night he died, clutching dramatically at his throat, behind a billboard in Chicago," continued the *Times.* "It's just that he strains the imagination a little trying to play both ends of the criminological scale.... (He) seems slightly miscast."

Several elements made the film quite entertaining: an energetic Big Apple dance routine between Wendy Barrie and Robinson; an even livelier fistfight sequence photographed with before-and-after shots for the newspapers, in which Robinson takes on not one but three thugs one by one in his living room; and *Thin Man*-style romantic banter, complete with Asta, the dog, between Robinson and his doting wife Barbara O'Neil. *The New York Herald-Tribune* acknowledged much of this but still gave a stereotypical negative review: "It seems evident that he is determined to make filmgoers forget that he was once the archetype of the genius gangster.... In *I Am the Law* he is at his best when he is mussing up three thugs to show his staff how yellow they really are. He delivers a number of speeches about law and order crisply if not very convincingly, dances the Big Apple to lead on the blondes, and acts extremely executive. It's still hard for me to keep in mind that he is a cleaner-upper rather than Little Caesar."

At least *Newsweek* saw the film simply as entertainment: "Robinson gives a typically vigorous and interesting performance [in a] fairly absorbing melodrama embellished with several fresh twists and considerable humor."

Robinson has fine support. Several actors — Otto Kruger, Douglas Wood, Louis Jean Heydt, Charles Halton, and Theodore von Eltz — all turned up two years later in the cast of *Dr. Ehrlich's Magic Bullet*. In fact, most of the cast appeared with Robinson more than once. Exceptions are John Beal and the two lovely actresses opposite him, Barbara O'Neil (as his wife) and Wendy Barrie. Barrie and Robinson rehearsed extensively with studio dance instructor Eddie Larkin on their Big Apple number.

Law professor John Lindsay hates the thought of taking a sabbatical year away from his classes. Instead, after he witnesses firsthand the mayhem caused by organized crime, he goes to a city council meeting to complain and is offered the task of wiping out the rackets. Lindsay does not know that Eugene Ferguson, a councilman who supported his appointment as special crimes commissioner, is one of the crime bosses. Ferguson's son, Paul, is one of Lindsay's best students and now his aide. Lindsay tries to glean information from Frankie Ballou, a former columnist with underworld ties. Lindsay goes to a nightclub and is dancing the Big Apple with her when Con Cronin, a mob rival, is gunned down. Lindsay tries to convince victims of crimes to speak up, but the mob assassination of one of them makes them more reticent than ever. Lindsay rounds up hundreds of crooks for identification by the victims. Lindsay has proof on film that Frankie murdered Moss Kitchell, one of the crime bosses, and he confronts Frankie and Eugene Ferguson with his evidence. A thug comes to warn Lindsay that his car has been rigged with a bomb, but Ferguson has borrowed the keys and is killed. Lindsay returns to his classes, having completed his job as crime commissioner.

Producer, Everett Riskin; director, Alexander Hall; screenplay, Jo Swerling; based on *Liberty* magazine articles by Fred Allhoff; music director, Morris Stoloff; camera, Henry Freulich; art directors, Lionel Banks, Stephen Goosson; set, Babs Johnstone; editor, Viola Lawrence; gowns, Kalloch; dance instructor, Eddie Larkin; cast: Edward G. Robinson (John Lindsay), Barbara O'Neil (Jerry Lindsay), Otto Kruger (Eugene Ferguson), John Beal (Paul Ferguson), Wendy Barrie (Frankie Ballou), Arthur Loft (Tom Ross), Marc Lawrence (Eddie Girard), Douglas Wood (Berry), Robert Middlemass (Moss Kitchell), Ivan Miller (Inspector Gleason), Charles Halton (Leander), Louis Jean Heydt (J. W. Butler), Emory Parnell (Brophy), Joseph Downing (Con Cronin), Theodore von Eltz (Martin), Byron Foulger (Simpson), Horace MacMahon (Prisoner), Frederick Burton (Governor), Lucien Littlefield (Roberts), Ed Keane, Robert Cummings, Sr., Harvey Clark, James Flavin, Harry Bradley (Witnesses), Fay Helm (Mrs. Butler), Kane Richmond, Robert McWade, Jr., Scott Colton, Gaylord [Steve] Pendleton, Anthony Nace, James Bush (Students), Walter Soderling (Professor Perkins), Ed Fetherstone (Austin), Bud Jamison (Bartender), Iris Meredith (Girard's girl), Lee

Shumway (Sergeant), Bess Flowers (Secretary), Bud Wiser, Lane Chandler (Policemen), Reginald Simpson, Cyril Ring (Photographers), James Millican, Lloyd Whitlock, J. E. MacMahon, Ernie Alexander, Eugene Anderson, Jr., Mary Brodel, Frank Bruno, Chick Collins, Joe DeStefan, Oliver Eckhardt, Allen Fox, Charles Hamilton, Russell Heustis, Scott Kolk, Edward LeSaint, Walter Merrill, Will Morgan, George C. Pearce, Phillips Smalley, Edward Thomas, George Turner, Jack Woody; Columbia; 83 minutes; August 1938

I Loved a Woman (Film, 1933) With *I Loved a Woman* Edward G. Robinson ap-peared in the second of several films in which his character had really lived or at least was based on a real person. Here its subject, meat tycoon J. Ogden Armour, was considerably fictionalized in David Karsner's novel *Red Meat*, the basis for the screenplay; in fact, the name Armour was avoided altogether in the script by calling Robinson's character John Hayden. Karsner also had written the biography of Horace Tabor on which the earlier *Silver Dollar* was based.

Leading ladies in the cast were Genevieve Tobin as Robinson's wife (she played his wife again in *Dark Hazard*) and Kay Francis. Producer Hal Wallis remembered in his memoir, *Starmaker*, that Robinson and Francis "were oddly matched. Kay was so tall that we had to put Eddie on a box in some scenes to bring him level with her and, understandably he was humiliated. Irritable and self-conscious, he argued with Kay frequently. But he ... gave credit to her fine acting."

"Eddie came in to discuss [the film] with me," Wallis continued, "and we made a number of changes in the dialogue. All of his suggestions were intelligent and to the point." Robinson's suggestions strengthened *I Loved a Woman* by following the character development in the novel more closely. He was pleased by the end result.

The reviews were good. *The New York Times* said, "Edward G. Robinson's latest picture ... is a worthy offering ... concerned with the crimes of Chicago meat-packers both during the Spanish-American and World Wars, and in it, Mr. Robinson has an excellent opportunity for a definite characterization, of which, it need hardly be said, this efficient actor takes full advantage.... [His] portrayal rivals his splendid interpretation in *Silver Dollar*." The *Sunday New York Times* said, "Mr. Robinson gives an excellent portrayal as a gentle and sympathetic individual who becomes a ruthless beef baron."

"A careful and conscious account of the life of a zestful American character, effectively acted by Edward G. Robinson," was the view of *The New York Herald-Tribune*; and the *New York Sun* did not disagree: "Mr. Robinson is never so admirable as in portraying what may be described as a ruthless rise to power, and thus he has another personal success on his hands." Dissenting, the *New York American* called *I Loved a Woman* "a dull and lifeless picture, with the virile Edward G. Robinson badly miscast."

In 1892 John Hayden is vacationing in Greece to get a last experience of cultural freedom. A telegram announcing his father's sudden death summons him back to Chicago to chair the family meat-packing business. On the way to his first board meeting he meets Martha Lane, who is making her way through mud and squalor to feed the tenement poor. Their relationship blossoms. Under the watchful eye of her father, Charles Lane, a business rival, they marry. As new chairman of the company, John sets a tone of liberal business practices. His relationship with his wife begins to deteriorate, particularly when he meets Laura McDonald, an aspiring opera singer. He spends a great deal of time with Laura and finances her European training. Martha hires a detective to gather evidence of John's infidelity, but Laura is involved with several men, and her interest in John is merely to inspire him, just as her ambition, with his help, has driven her. John ruthlessly drives his company, risking calamity, in order to gain power. The beef he sells to the United States forces fighting the Spanish American War is tainted, and more soldiers die of food poisoning than in battle, but John's profits soar. The war rages on. When Theodore Roosevelt is elected President, John is tried for manslaughter. Acquitted, he continues to take risks with the business. His books are examined, and he is indicted for fraud. Martha leaves him. Ruined, John returns to Athens. Laura visits him there, but he is aged and disoriented and doesn't recognize her.

Director, Alfred E. Green; screenplay, Charles Kenyon, Sidney Sutherland; based on the book by David Karsner; camera, James Van Trees; editor, Herbert Levy; supervisor, Henry Blanke; music director, Leo F. Forbstein; art director, Robert Haas; gowns, Earl Luick; cast: Edward G. Robinson (John Hayden), Kay Francis (Laura McDonald), Genevieve Tobin (Martha Lane Hayden), Robert Barrat (Charles Lane), J. Farrell MacDonald (Shuster), Henry Kolker (Sanborn), George Blackwood (Henry), Murray Kinnell (Davenport), Robert McWade (Larkin), Walter Walker (Oliver), Henry O'Neill (Farrell), Lorena Layson (Maid), Sam Godfrey (Warren), E. J. Ratcliffe (Theodore Roosevelt), Paul Porcasi (Hotel proprietor), William V. Mong (Bowen), Charles Coleman (Butler), Douglass Dumbrille (Auditor), William Worthington, Morgan Wallace, Harry Walker, Phil Tead, Edwin Stanley, Amy Rayan, Edwin Maxwell, Howard C. Hickman, Claude Gillingwater, James Donlan, Wallis Clark, Davison Clark; First National-Vitaphone; 90 minutes; September, 1933

I Will Not Go Back   (Television, 1970) Edward G. Robinson gave at least two public performances of this dramatic reading by Milton Geiger. The earlier performance was on *This Is Tom Jones*, an ABC-television variety show, in 1970, followed by a live reading at a "Musical Americana" program in 1971 by the United States Air Force Band in Washington, D. C. On the television show he also read Rudyard Kipling's *The Betrothed*. With the band, the following year he also narrated Carmen Dragon's *I Am an American*.

This Is Tom Jones; cast: Tom Jones, Edward G. Robinson, Liza Minelli, Ace Trucking Company; ABC-TV; 60 minutes; October 23 1970

"Musical Americana:" The United States Air Force Band and The Singing Sergeants; Colonel Arnald D. Gabriel (conductor); Edward G. Robinson (guest narrator); Sergeant Harry H. Gleeson (announcer); author, Milton Geiger (*I Will Not Go Back*); music, Sergeant John Caughman (*I Will Not Go Back*); Carmen Dragon (*I Am an American*); compositions and/or arrangements also by Joseph Willcox Jenkins, Henry Fillmore, Robert Russell Bennett, Sergeant Floyd E. Werle; Departmental Auditorium, Washington, D. C.; February 7, 1971

See ***I Am an American***; ***The Betrothed***; **United States Air Force Band**.

Ibsen, Henrik   (1828–1906), a Norwegian dramatist, wrote *A Doll's House, Hedda Gabler,* and *Ghosts*. At the American Academy of Dramatic Arts Edward G. Robinson acted in his *Pillars of Society,* and for the Theatre Guild he was in *Peer Gynt*. Ibsen was played by Frederick Jaeger in *Song of Norway*.

The Idle Inn   (Theater, 1921) Arthur Hopkins offered the part of Mendel in *The Idle Inn* to Edward G. Robinson, and he agreed to play in it, not knowing that Jacob Ben-Ami would have the lead. More consoling was the presence of his pal Sam Jaffe in the cast.

Young Maite is charmed by Eisik, an attractive rogue, but she is loyal to her family and intends to marry the man they have selected for her. During the wedding dance, however, Eisik and his companions abduct her. Reaching the "Idle Inn" on the high road, she tries to escape, but she cannot resist Eisik and surrenders to his charms.

Producer, director, Arthur Hopkins; playwright, Peretz Hirshbein; adaptation, Isaac Goldberg, Louis Wolheim; set, Robert Edmond Jones; choreography, Alexander Oumansky; cast: Jacob Ben-Ami (Eisik), Edward G. Robinson (Mendel), Louis Wolheim (Bendet), Sam C. Jaffe (Leibush), Eva MacDonald (Maite), Joanna Roos (Esther), Whitford Kane (Schakne), Mary Shaw (Hyenne), Margaret Fareleigh, Juliet Brennon, Bella Nodell, Ottie Wetter, Alice Kiesler, Daisy Rieger, Shirley Albert (Maidens), Elizabeth Hunt, Ellen Larned, Maud Sinclair, Gertrude Mann, Lucy English (Women), Andre Lensky, Leon Seidenberg (Eisik's Companions), William Schukin, Leo Witko (Peasant musicians), Jacob Kingsberry, George Casselberry, A. M. Bush, David Leonard, Bennie Wagschall, Philip Scherman, Julius Bleich, Henry Simons (Guests), Lionel Hogarth,

Stanley Howlett, Henry Sharp, Anton Grubman, Gregory Robbin, Boris Weiner, Frohman Foster (Merchants); opened at the Plymouth Theatre, New York; December 20, 1921.

The New York Times discussed the play's "somewhat muddled and perplexing proceedings ... and the company, too, can be no deep source of satisfaction."

"This was the most heterogeneous conglomerate company one could imagine," said Robinson. "There were Scotsmen, Irishmen, Cockneys, and Americans all trying to play Jews. It was a folk story, produced by Arthur Hopkins, but in the translation from the Yiddish, the last act was left out." — *The Cinema of Edward G. Robinson*

Illegal (Film, 1955) Author W. R. Burnett's association with Edward G. Robinson began with *Little Caesar*, which was adapted from his novel. Burnett teamed with James R. Webb to write the screenplay of *Illegal*. The film was the second remake of 1932's *The Mouthpiece,* based on the play of the same name by Frank J. Collins. A 1940 version was called *The Man Who Talked Too Much.*

Lewis Allen directed, reteaming with Robinson immediately following *A Bullet for Joey* the same year. Nina Foch, who was soon to play Moses' adoptive mother, Bithia, in *The Ten Commandments* with Robinson, had the female lead, and *Illegal* offered a good role to Jayne Mansfield in her first film.

Edward G. Robinson made paintings from his private collection available to the studio for use on the set — "$200,000 worth of well-guarded art," according to the fan magazine *Screen Stories*. In the film Robinson's character gazes at his own *Tahitian Flowers*, hanging on the wall in gangster Albert Dekker's foyer, and wonders, "Isn't that a Gauguin?"

Critically, *Illegal* fared well enough, given its history as old material now reworked as a vehicle for Robinson, whose offers in the 1950s were otherwise very slim. "[It] invades the higher echelons of crime, with a fast-thinking, double-dealing lawyer as its principal character," said *The New York Times*. "The fact that this hard-bitten lawyer is played by Edward G. Robinson in his old vein of stinging sarcasm is a clue to what you may expect."

The Monthly Film Bulletin liked the picture, calling it "hard-hitting stuff in the old gangster tradition." *The New York Herald-Tribune* saw Robinson as a "swivel-hipped lawyer who swings from the right side to the wrong side of the law and then reverses the field again to the right side."

Leslie Halliwell's *Film Guide* calls *Illegal* a "competent remake of *The Mouthpiece*, a good star melodrama," but *National Parent-Teacher* found it "a sleazy potboiler put together hurriedly for Edward G. Robinson," a view shared by *Newsweek*: "glimpses of a badly overcrowded stage."

District Attorney Victor Scott wins a first degree murder conviction against Ed Clary on circumstantial evidence. The night of the execution a deathbed confession clears Ed, but Scott's efforts to stop the electrocution are too late. He questions how many other innocent men he has sent to their death. Downing a bottle of Scotch, he cleans out his office files. He spends a night in jail on a charge of drunken and disorderly conduct. His court appearance the next day leads him to a lesser career — counselor to cheap hoods. When he defends a man who has embezzled thousands from a mob organization, Scott becomes the focus of gangster Frank Garland. He tells Garland he cannot be bought. However, Scott is surprised to learn that winning his next case becomes a victory for Garland. Ellen Miles, Scott's protégée when he was D.A., now works for the new D.A., Ralph Ford. Before Scott's downfall he and Ellen were to marry, but she marries co-worker Ray Borden instead. She discovers that Ray is the pipeline from the D.A.'s office to Garland. Confronting Ray, he tries to kill her, and she shoots him in self defense. Scott defends Ellen, on trial for Ray's murder and herself the suspected pipeline. Garland warns Scott that losing the case is necessary to protect his organization; a henchman attempts to kill Scott to prove the point. By presenting vital evidence — testimony from singer Angel O'Hara that Garland had talked on the phone to Ray Borden before he was killed — Scott is able to get Ellen exonerated.

Then he collapses from the wound inflicted by Garland's gunman.

Producer, Frank P. Rosenberg; director, Lewis Allen; screenplay, W. R. Burnett, James R. Webb; based on the play *The Mouthpiece* by Frank J. Collins; art director, Stanley Fleischer; music, Max Steiner; orchestra, Murray Cutter; sound, Stanley Jones; camera, J. Peverell Marley; editor, Thomas Reilly; make-up, Gordon Bau; costumes, Moss Mabry; assistant director, Phil Quinn; set, William Wallace; cast: Edward G. Robinson (Victor Scott), Nina Foch (Ellen Miles Borden), Hugh Marlowe (Ray Borden), Jayne Mansfield (Angel O'Hara), Ellen Corby (Miss Hinkel), Albert Dekker (Frank Garland), Edward Platt (Ralph Ford), Jay Adler (Joseph Carter), Howard St. John (E. A. Smith), DeForrest Kelley (Ed Clary), Robert Ellenstein (Joe Knight), James McCallion (Allen Parker), Lawrence Dobkin (Al Carol), Jan Merlin (Andy Garth), Clark Howat (George Graves), Henry Kulky (Taylor), Addison Richards (Harper), George Ross, Herb Vigran, Chris Alcaide (Policemen), Charles Meredith (Judge), John McKee, Barry Hudson (Detectives), Kathy Marlowe (Blonde), Ted Stanhope (Bailiff), Charles Evans (Judge), Jonathan Hale (Doctor), Marjorie Stapp (Night orderly), Fred Coby (Guard), Max Wagner (Bartender), John Cliff (Barfly), Henry Rowland (Jailer), Julie Bennett (Miss Worth), Pauline Drake (Woman), Roxanne Arlen (Miss Hathaway), Archie Twitchell (Mr. Manning), Stewart Nedd (Phillips), John Larch; Warner Bros.; 88 minutes; October 1955

Illnesses and accidents   During the run of *The Brothers Karamazov* on Broadway early in 1927, Edward G. Robinson was beset with several infirmities. In the first instance he was feverish and was advised to stay in bed, but he refused, continuing performances of the play. Later he required eleven stitches on his left hand following an accident on the set of the play. He had gripped the bannister of a large staircase and cut his hand on an exposed nail. Still later Robinson developed bursitis and was hospitalized briefly. To make matters worse, his father, Morris Goldenberg, died of a heart attack during the play's run.

On August 18, 1958, Robinson became ill on an American Airlines flight over Nevada. The plane made an emergency landing, and the actor was taken to a local hospital, where he had minor bladder surgery. The incident, according to *TV Guide*, caused a delay in the schedule of "Shadows Tremble," an original script on TV's *Playhouse 90*. The program aired two months later.

In June 1962, while filming *A Boy Ten Feet Tall* in the high altitude of Tanganyika, Africa, Robinson suffered a heart attack; he was rushed to a hospital for treatment, then to London for recuperation. The film was delayed, but he completed shooting after his recovery.

In June 1966, at the age of 72, he apparently fell asleep at the wheel of his car and hit a tree near his Beverly Hills home, causing major facial and abdominal injuries. Several weeks' recovery from four hours of surgery were followed by a get-well present from Frank Sinatra, a skateboard. With it, Robinson remembered, came the suggestion that it might be "an improvement over my driving."

During the 1960s and 1970s Robinson was faced with increasing deafness and recurring cancer. The latter, specifically cancer of the liver, claimed his life, after a month of hospitalization, on January 26, 1973.

"The Inner Voice"   (Radio, 1936) *The Standard Brands Hour*; cast: Edward G. Robinson, Ruth Easton, Len Hollister; NBC-radio; January 30, 1936

International players   Edward G. Robinson made several foreign films, gaining international status as an actor. He did a German version of *A Lady to Love* in 1930. In 1937 he went to England to star in *Thunder in the City*, the first of three British pictures he made (the others are *Journey Together* and *A Boy Ten Feet Tall*). In the 1960s and 1970s he went abroad to appear in such foreign-based projects as *Operation St. Peter, Peking Blonde, Grand Slam, Mad Checkmate,* and *Neither by Day Nor by Night*.

He acted with a number of players who appeared in a limited number of American films. Some were built up to become major stars, but, although not lacking in talent, few made a major impact. Cast in leading roles in mediocre films (to which Robinson nevertheless offered reliable support), many of these international players, some of them young and glamorous, disappeared almost immediately or lasted only a short time in films. Some simply returned to their homelands to work.

Lando Buzzanca (1935–) was the handsome Italian leading man of *Operation San Pietro*. In the 1970s he starred in such dubious titles as *Homo Eroticus, The Married Priest*, and *When Women Had Tails*.

Luli Deste (1902–51) was from Vienna. It was hoped she would become a new Dietrich. She was Robinson's love interest in *Thunder in the City* and appeared also in *She Married an Artist, South to Karanga,* and *Ski Patrol*.

Sergio Fantoni (1930–), a handsome Italian, appeared in American films beginning in 1960. His credits include *Esther and the King, The Prize* (with Robinson), *What Did You Do in the War, Daddy?* and *Von Ryan's Express*.

Dahlia Lavi (1940–) made her screen debut at the age of sixteen in her native Israel. Her first American film was *Two Weeks in Another Town* with Edward G. Robinson. Others were *Lord Jim, The Silencers,* and *Casino Royale*.

Toralv Maurstad (1926–) was considered Norway's leading actor at the time he acted with Robinson in Andrew Stone's *Song of Norway* (as Edvard Grieg). Perhaps the film's failure was one reason Maurstad did not appear in subsequent American films.

Christina Schollin (1937–), from Sweden, appeared with Robinson in *Song of Norway* as Grieg's patroness, Therese Berg, a singing role. In 1983 she was in the Oscar-winning foreign film *Fanny and Alexander*.

Camilla Sparv (1943–), a Swedish actress, is in *Mackenna's Gold*. Other films include *The Trouble with Angels, Murderer's Row, The Greek Tycoon, Caboblanco,* and *America 3000*.

Rose Stradner (1913–58) came from Austrian films to be in *The Last Gangster* as Robinson's wife; she was also in *Blind Alley* and *The Keys of the Kingdom*, and was married to director Joseph L. Mankiewicz.

An Intimate Dinner in Celebration of Warner Bros. Silver Jubilee (Short film, 1930) This short subject was produced to mark the studio's first twenty-five years.

Participants: Otis Skinner (Mr. W. B. Pictures), Beryl Mercer (Mrs. W. B. Pictures), Little Miss Vitaphone, Joan Blondell, Douglas Fairbanks, Jr., Oscar Hammerstein II, Otto Harbach, Lorenz Hart, Jerome Kern, Marilyn Miller, Edward G. Robinson, Richard Rodgers, Loretta Young; Warner Bros., 1930

"The Island in the Wilderness" (Radio, 1948) *The Eternal Light*; NBC-radio; March 14, 1948; Edward G. Robinson (Narrator)

Israel: Its Ancient Glories and Its Wonders of Today (Short film, 1959) While in Israel making this short documentary film, Edward G. Robinson visited with Prime Minister David Ben Gurion. *Israel* was shown in theaters during a re-release of *The Ten Commandments*.

Producer, writer, Leon Uris; director, Sam Zebba; music, Elmer Bernstein; Warner Bros.; WarnerScope, Technicolor; 29 minutes; 1959; Edward G. Robinson (Narrator); introducing the voice of Batya

"It Isn't Peanuts" (Radio) cast: Edward G. Robinson; Vincent Price (host); *Treasury Star Parade*; 1940s; radio; 15 minutes

It's a Great Feeling (Film, 1949) Edward G. Robinson was one of a dozen Warner stars and directors who played themselves in a musical spoof called *It's a Great Feeling*. In the story none of the top directors will work with Jack Carson because of his ego. So, for his next picture, which will also feature Dennis Morgan, Jack himself will be the director. The two discover Judy Adams, a waitress who wants to break into movies, and they sign her up to be their female lead. Various Hollywood stars turn up in the course of making the film, which includes several musical numbers. Both Jack and Dennis fall for Judy, but her heart belongs to Jeffrey Bushdinkel, her handsome beau back home in Wisconsin. After completing the film, she goes home to marry him.

Time magazine offered a negative among generally favorable reviews, saying the film was a "clownish musical ... the spoofing is hardly good enough to conceal the laborious spade work." *Newsweek*, calling it "as self-conscious as an after-dinner speaker who has forgotten his notes," at least found "parts of it extremely funny."

"A broad take-off on Broadway and picture making," according to *Variety*, "it has a gay, light air, color and a lineup of surprise guest stars that greatly enhance word-of-mouth values.... Edward G. Robinson gives a swell take-off on his stock hard-boiled gangster character in a sequence played for loud chuckles." *The New York Times* offered Robinson a second favorable review, stating that he "contributes a travesty on his hard-boiled gangster characterization."

There was an Oscar nomination for the title song by Sammy Cahn and Jule Styne.

Producer, Alex Gottlieb; director, David Butler; story, I. A. L. Diamond; screenplay, Jack Rose, Melville Shavelson; art director, Stanley Fleischer; set, Lyle B. Reifsnider; sound, Dolph Thomas, David Forrest; special effects, William McGann, H. F. Koenekamp; assistant director, Phil Quinn; choreography, LeRoy Prinz; songs, Sammy Cahn, Jule Styne; music director, Ray Heindorf; orchestra, Leo Shuken, Sidney Cutner; dialogue director, Herschel Daugherty; camera, Wilfrid M. Cline; editor, Irene Morra; costumes, Milo Anderson; makeup, Perc Westmore, Mickey Marcellino; Technicolor consultant, Natalie Kalmus; assistant, Mitchell Kovaleske; cast: Dennis Morgan (Himself), Jack Carson (Himself), Doris Day (Judy Adams), Bill Goodwin (Arthur Trent), Irving Bacon (Train clerk), Claire Carleton (Grace), Harlan Warde (Publicity man), Jacqueline DeWitt (Trent's secretary), Pat Flaherty (Studio guard), Gary Cooper, Joan Crawford, Sydney Greenstreet, Danny Kaye, Patricia Neal, Eleanor Parker, Ronald Reagan, Edward G. Robinson, Jane Wyman (Guest stars), David Butler, Michael Curtiz, King Vidor, Raoul Walsh (Themselves), Errol Flynn (Jeffrey Bushdinkel), Wilfred Lukas, Nita Talbot, Joan Vohs, Tom Dugan, Ralph Littlefield, Ray Montgomery, Forbes Murray, Maureen Reagan, Cosmo Sardo, Olan Soule, Wendy Lee, Eve Whitney, Carol Brewster, Sue Casey, Lois Austin, James Holden, Sandra Gould, Peter Meersman, Rod Rogers, Georges Renavent, Dudley Dickerson, Mel Blanc (Bugs Bunny), Jean Andren, Shirley Ballard, Mazzone-Abbott Dancers; Warner Bros.; 84 minutes; Technicolor; July 1949

It's Your Move see *Mad Checkmate*

Ivan, Rosalind (1884–1959) came to the New York stage from London in 1912. She acted with Edward G. Robinson in *The Night Lodging*, and translated *The Brothers Karamazov* from the Russian for the Theatre Guild. She was also with Robinson in *Arms and the Woman*, and thirty years later played his shrewish wife, Adele, in *Scarlet Street*. Her other films include *None but the Lonely Heart, The Corn Is Green,* and *The Robe*.

Jackson, Anne (1925–), the wife of actor Eli Wallach, appeared frequently with him on the New York stage (*The Typists and the Tiger, Luv*). She played Edward G. Robinson's daughter on Broadway in *Middle of the Night*. Her few films include *The Journey, Tall Story, The Angel Levine, Dirty Dingus Magee,* and *The Bell Jar*.

Jackson, Thomas E. (1886–1967) played cops in four films with Edward G. Robinson, most importantly as Lieutenant Flaherty, nemesis to *Little Caesar*, and as Inspector Jackson in *The Woman in the Window*. He was also in *Scarlet Street* and *The Amazing Dr. Clitterhouse*, as well as *Broadway, Good News, The Law of the Tropics,* and *Phone Call from a Stranger*.

Jaeckel, Richard (1926–97) began in films as a handsome juvenile in such World War II entries as *Guadalcanal Diary*. With Edward G. Robinson he plays Bobby Bronson, an aspiring ballplayer, in *Big Leaguer*, and Wade Matlock, a hired gun, in *The Violent Men*. He is in *Come Back Little Sheba* and *Sometimes a Great Notion*.

Jaffe, Bettye Ackerman (1928–) was on TV in *Ben Casey* and *Bracken's World*, and in the films *Face of Fire, Rascal,* and *M*A*S*H*. Her remembrances of her late husband, Sam Jaffe, and his lifelong relationship with Edward G. Robinson were included in the *A&E Biography* "Little Big Man." All three appear as themsleves in *Mooch*.

Jaffe, Sam (1891–1984) appeared onstage with Edward G. Robinson in *The Idle Inn* and *Samson and Delilah*. They also were together in a *For the Living* radio episode, "By-Products of the Atom," and on TV in *The Old Man Who Cried Wolf*. Jaffe was in *Gunga Din* (title role), *The Lost Horizon* (the High Lama), and *The Asphalt Jungle* (Doc Riedenschneider, Oscar nomination). Jaffe lived in the Robinson home for a time after the death of his first wife, Lillian Taiz, in 1941. His second wife, Bettye Ackerman, starred with Jaffe on TV's *Ben Casey*. He is on the BBC's *The Hollywood Greats: Edward G. Robinson*; the two were lifelong friends. In a letter to the author, Jaffe wrote, "He [Robinson] was a person of great integrity, a great actor and a rare friend. You've chosen well to emulate him."

Jaquet, Frank (1885–1958) appears in three films with Edward G. Robinson —*A Dispatch from Reuter's* (as Stein), *House of Strangers*, and *Tales of Manhattan*. Other films include *Crime School*, *Shine on Harvest Moon*, *D.O.A.*, and *Jupiter Darling*.

Jenkins, Allen (1900–1974) made a career of playing comic gangsters. He is in *The Stolen Jools* and four other features with Edward G. Robinson — Mike in *A Slight Case of Murder*, Okay in *The Amazing Dr. Clitterhouse*, Willie the Knife in *Brother Orchid*, and Vermin in *Robin and the 7 Hoods*. Other films include *42nd Street*, *Destry Rides Again*, *Ball of Fire*, and *Pillow Talk*.

Jenkins, Jackie "Butch" (1937–) made a handful of films as a child from 1943 (*The Human Comedy*) to 1948 (*Summer Holiday*). He plays Edward G. Robinson's young nephew, Arnold Hansen, in *Our Vines Have Tender Grapes*, and also has roles in *National Velvet* and *My Brother Talks to Horses*.

Jennings, DeWitt (1879–1937) played in three early films with Edward G. Robinson: *Outside the Law*, *The Night Ride*, and *Silver Dollar*. He also had roles in *Mystery of the Wax Museum* and *Mutiny on the Bounty*.

Jerusalem Is Her Name (Radio, 1953) This radio program was a taped broadcast from New York for the State of Israel Bonds.
 Cast: Edward G. Robinson, Paul Muni; Madison Square Garden; NBC; October 21, 1953

Jessel, George (1898–1981), songwriter, actor, and producer, was on Broadway in *The Jazz Singer* and in films from 1911: *Four Jills in a Jeep*, *The Busy Body*, etc. He was on TV with Edward G. Robinson on *Here Come the Stars*, on the radio in *The Roosevelt Special*, in a *Screen Snapshots* episode ("Hollywood Friars Honor George Jessel,") and the stage pageant *We Will Never Die*.

Jewelry Precious stones figure in the plots of Edward G. Robinson's films, from the diamond stick pin coveted by Rico in *Little Caesar* to diamond smuggling, the occupation of Cocky Wainwright in *A Boy Ten Feet Tall*. A robbery of diamonds from a vault is the subject of *Grand Slam*. The gang in *Peking Blonde* is seeking "The Blue Grape," a precious pearl. In *The Amazing Dr. Clitterhouse* Robinson, the doctor of the title, pulls off multiple jewelry heists in order to research criminology. Norma Shearer's pearls are stolen in the aptly named short film *The Slippery Pearls* (also known as *The Stolen Jools*). To raise money, his wife offers to pawn her jewels in *A Slight Case of Murder*, not realizing that Robinson's character, Remy Marco, has already done so. A jewel-encrusted dagger is a key prop in *The Outrage*.

 A pocket watch is given to Robinson at testimonials in *Little Caesar* (it is stolen) and *Scarlet Street*. A monogrammed watch is found on the murder victim in *The Woman in the Window*.

 For much of Robinson's career onscreen he wore his personal cats-eye ring on his left pinky finger. It is visible as early as 1939 in stills from *Blackmail*. In some films he wears a wedding ring instead. If his character were impoverished or otherwise would not wear it, it was missing. Offscreen Robinson also wore around his neck a charm that looked like a small red pepper.

Jewison, Norman (1926–) replaced Sam Peckinpah as director of *The Cincinnati Kid*, with Edward G. Robinson. Other films include *Send Me No Flowers, The Russians Are Coming ... The Russians Are Coming, The Thomas Crown Affair, Jesus Christ Superstar, Agnes of God, Moonstruck,* and the Oscar-nominated *Fiddler on the Roof* and *In the Heat of the Night*.

Jiminez, Soledad (1874–1966) played Edward G. Robinson's sweet Italian mother in *Kid Galahad*. She also played Paul Muni's mother in *Bordertown*, but was actually Spanish. Her other films include *In Old Arizona, Robin Hood of El Dorado, Black Bart,* and *Red Light*.

"Joe Doakes and the White Star" (Radio) *Treasury Star Parade*; Edward G. Robinson (host), Dinah Shore, Mabel Todd; 1940s; 15 minutes

Johann, Zita (1904–93) came to films from New York, where, with Edward G. Robinson, she had appeared in the Theatre Guild's production of *The Goat Song*. She was married to John Houseman at the time she was acting with Robinson in *Tiger Shark*. Other films include *The Mummy, The Man Who Dared,* and *Luxury Liner*.
See **Tiger Shark**.

Johnson, Ben (1919–96), an Oscar winner for *The Last Picture Show*, was in *Cheyenne Autumn* with Edward G. Robinson, as well as many of the other films of John Ford—*Three Godfathers, She Wore a Yellow Ribbon, Rio Grande*—plus *Shane, The Wild Bunch,* and *Red Dawn*.

Johnson, Russell (1924–) is known as The Professor on TV's *Gilligan's Island*. He was in several films, including *Black Tuesday* (with Edward G. Robinson), *It Came from Outer Space, A Distant Trumpet,* and *The Greatest Story Ever Told*.

Jones, Carolyn (1929–83) played Shirl in *A Hole in the Head*, with Edward G. Robinson, and also appeared with him paying tribute to Frank Capra on *This Is Your Life*. Her other films include *House of Wax, The Big Heat, King Creole, Ice Palace, Career,* and *The Bachelor Party*. She was Morticia on TV's *The Addams Family*.

Jones, Shirley (1934–), singer-actress, won the best supporting actress Oscar for *Elmer Gantry*. Earlier she played the Rodgers and Hammerstein heroines of *Carousel* and *Oklahoma!* on the screen. She appears with Edward G. Robinson as the female lead in *Pepe*, and is also featured in *Never Steal Anything Small* and *The Music Man*.

Jordan, Bobby (1923–65) was Angel, the youngest of the Dead End kids. He had a good comic role as Douglas Fairbanks Rosenbloom, a reform school kid, in *A Slight Case of Murder*, with Edward G. Robinson, and another, smaller role as a crying homesick sailor in *Destroyer*.

Jory, Victor (1902–82) was in *Cheyenne Autumn*, with Edward G. Robinson, as a stoic Indian chief; he was the voice-over narrator of *Mackenna's Gold*; and appeared also in TV's *Who Has Seen the Wind?* Other films include *A Midsummer Night's Dream* (as King Oberon), *The Adventures of Tom Sawyer, Dodge City, Gone with the Wind,* and *Papillon*.

Joslyn, Allan (1901–81), a comic actor, worked on the Broadway stage with Edward G. Robinson in *The Firebrand*. In Hollywood from 1936, he appeared in *They Won't Forget, Only Angels Have Wings, The Great McGinty, My Sister Eileen, The Horn Blows at Midnight,* and *Titanic*.

Journey Together (Film, 1945) "He chose to come to England in the middle of the war at his own expense, and for no salary whatsoever, to play this part in order to pay his own private tribute to this country's efforts during those frightening years," said Richard Attenborough. Edward G. Robinson and Attenborough appeared together in *Journey Together*. It was Robinson's second film made in England.

Producer, Royal Air Force Film Unit Ministry of Information; director, John Boulting; screenplay, Boulting; story, Terence Rattigan; music, Gordon Jacob; production designer, John Howell; special effects, Ray Morse; camera, Harry Waxman, Gilbert Taylor; editors, Michael Del Campo, Reginald Beck; cast: Richard Attenborough (David Wilton), Jack Watling (John Aynesworth), David Tomlinson (Smith), Stuart Latham (Flight sergeant fitter), Hugh Wakefield (Acting lieutenant), Sid Rider (A fitter), Z. Peromowski (Anson pilot), Bromley Challenor (A. C. 2 Jay), Edward G. Robinson (Dean McWilliams), Patrick Waddington (Flight Lt. Mander), Sebastian Shaw (Squadron Leader Marshall), Ronald Adam (Commanding Officer), Bessie Love (Mary McWilliams), Norvell Crutcher (Driver), George Cole, Rex Harrison, John Justin, Miles Malleson, Fletcher Markle, Jack Baker, Arthur Bolton, Stuart Dick, Jerry Fitzgerald, Michael McNeile, Peter Naglis, Hamish Nichol, Leslie Nixon, Nick Stuart, Tommy Tomlinson, Eric Worth, Ronald Squire (Guest stars), and Personnel of the Royal Air Force, Royal Canadian Air Force, and the United States Army; RKO British Films; 95 (or 80) minutes; March 1946

David Wilton and John Aynesworth are among recruits joining England's Royal Air Force. Their goal is to become pilots. In preliminary training in England they do well enough. Coming to the United States with a group for flight training in Arizona, the two come under the guidance of flight instructor Dean McWilliams. Through several missions it becomes increasingly apparent that being a pilot is not what Wilton is suited for. McWilliams takes him and Aynesworth to his ranch for a weekend with him and his wife, hoping that home-cooked meals and a less military-like atmosphere will have a calming effect. Aynesworth eventually becomes a pilot. But Wilton, discouraged, goes to navigator training in Canada. On active duty, when his crew's plane ditches in the sea during a reconnaissance mission over Germany, Wilton proves his ability in his new field by quickly reporting their life raft's location for rescue in the North Sea.

The New York Times called *Journey Together* "a dandy little picture about British airmen during the war, solidly authentic and full of character, action and suspense.... All of the cast—with the exception of Edward G. Robinson, who plays an instructor at the Arizona field, and Bessie Love, who plays his wife—were recruited from RAF personnel. It is no reflection on Mr. Robinson or Miss Love (and their roles are naturally brief) to say that the actual airmen are much more creditable in the film than they are."

The New York Herald-Tribune was not as impressed: "Edward G. Robinson has been dragged into the picture as an American pilot-training officer. He does his bit in a fatherly way." *Theatre Arts Magazine* said, "Mr. Robinson's role, although pivotal, is not large enough to draw attention from the agreeable playing of ... Attenborough ... and Watling."

Juarez and Maximilian (Theater, 1926)

Edward G. Robinson identified strongly with the historical character of Porfirio Diaz, whom he portrayed in Franz Werfel's *Juarez and Maximilian,* his seventh production for the Theatre Guild and his third teaming with Alfred Lunt. In his autobiography, however, his view of the script helps account for its imbalance. He felt that Werfel wrote Diaz as a kind of universal character—and the central focus of the script—while the play was attempting to tell the story of Emperor Maximilian. He noted further that the elaborate production values given the play by the Guild slowed down a much more dynamic drama which had been apparent in the rehearsal stages.

Produced by the Theatre Guild; playwright, Franz Werfel; director, Philip Moeller; settings and costumes, Lee Simonson; cast: Alfred Lunt (Maximilian), Edward G. Robinson (Porfirio Diaz), Dudley Digges (Archbishop Labastida of Mexico and Puebla), Clare Eames (Carlotta), Morris Carnovsky (Riva-Palacio; Canon Soria), Margalo Gillmore (Princess Agnes Salm), Earle Larimore (State Councillor Stephen Herzfeld), Sanford Meisner (Blasio), Erskine Sanford (Lawyer Siliceo; Jose Rincon Gallardo), Harold Clurman

(Mariano Escobedo; Polyphemie), Charles Allais (General Miramon), Albert Bruning (Dr. Basch), Cheryl Crawford (Madame Barrio), Arnold Daly (Francois Achille Bazaine), Stanley DeWolfe (Clarke; Corporal Winberger), Perry Ivins (Theodosio Lares), Philip Leigh (City Deputy of Chihuahua; Yapitan), Alfred Lewis (Iturbide), Philip Loeb (Elizea; General Tomas Mejia), Maurice McRae (Edouard Pierron), John Rynne (Grill), Roland Twombley (Official), Edward Van Sloan (Captain Miguel Lopez), Dan Walker (General Marquez); opened at the Guild Theatre, New York; October 11, 1926

The actor received better reviews than the play. "Robinson as Porfirio Diaz ... gives for the most part an admirable performance, acrid, savage, and exalted," said *The New Republic*. "The loose structure of the drama, rendered looser yet by a soft performance, blunts the point of the tragedy," noted *The New York Times*. "Little of the bitter irony [of the original] emerges.... Mr. Robinson conveys the fierce sincerity of Porfirio Diaz."

Best Plays 1926–27 noted that the play was presented in "pictures:" "The thirteen pictures are taken from scenes in and about the imperial palace in Mexico City, the pleasure palace at Chapultepec, and the headquarters of both armies in the field, covering that period of Maximilian's occupancy of the throne of Mexico from the autumn of 1865 to the summer of 1867."

Judaism Edward G. Robinson was born the fifth of six sons into a Jewish family in Bucharest, Rumania. Religious persecution (an older brother was injured in a pogrom) and the hopes for a better life prompted the family's move to the United States when he was ten.

Robinson played Jewish characters more often on the stage than in his films, where his Latinate presence seemed better suited to Italian gangsters. The plays include *The Idle Inn, The Goat Song, We Americans, The Kibitzer, Mr. Samuel,* and *Middle of the Night*. On television he was an impoverished Jewish grandfather in "The Messiah on Mott Street," and his characters were also Jewish in "Shadows Tremble," and "The Old Man Who Cried Wolf."

He also played Sol Roth in *Soylent Green*, Dr. Paul Ehrlich in *Dr. Ehrlich's Magic Bullet*, and Dathan, a skeptical Hebrew overseer in *The Ten Commandments*.

Robinson's first wife, Gladys Lloyd, was a Quaker, but his second, Jane Adler, was Jewish. His parents kept a kosher kitchen, but Robinson was a much more liberal Jew. One tradition he did uphold was the ritual of observing the *Jahrtzeit* on the anniversary of th e death of loved ones.

Karloff, Boris (1887–1969) The great English horror star supported Edward G. Robinson in two films among a dozen he made in 1931, the year he shot to fame as the *Frankenstein* monster. He was Sport Williams, a gambler, in *Smart Money*, and Rev. T. Vernon Isopod in *Five Star Final*. Karloff appeared on Broadway in *Arsenic and Old Lace* and lent his voice to the title role of the television cartoon *How the Grinch Stole Christmas*. Other films, from 1919, include *Scarface, The Old Dark House, The Mummy, The Black Cat, The Tower of London, The Body Snatchers, Unconquered, Comedy of Terrors,* and *Targets*.

Kate Smith's A & P Bandwagon see "Thunder in the City"

Kaye, Danny (1913–87), comedy star of *Hans Christian Andersen, The Secret Life of Walter Mitty, The Court Jester,* and TV's *The Danny Kaye Show*, was on several variety programs with Edward G. Robinson: *Hollywood Fights Back* and *The Roosevelt Special,* as well as "Victory Extra" on the radio, and on television in *Twelve Star Salute* and *Operation Entertainment*. Finally, the two guest-starred as themselves in the film *It's a Great Feeling*

Keane, Edward (1884–1959) appears in *Confessions of a Nazi Spy, I Am the Law,* and *Scarlet Street,* with Edward G. Robinson. He also is seen in *Charlie Chan in Panama, Mystery of the Wax Museum, G-Men,* and *Showboat*.

Keenan, Frank (1859–1929), New York actor, starred in a production of *The Pawn* in which Edward G. Robinson also appeared. He was in silent roles from 1915 — *The Bells, Hearts Aflame,* and *East Lynne.* His grandson was actor Keenan Wynn.

Keith, Brian (1921–97) played tough guys in two Edward G. Robinson films — as his younger brother, Cole, in *The Violent Men,* and as Vince, a crooked cop, in *Tight Spot.* He was popular on television in *Family Affair* and in such films as *The Parent Trap, Nevada Smith, The Russians Are Coming ... The Russians Are Coming, Reflections in a Golden Eye,* and *The Wind and the Lion.* His father was actor Robert Keith.

Kellaway, Cecil (1891–1973) was one of the floratian monks in *Brother Orchid,* with Edward G. Robinson. His other films include *Wuthering Heights, I Married a Witch, The Postman Always Rings Twice, Harvey, Hush Hush Sweet Charlotte, Guess Who's Coming to Dinner,* and *The Luck of the Irish,* receiving best supporting actor Oscar nominations for the latter two.

Kelley, Barry (1908–91) played attorney Dwight Foreman in *Vice Squad,* with Edward G. Robinson, and also was a police chief in *Robin and the 7 Hoods.* He had roles in *The Asphalt Jungle, The Manchurian Candidate,* and *The Love Bug,* among others.

Kelley, DeForrest (1915–99) was in films long before becoming *Star Trek's* Dr. Jim "Bones" McCoy. With Edward G. Robinson he was the wrongly executed Ed Clary in *Illegal.* Among his other films are *Fear in the Night* (remade as *Nightmare*), *House of Bamboo,* and *Gunfight at the OK Corral.*

Kelly, Jack (1927–92), known for his role as Bart in the *Maverick* series on television (James Garner was his brother, Bret), supported Edward G. Robinson in *The Glass Web, Black Tuesday,* and *The Violent Men.* He was also in *The Country Girl* and *Gunsmoke.*

Kelly, John (1901–47), who looked like a thug, acted with Edward G. Robinson in *Two Seconds, The Last Gangster, The Little Giant, Manpower, Tales of Manhattan,* and *Larceny, Inc.* Other films include *The Pittsburgh Kid, Little Miss Marker,* and *Bringing Up Baby.*

Kendall, Cy (1898–1953), heavy-set and mean-looking, was with Edward G. Robinson in *The Last Gangster, Blackmail* (as the sheriff), and *Scarlet Street* (Nick, the pawnbroker). They were on the radio together in "Kid Galahad" and episodes of *Big Town.* Other films include *Crime School, Billy the Kid,* and *Johnny Eager.*

Kennedy, Arthur (1914–90) played Doc Holliday in *Cheyenne Autumn.* On Broadway he acted in Arthur Miller dramas, notably in *All My Sons,* as Chris, *The Price,* and *The Crucible.* Other films include *High Sierra, Rancho Notorious, The Desperate Hours, Elmer Gantry,* and *Lawrence of Arabia.*

Kent, Barbara (1906–) was the leading lady in *Night Ride,* with Edward G. Robinson. In talking pictures from 1928 through 1941, she also was seen in Harold Lloyd's *Feet First* and *Welcome Danger,* and also *Lonesome, Chinatown After Dark, Emma, Vanity Fair,* and *Old Man Rhythm.*

Kerrigan, J. M. (1885–1964) came to films from the Abbey Players in Ireland. He was drunken Judge Harper in *Barbary Coast,* with Edward G. Robinson, and also appeared in *The Informer, Captains of the Clouds, The Long Voyage Home,* and *Gone with the Wind.*

Key Largo (Film, 1948) As if *Little Caesar* were not enough to establish Edward G. Robinson as America's definitive gangster star, the actor firmly reestablished his persona with a return to the fold nearly twenty years later. The resulting Johnny Rocco, as several critics have noted, was an older, wiser gangster than the Rico of *Little Caesar,* and *Key Largo* stands as a sort of bookend to the earlier film in his career. As Charles Matthews, in his book

Oscar A to Z, points out, "The only puzzle is why Robinson, who gives one of his finest performances as the gangster, failed to receive [an Academy Award] nomination."

Producer, Jerry Wald; director, John Huston; screenplay, Huston, Richard Brooks; based on the play by Maxwell Anderson; music, Max Steiner; orchestra, Murray Cutter; song, "Moanin' Low," Howard Dietz, Ralph Rainger; art director, Leo K. Kuter; set, Fred M. MacLean; sound, Dolph Thomas; continuity, Jean Baker; special effects, William McGann, Robert Burks; camera, Karl Freund; editor, Rudi Fehr; makeup, Perc Westmore, Frank McCoy; costumes, Marie Blanchard, Ted Schultz; wardrobe, Leah Rhodes; hairstyles, Betty Delmont; unit manager, Chuck Hansen; assistant directors, Art Lueker, John Prettyman; cast: Humphrey Bogart (Frank McCloud), Edward G. Robinson (Johnny Rocco), Lauren Bacall (Nora Temple), Lionel Barrymore (James Temple), Claire Trevor (Gaye Dawn), Thomas Gomez (Curley Hoff), John Rodney (Deputy Clyde Sawyer), Harry Lewis (Toots Bass), Dan Seymour (Angel Garcia), Marc Lawrence (Ziggy), Monte Blue (Sheriff Ben Wade), William Haade (Ralph Feeney), Jay Silverheels (Tom Osceola), Rodric Redwing (John Osceola), Pat Flaherty (Henchman), Joe P. Smith (Bus driver), Alberto Morin (Skipper), Jerry Jerome, Lute Crockett, John Phillips (Ziggy's men), Felipa Gomez (Old Indian Woman); Warner Bros., 101 minutes; July 1948

Frank McCloud comes to Key Largo to visit Nora, widow of one of the men under his command during the war, and her father-in-law, James Temple. The two manage the Largo Hotel. At the same time, notorious gangster Johnny Rocco and his men have arrived to complete a job. Rocco was deported but intends to make a comeback. The Temples are unaware who the men are until Sheriff Ben Wade and his deputy, Sawyer, come looking for the Osceola brothers, Indians who have broken out of jail. Wade has moved on, but Sawyer, curious, remains behind and is murdered, his body thrown in the ocean. Frank is reluctant to try stopping the gangsters, despite his chivalry toward Rocco's drunken mistress, Gaye Dawn. She is forced to sing to get a drink, and then it is refused because Rocco thinks she was "lousy"; Frank pours her a drink anyway. Later, the sheriff hunts down and kills the escaped Indians after Rocco lies, telling him that they killed Sawyer, whose body has washed ashore during a hurricane. Frank decides he must act. He pilots the gang aboard a cabin cruiser bound for Cuba, and with the help of a pistol smuggled to him by Gaye, he systematically does away with four of Rocco's henchmen. Rocco, alone now, tries to bargain with Frank. He throws out a gun to show he is unarmed, but, of course, he has another. He will split the money with Frank. Frank makes no response to Rocco. Infuriated, Rocco comes out, and Frank kills him. Wounded himself, he radios for help and heads back to Key Largo and Nora.

John Huston, who wrote and directed *Key Largo*, says in his memoir *An Open Book,* "Robinson accepted the part of the gangster with some reluctance. He had never cared for the gangster image.... I think *Key Largo* is best remembered by most people for the introductory scene, with Eddie in the bathtub, cigar in mouth. He looked like a crustacean with its shell off."

That image is an indelible one, of course; but in addition, the reviews Edward G. Robinson received for his acting were very enthusiastic. *The New York Times* commented on Huston's skills: "With remarkable filming and cutting, [he] has notably achieved a great deal of interest and tension in some rather static scenes — and scenes, too, that give the bald appearances of having been written for the stage." But the *Times* continued, "he has also got stinging performances out of most of his cast — notably out of Mr. Robinson, who plays the last of the red hot gangsters in top-notch style. Indeed, [his] performance is an expertly timed and timbered scan of the vulgarity, corruption and egoism of the criminal mind."

The New Yorker concurred, saying that the film was "livelier than [the play].... The leader of the ruffians has much in common with Lucky Luciano.... As played by Edward G. Robinson, this chap is in the great gangster tradition."

Newsweek said, "Huston and ... Brooks brought the 1939 drama up to date, also jettisoned Anderson's blank verse and most of his wordy preoccupation with the definition of honor.... *Key Largo* is a conventional gangster story raised by imagination and fine craftsmanship to a high level of excitement.... Relying on mood and accumulative tension, Huston, who also directed, has added another superior melodrama to [his] list. He is helped considerably by a first-rate cast. Bogart and Robinson, in roles that fit them as comfortably as old slippers, are as good as one might expect."

"Edward G. Robinson ... gave a splendid performance as a cynical and vicious gangster on the run," wrote Adam Garbicz and Jacek Klinowski in their book *Cinema, the Magic Vehicle: A Guide to its Achievement*

"*Key Largo* was Edward G. Robinson's last major gangster portrayal. He plays Johnny Rocco with the mannerisms and verve of his famous role in *Little Caesar*; but Rocco and his hoods are not young any more. They are clearly out of their time, relics of an old order that has passed.... Acting is low-keyed compared to Robinson's cigar-chomping, swaggering Rocco. The gangster is the complete antiromantic; a sadist and misogynist.... Robinson's performance during the storm scene, when he suffers uncontrollable shakes, is an example of broad physical acting to reveal the emotional stage of a character. His performance reflects the desperate nostalgia of one who has been 'a Somebody.'"—Joan Cohen, *Film Noir*

Robert Bookbinder praised "Robinson's marvelous character study," calling him "one of the truly great movie actors of the era, dazzling audiences and critics with his versatility and forever squelching the notion that gangster roles were his one and only forte.... As it turned out, the part of Rocco ... was simply too good to pass up, and it gave Robinson the greatest gangster characterization of his career ... virtuoso acting of the crude, malignant crime czar."—*Classics of the Gangster Film*

Who can argue with *The Commonweal's* assessment? "A topnotch movie ... Edward G. Robinson manages to make the character ... one of the most vicious in filmdom." Or with James Robert Parish in *The Tough Guys:* "[It is] one of Hollywood's superior gangster films, and Robinson's Johnny Rocco is one of the great celluloid gangsters.... In a seemingly perfect cast, Robinson's performance was the standout." Foster Hirsch called *Key Largo* "an ode to the vigorous Robinson madman ... a full-bodied character.... It's a broad, fulsome performance.... Robinson uses broad physical acting.... His electric presence subverts Maxwell Anderson's symbolic intentions...."—*Edward G. Robinson: A Pyramid Illustrated History of the Movies.*

And in a final summing up, *The New York Herald-Tribune* labeled *Key Largo* "a bowstring-tight humdinger of movie make-believe.... Robinson is *Little Caesar* all over again, terrorizing both his henchmen and the bystanders trapped with him in a lonely seaside hotel. In a story of modern crime, his acting might seem extreme, but here its touch of the twenties is exactly what is required of a brutish has-been who hopes that 'prohibition will come back in a couple of years.'"

"Robinson had wanted the part and $12,500 a week to play it," according to A. M. Sperber and Eric Lax in their book *Bogart*. "The way they [Bogart and Robinson] played off each other was a lesson in the art of film acting.... Huston let the two explore their ideas scene by scene before filming began. [Film editor Rudi] Fehr recalled that 'he just said to them, "Show me what you'd like to do here," and then he improved on that'.... Everyone knew that a good deal of the success of the interaction came from the high regard Bogart and Robinson had for each other.... 'They were delighted to be in the same picture,' Fehr said. 'They joked around. Watching them rehearse together was delightful because of their ability to create a scene and come up with a solution if a line didn't play or if one of them was uncomfortable sitting in a certain position or doing some bit of business....' Despite the commonly accepted story depicting both men as loftily indifferent to matters of status, it took months for their agents and the studio to agree on the placement of names and faces, type size, and other details of billing. Bogart, as the star, naturally got first place, but everything after that was negotiable. Sample layouts were made and given to all parties. At one point, Robinson's agent complained that Bogart's name was too big. At another, Bogart's complained that Robinson's head shot was too big. It wasn't just a question of ego; it was one of money, too. Billing determined earnings, negotiating power, and above all, one's place in the tightly hierarchic structure of studio Hollywood."

The film was released with Bogart, Robinson, and Lauren Bacall receiving first, second, and third billing, respectively, left-to-right, above the title. All three names were in the same size and type face in the posters and on the screen; however, Robinson's name, in the middle, was displayed higher than those of his two co-stars. For his part, Robinson felt fortunate even to be negotiating star billing. No longer under contract, he had been a freelance player away from Warner Bros. for six years. His age and political precariousness certainly didn't help the situation. On the set, however, everything was pleasant because everyone, including Lionel Barrymore and Claire Trevor, had the utmost respect for each other.

Lauren Bacall says in her autobiography *By Myself*, "The cast was fabulous — Eddie Robinson, Lionel Barrymore, Claire Trevor ... Eddie Robinson was a marvelous actor and a lovely, funny man.... We'd all gather round as [Barrymore] regaled us with theatrical stories. Eddie did 'Molly Malone' with a Yiddish accent which was wildly funny.... *Key Largo* was one of my happiest movie experiences ... to be able to work with such people. What a good time of life that was — the best people at their best. With all those supposed actors' egos, there was not a moment of discomfort or vying for position. That's because they were all actors, not just stars."

"Key Largo" (Radio, 1949) Robinson and Claire Trevor, along with co-players Dan Seymour and Harry Lewis, were heard on the radio in an adaptation of the film.

Director, Fred MacKaye; adaptation, Sanford Barnett; music director, Louis Silvers; sound, Charlie Forsyth; cast: Edward G. Robinson (Johnny Rocco); Claire Trevor (Gaye Dawn); Dan Seymour, Edmond O'Brien, Frances Robinson, Herb Butterfield, William Johnstone, Howard McNear, Edward Marr, Harry Lewis, Paul Dubov, Frank Richards, Jay Novello, Lou Krugman, Don Diamond, Dorothy Lovett (commercial), William Keighley (host), Debbie Reynolds (intermission guest), John Milton Kennedy (announcer); *Lux Radio Theatre*; CBS; 60 minutes; November 28, 1949

Kibbee, Guy (1882–1956) was in *Two Seconds* with Edward G. Robinson, and also had a cameo in *Dark Hazard*. He was also in *So Big, 42nd Street, Lady for a Day, Babbitt, Captain January, Mr. Smith Goes to Washington, Babes in Arms, Our Town,* and *Three Godfathers.*

Kibbee, Milton (1896–1970), brother of Guy Kibbee, was in five films with Edward G. Robinson — *The Man with Two Faces, Bullets or Ballots, Kid Galahad, Unholy Partners,* and *Scarlet Street.* He was also in *California Mail, The Greatest Show on Earth, Citizen Kane,* and *Strike Up the Band.*

The Kibitzer (Theater, 1927, 1929) This play is Edward G. Robinson's sole credit as a dramatic writer. Under not unsimilar circumstances, the making of *The Red House* was the only time he functioned as a film producer. He had no particular aspirations to be either a writer or a producer, much less a film director, like so many other actors of his time. Nevertheless, he *did* write *The Kibitzer* with Jo Swerling.

Swerling had written the play that Robinson played in Atlantic City in the summer of 1927. Robinson had high regard for Swerling's skill as a playwright, and he was pleased that the well-written character of Lazarus afforded him star billing for the first time. The script, unfortunately, wasn't strong enough to sustain a long run. Robinson was convinced that the play could be saved. Working with Swerling, he acted out various scenes while the author made changes. Ultimately the title page of the revised play bore the name of a co-author — a surprised Edward G. Robinson!

"Robinson loved doing a part that was both comic and sentimental," noted Foster Hirsch. "He thought it would be his insurance policy for years." But the stock market crash and the Depression, together with the exciting development of films that now could talk, lessened the play's impact. Robinson lost the role of Lazarus in the film to Harry Green.

1927 version: playwright, Jo Swerling; cast: Edward G. Robinson (Lazarus); Atlantic City, New Jersey; summer, 1927

1929 version: producer, director, Patterson McNutt; playwrights, Jo Swerling, Edward G. Robinson; director, Samuel T. Godfrey; technical director, Mildred Coughlin; publicist, Norman Furman; general manager, Thomas Kilpatrick; press representative, Henry Myers; set, Schaffner and Sweet; stage manager, Walter F. Scott; cast: Edward G. Robinson (Lazarus), Jeanne Greene (Josie), Hobart Cavanaugh (Emil Schmidt), Tom Fadden (Loomis), Samuel T. Godfrey (Briggs), Charles Hammond (Hanson), Travis "Weather" Hoke (A Barometer salesman), Nelan Jaap (Bill), Jacob Katzman (Yankel), Hunter Kaufman (Photographer), Louis LaBey (Sarnov), Alexis Polianov (Kikoupoupoulous), Michael Porter (Michaels), Al Roberts (Marks), Arthur S. Ross (Meyer), Walter F. Scott (Mullins), Vincent Strain (Reporter), James Whittaker (Nolan), Stanley G. Wood (Phillips), C. J. Williams (Wescott), George Spelvin, Jr., Lloyd Russell, Agnew T. Horine (Customers), Eugene Powers (James Livingston), George Spelvin, Sr. (An Officer), Henry Howard (First Kibitzer), Rex Boyd (Second Kibitzer), Fred M. Mitchell (A Butcher), Martha Edwards, Beatrice Bayard (Neighbors), Harry Carl (Florist's boy), Ford Bancroft (Ticker man), Alvah T. Posen, Oscar Mirantz, Phillip Pollumbaum, Abe Merrit; opened at the Royale Theatre, New York; February 18, 1929

Lazarus runs a cigar store in Amsterdam Avenue. He is chief adviser to the neighborhood, instructing everybody — from the pinochle players to the followers of the ponies and the stock market — how to place their wagers. He accidentally befriends James Livingston, a millionaire, and is given his choice between a bunch of stock and a cash reward. He takes the stock, installs a ticker in the cigar store and becomes in his own mind a heavy operator on the market. The stock soars ten points. Lazarus refuses to sell. The stock slides back and Lazarus thinks he is wiped out. But a daffy cousin had given the order to sell when the stock was at its peak.

The rewritten script was very successful. *The New York Times* said that "by virtue of [Robinson's] presence [it is] ... an enjoyable piece of theatre ... a mechanical, highly colored comedy which at times is more than a little preposterous. But it is also infectiously good-natured and human ... with a fair share of amusing lines and situations. The play is entirely Mr. Robinson and his performance. The portrayal ... by this actor of finish and variety is full length, revealing him in nearly all his moods and aspects. So credible an impersonation is it that you often wish that the play were a little more believable.... For Mr. Robinson it constitutes a minor sort of triumph, another scalp added to his list of histrionic achievements."

Theatre Arts Monthly commented, "Hardly a season fails to demonstrate Robinson's astonishing talents as a character actor." *The Nation* said, "Mr. Robinson brings his usual excellent technique and gift for characterization to *The Kibitzer*. He is so completely the shabby little trader ... that one begins to doubt if he were ever anyone else."

Kid Galahad (Film, 1937) *Film Daily* called *Kid Galahad* "easily one of the best fight pictures ever screened."

The casting of Bette Davis opposite Edward G. Robinson was a concession to his contractual demand that Warner Bros. not require him to carry a film by himself. She had just lost a landmark lawsuit in London against Warners wherein she had tried to get better roles than offered in her contract. In retrospect, Davis regarded *Kid Galahad* as important to her career if only in gaining for her the audience of a prizefighting film. "We co-starred Eddie with Bette Davis...." wrote Hal Wallis (with Charles Higham) in his memoir *Starmaker*. "After the first day's work, he said to me, 'This Davis girl. She's an amateur.

She's totally out of place in this picture.' I assured him that she would give a fine performance, but he did not warm to her, nor she to him. Neither recognized the other's talent."

"Neither performer was the type to walk through a role," noted James Robert Parish in *The Tough Guys*. "…When Edward G. Robinson's name is mentioned to Bette Davis, the first thing that comes to her mind is the death scene…. 'I remember a very powerful actor (she is usually careful not to divulge his name) who was doing a death scene. I was crying, and Janie Bryan was crying. I still remember his plaintive complaint to the director, "Don't you think the girls are crying too much?"'"

In his autobiography Robinson made no secret of his disdain for Bette Davis, although he later admitted an appreciation of her talent. Davis, less charitable, sophomorically pointed out Robinson's homeliness and voiced her distaste for having to kiss his purple lips during their scenes onscreen.

Robinson did not think of Nick as one of his anti-romantic roles. "It has softer moments," he said in a 1937 interview with Regina Carew in the *New York American*. "The romantic element is strongly stressed … there is an odd sort of romance between Nick and Fluff, but it is warm and sincere nevertheless."

Executive producer, Hal B. Wallis; associate producer, Samuel Bischoff; director, Michael Curtiz; screenplay by Seton I. Miller; based on the novel by Francis Wallace; assistant director, Jack Sullivan; special effects, James Gibbons, Edwin B. DuPar; music, Max Steiner, Heinz Roemheld; music director, Leo F. Forbstein; orchestra, Hugo Freidhofer; song, "The Moon Is in Tears Tonight," M. K. Jerome, Jack Scholl; art director, Carl Jules Weyl; sound, Charles Lang; camera, Tony Gaudio; editor, George Amy; gowns, Orry-Kelly; dialogue director, Irving Rapper; cast: Edward G. Robinson (Nick Donati), Bette Davis (Louise "Fluff" Phillips), Humphrey Bogart (Turkey Morgan), Wayne Morris (Ward Guisenberry / Kid Galahad), Jane Bryan (Marie Donati), Harry Carey (Silver Jackson), William Haade (Chuck McGraw), Ben Welden (Buzz Barrett), Soledad Jiminez (Mrs. Donati), Joe Cunningham (Joe Taylor), Joseph Crehan (Editor Brady), Veda Ann Borg (Redhead), Frank Faylen (Barney), Harland Tucker (Gunman), Bob Evans (Sam McGraw), Hank Hankinson (Jim Burke), Bob Nestell (Tim O'Brien), Jack Kranz (Denbaugh), George Blake (Referee), Charlie Sullivan (Second), Joyce Compton (Girl on phone), Eddie Foster (Louie, piano player), George Humbert (Barber), Emmett Vogan (Ring announcer), Don DeFore, Stan Jolley (Ringsiders), Harry Harvey, Don Brodie, Milton Kibbee, Horace MacMahon, John Shelton, Al Hill, Ralph Dunn (Reporters), Eddie Chandler (Title fight announcer), Lane Chandler (Timekeeper), Billy Arnold, Curtis Benton, Mary Doran, Max Hoffman, Edward Price, John Ridgely, Mary Sunde, Philip Waldron, Bess Flowers, Jack Adair, Don Barclay, Glen Cavender, Andre Chiron, Billy Coe, Irene Coleman, Virginia Dabney, Don Downen, Eddie Fetherston, Bud Geary, Eddie Graham, Kit Guard, Willard Hall, Kenneth Harlan, John Harron, Jack Hatfield, Ben Hendricks Jr., Stuart Holmes, Donald Kerr, Mike Lally, Frank Mayo, Tom McGuire, Carlyle Moore Jr., Edward Mortimer, Jack Mower, Louis Natheaux, Paul Panzer, Charles Randolph, Jack Richardson, Buddy Roosevelt, Ferdinand Schumann-Heink, John Sheehan, Elliott Sullivan, Huey White, Jeff York; Warner Bros.-First National; 101 minutes; May 1937

Celebrating the loss of their heavyweight championship contender, fight promoter Nick Donati and his girl, Fluff Phillips, discover the powerful right hook of Ward Guisenberry, a hotel bellhop helping to tend bar. Ward knocks down Chuck McGraw, who is managed by rival promoter Turkey Morgan. Ward is handsome, and the ladies at the party tease him, irritating their men. Nick and Turkey agree to get even by putting Ward in the ring against McGraw's brother, Sam. When the latter is knocked out, Turkey suspects a doublecross. Nick has Silver Jackson get Ward out of town. He takes him to Nick's mother's farm, where he meets Nick's sister, Marie. Furious that the fight game has gotten so close to his family, Nick retrieves Ward and brings him back to continue training. Fluff renames

Ward "Kid Galahad," and his popularity soars with each successive victory in the ring. Fluff falls in love with the Kid but learns he is in love with Marie. Fluff leaves Nick to return to singing in a nightclub. Marie comes to see the Kid fight and the two of them go to hear Fluff sing afterward. Marie's picture is published in the paper, and again Nick is angry. He doublecrosses the Kid in his championship bout, and for several rounds the Kid takes a beating, but after Fluff and Marie plead with him, Nick changes tactics. The Kid comes back and knocks out McGraw. Turkey comes gunning for Nick and is killed. Nick is also mortally wounded. Before he dies, he gives his blessing to Ward and Marie. Fluff is left alone.

The reviews, while favorable, generally focused on the excellent fight sequences. Foster Hirsch called "Robinson's performance ... tart," but found Bette Davis even more compelling. "[They] contribute steady impersonations that add immeasurably to its power," offered *The New York Herald-Tribune*. And *The New York Times,* noting "the comforting presence of Edward G. Robinson, Bette Davis and Harry Carey...." called it "lively, suspenseful, and positively echoing with the bone-bruising thud of right hooks to the jaw ... a good little picture ... [with] the consistently Napoleonic Mr. Robinson ... director and cast working smoothly to blend it into a sound drama."

"Robinson has here his best role since the *Little Caesar* days, that of Nick Donati, a racketeering fight promoter who insists upon being the brains of the boy he handles," said *The New York Journal-American*. "Edward G. Robinson's tough trainer/manager is well played, exhibiting some of the Levantine elegance which made him so memorable in Howard Hawks' *Barbary Coast*." — John Baxter, *Hollywood in the Thirties*

"In the scene Edward G. Robinson had to throw [Davis] bodily against a table. She struggled with Robinson, then fell back. Curtiz screamed at her, 'That's not the way to fight him, you goddam bum!' And Bette screamed back, 'You show me what you want me to do and I'll do it!'.... 'It's okay, Eddie, throw me,' Curtiz said. 'But if you struggle,' Robinson wailed, 'that's the end of me!' Bette had to laugh at the sight of the runtish actor trying to throw Curtiz's 195–pound body across the room.... Robinson pushed him. Curtiz ricocheted off the table and almost knocked Robinson over. Then he said to Bette, 'Goddamit, bum, this is what I want!' She nodded.... Robinson pushed her with all the strength he had used on Curtiz. As a result, she ricocheted so violently that she flew clean across the set and into Irving Rapper's lap."— Charles Higham, *Bette: The Life of Bette Davis*

Kid Galahad was remade in 1962 as a musical with Elvis Presley playing the Kid and Gig Young in the Robinson role. To avoid confusion, the Robinson film was retitled *The Battling Bellhop* for TV showings.

"Kid Galahad" (Radio, 1937, 1938) *Kid Galahad* was adapted for presentation on *Hollywood Hotel* and *Lux Radio Theatre*.

Cast: Edward G. Robinson (Nick), Joan Blondell (Fluff); *Hollywood Hotel;* CBS; June 4, 1937

Director, Frank Woodruff; adaptation, George Wells; sound, Charlie Forsyth; cast: Edward G. Robinson (Nick), Joan Bennett (Fluff), Wayne Morris (Kid), Andrea Leeds (Marie), Chester Clute, Cy Kendall, Edwin Max, Frank Nelson, Joe Cunningham, Lou Merrill, Louis Silvers, Ross Forrester, Galen Galt, David Kerman, Joe Franz, George Pembroke, Ruth Weston, Eddie Kane, Stewart Wilson, Cracker Henderson, Margaret McKay, Celeste Rush, Pauline Gould, George Webb, Alice Frost, Cecil B. DeMille (host), Melville Ruick (announcer), Jack Dempsey, Gene Tunney (intermission guests); *Lux Radio Theatre*, CBS; December 19, 1938

King, Zalman (1941–) was Edward G. Robinson's son in the Israeli film *Neither by Day Nor by Night*. His other motion pictures include *Stranger on the Run*, *The Dangerous Years of Kiowa Jones*, *The Ski Bum*, and *The Passover Plot*.

Kingsford, Walter (1882–1958) played Napoleon Bonaparte in *A Dispatch from*

Reuter's with Edward G. Robinson, and was his newspaper editor, Mr. Peck, in *Unholy Partners*. They are heard in the radio adaptation "The Criminal Code," and were also on Broadway together in *Under Sentence*. Films include *Captains Courageous, Algiers, Kitty Foyle,* and *My Favorite Blonde*.

Kingsley, Sidney (1906–95) won New York Drama Critics Circle Awards for *The Patriots* and his adaption of Arthur Koestler's novel *Darkness at Noon*. He directed that play's original run with Claude Rains and also the touring production with Edward G. Robinson. He won a Pulitzer Prize for *Men in White,* and also wrote and directed *Dead End, Detective Story,* and *Lunatics and Lovers*.

Kinski, Klaus (1926–91) was a character actor in international films, including three by Werner Herzog—*Aguirre: The Wrath of God, Fitzcarraldo,* and *Nosferatu the Vampyre,* plus *Dr. Zhivago* and *For a Few Dollars More*. With Edward G. Robinson he appeared as one of the gang members in *Grand Slam*. His daughter is actress Nastassja Kinski.

Kippen, Manart (1885–1947) appeared on Broadway with Edward G. Robinson in three plays—*Poldekin, Samson and Delilah,* and *Mr. Samuel*. He also had roles in films, notably as Stalin in *Mission to Moscow,* and also *Mildred Pierce* and *The Song of Bernadette*.

Kismet (Theater, 1911) Producers, Fiske, Klaw & Erlanger; playwright, Edward Knoblauch; cast: Charles Dalton (Hajj), Edward G. Robinson (Wazir Mansur), Leah Salisbury; Canadian tour; 1914 (autumn)

The three-act play was first produced in New York on Christmas Day, 1911. Hajj, a beggar and poet, is arrested in Baghdad. The Wazir will release him if he will kill the Caliph, Abdullah. He is put in jail again when the attempt fails, but he kills Sheik Jawan and escapes in his clothes. His daughter, Marsinah, has become part of the Wazir's harem. He drowns the Wazir and frees her to marry the Caliph. Although Hajj is banished, he returns home again.

Kitt, Eartha (1928–), singer-actress, appeared with Edward G. Robinson at Madison Square Garden in the *Chanukah Festival for Israeli* in 1962, 1963, and 1964. They were on TV in *Twelve Star Salute* and *All About People*. Her films include *New Faces, St. Louis Blues, Anna Lucasta,* and *Boomerang*. She was a 2000 Tony Award nominee for her role in the musical *The Wild Party*.

Knapp, Evalyn (1908–81) played Irene, Edward G. Robinson's blonde girlfriend, in *Smart Money*. She was in *Sinner's Holiday, Fifty Million Frenchmen, Fireman Save My Child, Big City Blues,* the serial *The Perils of Pauline,* and *Two Weeks to Live*, retiring from the screen in 1943.

Knox, Alexander (1907–95), nominated for an Oscar as *Wilson,* was Van Weyden in *The Sea Wolf,* with Edward G. Robinson, and was also on the radio in *Document A/777*. He was in *Sister Kenny* and *Sign of the Ram* (which he also wrote), *The Wreck of the Mary Deare, Khartoum, You Only Live Twice, Nicholas and Alexandra,* and TV's *Tinker, Tailor, Soldier, Spy*.

Kolker, Henry (1874–1947) appeared with Edward G. Robinson three times—*East Is West, I Loved a Woman,* and *Bullets or Ballots* (as the banker, Hollister). He is also in *Disraeli, Imitation of Life, Diamond Jim, Romeo and Juliet, Holiday, Union Pacific,* and *A Woman's Face*.

Komack, James (1930–77), also known as Jimmie, was in *A Hole in the Head* as Julius, Edward G. Robinson's dimwitted son with a hula hoop. He was also in *Damn Yankees* and worked in TV, notably in *The People's Choice* with Jackie Cooper, and producing *Chico and the Man*.

Kosleck, Martin (1907–94) portrayed Nazi propagandist Joseph Goebbels in three films—*Confessions of a Nazi Spy,* with Edward G. Robinson, *Hitler,* and *The Hitler Gang*. Among his other pictures are *Foreign Correspondent, The Frozen Ghost, 36 Hours,* and *Which Way to the Front?*

Kotto, Yaphet (1937–) played the title role in the *Night Gallery* episode "The Messiah on Mott Street," with Edward G. Robinson. His films include *The Thomas Crown Affair, Across 110th Street, Live and Let Die, Alien, The Star Chamber,* and *Freddy's Dead: The Final Nightmare.*

Kraft Music Hall (Radio, 1948) Edward G. Robinson made guest appearances on this program twice. In the first he appears in a sketch as Jolson's conscience and does a rendition of "April Showers."

Cast: Al Jolson, Oscar Levant, Edward G. Robinson, Lou Bring and His Orchestra, Ken Carpenter (announcer); 30 minutes; NBC-radio, March 18, 1948

The cast performs the life story of Little Asa, told in music.

Cast: Al Jolson, Oscar Levant, Edward G. Robinson, Lou Bring and His Orchestra, Ken Carpenter (announcer); 30 minutes; NBC-radio, October 7, 1948

Krasner, Milton (1901–88) photographed four films with Edward G. Robinson — *The Woman in the Window, Scarlet Street, House of Strangers,* and *Two Weeks in Another Town.* He won an Academy Award for his cinematography for *Three Coins in the Fountain,* and was nominated also for *Arabian Knights, All About Eve, Love with the Proper Stranger, An Affair to Remember, How the West Was Won,* and *Fate Is the Hunter.*

Kroeger, Berry (1911–91) was chauffeur Hugo Baumer, one of the *Seven Thieves,* with Edward G. Robinson. Onscreen from 1948, he also appeared in *Cry of the City, Blood Alley, The Mephisto Waltz,* and *The Man in the Glass Booth.*

Kruger, Otto (1885–1974), a Broadway actor, was with Edward G. Robinson in *I Am the Law, Dr. Ehrlich's Magic Bullet* (as Dr. Emil von Behring), *A Dispatch from Reuter's,* and "Bullets or Ballots" on the radio. Other films: *Treasure Island, Chained, They Won't Forget, The Saboteur, Murder My Sweet, High Noon,* and *Sex and the Single Girl.*

Lackteen, Frank (1894–1968) plays the Arab man bitten by a snake in *Dr. Ehrlich's Magic Bullet,* and a crew member aboard *The Ghost* in *The Sea Wolf.* He appears also in *The Ten Commandments,* as well as silent films, the *Jungle Girl* series, *Juarez,* and *Frontier Gal,* among others.

Ladd, Alan (1913–64) became a star playing tough guys and detectives — *This Gun for Hire, The Glass Key, The Blue Dahlia.* He played *Shane* and was also in *Hell on Frisco Bay* (with Edward G. Robinson), *The McConnell Story, The Proud Rebel,* and *The Carpetbaggers.*

Lady Esther's Screen Guild Theatre
This radio program featured dramatizations of screenplays on NBC. The title of the show was changed to *Lady Esther's Screen Guild Players* in 1945.

See "The Amazing Dr. Clitterhouse"; "Blind Alley"; "Flesh and Fantasy."

A Lady to Love (Film, 1930) Edward G. Robinson's fifth film, *A Lady to Love,* could and should have been better. Its basis was the 1925 Pulitzer Prize–winning play *They Knew What They Wanted,* by Sidney Howard. *A Lady to Love* was the second of three film versions of the story. In 1928 it was a silent film called *The Secret Hour,* with Jean Hersholt and Pola Negri, and in 1940 Charles Laughton and Carole Lombard remade it under the play's title. Frank Loesser's 1956 Broadway musical, *The Most Happy Fella,* is also based on Howard's story.

Victor Seastrom, an influential contributor to the development of the Swedish film industry, directed *A Lady to Love.* Leading lady Vilma Banky, a glorious and glamorous MGM silent star, was hardly up to the demands of sound and speaking English for the screen. The film was the second-to-last of her career, which had seen many non-dialogue romantic teamings with Ronald Colman and Gary Cooper. The picture was filmed simultaneously in German, wherein Banky's performance may have been more credible, and Robinson's friend, Joseph Schildkraut, replaced Robert Ames as Buck. Robinson had the opportunity to play the part in both languages.

Foster Hirsch noted that *A Lady to Love* gave him "one of the few romantic and sentimental characters that Robinson would ever play. His performance was animated.... Though Robinson performed with a flair, the film was ruined by a wildly miscast Vilma Banky."

In his autobiography, Robinson explained that although his leading lady was inexperienced in making the transition from silent films to sound, acceptable scenes were found, and to his surprise, a capable editor managed to help Banky's performance and the film.

Lena Schultz, a waitress in San Francisco, catches the eye of Tony, a middle-aged immigrant vineyard owner. He proposes marriage by letter and encloses a photo because they have not met. The photo is not Tony, however, but his handsome hired worker, Buck, since Tony fears Lena will reject him for his age and appearance. Lena accepts Tony's invitation and takes a train to the Napa Valley. When no one meets her, she goes to Tony's farm, only to find him being carried in on a stretcher, the victim of an accident on his way to meet her. She is taken aback by his initial deception, but ultimately his honesty and loving character impress her, and she marries him. She also has met Buck, however, and seeing him daily at the farm soon leads to a romance and seduction. Both Buck and Lena feel guilty, and it is not long before Tony discovers them. Angry at first, he forgives her. Lena decides to stay with Tony. Buck leaves the farm.

Director, Victor Seastrom; screenplay, Sidney Howard, based on his play *They Knew What They Wanted;* art director, Cedric Gibbons; sound, Douglas Shearer, J. K. Brock; camera, Merritt B. Gerstad; gowns, Adrian; editors, Conrad A. Nervig, Leslie F. Wilder; cast: Vilma Banky (Lena Schultz), Edward G. Robinson (Tony), Robert Ames (Buck), Richard Carle (Postman), Lloyd Ingraham (Father McKee), Anderson Lawler (Doctor), Gum Chin (Ah Gee), Henry Armetta (Angelo), George Davis (Georgie); German-language version, *Die Sehnsucht Jeder Frau*: Vilma Banky (Lena), Edward G. Robinson (Tony); Joseph Schildkraut (Buck); Frank Reicher, Conrad Seidemann, William Bechtel; MGM; 92 minutes; March 1930

Robinson's excellent personal reviews led to an offer of a long-term MGM contract, which he rejected because it contained no provision for time to perform on the New York stage.

"[It has] at least one performance, that of Edward G. Robinson, arising out of the mist of only fair direction, and a striving by the other players toward realism that just misses being excellent," said *The New York Times.* "As Tony, Mr. Robinson is capital. His happiness at discovering Lena and his joy at her willingness to remain ... are both ably portrayed with sufficient touches of pathos and imagination to bring him definitely forward as a player of no mean dramatic ability. The picture lacks mobility, but the range of acting, as offered by Mr. Robinson ... is most gratifying."

"Mr. Robinson is the life of the picture as the Italian grape-grower in search of a wife," according to *Cinema* magazine. "It is not a conventionally romantic role, but that of a man bubbling over with romance and Latin lovableness. It is hard to imagine it better acted."

"A somewhat effortful and highly seasoned performance by J. G. Robinson [sic] as the crippled, lovesick Italian, Tony."—*New York World*

See **Irving Thalberg**.

Laidlaw, Ethan (1900–63) began in silent westerns and had a career spanning thirty years. He appears in the Edward G. Robinson films *Little Caesar, The Whole Town's Talking, The Sea Wolf, The Violent Men,* and *The Ten Commandments.* Among 200 films from 1925 are *The Virginian, The Killers,* and *Alias Jesse James.*

LaMarr, Richard (1896–1975) was Edward G. Robinson's stand-in and played a small role as a neighbor in *All My Sons*. His film career dates from 1917 in *The Perils of Pauline* with Pearl White.

The Lambs   Edward G. Robinson joined The Lambs in New York after gaining stature as an actor. The supper club was formed in 1874 by actors, and soon its members began performing without fee in the annual "Lambs' Gambols," with proceeds going to charity.

Lancaster, Burt (1913–94) was Edward G. Robinson's son Chris in *All My Sons* on film and again on the radio. They were in *Hollywood Fights Back* (radio) together and narrate two short films—*All About People* and *The Heart of Show Business*. An Oscar winner for *Elmer Gantry*, Lancaster's other films include *From Here to Eternity*, *Birdman of Alcatraz* (nominations), *The Killers*, *Come Back Little Sheba*, *Trapeze*, *Judgment at Nuremberg*, *Tough Guys*, and *Field of Dreams*.

Landau, David (1878–1935) had one of his last roles as the detective in *The Man with Two Faces*, with Edward G. Robinson. He was also in *Arrowsmith*, *I Am a Fugitive from a Chain Gang*, and *Judge Priest*.

Landau, Martin (1931–) toured as George in *Middle of the Night*, with Edward G. Robinson. An Oscar winner for his role as Bela Lugosi in *Ed Wood*, he also appeared in *North by Northwest*, *Cleopatra*, *Nevada Smith*, *Crimes and Misdemeanors*, *Eye of the Stranger*, and *The Majestic*, as well as the long-running TV hit *Mission Impossible*.

Lane, Charles (1899–), a thin, banker-type character actor, appears in two Edward G. Robinson films, *Smart Money* and *Good Neighbor Sam*. He is also in *Mr. Deeds Goes to Town*, *Arsenic and Old Lace*, *It's a Wonderful Life*, *The Juggler*, and *The Gnome-Mobile*.

Lane, Richard (1900–82) is one of the gangsters, Mugsy O'Day, in *Brother Orchid* and also plays Sergeant "Alphabet" in *Mr. Winkle Goes to War*. Other appearances are in *Union Pacific*, *Meet Boston Blackie*, *Take Me Out to the Ballgame*, and *I Can Get It for You Wholesale*.

Lang, Fritz (1890–1976), a Viennese émigré, directed the *film noir* dramas *The Woman in the Window* and *Scarlet Street*, with Edward G. Robinson. Films after World War I include the German *Dr. Mabuse*, *Metropolis*, and *M*, and American features *Fury*, *You Only Live Once*, *Man Hunt*, *Ministry of Fear*, *Rancho Notorious*, *The Big Heat*, and *While the City Sleeps*.

Languages Edward G. Robinson spoke several languages. His native language was Rumanian, but, in American schools from the age of ten, he soon learned English. His Jewish studies fostered Yiddish. In addition, he was fluent in French, German, Spanish, Italian, Russian, and Hebrew.

His study of languages was a hobby. According to his widow, Jane, his library contained several volumes of grammar books. "He would go back over the French, go back over the German, and he knew how to conjugate.... When we went to Russia for the first film festival they ever had, he went up on the stage and spoke Russian."

He told *Parade* magazine in 1959, "Every man should have a sideline. You can never tell when it will help get you on the main track." His fluency earned him his first Broadway stage role, in 1915, for which actors who could speak with accents were needed. *Under Fire* had him in the roles of Frenchman, German, Belgian, and Cockney, and he was dubbed by co-workers as a "walking League of Nations."

In his performances he played a variety of European or Oriental characters: *The Pawn*, *The Little Teacher*, *Night Lodging*, *Poldekin*, *The Idle Inn*, *The Deluge*, *Peer Gynt*, *The Firebrand*, *The Man of Destiny*, *The Goat Song*, *Juarez and Maximilian*, *The Brothers Karamazov*, *Right You Are If You Think You Are*, and *Darkness at Noon* on the stage; and in films, a Cuban patriarch in *The Bright Shawl*, orientals in *East Is West* and *The Hatchet Man*, a Greek-American barber in *Smart Money*, a French impersonation in *The Man with Two Faces*, Italians in *Kid Galahad*, *Key Largo*, *House of Strangers*, and *Hell on Frisco Bay*, Norwegians in *Our Vines Have Tender Grapes* and *Song of Norway*, and a German professor in *The Prize*. Television roles in "Epitaph for a Spy" (*Climax!*), "Shadows Tremble" (*Playhouse 90*), and "Heritage" (*Zane Grey Theatre*) featured him with European accents.

Larceny, Inc. (Film, 1942) The last picture Edward G. Robinson made under his Warner Bros. contract before becoming a freelance actor was *Larceny, Inc.*, a comedy about a gangster who uses a luggage store as a front for drilling into the bank next door. It had funny moments but generally was not as successful as his earlier comedies, like *A Slight Case of Murder* and *The Whole Town's Talking*.

"You can't say that Edward G. Robinson doesn't try hard to go straight," noted *The New York Times*, adding, "it is a passing pleasure to see him back with the mob.... [The film is] somewhat forced, somewhat obvious ... but the characters are whimsically assorted and generally well-played.... Mr. Robinson, as usual, is a beautifully hard-boiled yegg. The principal joy is to watch him. His 'Pressure' cooks with gas."

"It has the ebullient Edward G. Robinson as star, a handsome production and a notable supporting cast ... [but] it has lost much of the Perelman nonsense humor.... Jack Carson and Edward Brophy go all the way in the mugging department, and so does Mr. Robinson on more than one occasion."—*New York Herald-Tribune*

Producer, Hal B. Wallis; associate producers, Jack Saper, Jerry Wald; director, Lloyd Bacon; screenplay, Everett Freeman, Edwin Gilbert; based on the play *The Night Before Christmas* by Laura and S. J. Perelman; camera, Tony Gaudio; art director, John Hughes; editor, Ralph Dawson; sound, Dolph Thomas; gowns, Milo Anderson; dialogue director, Hugh Cummings; music, Adolph Deutch; cast: Edward G. Robinson (Pressure Maxwell), Jane Wyman (Denny Costello), Broderick Crawford (Jug Martin), Jack Carson (Jeff Randolph), Ed Brophy (Weepy Davis), Anthony Quinn (Leo Dexter), Joseph Downing (Smitty), Jackie Gleason (Hobart), Barbara Jo Allen [Vera Vague] (Mademoiselle Gloria), Fortunio Bonanova (Anton Copoulos), John Qualen (Sam Bachrach), Harry Davenport (Homer Bigelow), Creighton Hale (Carmichael), Andrew Tombes (Oscar Engelhart), Grant Mitchell (Aspinwall), George Meeker (Jackson), Joseph Crehan (Warden), Jean Ames (Florence), William Davidson (McCarthy), Chester Clute (Buchanan), Emory Parnell (Officer O'Casey), Joe Devlin (Umpire), Jimmy O'Gatty, Jack Kenney (Convicts), John Kelly (Batter), Eddie Chandler, James Flavin (Guards), Dutch Hendrian (Chuck), William Phillips (Muggsy), Hank Mann, Eddie Foster, Cliff Saum, Charles Sullivan (Ballplayers), Charles Drake (Driver), Vera Lewis, DeWolfe Hopper, Ray Montgomery, Lucien Littlefield (Customers), Grace Stafford (Secretary), Pat O'Malley (Policeman), Harry Hayden (Salvation Army officer), Fred Kelsey, Roland Drew, Janice Ohman, Don Barclay, Arthur Q. Bryan, Frank Mayo, Jack Mower, Kitty Kelly, Philo Reh, Wallace Scott, Fred Walburn; Warner Bros.; 95 minutes; April 1942

Trying to go straight after their release from prison, J. Chalmers (Pressure) Maxwell and Jug Martin turn down an offer to be part of a bank robbery planned by Leo Dexter. They meet up with their buddy, Weepy Davis, and try to secure a bank loan to finance a racetrack. Unable to do so, the three use an old con game wherein Jug gets himself hit by a car and a frightened and embarrassed driver settles on the spot by writing a check. The check becomes down payment on the purchase of Bigelow's luggage shop, which conveniently adjoins a bank. Before long, Pressure, Jug, and Weepy are digging out its basement, removing the dirt via suitcases and trunks. Complications include the boys striking oil and water (furnace and utility pipes), people in the shop who thwart their efforts (including a variety of customers and Denny Costello, Pressure's adopted daughter, who has connected with Jeff Randolph, a luggage salesman). The local merchants are impressed by Pressure, who, despite his larcenous goals, manages to get improvements made in the neighborhood. Bank officials now want to examine the store. Worried, the boys hastily clean up and fill the hole in the floor with ... luggage. The bank, it turns out, wants to expand, and makes Pressure an offer of $15,000. Leo Dexter muscles in, taking over the robbery, adding dynamite. A fire starts in the shop, and Pressure rescues Mr. Bigelow. Dexter is caught, but Pressure, Jug, and Weepy are left free with a reprimand.

They are last seen running from another car-accident scam; their selected vehicle is a police car!

Lardner, Ring, Jr. (1915–2000) collaborated on the screenplay for *Woman of the Year* with Michael Kanin, and they won an Oscar. He was uncredited for work as a script doctor for *A Star Is Born, Nothing Sacred,* and *Laura*. As one of the Hollywood Ten, he was cited for contempt of Congress by the House Un-American Activities Committee and jailed. *The Cincinnati Kid*, with Edward G. Robinson, followed his blacklisting; he then won a second Academy Award for the script of *M*A*S*H*.

Larimore, Earle (1899–1947) appeared with Edward G. Robinson in Theatre Guild productions of *Ned McCobb's Daughter* and *Juarez and Maximilian*. His other New York credits include *The Silver Cord Strange Interlude,* and *Mourning Becomes Electra*. He was also in silent films.

The Last Gangster (Film, 1937) "By 1937 the original gangster formula had been so exhausted," wrote Foster Hirsch in his *Edward G. Robinson: A Pyramid Illustrated History of the Movies* "that Robinson made a tired movie at MGM (a studio singularly ill-equipped for the kind of hard-edged crime story that Warners turned out) called, significantly, *The Last Gangster*." Dissatisfied with roles being offered him, Robinson nonetheless shared the screen with James Stewart (in his eleventh picture in two years) and a strong Austrian actress named Rose Stradner.

Producer, J. J. Cohn; director, Edward Ludwig; screenplay, John Lee Mahin; story, William A. Wellman, Robert Carson; art directors, Cedric Gibbons, Daniel Cathcart, Edwin Willis; montages, Slavko Vorkapich; camera, William Daniels; editor, Ben Lewis; music, Edward Ward; cast: Edward G. Robinson (Joe Krozac), James Stewart (Paul North), Rose Stradner (Talya), Lionel Stander (Curly), Douglas Scott (Paul North, Jr.), John Carradine (Casper), Sidney Blackmer (Editor), Edward Brophy (Fats Garvey), Alan Baxter (Acey Kile), Grant Mitchell (Warden), Frank Conroy (Sid Gorman), Moroni Olsen (Shea), Ivan Miller (Wilson), Willard Robertson (Broderick), Louise Beavers (Gloria), Donald Barry (Billy Ernst), Ben Welden (Bottles Bailey), Horace MacMahon (Limpy), Edward Pawley (Brockett), John Kelly (Red), David Leo Tillotson, Billy Smith, Jim Kehner, Reggie Streeter, Dick Holland (Boys), Pierre Watkin, Cy Kendall, Frederick Burton (Editors), Douglas McPhail, Ernest Wood, Phillip Terry (Reporters), William Benedict (Office boy), Lee Phelps Guard on train), Larry Simms (Baby Joe), Wade Boteler (Turnkey), Walter Miller (Mike Kile), Victor Adams, Jerry Jerome, Shirley Chambers, Sammy Finn, Eddie Foster, Al Hill, Arthur Howard, Mitchell Ingraham, Priscilla Lawson, Edward Marr, Allen Mathews, Broderick O'Farrell, Eddie Parker, Lee Powell, Jack Raynold, Cyril Ring, Martin Turner, Huey White, Robert Neil Taylor, Priscilla Dean, Esther Muir, Billy Arnold, Nick Copeland, Paul Sutton, Jimmy Brewster, Gene Coogan, Mary Dees, Frank DuFrane, Allen Fox, Christian J. Frank, Bill Hutton, Harry Lash, Ralph McCullough, Bert Moorhouse, Don Roberts, Jack Stoney, E. Allyn Warren, Jimmy Zaner; MGM; December 1937

Gang leader Joe Krozac returns from a European trip with a beautiful wife named Talya. Her poor grasp of English keeps her ignorant of Joe's activities, such as his massacre of the Kile brothers (which is the reported on the front page of the morning paper). She tells Joe she will soon have his baby. But Joe is arrested and indicted for evasion of income tax, and his lawyer's efforts to keep him out of prison fail. Joe Jr. is born while Joe is aboard the train for Alcatraz. Talya brings the baby for visits. As a news angle, reporter Paul North gets a photo of the baby holding a gun. Talya complains to the editor but slowly learns who and what her husband really is. Paul befriends her and, after a time, she divorces Joe to marry Paul. Ten years pass, and Joe gets out of prison. Old gang members kidnap the boy and use him to force Joe to tell them where he has stashed his money. The police close in on the gang after Joe and the boy are freed. Making their way back to Talya and Paul, Joe tries to relate to his son but gets angry when the boy praises Paul as the only father he knows. Joe's embitteredness is softened by the realization that Talya and Paul have made a good home for his son. Joe leaves. Acey Kile, the surviving brother from the earlier shooting, now comes after Joe, and the two are killed in a shootout.

The reviews were good, considering the film was almost an anachronism. *The New York Times* discussed "Edward G., whose snarls and menace and brooding hate eminently qualify him to be not only 'The Last' but the very first gangster of filmdom," further stating that, "Mr. Robinson, in brief, is the gang cycle by himself. We refuse to believe that *The Last Gangster* is really his epitaph.... [He] plays it with an assurance born of long practice.... It has considerable interest, this facilely told and gliby presented fable."

Capitalizing on the real life parallel of Al Capone's incarceration for income tax evasion (hardly the worst crime of which he was guilty), the film errs in having Joe Krozac serve ten years at Alcatraz and be released in 1937, since the island was not used as a prison until 1933.

"His impersonation of a 1937 thug [is] as persuasive as was his portrait in that earlier classic of rats and rackets [*Little Caesar*]," offered *The New York Herald-Tribune*. "In the new offering, he creates a bitterly effective impersonation of a beaten hoodlum ... the film pivots surely around [his] performance.... [He] does a showy job with the role of Krozac, keeping the thug human, recognizable and pathological."

"Clear-cut star melodrama which suddenly turns sentimental," was the view of Leslie Halliwell in his *Film Guide*. And James Robert Parish, in *The Tough Guys*, said, "Robinson's role was that of the familiar gang boss, though the script ... provided considerable punch and some sympathy for the title character."

Laugh-In (Television, 1971) Edward G. Robinson was on the TV comedy show *Laugh-In* twice, contributing corny one-liners with the rest of the company. Asked by Dan Rowan what he thought of a current trend toward nudity in films, he growled, "I hate it. There's no place to hold a gun!"

Executive producer, George Schlatter; producer, Paul W. Keyes; production executive, Don von Atta; director, Mark Warren; associate director, John Kittleson; writers, Gene Farmer, Rowby Greeber, Allan Katz, Keyes, Marc London, Jim Mulligan, David Parrish, Gene Perret, John Rappaport, Don Reo, Bill Richmond, Stephen Spears, Jack Wohl; script supervisors, London, Parrish; stage managers, Ted Baker, Billy Barnes, Jerry Masterson; music, Jan Bernard; costumes, Michael Travis; cast: Dan Rowan, Dick Martin, Dennis Allen, Johnny Brown, Ruth Buzzi, Richard Dawson, Ralph Edwards, Liza Minelli, Gary Owens, Edward G. Robinson, Jill St. John, Barbara Sharma, Allan Sues, Lily Tomlin; CBS-TV; 60 minutes (date unknown)

Cast: Dan Rowan, Dick Martin, Ruth Buzzi, Tony Curtis, Frank Gorshin, Dean Jones, Edward G. Robinson, Buffalo Bob Smith & Howdy Doody, Lily Tomlin; October 11, 1971

Laughton, Charles (1899–1962) In *Tales of Manhattan* the segment in which Laughton energetically conducts a symphony in a tailcoat so small that it rips at the seams immediately precedes Edward G. Robinson's episode. They were together on the radio in *Document A/777* and guests on TV's *The Honeymooners*. An Oscar winner for *The Private Life of Henry VIII*, Laughton received nominations also for *Mutiny on the Bounty* and *Witness for the Prosecution*. Other films include *The Old Dark House, Les Miserables, They Knew What They Wanted, The Hunchback of Notre Dame, The Big Clock, Spartacus, Advise and Consent*, and, as director, *Night of the Hunter*.

Launzi (Theater, 1923) "It is a reverential occasion to which Arthur Hopkins invites the art loving public," said *The New York Times* about *Launzi*, but the play was not a hit. It reunited Edward G. Robinson with Arthur Hopkins and Pauline Lord.

Producer, director, Arthur Hopkins; playwright, Ferenc Molnar; adaptation, Edna St. Vincent Millay; cast: Pauline Lord (Launzi), Saxon Kling (Imre), Edward Robinson (Louis), Albert Bruning (Ivan), Christine Compton (Madame Ivan), Mary Hubbard

(Redempta), William J. McClure (Dr. Anton), Benedict McQuarrie (Policeman), Charles Millward (Frederick), Adrienne Morrison (Claire), Xenia Polinoff (Anna), Irene Shirley (Honorata), Edgar Stehli (Dr. Jeki), Lark Taylor (Dr. Barody), Edith Yaeger (Firmina), Mildred Whitney (Dativa); opened at the Plymouth Theatre, New York; October 10, 1923 (13 performances)

Launzi, an enchanting teenage girl, loves Imre, but he is in love with her mother. Throwing herself into the Danube, Launzi is rescued, but she asks that a bier be prepared for her funeral. This inspires Imre with pity but not love. Launzi has angel's wings strapped to her back in order to play out her life in death, and her family humors her. One night she tries to fly from her tower window, with disastrous results.

LaVerne, Lucille (1871–1945) was the voice of the witch in Disney's *Snow White*. She was also in the silents *Polly of the Circus*, *Orphans of the Storm*, and *Zaza*, and talkies *A Tale of Two Cities*, *The Devil's Holiday* and *Little Caesar*, with Edward G. Robinson, as the scheming Ma Magdalena.

Lawford, Peter (1923–84) shares no scenes with Edward G. Robinson in the first episode of *Flesh and Fantasy* as Pierrot during Mardi Gras; and he plays himself in the Las Vegas segment of *Pepe*. Other films include *Good News*, *Dead Ringer*, *Exodus*, and *They Only Kill Their Masters*.

Lawrence, Marc (1910–) recently in *The Big Easy* and *Newsies*, was with Edward G. Robinson in *I Am the Law*, as killer Eddie Girard; in *Tampico*, as Valdez, a mysterious shipmate; and in *Key Largo*, as Ziggy, a rival gangster. His other films include *Dr. Socrates*, *The Ox-Bow Incident*, *The Asphalt Jungle*, and *The Man with the Golden Arm*.

Leading Ladies True leading lady status belongs to those actresses who played opposite Edward G. Robinson when he was the male lead: Judith Anderson (*The Red House*), Jean Arthur (*The Whole Town's Talking*), Mary Astor (*The Little Giant*, *The Man with Two Faces*), Vilma Banky (*A Lady to Love*), Lynn Bari (*Tampico*), Wendy Barrie (*I Am the Law*), Joan Bennett (*Scarlet Street*, *The Woman in the Window*), Edna Best (*A Dispatch from Reuter's*), Joan Blondell (*Bullets or Ballots*), Mrs. Leslie Carter (*Stella Dallas*), Mady Christians (*All My Sons*), Virginia Christine (*Nightmare*), Claudette Colbert (*The Hole in the Wall*), Bebe Daniels (*Silver Dollar*), Bette Davis (*Kid Galahad*), Laraine Day (*Unholy Partners*), Luli Deste (*Thunder in the City*), Marlene Dietrich (*Manpower*), Ruth Donnelly (*A Slight Case of Murder*), Glenda Farrell (*Dark Hazard*), Nina Foch (*Illegal*), Kay Francis (*I Loved a Woman*), Mona Freeman (*Middle of the Night*), Paulette Goddard (*Vice Squad*), Ruth Gordon (*Dr. Ehrlich's Magic Bullet*), Jeanne Greene (*The Kibitzer*), Miriam Hopkins (*Barbary Coast*), Ruth Hussey (*Blackmail*), Diana Hyland (*The Mary Tree*), Frieda Inescourt (*The Taming of the Shrew*), Zita Johann (*Tiger Shark*), Anna Lee (*Flesh and Fantasy*), Aline MacMahon (*Five Star Final*, *Silver Dollar*), Agnes Moorehead (*Our Vines Have Tender Grapes*), Lois Nettleton (*Darkness at Noon*), Margaret O'Brien (*Our Vines Have Tender Grapes*), Barbara O'Neil (*I Am the Law*), Vivienne Osborne (*Two Seconds*), Jean Parker (*Black Tuesday*), Thelma Ritter (*A Hole in the Head*), Gena Rowlands (*Middle of the Night*), Ann Sothern (*Brother Orchid*), Rose Stradner (*The Last Gangster*), Genevieve Tobin (*I Loved a Woman*, *Dark Hazard*), Claire Trevor (*The Amazing Dr. Clitterhouse*), Helen Vinson (*The Little Giant*), Ruth Warrick (*Mr. Winkle Goes to War*), and Loretta Young (*The Hatchet Man*).

Edward G. Robinson worked with many other actresses who had major roles in his plays and films. Their scenes, however, either were played opposite others (i.e., Susan Hayward in *House of Strangers* was the leading lady, but her scenes in the film generally were with Richard Conte), or Robinson himself was not the leading player (as is the case of *The Ten Commandments*, in which Anne Baxter plays opposite Charlton Heston and Yul Brynner).

Lederer, Francis (1906–2000) was in French and German films before coming to Broadway and Hollywood. He played a Nazi in *Confessions of a Nazi Spy*, with Edward G. Robinson, and once again in *The Man I Married*. Other films include *Midnight, The Bridge of San Luis Rey, The Diary of a Chambermaid, Lisbon,* and *Terror Is a Man.*

Lee, Anna (1914–) was Edward G. Robinson's love interest, Rowena, in *Flesh and Fantasy*, and appears with him in *The Prize* as a reporter. She is also in *How Green Was My Valley, The Ghost and Mrs. Muir, Whatever Happened to Baby Jane?, The Unsinkable Molly Brown, The Man Who Shot Liberty Valance,* and *The Sound of Music.*

"The Legend of Jim Riva" (Television, 1961) Capitalizing on his long-standing image, Edward G. Robinson showed what could happen when gangsters grow old in his guest-star appearance on *Robert Taylor's Detectives*. Taylor, as the patient, righteous police captain, was in preliminary scenes, but he did not spar with Robinson's character. Here was an opportunity to speculate on the two actors' relationship with one another ten years following Committee hearings, wherein one of them was a friendly witness, convinced of a dangerous Communist element in Hollywood films.

A Four-Star/Bentley/Blackpool production; executive producers, Jules Levy, Arthur Gardner, Arnold Laven; producer, Arthur H. Nadel; teleplay, John K. Butler, Boyd Correll; story, Arthur Brown, Jr.; editors, Lyle Boyle, Bernard Barton; assistant producer, Marian Carpenter; art directors, Bill Ross, Gibson Holley; camera, Wilfrid M. Cline; production manager, Bruce Fowler; music, Herschel Burke Gilbert; music editor, Al Friede; makeup, Sid Perell; wardrobe, Robert B. Harris; set, James E. Roach; sound, Mandine Rogne, Don Rush; assistant director, Mike Salamunovich; casting, Stalmaster-Lister; cast: Edward G. Robinson (Jim Riva), Robert Taylor (Captain Matt Holbrook), Tige Andrews (Lt. Johnny Russo), Frank Sutton (Frankie Doyle), Oscar Beregi (Arnie), Joe DeSantis (Vince), Mark Goddard (Sgt. Chris Ballard), Rudy Solari (Nathan Riva), Naomi Stevens (Martha Riva), Butch Patrick (Bobby), William Sargent (Police officer), Sandra Warner (Miss Clark), Adam West (Sgt. Steve Nelson); *Robert Taylor's Detectives*, NBC-tv; 60 minutes; October 9, 1961

Jim Riva is released from prison after serving a fifteen-year sentence. Frank Doyle, a thug, breaks into his home following a family reunion and critically wounds Jim's wife. Jim believes the incident stems from a rivalry during the old days and takes matters into his own hands when the police do not solve the case quickly enough. He contacts former henchmen, not realizing every one has aged or died, and that the days of the mob are long gone. The police track Doyle, who wanted to make a name for himself in attacking the legendary Jim Riva. He is arrested, but not before Jim goes after Jake Ballinger, a former enemy. Seeing Jake elderly and helpless, sleeping in a wheelchair, makes Jim realize that the past has caught up with him.

Leigh, Janet (1927–) spoofed her *Psycho* shower murder scene in a bubble bath in *Pepe*. She appeared with Edward G. Robinson also in *Grand Slam*, and was in *Little Women, The Romance of Rosy Ridge, My Sister Eileen, Touch of Evil, Bye Bye Birdie,* and *The Manchurian Candidate*. Jamie Lee Curtis is her daughter by Tony Curtis.

Leigh, Philip (1880–1935) was a character actor with the Theatre Guild, appearing with Edward G. Robinson in five productions—*Androcles and the Lion, The Brothers Karamazov, Juarez and Maximilian, Ned McCobb's Daughter,* and *Right You Are If You Think You Are*. Onscreen he is in *The Virtuous Wives*, a silent film.

Lemmon, Jack (1925–2001) reprised his *Some Like It Hot* character (Oscar nomination) in *Pepe*. With Edward G. Robinson, he also was in *Good Neighbor Sam,* and he was on the 1964 and 1973 Oscar telecasts. He won for *Save the Tiger* and *Mister Roberts*, and was nominated for *The Days of Wine and Roses* and

The Apartment. Other films include *The Great Race, The Odd Couple, The China Syndrome, Glengarry Glen Ross, Grumpy Old Men,* and Kenneth Branagh's *Hamlet*.

LeRoy, Mervyn   (1900–87) began in Hollywood as an assistant cameraman and bit player. He directed four of Edward G. Robinson's films, beginning with *Little Caesar. Two Seconds, Five Star Final,* and *Unholy Partners* followed. They were also together in a Warner Bros. radio broadcast and the TV special *The Movie Crazy Years*. He was nominated for an Oscar for directing *Random Harvest*, and in 1975 he received the Irving Thalberg Award from the Academy. Other films include I Am a *Fugitive from a Chain Gang, The Wizard of Oz* (producer), *Thirty Seconds Over Tokyo, Quo Vadis, The Bad Seed,* and *Gypsy*.

Lesser, Sol   (1890–1980) produced *Tarzan* films, *Dick Tracy* serials, and westerns, plus *Our Town, Stage Door Canteen,* and, with Edward G. Robinson, *Vice Squad* and *The Red House*. Robinson co-produced the latter through their company The Film Guild Corporation.

Letter from Birmingham Jail   This dramatic reading about racism and civil rights was recorded at Steve Allen's home for presentation on the radio.

Steve Allen, Edward G. Robinson (participants); KABC radio; April 17, 1965

Letters   A piece of correspondence crucial to the plot is a letter revealed at the end of *All My Sons*. Larry, one of Joe Keller's two sons serving in the war, has written it to his fiancée, Ann, prior to going out on a flying mission. He has read in the newspapers about his and Ann's fathers, business partners, shipping defective cylinders from their plant to the Army Air Force. The shipment, once installed, resulted in the deaths of twenty-one pilots. Larry tells Ann in the letter that he is ashamed of his father and that he will not return from his mission. Larry's mother, Kate, believes her son will yet return from the war, but the letter is proof of his death. When Joe, played by Robinson, reads the letter, he realizes his guilt and commits suicide.

Delivery of the mail brings military orders in *Destroyer, Tampico,* and *Mr. Winkle Goes to War* (an induction notice), and, in *Tales of Manhattan*, an invitation to a law school reunion. Robinson sends a photo of his better looking best friend in order to win the hand of a mail order bride in *A Lady to Love*. In "The Messiah on Mott Street," as an elderly impoverished Jew he receives a letter from his brother in California with a $10,000 check.

Lewis, Harry   (1920–   )as Toots Bass, was the youngest of Johnny Rocco's henchmen in *Key Largo*, repeating his role on *Lux Radio Theatre*. He was in other films — *The Unsuspected, Gun Crazy*— but he had greater success in Hollywood in the restaurant business.

Lincoln, Abraham   (1809–65), sixteenth President of the United States, was portrayed onscreen by such luminaries as Walter Huston, Raymond Massey, and Henry Fonda. In TV's *The Right Man*, with Edward G. Robinson, Art Carney played him.

There are a number of references to Lincoln in Edward G. Robinson's films. In *Robin and the 7 Hoods* Peter Falk's character, Guy Gisborne, announces that, with the death of Robinson's character, Big Jim, he will be the new leader of the Chicago mobs, "kind of like when all the states got together and had a first President." Frank Sinatra, as Robbo, warns him, "Stay out of the North Side. You may have come in like George Washington, but you'll leave like Abraham Lincoln."

More seriously, Lincoln's death provided the climax for *A Dispatch from Reuter's*. Reuter's news service, newly upgraded to beat its competition, announces its first "scoop"— the assassination — in London, causing a near scandal until it can be verified.

When Robinson's young son in *The Last Gangster* proudly displays a Lincoln medal he earned "for outstanding achievement" during scouting with his stepfather (James Stewart), Robinson's character is unimpressed, suggesting Napoleon might have been a better role model. In *Cheyenne Autumn* Robinson plays a contemporary of Lincoln, Secretary of the Interior Carl Schurz. Troubled over the plight of the Indians of the film's title, Schurz gazes at a portrait of the dead President and asks, "What would you do, old friend? What would you do?"

"A Lincoln Portrait" Presented by The United States Air Force Band and The Singing Sergeants; Colonel Arnald D. Gabriel (conductor); written by Aaron Copland; Edward G. Robinson (guest narrator); 1970

Lindsay, Margaret (1910–81) was in films from 1932, including several *Ellery Queen* mysteries, *Garden of the Moon, The House of Seven Gables,* and *Please Don't Eat the Daisies.* She played Joan Bennett's girlfriend, Millie, in *Scarlet Street*, with Edward G. Robinson.

Litel, John (1894–1972) came to films from Broadway, appearing with Edward G. Robinson in *A Slight Case of Murder* and *The Amazing Dr. Clitterhouse.* Other films include *They Died with Their Boots On, Crime Doctor, Houseboat,* and *A Pocketful of Miracles.*

Literature Only a handful of major literary works became performance vehicles for Edward G. Robinson. Many of his projects were either written directly for the screen or adapted from current novels, plays, or the day's headlines. *The Sea Wolf* is an exception, with the 1904 novel by Jack London as its basis. Other instances include:

Stephen Vincent Benet's *The Devil and Daniel Webster*, adapted as a TV special, with Robinson as Webster; Henrik Ibsen's *Peer Gynt*, presented by the Theatre Guild, with Robinson as The Button Moulder and von Eberkopf; Luigi Pirandello's *Right You Are If You Think You Are,* presented by the Theatre Guild, with Robinson as Ponza; William Shakespeare's *The Taming of the Shrew*, adapted as an hour-long radio program, with Robinson as Petruchio; George Bernard Shaw's *Androcles and the Lion* and *The Man of Destiny,* presented by the Theatre Guild, with Robinson as Caesar and Giuseppe, respectively.

"Little Big Man" A recent treatment of Edward G. Robinson's life and career was on *A&E Biography* in 1996. The unavailability of a 1977 BBC documentary on Robinson in the United States made the A&E broadcast long overdue. A difference between the two programs was in the influence of Jane Robinson Sidney, the actor's widow, on the first program versus her absence (having died in 1991) from the second. According to Robinson's granddaughter, Francesca, who was interviewed for both programs, the more recent program allows for more favorable representation of Gladys Lloyd, Edward G. Robinson's first wife, whose erratic behavior over several years finally led to their divorce in 1956. A comment by narrator/producer Peter Jones is sympathetic: "Gladys was less plagued by demons in her later years...."

Biography, with Peter Graves; produced, written, and directed by Peter Jones (Peter Jones Productions, Inc., for the A&E Television Network); supervising producer, Andrew Tilles; associate producer, Genevieve Halili; directors of photography, Scott Judy, Bowden Hunt, Richard Westlein; editor, Ned Weisman; on-line editor, Scott Reynolds; production associate, Morgan Neville; music arranged by Robert Israel; music recorded at the Old Towne Music Hall, El Segundo, California; audio, John Scarpaci; makeup, Carolyn Brandon, Josephine Rosa Westlein; paintbox, Peter Keating; electronic graphics, Valerie Crane McCarthy; A&E supervising director, Carolanne Dolan; director of documentary programming, Bill Harris; executive producer, Michael Cascio; participants, Peter Graves, Charlton Heston, Bettye Ackerman Jaffe, Norman Lloyd, Patrice Marandel (curator, Los Angeles County Museum of Modern Art), John McCarty, Beulah Robinson, Francesca Robinson-Sanchez, Gena Rowlands, Claire Trevor (voice), Billy Wilder (voice), Peter Jones (narrator); special thanks to George Feltenstein, Susan Rubio, Francesca Robinson-Sanchez, Pamela Knowles, Charlene Green, Jeanie L. Constable, Joe Fronek, Jim Pascale, Ned Comstock, Ric Robertson (Academy of Motion Picture Arts and Sciences), Alexander Brun (Los Angeles County Museum of Art); film footage provided by Turner Entertainment Company, Warner

Bros., National Broadcasting Company Inc., Carson Productions Group, MCA Television LTD, Archive Films, BBC Worldwide America, Shokus Video, Coy Watson, Jr., The Library of Moving Images, Movietime Inc. Archives, Robinson home movies, c. 1996 Francesca Robinson-Sanchez, CMG Worldwide; still photographs, Francesca Robinson-Sanchez, USC Cinema Television Library, Bettye Ackerman Jaffe, Archive Photos-Bettman Archive, Collector's Book Store, City College of New York, Gena Rowlands, Kobal Collection; Audio Clips provided by Prof. Arthur B. Friedman, Marty Halperin; Academy Award audio clip courtesy of the Academy of Motion Picture Arts and Sciences, 1973; hotel accommodations provided by the Beverly Hilton Hotel (Beverly Hills) and the Carlyle Hotel (New York); 1996

Little Caesar (Film, 1931) By January 1931, Edward G. Robinson had been shuttling between Hollywood and New York for about a year. He made two films in Hollywood, went back to New York, and then came back to the West Coast to appear in *East Is West*, to redo scenes which Jean Hersholt had already filmed. He had played a gangster on Broadway and on tour in *The Racket*, and returned to New York again to appear in *Mr. Samuel* in the late fall. Hal Wallis of Warner Bros. was in the audience during one of the mere eight performances the play enjoyed, and he immediately offered Edward G. Robinson a film contract. In December Robinson was back in Hollywood again, and *The Widow from Chicago* was completed and released.

Suddenly, although not exactly overnight, Robinson achieved celebrity status with the next film offered under his new contract. The conditions were right: First, the movies had been talking now for about two years, and Robinson the actor, with his dynamic presence and stage training and his admittedly tough and homely looks, was an ideal talent to play gangsters; second, because the Depression and Prohibition, and Al Capone as the reigning underworld power, were victimizing America, gangster films were increasingly popular. Finally, W. R. Burnett had written a passionate and well crafted novel based on true events; a brutal gangland murder in Chicago had taken the life of a friend.

Here was an actor making an indelible impression on audiences with a single performance in a title role that would be identified with him for the rest of his life. Boris Karloff as the *Frankenstein* monster and Orson Welles in *Citizen Kane* come to mind, but otherwise such occurrences are rare.

Little Caesar made movie history. Gerald Peary, in an article titled "Rico Rising: Little Caesar Takes Over the Screen," comments: "The movie of *Little Caesar* was, at its release ... an instant popular success. 'Doors Are Smashed at Strand in Rush to See Gang Film' headlined a story in the New York *Daily Mirror*. 'Police reserves were summoned last night when a crowd of 3,000 persons stormed the doors.'" Peary notes also that, "According to Chicago Judge John Lyle in *The Dry and Lawless Years* (1960), 'Scarface [Capone] was ... 5 feet 8 inches, 190 pounds. He had a large flabby face with thick lips and coarse features. His nose was flat; his brows dark and shaggy, and a bullet shaped head was supported by a short thick neck.' All in all, a passable description of Robinson...."

In his autobiography *Starmarker*, Hal Wallis says, "I had intended to have Robinson play the small part of Otero in *Little Caesar*. But Eddie was determined to play Rico. He walked into my office one day wearing a homburg, heavy black overcoat, and white evening scarf, a cigar clenched between his teeth. He *was* Rico...." Robinson, in his autobiography *All My Yesterdays*, concurred: "I think Hal had always meant for me to play Rico.... And I do now what I have never done before. I thank him for *Little Caesar*."

Wallis continued, "I gave [Mervyn LeRoy] the script to read and he fell in love with it. (He ... pushed hard for a young actor named Clark Gable to play Joe Massara, but Jack Warner said no, he'd never amount to anything, his ears were too big.)" There are Hollywood stories that Gable, who had been a sensation onstage in the prison drama *The Last Mile*, tested instead for the role of Rico, but the truth is as Wallis states it.

"I had the pleasure of directing Mr. Robinson in *Little Caesar*, and we have been great friends for many years," commented Mervyn LeRoy. "He is one of the finest actors living and one of the finest gentlemen it has been my good fortune to know. I cannot say enough about him as an actor or as a person." Robinson also liked LeRoy. But he was cautious about his continual joking on the set. "Time after time I'd call the prop man over and have him nail Eddie's cigars down to something wooden on the set," admitted Leroy in his autobiography *Take One*. "The rest of the company would know what was going on and wait for Eddie's reaction. It's a simple little gag, perhaps silly, too, but it served the purpose — to keep the set light and the mood cheerful. The only problem I had with Eddie was his involuntary blinking when he fired his gun.... We tried everything we could think of—we even taped Eddie's eyelids — but nothing really worked...." Robinson said of the director, "More than any director I know, Mervyn is the audience. He is the man who goes to the box office and ... loves or hates a picture through his own emotions."—*All My Yesterdays*

Director, Mervyn LeRoy; producers, Jack L. Warner, Hal B. Wallis, Darryl F. Zanuck; associate producer, Robert Lord; screenplay, Francis Edward Faragoh, Robert N. Lee; based on the novel by W. R. Burnett; camera, Tony Gaudio; music, Erno Rapee; music director, Leo F. Forbstein; editor, Ray Curtiss; art director, Anton Grot; cast: Edward G. Robinson (Cesare Enrico Bandello, a.k.a. Rico and Little Caesar), Douglas Fairbanks, Jr. (Joe Massara), Glenda Farrell (Olga Stassoff), Sidney Blackmer (Big Boy), George E. Stone (Otero), Thomas Jackson (Flaherty), William Collier, Jr. (Tony Passa), Ralph Ince (Diamond Pete Montana), Stanley Fields (Sam Vettori), Maurice Black (Little Arnie Lorch), Noel Madison (Killer Pepi), Nick Bela (Ritz Colonna), Lucille LaVerne (Ma Magdalena), Landers Stevens (Commissioner McClure), Armand Kaliz (DeVoss), Ferike Boros (Tony's mother), Al Hill (Waiter), Gladys Lloyd, Larry Steers (Guests), George Daley (Machine gunner), Ernie S. Adams, Kernan Cripps, Ben Hendricks, Jr., Ethan Laidlaw, Louis Natheaux, Tom McGuire, Elmer Ballard; First National-Vitaphone; 80 (or 77) minutes; January 1931

After robbing a gas station, Cesare Enrico Bandello and his pal, Joe Massara, stop at a diner for spaghetti and coffee. "Rico" dreams of moving East, "where things break big!" He has no time for Joe's interests — women and dancing — and dismisses them. Rico joins Sam Vettori's mob, whose other members include Otero, Tony Passa, Scabby, Killer Pepi, and Kid Bean. When Rico tells Sam his full name, Sam snidely responds, "Oh, Little Caesar, eh?" Joe gets a job as dancing partner with Olga Stassoff at the Bronze Peacock, and thereby becomes a good inside man for a New Year's Eve holdup. Boss man Diamond Pete Montana warns Sam and his rival, Little Arnie Lorch, to avoid crimes that cannot be "fixed" by the Big Boy, such as killings. Despite this, on the night of the robbery Rico shoots McClure, the new crime commissioner. Tony, who drives the getaway car, panics; so Rico has Tony killed. His rise to power has begun. He takes over the gang from Sam, eliminates Arnie, and is invited by the Big Boy to take over the entire East Side. At a testimonial party Rico is presented a stolen watch as a gift from his gangland friends. Lt. Flaherty of the police force scowls at his success. Now living in the high style he always wanted, Rico expects Joe to continue as his right hand man, but Joe wants out. Rico goes after him at Olga's apartment, but at the crucial moment he cannot shoot Joe. Olga calls the police, and Rico escapes. Unable to return to his apartment to get his money, Rico hides out behind Ma Magdalena's store, but the old lady tricks him. Powerless now, Rico's downfall begins. In a few months most of the old gang is either dead or captured. Rico, living in a flophouse, reads a newspaper article calling him a coward. In a rage he telephones police headquarters, demanding to speak to Lt. Flaherty. His ranting gives the police time to trace the call. He is gunned down behind a billboard advertising Olga and Joe's new nightclub act. His uncomprehending dying words are, "Mother of Mercy, is this the end of Rico?"

Robinson garnered extraordinary personal reviews. Critical praise at the time of the film's release is borne out decades later. *The New York Herald-Tribune* said *Little Caesar* was "made important by the genuinely brilliant performance that Edward G. Robinson contributes to the title role.... Not even in *The Racket* was he more effective. Taking one of the most familiar roles in the universe, he makes it seem fresh and real. By a hundred details of characterization, he transforms a stock figure into a human being. And, heaven knows, he doesn't make Little Caesar human by suggesting any softness in him. Never does he cease being a savage and terrifying killer, a man who is all the more sinister because of his reality.... When you watch him writhing there in impotent rage ... and uttering grotesque animal outcries of pain and indignation, you are seeing a scene which almost any actor would ruin, but which Mr. Robinson makes the most effective current moment in the cinema."

Decades later, the promotional copy in the United Artists sixteen-millimeter rental catalogue reiterated the praise: "When Edward G. first snarled and swaggered his way across the screen, observing that 'this game ain't for guys that's soft,' his effects on the audiences of that grim winter of 1931 must have come with the jolt of an electric shock. Violent, out only for himself, Rico was perhaps a distasteful character, but forty years of imitation of the short man with the squashed face, the stogie firmly clenched between teeth, the growling voice, is eloquent testimony to his powerful and enduring allure. His body at last fatally torn by bullet wounds, Little Caesar cries out in disbelief, 'Mother of Mercy, is this the end of Rico?' The answer was of course no, for the legend of Robinson / Rico even now continues to grow with each passing year."

"*Little Caesar*, based on W. R. Burnett's novel of Chicago gangsterdom, was welcomed to the Strand yesterday by unusual crowds," wrote the *New York Times* reviewer. "The story deals with the career of Cesare Bandello, alias Rico, alias Little Caesar, a disagreeable lad who started by robbing gasoline stations and soared to startling heights in his 'profession' by reason of his high destiny. The production is ordinary and would rank as just one more gangster film but for two things. One is the excellence of Mr. Burnett's creditable and compact story. The other is Edward G. Robinson's wonderfully effective performance. Little Caesar becomes at Mr. Robinson's hands a figure out of Greek epic tragedy, a cold, ignorant, merciless killer, driven on and on by an insatiable lust for power, the plaything of a force greater than himself."

In retrospect, no less than the *Oxford Companion to Film* agreed: "Most outstanding is Edward G. Robinson's performance, which adds psychological complexity to Rico's vanity and ruthlessness."

In his study for the *Pyramid Illustrated History of the Movies: Edward G. Robinson*, Foster Hirsch comments: "Though contemporary critics praised him for playing a gangster realistically, Robinson, in fact, is highly mannered.... With broad ... strokes, he points up his character's foolish vanity, brute determination, and remarkable naiveté. Emphasizing the character's neurotic maladjustments, Robinson endows the role with some Freudian kinks that are only dimly present in W. R. Burnett's novel.... Without overdoing it, Robinson manages to elicit our sympathy for his antisocial, borderline psychopath.... Robinson doesn't make Little Caesar glamorous, but he does bring to the character a decidedly heroic presence. He gives Rico stature. He makes him a man to contend with."

Edward G. Robinson once remarked, "I loved the role — and still do, for that matter — but what I didn't love was the monotonous series of monotypes that followed." Robinson is credited with this additional telling comment: "In the light of his milieu and perhaps even in our light, [Rico] was kind, generous, and on the level."

Douglas Fairbanks, Jr., who co-starred in *Little Caesar*, commiserated with Robinson in his autobiography *The Salad Days*: "Poor Eddie Robinson was typecast for so long as 'the tough guy.' No gentler man ever walked. I enjoyed every minute of the film. I learned so much from the friendly Eddie Robinson...."

No one could have come close to challenging Eddie's classic performance."

More positive reviews, some from the time of the film's original release, and others in retrospective publications, are worth noting. In 1931 *The New Yorker* said, "Mr. Robinson's diagnosis ... is so simplified and so articulate as to be the outstanding characterization of the kind...." *The Commonweal* lauded *Little Caesar* for "irony and grim humor, and a real sense of excitement, and its significance does not get in the way of the melodrama."

An issue of *TV Guide*, covering a television broadcast of the film, said, "Robinson's portrait of the gangster — power-hungry, ruthless and surface sentimental — endures as a fundamental truth in its social and psychological implications, stripped of *The Godfather*'s romantic schmaltz, still chilling and topical in its implication."

"Any true distinction the film achieved was owed to the actor.... Robinson, with his short stature and a glower that seemed imbedded in his features ... made his performance all gestures and animal physicality."—*Crime Movies*

Bosley Crowther, in his book *The Great Films: Fifty Golden Years of Motion Pictures*, gave this praise: "It is a brilliant and chilling picture of a sardonic and sentimental Italian American, modeled more or less on Capone, [who] goes after power with a vengeance and is betrayed and destroyed in the end. Robinson's Rico may be a fictional character, skillfully realized by the actor from a script by W. R. Burnett, but he is believable."

An unknown piece of information concerns the actor who played the role of Scabby in *Little Caesar*. Scabby is a fairly important character. He is the one who makes the presentation of the stolen watch to Rico at his testimonial dinner. It is also he who patches up Rico's arm after he has been shot on the street. Sam Vettori says of Scabby when he is introduced to Rico for the first time, "What a clever guy he is!" John Cocchi, a noted film researcher, is among those unable to identify the actor, commenting, "I have long wondered who he is myself; others in the picture with less to do receive credit." A joint letter from the author to Douglas Fairbanks, Jr., and Mervyn LeRoy provided no answer. Fairbanks said, "I'm sorry, I just can't recall this fellow's name." LeRoy's assistant responded that the director didn't know the name; LeRoy died four days after the letter was sent.

"In 1931 the gangster film dominated the movies. By the middle of the next year it had entirely vanished from the screen, though not because of any lessened popularity. It was suppressed. That sensitive litmus paper, Will Hays, turned blue with alarm at the torrent of protest which the gangster pictures evoked from the Daughters of the American Revolution, the American Legion, and that greater legion of women's and business clubs which run the machinery of community life in the United States. It was useless for Mr. Hays to reply that the gangster films moralized against crime and were grim object lessons that it did not pay. The small-town civic leaders knew what indeed everybody knew, that Edward G. Robinson in the title role of *Little Caesar*, 1930, had become an ideal for emulation by hordes of young hero-worshipers. Nor did it help to argue that one of the purposes of the gangster films was to arouse the public to a consciousness of the prevalence of wrongdoing. There was in these topical films entirely too much evidence that existing government agencies weren't acting at all, perhaps because they were being paid off. But what probably most alarmed the respectable were certain assumptions, critical not of the breakdown of American institutions but of the institutions themselves."—Richard Griffith and Arthur Mayer in *The Movies*

The Little Giant (Film, 1933) The "little" in this film's title was no accident. The gritty gangster melodramas may have waned over two years, but Edward G. Robinson was still Little Caesar. Now Warners was looking for ways to put the gangster on display in different types of stories. Robinson had already played a gambler, a killer condemned to the electric chair, and gone "Oriental." Now it was time for comedy, and time for love. He got two leading ladies playing opposite him in *The Little Giant,* one of them the lovely Mary Astor.

"Eddie Robinson was the star, doing a kind of caricature of his tough gangster roles," she said in her book *A Life on Film*. "...The thing that was interesting to me was how TV had made so many things obsolete and absurd. Here was Eddie expressing comic wonderment at the way 'society' lived. Making cracks about thick rugs and slippery floors, the height of ceilings, silverware, and objets d'art. Seeing a small reproduction of the Venus de Milo on a table and remarking, 'With all her dough, you'd think she'd have the arms glued back on.' I suppose this was hilarious at the time. But since TV, there are few people who haven't seen beautiful homes or their reproductions as sets in a film. To make a whole picture on the social education of a hood — and a wealthy hood — who had never seen a game of polo or heard of it, who had never seen brandy served in a balloon glass ('Whyncha fill it up?') seems even more hilarious.... But to go back to 1933 and *Little Giant* with that little giant of an actor, Eddie Robinson, the two of us rather sadly doing a bad picture together, knowing it, telling each other, 'It might be funny.' It was. Sort of. But there was something wrong about Edward G. Robinson taking pratfalls from a polo pony."

Robinson, in turn, greatly admired Astor, feeling that her qualities as an actress were never fully appreciated. He warned television viewers that in *The Little Giant* could be seen the effects of a Los Angeles earthquake during the filming.

With the end of Prohibition, gangster Bugs Ahearn, who has run the Chicago beer rackets with his mob, now figures to go straight. He and his pal, Al Daniels, head for Santa Barbara to buy their way into society. He tries to help Polly Cass when he assumes she has fallen from her horse, but she merely got tired of riding. She accepts a ride back to town in Bugs' car and invites him to tea the next day. Trying to impress Polly and her parents, Bugs tells them he has just purchased an old mansion. Then he goes to an agent, Ruth Wayburn, and buys a house and hires her to manage its staff. He does not know that it was the Cass family that sold Ruth's father worthless bonds that caused him to lose everything, including the house, and die a broken man. The relationship develops between Polly and Bugs. She sees an opportunity to marry just long enough to collect alimony from him. Bugs wants to propose to her but becomes self-conscious and asks Ruth to coach him on what to say. Bugs announces his engagement to Polly. He offers to buy into Cass Winter & Company, and the directors are quick to sell him one hundred percent interest. This delights Polly, who now feels no obligation to marry Bugs. The Cass family is momentarily taken aback to learn who Bugs really is, but they condemn and shame him for not telling them the truth. Commiserating with Ruth and Al, Bugs tells them about his investment in the company. Horrified, Ruth tells Bugs all about the Casses. Bugs calls Chicago and orders his mob to California. They forcibly sell back the company to all the directors. Bugs confronts Polly and her family one last time to tell them off. He now settles down in his new house with Ruth, realizing it is she that he really loves. The gang members play polo outside on the grounds, riding horses, but shoot the ball with guns instead of using mallets.

Director, Roy Del Ruth; screenplay, Robert Lord, Wilson Mizner; story, Lord; supervisor, Ray Griffith; music, Leo F. Forbstein; art director, Robert Haas; camera, Sid Hickox; editors, Ray Curtiss, George Marks; gowns, Orry-Kelly; cast: Edward G. Robinson (James Francis "Bugs" Ahearn), Mary Astor (Ruth Wayburn), Helen Vinson (Polly Cass), Russell Hopton (Al Daniels), Kenneth Thomson (John Stanley), Shirley Grey (Edith Merriam), Donald Dillaway (Gordon Cass), Louise Mackintosh (Mrs. Cass), Berton Churchill (Donald Hadley Cass), Helen Mann (Frankie), Selmer Jackson (Announcer), Dewey Robinson (Butch Zanwutoski), John Kelly (Tim), Sidney Bracey (Butler), Bob Perry, Adrian Morris (Milano's hoods), Rolfe Sedan (Waiter), Charles Coleman (Charteris), Gordon "Bill" Elliott (Guest), Leonard Carey (Ingleby), Nora Cecil (Maid), Lester Dorr, Lorin Raker (Investment clerks), Guy Usher (Detective), John Marston (District attorney), Harry Tenbrook (Pulido), Ben Taggart (Cop); Loretta Andrews, Bonnie Bannon, Joan Barclay, Max Barwyn, Harry Bradley,

Lynn Browning, Joe Caites, Lew Harvey, William Worthington, Maxine Cantway, James H. Doyle, Al Hill, Ann Hovey, John Hyams, Alice Jans, Margaret LaMar, Frank Moran, Barbara Rogers, Matty Roubert, Renee Whitney, Jayne Shadduck, Pat Wing, Toby Wing, Tammany Young; First National-Warner Bros.; 74 minutes; May 1933

Reviews were generally positive. One, from *The Nation*, noted the film's social relevance: "Mr. Robinson's vicious little thug is presented with the greatest sympathy and good humor throughout, without the slightest insinuation of moral judgment ... [scenes] which reflect the increasing barbarism of the American cinema make *Little Giant* significant as well as amusing."

"Robinson reveals himself to be no mean comedian," said *The New York Times*. "...[He is] alert and forceful even in this light affair." *The Sunday New York Times* echoed that, "*The Little Giant* is an amusing bit of fluff which gives Mr. Robinson a chance to reveal unsuspected comedy talents.... [He] is as sure of his ground as a comedian as he has been in heavy roles. He makes Ahearn quick-witted and quite natural, so long as the story permits."

"This fast moving and thoroughly entertaining picture shows Mr. Robinson at his best and is one of the really worthwhile films that have come along during the last few weeks," commented *The New York World-Telegram*. "...[He] is excellent as the erstwhile racketeer." And *The New York Sun* agreed: "Edward G. Robinson undoubtedly finds himself with another success on his hands.... [He], it goes without saying, is forceful, right and genuinely amusing."

Finally, *The Indianapolis Star* hailed the film, saying, "A great deal of harmless fun as played by Edward G. Robinson, who reveals in this piece a gift for comedy characterization which hitherto had been only faintly suspected. His adventures into a plutocratic wonderland, in which all is not gold that glitters, we believe will amuse you."

The Little Teacher (Theater, 1918) At age 24 Edward G. Robinson began rehearsing his fifth Broadway play. It was his first comedy, called *The Little Teacher*, and it did well.

Producers, George M. Cohan, Sam Harris; playwright, Harry James Smith; director, Sam Forrest; cast: Mary Ryan, Edward G. Robinson (Batiste), Katherine Brewster, Paul Bryant, Curtis Cooksey, Florence Curran, Lillian Dix, James Giller, Thomas Giller, Harold Hartzell, Marie Haynes, Horace James, Viola Leach, Carolyn Lee, Kate Mayhew, Maxine Mazanovich, Nina Morris, William J. Phinney, Edward L. Snader, Waldo Whipple; opened at the Playhouse Theatre, New York; February 4, 1918

"The comedy is fresh and quite unforced, and the drama is as effective as it is veracious and simple," said *The New Republic*. "...As the Canuck friend of the hero, Edward G. Robinson had the best opportunity and made the most of it." *The New York Herald-Tribune* said that, "Robinson created an amusing role in Batiste."

Litvak, Anatole (1902–74) directed two films with Edward G. Robinson — *The Amazing Dr. Clitterhouse* and *Confessions of a Nazi Spy*. He was married to actress Miriam Hopkins. He worked in his native Russia, then in Germany, coming to the U.S. in 1937. Other films include *Tovarich, All This and Heaven Too, Anastasia,* and *The Journey*.

Lloyd, George (1892–1967) was a character actor who made five films with Edward G. Robinson — *Barbary Coast, Bullets or Ballots, Our Vines Have Tender Grapes, Scarlet Street,* and *A Slight Case of Murder*. He was also in *The Ox-Bow Incident, They Won't Forget,* and *Nightmare Alley*.

Lloyd, Gladys (1895–1971) was Edward G. Robinson's first wife. Her full name was Gladys Lloyd Cassell. She was the daughter of noted sculptor Clement Comley Cassell, and a direct descendant of the historical Ogden family, Pennsylvania Quakers who had owned George Washington's headquarters at Valley Forge. Gladys had appeared on Broadway with Fred and Adele Astaire in *Funny Face* and *Lady Be Good*. She also had been in *Apple Sauce* and with Robinson in *Henry, Behave* and *Mr. Samuel*. They met in 1924 and were married on January 21, 1927. In Hollywood she had small roles in Robinson's *Little Caesar, Smart Money, Five*

Star Final, Two Seconds, and *The Hatchet Man,* and appeared in *Clive of India* with Ronald Colman and Loretta Young. Edward G. Robinson, Jr., was born in 1933. For the war effort she distinguished herself with the organization of a group to boost troop morale known as "The Desert Battalion." They were the only girls brought in to cheer up troops training under General George S. Patton prior to their departure during the African campaign. During the 1940s Gladys was diagnosed with manic depression, hopsitalized, and given shock treatments. During this period she threatened divorce many times. After twenty-nine years, on August 6, 1956, she was granted a decree which awarded her half their property and 25 percent of Robinson's future earnings. She had an eye for art and helped amass the fabulous family collection. She did her own paintings and ceramics, eventually holding major one-woman shows of her work. The divorce meant the sale of the collection to comply with California's community property law. The bid of $3,125,000 paid for the art by Greek shipping magnate Stavros Niarchos made the front page of *The New York Times*. While attending the high school graduation of her granddaughter, Francesca, Gladys collapsed and went into a coma. She died on June 6, 1971.

Lobert, John B. "Hans" (1881–1968) was played by Edward G. Robinson in *Big Leaguer*. He was a third baseman for the Pittsburgh Pirates for fourteen years, beginning in 1903, then a coach at West Point from 1918 to 1925. He managed the Giants for several years before moving to Florida to head their recruitment and spring training programs.

Lockhart, Gene (1891–1957) could be sinister or sympathetic; he was in three films with Edward G. Robinson—as William Ramey, the antagonist of *Blackmail*; the banker, Herr Bauer, in *A Dispatch from Reuter's*; and the drunken Dr. "Louie" Prescott in *The Sea Wolf*. He is in the Christmas movies *Miracle on 34th Street* and *A Christmas Carol*, as well as *Algiers* (Oscar nomination), *Meet John Doe, Going My Way, The House on 92nd Street, Leave Her to Heaven,* and *Carousel*.

Lockheed's Ceiling Unlimited (Radio, 1943) Edward G. Robinson was on the program twice, as guest host on January 4, and in his *Big Town* role of Steve Wilson in an episode entitled "World of Tomorrow" in April.
See **"World of Tomorrow."**

Loeb, Philip (1894–1955) appeared with Edward G. Robinson in the Theatre Guild's *The Brothers Karamazov, The Goat Song, Juarez and Maximilian, Ned McCobb's Daughter,* and *Right You Are If You Think You Are*. He was on the screen opposite Gertrude Berg in *Molly,* and was also in *A Double Life* and *Room Service*.

Loft, Arthur (1897–1947), a stocky character actor, was in four films with Edward G. Robinson—*I Am the Law*, as editor Tom Ross; *The Woman in the Window*, as Claude Mazard; *Scarlet Street,* as Dellarowe, the art dealer; and *Flesh and Fantasy,* as a detective. Other pictures include *Blood on the Sun* and *Prisoner of Shark Island*.

Logan, Joshua (1908–88), a director and producer in Hollywood and New York, was responsible for both the stage and screen versions of *Mister Roberts, Picnic,* and *South Pacific*. He directed Edward G. Robinson's *Middle of the Night*, as well as *On Borrowed Time* and *Annie Get Your Gun*, and in Hollywood he helmed *Bus Stop, Sayonara,* and *Camelot*. He received Oscar nominations for *Picnic* and *Sayonara*. His faith in Robinson's work in *Middle of the Night* is evidenced in his comment to author Paddy Chayefsky, "He was created by God for this role."
See ***Middle of the Night***.

London, Julie (1926–92) made an early film appearance as Tibby Renton in *The Red House*, with Edward G. Robinson. Other pictures include *Jungle Woman, The Third Voice,* and *The George Raft Story*. Married to Jack Webb, she was on TV in his series *Emergency*.

Long, Richard (1927–74), as a juvenile, appeared in *The Stranger* with Edward G. Robinson; he was also on television as one of

Barbara Stanwyck's sons in *Big Valley*, and on the detective series *Bourbon Street Beat*. Other films include *The Egg and I, Criss Cross,* and *Home from the Hill*.

Lord, Marjorie (1922–) had a role in the first episode of *Flesh and Fantasy* and was also on TV with Edward G. Robinson in "Epitaph for a Spy." Her films include *Forty Naughty Girls, New Orleans,* and *Boy Did I Get a Wrong Number*. She was Danny Thomas' wife on TV's *Make Room for Daddy*.

Lord, Pauline (1890–1950) made her Broadway debut in *The Talker* in 1912. She worked with Edward G. Robinson five times, in *The Deluge* (as Sadie), *Drafted, Launzi* (title role), *Samson and Delilah* (as Dagmar Krumback), and *The Night Lodging* (as Nastya). She also played *Anna Christie*, Amy in *They Knew What They Wanted*, Nina in *Strange Interlude*, Abby in *The Late Christopher Bean*, Zenobia in *Ethan Frome*, and, on tour, Amanda Wingfield in *The Glass Menagerie*.

Lord, Robert (1900–76), writer/producer with Warner Bros., worked on Edward G. Robinson's *Five Star Final* and *The Little Giant* (screenplays), *Little Caesar, The Amazing Dr. Clitterhouse,* and *Confessions of a Nazi Spy* (as associate producer), and *The Man with Two Faces* (as supervisor). An Oscar winner for *One Way Passage* (original story), he was nominated also for *Black Legion*. Other films: *20,000 Years in Sing Sing, The Prince and the Pauper, The Letter,* and *In a Lonely Place*.

Lorre, Peter (1904–64) is caricatured, with Edward G. Robinson, in *Racket Rabbit*, a Bugs Bunny cartoon. They were together on tv's *The Ed Sullivan Show* and *The Honeymooners* and on the radio in *Hollywood Fights Back*. His films include *M, The Man Who Knew Too Much,* the *Mr. Moto* series, *The Maltese Falcon,* and *The Raven*.

Love, Bessie (1898–1986) was in films from 1915: *Intolerance, Sally of the Scandals,* as Edward G. Robinson's wife in *Journey Together,* singing and dancing in *The Broadway Melody* and *Good News,* and also *The Barefoot Contessa, The Loves of Isadora,* and *Sunday Bloody Sunday*.

Love, Montagu (1877–1943) was in *Dr. Ehrlich's Magic Bullet,* with Edward G. Robinson, as Prof. Hartmann, and played Delane of the *London Times* in *A Dispatch from Reuter's*. A silent screen villain, he was also in *Son of the Sheik, Don Juan, Lloyds of London, The Life of Emile Zola,* and *Gunga Din*.

Love Scenes Hardly what Edward G. Robinson was known for in his stage and screen performances, love scenes are present, nonetheless, in a number of his productions. Two early films with the "L" word in the titles are *I Loved a Woman* and *A Lady to Love*. The first has more to do with ambition, especially by the woman, whereas the latter is a genuinely romantic — if atypical — love triangle story in which Robinson wins the girl from a younger, handsomer man. That happened a quarter of a century later on Broadway, as well, when Robinson's character fell in love with a woman young enough to be his daughter in *Middle of the Night*.

Other examples where the film tough guy is chastened by love are *Silver Dollar* (he has not one, but two wives); *The Whole Town's Talking* (he wins Jean Arthur at the fadeout); *Bullets or Ballots* (Joan Blondell); *Thunder in the City* (Luli Deste); *Unholy Partners* (Laraine Day); *Flesh and Fantasy* (Anna Lee); and *Night Has a Thousand Eyes* and *Illegal* (although he loses Virginia Bruce and Nina Foch, respectively, in both). More telling, however, are these films that contain romantic interludes for the star:

**The Hatchet Man.* After a fling with a younger man, Loretta Young is rescued from him and realizes she loves Edward G.

**The Little Giant.* Robinson thinks he loves Helen Vinson and is coached in lovemaking by Mary Astor. Then he realizes *she* is the right one for him.

**I Am the Law.* By this time, Robinson is a domestic family man — well, at least a dog owner — and happily wed to Barbara O'Neil.

**Blackmail.* He and Ruth Hussey have an unusually sweet chemistry as husband and wife, and as parents of little Bobs Watson.

*Dr. Ehrlich's Magic Bullet. Ruth Gordon quietly and lovingly supports her husband's life's work as a medical researcher.

*A Dispatch from Reuter's. Part of the delightful courtship between Edna Best and Robinson is via carrier pigeon!

*Tampico. Again, the chemistry is good. Lynn Bari, who was a little more than half Robinson's age, plays a stowaway who falls in love with him as a wartime ship's captain.

He has loving wives in a number of films, but the emphasis is elsewhere: Margaret Seddon in *The Bright Shawl*; Ruth Donnelly in *A Slight Case of Murder*; Ruth Warrick in *Mr. Winkle Goes to War*; Agnes Moorehead in *Our Vines Have Tender Grapes*; Bessie Love in *Journey Together*; Dorothy Peterson in *The Woman in the Window*; Mady Christians in *All My Sons*; Esther Minciotti in *House of Strangers*; Nora Swinburne in *Operation X*; Virginia Christine in *Nightmare*; Thelma Ritter in *A Hole in the Head*; and Joanna Moore in *Never a Dull Moment*.

Love Triangles Although Edward G. Robinson's countenance tended to prevent him from being involved in love stories, in productions like *Middle of the Night*, *The Whole Town's Talking*, and *The Little Giant* the storyline has him falling in love and getting the girl. More often, however, he was the third party in a romantic triangle, as an obstacle to be removed to assure the happiness of others. The plot twists vary, but in these films Robinson is odd man out: *Barbary Coast* (Miriam Hopkins and Joel McCrea); *Night Has a Thousand Eyes* (Virginia Bruce and Jerome Cowan); *Brother Orchid* (Ann Sothern and Ralph Bellamy); *Manpower* (Marlene Dietrich and George Raft); *Illegal* (Nina Foch and Hugh Marlowe); *The Last Gangster* (Rose Stradner and James Stewart); *Scarlet Street* (Joan Bennett and Dan Duryea); *Tiger Shark* (Zita Johann and Richard Arlen); *Kid Galahad* (Bette Davis and Wayne Morris); and *The Violent Men* (Barbara Stanwyck and Brian Keith). In the last named, the lovers die and Robinson survives; and in *Kid Galahad*, after Robinson yields to Davis, she in turn yields to the romance between Morris and Jane Bryan.

He murders his girlfriend in *The Glass Web*, attempting to blame it on another of her lovers, John Forsythe. Robinson has a wife plus another involvement in *Two Weeks in Another Town*, *Dark Hazard*, *Silver Dollar*, and *I Loved a Woman*, but in none of the films does he "live happily ever after" with either. And despite the existence of a love triangles in *The Hatchet Man*, *A Lady to Love*, and *Thunder in the City*, he wins the girl!

There are romantic entanglements in each of the following, but Robinson's character is not directly involved: *The Man with Two Faces*, *Tales of Manhattan*, *Double Indemnity*, *House of Strangers*, *The Ten Commandments*, *A Hole in the Head*, *Pepe*, *The Prize*, *Cheyenne Autumn*, *The Cincinnati Kid*, *Mackenna's Gold*, *Song of Norway*, TV's *Who Has Seen the Wind?* and *U.M.C.*, and, in the theater, in *The Adding Machine*.

The Lower Depths see **The Night Lodging**

Lucas, Wilfred (1871–1940) began in silent films in 1907. With Edward G. Robinson he appears in *Silver Dollar*, *Brother Orchid*, and *The Sea Wolf* (and he is sometimes listed in the credits of *It's a Great Feeling*, despite having died nine years earlier). Other pictures include *The Man Without a Country*, *Pardon Us*, *Mary of Scotland*, and *Modern Times*.

Luciano, Lucky (1897–1962) Edward G. Robinson played Johnny Rocco in *Key Largo*, based loosely on this notorious gangster. Born in Sicily, his actual name was Charles Luciana. He was a leader in New York crime syndicates from the early 1930s. Convicted by Special Prosecutor Thomas E. Dewey in 1936 on charges of prostitution, Luciano was pardoned later by Governor Dewey because of the gangster's influence on the New York waterfront (from jail) in preventing wartime sabotage. He was deported to Europe in 1946. Seen in Cuba, he was thought to be mounting a return to the United States. This gave John Huston and Richard Brooks the idea to incorporate the Luciano legend into *Key Largo*. In an earlier film,

Marked Woman, Eduardo Ciannelli's gangster character was a thinly disguised Luciano; he was portrayed also by Vic Tayback in *Lepke* and Christian Slater in *Mobsters*. A documentary-style biography, *Lucky Luciano*, was produced in Italy in 1973.

The Lucky Strike Program Starring Jack Benny (Radio, 1946) Participants: Jack Benny, Edward G. Robinson, Eddie "Rochester" Anderson, Phil Harris, Jane Morgan, Dennis Day, the Sportsmen, L. A. "Speed" Riggs, F. E. Boone (tobacco auctioneers), Don Wilson (announcer); NBC-radio, 30 minutes; November 24, 1946.

"The cast does its version of *The Killers*, with guest Edward G. Robinson as a Little Caesar character," noted *Radio Yesteryear*.

"Lucy Goes to a Hollywood Premiere" (Television, 1966) Lucille Ball, Gale Gordon, Robert Foulk, Bert Freed, Reta Shaw, and Kirk Douglas, Anne Douglas, Jimmy Durante, Vincent Edwards, Edward G. Robinson, Jane Robinson (Guests); *The Lucy Show*, CBS-TV; February 7, 1966

Lukas, Paul (1894–1971) An Oscar winner for recreating his Broadway role as an anti–Nazi in *Watch on the Rhine*, he played one in *Confessions of a Nazi Spy*, with Edward G. Robinson. He came to Hollywood from Budapest in 1927. Films include *Little Women*, *Dodsworth*, *The Lady Vanishes*, *Kim*, *20,000 Leagues Under the Sea*, and *Lord Jim*.

Lund, John (1913–92) is in *Night Has a Thousand Eyes* with Edward G. Robinson, and appears also in *To Each His Own*, *A Foreign Affair*, *Brewster's Millions*, *High Society*, and *The Wackiest Ship in the Army*. He was a New York actor and writer on stage and radio.

Lunt, Alfred (1892–1980), a major figure of the New York stage, played the title role in *Clarence*, and was in *Outward Bound* in 1922. After marrying Lynn Fontanne, they appeared together almost exclusively. He and Edward G. Robinson were in five plays together — *Banco*, *Juarez and Maximilian*, *Ned McCobb's Daughter*, *The Goat Song*, and *The Brothers Karamazov* (the last two with his wife). "The Lunts," as they came to be known, were also in *The Guardsman* (also on film), *The Second Man*, *The Taming of the Shrew*, *Reunion in Vienna*, *Amphitryon 38*, *The Seagull*, *The Pirate*, *O Mistress Mine*, *I Know My Love*, *Quadrille*, and *The Visit*.

See **Lynn Fontanne**.

Lupino, Ida (1914–1995) was in "Only Yesterday" on *Lux Radio Theatre*, hosted by Edward G. Robinson. She was also with him on Eddie Cantor's March of Dimes Special on the Mutual Radio Network, and played Ruth Webster in *The Sea Wolf* on the screen. She was married to actors Louis Hayward and Howard Duff. Her credits, beginning in England in 1933, include, as actress, *Anything Goes*, *The Light That Failed*, *Devotion*, *The Hard Way*, *The Big Knife*, and *Junior Bonner*, and as director, *Outrage* and *The Trouble with Angels*.

Lux Radio Theatre Edward G. Robinson appeared in ten dramatizations on this CBS-radio series, which aired for fourteen years beginning in 1934.

See **"The Boss"**; **"Bullets or Ballots"**; **"The Criminal Code"**; **"Destroyer"**; **"Key Largo"**; **"Kid Galahad"**; **"The Maltese Falcon"**; **"Man on a Tightrope"**; **"Manpower"**; **"Only Yesterday"**; **"The Woman in the Window."**

Lux Video Theatre see **"Witness for the Prosecution"**

MGM Metro-Goldwyn-Mayer was one of the major film studios, founded in 1924 and headed by Louis B. Mayer. Edward G. Robinson worked there frequently, despite early differences with boss Irving Thalberg: *A Lady to Love*, *The Last Gangster*, *Blackmail*, *Unholy Partners*, *Our Vines Have Tender Grapes*, *Big Leaguer*, *The Prize*, *The Outrage*, *The Cincinnati Kid*, *Soylent Green*.

See **Irving Thalberg**.

MacArthur, Charles (1895–1956), screenwriter, playwright, and director, collaborated with Ben Hecht on the script of *Barbary Coast*. Other credits include Broadway's *The Front Page*, *Twentieth Century* (also onscreen), *Wuthering Heights*, and *I Take This Woman*. He was married to Helen Hayes; their son is James MacArthur of TV's *Hawaii Five-0*.

Macaulay, Richard   (1909–69) collaborated on the screenplays of Edward G. Robinson's *Brother Orchid*, *Manpower* and *Tampico*. His other works include *The Roaring Twenties*, *Torrid Zone*, and *Across the Pacific*. During the HUAC investigations he was a friendly witness, naming Communists in the film industry.

MacDonald, J. Farrell   (1875–1952) appeared with Edward G. Robinson in *I Loved a Woman* and *The Whole Town's Talking* (as the prison warden), and also in the short film *The Stolen Jools*. He acted and directed from 1914. His films include *Topper*, *A Tree Grows in Brooklyn*, and *It's a Wonderful Life*.

Mackendrick, Alexander   (1912–93) directed Edward G. Robinson in *A Boy Ten Feet Tall*. Starting as a screenwriter, he wrote and directed his first feature, *Whiskey Galore*, in 1949. His other films include *The Ladykillers*, *Sweet Smell of Success*, and *A High Wind in Jamaica*.

Mackenna's Gold   (Film, 1969) "A western of truly stunning absurdity" is what *The New York Times* called it, aptly summing up *Mackenna's Gold*. It had a distinguished cast of guest stars, but they were given little to do, "[including] such people as Cobb, Ciannelli, Massey, Meredith, Quayle, Robinson, and Wallach, each of whom does a sort of stagger-on and then dies." The exception, in fact, was Edward G. Robinson, who was given a juicy monologue. "When Edward G. Robinson went flawlessly through three pages of dialogue without a fluff, Gregory Peck applauded with the rest and said, 'You're the greatest of them all. I hope I'm as good as you.'"—Sheila Graham, *Confessions of a Hollywood Columnist*

A notorious outlaw named Colorado and his gang kidnap Sheriff Mackenna and Inga, the daughter of a local judge, as they search for lost Apache gold. In self defense Mackenna has killed Prairie Dog, an old Apache chief, and has memorized the map to the gold. Colorado forces Mackenna to follow the map. Six men from the nearby town of Hadleyburg join in the quest. One of them, Old Adams, saw the gold as a young man and was blinded by the Apaches. The Indians stage a massacre, killing nearly everyone. Sergeant Tibbs of the cavalry joins the search after shooting the men in his patrol one by one. Finding the lost canyon at last, everyone revels in the gold. The Apaches again attack. An earthquake obliterates the canyon, and only Colorado, Mackenna, and Inga escape. The two men have a fistfight, then part company, Mackenna vowing he will come back for Colorado. Mackenna and Inga ride off together with saddlebags full of gold.

A Highwood Production; producers, Carl Foreman, Dmitri Tiomkin; director, J. Lee Thompson; screenplay, Foreman; based on the novel by Will Henry; art directors, Geoffrey Drake, Cary Odell; set, Alfred E. Spencer; assistant director, David Salven; music, Quincy Jones; orchestra, Jack Hayes, Leo Shuken; song "Old Turkey Buzzard" by Freddie Douglas; sung by Jose Feliciano; special effects, Drake, John Mackey, Bob Cuff, Willis Cook, Larry Butler; camera, Joseph MacDonald; special effects camera, Farciot Edouart, Don Glouner, Richard Moore; sound, Derek Frye, William Randall, Jr.; second unit camera, Harold Wellman; second unit director, Tom Shaw; production manager, Ralph Black; hairstyles, Virginia Jones; costumes, Norma Koch; stunt coordinator, Buzz Henry; editor, Bill Lenny; stereophonic dubbing, Bob Jones, John Blunt; associate film editors, John Link, Jr., Raymond Poulton, Donald Deacon; first assistant film editor, Lois Gray; sound editor, Jeanne Henderson; assistant, Peter Bond; cast: Gregory Peck (Mackenna), Omar Sharif (Colorado), Telly Savalas (Sgt. Tibbs), Camilla Sparv (Inga), Keenan Wynn (Sanchez), Julie Newmar (Hesh-Ke), Ted Cassidy (Hachita), Eduardo Ciannelli (Prairie Dog), Dick Peabody (Avila), Rudy Diaz (Besh), Robert Phillips

(Monkey), Shelley Morrison (Pima squaw), J. Robert Porter (Young Englishman), John Garfield, Jr. (Adams' boy), Pepe Callahan (Laguna), Madeline Taylor Holmes (Old Apache woman), Duke Hobbie (Lieutenant), Victor Jory (Narrator), Trevor Bardette (Old man), and the gentlemen from Hadleyburg: Lee J. Cobb (Editor), Raymond Massey (Preacher), Burgess Meredith (Storekeeper), Anthony Quayle (Englishman), Edward G. Robinson (Old Adams), Eli Wallach (Ben Baker); Columbia, Super Panavision, Technicolor; 136 (or 128) minutes; June 1969

There were no positive reviews. *The New York Times* continued, "[It] is the work of J. Lee Thompson, a thriving example of that old Hollywood maxim about how to succeed by failing big.... Although it is set in the Old West, it actually has the shape of French farce: various groups of characters pursuing each other in and out of ambushes in the kind of circular action so dear to Feydeau...."

The Commonweal observed, "You have the feeling as you watch that no one is really directing [the] actors, most of whom seem to be on their own, just doing what they thought the scene was supposed to be about ... cliches and corn ... in this silly movie."

"Why study the psychology of gold fever in a mere handful of characters when you can hire everyone under the sun? Within minutes of their first appearance, Eli Wallach, Raymond Massey, Keenan Wynn, Burgess Meredith, Edward G. Robinson, and Lee J. Cobb are disposed of in order to litter the trail with celebrity cameos. It is the kind of movie that searches out spectacular locations in the wilderness, then spoils the physical splendor with phony process shots, trumped up melodrama, and such laughable special effects as an earthquake created in what appears to be a sandbox."—*Playboy*

Mackintosh, Louise (1864–1933) played the role of Mrs. Cass in *The Little Giant*. She was also in a 1926 silent film of the same name, as well as *Hard to Handle, Airmail,* and *Up the River.*

MacLaine, Shirley (1934–) An understudy for Carol Haney in Broadway's *The Pajama Game*, she went on when the star broke her leg, and was discovered by Hal Wallis. An Oscar winner for *Terms of Endearment*, she received nominations for *Some Came Running, The Apartment, Irma La Douce,* and *The Turning Point*. With Edward G. Robinson she starred in *My Geisha*, and they were on the 36th Annual Academy Awards. In 1999, when the American Film Institute named Robinson among the top fifty stars of all time, MacLaine, one of the hosts for the televised program, commented that onscreen Robinson could be both grandfatherly and sinister. "It all depended on what he was doing with his cigar," she said. Her other films include *The Trouble with Harry, The Children's Hour, Being There,* and *Steel Magnolias.*

MacLane, Barton (1902–69), Warner's tough guy, played racket boss Al Kruger in *Bullets or Ballots*, with Edward G. Robinson, and Smiley Quinn, who ran the clip joint in *Manpower*. He is also in *G-Men, The Maltese Falcon, The Prince and the Pauper, The Treasure of the Sierra Madre,* and *The Glenn Miller Story.*

MacMahon, Aline (1899–1991) played Edward G. Robinson's secretary in *Five Star Final*, and his first wife in *Silver Dollar* the following year. Among her other films are *The Mouthpiece, Babbitt, Ah Wilderness!, Dragon Seed* (Oscar nomination), *The Young Doctors,* and *All the Way Home.*

MacMahon, Horace (1906–71) has roles in *I Am the Law, The Last Gangster,* and *Kid Galahad* with Edward G. Robinson. He is also in *Susan Slept Here, My Sister Eileen,* and *Detective Story,* and on TV became a familiar face on the series *Naked City.*

MacMurray, Fred (1908–91) claimed to have had his best role as Walter Neff in Billy Wilder's *Double Indemnity*. He and Edward G. Robinson also appeared together on the 36th Annual Academy Awards broadcast. He was adept at comedy: *Murder He Says, The Egg and I, The Absent-Minded Professor,* and the TV series *My Three Sons*. Other films include

The Apartment, The Gilded Lily, The Caine Mutiny, The Oregon Trail, and *Follow Me Boys.*

Macready, George   (1909–73) is with Edward G. Robinson in *Two Weeks in Another Town.* He came from the stage, often playing villains. He is also in *The Commandos Strike at Dawn, A Song to Remember, Gilda, The Big Clock, The Desert Fox, Seven Days in May,* and *The Great Race.*

Mad Checkmate   (Film, 1968) This film has never been shown theatrically in the United States. It was sold to television and given the title *It's Your Move.* Also known as *Checkmate for MacDowall* and *Uno Scacco Tutto Matto,* it is one of a handful of European caper films Robinson made late in his career.

Producer, Franco Porro; director, Robert Fiz; screenplay, Fiz, Massimilliano Capriccoli, Ennio De Concini, Jose G. Maesso, Leonardo Martin, Juan Cesarbea; music, Manuel Asins Arbo; set, Rafael Ferri; camera, Antonio Macasoli; editor, Mario Morra; cast: Edward G. Robinson (MacDowell), Terry-Thomas (Jerome), Maria Grazia Buccella (Monique), Adolfo Celi, Manuel Zarzo, Jorge [George] Rigaud, Jose Bodalo, Loris Bazzocchi, Rossella Como, Rossella Bergamonti, Ana Maria Custodio, Franca Domenici, Gaetano Imbrio, Moises Menendez; Kinesis Films / Miniter / Tecisa; 89 minutes; color; 1968

Four people change places with look-alike counterparts at a bank in Majorca. It is part of a robbery plan organized by a man named MacDowell. The heist is pulled off successfully, but afterwards the four look-alikes become involved in complicated situations as they are mistaken for their doubles. The stolen money gets passed around from group to group. When MacDowell is questioned about bank employees being held in his cellar, he quickly sends them back to the bank to replace the impostors. Because the others looked just like them, the four have not been missed. The safe is opened, and to MacDowell's surprise, the money is there. Then four figures in dirty overalls clamor out a door, complaining they had been repairing the furnace and got locked in!

Madison, Noel   (1898–1975) had roles with Edward G. Robinson in *Little Caesar* (Killer Pepi) and *The Hatchet Man* (Charlie Kee). The son of actor Maurice Moscovitch, Madison also appears in *Sinner's Holiday, Manhattan Melodrama,* and *G-Men.*

Madison Square Garden   The New York auditorium known for prizefights and other major events was the site of Jewish programs in which Edward G. Robinson participated over the years. *We Will Never Die,* the pageant staged in 1943 to commemorate the lives lost in the Holocaust, was presented there, as were many *Chanukah Festivals for Israel.* Robinson made appearances in the latter over a twelve year period, 1956 to 1968.

Magrill, George   (1900–52), tough guy or cop, made four pictures with Edward G. Robinson: *Barbary Coast, The Sea Wolf, Double Indemnity,* and *House of Strangers.* He also was in *Meet Boston Blackie* and *The Flying Irishman,* as well as silent films.

Mail Call   (Radio) Participants: James Gleason, Lucille Gleason, Edward G. Robinson (Master of ceremonies), Dick Powell, Marion Hutton and the Modernaires, Ann Miller, Don Wilson (announcer); AFRS; date unknown; 30 minutes

Makeup   Edward G. Robinson had a character's face, and with his 5'8" height and slightly portly stature, he was never conventionally handsome.

For the first four decades of his career he was usually clean-shaven in his film roles, although beards, moustaches, and sideburns altered his look as the roles required. Gray hair for aging purposes, eyeglasses, and false noses also changed his appearance on the screen. Usually the whiskers were false in his early years. He grew his own black beard and moustache in the 1950s for *The Ten Commandments,* and in 1962 he again grew a moustache and beard for *A Boy Ten Feet Tall.* Described as grizzled, looking like a sort of junior Hemingway, he kept the look for the remainder of his life, except when he played small roles in *Good Neighbor Sam* and *Robin and the 7 Hoods* in 1964, when he was again temporarily clean-shaven. In his last decade Robinson usually looked dapper, professorial, and rather distinguished, with the beard neatly trimmed into a goatee. In *Mackenna's Gold* and *Soylent Green*, as in *A Boy Ten Feet Tall*, his beard was full, for a more weathered look.

He wore moustaches in the following: *A Lady to Love, Tiger Shark, Silver Dollar, A Dispatch from Reuter's, Our Vines Have Tender Grapes, House of Strangers, Operation X, The Violent Men,* and "Heritage." He sported a full beard in *The Goat Song, The Bright Shawl, The Man with Two Faces* (applied during the story as part of his impersonation of a Frenchman), *Dr. Ehrlich's Magic Bullet, The Ten Commandments, A Boy Ten Feet Tall,* and all films that followed. There were sideburns for *I Loved a Woman, Barbary Coast, The Sea Wolf, The Violent Men,* and *The Devil and Daniel Webster.* For the latter his nose was made more Roman by makeup man Dick Smith, to make him look more like the great orator.

Robinson's characters wore eyeglasses in *The Whole Town's Talking* and *The Woman in the Window.* He used a monocle as *A Man with Red Hair* and for *East Is West.* In the latter and *The Hatchet Man,* he wore Oriental eye makeup.

Malden, Karl (1914–) was in two films with Edward G. Robinson—*Cheyenne Autumn* (sharing no scenes) and *The Cincinnati Kid*, as The Shooter. On TV they were on *The Tonight Show* together. An Oscar winner for *A Streetcar Named Desire* (as Mitch, recreated from Broadway), Malden was nominated also for *On the Waterfront.* Other appearances were in *Baby Doll, Gypsy, How the West Was Won, Patton,* and TV's *The Streets of San Francisco* and *Skag.* He directed *Time Limit.* In October 2000 Malden, who is also a member of the U.S. Post Office Citizens Advisory Committee, spoke about Edward G. Robinson during the dedication of a 33–cent stamp in his honor.

See **The Cincinnati Kid**.

"The Maltese Falcon" (Radio, 1943) The popular film was adapted for presentation on *Lux Radio Theatre.*

Based on the novel by Dashiell Hammett and screenplay by John Huston; adaptation, George Wells; music director, Louis Silvers; sound, Charlie Forsyth; cast: Edward G. Robinson (Sam Spade), Gail Patrick (Brigid O'Shaughnessy), Laird Cregar (Caspar Guttman), Bea Benaderet, Charles Seel, Charlie Lang, Edward Marr, Fred MacKaye, Leo Cleary; Cecil B. DeMille (host); John Milton Kennedy (announcer); Norman Field, Warren Ashe, Duane Thompson, Paula Winslowe, Ann Tobin (commercials); *Lux Radio Theatre*; February 8, 1943

The Man of Destiny (Theater, 1925) This one-act play was the curtain-raiser for the longer Shaw comedy *Androcles and the Lion.* Robinson had always wanted to play Napoleon, either on the stage or screen, and lamented that here the role went to Tom Powers. According to Burns Mantle's *Best Plays of 1925–26,* "*The Man of Destiny* is the episode in which Napoleon, after Lodi, enjoys a battle of wits with a lady spy, succumbing with dignity to her charms while sharing honors with her in debate and defeating her mission."

The New York Times found *The Man of Destiny* "amusing," noting, however, that by comparison with *Androcles,* "the Guild did much less well, [although] Mr. Robinson made much of Giuseppe, the preternaturally wise innkeeper." *The New York Herald-Tribune* agreed, saying, "It was easily Edward G. Robinson as Giuseppe who carried off the histrionic honors."

Produced by the Theatre Guild; playwright, George Bernard Shaw; director, Philip Moeller; designer, Manuel Covarrubias; cast: Tom Powers (Napoleon), Clare Eames (Josephine), Edward Robinson (Giuseppe), Edward Reese (Lieutenant); opened at the Klaw Theatre, New York; November 23, 1925; 68 performances

"Man on a Tightrope" (Radio, 1953) Director, Earl Ebi; adaptation, Sanford Barnett; based on story by Neil Patterson and screenplay by Robert Sherwood; music director, Rudy Schrager; sound, Charlie Forsyth; cast: Edward G. Robinson, Terry Moore, Herb Ellis, Doris Singleton, Paul Frees, Parley Baer, William Conrad, Herb Butterfield, Shepard Menken, Lawrence Dobkin, Robert Boon, Leonard Penn, Joe Cranston, Robert Griffin, James Eagles, Dave Alpert, Edward Marr, Ken Carpenter (announcer), Irving Cummings (host); *Lux Radio Theatre*; CBS-radio; December 7, 1953; 55 minutes

"The Man Who Thought He Was Edward G. Robinson" (Radio, 1946) Producer, William Spier; writer, Leslie Raddis; cast: Edward G. Robinson, Verna Felton, Joseph Kearns, Jerry Hausner, Wally Maher; *Suspense*; CBS-radio; October 17, 1946; 30 minutes

"The Man Who Wanted to Be Edward G. Robinson" (Radio, 1948) This program, according to *Radio Yesteryear*, was different from "The Man Who Thought He Was Edward G. Robinson," airing nearly two years later on *Suspense*.

Cast: Edward G. Robinson; *Suspense*; CBS-radio; September 30, 1948

"The Man with Hope in His Hands" (Radio, 1946) Writer, Bernard Dryer; composer/conductor, Robert Armbruster; cast: Edward G. Robinson (Dr. Harvey Cushing), Ian Wolfe, Howard McNear, William Johnstone, Jack Moyles, George Sorel, Sammie Hill, Ann Tobin, Edwin Max, Jerry Hausncr, Ramsay Hill, Sidney Miller, James Eagles; Tom Collins (announcer); Gayne Whitman (host); *DuPont Cavalcade of America;* NBC-radio; March 11, 1946

A Man with Red Hair (Theater, 1928) Edward G. Robinson said that he watched lions being fed, noting the differences in their temperament — savage when hungry, and much gentler afterwards — and based his volatile characterization for *A Man with Red Hair* on his observations. "I chewed the scenery and had a ball," he said in his autobiography. The play was a success.

Producer, Charles L. Wagner; playwright, Benn W. Levy; based on a story by Hugh Walpole; director, John D. Williams; cast: Edward G. Robinson (Mr. Crispin), Harold Vermilyea, Henry Carvill, Kirby Hawkes, Mary Kennedy, Meayon Yon Kim, William Kim, Morris Lee, Barry O'Neill; Garrick Players; opened at the Ambassador Theatre, New York; November 8, 1928

Reviews were positive. "Robinson proves ... that he is without peer in this particular field on the legitimate stage," said *The New York Sun. The Nation* called his performance "horrible and powerful." *The New York Times* found *A Man with Red Hair* "not the high spot of his acting career, but it ranks well at the top. He brings out all the insane demoniacal qualities ... depicting the sadist as among the maddest and most horrific of men.... [It is] most effective."

The Man with Two Faces (Film, 1934) "Take off those whiskers, Robinson, I knew it was you all the time," wrote *Variety*'s reviewer. The trick to *The Man with Two Faces,* a film adaptation of George S. Kaufman and Alexander Woollcott's play *The Dark Tower,* was that Robinson's character, wearing elaborate makeup to disguise himself, murdered his brother-in-law and then took the makeup off and returned to being himself, the loving brother of Mary Astor.

Actress Jessica Wells makes a smash theatrical comeback in *The Dark Tower* with her brother, Damon. She had been sidelined for many months by a strange illness. Celebrating after the opening night performance at Aunt Martha's house are producer Ben Weston, playwright Barry Jones, actress Daphne Flowers, and Dr. Kendall. Unexpectedly, Stanley Vance shows up. He is Jessica's husband, who was thought dead. Immediately, Jessica's exhilaration turns to fear, and then total subservience to Vance, who has a Svengali-like control over her. Because his wife makes no protest while in this state, the others are powerless to stop him. After a few weeks there is a phone call from a Mr. Chautard, a Frenchman who is interested in investing in Jessica's play. The greedy Vance takes over negotiations and meets with Chautard at his hotel. Chautard kills Vance and puts his body in a closet. Then he goes to Ben Weston's office. Weston does not recognize him until Chautard removes elaborate makeup pieces, revealing that he is Damon. Inspector Curtis, investigating the murder, finds a moustache in a Gideon Bible in the hotel room and eventually deduces that Chautard must be Damon. Curtis suggests to Damon that defense by a good lawyer could probably save him.

Supervisor, Robert Lord; director, Archie Mayo; screenplay, Tom Reed, Niven Busch; based on the play *The Dark Tower* by George S. Kaufman and Alexander Woollcott; camera, Tony Gaudio; art director, John Hughes; makeup, Perc Westmore; editor, William Holmes; special effects, Fred Jackman; sound effects, Hal R. Shaw; music director, Leo F. Forbstein; songs "Stormy Weather" by Ted Koehler and Harold Arlen, "Am I Blue" by Harry Akst; cast: Edward G. Robinson (Damon Wells), Mary Astor (Jessica Wells), Ricardo Cortez (Ben Weston), Louis Calhern (Stanley Vance), Mae Clarke (Daphne Flowers), John Eldredge (Barry Jones), Arthur Byron (Dr. Kendall), Henry O'Neill (Inspector Crane), David Landau (William Curtis), Emily Fitzroy (Hattie), Margaret Dale (Martha Temple), Dorothy Tree (Patsy Dowling), Arthur Aylesworth (Morgue keeper), Virginia Sale (Peabody), Mary Russell (Debutante), Mrs. Wilfrid North (Matron), Howard Hickman (Mr. Jones), Maude Turner Gordon (Mrs. Jones), Dick Winslowe (Call boy), Frank Darien (Doorman), Bert Moorhouse (Driver), Ray Cooke (Bellboy), Jack McHugh (Newsboy), Douglas Cosgrove, Wade Boteler (Detectives), Guy Usher (Weeks), Milton Kibbee (Rewrite man), Joseph Crehan (Editor), Harry Tyler, Barbara Blair, and Anton Stengel (Chautard)*; First National; 72 minutes; July 1934

*Anton Stengel is listed onscreen in the credits, but it is actually Robinson in disguise as Chautard, the "second face" of the title.

"The brothers Warner blew the surprise at the start by changing the title to *The Man with Two Faces*," said Scott Meredith in *George S. Kaufman and His Friends*. "But this may have been because in their pragmatic way, they realized that there wasn't much chance of fooling movie audiences with the Max Sarnoff trick, not with the glaring eye of the camera picking up every blemish on the skin, and not with Edward G. Robinson playing the dual role.... 'I am not supposed to give away the identity of the mysterious murderer,' *Variety* said.... 'They can doll him up all they want to with a false goatee and a foreign accent, but they can't disguise that wide and unmistakable Robinson mouth and that broad Rumanian face of his....' It didn't really matter: the picture was a success, and the studio felt it had gotten its money's worth and more despite having paid $35,000 for the rights."

Generally the critics warmed to the film but accorded Robinson some ham-acting honors. "Mr. Robinson, as the self-confessed best actor in America and the self-appointed executioner of a first-class knave, maintains the comic mood successfully, which is a considerable help to the story," wrote *The New York Times*. "[He] concealed himself admirably behind a set of whiskers, a wig, false eyebrows, and a putty nose," said *The Sunday New York Times*, "but the snarl of Little Caesar occasionally slipped through his French accent."

The New York World-Telegram felt that, "Robinson's impression of Jessica's brother is a suave bit of acting, done in the best tradition of good actors impersonating good actors"; and *The New York American* called him "nothing if not versatile ... seen in the role of Damon Wells, the excellent and slightly egotistical actor. The role gives Robinson plenty of opportunity to exercise his recognized bent for character work and disguise."

The New York Herald-Tribune was less enthusiastic: "Robinson, Mary Astor, Louis Calhern and other members of the cast perform with moderate effectiveness."

The film was remade under the original title *The Dark Tower* in 1943. It had a circus theme and featured Ben Lyon and Herbert Lom.

The Man Without a Country (Recording, 1956)

Edward Everett Hale's patriotic story is about a fictional young Army lieutenant, Philip Nolan, who, at his court-martial for treasonous involvement with Aaron Burr, cried out, "Damn the United States!" As a result, he served a 56–year sentence aboard various Naval vessels, never venturing closer than one hundred miles from U.S. shores and never again hearing of the United States or his homeland. Originally published in 1863 in the *Atlantic Monthly*, *The Man Without a Country* helped strengthen the Union cause at the advent of the Civil War.

Written by Edward Everett Hale; Edward G. Robinson (reader); Caedmon Records; 1956

Mankiewicz, Joseph L. (1909–93), screenwriter, producer, director, won back-to-back directing Oscars for *A Letter to Three Wives* and *All About Eve*; was likewise nominated for *Five Fingers* and *Sleuth,* and for the screenplays of *Skippy* and *The Barefoot Contessa*. Other films include *The Three Godfathers, A Christmas Carol, The Philadelphia Story, Woman of the Year* (producer); *The Ghost and Mrs. Muir, Dragonwyck,* and, with Edward G. Robinson, *House of Strangers* (director); and *Julius Caesar, Guys and Dolls,* and *Cleopatra* (director-screenwriter).

Manny Raymond Serra wrote *Manny* as a fictional drama based on actual incidents and historical facts in the life of Edward G. Robinson. It did not fare well with the New York critics. Manny was short for Emanuel, Robinson's real given name, and it was also what he and his wife called their son, Edward G. Robinson (or Emanuel Goldenberg), Jr.

"The work is theatrically inadequate, and as presented, rarely rises above soap opera quality," said *Variety*. "Serra, who bears a slight physical resemblance to Robinson, tries occasionally to capture the late actor's speech patterns, and even his penchant for cigars, but he lacks the dynamic qualities that were Robinson's trademark."

The New York Times, noting that "Robinson was a serious, dedicated actor — with stage experience — and a cultured gentleman with a scholarly knowledge about fine art," lamented that, "instead of focusing on the contradiction between the man and his actor's identity, in his play *Manny* Raymond Sierra concentrates on the star's personal life…. He manages to reduce an interesting subject to a domestic soap opera…. Amateurish and obvious."

Questioned about the play (and her absence from it as a character), Robinson's widow, Jane, said, "I was not consulted nor did I care to be. I think the whole thing was ridiculous." — April 26, 1979

Playwright, Raymond Serra; producers, Robert R. Blume, Tony Conforti, Many Taustine; associate producers, Howard Effron, Michael E. Bash; director, Harold J. Kennedy; set design, John Kasarda; art director, Sam Harte; understudy, Suni Castrilli; lights, Rick Belzer; costumes, Bob Graham; hairstyles, Marylou Conforti; stage manager, Gary Stein; makeup, Ellen Tenoever; publicity, Max Risen; assistant stage manager, Paul Guskin; art consultant, John Panos; production associate, Joseph Peck; production assistants, Elizabeth Ottilie Preim, Toomas Rohtla, Lisa Sommerfield, Dierdre Taylor, Ed Schwartz, Molly Maginnis; cast: Raymond Serra (Manny), Hy Anzell (Voice of Hon. Francis Walters), Myra Chasen (Debbie), Pierre Epstein (Sam), Paul Guskin (Thalberg), Loren Haynes (Eddie, Jr.), Frances Helm (Gladys), Maxine Taylor-Morris (Margarita), Fredric Sirasky; filmed sequences-cinematography, John Annunziato, Nunzio Productions (multimedia); editor, Steve Sabato; opened at the Century Theatre, New York; April 18, 1979

Manpower (Film, 1941) The major excitement about *Manpower*— which didn't hurt its publicity — was the offscreen animosity between George Raft and Edward G. Robinson. It culminated in a physical altercation between the two on the set, captured by a *Life* magazine photographer. "In Hollywood April 26, Edward G. Robinson and George Raft were rehearsing a scene from their new picture, *Manpower*. Cast as pals, they profoundly dislike each other off location…. Raft was supposed to stop a quarrel between Robinson and Ward Bond by gently intervening. Instead he grabbed Robinson's arm, swung him around violently. Surprised, Robinson yelled, 'Not so rough, George,' and yanked his arm free. Raft retorted that Robinson could keep his directions to himself. As they started swinging a still photographer caught [an] exceptional picture. They were separated before damage was done." — *Life*

Hal Wallis had different thoughts on the matter. "On *Manpower* we had problems initially because Eddie was temperamentally unable to cope with Marlene Dietrich, whom he found cold and haughty. But he grew to respect her and discovered to his great delight that she was a lover of impressionist paintings. As shooting progressed he and George Raft both fell in love with Marlene." — Hal Wallis, with Charles Higham, *Starmaker*

Robinson downplayed any difficulties with Dietrich. He was impressed with her work ethic and her knowledge of filmmaking, feeling that they and Raft made a dynamic screen trio in a sometimes vacuous film. The troubles, he felt, were due to Raft's temperament; in later years the other tough guy actor was more conciliatory, Robinson noted.

Executive producer, Hal B. Wallis; producer, Mark Hellinger; director, Raoul Walsh; screenplay, Richard Macaulay, Jerry Wald; music, Adolph Deutsch; music director, Leo F. Forbstein; song "He Lied and I Listened" by Frank Loesser and Frederick Hollander; art director, Max Parker; sound, Dolph Thomas; costumes, Milo Anderson; dialogue director, Hugh Cummings; special effects, Byron Haskin, H. F. Koenekamp; camera, Ernest Haller; editor Ralph Dawson; technical adviser, Verne Elliott; assistant director, Russell Saunders; makeup, Perc Westmore; cast: Edward G. Robinson (Hank McHenry), Marlene Dietrich (Fay Duval), George Raft (Johnny Marshall), Alan Hale (Jumbo), Frank McHugh (Omaha), Eve Arden (Dolly), Barton MacLane (Smiley Quinn), Walter Catlett (Sidney Whipple), Joyce Compton (Scarlett), Lucia Carroll (Flo), Ward Bond (Eddie), Egon Brecher (Pop Duval), Cliff Clark (Cully), Joseph Crehan (Sweeney), Ben Welden (Al Hurst), Carl Harbaugh (Noisy Nash), Barbara Land (Marilyn), Barbara Pepper (Polly), Dorothy Appleby (Wilma), Ralph Dunn (Man at phone), Harry Strang (Foreman), Nat Carr (Waiter), John Kelly (Bouncer), Joan Winfield, Isabel Withers, Faye Emerson (Nurses), James Flavin (Orderly), Chester Clute (Drugstore clerk), Nella Walker (Floorlady), Harry Holman (Justice of the Peace), Dorothy Vaughan (Mrs. Boyle), Murray Alper, Dick Wessel (Linemen), Beal Wong (Singer), Jane Randolph (Hat check girl), Eddy Chandler, Lee Phelps (Detectives), Robert Strange (Bondsman), Dick Elliott (Drunk), Roland Drew, Eddie Fetherstone, Charles Sherlock, Jeffrey Sayre, DeWolfe Hopper, Al Herman, Arthur Q. Bryan, Harry Seymour, Joe Devlin, Lynn Baggett, William Royle; Warner Bros.; 105 minutes; July 1941

Buddies Hank McHenry and Johnny Marshall, who work on high tension power lines for the county, are called out with their team to make major repairs during a storm. When lightning strikes, Johnny is knocked unconscious. Hank saves him from falling but suffers a crippling jolt of electricity when his foot touches a wire. After he recovers, Hank, who now is confined to working on the ground, is made team foreman. Johnny accompanies team member Pop Duval to meet his daughter, Fay, when she is released from prison. On a later job, Pop is killed by a hot wire on the ground. As foreman of the team, Hank must tell Pop's next of kin. At first skeptical of Hank's kindness to her, Fay later agrees to marry Hank, even though she has told him she doesn't love him. Marriage frees her from her job in a sleazy clip joint where she has to deal with drunks and lowlife characters. Johnny now suffers a fall on the job and is brought to Fay and Hank's house to recuperate. Fay confesses to him that she has fallen in love with him, but Johnny rejects her. When the team goes away on a job for an extended period, she decides to leave Hank. She goes to the club to say goodbye to former coworkers and is caught in a raid. Johnny comes to town to bail her out. She returns with him to the camp and tells Hank she loves Johnny. It is another stormy night. Johnny is high up on a pole working on the power lines. Now in a violent rage, Hank climbs up and swings at Johnny with a wrench. Hank loses his balance. Johnny manages to catch his safety belt, but the belt breaks, and Hank falls. Dying, Hank asks Johnny to take care of Fay for him.

The New York Herald-Tribune review is typical: "Robinson, Raft, and Dietrich are no novices at handling conventional screen situations ... but ... the human drama which finds [them] forming a romantic triangle is never credible." The film rehashed the plot of the earlier melodrama *Tiger Shark,* in which Robinson, as odd man out in the triangle, conveniently died at the fadeout so that the lovers could live happily ever after. Raoul Walsh, director of *Manpower,* was grateful: "Many of my pictures would have fallen by the wayside without the help of ... the 'character men,' whose great talents helped me over many a rough spot over the years, [including] Edward G. Robinson."

"Manpower" (Radio, 1942) Director, Sanford Bennett; adaptation, George Wells; music director, Louis Silvers; sound, Charlie Forsyth; cast: Edward G. Robinson (Hank), Marlene Dietrich (Fay), George Raft (Johnny), Bea Benaderet, Charles Seel, Edwin Max, Frank Penny, Griff Barnett, Howard McNear; Cecil B. DeMille (host); E. H. Griffith, Mark Sandrich, George Stevens (guests, presenting DeMille a thirtieth anniversary award as a motion picture director); Melville Ruick (announcer); Torey Carleton, Warren Ashe, Stanley Farrar, Ann Tobin, Duane Thompson (commercials); *Lux Radio Theatre;* CBS-radio, March 16, 1942

Mansfield, Jayne (1933–67), a blonde bombshell, was in two films with Edward G. Robinson. In *Illegal* she played Angel O'Hara and sang "Too Marvelous for Words." Her role in *Hell on Frisco Bay* was smaller. Other films include *Pete Kelly's Blues, The Girl Can't Help It, Will Success Spoil Rock Hunter?, The Wayward Bus,* and *Kiss Them for Me.*

Marlowe, Hugh (1911–82) plays Ray Borden in *Illegal.* He is also the playwright Lloyd Richards in *All About Eve.* Formerly a radio announcer, his other film credits include *Meet Me in St. Louis, Monkey Business, Elmer Gantry, Birdman of Alcatraz,* and *Seven Days in May.*

Marsh, Mae (1895–1968) was a silent star in *The Birth of a Nation, Intolerance,* and *The White Rose.* More recently she played in *Tales of Manhattan* and *Hell on Frisco Bay* with Edward G. Robinson, *Jane Eyre, A Tree Grows in Brooklyn, The Robe,* and *Sergeant Rutledge.*

Marsh, Marian (1913–) played opposite John Barrymore in *Svengali* and was the ingenue Jenny Townsend in *Five Star Final,* with Edward G. Robinson. She appeared in *Whoopee, The Man I Married,* and *Adam Had Four Sons,* retiring from films in 1942.

The Martha Raye Show (Television, 1956) A gag used on this program has Edward G. Robinson leaping out of the audience to attack a Robinson impersonator.

Producers, Ed Simmons, Norman Lear, Karl Hoffenberg; director, Norman Lear; musical director, Carl Hoff; writer, Ed Simmons; cast: Martha Raye, Rocky Graziano, Edward G. Robinson (guest star); 1956

Martin, Dean (1917–95) plays himself in *Pepe,* and in *Robin and the 7 Hoods* he's a pool-playing version of Little John. With Edward G. Robinson he was also in a *Parade of Stars* telethon for the City of Hope. Once teamed with Jerry Lewis, Martin's films include *At War with the Army, Who Was That Lady?, The Sons of Katie Elder, The Silencers, Airport,* and *Something Big.*

"The Mary Tree" (Television, 1970) In this hour-long episode on *Bracken's World,* Edward G. Robinson played a writer being profiled in a television documentary. The significance of the title is that on the grounds of his estate a tree was planted the year his daughter, Mary, was born. "The Mary Tree" was telecast on NBC the same day and hour Robinson was appearing on ABC-TV on *This Is Tom Jones.*

Executive producer, Del Reisman; producer, Stanley Rubin; director, Paul Henreid; writer, Jerry Ziegman; creator, Dorothy Kingsley; theme song, Alan and Marilyn Bergman; sung by the Lettermen; music, David Rose, Jack Elliott, Robert Drasnin, Harry Geller, Lionel Newman, Warren Barker; cast: Edward G. Robinson (Elstyn Draper), Diana Hyland

(Mary Draper), Leslie Nielson (John Bracken), Peter Haskell (Kevin Grant), Elizabeth Allen (Laura Dean), Edward G. Robinson, Jr. (Bill Lawrence), Claudia Bryar (Housekeeper), Tim Herbert (Connie Rose), Jeff Donnell (Joan Elliott); *Bracken's World*; NBC-TV; 60 minutes; October 23, 1970

The Masquers A private men's club of Hollywood actors begun in the 1930s, the Masquers' members, together with a sister group for women known as the Dominoes, helped establish what is today the Screen Actors Guild.

In March 1969 Edward G. Robinson was honored by the Masquers with their George Spelvin Award, together with a citation by the California State Senators and a plaque from the city of Los Angeles. George Jessel hosted the evening. Those in attendance included Andy Albin, Jack Benny, Joan Blondell, George Burns, Pat Buttram, Senator Ralph C. Dills, Nanette Fabray, Henry Fonda, Allan Hersholt, Sam Jaffe and Bettye Ackerman, Mervyn LeRoy, Ranald MacDougal, Cesar Romero, George Seaton, James Stewart, Jack L. Warner, Richard Widmark, William Wyler, and Jane Robinson.

Massey, Raymond (1896–1983) alternated stage appearances—*John Brown's Body, Candida, Ethan Frome, J.B., Abe Lincoln in Illinois*—with films, recreating the last for an Oscar nomination; plus *The Old Dark House, The Scarlet Pimpernel, Things to Come, The Prisoner of Zenda, Arsenic and Old Lace, The Fountainhead, Prince of Players, East of Eden, Seven Angry Men,* and, with Edward G. Robinson, *The Woman in the Window* (as the D.A.) and *Mackenna's Gold* (the preacher).

Maté, Rudolph 1898–1964) began his film career in 1919 in European silent films. His U.S. films include *Come and Get It, Stella Dallas, The Real Glory,* and *Pride of the Yankees* (photography), and *D.O.A., When Worlds Collide, The Violent Men* (with Edward G. Robinson), *The 300 Spartans,* and *For the First Time* (as director).

Mathews, Carmen (1911–95) played Edward G. Robinson's wife on TV's *General Electric Theatre* drama, "The Drop-Out." She performed in films (*Butterfield 8, Rabbit Run, Sounder*) and on the Broadway stage (*Dear World, Copperfield*).

Maxwell House Coffee television commercial Barbara Stanwyck, Claudette Colbert, and Edward G. Robinson each plugged Maxwell House Coffee in different commercials in 1964. In perking the coffee, Robinson admonished his audience, "Now do it my way, see?" followed by a smile and, "You'll enjoy it."

"I hesitated about accepting the offer at first," Robinson admitted. "I had never done anything that commercial. But I saw nothing wrong in it, as long as the ad was in good taste and I believed in the article being sold. The fee was very good, and that is always a consideration. Everything was done with care. All in all, it was a pleasant experience."—quoted in the *St. Louis Post-Dispatch*

Mayer, Edwin Justus (1896–1960), playwright and screenwriter, had a Broadway success with *The Firebrand,* based on Benvenuto Cellini's autobiography, and in which Edward G. Robinson played Ottaviano. Mayer also wrote *Children of Darkness.* For the screen he wrote *The Unholy Night, Peter Ibbetson, Till We Meet Again, Desire,* and *To Be or Not to Be.*

McCallion, James (1918–91) was a character actor appearing in *Illegal,* with Edward G. Robinson, as an embezzler named Parker. He also appears in *North by Northwest* as a hotel valet, as well as in *Vera Cruz* and *Coogan's Bluff.* Earlier, as a child he was in *Boy Slaves.*

McCallister, Lon (1923–), a juvenile star, had non-speaking roles in *Romeo and Juliet, Stella Dallas,* and *Yankee Doodle Dandy,* then won important roles in *Stage Door Canteen, The Red House* (with Edward G. Robinson), *The Big Cat,* and *Combat Squad.* He retired from films in 1953.

McCarthy, Kevin (1914–) was in three films with Edward G. Robinson—

Nightmare, as his brother-in-law hypnotized into committing murder; *The Prize*, as a Nobel winner for medicine; and *U.M.C.*, as the prosecutor. Other films: *Death of a Salesman* (repeating his Broadway role as Biff), *Invasion of the Body Snatchers, The Misfits, The Best Man, Mirage, Kansas City Bomber*, and *Piranha*.

McClelland, Fergus (1955–), son of a British film producer, played the title role in the film adaptation of W. H. Canaway's novel *Sammy Going South*, which on the screen was entitled *A Boy Ten Feet Tall*.

McCrea, Joel (1905–90), a cowboy star, was in *Barbary Coast* with Edward G. Robinson, among other films for Samuel Goldwyn, such as *These Three*. He also appears in *Sullivan's Travels, Foreign Correspondent, The Palm Beach Story, The Virginian*, and *Ride the High Country*.

McDaniel, Sam (1896–1962), brother of Hattie McDaniel and also known as Deacon, plays roles in *Dark Hazard, Brother Orchid*, and *Double Indemnity*, although he shared no scenes with Edward G. Robinson. He is also in *Captains Courageous, Mr. and Mrs. North*, and *The Great Lie*.

McDonald, Francis (1891–1968) was Svenson in *The Sea Wolf*, and in *The Ten Commandments* he played a slave who dies in Moses' arms, unaware he has beheld the "Deliverer." Films include, from 1912, *The Prisoner of Shark Island, The Plainsman, If I Were King, Samson and Delilah*, and *Rancho Notorious*.

McHugh, Frank (1899–1981), Irish comic actor, is Slug O'Donnell in *The Widow from Chicago*, Herman in *Bullets or Ballots*, and Omaha in *Manpower*, all with Edward G. Robinson. They also appeared together in a radio adaptation of *The Great Man Votes*. Other pictures: *A Midsummer Night's Dream, The Front Page, The Crowd Roars, Going My Way, There's No Business Like Show Business, Mighty Joe Young*, and *The Last Hurrah*.

McKee, John (1870–1953) has roles in three films with Edward G. Robinson—*Big Leaguer* (as Dale Alexander), *Illegal* (as a detective), and *Cheyenne Autumn*. He is also in *MacArthur, Cape Fear*, and *The Professionals*.

McLaglen, Victor (1886–1959) was First Mate Fred Adamson in *Tampico*, with Edward G. Robinson, and they were also together in the short film *The Stolen Jools*. Best actor Oscar winner for *The Informer*, he was also nominated for *The Quiet Man*. Other films include *The Lost Patrol, Gunga Din, Rio, She Wore a Yellow Ribbon*, and *Around the World in Eighty Days*.

McQueen, Steve (1930–80) was *The Cincinnati Kid*, challenging The Man (Edward G. Robinson). Both were presenters on the 36th Annual Academy Awards telecast. Other credits: *The Blob, The Great St. Louis Bank Robbery, The Magnificent Seven, The Great Escape, The Sand Pebbles, Papillon, An Enemy of the People*, and the western TV series *Wanted: Dead or Alive*.

McRae, Maurice acted with Edward G. Robinson in three plays—*Juarez and Maximilian, Ned McCobb's Daughter*, and *Right You Are If You Think You Are*.

McVeagh, Eve (1919–97) plays one scene in *Tight Spot* as Ginger Rogers' scrappy sister, Clara. She also is featured with Edward G. Robinson in *The Glass Web*. A familiar 1950s character actress, she also is in *High Noon, I'll Cry Tomorrow, The Cobweb*, and *Crime and Punishment U.S.A.*

McWade, Edward (1872–1943) played the prison doctor in *Two Seconds*, Brother Sebastian in *Brother Orchid*, and a chemist in *A Dispatch from Reuter's*, all with Edward G. Robinson. His other films include *Arsenic and Old Lace* and *They Won't Forget*.

McWade, Robert (1882–1956) was on the New York stage with Edward G. Robinson in *The Deluge* and also played Larkin, a board member, in *I Loved a Woman*. Other films are *The First Year, Grand Hotel, Back Street,* and *42nd Street.* His son, Robert McWade, Jr., had a role in *I Am the Law.*

Meek, Donald (1880–1946), bald and befitting his name, was in four films with Edward G. Robinson — as Goofy in *The Hole in the Wall,* miner Sawbuck McTavish in *Barbary Coast,* Hoyt in *The Whole Town's Talking,* and Herr Mittelmeyer in *Dr. Ehrlich's Magic Bullet.* Other films: *Top Hat, Stagecoach, My Little Chickadee,* and *Magic Town.*

Megrue, Roi Cooper (1883–1927), playwright, authored Edward G. Robinson's first two Broadway plays. *Under Fire* was about the perils of war, and *Under Sentence* about prison reform. The penchant for "under" in the title was evident; his *Under Cover* ran for 349 performances in 1914. His other works include *It Pays to Advertise* and *Seven Chances.*

Memberships As a screen, stage, television, and radio performer, Edward G. Robinson was a member of several clubs and organizations, including the Actors Equity Association (AEA), the Associated Federation of Radio and Television Artists (AFTRA), the Screen Actors Guild (SAG), the Lambs, and the Masquers.
See **Lambs**; **Masquers**.

Mendes, Lothar (1894–1974) directed Edward G. Robinson in *Tampico* two years before retiring from films. A Viennese emigre, he directed in the U.S. and Britain from 1926, including *Paramount on Parade, Ladies' Man, Payment Deferred, Luxury Liner,* and *The Walls Came Tumbling Down,* his last.

Menken, Helen (1901–66), a stage actress, was once married to Humphrey Bogart. In the 1920 and 1921 summer seasons at Elitch's Gardens theater in Denver, she played opposite Edward G. Robinson in several productions, including *Enter Madame.* Her New York credits include *Three Wise Fools, Seventh Heaven, The Makropolous Secret, The Captive, Mary of Scotland,* and *The Old Maid.*

Mercer, Beryl (1882–1939) was Edward G. Robinson's mother-in-law in *Right You Are If You Think You Are,* and was with him also in *An Intimate Dinner in Celebration of Warner Bros. Silver Jubilee,* as Mrs. W. B. Pictures. Other films: *The Public Enemy, Outward Bound, Cavalcade,* and *Night Must Fall.*

Meredith, Burgess (1908–98) was with Edward G. Robinson in *Mackenna's Gold.* They also appeared together in the 1966 and 1967 *Chanukah Festivals for Israel.* His other films include *Idiot's Delight, Of Mice and Men, The Story of G.I. Joe, Advise and Consent,* and, earning supporting actor Oscar nominations, *The Day of the Locust* and *Rocky.* He played The Penguin on TV's *Batman.*

Meredith, Charles (1894–1970) plays a poker-playing business associate of Edward G. Robinson in *All My Sons* and a judge in the last scene of *Illegal.* A star of silents, including *Simple Souls* and *The Beautiful Liar,* he also appeared in *A Foreign Affair, Daisy Kenyon,* and *The Miracle of the Bells.*

Merivale, Philip (1887–1946) appeared with Edward G. Robinson as Judge Longstreet in *The Stranger,* one of his last roles. Married to Gladys Cooper, they were together in *This Above All* (screen), and *Othello* and *Macbeth* (stage). He was also in *Pygmalion, The Swan,* and *Mary of Scotland* (stage), and *Rage in Heaven* and *This Land Is Mine* (screen).

"The Messiah on Mott Street" (Television, 1971) This holiday story, presented on *Night Gallery,* earned an Emmy nomination for writer Rod Serling. In it, Edward G. Robinson played his final dramatic television role as the grandfather, Abe Goldman. To round the telecast to one hour, a fifteen-minute story with Zsa Zsa Gabor, Arthur O'Connell, and Rosemary DeCamp preceded "The Messiah on Mott Street."
According to *Rod Serling's Night Gallery, an After-Hours Tour,* by Scott Skelton and Jim Benson, "In the story's dignity and characterizations, it is among his (Serling's) very finest efforts. The germinal idea for 'Messiah' came

to Serling from screenwriter Sy Gomberg, whose stories about growing up in Newark, New Jersey, were legend at Hollywood parties ... NBC executives soon saw the potential of 'The Messiah on Mott Street' as an award winner ... assembled a magnificent trio of actors to essay the primary roles — Tony Roberts, Yaphet Kotto, and silver screen legend Edward G. Robinson ... No more apt performer (than Robinson) could have been chosen ... a brilliant actor but (he) also had a thorough knowledge of the religious subtext of Serling's script ... [Director Don] Taylor found ... that Robinson resisted playing the nuances of speech peculiar to the New York Jewish community. 'He had spent most of his career getting rid of the Jewish idiom,' Taylor says ... During the shooting, Robinson's presence on the set generated an atmosphere of respectful awe.

"'That was an overwhelming experience for me, working with one of my favorite actors....' admits costar Tony Roberts. 'On the first day that we worked together, Mr. Robinson asked me to come into his trailer and run some lines with him. Of course I was thrilled just to be anywhere near him! And as we started to go through the script, he revealed to me that he was very nervous — that he was *always* very nervous on the first day of shooting because he was fearful that he might be fired! Can you believe that? ... I remember an incident where he was lying in bed, doing one of his long monologues. It was his close-up, the very first take, and I was off-camera reading my lines for him right next to the lens, in the dark. He was about halfway through this very, very long speech that he had to deliver — it was riveting, just brilliant — and all of a sudden, he stopped.... The actor's concentration had been broken by the focus puller, whom Robinson could detect in the shadows next to the camera, mouthing his lines. 'He saw the kid's mouth moving while he was delivering his speech and it threw him off! ... [but] it caused no problem at all! We started from the top and he did the whole thing again, and it was even more brilliant than the first time! He didn't miss a beat. Not a line, not a comma, not a word, *nothing*!'

"As shooting progressed, issues of interpretation began to crop up ... In the end, Taylor was never entirely satisfied with Robinson's performance. 'He was very dear, but he took a [lot of work] ... And yet he turned out to be very good because he's a superb actor, a heavyweight....' Taylor's criticisms notwithstanding, the performances throughout 'The Messiah on Mott Street' are quite distinguished. Indeed the cast is perfect ... As Abraham Goldman, Robinson delivers a tour de force, investing his character with both wry humor and a Lear-like rage. Even in the depths of obvious illness, his passion for life radiates from him. His dialogue with the Angel of Death is vibrant with anger, his voice is music — and his handling of the idiom, despite Taylor's concerns, is thankfully not overdrawn. The actors' performances help make this segment one of *Night Gallery*'s most moving statements."

Abe Goldman is seriously ill and living in a tenement, caring for his grandson Mikey. His physician, Dr. Levine, and his faith in the Messiah sustain him. He does battle with the Angel of Death, who warns him he will return at midnight. Believing his grandfather's words, that "he will strike down our enemies, looming black against the sky," Mikey goes out to seek the Messiah and returns to the apartment with Mr. Buckner. At midnight there is commotion in Abe's room; an apparent miracle has occurred, as the Messiah's presence thwarts the Angel of Death, and Abe is well.

Producer, Jack Laird; teleplay, Rod Serling; director, Don Taylor; camera, Lionel Lindon; art director, Joseph Alves, Jr.; set, Chester Bayhi, John M. Dwyer; titles, Wayne Fitzgerald; music, Eddie Sauter, Paul Glass; theme song, Gil Melle; costumes, Bill Jobe; sound, David H. Moriarty, Roger A. Parish; unit manager, Burt Astor; editors, Richard Belding, Jean Berthelot; assistant producer, Anthony Redman; executive story consultant, Gerald Sanford; assistant director, Ralph Sariego; art work, Tom Wright, Logan Elston, Phil Bandierle; Universal Title; cast: Edward G. Robinson (Abe Goldman), Tony Roberts (Dr. Levine), Yaphet Kotto (Buckner), Ricky

Powell (Mikey), Joseph Ruskin (Prophet of doom), Anne Taylor (Miss Moretti), J. J. Fox; Rod Serling (Host); *Night Gallery*; NBC-TV; 40 minutes; December 18, 1971

Middle of the Night (Theater, 1956–1958) "It seems like old times to have Edward G. Robinson back," wrote Brook Atkinson in *The New York Times*. Robinson, who had spent the first fifteen years of his career on the New York stage, left to make cinema history as a tough guy. His return in the 1950s came about when the film community seemed to run out of work for him. To help offset accusations of Communism, he toured in a blatantly anti–Communist play, *Darkness at Noon*; and it helped artistically, at least, by way of some fine reviews. By 1955, after a dozen 'B' movies, he was ready to try Broadway again. Being cast in DeMille's *The Ten Commandments* certainly helped restore his 'A' status, but in the meantime, according to Leonard Spigelgass in *All My Yesterdays*, "he cheered when Joshua Logan sent him a script of Paddy Chayefsky's *Middle of the Night*."

"It was so truthful and touching and romantic and brave," said Logan. "…The only trouble was that Paddy had no third act…. I also knew who *had* to play the older Jewish man, and that was Edward G. Robinson." Logan maintains that Chayefsky "was terribly excited at the idea … as well he might have been, since Robinson was one of the greatest names and talents in our profession…. I had many visits with Eddie. I reminded him that this kind of part did not happen very often for a man in his full years…."—*Movie Stars, Real People and Me*

"Eddie was not only the most talented but the finest gentleman I ever met or worked with. The way he handled that rambunctious author while making his show a smash hit was one of the theatre's greatest untold stories."—Joshua Logan

"Paddy took on his star, Edward G. Robinson," noted Shaun Considine in *Mad as Hell, the Life and Work of Paddy Chayefsky*. "Along the Great White Way their frequent and colorful contests were referred to as 'the Bronx Bomber versus Little Caesar.' When Robinson had initially been suggested for his play, Chayefsky said he was a lousy choice. 'He's a gangster,' he said…. Onstage, his leading lady, Gena Rowlands, wearing high heels, towered above him. The sets, doorways, and other actors had to be scaled down to accommodate the star (Rowlands was told to wear flats). 'Paddy was the same height as Eddie,' said Wally Fried, the play's production manager…. 'Actually I think he enjoyed that Eddie insisted everybody come down to his size.' Along with his salary of $2,500 per week against 10 percent of the gross, Robinson was receiving out-of-pocket expenses (not to exceed $150 per week), first-class hotel accommodations at the Stanhope, a Cadillac (no earlier than a 1954 model), and a chauffeur who doubled as a masseur and dog walker. Robinson's contract also mandated that he receive a box-office statement of the attendance at each performance."

"When [it] opened in Wilmington, Delaware, Paddy was in a morose state," said director Logan in his book. "'They love it too much,' said Paddy. 'I don't like all those laughs … it's that Robinson….' Eventually he took out five or six of the biggest laughs in the play, and how I was able to persuade Eddie Robinson to give them up I don't know."

Shaun Considine: "Paddy would stand at the back of the theatre and make notes of the things that Eddie was doing which distracted from his play,' said Fried. 'Eddie would sometimes use his cigar as a prop, which Paddy felt was provoking the audiences to laugh at the wrong moments.'"

Leonard Spigelgass noted in *All My Yesterdays* that although *Middle of the Night* was threatened by the battles between writer, director, and star, the play made it to Broadway and became a hit. "When Eddie made his entrance, there was that marvelous, thrilling round of applause," he wrote, "and my friend, Eddie, just waited it out, playing the character, ignoring the applause, and then proceeding with the play."

"It ran well over a year and was a tremendous financial success," said Logan, "but Paddy kept saying to me on the side, 'Robinson's terrible; he's wrong for the part.' I would say, 'But, Paddy, he was made by God for this role. You'll never find anyone who's near him.' Paddy said, 'Well, he sure ain't going to be in the movie.'"

Shaun Considine notes that "in April 1956, three months after the play opened, Robinson informed Chayefsky and the producer-director, Logan, that he was leaving when his six-month contract was up.... Chayefsky was quoted as saying that he had three major studios bidding for it [the film] and that he wanted Spencer Tracy or Paul Muni to play Robinson's role."

Spencer Tracy, incidentally, had seen the play in the second month of its run, and wrote to Bert Allenberg of the William Morris Agency, "You know ... I've always considered myself among the best, but I can't touch Eddie Robinson." E. G. Marshall had played The Manufacturer in the original TV version, opposite Eva Marie Saint, but the film role went to Fredric March, much to Robinson's disappointment. In his autobiography he praised March, but felt that The Manufacturer needed to be played by a Jewish actor — like himself! Hollis Alpert, in the *Saturday Review*, may have supported that theory: "The story was more successful in the stage version. I suspect this was due to the playing of Edward G. Robinson and Gena Rowlands [and] Joshua Logan's direction...."

Walter Fried, according to Shaun Considine, said that Chayefsky's insensitivity in naming actor candidates for the film "forced Robinson to employ 'a face-saving device to offset the public rejection the announcement carried.' He gave his notice, declaring that he wanted to take on one of several movie offers that had come in for him. At Logan's request, Fried arranged a conciliatory meeting between Robinson and Chayefsky.... 'Paddy lost his temper and told Robinson that the movie was his business and that he did not feel obligated to talk to any actors about it.... Fried said that Paddy's dislike of Robinson would be something he would get over 'when he discovers years from now that Eddie is not his father.' Developing a bad cold 'augmented by prostate trouble,' Robinson informed Fried the next day that he did not want his condition aggravated ('so that the play would become distasteful to him and unconsciously — because Eddie is a pro — cause him to leave before his contract is up on June thirtieth,' said Fried to Logan). Showing he meant business, Robinson at the same time instructed his agent, Abe Lastfogel, to line up some definite movie work for him that summer.... On May 14, Mrs. Logan flew to New York to talk to the disgruntled Robinson and the querulous Chayefsky. Four days later, mission accomplished, she returned to California. At her urging, Chayefsky had agreed to curb his temper and ego and to make up with Robinson.... A new run-of-the-play contract was then offered to Robinson.... He would receive the same salary and perks, but his cut of the weekly gross would be raised from 10 to 15 percent. On June 1, Robinson signed the new contract."

According to Considine, Chayefsky continued trying to change the ending of the play well into its second year on Broadway. He quotes Martin Landau, who replaced Lee Philips in the role of George: "Chayefsky was constantly at the theatre during rehearsals with his revisions for the last scene ... between Eddie and Gena Rowlands's characters. Paddy wanted a deeper, more complex ending.... Even after we closed on Broadway and reconvened for the tour, he would come into the theatre with his new pages. While the rest of us were sitting in the audience, Paddy would be on stage with Robinson. He would hand him the pages. Eddie would read them, and say: 'Yass, very good. Yass! Yass!' And then he'd tap his cigar and say, 'Yass, waal, Paddy, we'll stick to the old one.' And Paddy would say frantically, 'But you don't understand. The old one ties it up too neatly.' And Eddie would say, 'We've done four hundred and seventy-five performances so far, and the audiences seem to like the play — so we'll stay with the old ending.'"

"When told by his understudy and road director, Curt Conway, that Chayefsky had performed onstage in England during the war, Robinson slapped his knee and said, 'I suspected he was a frustrated actor after all!' On the road in Washington, D.C., Robinson invited Chayefsky and Martin Landau to be his guests at the Press Club. 'On a napkin, I drew a caricature of Paddy and one of Eddie,' said Landau. 'And Eddie drew one of me, until we were all doing pictures of one another into the early hours of the morning.' The next day Chayefsky saw the matinee and evening performances. 'He still wanted to make changes,' said Landau, 'but Eddie wouldn't hear of it....' Robinson asked Chayefsky about his recreating his part on film. Nodding pensively, Chayefsky replied, 'We'll see, Eddie. We'll see....' Chayefsky proceeded to work on the screenplay.... The play was 'abysmally written — dreadful,' he said. 'I couldn't believe it had been a Broadway hit and was forced to come to the conclusion that it was really Edward G. Robinson, and not the play, that kept it going for two years.'"— Shaun Considine, *Mad as Hell, the Life and Work of Paddy Chayefsky*

Rowlands and Robinson worked together well and were fond of one another: "He was a quiet, gentle, scholarly man, with a sense of privacy about him," she was quoted in *TV Guide*. "He says of her, 'She was a bit confused by the direction at first, but then she found her own way of doing it. As for me at my age, she certainly was wonderful to make love to eight times a week.'"

Anne Jackson was also in the cast. "I learned a lot in that play," she commented. "For one thing I was still learning how to take advice. In one scene with Eddie Robinson, where he told me — I played his daughter — that he wanted to marry a young girl, it was supposed to be a blow to me. So I wanted to dramatize the fact that it was a blow. I wanted to walk away. Eddie said, 'No, she would never do that.' At first I was sore. He said, 'It's more effective if you don't show them. The cliché is to show them.' And he was right. Not because he was an older, more seasoned actor, but because he was an actor."

Producer, director, Joshua Logan; playwright, Paddy Chayefsky; settings and lighting, Jo Mielziner; stage managers, Neil Hartley, David Ford; costumes, Motley; wardrobe, Annette Kelly; music, Lehman Engel; sound, Sound Associates, Inc.; lighting, Century Lighting, Inc., City Knickerbocker; electric, Cliff Ashe, Joseph Maher; scenery, Imperial Studios; carpenters, Joe Cunningham, Edward Hauch; tour staging, Curt Conway; fabrics, Maharam, Inc.; drapes, J. Weiss & Sons; hairstyles and makeup, Ernest Adler; props, Herbert Gahagan, Martin Fontana, Jr.; general manager, Walter Fried; assistant to Mr. Logan, Joseph Curtis; assistant to Mr. Mielziner, John Harvey; press representatives, Frank Goodman, Ruth Cage, Leo Freedman, Abner D. Klipstein; cast: Edward G. Robinson (The Manufacturer [Jerry Kingsley]), Gena Rowlands (The Girl), Martin Balsam (The Son-in-law), Mona Freeman* (The Girl), Lee Philips (The Husband), Anne Jackson (The Daughter), Martin Landau* (The Husband), Nancy R. Pollock (The Sister), Norman Fell* (The Son-in Law), June Walker (The Mother), Betty Walker, Janet Ward, Effie Afton, Nellie Burt*, Doris Belack*, Patricia Benoit, Ethel Britton*, Joan Chambers (The Kid Sister), Marilyn Clark, Curt Conway, Sylvia Davis*, Ruth Masters, Peg Shirley*, Phyllis Wynn*, W. Zev Putterman, Barbara Bain, Nick Rosso (understudies); opened at the ANTA Theatre (managing director, Louis A. Lotito), New York; February 8, 1956; tour from October 9, 1957 (Shubert Theatre, New Haven, Connecticut) to March 29, 1958 (Curran Theatre, San Francisco); *National tour cast members

Gerald Bordman in *The Oxford Companion to American Theatre* sums up the story of the play: "When a rich, aging, and widowed manufacturer falls in love with his young, newly divorced receptionist, their liaison is opposed on both sides: by the mother of the girl and by the manufacturer's daughter. Only his son-in-law seems sympathetic. The girl returns briefly to her former husband, a coarse, oversexed musician. Finally the manufacturer and the girl reach their own understanding...." The play "divided the New York critics, some seeing it as a sensitive character study, others as soap opera. The magnificent, understated performance of Robinson was the main reason for the play's success."

Virtually all the reviews praised Robinson's performance, but not the play: "The first Broadway play by TV's star playwright, Paddy

Chayefsky, was — even with Edward G. Robinson's fine performance to aid it — decidedly disappointing," said Louis Kronenberger in *The Best Plays of 1955–1956.*

John McClain in *New York Journal American* countered with praise for Chayefsky, calling *Middle of the Night* "arresting, brilliant, and often great [with a] thoughtful and commanding performance by Mr. Robinson."

"It's not a great play, but it is an appealing one," said the *St. Louis Post-Dispatch,* "and it furnishes an excellent vehicle for Edward G. Robinson in a true and touching portrayal [which is] remarkably perceptive. It is sensitive, very human, warmly sympathetic, and skillfully underplayed."

Brooks Atkinson in *The New York Times* said that Robinson "gives a winning and skillful performance. No one could be more relaxed about a part. But no one could give the character more warmth or tenderness, or make an undistinguished man seem so notable.... Although Mr. Robinson does not make the manufacturer extraordinary, he makes him human and disarming, and very pleasant company.... Mr. Chayefsky's intentional cultivation of the average and the obvious has its own limitations.... What saves it is Mr. Robinson's quiet authority as an actor. It is good to be reminded of his easy skill and to have him back with us again."

In *The Sunday New York Times,* Atkinson embellished his praise for the actor: "If the years have done nothing else to him, they have supplied a quarter of a century of living, which leaves its mark on the soul of everyone who is perceptive. If there is any technical difference that can be noted by a theatregoer with a short memory, it is a deepening of authority. His acting seems to be effortless. The round, scowling, weary face is the same. So is the voice that just escapes sounding plaintive. As usual, he wears a soft hat carelessly jammed on one side of his head; he walks with his familiar loose motion, and he smokes a cigar that is as big as he is. But he absorbs the role without seeming to be acting it, not because it represents typecasting ... but because his acting is spontaneous and magnetic.... There is also a basic decency in the character he is acting. Mr. Robinson did not have to learn that anywhere.... He has always been a good actor."

"He is still a very good actor," echoed John Chapman in *The New York Daily News.* "Robinson is a dynamic and convincing actor and Logan is a dynamic and convincing producer-director, so *Middle of the Night* has been given a much better production than it deserves."

Life said, "Most people forget what a fine and versatile actor [he] really is. This month, after 25 years in Hollywood, he has returned to the Broadway theatre where his career began and, without a cop on his trail or a gat on his hip, gives a touching performance as a lovelorn widower."

"Thanks in great part to the superb and moving performance of Edward G. Robinson in the leading role, the result is a touching and interesting drama," said Richard Watts in *The New York Post.* "...The veteran actor has lost none of his theatrical cunning ... and he has gained, I think, new depths and compassion. There is great tenderness in his playing ... as well as tact and restraint, and he succeeds in being deeply poignant without ever slopping over into saccharinity."

"Robinson plays ... with a soft glow and the most effective relaxation. He is believable and sympathetic, and makes you feel he has something at stake for which you urgently hope he will find a resolution," observed William Hawkins in *The New York World-Telegram.*

"Edward G. Robinson takes that cigar out of his mouth long enough to hoist a blanketed baby onto his shoulder," began Walter Kerr in *The New York Herald-Tribune.* "On him the baby looks great.... [He is given] a chance to work in gentle, quiet depth. The brass has been temporarily muted, the snarl splits the evening just once.... In every conscience-stricken twist and turn ... Mr. Robinson is precise, honest, warmly affecting. The images are always humbly accurate.... And throughout the evening the alert, snappish, no-nonsense intelligence that glints from behind those puffy, glowering eyes is shrewdly on display. Mr. Robinson gets, in addition, an opportunity to do something he does almost better than any other working actor: describe a longish situation we never see, and make us see it with sizzling clarity. It's a beautifully controlled, absolutely direct performance."

"Even in Hollywood he has varied his tough guy roles with any number of characterizations demanding the discipline and authority of a genuine actor. This is the kind of role Robinson has in *Middle of the Night*.... His love scenes are tentative and gentle.... It is a fine and wise performance."—*Time*

"Robinson gives a direct and touching performance ... modulated with great tact ... though the part taps nothing like his full resources."—*The Commonweal*

"Robinson is superb.... He is gentle, understanding.... So intense is his performance that the first-nighters were tremendously moved by it."—Robert Coleman, *Daily Mirror*

"Edward G. Robinson returns triumphantly to the stage.... [He] plays The Manufacturer with remarkable restraint and intelligence," said *The New Yorker*.

Middleton, Charles (1879–1949), often sinister, made five films with Edward G. Robinson—*East Is West, The Hatchet Man, Silver Dollar, Blackmail,* and *Our Vines Have Tender Grapes.* In the *Flash Gordon* serial he was Ming the Merciless. Films include *Duck Soup, Show Boat, An American Tragedy, Alexander Hamilton,* and *Abe Lincoln in Illinois*.

Mielziner, Jo (1901–76), "the leading set designer of his era," according to *The Oxford Companion to American Theatre*, was responsible for the double interior set and lighting design for *Middle of the Night*. Fifty years of Broadway hits include *Strange Interlude, Street Scene, Of Thee I Sing, Winterset, The Glass Menagerie, Annie Get Your Gun, A Streetcar Named Desire, Mister Roberts, Death of a Salesman, South Pacific, Guys and Dolls, The King and I, Cat on a Hot Tin Roof, Gypsy,* and *1776*.

Miller, Arthur (1915–) His *All My Sons* won the 1947 New York Drama Critics Award; it was his first Broadway success. Edward G. Robinson, playing the lead in the film, was a fan of Miller and had hoped to play Willy Loman in *Death of a Salesman*. He was offered the role of the octogenarian Solomon, the furniture dealer in *The Price*. Miller's other works include *The Crucible* (a veiled attack on the House Un-American Activities Committee), *Incident at Vichy, A View from the Bridge,* and *Broken Glass*.

Miller, Ivan (1889–1967) appeared onscreen in *Blackmail, I Am the Law,* and *The Last Gangster*, all with Edward G. Robinson. He was also seen in *Dr. Socrates, Call of the Yukon,* and *Geronimo*.

Miller, Seton I. (1902–74) began as an actor in silents, then turned to writing. His screenplays include *Bullets or Ballots* and *Kid Galahad* (both with Edward G. Robinson), *The Criminal Code* (Oscar nomination), *Scarface, The Adventures of Robin Hood, Here Comes Mr. Jordan* (Oscar), *The Ministry of Fear, The Mississippi Gambler,* and *The Last Mile*.

Minciotti, Esther (1883–1962) played Edward G. Robinson's long-suffering wife in *House of Strangers*. Her husband, Sylvio, was also in the film. She played Ernest Borgnine's mother in *Marty*, and was also in *The Undercover Man, Strictly Dishonorable,* and *The Wrong Man*.

Minelli, Liza (1946–), daughter of Judy Garland and Vincente Minelli, appeared on TV with Edward G. Robinson on *Laugh-In* and *This Is Tom Jones*. On the *45th Annual Academy Awards*, when he was honored posthumously, she won an Oscar for *Cabaret*. Her other films include *The Sterile Cuckoo* (Oscar nomination), *Lucky Lady,* and *New York, New York*

Minelli, Vincente (1910–86), known for his MGM musicals, directed *Two Weeks in Another Town*, with Kirk Douglas and Edward G. Robinson. His films include *Cabin in the Sky, Meet Me in St. Louis, Father of the Bride, An American in Paris* (Oscar nomination), *Lust for Life, Tea and Sympathy, Gigi* (which earned nine Oscars, including picture and director), and *Some Came Running.*

Mineo, Sal (1939–76) began in films playing juvenile roles—*Giant, Dino, Rebel Without a Cause* (Oscar-nominated for the latter, and for *Exodus*). He was also in *The Gene Krupa Story, The Longest Day, The Greatest Story Ever Told,* and, with Edward G. Robinson, *Cheyenne Autumn.*

Mirrors In *Two Weeks in Another Town* Edward G. Robinson stops his wife (Claire Trevor) from overdosing on pills by breaking down the bathroom door, shattering the mirror. At the climax of *Operation X* he shatters a mirror by flinging at it a framed photograph of his daughter (Peggy Cummins). In *Key Largo,* as Johnny Rocco, he catches a glimpse of Lauren Bacall in the mirror as he nurses the scratch she has just given him; and in various gangster movies, such as *Little Caesar, The Little Giant,* and *Brother Orchid,* he preens before the mirror like a peacock.

A through-the-looking-glass effect was achieved in several of Edward G. Robinson's films by using mirrors; that is, they enhanced the idea of dreams, multiple images, and mystery. Reflections are evident in window glass, spectacles, polished table tops, and pools of water. In *Woman in the Window,* reflections are used to create not only double but distorted images to suggest — at least subliminally — the quality of a dream Professor Wanley is having. Similarly, in *Nightmare* the murder by hypnosis occurs in a multi-mirrored closet. Mirrors used cleverly in *The Whole Town's Talking* heighten the uniqueness of twin images, as played by Robinson; and finally, Robinson's mirror image (his conscience?) responds in a dialogue about murder in *Flesh and Fantasy.*

Mr. Samuel (Theater, 1930) This play was a turning point in Edward G. Robinson's career. After this production, it was over twenty years before he acted in the live theater again. Although *Mr. Samuel* received creditable reviews, audiences dwindled nightly and it closed after one week. Robinson's rationale, as stated in his autobiography, was, "I've been true to the theatre, but who's been true to me?"

The Commonweal called *Mr. Samuel* "a genuinely amusing — if not vastly important play in which Edward G. Robinson gave us one more of his inimitable character portraits.... As interpreted by Mr. Robinson — undoubtedly one of the most authentic and versatile actors on our stage today — Samuel never becomes actually monotonous. But he so far outdistances all the other characters in delineation and interest that the play becomes monologue rather than drama."

Samuel Brisach is a domineering businessman. His brothers and his son, who work for him, turn on him and try to take controlling interest of the company. Brisach suffers a heart attack and collapses, but the next day, by telephone, he is able to stage a buy-out that saves the firm and increases profits.

A comedy in three acts; producer, George C. Tyler, Erlanger Productions; playwright, Edmond Flege; adaptation, Winthrop Ames; director, Clifford Brooke; cast: Edward G. Robinson (Samuel Brisach), Gladys Lloyd (Maud Ruben), Manart Kippen (Joseph), Alexis M. Polianov (Head Waiter), France Bendtsen (Dr. Weil), Fairfax Burgher (Philip Baird), Kate Byron (Anna), Wallis Clark (Simon), Thomas Coffin Cooke (Russell), Teresa Dale (Estelle), Charles H. Doyle (Cato), Betty Hanna (Lillian Baird), Geneva Harrison (Miss Rosenthal), Harry Joyner (Nathan), Henry Mortimer (Senor Pradella), Adelaide Prince (Judith), Harry Redding (White), Charles Ritchie (Kasen), Brinsley Shaw (Harris), Sam Silverbush (Lemler), Jeanne Wardley (Maid), Eddie Wragge (Junior Baird), Robert Hudson (Roland), H. Dudley Hawley (Irving Van Ingen); opened at the Little Theatre, New York; November 10, 1930

The play closed, and before the end of the year Edward G. Robinson was back in Hollywood—filming *Little Caesar*!

Mr. Winkle Goes to War (Film, 1944) Among Edward G. Robinson's war films, this suffered in the credibility department. He played against type as a henpecked hypochondriac. Yet, the fact of the matter is that Robinson, an actor, was playing a role. *The New York Times* summed it up: "A fair lot of leisurely humor has been caught in this unpretentious tale of a 44–year-old draftee's troubles … it is sure-fired humor, a non-violent form of slapstick.… Robinson does everything in his power to give a comic simulation of Caspar Milquetoast turned G.I. … and some of his flashes of bewilderment are amusing, too. But … it is hard to believe that Mr. Robinson would take what he does lying down."

Wilbert Winkle hates his desk job at the bank, and on June 1 he resigns in order to devote himself full-time to the "fix-it" shop in his garage. He is helped by Barry, a boy from the orphanage. Amy, Wilbert's wife, is concerned about what people will think and argues with Wilbert to reconsider. Wilbert receives a draft notice. He reports for his physical, and to everyone's surprise, although he is 44, he goes on to basic training. The physical regimen is strenuous, but Wilbert perseveres. Given a desk job based on his civilian experience, he requests the motor pool, which will allow him to work with his hands. Along with Sgt. "Alphabet" (so nicknamed because his Polish name is unpronounceable), Jack Pettigrew, and Tinker, Wilbert goes overseas to fight the Japanese. During combat, with his unit pinned down by enemy fire, he commandeers a bulldozer that is out of commission and overruns the enemy camp. Recovering at a hospital from injuries, he learns from Jack that Tinker and Alphabet were killed. He goes home to a hero's welcome but is too shy to face the crowds. At home, Amy has had a change of heart; Barry has helped put a gate in the back fence so Wilbert can go directly from the house to work in his shop.

Producer, Jack Moss; associate producer, Norman Deming; director, Alfred E. Green; screenplay, Waldo Salt, George Corey, Louis Solomon; based on the novel by Theodore Pratt; assistant director, Earl Bellamy; music score, Carmen Dragon; music, Paul Sawtell, M. W. Stoloff; art director, Lionel Banks; set, George Montgomery, Rudolph Sternad; camera, Joseph Walker; editor, Richard Fanite; technical adviser, Robert Albaugh; sound, Lambert Day; cast: Edward G. Robinson (Wilbert Winkle), Ruth Warrick (Amy Winkle), Ted Donaldson (Barry), Bob Haymes (Jack Pettigrew), Richard Lane (Sgt. "Alphabet"), Robert Armstrong (Joe Tinker), Richard Gaines (Ralph Wescott), Walter Baldwin (Plummer), Art Smith (McDavid), Ann Shoemaker (Martha Pettigrew), Paul Stanton (A. B. Simkins), Buddy Yarus (Johnson), William Forrest, Warren Ashe (Captains), Bernardine Hayes (Gladys), Jeff Donnell (Hostess), Howard Freeman (Mayor), Nancy Evans, Ann Loos, Early Cantrell (Girls), Larry Thompson, Terry Frost (M.P.s), James Flavin, Fred Kohler, Jr., Dennis Moore (Sergeants), Bob Mitchum (Corporal), Herbert Hayes, Ben Taggart, Sam Flint, Nelson Leigh, Forbes Murray, Ernest Hilliard (Doctors), Fred Lord, Cecil Ballerino, Ted Holley, Les Sketchley, Ed Jenkins, Paul Stupin (Draftees), Hugh Beaumont (Range Officer), Emmett Vogan (Barber), Tommy Cook (Kid); Columbia; British title: *Arms and the Woman*; 80 minutes; August 1944

Reviews of the film were mixed. "He never succeeds in being either meekly amusing or properly courageous," said *The New York Herald-Tribune*. "He merely walks through his role." Retrospective accounts were no more favorable. Leslie Halliwell, in his *Film Guide*, called *Mr. Winkle Goes to War* an "agreeable, forgettable propaganda comedy-drama." James Robert Parish, in *The Tough Guys,* said, "Promoted by Columbia Pictures as 'in the great *Mr. Deeds* tradition' … [it is] an unsuccessful melding of comedy and drama."

Mitchell, Grant   (1874–1957) was on Broadway for thirty years before coming to films. He was in *Dinner at Eight, The Life of Emile Zola, Mr. Smith Goes to Washington, The Grapes of Wrath, Laura,* and two with Edward G. Robinson—*The Last Gangster,* as the prison warden, and *Larceny, Inc.,* as Mr. Aspinwall, the banker.

Mitchell, Howard   (1888–1958) began in silents in 1914. He has roles in three films with Edward G. Robinson—*Bullets or Ballots, Scarlet Street,* and *House of Strangers*. He appears also in *Queen of the Mob* and *The Mad Doctor.*

Mitchell, Thomas (1895–1962) worked with Edward G. Robinson four times: in *Under Sentence*, *Tales of Manhattan*, *Flesh and Fantasy*, and *The Right Man*. The first was a Broadway play; in the second, a film, they shared no scenes. In the third (a film) they played victim and murderer, respectively, and in the fourth (on television), U.S. Presidents Grover Cleveland and Theodore Roosevelt. Mitchell is remembered as Scarlett O'Hara's father in *Gone with the Wind* and as Uncle Billy in *It's a Wonderful Life*. He won a best supporting actor Oscar for *Stagecoach* and earned another nomination for *The Hurricane*. Other films include *Lost Horizon*, *Mr. Smith Goes to Washington*, *Our Town*, *The Outlaw*, *The Sullivans*, and *High Noon*.

Mitchum, Robert (1917–97) played a bit in *Mr. Winkle Goes to War*, with Edward G. Robinson. Oscar-nominated for *The Story of G. I. Joe*, he was in *Out of the Past*, *Night of the Hunter*, *Heaven Knows Mr. Allison*, *The Sundowners*, *Ryan's Daughter*, *Farewell My Lovely*, and TV's *The Winds of War*.

Moeller, Phillip (1880–1958) staged plays for the Theatre Guild, including *They Knew What They Wanted*, *Strange Interlude*, *Elizabeth the Queen*, and *Mourning Becomes Electra*, plus eight featuring Edward G. Robinson: *The Adding Machine*, *Androcles and the Lion*, *The Man of Destiny*, *The Brothers Karamazov*, *The Chief Thing*, *Juarez and Maximilian*, *Ned McCobb's Daughter*, and *Right You Are If You Think You Are*.

Montalban, Ricardo (1920–) was Mr. Roarke on the TV series *Fantasy Island*. He worked in New York and his native Mexico, then in Hollywood in *The Kissing Bandit*, *Sayonara*, *Madame X*, *Sweet Charity*, and *Star Trek: The Wrath of Khan*. He plays an Indian in *Cheyenne Autumn*, with Edward G. Robinson.

Montand, Yves (1921–91) brought his one-man revue from Europe to Broadway. He is in the French films *Wages of Fear*, *The Sleeping Car Murders*, *State of Siege*, and *Z*, and in the U.S., *Let's Make Love*, *My Geisha* (with Edward G. Robinson), *On a Clear Day You Can See Forever*, and *Grand Prix*. He was married to Simone Signoret.

Montgomery, Ray (1919–98) is with Edward G. Robinson in *Larceny, Inc.*, *It's a Great Feeling*, and TV's "The Drop-Out." Other films are *The Hard Way*, *Johnny Belinda*, *Action in the North Atlantic*, and *A Private Affair*.

Mooch (Short film, 1971) Encountering stars and producers along the way, a dog tries to make it in show business.

Director, Richard Edman; screenplay, Jerry Divine, Jim Backus; music, Don Piestrup; title song sung by Sonny Curtis; lyrics by Ann Nicolaysen; director of photography, Allen Daviau; associate producer, Andrew Babbish; editor, Larry Heath; animals supplied and trained by Frank Inn; costumes, Frederick's of Hollywood; art director, Michael Divine; assistant director, Ray Gosnell; gaffer, Glenn Rowland Jr.; wardrobe, Lynn Divine; makeup, Scott Hamilton; assistant cameraman, Mike Chevalier; effects cutter, Jeff Bushelman; assistant editor, Tom Bernardi; titles and optical effects, Pacific Title; sound, Ryder Sound Services; cast: John Harding (Dr. Hackett), Kim Hamilton (Nurse); Gino Conforti (Hairdresser), Jerry Hausner (Producer), Bert Holland (Attendant), Grace Albertson (Lady with cat), Jay Jostyn (Man with duck), Lynne Lipton (Voice of Mooch), Zsa Zsa Gabor, Richard Burton (Narrators), Vincent Price, James Darren, Jill St. John, Jim Backus, Mickey Rooney, Phyllis Diller, David Wayne, Darren McGavin, Rose Marie, Cesar Romero, Edward G. Robinson, Sam Jaffe, Bettye Ackerman, Jay C. Flippen, Dick Martin, Marty Allen, and the voices of Rex Harrison, Jack Benny, Dean Martin (Themselves); a Jerry Divine-Jim Backus production, 1971; a.k.a. *Mooch Goes to Hollywood*

Moore, Joanna (1934–97) Mother of Tatum O'Neal, and once married to Ryan O'Neal, she played Melanie Smooth, Edward G. Robinson's wife, in *Never a Dull Moment*.

Other films include *Touch of Evil, Son of Flubber, The Last Angry Man,* and *The Hindenburg.*

Moore, Owen (1886–1939) appeared in nearly two hundred films beginning with silents in 1908. He is Fingers O'Dell in *Outside the Law* with Edward G. Robinson and appears also in *A Star Is Born* and *She Done Him Wrong.*

Moorehead, Agnes (1906–74) lost the role of the war crimes investigator in *The Stranger* to Edward G. Robinson. She played his wife in *Our Vines Have Tender Grapes.* Starting with Orson Welles' Mercury Theatre, she had roles in his *Citizen Kane, Journey Into Fear,* and *The Magnificent Ambersons,* receiving Oscar nominations for the latter, and also for *Mrs. Parkington, Johnny Belinda,* and *Hush Hush Sweet Charlotte.* Other films include *Jane Eyre, Show Boat, Caged, Raintree County,* and *The Bat.* On the radio she was in *Sorry, Wrong Number,* and was delightful as Endora on TV's *Bewitched.*

Morgan, Dennis (1910–94) was the lead in *It's a Great Feeling,* in which Edward G. Robinson was a guest star. A former announcer and opera singer, he also was in *The Great Ziegfeld, The Fighting 69th, The Hard Way, Thank Your Lucky Stars,* and *Christmas in Connecticut.*

Morgan, Frank (1890–1949) was the Duke of Florence in *The Firebrand* (Edward G. Robinson played his brother), and reprised the role in the film *The Affairs of Cellini.* He was also in *The Shop Around the Corner, Boom Town, Tortilla Flat, The Human Comedy, Courage of Lassie,* and *The Three Musketeers,* but is best remembered as *The Wizard of Oz.*

Morgan, Harry (1915–), in several TV series (*Pete and Gladys, Dragnet, M*A*S*H*), played in films from 1942: *To the Shores of Tripoli, The Ox-Bow Incident, Dragonwyck, All My Sons* (with Edward G. Robinson), *High Noon, The Glenn Miller Story, Inherit the Wind, Support Your Local Sheriff, The Apple Dumpling Gang,* and *The Shootist.*

Morin, Alberto (1902–89) was in three films with Edward G. Robinson — as a boat captain in *Key Largo,* Victoro in *House of Strangers,* and a cameraman in *Two Weeks in Another Town.* He is also in *Gone with the Wind, My Sister Eileen,* and *The Cheyenne Social Club.*

Morley, Robert (1908–92), a rotund English actor and playwright (*Edward My Son*), was in the films *Major Barbara, The African Queen, Topkapi, The Loved One, Theatre of Blood,* and *Who is Killing the Great Chefs of Europe?* He shared no scenes in *Song of Norway* with Edward G. Robinson.

Morris, Frances (1908–) appeared onscreen with Edward G. Robinson in *Bullets or Ballots, Night Has a Thousand Eyes,* and *The Woman in the Window.* She is also in *My Son John* and *Carrie.*

Morris, Wayne (1914–59), his career interrupted by service in World War II and several decorations, appeared in the films *China Clipper, Kid Galahad* (title role, with Edward G. Robinson), *The Voice of the Turtle, The Time of Your Life,* and *Paths of Glory.* He was with Robinson in the radio adaptation of *Kid Galahad.*

Moscow Strikes Back (Documentary, 1943) Edward G. Robinson was narrator of this Oscar-winning documentary film. *The New York Times* said, "We have not seen a film to equal it."

The New York Daily News reviewer called *Moscow Strikes Back* "a savagely stirring movie. Here in living terms is a real people's war. Truly great ... I beg you to see it!"

"It's about how Russia hurled back the Nazis in December, 1941," said *Photoplay.* "Don't be afraid to see this slice of history in the raw because you think you'll be shocked and horrified. You will be, but it's the sort of shock that carries with it tremendous vitalization.... You'll see the home of Tolstoy with scarcely a piece of furniture remaining because the Nazis used it for firewood. 'And this,' says the effective voice of Edward G. Robinson, narrator, 'in a house surrounded by forests!' You'll see the home of Tchaikovsky reduced to a shambles, his priceless musical scores pitched out into the snow.... And you'll see the frozen mutilated bodies of little girls raped by the Nazis. We recommend that every man in the armed forces of Uncle Sam be shown this picture. He won't need any lectures on what we're fighting for."

Edward G. Robinson (Narrator); commentary, Albert Maltz; music, Dmitri Tiomkin; editor, Slavko Vorkapich; Art Kino; 1943

Motion Picture Alliance for the Preservation of American Ideals

This group, founded in February 1944, included Ward Bond, Clarence Brown, Gary Cooper, Victor Fleming, Hedda Hopper, Adolphe Menjou, Norman Taurog, Robert Taylor, King Vidor, John Wayne, and Sam Wood. They were convinced that Hollywood was dominated by Communists and that the Roosevelt administration was not doing enough to protect the country against infiltration.

"The Movie Crazy Years"

(Television, 1971) Joan Blondell, Busby Berkeley, John Bright, Bette Davis, Olivia deHavilland, Mervyn LeRoy, Pat O'Brien, Edward G. Robinson, Hal B. Wallis, William A. Wellman (interviews); *N.E.T. Playhouse on the Thirties*; PBS-TV; 1971

Mower, Jack

(1891–1965), a Hawaiian, was in silent serials and westerns, and was in five sound films with Edward G. Robinson — *A Slight Case of Murder, Confessions of a Nazi Spy, Kid Galahad, The Whole Town's Talking,* and *Larceny, Inc.* Other films include *Torrid Zone* and *County Fair.*

Muni, Paul

(1895–1967) appeared with Edward G. Robinson four times: once when they narrated the pageant in tribute to the victims of the Holocaust, *We Will Never Die,* and three times on the radio — a Warner Bros. broadcast, *The Roosevelt Special,* and on *Jerusalem Is Her Name* on NBC. They competed for the 1956 Tony Award for best actor (Muni won for *Inherit the Wind*). An Austrian emigre to the Yiddish Theatre, Muni replaced Robinson when *We Americans* went to Broadway. He was nominated for an Oscar for *The Valiant*, his first film, and for *I Am a Fugitive from a Chain Gang, The Life of Emile Zola,* and *The Story of Louis Pasteur* (winning for the last). He received a final nomination for *The Last Angry Man*. Other films include *Scarface, The Good Earth,* and *A Song to Remember.*

Munson, Ona

(1906–55) replaced Claire Trevor as Lorelei Kilburn opposite Edward G. Robinson in *Big Town*. She appeared in *Five Star Final* with him, as a reporter, and also played Lon McCallister's mother in *The Red House*. She was in vaudeville and on Broadway before coming to films, which include *Going Wild, Scandal Sheet, Lady from Louisiana, The Shanghai Gesture,* and — in perhaps her best known role — *Gone with the Wind*, as madame Belle Watling.

Murder / attempted murder

Despite his indelible image as a gangster and/or criminal in film, Edward G. Robinson's characters were not generally cold-blooded murderers on the screen, but they were culpable. If some of the killings were premeditated, there are more instances of accidental death and self defense.

In *All My Sons*, Robinson's poor quality control when manufacturing airplane engines results in 21 flyers going down during the war. This is not unlike his disregard for standards in meat-packing in *I Loved a Woman*, which results in the food poisoning deaths of soldiers in the field. As editor of a muckraking tabloid newspaper in *Five Star Final*, he shares the responsibility for two suicides.

In *The Amazing Dr. Clitterhouse* he studies the clinical art of murder when he poisons Humphrey Bogart. As boss of San Francisco in *Barbary Coast* he is responsible for the murders of characters played by Frank Craven, Donald Meek, and Roger Gray. Robinson is prevented from killing Gene Lockhart at the conclusion of *Blackmail*, but he successfully goads the same actor to suicide in *The Sea Wolf*. He investigates murder in *Double Indemnity*.

In *Flesh and Fantasy* he strangles Thomas Mitchell after earlier murder attempts on Dame May Whitty and C. Aubrey Smith have failed. He strangles Kathleen Hughes in *The Glass Web*. He orders the killing of his nephew, played by Perry Lopez, and guns down Paul Stewart in *Hell on Frisco Bay*. Robinson also guns down deputy sheriff John Rodney in *Key Largo*. In the same film he allows the Osceola brothers to be shot.

Robinson dispatches both J. Carroll Naish and Leslie Fenton as *The Hatchet Man* and poisons Louis Calhern in *The Man with Two Faces*. In the love triangle dramas *Manpower* and *Tiger Shark* (the latter actually being the original story recycled), following attempts to kill Richard Arlen and George Raft, respectively, he dies, victim of a fall in the former and a shark attack in the latter.

Robinson's murder of Allene Roberts' parents before the film begins is the cause of his mental instability in *The Red House*. In *Scarlet Street* he stabs Joan Bennett repeatedly with an ice pick. Gangster Joseph Downing does the four killings of the title in *A Slight Case of Murder*. Robinson's fistfight with James Cagney in *Smart Money* results in the latter's death. Self defense causes Victor McLaglen's death in *Tampico*, Edward Arnold's in *Unholy Partners*, and Arthur Loft's (stabbed with scissors) in *The Woman in the Window*. Robinson conspires with Joan Bennett to poison blackmailer Dan Duryea in the latter film. Ed Brophy is dispatched by Robinson offscreen in *The Whole Town's Talking*.

Murray, Forbes He appeared in four films with Edward G. Robinson: *Tales of Manhattan, Larceny, Inc., It's a Great Feeling,* and *Mr. Winkle Goes to War*. Other films include *Imitation of Life, Gilda, The Razor's Edge,* and *Monkey Business*.

Muse, Clarence (1899–1979) was in *Huckleberry Finn, Show Boat, Cabin in the Cotton, Watch on the Rhine, Porgy and Bess,* and, with Edward G. Robinson, *Tales of Manhattan, Flesh and Fantasy, Double Indemnity,* and *Scarlet Street*. They were also together on radio's *The Roosevelt Special*.

Music / Singing Edward G. Robinson appears in four musical films: *Robin and the 7 Hoods, Song of Norway, It's a Great Feeling,* and *Pepe,* featuring dozens of songs and dances performed by, among others, Frank Sinatra, Dean Martin, Sammy Davis, Jr., Bing Crosby, Florence Henderson, Harry Secombe, Doris Day, Dennis Morgan, Jack Carson, Judy Garland, Dan Dailey, Shirley Jones, Maurice Chevalier, and Cantinflas. Robinson himself does not sing in these films. The title song from *It's a Great Feeling,* "The Faraway Part of Town" (Judy Garland in *Pepe*), and "My Kind of Town" (Sinatra, *Robin and the 7 Hoods*) all received Oscar nominations, and the latter two films were nominated for their musical scores. The dramatic score of *The Woman in the Window* was nominated; and, of course, *A Hole in the Head* won the Oscar for James Van Heusen and Sammy Cahn with their song "High Hopes."

Other Robinson films include Kay Francis singing "Home on the Range" in *I Loved a Woman*; Marsha Hunt, "After You've Gone" (*Unholy Partners*); Claire Trevor, "Moanin' Low" (*Key Largo*); Marlene Dietrich, "He Lied and I Listened" (*Manpower*); Bette Davis, "The Moon Is in Tears Tonight" (*Kid Galahad*); Mae Clarke, "Stormy Weather" (*The Man with Two Faces*); Connie Russell, "The Last I Ever Saw of My Man" and "What's Your Sad Story?" (*Nightmare*); Jayne Mansfield, "Too Marvelous for Words" (*Illegal*); Joanne Dru, "The Very Thought of You" (*Hell on Frisco Bay*); Frank Sinatra, "All My Tomorrows" and "High Hopes" with Eddie Hodges (*A Hole in the Head*); Jose Feliciano, "Old Turkey Buzzard" (*Mackenna's Gold*); and Johnny Mathis, the title song of *The Biggest Bundle of Them All*.

A singer at the piano does a medley of songs—"It Had to Be You," "Shine on Harvest Moon," "I'm Dancing with Tears in My Eyes," "Melancholy Baby," and "The Music Goes Round and Round"—in *A Slight Case of Murder*. "Melancholy Baby" is the major theme of the musical score of *Scarlet Street*. "You'll Never Know" is played during *All My Sons*. "Temptation" is on the phonograph during the murder in *The Glass Web*. "Tangerine" haunts the final moments of *Double Indemnity*, while the film also features a segment of Schubert's "Unfinished Symphony" at the Hollywood Bowl. Other classical music includes "The Pilgrim's Chorus" from Wagner's *Tannhauser*, a theme used in *Silver Dollar*. The entire score of *Song of Norway* is by Edvard Grieg; while much of *My Geisha* features Puccini's *Madama Butterfly*. *Soylent Green* features Beethoven's "Pastorale" and selections from Grieg. *Dr. Ehrlich's Magic Bullet* features well-known German waltzes, including "The Blue Danube." Turn of the century music hall songs "Hello, My Baby," "Oh, Susannah," and "Camptown Races" are featured in *The Sea Wolf* and *Barbary Coast*. "For He's a Jolly Good Fellow" is sung to Edward G. Robinson at testimonial banquets in *Scarlet Street* and *Robin and the 7 Hoods*.

Robinson himself sings in *I Loved a Woman*, with Genevieve Tobin ("Little Annie Rooney"); in an impromptu quartet of Army buddies in *Mr. Winkle Goes to War* ("Oh, Genevieve"); in *House of Strangers* (along with a Lawrence Tibbett opera recording); in *The Little Giant,* Wagner's *Tannheuser* again; and, with Kirk Douglas, briefly in *Two Weeks in Another Town* ("Auld Lang Syne"). On the radio he was heard in a rendition of "April Showers" on *Kraft Music Hall*, with Al Jolson.

Grand pianos were evident in *All My Sons* and *Song of Norway*, and an upright — on wheels — was used in *Thunder in the City*. *Tales of Manhattan* involves a symphony orchestra in the Charles Laughton segment. A still from *Mr. Winkle Goes to War* shows Robinson playing a trumpet, but the scene does not appear in the film.

See **Dancing**.

"Musical Americana" Presented by The United States Air Force Band and The Singing Sergeants; Colonel Arnald D. Gabriel (conductor); Edward G. Robinson (guest narrator); Sergeant Harry H. Gleeson (announcer); author, Milton Geiger (*I Will Not Go Back*); music, Sergeant John Caughman (*I Will Not Go Back*), Carmen Dragon (*I Am an American*); additional compositions and/or arrangements by Joseph Willcox Jenkins, Henry Fillmore, Robert Russell Bennett, Sergeant Floyd E. Werle; Departmental Auditorium, Washington, D.C., February 7, 1971

My Daughter Joy see **Operation X**

My Geisha (Film, 1962) Shirley MacLaine and Edward G. Robinson shared several scenes in *My Geisha*, a comedy filmed on location in Japan in 1961. "Mr. Robinson is not only a brilliant actor but a generous, nice man who spent much of his off-camera time working with the young actors in our picture," wrote MacLaine in a letter to the editor of *Cosmopolitan* magazine. The film loosely deals with motion picture–making, with MacLaine appearing as a comedienne and Robinson as her studio producer. "Much of it reminds you of television situation comedy, which is endurable only to those fascinated by the personalities of the performers," suggested *The New York Herald-Tribune*.

A Sachiko production; producer, Steve Parker; director, Jack Cardiff; screenplay, Norman Krasna; art directors, Hal Pereira, Arthur Lonergan, Makoto Kikuchi; music, Franz Waxman; sound, Harold Lewis, Charles Grenzbach; camera, Shunichiro Nakao, Stanley Sayer; 2nd unit director, Ikuo Kobayashi; editor, Archie Marshek; production manager, Harry Caplan; orchestrations, Leonid Raab; song, Hal David; costumes, Edith Head, Seibu (kimonos), Frank Somper (furs); makeup, Wally Westmore, Shu Uemura; wigs, Junjiro Yamada; Technicolor consultant, Ron Thompson; assistant director, Harry Katz; cast: Shirley MacLaine (Lucy Dell/Yoko Mori) Yves Montand (Paul Robaix), Edward G. Robinson (Sam Lewis), Bob Cummings (Bob Moore), Yoko Tani (Kazumi Ito), Tatsuo Saito (Kenichi Takata), Tamae Kyokawa (Amatsu Hisako), Ichiro Hayakawa (Kaida), Alex Gerry (Leonard Lewis), Tsugundo Maki (Shig), Satoko Kuni (Maid), Nariko Muramatsu, Akiko Tsuda (Head waitresses), Kazue Kaneoko, Junko Aoki, Akemi Shimomura, Maymi Momose, Kyoko Takeuchi (Geishas), Marion Furness (Bob's girlfriend), George Furness (George); Paramount; Technirama and Technicolor; 120 minutes; June 1962

Paul Robaix, a film director, does most of his movies with his wife, Lucy Dell, a comedy star. He plans to make a film of *Madama Butterfly* on location in Japan without her in order to prove his ability on his own. But without her name on the film, the budget will allow only a mediocre production. As a gag, Lucy follows Paul to Japan and dresses up as a geisha, betting producer Sam Lewis that Paul will not recognize her. When Lucy wins the bet, she gets the idea to audition for the part. But Paul is not told the truth for fear it will hurt his pride. Under the name Yoko Mori, Lucy stars in the film. Bob Moore, Lucy's usual costar, falls in love with Yoko and wants to make her his fourth wife. Paul, meanwhile, discovers Lucy's deception while viewing negatives of the film. Hurt, he attempts to make love to Yoko; Lucy, who never doubted her husband's faithfulness, now feels their marriage is over. At the premiere of the finished *Madama Butterfly*, the studio's plan is to have Yoko appear onstage to take a bow and then remove her wig to become Lucy Dell. However, Lucy decides instead to come onstage without the geisha makeup and announce that Yoko has entered a convent. Paul, grateful to have succeeded on his own, lets Lucy know he found out who Yoko really was before he tried to seduce her.

"It is perhaps a tribute to the cast that the film often appears less crass and vulgar than it might have been," wrote the *Monthly Film Bulletin*. "Edward G. Robinson gives his customary relaxed and beautifully timed performance." *The New York Times* called *My Geisha* "a visually beautiful if only temporarily convincing romantic comedy drama … amiable and easy on the eyes and ears, but unfortunately it does not have too much to say … Edward G. Robinson takes the role of [an] understanding producer-mentor in casual but effective stride."

"My Wife, Geraldine" (Radio, 1945) On this radio broadcast, according to *Radio Yesteryear,* "a meek man seeks the ideal woman to be his fictitious wife, and then is accused of her murder."

Producer, director, editor, William Spier; story, Robert Tallman; adaptation, Gerald Marcus; introduced by "The Man in Black"; cast: Edward G. Robinson, Jeanette Nolan, Elliott Lewis, Joseph Kearns, John McIntire, Howard McNear, Harry Lang, Wally Maher; Truman Bradley (announcer); *Suspense*; CBS; March 1, 1945; 30 minutes.

Myerson, Bess (1924–) was Miss America of 1945 and was on TV in *The Big Payoff* and *I've Got a Secret*. She appeared with Edward G. Robinson in four consecutive *Chanukah Festival for Israel* programs from 1964 to 1967. She was cultural affairs commissioner of New York City.

NBC Star Playhouse see "A Slight Case of Murder"

N. E. T. Playhouse on the Thirties see "The Movie Crazy Years"

Naish, J. Carroll (1900–73) made three films in a row with Edward G. Robinson — as Sun Yat Ming, victim of *The Hatchet Man*; Tony, the dance hall proprietor in *Two Seconds*; and *Tiger Shark*. They shared no scenes in *Tales of Manhattan* but wore the same tailcoat. He played all ethnic types but was a descendant of Irish peers. There were Oscar nominations for *Sahara* and *A Medal for Benny*. Other films include *Beau Geste, Blood and Sand, Humoresque,* and *Annie Get Your Gun* (as Chief Sitting Bull). He died two days before Robinson.

Name Emanuel Goldenberg probably never would have been a proper marquee name for a leading man of the theater or the movies. Early on, Edward G. Robinson was encouraged to change his real name. He felt he was being asked to find something that sounded more Anglo-Saxon. He tried various translations, and wound up with "Edward," then King of England, in place of Emanuel; "G" for Goldenberg (but in interviews he'd say it stood for "God only knows!" or "gangster"); and "Robinson." The surname with no apparent connection came from a play — an unseen character announced by a butler, "A Mr. Robinson to see you." Robinson thought that had dignity. Yet the actor often said if he had it all to do over again, he'd choose something shorter. "You have no idea how long it takes to write 'Edward G. Robinson' for a flock of autograph hunters!"

Robinson was billed under his new name virtually from the beginning of his career, although on some occasions without the "G," and sometimes with an arbitrary change, as in Edward *Gould* Robinson. During his early years onscreen, even with star billing, the first name was abbreviated as "Edw." or "Ed." Friends called him Eddie. By the time he was a celebrity, Robinson had arranged to change his name permanently, legally. In 1933, when his son was born, he was Edward G. Robinson, Jr., and both father and son were known as "Manny." Several family members changed the Goldenberg surname to Robinson as well.

Napoleon Bonaparte (1769–1821), as Napoleon I, was Emperor of France from 1804 to 1815. After military victories, he centralized the local government, adopted a civil code of law, created the Bank of France, and strengthened bridges and roads. His reign saw renewed battles with Spain, Britain, Russia. He divorced his wife, Josephine, to form an alliance with the Habsburgs by marrying Marie Louise, daughter of the emperor of Austria. Charles Louis Napoleon Bonaparte (Napoleon III, 1808–1873) was nephew to Napoleon I and ruled France from 1852 to 1870.

Edward G. Robinson always wanted to play Napoleon I on the stage or screen, maintaining that he was the right height and size. The closest he came was with the Theatre Guild, which produced Shaw's *The Man of Destiny* (but in which Tom Powers played the Emperor). There were negotiations with studios in the early 1930s, with such suggested actresses as Gloria Swanson, Bette Davis, and Barbara Stanwyck as possible Josephines, but apparently Robinson, who had script approval, was never happy with adaptations that were presented.

Robinson and his wife Gladys once attended a Hollywood costume party dressed as Napoleon and Josephine. The host was Basil Rathbone; the couple benefited from the makeup man at Warners.

Napoleon III is played by Walter Kingsford in Edward G. Robinson's *A Dispatch from Reuter's*. His speech is the first news item sent via telegraph by the Reuter system from France to England. In *The Last Gangster* Robinson's character admires Napoleon, suggesting to his son that he would make a better role model than Abraham Lincoln, whose likeness is on a medal the boy has won in scouting.

Nash, Mary (1885–1976) was on the stage from 1904 in *The City, The Man Who Came Back, Captain Applejack,* and *The Two Orphans.* She was the lead in *Arms and the Woman,* Edward G. Robinson's silent debut, filmed in New York, and was also in *Heidi, Come and Get It, The Philadelphia Story, The Human Comedy,* and *Till the Clouds Roll By.*

National Board of Review The National Board of Review cited these among Edward G. Robinson's films: *Two Seconds,* one of the year's ten best in 1932; *Confessions of a Nazi Spy,* the best out of ten selected in 1939 (also cited were actors Francis Lederer and Paul Lukas); *Tales of Manhattan*—Robinson was one among thirty performers cited for excellence in 22 films in 1942; *The Ten Commandments*—in 1956 Yul Brynner was cited (including also his work in *Anastasia* and *The King and I*); and *The Cincinnati Kid,* 1965—Joan Blondell was named as best supporting actress.

Nazism The most obvious elements of Nazism in Edward G. Robinson's works were in the films where he played government agents on their trail. In *Confessions of a Nazi Spy* the plot of the film dealt with detecting, tracking, apprehending, and bringing Nazis to justice in the United States courts. Actual footage of Hitler and public events in Europe were part of the film, but in particular the performance of Paul Lukas as Dr. Kassel, ranting and declaiming the party propaganda, was vividly reminiscent of Der Fuhrer's passion and strength.

That passion was somewhat more controlled but equally insidious in Orson Welles' portrait of Franz Kindler in *The Stranger*. Believing himself safe in New England after the war, it wasn't necessary for him to show his true colors until war crimes investigator Wilson, played by Robinson, came to town to trap him. From that point, cold-blooded murder, clever lies and coverup, and a plot to murder his new wife were the focal point. As in *Confessions of a Nazi Spy*, the film featured documentary footage — this time of gas chambers and concentration camps.

In *Tampico* Robinson played a ship's captain who comes under attack by the Germans, but the emphasis was on spy-chasing and action rather than Nazi character and ideology. Robinson's other films that touched on the war — *Destroyer, Mr. Winkle Goes to War, Journey Together, Our Vines Have Tender Grapes, All My Sons* — dealt with the Pacific front, or the R.A.F., or the impact of the war at home. Robinson felt that Wolf Larsen in *The Sea Wolf* was a Nazi in everything but name, and as a result the filming in 1941 had political relevance. Episodes of *Big Town* on the radio eventually had Robinson's character, editor Steve Wilson, battling the Nazis.

Philosophically, the most interesting commentary about Nazism in Robinson's performances came in *Dr. Ehrlich's Magic Bullet*. As with *The Sea Wolf*, the time of the story preceded Hitler by several decades. Dr. Paul Ehrlich was a German Jew, and one of the reasons Warner Bros. took on the project of filming his story was to refute Hitler's statement at the time that "scientific discovery by a Jew is worthless." The script writers had Ehrlich presage future events in his deathbed speech to his medical colleagues:

"There are a few things I want to talk over. 606 works, we know. The magic bullet will cure thousands. The principle on which it works will serve against other diseases ... many others, I think. But there can be no final victory over diseases of the body unless the diseases of the soul are also overcome. They feed upon each other ... diseases of the body, diseases of the soul. In days to come there will be epidemics of greed ... hate ... ignorance. We must fight them in life as we fought syphilis in the laboratory. We must fight, fight ... we must never, never stop fighting."

In 1943 Edward G. Robinson joined Paul Muni to narrate *We Will Never Die* at Madison Square Garden, paying tribute to the six million Jews of Europe who perished in the Holocaust at the hands of the Nazis.

Ned McCobb's Daughter

(Theater, 1926) The plot of this play, as outlined by Gerald Bordman in *The Oxford Companion to American Theatre*, has "Carrie, daughter of Captain Ned McCobb ... married into the good-for-nothing Callahan family. Her faithless husband, George, has forced McCobb to mortgage his farm to pay for an abortion for George's mistress. George has also been stealing money from the local ferry company. When he is arrested, his bootlegger brother, Babe, offers Carrie the money to pay off the mortgage and to provide George's legal fees in return for allowing him to store his whiskey in her barn. Carrie accepts the money, but then cooperates with the authorities to rid herself of both brothers."

Produced by the Theatre Guild; playwright, Sidney Howard; director, Philip Moeller; set, Aline Bernstein; stage manager, Maurice McRae; assistant, Barbara Bruce; technical director, Kate Lawson; costumes, Eaves Costumes, Inc.; scenery, Cleon Throckmorton, Inc.; cast: Alfred Lunt (Babe Callahan), Clare Eames (Carrie Callahan), Edward G. Robinson (Lawyer Grover), Earle Larimore (George Callahan); Morris Carnovsky (Second Federal Man), Dudley Digges (Captain Ned McCobb), Margalo Gillmore (Jenny), Philip Leigh (Ben McCobb), Philip Loeb (Nat Glidden), Maurice McRae (First Federal Man), Albert Perry; opened at the John Golden Theatre, New York; November 29, 1926 (132 performances)

Reviews of *Ned McCobb's Daughter* favored performance over story quality. Gerald Bordman commented that "sharply etched character studies elevated this work above the run of contemporary melodramas."— *The Oxford Companion to American Theatre*

"Mr. Howard's play has 'character,'" said *The New York Times*. "One might wish that the drama were more shapely and economical." *The Nation* said, "On the whole the production ... is more consistently good than the play."

Robinson played Lawyer Grover, one of his few American characterizations on the Broadway stage. Playwright Sidney Howard complimented him on the hinted New England accent he developed for the role.

Neither by Day Nor by Night (Film, 1972) An MPI/Mordechai Slonim Films Production; producer, Mordechai Slonim; associate producer, Mischa Asheroff; director, Steven Hilliard Stern; screenplay, Stern, Gisela Slonim; based on a play by Avraham Raz; camera, Gadi Danzig, Amnon Salamon; production manager, Nachman Tservanitsev; assistant directors, Naomi May-Bar, Eli Cohen; music, Vladimir Cosma; songs "Time" and "Innocent Friends" by Stern, Cosma, George and Michel Costa, Derrick Leather, John Stevenson; set, Gidi Levi; location manager, Chaim Mutchnik; editors, Eve Newman, Alain Jacobavitch; assistants, Omna Cohen, Michael Karr; makeup, Aniko Schik; wardrobe, Marjorie Gershon; continuity, Shoshana Rosen; special effects, LeGrand Sounds for Sight; crew, Moshe Fletcher, Shmuel Levy, Ovadia May-Bar, Eitan Tsur, Loui Yisacher; cast: Zalman King (Adam), Edward G. Robinson (The Father), Miriam Bernstein-Cohen (Hannah Sokolova), Chaim Amitar (Akira), Mischa Asheroff (Doctor), Shmuel Calderon, Dalia Friedland (Yael), Eli Cohen, Zicha Gold, Zalmen Hirshfield, Zeev Pa-amoni, Rachel Ravid, Mona Silberstein, David Smadar, Jetta Luka; Motion Pictures International-Monarch Films; Eastman color; 95 minutes; 1972

Adam is an American expatriate living on a kibbutz in Tel Aviv. While he is picking oranges, there is a bomb attack and he is injured. In the hospital he is visited by his father, but their meeting is short and strained. Adam will soon go blind. During his stay at the hospital he falls in love with Yael, his nurse, whose parents perished at Auschwitz. Adam's other friend at the hospital is Hannah Sokolova. She is an elderly lady whose own blindness allows her to be disillusioned into believing Adam is an Israeli soldier she loved in her youth. Adam enjoys Hannah's companionship and does not discourage her fantasy. She will have a cataract operation to restore her sight; Adam, through his loss, learns compassion.

"The Berlin [Film Festival] audiences gave the Israelis a warm reception, there was much praise of the veteran actress Miriam Bernstein-Cohen.... The International Writers Guild honored the film for its 'humanity in a time of excessive brutality,'" commented *Film Society*. "Robinson's neatly etched cameo provides a morsel of pleasure," said the *Monthly Film Bulletin*

Nettleton, Lois (1930–) was a leading lady in films (*Period of Adjustment, Dirty Dingus Magee, The Best Little Whorehouse in Texas, Deadly Blessing*) and TV miniseries (*Centennial, Washington: Behind Closed Doors*). Early in her career she played opposite Edward G. Robinson as Luba in the touring production of *Darkness at Noon*.

Network of the Americas (Radio, 1942) Participants (many speaking in both Spanish and English): Dick Powell, Melvyn Douglas (narrators), Edward G. Robinson, Henry Wallace, Jinx Falkenberg, Lauritz Melchior, Nelson Rockefeller, Rita Hayworth, Ronald Colman, William S. Paley; CBS-radio; 90 minutes; May 19, 1942

Never a Dull Moment (Film, 1968) "Edward G. Robinson at his too-rarely-seen best" was *The New Yorker*'s assessment of his sole venture for Walt Disney Productions.

It is possible that Walt Disney was aware that Robinson had signed to appear in *Never a Dull Moment* despite his having died a year and a half before the film opened. In recent years an increasing number of adult-themed projects have been produced by the Disney organization—*Fatal Attraction*, to name one example—but in 1968 the hiring of Edward G. Robinson may have been thought tame, or even conciliatory, remembering that Walt Disney was an outspoken conservative witness before the House Un-American Activities Committee.

"With no pretensions to being anything but a rollicking farce, this slight but intermittently amusing comedy largely succeeds on its own modest level," said the *Monthly Film Bulletin*. "Edward G. Robinson, nostalgically cast as an art-loving racketeer, plays the part as straight as a die, and happily avoids the temptations offered by a zany action painting sequence."

Producer, Ron Miller; director, Jerry Paris; screenplay, A. J. Carothers; based on the novel *A Thrill a Minute with Jack Albany,* by John Godey; art directors, Carroll Clark, John B. Mansbridge; matte artist, Alan Maley; set, Emile Kuri, Frank R. McKelvey; special effects, Eustace Lycett, Robert A. Mattey; assistant director, John C. Chulay; sound mixer, Dean Thomas; music, Robert F. Brunner; music editor, Evelyn Kennedy; orchestrator, Cecil A. Crandall; camera, William Snyder; editor, Marsh Hendry; makeup, Gordon Hubbard; costumes, Bill Thomas, Chuck Keehne, Neva Rameo; hairstyles, Laure Matheron; assistant to the producer, Tom Leetch; script supervisor, Robert O. Cook; cast: Dick Van Dyke (Jack Albany), Edward G. Robinson (Leo Joseph Smooth), Dorothy Provine (Sally Inwood), Henry Silva (Frank Boley), Joanna Moore (Melanie Smooth), Tony Bill (Florian), Slim Pickens (Cowboy Schaeffer), Jack Elam (Ace Williams), Ned Glass (Rinzy Tobreski), Richard Bakalyan (Bobby Macoon), Mickey Shaughnessy (Francis), Philip Coolidge (Fingers Felton), James Milhollin (Museum director), Johnny Silver (Prop man), Anthony Caruso (Tony Preston), Paul Condylis (Lenny), Bob Homel (Captain Jacoby), Dick Winslow (Actor), Jackie Russell (Sexy girl), Rex Dominick (Sam), Eleanor Audley (Woman at museum), Ken Lynch (Police lieutenant), John Cliff, John Dennis (Museum guards), Tyler McVey (Chief Grayson), Jerry Paris (Police photographer); Buena Vista (Walt Disney Productions); 100 minutes; Technicolor; August 1968

Jack Albany, a TV actor, is picked up on a dark night by Florian, the nephew of Leo Joseph Smooth, a prominent retired gangster. Jack has been mistaken for professional killer Ace Williams. Fearing for his life, instead of revealing who he really is, he does all he can to convince Smooth and his gang that he really is Ace. He would enlist the help of Sally Inwood, Smooth's painting instructor, to escape, but she will not believe he is *not* Ace. Smooth has a master plan to steal a huge painting, *Field of Sunflowers*, from the local museum. He needs Ace to dispose of guards while his gang heists the painting. When the real Ace shows up, Jack manages, with Sally's help, to knock him out and stash him in the basement. At the museum Jack finally rebels when it is time to kill the guards. There is a climactic chase through the modern art section of the museum, and Jack manages to trap nearly all the gang on an oversized mobile. The police come, and with Jack they return to a warehouse to arrest Smooth. Sally decides to stay with Jack to help him with his acting career.

Although Leslie Halliwell in his *Film Guide* said the film had "vigor, but not much flair," most critics enjoyed Robinson's performance in particular. "Edward G. Robinson once again gives an effortless interpretation of a top criminal," said the *Daily News*, "[with] lines like: 'Keep your hands to yourself or I'll take them away from you.'" *The New York Times* agreed, saying, "The idea of the theft itself has possibilities, with the gang masterminded by an old hand, Edward G. Robinson, as an art authority.... [He] plays it cool and casual, wisely, and his hoodlums rough it up with Keystone Kops subtlety."

New York Drama Critics Circle Award
Broadway productions of Arthur Miller's *All My Sons* and Sidney Kingsley's *Darkness at Noon* won the New York Drama Critics Circle Awards in 1946–47 and 1950–51, respectively. Edward G. Robinson played in the film version of the former and was in the national tour of the latter. The awards were begun in 1935.

Newman, Paul (1925–) made two films with Edward G. Robinson — *The Prize* and *The Outrage*. They also narrate the short film *All About People*. Newman won the best actor Oscar for *The Color of Money* and received seven other nominations: *Cat on a Hot Tin Roof, The Hustler, Hud, Cool Hand Luke, Absence of Malice, The Verdict,* and *Nobody's Fool.* He was on Broadway in *Picnic*; other pictures include *Rachel, Rachel* (as director), *Somebody Up There Likes Me, Harper, Butch Cassidy and the Sundance Kid, The Sting,* and *Message in a Bottle.*

Newspapers A staple of the 1930s dramas was the newspaper headline swirling into view to announce events in the story, especially with such headlines as "War Declared!" or "Mobster Convicted." The technique, using dozens of headlines, was used to chronicle plot developments in *Confessions of a Nazi Spy,* including news of the war in Europe, and finally "Nazi Spies Convicted."

The swirling headlines are featured also in *The Last Gangster, Kid Galahad, Dr. Ehrlich's Magic Bullet, Destroyer,* and *Brother Orchid,* among others; and, naturally, newspapers are props in many films and plays.

Newspaper publication is featured in *Five Star Final,* wherein Robinson, as editor Randall, dredges up a twenty-year-old murder case to boost circulation; in *Unholy Partners,* as Robinson, returning from World War I, has an idea for a new kind of paper and enlists the help of gangster Edward Arnold for financing; in *Barbary Coast,* where editor Marcus Aurelius Cobb (Frank Craven) starts a newspaper, *The Clarion,* exposing San Francisco's corruption, only to be stopped by Robinson, who owns the town. Finally, *A Dispatch from Reuter's,* while not about the newspaper business, tells the story of the founding of the news gathering agency in Europe that still bears the Reuter's name today.

Edward G. Robinson's most famous connection to newspapers is his starring role as Steve Wilson, editor of *The Illustrated Press,* on radio's *Big Town* for four years.

Newsreels see **Film Within a Film**

Niarchos, Stavros (1909–96) was a Greek shipping tycoon, owner of one of the largest privately held tanker fleets in the world, begun in 1939. He conducted business from many offices around the world, including his luxury yacht *The Creole,* which sailed the Mediterranean. Following Edward G. Robinson's divorce from Gladys Lloyd, Niarchos purchased their joint art collection for $3,125,000 in 1957. "I want the paintings to bring me joy," he said. Robinson was frustrated in his attempts to buy back any of the 58 paintings and ultimately never met Niarchos. He further lamented the potential damage of salt air to the oil canvases housed on the yacht. Niarchos, married five times, became brother-in-law to rival shipping magnate Aristotle Onassis, and later, grandson to Henry Ford.

Nielsen, Leslie (1926–) played John Bracken, film producer, on TV's *Bracken's World.* Edward G. Robinson was guest star in an episode called "The Mary Tree" and played a cameo as himself in "Panic." Nielson played serious roles—*Tammy and the Bachelor, The Poseidon Adventure*—but more recently he has done comic turns in *The Naked Gun, Airplane,* and *Dracula—Dead and Loving It.*

The Night Before Christmas see ***Larceny, Inc.***

Night Gallery see **"The Messiah on Mott Street"**

Night Has a Thousand Eyes (Film, 1948) This was Edward G. Robinson's third film in 1948, and, as in the other two—*Key Largo* and *All My Sons*—he was dead of a gunshot wound at the fadeout. The *New York Times* critic described the film as "unadulterated hokum … done in somber fashion with Edward G. Robinson playing the gent as a figure of tragic proportions." Robinson apparently agreed, using the first two words of the review in his memoirs as his comment on the film.

John Triton once had a mental telepathy vaudeville act with his fiancée, Jenny, and Whitney Courtland. However, he started having visions of the future, which disrupted the act. Sometimes he was able to be of help through the visions, but always, whether he intervened or not, they came true. He left his partners one night when a vision of Jenny's death in childbirth came to him. And so it was Courtland, not John, who married Jenny and became wealthy on a tip from John on an oil deal. Then their daughter, Jean, was born, and Jenny died. John now reenters the Courtlands' lives years later to warn against an air disaster he has "seen" that will kill Whitney Courtland. But the warning comes too late. John foresees Jean's death. The police and her fiancée, Elliott Carson, are skeptical. A series of John's visions—flowers being stepped on, the feet of a lion, a gun misfiring—all come to pass. Then a corporate partner is discovered as the would-be killer. The only vision that failed to come true was Jean's death "under the stars," because in saving her life, John gave up his own.

Producer, Endre Bohem; director, John Farrow; screenplay, Barre Lyndon, Jonathan Latimer; based on the novel by Cornell Woolrich; music, Victor Young; art directors, Hans Dreier, Franz Bachelin; set, Sam Comer, Ray Moyer; camera, John F. Seitz; process photography, Farciot Edouart; sound, Gene Garvin, Hugo Grenzbach; costumes, Edith Head; script supervisor, Irving Cooper; editor, Eda Warren; makeup, Wally Westmore; assistant director, William Coleman; cast: Edward G. Robinson (John Triton), Gail Russell (Jean Courtland), John Lund (Elliott Carson), William Demarest (Lt. Shawn), Virginia Bruce (Jenny), Jerome Cowan (Whitney Courtland), Richard Webb (Peter Vinson), Onslow Stevenson (Dr. Walters), John Alexander (Mr. Gilman), Roman Bohnen (Melville Weston), Luis Van Rooten (Mr. Myers), Henry Guttman (Butler), Mary Adams (Miss Hendricks), Philip Van Zandt (Chauffeur), Douglas Spencer (Dr. Ramsdell), Jean King (Edna, the maid), Dorothy Abbott (2nd maid), Bob Stephenson (Bertelli), William Haade (Gowan), Stuart Holmes (Scientist), Jean Wong, Anna Tom (Chinese women), Weaver Levy (Chinese man), Atarne Wong (Waiter), Jane Crowley (Woman at newsstand), Joey Ray (Announcer), Eleanor Vogel (Scrubwoman), Minerva Urecal (Italian woman), Renee Randall, Marilyn Gray, Betty Hannon (Secretaries), Lester Dorr (Mr. Byers), Violet Goulet, Major Sam Harris (Deb's parents), Margaret Field (Agnes), John Sheehan (Doorman), James Davies (Jailer), Harland Tucker (Husband of frantic woman), Harry Allen, Gladys Blake, Billy Burt, Helen Chapman, Walter Cook, Jim Drum, Jimmie Dundee, Edward Earle, Julia Faye, Antonio Filauri, Len Hendry, Jerry James, Lyle Latell, Frances Morris, George Nokes, Rae Patterson, Albert Pollet, Audrey Saunders, Raymond Saunders, Russell Saunders, Marie Thomas, Regina Wallace, Ruth Roman; Paramount; 80 minutes; October 1948

"The film's strong points are Farrow's stylish direction and Robinson's fine performance as a sort of Woolrich surrogate," said Francis M. Nevins, Jr., in *Cornell Woolrich: First You Dream, Then You Die.* Leonard Maltin, in *TV Movies*, noted that despite a sometimes corny script, *Night Has a Thousand Eyes* was an "intriguing story of a magician who has uncanny power to predict the future."

"The build-up in the earlier part is superb of its kind, and Robinson's acting, even under the stars, is a pleasure to note," wrote Gordon Gow in *Suspense in the Cinema,* noting his "splendidly controlled expressions of interior disquiet. A big personality actor, he knew how to rein in the histrionics; and with such a face as his, the minimal expression in front of the camera was enough to register strongly in the magnified image that would reach the screen."

The Commonweal said simply, "Edward G. Robinson is excellent," while *The New York Herald-Tribune* admitted that, "Robinson labors diligently and sometimes effectively in the part of the crystal ball gazer."

See **John Seitz**.

"Night Has a Thousand Eyes" (Radio, 1949) Producer, Howard Wiley; director, Bill Cairn; adaptation, Milton Geiger; composer/bconductor, Henry Russell; cast: Edward G. Robinson, Paul Frees, William Demarest, Frank Barton (announcer); *Screen Director's Playhouse*; NBC; February 27, 1949; 30 minutes

The Night Lodging (Theater, 1919, 1920) This play was Edward G. Robinson's second venture with producer Arthur Hopkins. Written in 1902 and presented by the Moscow Art Theatre, it has become a classic of Russian literature under its better known title *The Lower Depths*. Burns Mantle's *Best Plays of 1919–1920* called it "a series of detached but arresting incidents in the lives of Russia's submerged poor."

Alexander Bakshy, a translator of the play, observes that, "three of the characters (the Baron, Satin, and Peppel) are former jailbirds, and Luka ... is one of them, too, though obviously reformed. Three other characters ... Klestch, and the two longshoremen, the Tartar and the Goiter, typify the conscientious, upright working man.... But it is Satin, Luka, and Peppel through whom the moral message of the play is most conveyed."—*Masters of Modern Drama*, by Haskell M. Block and Robert G. Shedd. Robinson played the role of Satin (a role undertaken by no less than Stanislavsky during a revival in Moscow in 1923).

"The play gave only a few matinee performances, then closed, but necessity saw it revived later in the season for a short run," according to Gerald Bordman, *American Theatre: A Chronicle of Comedy and Drama, 1914–1930*. (When it reopened in the spring of 1920, Richard Dix, Phoebe Hunt, and Clyde North had joined Robinson and the company.)

A drama in four acts; producer, Arthur Hopkins; playwright, Maxim Gorky; director, William Harris, Jr.; cast: Pauline Lord (Nastya), Edward G. Robinson (Konstantin Satin), E. J. Ballantine (Alyoshka), Alan Dinehart (Vassily Peppel), Rosalind Ivan (Anna) Gilda Varesi (Vassilissa Karpovna Kostylyova), Hans Robert (Andrey Dmitrich Kletsch), Alexis M. Polianov (Assan, the Tartar), William E. Hallman (Mikhail Ivanovich Kostylyov), Eva MacDonald (Natasha), Charles Kennedy (Abram Ivanych Medvedev), Cecil Yapp (Bubnov), Lillian Kingsbury (Kvashnya), W. H. Thompson (Luka), Edwin Nicander (The Actor), Louis Alter (Krivoy Zob, the Goiter), Cecil Clovelly (The Baron); opened at the Plymouth Theatre, New York; December 22, 1919

"The present company, assembled by William Harris, Jr., is quite hopelessly handicapped, so that only Edward G. Robinson flares up in one scene of drink befuddled oratory," said *The New York Times*. And yet Alexander Woollcott, writing in the *Times*, expanded on that praise, mentioning the play's "extraordinary vitality ... a thoughtful, suggestive, enriching, exultant play, superbly acted ... Gilda Varesi, who has a role full of passion, and jealousy, and hate, and who reveals once more that something of the real flame is in her. A little of it is in Edward Robinson, too. You have only to see his performance as Satin to realize it and to realize, too, how all-compensating is the real fire. Here is a young actor without an atom of what is feebly called 'personal distinction.' His speech ... is what Mrs. Sanders used to call 'barbarous.' He takes the keynote speech of the play where Satin cries out, 'What is truth? Human beings—that's the truth,' and devastates it by saying, 'youman beans'...."

Robinson was shocked and embarrassed by Woollcott's comments. "[He] stood me on ear ... devastated me, and I don't think I've ever said 'youman beans' since," he declared in *All My Yesterdays*. But there had been more to Woollcott's review: "...Yet he might befoul a hundred speeches and still be worth his weight in gold. For the meaning of the role is in his mind and the glow and spirit of it comes forth from him. It is just such playing as his that answers best all the pishposh written in the critiques of the puppet school."

Other reviews were just as glowing. *The New York Herald-Tribune* said, "Robinson carried off a scene in the last act with a true spirit of fire." Said *The Nation*, "The players, accustomed to the false and the flashy, literally surpass themselves.... Mr. Edward G. Robinson as Satin sulks and smoulders until the word of liberation comes to him and then rises to his great moment with a fervor not less convincing for its almost lyrical touch." Finally, *The New Republic* added, "It is a strong, firm, spacious, capable performance resting ... on a general level of excellence.... Much could be said [of the actors] ... particularly Mr. E. G. Robinson as the devil-may-care."

The Night Ride (Film, 1930) "There was the part of a Capone-like gangster in the picture [*The Night Ride*]," noted Joseph

Schildkraut in his autobiography *My Father and I,* "and I suggested my good friend and former classmate at the American Academy of Dramatic Arts, Edward G. Robinson, for the role. Carl Laemmle, Jr., had never heard of him, and it took all of my persuasion to make Universal engage him. Robinson was magnificent, perfectly cast, and he played me right off the screen, as the saying goes."

Producer, Carl Laemmle, Jr.; director, John S. Robertson; based on a story by Henry LaCossitt; screenplay, Edward T. Lowe, Jr.; dialogue, Tom Reed, Lowe; titles, Charles Logue; camera, Alvin Wyckhoff; sound, C. Roy Hunter; editors, Milton Carruth, A. Ross; cast: Joseph Schildkraut (Joe Rooker), Barbara Kent (Ruth Kearns), Edward G. Robinson (Tony Garotta), Harry Stubbs (Bob O'Leary), DeWitt Jennings (Captain O'Donnell), Ralph Welles (Blondie), Hal Price (Mac), George Ovey (Ed); Universal; 80 minutes (6 reels); 1930

On his wedding night, reporter Joe Rooker is called away to cover a bank robbery and murder. He suspects gangster Tony Garotta and writes a story for his paper implicating him. Garotta kidnaps Joe, intending to kill him. He tells Joe that his bride and mother-in-law were killed in a bombing. Garotta is caught in a police trap. Joe gets the exclusive story and learns that his family is safe.

The New York Times called the film "a thrilling tale ... Edward G. Robinson is excellent." *The Commonweal* liked the actor better than the picture: "The impeccable work of Mr. Robinson is the only redeeming feature." And finally, *Variety* said, "Edward G. Robinson is a finished and polished actor, ideal for the character he creates."

Nightmare (Film, 1956) This picture was "a remake of [Maxwell] Shane's 1947 adaptation of [Cornell] Woolrich's story, entitled *Fear in the Night*. The remake benefits from superior acting, particularly by [Kevin] McCarthy, a bigger budget, and inventive jazz score, and the use of New Orleans locations. The photography is this film, from the opening credits done in wax over McCarthy's eyes illuminated by candle, is markedly more expressionistic and is aptly reinforced by the score. The use of McCarthy's narration, the exotic bayous and strange nocturnal odyssey down Bourbon Street, combine with the mutated version of the jazz piece and contribute to the film's oneiristic tone."—Robert Porfirio, *Film Noir*

A Pine/Thomas/Shane production; producers, William Thomas, Howard Pine; director, Maxwell Shane; based on a novel by Cornell Woolrich [William Irish]; screenplay, Shane; art director, Frank Sylos; set, Edward Boyle; special effects, Howard A. Anderson; music, Herschel Burke Gilbert; song, Gilbert, Doris Houck, Dick Sherman; vocal and instrumental arrangements, Billy May; sound, Jack Solomon, Roger Heman, Paul Wolff; camera, Joseph Biroc; wardrobe, Fay Moore, Frank Beetson; hairstyles, Myrl Stoltz; makeup, Norman Pringle; editor, George Gittens; assistant director, Robert Justman; cast: Edward G. Robinson (Rene), Kevin McCarthy (Stan Grayson), Connie Russell (Gina), Virginia Christine (Sue), Rhys Williams (Torrence), Gage Clarke (Belnap), Barry Atwater (Warner), Marian Carr (Madge), Billy May (Louie Simes) and his Orchestra, Meade "Lux" Lewis; United Artists; 89 minutes; May 1956

Stan Grayson, a New Orleans jazz musician, awakens from a nightmare in a cold sweat. He dreamed he killed a man in a strange mirrored closet. Unnerved by the presence of a strange key and a button and bruises on his neck where the man had tried to strangle him, he is also haunted by the strains of eerie, unidentifiable music. He goes to Rene, his brother-in-law, a police inspector. Rene is skeptical. He suggests that Stan relax and go with him and his wife, Sue, and Stan's singer girlfriend, Gina, on a picnic. Caught in a sudden cloudburst, they retreat to the car. Stan directs them to shelter at an old mansion but is powerless to explain how he knows all about the house. Discovery of bloodstains in a mirrored closet upstairs convinces Rene that Stan is involved in more than a dream. The police interrupt them but soon are telling Rene and Stan about an unsolved murder. Rene gets tough with Stan, demanding to know the truth, and again Stan is helpless. Back at his hotel he is about to jump from the window ledge. Rene gets to him just in time and, accepting his piecemeal story, begins his own investigation. He questions Stan about a man down the hall whose oddly pushy behavior Stan mentions. After returning to the mansion, Rene deduces that its owner, a psychiatrist named Belnap, hypnotized Stan into killing his wife's lover. Stan identifies a portrait of Belnap as the man at the hotel. Rene has Stan confront Belnap and be hypnotized again in order to prove that it could be done. Belnap hypnotizes Stan and suggests he drown himself, but Rene rescues him. Belnap is shot trying to escape. Stan returns to play the trumpet in his jazz band, with Gina singing.

Reviews for *Nightmare* were mixed. "Mr. Robinson does the best he can, as usual, with his lean material," said *The New York Herald-Tribune*, "but the fact is good acting does little more than remind one of the waste." Leslie Halliwell's *Film Guide* agreed, calling the film a "lethargic remake of the ingenious *Fear in the Night*. Watchable."

A more upbeat review came from *Box Office* magazine: "Slick, spine-tingling mystery. Goose-pimply screenplay. Suspense and excitement; competent cast. Timely, engrossing." And *The New York Times* called it "a modest melodrama with some crooked turns, but [with] neat performances by Messrs. Robinson and McCarthy and Connie Russell and Virginia Christine."

Niven, David (1909–83) had his first film role (a bit) in *Barbary Coast* as a sailor thrown out of a saloon. His other films include *Wuthering Heights, The Bishop's Wife, Around the World in Eighty Days,* and *The Pink Panther*. He won an Academy Award for *Separate Tables*.

Nolan, Jeanette (1911–98), married to character actor John McIntire, appeared with him and Edward G. Robinson in the title role in the radio drama *My Wife Geraldine*. Her films include *Macbeth, The Happy Time, The Big Heat, The Great Impostor,* and *The Man Who Shot Liberty Valance*.

Nolan, Mary (1905–48), a former Ziegfeld girl, played roles in German films from 1925, then returned to America to appear in *West of Zanzibar, Shanghai Lady, X Marks the Spot,* and, opposite Edward G. Robinson, *Outside the Law*.

Nugent, Elliott (1899–1980), actor, director, writer, collaborated with James Thurber and starred in *The Male Animal* on Broadway, and adapted it for the screen. He also wrote *The Poor Nut* and *Father's Day,* directed *The Mouthpiece, Enter Madame,* and *The Cat and the Canary,* and acted onscreen with Edward G. Robinson in *Thunder in the City*.

Number 37 (Theater, 1913) The only Yiddish play Edward G. Robinson appeared in was *Number 37*, in which the lead role was played by Joseph Schildkraut's father. Cast: Rudolph Schildkraut, Edward G. Robinson; West End Theatre, New York; 1913

Numbers Numbers in the titles of Edward G. Robinson's films, plays, television and radio appearances include *One Touch of Nature, First Is Last, The Man with Two Faces, Two Seconds, Two Weeks in Another Town, Double Indemnity, Five Star Final, Robin and the 7 Hoods, Seven Thieves, A Boy Ten Feet Tall, The Ten Commandments, Number 37, Document A/777, Night Has a Thousand Eyes,* and *The $64,000 Challenge*.

O'Brien, Margaret (1937–) received a special Oscar in 1944 as an outstanding child actress. She appeared in *Journey for Margaret, Thousands Cheer, Jane Eyre, The Canterville Ghost, Meet Me in St. Louis, Our Vines Have Tender Grapes* (as Edward G. Robinson's daughter, Selma), *The Secret Garden,* and *Heller in Pink Tights*.

O'Brien, Pat (1899–1983) appeared with Edward G. Robinson on Broadway in *Henry, Behave,* on the radio drama *Ship Forever Sailing,* and in the TV specials *Operation Entertainment* and *The Movie Crazy Years;* they never made a film together. O'Brien's films include *The Front Page, Garden of the Moon* (a

Busby Berkeley musical in a role for which Robinson was considered!), *'Til We Meet Again*, *Knute Rockne — All American* (title role), *The Last Hurrah*, *Some Like It Hot*, and *Ragtime*.

Occupations Doubtless the gangster was Edward G. Robinson's most common occupation among the characters he played. He frequently played policemen and investigators, lawyers, doctors, and businessmen, as well as such varied character types as gamblers, blue collar workers, farmers, military men, politicians, clerks, and, of course, actors. Titles of his films, plays, and television shows are listed below under various professions (listed alphabetically).

Actor (or some other show business type): *The Man with Two Faces*, *Actors and Sin*, *The Prize*, and, of course, productions in which he appeared as himself: *Pepe*, *It's a Great Feeling*, TV's "Batman's Satisfaction," "Panic," and *The Lucy Show* (actors); *Night Has a Thousand Eyes*, (mentalist); *Samson and Delilah*, *The Chief Thing* (stage directors); *My Geisha*, *Two Weeks in Another Town*, and *Pepe* (film executives); Author: *The Mary Tree*; Banker: *House of Strangers*; Barber: *Smart Money*, *House of Strangers*; Baseball trainer: *Big Leaguer*; Beer baron: *The Little Giant*, *A Slight Case of Murder*; Clerk: *The Whole Town's Talking*, *Mr. Winkle Goes to War*, *Scarlet Street*; Construction worker: *Two Seconds*; Detective, investigator, or policeman: *A Royal Fandango*, *Bullets or Ballots*, *Confessions of a Nazi Spy*, *Double Indemnity*, *The Stranger*, *Vice Squad*, *A Bullet for Joey*, *Nightmare*, *Peking Blonde*; Editor or news gatherer: *Five Star Final*, *Unholy Partners*, *A Dispatch from Reuter's*, *Big Town*; Educator: *The Woman in the Window*, *I Am the Law*, *Seven Thieves*, *Grand Slam*; Electric linesman: *Manpower*; Farmer or rancher: *A Lady to Love*, *Our Vines Have Tender Grapes*, *The Red House*, *The Violent Men*, "Heritage," *Good Neighbor Sam*; Fisherman or sea captain: *Tiger Shark*, *The Sea Wolf*, *Who Has Seen the Wind?*, *Tampico*, *Destroyer*; Gambler: *The Kibitzer*, *Smart Money*, *Dark Hazard*, *The Cincinnati Kid*; Gangster: *The Racket*, *The Hole in the Wall*, *The Night Ride*, *Outside the Law*, *East Is West*, *The Widow from Chicago*, *Little Caesar*, *The Hatchet Man* (Chinese Tong leader), *The Little Giant* (beer baron), *The Whole Town's Talking*, *Barbary Coast*, *Kid Galahad* (fight manager), *The Last Gangster*, *A Slight Case of Murder* (beer baron), *Brother Orchid*, *Larceny, Inc.*, *Key Largo*, "A Set of Values," *Black Tuesday*, *Hell on Frisco Bay*, "The Legend of Jim Riva," *Robin and the 7 Hoods*, *Operation San Pietro*, *The Biggest Bundle of Them All*, *Never a Dull Moment*; Innkeeper: *The Man of Destiny*; Lawyer: *Ned McCobb's Daughter*, *Tales of Manhattan*, *Flesh and Fantasy*, *Tight Spot*, *Illegal*, *The Case of Kenny Jason*, *The Devil and Daniel Webster*; Manufacturer: *All My Sons*, *Middle of the Night*, "A Good Name"; Meat packer: *I Loved a Woman*; Merchant: *Silver Dollar*, *A Hole in the Head*, *Mr. Samuel*, *The Kibitzer*; Military: *Under Fire*, *Juarez and Maximilian*, *Tampico*, *Destroyer*, *Mr. Winkle Goes to War*, *Journey Together*, *Darkness at Noon*; Oil fire fighter: *Blackmail*; Overseer: *The Ten Commandments*; Physician: *The Amazing Dr. Clitterhouse*, *Dr. Ehrlich's Magic Bullet*, *U.M.C.*; Piano seller: *Song of Norway*; Politician or promoter: *Silver Dollar*, *Thunder in the City*, *Operation X*, *Mad Checkmate*; Prisoner: *Larceny, Inc.*, *Under Sentence*, *The Last Gangster*, *Black Tuesday*, "The Legend of Jim Riva"; Prospector: *Mackenna's Gold*, *A Boy Ten Feet Tall* (diamond smuggler); Realtor: *Henry, Behave*; Researcher: *The Glass Web*, *Soylent Green*; Retired: *The Old Man Who Cried Wolf*, "The Messiah on Mott Street"; Royalty: *The Firebrand*, *Androcles and the Lion*; Salesman: "The Drop-Out"; Scientist: *Dr. Ehrlich's Magic Bullet*, *Seven Thieves*; Spy: "Epitaph for a Spy," *Darkness at Noon*.

O'Connor, Tim (1925–) played the part of Jabez Stone in the TV special *The Devil and Daniel Webster*, in which Edward G. Robinson starred as Webster. He also has roles in *Incident in San Francisco*, *Across 110th Street*, *Buck Rogers in the 25th Century*, and *Black Jack*.

O'Herlihy, Dan (1919–) started with Dublin's Abbey Players. Nominated for an Oscar for *The Adventures of Robinson Crusoe*, he was in *Macbeth*, *The Desert Fox*, *Imitation* *of Life, Fail Safe, MacArthur, Robocop,* and *The Last Starfighter* (as Grig, the lizard). He narrated *Actors and Sin*, in which he played Edward G. Robinson's son-in-law, a playwright.

The Old Man Who Cried Wolf (Television, 1970) Edward G. Robinson made one major dramatic television appearance that was not on a special program or one that featured him as a guest star. It was *The Old Man Who Cried Wolf,* an ABC-TV *Movie of the Week.* Robinson commented at the time, "I decided to make the big plunge, do a 'Movie of the Week,' to see if I could stand the gaff. Well, we worked on it for ten days, and when I say 'work,' I mean it. We worked days and nights, long hours. It was a little too much, I thought, but we got it done." He said later, "Playing in *The Old Man Who Cried Wolf* was a most rewarding experience, one which I thoroughly enjoyed.... I'm happy the film was so well received."

Reviews for *The Old Man Who Cried Wolf* were excellent. "Robinson's performance is strong and moving," said *The Hollywood Reporter*. James Robert Parish and Alvin H. Marill, in *The Cinema of Edward G. Robinson,* championed his work, saying he "acted circles around the rest of the cast." And finally, "Robinson's articulate, impressive performance at communicating fear on one hand and determination to see justice done on the other provided a fresh and extremely fascinating look for an oft-told suspense tale," wrote Pete Rahn in the *St. Louis Globe Democrat.* "Robinson's splendid work in that play will very likely put him in the running for an Emmy award." Unfortunately, there was no nomination.

The television project reunited Edward G. Robinson with several performers — Diane Baker from *The Prize,* Martin Balsam from *Middle of the Night,* and, most happily, Sam Jaffe, his lifelong friend, who played such a role in the film. Ironically, two actresses who played Robinson's loving wives in other projects were also in the film — Virginia Christine as a no-nonsense nurse, and Naomi Stevens as a witness who thinks his character is crazy.

A retired furniture maker, Emile Pulska, visits Abe Stillman in his small store and witnesses his murder by Frank Jones, a gangster to whom Abe owes money. Knocked unconscious at the time, Emile is later unable to convince the police that he saw the murder. Emile seeks out witnesses — Louis, a boy who had been in the store, and Mrs. Raspili, but they will not corroborate his story. Frank Jones appears and warns Emile to cease being involved. Stanley and Peggy, Emile's son and daughter-in-law, fearing the onset of senility when Emile's story seems far-fetched, reluctantly place Emile under the observation of Dr. Morheim at a hospital. Emile, determined to prove the truth of what he saw, flees and encounters detectives, his city councilman, and, eventually, Jones, who shoots him. He dies in Stanley's arms, having finally proved he was right.

Executive producer, Aaron Spelling; producer, director, Walter Grauman; teleplay, Luther Davis; story, Arthur Horwitt; assistant, Edward G. Robinson, Jr.; camera, Arch R. Dalzell; music, Robert Drasnin; editor, Art Seid; assistant director, Max Stein; art director, Paul Sylos; cast: Edward G. Robinson (Emile Pulska), Martin Balsam (Stanley), Diane Baker (Peggy), Percy Rodrigues (Frank Jones), Ruth Roman (Lois), Ed Asner (Dr. Morheim), Martin E. Brooks (Hudson Ewing), Paul Picerni (Detective Green), Sam Jaffe (Abe Stillman), Robert Yuro (Detective Seroly), Bill Elliott (Carl), James A. Watson (Leon), Naomi Stevens (Mrs. Raspili), Virginia Christine (Miss Cummings), Jay C. Flippen (Pawnbroker), Jason Wingreen (Arthur), Pepe Brown (Louie); *ABC Movie of the Week*; 90 minutes; ABC-TV; October 13, 1970

Olivier, Sir Laurence (1907–89), actor and director, was named as possible presenter of the honorary Academy Award to Edward G. Robinson when it was hoped that he would lived to attend the ceremonies. Both actors were heard on the radio drama *Document A/777.* Olivier won an Oscar for *Hamlet* and received nominations for *Wuthering Heights, Rebecca, Henry V, Richard III, The Entertainer, Othello, Sleuth,* and *Marathon Man.* He was in

Pride and Prejudice, Carrie, Spartacus, and *Clash of the Titans* on the screen, and in *Private Lives, Uncle Vanya,* and *Becket,* among others, on Broadway.

Olsen, Moroni (1889–1954) was onscreen with Edward G. Robinson in *The Last Gangster* and *I Am the Law*. He was also in *The Three Musketeers, Annie Oakley, Seven Keys to Baldpate, Plough and the Stars, The Glass Key, Life with Father, Notorious, Samson and Delilah,* and *Father of the Bride.*

One Touch of Nature (Theater, 1906) This production, according to Edward G. Robinson's autobiography *All My Yesterdays,* was his first experience on the stage, at the age of thirteen. He had a mad crush on Sadie Bodner, a young lady, also thirteen, who played his daughter. Cast: Sadie Bodner, Emanuel Goldenberg (Edward G. Robinson); produced by the University Settlement House, New York; 1906

O'Neil, Barbara (1909–80) played Edward G. Robinson's wife in *I Am the Law.* She received an Oscar nomination as the Duchess De Praslin in *All This and Heaven Too.* Her other films include *Stella Dallas, Tower of London, Gone with the Wind* (as Scarlett O'Hara's mother), *The Secret Beyond the Door, I Remember Mama,* and *The Nun's Story.*

O'Neill, Henry (1891–1961) played in six films with Edward G. Robinson — as a private detective in *I Loved a Woman*; a police inspector in *The Man with Two Faces*; Bryant, a crusading editor in *Bullets or Ballots*; the trial judge in *The Amazing Dr. Clitterhouse*; the prosecutor in *Confessions of a Nazi Spy*; and Dr. Lentz in *Dr. Ehrlich's Magic Bullet.* Other films: *The Story of Louis Pasteur, The Life of Emile Zola, A Guy Named Joe, Anchors Aweigh,* and *The Wings of Eagles.*

"Only Yesterday" (Radio, 1945) Edward G. Robinson hosted this episode of *Lux Radio Theatre* and, according to *Radio Yesteryear,* "spoke briefly about the death of President Roosevelt prior to introducing the story, which had to do with a spurned wife during the time of the stock market crash."

Director, Fred MacKaye; adaptation, George Wells; music director, Louis Silvers; sound, Charlie Forsyth; cast: Ida Lupino, Robert Young, Edward Marr, Howard McNear, Lois Corbett, Lurene Tuttle, Tommy Cook, Charles Seel, Norman Field, Ferdinand Munier, Doris Singleton, Regina Wallace, Janet Scott, Truda Marson, Julie Bannon, Betty Jean Hainey, Ann Tobin, Virginia Gregg, Edward G. Robinson (host); John Milton Kennedy (announcer); *Lux Radio Theatre*; CBS; April 16, 1945

Operation Entertainment (Television, 1952) This special program was one of Edward G. Robinson's earliest television appearances.

Producers, Robert Welch, William Kayden; director, William Bennington; music, Von Dexter, Robert Armbruster; writer, Glenn Wheaton; cast: Bell Sisters, Ray Bolger, Jack Carson, Jerry Colonna, Eddie Fisher, Connie Haines, Jack Haley, William Holden, Bob Hope, Danny Kaye, George Meany, Terry Moore, Pat O'Brien, Tyrone Power, Ronald Reagan, Debbie Reynolds, Gen. Matthew B. Ridgeway, Edward G. Robinson, Tony Romano, Dinah Shore, Danny Thomas, Patti Thomas, Audrey Totter, Keenan Wynn; NBC-TV, 60 minutes; September 20; 1954

Operation San Pietro (Film, 1968) Capitalizing on his nearly forty years as a cinema icon, the producers of *Operation San Pietro* cast Edward G. Robinson as Joe Ventura, a wealthy gangster living in Europe. Unfortunately, the story was of questionable taste, dealing with the theft of Michaelangelo's *Pietà* from the Vatican. Released in Europe, *Operation San Pietro* was sold directly to television in the United States.

Motion Picture Guide called *Operation San Pietro* "a very weak comedy," adding that, "Robinson made several films in Europe during the mid–1960s, none of them particularly memorable, but this was surely one of the worst."

Robinson commented, "I have no idea whatever happened to *Peking Blonde* and

Operation San Pietro. Perhaps they were not considered worthy enough for an American release. I was not particularly pleased with either story, and accepted the engagements as a matter of therapy. They kept me occupied after a recent illness." This, perhaps, was reason enough for Robinson to appear in such films. However, Rome and other European locations also gave him the opportunity also to travel and see the great museums.

A co-production of Ultra Film (Rome)/Marianne Productions (Paris)/Roxy Films (Munich); Producer, Turo Vasile; director, Lucio Fulci; screenplay, Ennio De Concini, Adriano Baracco, Roberto Gianviti, Paul Hengge, Fulci; assistant director, Francesco Massaro; music, Ward Swingle, Armando Trovaioli; art director, Giorgio Giovannini; camera, Erico Menczer, Alfio Contini; cast: Lando Buzzanca (Napoleon), Edward G. Robinson (Joe Ventura), Heinz Ruhmann (Cardinal Braun), Jean-Claude Brialy (Cajella), Pinuccio Ardia (Baron), Dante Maggio (Captain), Ugo Fancareggi (Agonia), Uta Levka (Samantha), Marie-Christine Barclay (Marisa), Antonella Delle Porte (Cesira); Wolfgang Kieling (Poulain), Herbert Fux (Targout) Jed Curtis (Courier), Giovanni Ivan Scratuglia; Paramount; Eastman Color; 96 (or 88) minutes 1968; alternate titles: *Operazione St. Peter's, Die Abenteure des Kardinal Braun*.

Four thieves steal Michaelangelo's *Pietà* from the Vatican but realize they have no fence for the statue and no way of getting rid of it. Joe Ventura, a gangster, buys the *Pietà* for $40 and a plate of spaghetti. Joe plans to store the statue on a boat offshore in international waters and eventually sell it back to the church. Meanwhile, hoping to minimize adverse publicity, the Vatican has local priests track Joe down. At the dock, Cardinal Braun leads an attack on the boat. The crew is quickly disarmed, the gangsters are tossed overboard, and Michaelangelo's masterpiece is saved.

Operation X (Film, 1950) Edward G. Robinson's political difficulties kept him from better film offers, and his struggles continued with his wife Gladys's ongoing mental condition. He went to Europe in 1949, where he starred in Gregory Ratoff's film *Operation X*, about a man obsessed with both his daughter and with world power. The film, also called *My Daughter Joy,* was not successful.

Despite generally unfavorable reviews for the picture, Robinson's performance was praised: "Robinson strides through the leading role in a suitable imitation of megalomania," said *The New York Herald-Tribune*; and "[he] gives the film's solitary rounded performance," according to *The New York Times*.

Producer, director, Gregory Ratoff; associate producer, Phil Brandon; screenplay, Robert Thoeren, William Rose; based on the novel *David Golder* by Irene Nemirowsky; set, Andre Andrejew; set dressing, Dario Simone; production manager, T. S. London Haynes; sound, Jack Drake; sound recording, H. C. Pearson, W. Salter; assistant director, Cliff Brandon; camera, Georges Perinal; camera operation, Denys Coop; Italian sequences filmed by Andre Bac; music director, Dr. Hubert Clifford; music, R. Gallois-Montbrun; played by the London Symphony Orchestra; continuity, Maisie Kelly; makeup, U. P. Hutchinson; hairdresser, Joe Shear; editor, Raymond Poulton; cast: Edward G. Robinson (George Constantin), Peggy Cummins (Georgette), Richard Greene (Larry Boyd), Nora Swinburne (Ava Constantin), Finlay Currie (Sir Thomas McTavish), Gregory Ratoff (Marcos), Ronald Adam (Col. Fogarty), Walter Rilla (Andreas), James Robertson Justice (Prof. Karol), David Hutcheson (Ennix), Dod Nehan (Polato), Peter Illing (Sultan), Ronald Ward (Dr. Schindler), Roberto Villa (Prince Alzar), Harry Lane (Barboza); Columbia; 79 minutes; December 1950; a.k.a. *My Daughter Joy*.

George Constantin's ambition is to rule the world, and through his project, Operation X, his goal is in sight. To complete the project he must acquire a material controlled by a middle eastern sultan. Driven by memories of his impoverished childhood, Constantin has become brilliant and ruthless in his business dealings. As a measure of his character, he is prepared now to marry off his daughter,

Georgette, to the sultan's son in exchange for the needed substance. Next to power, Georgette is the one thing Constantin adores. Larry Boyd, a reporter, discovers Constantin's intent to exploit the world through Operation X and becomes involved with Georgette. Angered, Constantin will not let Boyd stay. Ava, Constantin's wife, intercedes on behalf of Georgette and her happiness. When Constantin will not yield, Ava reveals to him that Georgette is not his daughter. The shock all but destroys her husband and dooms Operation X.

The Orient Late in his career, Edward G. Robinson traveled to Japan to be in *My Geisha*, playing an American producer making a film of *Madama Butterfly*. Shirley MacLaine spent most of her time in the film made up as a geisha. Robinson played Asians in several projects. He was a Filipino named Hushmaru onstage in *The Pawn*. During World War II, for a Los Angeles stage pageant for the United China Relief Fund, he impersonated Chiang Kai-shek. He enacted Asian characters in *Outside the Law, East Is West*, and *The Hatchet Man*, and Asian characters are featured in *Barbary Coast, Dr. Ehrlich's Magic Bullet, Destroyer, Mr. Winkle Goes to War, My Geisha*, and *Peking Blonde*.

Osborne, Vivienne (1896–1961) played Edward G. Robinson's trampy wife in *Two Seconds*. She started in silent films in 1920 following a Broadway career as a dancer and leading lady. Her other films include *Life Begins, Luxury Liner, Wives Never Know, No More Ladies,* and *Dragonwyck*.

Oscars see **Academy of Motion Picture Arts and Sciences Awards**

Our American Scriptures (Radio, 1943) On Independence Day, two years before the end of World War II, a program of dramatic readings was broadcast on CBS-radio. The text consisted of the letters of Thomas Jefferson and the United States Constitution.

Cast: Edward G. Robinson (Reader); *U.S. Rubber Hour*; CBS-radio; July 4, 1943

Our Vines Have Tender Grapes (Film, 1945) Near the end of World War II, and in the middle of his newfound success in the gloomy and cynical world of *film noir*, Edward G. Robinson went to MGM to appear in a sentimental family film about farm life called *Our Vines Have Tender Grapes*. Cast decidedly against type as the gentle and practical Norwegian parents of young Margaret O'Brien, both Robinson and Agnes Moorehead were a little too old for their roles, but they both gave the film strength. The picture achieves a balance between sweetness and irony as it focuses on the elements of nature as backdrop to a young girl's growing up.

The New York Times led the praise for both the film and Robinson's performance: "A charming pastoral … tenderly sentimental vignettes of family life … sketched with loving care and understanding by a knowing group of players in this beautifully made MGM production…. Edward G. Robinson is stolid and loveable as Martinius, and in this role gives one of the finest performances of his long and varied career."

Both *The New Yorker* and *Variety* concurred. The former announced, "Robinson and Agnes Moorehead as his wife perform as well as they ever have in their careers." And *Variety* said, "Robinson gives a deft study of the farmer, an inarticulate, soil-bound man…. His groping for answers to his daughter's questions and drawing on parallels from farm life for explanations make empathetic points to the script's philosophy of simplicity."

Retrospective writing about the film was mixed. Foster Hirsch, in his *Edward G. Robinson: A Pyramid Illustrated History of the Movies*, said, "With a snarl or a mean look, Robinson subverts the goody-goody atmosphere…. [In] two especially revealing scenes, one in which Martinius snaps at his daughter, ordering her to go to bed, and another in which, gun in hand, he goes to shoot cattle who are trapped in a burning barn … the actor responds to his role with an enthusiasm that the material has not encouraged."

Leslie Halliwell dismissed the film in his *Film Guide* as an "unexceptional family picture produced in MGM's best manner." *TV Key*

Movie Guide was not as critical, calling *Our Vines Have Tender Grapes* a "warm, moving, well-played story…. It's a touching theme, and it's delivered with a minimum of corn." Of Robinson's performance, James Robert Parish said in *The Tough Guys,* "Behind a full moustache, and with a Scandinavian accent and soiled farmer clothes, he effectively portrayed a soft, warm character."

At Edward G. Robinson's death, a contributor to the monthly publication *Movie Maker* cited *Our Vines Have Tender Grapes* in a eulogy to the actor. "Robinson's performance is absolutely superb, and the tenderness he brings to the part could hardly be further removed from his tough hoodlum portrayals…. [He was] a very great professional." *Movie Maker,* April 1973

Producer, Robert Sisk; director, Roy Rowland; screenplay, Dalton Trumbo; based on the novel *For Our Vines Have Tender Grapes* by George Victor Martin; music Bronislau Kaper; art directors, Cedric Gibbons, Edward Carfagno; set, Edwin B. Willis, Hugh Hunt; sound, Douglas Shearer; camera, Robert Surtees; special effects, Danny Hall, A. Arnold Gillespie; costumes, Kay Carter, Irene; makeup, Jack Dawn; editor, Ralph E. Winters; assistant director, Horace Hough; cast: Edward G. Robinson (Martinius Jacobson), Margaret O'Brien (Selma Jacobson), James Craig (Nels Halverson), Agnes Moorehead (Bruna Jacobson), Frances Gifford (Viola Johnson), Jackie "Butch" Jenkins (Arnold Hanson), Morris Carnovsky (Bjorn Bjornson), Sara Haden (Mrs. Bjornson), Louis Jean Heydt (Mr. Faraasen), Francis Pierlot (Minister), Greta Granstedt (Mrs. Faraasen), Arthur Space (Peter Hanson), Arthur Hohl (Dvar Svenson), Elizabeth Russell (Kola Hanson), Dorothy Morris (Ingaborg Jensen), Charles Middleton (Kurt Jensen), Abigail Adams (School girl), Johnny Berkes (Driver), Rhoda Williams (Marguerite Larsen), George Lloyd (Farmer); MGM; 105 minutes; September 1945

Selma lives on a farm with her parents, Martinius and Bruna Jacobson, in a Norwegian community in Wisconsin. On the way home to supper, she and her cousin, Arnold Hanson, are given a lift by Nels Halverson, editor of the newspaper, and Viola Johnson, the new schoolteacher. Selma is given a newborn calf to care for. Martinius and Selma go to see Bjorn Bjornson's new barn, which has all the latest milking equipment and nameplates for each cow. Selma and Arnold fight one day over her new skates. Martinius punishes Selma for selfishness by giving her skates to Arnold and sending her to bed without supper. To ease his parental guilt, Bruna tells Martinius that a circus will pass through town at four a.m. He wakes his daughter, they go to meet the circus, and for a modest fee Selma gets a ride on an elephant. Arnold is left alone as Selma starts school. At Christmas Selma does a recitation at church, and the Jacobsons are joined by the Bjornsons, the Faraasens, Arnold, and the Hansons. Arnold returns Selma's skates. With the winter thaw, the children use a large metal bathtub from the barn to play boat in the back yard. Puddles on the farm lead to ponds and streams and ultimately the river. The children lose control of the tub in the raging waters, and townspeople race to the bridge to grab the tub before it passes under, and the children are saved. Later in the season there is a storm, and lightning strikes Bjornson's barn. The Jacobsons join the rest of the community to try to put out the fire, but it becomes necessary for Martinius to use his pistol to shoot the cattle. Mrs. Bjornson laments that they lost everything and had no insurance. It is now springtime. After church one Sunday, Nels announces that publication of the paper will be interrupted as he joins the army. He solicits the congregation for assistance for the Bjornsons, and the response is meager — just coins in the collection plate — until Selma offers her calf, Elizabeth. Others come forth with generous contributions of pigs, cows, hay, silage. The community spirit convinces Viola, who has fallen in love with Nels, to stay on as teacher. She will also be interim editor of the paper.

Oury, Gerard (1919–) acted in, wrote, and directed French films from 1947 and began in English-speaking features in 1953, including *The Journey* and *The Sword and the*

Rose. He plays Dr. Claude Marceau in *The Prize*, with Edward G. Robinson.

Ouspenskaya, Maria (1876–1949) plays Frau Speyer, a research benefactor, in *Dr. Ehrlich's Magic Bullet*. She came to the U.S. from Russia with the Moscow Art Theatre and began her Hollywood career in 1936. Her other films include *Dodsworth, The Rains Came, Waterloo Bridge, The Wolf Man, Kings Row,* and *A Kiss in the Dark*.

The Outrage (Film, 1964) In 1959 screenwriters Fay and Michael Kanin had successfully adapted Akiro Kurosawa's 1951 Japanese film classic *Rashomon* for the Broadway stage. It starred Claire Bloom and Rod Steiger as the wife of a Samurai officer and a bandit who rapes her. Five years later Michael Kanin transferred the story to film again, setting it in the American West. In *The Outrage* Claire Bloom recreated her stage role as the wife and Paul Newman became the bandit, now a Mexican, Juan Carrasco. Laurence Harvey played the husband (now a Southern Army colonel), and Edward G. Robinson was a con man. Newman has stated that *The Outrage* undoubtedly is his best acting work but that the film received poor distribution. In her book *Icons: Intimate Portraits*, Denise Worrell quotes him on *The Outrage*: "I liked that a lot."

The *St. Louis Post-Dispatch* offered praise. "This study of the nature of truth as presented in four widely disparate accounts of an alleged murder and rape by a bandit is still ironic, stimulating, and intriguing.... [Director Martin] Ritt has given the film conviction and enough realism for his purpose.... Robinson as the con man, Howard DaSilva as the prospector, and William Shatner as an itinerant preacher, offer succinct character work. The visual composition and photography are outstanding."

"Edward G. Robinson's portrayal of the bearded, seedy, cocky con artist is earthy and direct," said *The New York Times*. "In focusing cynically on 'truths' that remain a mystery at the film's end, Martin Ritt and his willing company have done nobly by the original in their provocative and engrossing drama." *The Commonweal* called *The Outrage* "an absorbing adult film, the kind that Hollywood makes too seldom."

Commenting in his *Edward G. Robinson: A Pyramid Illustrated History of the Movies:* Foster Hirsch sounded two notes typical of some of the film's reviews: "The attempt to transfer *Rashomon* to the American West was strained ... [yet, in] one of the strongest performances of his last decade ... Robinson performs with a sincerity that softens the sharp edges ... [and] delivers his speeches ... with a neat oratorical flourish."

"Robinson is delightful as the cruddy old con man," wrote the *Daily News*. "[He plays] a cynic who hears the various versions of the crimes and believes none." *Variety* said, "Robinson displays earthy humor." And *The New York Herald-Tribune* was simple and direct: "Robinson shows up as a *Little Caesar*ized hobo con man."

A Martin Ritt production; producer, A. Ronald Lubin; associate producer, Michael Kanin; director, Martin Ritt; screenplay, Kanin; based on the Japanese film *Rashomon* by Akiro Kurosawa; from stories by Ryunosuke Akutagawa and the play *Rashomon* by Fay and Michael Kanin; music, Alex North; art directors, George W. Davis, Tambi Larsen; set, Henry Grace, Robert R. Benton; second unit director, Lesley Selander; special effects, J. McMillan Johnson, Robert R. Hoag; costumes, Donfeld; makeup, William Tuttle; assistant director, Daniel J. McCauley; camera, James Wong Howe; editor, Frank Santillo; cast: Paul Newman (Juan Carrasco), Laurence Harvey (The Husband), Claire Bloom (The Wife), Edward G. Robinson (The Con Man), William Shatner (The Preacher), Howard DaSilva (The Prospector), Albert Salmi (Sheriff), Thomas Chalmers (Judge), Paul Fix (Old Indian); MGM; 97 minutes; October 1964

A disillusioned preacher meets a weary prospector at a tumbledown railway stop in the desert. He plans to leave town because of the outrage of recent days — a killing, rape, and apparent lies at a trial, which left everyone guessing. Their talk rouses a seedy old con man sleeping in a back room. Several versions of the story are retold: Juan Carrasco, a notorious bandit, encounters a lovely lady and her Southern army colonel husband traveling by buggy in the desert and detains them with talk of Aztec jewelry. He later ties the husband to a tree and rapes the wife. The husband dies from a stab wound after fighting to avenge his family honor. In the first version of the story, Carrasco's own, he is a macho outlaw, brave, heroic. He kills the husband as a final victory. The second version, the wife's story, has her as a delectable plaything that the two men vie for, then spurn; then she stabs her husband after he rejects her. An old Indian happened to hear the "husband's dying words," and in this third version, he is a martyr — unappreciated by his wife and doomed to self-sacrifice and suicide. Finally, the prospector relates a fourth version of the story *he* claims to have witnessed coming on the scene: The wife is a scatterbrained Southern coquette, the men are bumbling duelists, and the husband, unfortunately, trips on the Aztec dagger. The prospector confesses to stealing the dagger, so perhaps his story has some truth to it, but as the con man phrases it, "People see what they wanna see and say what they wanna hear. The truth is like that little ball under the three shells — now you see it, now you don't." From within the station crying is heard. It is an abandoned infant, and its presence is seen as an omen. The preacher decides to stay; the prospector agrees to care for the child. The con man is left alone to hail the approaching train.

Outside the Law (Film, 1930) Lon Chaney had success playing an Oriental named Ah Wing in the 1920 original silent version of *Outside the Law*, which was directed by Tod Browning. Ten years later Browning wanted to remake the film as a talkie. Chaney, who was dying of bronchial cancer, had just completed the only talking film in his career — a remake of his *The Unholy Three*. Edward G. Robinson undertook the Chaney role, now named Cobra Collins. Robinson was disenchanted with his work in Hollywood at this point; his overnight stardom in *Little Caesar* was still a few months in the future. He was greatly frustrated by the process of filmmaking.

A favorable review of *Outside the Law* came from *The New York Times:* "Edward G. Robinson imparts a good deal of strength to his interpretation of Collins." But *Variety* assessed the film's weaknesses with these words: "The acting may be summed up as 90 percent pitiful.... As the result, Robinson, Miss Nolan and Owen Moore work the angle of talking out of the corner of the mouth with such consistency and such exaggerated gusto as to provoke the sensibilities and patience of the most easygoing fan."

Producer, Carl Laemmle, Jr.; associate producer, H. M. Asher; director, Tod Browning; screenplay, Browning, Garrett Fort; art director, William R. Schmitt; sound, C. Roy Hunter; synchronization/score, David Broekman; costumes, Juliann Mathieson; camera, Roy Overbaugh; editor, Milton Carruth; supervising editor, Maurice Pivar; cast: Mary Nolan (Connie), Edward G. Robinson (Cobra Collins), Owen Moore (Fingers O'Dell), Eddie Sturgis (Jake), John George (Humpy), Delmar Watson (The Kid), Rockcliffe Fellowes (Captain O'Reilly), Louise Beavers (Judy), DeWitt Jennings (Police chief), Frank Burke, Sidney Bracey, Rose Plummer, Mathew Betz, Rodney Hildebrand, James Leong, Charles "Buddy" Rogers (Cigar clerk); Universal; 76 minutes; September 1930

Cobra Collins, a gang leader, hears about plans for a $500,000 bank robbery and demands a fifty-fifty cut. The plan involves Fingers O'Dell posing as a mannequin in the bank's window so the police will recognize him. Connie, Fingers' girlfriend, tries to get around Cobra's demand by telling him the robbery won't be for another week, but Cobra doesn't believe her. Fingers completes the robbery, having hidden after hours one night in a locker room in the building. He escapes, but unfortunately his hideout is an apartment across from a policeman's. The crime is resolved in a shootout with the police, wherein Cobra is killed. Fingers and Connie go to jail.

P. Lorillard Comedy Theatre see "**A Slight Case of Murder**"

Page, Gale (1913–83) played Nurse Randolph to *The Amazing Dr. Clitterhouse* (Edward G. Robinson). She was suggested by Jack L. Warner to play Robinson's wife in *Dr. Ehrlich's Magic Bullet,* but the role went to Ruth Gordon. She retired from films in 1954, after appearing in *Crime School, Knute Rockne — All American, The Time of Your Life, Anna Lucasta,* and *About Mrs. Leslie.*

Paget, Debra (1933–) a beautiful ingenue in films, beginning with *Cry of the City* in 1948, appeared twice with Edward G. Robinson, as Maria Delmonico in *House of Strangers* and Lilia, the water girl, in *The Ten Commandments.* Other films include *Broken Arrow, 14 Hours, Stars and Stripes Forever, Demetrius and the Gladiators, Seven Angry Men, Love Me Tender,* and *Tales of Terror.*

Paid in Full (Theater, 1913) Virtually all references correctly record his appearance in *Paid in Full* in 1913 as Edward G. Robinson's professional debut. The references also list Binghamton, New York, as the city. However, according to his autobiography, the stock company producing the play was in Albany, which is more than a hundred miles to the northeast. Binghamton, according to the actor, was where during that time he ventured for his first sexual encounter!

He learned an important early lesson while working with the S. M. Stainach Stock Company. In addition to performing apprenticeship duties backstage, at one performance he got the opportunity to act the small role of Sato in *Paid in Full.* Onstage, he found himself immediately slighted by the arrogant leading man. Robinson decided then and there that all future performers with whom he worked would receive due respect.

In its first Broadway run in 1908, *Paid in Full* played 167 performances. Walter Prichard Eaton commented that it "has a purpose above the mere trickle of a story, the rehashing of conventional situations — that is searching for truth."

Joseph Brooks expects that his wife Emma will help him avoid embezzlement charges with his company. She has been blindly obedient to him, but ultimately leaves him when she realizes how shameless and worthless he really is.

Produced by S. M. Stainach Stock Company; playwright, Eugene Walter; cast included Edward G. Robinson (Sato); Albany, New York; April 1913

Paiva, Nestor (1905–66), a bald, Italian character actor, appears with Edward G. Robinson as a Naval investigator in *Tampico* and as retired gangster Lou Fisachetti in *Hell on Frisco Bay.* He was in over 100 films, including *Beau Geste, Johnny Eager, The Song of Bernadette, Road to Rio, Mighty Joe Young, Young Man with a Horn, Call Me Madam,* and *The Left-Handed Gun.*

"Panic" (Television, 1969) A year prior to his guest-starring appearance in "The Mary Tree" on *Bracken's World,* an NBC-TV series about the film industry, Edward G. Robinson played a cameo role as himself in a scene with Eleanor Parker at the end of an episode called "Panic."

Executive producer, Del Reisman; producer, Stanley Rubin; director, Ted Post; teleplay, Oliver Hailey; creator, Dorothy Kingsley; theme song, Alan and Marilyn Bergman, sung by The Lettermen; cast: Eleanor Parker, Elizabeth Allen, Scott Brady, Peter Haskell, Judson Pratt, Karen Jensen, Laraine Stephens, Tod Andrews, Dennis Cole, Pilar Del Rey, Diana Dye, Dick Whittington, Edward G. Robinson (Himself); *Bracken's World*; NBC-TV; 60 minutes; September 26, 1969

Parade of Stars (Television, 1957) This special, a nineteen-and-a-half hour telethon headlined by Dean Martin for the City of Hope, was called "vulgar" by columnist Dorothy Kilgallen. — Nick Tosches, in *Dino: Living High in the Dirty Business of Dreams*

Producers, Martin Tannenbaum, Arthur Kovitz; participants: Dean Martin, Captain Video, Carmine DeSapio, Sammy Davis, Jr., Ethel Waters, Edward G. Robinson, Perry Como, Floyd Patterson, Jackie Gleason, Murray Kaufman; WABD-TV, New York; May 1957

Paramount Pictures The company was started in 1916 when Adolph Zukor's Famous Players merged with Jesse Lasky's Feature Play company to form Famous Players–Lasky. The name was not changed to Paramount until 1927, following another merger with a distributor. Edward G. Robinson made his first talking picture, *The Hole in the Wall*, for Paramount. Other films he made there were *Double Indemnity, Night Has a Thousand Eyes, The Ten Commandments, My Geisha, A Boy Ten Feet Tall, Peking Blonde, Grand Slam,* and *Operation San Pietro*.

Paris, Jerry (1925–86) acted in *Cyrano de Bergerac, The Caine Mutiny, Marty,* and *The Great Impostor*, then TV's *The Dick Van Dyke Show*, for which he later won a directing Emmy. His first feature was *Never a Dull Moment* for Disney, with Van Dyke and Edward G. Robinson. Other films include *Star-Spangled Girl* and two *Police Academy* features.

Parker, Eleanor (1922–) received Oscar nominations for *Caged, Detective Story,* and *Interrupted Melody*. She is Miss Rogers in *A Hole in the Head*, with Edward G. Robinson. They also are guest stars in *It's a Great Feeling*, and she was a series star of *Bracken's World* when Robinson played himself in cameo in the episode "Panic." Her other films include *The Voice of the Turtle, Valentino, The King and Four Queens, Home from the Hill, The Sound of Music* (as the Baroness), and *Eye of the Cat*.

Parker, Jean (1912–) was Edward G. Robinson's moll in *Black Tuesday*. Her film career began in 1932; she was Beth in *Little Women* and also appeared in *Rasputin and the Empress, Lady for a Day, The Ghost Goes West, The Arkansas Traveler, Deerslayer, Dead Man's Eyes, Bluebeard, Those Redheads from Seattle,* and *Apache Uprising*.

Parker, Willard (1912–96) played Edward G. Robinson's future son-in-law, a state trooper, in *A Slight Case of Murder*. He was also in *That Certain Woman, Apache Drums, The Naked Gun, Young Jesse James, Air Patrol,* and *Waco*, and he was on TV in the 1950s in *Tales of the Texas Rangers*.

Parks, Larry (1914–75) may be the actor most closely associated with the embarrassment of the House Un-American Activities Committee's hunt for Communists in the film industry. In March 1951 Parks was questioned in several sessions by the Committee. He admitted being recruited into party membership in 1941, calling it a "mistake of judgment" on the part of an idealistic 25-year-old. Pressed further by the Committee, he felt forced into having to choose between being held in contempt of Congress and naming names. Later, in a closed evening session, he did name names. In his testimony he also said, prophetically, "I think my career has been ruined because of this." Although he was never officially blacklisted, his contract with Columbia was cancelled and he was not hired by other studios. Parks' film career began in 1941 with *Mystery Ship*. He also was in *Canal Zone, Reveille with Beverly, Deerslayer, Destroyer* (as Ensign Johnson, with Edward G. Robinson), and *Counter-Attack* before scoring a sudden hit in 1946 playing Al Jolson in *The Jolson Story*. Seven other films, including *Jolson Sings Again*, followed prior to his Congressional testimony, but then there were only two more. His last film was *Freud* in 1962.

Parnell, Emory (1894–1979) plays pleasant, if not-too-bright, cops in three films with Edward G. Robinson: *I Am the Law, Larceny, Inc.,* and *A Hole in the Head*. In *Unholy Partners* he is Colonel Mason. Other films: *The Miracle of Morgan's Creek, Mr. Blandings Builds His Dream House, Call Me Madam, Sabrina,* and *The Andromeda Strain*, plus TV roles in *The Life of Riley* and *Lawman*.

Pawley, William (1906–52) played the gangster thrown out of Joan Blondell's club by Edward G. Robinson in *Bullets or Ballots*. He turned up as a hood the following year in *The Last Gangster*. His other films include *G-Men, White Banners,* and *Union Pacific*. In 1942 he replaced Robinson as crusading editor Steve Wilson on the radio in *Big Town*.

The Pawn (Theater, 1917) Edward G. Robinson's third Broadway play was called *The Pawn*. Apparently, according to his autobiography *All My Yesterdays*, the play was also his *fourth*. The first engagement came shortly after his run in *Under Sentence*, but it closed in two weeks, preceding an April 1917 declaration of war by President Woodrow Wilson. In the fall, while waiting to be drafted, Robinson was cast as an Oriental in another engagement of the play.

Cast: Frank Keenan, Edward G. Robinson; spring, 1917

Producers, Messrs. Shubert; cast: Walker Whiteside, Edward G. Robinson (Hushmaru), K. Arashi, Isa Aoki, James L. Crane, Gertrude Dallas, Malcolm Duncan, S. Furusho, Ione McGrane, C. Miyaki, Charles A. Sellon, Joseph Selman, K. Takemi, G. Tatsuno, Marjorie Wood; September 1917

"For two acts [it] ... is as slow as it is preposterous," wrote *The New York Times*, "and though the third act strikes a livelier pace, the improvement comes too late and at best seems too slight to save the evening."

Peck, Gregory (1916–) received Oscar nominations for *Keys of the Kingdom, The Yearling, Spellbound, Gentleman's Agreement,* and *Twelve O'Clock High*, and won for *To Kill a Mockingbird*. Other films: *Duel in the Sun, Roman Holiday, The Big Country, The Guns of Navarone, Mackenna's Gold* (with Edward G. Robinson), *MacArthur, The Boys from Brazil,* and *Other People's Money*. He and Robinson were also on TV together on *The Ed Sullivan Show* and the *36th Annual Academy of Motion Picture Arts and Sciences Awards* telecast.

Peer Gynt (Theater, 1923) Early in 1923 Edward G. Robinson debuted with the Theatre Guild in Henrik Ibsen's *Peer Gynt*, in the role of the Button Moulder and a smaller role, Herr von Eberkopf. It was the first of his ten plays with that organization. The title role was played by Joseph Schildkraut, Robinson's friend from the American Academy of Dramatic Arts.

Written in 1867, the play is, according to *Masters of Modern Drama*, "Ibsen's ... most exuberant and most poetic drama. The last of his plays to be written in verse, it blends a capricious and free-wheeling fantasy with spirited satire and deep philosophical implications. Less solemn by far than Goethe's *Faust*, it embodies the same conception of drama as a vast cosmic quest, a revelation of the mystery and meaning of human existence. Ibsen found the wonderful adventures of *Peer Gynt* in traditional folklore, notably in Asbjornsen's *Norwegian Fairy-Stories*, and combined them with recollections of his childhood in the mountains and valleys of central Norway.... The first line of the play, 'Peer, you're lying,' sets the tone of the whole piece. An attractive but utterly unprincipled rogue, Peer never sees himself as he really is. Attracted to Solveig, he woos a troll, and follows the counsel of the Great Boyg, to 'go round about.' Peer's way becomes that of evasion and compromise. His complete dedication to the Gyntian Self transforms him into a troll without his knowing it. Whether in the north or south, in the ancient or modern world, Peer's code and conduct remain the same. At the final return home he gains a measure of insight into his condition, but it comes almost too late; the Button Moulder will be waiting at the third crossroads.... The plight of the hero is that of Ibsen's countrymen and of all mankind, but Peer's imaginative vitality, his quick tongue and ready wit, his fanciful idealism and lively adaptability, make him a vigorous and wholly individual personality as well as a great symbolic creation.... The music of Edvard Grieg, composed in 1874, captures some but not all of the intoxication and frenzy of Ibsen's turbulent play. The wild phantasmagoria of *Peer Gynt* points directly to Strindberg's expressionism."— Haskell M. Block and Robert G. Shedd, *Masters of Modern Drama*

Alexander Woolcott in *The New York Times* praised the Theatre Guild's production of *Peer Gynt*, saying that, "a triumph for expressionism came to life as never before, at least in America," and, in particular, "there must be a word for the telling performance of Edward G. Robinson as the Button Moulder in the superb last act."

A dramatic poem produced by the Theatre Guild; playwright, Henrik Ibsen; translation,

William and Charles Archer; director, Theodor Komisarjevsky; music, Edvard Grieg; cast: Joseph Schildkraut (Peer Gynt), Dudley Digges (The Troll King), Helen Westley (The Troll King's Daughter), Edward G. Robinson (The Button Moulder; Herr von Eberkopf), Armina Marshall (Kari), Louise Closser Hale (Ase), C. Porter Hall (Old Man of Hegstad), Charles Halton (Begriffenfeldt), Elise Bartlett, Eve Casanova, Helen Sheridan (Herd Girls), Romney Brent (Thief), William W. Griffith (Solveig's Father, Troll Courier), Stanley G. Wood (Aslak, Troll Courier, Mr. Cotton), Stanley Howlett (Bride's Father; Hussein; The Lean One), Lillebil Ibsen (Anitra), Philip Leigh (Bridegroom's Father, Troll Courier; Trumpeterstrale; Peer's Son), Selena Royle (Solveig), Alfred Alexandre (Receiver), Bertha Broad (Ingrid), Albert Carroll (Monsieur Ballon, Dancer), Barbara Kitson (Dancer), William Franklin (Mads Moen; Troll Chamberlain; Fellah), J. Andrew Johnson (Second Old Man), Charles Tagewell (Officer), Francine Wouters (Helga; Ugly Brat), Elizabeth Zachry (Solveig's Mother), Ellen Larned (Bridegroom's Mother); opened at the Garrick Theatre, New York; February 5, 1923

Peerce, Jan   (1904–84), Metropolitan Opera tenor, appeared on stage at four *Chanukah Festivals for Israel* with Edward G. Robinson, from 1963 through 1966. They also appeared together on a TV special, *Twelve Star Salute*. Peerce played roles in *Rigoletto*, *La Traviata*, and *La Boheme*.

Peking Blonde   (Film, 1967) This was the first of several pictures in which Edward G. Robinson appeared during the late 1960s, made by European production companies capitalizing on his name and presence. Seldom were the films of any distinction, nor were his roles in them. He did not usually play the leads. In *Peking Blonde* Robinson is one of the few actors who dubbed his own English, while the lip movements of other players do not match, giving the film an odd corniness. Robinson said of this and another picture he made shortly thereafter, "I have no idea whatever happened to *Peking Blonde* and *Operation San Pietro*. Perhaps they were not considered worthy enough for an American release. I was not particularly pleased with either story and accepted the engagements as a matter of therapy. They kept me occupied after a recent illness." *Peking Blonde* has been shown on television in the United States, but it never played in theaters.

"Spy shenanigans concern Chinese, Russian and Yank spies seeking errant Red Chinese missile data plus a priceless jewel. But all this does not quite have the verve, ironic comic twists or sheer suspense and action flair to bring it off. It emerges possibly ... on the color, scope and lure of the Edward G. Robinson name, albeit he has a small role in the affair ... [as] the shrewd CIA chief." —*Variety*

Christine Olsen turns up in Paris, an amnesiac and bearing the tattoo of a powerful Chinese crime lord. Gandler, a struggling actor, is hired by CIA agent Douglas to impersonate Christine's husband in order to pick up information, but specifically to find a missing gem, the legendary Blue Grape. Christine recovers and there are several attempts made on her life by Russian agents. The story shifts to Hong Kong, where Christine's sister Erika has possession of the gem. Erika is killed when her boat is firebombed. Christine is taken to Peking. Gandler now has the Blue Grape. He and a Russian agent are pulled from the water by Douglas and his men. Christine is traded for the gem, and when she is released to Gandler, she shows him a notebook full of scientific data she has lifted, which should be worth millions.

A co-production of Hans Eckelkamp Films (West Germany) / Copernic Films (France) / Clesi Cinematografica (Italy); producers, Raymond Danon, Maurice Jacquin; director, Nicolas Gessner; screenplay, Gessner, Mark Behm; based on the novel by James Hadley Chase; adaptation, Jacques Vilfrid; music, Francois de Roubaix; art director, Georges Petitot; sound, Joseph Giaume; camera, Claude Lecomte; editor, Jean-Michel Gauthier; assistant directors, Alan Mylonas, Claude Vitale, Michel Lang, Marcello Crescenzi, Charles Dubosc; cast: Mireille Darc (Christine), Claudio Brook (Gandler), Edward G. Robinson (Douglas), Pascale

Roberts (Secretary), Francois Brion (Erika), Joe Warfield (Doctor), Giorgia Moll, Karl Studer, Yves Elliot, Valery Inkjinoff, Tiny Young, Aime DeMarch, Jean-Jacques Delbo, Annie Marie Blanc, Guido Celano, Mario Hindermann, Helmut Lange, Gunter Luecke, Mei-Chen, Werner Schwier; Paramount; a.k.a. *The Blonde from Peking* and *Une Blonde de Pekin*; 80 (or 95) minutes; Transcope, Eastman color; January 1968

People Are Like That (Radio, 1949) Edward G. Robinson (narrator); a radio program about polio; July 1949; 30 minutes

Pepe (Film, 1960) "The rare and wonderful talents of Mexican comedian Cantinflas ... are pitifully spent and dissipated amid a great mass of Hollywood dross in the over-sized, over-peopled *Pepe*," said the review in *The New York Times*. Leonard Maltin in *TV Movies* called the film a "bomb. This one's only if you're desperate."

Despite the fact that the reviews gave a fairly accurate assessment of the film, *Pepe* received seven Academy Award nominations — for its color cinematography, art direction, and costume design, and for its sound, editing, song, and music score.

On the plus side, the film's participants seemed to be having a wonderful time. As Jane Robinson Sidney commented in 1990, "Locations were great and *Pepe* even better, as George was such great host to his actors." Producer-director George Sidney followed Cantinflas from Mexico to Hollywood to Las Vegas and back again. Familiar faces recreated familiar scenes — Jack Lemmon in drag shooting retakes for *Some Like It Hot*; Janet Leigh, fresh from her demise in *Psycho*, playing comedy in the bathtub; TV's Donna Reed and *Dennis the Menace* (Jay North), Bing, Maurice, and Judy all singing away; and Frank, Dean, and Sammy holding court with the Rat Pack. Dan Dailey, the featured leading man, danced a little, and Shirley Jones, playing opposite him, sang. She won her best supporting actress Oscar for *Elmer Gantry* the same year.

In the film Jane Robinson is credited with a guest appearance, but it is difficult to find her if she is present. Robinson appears in several scenes as himself, but the plot has him playing a film producer, which was fictionalized.

There were more negative reviews. *The New York Herald Tribune* said, "When Robinson sees the completed film [within a film], he assures Dailey: 'Nothing to worry about. Pure entertainment.' Which may hint at the credos of screen writers Dorothy Kingsley and Claude Binyon and of producer-director George Sidney." And Maltin, in his *Film Guide*, called *Pepe* a "feeble and seemingly endless extravaganza…. Few of the guests have anything worthwhile to do."

Producer-director, George Sidney; associate producer, Jacques Gelman; based on a play by Ladislas Besh-Fekete; story, Leonard Spigelgass, Sonya Levien; screenplay, Dorothy Kingsley, Claude Binyon; assistant director, David Silver; sound, Charles J. Rice, James Z. Flaster; art director, Ted Haworth; set, William Kiernan; music, Sammy Cahn, Andre Previn, Johnny Green; songs, Roger Edens, Hans Wittstatt, Dory Langdon, Augustin and Maria Teresa Lara; choreography, Eugene Loring, Alex Romero; costumes, Edith Head; makeup, Ben Lane; camera, Joe MacDonald; editors, Viola Lawrence, Al Clark; cast: Cantinflas (Pepe), Dan Dailey (Ted Holt), Shirley Jones (Suzy Murphy), Joey Bishop, Billie Burke, Michael Callan, Maurice Chevalier, Charles Coburn, Richard Conte, Bing Crosby, Tony Curtis, Bobby Darin, Sammy Davis, Jr., Jimmy Durante, Zsa Zsa Gabor, Judy Garland (Singing voice), Greer Garson, Hedda Hopper, Ernie Kovacs (Immigration inspector), Peter Lawford, Janet Leigh, Jack Lemmon, Dean Martin, Jay North, Kim Novak, Andre Previn, Donna Reed, Debbie Reynolds, Edward G. Robinson, Cesar Romero, Frank Sinatra (Guest stars), Stephen Bekassy (Jeweler), Ann B. "Schultzy" Davis (Robinson's secretary), William Demarest (Studio guard), Vicki Trickett (Lupita), Hank Henry (Manager), Joe Hyams (Charro), Suzanne Lloyd (Carmen), Matt Mattox (Dancer), Jack Entratter, Buddy Fogelson, Carlos Montalban, Carlos Rivas, Jane Robinson, Bunny Waters, Dorothy Abbott, Jim Bacon, Steve

Baylor, Lela Bliss, John Burnside, Steve Carruthers, Jimmy Cavanaugh, Shirley DeBurgh, Carol Douglas, Bonnie Green, Kenner C. Kamp, David Landfield, Jeanne Manet, Margie Nelson, Francisco Reguerro, Fred Roberts, Billy Snyder, Ray Walker, Jim Waters; Columbia; 195 minutes; December 1960

Pepe, a Mexican ranch hand, adores his white stallion, Don Juan. When film director Ted Holt buys the horse at an auction, Pepe comes to Hollywood to find him. At the studio he sings with Bing Crosby and wrecks Jack Lemmon's car. He befriends Suzy Murphy, a talented singer-dancer with no delusions about stardom. Invited to a club to see her perform, Pepe gets mixed up in the realistic action of the number, and Suzy is fired. Ted hopes to sell Don Juan to Edward G. Robinson in order to raise funds to produce a musical on location in Mexico. Pepe brings Suzy to Ted's rundown mansion, and Ted is impressed enough with her to put her in the film. Pepe goes to Las Vegas and wins big at a casino, much to the surprise of Frankie, Dino, Sammy, et al. Ted and Suzy fall in love, but Pepe mistakes Maurice Chevalier's advice on the subject and believes Suzy loves him. All ends happily when the film is a success, Suzy and Ted are together, and Don Juan is given back to Pepe.

Perelman, S. J. (1904–79), a New York humorist, wrote, with his wife Laura, *The Night Before Christmas* (filmed as *Larceny, Inc.*, with Edward G. Robinson) and *All Good Americans*. He collaborated with Ogden Nash on *One Touch of Venus*, and also wrote *The Beauty Part*.

Performances, Good and Bad The author has a bias about Edward G. Robinson's performances, maintaining that he never really gave a bad one. Foster Hirsch, the actor's biographer for the *Pyramid Illustrated History of the Movies*, feels his performances ranged from *All My Sons* (the best) to *The Ten Commandments* (the worst), blaming the latter on Robinson's image as a contemporary urban type being a poor fit for the Biblical epic.

Inarguably, Robinson's performances were always as good or better than the films themselves. Pressed to identify performances that are low on the spectrum, a concession might be made about his work in *Actors and Sin, The Glass Web,* and *My Geisha*, to pry three out of a career of excellent work. Maybe an awkwardness about these performances lies in their connection to show business — the theater, television, and filmmaking.

In *Actors and Sin*, as in the other three, Robinson is restricted by the script, as a doting Shakespearean father of a temperamental Broadway star, played by Marsha Hunt. But he is also hammy and morose. Unlike the typical Robinson film, in this he is unable to arouse much audience sympathy.

Though he was never a romantic lead, in *The Glass Web* we are asked to believe him (at nearly sixty!) the lover of a 24–year-old starlet. Surprised when she rejects him, he murders her and covers up the crime; yet he also has the preposterous idea that the whole thing would make a viable project for the TV show he writes, "Crime of the Week."

Finally, in *My Geisha* Robinson plays a film producer who must mouth such embarrassing dialogue that it undermines his credibility. Shirley MacLaine (cast logically as a comic film star) asks him if film producers are born devious or are taught it at the studio, and Robinson responds with a smile, "Like the man said who was asked if he was a Communist: 'We're not allowed to tell.'" He assesses her cardboard film-within-a-film performance as *Madama Butterfly* as Oscar-worthy.

It would be much easier to complain about the performances of others in Robinson's films. He complained about Vilma Banky and Alice White in early talkies, as well as Miriam Hopkins in *Barbary Coast,* who is admittedly difficult to watch for as much screen time as she is given; Yvonne DeCarlo and John Derek in *The Ten Commandments* are only slightly worse than Charlton Heston and Anne Baxter; and the majority of the casts of *Pepe, Cheyenne Autumn, Mackenna's Gold,* and *Song of Norway* should have known better.

Wonderful, excellent performances are plentiful. While Robinson himself was always good, the author will stop with a list of fifteen films: *Little Caesar, Five Star Final, The Whole*

Town's Talking, Dr. Ehrlich's Magic Bullet, The Sea Wolf, Tales of Manhattan, Double Indemnity, The Woman in the Window, Our Vines Have Tender Grapes, Key Largo, All My Sons, House of Strangers, A Hole in the Head, Soylent Green, and, finally, *The Cincinnati Kid,* in which the ensemble playing simply is as good as it gets in films, and Edward G. Robinson still walked off with the acting honors.

Others who do simply splendid work with Robinson include Aline MacMahon in *Five Star Final* and *Silver Dollar;* Mary Astor in *The Little Giant;* Jean Arthur, Etienne Girardot, and Donald Meek in *The Whole Town's Talking;* Ruth Donnelly, Allen Jenkins, and Ed Brophy in *A Slight Case of Murder;* Gene Lockhart in *Blackmail;* Ruth Gordon in *Dr. Ehrlich's Magic Bullet;* Alexander Knox in *The Sea Wolf;* Thomas Mitchell in *Flesh and Fantasy;* Lynn Bari in *Tampico;* Barbara Stanwyck and Fred MacMurray in *Double Indemnity;* Joan Bennett and Dan Duryea in *The Woman in the Window* and *Scarlet Street;* Billy House and Konstantin Shayne in *The Stranger;* Humphrey Bogart, Lauren Bacall, Lionel Barrymore, Thomas Gomez, and Oscar-winner Claire Trevor in *Key Largo;* Fay Wray in *Hell on Frisco Bay;* Yul Brynner and Sir Cedric Hardwicke in *The Ten Commandments;* Thelma Ritter in *A Hole in the Head;* Eli Wallach in *Seven Thieves;* Paul Newman in *The Prize* and *The Outrage;* and Martin Balsam in *The Old Man Who Cried Wolf.*

Perlman, Itzhak (1945–), a concert violinist and soloist, was born in Tel Aviv, Israel. With Edward G. Robinson he appeared in three successive *Chanukah Festivals for Israel* held at Madison Square Garden from 1965 to 1967.

Peters, Roberta (1930–), an operatic soprano, appeared with Edward G. Robinson at Madison Square Garden for the *Chanukah Festivals for Israel* from 1962 to 1964, and in 1967. She is known for her performances in *The Barber of Seville, Don Giovanni,* and *Lucia di Lammermoor.*

Peterson, Dorothy (1900–79) played Edward G. Robinson's wife in The *Woman in the Window.* Her other films, from 1930, include *Dark Victory, Saboteur, Mr. Skeffington,* and *Sister Kenny.* She also appeared on such television soap operas as *Secret Storm* and *The Edge of Night.*

The Petrified Forest Edward G. Robinson never played in this Robert Sherwood story, either on the stage or the screen, but he did figure in the story of how Humphrey Bogart won the film role. Bogart had been in Hollywood and made several less than memorable films. Returning to New York, he was offered the role of gangster Duke Mantee in *The Petrified Forest* and was an immediate success. Producer/star Leslie Howard promised him he would repeat the role on film.

Warner Bros. had other ideas. *Variety* reported in 1935 that Robinson would play the part. "A script of *The Petrified Forest* was rushed to Robinson, who knew a great role when he read one," wrote A. M. Sperber and Eric Lax in *Bogart.* "If questions of billing could be worked out, the answer was definitely yes." Bogart called Leslie Howard in Scotland; then Howard cabled Warner: "INSIST BOGART PLAY MANTEE. NO BOGART NO DEAL.... Robinson [was] odd man out. His insistence on co-star billing would make it hard to sell (what the studio wanted to promote as) the greatest Howard–[Bette] Davis vehicle ever if the top credits read 'Leslie Howard–Edward G. Robinson.' An obscure actor with an impossible name like Humphrey Bogart posed no such problem."

That Robinson rejected the role of Duke Mantee because he was tired of playing so many gangster roles is a less likely story, but it satisfied the publicists.

Phelps, Lee (1893–1959) was in eight films with Edward G. Robinson. He played policemen *(Brother Orchid* and *Scarlet Street),* detectives *(Manpower, Flesh and Fantasy,* and *Vice Squad),* or guards *(Blackmail* and *The Last Gangster),* but in *Unholy Partners* he was a mechanic. He was also in *Anna Christie, Trade Winds,* and a number of B Westerns.

"The Philippines Never Surrendered" (Radio, 1945) program with an obvious message about the war was the story of Edward Kuder, a school superintendent who built an underground movement in the Philippines during the Japanese Occupation.

DuPont Cavalcade of America; NBC; cast: Edward G. Robinson (Kuder); Gayne Whitman (host); Robert Armbruster (announcer); writer, Arthur Miller; April 30, 1945; 30 minutes

Philips, Lee (1927–99) played the musician husband of the girl Edward G. Robinson's character falls in love with in *Middle of the Night.* He recreated his role on the screen, and also played Robinson's son in the TV drama *A Good Name.* After a few more roles in films (*Peyton Place, Tess of the Storm Country*), he became a television director.

Photography News photography figures in *Blackmail, I Am the Law, Unholy Partners,* and *Five Star Final.* The latter two films have to do with the newspaper business; *I Am the Law* has three gangsters photographed for the press in "before and after" shots when they are matched in fistfights against special investigator Edward G. Robinson. In *Blackmail* Robinson is caught by a newsreel crew after putting out an oil fire.

In *A Slight Case of Murder,* Robinson's portrait is found on bottles of Gold Velvet beer, a ghastly product his company produces during Prohibition. His character in *A Lady to Love* substitutes the more handsome photograph of his friend for himself while squiring a waitress to be his bride. In an effort to locate a former commandant, now in hiding, Nazi war criminal Konrad Meinike (Konstantin Shayne) is sent by the passport photographer to Connecticut in *The Stranger.* Lynn Bari objects when she and Robinson are snapped by a photographer in *Tampico;* similarly, he objects to being photographed in *The Prize.* In *Little Caesar* Rico loves having his picture taken. When facing flashbulbs as lookalike for Public Enemy No. 1 in *The Whole Town's Talking,* he faints. Police detective Robinson discovers the identity of the murderer in *Nightmare* by doctoring an eight-by-ten photograph with a marker. An eight-by-ten of Robinson from *The Widow from Chicago* is on the set of "The Legend of Jim Riva," delineating his character's past as a crime lord.

Physical Characteristics Edward G. Robinson was one of the most readily identifiable personalities in movies, and one of the most imitated. Never handsome, his face was sometimes compared to that of a bulldog, with a wide and gaping mouth. Bette Davis once crudely announced her distaste for kissing his purplish lips. Short, at five-feet, eight inches, but self-aware, he developed a credo early in his stage career as he made the rounds of producers looking for work: "Not much face value, but when it comes to stage value, I'll deliver."

In the middle of Robinson's right cheek was a mole, an inherited feature. In early publicity stills the mole was often removed via airbrush. He added moustaches, sideburns, and beards to his face in order to delineate his characters. In the 1960s he began to sport a real goatee and mustache, which softened his otherwise homely features, and he became a very distinguished looking senior citizen.

Robinson's voice was slightly nasal, but rich in tone. No trace of his European beginnings was discernible in his speech, although he was unable to deny the influence of the Bronx. He was a chain cigarette and cigar smoker onscreen and off, and he was often seen with a pipe.

Pickens, Slim (1919–83), tall, gangly, and usually comic, he is best remembered in *Dr. Strangelove* as the soldier who rides an atomic bomb like a bucking bronco as it drops out of the plane. He was a rodeo clown before coming to films, and appears in several westerns. With Edward G. Robinson, he plays Cowboy in *Never a Dull Moment.*

Pillars of Society (Theater, 1912) While he was a student at the American Academy of Dramatic Arts, Edward G. Robinson performed in Henrik Ibsen's play, which was written in 1874. In *Masters of Modern Drama* the play is called a "harsh indictment of moral corruption and crime for the sake of money and power."

Produced by the American Academy of Dramatic Arts; playwright, Henrik Ibsen; cast: Edward G. Robinson; Carnegie Lyceum Theatre, 1912.

Places Since his typical roles were contemporary urban characters, it is not unusual that the settings for many of Edward G. Robinson's films and plays were in New York, Los Angeles, or other major cities. Chicago, for example, would be the expected locale for *The Widow from Chicago,* as it is for *Robin and the 7 Hoods,* which introduced Sinatra's new anthem, "My Kind of Town." The old musical standard "Chicago" was heard in *The Little Giant,* and *I Loved a Woman* was also set in that city.

New York is the setting for *Henry Behave, The Kibitzer, The Hole in the Wall, The Man with Two Faces, Bullets or Ballots, Kid Galahad, A Slight Case of Murder* (Saratoga), *Confessions of a Nazi Spy, Larceny, Inc., Tales of Manhattan, Scarlet Street* (Greenwich Village), *House of Strangers, Actors and Sin, Middle of the Night, Grand Slam,* and "The Messiah on Mott Street."

These stories take place in California — Los Angeles: *Tiger Shark, The Little Giant* (Santa Barbara), *Manpower, Destroyer, Double Indemnity, It's a Great Feeling, Vice Squad, Tight Spot,* "The Legend of Jim Riva," *Never a Dull Moment, U.M.C.,* "The Mary Tree," and *The Old Man Who Cried Wolf;* San Francisco: *A Lady to Love* (the Napa Valley), *East Is West, The Hatchet Man, Barbary Coast, The Last Gangster* (including Alcatraz), *The Sea Wolf, Night Has a Thousand Eyes, Hell on Frisco Bay, Good Neighbor Sam.*

Other settings include Africa for *The Ten Commandments* (Egypt) and *A Boy Ten Feet Tall;* Cuba for *The Bright Shawl;* England for *Thunder in the City, A Dispatch from Reuter's, Flesh and Fantasy,* and *Journey Together;* France for "Epitaph for a Spy" and *Seven Thieves;* Germany for *Confessions of a Nazi Spy, A Dispatch from Reuter's, Dr. Ehrlich's Magic Bullet,* and *The Stranger;* Greece for *I Loved a Woman;* Israel for *The Ten Commandments* and *Neither by Day Nor by Night;* Italy for *The Firebrand, Androcles and the Lion, Right You Are If You Think You Are, Two Weeks in Another Town, Grand Slam, Operation San Pietro, The Biggest Bundle of Them All,* and "The Taming of the Shrew"; Mexico for *Juarez and Maximilian, Tampico, Who Has Seen the Wind?* and *Pepe;* Miami for *A Hole in the Head, Kid Galahad, Key Largo,* and *Big Leaguer;* Montreal for *A Bullet for Joey;* New England for *Ned McCobb's Daughter, The Stranger* (Connecticut), "Shadows Tremble," and *The Devil and Daniel Webster;* New Orleans for *Nightmare, The Cincinnati Kid,* and *Flesh and Fantasy;* Oklahoma for *Blackmail;* the Orient for *The Hatchet Man, My Geisha,* and *Peking Blonde;* Rio de Janiero for *Grand Slam;* Russia for *The Night Lodging, The Brothers Karamazov,* and *Darkness at Noon;* Scandinavia for *Peer Gynt, The Prize* (Stockholm), and *Song of Norway;* the American West for *Silver Dollar* (Denver), *The Violent Men,* "Heritage" (Missouri), *The Outrage, Cheyenne Autumn,* and *Mackenna's Gold;* and Wisconsin for both *It's a Great Feeling* and *Our Vines Have Tender Grapes.* Films that featured scenes at sea include *The Little Giant, Confessions of a Nazi Spy, The Sea Wolf, Destroyer, Tampico, Journey Together,* and *Who Has Seen the Wind?*

Places in the titles of his films include *The Widow from Chicago, Barbary Coast, Tales of Manhattan, Tampico, Key Largo, Hell on Frisco Bay, The Cincinnati Kid, Peking Blonde,* and *Song of Norway,* plus radio's *Jerusalem Is Her Name* and *Letter from Birmingham Jail,* as well as such non-specific places as *Big Town, The Hole in the Wall, East Is West, The Whole Town's Talking, Scarlet Street, Thunder in the City, Two Weeks in Another Town,* and "Blind Alley."

Planet of the Apes Edward G Robinson made a six-minute screen test in full simian makeup as ape scientist Dr. Zaius in anticipation of playing the role in *Planet of the Apes.* He was forced to withdraw from the project, however, because of the claustrophobic effects of Ben Nye's latex prosthetic makeup, which aggravated his heart condition. A brief story in *Variety*, however, reported that Robinson withdrew because of his commitment to filming *Mackenna's Gold* and an inability to reconcile the schedules.

In the film Robinson was replaced by Maurice Evans. Charlton Heston's character, called Thomas in the test, was changed to Taylor. For the test, James Brolin and Linda Harrison played small roles as younger apes; their makeup was simply whitened faces. Roddy McDowall and Kim Hunter, however, played their expanded roles in the feature film, while Harrison played not an ape, but Nova, Heston's human love interest.

Screen test: director, Franklin Shaffner; script by Rod Serling and Michael Wilson, based on the novel *Monkey Planet*, by Pierre Boulle; music, Jerry Goldsmith; camera, Leon Shamroy; makeup, Ben Nye, Dan Striepeke; cast: Charlton Heston (Thomas); Edward G. Robinson (Dr. Zaius); James Brolin (Cornelius); Linda Harrison (Zira); 1968

See **Unrealized Projects**.

Platt, Edward (1916–74) played Ralph Ford, who succeeds Edward G. Robinson as D. A. in *Illegal*. Known as The Chief in the television series *Get Smart*, Platt's other films include *Rebel Without a Cause*, *The Helen Morgan Story*, *North by Northwest*, and *Atlantis, the Lost Continent*.

Playhouse 90 see **"Shadows Tremble"**

Plays / Theater Appearances Gerald Bordman's *The Oxford Companion to the American Theatre* cites Edward G. Robinson as "an actor of great range, depth, and promise," and laments his having been lured to "a long career in Hollywood." He made his first appearance on the stage with the University Settlement House at the age of thirteen in *One Touch of Nature* in 1906. More than a half dozen productions followed, including *Paid in Full* in 1913 in Albany, New York, his professional debut. First appearing on Broadway in *Under Fire* in 1915, he soon worked for producer Arthur Hopkins in six plays from 1917 to 1923, including *The Night Lodging,* better known as *The Lower Depths*. More than two dozen appearances on Broadway, including ten with the Theatre Guild, followed. Robinson had a major success playing his first gangster role in Bartlett Cormack's *The Racket* in 1927. It was timely that, after the play was banned in Chicago, the tour diverted to California, where film executives first noticed him. He helped Jo Swerling rewrite *The Kibitzer* after its first run failed, and Swerling gave Robinson co-authorship credit when it was revived in 1929. Robinson did not appear on stage in plays after 1930 until he undertook the national tour of *Darkness at Noon* twenty years later in 1951–52. His only other Broadway engagement came five years later in *Middle of the Night* in 1956. Robinson was, however, one of the narrators in 1943 for *We Will Never Die*, a pageant staged at Madison Square Garden commemorating the loss of six million Jews in the Holocaust, and he appeared in *Chanukah Festivals for Israel* at the Garden regularly from 1956. At the Festival in 1968 he was honored on his 75th birthday with a performance dedicated to him by the Sophie Maslow Dance Company.

Among personalities Edward G. Robinson worked with in his theater career were:

<u>actors</u> George Arliss, Martin Balsam, Ethel Barrymore, Ed Begley, Jacob Ben-Ami, Morris Carnovsky, Leo Carillo, Mrs. Leslie Carter, Harold Clurman, Elisha Cook, Jr., Frank Craven, Laura Hope Crewes, Dudley Digges, Richard Dix, Clare Eames, Lynn Fontanne, Mona Freeman, Anne Jackson, Sam Jaffe, Zita Johann, Allyn Joslyn, Martin Landau, Earle Larimore, Pauline Lord, Alfred Lunt, Sanford Meisner, Thomas Mitchell, Frank Morgan, Lois Nettleton, Pat O'Brien, Tom Powers, Gena Rowlands, Erskine Sanford, Joseph and Rudolph Schildkraut, Lee Strasberg, Spencer Tracy, Henry Travers, Helen Westley, and Margaret Wycherly; <u>producers</u> George M. Cohan, Abe Erlanger, Harrison Grey Fiske, Sam Harris, William Harris, Jr., Arthur Hopkins, Marc Klaw, Joshua Logan, Arch and Edgar Selwyn, the Messrs. Shubert, and George C. Tyler; <u>directors</u> Sam Forrest,

Arthur Hurley, Theodore Komisarjevsky, Joshua Logan, and Philip Moeller; authors of plays he appeared in include Zoe Akins, Henning Berger, Paddy Chayefsky, Bartlett Cormack, Irvin S. Cobb, Maxim Gorky, Sidney Howard, Henrik Ibsen, Sidney Kingsley, Edward Knoblauch, Benn W. Levy, Roi Cooper Megrue, Ferenc Molnar, Luigi Pirandello, Elmer Rice, George Bernard Shaw, Jo Swerling, Booth Tarkington, and Franz Werfel.

Edward G. Robinson's complete stage appearances:

1906: *One Touch of Nature*
1912: *Pillars of Society*
1913: *The Bells of Conscience; Number 37; Paid in Full; The Gambler; Alias Jimmy Valentine*
1914: *Kismet; Electrocution*
1915: *Under Fire*
1916: *Under Sentence*
1917: *The Pawn* (two productions); *The Deluge; Drafted*
1918: *The Little Teacher; Polly with a Past*
1919: *First Is Last; The Night Lodging*
1920: *Enter Madame; Poldekin; Samson and Delilah*
1921: *Eyvind of the Hills; The Idle Inn*
1922: *The Deluge* (revived); *Banco*
1923: *Peer Gynt; The Adding Machine; The Voice; A Royal Fandango*
1924: *Stella Dallas; The Firebrand*
1925: *The Man of Destiny; Androcles and the Lion*
1926: *The Goat Song; The Chief Thing; We Americans; The Stolen Lady; Henry Behave; Juarez and Maximilian; Ned McCobb's Daughter*
1927: *The Brothers Karamazov; Right You Are If You Think You Are; The Kibitzer; The Racket*
1928: *A Man with Red Hair; The Kibitzer* (revived)
1930: *Mr. Samuel*
1943: *We Will Never Die*
1951: *Darkness at Noon*
1956: *Middle of the Night; Chanukah Festival for Israel*
1957: *Chanukah Festival for Israel; Middle of the Night* (tour)
1960: *Chanukah Festival for Israel*
1962: *Chanukah Festival for Israel*
1964: *Chanukah Festival for Israel*
1965: *Chanukah Festival for Israel*
1967: *Chanukah Festival for Israel*
1968: *Chanukah Festival for Israel*

Films in which Robinson played that were based on plays include *The Hole in the Wall, A Lady to Love* (*They Knew What They Wanted*), *East Is West, Five Star Final, The Hatchet Man* (*The Honorable Mr. Wong*), *Two Seconds, The Man with Two Faces* (*The Dark Tower*), *A Slight Case of Murder, The Amazing Dr. Clitterhouse, Larceny, Inc.* (*The Night Before Christmas*), *Scarlet Street* (*La Chienne*), *All My Sons, Key Largo, Tight Spot* (*Dead Pigeon*), *Illegal* (*The Mouthpiece*), *A Hole in the Head, Pepe* (*Broadway Magic*), *The Devil and Daniel Webster, The Outrage* (*Rashomon*), *Song of Norway,* and *Neither by Day Nor by Night.*

Poldekin (Theater, 1920) Distinguished actor George Arliss had delivered the commencement address at Edward G. Robinson's graduation ceremonies at the American Academy of Dramatic Arts in 1913, and he later responded to a letter from Robinson advising him that the key to a theater career was planning. Robinson joined Arliss on Broadway in the anti–Bolshevik comedy *Poldekin*, but, unfortunately, it closed within a month.

Producer, George C. Tyler; playwright, Booth Tarkington; cast: George Arliss, Edward G. Robinson (Pinsky), Sidney Toler, Manart Kippen, Carl Anthony, William H. Barwald, Julia Dean, Emil Hoch, Elsie Mackay, Hubert Wilke; opened at the Park Theatre, New York; September 9, 1920

The New York Times said that *Poldekin* was "not much more than an informal debate … its people are but embodied points of view…. It may be guessed that the play is not Mr. Tarkington's best."

Politics In December 1938 a "Committee of 56" members was formed to sign a letter to President Roosevelt urging a boycott on trade with Nazi Germany. Meeting at Edward G. Robinson's home, the Committee heard a speech by Clark M. Eichelberger, director of the League of Nations Association. Present were Don Ameche, Fay Bainter, Lucille Ball, Joan Bennett, Abner Biberman, George Brent, Bruce Cabot, James Cagney, Charles Chaplin, Joan Crawford, Donald Crisp, Bette Davis, Melvyn Douglas, Alice Faye, Henry Fonda, John Ford, Ben Hecht, Jean Hersholt, Miriam Hopkins, Priscilla Lane, Myrna Loy, Aline MacMahon, Tony Martin, Groucho Marx, Burgess Meredith, Paul Muni, Elliott Nugent, Pat O'Brien, Dennis O'Keefe, Dick Powell, Claude Rains, Rosalind Russell, Ann Sheridan, Gale Sondergaard, Spencer Tracy, and Jack L. Warner, among others.

On April 14, 1943, a pageant was staged at the Hollywood Bowl to benefit the China Relief Fund, featuring a 36–minute speech by Madame Chiang Kai-shek. It was produced by David O. Selznick, directed by William Dieterle, decorated by Cedric Gibbons, scripted by Henry Kronman, and featured music by Herbert Stothart and the Los Angeles Philharmonic Orchestra. Participants included Spencer Tracy, Walter Huston, Henry Fonda, Dr. Corydon M. Wassell, and Edward G. Robinson (made up to look like Generalissimo Chiang Kai-shek himself).

In the late 1940s, as a protest to the actions of the House Un-American Activities Committee investigating Communism in the film industry, a group including Judy Garland, Burt Lancaster, William Wyler, John Huston, Billy Wilder, Phillip Dunne, Danny Kaye, Gene Kelly, Lauren Bacall, Humphrey Bogart, Ira Gershwin, and Edward G. Robinson helped form the Committee for the First Amendment.

Appearing at the 1960 Democratic party convention, Edward G. Robinson was among thirty or more celebrities, notably Frank Sinatra and his "Rat Pack," who supported John F. Kennedy. When introduced to the delegates at the convention, Robinson's ovation was among the strongest. He was a lifelong Democrat who campaigned actively for both Kennedy and Franklin Roosevelt.

See **Franklin Roosevelt**; **William Randolph Hearst**.

Polito, Sol   (1892–1960) became a lighting cameraman in 1917, and had a long career as a cinematographer, receiving Oscar nominations for *The Private Lives of Elizabeth and Essex, Sergeant York,* and *Captains of the Clouds.* Among his other pictures are *Alias Jimmy Valentine, I Am a Fugitive from a Chain Gang, The Petrified Forest, Dodge City, The Sea Hawk, The Corn Is Green, Rhapsody in Blue, Sorry Wrong Number, The Voice of the Turtle,* and — with Edward G. Robinson — *The Widow from Chicago, Five Star Final, Two Seconds, Dark Hazard, Confessions of a Nazi Spy,* and *The Sea Wolf.*

Polly with a Past   (Theater, 1919) After being discharged from Navy service during the first World War, Edward G. Robinson appeared in a stock production of *Polly with a Past*, which originally had been produced in New York by David Belasco in the summer of 1917.

Polly, a minister's daughter from Ohio, is studying music in New York and gets a job as a maid to help support herself. When Rex Van Zile becomes disillusioned with his life, his friends ask Polly to impersonate a French adventuress and play up to him. The two fall in love.

Produced by the Garrick Players; a three-act comedy by George Middleton and Guy Bolton; cast included Edward G. Robinson (A Stranger); Washington, D.C.; 1919

Polo with the Stars   (Short Film, 1941) Cast: Joe E. Brown, Jack Holt, Charles "Buddy" Rogers (Players), Edward G. Robinson, Jack Oakie (Spectators), Knox Manning (Commentator); WB Hollywood Novelty Series, #7301.

Porcasi, Paul   (1880–1946), an Italian character actor, played in *Smart Money* (as Mr. Amenoppopolus) and *I Loved a Woman* with Edward G. Robinson. His other films include *Flying Down to Rio, Footlight Parade, Devil and the Deep,* and *Maytime.*

Porky's Tire Trouble   In this cartoon, Porky Pig's dog, Flat Foot Flookey, falls into a vat of rubberizing solution at walrus boss Bletcher's factory and morphs into Edward G. Robinson, Edna Mae Oliver, and Clark Gable.

Supervisor, Robert Clampett; story, Warren Foster; animation, Norman McCabe; musical director, Carl W. Stalling; Looney Tunes, 1939; 7 minutes

Portraits Paintings of Edward G. Robinson were used in several of his films—*East Is West, House of Strangers, Never a Dull Moment,* and *Robin and the 7 Hoods.* For the latter, two portraits were hanging in various scenes in the film following his two-minute cameo when he is shot to death at his birthday celebration.

A portrait of Abraham Lincoln provides a poignant moment in *Cheyenne Autumn,* when Robinson's character, Carl Schurz, wonders how to handle a situation with the Indians of the title. Joan Bennett's portrait is key to both *The Woman in the Window* and *Scarlet Street.* In the first, the picture is hanging in a gallery outside Robinson's club and is admired by him and his friends. In the latter she is a subject that Robinson paints, later claiming it is a self-portrait. A painting of Marsha Hunt is slashed in *Actors and Sin.*

Edward G. Robinson did two self-portraits, excellent likenesses, which he claimed kept him occupied at a time when film offers were in short supply due to his political difficulties.

Postage Stamp In April 2000 the United States Post Office announced that Edward G. Robinson would become the sixth honoree in their "Legends of Hollywood" series. Previous honorees were Marilyn Monroe, James Dean, Humphrey Bogart, Alfred Hitchcock, and James Cagney. A 33–cent stamp with Robinson's likeness, rendered by Drew Struzan from a photograph by Elmer Fryer, became available at ceremonies at Grauman's Egyptian Theatre on October 24.

The event was emceed by TV host and author Robert Osborne. Jean Firstenberg, director of the American Film Institute, also spoke. Dedication of the stamp was by Karl Malden, who also is a member of the Citizens' Stamp Advisory Committee of the post office. Unveiling was by Francesca Robinson-Sanchez, the actor's granddaughter, and her son, Adam. Personal remembrances were offered by Malden, Charlton Heston, Nanette Fabray, Florence Henderson, Norman Lloyd, and Rich Little. The late Steve Allen also spoke after playing Gershwin's "Our Love Is Here to Stay" on Robinson's autographed concert Steinway piano, which, having been willed to the UCLA music department, was on loan for the event. (Allen died of a heart attack six days later.) Speakers for the U.S. Postal Service were Kerry Wolny, Los Angeles district postmaster, and the Honorable Tirso del Junco, M.D., a member of the board of governors.

During the week, the American Film Institute screened over one hundred new films as part of its AFI Fest 2000. In conjunction with the unveiling of the stamp, the AFI also showed Robinson's *The Cincinnati Kid.* Guests at the dedication reconvened for a luncheon reception at the nearby Cafe des Artistes. Attending were Dick Van Patten, producer Stanley Rubin and his wife, the former Kathleen Hughes, Peter Mark Richman, and Robinson family members Marian Parker, Beulah Robinson, Jeanne Kroman, Willary Scatchard, Eric Loebel, and Peter Robinson.

Potter, H. C. (1904–77) directed films and Broadway shows (*A Bell for Adano*). His only picture with Edward G. Robinson was *Blackmail.* Other features, beginning in 1936, include *The Shopworn Angel, Mr. Lucky, The Farmer's Daughter, Mr. Blandings Builds His Dream House,* and *The Time of Your Life.*

Powell, William (1891–1984) was a classmate of Edward G. Robinson's at the American Academy of Dramatic Arts. They appeared together in *The Bright Shawl.* He is remembered for *The Thin Man* series with Myrna Loy, as well as for *The Great Ziegfeld, My Man Godfrey, Life with Father, How to Marry a Millionaire,* and *Mister Roberts.*

"The Power of the X-Ray" (Radio, 1950) *For the Living*; sponsored by the American Cancer Society; cast: Edward G. Robinson, Verna Felton, Gerald Mohr; 1950; Episode J, 15 minutes

Powers, Tom (1890–1955) appeared with Edward G. Robinson in the George Bernard Shaw double bill of *Androcles and the Lion* (as the Captain) and *The Man of Destiny* (as Napoleon). In Hollywood he was the murdered husband in *Double Indemnity.* He appeared in silents from 1912, as well as *The Blue Dahlia, The Farmer's Daughter,* and *Julius Caesar.*

Presidents Edward G. Robinson was a lifelong Democrat, despite having stumped for William Randolph Hearst, a Republican, early in the last century. He campaigned for Presidents Franklin Roosevelt and John F. Kennedy. A congratulatory telegram from President Lyndon B. Johnson was read at Madison Square Garden during a *Chanukah Festival for Israel* on the occasion of Robinson's 75th birthday. During his career Robinson had several professional associations with Ronald Reagan prior to Reagan's ascendancy to the White House via the California governorship.

Several United States Presidents figured in the storylines of Robinson's dramatic works. The Lincoln assassination leads to the climax in *A Dispatch from Reuter's,* and his portrait is a presence as old friend to Secretary of the Interior Carl Schurz (Robinson) in *Cheyenne Autumn.* President Chester A. Arthur attends Robinson's wedding in *Silver Dollar.* The McKinley assassination and the inauguration of Theodore Roosevelt are included in *I Loved a Woman.* Robinson portrayed Roosevelt in the TV special *The Right Man.* Herbert Hoover and Franklin Roosevelt are referred to in *The Little Giant* as Prohibition comes to an end. Nineteenth-century presidents Andrew Jackson and Abraham Lincoln are mentioned in Edward Everett Hale's short story *The Man Without a Country,* which Robinson recorded for Caedmon Records. Milton Geiger's dramatic reading *This Is It,* read by Robinson on TV's *The Hollywood Palace,* refers to critical decisions made by such Presidents as Jefferson, Jackson, Lincoln, Wilson, Roosevelt, Truman, and Kennedy.

Presle, Micheline (1922–) debuted in films in her native France at the age of 16. She appears with Edward G. Robinson in *The Prize,* one of only a handful of American films she made from 1948 (*If a Man Answers, King of Hearts, Nea: A new Woman*).

Price, Vincent (1911–93) was for several decades the chief villain in the films of Roger Corman (often Edgar Allan Poe stories). With Edward G. Robinson, he was featured in *The Ten Commandments* as master builder Baka, the Egyptian slain by Moses. Fellow art lovers, Price and Robinson tested each other's knowledge for six weeks on television's *The $64,000 Challenge.* They also appeared together on *The Ed Sullivan Show* and on several radio programs — *Hollywood Fights Back, Document A/777, It Isn't Peanuts,* and an adaptation of *Flesh and Fantasy.* Price was interviewed on the BBC's biography *The Hollywood Greats: Edward G. Robinson* and they appear as themselves in *Mooch.* Other films include *Laura, House of Seven Gables, House of Wax,* the *Dr. Phibes* films, *The Whales of August, Edward Scissorhands,* and Michael Jackson's video, *Thriller.* Victoria Price, in her book *Vincent Price: A Daughter's Biography*, quotes her father: "When I first came out here, I met Eddie, and thank God I met him. Actually I had known him slightly in New York, because I used to follow him around the galleries because I knew he had money. But I had knowledge, and I was interested in what he would buy — and he bought superb things."

Prison Robinson's second Broadway play, *Under Sentence,* dealt with prison reform. However, given his tough guy image, it is surprising how few of Edward G. Robinson's movies actually have a prison setting. In *Two Seconds* he faces the electric chair for murdering his wife. In *The Whole Town's Talking* he visits prison just long enough to bump off an enemy (Ed Brophy). He is sent to Alcatraz for a ten-year sentence for income tax evasion in *The Last Gangster. Blackmail* has innocent man Robinson sentenced to the chain gang. He is paroled from Sing Sing at the beginning of *Larceny, Inc.* With gang members, he breaks out of jail on *Black Tuesday* — the day the killers die in the electric chair. He is released from prison after fifteen years at the beginning of television's *The Legend of Jim Riva.*

Other characters in Robinson films spend time in prison. Claudette Colbert and Alan Ladd in *The Hole in the Wall* and *Hell on Frisco Bay,* respectively, have just been released. Richard Conte serves seven years for attempting to bribe a juror in *House of Strangers.*

Ginger Rogers gets out of prison to serve as a state's witness in *Tight Spot*. Fred MacMurray's execution scene in the gas chamber at Folsom Prison was deleted from the finished film of *Double Indemnity*. Another deleted scene—from *Scarlet Street*—had Robinson climbing a telephone pole to get a look over the prison wall at Dan Duryea's execution. The denouement of *All My Sons* has Robinson's character agreeing to be taken to prison, but he shoots himself instead. Earlier in the same film Burt Lancaster learns the truth about his father by going to prison to talk with Robinson's former business partner (played by Frank Conroy).

The Prize (Film, 1963) Multiple roles played by one actor have been a Hollywood staple for decades. Edward G. Robinson had already made a deft contribution to the form in the gangster comedy *The Whole Town's Talking* in 1935. Nearly thirty years later, the casting for a film adaptation of Irving Wallace's best-selling novel *The Prize* offered Robinson a second dual role. In the novel the two characters were Professor Max Stratman, a Nobel laureate in physics, and his older brother Walther, who had been brainwashed by Communists and defected to the East. Ernest Lehman's screenplay not only changed the characters to have Walther be a twin, but the role is actually that of an actor doing an impersonation. Walther never appears, having died years earlier. Unlike *The Whole Town's Talking*, which employed several trick screen confrontations between its two Robinson characters, *The Prize* has only one scene (at the end of the film) where the two characters meet and Robinson is actually onscreen with himself.

The Prize was a lightweight MGM mystery that afforded superstar Paul Newman opportunities to play comedy and show off his physique. In Denise Worrell's *Icons: Intimate Portraits*, Newman referred to the film as "a lark." Leslie Halliwell said of the picture in his *Film Guide*, "Whatever the original novel is like, the film is a Hitchcock pastiche which works better than most Hitchcocks: suspenseful, well-characterized, fast-moving and funny from beginning to end."

Screenwriter Lehman commented that the picture "did quite well at the box office. It was difficult for me to write simply because—wisely or unwisely—I decided to make a fun-and-games, *North by Northwest* type of entertainment out of it. I felt that was what the public wanted at the time.... I would say that Wallace's novel was far more sensibly serious than my capricious approach, and though the picture got many very good reviews, it also got some indifferent ones. I blame that on myself; if people failed to notice the tongue in my cheek, it was my fault as a writer, not theirs for dim vision...."—quoted in *Showcase*, by Roy Newquist.

Lehman's "fun-and-games" included a scene at a nudist colony similar to one at an art auction in his *North by Northwest*, wherein the hero, surrounded by the bad guys, is safe in a crowd but cannot escape. He "summons" the police through deliberate disorderly conduct.

Some of the reviews were almost as entertaining as the film. "You and I already know this," said *The New York Herald-Tribune*. "Good old Edward G. Robinson, playing an umlaut-accented physicist, has had a meeting with a queer Iron Curtain type ('So we meet again, Eckart!') and has been kidnapped after he refuses to defect to the East—and good old Edward G. Robinson, with a slightly lighter umlaut-accent, is busy impersonating himself in order to make un–American remarks at the Nobel ceremonies while the real Edward G. Robinson is being shanghaied to Leningrad aboard a freighter." According to *Newsweek*: "*The Prize* is the Nobel Prize. In this picture ... it is awarded to Edward G. Robinson, the well-known physicist. The minute the old dear arrives in Stockholm to get his check, he is abducted by some Russian agents who look as if they took sneering lessons from Little Caesar.... But now and then there are some funny lines. There is plenty of fast action, too."

The New York Times complained, "This florid farrago of fiction ... plays fast and loose not only with the prestige of the Nobel affair but also with simple conventions of melodrama and with the intelligence of the customers. It gathers together as recipients of Nobel awards about as lurid a lot of performers as might walk up to receive Oscars at one of those Academy Award nights in Hollywood." But the review added, "Mr. Robinson in both of his roles is good." *The New York Daily News* agreed, saying, "The able old pro, Edward G. Robinson, seen briefly as Dr. Max Stratman, gives a performance of strength and dignity, the best in the film." James Robert Parish, in *The Tough Guys,* simply referred to *The Prize* as one of Robinson's "solid film roles ... a lavishly mounted espionage thriller."

A Roxbury production; producer, Pandro S. Berman; associate producer, Kathryn Hereford; director, Mark Robson; screenplay, Ernest Lehman; based on the novel by Irving Wallace; assistant director, Hank Moonjean; art directors, George W. Davis, Urie McCleary; set, Henry Grace, Dick Pefferie; special effects, J. McMillan Johnson, A. Arnold Gillespie, Robert R. Hoag; music, Jerry Goldsmith; camera, William H. Daniels; editor, Adrienne Fazan; sound, Franklin Milton; wardrobe, Bill Thomas; makeup, William Tuttle; hairstyles, Sydney Guillaroff; cast: Paul Newman (Andrew Craig), Edward G. Robinson (Dr. Max Stratman / Impersonator), Elke Sommer (Inger Lisa Andersen), Diane Baker (Emily Stratman), Micheline Presle (Dr. Denise Marceau), Gerard Oury (Dr. Claude Marceau), Sergio Fantoni (Dr. Carlo Farelli), Kevin McCarthy (Dr. John Garrett), Leo G. Carroll (Count Bertil Jacobsson), Sacha Pitoeff (Daranyi), Jacqueline Beer (Monique Souvir), John Wengraf (Hans Eckart), Don Dubbins (Ivar Kramer), Virginia Christine (Mrs. Bergh), Rudolph Anders (Mr. Bergh), Martine Bartlett (Saralee Garrett), Karl Swenson (Hilding), John Qualen (Oscar), Ned Wever (Clark Wilson), Martin Brandt (Steen Ekberg), Ivan Triesault (Hotel clerk), Grazia Narciso (Mrs. Farelli), Larry Adare, Robin Adare (Garrett children), Lester Mathews, John Banner, Teru Shimada, Jerry Dunphy, Michael Panaieff (News correspondents), Edith Evanson (Mrs. Ahlquist), Queenie Leonard (Miss Fawley), Ben Wright, Anna Lee, Sam Edwards, Lyle Sudrow, Albert Carrier, Gregory Gaye (Reporters), Erik Holland (Photographer), Alice Frost (Swedish woman), Sven-Hugo Borg (Lindbloom), Ike Ivarsen (Speaker), Carl Rydin, Ronald Nyman (Burly Swedes), Sven Peterson, Ellie Ein, Raanheld Vidar (Bellboys), Peter Coe, Dr. Harold Dyrenforth, Fred Holliday (Officers), Noel Drayton (Constable Strohm), Gene Roth (Swedish man on phone), Carol Byron (Stewardess), Sid Raymond (Actor), Carl Carlsson (Swedish visitor), Karen Van Unge (Receptionist), Gregg Palmer (Swedish commentator), Donald Ein, Sigfried Tor (Waiters), Otto Reichow (Seaman), Robert Garrett, Paul Busch, Danny Klega, Fred Scheiwiller (Deck Hands), John Holland, Mauritz Hugo (Speakers), Anna Lena Lund (Blonde), Peter Bourne, Bjorn Foss (Swedish men), Margareta Lund, Felda Ein, Brigitta Engstrom (Women), Britta Eckman, Maiken Thornberger, Maria Schroeder, Jill Carson, Pam Peterson, Sigrid Petterson, Margareto Sullivan (Nudists); MGM; 136 minutes; Panavision, MetroColor; January 1964

Six Nobel winners gather at the Grand Hotel in Stockholm: Dr. Carlo Farelli and Dr. John Garrett, medicine; Drs. Claude and Denise Marceau, chemistry; Dr. Max Stratman, physics; and Andrew Craig, literature. Stratman chats briefly with Craig prior to going to meet with Dr. Eckart, a Communist who wants Stratman to denounce the West and rejoin old colleagues. The next day Craig thinks Stratman seems subtly different. A phone call summons Craig to an address in Stockholm, where he finds a man dying. He is pursued by a man who pushes him into a canal. Later, learning from Dr. Garrett that Dr. Stratman had been seen at an area hospital, Craig investigates. He runs into Dr. Eckart and discovers a hospital room that has only recently been vacated. Eckart's men follow Craig and try to run him down in a car. He retreats to a meeting at a nudist camp, where, by causing a scene he "summons" a police escort back to his hotel. Craig traces the kidnaped Stratman and Craig's lovely escort, Inger Lisa Andersen, to a steamer where they are being held hostage; the ship is bound for Leningrad. The three escape, but at the hotel Stratman suffers a heart seizure. Drs. Farelli and Garrett improvise a shock treatment to revive him. Everyone heads to the ceremonies, where briefly there are *two* Stratmans. The impostor flees but is killed. Craig chases the killer to the roof of the building, where the latter is shot by the police. Craig returns inside and accepts his Nobel Prize. Count Bertil Jacobsson, who has long been in charge of the annual proceedings, muses that because nothing ever goes wrong he is always foolish to worry.

Procter & Gamble's This Is Hollywood see "The Stranger"

Producers Every theatrical project has a producer, whether for the stage, film, television, a recording, or radio. He is the individual who has the ultimate responsibility, financially and developmentally, from script selection to final form. Producers range in authority from associates assigned to projects within a studio or theatrical organization to free-lance or often visionary creators who operate independently of the system.

Brothers Edgar and Arch Selwyn (Selwyn and Co.) were the producers of Edward G. Robinson's first two Broadway plays, *Under Fire* and *Under Sentence*. Several years later they mounted a production of *Stella Dallas* in which Robinson appeared. The producer Robinson most frequently worked for (discounting ten projects at the Theatre Guild) was Arthur Hopkins, in six productions from 1917 to 1923. In 1916 the Selwyns and Hopkins joined with Samuel Goldfish (changed to Goldwyn) to form Goldwyn Pictures. In 1920 Robinson was hired to be in the Goldwyn film *Fields of Glory*, but on seeing himself in some of the results, he begged to be let out of the contract. Goldwyn Pictures was destined to evolve into Metro-Goldwyn-Mayer in 1924, but Goldwyn already had been ousted, and in 1923 formed the new company, Samuel Goldwyn, Inc. Robinson worked for Goldwyn in *Barbary Coast*.

While Robinson was under contract at Warner Bros. from 1930 to 1942, Jack L. Warner was production chief; executive producers were Hal B. Wallis and (until 1933) Darryl F. Zanuck. Among associate producers were Henry Blanke and Robert Lord. Each received screen credit for a number of Robinson's films, Blanke as supervisor for *I Loved a Woman* and associate producer for *A Dispatch from Reuter's* and *The Sea Wolf*, and Lord, similarly, as supervisor for *Dark Hazard* and associate producer for both *The Amazing Dr. Clitterhouse* and *Confessions of a Nazi Spy*. The screen credits for *Dr. Ehrlich's Magic Bullet* and *The Sea Wolf* read "Jack L. Warner in charge of production" and "Hal B. Wallis, executive producer." They and Zanuck all claimed responsibility for the success of *Little Caesar*. On eight other films Wallis was listed as either executive producer (*Kid Galahad, Brother Orchid, Manpower*) or simply producer (*Five Star Final, Two Seconds, The Hatchet Man, A Dispatch from Reuter's, Larceny, Inc.*)

Directors of several of Edward G. Robinson's films doubled also as producers—Frank Capra, Cecil B. DeMille, Ben Hecht (also as writer), Gregory Ratoff, Fritz Lang, David Swift, Andrew L. Stone, and George Sidney (who also produced the *36th Academy Awards* and *Who Has Seen the Wind?* on TV). Actors serving as producers include Frank Sinatra (with Capra), *A Hole in the Head*; Charles Boyer, *Flesh and Fantasy*; and John Houseman (prior to his acting career), *Two Weeks in Another Town*.

Robinson himself was reluctant producer of one of his films, joining Sol Lesser to obtain financing for *The Red House*. Onscreen Robinson acted the role of film producer in *Pepe* and *My Geisha*. The latter's actual producer was Steve Parker, husband of star Shirley MacLaine. Diana Productions was formed by Joan Bennett and her husband, Walter Wanger, to produce *Scarlet Street*.

In the theater Joshua Logan, director of *Middle of the Night* on Broadway, was also its producer. Himan Brown produced all of the *Chanukah Festivals for Israel* at Madison Square Garden in which Robinson took part over a twelve-year period, and also two television specials in which he appeared for the Jewish Federation—*Stars Salute '64* and *Twelve Star Salute*.

Prohibition From 1920 to 1933 federal legislation prevented the manufacture, sale, and consumption of alcohol in the United States. It was a "noble experiment" that failed, since immediately the "bootlegger" began to make the stuff; the "speakeasy" sold it; and Americans drank it. Prohibition provided newfound success for crime lords like Al Capone. And in films the gangster was in his heyday. Edward G. Robinson plays "beer barons" in *The Little Giant, A Slight Case of Murder,* and, briefly, *Robin and the 7 Hoods.* In *Two Seconds* he gets drunk at a speakeasy and ends up married.

Projection of America (Short, 1943) This film was produced by the overseas division of the Office of War Information. Edward G. Robinson discussed life in America. Edward G. Robinson (Narrator); Office of War Information; 1943

Provine, Dorothy (1937–) was a success on the 1960s TV show *The Roaring Twenties.* She played the title role in *The Bonnie Parker Story,* and was also in *It's a Mad, Mad, Mad, Mad World, The Great Race,* and two with Edward G. Robinson—*Good Neighbor Sam,* as Jack Lemmon's wife, and *Never a Dull Moment,* as art instructor Sally Inwood.

Qualen, John (1899–1987), a diminutive Norwegian, was in the Broadway and screen versions of *Street Scene.* Other films include *His Girl Friday, The Grapes of Wrath, The Long Voyage Home, Casablanca, The High and the Mighty, Anatomy of a Murder, The Man Who Shot Liberty Valance,* and four with Edward G. Robinson—*Brother Orchid, Larceny, Inc., Cheyenne Autumn,* and *The Prize.*

Quayle, Sir Anthony (1913–89), an English actor, was with Edward G. Robinson in *Mackenna's Gold.* Trained at the Royal Academy of Dramatic Arts, he performed at the Old Vic. Other films: Olivier's *Hamlet, The Wrong Man, The Guns of Navarone, Lawrence of Arabia,* and *Anne of the Thousand Days* (Oscar nomination).

Quinn, Anthony (1915–2001) won supporting Oscars for *Viva Zapata* and *Lust for Life,* and received best actor nominations for *Zorba the Greek* and *Wild Is the Wind.* Other films include *Larceny, Inc.* (with Edward G. Robinson), *La Strada, The Buccaneer* (director), *The Guns of Navarone, Lawrence of Arabia,* and *Requiem for a Heavyweight.* He appeared with Robinson also in the *Chanukah Festival for Israel* in 1965.

Quotes "Some people have youth, some have beauty. I have menace." The quote refers to Edward G. Robinson's philosophy of success in being a film star.

Edward G. Robinson's final line in *Little Caesar* is as recognizable as the film itself as one of the screen's most famous quotations. Robinson utters the line in disbelief as he lies dying behind a billboard, mowed down by machine gun bullets from his nemesis, Sergeant Flaherty: "Mother of Mercy, is this the end of Rico?" Various sources refer to the line beginning, "Mother of God...." and *Little Caesar* may have been filmed with both versions.

Another well remembered line from the film comes during Rico's ascent to power, as he tells his boss, "Y'know Sam, you can dish it out, but you're gettin' so's you can't take it no more." A third household phrase of the time, "Take him for a ride," is not heard in the film.

Thirty-five years after *Little Caesar,* Robinson's standing as The Man is challenged by an upstart young poker player, and Edward G. Robinson's Lancey Howard bests *The Cincinnati Kid*'s aces-and-tens full house with a diamond straight flush, delivering this steely ultimatum: "You're good, Kid. But as long as I'm around, you're second best. You might as well learn to live with it." Punctuated by Robinson striking a match and gesturing with it in the Kid's direction, Robinson lights his cigar when he has finished the speech.

Other memorable lines spoken by Robinson on the screen include his deathbed plea in *Dr. Ehrlich's Magic Bullet,* added by the screenwriters with an awareness of what was happening in Nazi Germany at the time (1940, although the time of the film is 1912): "In days to come there will be epidemics of greed … hate … ignorance. We must fight them in life as we fought syphilis in the laboratory.…"

Aware that he was no matinee idol, in the early days of his theater career Robinson came up with a line to help him win parts from Broadway producers: "Not much face value, but when it comes to stage value, I'll deliver."

Robinson on acting: "An audience identifies with the actor of flesh and blood and heartbeat as no reader or beholder can identify with even the most artful photographs, books, or the most inspired paintings. There, says the watcher, but for some small difference in time, or costume, or inflection or gait, go I. And so the actor becomes a catalyst: he brings to bright ignition that spark in every human being that longs for the miracle of transformation."—March, 1969, as recipient of the George Spelvin Award from the Masquers

"I think I have not only been a good citizen. I think I have been an extraordinarily good citizen and I value this above everything else.… I think I may have taken money under false pretenses in my own business, and I may not have been as good a husband or father or friend as I should have been, but I know my Americanism is unblemished and fine and wonderful, and I am proud of it, and I don't feel it is conceit on my part to say this, and I stand on my record or fall on it.…" This quote is in the Congressional Record as part of Edward G. Robinson's testimony before the House Un-American Activities Committee in an effort to clear his name from Communist accusations.

"To Edward G. Robinson, who achieved greatness as a player, a dedicated citizen and patron of the arts, in sum a Renaissance man … from his friends in the industry he loves," is inscribed on the Academy Award statuette awarded to Edward G. Robinson posthumously in 1973, recognizing his life's work.

"It couldn't have come at a better time in a man's life," voiced Robinson through his widow, as she accepted his honorary Oscar on the ABC-tv telecast of the *45th Academy Awards*. His words continued, "Had it come earlier, it would have aroused deep feelings in me. Still, not so deep as now. I am so very grateful to my rich, warm, creative, talented, intimate colleagues who have been my life's associates. How much richer can you be?"

See **Academy Awards**; **Nazism**.

R K O   The initials stand for Radio-Keith-Orpheum, a film company that produced such classics as the musicals of Fred Astaire and Ginger Rogers, *The Informer, Citizen Kane, Suspicion,* and *The Woman in the Window* and *The Stranger,* with Edward G. Robinson. The company evolved out of corporate mergers in 1928. Howard Hughes acquired controlling interest in RKO in 1948, but film production ceased shortly thereafter.

Rachmil, Lewis J.   (1908–84) produced two of Edward G. Robinson's films in a row — his first Western, *The Violent Men,* and *Tight Spot.* Other films include *Gidget, Hawaii, Trader Horn, Footloose,* and *Protocol.*

The Racket   (Theater, 1928) Edward G. Robinson's very first gangster role was in 1927 in *The Racket*. The play opened on Broadway a full three years before *Little Caesar*. Robinson's character is listed in the playbill as "An Unidentified Man," but actually is a celebrated mobster named Nick Scarsi. Discussed at length during the first two acts of the three-act melodrama, Scarsi makes his first entrance late in the second act, killing a policeman. He escapes and is captured before Captain McQuigg, his adversary, finally identifies him for the audience.

The playwright, Bartlett Cormack, describes the character: "A man comes in from the street, hesitating at the door for a quick glance about the room. He is a muscular, hard-bodied, Americanized Italian of thirty-eight, in a slightly form-fitted brown topcoat and soft hat. He is smartly dressed, but under the knot of his necktie his soft colored shirt collar is fastened with a diamond bar pin." Since there were obvious parallels between Nick Scarsi and Chicago's then reigning underworld power Al Capone, Cormack added a preface to the script that included this disclaimer: "The game of identifying certain characters of the following play with living persons whose individuality in action and effect has made them well-known in Chicago, where the play is laid, and by grace of the press familiar to the outside world, has been pursued with such gossipy enthusiasm since the production of the play in New York that it perhaps behooves me to state that the names, the characters themselves, and the story of *The Racket* are imaginary...."

Chicago authorities nonetheless felt compelled to cancel the play's run there. Edward G. Robinson has noted that the aborted tour of *The Racket* took him to San Francisco and Los Angeles. And there the movie producers witnessed his powerful performance. He didn't much care for the role, taking it rather reluctantly, but, "Boy, did that play change my life," he commented in *All My Yesterdays*.

Robinson also had valuable advice for future actors, based on an embarrassing situation that arose during a performance of *The Racket* when his co-player was to shoot him dead in the last act of the play. As there were no blanks in the gun, it became necessary for Robinson to suffer an improvised heart attack to end the scene. His advice? "No matter how big you get, check out all the props."

Producer, Alexander McKaig; playwright, Bartlett Cormack; sets, Livingston Platt; costumes, Revellion Freres, Jay-Thorpe; company manager, Warren Lemon; press representative, John Peter Toohey; cast: Edward G. Robinson (An Unidentified Man [Nick Scarsi]), John Cromwell (Captain McQuigg), Edward Eliscu (Joe Scarsi), Marion Coakley (Irene Hayes), Romaine Callender (State's Attorney Welch), Willard Robertson (Pratt), Norman Foster (Dave Ames), Ralph Adams (Sam Meyer), Jack Clifford (Det. Clark), G. Pat Collins (Johnson), Harry English (Lt. Gill), Michael Flanagan, Charles O'Connor, (Patrolmen), Louis Frohoff (Alderman Kublacek), Mal Kelly (Sgt. Sullivan), Robert LeSeuer / Charles Peyton (Glick), Fred Irving Lewis (Det. Sgt. Delaney), Harry McCoy (Turck), Hugh O'Connell (Miller), C. E. Smith (Sgt. Schmidt); opened at the Ambassador Theatre, New York; November 22, 1927 (119 performances)

Both Robinson and *The Racket* received good reviews from the critics. *Theatre Magazine* called his performance "a masterly creation of character." *The New York Times* offered that the play was "a new melodrama ... a rattling good one.... [It] tells a sizzling story.... Edward G. Robinson makes a sinister figure out of the powerful Italian."

His work was singled out in *The New York Herald-Tribune*: "Robinson as the villainous boss was the only one whose makeup and manner clicked with 'theatre' the instant he stepped on the scene. He was quite wicked enough to satisfy the hungriest melodrama fan." This opinion was echoed by *The New York World:* "Robinson as the crook, stopping at nothing, was great, especially at the last when driven into a corner, threatening, desperate, but cold and calculating." Finally, Burns Mantle noted that the play "bears unmistakably the stamp of authenticity in character, scene and speech and reflects vividly a phase of civic life in America."

Racketeer Rabbit One rainy night in an abandoned house Bugs Bunny takes on Rocky (Edward G. Robinson) and Hugo (Peter Lorre).

Director, Friz Freleng; story, Michael Maltese; animation, Gerry Chiniquy, Manny Perez, Ken Champin, Virgil Ross; layouts and backgrounds, Hawley Pratt, Paul Julian; voices, Mel Blanc; musical director, Carl W. Stalling; Looney Tunes, 1946; 7 minutes

Radio Edward G. Robinson's most significant contribution to the medium was his series *Big Town*, in which he played Steve Wilson, managing editor of *The Illustrated Press* for four years on CBS. He also gave more than one hundred additional performances on the radio over a thirty-four-year span. The chronological listing below is the most complete available:

1931	August 8	*Radio Newsreel of Hollywood*
1932		Warner Bros. radio broadcast
1933	April 21	*The Chevrolet Program*
	November 7	*California Melodies*
1935	February 1	*Hollywood Hotel*: "The Whole Town's Talking"
1936	January 13	*Lux Radio Theatre*: "The Boss"
	January 30	*The Standard Brands Hour*: "The Inner Voice"
	April 17	*Lux Radio Theatre*: "Bullets or Ballots"
	May 8	*Hollywood Hotel*: "Bullets or Ballots"
1937	January 18	*Lux Radio Theatre*: "The Criminal Code"
	April 29	*Kate Smith's A & P Bandwagon*: "Thunder in the City"
	June 4	*Hollywood Hotel*: "Kid Galahad"
	July 3	*CBS Shakespeare Theatre*: "The Taming of the Shrew" (a.k.a. *Columbia's Shakespeare*, *1937 Shakespeare Festival*, and *The Shakespeare Cycle*)
	October 19 to June 2, 1942	*Big Town*: "The Case of the Missing Milk," "Death Rides the Highway," "Every Eighteen Hours," "The Million-Dollar Dog Stealing Racket," among many other episodes
1938	March 10	*Hollywood Showcase*
	December 19	*Lux Radio Theatre*: "Kid Galahad"
	December 24	*America Calling*: "Ship Forever Sailing"
1940	February 25	*Gulf Screen Guild Theatre*: "Blind Alley"
	April 30	*Children's Crusade for Children*
1941	November 2	*Gulf Screen Guild Theatre*: "The Amazing Dr. Clitterhouse"
	December 15	*We Hold These Truths*
1942	March 16	*Lux Radio Theatre*: "Manpower"
	May 19	*Network of the Americas*
1942–1944	(exact dates unknown)	*Treasury Star Parade*: "The Checker Player," "It Isn't Peanuts," "Joe Doakes and the White Star"
1943	January 4	*Lockheed's Ceiling Unlimited*
	February 8	*Lux Radio Theatre*: "The Maltese Falcon"
	March 15	*DuPont Cavalcade of America*: "A Case for the F.B.I."
	April 18	*Radio Readers Digest*
	April 26	*Lockheed's Ceiling Unlimited*: "World of Tomorrow"
	June 30	Hollywood War Savings radio program
	July 4	*U.S. Rubber Hour*: "Our American Scriptures"
	December 31	*Amos 'n' Andy*
1944		*Too Long, America*
	January 23	*Eddie Cantor's March of Dimes Special*
	April	United Nations radio program
	April 3	*Lux Radio Theatre*: "Destroyer"
	June 5	*Lady Esther's Screen Guild Theatre*: "The Amazing Dr. Clitterhouse"
	October 2	*Suspense*: "The Voice on the Stairs"
	November 6	*The Roosevelt Special*
1945	March 1	*Suspense*: "My Wife Geraldine"
	April 8	*P. Lorillard Comedy Theatre*: "A Slight Case of Murder"

	April 16	*Lux Radio Theatre*: "Only Yesterday"
	April 19	*Command Performance*
	April 30	*DuPont Cavalcade of America*: "The Philippines Never Surrendered"
	June 25	*Lux Radio Theatre*: "The Woman in the Window"
	July 16	*Lady Esther's Screen Guild Theatre*: "Flesh and Fantasy" (also dated October 13)
	August 14	*Command Performance*: "Victory Extra"
	September 29	Victory Chest program
1946	March 11	*DuPont Cavalcade of America*: "The Man with Hope in His Hands" (a.k.a. "The Doctor with Hope in His Hands")
	March 26	*Colgate Theatre of Romance*: "The Woman in the Window"
	October 7	*The Victor Borge Show*
	October 17	*Suspense*: "The Man Who Thought He Was Edward G. Robinson"
	November 18	*Lady Esther's Screen Guild Theatre*: "Blind Alley"
	November 24	*The Lucky Strike Program Starring Jack Benny*
	December 7	*Procter & Gamble's This Is Hollywood*: "The Stranger"
1947	October 26	*Hollywood Fights Back*
	?	*Family Theatre*
1948	March 14	*The Eternal Light*: "Island in the Wilderness"
	March 18	*Kraft Music Hall*
	April 11	*Sealtest Variety Theatre*: "Sleight of Hand"
	April 12	*Camel's Screen Guild Players*: "The Great Man Votes"
	September 30	*Suspense*: "The Man Who Wanted to Be Edward G. Robinson"
	October 7	*Kraft Music Hall*
	November 11	*Camel's Screen Guild Players*: "All My Sons"
1949	January 28	*Ford Theatre*: "The Woman in the Window"
	February 27	*NBC Playhouse*: "Night Has a Thousand Eyes"
	March 31	*Suspense*: "You Can't Die Twice"
	May 16	Savings Bond radio show
	July	*People Are Like That*
	November 28	*Lux Radio Theatre*: "Key Largo"
	December 2	*Screen Directors Playhouse*: "All My Sons"
1940's	(dates unknown)	*Mail Call* Red Cross radio show
1950	February 3	*Screen Directors Playhouse*: "The Sea Wolf"
	March 26	*Document A/777*
	June 1	*Suspense*: "A Case of Nerves"
	October 23	*Voice of America*
	October 25	*Voice of America*
	December	*Voice of America* (two programs)
	(dates unknown)	*For the Living*: "By-Products of the Atom," "Cancer, Cause for Hope," "Cancer in Men," "Cancer in Women," "Frauds and Superstitions," "Power of the X-Ray," "Radium Against Cancer," "The Seven

		Symptoms," "The Weapon of Surgery," "What Are We Fighting?," "The Why of Cancer," and two untitled episodes
1951	January 25	*Screen Directors Playhouse*: "House of Strangers"
1952	December 7	*The Eternal Light*: "Trial and Error"
1953	October 6	*The Buick-Berle Show*
	October 21	*Jerusalem Is Her Name*
	December 7	*Lux Radio Theatre*: "Man on a Tightrope"
	December 20	*The Eternal Light*: "Face to Face with Gabriel"
1954	January 24	*NBC Star Theatre*: "A Slight Case of Murder"
	December 26	*Guest Star*: "The Blue Albatross"
1963	December 1	*The World's Greatest Showman*
1965		*Letter from Birmingham Jail*

Radio Newsreel of Hollywood   Edward G. Robinson; August 17, 1931

Radio Readers Digest   Edward G. Robinson; ABC-radio; April 18, 1943

"Radium Against Cancer"   (Radio, 1950) *For the Living*, radio; sponsored by the American Cancer Society; cast: Edward G. Robinson, Anne Revere; episode E; 15 minutes; 1950

Raft, George   (1895–1980) was with Edward G. Robinson in *Manpower*, during which their on-set animosity made headlines. A radio version on *Lux Radio Theatre* followed, and they appeared together in *The Roosevelt Special*. They were together again in the film *A Bullet for Joey* eleven years later. Raft also was interviewed by the BBC for *The Hollywood Greats: Edward G. Robinson*. At the time he said of his co-star, "He was no tough guy, he didn't want to play tough guys — originally — but when he made *Little Caesar*, it made him a great reputation...." Raft and Robinson danced in each other's arms during a ship's concert aboard the *S.S. Normandie* in a transatlantic crossing in 1939. He turned down good pictures, i.e., *The Maltese Falcon* (Bogart) and *Double Indemnity* (Fred MacMurray); his other films include *Scarface, Bolero, Each Dawn I Die, They Drive by Night, Johnny Allegro, Black Widow*, and *Some Like It Hot*.

Ratoff, Gregory   (1897–1960) came to films via the Moscow Art Theatre, the Yiddish Players (New York), and Broadway. He directed and appeared in *Operation X*, with Edward G. Robinson. He also directed *Intermezzo, Adam Had Four Sons,* and *The Corsican Brothers,* and he appeared in *The Road to Glory, Seventh Heaven, All About Eve,* and *Exodus*.

Raye, Martha   (1916–94), a comedienne with trademark large mouth, was known for her work entertaining the troops from World War II through the Vietnam conflict, for which she received the Jean Hersholt Humanitarian Award. Edward G. Robinson was a guest on her TV variety show in 1956. Her films include *Rhythm on the Range, The Farmer's Daughter, The Boys from Syracuse, Four Jills in a Jeep, Monsieur Verdoux,* and *Jumbo*.

Reagan, Ronald   (1911–) was, of course, governor of California and the fortieth President of the United States, following a twenty-five year career in Hollywood. His films include *Dark Victory, Kings Row, Knute Rockne — All American, The Voice of the Turtle, Bedtime for Bonzo,* and, with Edward G. Robinson, (as a radio announcer) *The Amazing Dr. Clitterhouse* and *It's a Great Feeling* (as himself). On TV they were together in *Operation Entertainment,* and Reagan hosted TV's *General Electric Theatre,* presenting Robinson in the episode "The Drop-Out."

Red Channels This pamphlet, published in June 1950, listed the names of performers, writers, composers, and producers, with brief dossiers on each. It was the start of Edward G. Robinson's troubles with the House Un-American Activities Committee. The document cited organizations considered subversive or Communist fronts. Subtitled "The Report of Communist Influence on Radio and Television," *Red Channels* served to damage many careers during a period of mounting hysteria over infiltration by the Communists in the media.

The Red Cross at War (Documentary Film, 1943) Edward G. Robinson was narrator for this documentary film in 1943; date unknown

Red Cross Radio Show (Radio) Cast: Don Ameche, George Burns, Edward G. Robinson; date unknown

The Red House (Film, 1947) In 1947 producer Sol Lesser approached Edward G. Robinson with a screenplay by Delmer Daves based on a dark novel by George Agnew Chamberlain, *The Red House*. Robinson learned that his star name was needed to finance the production. With Lesser he formed the Film Guild Corporation / Thalia Productions to produce the film. According to Robinson, "It was a moody piece, got moody notices, but I think it made a few bucks."—*All My Yesterdays*

Generally the reviews were excellent for the film and its star. "An ordinary mystery story has received a booster charge of good direction in *The Red House*, and the result is a moody hair-raiser of a melodrama," said *The New York Herald-Tribune*. "With veterans Edward G. Robinson and Judith Anderson pacing four newcomers to a round of convincing performances, this ... production is a taut and steady item of menacing make-believe.... Daves' direction has brought the scenery so much to life that it becomes the most important character of the piece."

The New York Times advised that it "should supply horror-hungry audiences with the chills of the month.... Edward G. Robinson is excellent as crippled Pete, whose mind is cracking under the thrall of the horrible secret of the red house." In his *Film Guide* Leslie Halliwell referred to the film's "*Psycho*-like suspense melodrama [as] too extended for comfort and too restricting for the actors, but effective in spurts."

"Edward G. Robinson contributes another genuinely outstanding performance to his inspiring list of achievements. Only an actor of Robinson's skill and experience could withhold from overplaying so tempting a role," said *Modern Screen*. And finally, "1947 will probably see no film with suspense more chilling."—*Life*

Produced by the Film Guild Corporation / Thalia Productions; producers, Sol Lesser, Edward G. Robinson; director, Delmer Daves; based on the novel by George Agnew Chamberlain; screenplay, Daves; music, Miklos Rozsa; art director, McClure Capps; set, Dorcy Howard; camera, Bert Glennon; sound, Frank McWhorter; editor, Merrill White; production manager, Clem Beauchamp; costumes, Frank Beetson; makeup, Irving Berns; assistant director, Robert Stillman; cast: Edward G. Robinson (Pete Morgan), Lon McCallister (Nath Storm), Judith Anderson (Ellen Morgan), Allene Roberts (Meg Morgan), Julie London (Tibby), Rory Calhoun (Teller), Ona Munson (Mrs. Storm), Harry Shannon (Dr. Byrne), Walter Sande (Don Brent), Arthur Space, Pat Flaherty (Policemen); United Artists; 100 minutes; March 1947

Young Meg Morgan arranges to have her friend, Nath Storm, work part time to help Pete Morgan and his sister, Ellen, on their farm. Pete is Meg's guardian since the death of her parents several years earlier. Although Pete warns Nath to stay away from a red house in the Oxhead Woods, he and Meg spend the following Sunday searching for it. Pete instructs Teller, a caretaker he has hired, to fire his rifle at trespassers. Meg is running from Teller when she falls and breaks her leg. As weeks pass and Meg recovers, Pete's strange behavior increases. Ellen decides it is time to burn the red house, but she is shot by Teller.

Meg runs to Pete for help, but Ellen is dead. Pete takes Meg to the red house, where his mind reverts to the past, and Meg becomes her mother in his eyes. He loves her, he says. She screams, and to stop her he must kill her, as he killed her mother and father fifteen years earlier. Nath arrives with the police, and Pete runs. He drives his truck through a shed next to the red house, into a bog, where it sinks from view.

Redwing, Rodd (1905–1971), a Chickasaw Indian also known as Rodric, appears with Edward G. Robinson as one of the Osceola brothers in *Key Largo* and also has a role in *The Ten Commandments*. His other films include *Copper Sky, Lives of a Bengal Lancer, Elephant Walk, Gunga Din, The Naked Jungle,* and *Shalako*.

Reicher, Frank (1875–1965), a German emigre, acted and directed in the American theater and silent films. He appeared with Edward G. Robinson in *The Goat Song* and in the films *A Lady to Love* (in the German version), *The Amazing Dr. Clitterhouse* (as a psychiatrist), and *Dr. Ehrlich's Magic Bullet* (as Ehrlich's physician). Others among 200 films include *King Kong, Stage Door, To Be or Not To Be, Song of Bernadette,* and *Samson and Delilah*.

Reis, Irving (1906–53) directed Edward G. Robinson in *All My Sons*. He was founder of CBS Radio's *Columbia Workshop*, and became a Hollywood screenwriter in 1938 and a director two years later. His films include several in *The Falcon* series, as well as *The Bachelor and the Bobby-Soxer, Enchantment, Dancing in the Dark,* and *The Fourposter*.

Religion "Mother of Mercy, is this the end of Rico?" was not uttered in a church, but as the famous last line of *Little Caesar*, it perhaps was evidence of the main character's belief in a higher power. Rather, Rico used the church setting to eliminate an unreliable member of the gang, mowing him down on the front steps after he has been to confession!

The church figures in only a few of Edward G. Robinson's films. As the one real Jewish member of the all-star cast of *The Ten Commandments*, he is a skeptic, turning on Moses and his "desert God." In gangster roles in *Hell on Frisco Bay* and *Black Tuesday* his attitude is cynical at best. In the former he complains about the number of crucifixes his wife keeps in the house; in the latter he is not above killing a priest he is holding hostage.

In *Soylent Green* a priest is murdered for knowledge he gained in confession. But the way of the future, as depicted in that film, is pretty grim; one character laments as a character dies, "I think for my grandmother they had a service or something." *Operation San Pietro* has as its lame premise the theft of Michelangelo's *Pietà* from the Vatican and an army of priests giving chase.

A disillusioned preacher in *The Outrage* (William Shatner) experiences newfound faith with the discovery of an abandoned baby; and church-going has its respectable moments in *Our Vines Have Tender Grapes*, as Robinson is seen at services at Christmastime and later, in the spring, as the townspeople take up a collection to help a farmer whose barn was destroyed by fire. In the comedy *Brother Orchid* he joins an order of monks after having traveled the world, now declaring that here he has found "the real class."

Remakes Edward G. Robinson was in a number of films that were remakes of earlier silent works, notably *East Is West* and *Outside the Law* (wherein his roles originally were played by Warner Oland and Lon Chaney, respectively) and, of course, Cecil B. DeMille's epic version of his silent *The Ten Commandments*.

A Lady to Love, based on Sidney Howard's play *They Knew What They Wanted,* was the second of its four film versions, the first being the silent *The Secret Hour* (Pola Negri, Jean Hersholt). It was later remade under the play's title (Carole Lombard, Charles Laughton) and as *The Unholy Wife* (Diana Dors, Rod Steiger).

The Mouthpiece (Warren William) had a second incarnation, following *The Man Who Talked Too Much* (George Brent), as *Illegal,* with Robinson. *The Sea Wolf* had been done as a silent film three times and once as a talkie (Hobart Bosworth, Noah Beery, Ralph Ince, and Milton Sills); following Robinson's version, it was remade as *Barricade*, a western (Raymond Massey), *Wolf Larsen* (Barry Sullivan), and a TV feature (Charles Bronson). Robinson appeared in *The Outrage*, a Westernized reworking of the Japanese play and film *Rashomon*. (His counterpart in the Japanese film, a wigmaker, was played by Kichijiro Uedo.)

Five of his early features were remade. *Dark Hazard* became *Wine, Women and Horses* (Barton MacLane, Ann Sheridan); *Five Star Final* evolved into *Two Against the World* (Humphrey Bogart); *A Slight Case of Murder* was adapted into the musical *Stop, You're Killing Me* (Broderick Crawford, Claire Trevor); and *Kid Galahad* was remade as *The Wagons Roll at Night* (Bogart, Sylvia Sidney, Eddie Albert) and as a musical called *Kid Galahad* (Gig Young, Elvis Presley). For the last, the Robinson version was retitled *The Battling Bellhop* to avoid confusion when shown on television.

Tiger Shark had four versions in ten years — *Bengal Tiger* (Barton MacLane); *Slim* (Pat O'Brien, Henry Fonda, Margaret Lindsay); *King of the Lumberjacks* (Stanley Fields, John Payne); and, finally, *Manpower*, in which Robinson redid his role opposite Marlene Dietrich and George Raft.

Double Indemnity was remade for television with Richard Crenna, Lee J. Cobb, Samantha Eggar, and Robert Webber. *House of Strangers* reappeared as *Broken Lance*, and *Nightmare* is a remake of *Fear in the Night*. Robinson's projects *Grand Slam, The Little Giant*, and *A Slight Case of Murder*, should not be confused with other films of the same name.

Remley, Ralph M. (1894–1939) played in *The Whole Town's Talking* (an office wiseacre) and *Bullets or Ballots* (a veteran cop) with Edward G. Robinson. His other pictures include *The Story of Alexander Graham Bell*, *Make Way for Tomorrow*, *Princess O'Hara*, and *King of the Underworld*.

Rennie, James (1890–1965) played the hard-drinking alumnus Hank Bronson in *Tales of Manhattan*, with Edward G. Robinson. From the Broadway stage to silent pictures, he played opposite (and married) Dorothy Gish. Sound films include *A Bell for Adano*, *Wilson*, and *Now, Voyager*.

Restaurants A variety of night spots with music were backgrounds for Robinson films. In *Dr. Ehrlich's Magic Bullet* he and his wife and two doctor friends are celebrating his new appointment with the Koch Institute when he collapses during a waltz, the victim of tuberculosis. In *All My Sons* the Keller family goes out on the town for a lobster dinner, which is cut short by a drunken lady sauntering up to Robinson to call him "murderer."

An hilarious eating scene in *The Biggest Bundle of Them All* features the huge Francesco Mule gorging himself at a restaurant and telling a friend, "Wait, there is more!" Coffee shops are frequent settings, as in the beginning of *Little Caesar* when Rico and his buddy, Joe (Douglas Fairbanks, Jr.), have spaghetti and coffee after robbing a gas station. In *The Whole Town's Talking* Robinson and Jean Arthur have lunch at the Blue Bird Café, and he is spotted and reported, mistakenly, as Public Enemy No. 1. *Larceny, Inc.* and *Night Has a Thousand Eyes* also have coffee shop settings.

Robinson's character owns and runs the Bella Donna, a hotel-casino on the *Barbary Coast*. Other night clubs are featured in *I Am the Law* (Robinson dances the Big Apple with Wendy Barrie), *Kid Galahad* (Bette Davis sings "The Moon Is in Tears Tonight"), *Manpower* (Marlene Dietrich sings "He Lied and I Listened"), *Unholy Partners* (Marsha Hunt sings "After You've Gone"), *Bullets or Ballots* and *Brother Orchid* (clubs owned by Joan Blondell and Ann Sothern, respectively), *Two Seconds, Robin and the 7 Hoods, Nightmare*, and *Pepe*. Musical revues are featured.

Sidewalk or outdoor cafes are used for scenes in *A Dispatch from Reuter's, Seven Thieves, Scarlet Street, Grand Slam*, and *Two Weeks in Another Town*. Barrooms are settings in *House of Strangers, Tampico, Illegal, The Sea*

Wolf, Tales of Manhattan, and *The Woman in the Window.*

Reuter, Paul Julius Baron von (1816–99) His enterprise of transmitting stock prices from London via telegraph in 1851 grew into an international service. News of events in Europe still bears the Reuters name as disseminator of information to the world press, not unlike UPI (United Press International) and AP (Associated Press) in this country. Edward G. Robinson portrayed Reuter onscreen in *A Dispatch from Reuter's;* the film delineates his beginnings with a pigeon post and chronicles, among other events, a speech by Napoleon sent via telegraph, plus news of the Lincoln assassination. Reuter was born in Germany but became a naturalized British subject in 1871.

Reviews Edward G. Robinson's track record is excellent among reviewers. Often enough, his films were not as good as his performances in them. Early in his career he was often cited for his dynamic personality and superior acting ability. Later he was regarded among the best of the "old pros." His own assessment of his abilities sometimes followed no less respected commentary of the day than *The New York Times,* particularly if the review was less than praiseworthy. For example, the *Times* called *Night Has a Thousand Eyes* "unadulterated hokum," and that's what Robinson echoed in his autobiography. When the same paper found his performance in *Scarlet Street* "monotonous," that word was also used in his memoirs, as was "bloodless" from the *Times* review of *The Stranger.*

Among the more amusing reviews are two from the 1950s: "An actor who had developed well-nigh infinite modulations of the sneer, Robinson, after thirty years of practice, has at last produced his masterpiece. In *Vice Squad,* he displays a sneer so spectacular that he can almost be said to smile." And, of performances in *A Bullet for Joey:* "These are the things Mr. Raft and Mr. Robinson can act with their eyes shut—and sometimes do."

Reynolds, Debbie (1932–), singer-dancer-comedienne, was memorable in *Singin' in the Rain, The Tender Trap, Tammy and the Bachelor, The Mating Game, The Unsinkable Molly Brown* (Oscar nomination), and the more recent *Mother* and *In and Out.* She was a buddy of Edward G. Robinson's; they were in the TV special, *Operation Entertainment* and (sharing no scenes) *Pepe.*

Rice, Elmer (1892–1967) wrote the masterpiece of expressionist drama *The Adding Machine,* in which Edward G. Robinson appeared as the confused Shrdlu in the original production. With Robinson he appeared on the radio in *The Roosevelt Special.* Others among his 24 plays include *Street Scene, Counsellor-at-Law, Between Two Worlds,* and *Dream Girl.* He was married to actress Betty Field.

Richards, Addison (1887–1964) appeared in four films with Edward G. Robinson—*Bullets or Ballots, Destroyer, Illegal,* and *The Ten Commandments.* Other pictures include *My Little Chickadee, Pride of the Yankees, A Guy Named Joe, Spellbound, Leave Her to Heaven,* and *Anna and the King of Siam.*

Richards, Jeff (1922–89), a former professional ball player, was appropriately cast as a New York Giants rookie in *Big Leaguer,* with Edward G. Robinson. He was also in *Kill the Umpire, Angels in the Outfield, Seven Brides for Seven Brothers, Don't Go Near the Water,* and *Secret of Purple Reef.*

Richardson, Sir Ralph (1902–83), one of England's finest actors, appeared with Edward G. Robinson in *Thunder in the City.* He was also in *The Four Feathers, The Heiress* (Oscar nomination), *Richard III, Our Man in Havana, Long Day's Journey Into Night, Dr. Zhivago, Lady Caroline Lamb,* and *Greystoke* (Oscar nomination).

Rigaud, George (1905–84) Sometimes billed as Jorge, he appears in two films with Edward G. Robinson—*Grand Slam* and *Mad Checkmate.* Active since the 1930s, his films include *Paris Underground, I Walk Alone, The Happy Thieves,* and *Guns of the Magnificent Seven.*

The Right Man (Television, 1960) In 1960, the election year in which John F. Kennedy defeated Richard Nixon for the Presidency, CBS produced a special about famous candidates, real and fictional. The tone was lighthearted and bipartisan, with comic contributions from Tom Bosley and Paul Ford. Ironically, John Alexander, who was known for his comic portrait of Teddy Roosevelt in *Arsenic and Old Lace* on the stage and screen, here played Wendell Willkie, yielding the Roosevelt role to Edward G. Robinson.

Producer, Fred Freed; director, Burt Shevelove; music, George Kleinsinger; cast: Edward G. Robinson (Theodore Roosevelt), Thomas Mitchell (Grover Cleveland), Richard Boone (Abraham Lincoln), Art Carney (Franklin D. Roosevelt), Tom Bosley (Throttlebottom), Celeste Holm (Victoria Woodhull), Paul Ford (The Perfect Candidate), Martin Gabel (William Jennings Bryan), Loring Smith (Harry Daugherty), Tom Gorman (Joseph Medill), Kevin Patrick (Isbill), Alan Bunce (Al Smith), John Alexander (Wendell Wilkie), Mort Marshall (Lippman), Walter Klavin (Gilhooley), David Doyle (Fulton), Luis Van Rooten (Croker), Garry Moore (Narrator); CBS-TV; 60 minutes; October 24, 1960

Right You Are If You Think You Are (Theater, 1927) Edward G. Robinson enjoyed playing the matinees of *Right You Are If You Think You Are* and garnered favorable reviews. "Mr. Robinson plays Ponza ... with fine concentration and unity," said *The New Republic*. *The New York Times* called the play "a thoroughly delightful metaphysical melodrama ... mounted with superb skill.... Mr. Robinson as the husband act[s] capitally."

Produced by the Theatre Guild; playwright, Luigi Pirandello; director, Philip Moeller; cast: Edward G. Robinson (Ponza), Henry Travers (Sirelli), Morris Carnovsky (Commendatore Agazzi), Laura Hope Crewes (Amalia), Beryl Mercer (Signora Frola), Elisabeth Risdon (Signora Sirelli), Armina Marshall (Signora Ponza), Helen Westley, (Signora Cini), J. W. Austin (The Prefect), Philip Loeb (Centuri), Dorothy Fletcher (Signora Nenni), Maurice McRae (Butler), Phyllis Connard (Dina), Reginald Mason (Lamberto Laudisi), Philip Leigh (Gentleman); opened at the Guild Theatre; March 2, 1927 (48 performances)

Ponza, his wife, and mother-in-law, Signora Frola, live in separate apartments in a small Italian town, where explanations to gossips are different from each of them. Ponza says his mother-in-law insanely believes her daughter is his wife, but her daughter is deceased. The Signora claims Ponza is insane, believing his first wife has died. Signora Ponza says that the three of them live separately for reasons that need not be explained.

Ritt, Martin (1920–90) began his career as a stage actor, then directed on Broadway and for television. He taught at the Actors Studio and since 1957 has directed films: *The Sound and the Fury, The Spy Who Came in from the Cold, The Great White Hope, Sounder, Pete 'n' Tillie, The Front, Norma Rae,* and several with Paul Newman — *The Long Hot Summer, Paris Blues, Hud, The Outrage* (featuring Edward G. Robinson), and *Hombre*.

Ritter, Thelma (1905–1969), often a wisecracking comedienne, played in *A Hole in the Head* as Edward G. Robinson's wife, Sophie. Earlier, on radio, she appeared with him on *Big Town*. She received six Academy Award nominations — for *All About Eve, The Mating Season, With a Song in My Heart, Pickup on South Street, Pillow Talk,* and *Birdman of Alcatraz*. She also was in *Miracle on 34th Street, Titanic* (1953, as Molly Brown), *Daddy Long Legs,* and *The Misfits*.

Robert Taylor's Detectives see "The Legend of Jim Riva"

Roberts, Allene (1928–) played Meg, the young girl who searched the Oxhead Woods for *The Red House*, which starred Edward G. Robinson. Subsequently she was seen in *Knock on Any Door* with Humphrey Bogart and in the police drama *The Hoodlum, Sign of the Ram, Santa Fe,* and *Union Station*.

Roberts, Tony (1939–) was on Broadway in Woody Allen's *Play It Again, Sam*, repeating the role onscreen. He also appeared in *Star-Spangled Girl, Serpico, The Taking of Pelham 1–2–3,* and *Annie Hall.* He was Dr. Levine in "The Messiah on Mott Street" on *Night Gallery,* with Edward G. Robinson.

See **"The Messiah on Mott Street."**

Robertson, John S. (1878–1964) directed two of Edward G. Robinson's early films, the silent *The Bright Shawl* and *The Night Ride.* He directed over forty films from 1917 to 1935, including John Barrymore's *Dr. Jekyll and Mr. Hyde, Tess of the Story Country, The Enchanted Cottage, The Crime Doctor,* and *Captain Hurricane.*

Robertson, Willard (1886–1948) went from the stage to films, appearing with Edward G. Robinson in *The Racket, Dark Hazard,* and *The Last Gangster.* His other screen credits include *Skippy, The Gorgeous Hussy, Winterset, Kentucky, The Cat and the Canary,* and *Air Force.*

Robeson, Paul (1898–1976) made only ten films, the last being *Tales of Manhattan,* which also featured Edward G. Robinson. Among the others were *The Emperor Jones* and *Showboat,* the former also a Broadway success, as was his *Othello.* He visited the Soviet Union and embraced Communism in an effort to thwart racial discrimination, but he remained an American citizen.

Robin and the 7 Hoods (Film, 1964)

This was the only feature film Edward G. Robinson made in which his star presence spoke for itself—as the quintessential Warner Brothers gangster icon. In *Robin and the 7 Hoods,* a Rat Pack musical based loosely and farcically on the Robin Hood legend, he appears only in the first three minutes of the picture prior to gangland assassination—and without billing.

Thereafter his presence in the film is in the form of two portraits that hang prominently on the walls of the set. "Edward G. Robinson does an imitation of Edward G. Robinson, which is lots of fun," said *Newsweek.* James Robert Parish, in *Great Gangster Pictures,* noted that "the best bit in the film occurs at the outset. In 1928, a party is thrown for Big Jim (Robinson), a *Little Caesar*–style hood. At this birthday party he is gunned down a la George Raft in *Some Like It Hot.*"

"It's shades of *Little Caesar* and *Guys and Dolls* and every orphanage musical Crosby ever enhanced—but how wrong can it go when you start out with Edward G. Robinson as the top hood of 'em all?"—*The New York Herald-Tribune*

The New York Times thought less of the film, saying it was "almost as strained and archaic in the fable it has to tell of Prohibition-era gangsters in Chicago as the fable of Robin Hood it travesties.... For all those magnificent talents, it is an artless and obvious film. The brightest thing about it is its color photography." But *Variety* felt that, "the spirit of a hit is apparent and picture stacks up nicely as mass entertainment.... [It] opens in 1928 with the gangster kingpin of the day—Edward G. Robinson doing a cameo bit here—guest of honor at a birthday party. After a sentimental rendition of *For He's a Jolly Good Fellow,* they shoot Robinson dead."

Richard Schickel, writing in *Life,* said, "Robinson makes a brief but hilarious reappearance as a Little Caesar at a testimonial dinner that turns into his own wake.... Part of *Robin*'s charm is its adroit use of the unexpected—as when Robinson's boys wind up a chorus of *For He's a Jolly Good Fellow* with a salvo of bullets aimed at his heart; or the solemn moment at Robinson's funeral, when the bugler steps up at the grave and out comes not *Taps,* but *Last Call....* With this off-gait, off-beat film, Sinatra and the Clan have finally made their point. I sincerely hope that they will stop, now that they're ahead. As any seasoned crap player can tell them, the odds against making a point twice in a row are 12 to 7."

A P-C production; executive producer, Howard W. Koch; producer, Frank Sinatra; associate producer, William H. Daniels; director, Gordon Douglas; screenplay, David R. Schwartz; camera, Daniels; art director, LeRoy Deane; set, Ralph Bretton; assistant directors, David Salven, Lee White; dialogue supervisor, Thom Conroy; music, Nelson Riddle; songs, Sammy Cahn, James Van Heusen;

orchestra, Gilbert C. Grau; choreography, Jack Baker; costumes, Donfeld; hairstyles, Jean Burt Reilly; makeup, Gordon Bau; sound, Everett Hughes, Vinton Vernon; editor, Sam O'Steen; cast: Frank Sinatra (Robbo), Dean Martin (Little John), Sammy Davis, Jr., (Will), Bing Crosby (Allen A. Dale), Peter Falk (Guy Gisborne), Barbara Rush (Marian), Victor Buono (Deputy Sheriff Potts), Hank Henry (Six Seconds), Robert Carricart (Blue Jaw), Allen Jenkins (Vermin), Jack LaRue (Tomatoes), Sonny King, Phil Crosby, Richard Bakalyan (Robbo's men), Robert Foulk (Sheriff Glick), Hans Conried (Mr. Ricks), Sig Rumann (Hammacher), Phil Arnold (Gimp), Harry Swoger (Soup Meat), Joseph Ruskin (Tick), Bernard Fein (Liver Jackson), Harry Wilson, Joe Brooks, Barry Kelley (Police chief), Maurice Manson (Dignitary), Chris Hughes (Judge), Ron Dayton (Man), Larry Mann (Workman), Richard Simmons, Roger Creed (Gisborne's Men), Caryl Lee Hill (Waitress), Carolyn Morin (House girl), Al Silvani, Joe Gray, John Delgado, Boyd "Red" Morgan, John Pedrini, Al Wyatt, Chet Allen, Tony Randall (Hoods), Bill Zuckert (Prosecuting attorney), Milton Rudin (Judge), Ed Ness, Frank Scannell (Lawyers), Thom Conroy, Joey Jackson (Butlers), Linda Brent (Woman derelict), Jerry Davis, Manuel Padilla, Mark Sherwood (Boys), Mickey Finn (Bartender), Billy Curtis, Eve Bernhardt, Anne D'Aubray, Leslie Perkins, Chuck Hicks, Paul Frees (Announcer), and, unbilled, Edward G. Robinson (Big Jim); Warner Bros.; 123 (or 103) minutes; August 1964

At his birthday party, Big Jim, who runs the Chicago mobs, is shot dead by Guy Gisborne's gang, while Robbo, a rival, is out of town on business. A subtle gang war ensues with Guy and Robbo destroying each other's nightclubs. Robbo is joined by Will Scarlet and Little John. When Marian, Big Jim's daughter, gives Robbo $50,000 to find her father's killers, he gets rid of it by giving the money to an orphanage. The publicity turns Robbo into a hero. Allan A. Dale, of the orphanage, is added to Robbo's staff to run public relations. One by one, Marian uses Robbo, John, Guy, and even Sheriff Potts to gain control of gang operations. Guy and the Sheriff end up in the cornerstones at dedications of new buildings. When Robbo's organization is wrecked after a trial, Robbo, John, and Will are left out in the cold as street corner Santas. Marian, meanwhile, has hooked up with Dale.

Robinson, Dewey (1898–1950) is in three films with Edward G. Robinson — as one of the henchmen in *The Little Giant*; running the pub where Charles Laughton plays honky tonk piano in *Tales of Manhattan*; and saving Robinson from hanging himself in *Scarlet Street*. He is also in *Enemies of the Law, A Midsummer Night's Dream,* and *Dillinger*.

Robinson, Edward G., Jr. (1933–74) was the only child of Edward G. Robinson and his first wife, Gladys, and was called Manny. He had a sometimes troubled life, which was chronicled in an autobiography, *My Father—My Son*, published in 1958. The book discusses his difficulties growing up in the shadow of his famous but loving parents and incidents of drunk driving and a denied suicide attempt, among other brushes with the law. In 1952 he married Frances Chisholm, a model and actress; their daughter, Francesca, was born the following year. They were divorced in 1955. Later marriages were to Elaine Conte and Non Morris. A book on Marilyn Monroe, *The Marilyn Encyclopedia*, mentions their affair when Manny was nineteen and she was 25. He had roles in her films *Some Like It Hot* and *Bus Stop* and was also onscreen in *Screaming Eagles, Tank Battalion, Invasion U.S.A.,* and TV's *City Beneath the Sea*. Following brief periods of estrangment, he reconciled with his parents and worked with his father on television (*Zane Grey Theatre, Bracken's World*), both on camera and as an assistant director. He appeared in stage productions of *A Streetcar Named Desire* and *The Time of Your Life*. Father and son did a radio presentation of a scene from *All My Sons*. Robinson Jr. died thirteen months to the day after his father, on February 26, 1974.

Rod Serling's Night Gallery see "The Messiah on Mott Street"

Rogers, Ginger (1911–95) starred in *Tight Spot* and *Tales of Manhattan* (second episode) with Edward G. Robinson. An Oscar winner for *Kitty Foyle*, she sang and danced with Fred Astaire in *Flying Down to Rio, The Gay Divorcee,* and *Top Hat,* and was also in *42nd Street, Stage Door, Roxie Hart, Lady in the Dark, The Major and the Minor,* and *Black Widow*.

Roland, Gilbert (1905–94), a dashing Mexican-born silent star in *Camille*, played an Indian in *Cheyenne Autumn*, with Edward G. Robinson. Other pictures include *She Done Him Wrong, Juarez, The Tall Men, The Bad and the Beautiful, The Big Circus,* and *Islands in the Stream*.

Roman, Ruth (1924–99) played in *The Jungle Queen* series in the 1940s, also *Stage Door Canteen, Since You Went Away, Good Sam, Champion, Three Secrets, Strangers on a Train, The Far Country, Love Has Many Faces*, and, with Edward G. Robinson, a bit role in *Night Has a Thousand Eyes* and a co-starring part in *The Old Man Who Cried Wolf* on TV.

Romero, Cesar (1907–94) is in three films with Edward G. Robinson, but they share no scenes: *Tales of Manhattan* (second episode) *Mooch*, and *Pepe* (as himself in the Las Vegas sequence). His other films include *Clive of India, Diamond Jim, Julia Misbehaves, Vera Cruz, Around the World in 80 Days, Batman* (as the Joker in the TV series), and *Hot Millions*.

Roos, Joanna (1901–89) played the role of Esther onstage with Edward G. Robinson in *The Idle Inn*, and forty years later was Janet, his production assistant, in *Two Weeks in Another Town*, one of her first film roles. A New York actress, she also appeared in *Splendor in the Grass*.

Roosevelt, Franklin D. (1882–1945) was the 32nd President of the United States and the only chief executive to serve more than three terms of office. Prior to his election in 1932 he had been Secretary of the Navy (during World War I) and, later, Governor of New York. As President, he fought the Depression with his campaign, the New Deal, saw America through World War II, and began efforts toward organizing the United Nations.

Roosevelt's fight against paralyzing polio was dramatized by Dore Schary in the play and film *Sunrise at Campobello*, in which he was portrayed by Ralph Bellamy. Edward Herrman has played him in recent productions, and in TV's *The Right Man*, with Edward G. Robinson as his cousin, Theodore, he was played by Art Carney.

Robinson campaigned for Roosevelt in his re-elections. With Melvyn Douglas, he auctioned off the President's dun-colored fedora hat to raise $3,200 in campaign funds, and in another ploy, he joined Walter Huston, Groucho Marx, and Robert Benchley in a drag variety show, wearing Southern Belle dresses and banana curls. Jane Wyman and other female stars donned tuxes to be the "ladies'" escorts. The 1940 Hollywood-for-Roosevelt committee included Pat O'Brien, Joan Bennett, Douglas Fairbanks, Jr., Alice Faye, Robinson, Rosalind Russell, and Henry Fonda. With other celebrities, Robinson worked for re-election on radio in *The Roosevelt Special* in 1944.

The President himself was heard at the conclusion of the radio broadcast *We Hold These Truths*, which commemorated the 150th anniversary of the Bill of Rights. It was broadcast exactly one week after the attack on Pearl Harbor in December 1941.

Roosevelt, Theodore (1858–1919) was an attorney and member of the New York state legislature from 1881, and president of the police board. After serving as assistant secretary of the Navy, he formed the "Rough Riders" during the Spanish-American war and subsequently became mayor of New York. He became the 26th President of the United States as Vice President under assassinated William McKinley. He helped settle the great coal strike, fought monopolies through "trust-busting," and was vigorously active in international politics, notably in building the Panama Canal and in ending the Russo-Japanese war. He won the Nobel Peace Prize in 1906. His best known impersonation is that of John Alexander as "Teddy" Brewster on stage and screen in the comedy *Arsenic and Old Lace.* He was portrayed by Edward G. Robinson on TV in *The Right Man*, and in *I Loved a Woman*, by E. J. Ratcliffe, confronting Robinson's character about the ethics of selling tainted meat to the Army. A real life result was the pure food act of 1906.

The Roosevelt Special (Radio, 1944) More than thirty film stars and other luminaries appeared on a radio election eve special for Franklin Roosevelt's last term of office. It included "a 94-year-old Republican who shook the hand of Abraham Lincoln, 'the greatest Republican of them all,' [who] tells why he's voting for Roosevelt," according to *Radio Yesteryear*, which calls this program a "fascinating, albeit low point in American political broadcasting." *The Roosevelt Special* may have been the only time the six major Warner Bros. gangster stars—Bogart, Cagney, Garfield, Muni, Raft, and Robinson—ever appeared together!

CBS-radio; writer, Norman Corwin; music, E. Y. Harburg, Earl Robinson; participants: Lucille Ball, Tallulah Bankhead, Constance Bennett, Joan Bennett, Gertrude Berg, Milton Berle, Mr. and Mrs. Irving Berlin, Humphrey Bogart, Charles Boyer, Virginia Bruce, James Cagney, Harry Carey, Bennett Cerf, Claudette Colbert, Marc Connelly, Joseph Cotten, Russell Crouse, Linda Darnell, John Dewey, Eddie Dowling, Olin Downes, Edna Ferber, John Garfield, Judy Garland, James Gleason, Paulette Goddard, John Gunther, Averell Harriman, Betty Hall, Susan Hayward, Rita Hayworth, Fannie Hurst, Walter Huston, Rex Ingram, the Ink Spots, George Jessel, Danny Kaye, Gene Kelly, Evelyn Keyes, Groucho Marx, Dorothy Maymor, Paul Muni, Clarence Muse, Alonzo Myers, Cliff Nazarro, Julius Oscar, Dorothy Parker, Waldo Pierce, George Raft, Quentin Reynolds, Elmer Rice, June Richmond, Edward G. Robinson, President Franklin D. Roosevelt, Barney Ross, Vincent Sheehan, Frank Sinatra, Gale Sondergaard, Vilhjalmur Stafansson, Paul Strand, Franchot Tone, Lana Turner, Louis Untermeyer, Benay Venuta, Richard Whorf, Monty Woolley, Fay Wray, Jane Wyman, Keenan Wynn; November 6, 1944

Rosenbloom, "Slapsie" Maxie (1903–76) was a prizefighter who held the light-heavyweight world championship for four years. He turned to films and TV, playing comic streetwise hoods. In *The Amazing Dr. Clitterhouse*, with Edward G. Robinson, he plays Butch, and he also has roles in *Mr. Broadway, Each Dawn I Die, To the Shores of Tripoli,* and *The Beat Generation.*

Rowlands, Gena (1934–) understudied for *The Seven-Year Itch* on Broadway, then played in *Middle of the Night* opposite Edward G. Robinson, whom she called "a gentle, scholarly man with a sense of privacy about him." They performed a segment of the play on *The Ed Sullivan Show*. In Hollywood she was Oscar-nominated for two films directed by her husband, the late **John Cassavetes** (1929–89)—*A Woman Under the Influence* and *Gloria*. More recently, she appears in *Another Woman, Once Around,* and *Hope Floats*, as well as the A&E *Biography* about Robinson, "Little Big Man," in which she talked about his respect for acting. "He said, 'It's not just a vanity thing that you go up and show off, and everybody applauds and says isn't that nice? You are communicating with the audience—your pain, the experiences that you've had, and that you've survived. And you take that to your character and through your character to your audience. And then your audience starts sending it back. It's a rather magical thing that happens.' But it is not a shallow thing with him. He felt that you really had that duty and that it was not only—it was your great joy and pleasure. And it was wonderful to be around someone who thought in those terms and lived in those terms."

A Royal Fandango (Theater, 1923) *A Royal Fandango* was Edward G. Robinson's sixth and final play in association with producer-director Arthur Hopkins. During this venture he became upset that the director initially entrusted the actors to stage the play all on their own, with star Ethel Barrymore naturally always gravitating to center stage. Although conceding that the audience would pay to see the star, Robinson nonetheless asked Hopkins to be let out of his contract. Hopkins' counter was to subtly restage the scenes, and Robinson stayed, but the play, which ran 24 performances, was not successful, despite mild praise from *The New York Times:* "There is a certain charm and humor, an originality of humoresque fancy."

Producer-director, Arthur Hopkins; playwright, Zoe Akins; cast: Ethel Barrymore (H.R.H. Princess Amelia), Spencer Tracy (Holt), Edward G. Robinson (Pascual), Jose Allesandro (Chucho Panez), Frank Antiseri (Skelly), Virginia Chauvenet (Lady Lucy Rabid), Denise Corday (Henriette), Drake DeKay (Arthur), Charles Eaton (Prince Alexander), Walter Howe (Parrish), Teddy Jones (Prince Michael), Cyril Keightley (H.R.H. Prince Peter), Aileen Poe (Pilar), Beverly Sitgreaves (Ampero), Lorna Volare (Princess Titania), Harold Webster (Mr. Wright); opened at the Plymouth Theatre, New York; November 12, 1923

Her Royal Highness Princess Amelia is given to occasional attacks of love madness and falls for a handsome matador, Chucho Panez. On a visit to the mountains to tend him during an illness, she learns of a plot to assassinate her husband, Prince Peter, and, shaken, she returns to him and their three children.

A Royal Fandango was the only time Edward G. Robinson worked with Spencer Tracy. Both were virtually unknown actors who were only a few years from making their respective marks on the stage and screen.

"An unsigned review in the old *New York World* mentioned Tracy and Robinson: 'They looked as though they had been picked up by the property man.'"— Bill Davidson, *Spencer Tracy, Tragic Idol*

Rub, Christian (1887–1956) is in *Silver Dollar*, with Edward G. Robinson, as Hook, a miner, and in *Tales of Manhattan* as a musician in the Laughton episode. His is the voice of Gepetto in Disney's *Pinocchio*, and he also appears in *Heidi, You Can't Take It with You, Captains Courageous,* and *The Great Waltz.*

Rubin, Benny (1899–1986), a Jewish comic, had roles with Edward G. Robinson in *The Glass Web* (as a clown) and *A Hole in the Head* (as Abe Diamond). Other films include *Here Comes Mr. Jordan* and *Thoroughly Modern Millie.*

Ruhmann, Heinz (1902–94) was a German actor who appeared, with Edward G. Robinson, as Cardinal Braun in *Operation San Pietro.* He was also in *Ship of Fools, The Man Who Thought He Was Sherlock Holmes,* and several films in his native country from the silent era.

Rumann, Sig (1884–1967), a German character actor, made three films with Edward G. Robinson: *Confessions of a Nazi Spy* (as Krogman, a Nazi lawyer); *Dr. Ehrlich's Magic Bullet* (as Dr. Wolfert); and *Robin and the 7 Hoods* (as Hammacher, owner of a pretzel factory). He is also in *Ninotchka, A Night at the Opera, Stalag 17,* and *The Glenn Miller Story.*

Runyon, Damon (1884–1946), with Howard Lindsay, wrote the play *A Slight Case of Murder,* on which the Edward G. Robinson film of the same name is based. Once a sports writer, he turned to satirical comedies about the New York underworld. The most successful adaptation of his work is the musical *Guys and Dolls.*

Rush, Barbara (1927–) came to films from the Pasadena Playhouse. She was in *Robin and the 7 Hoods,* as Edward G. Robinson's daughter, Marian, though they shared no scenes, and also *The Young Lions, The Bramble Bush, Come Blow Your Horn, The Young Philadelphians,* and *The Man.*

Russell, Connie (1923–90) appeared with Edward G. Robinson as a singer in *Unholy Partners,* and in a singing and acting role in *Nightmare.* Onscreen from 1937, her other films include *Melody and Romance, Lady Be Good, This Is My Love,* and *Ship Ahoy.*

Russell, Gail (1924–61), onscreen from 1943, played Jean Courtland, the ingenue in *Night Has a Thousand Eyes,* with Edward G. Robinson. She also appears in *Lady in the Dark, Our Hearts Were Young and Gay, Angel and the Badman, The Uninvited,* and *The Wake of the Red Witch.*

Ruysdael, Basil (1888–1960) was in *The Violent Men,* with Edward G. Robinson, as Tex Hinkleman. Among his other films, from 1929, are *The Cocoanuts, Pinky, Broken Arrow, Carrie, The Blackboard Jungle,* and *The Story of Ruth.* He was a former announcer and opera singer.

Ryan, Mary (1886–1948), a New York actress, appeared with Edward G. Robinson in *The Little Teacher.* She appeared in the silent films *The Blind Cattle King, The Power of Silence,* and *Who Is the Savage?*

Ryan, Robert (1909–73) was on the radio with Edward G. Robinson in *Document A/777* and *Hollywood Fights Back.* In New York at Madison Square Garden they appeared together in the *Chanukah Festival for Israel* in 1963. Films include *The Set-Up, Crossfire* (best supporting actor Oscar nomination), *The Professionals,* and *The Iceman Cometh.*

Sammy Going South see ***A Boy Ten Feet Tall***

Samson and Delilah (Theater, 1920) This play within a play is an allegorical work. Art and the theater are personified as Samson and Delilah, respectively, with the public symbolized as the Philistines. Art is betrayed by the theater in a parallel to the Samson story. Peter Krumback, who wrote the play, dismisses the actor playing Samson and takes on the role himself opposite his wife Dagmar, as Delilah. But Dagmar is secretly in love with Sophus Meyers, a furniture dealer. When Peter discovers the two, he intends to shoot them both, but instead kills himself.

Producer, Arthur Hopkins; playwright, Sven Lange; translated by Samuel S. Grossman; cast: Jacob Ben-Ami (Peter Krumback), Pauline Lord (Dagmar Krumback), Edward G. Robinson (The Director), Samuel Jaffe (Kristensen), Manart Kippen (Lundberg), Jacob Kingsberry (Olson), Alexis M. Polianov (Nagel), Robert T. Haines (Sophus Meyers), Marie Bruce (Laura), Thomas Meegan (Munson), A. W. Reno (Frederick), Robert Harrison (Dukar), Olga Olonova (Milka), Stella Larimore (Pila); opened at the Greenwich Village Theatre, New York; November 17, 1920

Edward G. Robinson had mixed feelings about *Samson and Delilah* due to the personality of Russian-Yiddish star Jacob Ben-Ami, whose talent, in Robinson's opinion, was counter-balanced by a stubborn temperament. Appearing in his first English-speaking role, Ben-Ami garnered the best reviews. On the other hand, Robinson had great respect for producer Arthur Hopkins, was enamored of leading lady Pauline Lord, and was happy to be working for the first time with his lifelong friend Sam Jaffe.

The New York Times found *Samson and Delilah* "a showy and interesting, but intrinsically important play.... There must be a word for the helpful work of Robert T. Haines, Edward G. Robinson (a fine performance), Manart Kippen, and Marie Bruce."

Sanchez, Adam Edward (1983–), son of Edward G. Robinson's only granddaughter — by his only son, Edward G. Robinson, Jr. — he is named after the actor. Formerly a four-year varsity football player at Malibu High School, he currently studies history and policitical science on scholarship at California Lutheran University.

Sanchez, Francesca Gladys Robinson (1953–), the only daughter of Edward G. Robinson, Jr., is Robinson's only grandchild.

She was educated at Marymount High School, U.C.L.A., and Imaculate Heart College, where she earned a fine arts degree. Today she is an art consultant. In the 1960s her grandfather escorted her and her teen friends to Beatles concerts on the west coast. Francesca married Ricardo Sanchez in 1977, and their son, Adam Edward was named for his great-grandfather. Francesca appears on two biographical specials—the BBC's *The Hollywood Greats: Edward G. Robinson*, and "Little Big Man," produced for the *A&E Biography* series.

Sanchez, Ricardo Adan   (1940–99), a friend of Edward G. Robinson, Jr., married his daughter Francesca in 1977. He was part of the Southern California community as a property manager in Malibu. He held an engineering degree from U.C.L.A. and earlier had worked in films at MGM for producer Arthur Freed.

Sanders, George   (1906–72) won a best supporting actor Oscar for *All About Eve*. His other films include *The Moon and Sixpence, Rebecca, Foreign Correspondent, Man Hunt, While the City Sleeps, Village of the Damned*, and, with Edward G. Robinson, *Confessions of a Nazi Spy* (as Nazi Franz Schlager) and *Tales of Manhattan* (as Williams).

Sanford, Erskine   (1880–1950) plays a small role in *The Stranger* and several others of Orson Welles' films. He was with the Theatre Guild and acted with Edward G. Robinson in *Juarez and Maximilian* and *The Goat Song*.

Savalas, Telly   (1924–94) was best known for his role as television detective *Kojak*. He appeared as Kojak on TV's *The Marcus Nelson Murders*, and also was in *Birdman of Alcatraz, The Slender Thread, The Dirty Dozen*, and *Mackenna's Gold* (as Sergeant Tibbs) with Edward G. Robinson.

Savings Bond Show   (Radio, 1949) Producers, Cornwell Jackson, William Wildiss; writers, Hugh Wedlock, Howard Schneider, Ed Hellwig, John Fenton Murray; participants: Eddie "Rochester" Anderson, Edward Arnold, Lionel Barrymore, Jack Benny, Irene Dunne, Verna Felton, Betty Garrett, Bob Hope, Al Jolson, Gene Kelly, Alan Ladd (Master of ceremonies), Jules Munshin, Edward G. Robinson, Roy Rogers, Frank Sinatra, Red Skelton, John Snyder (Secretary of the Treasury), Jo Stafford, President Harry S. Truman, Fred Waring, Esther Williams, the Riders of the Purple Sage, Robert Armbruster and His Orchestra, Ken Carpenter (announcer); 60 minutes; ABC-radio, May 16, 1949

Sawyer, Connie   repeated her stage role on film as the drunken Miss Wexler in *A Hole in the Head*. She was onscreen also in *Ada, Oh God!, True Grit, When Harry Met Sally*, and *Dumb and Dumber*.

Sawyer, Joseph   (1901–82) is one of Killer Mannion's henchmen in *The Whole Town's Talking* and an unwitting conspirator in *Confessions of a Nazi Spy*, with Edward G. Robinson. Other credits include *The Informer, The Petrified Forest, The Grapes of Wrath, Sergeant York, A Double Life, Gilda*, and the TV series *Rin Tin Tin* (as Sergeant O'Hara).

Saylor, Syd   (1895–1962) was in silent two-reel comedies and, in his later years, often played a stuttering cowboy, as in *Cheyenne Autumn*. In *Scarlet Street* he is a reporter covering an execution. Among his other films are *Little Miss Broadway, Arizona, Sitting Pretty, Mule Train*, and *Big Jack*.

Scarlet Street   (Film, 1946) The success of *The Woman in the Window* the year before prompted several of its participants to reunite for another *film noir* venture. Director Fritz Lang teamed again with Edward G. Robinson, Joan Bennett, Dan Duryea, and several character players to make *Scarlet Street*. Diana Productions was comprised of Lang, Bennett, and her husband, Walter Wanger. The French play *La Chienne* (*The Bitch*), on which the film is based, told the story of a love triangle from the points of view of its three principals. It was filmed in 1931 as *La Chienne* by Jean Renoir.

Lang's production met with censorship problems. Robinson stabs Bennett several times, which was objectionable, and Robinson's character goes free at the fade-out. Some of the stabs were deleted, but the film has many more than just the one that several sources say was left after editing. And the ending stood, doubtless because, even in his freedom, Robinson's character would be tortured by the memory of his victims for the rest of his life.

On his way home from a party in tribute to his years of service as a cashier for J. J. Hogarth & Company, Christopher Cross sees a man slapping a woman in the street. He knocks the man unconscious with his umbrella. The woman, Kitty March, lets him buy her a drink, and he becomes infatuated. Chris's wife, Adele, hates his Sunday painting. He rents an apartment for Kitty where he also can paint, and eventually he embezzles from the firm for her. Johnny, Kitty's boyfriend, doubts Chris's talent, although Kitty believes Chris is a known artist. When Johnny takes two works to a dealer in Greenwich Village, they are bought by art critic Elliot Janeway through the Dellarowe Gallery. Johnny, fearing Janeway and Dellarowe are the police, lies, saying the works are Kitty's. Horrified, she signs several works, which go on display. Adele sees them and accuses Chris of forgery! More confused than angry, Chris confronts Kitty. She tells him she was desperate for money. Thrilled that his work is being recognized, Chris has Kitty pose for a "self portrait." Adele's first husband turns up and demands money from Chris to stay missing. Chris, however, seizes the opportunity to be rid of his shrewish wife. His embezzling is discovered, but Chris is not prosecuted. He goes to the apartment and sees Kitty embracing Johnny. Johnny leaves. Kitty laughs at Chris, calling him old and ugly. He stabs her repeatedly with an ice pick. Johnny is tried for her murder and executed. Chris is now homeless and without a job, haunted by the voices of Kitty and Johnny. He unsuccessfully tries suicide. Years pass; the voices continue. Routed from sleeping on a bench in Central Park, Chris shuffles past Dellarowe's window, where Kitty's portrait is being carried out, having been sold for $10,000.

A Diana/Fritz Lang Production; executive producer, Walter Wanger; producer-director, Fritz Lang; screenplay, Dudley Nichols; based on the novel and play *La Chienne* by Georges de la Fouchardiere, Mouzey-Eon; camera, Milton Krasner; art director, Alexander Golitzen, John B. Goodman; sound, Glenn E. Anderson, Bernard B. Brown; costumes, Travis Banton; paintings, John Decker; makeup, Jack P. Pierce; hairstyles, Carmen Dirigo; assistant director, Melville Shyer; special effects, John Fulton; set, Russell A. Gausman, Carl Lawrence; music, Hans J. Salter; editor, Arthur Hilton; cast: Edward G. Robinson (Christopher Cross), Joan Bennett (Katherine "Kitty" March), Dan Duryea (Johnny Prince), Margaret Lindsay (Millie), Rosalind Ivan (Adele), Jess Barker (Janeway), Samuel S. Hinds (Charlie), Russell Hicks (J. J. Hogarth), Arthur Loft (Dellarowe), Charles Kemper (Homer Higgins), Vladimir Sokoloff (Pop Lejon), Cy Kendall (Nick), Thomas Jackson (Inspector), Fred Essler (Marchetti), Anita Bolster (Mrs. Michaels), Byron Foulger (Jones), George Lloyd, Joe Devlin, Syd Saylor (Reporters), Lou Lubin (Tiny), Edgar Dearing, Tom Dillon, Lee Phelps, Matt Willis, Robert Malcolm (Policemen), Chuck Hamilton (Chauffeur), Gus Glassmire, Ralph Littlefield, Sherry Hall, Howard Mitchell, Jack Statham (Employees), Rodney Bell (Barney), Henri DeSoto (Waiter), Milton Kibbee (Saunders), Tom Daly (Penny), George Meader (Holliday), Clarence Muse (Ben), John Barton (Hurdy gurdy), Emmett Vogan (Prosecutor), Horace Murphy (Milkman), Will Wright (Loan manager), Dewey Robinson (Derelict), Fritz Leiber (Evangelist), Dick Wessel, Dick Curtis (Detectives), Richard Abbott, Richard Cramer, Rev. Neal Dodd, Ralph Dunn, Arthur Gould Porter, William Hall, Herbert Heywood, Boyd Irwin, Edward Keane, Constance Purdy, Beatrice Roberts, Wally Scott, Kerry Vaughn, Charles C. Wilson; Universal; 103 minutes; January 1946

"Six weeks before its scheduled New York opening ... it was slapped with a ban by the Motion Picture Division of the New York State Department of Education. Rather than request certain deletions in the 'adult drama,' the Board of Review banned the entire film, an action taken only rarely against a major Hollywood production (like *The Outlaw*). On appeal the Board announced that, in consideration of public opinion and the seriousness of the film's intentions(!), the motion picture would be licensed for exhibition if certain cuts were made — like, allegedly, elimination of six of the seven stabs which Christopher Cross (Robinson) inflicts on Kitty March (Bennett) with an ice pick, as well as certain isolated lines of dialogue. The cuts were made." — James Robert Parish and Alvin H. Marill, *The Cinema of Edward G. Robinson*

"*Scarlet Street* was not only Fritz Lang's favorite American film," noted Robert Ottoson in his book *A Reference Guide to the American Film Noir: 1940–1958*, "but it contains one of the most typical noir themes — the weak-willed male who becomes involved with a *femme fatale*, which eventually leads to his downfall.... One cannot forget the penultimate scene, when Robinson staggers into his dark, dingy tenement room. Neon lights flashing outside, Hans Salter's throbbing music on the soundtrack, and Robinson climbing on a chair in an attempt to hang himself convey everything one needs to know about the forties *film noir*."

"Lang employed John Decker to paint fourteen 'primitives' in the tradition of Henri Rousseau and Camille Bombois for *Scarlet Street*. Decker, who also served as a technical advisor, patiently instructed Robinson in the processes that would be followed by an amateur painter.... According to an observer who visited Lang at Sound Stage Nine at Universal, the director 'got up on chairs and examined the pictures....' He squinted through his range-finder and conferred volubly with Robinson.... After several hours ... Lang announced that it would not be necessary for Decker to repaint any of the canvases." — *The Films of Fritz Lang* by Frederick W. Ott

"It may have a nightmarish quality, but that was intentional after he committed the murder.... I even had a scene (which I myself cut out — it didn't click, it was comic to me): the evening Dan Duryea was to be electrocuted in Sing-Sing, I had Robinson climbing up a telegraph pole on a hill overlooking the prison to watch the glare of the light in the death house. It was too much. But what you call stylized is something else. Perhaps it comes from the fact that everything was shot in the studio." — Fritz Lang

Atypically, Robinson's reviews were weak. *The Sunday New York Times* said, "It seems a sluggish and manufactured tale.... Edward G. Robinson performs monotonously." *The New York Herald-Tribune* was not much more favorable, commenting that, "Robinson, who is no mean art connoisseur, must have had a field day acting the part of the cashier who discovers that he has real talent in a thwarted love affair. He gives his all to the portrayal, sometimes a bit too much."

The New Yorker allowed that, "Robinson conducts himself with a kind of weary competence," while *Variety* actually offered praise: "Script is tightly written by Dudley Nichols and is played for sustained interest by the cast. Two stars turn in top work to keep the interest high."

Schell, Maria (1926–) was the mother in *Who Has Seen the Wind?*, a TV special about a family without a country in which Edward G. Robinson plays the ship's captain. She won international acting awards for *The Last Bridge* (Cannes) and *Gervaise* (Venice). Her American films include *The Brothers Karamazov, The Hanging Tree,* and *Superman*.

Schildkraut, Joseph (1895–1964), Edward G. Robinson's classmate at the American Academy of Dramatic Arts, appeared with him on Broadway in *Peer Gynt*. On the screen they were together in *The Night Ride* and the German version of *A Lady to Love* (*Die Sehnsucht Jeder Frau*). Other films include *King of Kings, The Life of Emile Zola* (best supporting actor Oscar as Captain Dreyfus), and *The Diary of Anne Frank*, as Otto Frank, a role he recreated following a long Broadway run.

Schildkraut, Rudolph (1865–1930), the actor's father, starred in the Yiddish play *Number 37*, in which Edward G. Robinson had an early featured role.

Schneider, Romy (1938–82), the daughter of Austrian screen actors, was a star for ten years in Europe before making American films, including *The Victors, The Cardinal, Good Neighbor Sam* (with Edward G. Robinson), and *What's New Pussycat?* She then returned to European films.

Schurz, Carl (1829–1906) was a Prussian-born editor, soldier, and political leader in the United States. Among the literary works he edited were the New York *Evening Post* and *Harper's Weekly*. He had been a republican senator from Missouri and minister to Spain prior to being appointed Secretary of the Interior by President Lincoln in 1877. He is depicted on the film *Cheyenne Autumn* (and played by Edward G. Robinson) as having intervened on behalf of the Indians. Historically that never happened, although he was sympathetic to their cause, arguing for fair treatment. He was also a leader of the anti-slavery movement.

Science Fiction *Soylent Green*, Edward G. Robinson's last film, ventures into the realm of science fiction in its grim outlook on the future. But rather than depicting alien beings or a connection between the earth and some strange new world, at issue is the horrific change possible if more isn't done in the way of conservation of the planet — waste, destruction, overpopulation, and cannibalism.

The occult is represented in *Night Has a Thousand Eyes* and *Flesh and Fantasy* (the mysteries of clairvoyance), resulting in some otherwise impossible events in the stories. *Nightmare* and *The Hole in the Wall* deal with crime by hypnotism and fortune telling, respectively. TV's *The Devil and Daniel Webster* involved the supernatural element of calling up the dead.

Scourby, Alexander (1913–85) was narrator for *Victory at Sea*, among other documentary films, and played roles in *Affair in Trinidad, Because of You, The Big Heat, Man on a String, The Devil at 4 O'Clock*. With Edward G. Robinson, he played Raymond LeMay, one of the *Seven Thieves*.

Screen Actors Guild Edward G. Robinson was a longtime member of the Screen Actors Guild, a union formed in 1933. He and other liberal members, such as Katharine Hepburn, Alexander Knox, and Paul Henreid, were vocal in their campaigns, notably in dealing with striking actors. Members of the conservative opposition included Ronald Reagan, George Murphy, Edward Arnold, and Robert Montgomery.

On November 16, 1969, Robinson received the Guild's annual award "for outstanding achievement in fostering the finest ideals of the acting profession." The award was presented by president Charlton Heston and board member Karl Malden at the Guild's annual membership meeting at the Hollywood Palladium. Previous recipients were Bob Hope, Barbara Stanwyck, William Gargan, and James Stewart.

Screen Director's Playhouse (Radio) This program aired from January 1949 through September 1951 on NBC and ABC-radio. It presented Edward G. Robinson in shortened adaptations of four of his films: *The Sea Wolf, Night Has a Thousand Eyes, House of Strangers,* and *All My Sons.*

Creator, Don Sharpe; producer, Howard Wylie; announcer, Jimmy Wallington; orchestra, Henry Russell; director, Bill Cairn; writers, Dick Simmons, Milton Geiger

See **"All My Sons"**; **"House of Strangers"**; **"Night Has a Thousand Eyes"**; **"The Sea Wolf."**

Screen Snapshots (Short films) Edward G. Robinson appeared in six documentary film short subjects about Hollywood, produced by Columbia Pictures.

"Russian Music" (Series #21); with Edward G. Robinson; 1942

"Golden Jubilee of Film" (Series 23); participants: Fred Astaire, John Barrymore, Lionel Barrymore, Wallace Beery, Humphrey Bogart, Irene Dunne, Lillian Gish, Cary Grant, Rita Hayworth, Hedy Lamarr, Carole Lombard, Mary Pickford, Edward G. Robinson, Rosalind Russell; 1944

"Hollywood Honors Hersholt" (Series 27); participants: Edward G. Robinson, Jean Hersholt; 1948

"Hollywood Friars Honor George Jessel" (Series 27); participants: Edward G. Robinson, George Jessel; 1948

"Ice Capades" (Series 29); participants: Dana Andrews, Dan Duryea, Wanda Hendrix, Edward G. Robinson; 1950

"Hollywood Memories" (Series 30); with Edward G. Robinson; 1951

The Sea Wolf (Film, 1941) Edward G. Robinson first read Jack London's novel *The Sea-Wolf* as serialized in *The Saturday Evening Post* in 1904. Thirty-seven years later on the screen, the role of Wolf Larsen was well suited to Robinson's tough guy image. Though the story was from the turn of the century, the film, with its Nietzschean dictatorial villain, had a timely parallel with World War II.

Three silent versions of the story, and one with sound, had already been made. Hobart Bosworth in 1913, Noah Beery in 1920, Ralph Ince in 1925, and Milton Sills in 1930 had all played Wolf Larsen. Following Robinson's fifth version, there were three others — a disguised western, *Barricade*, with Raymond Massey, in 1950; *Wolf Larsen*, with Barry Sullivan, in 1957; and finally, a cable television movie in 1993 with Charles Bronson and Christopher Reeve. "Some of the [Robinson] film's footage was reused, in a colorized version," for the latter, according to Charles Matthews in his book *Oscar A to Z*. In fact, the special effects for Robinson's version of *The Sea Wolf* were nominated for an Oscar, but the winner was *I Wanted Wings*.

Charles Higham and Joel Greenberg, in *Hollywood in the Forties*, praised "Michael Curtiz' magnificent 1941 version ... full justice was for once done to London's text, here adapted by Robert Rossen. With the aid of models, newly introduced fog machines, and a studio tank, the film hauntingly captured an eerie malevolent atmosphere, brooding and full of terror.... From its economic opening scenes ... to its powerful climax ... it gripped consistently. Throughout, Curtiz provided object lessons in the use of sound — the groaning timbers of the ship, creaking footsteps, the wind — and closeup, while the art direction of Anton Grot, Sol Polito's bravura low-key camerawork, and the masterfully understated music of Erich Wolfgang Korngold helped make *The Sea Wolf* a triumph of Warner's craftsmanship. The performances were faultless: Edward G. Robinson's Wolf Larsen, obsessed, satanic, played to the hilt as a demoniac descendent of Captain Ahab, a tormented Nietzschean figure who delights equally in inflicting cruelty on his underlings and reading the works of Milton and Shakespeare...."

"Robinson is not content to play the sea wolf as a grotesque," stated to Foster Hirsch. "He makes him a cripple rather than a fiend, a man in the grip of some powerful undefined force.... It's a vibrantly physical performance, Robinson fiercely rubbing his aching skull, stomping magisterially on the deck.... What gives the performance its particular tension is the possibility Robinson suggests that Larsen might have been normal ... there are flashes of the brilliant and cultivated gentleman that might have been.... Robinson vividly conveys the character's crude yet genuine intellect, his strong yearning for self-knowledge. And yet he conveys as well the character's underlying helplessness.... One of the great psychotics in American films."— Foster Hirsch, *Edward G. Robinson: A Pyramid Illustrated History of the Movies*

Reviews were generally positive, although some felt Robinson went overboard. "We don't recall that he has ever been presented with such scrupulous psychological respect as he is in [this] version of *The Sea Wolf*," reported *The New York Times*. "This time his monstrous sadism is explored, and the mind of the

Wolf is exposed as just a bundle of psychoses. With Edward G. Robinson playing him, the expose is vivid indeed.... Some of *The Sea Wolf* is too heavily drenched with theatrical villainy, and Mr. Robinson occasionally overacts the part. But on the whole, the slapping and cuffing are done with impressive virility and in a manner distinctive to Warner films."

"On the whole, the cast is first rate," said *The New York Herald-Tribune*. "Robinson gives to a few moments of overacting as the tyrannical captain of the *Ghost*, but he is generally helpful to the melodramatic scheme of things." *Variety* cited the "marquee voltage" of Robinson, John Garfield, and Ida Lupino in the "strong adventure drama," and added that, "Robinson provides plenty of vigor and two-fisted energy to the actor-proof role of Wolf Larsen and at times is over-directed."

"At the head of the splendid acting team is Edward G. Robinson," wrote Tony Thomas in *Films of the Forties*. "[He] thoroughly exploits the rich possibilities of his role.... The film allowed Robinson something he richly deserved but seldom got — top billing and a major characterization ... his acting develops the role fully."

And lastly, according to R.A.E. Pickard, "the fine performance of Edward G. Robinson stands out in this technically expert, finely written version of Jack London's turn-of-the-century sea drama."—*The Oscar from A to Z*

Producers, Jack L. Warner, Hal B. Wallis; director, Michael Curtiz; screenplay, Robert Rossen; based on the novel by Jack London; associate producer, Henry Blanke; camera, Sol Polito; art director, Anton Grot; special effects, Byron Haskin, H. F. Koenekamp (Oscar nomination); music, Erich Wolfgang Korngold; music director, Leo F. Forbstein; orchestra, Hugo Friedhofer, Ray Heindorf; sound, Oliver S. Garretson; dialogue director, Jo Graham; editor, George Amy; makeup, Perc Westmore; cast: Edward G. Robinson (Wolf Larsen), Ida Lupino (Ruth Brewster), John Garfield (George Leach), Alexander Knox (Humphrey Van Weyden), Barry Fitzgerald (Cooky), Gene Lockhart (Dr. "Louie" Prescott), Stanley Ridges (Johnson), Howard DaSilva (Harrison), Francis McDonald (Svenson), David Bruce (Young sailor), Ralf Harolde (Agent), Frank Lackteen (Smoke), Louis Mason, Dutch Hendrian (Crew members), Cliff Clark, William Gould (Detectives), Charles Sullivan (First mate), Ernie Adams (Pickpocket), Jeane Cowan (Singer), Wilfred Lucas (Helmsman), Ethan Laidlaw, George Magrill; Warner Bros.; 100 minutes; March 1941

Captain Wolf Larsen of the sealing schooner *Ghost* picks up two survivors of a ferry disaster—Ruth Webster, an escaped convict, and Humphrey Van Weyden, a writer. Van Weyden, shocked at the brutality aboard the *Ghost*, is forced to serve as cabin boy. Cooky steals Van Weyden's notes and turns them over to Larsen, who enjoys the writings and urges Van Weyden to write about him. Self-educated, Larsen believes in the philosophy of John Milton's *Paradise Lost*: "Better to reign in hell than serve in heaven." Van Weyden learns that the Captain suffers headaches and is going blind. George Leach, another convict who signed on in San Francisco to escape the police, gives blood to save Ruth, who is delirious in a cabin below. Louie, the ship's drunken doctor, enjoys a brief moment of pride in restoring her health, but, ridiculed by Larsen and the crew, he leaps to his death from the topmast. Leach, Ruth, and Van Weyden escape in a dinghy. Larsen tells the crew that Cooky informed on them about an attempted mutiny, and he is keelhauled. A shark attacks, and Cooky loses his legs before he can be rescued. The *Ghost* begins sinking, having been fired upon by the Captain's brother, Death Larsen. The escapees meet up with the ship and try to pick up supplies, but Larsen locks Leach in the storeroom. Almost completely blind now, Larsen shoots at Van Weyden. The writer pretends Larsen missed and nobly offers to go down with the ship instead of Leach. When Larsen hears Van Weyden's body fall, he realizes the trick, but Ruth and Leach escape as the ship goes under. They row to an island and freedom.

"The Sea Wolf" (Radio, 1950) The script of *The Sea Wolf* was adapted for presentation on *Screen Director's Playhouse*.

Creator, Don Sharpe; producer, Howard Wylie; announcer, Jerry Wallington; orchestra, Henry Russell; director, Bill Cairn; writers, Dick Simmons, Milton Geiger; cast: Edward G. Robinson (Wolf Larsen), Paul Frees, Lurene Tuttle, Lou Merrill, Wilms Herbert, Herb Butterfield; NBC-radio; February 3, 1950

Sealtest Variety Theatre (Radio, 1948) Writer, Milton Geiger; continuity, Howard Harris; director, Glenhall Taylor; cast: Dorothy Lamour, Edward G. Robinson, Jimmy Durante, Henry Russell and His Orchestra, Carlton KaDell (announcer); the Crew Chiefs; NBC-radio; April 11, 1948

Dorothy Lamour and Edward G. Robinson appear in a drama called "Sleight of Hand."

Seastrom, Victor (1879–1960) [Sjostrom] was in Hollywood for five years, having directed Swedish films, then returned home. Among his U.S. films are *He Who Gets Slapped, The Tower of Lies, The Scarlet Letter, The Divine Woman, The Wind,* and, with Edward G. Robinson, *A Lady to Love.* Late in his career he acted in Ingmar Bergman's *Wild Strawberries.*

Secombe, Sir Harry (1921–2001), a heavyset tenor, made his first film impact as Mr. Bumble, who runs the orphanage in *Oliver!* He plays Bjornsterne Bjornson, a Norwegian playwright, in *Song of Norway*, with Edward G. Robinson. He is also in *Svengali, Davy,* and *The Bed Sitting Room.*

Die Sehnsucht Jeder Frau see *A Lady to Love*

Seitz, John (1893–1979), cinematographer, is the inventor of the matte shot, (in which images are blocked out or replaced as a trick effect). He received seven Oscar nominations — for *Double Indemnity* (starring Edward G. Robinson), *The Divine Lady, Five Graves to Cairo, The Lost Weekend, Sunset Boulevard, When Worlds Collide,* and *Rogue Cop.* Also with Robinson he worked on *Hell on Frisco Bay* and *Night Has a Thousand Eyes.* On the latter film, Seitz commented in *Film Noir Reader 3*, "Eddie Robinson had a good chance to win the [Academy] Award for that one. He was so moving…"

Selwyn and Company produced *Under Fire*, Edward G. Robinson's first Broadway play, and also his second, *Under Sentence*, and yet another, a touring production of *Stella Dallas.* The production company was comprised of Arch Selwyn (1877–1959) and his brother Edgar (1875–1944); their successes continued for a dozen years: *Under Cover, Why Marry?, Smilin' Through, The Circle,* and *Romeo and Juliet.* Their All-Star Feature Films Company merged with Goldwyn, becoming a forerunner of MGM. They produced plays separately (*Bitter Sweet, Gentlemen Prefer Blondes, Strike Up the Band*), and Edgar directed for the screen (*The Sin of Madelon Claudet*), wrote, and produced films.

Selzer, Milton (1918–) was Doc, one of the poker players in *The Cincinnati Kid*, with Edward G. Robinson. He worked in television and films: *The Young Savages, In Enemy Country,* and *The Legend of Lylah Clare,* among others.

Serra, Raymond An actor and more or less a lookalike for Edward G. Robinson, he wrote a play produced on Broadway in 1978 called *Manny*, which chronicled Robinson's life and career. Serra also played the title character. The play was not well received by the critics. Serra also appeared on television, notably *Contract on Cherry Street*, a police drama starring Frank Sinatra, whom he admired, and in the films *Marathon Man, Dog Day Afternoon, Prizzi's Honor,* and *Wolfen.*

"A Set of Values" (Television, 1955) This was the second of Edward G. Robinson's two appearances on *Ford Theatre.*

Producer, Irving Starr; cast: Edward G. Robinson (Baron Carter), Ann Doran (Sue Carter), Tommy Cook (Jerry Carter), Paul Fix (Franklin), Joseph Downing (Arnie); *Ford Theatre*, NBC-TV; 30 minutes; December 29, 1955

"The Seven Symptoms" (Radio, 1950) Sponsored by the American Cancer Society;

Edward G. Robinson (narrator); radio; *For the Living*, sequence F; 15 minutes; 1950

Seven Thieves (Film, 1960) This film, only the fourth that Edward G. Robinson made for 20th Century–Fox, used process photography to suggest European locations in Cannes and Monte Carlo, where the thieves of the title plot to rob the casino of $4 million in francs. The screenplay was by a gin-rummy-playing pal of Robinson's, Sydney Boehm, who had earlier written the scripts for both *Black Tuesday* and *Hell on Frisco Bay*. Boehm also produced.

Robinson was now 66 years old, and, perhaps appropriately, *Seven Thieves* began a series of films in which the actor masterminded elaborate schemes in which younger gang members carried out the greater share of the physical activity. Rod Steiger co-starred as an old friend who turns out to be Robinson's son and the power behind "Professor" Robinson's brains. The ads for the film had "Little Caesar" joining "Al Capone" to "pull off Monte Carlo's biggest heist!"

The director was Henry Hathaway, who did not always see eye to eye with Steiger's method acting and intensity. "Christ, it was supposed to be a fun film," said Hathaway, "and Steiger is far from having a sense of humor." Apparently, the "fun film" idea was to translate into a lightweight caper film; earlier stars suggested were William Powell and Dean Martin. Joan Collins and Eli Wallach provided good support. The reviews were mixed, but *Seven Thieves* was solid entertainment and received an Academy Award nomination for Bill Thomas's costume designs.

Producer, Sydney Boehm; director, Henry Hathaway; screenplay, Boehm; based on the novel *Lions at the Kill* by Max Catto; art directors, Lyle R. Wheeler, John DeCuir; set, Stuart A. Reiss, Walter M. Scott; sound, Harry M. Leonard, Charles Peck; music, Dominic Frontiere; orchestra, Edward B. Powell; camera, Sam Leavitt; editor, Dorothy Spencer; makeup, Ben Nye; costumes, Bill Thomas; hairstyles, Myrl Stoltz; assistant director, Al Schaumer; cast: Edward G. Robinson (Theo Wilkins), Rod Steiger (Paul Mason), Joan Collins (Melanie), Eli Wallach (Pancho), Michael Dante (Louis), Alexander Scourby (Raymond LeMay), Berry Kroeger (Hugo Baumer), Sebastian Cabot (Casino director), Marcel Hillaire (Duc de Salins), John Berardino (Chief of detectives); Alan Caillou (Sir Gerald), Alphonse Martell (Governor), Marga Ann Deighton (Governor's wife), Maurice Manson (Croupier), Jonathan Kidd (Seymour), Ida Augustian (Claire), Luis Mata Jr. (Sandy), Eugene Borden, Peter Camlin, Marcel De La Brosse, Donald Lawton, Eddie LeBaron, Jeffrey Sayre, Joe Romantini, Louis Mercier, George Nardelli, Andre Phillipe, Frances Ravel; 20th Century–Fox; Cinemascope; 102 minutes; March 1960

Paul Mason joins Theo Wilkins' scheme to rob the Monte Carlo casino of $4,000,000. Melanie, a dancer; Pancho, a saxophonist; Louis, a safecracker; Hugo, a chauffeur-mechanic; and Raymond LeMay, secretary to the casino director, are also involved. Raymond arranges invitations to the Governor's Ball. Pancho impersonates a wheelchair-ridden baron, with Theo his physician. Paul, Melanie, and Louis also are on the guest list. Paul and Louis climb via a window ledge to an apartment with an elevator that leads to the vault two stories below. They crack the safe and take the money up to the apartment, which adjoins the director's office. Theo substitutes an injection when Pancho hesitates in taking the cyanide capsule that will produce the effect of a seizure. Pancho is taken to the casino director's office, where Theo pronounces his patient dead. Theo deftly puts off a curious doctor who witnessed the "seizure." Paul and Louis put the money in Pancho's wheelchair, then retrace their steps back to the ballroom. Despite setbacks — Pancho's fear of the capsule, Raymond's nervousness, Louis' fear of heights, and a man recognizing Melanie — the robbery is successful. The escape is made in an ambulance driven by Hugo. Theo is happy, having at last "made the world gasp a little." In the back of the ambulance he dies in his sleep as the seemingly lifeless Pancho awakens. At first alarmed, the gang reasons that Theo's age is a factor, and the money now divides only six ways. Paul suffers the most; Melanie realizes that Theo was his father. Discovering the money has been marked by the Bank of France, Paul and Melanie decide to return it to the casino. Then they win at roulette!

The New York Herald-Tribune said that the film "does not come up to the expectations one would reasonably have of a crime suspense movie aided by Edward G. Robinson, Rod Steiger and Eli Wallach." But other periodicals lavished praise. *Newsweek* felt it had "as humorous and entertaining a bunch of crooks as the screen has offered in years ... [and] more than an hour of tense, funny, understated entertainment built around a slick $4 million robbery ... a winning combination."

"So skillfully is the first part of *Seven Thieves* done," according to *The Commonweal*, "that the second part ... builds up a suspense that is almost unbearable.... [It is] expertly directed by Henry Hathaway, [and] it is fairly absorbing cinema fare." *The New York Times* agreed, saying the film was "well-conceived for suspense and excitement, well directed by Henry Hathaway, and well played."

Playboy complimented Robinson's work: "As the master criminal [he] is quietly effective at managing the details." But the reviewer pointed out the weakness in the cinematography, saying, "The film makes use of process shots of the principals superimposed against Riviera backgrounds, and if the technique were used more convincingly, it might well lead the way toward trimmer budgets. However, the trickery is occasionally too transparent."

Perhaps the best compliment came from Lee Mortimer in *Mirror Magazine*: "The most breathtaking suspense since *Rififi*."

"Shadows Tremble" (Television, 1958) Producers, Fred Coe, Herbert Brodkin; director, Herbert Hirshman; teleplay, Ernest Kinoy; music, Robert Allen, George Smith; cast: Edward G. Robinson (Oscar Bromek), Ray Walston (Partridge), Beatrice Straight (Grace Tyburn), Frank Conroy (John Tyburn), Parker Fennelly (George Putnam), Robert Webber (Malcolm Field); *Playhouse 90*; CBS-TV; 90 minutes; October 23, 1958

The Shakespeare Cycle (Radio) see *Columbia's Shakespeare* and "The Taming of the Shrew"

Shakespeare Festival (1937, Radio) see *Columbia's Shakespeare* and "The Taming of the Shrew"

Shannon, Harry (1890–1964) is in two films with Edward G. Robinson—*The Red House* (Dr. Byrne) and *The Violent Men* (Perdue). He is also in *Citizen Kane, Once Upon a Honeymoon, The Sullivans, Captain Eddie, Mr. Blandings Builds His Dream House, The Tall Men,* and *Gypsy.*

Sharif, Omar (1932–) was a star in Egyptian films for several years before playing in *Lawrence of Arabia* (Oscar nomination for best supporting actor). Subsequent English-language films include *Doctor Zhivago, Funny Girl,* and *Mackenna's Gold* (with Edward G. Robinson).

Shatner, William (1931–) became a major star as Captain Kirk in the popular *Star Trek* TV series, which spawned several movies. His other credits include *The Brothers Karamazov, Judgment at Nuremberg, Go Ask Alice,* and, with Edward G. Robinson, *The Outrage* (as a preacher).

Shaughnessy, Mickey (1920–85) played comic mugs very effectively. He was Francis, the butler, in *Never a Dull Moment,* with Edward G. Robinson, and was also in *From Here to Eternity, Don't Go Near the Water, The Adventures of Huckleberry Finn,* and *Jailhouse Rock.*

Shaw, George Bernard (1856–1950), an Irish playwright known for his wit and social commentary, wrote *Arms and the Man, Candida, Pygmalion* (the basis for the musical *My Fair Lady*), *Man and Superman, Heartbreak House,* and two short plays done by the Theatre Guild with Edward G. Robinson: *Androcles and the Lion* (Robinson played Caesar) and *The Man of Destiny.*

Shayne, Konstantin (1888–1974) With Edward G. Robinson, he was Nazi war criminal Konrad Meineke, who was permitted to escape in order to lead authorities to bigger prey in *The Stranger*. His other films include *Five Graves to Cairo, Till We Meet Again, None but the Lonely Heart, The Secret Life of Walter Mitty, Song of Love,* and *Vertigo*.

"Ship Forever Sailing"   (Radio, 1938) *America Calling*; director, Frank Capra; cast: Edward Arnold, Lionel Barrymore, James Cagney, Walter Connolly, Donald Crisp, Pat O'Brien, Edward G. Robinson; NBC-radio; December 24, 1938

Short films   Edward G. Robinson appeared in the following short films, considered either short subjects or documentaries. (*Moscow Strikes Back*, which he narrated, was about wartime Russia; it won an Academy Award as best documentary in 1943.)

1930	*An Intimate Dinner in Celebration of Warner Bros. Silver Jubilee*
1931	*How I Play Golf*
1932	*The Slippery Pearls* (a.k.a. *The Stolen Jools*) with an all-star cast to benefit tuberculosis research
1935	*A Day at Santa Anita*
1939	*Verdensberomtheder I Kobenhaven* (Danish film)
1941	*Polo with the Stars*
1942	*Screen Snapshots* (Russian music)
1943	*Moscow Strikes Back*
	Projection of America (produced by the Office of War Information)
	The Red Cross at War
1944	*Screen Snapshots* (Golden Jubilee of Film)
1946	*The American Creed* (produced for Brotherhood Week)
1948	*Screen Snapshots* (honoring Jean Hersholt)
	Screen Snapshots (The Friars honoring George Jessel)
	Where Do You Get Off? (produced for the United Jewish Appeal)
1950	*Screen Snapshots* (Ice Capades)
1951	*Screen Snapshots* (Hollywood Memories)
1957	*The Heart of Show Business* (produced by Variety Clubs International)
1959	*Israel: Its Ancient Glories and Its Wonders of Today*
1967	*All About People* (produced by the United Jewish Welfare Fund)
1971	*Mooch*

Shumway, Lee   (1884–1959), onscreen from 1909, was in *The Widow from Chicago, The Whole Town's Talking,* and *I Am the Law* with Edward G. Robinson. In *Double Indemnity* his scenes as a guard in the final execution scene were deleted. He appears also in *Men of the Night* and *The Leathernecks*.

Sidney, George   (1916–2002), Oscar-winning director of the short subjects *Quicker 'n a Wink* and *Of Pups and Puzzles*, directed Edward G. Robinson in *Pepe* and *Who Has Seen the Wind?* He also was director for the *36th Annual Academy Awards* broadcast on which Robinson appeared to present the screenplay Oscars. Sidney's first wife was drama coach Lillian Burns, mentor to Debbie Reynolds, among others. Sidney married Jane Adler Robinson, Edward G. Robinson's second wife and widow, in 1978. A photographer, he is credited with assistance on the two books *Edward G. Robinson's World of Art* and the autobiography, *All My Yesterdays*. Following Jane Sidney's death in 1991, George Sidney married columnist Corinne Entratter. His feature films include *Anchors Aweigh, The Harvey Girls, The Three Musketeers, Annie Get Your Gun, Show Boat, Kiss Me Kate, Pal Joey,* and *Bye Bye Birdie*.

Sidney, Jane Adler Robinson   (1919–91) A New York couturiere and artist, she came to Hollywood in connection with the first Mrs. Edward G. Robinson's (Gladys Lloyd) purchase of fashions. She was associated with the New York production of *Middle of the Night*. On January 16, 1958, while the play was on tour in Washington, D.C., she became the second Mrs. Robinson. In 1971 she wrote *Edward G. Robinson's World of Art*, featuring photos of much of their art collection, as "a gift to my husband." She appeared in the movie *Pepe* with Robinson for director

George Sidney in 1960. In 1978, five years after Robinson's death, she married George Sidney. Suffering from lupus disease for several years, she died on July 21, 1991.

Sidney, Sylvia (1910–99), with her husband Luther Adler, participated in *We Will Never Die* with Edward G. Robinson, and also the 1960 *Chanukah Festival for Israel.* Her films range from *Dead End* through *Summer Wishes Winter Dreams* (Oscar nomination), *Beetlejuice,* and *Mars Attacks*

Silent films In *Arms and the Woman* in 1916 Edward G. Robinson was an extra. The film was made in New York while Robinson was on the stage in *Under Sentence,* and he did not remember making the movie. His appearance was discovered by author Kevin Brownlow, whose book book, *The War, the West, and the Wilderness* clearly shows a still of the 23–year-old actor.

According to *All My Yesterdays*, Robinson worked for Samuel Goldwyn in a film called *Fields of Glory*, written by Irvin S. Cobb and starring Dorothy Gish. But Robinson disliked the project, asked to be let out, and his scenes were not used. With or without him, there does not seem to be documentation of a finished film.

For *The Bright Shawl* in 1923, Robinson's only other silent feature, director John Robertson suggested that he might be good as a Spanish Don named Domingo Escobar because of his resemblance (with beard and moustache) to Oscar Hammerstein. For Robinson it meant, in addition to a better salary than the theater was offering, a chance to see Havana (with access to great cigars). He played Mary Astor's father in the film, which also starred Richard Barthelmess, Dorothy Gish, William Powell, and Jetta Goudal.

Silver Dollar (Film, 1932) "Little seen in recent years, this fine epic drama attests to the superb range of Edward G. Robinson ... the well-crafted screenplay changed the names of its protagonists, with the silver tycoon here rechristened 'Yates Martin,' his first wife Augusta now called 'Sarah,' and Mrs. Doe alias 'Lily Owens.' *Silver Dollar* remains faithful to the essence of Horace Tabor's story ... with a blonde-wigged Bebe Daniels as the rejuvenating second wife and Aline MacMahon in a superbly detailed characterization as the discarded Sarah/Augusta."— Jerry Vermilyea, *Films of the Thirties*

Director, Alfred E. Green; screenplay, Carl Erickson, Harvey Thew; based on a biography of H. A. W. Tabor by David Karsner; camera, James Van Trees; art directors, Anton Grot, Robert Haas; editor, George Marks; costumes, Orry-Kelly, Cheney Brothers; cast: Edward G. Robinson (Yates Martin), Bebe Daniels (Lily Owens), Aline MacMahon (Sarah Martin), Jobyna Howland (Poker Annie), DeWitt Jennings (Foreman), Robert Warwick (Col. Stanton), Russell Simpson (Hamlin), Harry Holman (Adams), Charles Middleton (Jenkins), John Marston (Gelsey), Marjorie Gateson (Mrs. Adams), Emmett Corrigan (President Arthur), Wade Boteler, William LeMaire (Miners), David Durand (Mark), Lee Kohlmar (Rische), Teresa Conover (Mrs. Hamlin), Leon Waycoff [Ames] (Secretary), Virginia Edwards (Emma Abbott), Christian Rub (Hook), Walter Rogers (General Grant), Niles Welch (William Jennings Bryan), Wilfred Lucas, Alice Wetherfield, Herman Bing, Bonita Granville, Walter Long, Willard Robertson, Frederick Burton, Charles Coleman; First National; 84 minutes; December 1932

Yates Martin is looking for gold in Colorado. When he and his wife, Sarah, set up a general store, they extend credit to miners and nearly go broke. Silver is discovered by two men, and they share their find with the Martins for his past generosity. Yates becomes rich and prominent in the new town of Denver. He runs for lieutenant governor. He builds an opera house and falls in love with Lily Owens, a socialite. Winning a vacant seat in the United States Senate, Yates leaves Sarah to marry Lily, and the wedding in Washington is attended by president Chester A. Arthur. Returning to Colorado, Yates is wiped out when silver is demonetized in favor of the gold standard. Old and destitute, Yates goes back to the opera house, remembering grander days. He collapses of a heart attack and dies. Both Sarah and Lily attend his funeral.

"Edward G. Robinson gave a conspicuously able performance," said *The New York Times*. "The role ... is especially well-suited to Mr. Robinson's talent. His characterization is compelling and convincing, and he succeeds admirably in delivering the complex nature of the man who, in the film, is invariably more fortunate than clever." *The Sunday New York Times* added, "Whatever Mr. Robinson did in *Little Caesar* is even more convincing here."

"The picture provides Edward G. Robinson with one of the most vibrant of all the lively parts he has portrayed," said *The New York American*. "And needless to say, he creates a character rich and full and colorful, vivid in all its dimensions. It is an achievement, perhaps the finest in all his cinematic career."

"Directed and written with the proper vigor and quite brilliantly played by Edward G. Robinson, the film presents what is perhaps a fairly neglected period in the national life with raciness and authenticity."—*The New York Herald-Tribune*

James Robert Parish, in *The Tough Guys*, observed that, "Robinson enjoyed a meaty role, one that allowed him an expansive death scene.... The top accolade came from ex–New York governor Alfred E. Smith, who wired Warner Brothers, 'Robinson is more Haw Tabor than Tabor himself could have been.'"

The film was one of Robinson's favorites.

Silverheels, Jay (1919–80) played Indian sidekick Tonto in the long-running TV western *The Lone Ranger*. With Edward G. Robinson, he appears in *Key Largo* as one of the doomed Osceola brothers. He was Geronimo in *Broken Arrow* and *Walk the Proud Land*, and was also in *Yellow Sky*.

Simonson, Lee (1888–1967), designer for the Theatre Guild, of which he was a founder, created sets for *The Adding Machine*, *Peer Gynt*, and *The Goat Song*, all with Edward G. Robinson. His other productions include *R.U.R.*, *Liliom*, *Marco Millions*, *Idiot's Delight*, and *Joan of Lorraine*

Sinatra, Frank (1915–98), legendary singer and popular actor from the 1940s, won an Oscar as best supporting actor for *From Here to Eternity*. Edward G. Robinson appears with him in three films: *A Hole in the Head* (as his elder brother), *Pepe* (the two are among the more than thirty guest stars), and *Robin and the 7 Hoods*. They were also together at Madison Square Garden for the stage pageant *We Will Never Die* and on several radio broadcasts, including a Savings Bond show, *The Victory Chest Program,* "Victory Extra," and *The Roosevelt Special*. Sinatra also appeared on the *36th* and *45th Academy Awards* telecasts. The Robinson screen persona of the 1930s was a hero to the young Sinatra, according to Richard Gehman's biography *Sinatra and His Rat Pack*. The two shared the same birthday, December 12, and began exchanging elaborate gifts when filming *A Hole in the Head*. For a time they also shared liberal political beliefs and, with several other celebrities, appeared at the 1960 Democratic National Convention to nominate John F. Kennedy. In 1966, when Robinson had a near-fatal auto accident, Sinatra sent a get-well present—a skateboard—intended "as an improvement over my driving."

The Singers (Television, 1969) Executive producer, Mel Torme; producer-director, Bill Foster; musical director, Billy May; writers, Bill Richmond, Elias Davis, David Pollock, David Finkle, Bill Weeden, Mel Torme; featuring: John Byner, Phyllis Diller, James Farentino, Gerri Granger, Jack Jones, Frankie Laine, Lynne Lipton, Marilyn Michaels, Ricardo Montalban, Louisa Moritz, Harve Presnell, Charles Nelson Reilly, Cliff Robertson, Edward G. Robinson, Bobby Van, Jonathan Winters; Michele Lee (Host); CBS-TV; 60 minutes; September 8, 1969

The $64,000 Challenge (Television, 1956) On this game show, a follow-up to *The $64,000 Question*, Edward G. Robinson and Vincent Price vied in the category of fine art.

Producers, Joe Cates, Ed Jurist; directors, Cates, Seymour Robbie; set, Eddie Gilbert, Charles Lisanby; music director, Norman Leyden; announcer, Bill Rogers; commercials, Barbara Britton, Jonathan Blake; CBS-TV; 30

minutes; September 30, October 7, 14, 21, and 28, 1956; Vincent Price, Edward G. Robinson; Ralph Storey (host)

"The producers of the TV show had found the Price–[Billy] Pearson match among their most popular, and now recruited the old Hollywood 'gangster' [Robinson] to show his cultured side on the air. It was the perfect competition in many ways…. In real life, the two were probably the most gentle and cultured men in the motion picture industry!…. The two actors battled for six weeks, reaching the $64,000 questioning on the last night. Instead of having a tie, the two men drew the match when both gave wrong answers…. The two movie stars split the top prize, $32,000 to each, and the match was over."—*Vincent Price Unmasked*, by James Robert Parish and Steven Whitney.

Victoria Price notes, in her book about her father, *Vincent Price: A Daughter's Biography*, "As a champion, Vincent was given the opportunity to choose a challenger. He suggested his good friend, Edward G. Robinson. The two proved the most popular team ever. Between thirty-five and fifty million viewers tuned in each Sunday for six weeks. On the final week Robinson was asked his four-part $64,000 question first and incorrectly answered the third part, mistaking a painting by Bellini for a Van Eyck. Vincent then had the chance to win it all. He was asked to name every artist who had worked on the Sistine Chapel. He named all nine, but left out Daniel de Volterra, who was brought in by a conservative eighteenth century pope to paint fig leaves over all of the nudes. The next day the press went wild, some grumbling that he had lost by a fig leaf, others accusing him of taking a dive for his friend, Robinson, so that the two could split the prize—a charge Vincent strongly denied…. For Vincent Price and Edward G. Robinson *The $64,000 Challenge* represented simply another more public chapter in their long friendship."

Slang   Gangster films have provided the English language with colorful slang and idiom. Catch phrases such as "You can dish it out, but you can't take it" were present as early as 1931 in *Little Caesar*.

A gangster's chief weapon was his gun, sometimes called a *gat* or a *rod* or a *heater*. A machine gun has been referred to as a *Chicago typewriter*. Odd vernacular was more likely to occur in comedies, such as Robinson's *The Whole Town's Talking, Brother Orchid,* or *The Little Giant*. Choice verbiage includes "a bunch of *molokeys*" (gang members), or *mugs*, and "a lot of *kopecks* [money]—no, *mazuma*—that's better English." In more serious treatments, such words seemed corny at best and were used less.

A gangster's girlfriend was known as his *moll*, and a *fence* was someone who could dispose of hot (stolen) goods. Detectives became *dicks*, and sometimes *bulls,* if they were a particularly stubborn challenge to the mob.

Futuristic usage was developed for *Soylent Green*, itself coined to delineate mass-produced 21st-century food, a bland combination of soybeans and lentils. *Soylent Yellow* is mass produced bread, whereas the green element, purporting to be derived from algae and seaweed from the ocean floor, finally proved to be of more grisly content. In the film, Edward G. Robinson's character, an aged police researcher/professor, is called a *book* in the new language. Similarly, girls available for companionship to the rich as live-in residents at a posh apartment were demeaningly referred to as *furniture*.

"Sleight of Hand" see *Sealtest Variety Theatre*

A Slight Case of Murder   (Film, 1938) This film was not Edward G. Robinson's first gangster comedy, but arguably it was his funniest. It made *The New York Times* Ten Best list for 1938. "We haven't laughed so much since Remy Marco's Mike found four parties shot to death in the back bedroom of the Saratoga house his boss had rented for the season," said the reviewer. "For a Runyonesque panel, the casting director had the marvelous good fortune to find Edward G. Robinson and Ruth Donnelly to play Mr. and Mrs. Marco. If you're not too squeamish, you should have a round of chuckles on the house." As Graham Greene noted, "The complications crazily mount, sentiment never raises its ugly head, and a long nose is made at violence and death."

The New York Herald-Tribune called the film "one of the funniest and most satisfying farces which has come out of Hollywood in some time. For Mr. Robinson, the show is a major dispensation. After *The Last Gangster*, it was fairly obvious that straight variations on the Little Caesar role had been exhausted. *A Slight Case of Murder* gives him a burlesque underworld bigshot to portray, and he handles the assignment with comical efficiency. As a Prohibition-needled beer baron who turns square but forgets to stop needling his beer, he realizes a nice blend of ruthlessness and clowning.... Little Caesar has died hard but his passing shouldn't grieve Mr. Robinson unduly if he can get more scripts like this one."

Producer, Hal B. Wallis; associate producer, Sam Bischoff; director, Lloyd Bacon; screenplay, Earl Baldwin, Joseph Schrank; based on the play by Damon Runyon and Howard Lindsay; music/lyrics, M. K. Jerome, Jack Scholl; art director, Max Parker; camera, Sid Hickox; editor, James Gibbon; music director, Leo F. Forbstein; sound, Stanley Jones; gowns, Howard Shoup; cast: Edward G. Robinson (Remy Marco), Jane Bryan (Mary), Ruth Donnelly (Nora), Allen Jenkins (Mike), Willard Parker (Dick Whitewood), Ed Brophy (Lefty), Harold Huber (Giuseppe), Paul Harvey (Whitewood), Bobby Jordan (Douglas Fairbanks Rosenbloom), Margaret Hamilton (Mrs. Cagle), John Litel (Post), Eric Stanley (Ritter), Joseph Downing (Innocence), George E. Stone (Kirk), Bert Hanlon (Sad Sam), Jean Benedict (Remy's secretary), Harry Seymour (Singer), Betty Compson (Loretta), Carole Landis (Blonde), Joe Caites (No Nose Cohen), George Lloyd (Little Butch), John Harmon (Blackhead Gallagher), Harry Tenbrook (Stranger), Duke York (Champ), Pat Daly (Manager), John Hiestand (Announcer), Bert Roach (Speakeasy proprietor), Harry Cody (Pessimistic patron), Al Hill, Ben Hendricks, Ralph Dunn, Wade Boteler (Policemen), Myrtle Stedman, Lola Cheeney (Nurses), Isabel La Mal, Alan Bridge, Tommy Bupp, Anne O'Neal, Al Herman, John Harron, Jack Mower, Elliott Sullivan; Warner Bros.; 85 minutes; February 1938

With the repeal of Prohibition, beer baron Remy Marco decides to go legitimate. It costs him profits, though, because his awful-tasting beer can no longer compete with quality brews. Bankers Ritter and Post want Remy's brewery for themselves rather than renew his note. Remy, his wife Nora, and their daughter Mary take an orphan — Douglas Fairbanks Rosenbloom — with them to their summer place in Saratoga. Before they arrive, a mobster named Innocence kills four men who helped him rob a racetrack, then hides upstairs. Mary's boyfriend, Dick Whitewood, has gotten a job as a state trooper and calls on the Marcos, but he is dismissed because Remy hates cops. Remy's boys dispose of the dead gangsters on neighboring lawns. Nora tells Remy about Mary and Dick, and Dick's father is invited to a party that evening. Douglas finds the stolen money under his bed. Remy's boys, discovering there is a reward, retrieve the four bodies and hide them in an upstairs closet. Mr. Whitewood, who is feeling ill, goes upstairs, sees them, and, not realizing they are dead, runs downstairs declaring that crooks with guns are after him. Remy makes a hero out of Dick by sending him to "kill" the crooks and solve the robbery. Dick shoots wildly, and a stray bullet even wings Innocence, now trying to escape. Dick faints, and Remy, amazed at Dick's luck, joins him.

While in his autobiography Robinson was generous in his praise for the film's comedy, in a 1971 *Films in Review* article that praise was muted: "After the screening of *A Slight Case of Murder*... Edward G. Robinson, ably assisted by his good friend, Sam Jaffe, *did* sparkplug a lively and amusing, and at times informative Q-&-A session. Robinson had wit, total recall and stage presence, despite a hearing infirmity. He admitted *A Slight Case of Murder* doesn't now seem as funny as he had remembered it and partly blamed director Lloyd Bacon for not taking more time filming it and getting more out of the comedy potential (he said it had been made in about seven weeks)."

In retrospect, James Robert Parish, in *The Tough Guys,* said, "Robinson thoroughly approved of the script and had no qualms about burlesquing his standard cinema image."

"A Slight Case of Murder" (Radio, 1945; 1954) *A Slight Case of Murder* was adapted for radio presentation on *P. Lorillard Comedy Theatre* in 1945 and *NBC Star Playhouse* in 1954.

Cast: Edward G. Robinson (Remy Marco); *P. Lorillard Comedy Theatre*; NBC-radio; April 8, 1945

Cast: Edward G. Robinson (Remy Marco), Elspeth Eric, Pat Hosley, William Redfield, Wendell Holmes, Larry Haines; *NBC Star Playhouse*; NBC-radio; January 24, 1954

The Slippery Pearls see *The Stolen Jools*

Smart Money (Film, 1931) "In my second Hollywood year, 1931," wrote James Cagney, "came *Smart Money*, the only picture I ever made with that fine gentleman and splendid actor, Edward G. Robinson. Again Eddie was a gangster, again I was a pal.... I saw *Smart Money* not long ago because I was curious about it. A solid number of my pictures I've never seen, and some of the ones I have seen satisfy my curiosity about them in a single showing or even halfway through. Anyway, looking at *Smart Money* gave me the pleasure of seeing Eddie as his usual sharp self, that always reliable self."—*Cagney by Cagney*

"That natural graciousness, verging on the courtly, that marked Robinson's mature style begins to emerge here [at the time of *Smart Money*]," noted Richard Schickel in his book *James Cagney, a Celebration*. "No more than Cagney was he merely a hard guy. And he was perhaps quicker to shed that image than Cagney."

Cagney and Robinson had each had watershed successes in 1931 with *The Public Enemy* and *Little Caesar*, respectively. *Smart Money* was the next film for both, but while Robinson had the lead as gambler Nick Venizelos, Cagney was given not much more than a supporting role.

Director, Alfred E. Green; screenplay, Kubec Glasmon, John Bright, Lucien Hubbard, Joseph Jackson; story, Hubbard, Jackson; camera, Robert Kurrle; art director, Robert Haas; editor, Jack Killifer; makeup, Perc Westmore; gowns, Earl Luick; cast: Edward G. Robinson (Nick Venizelos), James Cagney (Jack), Evalyn Knapp (Irene), Ralf Harolde (Sleepy Sam), Noel Francis (Marie), Margaret Livingstone (D.A.'s girl), Maurice Black (Greek barber), Boris Karloff (Sport Williams), Morgan Wallace (Black), Billy House (Salesman gambler), Paul Porcasi (Amenoppopolus), Polly Walters (Lola), Ben Taggart (Hickory Short), Gladys Lloyd, Wallace MacDonald (Cigar stand clerks), Clark Burroughs (Back-to-back Schultz), Edwin Argus (Two-time Phil), John Larkin (Snake Eyes), Walter Percival (Barnes), Mae Madison (Small town girl), Allan Lane (Suicide), Eulalie Jensen (Matron), Charles Lane (Desk clerk), Edward Hearn (Reporter), Eddie Kane (Tom), Clinton Rosemond (George), Charles O'Malley (Machine gunner), Gus Leonard (Joe), John George (Dwarf), Nick Bela, Harry Semels, Charlotte Merriam, Larry McGrath, Spencer Bell; Warner Bros.; 90 (or 83) minutes; June 1931

Nick Venizelos, a barber from Irontown, is a lucky gambler. Pals in his shop stake him to try his luck in the big city. He plays dice with Marie, who works at the hotel cigar stand. She tips him off about a big poker game with Hickory Short. Nick joins the game but loses everything. He sees a photo of the real Hickory in the paper the next day and realizes he has been hustled. Seeking revenge, he fights with Sleepy Sam, the impersonator, and loses Marie to him. Nick takes a job as a barber and soon is successfully gambling again. He sets up his own club and is joined by his buddy, Jack, from Irontown. The District Attorney, hoping to nail Nick, sends a blonde to see him. Nick is wise to her, however, and while charming her, gives her a kick in the seat. One night Jack and Nick rescue a woman about to jump off a bridge. Jack is immediately suspicious of Irene, but Nick takes her in and cares for her. The D.A. forces Irene to plant a racing form in Nick's jacket. Jack sees her, and he tries to warn Nick, who misunderstands. There is a fight. The casino is raided, and Nick is arrested and about to be taken away when it is discovered Jack has been killed. Sentenced to ten years in prison for manslaughter, Nick is met at the train station by Marie. Still the cheerful gambler, Nick bets her he will be out of prison in five years.

The New York Times called *Smart Money* "fast-moving and fairly entertaining. Mr. Robinson gets all that is humanly possible out of the part of Nick the Barber ... leaves no stone unturned to attract the spectator's attention." *Time* saw in Robinson "an actor with the face of a depraved cherub and a voice which makes everything he says seem violently profane."

With the passage of time the film and its stars have held up well. Patrick McGilligan in *Cagney, the Actor as Auteur* referred to "frequent flashes of brilliant acting from the two principals, Robinson and Cagney." Carlos Clarens in *Crime Movies* noted that screenwriters "Glasmon and Bright spiced up the Runyonesque yarn with black jokes, Jewish jokes, Greek jokes, and some relaxed (perhaps never so relaxed) camping around between Robinson and Cagney."

Smith, Sir C. Aubrey (1863–1948), a tall Englishman, was the Dean of Norwalk, Edward G. Robinson's intended murder victim, in *Flesh and Fantasy*. Twenty years on the stage (*The Light That Failed*, *The Constant Wife*) preceded his film career, which included *Love Me Tonight*, *Romeo and Juliet*, *The Hurricane*, *The Four Feathers*, *Rebecca*, and *Little Women*.

Smith, Harry James (1880–1918) wrote *The Little Teacher*, Edward G. Robinson's fifth Broadway play. Other works include *Mrs. Bumpstead-Leigh* and *A Tailor Made Man*. He was an editor at *Atlantic Monthly*.

Smoking Edward G. Robinson, along with such notables as Winston Churchill, Groucho Marx, George Burns, and Ernie Kovacs, was "one of the great cigar people of the world." Shirley MacLaine, a host on the American Film Institute's special TV program *100 Years, 100 Stars* in 1999, noted that Robinson (who on the show ranked 24th among male stars in Hollywood through 1950) could appear either menacing or grandfatherly. "I think it depended on what he was doing with his cigar," she observed. In addition to cigars, Robinson frequently smoked pipes and cigarettes onscreen and onstage. He had a fine personal collection of pipes, and even had tobacco bearing his name — "Edward G. Robinson's Blend." For the silent film *The Bright Shawl* in 1923, he was delighted to travel to Cuba for the location work in order to experience the cigars firsthand.

His is a cigar-smoking presence in *Little Caesar*, *Key Largo*, *Never a Dull Moment*, *Operation San Pietro*, *Good Neighbor Sam*, *It's a Great Feeling*, *Dr. Ehrlich's Magic Bullet*, and *The Cincinnati Kid*, among many others. Films in which smoking is more than just occasional include: *Double Indemnity*, in which a running bit is made of Fred MacMurray lighting matches for him — "They explode in my pocket," Robinson's character says; *The Whole Town's Talking*, in an hilarious scene where he coughs and sputters while experiencing both cigars and alcohol for the first time; and *Cheyenne Autumn*, where he substitutes long stogies for the Indians' peace pipe when they have no tobacco. In *The Stranger* his offscreen presence is noted in the form of a shadow or even a puff of smoke, as he covertly trails a war criminal from Europe to Connecticut. His mishaps include breaking his pipestem in that film; in *I Am the Law* he invariably leaves a lit pipe in his coat pocket, which begins smoking on its own.

Soderling, Walter (1892–1968) appears with Edward G. Robinson in *I Am the Law* (Professor Perkins) and *All My Sons* (Charlie). He also plays roles in *Maid of Salem*, *Penny Serenade*, *Mr. Smith Goes to Washington*, *Meet John Doe*, and *Rhapsody in Blue*.

Sokoloff, Vladimir (1889–1962), diminutive actor from the Moscow Art Theatre, is in *The Amazing Dr. Clitterhouse*, with Edward G. Robinson, as Popus, evaluating stolen jewels, and as Pop Lejon, Greenwich Village art dealer, in *Scarlet Street*. Other films include *The Story of Louis Pasteur*, *For Whom the Bell Tolls*, and *The Magnificent Seven*.

Sommer, Elke (1940–) made movies in her native Germany, then, via England, came to American films of the 1960s: *The Victors*, *A Shot in the Dark*, *The Prize* (with Paul

Newman and Edward G. Robinson), and *The Wicked Dreams of Paula Schultz*, exploiting her image as a sexy blonde.

Song of Norway

(Film, 1970) Artistically, this film is not at the top of Edward G. Robinson's "A" list. "The movie is of unbelievable badness; it brings back clichés you didn't know you knew," said Pauline Kael in *The New Yorker*. "...It seems to have been made by trolls." *Time* magazine commented that, "adapted by [Andrew] Stone from the highly successful 1944 Broadway operetta and filmed in Scandinavia and England at a cost of about $4,000,000, *Song of Norway* is a wildly romanticized biography of Edvard Grieg.... By comparison, *The Sound of Music* is not only trenchant social drama but a symphonic tour de force."

According to *The New York Times*, "*Song of Norway* is no ordinary movie kitsch, but a display to turn Guy Lombardo livid with envy.... Robert Morley, Edward G. Robinson and Oscar Homolka appear in non-singing roles. That they ... appear to be a little more foolish than they need be is not only because of the scenario, but also because of Stone's pursuit of realism, in this case, of scenery, which is so overwhelming that the people are reduced to being scenic obstructions."

Producers, Andrew L. Stone, Virginia Stone; director, screenplay, Andrew L. Stone; suggested by the stage play with book by Milton Lazarus, music and lyrics (based on the works of Edvard Grieg) by Robert Wright and George Forrest, from a play by Homer Curran; choreography, Lee Theodore, Avind Harum, Larry Oaks; assistant director, John O'Connor; art director, William Albert Havemeyer; second unit director, Yakima Canutt; assistants, Bill Graf, Paul Cowan; sound, John Purchese; animation sequences, Kinney-Wolf, Leif Jul, Jack Kinney, based on drawings by Theodore Kittelson; camera, Davis Boulton, Kelvin Pike, Stan Mestel; editor, Virginia Stone; assistant, Peter Halsey; production supervisor, John Benson; hairstyles, Jan Dorman; makeup, Kay Freeborn; costumes, Fiorela Mariani, David Walker; wardrobe, Dora and Ralph Lloyd; musical supervisor / orchestrater / conductor, Roland Shaw; concerto conductor, Oivin Fjeldstad; piano, John Ogden; piano soloist, Brenda Lucas; London Symphony Orchestra; cast: Florence Henderson (Nina Hagerup Grieg), Toralv Maurstad (Edvard Grieg), Christina Schollin (Therese Berg), Frank Poretta (Rikard Nordraak), Robert Morley (Berg), Edward G. Robinson (Krogstad), Harry Secombe (Bjornsterne Bjornson), Oscar Homolka (Engstrand), Elizabeth Larner (Mrs. Bjornson), Frederick Jaeger (Henrik Ibsen), Henry Gilbert (Franz Liszt), Richard Wordsworth (Hans Christian Andersen), Bernard Archard (George Nordraak), Susan Richards Chitty (Aunt Aline), John Barrie (Hagerup), Wenke Foss (Mrs. Hagerup), Ronald Adam (Gade), Carl Rigg (Captain Hansen), Aline Towne (Mrs. Thoresen), Nan Munro (Irate woman), James Hayter (Berg's butler), Erik Chitty (Helsted), Manoug Parikian (Violinist), Richard Vernon, Ernest Clark (Councilmen), Eli Lindtner (Bjornson's secretary), Rolf Berntzen (Doctor), Ros Drinkwater, Rosalind Speight (Liszt's friends) Charles Lloyd Pack (Chevalier), Cyril Renison (Butler), Robert Rietty (Winding), Ilse-Nore Tromm (Girl's mother), Tordis Maurstad (Mrs. Schmidt), Avind Harum, Susan Claire, Gordon Coster, Jane Darling, Hermione Farthingale, Michele Hardy, Roy Jones, Robert Lupone, Matt Mattox, Paddy McIntyre, Denise O'Brien, Stephen Reinhardt, Peter Salmon, Jeffrey Taylor, Jennie Walton, Barbara von der Heyde, Barrie Wilkinson (Dancers); ABC Pictures Corp./Cinerama Releasing Corp.; Super Panavision & Deluxe Color; 142 minutes; November 1970

The story of Edvard Grieg's becoming the foremost composer of Norway involves several figures — Rikard Nordraak, a fellow composer and close friend; Therese Berg, who loved him but aided his career, avoiding romance, in a bargain with her father; and Nina Hagerup, Grieg's cousin, whom he married. Through Nordraak, Grieg meets Hans Christian Andersen, for whom Nina sings compositions based on Andersen's works. When Grieg fails to obtain a conducting post at the National Theater in Christiania, he struggles to support his wife by giving music lessons. He agrees to collaborate with Bjornson, Nordraak's cousin, on an opera based on

Norway's legendary trolls. Therese Berg presents Grieg with a grand piano, which humiliates Nina, who has sold her old cottage in order to buy a piano from Krogstad, a local dealer. Grieg goes to Rome on a small stipend at the urging of both Therese and Franz Liszt. He meets Henrik Ibsen and impulsively agrees to write a score for *Peer Gynt*, which hurts his relationship with Bjornson. Greig's career advances as he gives several important concerts in an extended stay in Rome. However, he learns from Krogstad that Nina is impoverished at home. Also, Nordraak has died. Grieg returns home to commit himself to Nina and the writing of his country's music.

The reviews were not all negative. *Variety* called *Song of Norway* "a magnificent motion picture," noting that "unfortunately Stone's screenplay imparts a frequently banal, two-dimensional note…. Edward G. Robinson is kindly and concerned as the kindly concerned old piano dealer."

The *St. Louis Post-Dispatch* said, "Visually and musically, *Song of Norway* is remarkably beautiful and enchanting. The story, although the acting is fairly good, gets a bit tedious in the second half, as producer-director Andrew Stone insists on sticking literally to the facts of the life of nineteenth century Norwegian composer Edvard Grieg. But on the whole the virtues outweigh the defects…. There are such familiar character actors as Edward G. Robinson, Robert Morley, Harry Secombe and Oscar Homolka to bolster the cast."

In his *Film Guide*, Leslie Halliwell called *Song of Norway* a "multinational hodgepodge, mostly in the *Sound of Music* style, but with everything from cartoons to Christmas cracker backgrounds. Quite watchable and the landscapes are certainly splendid."

The Sophie Maslow Dance Company The group performed regularly during several *Chanukah Festivals for Israel* at Madison Square Garden. Edward G. Robinson appeared with them in nine programs, in 1956, 1960, and 1962 through 1968. The final year, their ballet *Scenes from the Yiddish Theatre* was dedicated to him as part of his 75th birthday tribute.

Sorel, George (1899–1948) played in three films with Edward G. Robinson — as an Italian salesman in *Brother Orchid*, a spy in *Tampico*, and a headwaiter in *All My Sons* and on the radio in "The Man With Hope in His Hands." He once commented that he learned English watching Robinson's gangster films. Other films include *Swiss Miss, Hitler — Dead or Alive, Once Upon a Honeymoon, To Have and Have Not,* and *Casablanca*.

Sothern, Ann (1909–2001) had a long career as a comedienne in films and on TV. She is Flo Addams, Edward G. Robinson's leading lady, in *Brother Orchid*, and also starred in the *Maisie* series. Other films are *Lady Be Good, Panama Hattie, Cry Havoc,* and, more recently, *The Whales of August* (Oscar nomination). Her TV series was called *Private Secretary*.

Soule, Olan (1910–94) was with Edward G. Robinson in *The Cincinnati Kid* and *It's a Great Feeling*, also on TV in *A Good Name*. His other films include *Call Me Madam, North by Northwest, Queen Bee,* and *The Towering Inferno*. Prior to coming to films, he was on radio in *The First Nighter*.

Sovey, Raymond (1897–1966), a Broadway designer, created a set for *The Brothers Karamazov* featuring a high staircase, which was used to great effect at the climax of the play by Edward G. Robinson as the epileptic brother. Sovey's other shows include *The Front Page, Green Grow the Lilacs, The Petrified Forest, Our Town, Gigi,* and *Witness for the Prosecution*.

Soylent Green (Film, 1973) This was Edward G. Robinson's final film, completed in October 1972 and released the following April. Robinson was hospitalized over New Year's and died on January 26. The honorary Oscar voted him by the motion picture academy was announced only two weeks before and was presented posthumously in March to Robinson's widow, Jane, by Charlton Heston, the film's star. A clip from *Soylent Green* was shown on the broadcast.

The film has gained a cult following in the three decades since it was first shown. Its message, showing that society had squandered natural resources to the point of needing to rely on cannibalism for survival, was flawed at best. The horror that "Soylent green is people!" ought to have been secondary to the idea that a society could sink so low. But the film was popular. One dubious distinction is that the film was considered *the* movie to see when "stoned." *Soylent Green* was redeemed by Robinson's presence in his final role. Debate over his character's euthanasia, in view of his having succumbed to cancer two months earlier, made great press.

"There is a ghoulishness to *Soylent Green* even beyond its cannibalistic theme," wrote Frederik Pohl and Frederik Pohl IV in their book *Science Fiction: Studies in Film*. "Edward G. Robinson, dying while he made it, portrays a dying man in the film. When his actual death occurred, it gave an ugly little tweak to the publicity. The film does not have a great deal beyond ghoulishness to offer, and almost all of that was injected by the film people. [Harry] Harrison's novel was a purely cautionary tale about overpopulation; his word 'soylent' was a coinage from 'soy beans' and 'lentils.' The cannibalism was an inspiration from Hollywood."

In the year 2022, pollution and overpopulation have turned New York City into a police state. Natural resources are depleted. The food supply is largely synthetic, made by the Soylent Company. Their latest product, soylent green, is said to be made from algae and seaweed from the ocean floor. When a wealthy business executive named Simonson is butchered, the case goes to Detective Thorn and his researcher, or "book," Sol Roth. Thorn meets Shirl, Simonson's mistress, called "furniture" because she comes with the apartment, and Tab Fielding, a bodyguard. To Sol's delight, Thorn also appropriates from Simonson's apartment such rare commodities as fresh vegetables, beef, liquor, soap, pencils, paper, and reference books. Sol learns that Simonson was on the board of the Soylent Company. Thorn falls for Shirl, and he suspects Tab of the murder. Hatcher, Thorn's superior, tells him that higher-ups want the case closed, but Thorn refuses, fearing the loss of his job. The populace starts a riot when the food supply runs low. While on riot control, Thorn is shot by Simonson's assassin, who in turn is crushed under a large "scoop," a special means of crowd control. Sol goes to the Exchange, where other "books" confirm his fear of the truth. Devastated, he decides he will "go home." A euthanasia center shows films of the earth's long-decimated wildlife, fresh streams, and other beauties of nature, all to the strains of light classical music. Before he dies, Sol tells Thorn what he has learned, but that there is no proof. Thorn follows Sol's body from the suicide center to a factory outside the city, where he sees production of the soylent wafers made from the reconstituted dead! Tab has tailed Thorn and shoots him, but Thorn kills Tab. Hatcher promises a badly wounded Thorn that he will tell the world the truth about soylent green.

Producers, Walter Seltzer, Russell Thacher; director, Richard Fleischer; screenplay, Stanley R. Greenberg; based on the novel *Make Room, Make Room!* by Harry Harrison; camera, Richard H. Kline; art director, Edward C. Carfagno; set, Robert Benton; costumes, Pat Barto, Betsy Cox, Norman Burza; music, Fred Myrow; symphony conductor, Gerald Fried; action scenes, Joe Canutt; production manager, Lloyd Anderson; special effects, Robert R. Hoag, Matthew Yuricich, A. J. Lohman; special camera sequences, Braverman Productions; prologue photos, Magnum; sound, Charles M. Wilborn, Harry W. Tetrick; editor, Samuel E. Beetley; technical consultant, Frank A. Bowerman; props, Terry Ballard; casting, Jack Baur; assistant directors, Daniel S. McCauley, Gene Marum; makeup, Bud Westmore; hairstyles, Sherry Wilson; cast: Charlton Heston (Detective Thorn), Edward G. Robinson (Sol Roth), Leigh Taylor-Young (Shirl), Joseph Cotten (William R. Simonson), Chuck Connors (Tab Fielding), Brock Peters (Hatcher), Paula Kelly (Martha), Stephen Young (Gilbert), Whit Bissell (Governor Santini), Lincoln Kilpatrick (Priest), Mike Henry (Kulozik), Roy Jenson (Donovan), Leonard Stone (Charles), Celia Lovsky

(Exchange leader), Dick Van Patten (Usher), Cyril Delevanti, Morgan Farley, Belle Mitchell (Books), Jane Dulo (Mrs. Santini), Forrest Wood, Faith Quabius (Attendants), Tim Herbert (Brady), John Dennis (Wagner), Jan Bradley (Bandana woman), Carlos Romero (New tenant), Pat Houtchens (Fat guard), Joyce Williams, Erica Hagen, Beverly Gill, Suesie Eejima, Cheri Howell, Kathy Silva, Jennifer King, Marion Charles (Furniture girls), Ida Mae McKenzie; MGM; Panavision; MetroColor; 97 minutes; April 1973

The film received some favorable reviews, generally with praise going to Robinson. In fact, *Soylent Green* is memorable chiefly because it is Robinson's final film. A summary of reviews appeared in *Film Facts*: "A source of controversy ... was Edward G. Robinson's final film appearance — which ironically culminated in a lengthy death scene.... *The San Francisco Chronicle* praised the actor's 'sad and eloquent' farewell in the 'better than average thriller,' and the *Chicago Sun Times* singled out Robinson's 'tremendously dignified and poignant death scene' as 'the most impressive' in the 'good, solid science fiction movie.' But the same scene either disturbed or disgusted [others].... The *New York Daily News*, though acknowledging that 'Robinson does the death scene with touching dignity,' felt that 'such a scene seems a terrible indignity in the light of his own passing....' The *New Yorker* thought the 'shudderingly cruel' sequence that 'exploits the mock-dead face...' was in gruesome taste.... Somebody might have tried quite hard not to use shots of Robinson heroically choosing death when he looked so distressingly close to it.'"

Praise came from *Variety*. "To the late Edward G. Robinson went the best part, to which he gave a fine display of his talents in what turned out to be a valedictory performance."

"Robinson's performance is among his best — warm, colorful, and humanistic," agreed *The Los Angeles Times* reviewer. "The plot, agonizingly, calls for us to watch him die, and the sequence is acutely uncomfortable and embarrassing to see, the more so because Robinson does it — as he did everything — with heartbreaking dignity. I would as soon not have seen it."

John Brosnan, in his book *Future Tense: The Cinema of Science Fiction*, calls *Soylent Green* "the best film to date dealing with overpopulation.... No one cares, or should care, about the dumb little story rattling around ... no one cares what soylent green is either as it's pretty obvious from the beginning, but what they're really looking at is that terrible world.... It certainly succeeded as a commercial picture.... By July 1974 Charlton Heston had made a million dollars out of it...."

Brosnan quotes Harry Harrison, author of *Make Room, Make Room!*, on which the screenplay was based: "I was watching a scene with Edward G. Robinson being shot — it was a closed set but they let me stay — and I heard Robinson complain to Fleischer that he didn't know what his role was supposed to be, so I got him aside and said that I was the guy who wrote the book and gave him a copy, and I said, 'Do you mind if I explain a bit about what your role is supposed to be?' And he said: 'Sure, come to my dressing room and have some lunch.' So, over a sandwich I told him: 'Very simply, you are *me* in this story. I'll be your age at the time when all the events of the film are taking place. You are the only living connection with the old world — you are the only person in the whole film who lived in a world of plenty — you are the link that connects our world with the world in the film.' And he said: 'Thank you very much for your help.' And once he knew what he was doing he put a lot of color into his scenes, inventing lots of bits of extra business. Heston was the same — he embellished his role in the same way. Like the eating scene where they're both eating some horrible cracker made of seaweed — in the original scene they just ate while they were talking, but both of them invented little schticks as the scene was shot...."

Finally, the words of director Richard Fleischer: "I think what we showed was a very accurate extrapolation of our time because if we go on as we're going that picture will come true. But even though it was an honest look at the future, it was also an entertaining one with some wonderful actors in it. I think Eddie Robinson in particular was marvelous, and Chuck Heston's performance was a different type of one for him."

Numerous reviews offered questionable praise. "For a film so devoid of any thematic strategy or even plain story-telling flair," the *Monthly Film Bulletin* began, "*Soylent Green* does turn up the occasional delight…. [One is] a scene where the grim warning note for the rest of the film is given an edge of delirious fantasy as Sol, a crumpled survivor from another world, gruffly personified by Edward G. Robinson in his last appearance, gives himself up to death in a strongly affecting moment of romantic kitsch."

The New York Times said, "New Yorkers certainly have problems these days … but nothing like the horrors due in 2022 as depicted in *Soylent Green*…. Unfortunately the script, direction and the principals involved in this struggle for survival often are as synthetic as *Soylent Green*, [which] projects essentially simple, muscular melodrama a good deal more effectively than it does the potential of man's seemingly witless destruction of the earth's resources…, Mr. Robinson is pitiably natural as the realistic, sensitive oldster facing the futility of living in dying surroundings."

"Watching Edward G. Robinson appear posthumously in *Soylent Green* is rather a chilling experience," said the *St. Louis Post-Dispatch*. "The very knowledge that he is dead produces some sadness, of course, but to see him portray an old man who is a living anachronism and then to die at his own request produces an impact that the filmmakers did not expect. The combination of science fiction and murder mystery, with some crooked politicians thrown in for luck, is a pretty good yarn."

"Robinson's role is a parody of the last cultured man," wrote *Newsweek*. "We are asked to feel a sense of loss at the death of this brave little bookworm. But who can feel anything but gloom that this should, in fact, be the end of Little Caesar, that Edward G. Robinson's last role should be that of a two-bit character in a film with a mechanical heart? It's sad to see him playing second fiddle to Charlton Heston…."

"Robinson … lends a desperately needed bit of humanity, but it's depressing to see that his last scene turns out to be a protracted, albeit peaceful death scene."—*The Washington Post*

"In a rueful irony, his death scene is the best in the film."—*Time*

Following are comments by Joseph Cotten and Charlton Heston about Robinson at the time of filming. "It was nice working with Eddie Robinson," commented Cotten. "He was a sweet man. I don't think he was very well making the movie, and I don't think somehow he'd had a very happy life. But he was nice."

Heston, whose work with Robinson also included *The Ten Commandments*, as well as being the presenter of the Oscar to his widow and speaker of a eulogy at his funeral, had much to say about his colleague in two books. In *The Actor's Life* in 1976 were published portions of his diary of the filming: "August 4, 1972: MGM's offer to Eddie Robinson of $25,000 plus $25,000 deferred elicited his inarguable response, 'At 79 I'm not much interested in deferrals.' I hope they'll pay whatever it takes to get him…. September 7: Eddie Robinson's a lovely actor to work with. The chemistry between us is good…. He knew while we were shooting, though we did not, he was terminally ill. He never missed an hour of work nor was late to call. He was never less than the consummate professional he had been all his life. I'm still haunted, though, by the knowledge that the very last scene he played, which he knew would be the last day's acting he'd ever do, was his death scene. I know now why I was so overwhelmingly moved playing it with him…. October 3: Finished shooting…." Twenty years later, Heston adds in *In the Arena*, "He sat in a chair on the sound stage all day, seldom going back to his trailer, talking to the other actors, the crew people, Dick and Walter. I think he wanted to feel the banter behind the cameras once more too, not just the words. I remember him listening to a couple of young actors bitching about the boring waits between setups while the shot's laid out and lit. He grinned. 'You know, I've always figured the waiting is what they pay me for. The acting I do free.' The acting was also very fine. His Sol was quirky and wary without falling into the standard oddball old geezer that actors so often use…. I've never heard of an actor playing a death scene in terms of his own true and imminent death. It was an awesome experience."

Time has been kind to *Soylent Green*. In the October 1998 issue of *Entertainment Weekly*, the film is in "The Galaxy's Top 100" works of science fiction, which included "books, movies, TV shows, comics, and even videogames ... chosen and judged not just by quality and their influence on pop culture but also by their impact on the collective imagination." The ten front-runners are legends: *Star Wars, Star Trek, The Twilight Zone, Frankenstein, 2001: A Space Odyssey, Metropolis, War of the Worlds, Invasion of the Body Snatchers, Alien/Aliens,* and *Superman*. Other classics like *The Day the Earth Stood Still, Close Encounters of the Third Kind, 1984, The X-Files, Planet of the Apes, E.T., Brave New World, The Fly,* the *Back to the Future* trilogy, *Godzilla, Jurassic Park, The Thing,* and *The Incredible Shrinking Man* also precede *Soylent Green*, which ranked number 38*. But listed *after* it are such works as *V, Forbidden Planet, The Martian Chronicles,* the *Flash Gordon* serials, *RoboCop, The Jetsons, Things to Come, Dr. Who, The Rocky Horror Picture Show, Them!, Dr. Jekyll and Mr. Hyde, The Incredible Hulk, Dune, Max Headroom, The Six Million Dollar Man,* and, at number 100, *Independence Day*.

*Also placing 38th, ironically, among the American Film Institute's "100 Greatest Movies of All Time" in 1998 was *Double Indemnity*.

Space, Arthur (1908–83), in films and TV since 1941, plays policemen in *The Woman in the Window* and *The Red House,* and is Edward G. Robinson's brother-in-law, Peter Hanson, in *Our Vines Have Tender Grapes*. He is also in *Tortilla Flat, Wilson, Leave Her to Heaven, The Spirit of St. Louis,* and *The Shakiest Gun in the West*.

Special Appearances Fourteen Warner Bros. players were in the stands playing extras in a racetrack scene in *Dark Hazard*. Baseball's Carl Hubbell, Al Campanis, Bob Trocolor, and Tony Ravish played themselves in *Big Leaguer*. English players Rex Harrison and George Cole are listed in the credits of *Journey Together*. The singing group the Hi-Lo's, and director David Swift, appear as themselves in *Good Neighbor Sam*; jazz musician Sweet Emma Barrett sings and plays the piano briefly as herself in *The Cincinnati Kid*.

Special Effects Special effects in films are artificial photographic illusions which usually are created by means other than live filming. Today the development of highly sophisticated computer-generated images dramatically increases the possibilities for believability in films. Examples of special effects in Edward G. Robinson's pictures include the depiction of the Biblical plagues, the burning bush, the pillar of fire, inscribing the tablets, and, of course, the parting of the Red Sea in *The Ten Commandments*. John Fulton, who was in charge of special effects for the film, won an Oscar for his work. Byron Haskin and Nathan Levinson at Warner Bros. also received a nomination for their special effects in *The Sea Wolf,* which included the use of fog and wind machines, a studio tank to represent the ocean, and sound effects that were innovative for the time. Split-screen techniques to make Edward G. Robinson into twin characters were employed in *The Whole Town's Talking* and *The Prize*. Microscopic photography was used in *Dr. Ehrlich's Magic Bullet*.

Spiegel, Sam (1903–85) produced the first two of his fourteen films, *Tales of Manhattan* and *The Stranger,* under the pseudonym S. P. Eagle. Also with Edward G. Robinson he appeared on the *36th Academy of Motion Picture Arts and Sciences Awards* to accept a best picture Oscar — his third — for *Lawrence of Arabia*. Others were for *On the Waterfront* and *The Bridge on the River Kwai*; *Nicholas and Alexandra* earned him a fourth nomination. Spiegel also produced *The African Queen* and *Suddenly Last Summer*.

Spigelgass, Leonard (1908–85) was a writer for the stage and screen who collaborated on the screenplay for *Pepe*. More importantly, he was Edward G. Robinson's friend and, working with him, completed the manuscript of *All My Yesterdays* after Robinson's death. He was interviewed on the BBC special *The Hollywood Greats: Edward G. Robinson*. His plays include *A Majority of One* and *Dear Me, the Sky Is Falling*.

Sports Unathletic as a youth, Edward G. Robinson turned to oratory and the stage. But he was a fan of baseball. In films he played Hans Lobert, former third baseman and manager of the New York Giants recruiting program in *Big Leaguer*. In *Larceny, Inc*. he plays baseball on the prison team prior to his release. He managed prizefighters (boxing) in *Kid Galahad*, a film that contains some of the best fight sequences ever seen in American cinema. Additional boxing scenes are found in *House of Strangers*. In *The Little Giant* he tries polo — without much success. His gang seems to have better luck shooting at the ball than hitting it with a mallet.

Stafford, Grace (1903–92) plays roles in the Edward G. Robinson films *Confessions of a Nazi Spy* (as Mrs. Schneider, Francis Lederer's wife) *A Dispatch from Reuter's*, and *Larceny, Inc.* The wife of cartoonist Walter Lantz, hers was the voice of Woody Woodpecker!

Stander, Lionel (1908–94), often a comic tough guy (as in *The Last Gangster*, with Edward G. Robinson), was a victim of the HUAC witch hunt, but he later became popular as the butler on the TV series *Hart to Hart*. Other films include *Mr. Deeds Goes to Town, A Star Is Born, Call Northside 777, Once Upon a Time in the West,* and *New York New York*.

Stanley, Kim (1925–2001) played on Broadway in *Picnic, Bus Stop, A Touch of the Poet,* and *The Three Sisters,* the last also on the screen. She was nominated for Oscars for *Seance on a Wet Afternoon* and *Frances,* and appeared most recently in *The Right Stuff*. She was in the TV movie *U.M.C.* but shared no scenes with Edward G. Robinson.

Stanwyck, Barbara (1907–91) A star from the 1930s, she appeared in three films with Edward G. Robinson — *Flesh and Fantasy* (separate episodes), *Double Indemnity* (one of her four Academy Award nominations), and *The Violent Men* (a western). She and her first husband, Frank Fay, are in *The Stolen Jools* with Robinson, and she was among those named to appear in a biography of Napoleon opposite Robinson, but the film never materialized. She and Robinson paid tribute to Cecil B. DeMille on television in *The World's Greatest Showman,* and, like Robinson, she pitched Maxwell House Coffee in a commercial. Her other films include *Miracle Woman, The Bitter Tea of General Yen, Annie Oakley, The Lady Eve, Meet John Doe, The Strange Love of Martha Ivers, Walk on the Wild Side,* and — with Oscar nominations — *Ball of Fire, Stella Dallas,* and *Sorry, Wrong Number*. She was awarded an honorary Academy Award in 1981. On television she played in *The Thorn Birds* and in her western series *The Big Valley*. Her second husband was Robert Taylor.

Starr, Frances (1881–1973), a Broadway actress for forty years (*The Easiest Way, Claudia*), was in *Five Star Final*, with Edward G. Robinson, as Nancy Voorhees, whose past, exploited by the press, causes her suicide. She was also in *This Reckless Age* and *The Star Witness*.

Stars Salute '64 (Television, 1964) This special was produced in New York as a fundraiser for the Jewish Federation.

Producer-director, Himan Brown; writer, Alvin Boretz; participants: Louis Armstrong, Theodore Bikel, Julie Harris, Steve Lawrence, Robert Merrill, Sidney Poitier, Edward G. Robinson, Peter Sellers, Barbra Streisand; 1964

State of Israel Bond Organization

In addition to his participation in several annual *Chanukah Festivals for Israel* at Madison Square Garden, Edward G. Robinson was honored by the State of Israel Bond Organization on July 14, 1968, at a "Salute to Israel" at the Beverly Hilton Hotel in Los Angeles. He was cited for his contribution to the promotion of understanding between the peoples of the United States and Israel. Past recipients include Shelley Winters, Herschel Bernardi, Sam Jaffe, Elmer Bernstein, Lorne Greene, and Simon Wincelberg.

Steers, Larry (1881–1951) played in *Little Caesar, The Whole Town's Talking, The Amazing Dr. Clitterhouse,* and *The Woman in the Window* with Edward G. Robinson. Beginning in silent films, he also was in *New Brooms, Bride of the Storm, If I Had a Million,* and *The Gangster.*

Steiger, Rod (1925–) Nominated for Oscars for *On the Waterfront* and *The Pawnbroker*, he won for *In the Heat of the Night.* A method actor, he plays Edward G. Robinson's son in *Seven Thieves.* His other films include *The Big Knife, Oklahoma!, The Harder They Fall, Al Capone, W. C. Fields and Me,* and *Mars Attacks.* He was married to Claire Bloom.

Stella Dallas (Theater, 1924) Produced by Selwyn & Company; playwrights, Henry Gribble and Gertrude Purcell; based on the novel by Olive Higgins Prouty; stage manager, George Cukor; cast included: Mrs. Leslie Carter (Stella), Edward G. Robinson (Ed Munn); 1924

Mrs. Leslie Carter, a legendary American stage actress, was past sixty when she undertook the title role in *Stella Dallas* for Selwyn and Company in 1924. Nearly fifty years later, when he was writing his memoirs, Robinson (who was half her age when he appeared opposite her in the role of Ed Munn), commented, "It had never occurred to me that she had aged…. On the stage Mrs. Carter would doze, waking just in time to step on my line…. Playing with her was so difficult…. I am sorry I did not understand [her] then. I understand her now. She had been playing all her life; she was determined to go on with it. As I am now."

Stephenson, Henry (1871–1956) went from London to the New York stage, acting in Edward G. Robinson's first play, *Under Fire.* In Hollywood he was in *A Bill of Divorcement, Little Women, Mutiny on the Bounty, Captain Blood, Suez, Little Old New York, Mr. Lucky,* and *The Locket.*

Stephenson, James (1889–1941), an English leading man, was in *Confessions of a Nazi Spy* and *A Dispatch from Reuter's* with Edward G. Robinson, as well as *Boy Meets Girl, The Letter* (Oscar nomination), *The Old Maid, South of Suez, Beau Geste,* and *Shining Victory.*

The Steve Allen Show (Television, 1957) Steve Allen (host), Marilyn Jacobs, Louis Nye, Skitch Henderson, Don Knotts, Tom Poston, Bill Dana (regulars); Edward G. Robinson; NBC-TV, 1957

Stevens, K. T. (1919–94) played Edward G. Robinson's secretary in *Vice Squad.* The daughter of director Sam Wood, she was married to actor Hugh Marlowe. Her other films include *Peck's Bad Boy, Kitty Foyle, The Great Man's Lady,* and *Bob & Carol & Ted & Alice.*

Stevens, Landers (1877–1940), the father of director George Stevens, appeared as Crime Commissioner McClure, shot by Rico during the robbery in *Little Caesar.* Among his other films are *The Trial of Mary Dugan, Hell Divers,* and *Swing Time.*

Stevens, Naomi An Italian matron, she was in two TV shows with Edward G. Robinson — as his wife in "The Legend of Jim Riva" on *Robert Taylor's Detectives,* and as Mrs. Raspili in *The Old Man Who Cried Wolf.* Her films include *The Apartment, Valley of the Dolls,* and *Buena Sera, Mrs. Campbell.*

Stevens, Risë (1913–), Metropolitan Opera star, appeared with Edward G. Robinson in the *Chanukah Festival for Israel* in 1960. Her operas include *Carmen, Mignon, Die Fledermaus* and *Der Rosenkavelier,* and she had a featured role in *Going My Way.*

Stevens, Warren (1919–) played gangster Joey Stewart in *Black Tuesday*, with Edward G. Robinson. He also had roles in *The Frogmen, Deadline U.S.A., The Barefoot Contessa, Forbidden Planet, Madigan,* and on *The Richard Boone Show,* a TV anthology.

Stewart, James (1908–98), a star from the 1930s, appeared in two films with Edward G. Robinson — *The Last Gangster* and *Cheyenne Autumn.* They were narrators for

TV's *The World's Greatest Showman*, and appeared together in the short film *The American Creed*, and on the radio drama *We Hold These Truths*. He received Oscar nominations for *Mr. Smith Goes to Washington*, *It's a Wonderful Life*, *Harvey*, and *Anatomy of a Murder*, and won for *The Philadelphia Story*, plus an honorary award in 1984. Other films include *You Can't Take It with You*, *Destry Rides Again*, *Winchester '73*, *Rear Window*, *The Glenn Miller Story*, *The Spirit of St. Louis*, and *Shenandoah*.

Stewart, Paul (1908–86) came to films via Orson Welles' Mercury Theatre, having been heard on radio in *The War of the Worlds*. He was first onscreen in *Citizen Kane*. With Edward G. Robinson he is in *Hell on Frisco Bay*, as Joe, the lead henchman. Other films include *Champion*, *The Window*, *In Cold Blood*, and *W. C. Fields and Me*.

The Stolen Jools (Short film, 1931) This two-reeler, also known as *The Slippery Pearls*, features an all-star cast. It was produced by Pat Casey for National Variety Artists to raise funds for the Tuberculosis Sanitarium (now the Will Rogers Memorial Hospital for Respiratory Diseases) in Saranac Lake, New York.

Distributor, Paramount Pictures & National Screen Service; production financing, Chesterfield (cigarettes); director, William McGann; producer, Pat Casey; cast: Robert Ames, Richard Barthelmess, Warner Baxter, Wallace Beery, Joe E. Brown, Charles Butterworth, Claudette Colbert, Joan Crawford, Maurice Chevalier, Gary Cooper, Bebe Daniels, Richard Dix, Fifi Dorsay, Irene Dunne, Stuart Erwin, Douglas Fairbanks, Jr., Frank Fay, Louise Fazenda, Skeets Gallagher, Oliver Hardy, George "Gabby" Hayes, Hedda Hopper, Allen Jenkins, Eddie Kane, Buster Keaton, the Keystone Kops, Stan Laurel, Winnie Lightner, Edmund Lowe, Ben Lyon, J. Farrell MacDonald, Victor McLaglen, Polly Moran, Jack Oakie, Eugene Pallette, Edward G. Robinson, Charles "Buddy" Rogers, Norma Shearer, Lowell Sherman, George Sidney, Barbara Stanwyck, George E. Stone, Bert Wheeler, Robert Woolsey, Fay Wray, Loretta Young, Matthew Beard (Stymie), Little Betty the Midget, Little Billy, Ed Brendel, Norman Chaney (Chubby), Dorothy Deborba (Echo), Claudia Dell, Wynne Gibson, Mitzi Green, William Haines, Jack Hill, Alan Hoskins (Farina), Bobby Hutchins (Wheezer), Mary Ann Jackson, Dorothy Lee, Charlie Murray, Shirley Jean Rickert, and Pete the Pup; April 1931

The Stolen Lady (Theater, 1926) In 1926, between seasons of the Theatre Guild, Edward G. Robinson appeared in three plays — *We Americans*, *The Stolen Lady*, and *Henry Behave*. *The Stolen Lady* was a flop that failed to make it to Broadway.

Cast: Edward G. Robinson (Col. Virgilio Hermanos Barroso), Leo Carillo; New York; July 1926

Stone, George E. (1903–67) is in five films with Edward G. Robinson: *Little Caesar*, as Otero (a role originally intended for Robinson); *Five Star Final* (Ziggie Feinstein); *Bullets or Ballots* (Wires); *A Slight Case of Murder* (Kirk, an ex-jockey); and the short *The Stolen Jools*. He is also in *The Last Mile*, *Alias Boston Blackie* (and ten others in that series), *The Man with the Golden Arm*, *Guys and Dolls*, and *Some Like It Hot*.

Stone, Milburn (1904–80) was Doc on TV's *Gunsmoke*, for which he won an Emmy Award. In *Black Tuesday*, with Edward G. Robinson, he played Fr. Slocum, a hostage whose life is threatened. Other films include *China Clipper*, *Young Mr. Lincoln*, *Corvette K-225*, and *Drango*.

Straight, Beatrice (1916–2001) won a best supporting actress Oscar for *Network*. She also appeared onscreen in *Phone Call from a Stranger*, *Patterns*, *The Nun's Story*, *Bloodline*, *Poltergeist*, and on TV as Grace Tyburn in "Shadows Tremble" on *Playhouse 90* with Edward G. Robinson.

Strange, Robert (1881–1952) made four appearances with Edward G. Robinson, on the Broadway stage in *First Is Last* and *Banco*, and in the films *Dr. Ehrlich's Magic Bullet* and *Manpower*. He played in the serials *King of the*

Royal Mounted and *Adventures of Captain Marvel*, and was also in *All That Money Can Buy, High Sierra,* and *The Smiling Lieutenant.*

The Stranger (Film, 1946) Independent Releasing Company; producer, S. P. Eagle (Sam Spiegel); director, Orson Welles; screenplay, Anthony Veiller, John Huston, Welles; based on a story by Decla Dunning, Victor Trivas; assistant director, Jack Voglin; dialogue director, Gladys Hill; sound, Arthur Johns, Corson F. Jowett; music, Bronislau Kaper; orchestra, Harold Byrnes, Sydney Cutner; art director, Perry Ferguson; camera, Russell Metty; editor, Ernest Nims; makeup, Bob Cowan; costumes, Michael Woulfe; cast: Edward G. Robinson (Wilson), Loretta Young (Mary Longstreet), Orson Welles (Franz Kindler/Charles Rankin), Richard Long (Noah), Philip Merivale (Judge Longstreet), Byron Keith (Dr. Jeff Lawrence), Billy House (Potter), Martha Wentworth (Sara), Konstantin Shayne (Konrad Meinike), Isabel O'Madigan (Mrs. Lawrence), Pietro Sosso (Mr. Peabody), Erskine Sanford (Professor), Theodore Gottlieb; RKO-International; 94 minutes; July 1946

On the insistence of Wilson, an American war crimes investigator, condemned Nazi Konrad Meinike is allowed to escape from prison to lead authorities to his superior, Franz Kindler. Kindler has settled in the small town of Harper, Connecticut. Wilson trails Meinike, but Meinike tries to kill his pursuer. Meinike meets Mary Longstreet, who is to marry Charles Rankin, a history professor at the local college. Rankin (who is Kindler) is suspicious about Meinike's escape and strangles him. Wilson begins putting pieces together. He knows the man he is looking for as Kindler has a passion for clocks; and the church tower in the town square has a large clock in disrepair. He places Charles Rankin above suspicion at first, after meeting him at a dinner party. Then, remembering a comment Rankin made that Karl Marx was not a German but a Jew, he reconsiders. Mary's dog, Red, is found poisoned; then Meinike's body is discovered. Rankin now lies to Mary, admitting he killed Meinike, telling her that Meinike had been blackmailing him. When Wilson and Judge Longstreet, Mary's father, tell her the truth about Kindler, she rages at them, denying her husband could be a Nazi. Her emotional state concerns Rankin such that he plans her "suicide." He saws through a rung of the ladder leading up into the clock tower and then asks her to meet him there. Sara, the housekeeper, fakes a heart attack to keep Mary from leaving the house. Mary calls her brother, Noah, to keep her appointment at the tower. At this, Wilson rushes to the tower and nearly falls from the ladder. Rankin returns home and is shocked to see Mary there, alive. She denounces him as Kindler, and he runs. Later that night Mary goes to the tower; Rankin is there. She has a gun and intends to kill him. Wilson arrives. Mary shoots and hits the clock mechanism, setting it in motion. Wilson grabs the gun and shoots Rankin, who falls onto the platform in front of the clock, where he is impaled on the sword of a large angel. Screaming, he falls to his death.

Both Orson Welles and Edward G. Robinson dismiss this film. The Welles argument is summed up by Carl Macek in *Film Noir:* "*The Stranger* exists as an answer to the critics who complained that Welles could not make a 'program' picture. He did, and it has found a niche in the canon of the *film noir.*" Robinson, in his memoirs, fell victim once again to reiterating *The New York Times'* assessment of his work, that "the whole film comes off a bloodless, manufactured show."

The opinions of Welles and Robinson notwithstanding, the fact is that *The Stranger* is a very well made and very entertaining melodrama. One observation fifty years after all the arguments about the film's quality and performances had been voiced is fascinating to ponder—the premise of Robinson, who had built his career on playing psychological villains and who also was Jewish, switching roles with Welles! "I can only agree ... that Edward G. Robinson would have been much more effective in that role—restrained, stealthy, anxious, guilty," commented David Thomson in *Rosebud, the story of Orson Welles.* "Done that way, Kindler could have been more frightening and more sympathetic."

The *Times* review continued, "It is true that Mr. Welles has directed his camera for some striking effects, with lighting and interesting angles much relied on in his technique. The fellow knows how to make a camera dynamic in telling a tale. And it is true, too, that Edward G. Robinson is well restrained as the unrelenting sleuth." And the *Sunday New York Times* added that "two very good performances in the picture, by Edward G. Robinson as the sleuth and by Billy House as a small-town meddler, are ... partial tribute to Mr. Welles."

"Edward G. Robinson matches staccato line for staccato line with Welles as his nemesis, charged with bringing Nazi criminals to justice," said *The New York Herald-Tribune*. Leslie Halliwell's *Film Guide* called *The Stranger* "highly unconvincing and artificial melodrama, enhanced by directorial touches, splendid photography, and no-holds barred climax involving a church clock."

James Robert Parish in *The Tough Guys* maintains that *The Stranger* contains "one of [Robinson's] most underrated performances.... Orson Welles' flamboyant post–World War II melodrama of a notorious Nazi killer of Jews.... The war crimes agent was originally intended for ... Agnes Moorehead. However, for box office value she was replaced by Robinson.... Some of the role's effectiveness — a woman telling another woman that her husband is a monster — was lost in the marquee shuffle. At the same time the fact that Robinson in real life was a Jew helped the role take on a new kind of dimension and excitement. Welles pulled out all the stops ... his work is both clever ... and grandiose.... The climax is theatrical, exciting, and totally representative of the director's flair for the dramatic.... Robinson plays his part with a determined, mordant humor."

Welles once called Robinson "an immensely effective actor." And he is quoted by Peter Bogdanovich in his book *Orson Welles*:

WELLES: I think Robinson is one of the best movie actors of all time.
BOGDANOVICH: Was the Billy House character in *The Stranger*, the druggist who played checkers, based on your experience somewhere?
WELLES: No, I invented him. He was mostly written on the set. Had great trouble with Eddie Robinson — he went to the front office about it.
BOGDANOVICH: Why?
WELLES: You know: 'I'm a star and who's this fellow Billy House.'
BOGDANOVICH: That was the best stuff in the picture, I thought.
WELLES: So maybe Eddie was right. It's the only stuff I really liked....
BOGDANOVICH: It's an interesting thing about your playing heavies — you're always so sympathetic. In *The Stranger* I find myself rooting for you instead of Robinson, which throws the picture into a kind of ambiguous —
WELLES: Well, I think it was intentional even in the script. But I think *most* heavies *should* be played for sympathy. All the good ones in the theatre are.

There were positive reviews. *Theatre Arts Magazine* said, "The first half of Orson Welles' *The Stranger* pursues its ominous course with the tension of a taut rubber band.... Edward G. Robinson supports solidly throughout." And *Variety* noted the film's "fine production, strong direction and playing, and clever writing [which] shape the ingredients to concentrate interest on as deadly a manhunt as has ever been screened.... A uniformly excellent cast gives reality to events that transpire.... The three stars ... turn in some of their best work."

"Robinson [gives] ... a thoughtful, selfless performance," thought Foster Hirsch, "and his solid presence counters Welles' sometimes operatic excesses as actor and director. Quietly smoking his pipe, sedately drinking coffee, explaining to Young the situation she's in, and playing a sly teasing game with Welles, Robinson gives the film the firm center it needs.... The film has a quietly sinister atmosphere that's very effective, and it's filled with eccentric touches...." — *Edward G. Robinson: A Pyramid Illustrated History of the Movies*

Finally, James Naremore in *The Magic of Orson Welles* said that Robinson "manages to charm audiences despite the relative colorlessness of his role."

"The Stranger" (Radio, 1946) Cast: Edward G. Robinson, Ruth Hussey; *Procter and Gamble's This Is Hollywood*; CBS-radio; December 7, 1946

Strasberg, Lee (1901–82) acted with the Theatre Guild in *The Chief Thing* with Edward G. Robinson. He co-founded the Group Theatre with Harold Clurman and Cheryl Crawford in 1931 and became an advocate of method acting, heading the Actors Studio beginning in 1948. He acted in the films *The Godfather Part II* (Oscar nomination), *And Justice for All,* and *Going in Style.*

Studios Edward G. Robinson's early films were made at Paramount, MGM, Universal, and First National (later Warner Bros., or a division thereof). He subsequently worked for Columbia, United Artists, 20th Century–Fox, Disney, and a number of other independent production companies.
See names of individual studios.

Styne, Jule (1905–94), composer of such Broadway fare as *Peter Pan, Gentlemen Prefer Blondes, Bells Are Ringing, Gypsy, Funny Girl,* and *Sugar,* he music for films as well, including the adaptation of some of his stage successes, as well as *Three Coins in the Fountain* (Oscar for the title tune) and *Anchors Aweigh.* He received many other nominations, including one for the title song from *It's a Great Feeling,* written with Sammy Cahn.
See **Sammy Cahn.**

Suicide *Soylent Green, All My Sons, The Red House,* and *Unholy Partners* all ended with Edward G. Robinson's suicide, as does *The Woman in the Window*— until its trick ending is revealed; he accepts the inevitability of death at the end of *Night Has a Thousand Eyes, The Sea Wolf,* and *Barbary Coast.* His monologue on "suicide — how committed" in *Double Indemnity* is a classic.

Muck-raking journalism drives two characters in *Five Star Final* to suicide.
See **Death Scenes.**

Sullivan, Charles (1899–1972) appears in six films with Edward G. Robinson — *The Whole Town's Talking, Kid Galahad, The Sea Wolf, Larceny, Inc., Manpower,* and *The Last Gangster.* He is also in *Girl in Every Port* and *The Lash Hurrah.*

Sullivan, Ed (1901–73), former newspaperman, hosted an hour-long weekly variety program on CBS-TV. Edward G. Robinson appeared twice — in a cutting from *Middle of the Night* with co-star Gena Rowlands, and also in a tribute to director John Huston. Sullivan appeared with Robinson in the *Chanukah Festival for Israel* in 1964 and played himself in the film *Bye Bye Birdie.*

Surprise Endings *The Woman in the Window,* one of Edward G. Robinson's finest melodramas, has been both criticized and defended for its ending, in which the whole murder-adventure turns out to be a dream. We may have forgotten that in an early scene Robinson had asked the porter at his club to remind him when it is 10:30 p.m. When he does, Robinson's character has fallen asleep, and the porter nudges him awake. At the end of the film, to escape his fate of being blackmailed for murder, Robinson takes an overdose of sleeping pills and falls asleep in a chair. Presumably dead, he is now awakened by the porter a second time. The trick ending is effective; it made people talk.

In the subsequent *film noir* with the same leads, *Scarlet Street,* Robinson is a murderer who is expected to be brought to justice in some way. The "justice" imposed on him is to live, haunted by the memories and voices of the lovers he killed.

No one expects Steve McQueen's character as *The Cincinnati Kid* to lose, and no one expects Edward G. Robinson's character, The Man, to win in their climactic poker game. But it happens in a surprise ending that leaves audiences identifying strongly with Mc-Queen's loss. Other surprise film endings include:

**Grand Slam.* After making a complicated robbery scheme work, supposed victim Janet Leigh unites with mastermind Robinson, having cleverly switched bags to gain the diamonds. But a purse snatcher steals the bag from Janet in the last moments of the movie.

A Hole in the Head. Robinson, a tightwad businessman, decides to forgo returning to New York and his millinery store, and instead takes a Miami vacation with his wife.

Seven Thieves. There are several trick endings. As in *Grand Slam*, success in the elaborate robbery scheme is short-lived. The $4 million in francs is marked money. Moreover, Robinson's character dies of a heart attack moments after the thieves' getaway. And when Rod Steiger and Joan Collins decide to return the money anonymously, they win at roulette!

The Amazing Dr. Clitterhouse is so named because at his murder trial he is acquitted on the grounds of insanity.

*Barbara Rush (Marian in *Robin and the 7 Hoods*) ends up, not with Frank Sinatra or Dean Martin, but with Bing Crosby, while the other characters are literally left out in the cold.

The Survivor from Warsaw (Narration, 1969) Arnold Schoenberg's symphony had Edward G. Robinson as narrator for two performances at the Music Center Pavilion in Los Angeles.

Edward G. Robinson (narrator); Los Angeles Philharmonic Orchestra, Men's Chorus of the Los Angeles Master Chorale, Roger Wagner, director; Zubin Mehta, conductor; composer, Arnold Schoenberg; November 7 and 8, 1969

Suspense This program featuring hour-long mystery stories was broadcast on CBS-radio.

See **"A Case of Nerves"**; **"The Man Who Thought He Was Edward G. Robinson"**; **"The Man Who Wanted to Be Edward G. Robinson"**; **"My Wife, Geraldine"**; **"You Can't Die Twice."**

Sutton, Frank (1923–74) is known for his role as the sergeant on TV's *Gomer Pyle, USMC*. With Edward G. Robinson, he played Frank Doyle, a would-be killer, in "The Legend of Jim Riva" on *Robert Taylor's Detectives*. His films include *Marty*, *Town Without Pity*, and *The Satan Bug*.

Swerling, Jo (1893–1964) wrote *The Kibitzer*, a moderately successful play in its first run. Edward G. Robinson, who had played the lead, worked with him, acting out scenes to improve it, and when it reopened two years later, he was given co-authorship credit. Swerling collaborated also on the book of *Guys and Dolls* and the screenplays of Robinson's *The Whole Town's Talking* and *I Am the Law*, as well as *Dirigible*, *Platinum Blonde*, *The Westerner*, *Lifeboat*, *The Pride of the Yankees*, and *It's a Wonderful Life*.

Swinburne, Nora (1902–2000) played Edward G. Robinson's wife in *Operation X*. She was in silent films in her native England and also appeared in *Dinner at the Ritz*, *Quo Vadis*, *Third Man on the Mountain*, and *Anne of the Thousand Days*.

Tabor, Horace Austin Warner (Haw) (1830–99) was played onscreen by Edward G. Robinson in *Silver Dollar*. He was "a Vermont-born Western prospector ... who gained his considerable wealth mining silver from his Matchless Mine in Leadville, Colorado. In 1878, Tabor became Leadville's first mayor, served five years as Colorado's lieutenant governor, and briefly occupied a U.S. Senate seat. But before his death, Tabor lost his fortune ... attributable [in part] to society's refusal to accept his second wife, for scandal surrounded Tabor's affair with this vivacious young woman ... for whom the tycoon divorced the mother of his children. But 'Baby Doe' remained faithful to Horace's memory, and when she died a recluse in 1935, it was in a shack near the mine...."—Jerry Vermilyea, *Films of the Thirties*

Taggart, Ben (1889–1947), a heavyset character who often played cops, appears in four films with Edward G. Robinson—*Smart Money* (as gambler Hickory Short), *The Little Giant*, *The Whole Town's Talking*, and *Mr. Winkle Goes to War*. Other films include *Horse Feathers* and *Penny Serenade*.

Tales of Manhattan (Film, 1942) *The New York Journal American* took a practical approach in commenting about the all-star cast of *Tales of Manhattan*, saying the film "boasts a cast glittering enough to interest everyone but the lads who have to figure out the electric lightbulbs on theatre marquees."

According to *The Films of Rita Hayworth*, by

Gene Ringgold, "The idea of using a dress tailcoat as the gimmick on which each story is hung is said to have come from Alan Campbell (Dorothy Parker's husband). The first episode filmed starred Charles Laughton and the last one to be written and filmed starred Edward G. Robinson. A sequence filmed which was to immediately precede the finale starred W. C. Fields, but it was deleted after several previews when audience reaction made it apparent that it was not in keeping with the generally dramatic tone of the other sequences." With the release of the film, five stars added their footprints, hand prints, and signatures to cement blocks outside Grauman's Chinese Theater. Present along with Sid Grauman were Hayworth, Laughton, Robinson, Henry Fonda, and Charles Boyer. A dozen more familiar faces in the picture made it truly an all-star company. The fifth episode of the film, starring Ethel Waters and Paul Robeson, became a problem. Robeson, appearing in what would be the last film of his career, denounced his participation in it because the scenes demeaned blacks. With the advent of television, there were fewer showings, or in some cases the episode was deleted. Leslie Halliwell noted in *The Filmgoer's Companion, Sixth Edition*, that, "the Negro sequence was incredibly 'Uncle Tom.'"

Producers, Boris Morros, S. P. Eagle (Sam Spiegel); director, Julien Duvivier; stories/screenplays, Ben Hecht, Ferenc Molnar, Donald Ogden Stewart, Samuel Hoffenstein, Alan Campbell, Ladislas Fodor, Laslo Vadnay, Laszlo Gorog, Lamar Trotti, Henry Blankfort; assistant directors, Robert Stillman, Charles Hall; music, Sol Kaplan; orchestra, Charles Bradshaw, Clarence Webster; songs, Ralph Rainger, Leo Robin, Saul Chaplin, Paul Francis Webster; music directors, Edward Paul, Hugo Friedhofer; arrangements, Hall Johnson; art directors, Richard Day, Boris Leven; set, Thomas Little; sound, W. D. Flick, Roger Heman; camera, Joseph Walker; editor, Robert Bischoff; makeup, Guy Pearce; costumes, Irene, Bernard Newman, Dolly Tree, Gwen Wakeling, Oleg Cassini; unit manager, J. H. Nadel; cast: Charles Boyer (Orman), Rita Hayworth (Ethel), Ginger Rogers (Diane), Henry Fonda (George), Charles Laughton (Charles Smith), Edward G. Robinson (Larry Browne), Paul Robeson (Luke), Ethel Waters (Esther), Eddie "Rochester" Anderson (Lazarus), Thomas Mitchell (Halloway), Eugene Pallette (Luther), Cesar Romero (Harry), Gail Patrick (Ellen), Roland Young (Edgar), Elsa Lanchester (Mrs. Smith), Victor Francen (Arturo Bellini), George Sanders (Williams), James Gleason (Father Joe), Harry Davenport (Prof. Lyons), J. Carroll Naish (Costello), Helene Reynolds (Actress), Christian Rub (Wilson), Adeline De Walt Reynolds (Grandmother), Sig Arno (Piccolo player), Will Wright (Skeptic), Dewey Robinson (Proprietor), Tom O'Grady (Latecomer), Forbes Murray (Dignified man), James Rennie (Hank Bronson), Harry Hayden (Soupy Davis), Morris Ankrum (Judge), Don Douglas (Henderson), Mae Marsh (Molly), Barbara Lynn (Mary), Hall Johnson Choir (Townspeople), Clarence Muse (Grandpa), George Reed (Old Christopher), Cordell Hickman (Nicodemus), John Kelly (Monk), Rene Austin, Olive Bell, Joseph Bernard, Buster Brodie, Don Brodie, Jack Chefe, Rita Christiani, Gus Corrado, Frank Dae, Frank Darien, Maggie Dorsey, Alberta Gary, Charles Gray, Robert Grieg, William Halligan, Esther Howard, Philip Hurlie, Frank Jaquet, Ella Mae Lashley, Johnny Lee, Connie Leon, Marian Martin, Lonnie Nichols, Frank Orth, Alex Pollard, Paul Renay, Archie Savage, Ted Stanhope, Charles Tannen, Curly Twyfford, Laura Vaughn, Blue Washington, Charles Williams, Eric Wilton; 20th Century–Fox; 118 minutes; September 1942

Broadway star Paul Orman races to the country home of Ethel Halloway. Her husband suspects her of infidelity. While cleaning The Colonel, the pride of his gun collection, Halloway taunts Orman, then shoots him. Ethel quickly asserts it was an accident. Orman puts on an act—first a death scene; then, pretending that Halloway missed, dismissing Ethel and chiding Halloway for doubting her. Luther, his chauffeur, takes Orman to the hospital and the tailcoat (with bullet hole) to Edgar, Harry's manservant. Diane, who is engaged to Harry, finds a letter in the coat from "Squirrel" to her "Lion." Harry tells her the tailcoat belongs to his friend, George, who wore it home by mistake. George covers for Harry, saying he is the Lion, but Squirrel appears, and Harry is caught. The marriage is off, but no matter; Diane has fallen for George. The tailcoat goes to a pawnshop. Charles Smith is invited by Maestro Bellini to conduct his new symphony. Charles wears the tailcoat, but it is too tight. On each wave of his baton, the coat rips. The audience laughs, and Charles stops, humiliated. Bellini, seated in a box, removes his tailcoat and bids Charles continue, which he does with great success. The tailcoat is given to a mission. Larry Browne, a derelict in Chinatown, wears it to his 25–year law school reunion at the Waldorf Astoria. He meets old friends, including Professor Lyons, Soupy Davis, and Hank Bronson. When Henderson misplaces his wallet, everyone jokingly surrenders to a search except Larry. Williams, a rival, knows that Larry had been disbarred, and during a mock trial over the theft, Larry bitterly "throws himself on the mercy of the court." He returns to the mission more pitiable than ever, not counting on Soupy and Hank, who drop by to reassure him that the offer of a new job holds good. Costello steals the tailcoat and wears it to hold up a nightclub, then flies to Mexico. When the money and coat catch fire, he throws it from the plane. It lands in a rural black community, where it is thought to be a gift from heaven. Reverend Lazarus distributes the cash in answer to each person's prayers. Children are given money for shoes, Esther wants a cow. An old gentleman has prayed for money for a coffin — a mahogany one. Esther remembers Old Christopher, the poorest among them, who, if he prayed for all the money, should receive it. He admits he prayed for a scarecrow, which seems the perfect use for an old tailcoat.

The reviews were mixed to good, favoring Robinson's performance, which was cited by the National Board of Review as one of the year's best. *The New York Times* said, "*Tales of Manhattan* is one of those rare films.... Neither profound nor very searching, it nevertheless manages to convey a gentle, detached comprehension of the irony and pity of life.... A tricky departure from the norm, which in spite of its five-ring circus nature, achieves an impressive effect.... Edward G. Robinson gives a masterful performance as the bum who has seen better days." Further comment in *The Sunday New York Times*: "Mr. Robinson fills the bill superbly, but the writers let him down in the end."

"Of the series, this corner may be put down as preferring the Robinson episode above all else," wrote the *New York Morning Telegraph*, "with Robinson himself giving a superb performance."

The New York Herald-Tribune said, "An impressive lineup of stars is to be found in *Tales of Manhattan*. High-ranking scenarists have spun the plot. The distinguished French director Julien Duvivier has staged the show. If it is big movie names you want, [it] is a prodigal offering. Obviously they lend an aura of glamor and fascination to the proceedings. What they fail to do is make *Tales of Manhattan* more than a disjointed and pretentious picture."

"The Taming of the Shrew"   (Radio, 1937) Author, William Shakespeare; adaptation, Gilbert Seldes; director, Brewster Morgan; orchestra, Victor Bay; announcer, Conway Tearle; cast: Edward G. Robinson (Petruchio), Frieda Inescourt (Katherina), Eric Snowden, Phillip Terry, Charles D. Brown, Morris Ankrum, Lionel Pape, William Austin, Ernestine deBecker, Jack Smart, Robert Frazer, Ethel Mantell; *CBS Shakespeare Theatre*, CBS-radio; August 2, 1937 (also dated July 3, 1937)

"Easily the most enjoyable hour in the series is provided by Edward G. Robinson — the onetime Little Caesar — as Petruchio, who's come to wive it wealthily in Padua in 'The Taming of the Shrew.' The play is the simplest in the series to keep up with, being primarily the confrontations of one man and one woman, and Mr. Robinson races through it with gusto. He is aggressive, virile, boisterous and funny. He roars but never hams, he sings a bit, he kisses big juicy kisses, he has the studio audiences laughing out loud."—*The New York Times*, December 13, 1981, in a review of Ariel Records' release of the radio broadcast recordings.

Tampico   (Film, 1944) In *Tampico* Lynn Bari was twenty years younger than Edward G. Robinson, but they made an agreeable romantic couple in this modest war melodrama.

Captain Bart Manson picks up survivors from a torpedoed ship in Mexican waters. Among them is Kathy Hall, who has lost all her identification. She and Bart become acquainted when she uses his cabin during the overcrowded conditions aboard the ship. Once ashore in Tampico, Bart agrees to vouch for her so that she will not be deported back to Europe. Because he must know her whereabouts at all times, they go out on the town together. They hit it off and, on a whim, decide to marry. Kathy finds a house for them overlooking the water and a reception is held. Bart's first mate, Fred Adamson, disapproves of the marriage, and he and Bart argue. Secret orders for Bart's crew arrive, and he leaves in the middle of the night. Kathy goes down to the ship to see him off, and he warns her she should not have come. At sea Bart's ship is torpedoed, and Fred is among those missing in action. In an investigation, Kathy comes under suspicion as a spy. When she admits to Bart that she had no papers or passage, but stowed away on the ship that was lost, his suspicion grows, and they have a falling out. He is seen frequently in the Tampico bars, giving the appearance of one drowning his troubles in liquor, but actually he is setting himself up to be contacted by the spy organization. Once approached, he is asked to supply vital information about the U.S. ships in the area. He reports to the authorities and then returns to the spy headquarters with his information. As the spy ring is being captured, one man escapes, and Bart follows him, only to encounter Fred, who has been working with the enemy. Bart is forced to shoot Fred in self defense. He returns to apologize to Kathy and to say goodbye, but they decide to stay together.

Producer, Robert Bassler; director, Lothar Mendes; screenplay, Kenneth Gamet, Fred Niblo, Jr., and Richard Macaulay; story, Ladislas Fodor; special effects, Fred Sersen; art directors, James Basevi, Albert Hogsett; set, Thomas Little, Al Orenbach; camera, Charles Clarke; editor, Robert Fritch; music director, Emil Neuman; choreography, Geneva Sawyer; assistant director, Jasper Blystone; cast: Edward G. Robinson (Captain Bart Manson), Lynn Bari (Kathy Hall), Victor McLaglen (Fred Adamson), Mona Maris (Dolores), Robert Bailey (Watson), Marc Lawrence (Valdez), E. J. Ballantine (Silhouette man), Tonio Selwart (Kruger), Nestor Paiva (Naval commander), Daniel Ocko (Immigration inspector), Ben Erway (Dr. Brown), Helen Brown (Mrs. Kelly), Roy Roberts (Crawford), George Sorel (Stranger), Carl Ekberg (Mueller), Charles Lang (Naval officer), Ralph Byrd (O'Brien), Karen Palmer (Bit), David Cota (Messenger), Muni Seroff (Rodriguez), Juan Varro (Photographer), Antonio Moreno (Justice of the Peace), Martin Garralaga (Serra), Martin Black (Steward), Trevor Bardette, Chris-Pin Martin (Waiters), Margaret Martin (Proprietor), Virgil Johansen (Seaman), Arno Frey (Navigator), Jean Del Val (Pilot), Ludwig Donath, Constantine Romanoff, Martin Cichy, Peter Helmers, Paul Kruger, Rudolph A. Lindau, Otto Reichau, Hans von Morhart; 20th Century–Fox; 75 minutes; June 1944

"It has all the elements of a good suspenseful drama," said *The New York Times,* "but it becomes increasingly obvious that nothing unlooked for is going to come about…. Mr. Robinson's role as a love-chastened ship's captain is carried off in his usual businesslike manner, although his admirers will likely feel that the chastening isn't particularly advantageous to his traditional characterization."

And *The New York Herald-Tribune* felt that, "if the film has any virtue at all, it is that of underplaying, but while this has proved to be the outstanding feature of many of our most exciting pictures, this quality in itself is not sufficient…. Wearing the four stripes of the merchant marine, Edward G. Robinson comes off with most of the acting honors."

Tani, Yoko   (1932–99) plays a Japanese geisha who gives crash-course instruction to Shirley MacLaine in *My Geisha*. She also appears in *The Quiet American, Who's Been Sleeping in My Bed?,* and *The Savage Innocents*.

Tarkington, Booth   (1869–1946), novelist-turned-playwright with *Monsieur Beaucaire,* authored *Poldekin,* in which Edward G. Robinson appeared with George Arliss. Other plays include *Clarence* and *Intimate Strangers*. His novel *Seventeen* was adapted for the stage for Ruth Gordon.

Taylor, Dub   (1907–94) was in Capra's *You Can't Take It with You,* playing the xylophone, and *A Hole in the Head,* with Edward G. Robinson. He is also a poker dealer in *The Cincinnati Kid*. Other films include *Riding High, No Time for Sergeants,* and *Bonnie and Clyde.*

Taylor, Robert   (1911–69) and Edward G. Robinson were in *Verdensberomtheder I Kobenhaven*, a Danish film short, and on TV's *Robert Taylor's Detectives* in "The Legend of Jim Riva." Once married to Barbara Stanwyck, Taylor was a friendly witness during House Un-American Activities Committee hearings. His films include *Camille, Magnificent Obsession, A Yank at Oxford, Waterloo Bridge, Bataan, Quo Vadis,* and *Ivanhoe.*

Taylor, Rod   (1929–), prior to becoming a leading man in *The Birds* and *The Time Machine*, played a hood, Brody Evans, in *Hell on Frisco Bay*, with Edward G. Robinson. Other films include *Raintree County, Sunday in New York, The V.I.P.s, Fate Is the Hunter,* and *Young Cassidy.*

Tedrow, Irene   (1907–95), onscreen from 1937, played Tuesday Weld's mother in *The Cincinnati Kid*, had a role in *The Ten Commandments*, and was on the radio as Edward G. Robinson's wife in an adaptation of *All My Sons*. Her other films include *Journey Into Fear, Please Don't Eat the Daisies, The Parent Trap,* and *The Greatest Story Ever Told.*

Telephones   There are many of Edward G. Robinson's performances in which the telephone is used routinely, but more interesting is how the instrument figures in some of the storylines. Its most dramatic use, perhaps, is in *Five Star Final*, at the film's climax, when Robinson's character, a newspaper editor named Randall, announces that his boss "can go to....!" and punctuates the remark by throwing his ringing telephone through a glass door. In the same film, telephone conversations and their connections through the operator are shown in an early version of split-screen photography. Split screen conversations occur also in both *A Hole in the Head* and *My Geisha.*

The use of the phone is key to the plot of several films. Gangster Humphrey Bogart learns Robinson's identity as *The Amazing Dr. Clitterhouse* via a gadget he has devised to "trace" a call on the phone dial. A last-minute phone call from the district attorney (Robinson) is too late to save a death-row inmate from execution in *Illegal*, beginning the D.A.'s fall from grace. *The Man with Two Faces* is first heard on the telephone (Robinson with a French accent); later he appears in goatee, monocle, and false nose. The planning of the murder in *Double Indemnity* is done via pay phone; Paul Newman's hunt for a murderer in *The Prize* begins with a mysterious phone call from the dying man.

That "you can deny a phone call in court" was Robinson's alibi in *All My Sons*. His partner, sentenced to prison for shipping defective airplane cylinders, testified that Robinson's character, Joe Keller, had told him over the phone to "ship them." Denying that, Keller was exonerated. At the end of *The Woman in the Window*, Joan Bennett is desperately trying to reach Robinson by phone to tell him that their blackmailer is dead, but it is too late—Robinson has taken sleeping pills. Emergencies are telephoned in *Our Vines Have Tender Grapes* and *The Stranger*. In the latter film Robinson, talking with government authorities in Washington, has the telling line, "Who but a Nazi would deny that [Karl] Marx was a German because he was a Jew?"

Most entertaining is Robinson's swallowing oysters in *The Cincinnati Kid* while discussing an upcoming poker match on the phone with Rip Torn. Finally, *Little Caesar* is memorable for its scene of Robinson on the phone bellowing at Inspector Flaherty, "This is Rico! R-I-C-O. Rico, that's who!" Flaherty has called Rico "yellow" in the newspapers, and Rico's vanity won't stand for it. He telephones to tell off the inspector; the call is traced, and … "Mother of Mercy, is this the end of Rico?"

Television   In addition to appearing on several dozen programs, nearly all of Edward G. Robinson's films have been shown on television. It has proved an excellent way to keep his image in the public eye, but as he once lamented, "I wish I were getting residuals." *The Ten Commandments,* among many of the feature films he appeared in, makes at least an annual appearance during the Easter / Passover season.

The medium itself (or the presence of a television set) was also part of Robinson's projects. Notably, *The Glass Web*, filmed in 3–D, had as its premise "Crime of the Week," a television program dramatizing real murders, and, in particular, the murder of a young starlet who had acted on the show. At the time, in 1953, the movies were still chafing at the growing presence of television sets in American homes. It was also the year of Cinerama, which it was hoped would curtail interest in TV. The use of 3–D and the linking of television to crime were interesting ploys to draw the public back out of their houses and into movie theaters, but they met with little success.

Other Robinson films in which television figured include *The Prize* (a murder victim is watching the Nobel press conference); *Tight*

1952	June 21	*U.S. Olympic Committee Telethon*
1953	September 17	*Lux Video Theatre*: "Witness for the Prosecution"
	(date unknown)	*What's My Line?*
1954	(date unknown)	*For the Defense*: "The Case of Kenny Jason"
	September 20	*Operation Entertainment*
	December 9	*Climax!*: "Epitaph for a Spy"
1955	January 13	*Ford Theatre*: "…And Son"
	December 29	*Ford Theatre*: "A Set of Values"
1956	(date unknown)	*The Ed Sullivan Show* (two segments)
	(date unknown)	*The Honeymooners*
	(date unknown)	*The Martha Raye Show*
	September 30– October 28	*The $64,000 Challenge*
1957	(date unknown)	*The Steve Allen Show*
1957	May	*Parade of Stars Telethon*
1958	(date unknown)	*This Is Your Life, Frank Capra*
	October 23	*Playhouse 90*: "Shadows Tremble"
1959	(date unknown)	*This Is Your Life, Mervyn LeRoy*
	March 2	*Goodyear Theatre*: "A Good Name"
	April 2	*Zane Grey Theatre*: "Heritage"
1960	February 14	*Breck Golden Showcase: The Devil and Daniel Webster*
	October 24	*The Right Man*
	(date unknown)	*What's My Line?*
1961	(date unknown)	*Here's Hollywood*
	January 29	*General Electric Theatre*: "The Drop-Out"
	October 9	*Robert Taylor's Detectives*: "The Legend of Jim Riva"
	December 9	*Twelve Star Salute*
1962	March 18	*DuPont Show of the Week*: "Cops and Robbers"
1963	December 1	*The World's Greatest Showman*
1964	(date unknown)	*Stars Salute '64*
	(date unknown)	Maxwell House Coffee commercial
	April 13	*36th Annual Academy of Motion Picture Arts and Sciences Awards*
1965	January 9	*Hollywood Palace*: This Is It
	February 19	*Xerox Special: Who Has Seen the Wind?*
	June 17 & 24	*Eye on Art*
1966	February 7	*The Lucy Show*: "Lucy Goes to a Hollywood Premiere"
1967	March 2	*Batman*: "Batman's Satisfaction"
1968	September 15	*Here Come the Stars*
	September 25	*The Tonight Show with Johnny Carson*
1969	(date unknown)	*Bracken's World*: "Panic"

	April 17	*World Premiere Movie*: U.M.C.
	September 8	*The Singers*
1970	(date unknown)	*Laugh-In*
	June-August	*Happy Days*
	October 13	*ABC Movie of the Week*: *The Old Man Who Cried Wolf*
	October 23	*Bracken's World*: "The Mary Tree"
	October 23	*This Is Tom Jones*: "The Betrothed," "I Will Not Go Back"
1971	(date unknown)	*N.E.T. Playhouse on the Thirties*: "The Movie Crazy Years"
	May 4	*Hollywood Television Theatre*: U.S.A.
	October 11	*Laugh-In*
	December 18	*Rod Serling's Night Gallery*: "The Messiah on Mott Street"

Posthumous telecasts:

1973	March 18	*The American Idea*: *The Land*
	March 27	*45th Annual Academy of Motion Picture Arts and Sciences Awards*
1979	August 3	*The Hollywood Greats: Edward G. Robinson*
1996	(date unknown)	*A&E Biography*: "Little Big Man"

Spot, in which the characters watch a musical variety telethon; *Vice Squad*, in which Robinson, as a police captain, is interviewed live on a program and is interrupted to deal with a bank robbery; and *Soylent Green*, in which the Governor (played by Whit Bissell) talks to the people of New York in the year 2022.

Television Programs   Edward G. Robinson appeared on the following programs over a twenty-year period:

The Ten Commandments   (Film, 1956) In the 1950s Edward G. Robinson's career foundered as he played roles in several "B" films, the result of adverse publicity from the House Un-American Activities Committee's investigations into Communist ties in the film community. Although Robinson testified voluntarily before Congress on three occasions and thought he had cleared his name, it wasn't until Cecil B. DeMille, who wanted him for the role of Dathan in *The Ten Commandments*, demanded to know why Robinson was "unacceptable." DeMille had Robinson investigated, and ultimately found no reason not to hire him. DeMille's decision restored Robinson's status in Hollywood.

DeMille began working on *The Ten Commandments* at the end of a long and colorful career. His 1923 silent version of the film had employed a modern story as its second half that paralleled the Biblical tale. The new film, which was shot in VistaVision and Technicolor, ran nearly four hours. Along with such movies as *Gone with the Wind*, it became a prototype of the blockbuster epic. *The Ten Commandments* was a popular commercial success whose merits were strongest in the magnitude and sweep of the story and the technical effects incorporated in its telling.

The edict of Egyptian Pharaoh Rameses I that male Hebrew children be slaughtered to prevent the emergence of their Deliverer prompts Yochabel to save her infant son, Moses, by setting him adrift in a basket down the Nile. Bithia, sister of Sethi, now Pharaoh, discovers the baby and raises him as her own son. Moses falls in love with Nefretiri, who will be queen to the next pharaoh. While Moses builds Sethi's treasure city in Goshen, his son, Rameses II, is given the task of finding the Deliverer. Nefretiri murders her servant, Memnet, after she reveals Moses' identity. Moses learns he has a brother, Aaron, and a sister, Miriam. He takes his place in the brick pits as a slave. Moses kills Baka, the Egyptian master builder, in order to save Joshua, who now proclaims Moses their people's Deliverer. This is overheard by Dathan, a Hebrew overseer, who reports it to Rameses. Moses is banished to the desert. He survives the ordeal and, staying in the tents of Jethro, eventually chooses Sephora for his wife. Several years pass. Moses climbs to the top of Mount Sinai, where the Voice of God commands him to go to Egypt to free the slaves. Rameses has succeeded his father on the throne, with Nefretiri as his queen. Rameses dismisses Moses twice. After a third visit, following hail, pestilence, and disasters, Rameses decrees death to the firstborn of the slaves. Nefretiri sends Moses' son and Sephora away; however, Moses cannot alter the fate of Rameses' firstborn son, nor all firstborn in Egypt. Only those who smeared lambs' blood on their doors as an indication for God to "pass over" their house are saved. Pharaoh lets the slaves go. All of Israel, led by Moses, marches out of Egypt in the great exodus. Taunted by Nefretiri, Rameses reneges and takes his army to slaughter the fleeing Hebrews; the warriors are blocked by a pillar of fire as Moses stretches his staff across the waters. The sea parts, and the Hebrews proceed on dry land. The pillar of fire dissipates and Pharaoh's soldiers advance, only to be drowned as the sea closes in over them. At the foot of Mount Sinai, the Israelites, awaiting Moses' return, are stirred up by Dathan's skepticism and his reasoning that they would be better off returning to Egypt, where at least there is food. Moses asks God for guidance. Again the pillar of fire materializes. The flames sear the Ten Commandments into the wall of stone, which is then separated into tablets that Moses carries down the mountain. He meets an ungrateful mob of his people who, at Dathan's urging and through Aaron's craftsmanship, now have a golden calf, an idol, to worship and to parade before them back to Egypt. They have spent days drinking and reveling. Denouncing them, Moses throws the stone tablets at the golden calf. The ground opens and swallows up Dathan and the other evildoers. The Hebrews wander forty years in the wilderness until the generations that did the evil are consumed. Quite aged now, Moses consecrates Joshua, who leads the Israelites across the River Jordan to the Promised Land.

Producer-director, Cecil B. DeMille; based on the novels *Prince of Egypt* by Dorothy Clarke Wilson, *Pillar of Fire* by Rev. J. H. Ingraham, and *On Eagle's Wings* by Rev. G. E. Southon, in accordance with Holy Scriptures and the ancient texts of Josephus, Eusebius, Philo, and the Midrash; screenplay, Aeneas MacKenzie, Jesse L. Lasky, Jr., Jack Gariss, Fredric M. Frank; associate producer, Henry Wilcoxon; music, Elmer Bernstein; camera, Loyal Griggs, J. Peverell Marley, John Warren, Wallace Kelly; special effects, John P. Fulton (Oscar winner); process photography, Farciot Edouart; optical photography, Paul Lerpae; art directors, Hal Pereira, Walter Tyler, Albert Nozaki; set, Ray Moyer, Sam Comer; costumes, Edith Head, Arnold Friberg, Dorothy Jeakins, Ralph Jester, John Jenson; sound, Gene Garvin, Harry Lindgren, Louis H. Mesenkop, Loren Ryder; editor, Anne Bauchens; assistant directors, Fouad Aref, Francisco Day, Michael Moore, Daniel McCauley, Edward Salven; construction, Jerry Cook; production manager, Kenneth DeLand, Donald Robb, Frank Caffey; dialogue supervisors, Donald MacLean, Frances Dawson; choreography, Leroy Prinz, Ruth Godfrey; hairstyles, Nellie Manley; makeup, Wally Westmore, Frank Westmore, Frank McCoy; props, Gordon Cole, Robert Goodstein; research, Henry Noerdlinger, Gladys Percey; Technicolor consultant, Richard Mueller; unit director, Arthur Rossen; cast: Charlton Heston (Moses), Yul Brynner (Rameses), Anne Baxter (Nefretiri), Edward G. Robinson (Dathan), Yvonne DeCarlo (Sephora), Debra Paget (Lilia), John Derek (Joshua), Sir Cedric Hardwicke (Sethi), Nina Foch (Bithia), Martha Scott (Yochabel), Judith Anderson (Memnet), Vincent Price (Baka), John Carradine (Aaron), Eduard Franz (Jethro), Olive Deering (Miriam), Donald Curtis (Mered), Douglass Dumbrille (Jannes), Lawrence Dobkin (Hur Ben Caleb), Frank DeKova (Abiram), H. B. Warner (Amminadab), Henry Wilcoxon (Pentaur), Julia Faye (Elisheba), Diane Hall, Joanna Merlin, Lisa Mitchell, Pat Richard, Joyce Vanderveen, Noelle Williams (Jethro's daughters), Joan Woodbury (Korah's wife), Francis J. McDonald (Simon), Ian Keith (Rameses I), John Miljan (Blind One), Woody Strode (King of Ethiopia), Dorothy Adams (Slave woman), Henry Brandon (Commander of the Hosts), Michael Connors (Amalekite), Gail Kobe (Slave girl), Fred Kohler, Jr. (Foreman), Frankie Darro, Kenneth MacDonald, Carl Switzer (Slaves), Addison Richards (Fanbearer), Onslow Stevens (Lugal), Clint Walker (Sardinian captain), Frank Wilcox (Wazir), Luis Alberni (Old Hebrew), Michael Ansara (Taskmaster), Zeev Bufman,

Robert Vaughn (Hebrews at Golden Calf), Franklin Farnum (Official), Kathy Garver (Child), Walter Woolf King (Herald), Frank Lackteen (Old man praying), John Hart (Cretan ambassador), Esther Brown (Princess Tharbis), Kem Dibbs (Guard), Abbas El Boughdadly (Rameses' charioteer), Fraser Heston (Infant Moses), Eugene Mazzola (Pharaoh's son), Ramsay Hill (Korah), Paul DeRolf (Eleazar), Tommy Duran (Gershom), Rushti Abaza, Eric Alden, E. J. Andre, Babette Bain, Vicki Bakken, Baynes Barron, Kay Bell, Mary Benoit, Dehl Berti, Michael Burden, Robert Carson, Ken Christy, Robert Clark, Fred Coby, Peter Coe, Rus Conklin, Edna Mae Cooper, Henry Corden, Tony Dante, Terence DeMarney, Adeline DeWalt Reynolds, Edward Earle, Richard Farnsworth, Maude Fealy, Mimi Gibson, Diane Gump, Frank Hagney, Nancy Hale, Kay Hammond, Peter Hanson, Paul Harvey, Donald Hayne, Ed Hinton, June Jocelyn, Mary Ellen Kay, Richard Keane, Ethan Laidlaw, Emmett Lynn, Herbert Lytton, Barry Macollum, Peter Mamakos, Irene Martin, Beverly Mathews, George Melford, John Merrick, John Merton, Amena Mohamed, Paula Morgan, Amadeo Nazzari, Dorothy Neumann, Ron Nyman, John Parrish, Edmund Penney, Jon Peters, Stanley Price, Rodric Redwing, Keith Richards, Carlos Rivas, Ric Roman, Joan Samuels, Archie Savage, Naomi Shaw, Marcoreta Stanley, Irene Tedrow, Amanda Webb, Jean Wood, Lillian Albertson, Joel Ashley, Robert Bice, Tim Cagney, Steve Darrell, Anthony Eustrel, Matty Fain, Vernon Rabar, Anthony George, Dawn Richard; Paramount, Technicolor, VistaVision; 221 minutes; October 1956

The film has been equally hailed and derided, and so has Robinson's performance in it. On the plus side, *The New York Times* called *The Ten Commandments* "a moving story of the spirit of freedom rising in man under the divine inspiration of his maker...." and continued, "Mr. DeMille has worked photographic wonders. And his large cast of characters is very good, from Sir Cedric Hardwicke as a droll and urbane Pharaoh to Edward G. Robinson as a treacherous overlord."

Charlton Heston commented on the acting in his memoir *In the Arena*: "John Carradine was extraordinary as Aaron ... as was Edward G. Robinson in a difficult composite drawn from several faint-hearted Israelites featured in the book of Exodus. Eddie's Dathan mixes them all into one wonderfully unpleasant man." "[Robinson] is splendidly decadent," noted James Robert Parish in *The Tough Guys*.

Jesse L. Lasky, Jr., one of the film's screenwriters, commented on Robinson's reliable performance. "Edward G. Robinson, an old friend of mine, was playing Dathan, the dissembler, which saddled him with the most difficult moment in the film.... The Children of Israel have, by the will of God and the intercession of Moses, escaped from bondage. They have seen the sea opened for them.... And they have been promised by their unfailing leader that he will descend from Mount Sinai to bring them God's law.... Yet, after all that has happened, in a mere thirty days ... they lose their faith.... [Dathan] sells them the preposterous idea that the return to slavery in Egypt as worshipers of the golden calf is their only salvation.... Such chronicles are very well when bound in a holy book, but the screen is something else: a magnifying glass for skepticism. Eddie accomplished the impossible with the reading of that speech.... He [later] said, 'You gave me the greatest exit a heavy ever had ... created a tempest, then an earthquake, then opened a fissure and had me fall through into hell. Even in *Little Caesar* I never had an exit as good as that.'"—Jesse L. Lasky, Jr., *Whatever Happened to Hollywood?*

Foster Hirsch disagrees with Lasky: "His performance ... may well be the poorest of his long career." Hirsch found Robinson guilty of "scowling on the sidelines, pointing rhetorically to the heavens, playing up the role of the traditional skeptic...."—*Edward G. Robinson: A Pyramid Illustrated History of the Movies.*

Robinson's presence in the film has been the target of jokes because he stands out as an icon of urban crime as Little Caesar. As recently as November 1996, *Movieline* quoted comedian Arsenio Hall tongue-in-cheek on the movie that influenced him most: "*The Ten Commandments* ... The casting of legendary screen gangster Edward G. Robinson in a Biblical film damaged me severely. It changed my life. I've been in therapy ever since." Similar humor was used on television's *The Golden Girls*, in which Estelle Getty's character contemplates becoming a nun. Before taking her vows, she seeks answers to three theological puzzles, two regarding the church, and the third, wondering what Robinson was doing in that film. Finally, comedian Billy Crystal has used his Robinson impersonation from the film many times: "Where's your Moses now? Nyaaah!"

Today's mainstream criticism puts *The Ten Commandments* in perspective. Leslie Halliwell refers to it as "popular but incredibly stilted and verbose Bible-in-pictures spectacle. A very long haul along a monotonous route, with the director at his pedestrian worst." But Richard Schickel in *The Movies* favors it as "spectacular brimming over with gorgeously photographed calamities, man made and God-made."

"This new version of DeMille's silent ... saga, *The Ten Commandments*, overwhelms its audience, it's that big," claimed *Variety*. "Pictorially it is greatly impressive, dwarfing all cinematic things that have gone before it. It is unlikely that any other producer than DeMille would have attempted such a mammoth production and it's to be doubted that many others could have held the extraordinary project under control.... Competent work is done by Edward G. Robinson as the evil Hebrew."

Cue magazine concurred: "Upon the second book of the Old Testament veteran moviemaker Cecil B. DeMille has built himself a towering monument, the biggest, the most spectacular, and by all means the most impressive of all his works."

The Ten Commandments won an Academy Award for its special effects.

Tenbrook, Harry (1887–1960) was in three pictures with Edward G. Robinson—*The Little Giant*, *Barbary Coast*, and *A Slight Case of Murder*. In the latter he played the stranger among the four gangsters who ended up as corpses. He is also in *Scarface*, *Destry Rides Again*, and *Mister Roberts*.

Terry-Thomas (1911–90), a gap-toothed Englishman, often played comic butlers, as in *Mad Checkmate* (a.k.a. *It's Your Move*) with Edward G. Robinson. Onscreen from 1949, he was also in *I'm All Right Jack*, *It's a Mad, Mad, Mad, Mad World*, and *How to Murder Your Wife*.

Thalberg, Irving G. (1899–1936), vice president and supervisor of production at MGM, offered Edward G. Robinson a million-dollar contract in 1930, but Robinson turned it down because it did not afford him time off to return to the New York stage. Leaving Thalberg's office, he promptly threw up. Thalberg was known as the "boy wonder," having begun working at Universal at the age of twenty. His film credits include *The Merry Widow*, *Ben-Hur*, *Anna Christie*, *Freaks*, *The Barretts of Wimpole Street*, *Mutiny on the Bounty*, *A Night at the Opera*, *The Good Earth*, and *Romeo and Juliet*. He was married to Norma Shearer.

The Theatre Guild The company produced ten plays that featured Edward G. Robinson, who was a member of the acting company for four years:

1923	February	*Peer Gynt*
	March	*The Adding Machine*
1925	November	*Androcles and the Lion* and *The Man of Destiny*
1926	January	*The Goat Song*
	March	*The Chief Thing*
	October	*Juarez and Maximilian*
	November	*Ned McCobb's Daughter*
1927	January	*The Brothers Karamazov*
	March	*Right You Are If You Think You Are*

Among its players during that time were Alfred Lunt and Lynn Fontanne, Morris Carnovsky, Dudley Digges, Laura Hope Crewes, Clare Eames, Margalo Gillmore, Earle Larimore, Armina Marshall, Beryl Mercer, Elisabeth Risdon, Erskine Sanford, Joseph Schildkraut, Henry Travers, Helen Westley, and Margaret Wycherly. Character actors with the Guild who later appeared onscreen with Robinson include Louise Closser Hale, Porter Hall, Charles Halton, Zita Johann, and Tom Powers. Two performers—G. Wood and Judith Lowry—who became better known in film and television as they aged, also were in the company with Robinson, as were the notable Harold Clurman, Lee Strasberg, and Sanford Meisner.

Organized in 1919, the Theatre Guild has been called by Gerald Bordman in *The Oxford Companion to American Theatre,* "the most exciting and responsible producing organization of the 1920s and 1930s." Before Robinson joined the company, the Guild had produced Shaw's *Heartbreak House, Mr. Pim Passes By,* and *Liliom,* and during Robinson's association, also *The Guardsman, They Knew What They Wanted, The Garrick Gaieties, The Silver Cord, Porgy,* and *Marco Millions.* Successes during its last thirty years (1928–1958) include *Strange Interlude, Elizabeth the Queen, Mourning Becomes Electra, Ah, Wilderness!, Mary of Scotland, Porgy and Bess, Idiot's Delight, The Philadelphia Story, The Time of Your life, Oklahoma!, Carousel, The Iceman Cometh, Come Back Little Sheba,* and *Sunrise at Campobello.*

"This Is It" (Television, 1965) Edward G. Robinson was guest star on the weekly variety show *Hollywood Palace,* doing a dramatic reading by Milton Geiger called "This Is It."

See **Hollywood Palace**.

This Is Tom Jones (Television, 1970) Edward G. Robinson gave two dramatic readings on Tom Jones' variety show — Rudyard Kipling's "The Betrothed" and Milton Geiger's "I Will Not Go Back." (As rare as Robinson's television appearances were, this program aired coincidentally on the same day and hour as his appearance in "The Mary Tree" on *Bracken's World.*)

Tom Jones, Edward G. Robinson, Liza Minelli, Ace Trucking Company; ABC-TV; 60 minutes; October 23, 1970.

This Is Your Life (Television, 1958, 1959) Film directors Frank Capra and Mervyn LeRoy were honored guests on separate segments of *This Is Your Life.* Capra was producing and directing the feature *A Hole in the Head.* At the beginning of the program Edward G. Robinson appeared to surprise Capra, along with Carolyn Jones and Edith Head.

Producer, Alex Gruenberg; executive producer, Ralph Edwards; director-writer, Richard Gottlieb; music, Von Dexter; research, Janet Tighe; staff, John Crouch, Barbara Dunn-Leonard, Gary Edwards, Pat Gleason, George Moore; participants: Frank Capra, Edward G. Robinson, Carolyn Jones, Eddie Hodges, Dub Taylor, Edith Head, Sam Briskin, Emil Levine, Turner Shelton, Joseph Walker, Lucille Capra, Tom Capra, Lulu Capra, and Frank Capra, Jr.; Ralph Edwards (host); *This Is Your Life*; NBC-TV; 1958

Participants: Mervyn LeRoy, Edward G. Robinson; Ralph Edwards (host); *This is Your Life*; NBC-TV, 1959

Thugs with Dirty Mugs This cartoon is a parody of Warner Bros. 1930s gangster films, in which "Ed G. Robemsome" plays bank robber Killer Diller.

Supervisor, Fred (Tex) Avery; story, Jack Miller; animation, Sid Sutherland; musical direction, Carl W. Stalling; Merrie Melodies, 1939; 7 minutes

Thunder in the City (Film, 1937) In 1937 Edward G. Robinson went abroad on loanout from Warners to Columbia Pictures to make a comedy called *Thunder in the City.* In London he met an old friend, playwright Robert Sherwood, and asked him to help fix the predictable script. Sherwood tried his best, but the resulting satire was not very successful. The trip to England afforded Robinson the opportunity to see the art galleries, both in London and Paris, and to purchase works by Renoir, Morisot, Gauguin, Daumier, Gericault, Cezanne, and Corot to add to the reproductions and paintings in his collection.

Thunder in the City was an odd success. "The film has the superficial smoothness and pace that might have been expected from so much American collaboration," said *The New York Times.* "Mr. Robinson is too deliciously American, but never less than Napoleonic." *The New York Herald-Tribune* found Robinson "brilliantly comic ... as he was sinisterly forbidding in his memorable gangster roles." And James Robert Parish in *The Tough Guys* praised him for "offering one of his razzle-dazzle performances and even managing to instill a bit of romanticism into his characterization."

Liberty magazine said, "Actually the proceedings have a diverting quality.... Eddie Robinson gives a sharp, vigorous performance of the Yankee stunt man."

Dan Armstrong is sent to England by Mr. Snyderling, his boss, hopefully to learn more low-key methods in auto sales. His cousins, Lord and Lady Challenor, invite him to spend the weekend with them at Challenor Hall, where other guests include the Duke and Duchess of Glenavon, their daughter, Patricia, and a stockbroker named Manningdale. Dan helps set up a company to develop a rare metal, magnalite. The Duke is made chairman. Magnalite is available in large deposits on property owned by the Duke and Duchess in Rhodesia. However, Manningdale, who is interested in Patricia, acquires the rights to the only method of processing the raw mineral, so that Dan must sacrifice his interest in the company in order to avoid bankruptcy. Preparing to return to America, Dan is greeted at the airport by a large crowd of well-wishers, led by the Duke and Duchess and Patricia, who has left Manningdale because she really loves Dan.

An Atlantic Hoffberg production; producers, Akos Tolnay, Alexander Esway; assistant producer, Richard Vernon; director, Marion Gering; screenplay, Robert Sherwood, Aben Kandel, Tolnay, Walter Hackett; additional dialogue, Dudley Storrich; scenario, Jack E. Jewell; art director, George Ramon; camera, Al Gilks, Gus Drisse; special effects, Ned Mann; music, Muir Matheson, Miklos Rozsa; production manager, Hal Richmond; sound, Terry Cotler; recording director, A. W. Watkins; editor, Arthur Hilton; cast: Edward G. Robinson (Dan Armstrong), Luli Deste (Lady Patricia), Nigel Bruce (Duke of Glenavon), Constance Collier (Duchess of Glenavon), Ralph Richardson (Henry Manningdale), Annie Esmond (Lady Challenor), Arthur Wontner (Sir Peter Challenor), Elizabeth Inglis (Dolly), Cyril Raymond (James), Nancy Byrne (Edna), Billy Bray (Bill), James Carew (Snyderling), Everley Gregg (Millie), Elliott Nugent (Casey), Terence DeMarney (Reporter), Roland Drew (Frank), Donald Cathrop (Dr. Plumet); Columbia, 76 minutes; April 1937

"Thunder in the City" (Radio, 1937) *Thunder in the City* was adapted for radio immediately after it opened in theaters.

Cast: Edward G. Robinson; *Kate Smith A & P Bandwagon*; CBS-radio; April 29, 1937

Tiger Shark (Film, 1932) The third of Edward G. Robinson's four films in 1932 offered him the change of pace of a fishing story, based on the novel *Tuna* by Houston Branch. The plot was a familiar triangle — two buddies meet a girl, one marries her, then she falls in love with the other, more handsome man. The husband conveniently dies at the fadeout, allowing the two lovers to live happily ever after. Robinson played the odd man out, repeating the role when the plot was recycled into *Manpower* nine years later.

Fortunately, *Tiger Shark* turned out well. The director was Howard Hawks. "At the end of the first day I said to Eddie Robinson, 'This is going to be the dullest picture that's ever been made....' And he said, 'What can we do?' I said, 'Well, if you're willing to try it with me, why, let's make him happy-go-lucky, talkative ... you're going to have to keep talking all through the picture.' He said, 'Fine, let's do it.'"— Howard Hawks, quoted in *The World of Howard Hawks* by Andrew Sarris

"I went down to the San Diego docks and talked to some living originals," said screenwriter Wells Root. "Their lingo was so strange, so specialized, that I knew we would never get it right on the set. So the studio hired a real Portuguese tuna captain to edit the script with me and to stand by Robinson throughout shooting. The three of us worked over every speech. The tuna man's job was to make it authentic, mine to make it comprehensible."

Robinson enjoyed working on the film, except for his fear of water in the ocean scenes, which were filmed on location at Catalina Island. Fortunately, a double was used in major action scenes. The problem was that Robinson couldn't swim! He said he was fond of Howard Hawks as a director despite the political tensions that developed on the set of their next film three years later. Andrew Sarris quotes Hawks on Robinson: "He's a fine actor, and I thought he did a great job. But I hate to think of what the picture would have been ... because the whole tenor of the picture changed."

Robinson's leading lady, Zita Johann, had a much different opinion about working with Robinson. "Eddie was *very* difficult," she said. "He refused to allow me to have co-star billing with him. He went to the front office and complained bitterly that I was getting too much footage and too many closeups. He refused to line-rehearse with me. In one scene, Eddie came barging in with this phony accent (there was very little authenticity in those days), overacting madly. I realized, 'I can take this scene away from him by cutting under him.'—And I did! Well, Eddie was in a rage!"—quoted in *Women in Horror Films, 1930s*, by Gregory W. Mank

Director, Howard Hawks; supervisor, Ray Griffith; screenplay, Wells Root; based on the story *Tuna* by Houston Branch; art director, Jack Okey; assistant director, Richard Rosson; camera, Tony Gaudio; editor, Thomas Pratt; music director, Leo F. Forbstein; cast: Edward G. Robinson (Mike Mascarena), Richard Arlen (Pipes Boley), Zita Johann (Quita), Vince Barnett (Engineer), J. Carroll Naish (The man), Leila Bennett (Barber), William Ricciardi (Manuel), Edwin Maxwell; First National; 80 minutes; September 1932

Mike Mascarena, a Portuguese tuna fisherman, and his buddy, Pipes Boley, are lost at sea in a small dinghy. Mike loses his hand to a tiger shark after saving Pipes' life. After they are rescued, Mike makes the adjustment with a hook in place of the missing hand. Back at sea once again, an old fisherman, Manuel, a member of Mike's crew, is killed when he accidentally falls overboard and is attacked by a shark. Mike goes to his house to tell Manuel's daughter, Quita. Eventually the two get to know each other, and when Mike proposes marriage, she tells him she doesn't love him but accepts because he has been so kind to her. Time passes. Quita confesses to Pipes that she cannot stay with Mike because she loves Pipes. During a marathon fishing session, Pipes is seriously injured by a hook and is taken to Mike's house to recover. Quita decides to accompany the men on the next voyage, fearful of losing Pipes. Mike discovers them in an embrace in the cabin and attacks Pipes, then throws him into a dinghy and tries to sink it by harpooning a hole in it. The sharks, he says, will judge. As they draw near, a rope catches Mike's leg, he is thrown overboard, and the shark attacks. By the time he is pulled from the water, it is too late. He gives Quita and Pipes his blessing and dies.

Reviews of the film mentioned the quality of Robinson's acting. "Mr. Robinson gives a fine, finished performance as Mike, blending love and hatred in exactly the right manner," said *The New York World-Telegram*. "This fisherman is portrayed splendidly by Edward G. Robinson, who makes the character both sympathetic and fearsome," wrote *The New York Times*.

"The film is driven beyond its plot level by the larger-than-life characters and the symbolism of the sharks," notes Andrew Sarris. "However there is another, more Hawksian, aspect to the symbolism.... Ultimately it is Robinson who is unnatural in attempting to defeat the inexorable sexual attractions of nature.... Hawks remorselessly applies the law of nature to sex. The man who is flawed by age, mutilation, or unpleasing appearance ... inevitably loses the woman to a flawless rival.... One scene in *Tiger Shark* deserves special attention for its technical brilliance. Arlen and the girl have a single-take love scene in the ship's cabin to the sound of shots from the deck as Robinson fires gratuitously at sharks. As the scene rises in intensity, the firing stops, and the girl registers the appearance of Robinson in the doorway in a turning shot of slow horror. While Robinson advances on the adulterous couple, the camera closes in until he dominates the screen...."

Future actor-director-producer John Houseman was married to Robinson's leading lady, Zita Johann, at the time of filming. "Through the influence of Zita's agent, [I] became one of five writers whom Hawks kept in various hotel rooms.... Not one word of mine was ever used and I soon stopped trying.... The company moved ... to Catalina Island ... I continued to spend my days on the set, learning what I could about the making of motion pictures until one day, in the Catalina channel, while Robinson was playing his final sequence on the deck of the tuna boat (after the tiger shark had chewed off his remaining leg), he refused to continue his death scene with Zita until I had been removed and rowed ashore." — John Houseman, *Runthrough*

Robinson "quite properly" had him removed from the set, explained Houseman, admitting that playing a death scene while the husband of the leading lady watched from the sidelines would be difficult. He is incorrect, however, in the reference to Robinson's "remaining leg," since his character had instead lost a hand to the shark.

Tight Spot (Film, 1955) *The New York Times* said, "*Tight Spot* is a pretty good little melodrama, the kind you keep rooting for as generally happened when Lenard Kantor's *Dead Pigeon* appeared on Broadway a while back.... Mr. Keith and Mr. Robinson are altogether excellent. If Academy Awards aren't in order, neither are apologies."

"Eddie Robinson, in the relatively quiet role of the district attorney, once more proves what a really expert trouper he is," said *The Hollywood Reporter*. "He has a wonderful authority in the scenes requiring it, but it's even more exciting to watch the skill with which he supports and builds the effects of the actors he's working with. His listening helps the audience to listen, and the subtle methods by which he directs spectator attention make him the all-important underscoring in many of Ginger's big scenes."

Producer, Lewis J. Rachmil; director, Phil Karlson; screenplay, William Bowers; based on the novel and play *Dead Pigeon* by Lenard Kanter; art directors, Carl Anderson, Ross Bellah; set, Louis Diage; music director, Morris Stoloff; orchestra, Arthur J. Norton; musical score, George Duning; sound, Lambert Day, John Livadary; camera, Burnett Guffey; editor, Viola Lawrence; assistant director, Milton Feldman; costumes, Jean-Louis; hairstyles, Helen Hunt; still photography, Lippman & Croneworth; cast: Ginger Rogers (Sherry Conley), Edward G. Robinson (Lloyd Hallett), Brian Keith (Vince Striker), Lorne Greene (Benjamin Costain), Katherine Anderson (Willoughby), Allen Nourse (Rickles), Peter Leeds (Fred Packer), Doye O'Dell (Mississippi Mac), Eve McVeagh (Clara Moran), Lucy Marlowe (Prison girl), Helen Wallace (Warden), Frank Gerstle (Jim Hornsby), Gloria Ann Simpson (Miss Masters), Robert Shields (Carlyle), Norman Keats (Arny), Kathryn Grant (Honeymooner), Ed "Skipper" McNally (Harris), John Marshall, John Larch, Ed Hinton (Detectives), Joseph Hamilton (Judge), Tom DeGraffenried (Doctor), Alan Reynolds (Bailiff), Alfred Linder (Tonelli), Will J. White (Plainclothesman), Bob Hopkins (TV salesman), Robert Nichols, Erik Paige, Kevin Enright, Tom Greenway, Dean Cromer, Kenneth N. Mayer, John Zaremba; Columbia; 97 minutes; March 1955

Sherry Conley is moved from prison to a hotel suite by attorney Lloyd Hallett, prosecutor at the trial of mobster Benjamin Costain. Hallett hopes that Sherry, who was on a private cruise in the West Indies with Costain, will testify against him. Unfortunately, no witnesses against him have survived Costain's efforts to silence them. At first Sherry is delighted to be in such pleasant surroundings, with room service and a new dress, but she has no intention of testifying. She spars with Vince, a tough cop assigned to protect her, and the two become attracted to each other. Hallett brings in Sherry's sister, Clara, to help convince her to change her mind, but their reunion turns into a bitter shouting match. In an attempt on Sherry's life by a hired gun, Willoughby, the prison matron staying with her is killed. For the first time Sherry is angry enough to fight back. This is distressing to Vince because, reluctantly, he has been coerced into working for Costain and now must see to it that Sherry dies. At the last minute he changes his mind and is gunned down protecting her. Sherry appears in court. When asked her occupation, she replies, "Gang buster."

Variety said, "Robinson is very good as the Fed down to his last witness." *Newsweek* called the film "a modest bit of movie-making, which adds up to a good deal more than the sum of its parts. What makes the film surprisingly effective is the neat coordination of all its elements — a tidy interplay of individual styles of acting, timely changes of focus, element, and mood.

"Thanks to Ginger's emoting and Edward G. Robinson's brilliant dramatics, [it] is a first-rate film in its category," said the *Hollywood Citizen News*. And *TV Key Movie Guide* called *Tight Spot* a "well-acted crime drama … [with] witty dialogue."

Less enthusiastically, Leslie Halliwell's *Film Guide* rated the picture a "fairly routine crime melodrama with unexciting star performances," and the *St. Louis Post-Dispatch* called it "a sortie into potboiler melodramatics in which Edward G. Robinson is a district attorney.… Some of its narrative twists are interesting enough."

Tobacco see **Smoking**

Tobin, Genevieve (1901–95) played opposite Edward G. Robinson twice as his long-suffering wife — in *Dark Hazard* and *I Loved a Woman*. Married to director William Keighley, she also was in *Easy to Love, The Goose and the Gander, The Great Gambini,* and *The Petrified Forest*. On Broadway she appeared in *Little Old New York* and *King Lear*.

Toler, Sidney (1874–1947) was in *Dark Hazard* with Edward G. Robinson and also on Broadway in *Poldekin*. Remembered (with Warner Oland) as one of the screen's Charlie Chans, he is also in *Call of the Wild, The Gorgeous Hussy, If I Were King,* and *A Night to Remember*.

Tomlinson, David (1917–2000), who became a familiar face in Disney films (the father in *Mary Poppins, The Love Bug*), was in the British R.A.F. propaganda film *Journey Together* with Edward G. Robinson. He also is in *Carry On Admiral, Tom Jones,* and *The Liquidator*.

The Tonight Show with Johnny Carson (Television, 1968) Jane Robinson, in her book, *Edward G. Robinson's World of Art*, discusses her husband's appearance on the show:

"When Johnny Carson's *Tonight* show was being taped on the West Coast the producer made his usual inquiry, 'Would Eddie appear?' His answer was, 'Thank you, no.' The producer called and tried to persuade him once more; I answered the phone and committed him to the show.… I mentioned that Eddie was a painter and asked whether it might be arranged that his own pictures be exhibited on the show … I began to steal original EGRs from our own home; I stealthily crept down the stairs, hoping that Eddie would not see me. My plan was to have the pictures framed and to show them on the program; also to get Eddie to the NBC Studios without his knowledge.… I decided to give a party the same night; it was to be my shield against his disapproval. Having now involved myself in this plot, it was necessary to have co-conspirators. My partners in crime were Sam Jaffe, George Burns, Karl Malden, and Debbie Reynolds. One might say that we were the mob and Eddie the victim. I was nearly caught a thousand times.… We had never been to the NBC Burbank studios where Eddie's paintings now were. Georgie Jessel had invited us there for a taping of his show the night before Eddie was to appear. And because Eddie is devoted to George, he decided to go.… Then came *the* day — I was prepared to be the second ex–Mrs. Edward G. I had sent my wedding ring to the scene of the crime; he was to return it if I was forgiven. The surprise worked. The audience loved Eddie; he loved them. Suddenly he was home again and returned the ring; all was forgiven. He enjoyed the party. Alone and quietly the following evening, we watched the program. I particularly liked Eddie's reaction when his paintings came into view. I remember so well his comment on seeing his own work: 'I realized when I began painting myself, that I didn't pay enough for the pictures I purchased.…'"

Participants: Johnny Carson, George Burns, Edward G. Robinson, Karl Malden; September 25, 1968

Tony Awards see **Antoinette Perry (Tony) Awards**

Too Long, America (Radio, 1944) was a radio program about racial intolerance. Edward G. Robinson (narrator); 1944

Toomey, Regis (1902–91) plays Commander Clark, skipper of the John Paul Jones II, in *Destroyer*, with Edward G. Robinson, and he is also in *Confessions of a Nazi Spy*. Other films include *Union Pacific, His Girl Friday, Meet John Doe, Spellbound, The Big Sleep, Show Boat,* and *Guys and Dolls*.

Torn, Rip (1931–) plays Slade, a wealthy Southerner, in *The Cincinnati Kid*. He is also in *Baby Doll, A Face in the Crowd, Cat on a Hot Tin Roof, Sweet Bird of Youth, Men in Black,* and *The Insider*. He was married to Geraldine Page and appeared with her on the stage and in films.

Totter, Audrey (1918–) is the love interest of kidnap victim George Dolenz in *A Bullet for Joey* and is seen fleetingly in *U.M.C.* (she later became a regular cast member in the *Medical Center* TV series). She also appeared with Edward G. Robinson on TV in *Operation Entertainment*. Other films include *The Postman Always Rings Twice, The Set-Up,* and *The Blue Veil*.

Tracy, Spencer (1900–67) A two-time Oscar winner (for *Captains Courageous* and *Boys Town*), he and Edward G. Robinson had small roles onstage in *A Royal Fandango*. One review of their performances said they looked as though they had been picked up by the prop man. They also appeared live onstage together in a benefit for the United China Relief Fund. Tracy was scheduled to appear in both *Cheyenne Autumn* and *The Cincinnati Kid*, but Robinson replaced him because of Tracy's ill health. His other films include *San Francisco, Test Pilot, Young Tom Edison, Inherit the Wind, The Old Man and the Sea, Judgment at Nuremberg,* and nine with Katharine Hepburn.

Trains Edward G. Robinson's first entrance in *The Cincinnati Kid* is through a cloud of steam as he disembarks from a passenger train arriving in New Orleans. Others among his films in which trains are part of the action include *The Woman in the Window* (his family is departing on a summer vacation); *Kid Galahad* (a trip from Miami to New York); *The Biggest Bundle of Them All* (robbery of a $5 million shipment of platinum); and *Scarlet Street* (reporters discussing the nature of murder and conscience on the way to cover an execution).

He is on a cross-country train ride to San Francisco, then Alcatraz, in *The Last Gangster*. He boards a train taking him to prison at the conclusion of *Smart Money*. He and two others await a train that finally pulls into the station at the end of *The Outrage*. In *Night Has a Thousand Eyes* the railroad represents danger, as Gail Russell's character attempts suicide; similarly, in *Double Indemnity* the train is part of the murder plot, and the victim's body is found on the tracks. An elevated train crashes in *The Hole in the Wall*, and in *The Widow from Chicago* a character disappears by jumping off a moving train.

Travers, Henry (1874–1965) appeared with Edward G. Robinson in the Theatre Guild plays *Androcles and the Lion* (as Androcles), *The Chief Thing,* and *Right You Are If You Think You Are*. In films he is known as the angel Clarence in *It's a Wonderful Life*. Others include *The Invisible Man, Ball of Fire, High Sierra,* and *Shadow of a Doubt*.

Treasury Star Parade (Radio) According to an encyclopedia of "old-time radio," "Edward G. Robinson played a man unconcerned by gasoline rationing until the gas turned into blood as he pumped it into his car." This was rather powerful and symbolic radio for wartime America. The broadcasts, in which major stars participated, donating their services, were fifteen minutes long.

Hosts, Henry Hull, Paul Douglas; announcers, Larry Elliott, David Broekman; director, William A. Bacher; writers, Neil Hopkins, Norman Rosten, Violet Atkins; music theme "Any Bonds Today?" by Irving Berlin; cast: Edward G. Robinson; date of appearances unknown.

See "The Checker Player"; "Joe Doakes and the White Star"; "It Isn't Peanuts."

Trevor, Claire (1909–2000) played opposite Edward G. Robinson as Jo Keller in *The Amazing Dr. Clitterhouse*, as Gaye Dawn in *Key Largo* (Academy Award as best supporting actress), radio adaptations of both, and as Clara Kruger in *Two Weeks in Another Town*. Also on the radio, they were together on *Big Town* for several seasons, and they appeared on the *Ed Sullivan Show* on TV. She was heard briefly in the *A&E Biography* on Robinson, "Little Big Man." She received Oscar nominations for *Dead End* and *The High and the Mighty*, and acted in *Stagecoach, Murder My Sweet,* and *How to Murder Your Wife*.

"Trial and Error" (Radio, 1952) This half hour radio program was presented on *The Eternal Light*, produced by NBC and the Jewish Theological Seminary. Its basis was the writings of Chaim Weizmann.

Producer, Milton E. Krents; directors included Frank Papp, Anton M. Leader, Andrew C. Love; research, Dr. Moshe Davis; supervisor, assistant producer, Barbara Gair; music score, Morris Mamorsky; orchestra, Milton Katima, Robert Armbruster; cantors, Robert E. Seigal, David Patterman; writers included Morton Wishengrad; cast: Edward G. Robinson (Chaim Weizmann); NBC-radio; December 7, 1952

Triesault, Ivan (1902–80), often a villain, was the Grand Hotel desk clerk who introduces *The Prize* Nobel winners played by Newman and Robinson. He also worked with Robinson on TV in "Epitaph for a Spy." A dancer and mime, he came to films via Europe and Broadway. His films include *Mission to Moscow, The Hitler Gang, Notorious, Golden Earrings, Kim,* and *Von Ryan's Express*.

Trowbridge, Charles (1882–1967) played an intelligence officer in *Confessions of a Nazi Spy*, with Edward G. Robinson, and had also acted with him at Elitch Gardens in summer stock. His other films include *Sergeant York* and *Mission to Moscow*.

Trumbo, Dalton (1905–76) wrote the screenplay for *Our Vines Have Tender Grapes*, as well as for *Kitty Foyle* and *A Guy Named Joe*. He served a prison sentence as one of the Hollywood Ten, was blacklisted, and later — writing under the pseudonym Robert Rich — won an Oscar for *The Brave One*. He later wrote *Spartacus, Exodus, Hawaii,* and *Johnny Got His Gun*.

Tucker, Harland (1893–1949) appears onscreen in *Kid Galahad* and *Night Has a Thousand Eyes* with Edward G. Robinson. Decades earlier, on the Broadway stage, they appeared together in *Under Fire*. His other films include *Desert Fury, A Foreign Affair,* and *The Big Clock*.

Turrou, Leon G. He was the author of *The Nazi Spy Conspiracy in America*, which Warner Bros. filmed as *Confessions of a Nazi Spy*. Turrou was portrayed in the film, under the pseudonym of Ed Renard, by Edward G. Robinson.

Tuttle, Frank (1892–1963), admitting past Communist party membership and naming names of "fellow travelers," was a friendly witness for the House Un-American Activities Committee investigations. His writing and directing career, which had begun in 1922, suffered as a result. *Hell on Frisco Bay*, with Edward G. Robinson, was one of his last films. Others include *The Cradle Buster, The Big Broadcast, The Glass Key,* and *This Gun for Hire*.

Twelve Star Salute (Television, 1961) A music and comedy salute to the Federation of Jewish Philanthropies; producer, Hiram Brown; participants: Danny Kaye (host); Anna Maria Alberghetti, Lucille Ball, Benny Goodman, Morton Gould, Charlton Heston, Eartha Kitt, Tony Martin, Mitch Miller, Jan Peerce, Edward G. Robinson; ABC-TV; December 9, 1961

20th Century–Fox The company was formed through merger in 1935 of the Fox Film Corporation (founded in 1912 by

William Fox) with Twentieth Century (formed two years earlier by Darryl F. Zanuck and Joseph Schenk). 20th Century–Fox copyrighted CinemaScope. Edward G. Robinson made only four films at the studio — the fewest of his career: *Tampico, Tales of Manhattan, House of Strangers,* and *Seven Thieves.*

Twins Edward G. Robinson played identical double characters in both *The Whole Town's Talking* and *The Prize,* although in neither case were the characters natural twins. In the former film, Robinson is meek clerk Arthur Ferguson Jones, who is mistaken for Public Enemy No. 1, Killer Mannion. In the latter he plays Nobel Prize–winning Dr. Max Stratman and an actor made up to impersonate him when the doctor is kidnaped by Russian agents. In both films the unsavory double is killed by the bad guys who mistakenly believe he is the virtuous double. In *The Whole Town's Talking* the dual characters are the leads in the film, whereas the doctor in *The Prize* is not much more than a supporting role, and Robinson's two characters (the doctor and his actor-double) share little screen time together.

Two Seconds (Film, 1932) In 1996 Dale Thomajan wrote in *Film Comment,* "Hollywood is not and never has been in the business of making masterpieces, so it's always a pleasant surprise when one rolls off the assembly line. Amidst the wealth of very good and near-great WB pre-code movies, a masterpiece did emerge in 1932. *Two Seconds,* a recreation of what a condemned murderer (Edward G. Robinson) recalls just before the switch is thrown, is like an off–Broadway play in which everything unaccountably goes right. Easily one of the deftest, darkest, and most powerful movies Hollywood ever gave us...."

"His performance here offers a reconciliation of the sometimes unsettled marriage in his screen personality: the rasping vehemence and oratorio fervor with which his viewers became familiar almost from the start; and, the precise, musing intelligence that often overhangs his performances of flat-out brutes, lending these portrayals a kind of glib dispatch.... He was an outstanding *reader,* excelling at set-pieces of declamation; and this accorded with his frequent castings as a loner and/or exile. The enigmatic pioneer, the gang leader who is eased out of his leadership, the skipper ill at ease with his private reflections — all are pensive men of affairs.... Robinson may have been the first of the starring gun butts to portray the gangster protagonist as an alien." — Donald Phelps, "On the Spot," *Film Comment,* March-April 1996

Producer, Hal B. Wallis; director, Mervyn LeRoy; screenplay, Harvey Thew; based on the play by Elliott Lester; camera, Sol Polito; art director, Anton Grot; editor, Terrill Morse; music director, Leo F. Forbstein; cast: Edward G. Robinson (John Allen), Preston Foster (Bud Clark), Vivienne Osborne (Shirley Day), J. Carroll Naish (Tony), Guy Kibbee (Bookie), Gladys Lloyd (Annie), Frederick Burton (Judge), Dorothea Wolbert (Lizzie), Edward McWade (Prison doctor), Berton Churchill (Warden), William Janney (College student), Lew Brice, Franklin Parker, Frederick Howard (Reporters), June Gittelson (Fat girl), Jill Bennett, Luana Walters (Tarts), Otto Hoffman (Justice of the Peace), Harry Beresford (Doctor), John Kelly, Matt McHugh (Mashers), Harry Woods (Executioner), Charles E. Evans (Priest), Helena Phillips Evans (Landlady), Sam Rice (Bald dancer), Adrienne Dare; First National; 68 minutes; May 1932

John Allen is escorted to the electric chair. Onlookers assembled to witness his execution have been told that once the switch is thrown, it will take two seconds for him to die. One witness comments that those will probably be the longest two seconds of his life. The story flashes back to an earlier time, when John and his roommate, Bud, are construction workers high above the city on a skyscraper. John rejects a blind date with Bud and his girl, Annie, and instead goes to a dance hall. He meets Shirley Day, and although she gets fired that evening because of trouble with rough customers, she and John get along. Bud is skeptical of their relationship, certain that Shirley is no good. John gets drunk one night and he and Shirley get married. On the job Bud tries to warn John about Shirley, telling him that she continues to see Tony, who manages the dance hall. John takes a swing at Bud, who loses his balance and falls to his death. John becomes ill with remorse and is unable to work. Winning a few dollars through a bookie, he pays off the doctor bills, rent, and finally a debt to Tony from Shirley's borrowing. Then he shoots her. At his trial, John maintains he deserves the death sentence not for killing Shirley but for causing Bud's death. But now the switch has been thrown and John's two seconds are over.

Most of the original reviews were favorable. "Edward G. Robinson contributes a remarkably forceful portrayal in the picture version of Elliott Lester's play," said *The New York Times*. "…When Mr. Robinson depicts the nerve-racked condition of Allen or delivers a heated talk to the judge who sentences him, his acting is unusually impressive…. [It is] a film that compels attention." *The Los Angeles Express* claimed *Two Seconds* was "far superior to *Little Caesar*…. I bow, Mr. Robinson, in tribute to an excellent performance." And John Baxter in *Hollywood in the Thirties* called the film "one of the more unusual Warners lowlife dramas … strongly biased towards social comment…. Vicious and disenchanted, [it] is unrelieved in its black mood."

The quality of the film was lost on some. Indeed, Robinson in his autobiography was at best indifferent. The reviewer for *The New York World-Telegram* said, "With *Two Seconds* … the distinguished screen career of Edward G. Robinson encounters a temporary lapse. With the excellent Mervyn LeRoy as director, and with several experienced players to support him, Mr. Robinson, whose *Little Caesar* still stands as his finest screen portrayal, moves indifferently, and at times almost amateurishly, through a picture of incredibly meager purpose…. I had no idea that Mr. Robinson, whose flair for choosing good parts for himself is well known, could be caught so empty handed and that he would ever allow himself to indulge in such overacting as he does here."

Two Weeks in Another Town (Film, 1962) *Two Weeks in Another Town* was Edward G. Robinson's third (and last) film opposite Claire Trevor. And for the first time in their long association, through radio's *Big Town* and the features *The Amazing Dr. Clitterhouse* and *Key Largo*, Robinson finally "made an honest woman of her," as noted in the film's pressbook; she had been his star reporter, fenced his stolen jewels, and boozed her way to an Oscar as his mistress, but Trevor had never portrayed Robinson's wife. Matrimonial joy was in short supply, however, in *Two Weeks in Another Town*. Trevor drinks as of old, shrieks, and nags. Robinson's character refers to her as his "lawful wedded nightmare."

This also was Robinson's third film in two years about moviemaking. In the earlier comedies *Pepe* and *My Geisha* his roles were as producers; now he was in a drama, playing a has-been director named Maurice Kruger. (The surname was originally Delaney in the novel by Irwin Shaw.) Location work in Rome doubtless offered Edward G. Robinson consolation, because of the European travel and art treasures. At the time, shooting was also in progress on *Cleopatra*, the Elizabeth Taylor–Richard Burton spectacle, and the evenings were full of celebrity parties.

Two Weeks in Another Town did not fare well. Kirk Douglas said in his autobiography *Ragman's Son*, "Now, suddenly a new head of the studio took over, Joseph Vogel. He decided that MGM should make only family pictures. Now, one thing *Two Weeks in Another Town* was not, was a family picture. It was very sexy, had some wild scenes. But he decided that the film would be edited differently — he was determined to make a family picture out of what we had shot. In the middle of these discussions, I wondered where John Houseman, the producer, was. When I saw them emasculate the film, I wrote to Vogel, even though I was just an actor in it. I implored him, argued with him, told him that if he had wanted to make a family picture, he never should have made *Two Weeks in Another Town*. They cut out the most exciting scenes. I felt this was such an injustice to Vincente Minelli, who'd done a wonderful job with the film."

Producer, John Houseman; associate producer, Ethel Winant; director, Vincente Minelli; screenplay, Charles Schnee; based on the novel by Irwin Shaw; assistant director, Erich von Stroheim, Jr.; art directors, George W. Davis, Urie McCleary; set, Keogh Gleason, Henry Grace; visual effects, Robert R. Hoag; music, David Raksin; sound, Franklin Milton; camera, Milton Krasner; editors, Adrienne Fazan, Robert J. Kern, Jr.; gowns, Pierre Balmain; wardrobe, Walter Plunkett; makeup, William Tuttle; hairstyles, Sydney Guillaroff; color consultant, Charles K. Hagedon; cast: Kirk Douglas (Jack Andrus), Edward G. Robinson (Maurice Kruger), Cyd Charisse (Carlotta), George Hamilton (Davie Drew), Claire Trevor (Clara), Dahlia Lavi (Veronica), James Gregory (Brad Byrd), Rossanna Schiaffino (Barzelli), Joanna Roos (Janet), George Macready (Lew Jordan), Mino Doro (Tucino) Stefan Schnabel (Zeno), Vito Scotti (Assistant director), Tom Palmer (Dr. Cold Eyes), Erich von Stroheim, Jr. (Ravinski), Leslie Uggams (Chanteuse), Janet Lake (Noel O'Neill), Joan Courtenay (Signora Tucino), Alberto Morin (Cameraman), Margie Liszt (Liz), Franco Corsaro, Edward Comans (Henchmen), Edit Angold (German tourist), Don Orlando, James Garde (Sound engineers), Red Perkins (George Jarrett), Albert Carrier (Electrician), Beulah Quo (Nun), Cilly Feindt (Lady Godiva), Lilyan Chauvin, Ann Molinari (Bar girls), Charles Horvath, John Indrisano (Bouncers), Benito Frezie, Tony Randall, Joe Dante (Men in lounge); MGM; CinemaScope, Metrocolor; 107 minutes; August 1962

Jack Andrus, an actor recovering from a nervous breakdown, gets a telegram from Maurice Kruger, his old director, saying he should come to Rome to play a key role in a new film. When he gets there, Jack learns there really is no part for him — maybe he could supervise the dubbing? Really, Kruger tells him, the sanitarium called and asked that he be offered a job. Jack stays in Rome, getting involved with Veronica, a friend of Davie Drew, a confused young actor in the film. The female lead, an Italian bombshell named Barzelli, is carrying on with Kruger, right under his wife Clara's nose. Also complicating things is the presence in Rome of Carlotta, Jack's ex-wife. When Kruger suffers a heart attack, Jack completes the film — on schedule. Driven by Clara, Kruger denounces Jack for trying to steal his picture. Jack is disbelieving and angry. He ends up at a party. Carlotta is there and begins to taunt him. Drunk, he leaves with her in a sports car and reenacts a near-fatal collision with a stone wall that led to his eventual breakdown. This time, however, he is in control. He has learned to survive — without Carlotta, without Kruger. He even gives Veronica back to Davie as he runs to catch his plane home.

Cyd Charisse shared Kirk Douglas's concern about the finished film, saying, "The picture should have been better than it was. After Vincente [Minelli] finished his cut, somebody else took over and chopped it to shreds. When I finally saw [it] I couldn't make heads or tails of the story — it was so disconnected — and I'd been in it. It was a shame, yet I had some very good scenes and certainly enjoyed working with the talented Kirk Douglas.... It was fun to make, whatever the result, primarily because it was shot on location in Rome and Paris, and I had a fabulous Pierre Balmain wardrobe to wear.... And dear, brilliant Edward G. Robinson was in the movie, and he was always taking off, when he had even an hour free, rushing to one art gallery after another to add to his fabulous collection of paintings."— *The Two of Us*, by Tony Martin and Cyd Charisse

"When a group of top American filmmakers goes all the way to Rome to make a picture about the sort of Hollywood rejects who sometimes get involved in this sort of trash and then make it as trashy as the worst stuff, it is time for a loud and pained complaint," wailed *The New York Times*. "*Two Weeks in Another Town* [is] a drippy drama on a theme of degradation.... As the expatriate American director ... Edward G. Robinson snarls familiarly and gives but the barest impression of a man being in genuine distress."

Newsweek agreed: "Irwin Shaw's sticky bestseller ... has been kneaded into an equally gummy film of considerable embarrassment." And *The New York Herald-Tribune* slammed Robinson: "[As] the once great director ... his performance makes it hard to believe that the man ever directed a pedestrian successfully across a street."

There was, thankfully, some recognition of the effort behind the finished product. Peter Bogdanovich wrote in *Film Culture*, "Minelli's flair for melodrama and heightened characterization has never been more apparent: Robinson and Trevor squabbling with each other, acidly cutting at every opportunity; and then, in bed at night, he starts to weep self-pityingly and she mothers him like a small child — it is a devastating scene."

Variety noted that the "only remotely lifelike characters in the story are Robinson and Claire Trevor as an ambiguous married couple whose personalities transform under the secretive cover of night. But the characters are as despicable as they are complex, and the film is desperately in need of simpler, nicer people. Robinson and Miss Trevor, two reliable performers, do all they can with their roles." The *St. Louis Post-Dispatch* felt that, "Douglas and Robinson are good enough to give any picture character, so any deficiencies probably can more correctly be laid at the door of the script and director."

"The 'other town' is Rome," said *The Saturday Review*, "where an Italo-American co-production is under way — a penny-pinching, coldly calculated affair that is being ineptly directed by a frightened has-been ... tellingly played by Edward G. Robinson [who] grinds out footage to the best of his dwindling ability, [and] knows that his work can be taken away from him at any time and completed by other, unsympathetic hands."

Finally, from *Hollywood on Hollywood*, by James Robert Parish, Michael Pitts, and Gregory Mank: "As always, Robinson was a delight."

Tyler, George C. (1867–1946) produced over 200 plays in New York, among them *Mr. Samuel* and *Poldekin* featuring Edward G. Robinson, as well as *The Squaw Man, Alias Jimmy Valentine, The Garden of Allah, Clarence, Dulcy, Merton of the Movies, The Plough and the Stars,* and revivals of *She Stoops to Conquer, The Beaux' Stratagem,* and *Macbeth.*

U. M. C. (Television, 1969) The initials stand for University Medical Center. This *CBS World Premiere Movie* was the pilot film for the *Medical Center* series, which ran for seven years, through 1976. Dr. Joe Gannon was played by Chad Everett in the series, replacing Richard Bradford, but James Daly continued his role as Dr. Lochner. Alvin H. Marill's assessment in *Movies Made for Television* focused on Robinson: "[His] dignified performance ... highlights this pilot movie for the popular ... series."

Two parallel stories converge. Dr. Lee Forestman has an attack while performing surgery; his heart is failing. Raymond Hanson, a patient of Dr. Joe Gannon, suffers a fall, checks into the hospital, and subsequently dies of abdominal injuries. After agreeing that Hanson's heart may be used in a transplant operation for Dr. Forestman, Hanson's wife Joanna reconsiders and sues the hospital and Gannon, alleging a conflict of interest — that her husband's death was allowed in order to obtain a donor heart. During a trial, Dr. Gannon is vindicated. Dr. Forestman recovers.

CBS World Premiere Movie; producer, A. C. Ward, Frank Glicksman; director, Boris Sagal; teleplay, Ward; art directors, George W. Davis, Marvin Summerfield; editor, Henry Batista; camera, Joseph LaShelle; cast: Richard Bradford (Dr. Joe Gannon), Edward G. Robinson (Dr. Lee Forestman), James Daly (Dr. Paul Lochner), Kim Stanley (Joanna Hanson), Maurice Evans (Dr. Easler), Kevin McCarthy (Coswell), J. D. Cannon (Jarris), William Windom (Raymond Hanson), Don Quine (Martin), Shelley Fabares (Mike), James Shigeta (Chief resident), William Marshall (Dr. Tawn), Alfred Ryder (Dr. Corlane), Robert Emhardt (Judge), Herb Angren, Mel Carter, Michael Evans, Marianne Gordon, Billy Gray, Karen Norris, Tim O'Kelley, Audrey Totter, Christopher West, Jason Wingreen; CBS-TV; 120 minutes; April 17, 1969; also known as *Operation Heartbeat*

U.S.A. (Television, 1971) Edward G. Robinson delivered the opening and closing speeches of this televised "dramatic revue," which had been produced theatrically in New

York in 1959. The *Samuel French Basic Catalogue of Plays and Musicals* calls *U.S.A.* "a superbly woven and exciting cavalcade of America in the first third of the twentieth century ... a striking panorama of an era, a masterful use of biography, news, and fiction."

Hollywood Television Theatre; producer-director, George Schaefer; authors, Paul Shyre, John Dos Passos; based on the novel by Dos Passos; cast: Michele Lee, John Davidson, James Farentino, Joan Hackett, Peter Bonerz, Shirley Knight, Edward G. Robinson; PBS; 150 minutes; May 4, 1971

U.S. Olympic Committee Telethon (Television, 1952) Participants: Bing Crosby, Edward G. Robinson; Bob Hope (Host); NBC-tv; June 21, 1952

Uggams, Leslie (1943–) sang the blues number "Don't Blame Me" at the end of *Two Weeks in Another Town*. She was in *Roots* and *Backstairs at the White House* on television, and also *Skyjacked* and *Black Girl*.

Uncredited appearances Edward G. Robinson played Big Jim in the musical *Robin and the 7 Hoods* with no billing, trading on his three-plus decades as a Warner Bros. tough guy. Hans Conried plays an unbilled role as an architect in the same picture. On television Robinson turned up as himself at the fadeout of a *Batman* episode. Others uncredited on the screen include Tony Curtis and Dean Martin in *Pepe*, but such Hollywood in-jokes were a rare occurrence in Edward G. Robinson's films.

See **Billing**; **Bit parts**; **Dual roles**; **Guest stars**; **Special appearances**.

Under Fire (Theater, 1915) This play marked Edward G. Robinson's first Broadway appearance. According to his autobiography he landed not one but four roles — a Belgian spy, a Belgian peasant, a German officer, and a Cockney soldier — due to his gift with languages. Eventually he replaced other actors, doubling in several of the 31 European-accented roles of the play.

"In minor roles, exceedingly good work is done by Robert Fischer, Norman Tharp, E. G. Robinson, and Henry Stephenson," said *The New York Times*; and *The Nation* called *Under Fire* "the best of the 'war' plays that have yet been seen. It is, on the whole, good melodrama, well-staged, and generally well-acted."

Producer-director-playwright, Roi Cooper Megrue; director, William Courtenay; produced by Selwyn & Co.; Adolph Klauber, general manager; cast: William Courtenay (Captain Redmond), Frank Craven (Charlie Brown), Violet Heming (Ethel Willoughby), Edward G. Robinson (Andre LeMaire), Henry Stephenson, Robert Fischer, Phoebe Foster, H. M. Harvey, Edward Hicks, Walter Kingsford, Felix Krembs, Edward Mawson, McKay Morris, Dorothy Abbott, Sydney Chon, Malise Sheridan, Norman Tharp, Harland Tucker, Jack Wessel; Hudson Theater, New York; August 11, 1915

Under Sentence (Theatre, 1916) Robinson commented that the playwright Roi Cooper Megrue apparently had a fascination for titles that started with 'under,' since his second Broadway role was in *Under Sentence* — and he was right; an earlier Megrue success, in 1914, was called *Under Cover*. Originally titled *John W. Blake*, *Under Sentence* dealt with prison reform.

Producer-director-writer, Roi Cooper Megrue; producer-writer, Irwin S. Cobb; produced by Selwyn & Co.; cast: Edward G. Robinson (Fagan), Thomas Mitchell, Janet Beecher, John A. Boon, Harry Crosby, Stephen Denbeigh, E. H. Dresser, Lawrence Eddinger, T. P. Gunn, Felix Krembs, George MacQuarrie, George Nash, H. W. Pemberton, Joseph Slaytor, Gerald Oliver Smith, George Wright, Jr.; Harris Theatre, New York; October 3, 1916

The New York Times called *Under Sentence* "a crowded and curious play ... the first part is a bald, unvarnished, and continuously interesting melodrama, the second, which begins with the third act ... is a lively treatment of prison reform that borders on extravaganza.... Nash ... and Miss Beecher help a lot, as do Felix Krembs, E. G. Robinson, and Joseph

Slaytor. At concert pitch they keep the melodramatic scenes ... thoroughly interesting and do nothing to prevent the last act from being amusing."

Unholy Partners (Film, 1941) The fourth and final film Edward G. Robinson made with director Mervyn LeRoy was *Unholy Partners.* He was the good guy for a change, and Edward Arnold the gangster, with Laraine Day and Marsha Hunt as co-stars.

Producer, Samuel Marx; director, Mervyn LeRoy; screenplay, Earl Baldwin, Bartlett Cormack, Lesser Samuels; art director, Cedric Gibbons; associate, Urie McCleary; set, Edwin B. Willis; sound, Douglas Shearer; camera, George Barnes; editor, Harold F. Kress; technical adviser, Duffy Cornell; music, Daniele Amfitheatrof, David Snell; song "After You've Gone," by Henry Creamer, Turner Layton; musical arrangements, Lenny Hayton; vocal, Al Siegel; orchestra, Wally Heglin; cast: Edward G. Robinson (Bruce Corey), Edward Arnold (Merrill Lambert), Laraine Day (Miss Cronin), Marsha Hunt (Gail Fenton), William T. Orr (Tommy Jarvis), Don Beddoe (Mike Reynolds), Charles Dingle (Clyde Fenton), Robert Homans (Inspector Brody), Walter Kingsford (Editor Peck), Charles Halton (Kaper), Clyde Fillmore (Jason Grant), Marcel Dalio (Molyneaux), Frank Faylen (Roger Ordway), Joseph Downing (Jerry), Connie Russell (Singer), William Benedict (Boy), Charles B. Smith, Marvin Stevens (Copy boys), Frank Dawson, George Ovey (Old men), Tom Seidel (Reporter), Tom O'Rourke (Young man), Emory Parnell (Colonel Mason), Al Hill (Rector), Jay Novello (Stick man), John Lilson (Circulation man), Billy Mann (Barber), Ann Morrison (Hazel), Lester Scharff (Tony), June MacCloy (Glamor girl), Don Costello (Pelotti), Larraine Krueger, Natalie Thompson (Girls at party), Florine McKinney (Mary), Charles Jordan (Gorilla), Ann Pennington (Operator), Lee Phelps (Mechanic), Lester Dorr (Circulation manager), Gertrude Bennett, Estelle Etterre (Newspaper women), Milton Kibbee (Drunk), Elliott Sullivan (Eddie), Buster Slaven (News boy), James P. Spencer (Druggist), Ray Teal (Waiter), Gino Corrado, Frank Orth, Walter Sande, Frank Puglia, Tom Neal; MGM; 94 minutes; December 1941

Newspaperman Bruce Corey returns from World War I with an idea for a paper with a smaller format. Seeking backing, he gambles with gangster Merrill Lambert, who expects that his support for the new venture will give him power over content. Corey, however, uses the paper to expose graft, and he comes close to exposing Lambert's operations to the law. Lambert kidnaps Tommy Jarvis, who works for Corey, in order to take control. Corey rescues Jarvis, then kills Lambert in self defense. Miss Cronin, Corey's secretary, takes his confession down in dictation; then Corey goes on a transatlantic flight sponsored by the paper, from which he knows he will not return. Cronin and Jarvis vow to continue publishing.

Variety gave the film a negative review: "Both Robinson and Arnold play the leads with the snarling bravado reminiscent of the gangster style of films. In fact, it all seems like a reissue." But *The New York Times* praised the picture, calling it "a hardbitten melodrama of a tabloid editor during the twenties when 'death and emotions were cheap.' They have brought in Edward G. Robinson to play the editor, and he knows how to make a caustic line flip like the tip of a bullwhip.... Credit much of the film's intermittent excitement to Mr. Robinson, who still packs more drive than almost any six actors one could name."

United Artists In 1919 four stars — Charlie Chaplin, D. W. Griffith, Mary Pickford, and Douglas Fairbanks — founded United Artists to produce, release, and distribute films. The company was unique in that it had no studios of its own. Edward G. Robinson made eight films for UA over twenty-five years. Major producers were involved in several: *Barbary Coast* (Samuel Goldwyn); *The Red House* and *Vice Squad* (Sol Lesser); *Actors and Sin* (Ben Hecht); *A Hole in the Head* (Frank Capra and Frank Sinatra). Other films were *Black Tuesday, Nightmare,* and *A Bullet for Joey.*

United China Relief Fund Benefit (Theater, 1943) Producer, David O. Selznick; director, William Dieterle; writer, Henry Kronman; set decorator, Cedric Gibbons; music, Herbert Stothart; Los Angeles Philharmonic Orchestra; participants: Spencer Tracy, Henry Fonda, Dr. Corydon M. Wassell, Madame Chiang Kai-shek, Walter Huston, Edward G. Robinson (as Generalissimo Chiang Kai-shek); Hollywood Bowl, Los Angeles, April 14, 1943

United Nations radio Ben Hecht wrote a radio play for the opening session of the United Nations. Cast: Edward G. Robinson, Harold Stassen; Mutual Network; April 1944

United States Air Force Band Edward G. Robinson did dramatic readings with the United States Air Force Band, including Milton Geiger's *I Will Not Go Back* and *I Am an American*, and Aaron Copland's *A Lincoln Portrait*. The band, known as "America's International Musical Ambassadors," was formed in 1941. Its official choral group is called The Singing Sergeants. It has performed many concerts on radio and television and in over fifty countries of the world. Edward G. Robinson appeared as guest artist on at least three occasions, from 1965 to 1971. The conductor was Colonel Arnald D. Gabriel.

On May 24, 1965, Robinson narrated Aaron Copland's *A Lincoln Portrait* during the *America the Beautiful Concert* at the Watergate Hotel on the Potomac at the Lincoln Memorial in Washington, D.C. The evening concert was part of President Lyndon B. Johnson's two-day White House Conference on Natural Beauty. Featured were panels on landscaping, parks, highways, waterways, billboards, underground utilities, and suburbia, among others, and an open meeting at which most cabinet members were present. Robinson served also as master of ceremonies at the evening concert and delivered opening remarks. The concert's musical program included *American Overture for Band* by Joseph Jenkins; *America the Beautiful* by Samuel Augustus Ward, arranged by Carmen Dragon; *American Salute* by Morton Gould; a performance by The Singing Sergeants in *A Musical Tour of the U.S.A.*, arranged by Sergeant Floyd Werle; *Americans We*, a march by Henry Fillmore; *A Lincoln Portrait*; and *The Stars and Stripes Forever* by John Philip Sousa.

Robinson appeared again with the United States Air Force Band on its fall tour in Southern California, on November 5, 1965, at MacArthur Park in Los Angeles, and also on November 6 at Anaheim.

On February 7, 1971, the United States Air Force Band and The Singing Sergeants presented a *Musical Americana* concert in Washington, D.C. at the Departmental Auditorium on Constitution Avenue, with Robinson serving as guest narrator. He read Milton Geiger's *I Will Not Go Back*, with music by Sergeant John Caughman, and Carmen Dragon's *I Am an American*. The musical program also included *American Overture for Band* by Joseph Willcox Jenkins; *Americans We* by Henry Fillmore; *A Suite of Old American Dances*, arranged by Robert Russell Bennett; and The Singing Sergeants performing their transcontinental tour, arrangements by Sergeant Floyd Werle.

Universal Studios Universal was responsible for several of Edward G. Robinson's early features — *The Night Ride, East Is West, Outside the Law*. Later films were *Flesh and Fantasy, Scarlet Street, All My Sons*, and *The Glass Web*. Founded by Carl Laemmle in 1912, the studio — also known for a time as Universal-International — continues today with such successes as *Jaws* and *American Graffiti*.

Uno Scacco Tutto Matto see **Mad Checkmate**

Unrealized projects Once he was an established star, Edward G. Robinson's name was mentioned for a number of projects. Some were begun, some were not. But long before he had the power to decline a film, he was involved in a silent picture called *Fields of Glory*. Hired by Samuel Goldwyn and working with Dorothy Gish, he asked to be let out of his contract after he saw what he looked like on the screen. It is unknown whether the picture was ever completed, as it does not appear in Goldwyn filmographies or those of Miss Gish.

As early as 1933 Edward G. Robinson was interested in doing a film on the life of Napoleon. At different times, suggested co-stars to play Josephine were Gloria Swanson, Barbara Stanwyck, Kay Francis, and Bette Davis; Reginald Owen was suggested for the role of Talleyrand. The biography never materialized because Robinson did not approve a script.

Robinson did not play Duke Mantee in the film of Robert Sherwood's *The Petrified Forest*. He rejected the role because it was another gangster story, but Leslie Howard (who was recreating his Broadway role) demanded that Humphrey Bogart, who had played Mantee on Broadway, be cast. Another Bogart hit, *High Sierra*, had first been offered to Robinson, Cagney, and George Raft.

Robinson turned down the role of Don Luis in 1938's *Anthony Adverse*; the part went to Claude Rains. He was considered for a song-and-dance role in Busby Berkeley's *Garden of the Moon* the same year. Similarly, he, along with Thomas Mitchell and Frank Morgan, was considered for the role of Captain Andy in George Sidney's remake of *Showboat*, but Joe E. Brown was cast.

The Wayfarers, a novel by Dan Wickenden, had been adapted into a screenplay by Abraham Polonsky, an Oscar-nominated writer-director. Norris Bryant, the leading character, was a newspaper editor who had been driven to alcoholism by the death of his wife in childbirth ten years earlier. The role was offered to Edward G. Robinson through Paramount, and he accepted it, but in the mid-1940's the studio declined to produce the film because of its a Depression theme.

In the late 1960s he was offered stage roles — as Solomon, the furniture dealer, in Arthur Miller's *The Price*, and in *Scratch* (a musical version of *The Devil and Daniel Webster*, with book by Archibald Macleish) — but he turned down both for reasons of age and health. Edward G. Robinson was considered for but did not appear in the more recent films *Cervantes, the Proud Rebel*; *Planet of the Apes*, *The Angel Levine*; *The Paper Chase*; *I Never Sang for My Father*; and *The Godfather*.

Vacations   Edward G. Robinson's characters generally were not the kind to take vacations. In *Brother Orchid* and *The Little Giant* his gangsters go off looking for class, to Europe and to Southern California, respectively, but the journeys represent career change as well. His over-aggressive car salesman is sent to England "to learn restraint" in *Thunder in the City*.

A sabbatical from teaching makes his law professor in *I Am the Law* eligible for the job of racket buster. It is his family's summer vacation *without* him in *The Woman in the Window* that allows him the freedom for that film's adventure. In *Dr. Ehrlich's Magic Bullet* he takes a rest cure in Egypt to overcome a bout with tuberculosis. He goes on vacation to Saratoga at his summer house, only to discover *A Slight Case of Murder*. Following the events of *A Hole in the Head* and *The Whole Town's Talking* he vacations at Miami Beach and in Shanghai, respectively. One story in which Robinson's character actually is on vacation is "Epitaph for a Spy," a drama presented on TV on *Climax!* He unwittingly becomes involved with foreign spies and works toward their capture.

Valentine, Paul   (1919–) played the part of Pietro, the prizefighter, one of Edward G. Robinson's four sons in *House of Strangers*. He also appears in *Out of the Past, La Passione, Against All Odds, The Man Who Saw Tomorrow, Yes Giorgio, Pennies From Heaven,* and on tv's *Naked City*.

Van Cleef, Lee   (1925–89) became a star of "spaghetti" (Italian-made) westerns: *For a Few Dollars More, The Good the Bad and the Ugly*. He was one of the bank robbers in *Vice Squad*, with Edward G. Robinson, and also appeared in *High Noon* and *The Man Who Shot Liberty Valance*.

Van Dyke, Dick   (1925–) recreated his Broadway role in the film of *Bye Bye Birdie,* and was also in *Mary Poppins* and *Chitty Chitty Bang Bang*. With Edward G. Robinson he was in *Never a Dull Moment*, and they also narrated *The American Ideal: The Land*. He had success on TV with *The Dick Van Dyke Show* and more recently, *Prescription: Murder*.

Van Eyck, Peter (1913–69), a German actor, masterminded the kidnaping scheme in *A Bullet for Joey*. His other roles, from 1943, include *The Moon Is Down*, *The Wages of Fear*, *The Spy Who Came in from the Cold*, and *Station Six—Sahara*.

Van Heusen, James (1919–90) was a four-time Oscar winner. "High Hopes," sung by Frank Sinatra and Eddie Hodges in *A Hole in the Head*, "All the Way," from *The Joker Is Wild*, and "Call Me Irresponsible," from *Papa's Delicate Condition*, were written with Sammy Cahn; while "Swinging on a Star," from *Going My Way*, had lyrics by Johnny Burke. There were a dozen other nominations, including "My Kind of Town," also with Cahn, from *Robin and the 7 Hoods*.
See **Sammy Cahn**.

Van Patten, Dick (1928–) was a child actor on Broadway (*I Remember Mama*) and appeared in films from the 1960s: *Charley*, *Snowball Express*, *Soylent Green* (with Edward G. Robinson), *Westworld*, *The Shaggy D.A.*, and *High Anxiety*. On TV he was in the comedy *Eight Is Enough*.

Varesi, Gilda (1887–?) She appeared on Broadway in *The Night Lodging* with Edward G. Robinson in 1919. The following year her comedy *Enter Madame*, written with Dorothy Byrne, opened. It was based in part on her memories of her opera star mother, Elena Varesi, and was subsequently produced in stock at the Elitch Gardens in Denver, with Robinson as the male lead.

Vaughn, Robert (1932–) played a Hebrew at the Golden Calf in *The Ten Commandments*, with Edward G. Robinson, and was popular on TV as *The Man from U.N.C.L.E.* Other films include *Bullitt*, *The Magnificent Seven*, and *The Towering Inferno*. He wrote a book, *Only Victims*, about the effects of the House Un-American Activities Committee investigations.

Velez, Lupe (1908–44), a Mexican comedienne, played opposite Edward G. Robinson as Ming Toy in *East Is West*. She started out as a fiery dancer in nightclubs and later played in the *Mexican Spitfire* series. Other films include *The Gaucho*, *Lady of the Pavements*, *Tiger Rose*, *The Squaw Man*, and *Strictly Dynamite*.

Vera-Ellen (1926–81) was a dancer in MGM musicals. Her films include *Wonder Man*, *Words and Music*, *On the Town*, *Three Little Words*, *Call Me Madam*, *White Christmas*, and, in a non-musical role, *Big Leaguer*, as Edward G. Robinson's niece, Christy.

Verdensberomtheder I Kobenhaven
(Short film, 1939) Participants in this short film were Duke Ellington, Charles Lindbergh, Myrna Loy, Alice Babs Nillson, Edvard Persson, Edward G. Robinson, and Robert Taylor; Dansk Films, Denmark; 1939

Vice Squad (Film, 1953) Gallows humor might have been better than none at all for Edward G. Robinson in 1953. *Time* magazine's review of this film, calling him "monotonous and entertaining as ever," offered an endearing portrait: "An actor who had developed well-nigh infinite modulations of the sneer, Robinson, after thirty years of practice, has at last produced his masterpiece. In *Vice Squad*, he displays a sneer so spectacular that he can almost be said to smile."

The New York Times offered no criticism: "Edward G. Robinson, who hasn't been around lately to glower at movie audiences, is back in harness, this time as a captain of detectives plagued by a variety of cons, stoolies, gunmen and molls, and the problems of running down a cop-killing gang of robbers."

Police Captain Barnaby's day begins with the shooting of an officer during a car theft. His witness, funeral director Jack Hartrampf, is married and reluctant to speak up, since he was leaving Vickie's apartment at the time—

2:00 a.m. Other cases concern a young lady convinced that a bogus Italian count is after her mother's money; Mr. Jenner, who is referred to the state hospital because television shadows are chasing him; and a hood named Frankie who has a tip that a bank robbery is due to happen. The men who stole the car, Al Barkis and Pete, are part of the gang about to rob the bank. The police put plainclothesmen behind teller's windows, there is a shootout, and the gang takes a young bank teller named Carol hostage. Marty Kusalich, a gang member who had second thoughts and fled from the robbery, is caught through his association with one of the girls in Mona Ross's escort service. Under police questioning, and fearful that Hartrampf will identify him, Marty reveals the gang's hideout, a warehouse. Barnaby and his men close in and rescue the girl, and the gang members are killed or arrested.

Producers, Sol Lesser, Jules V. Levy, Arthur Gardner; director, Arnold Laven; screenplay, Lawrence Roman; based on the novel *Harness Bull* by Leslie T. White; art director, Carroll Clark; set, Raymond Blotz, Jr.; sound, Harry Lindgren; music, Herschel Burke Gilbert; orchestra, Joseph Mullendore; camera, Joseph C. Biroc; editor, Arthur H. Nadel; assistant director, Nathan Barragar; production assistant, Pat Fielder; dialogue director, Harlan Warde; script supervisor, Leslie Martinson; makeup, Gustaf M. Norin; costumes, Norma; hairstyles, Lillian Shore; furs, Al Teitelbaum; cast: Edward G. Robinson (Captain Barnaby), Paulette Goddard (Mona), K. T. Stevens (Ginny), Porter Hall (Jack Hartrampf), Adam Williams (Marty Kusalich), Edward Binns (Al Barkis), Lee Van Cleef (Pete), Jay Adler (Frankie), Joan Vohs (Vickie), Dan Riss (Lieutenant Imlay), Mary Ellen Kay (Carol), Barry Kelley (Dwight Forman), Percy Helton (Jenner), John Verros (Montoya), Harlan Warde, Murrap Alper, Russ Conway, Robert Karnes, Charles Tannen, Lewis Martin, Lee Phelps, George Eldredge, Lennie Bremen, Paul Bryar, Byron Kane; United Artists; 88 minutes; August 1953

Reviews of *Vice Squad* were mixed to negative. "There are competent performances from the supporting cast, but it is surprising," said the *Monthly Film Bulletin*, "to find Edward G. Robinson wasting his talent in the unrewarding role of Captain Barnaby." The real surprise is that the *Monthly Film Bulletin* wasn't more aware of the difficulties Hollywood was having with Washington at the time. "Robinson plays the tired captain with conviction and sour patience," said *The New York Herald-Tribune*.

The *St. Louis Post-Dispatch* was kinder: "Robinson is credible and creditable.... [The film has] a fast-paced plot." In retrospect, Leslie Halliwell was closer to the truth, saying *Vice Squad* is "quite watchable, but scarcely entertaining."

The Victor Borge Show (Radio, 1946) On this radio comedy show, guest star Edward G. Robinson was involved in finding hidden art and having his insomnia cured.

Participants: Victor Borge, Benny Goodman and his Orchestra, Edward G. Robinson, Art Lund, Don Wilson (announcer); NBC-radio; October 7, 1946

The Victory Chest Program (Radio, 1945) Producer-directors, Howard Wiley, Carlton E. Morse; writers, Morse, Arch Oboler; conductor, Meredith Willson; participants: Edward G. Robinson (Voice of the Fathers of America), Admiral William F. Halsey, Bob Hope (Ronald Rigor), Kay Kyser (Tyrone Mortis), Gov. Earl Warren, Gene Autry, Lionel Barrymore, Eddie Cantor, Jack Carson, Jerry Colonna, Tommy Cook, Bill Johnson, Frances Langford, Harold Peary, Dinah Shore, Frank Sinatra, Orson Welles, Margaret Brayton, Hal Gerard, Preston Hotchkiss, Patricia Lowery, Shirley Mitchell, Robert Regent, Tony Romano, Leonard Sues, Lee Sweetland, Paul Theodore, James Powell (announcer), the Norwegian Victory Chorus, the Ken Darby Chorus, the Victory War Chest Orchestra; September 29, 1945

"Victory Extra" (Radio, 1945) Participants: Bing Crosby (host), Lucille Ball, Lionel Barrymore, Janet Blair, Bette Davis, Claudette Colbert, Marlene Dietrich, Jimmy Durante,

Ed Gardner, Greer Garson, Cary Grant, Lena Horne, Jose Iturbi, Danny Kaye, the King Sisters, Herbert Marshall, Marilyn Maxwell, Johnny Mercer, Burgess Meredith, Carmen Miranda, Robert Montgomery, William Powell, Edward G. Robinson, Lina Romay, Dinah Shore, Ginny Simms, Frank Sinatra, Harry Von Zell, Orson Welles, Martha Wilkerson; Ken Carpenter (announcer); *Command Performance;* AFRS; 97 minutes; August 17, 1945

Vigran, Herbert (1910–96) had roles in four films with Edward G. Robinson — *All My Sons, House of Strangers, Illegal,* and *Hell on Frisco Bay.* Other films, from 1940, include *It All Came True, Bedtime for Bonzo, Susan Slept Here, First Monday in October,* and *The Shaggy D.A.*

Vinson, Helen (1907–99) was Polly Cass in *The Little Giant,* with Edward G. Robinson, and she appeared with him in an early Warner Bros. radio broadcast. She appeared onscreen in *Two Against the World, I Am a Fugitive from a Chain Gang, The Kennel Murder Case, Broadway Bill, The Wedding Night, In Name Only,* and *Torrid Zone* before retiring in 1945.

The Violent Men (Film, 1954) This was Edward G. Robinson's first western — "a species I loathe," he said — and also his first CinemaScope-Technicolor feature (discounting a cameo in *It's a Great Feeling*). Barbara Stanwyck played his wife — with a personality not unlike Phyllis Dietrichson from their earlier film together, *Double Indemnity.* Glenn Ford had the lead. "Mr. Robinson is spared destruction, possibly because his performance is the best," said *The New York Times,* noting that he "and Miss Stanwyck have been twisted by cupidity into villains of more than routine blackness."

To please his wife Martha, Lew Wilkison grabs all the land in the valley to add to Anchor, his ranch, either by buying out or driving out the smaller-scale ranchers and farmers. Lew lost the use of his legs in a range war twelve years earlier and now has brought in his brother, Cole, to help him. Cole, however, is carrying on with Martha behind Lew's back. Their daughter, Judith, knows but cannot tell her father. John Parrish will not be bought out nor driven from his ranch and decides to fight back. He kills Wade Matlock, a young hired gun working for Wilkison, after Matlock gunned down the town sheriff and Bud Hinkleman, who works for Parrish. Parrish's men ambush the Anchor forces and set fire to the house. Martha throws Lew's crutches into the blaze, certain he will be unable to escape, then seeks revenge on Parrish, whom she claims killed her husband. But Lew has survived. Cole is killed by Parrish in a shootout, and Martha is gunned down by Elena, a Mexican girl who was in love with Cole. Parrish stays on to be with Judith, with whom he has fallen in love.

Producer, Lewis J. Rachmil; director, Rudolph Maté; screenplay, Harry Kleiner; based on the novel *Smoky Valley* by Donald Hamilton; music, Max Steiner; camera, Burnett Guffey, W. Howard Greene; art director, Carl Anderson, Ross Bellah; set, Louis Diage; sound, Lambert Day; recording supervisor, John Livadary; editor, Jerome Thoms; color consultant, Francis Cugat; makeup, Clay Campbell; hairstyles, costumes, Jean-Louis, Helen Hunt; assistant director, Sam Nelson; music director, Morris Stoloff; cast: Glenn Ford (John Parrish), Barbara Stanwyck (Martha Wilkison), Edward G. Robinson (Lew Wilkison), Dianne Foster (Judith Wilkison), Brian Keith (Cole Wilkison), May Wynn (Caroline Vail), Warner Anderson (Jim McCloud), Basil Ruysdael (Hinkleman), Lita Milan (Elena), Richard Jaeckel (Wade Matlock), James Westerfield (Magruder), Jack Kelly (Derosa), Willis Bouchey (Sheriff Kenner), Harry Shannon (Purdue), Peter Hanson (George Menefee), Don C. Harvey (Jackson), Robo Bechi (Tony), Carl Andre (Dryer), James Anderson (Hank Purdue), Katharine Warren (Mrs. Vail), Tom Browne Henry (Mr. Vail), Bill Phipps (Bud Hinkleman), Edmund Cobb (Anchor rider), Frank Ferguson (Mahoney), Raymond Greenleaf (Dr. Crowell), Ethan Laidlaw (Barfly); Columbia; CinemaScope/Technicolor; 96 minutes; January 1955

Most reviews focused on Robinson's anachronistic presence in a western. "Robinson plays Little Caesar in buckskin," said *The New York Herald-Tribune*. "He has moved from urban vice dens to the wide open spaces, but henchmen still jump to do his bidding. Where once the command was 'Put the body in cement and drop it in the East River!' now it's 'Clean out the valley! I don't care if you have to burn every ranch and string up all the ranchers!'" *Newsweek* claimed that "the most ornery varmint around [was] Edward G. Robinson, a crippled cattle baron, full of Colt slugs from the old range wars, but still stuffed also with greed and pride…. The cattle stampeding gets just about as vast as CinemaScope can get. The skies light up with Technicolor arson, and the falling bodies are of both sexes, with chivalry barely skinning through."

"So much snarling goes on that this seems like a gangster film in fancy dress, but it does hold attention," allowed Leslie Halliwell's *Film Guide*.

Vogan, Emmett (1893–1969) is in five films with Edward G. Robinson—*The Whole Town's Talking, Kid Galahad, Confessions of a Nazi Spy, Mr. Winkle Goes to War,* and *Scarlet Street*. He played in many "B" westerns and was also seen in *Whistling in Dixie* and *Sorrowful Jones*.

The Voice (Theater, 1923) Edward G. Robinson went to Chicago in the spring of 1923 after doing his first two plays with the Theatre Guild. During rehearsals for *The Voice*, he and the company hoped the play would improve, but it failed.

Playwright, Frederic Arnold Kummer; presenter, H. H. Frazee; cast: William Courtenay, Edward G. Robinson, Philip Lord, Pierre Watkin, Alice Buchanan, Conrad Cantzen, Monroe Childs, Virginia Hammond, Bryce Kennedy, John Milton, Henry Mortimer, George Parsons; opened at the Cort Theatre, Chicago; May 27, 1923

Voice of America (Radio, 1950) In 1950 Edward G. Robinson was heard on at least four New York broadcasts of this radio program. On October 23 he appeared as Molotov, a Soviet leader, and on October 25 he did a broadcast in his native Rumanian. Two programs in Italian followed in December.

"The Voice on the Stairs" (Radio, 1944) Edward G. Robinson; Walter Huston (Narrator); *DuPont Cavalcade of America*; NBC-radio; October 2, 1944

Voices from the Hollywood Past (Recording, 1964) Author-journalist Tony Thomas presents interviews with Walt Disney, Buster Keaton, Harold Lloyd, Stan Laurel, Basil Rathbone, and Edward G. Robinson. Separate interviews were done beginning in 1959; Robinson's seven-minute segment was recorded at his home in March 1964.

Thomas comments, "Robinson … was an easy man to interview. He was a gentleman. He had a gentle humor, a cultivated interest in the arts, and a genuine compassion for humankind. All of which was in addition to his skill as an actor and all of which enabled him to expand and refine that skill…. That such a dignified and non-violent man should become popular playing ranting, snarling villains is one of the ironies of the picture business. But, as he said in our interview, there were compensations. They were visible to anyone who had the pleasure of visiting him in his home in Beverly Hills, which was a treasure trove of objets d'art, replete with an enviable collection of French oil paintings…. I look back on [our interview] as one of the most interesting afternoons I have ever spent."

Producer, Tony Thomas; executive producer, Amelia S. Haygood; engineer, Hildegard Hendel; Neumann Mastering, Kenneth R. Perry; art direction and design, Tri-Arts, Inc.; 53 minutes; Delos Records, Inc.; 1975

Voigt, John (1900–90) A German actor, known also as Paul Andor and Wolfgang Zilzer, he is featured in *Confessions of a Nazi Spy* as Westphal, *Dr. Ehrlich's Magic Bullet* as Kellner (whose treatment for syphilis restores his eyesight), and *A Dispatch from Reuter's* as a telegraph agent.

von Eltz, Theodore (1894–64) was in silent pictures, including *The Sea Wolf* and *The Four Feathers*, plus *Bright Eyes*, *Magnificent Obsession*, *Topper*, *Rhapsody in Blue*, and *The Big Sleep*. He appears with Edward G. Robinson in *I Am the Law* as nightclub owner Martin, and *Dr. Ehrlich's Magic Bullet* as Dr. Kraus.

Wagner, Robert (1930–) plays Harry Price in *The Biggest Bundle of them All*, with Edward G. Robinson. His credits include *Stars and Stripes Forever*, *Broken Lance*, *The Pink Panther*, *Harper*, and, on TV, *It Takes a Thief*, *Switch*, and *Hart to Hart*. He was married to Natalie Wood and appeared with her in *All the Fine Young Cannibals*.

Wald, Jerry (1911–62) collaborated on the screenplay of *Manpower*, was associate producer for *Larceny, Inc.*, and produced *Key Largo*. Among his other credits as producer are *Destination Tokyo*, *Pride of the Marines*, *George Washington Slept Here*, *Mildred Pierce*, *The Lusty Men*, *Peyton Place*, *Mr. Hobbs Takes a Vacation*, and *Sons and Lovers*.

Wallach, Eli (1915–) plays Pancho in *Seven Thieves*, with Edward G. Robinson, and Ben Baker in *Mackenna's Gold*. They were participants in the Madison Square Garden *Chanukah Festival for Israel* in 1964 and 1967. Wallach and his wife, Anne Jackson, acted on Broadway in *Rhinoceros*, *The Typists and the Tiger*, and *Luv*. Other films include *Baby Doll*, *The Magnificent Seven*, *The Misfits*, *The Angel Levine*, *Movie Movie*, *Nuts*, *Tough Guys*, and *The Godfather Part III*.

Wallis, Hal B. (1899–1986), a producer at Warner Bros., then independently, was responsible for *A Dispatch from Reuter's*, *Dr. Ehrlich's Magic Bullet*, *Five Star Final*, *The Hatchet Man*, *Larceny, Inc.*, *Little Caesar*, *The Sea Wolf*, *A Slight Case of Murder*, and *Two Seconds*, and received screen credit as executive producer for *Brother Orchid*, *Kid Galahad*, and *Manpower*. Among these, *Five Star Final* was a best picture Oscar nominee, as were *I Am a Fugitive from a Chain Gang*, *Flirtation Walk*, *Captain Blood*, *The Adventures of Robin Hood*, *Four Daughters*, *Jezebel*, *All This and Heaven Too*, *The Letter*, *The Maltese Falcon*, *One Foot in Heaven*, *Sergeant York*, *Kings Row*, *Yankee Doodle Dandy*, *Watch on the Rhine*, *The Rose Tattoo*, *Becket*, *Anne of the Thousand Days*, and *Casablanca* (which won). He was on TV's "The Movie Crazy Years," an early Warners radio broadcast, and the BBC's *The Hollywood Greats: Edward G. Robinson*.

Walsh, Raoul (1887–1981) began as an assistant to D. W. Griffith. In *The Birth of a Nation* he plays John Wilkes Booth. His directing credits include *Pillars of Society*, *The Thief of Baghdad*, *The Big Trail*, *They Drive by Night*, *Manpower* (with Edward G. Robinson), *The Horn Blows at Midnight*, *Objective Burma*, *White Heat*, and *The Tall Men*.

Walston, Ray (1918–2000) appeared on Broadway (*Damn Yankees*) prior to coming to films (*South Pacific*, *Tall Story*, *The Apartment*, *Portrait in Black*, *The Sting*, *Fast Times at Ridgemont High*), but he is best remembered as the title character on TV's *My Favorite Martian*. He was on *Playhouse 90* with Edward G. Robinson in "Shadows Tremble."

Walter, Eugene (1874–1941) wrote *Paid in Full*, in which Edward G. Robinson made his first professional appearance. Walter's other works include *The Easiest Way*, *Trail of the Lonesome Pine*, and *Fine Feathers*.

War Edward G. Robinson served in the United States Navy during World War I, but he never left Pelham Bay in New York while on active duty. Decades later he took great pride in being the first actor to entertain troops in Europe after D-Day. He made speeches on the radio, broadcasting Allied propaganda in foreign languages as part of his efforts with the Office of War Information.

His first Broadway play, *Under Fire*, dealt with the first world war in Europe. Films that dealt with war (at least in part) include: *I Loved a Woman* (Spanish American War), *The Bright Shawl* (war between Cuba and Spain), *Arms and the Woman*, *Unholy Partners* (World

War I), *Confessions of a Nazi Spy, Tampico, Destroyer, Mr. Winkle Goes to War, Our Vines Have Tender Grapes, The Stranger, Key Largo,* and *All My Sons* (World War II), and *A Bullet for Joey* and *The Prize* (the Cold War).

The war on crime in the United States is tangent to virtually every Robinson gangster film, but in particular it is the focus of *Bullets or Ballots* and *I Am the Law.* Gang wars are peripherally evident in *The Last Gangster* and the comedies *Brother Orchid* and *Robin and the 7 Hoods.*

See **Nazism**.

Warner, H. B. (1876–1958) came from the London and Broadway stages to Hollywood, where he played Christ in *King of Kings.* He was in *Five Star Final* and *The Ten Commandments* with Edward G. Robinson, but they shared no scenes. Other films include *The Lost Horizon* (an Oscar nomination as Chang) and *It's a Wonderful Life* (Mr. Gower).

Warner, Jack L. (1892–1978) and his brothers Harry, Albert, and Sam founded the film production company which bears their name. Jack became head of production and was active for over forty years as a producer, receiving best picture Oscar nominations for *Disraeli, Flirtation Walk, Yankee Doodle Dandy, Auntie Mame,* and *My Fair Lady,* the last winning eight awards. His name is listed as producer on Edward G. Robinson's *Dr. Ehrlich's Magic Bullet, Little Caesar,* and *The Sea Wolf.* Warner and Robinson appeared together in an early radio broadcast.

Warner Bros. / First National The company, incorporated in 1923, twenty years following its start with a nickelodeon, grew with the acquisition of First National Pictures and Vitagraph, and made history with its development of sound for *The Jazz Singer* in 1928. In the 1930s and 1940s the studio produced gangster films and social dramas, as well biographies, in which Edward G. Robinson was a major performer. He was among a number of players from the stage whose voice lent itself to the naturalism of the films of the sound era.

Robinson's Warner films (before 1936 called First National–Vitaphone) are *The Bright Shawl* (silent), *The Widow from Chicago, Little Caesar, Smart Money, Five Star Final, The Hatchet Man, Two Seconds, Tiger Shark, Silver Dollar, I Loved a Woman, Dark Hazard, The Man with Two Faces, Bullets or Ballots, Kid Galahad, A Slight Case of Murder, The Amazing Dr. Clitterhouse, Confessions of a Nazi Spy, Dr. Ehrlich's Magic Bullet, Brother Orchid, A Dispatch from Reuter's, The Sea Wolf, Manpower,* and *Larceny, Inc.,* all made under contract, plus six more after Robinson became a freelance actor in 1942: *Key Largo, It's a Great Feeling, Illegal, Hell on Frisco Bay, Robin and the 7 Hoods,* and *Cheyenne Autumn.*

Other major players in the Warner roster included Dick Powell, Ruby Keeler, Bette Davis, Errol Flynn, Olivia deHavilland, Humphrey Bogart, James Cagney, Paul Muni, and Bugs Bunny.

Through the decades the company produced Busby Berkeley musicals, adventure films, women's melodramas, mysteries, and blockbusters, enduring corporate mergers into Warner-Seven Arts and Time-Warner. There is a successful TV network, and feature films still bear the famous WB shield.

Warner Bros. Radio Broadcast (Radio, 1932) Participants: Lloyd Bacon, Joe E. Brown, Bebe Daniels, Glenda Farrell, Robert Goldstein, Mervyn LeRoy, Paul Muni, Ken Murray, Edward G. Robinson, Helen Vinson, Jack L. Warner; 1932

Warrick, Ruth (1915–), known for her role as Phoebe Tyler on the daytime soap opera *All My Children*, began with Orson Welles and the Mercury Theatre and was in his *Citizen Kane* and *Journey Into Fear*. In *Mr. Winkle Goes to War* she played Edward G. Robinson's henpecking wife, and she also appeared in *China Sky, Daisy Kenyon,* and *Ride Beyond Vengeance.*

Washington, Blue (1898–1970), a black actor, was in two films with Edward G. Robinson — as a nervous bank guard in *The Whole Town's Talking,* and in the final segment of *Tales of Manhattan*. Other films include *Road to Morocco, Gone With the Wind*, and *Prisoner of Shark Island*.

Water   Edward G. Robinson could not swim. He had the pool at his Beverly Hills mansion replaced with an art gallery. Scenes in such films as *Tiger Shark, The Sea Wolf,* and *Tampico* that showed him overboard in the water were completed either with a double or in closeups that did not require him to be in very deep. Several films featured scenes on the beach — *A Hole in the Head, Seven Thieves, Pepe, Key Largo*. Doubtless the most impressive display of water in a Robinson film is the parting of the Red Sea in *The Ten Commandments*.

Waters, Ethel   (1896–1977), in *Cabin in the Sky* and *Member of the Wedding* on Broadway and on the screen, became the first black woman to receive star billing in either medium. She was nominated for an Oscar for *Pinky*. She and Edward G. Robinson share no scenes in *Tales of Manhattan*, but both participated in a *Parade of Stars* telethon for the City of Hope.

Watling, Jack   (1923–2001), a British juvenile, was one of the R.A.F. air crew in *Journey Together*, with Edward G. Robinson. He also had roles in *Quartet, The Winslow Boy, The Admirable Crichton,* and *11 Harrowhouse*.

Watson, Bobs   (1930–99) played tykes in many films of the 1930s. He was Peewee in *Boys Town*, Pud in *On Borrowed Time*, and Hank, Edward G. Robinson's son, in *Blackmail*. He left films to become a Methodist minister. Other pictures include *Dodge City* and *In Old Chicago*.

Wayne, David   (1914–95) played major roles on Broadway (Sakini in *The Teahouse of the August Moon*, Og in *Finian's Rainbow*, Ensign Pulver in *Mister Roberts*) and on the screen (*Adam's Rib, The Three Faces of Eve, The Last Angry Man*). In the TV special *The Devil and Daniel Webster* he was Mr. Scratch, opposite Edward G. Robinson's Webster. They were both in *Mooch*.

We Americans   (Theater, 1926) This play, in which Edward G. Robinson appeared in Atlantic City, was destined for a successful Broadway run, but his commitment to the Theatre Guild's 1926–27 season prevented him from continuing in it. He was succeeded in his role by Paul Muni.

Producer, John Golden; playwrights, Milton Herbert Gropper, Max Siegel; director, Sam Forrest; cast: Edward G. Robinson, Clara Langsner; opened in Atlantic City, New Jersey; 1926

We Hold These Truths   (Radio, 1941) Norman Corwin's radio drama *We Hold These Truths* was broadcast on the four major networks only eight days after the Japanese attack on Pearl Harbor. Presented live from Los Angeles, New York, and Washington, it became a wartime call to arms and also a radio classic.

A special program commissioned to commemorate the 150th anniversary of the Bill of Rights; writer, Norman Corwin; music, Bernard Herrmann; Leopold Stokowski, conducting the NBC Symphony Orchestra; participants: Edward Arnold, Lionel Barrymore, Walter Brennan, Bob Burns, Norman Corwin, Walter Huston, Elliott Lewis, Marjorie Main, Edward G. Robinson, President Franklin D. Roosevelt, James Stewart (narrator), Rudy Vallee, Orson Welles; NBC (red and blue networks), CBS, MBS (Mutual) network; December 15, 1941

We Hold These Truths had been planned weeks before the Pearl Harbor attack. Scheduled to air on the anniversary of the Bill of Rights, it was completed by writer Corwin on the train from the east coast to Hollywood only days before and had even greater impact under the circumstances.

According to R. LeRoy Bannerman's book on Corwin, *On a Note of Triumph*, "coverage reached half the population of the United States, the largest audience ever to hear a dramatic performance." Bannerman notes further that President Roosevelt, learning the following day that the program — which ended with his eight-and-one-half minute talk — had been such a success, joked to Archibald MacLeish, "So, you've made an actor of me!"

The radio program was the first of three in which Robinson worked with Corwin. An election eve program, *The Roosevelt Special,* followed in 1944, and *Document A/777,* a drama about the United Nations, was presented in 1950.

We Will Never Die (Theater, 1943) Ben Hecht, in his autobiography *A Child of the Century*, states, "*We Will Never Die* played two performances in its one night in Madison Square Garden. Some forty thousand people squeezed in to witness it. Another twenty thousand crowded the streets outside and listened to the performance and Kurt Weill's great music piped over loud speakers.... Our victory was more than weeping and cheering audiences. The news and pictures of our pageant in the press were the first American newspaper reports on the Jewish massacre in Europe."

"The Garden was filled long before the lights went down at 8:45 p.m., and crowds assembled outside for the second performance, which started at 11:15 p.m.," according to *The New York Times.* "Each performance ran ninety minutes.... The actors moved against towering tablets, as of stone, engraved with the Ten Commandments. The stage was a gray stone escarpment with steps leading down. Massed choirs sang behind dark blue curtains.... Onto the stage shuffled and walked twenty of the rabbinate saved from European ghettos, most of them bearded patriarchs clad in black gowns and white prayer shawls.... Paul Muni and Edward Robinson, dwarfed by the great stone tablets, came through the space between the Ten Commandments. Muni moved to a pulpit on the right, Robinson to the left. Alternately, they recited the record that Jews have written into world history, from Abraham and Moses down to our time."

"A Memorial to the Two Million Jewish Dead of Europe"; producer, Billy Rose; director, Moss Hart; written by Ben Hecht; music, Kurt Weill; conductor, Isaac Van Grove; scenic designer, Lemuel Ayres; committee, Mike Ben-Ami, Peter Bergson, Sam Merlin; participants: Luther Adler, Stella Adler, Ralph Bellamy, Jacob Ben-Ami, Leonard Bernstein, Marlon Brando, John Garfield, George Jessel, Paul Muni, Edward G. Robinson, Sylvia Sidney, Frank Sinatra; Madison Square Garden, New York; 90 minutes; March 9, 1943 (two performances)

"The Weapon of Surgery" (Radio, 1950) Sponsored by the American Cancer Society; *For the Living,* radio; episode G; cast: Edward G. Robinson, John Brown, Lurene Tuttle; 15 minutes; 1950

Weather When gangsters hold people hostage at the Largo Hotel, the one thing that almost saves them, ironically, is a hurricane. It is the one force that Johnny Rocco in *Key Largo* is afraid of. But it passes. Weather, rain in particular, is a plot element in several Robinson films, such as *The Last Gangster, The Woman in the Window, Nightmare,* and *The Outrage. Manpower* contains heavy rain and ice storms, which guarantees the power linesmen plenty of dangerous work.

Characters in the stage play *The Deluge* await the end of a rainstorm. *Middle of the Night* on the stage had its leading character walk several blocks in the snow in Manhattan. The Indians of *Cheyenne Autumn* must endure a bitter winter during their trek to their homeland. All four seasons are depicted in *Our Vines Have Tender Grapes*, but it is the weather — rain, an electrical storm, and flooding — that causes the greatest calamities in the film. Biblical hail that turns to fire was realistically depicted in *The Ten Commandments.* The title *Thunder in the City* is misleading — there is no thunder in the film.

Webster, Daniel (1782–1852) Stephen Vincent Benet's short story *The Devil and Daniel Webster*, featured the celebrated statesman in a mythical confrontation with Mr. Scratch — the devil — in the successful defense of a New England farmer. Edward G. Robinson impersonated Webster in a live television adaptation. The real Webster, who has been called America's greatest orator, began his career as a lawyer in his native New Hampshire and subsequently served for twenty-five years in both houses of Congress and as

Secretary of State under Presidents William Henry Harrison and John Tyler.

Weizmann, Chaim (1874–1952) was the first president of the State of Israel, which he helped to establish in 1948 through his work with the World Zionist Organization. Born in Poland, he became a biochemistry instructor in England and gained recognition for his Zionist views through his service during World War I. His book *Trial and Error* was dramatized as a radio program on *The Eternal Light* the year of his death. He was portrayed by Edward G. Robinson.

Welch, Raquel (1940–) played sexpot roles in *One Million Years B.C.*, *Myra Breckenridge*, and *The Biggest Bundle of Them All*, in which she danced the watusi with Edward G. Robinson. She appeared on the telecast of the *45th Academy Awards* when Robinson was honored posthumously, and she performed on Broadway in the musical *Woman of the Year*.

Weld, Tuesday (1943–) played ingenues, then mature women in *Wild in the Country*, *Rally Round the Flag Boys*, *The Cincinnati Kid* (Steve McQueen's girlfriend), *Looking for Mr. Goodbar* (Oscar nomination), and *Once Upon a Time in America*. She and Edward G. Robinson also appeared on the *36th Academy Awards* broadcast. Her husband is violinist Pinchas Zuckerman; she was formerly married to Dudley Moore.

Welden, Ben (1901–97) a swarthy, balding tough guy, appeared in three films with Edward G. Robinson — *The Last Gangster*, *Manpower*, and *Kid Galahad*. He also was in *Hollywood Cavalcade*, *Angel on My Shoulder*, and *The Lemon Drop Kid*.

Welles, Orson (1915–85) wrote, acted in, and directed his first film, *Citizen Kane*, at the age of 26. His Mercury Theatre yielded major names to films (Agnes Moorehead, Joseph Cotten), and the group made a fateful radio broadcast of *War of the Worlds*. He and Edward G. Robinson were on the radio in Welles' *Ceiling Unlimited*, *The Victory Chest Program*, "The Victory Extra," and *We Hold These Truths*; as well as TV's *Ed Sullivan Show*, paying tribute to John Huston. Welles directed and starred as Franz Kindler / Charles Rankin in *The Stranger*, with Robinson. His other films include *The Magnificent Ambersons*, *The Lady from Shanghai*, *Touch of Evil*, *The Trial*, *Chimes at Midnight*, and *A Man for All Seasons*.

Wellman, William A. (1896–1975) directed *The Hatchet Man*, with Edward G. Robinson; his story was used for *The Last Gangster*; and they were also on TV in "The Movie Crazy Years." Other films: *Public Enemy*, *Nothing Sacred*, *Beau Geste*, *The Story of G.I. Joe*, *Roxie Hart*, *A Star Is Born*, *Battleground*, and *The High and the Mighty*. He was Oscar-nominated for the last three.

Wengraf, John (1897–1974) was with Edward G. Robinson in *The Prize* as Dr. Eckart, heading the gang of kidnapers. Among his other film credits are *Mission to Moscow*, *The Seventh Cross*, *Call Me Madam*, *Weekend at the Waldorf*, *The Pride and the Passion*, and *Judgment at Nuremberg*.

Werfel, Franz (1890–1945), a Jewish author, was born in Austria. He wrote the novels *The Song of Bernadette* and *Jacobowsky and the Colonel*, and, for the stage, *The Goat Song* and *Juarez and Maximilian*. The latter were produced by the Theatre Guild and featured Edward G. Robinson in major roles. Werfel came to the United States after fleeing the Nazi occupation of France.

Wessel, Dick (1910–65) appears with Edward G. Robinson, notably as Buffalo Burns in *Brother Orchid*, but also in *Manpower* and *Scarlet Street*. His other films include *They Made Me a Criminal*, *Action in the North Atlantic*, *Calamity Jane*, and *The Ugly Dachshund*.

Westerfield, James (1912–71) played Deputy Sheriff Magruder in *The Violent Men*, with Edward G. Robinson. Other credits include *Undercurrent, On the Waterfront, The Shaggy Dog, Homicidal,* and *Birdman of Alcatraz.*

Westerns Edward G. Robinson referred to the Western film as "a species I loathe." He was in *The Outrage, Cheyenne Autumn, Mackenna's Gold, Silver Dollar, The Violent Men,* and TV's *Zane Grey Theatre* ("Heritage"). In the first three films listed, ironically, the plots involve the death of an old Indian (played by Paul Fix, Victor Jory, and Eduardo Ciannelli, respectively). If Robinson appears on horseback, the character he is playing is either blind or crippled, except in *Cheyenne Autumn;* in that film the riding was done by a double in a long shot.

Westley, Helen (1879–1942), one of the founders of the Theatre Guild in 1918, acted there with Edward G. Robinson in *The Adding Machine* (as Mrs. Zero), *The Chief Thing, The Goat Song, Peer Gynt,* and *Right You Are If You Think You Are.* In Hollywood from the 1930s, she played in *Death Takes a Holiday, Banjo on My Knee, Zaza,* and *Lillian Russell.*

Weston, Jack (1925–96) played the role of Pig, a poker player in *The Cincinnati Kid,* with Edward G. Robinson. Heavyset and usually comic, he came to films via Broadway and TV. Films include *Please Don't Eat the Daisies, Wait Until Dark, The Ritz, Dirty Dancing,* and *The Four Seasons.*

Wexley, John (1907–85), wrote the prison play *The Last Mile.* In Hollywood he collaborated on the screenplays of *The Amazing Dr. Clitterhouse* and *Confessions of a Nazi Spy,* both featuring Edward G. Robinson. Other Broadway works include *Steel* and *They Shall Not Die.*

Weyl, Carl Jules (1890–1948) was art director for five of Edward G. Robinson's Warner Bros. films: *The Amazing Dr. Clitterhouse, Bullets or Ballots, Confessions of a Nazi Spy, Dr. Ehrlich's Magic Bullet,* and *Kid Galahad.* He won an Oscar for *The Adventures of Robin Hood,* and was nominated for *Mission to Moscow.* Other films include *Casablanca, The Big Sleep,* and *The Corn Is Green.*

"What Are We Fighting?" (Radio, 1950) Sponsored by the American Cancer Society; radio; cast: Edward G. Robinson, Donald Woods, Ed Begley; *For the Living,* segment K; 1950

What's Cookin' Doc? Bugs Bunny competes with James Cagney for an Oscar, doing impersonations of Bing Crosby, Cecil B. DeMille, Carmen Miranda, and Edward G. Robinson.

Supervisor, Bob Clampett; story, Michael Sasanoff; animation, Bob McKimson; musical direction, Carl W. Stalling; Merrie Melodies, 1944; 7 minutes

What's My Line? (Television, 1953, 1960) Edward G. Robinson was the mystery guest twice on this popular game show. In his book *What's My Line?* producer Gil Fates gives this account of Robinson's appearance in 1960: "Robinson had the audience convulsed with a Cherman Mr. Kitzel accent, in which he agreed with Arlene Francis that he was indeed 'adorable.'"

A Mark Goodson-Bill Todman production; producers, Gil Fates, Bob Bach; directors, Paul Monroe, Franklin Heller, Frank Satenstein; set, Manuel Essman, John Ward, Robert Rowe Paddock, Willard Levitas; music, Milton DeLugg; theme song "Roller Coaster" by DeLugg and Lou Burch; announcers, Lee Vines, Hal Simms; commercials, Dennis James; John Daly (host); Arlene Francis, Bennett Cerf, Fred Allen*, Dorothy Kilgallen (panelists); Edward G. Robinson (mystery guest); CBS-TV; 30 minutes; 1953 and 1960.
*Allen died in 1955.

Where Do You Get Off? (Short film, 1948) Edward G. Robinson; United Jewish Appeal, 1948

White, Alice (1907–83) played the title role in *The Widow from Chicago,* with Edward G. Robinson. Onscreen from 1927, her other films include *The Sea Tiger, Gentlemen Prefer*

Blondes, Luxury Liner, Jimmy the Gent, and *Flamingo Road.*

Whitehead, Augustine (1893–1976), a close Robinson family friend, she was the Strasbourg-born daughter of Perillon, a preeminent French candle maker and was governess to Edward G. Robinson, Jr., in his early years. She later became a devoted traveling companion, influential figure, confidante, and guardian to Francesca, Edward G. Robinson's granddaughter.

Whitty, Dame May (1865–1948) is Lady Pamela Hardwick in *Flesh and Fantasy,* with Edward G. Robinson, and repeated her role on the radio. Oscar-nominated for her first sound film, *Night Must Fall* (recreated from Broadway), and for *Mrs. Miniver,* she was also in *The Lady Vanishes, Suspicion, Lassie Come Home, Madame Curie,* and *Gaslight.*

Who Has Seen the Wind? (Television, 1965) Xerox Special; a Telsun Foundation Production; producer-director, George Sidney; executive producer (Telsun), Edgar Rosenberg; associate producer (Telsun), C. O. Erickson; teleplay, Don M. Mankiewicz; story, Tad Mosel; cinematography, Joseph MacDonald; art director, Robert Luthardt; production designer, Ted Haworth; editor, Frank Santillo; assistant editor, Frank Unoste, Jr.; composer/conductor, Johnny Green; song "Who Has Seen the Wind?" by Green, Christina Rossetti; sung by Nancy Wilson; sound director, Clarence Peterson; assistant director, Bob Anderson; technical adviser, Carl Morrison; costume designer, Edith Head; costume supervisor, Paul Tetrick; makeup supervisor, Louis LaCava; cast: Edward G. Robinson (Captain), Stanley Baker (Janos), Maria Schell (The Mother), Theodore Bikel (The Father), Veronica Cartwright (Kiri), Gypsy Rose Lee (Proprietress), Lilia Skala (Nun), Simon Oakland (Inspector), Paul Richards (Father Ashton), Victor Jory (Peralton); Monica Keating, Ford Dunhill, Milton Frome, Steven Geray, Gil Perkins; ABC-TV; 90 minutes; February 19, 1965

Who Has Seen the Wind? was nominated for an Emmy award for outstanding program achievement. Shooting began in July 1964. According to Eric Monder in *George Sidney: A Bio-Bibliography,* "Edward G. Robinson comes across like a seedy, run-down version of Captain Andy." *Life* magazine called *Who Has Seen the Wind?* "soap opera; good intentions have not been enough to produce a good show."

Josef and Maria Radek have lived as refugees with their daughter, Kiri, aboard the tramp steamer *Hirundo* since the end of World War II. Their country was written out of existence and they have been awaiting their official release from the ship for twelve years. In Manzanillo, Janos, a radio operator escaping political persecution, jumps from the *Margit,* a freighter, and swims to the Mexican shore. A United States policeman catches him in a bar. Janos pleads his case from prison and is allowed to flee to the *Hirundo.* Janos is attracted to Maria, the cook, and to her flirtatious young daughter. Maria sends Kiri to live at a convent. Josef fights with Janos and ultimately commits suicide in despair over his family's separation. Too late, the United Nations arranges the family's asylum in Holland.

"The filming was not without danger," according to Theodore Bikel. "A storm at sea brought us perilously close to capsizing as we were being shuttled in a small tender. But the project was exhilarating all the same. We were in Mazatalan, Mexico, at that time off the beaten track, and out of season as well."— *Theo, the Autobiography of Theodore Bikel*

When asked why Edward G. Robinson received no mention in *Theo,* Bikel said, "It was an omission.... He was a lovely man— who spoke Yiddish!"

The Whole Town's Talking (Film, 1935) "A dizzy delight ... pungently written, wittily produced," is what *The New York Times* had to say about this film, "and topped off with a splendid dual performance by Edward G. Robinson, it may be handsomely recommended as the best of the new year's screen comedies.... Mr. Robinson, while he succeeds in being unbelievably downtrodden in the wistful little man who looks like Public Enemy No. 1, has not forgotten how to play Little Caesar, and he stifles the laugh in your throat when he is being Killer Mannion…. With a splendid narrative like this, he returns with a rush to the front line of film players."

Robinson received uniformly good notices for the film and his performance. He also had a good time making the picture because he had confidence in director John Ford, and he admired both his co-star Jean Arthur and screenwriter Jo Swerling.

Producer, Lester Cowan; director, John Ford; screenplay, Jo Swerling, Robert Riskin; based on a novel by W. R. Burnett; assistant director, Wilbur McGaugh; camera, Joseph August; editor, Viola Lawrence; cast: Edward G. Robinson (Arthur Ferguson Jones / Killer Mannion), Jean Arthur (Wilhelmina "Bill" Clark), Wallace Ford (Healy), Donald Meek (Hoyt), Edward Brophy (Bugs Martin), Arthur Byron (District Attorney Spencer), James Donlan (Det. Sgt. Pat Howe), Etienne Girardot (Seaver), Paul Harvey (J. G. Carpenter), Arthur Hohl (Det. Sgt. Mike Boyle), J. Farrell MacDonald (Warden), Ralph M. Remley (Sam Dixon), Blue Washington (Bank guard), Effie Ellsler (Aunt Agatha), Robert Emmett O'Connor (Lt. Mac), John Wray (Harry), Joseph Sawyer (Nick), Frank Sheridan (Russell), Clarence Hummel Wilson (Chamber of Commerce president), Virginia Pine (Seaver's secretary), Ferdinand Munier (Mayor), Cornelius Keefe (Radio man), Francis Ford, Emmett Vogan (Reporters), Lucille Ball, Charles King, Gordon DeMain (Bits), Robert Homans (Detective), Grace Halo (Sob sister), Walter Long (Convict), Ben Taggart (Cop), Al Hill (Gangster), Sam Flint (City official), Bess Flowers (Secretary), Mary Gordon (Landlady), Tom London (Guard); Jack Mower, Ernie Adams, Don Brodie, Eddie Chandler, Jules Cowles, Kernan Cripps, Eddie Fetherston, Roger Gray, Kit Guard, Bernardine Hayes, Sherry Hall, Edward Hearn, Dutch Hendrian, Rodney Hildebrand, John Ince, Bud Jamison, Edward Davis, Pat O'Malley, Steve Pendleton, Charles Sherlock, Lee Shumway, Charles Sullivan, Harry Tenbrook, Harry Abrahams, Carmen Andre, Charles A. Bachman, Brooks Benedict, Joe E. Bernard, Stanley Blystone, Harry Bowen, Edward Brady, Lynton Brent, Maurice Brierre, Vance Carroll, Monte Carter, Nancy Caswell, Allen Cavan, Steve Clark, Ivan Christy, Nick Copeland, Floyd Criswell, Charles Cross, Alice Dahl, Sidney D'Albrook, Bobbie Dale, Lew Davis, Sidney DeGray, Rita Donlin, Allyn Drake, Lowell Drew, Harry Dunkinson, Jay Eaton, Pearl Eaton, Budd Fine, Larry Fisher, Mary Foster, Rosita Foucher, Christopher J. Frank, Desmond Gallagher, Robert Graves, Jack Gray, Maurine Gray, Carlton Griffin, Arthur Stuart Hall, Pat Hartigan, Ed Hart, Charles Hickman, Pauline High, Carol Holloway, Mitchell Ingraham, Sunny Ingraham, John Irwin, Gladden James, William Jeffrey, Pardner Jones, Frank Marlowe, Hal Price, Edward Keane, Brady Kline, W. E. Lawrence, Peggy Leon, Stanley Mack, Charles McAvoy, Charles McMurphy, Philip Morris, Harry Mount, Irving Newhoff, Ned Norton, Frank O'Connor, Ted Oliver, Jimmy Phillips, Richard Powell, Hal Price, James Quinn, Arthur Ranken, Jack Richardson, Oscar Rudolph, Dick Rush, Jack Santoro, Allan Sears, Reginald Simpson, Phillips Smalley, Robert Stanley, Arthur Thalasso, William L. Thone, John Tyke, Billy West, Lloyd Whitlock, Robert Wilber, Corinne Williams, Maston Williams, William A. Williams, Harry Wilson, Ernest F. Young; Columbia; 93 minutes; March 1935; working title, *Passport to Fame*

The first morning in eight years on the job that Arthur Ferguson Jones oversleeps is the day his boss, Mr. Seaver, has been instructed by the boss, J. G. Carpenter, to give him a raise for never having been late. Carpenter also tells Seaver to fire the next employee who comes in late. The dilemma of Jones being both is nothing compared to the discovery among his office associates that he is a dead ringer for Public Enemy No. 1, Killer Mannion, whose breakout from jail is all over the front page of the papers. Jones goes to lunch at the Blue Bird Cafe and is recognized immediately—as Mannion—by Hoyt, who calls the police. They arrive in squads with sirens blaring and arrest Jones and Wilhelmina "Bill" Clark, a co-worker who infatuates Jones and who has joined him for lunch. A thorough grilling by detectives nearly convinces everyone that Jones is Mannion. District Attorney Spencer dictates a letter for Jones to carry, clearing him should he be mistakenly picked up as Mannion again. That night Mannion shows up at Jones' apartment, borrows the letter, goes on a crime spree, then returns the letter so Jones can use it during the day. Mystified by the ongoing crime, the authorities decide to lock Jones up in prison for his own safety. Mannion goes in his place, however, so he can bump off Slugs Martin. Then Mannion kidnaps Seaver and Miss Clark, along with Aunt Agatha, who has come to visit Jones. Mannion plans to have Jones killed by the police when he delivers a packet of money to the bank. Jones misplaces the package, though, and returns to the hideout for it and overhears the plot to have him killed. When the gang members see him, they mistake him for Mannion. Jones, affecting Mannion's gruff voice, orders the gang to eliminate the double, and they machine-gun Mannion. Jones gives himself away by fainting, but, fortunately, the police arrive. He collects a large reward and proposes to Miss Clark, and they leave on a cruise to Shanghai.

"Edward G. Robinson, who has been suffering from a succession of weak roles, registers an impressive return to his old-time form in a brace of parts in an amusing combination of farce and melodrama," said the *Literary Digest*. "...*The Whole Town's Talking* is not long on plausibility.... But the pace is fast, and the fun and thrills are reasonably frequent, and the photoplay becomes genuinely good fun. With two roles to handle — and handle with ability and resource — Mr. Robinson, of course, is pretty much the whole show, but there is an excellent supporting cast. Jean Arthur ... is forthright, charming, and real ... and help is provided by Etienne Girardot, Donald Meek, Paul Harvey, and others."

The New York Herald-Tribune noted that, "after a number of recent cinema adventures in a minor key, Edward G. Robinson returns to the days of his Hollywood glory in a lively and satisfactory combination of farce and melodrama.... The work manages to supply a one-man carnival for its star, and with Mr. Robinson taking every advantage of its sideshow possibilities, you have the opportunity to enjoy good acting and to have the soul-satisfying pleasure of watching the shrewd and resourceful performer on one of the happiest times of his life. Here, Mr. Robinson enjoys the vast blessing of a picture which enables him to perform in two contrasting roles without the necessity of a scene wherein he must pretend to make embarrassed love to the wife of his double.... The picture is, of course, always a Robinson field day, and the star takes proper and unashamed advantage of all his opportunities."

"Mr. Robinson, turning in a performance that goes up near the top of the comedy list for this year, plays a dual role," said *The New York Sun*; and William K. Everson in *The Bad Guys* called the film "an exciting — and amusing — semi-lampoon of gangster movies made by John Ford."

The New York American labeled *The Whole Town's Talking* "the best thing Mr. Robinson has done since the unforgettable *Little Caesar*.... [He] is twin star of the picture, for he portrays both clerk and killer, and delivers two separate and distinct characterizations which never once overlap or intrude one upon another. No one need be told how thrillingly [he] can impersonate an underworldling, and his Killer Mannion ranks with the finest of these conceptions.... The entire piece is a field day for Robinson."

Variety said, "Robinson will derive a heap of benefits from this assignment. It hands him some dazzling moments of acting ... notably, his characterization of the submerged, overpolite and indecisive office worker is human and believable. Always having been a swell actor, because he makes you believe him in various roles, this picture is a great break for him."

"The Whole Town's Talking" (Radio, 1935) Robinson and Jean Arthur repeated their roles in a radio adaptation of their hit film.

Cast: Edward G. Robinson (Arthur Ferguson Jones/Killer Mannion), Jean Arthur (Bill Clark); *Hollywood Hotel*; CBS; February 1, 1935

"The Why of Cancer" (Radio, 1950) Sponsored by the American Cancer Society; radio; cast: Edward G. Robinson, Gene Lockhart; *For the Living*, segment C; 15 minutes; 1950

Widmark, Richard (1914–) came to films after a time in radio and on Broadway. He played a villain in *Kiss of Death* (Oscar nomination), and he is Captain Archer in *Cheyenne Autumn*, with Edward G. Robinson. Other films include *Slattery's Hurricane, The Cobweb, Time Limit, Murder on the Orient Express, Madigan, The Alamo,* and *True Colors*.

The Widow from Chicago (Film, 1930) This was Edward G. Robinson's first sound feature at Warner Bros.-First National, immediately preceding *Little Caesar*. In his autobiography he dismisses the film because he saw little talent in either his leading lady, Alice White, or the director, Edward Cline, noting, "I liked him, but I liked my mother better, and I wouldn't let her direct a picture." Even with that grim assessment of the film, Foster Hirsch points out insightfully that Robinson's "star presence is unmistakable."

Director, Edward Cline; screenplay, story, Earl Baldwin; camera, Sol Polito; art director, Anton Grot; editor, Edward Schroeder; sound, Clifford A. Ruberg; music, Erno Rapee; orchestra, Leo F. Forbstein; cast: Alice White (Polly Henderson), Neil Hamilton (Swifty Dorgan), Edward G. Robinson (Dominic), Frank McHugh (Slug O'Donnell), Lee Shumway (Chris Johnston), Brooks Benedict (Mullins), John Elliott (Det. Lt. Finnegan), Dorothy Mathews (Cora), Ann Cornwall (Mazie), E. H. Calvert (Captain Davis), Betty Francisco (Helen), Harold Goodwin (Jimmy Henderson), Mike Donlin (Desk man), Robert Homans (Patrolman), Al Hill (Johnston), Mary Foy (Neighbor woman), Allan Coran (Sergeant Dunn); First National; 64 minutes; December 1930

The New York Times recognized the film's quality. "The endless variety of Edward G. Robinson's particular world of make believe is demonstrated once again in *The Widow from Chicago*, which presents him as an agreeably despicable gang leader in the metropolitan beer racket…. Mr. Robinson gives an interesting and authentic characterization as Dominic, a resourceful and intelligent underworld power. It is not his fault that he is made to provide a denouement by falling into the most puerile of traps."

Variety disagreed: "Robinson's gang leader is the poorest such characterization he has turned in…. Some of the things Robinson has to say sound all out of proportion. Miss White's exaggerated eye-rolling is just as bad. Neil Hamilton is miscast." *The New York Herald-Tribune* praised the film: "Mr. Robinson plays the underworld king in the best Nick Scarsi [*The Racket*] manner and, as usual, presents a vivid and striking portrait of a coldly malignant killer."

Jimmy Henderson, a New York detective, joins Dominic's gang by posing as Swifty Dorgan. The real Swifty escaped from Henderson by jumping off a moving train, disappeared, and is presumed dead. Outside his apartment Henderson is gunned down as his sister, Polly, watches from an upstairs window. Polly goes to Dominic to get a job at his nightclub, determined to avenge her brother's death. She introduces herself as Swifty's widow. When the real Swifty turns up she convinces him not to reveal her cover. They fall in love. Following an attempt by Dominic's gang to rob a rival club, Polly listens to Dominic talk about killing policemen, including one named Henderson. Detectives hear the "confession" over the telephone. Noticing the phone off the hook, Dominic tries to escape but finally surrenders to the police as Swifty and Polly go off together.

Wilcoxon, Henry (1905–84) came from the London stage and films to play in Cecil B. DeMille's *Cleopatra* (Marc Antony) and *The Crusades* (King Richard). He was associate producer for *The Ten Commandments* and also played Pentaur. His other films include *Last of the Mohicans, The Greatest Show on Earth, Man in the Wilderness,* and *F.I.S.T.*

Wilder, Billy (1906–2002), a Viennese emigre, was a screenwriter in collaboration with Charles Brackett, Raymond Chandler, and/or I.A.L. Diamond, as well as a director. He won best picture, direction, and writing Oscars for *The Lost Weekend* and *The Apartment,* and received similar nominations for both *Sunset Boulevard* (writing win) and *Double Indemnity.* In addition, *Witness for the Prosecution* and *Some Like It Hot* were named for direction and writing, respectively. *Sabrina* was nominated for its directing and writing, and *Stalag 17* for directing alone. Finally, there were screenplay nominations for *Ninotchka, Ball of Fire, A Foreign Affair, The Big Carnival,* and *The Fortune Cookie.* Sharing a love for Impressionist art, Wilder commented about Robinson on *A&E Biography*'s "Little Big Man": "He was the guy who introduced us to new painters that we did not know." He called Robinson's collection "phenomenal."

Will Edward G. Robinson left an estate of more than $2,250,000. His will, written February 15, 1972, was admitted to probate in Superior Court. It stipulated that his art collection be sold, and in March 1973 it was purchased by corporate executive Armand Hammer for $5,125,000. The will named his widow, Jane, to receive fifty percent of the estate and Edward, Jr., and Francesca twenty-five percent each, in trusts, following provisions in five percent shares to the City College of New York, the Actors Fund of America, the Motion Picture Relief Fund, the American Academy of Dramatic Arts, the Jewish Federation, and the N.A.A.C.P. Legal Defense and Educational Fund. His papers, scripts, photos, and mementos, including the Oscar, were also left to Jane, who later turned them over to the University of Southern California.

Williams, Adam (1929–) is in *Vice Squad,* with Edward G. Robinson, as Marty Kusalich, one of the bank robbers. He is also in *Without Warning, The Big Heat, Fear Strikes Out, North by Northwest,* and *The Last Sunset.*

Williams, Guinn "Big Boy" (1899–1962) played big, goodhearted lunks onscreen, including Moose McCarthy in *Blackmail,* with Edward G. Robinson. Will Rogers gave him the nickname "Big Boy." Other films, from 1919, include *The Jack Rider, Liliom, Flirtation Walk, Virginia City, The Littlest Rebel, A Star Is Born, Swamp Water,* and *The Alamo.*

Williams, Rhys (1897–1969), a Welshman onscreen from 1941, was a dialect coach for *How Green Was My Valley.* His films include *Mrs. Miniver, The Bells of St. Mary's, The Farmer's Daughter, The Spiral Staircase, The Corn Is Green, Raintree County, The Sons of Katie Elder,* and *Our Man Flint.* With Edward G. Robinson, he plays a detective in *Nightmare.*

"Witness for the Prosecution" (Television, 1953) This hour-long drama was Edward G. Robinson's first dramatic television appearance. It was based on the Agatha Christie mystery of the same name.

Producer, Calvin Kuhl; adapted for television by Anne Howard Bailey; based on the novel by Agatha Christie; director, Richard Goode; music, Milton Weinstein, Vladimir Selinsky; cast: Edward G. Robinson (A. J. Mayherne), Andrea King (Romaine Vole), Tom Drake (Leonard Vole), Leo Curley (Judge), Thomas Browne Henry (Judge), Blaine Williams, Roy Darmour, Leslie Turner, William O'Brien, Bryan Davis; *Lux Video Theatre,* September 17, 1953

Wives Gladys Lloyd Cassell, born in 1895, married Edward G. Robinson on January 21, 1927; they had one son, Edward G. Robinson, Jr., born in 1933, and were divorced in August 1956. She also had a daughter, Jeanne, by a previous marriage. Gladys died in June 1971.

Jane Bodenheimer Adler, born in 1919, married Robinson on January 16, 1958; she was widowed when he died on January 26, 1973. She married George Sidney in 1978. When Jane died in 1992, George, who had been married previously to Lillian Burns, married Corinne Entratter.

Robinson's onscreen wives included his real wife, Jane, in *Pepe,* playing herself. Gladys appeared in several films with Robinson in the early 1930s but never played the role of his wife.

Several actresses named Ruth played Robinson's wife onscreen: Ruth Donnelly, *A Slight Case of Murder;* Ruth Hussey, *Blackmail;* Ruth Gordon, *Dr. Ehrlich's Magic Bullet;* and Ruth Warrick, *Mr. Winkle Goes to War.*

Onscreen wives also include Jean Arthur, *The Whole Town's Talking;* Mary Astor, *The Little Giant;* Elsie Baker, *Good Neighbor Sam;* Lynn Bari, *Tampico;* Edna Best, *A Dispatch from Reuter's;* Mady Christians, *All My Sons;* Virginia Christine, *Nightmare;* Bebe Daniels, *Silver Dollar;* Luli Deste, *Thunder in the City;* Marlene Dietrich, *Manpower;* Rosalind Ivan, *Scarlet Street;* Zita Johann, *Tiger Shark;* Bessie Love, *Journey Together;* Aline MacMahon, *Silver Dollar;* Esther Minciotti, *House of Strangers;* Joanna Moore, *Never a Dull Moment;* Agnes Moorehead, *Our Vines Have Tender Grapes;* Vivienne Osborne, *Two Seconds;* Dorothy Peterson, *The Woman in the Window;* Thelma Ritter, *A Hole in the Head;* Margaret Seddon, *The Bright Shawl;* Barbara Stanwyck, *The Violent Men;* Nora Swinburne, *Operation X;* Genevieve Tobin, *I Loved a Woman* and *Dark Hazard;* Claire Trevor, *Two Weeks in Another Town;* Renata Vanni, *Hell on Frisco Bay;* and Loretta Young, *The Hatchet Man.*

On the stage Robinson was married to Armina Marshall in *Right You Are If You Think You Are,* and Gena Rowlands in *Middle of the Night.* On the radio he was married to Verna Felton in *The Man Who Thought He Was Edward G. Robinson,* Frieda Inescort in "The Taming of the Shrew," and Jeannette Nolan in *My Wife, Geraldine.* Television wives include Ann Doran in "A Set of Values," Carmen Mathews in "The Drop-Out," and Naomi Stevens in "The Legend of Jim Riva."

Wolheim, Louis (1880–1931) was on Broadway in *The Jest, The Hairy Ape, What Price Glory?* and, with Edward G. Robinson, *The Idle Inn,* adapting the script from its original Yiddish. His films include *Dr. Jekyll and Mr. Hyde, Orphans of the Storm,* and *All Quiet on the Western Front.*

The Woman in the Window (Film, 1945) Following the success of Billy Wilder's *Double Indemnity,* Edward G. Robinson began a two-film association with another German director, Fritz Lang, and the initial result, *The Woman in the Window,* was another triumph of *film noir.*

The reviews were uniformly excellent, with *The New York Times* calling the film "a humdinger of a mystery melodrama. [It is] ... superlatively directed by Fritz Lang, and we couldn't imagine a better set of performers than the cast this picture boasts. Each player ... is almost letter perfect.... Mr. Robinson, who was so good as the insurance investigator of *Double Indemnity,* gives a masterly performance as the professor."

The cast featured Joan Bennett (replacing Merle Oberon), Raymond Massey, and Dan Duryea in their first of two appearances each with Robinson. Two child actors from *Our Gang* had small roles. Spanky McFarland played a boy scout who finds a dead man's body in the woods, telling the world about the incident via newsreel, and Robinson's son was played by Bobby Blake.

Producer, screenplay, Nunnally Johnson; director, Fritz Lang; based on the novel *Once Off Guard* by J. H. Wallis; assistant director, Richard Harlan; art director, Duncan Cramer; music, Arthur Lang; special effects, Vernon Walker; camera, Milton Krasner; editor, Marjorie Johnson, Gene Fowler Jr., Paul Weatherwax; set director, Julia Heron; costumes, Muriel King; stills, Ed Henderson; cast: Edward G. Robinson (Professor Richard Wanley), Joan Bennett (Alice Reed), Raymond Massey (Frank Lalor), Dan Duryea (Heidt), Edmond Breon (Dr. Barkstone), Thomas E. Jackson (Inspector Jackson), Dorothy Peterson (Mrs. Wanley), Spanky McFarland (Boy Scout), Arthur Space (Captain Kennedy), Arthur Loft (Claude Mazard), Frank Dawson (Steward), Claire Carleton (Blonde), Carol Cameron (Elsie), Bobbie Blake (Dickie), Harry Hayden (Pharmacist), Joe Devlin (Toll collector), Iris Adrian (Hooker), Alec Craig

(Garage attendant), Eddy Chandler (Police driver), Ralph Dunn (Traffic cop), Bess Flowers (Bar extra), Fred Graham (Motorcycle cop), Tom Hanlon (Radio announcer), Ruth Valmy (Glamor model), Tom Dillon (Officer Flynn), Larry Steers, Brandon Beach, James Beasley, Austin Bedell, Al Bensalt, Paul Bradley, Don Brodie, James Carlisle, Fred Chapman, Hal Craig, Thomas P. Dunn, William Dyer, Calvin Emery, Jack Gardner, Jack Gargan, James Harrison, William Holmes, Fred Hueston, Sheldon Jett, J. W. Johnston, Donald Kerr, Lawrence Lathrop, Ann Loos, Frank McClure, Joel McGinnis, Harold McNulty, Charles Meakin, Frank Melton, Frank Mills, Harold Minjer, Francis Morris, Ralph Norwood, Wedgewood Nowell, Ann O'Neal, Louis Payne, David Pepper, Alex Pollard, Fred Rapport, Ray Saeger, Scott Seaton, Wyndham Standing, Lane Watson; RKO; 99 minutes; December 1944

With his wife and children away from New York on a summer vacation, Professor Richard Wanley muses about middle-aged flings with his friends, District Attorney Frank Lalor and Dr. Barkstone. Following a final round of after-dinner drinks at their club, the others leave and Wanley begins reading *The Song of Solomon* in the club library, asking the steward to remind him when it is 10:30. Leaving the club, he pauses to admire a painting in the art gallery window next door. When the model for the painting, Alice Reed, appears, they strike up a conversation, go for a drink, and then to her apartment where Wanley is shown other sketches by the painter of the portrait. A man bursts in the room and, in a jealous rage, attacks Wanley. Wanley stabs the man in self defense. Alice and Wanley are stunned for a moment but then develop a plan as an alternative to going to the police, which under the circumstances would ruin them both. Wanley goes to get his car, then wraps the body in a blanket and dumps it in the woods. They hope this ends the incident. However, the dead man turns out to be a famed promoter, Claude Mazard. Through Lalor, Wanley is kept up to date on the investigation, and alarming circumstantial evidence mounts up. Alice and Wanley manage to escape detection, however, and think themselves safe until Heidt, who was Mazard's bodyguard, calls on Alice and demands money. They attempt to murder Heidt but fail. Wanley decides to take his own life, unaware that the police have tracked Heidt, gunned him down, and found Mazard's watch on his body. Wanley slumps over in his chair to die. At this point the club steward awakens him to tell him it is 10:30. Wanley is dumbfounded; he has dreamed the entire episode! Leaving the club, he tips Charley, the hat check man—who was Mazard in his dream! Outside, the doorman is—Heidt! Pausing for a moment to gaze at the portrait of the woman in the window, he is startled by a streetwalker who asks for a light for her cigarette. Wanley tells her no and runs away.

In his column, Walter Winchell led the praise for the picture, claiming it "rates three cheers and four screams!" *The New York Herald-Tribune* singled out the acting, saying, "Edward G. Robinson has seldom, if ever, been better than he is as the professor whose logical and ultimately desperate attempts to cover up his act are foiled at every turn."

"[He] gives everything he has to the role as the reserved and reticent professor, scoring solidly," said *Variety,* which also had praise for the screenplay: "Nunnally Johnson whips up a strong and decidedly suspenseful murder melodrama in *The Woman in the Window.*" Johnson, in turn, credited Robinson: "Eddie played it so beautifully that you accepted the fact that he had had a dream and that it embodied people that he knew."

Fritz Lang paid this tribute: "Each part he plays he enriches with deep and warm understanding of human frailties and compels us to pity rather than condemnation, always adding vivid color to the intricate mosaic of motion picture reality. The most cherished memories of my career in motion pictures, which spans more than forty years, are working with Edward G. Robinson."

"Once during *Woman in the Window* [Lang] spent a whole hour rearranging Joan Bennett's negligee so that she would cast a certain shadow he wanted," said Robinson in an interview in *Take One.* "That kind of perfectionism seems great now, and it helps the film when you see the finished picture, but at the time, well.... *Woman in the Window* was extraordinary. We started out, of course, with one of the most perfect scripts I have ever been associated with, by Nunnally Johnson.... Fritz was an innovator, of course, and that scene in which the character seems to die, then the camera comes in for a close-up and immediately pulls back to reveal him just asleep in a different costume in a different room was extraordinary. There was no cut at all. I was wearing a second costume under the first which grips pulled away as the camera came in, and the entire room also split in half and was pulled away to reveal a second set. No cut. Extraordinary."— Interviewed by D. Overbey

In *Films in Review* Joan Bennett commented about her co-star: "He was going through a terrible time with his wife, Gladys. She was being given shock treatments, and despite his personal problems, he was always a sweet, kind man."

"The Woman in the Window" (Radio, 1945) The 1944 film was adapted and presented on the radio three times — on *Lux Radio Theatre, Colgate Theatre of Romance,* and *Ford Theatre*.

Director, Fred MacKaye; adaptation, Sanford Barnett; music director, Louis Silvers; sound, Charlie Forsyth; cast: Edward G. Robinson (Professor Wanley), Joan Bennett (Alice Reed), Dan Duryea (Heidt), Charles Seel, Herbert Rawlinson, Norman Field, Edward Marr, Stanley Farrar, Ed Emerson, Haskell Coffin, Franklyn Parker, Duane Thompson, Lester Matthews, Mark Hellinger (host); John Milton Kennedy (announcer); Janet Russell, Doris Singleton, Ann Tobin, Betty Jean Hainey, Truda Marson, Ralph Lewis, Julie Bannon, Virginia Gregg (Commercials); *Lux Radio Theatre*, CBS-radio, 60 min.; June 25, 1945

"The Woman in the Window" (Radio, 1946) Cast: Edward G. Robinson (Professor Wanley); *Colgate Theatre of Romance*; CBS-radio; March 26, 1946

"The Woman in the Window" (Radio, 1949) Producer-director, Fletcher Markle; script editor, Vincent McConnor; writer-adaptors, Brainerd Duffield, Hugh Kemp; music, Cy Feuer; cast: Edward G. Robinson (Professor Wanley), Linda Darnell (Alice Reed); announcer, Nelson Case; *Ford Theatre*; CBS-radio; 60 min.; January 28, 1949

Wood, Douglas (1880–66), an English actor, plays in *I Am the Law* as Berry and *Dr. Ehrlich's Magic Bullet* as Speidler, with Edward G. Robinson. His other credits include *This Is My Affair, The Prisoner of Shark Island, H.M. Pulham Esq., Sergeant York,* and *Harriet Craig*.

Wood, Stanley G. (1919–2000) was on Broadway in *The Chief Thing, The Kibitzer, The Goat Song,* and *Peer Gynt* with Edward G. Robinson. In later years he appeared with the National Repertory Theatre under the shorter name G. Wood, and in films, such as *M*A*S*H* and *Harold and Maude*.

Woolrich, Cornell (1903–68), also known as William Irish, wrote several mystery novels that became films, including *Rear Window,* and, with Edward G. Robinson, *Night Has a Thousand Eyes* and *Nightmare*.

"World of Tomorrow" (Radio, 1943) Producer-director, Thomas Freebairn-Smith; music, Lud Guskin, Anthony Collins; cast: Edward G. Robinson (Steve Wilson); narrator, Patrick McGeehan; *Lockheed's Ceiling Unlimited*; CBS-radio; April 26, 1943

World Premiere Movie see *U.M.C.*

The World's Greatest Showman (Television & Radio, 1963) This special television program was a tribute to film director Cecil B. DeMille.

Participants: Yul Brynner, Cecil B. DeMille, Samuel Goldwyn, Rev. Billy Graham, Charlton Heston, Bob Hope, Edward G. Robinson, Barbara Stanwyck, James Stewart, Gloria Swanson, Cornel Wilde; NBC-tv; 90 minutes; December 1, 1963

Excerpts of the program were also broadcast on NBC-radio the same date.

Wray, Fay (1907–) is remembered as *King Kong*'s leading lady. Her other films, from 1923, include *The Four Feathers, The Mystery of the Wax Museum, The Affairs of Cellini, Adam Had Four Sons, The Cobweb, Queen Bee, Tammy and the Bachelor*, plus, with Edward G. Robinson, the short film *The Stolen Jools* and *Hell on Frisco Bay*, and on radio in *The Roosevelt Special*.

Wray, John (1888–1940) plays a henchman in *The Whole Town's Talking*, with Edward G. Robinson, and in *Blackmail* he is Diggs, who tries to escape with Robinson from the chain gang. Wray directed the silent films *Anna Christie* and *Human Wreckage*, and acted in *Quick Millions, All Quiet on the Western Front, The Mouthpiece*, and *Mr. Smith Goes to Washington*.

Wycherly, Margaret (1881–1956) played the mothers of Gary Cooper in *Sergeant York* (Oscar nomination) and James Cagney in *White Heat*. She acted with Edward G. Robinson, as Daisy Diana Dorothea Devore, in *The Adding Machine*, and as Halla in *Eyvind of the Hills*. Other Broadway credits include *Six Characters in Search of an Author, Tobacco Road*, and *The Glass Menagerie*; her films include *Crossroads* and *The Yearling*.

Wyman, Jane (1914–), first wife of Ronald Reagan, was on the radio in *The Roosevelt Special* and onscreen in *Larceny, Inc.*, with Edward G. Robinson, and they all three play cameos in *It's a Great Feeling*. She won an Oscar for *Johnny Belinda*, and was nominated for *The Yearling, The Blue Veil*, and *The Magnificent Obsession*. Other credits include *The Lost Weekend* and, more recently, TV's *Falcon Crest*.

Wynn, Keenan (1916–86), son of comic Ed Wynn and grandson (on his mother's side) of silent film actor Frank Keenan, is in *A Hole in the Head* and *Mackenna's Gold* with Edward G. Robinson. They were on the radio together in *The Roosevelt Special* and *Hollywood Fights Back*, and on TV in *Operation Entertainment*. Other films include *See Here Private Hargrove, Kiss Me Kate, Requiem for a Heavyweight, Dr. Strangelove*, and Disney's *The Absent-Minded Professor* and *The Shaggy D.A.*

"You Can't Die Twice" (Radio, 1949) Producer-director, Anton M. Leader; cast: Edward G. Robinson (Sam Brown), Harlow Wilcox (announcer); *Suspense*; CBS-radio; 30 min.; March 31, 1949

Young, Carleton (1907–71) came to films from radio (as *Ellery Queen* and *The Count of Monte Cristo*). He appears with Edward G. Robinson in *Cheyenne Autumn* as his aide, and also in the television drama *A Good Name*. Young's other films include The *Kissing Bandit, Deadline U.S.A.*, and *The Last Hurrah*.

Young, Loretta (1913–2000) won an Oscar for *The Farmer's Daughter*, and from 1953 to 1961 had her own dramatic TV show. She starred with Edward G. Robinson twice — in *The Hatchet Man* and *The Stranger*, and they were in the short films *The Stolen Jools* and *An Intimate Dinner in Celebration of Warner Bros. Silver Jubilee*. Sally Blane, her elder sister, appears in *A Bullet for Joey*. Other films include *Call of the Wild, Rachel and the Stranger, Come to the Stable*, and *A Night to Remember*.

Young, Robert (1907–98) played in films long before his memorable TV work on *Father Knows Best* and *Marcus Welby, M.D.* He was on radio three times with Edward G. Robinson, in *Document A/777, Hollywood Fights Back*, and "Only Yesterday" on *Lux Radio Theatre*. His films include *Crossfire, Secret Agent, Claudia*, and *H. M. Pulham, Esq.*

Zane Grey Theatre see **"Heritage"**

Zanuck, Darryl F. (1902–79) began working in films at Warner Bros. as a screenwriter in 1923 on several stories for Rin Tin Tin. He was put in charge of production during the transition to sound and contributed to the writing and production of *Little Caesar*. As chief of production at 20th Century–Fox for thirty-five years, his major successes included *The Grapes of Wrath, How Green Was My Valley, The Razor's Edge, Gentleman's Agreement, All About Eve,* and *The Longest Day.*

Zimbalist, Efrem, Jr. (1923–) had two successful TV series, *77 Sunset Strip* and *The F.B.I.* The son of a concert violinist and opera singer, and father of actress Stephanie Zimbalist, his first film was *House of Strangers*, as Tony, one of Edward G. Robinson's four sons. Other films include *By Love Possessed, Wait Until Dark,* and *Airport 1975.*

Bibliography

"Actor-Collector." *Literary Digest*, January 9, 1937.

"Actor Robinson's Wife Names 'Other' Woman." *Los Angeles Examiner*, June 30, 1956.

"Actor's Son Gets 60 Days." *The New York Times*, June 4, 1957.

Aman, Libby. "Little Caesar Is Surviving Beautifully." *The Washington Star*, March 23, 1971.

Armstrong, Richard B. & Mary Willem. *The Movie List, A Reference Guide to Film Themes, Settings and Series*. Jefferson, North Carolina: McFarland, 1990.

Astor, Mary. *A Life on Film*. New York: Delacorte Press, 1971.

Astor, Mary. *My Story*. New York: Dell, 1959.

Bacall, Lauren. *By Myself*. New York: Knopf, 1978.

Bacon, James. *Made in Hollywood*. New York: Warner Books, 1978.

Baker, Gretta. "Here's My Favorite." *Scholastic*, March 16, 1942.

Bannerman, R. LeRoy. *On a Note of Triumph*. New York: Carol Publishing Group, 1986.

Barr, Tony. *Acting for the Camera*. New York: Harper & Row, 1982.

Baxter, John. *Hollywood in the Thirties*. New York: Paperback Library Edition, Cororet Communications, 1970.

Behlmer, Rudy. *Inside Warner Bros. (1935–1951)*. New York: Viking Penguin, 1985.

Bentley, Eric. *Are You Now or Have You Ever Been*. New York: Harper Colophon Books, 1972.

Beylie, Claude. "Ave, Little Caesar." *Ecran*, March, 1973.

"Big Little Caesar." *Time*, February 5, 1973.

Bikel, Theodore. *Theo, the Autobiography of Theodore Bikel*. New York: Harper/Collins, 1994.

Billips, Connie, and Arthur Pierce, *Lux Presents Hollywood*. Jefferson, North Carolina: McFarland, 1995.

Block, Haskell M., and Robert G. Shedd. *Masters of Modern Drama*. New York: Random House, 1962.

Blum, Daniel, and John Kobal. *A New Pictorial History of the Talkies*. New York: Perigree Books / G. P. Putnam's Sons, 1982.

Bookbinder, Robert. *Classics of the Gangster Film*. Secaucus, New Jersey: Citadel Press, 1985.

Bogdanovich, Peter. *This Is Orson Welles*. New York: Harper/Collins, 1992.

Bordman, Gerald. *American Theatre: A Chronicle of Comedy and Drama, 1914–1930*. New York: Oxford University Press, 1995.

Bordman, Gerald. *The Oxford Companion to American Theatre*. New York: Oxford University Press, 1992.

Brockman, Alfred. *The Movie Book: The 1930s*. New York: Crescent Books, 1987.

Brosnan, John. *Future Tense: The Cinema of Science Fiction*. New York: St. Martin's Press, 1978.

Brown, Gene. *Movie Time*. New York: Macmillan, 1995.

Brownlow, Kevin. *The War, the West, and the Wilderness*. New York: Knopf, 1978.

Cagney, James. *Cagney by Cagney*. Garden City, New York: Doubleday, 1976.

Capra, Frank. *The Name Above the Title*. New York: Macmillan, 1971.

Ceplair, Larry, and Steven Englund. *The Inquisition in Hollywood — Politics in the Film Community 1930–1960*. Berkeley California: University of California Press, 1979.

Chaneles, Sol, and Albert Wolsky. *The Movie Makers*. Secaucus, New Jersey: Derbibooks, 1974.

Charity, Tom. *John Cassavetes: Lifeworks*. London, England: Omnibus Press, 2001.

Clarens, Carlos. *Crime Movies*. New York: W. W. Norton, 1980.

Bibliography

Cogley, John. *Report on Blacklisting: Movies.* New York: Fund for the Republic, 1956.

"Collectors at Work." *Time,* February 5, 1951.

Collins, William B. "A Legend the New Generation Wants to Know." *Philadelphia Enquirer,* December 2, 1973.

Considine, Shaun. *Mad as Hell: The Life and Work of Paddy Chayefsky.* New York: Random House, 1994.

Cormack, Bartlett. *The Racket.* New York: Vail-Ballou Press, 1927.

Cowie, Peter. *Seventy Years of Cinema.* Cranbury, New Jersey: A. S. Barnes, 1969.

Crowther, Bosley. *The Great Films: 50 Golden Years of Motion Pictures.* New York: Putnam, 1967.

Current Biography. January 1950.

Curtis, Tony, with Barry Paris. *Tony Curtis, The Autobiography.* New York: William Morrow, 1993.

Darvid, Diana Douglas. *In the Wings.* New York: Barricade Books, 1999.

Davidson, Bill. *Spencer Tracy, Tragic Idol.* New York: Dutton, 1987.

Douglas, Kirk. *Ragman's Son.* New York: Simon & Schuster, 1988.

Dowdy, Andrew. *Films of the Fifties.* New York: William Morrow, 1973.

Ducas, Dorothy, and Adele Brown. "The Men Mix It." *Colliers,* September 2, 1939.

"E. G. Robinson Reweds." *The New York Times,* January 17, 1958.

"E. G. Robinson Jr. Dies in Sleep at 40." *St. Louis Post-Dispatch,* February 27, 1974.

"E. G. Robinson Jr. Felled by Overdose of Sleeping Pills." *New York Post,* April 25, 1956.

"Ed. G. Robinsons Settle Battle Over $3,500,000." *Los Angeles Evening Herald Express,* August 3, 1956.

"Edward G. Robinson Banishes Son from Home in Love Row." *Los Angeles Evening Herald Express,* February 15, 1952.

Eiselen, Frederick Carl, Edwin Lewis, and David G. Downey. *The Abingdon Bible Commentary* New York: The Abingdon Press, 1929.

Everson, William K. "Portrait." *Show,* April, 1973.

Everson, William K. *The Bad Guys: A Pictorial History of the Movie Villain.* New York: Cadillac, 1964.

Eyles, Allen. "Edward G. Robinson." *Films and Filming,* January 1964.

Fairbanks Jr., Douglas. *The Salad Days.* Garden City, New York: Doubleday, 1988.

Fates, Gil. *What's My Line?* Englewood Cliffs, New Jersey: Prentice-Hall, 1978.

"Film Star's Son Arrested." *The New York Times,* July 21, 1954.

"The First Flickers," *Newsweek.* November 23, 1959.

Fishbein, Ed. "Ed. G. Robinson Is Remembered at a Sale." *The Washington Star,* August 3, 1977.

Fishgall, Gary. *Against Type: The Biography of Burt Lancaster.* New York: Scribner, 1995.

Fleischer, Richard. *Just Tell Me When to Cry.* New York: Carroll & Graf, 1993.

Frank, M. "Sterling Collection for the Star of *Little Caesar* and *Double Indemnity.*" *Architectural Digest,* April 1990.

Freedland, Michael. *All the Way, a Biography of Frank Sinatra, 1915–1998.* New York: St. Martin's Press, 1997.

Gabler, Neal. *An Empire of Their Own.* New York: Crown, 1988.

Gabree, John. *Gangsters, from Little Caesar to The Godfather: Pyramid Illustrated History of the Movies.* New York: Pyramid, 1973.

Gansberg, Alan L. *Little Caesar: A Biography of Edward G. Robinson.* Kent, England: Sevenoaks, 1983.

Garbicz, Adam, and jack Klinowski. *Cinema, the Magic Vehicle: A Guide to Its Achievement.* Metuchen, New Jersey: Scarecrow Press, 1975.

Gassner, John, and Dudley Nichols. *20 Best Screenplays.* New York: Crown, 1943.

Gehman, Richard. *Bogart.* Greenwich, Connecticut: Gold Medal Books / Fawcett, 1965.

Gehman, Richard. *Sinatra and His Rat Pack.* New York: Belmont Books, 1961.

Geist, Kenneth L. *Pictures Will Talk: The Life and Films of Joseph L. Mankiewicz.* New York: Scribner, 1978.

Gianetti, Louis D. *Understanding Movies.* Englewood Cliffs, New Jersey: Prentice-Hall, 1972.

Giesler, Jerry, and Pete Martin. *Hollywood Lawyer: The Jerry Giesler Story.* New York: Simon & Schuster, 1960.

Golden, J. David. *The Golden Age of Radio.* Sandy Hook, Connecticut: Yesteryear Press, 1998.

Goldman, William. *The Season.* New York: Harcourt, Brace & World, 1969.

Gordon, Ruth. *An Open Book.* Garden City, New York: Doubleday, 1980.

Gow, Gordon. *Suspense in the Cinema.* New York: Paperback Library Edition, Coronet Communications, 1971.

Green, Lee. "Edward G. Robinson—He Lived with Gentleness—He Died with Strength." *Motion Picture,* April 1973.

Griffith, Richard, and Arthur Mayer. *The Movies.* New York: Simon and Schuster, 1970.

Grobel, Lawrence. *The Hustons*. New York: Avon, 1989.

Halliwell, Leslie. *Film Guide*. New York: Charles Scribner's Sons, 1977.

Halliwell, Leslie. *The Filmgoer's Companion*, sixth edition. New York: Hill and Wang, 1977.

Halliwell, Leslie, and John Walker, ed. *The Filmgoer's and Video Viewer's Companion*. New York: Harper Perennial / Harper Collins, 1993.

Harmon, Jim. *The Great Radio Heroes*. Garden City, New York: Doubleday, 1967.

Haun, Harry. *The Movie Quote Book*. New York: Lippincott & Crowell, 1980.

Hecht, Ben. *A Child of the Century*. New York: Signet Books / The New American Library, 1955.

Helburn, Theresa A. *A Wayward Quest*. Boston, Massachusetts: Little, Brown, 1960.

Heston, Charlton. *The Actor's Life*. New York: E. P. Dutton, 1976.

Heston, Charlton. *In the Arena*. New York: Simon & Schuster, 1995.

Higham, Charles. *Bette: The Life of Bette Davis*. New York: Macmillan, 1981.

Higham, Charles. *Warner Brothers*. New York: Charles Scribner's Sons, 1975.

Higham, Charles, and Joel Greenberg. *Hollywood in the Forties*. New York: Paperback Library Edition / Coronet Communications, 1968.

"Highest Bidder." *Newsweek*, February 4, 1957.

Hirsch, Foster. *The Dark Side of the Screen: Film Noir*. San Diego, California: A. S. Barnes, 1981.

Hirsch, Foster. *Edward G. Robinson: A Pyramid Illustrated History of the Movies*. New York: Pyramid, 1975.

Hope, Bob. *Have Tux, Will Travel*. New York: Simon & Schuster, 1954.

Houseman, John. *Runthrough*. New York: Simon & Schuster, 1972.

Huston, John. *An Open Book*. New York: Knopf, 1980.

Hyams, Joe. *Bogie: The Definitive Biography of Humphrey Bogart*. New York: Signet Books / The New American Library, 1967.

Jackson, Kenneth T., editor-in-chief. *Dictionary of American Biography, Supplement Nine, 1971–1975*. New York: Charles Scribner's Sons, 1994.

Jay, Michael, ed., and Colin McArthur. *Heroes of the Silver Screen*. New York: Galahad Books, 1975.

Jerome, Stuart. *Those Crazy, Wonderful Years When We Ran Warner Bros*. Secaucus, New Jersey: L. Stuart, 1983.

Jones, Barry, and M. V. Dixon. *The MacMillan Dictionary of Biography*. London, England: Papermac, a Division of Macmillan, 1981.

Josefsberg, Milt. *The Jack Benny Show*. New Rochell, New York: Arlington House, 1977.

Kael, Pauline. *Kiss Kiss Bang Bang*. Boston, Massachusetts: Little, Brown, 1968.

Kaminsky, Stuart M. *American Film Genres*. New York: Dell, 1977.

Karney, Robyn, ed., and Joel W. Finley. *The Movie Stars Story*. New York: Crescent Books / Crown, 1984.

Katz, Ephraim. *The Film Encyclopedia*. New York: Perigee Books / The Putnam Publishing Group, 1979.

Kennedy, J. B. "Tough as Velvet." *Colliers*, January 2, 1932.

Knox, Sanka. "E. G. Robinson Art Brings $3,000,000." *The New York Times*, February 26, 1957.

Kronenberger, Louis. *The Best Plays of 1955–1956*. New York: Dodd, Mead, 1956.

Lasky, Jesse L. *Whatever Happened to Hollywood?* New York: Funk & Wagnalls, 1975 .

Lawson, John Howard. *Film: The Creative Process*. New York: Hill and Wang, 1967.

LeRoy, Mervyn. *Take One*. New York: Hawthorn Books, 1974.

Lewis, Arthur H. *It Was Fun While It Lasted*. New York: Trident Press, 1973.

Logan, Joshua. *Movie Stars, Real People, and Me*. New York: Delacorte Press, 1978.

Loggia, Marjorie, and Glenn Young, ed. *The Collected Works of Harold Clurman*. New York: Applause Books, 1994.

Lorentz, Pare. *Lorentz on Film: Movies to 1927 to 1941*. New York: Hopkinson and Blake, 1975.

Lyman, Darryl. *Great Jews on Stage and Screen*. Middle Village, New York: Jonathan David Publishers, 1987.

McAdams, William. *Ben Hecht, a Biography*. New York: Barricade Books, 1990 .

McBride, Joseph, and Andrew Sarris (contributor). *Focus on Howard Hawks*. Englewood Cliffs, New Jersey: Prentice-Hall, 1972.

McCarty, Clifford. *Bogey: The Films of Humphrey Bogart*. New York: Citadel Press, 1965.

McCarty, John. *Hollywood Gangland*. New York: St. Martin's Press, 1993.

McClelland, Doug. *Hollywood Talks Turkey, The Screen's Greatest Flops*. Boston, Massachusetts: Faber and Faber, 1989.

McCoy, Malachy. *Steve McQueen*. London, England: W.H. Allen, 1975.

McDowall, Roddy. *Double Exposure*. New York: Delacorte Press, 1966.

Bibliography

McGilligan, Patrick. *Cagney, the Actor as Auteur.* San Diego: A. S. Barnes, 1982.

MacLaine, Shirley. *My Lucky Stars, a Hollywood Memoir.* New York: Bantam, 1995.

Magill, Frank N., editor. *Magill's Survey of Cinema: Silent Films.* Englewood Cliffs, New Jersey: Salem Press, 1982.

Malden, Karl, with Carla Malden. *When Do I Start?* New York: Simon & Schuster, 1997.

Maltin, Leonard, editor. *Leonard Maltin's TV Movies and Videoguide.* New York: New American Library, 1987.

Maltin, Leonard, editor. *TV Movies, 1970–80 Edition.* New York: New American Library, 1978.

Mank, Gregory W. *Women in Horror Films, 1930s.* Jefferson, North Carolina: McFarland, 1999.

Mantle, Burns. *The Best Plays of 1919–1969/70.* Boston and New York: Dodd, Mead, 1928–1978.

Marill, Alvin H. *The Complete Films of Edward G. Robinson.* New York: Carol Publishing Group, 1990.

Marill, Alvin H. *Movies Made for Television.* New York: Da Capo Press / Plenum, 1981.

Marill, Alvin H. *Samuel Goldwyn Presents.* South Brunswick, New Jersey: A. S. Barnes, 1976.

Martin, Tony, and Cyd Charisse. *The Two of Us.* New York: Mason/Charter, 1976.

Matthews, Charles E. *The Oscar A to Z.* New York: Doubleday, 1995.

Meredith, Scott. *George S. Kaufman and His Friends.* Garden City, New York: Doubleday, 1974.

Meyer, William R. *Warner Brothers Directors.* New Rochelle, New York: Arlington House, 1978.

Michael, Paul, ed. *Movie Greats.* New York: Garland Books, 1969.

Millier, Arthur. "Living Art Radio Program." *Magazine of Art,* November 1942.

Mr. Samuel. The Commonweal, November 26, 1930.

Monder, Eric. *George Sidney, a Bio-Bibliography.* Westport, Connecticut: Greenwood Press, 1994.

Mordden, Ethan. *The Hollywood Studios.* New York: Simon & Schuster, 1989.

Naremore, James. *The Magic World of Orson Welles.* New York: Oxford University Press, 1978.

Nast, Herbert E., Esq. *Wills of the Rich and Famous.* New York: Warner Books, 1991.

Neibaur, James L. *Tough Guy: The American Movie Macho.* Jefferson, North Carolina: McFarland, 1989.

Nevins, Francis M. *Cornell Woolrch — First You Dream, Then You Die.* New York: Mysterious Press, 1988.

Newquist, Roy. *Showcase.* New York: William Morrow, 1966.

"Niarchos Named as Buyer of Art." *The New York Times,* February 28, 1957.

Niderost, E. "Edward G. Robinson: The Classic Gangster." *Classic Image,* May 1993.

Nowlan, Robert A., and Gwendolyn W. Nowlan. *Film Quotations.* Jefferson, North Carolina: McFarland, 1994.

Osborne, Robert. *50 Golden Years of Oscar.* LaHabra, California: ESE California, 1979.

Othman, Frederick C. "Art Is a Tough Racket, Pal." *Saturday Evening Post,* July 1, 1944.

Ott, Frederick W. *The Films of Fritz Lang.* Secaucus, New Jersey: Citadel Press, 1979.

Ottoson, Robert. *A Reference Guide to the American Film Noir, 1940–1958.* Metuchen, New Jersey: Scarecrow Press, 1981.

Overbey, D. Interview. *Take One,* May 1978.

Parish, James Robert. *The Great Gangster Pictures.* Metuchen, New Jersey: Scarecrow Press, 1987.

Parish, James Robert, *The Tough Guys.* New Rochelle, New York: Arlington House, 1976.

Parish, James Robert, and Alvin H. Marill. *The Cinema of Edward G. Robinson.* New York: A. S. Barnes, 1972.

Parish, James Robert, and Don E. Stanke. *The Leading Ladies.* New Rochelle, New York: Arlington House, 1977.

Parish, James Robert, and Michael R. Pitts, with Gregory W. Mank. *Hollywood on Hollywood.* Metuchen, New Jersey: Scarecrow Press, 1978.

Parish, James Robert, and Steven Whitney. *Vincent Price Unmasked.* New York: Drake, 1974.

Parsons, Louella. "Portrait of an Artist." *New York Journal-American,* March 22, 1959.

Peary, Dany, ed., and Leonard Spigelgass. *Close Up, the Movie Star Book.* New York: Workman Publishing, 1979.

Peary, Gerald, ed. *Little Caesar.* Madison, Wisconsin: University of Wisconsin Press, 1981.

Penzler, Otto. *101 Greatest Films of Mystery and Suspense.* New York: Simon & Schuster, 2000.

Phillips, Dee. "Little Caesar Was a Big Man." *Photoplay,* June 1973.

Pickard, Roy. *The Award Movies.* New York: Schocken Books, 1981.

Pickard, Roy. *The Oscars from A to Z.* New York: Taplinger Publishing Company, 1978.

Pohl, Frederik, and Frederik Pohl IV. *Science Fiction: Studies in Film.* New York: Ace Books, 1981.

Porfirio, Robert, Alair Silver, and James Ursini, editors. *Film Noir Reader 3.* New York: Limelight Editions, 2002.

Portrait. *Life,* March 1, 1948.

Portrait. *Saturday Review*, April 13, 1957.

Portrait. *Theatre Arts Monthly*, April, 1929.

Price, Victoria. *Vincent Price: A Daughter's Biography.* New York: St. Martin's Griffin, 1999.

Quirk, Lawrence J. *Claudette Colbert, an Illustrated Biography.* New York: Crown, 1985.

Ragan, David. *Who's Who in Hollywood 1900–1976.* New Rochelle, New York: Arlington House, 1976.

"Return of Robinson." *Life*, February 27, 1956.

Ringgold, Gene. *The Films of Rita Hayworth.* Secaucus, New Jersey: Citadel Press, 1974.

Robinson, Edward G. "A Lesson I learned from Life." *Parade*, April 25, 1965.

Robinson, Edward G. "A Man Should Have a Sideline." *Parade*. November 22, 1958.

Robinson, Edward G., with Leonard Spigelgass. *All My Yesterdays.* New York: Hawthorn Books, 1973.

Robinson, Edward G., Jr., with William Dufty. *My Father — My Son.* New York: Frederick Fell, 1958.

Robinson, Jane. *Edward G. Robinson's World of Art.* New York: Harper & Row, 1971.

"Robinson Pictures." *Newsweek*, January 21, 1956.

"Robinson Wins Film Guild Award." *Los Angeles Times*, November 12, 1969.

"Robinsons Arrange Settlement." *The New York Times*, August 4, 1956.

"Robinsons Divorced." *The New York Times*, August 7, 1956.

Roman, Robert. "Edward G. Robinson." *Films in Review,* August-September 1966.

Rose, Frank. *The Agency, William Morris and the Hidden History of Show Business.* New York: Harper/Collins, 1995.

Rosow, Eugene. *Born to Lose: The Gangster Film in America.* New York: Oxford University Press, 1978.

Royce, Brenda Scott. *Lauren Bacall, a Bio-Bibliography.* Westport, Connecticut: Greenwood Press, 1992.

Scherle, Victor, and William Turner Levy. *The Films of Frank Capra.* Seacaucus, New Jersey: Citadel Press, 1977.

Scheuer, Steven H., ed. *TV Key Movie Guide.* New York: Bantam Books, 1966.

Schickel, Richard. *James Cagney, a Celebration.* Boston, Massachusetts: Little, Brown, 1985.

Schickel, Richard. *Movies: The History of an Art and an Institution.* New York: Basic Books, 1964.

Schildkraut, Joseph. *My Father and I.* New York: Viking Press, 1959.

Sennett, Ted. *Great Movie Directors.* New York: Harry N. Abrams / AFI Press, 1986.

Shipman, David. *The Great Movie Stars.* New York: St. Martin's Press, 1969.

Silver, Alain, and James Ursini. *Film Noir Reader.* New York: Limelight Editions, 1996.

Silver, Alain, and Elizabeth Ward, editors, and Robert Porfirio, Joan Cohen, and Carl Macek (contributors). *Film Noir: An Encyclopedic Reference to the American Style.* Woodstock, New York: Overlook Press, 1979.

Sinclair, Andrew. *John Ford.* New York: Dial press, 1979.

Skelton, Scott, and Jim Benson. *Rod Serling's Night Gallery, an After-Hours Tour.* Syracuse, New York: Syracuse University Press, 1999.

Skinner, R. Dana. "*Little Giant* and Mr. Robinson." *The Commonweal*, June 16, 1933.

Smith, Ella. *Starring Miss Barbara Stanwyck.* New York: Crown, 1985.

Sperber, A.M., and Eric Lax. *Bogart.* New York: William Morrow, 1997.

Sperling, Cass Warner, and Cork Millner, with Jack Warner, Jr. *Hollywood Be Thy Name: The Warner Brother Story.* Rocklin, California: Prima Publishing, 1994.

Steinberg, Cobbett. *Reel Facts: The Movie Book of Records.* New York: Random House, 1978.

Strout, Dick. Interview. *Touch*, February 1974.

Taylor, Al, and Sue Roy. *Making a Monster.* New York, Crown, 1980.

Terrace, Vincent. *Television Specials.* Jefferson, North Carolina: McFarland, 1995.

Thomas, Tony. *The Films of the Forties.* Seacaucus, New Jersey: Citadel Press, 1975.

Thomson, David. *A Biographical Dictionary of Film.* New York: William Morrow, 1976.

Thomson, David. *Rosebud, the Story of Orson Welles.* New York: Alfred A. Knopf, 1996.

Tosches, Nick. *Dino: Living High in the Dirty Business of Dreams.* New York: Doubleday, 1992.

Truitt, Evelyn Mack. *Who Was Who On Screen.* New York: R.R. Bowker, 1983.

Tuska, Jon. *The American West on Film.* Westport, Connecticut: Greenwood Press, 1985.

Vermilye, Jerry. *The Fillms of the Thirties.* Seacaucus, New Jersey: Citadel Press, 1982.

Victor, Adam. *The Marilyn Encyclopedia.* Woodstock, New York: Overlook Press, 1999.

Wallis, Hal, and Charles Higham. *Starmaker.* New York: Macmillan, 1980.

"Wasn't Suicide Try: Robinson." *New York Daily Mirror,* April 26, 1956.

Whitman, Alden. "Passing of a Gentle Tough Guy." *The New York Times*, February 3, 1973.

"Wife Granted Divorce from Robinson Jr." *Los Angeles Times*, October 15, 1955.

Wilde, Oscar. *Complete Shorter Fiction*. Oxford, England: University Press, 1979.

Williams, Lucy Chase. *The Complete Films of Vincent Price*. New York: Carol Publishing Group, 1995.

Willis, John, editor. *John Willis' Screen World, 1974*. New York: Crown, 1974.

Wlaschin, Ken. *The Illustrated Encyclopedia of the World's Great Movie Stars and Their Films — from 1900 to the Present Day*. New York: Salamander / Harmony Books, 1979.

Worrell, Denise. *Icons: Intimate Portraits*. New York: Atlantic Monthly, 1988.

Yurka, Blanche. *Bohemian Girl*. Athens, Ohio: Ohio University Press, 1970.

Zolotow, Maurice. *Billy Wilder in Hollywood*. New York: G. P. Putnam's Sons, 1977.

Index

A&E Biography (with Peter Graves) 15, 17, 48, 140, 159, 167, 189, 273, 274, 277, 311, 321, 344
Abaza, Rushti 313
Abbey Players 123, 172, 235
Abbott, Dorothy 231, 247, 326
Abbott, L. B. 42
Abbott, Michael 35
Abbott, Richard 88, 278
ABC 14, 29, 35, 154, 158, 163, 208, 236, 261, 265, 273, 277, 280, 315, 321, 340
ABC Movie of the Week 17, 236, 311
ABC Pictures Corporation/Cinerama 121, 293
ABC Savings Bond 89
ABC Theatre Company 21
Abdulla, Achmed 144
Abe Lincoln in Illinois 88, 93, 159, 209, 217
Die Abenteure des Kardinal Braun 238
The Abingdon Bible Commentary 93
The Abominable Dr. Phibes 87, 256
About Mrs. Leslie 243
Abraham Lincoln 32, 160
Abrahams, Harry 341
Absence of Malice 230
The Absent-Minded Professor 201, 348
Academy of Motion Picture Arts and Sciences 8, 10, 12, 15, 17, 18, 19, 24, 31, 36, 38, 40, 41, 43, 46, 53, 54, 56, 61, 64, 65, 66, 68, 72, 80, 83, 86, 88, 89, 90, 93, 97, 99, 104, 107, 116, 118, 123, 128, 129, 134, 135, 137, 138, 141, 142, 143, 146, 148, 149, 155, 156, 159, 160, 166, 167, 168, 169, 172, 173, 180, 182, 184, 185, 187, 188, 189, 190, 196, 197, 199, 201, 203, 206, 209, 211, 217, 218, 220, 221, 222, 223, 225, 229, 234, 236, 237, 239, 244, 245, 247, 248, 249, 254, 258, 260, 261, 269, 270, 273, 274, 276, 277, 279, 281, 282, 283, 284, 285, 286, 288, 294, 297, 298, 299, 300, 303, 310, 312, 314, 318, 320, 321, 329, 330, 335, 336, 338, 339, 340, 344, 348
Academy of Motion Picture Arts and Sciences Awards (36th) 12, 18, 34, 35, 93, 187, 201, 210, 245, 259, 286, 288, 298, 338
Academy of Motion Picture Arts and Sciences Awards (45th) 18, 19, 24, 65, 134, 145, 187, 217, 261, 288, 311, 338
Accident 38
Ace in the Hole 131, 142
Ace Trucking Co. 163, 314
Across 110th Street 180, 235
Across the Pacific 200
Act One 142
The Acting Company 159
Acting for the Camera 115
Action in the North Atlantic 220, 338
Actors and Sin 11, 20, 21, 24, 29, 31, 37, 75, 76, 94, 121, 146, 159, 235, 236, 248, 251, 255, 327
"Actor's Blood" 10, 21, 31
Actors Equity Association 211
Actors Fund of America 344
The Actor's Life, Journals 1956–1976 148, 297
Actors Studio 75, 270, 304
Acuff, Eddie 126
Ad Ogni Costo 22, 26, 139
Ada 277
Adair, Jack 177
Adam Had Four Sons 97, 208, 265, 348
Adam, Ronald 22, 170, 238, 293
Adams, Abigail 240
Adams, Bill 45
Adams, Dorothy 312
Adams, Ernie 88, 191, 282, 341
Adams, Mary 231
Adams, Mason 45
Adams, Maude 65
Adams, Ralph 262
Adams, Stanley 22, 147
Adams, Victor 184
Adam's Rib 115, 138, 148, 336
Adamson, James 108
Adare, Larry and Robin 76, 258
The Addams Family 169
The Adding Machine 5, 22, 41, 94, 101, 118, 140, 141, 198, 220, 253, 269, 288, 314, 339, 348
Adler, David 117
Adler, Ernest 215
Adler, Jacob 23
Adler, Jane *see* Sidney, Jane
Adler, Jay 22, 23, 165, 331
Adler, Luther 10, 23, 41, 76, 157, 158, 287, 337
Adler, Stella 23, 337
The Admirable Crichton 336
Adonis 103
Adrian 181
Adrian, Iris 345
Adventures of Captain Marvel 302
Adventures of Don Juan 57
The Adventures of Huckleberry Finn 223, 285
The Adventures of Marco Polo 118
The Adventures of Robin Hood 90, 142, 217, 334, 339
Adventures of Robinson Crusoe, The 235
The Adventures of Tom Sawyer 169
Advise and Consent 29, 36, 128, 185, 211
Affair in Trinidad 280
An Affair to Remember 180
Affairs of Cellini 221, 348
AFI Fest 2000 255
The African Queen 46, 54, 148, 221, 298
AFRS (Armed Forces Radio Station) 82, 202, 332
"After You've Gone" 223, 268, 327
Afton, Effie 215

357

Index

Against All Odds 329
Agee, James 41, 109
Agnes of God 169
The Agony and the Ecstasy 149
Aguirre: The Wrath of God 179
Ah, Wilderness! 201, 315
Ainsley, Norman 103
Air Force 58, 144, 159, 271
Air Patrol 244
Airmail 201
Airplane 57, 230
Airport 49, 146, 208
Airport 1975 349
Akins Zoe 253, 275
Akst, Harry 205
Akutagawa, Ryunosuki 241
Al Capone 38, 283, 300
The Alamo 143, 343, 344
Alaska Patrol 143
Albaugh, Robert 219
Alberghetti, Anna Maria 321
Alberni, Luis 23, 57, 312
Albert, Eddie 19, 21, 24, 103, 268
Albert, Edward 19, 24
Albert, Shirley 163
Alberts, Mal 62
Albertson, Frank 52
Albertson, Grace 220
Albertson, Lillian 313
Albin, Andy 78, 209
Alcaide, Chris 165
Alcatraz 37, 184, 185, 256, 320
Alden, Eric 313
Alden, Hortense 122
Aldon, Louis 86
Aldrich, Robert 24, 43, 44
Alex Reid & Levevre Gallery 33
Alexander, Ernie 162
Alexander Hamilton 217
Alexander, J. Grubb 144
Alexander, Jeff 129
Alexander, John 24, 231, 270, 274
Alexander the Great 38
Alexander's Ragtime Band 88
Alexandre, Alfred 246
Algiers 56, 61, 118, 159, 179, 196
Alias Boston Blackie 301
Alias Jesse James 181
Alias Jimmy Valentine 4, 24, 253, 254, 325
Alias Nick Beal 117
Alice Adams 148
Alien 180, 298
Aliens 298
Alison, David 98
All About Eve 93, 155, 180, 206, 208, 265, 270, 277, 349
All About People 24, 38, 43, 64, 128, 149, 179, 182, 229, 286
All Good Americans 248
All My Children 156, 335
All My Sons 10, 15, 18, 24, 25, 26, 61, 66, 71, 76, 83, 86, 87, 89, 94, 111, 112, 115, 121, 125, 128, 129, 130, 133, 141, 156, 172, 181, 182, 186, 188, 198, 210, 217, 221, 222, 223, 224, 227, 229, 230, 235, 248, 249, 253, 257, 267, 268, 280, 292, 294, 304, 309, 328, 332, 335, 345
All My Sons (Broadway) 79
"All My Sons" (radio) 26, 264, 272, 280
"All My Tomorrows" 152, 223
All My Yesterdays 1, 19, 26, 47, 54, 58, 59, 63, 77, 83, 92, 100, 122, 124, 157, 177, 181, 189, 191, 213, 232, 237, 245, 262, 266, 286, 287, 290, 299
"All of Me" 80
All Quiet on the Western Front 36, 40, 57, 345, 348
All-Star Feature Films Company 283
All That Money Can Buy 88, 99, 160, 302
All the Fine Young Cannibals 334
All the King's Men 80, 88, 97, 112, 141
All the President's Men 38
"All the Way" 65, 330
All the Way—A Biography of Frank Sinatra 151
All the Way Home 201
All This and Heaven, Too 56, 195, 237, 334
Allais, Charles 171
Allen, Barbara Jo 183
Allen, Casey 45
Allen, Chet 45
Allen, Dennis 185
Allen, Elizabeth 74, 209, 243
Allen, Frank 96
Allen, Fred 113, 339
Allen, Gracie 64
Allen, Harry 231
Allen, Jared 55
Allen, Lewis 26, 62, 101, 165
Allen, Marty 220
Allen, Robert 285
Allen, Steve 131, 188, 255, 300
Allen, Woody 119, 270
Allenberg, Bert 214
Allesandro, Jose 275
Allhoff, Fred 161
Alper, Murray 207, 331
Alpert, Dave 204
Alpert, Herb 49
Alpert, Hollis 214
Alter, Louis 232
Altfield, Sheldon I. 149
Alves, Joseph, Jr. 212
Alvin, John 62
"Am I Blue?" 205
The Amazing Dr. Clitterhouse 8, 27, 28, 37, 49, 53, 54, 55, 66, 72, 87, 89, 94, 106, 120, 129, 132, 134, 141, 142, 143, 145, 155, 156, 160, 167, 168, 186, 189, 195, 197, 222, 237, 243, 253, 259, 267, 274, 292, 300, 305, 309, 321, 323, 335, 339
"The Amazing Dr. Clitterhouse" (radio) 28, 159, 180, 263
Ambassador Theatre 204, 262
Ambler, Eric 115
Ameche, Don 254, 266
America Calling 28, 263, 286
America the Beautiful 328
America 3000 166
American Academy of Dramatic Arts 4, 20, 28, 32, 57, 111, 122, 138, 163, 233, 245, 250, 251, 253, 255, 279, 344
American Airlines 165
American Cancer Society 35, 65, 66, 129, 130, 255, 265, 283, 337, 339, 343
The American Creed 28, 148, 286, 301
American Film 43, 109
American Film Institute 3, 53, 93, 107, 255, 292, 298
American Graffiti 328
American Idea: The Land 29, 128, 311, 330
An American in Paris 128, 135, 217
American-International Pictures 29, 121
American Legion 82, 193
American Nazi Bund 85
American Overture for Band 328
American Red Cross 264, 266
American Salute 328
American Stair-Glide Corporation 23, 145
American Theatre: A Chronicle of Comedy and Drama, 1914–1930 232
An American Tragedy 217
American West on Film 74
American Youth for Democracy 110
Americans We 328
Ames, Jean 183
Ames, Leon 287
Ames, Robert 29, 181, 301
Ames, Winthrop 218
Amfitheatrof, Daniele 157, 327
Amitar, Chaim 228
Amos 'n' Andy 29, 263
Amphitryon 38 199
Amy, George 177, 282
Anastasia 61, 195, 226
Anatomy of a Murder 32, 260, 301
Anchors Aweigh 79, 237, 286, 304
Ancona, Tony 92
And Justice for All 304
"...And Son" 11, 29, 55, 71, 129, 310
And Then There Were None 123, 160
Anders, Rudolph 21, 29, 85, 258
Andersen, Hans Christian 293
Anderson, Bob 340

Index

Anderson, Carl 318, 332
Anderson, Eddie "Rochester" 29, 199, 277, 306
Anderson, George 109
Anderson, Glenn E. 278
Anderson, Herbert 105
Anderson, Howard A. 233
Anderson, James 332
Anderson, Judith 10, 11, 29, 186, 266, 312
Anderson, Katherine 318
Anderson, Lindsay 22
Anderson, Lloyd 295
Anderson, Mary 103
Anderson, Maxwell 10, 83, 173
Anderson, Milo 27, 167, 183, 207
Anderson, Warner 29, 332
Andor, Paul 85, 333; see also Voigt, Jon
Andre, Anthony 137
Andre, Carl 332
Andre, Carmen 341
Andre, E. J. 313
Andrejew, Andrew 238
Andren, Jean 167
Andrews, Clark 45
Andrews, Dana 280
Andrews, Edward 29, 138
Andrews, Julie 18, 19
Andrews, Loretta 194
Andrews, Tige 187
Andrews, Tod 243
Androcles and the Lion 5, 30, 49, 57, 65, 82, 87, 113, 115, 140, 150, 155, 187, 189, 220, 234, 235, 251, 253, 255, 285, 314, 320
The Andromeda Strain 244
The Angel and the Badman 276
The Angel Levine 167, 329, 334
Angel on My Shoulder 338
Angels in the Outfield 269
Angels Over Broadway 41, 146
Angels with Dirty Faces 65, 90, 111, 138
Angiolillo, Luciana 139
Angold, Edit 324
Angren, Herb 235
Angus, Donald 75
Anheuser-Busch, Inc. 23, 47
Animal Crackers 143
The Animals 46
Ankrum, Morris 31, 69, 306, 307
Ann-Margret 13, 31, 76, 78
Anna and the King of Siam 269
Anna Christie 90, 128, 156, 197, 249, 314, 348
Anna Karenina 130
Anna Lucasta 93, 179, 243
Annabella 18
Annakin, Ken 46
Anne of the Thousand Days 260, 305, 334
Annie Get Your Gun 33, 65, 79, 196, 217, 225, 286
Annie Hall 271

Annie Oakley 130, 237, 299
Annunziato, John 206
Another Woman 274
Another World 42
Ansara, Michael 49, 312
ANTA Theatre 100, 215
Anthiel George 21
Anthony, Carl 253
Anthony, Frank 27
Anthony, Tom 138
Anthony Adverse 23, 134, 141, 329
Antiseri, Frank 275
Antoinette Perry (Tony) Awards 18, 31, 32, 36, 37, 38, 130, 179, 222, 319
Antony and Cleopatra 142
"Any Bonds Today?" 320
Any Given Sunday 149
Anything Goes 134, 199
Anzell, Hy 206
Aoki, Isa 245
Aoki, Junko 224
Apache 31
Apache Drums 130, 244
Apache Uprising 244
The Apartment 188, 201, 202, 300, 334, 344
Apfel, Oscar 32, 125
Appel, Victor 21
Applause 37
The Apple Dumpling Gang 221
Apple Sauce 195
Appleby, Dorothy 207
Appointment in Berlin 71
"April Showers" 180, 224
Arabian Knights 180
Aragno, Riccardo 46
Arashi, K. 245
Arbo, Manuel Asins 202
L'Arbre Mort 33
Arbury, Guy 92
Archer, William and Charles 246
Archerd, Bernard 293
Archive Films 190
Arco, Louis 104
Ardell, Franklyn 123, 158
Ardell, Maxine 158
Arden, Eve 32, 207
Ardia Pinnucia 238
Aref, Fouad 312
Argus, Edwin 291
Ariel Records 307
Arizona 277
The Arkansas Traveler 79, 244
Arkoff, Samuel Z. 29
Arlen, Harold 32, 205
Arlen, Richard 198, 223, 317
Arlen, Roxanne 165
Arliss, George 5, 20, 28, 32, 83, 94, 102, 252, 253, 308
Armbruster, Robert 78, 204, 237, 250, 277, 321
Armetta, Henry 181
Armour, J. Ogden 32, 48, 162
Armour, Philip Danforth 32

Armour and Company 32
Arms and the Man 4, 27, 32, 47, 49, 57, 58, 69, 120, 141, 143, 167, 226, 286, 334
Arms and the Woman 27, 219, 287; see also *Mr. Winkle Goes to War*
Armstrong, Louis 299
Armstrong, Paul 24
Armstrong, Robert 33, 219
Army Air Force 87
Arno, Sig 306
Arnold, Billy 177, 184
Arnold, Edward 9, 33, 223, 230, 277, 280, 286, 327, 336
Arnold, Frank 126
Arnold, Jack 135
Arnold, Phil 272
Around the World in 80 Days 67, 210, 234, 273
Arrowsmith 137, 182
Arsene Lupin 87
Arsenic and Old Lace 24, 136, 171, 182, 209, 210, 270, 274
Arthur, Beatrice 19
Arthur, Chester A. 256, 287
Arthur, Jean 7, 34, 81, 186, 197, 249, 268, 341, 342, 343, 345
Artists and Models 32
Artkino 17, 222
As Thousands Cheer 72
Asbjornsen 245
Asbury, Herbert 40
Ash, Jerry 113
Ashby, Hal 78
Ashe, Cliff 215
Ashe, Warren 97, 203, 208
Asher, H. M. 113, 242
Asheroff, Mischa 34, 228
Ashkenzai, Schmuel 70
Ashley, Joel 313
Ashton, Herbert 60
Asner, Edward 14, 34, 236
The Asphalt Jungle 64, 65, 160, 168, 172, 186
Associate Federation of Radio and Televison Artists (AFTRA) 211
Associated First National 120, 123
Associated Press (AP) 50, 269
Asta 30, 161
Astaire, Adele 195, 280
Astaire, Fred 69, 72, 195, 261, 273
Astor, Burt 212
Astor, Mary 5, 7, 34, 35, 57, 64, 72, 76, 81, 86, 113, 186, 193, 194, 197, 204, 205, 249, 287, 345
Astoria Studios 6
Astra Film Corporation 32
At This Very Moment 35, 156
At War with the Army 208
Atkins, Norma 70
Atkins, Violet 320
Atkinson, Brooks 213, 216
Atlantic Films 120, 316
Atlantic Monthly 206, 292

Index

Atlantis the Lost Continent 252
Attenborough, Richard 9, 35, 169, 170
Atwater, Barry 233
Audley, Eleanor 229
August, Joseph 341
Augustian, Ida 76, 284
"Auld Lang Syne" 224
Auntie Mame 335
Aureli, Andrea 46
Austin, J. W. 270
Austin, Lois 167
Austin, Rene 306
Austin, Tracy 49
Austin, William 307
The Autobiography of Theodore Bikel 340
Autry, Gene 331
Avant le Theatre 7
Avery, Fred (Tex) 155
Awake and Sing! 68
The Award Movies 66
The Awful Truth 90
Axelrod, George 18
Aylesworth, Arthur 205
Ayres, Lemuel 337
Ayres, Lew 36, 113

"B" Pictures 11, 36, 50, 62, 83, 146, 213, 311
Babbish, Andrew 220
Babbitt 175, 201
Babes in Arms 90, 175
Baby Doll 203, 320, 334
Baby Face Nelson 114
Bac, Andre 238
Bacall, Lauren 10, 28, 37, 54, 154, 173, 175, 218, 249, 254
Bach, Bob 339
Bachelin, Franz 231
The Bachelor and the Bobby Soxer 267
Bachelor Father 129
Bachelor Mother 54
The Bachelor Party 169
Bachman, Charles A. 341
Back Street 56, 211
Back to the Future 298
Backer, William A. 320
Backstairs at the White House 326
Backus, Jim 220, 247
Bacon, Irving 27, 37, 104, 167
Bacon, James 50, 51
Bacon, Lloyd 37, 59, 101, 183, 290, 335
The Bad and the Beautiful 110, 119, 135, 273
The Bad Guys 62, 342
The Bad Seed 79, 188
Baer, John 29
Baer, Parley 137, 204
Baggett, Lynn 207
Bailey, Anne Howard 344
Bailey, Robert 308

Bain, Babette 313
Bain, Barbara 215
Bainter, Fay 113, 254
Bakalyan, Richard 229, 272
Baker, Carroll 13, 38, 73, 74
Baker, Diane 13, 14, 37, 102, 236, 258
Baker, Elsie 38, 138, 345
Baker, Herbert 44
Baker, Jack 170, 172
Baker, Jean 173
Baker, Stanley 38, 340
Baker, Ted 185
Baker, Tommy 60
Bakken, Vicki 313
Bakshy, Alexander 232
Balcon, Sir Michael 55
Baldwin, Earl 59, 290, 327, 343
Baldwin, Walter 38, 74, 99, 111, 219
Ball, Lucille 24, 38, 49, 97, 154, 199, 254, 274, 321, 331, 341
Ball of Fire 112, 130, 137, 144, 168, 299, 320, 344
Ballantine, E. J. 38, 232, 308
Ballard, Elmer 191
Ballard, Shirley 167
Ballard, Terry 295
Ballerino, Cecil 219
Balmain, Pierre 324
Balsam, Martin 11, 14, 76, 215, 236, 249, 252
Banco 5, 38, 57, 71, 82, 199, 253, 300
Bancroft, Anne 18
Bancroft, Ford 176
The Band Wagon 72
Bandierle, Phil 212
Banjo on My Knee 339
The Bank Dick 149
Bankhead, Tallulah 274
Banks, Lionel 97, 161, 219
Banky Vilma 6, 38, 41, 180, 181, 186, 248
Banner, John 258
Bannerman, R. Leroy 106, 336
Bannon, Bonnie 194
Bannon, Jim 138
Bannon, Julie 237, 347
Banton, Travis 278
Baracco, Adriano 238
Baragli, Nino 139
Barbary Coast 7, 17, 18, 26, 38, 39, 40, 47, 49, 53, 57, 66, 71, 83, 87, 88, 97, 100, 107, 120, 128, 132, 133, 134, 137, 144, 146, 155, 156, 172, 178, 186, 195, 198, 200, 202, 203, 210, 211, 222, 224, 230, 234, 235, 239, 248, 251, 259, 268, 304, 314, 327
The Barber of Seville 28, 249
Barclay, Don 177, 183
Barclay, Joan 194
Barclay, Marie-Christine 238
Bardette, Trevor 52, 201, 308

The Barefoot Contessa 54, 197, 206, 300
Barefoot in the Park 56
Baretta 52
Bar-Illan, David 70, 71
Bari, Lynn 9, 40, 186, 198, 249, 250, 307, 345
Barker, Bob 49
Barker, Jess 40, 145, 278
Barker, Warren 208
Barnes, Billy 185
Barnes, George 53, 327
Barnett, Griff 208
Barnett, Sanford 98, 175, 203, 347
Barnett, Vince 40, 317
Barr, Byron 40, 108
Barr, Ken 92
Barr, Tim 126
Barr, Tony 115
Barragar, Nathan 331
Barrat, Robert 41, 91, 163
Barrett, Beatrice 126
Barrett, Sweet Emma 78, 298
The Barretts of Wimpole Street 314
Barricade 268, 281
Barrie, John 293
Barrie, Wendy 90, 161, 186, 268
Barrier, Edgar 126
Barrington, Lewis 22
Barron, Baynes 313
Barron, Jack 111
Barron, Patricia 75
Barry, Donald 184
Barrymore, Ethel 5, 41, 82, 156, 252, 275
Barrymore, Georgiana Drew 41
Barrymore, John 41, 80, 140, 156, 208, 271, 280
Barrymore, Lionel 10, 37, 41, 154, 156, 173, 175, 249, 277, 280, 286, 331, 336
Barrymore, Maurice 41
Barsha, Leon 62
Bartell, Harry 51
Barthelmess, Richard 5, 41, 57, 159, 287, 301
Bartlett, Elise 22, 41, 123, 246
Bartlett, Martine 258
Barto, Pat 295
Barton, Bernard 187
Barton, Dan 148
Barton, Frank 98, 231
Barton, John 277
Barwald, William H. 253
Basehart, Richard 106
Basevi, James 308
Bash, Michael E. 206
Bassermann, Albert 41, 102, 103, 104
Bassing, Robert 29
Bassler, Robert 308
The Bat 221
Bataan 309
Bates, Charles P. 116

Bates, Granville 59
Batista, Henry 325
Batman 14, 41, 42, 142, 211, 273, 310, 326
"Batman's Satisfaction" 41, 42, 234, 310
Battle Cry 130
Battleground 338
Battlestar Gallactica 140
The Battling Bellhop 26, 178, 268
Batya 166
Bau, Gordon C. 147, 165, 272
Bauchens, Anne 17, 312
Baur, Frank 148
Baur, Jack 295
Baxter, Alan 184
Baxter, Anne 11, 18, 42, 186, 248, 312
Baxter, George 21
Baxter, John 178, 323
Baxter, Les 55
Baxter, Warner 301
Bay, Victor 307
Bayard, Beatrice 176
Bayhi, Chester 42, 212
Baylor, Hal 51
Baylor, Steve 247, 248
Bazzocchi, Loris 202
BBC (British Broadcasting Corporation) 15, 48, 154, 160, 168, 189, 190, 256, 265, 277, 299, 334
Beach, Brandon 346
Beal, John 42, 66, 154, 161
Beal, Royal 99
Beard, Matthew 301
Beasley, Byron 116
Beasley, James 346
The Beat Generation 274
The Beatles 277
Beau Geste 51, 88, 107, 142, 225, 243, 300, 338
Beauchamp, Clem 266
Beaumont, Hugh 219
The Beautiful Liar 211
The Beauty Part 248
The Beaux' Stratagem 325
Beavers, Louise 42, 63, 184, 242
"Because of You" 280
Bechi, Robo 332
Bechtel, William 181
Beck, A. S. 92
Beck, Reginald 170
Becket 237, 334
Beckman, John 147
Becky Sharp 61, 80, 156
The Bed Sitting Room 283
Beddoe, Don 327
Bedell, Austin 346
Bedtime for Bonzo 265, 332
Beecher, Janet 42, 76, 326
Beer, Jacqueiline 258
Beery, Noah 268, 281
Beery, Wallace 97, 280, 301
Beethoven, Ludwig van 224

Beetlejuice 287
Beetley, Samuel E. 295
Beetson, Frank 74, 233, 266
Begley, Ed 18, 42, 116, 339
Begley, Ed, Jr. 42
Behm, Mark 246
Behring, Dr. Emil von 215 104, 105, 180
Being There 201
Bekassy, Stephen 247
Bela, Nick 191, 291
Belack, Doris 215
Belafonte, Harry 35, 146
Belarsky, Sidor 70
Belasco, David 144, 254
Belding, Richard 212
Bell, James 51
Bell, Kay 313
Bell, Monta 113, 153
Bell, Olive 306
Bell, Rodney 277
Bell, Spencer 291
A Bell for Adano 86, 255, 268
The Bell Jar 167
Bell Sisters 237
Bellah, Ross 42, 318, 332
Bellamy, Earl 219
Bellamy, Ralph 8, 58, 59, 70, 81, 198, 273, 337
Bellini 289
The Bells 4, 43, 172
Bells Are Ringing 304
The Bells of Conscience 4, 43, 253
The Bells of St. Mary's 344
Belzer, Rick 206
Ben-Ami, Jacob 5, 43, 101, 136, 163, 276, 337
Ben Casey 167
Ben Gurion, David 70, 166
Ben-Hur 148, 314
Benaderet, Bea 203, 208
Benchley, Peter 43
Benchley, Robert 43, 126, 273
Bendtsen, France 218
Benedict, Brooks 341
Benedict, Jean 290
Benedict, William 184, 327, 343
Benet, Stephen Vincent 99, 189, 337
Bengal Tiger 268
Bennett, Barbara 43
Bennett, Constance 43, 274
Bennett, Gertrude 327
Bennett, Jill 322
Bennett, Joan 9, 10, 34, 36, 43, 67, 141, 178, 186, 189, 198, 223, 249, 254, 255, 259, 273, 274, 277, 278, 309, 345, 346, 347
Bennett, Julie 165
Bennett, Leila 317
Bennett, Richard 43
Bennett, Robert Russell 163, 224, 328
Bennett, Russell 122
Bennett, Sanford 208

Bennington, William 237
Benny, Jack 24, 29, 43, 72, 131, 148, 199, 209, 220, 277
Benny the Gouge 63
Benoit, Mary 313
Benoit, Patricia 215
Bensalt, Al 346
Benson, Archie 92
Benson, Frank 40
Benson, Jim 211, 212
Benson, John 293
Benson & Hedges 92
Bentley Productions 187
Benton, Curtis 177
Benton, Dean 98
Benton, Robert R. 241, 295
Benussi, Femi 46
Berardino, John 43, 284
Beregi, Oscar 43, 187
Beregi, Oscar, Sr. 43
Berenson, Marisa 19
Beresford, Harry 322
Berg, Gertrude 196, 274
Bergamonti, Rossella 202
Bergen, Candice 19
Bergen, Edgar 99, 146
Berger, Henning 96, 253
Bergere, Ouida 32
Bergman, Alan & Marilyn 208, 243
Bergman, Hjalmar 79, 96
Bergman, Ingmar 283
Bergman, Ingrid 28
Bergson, Peter 337
Berkeley, Busby 14, 222, 235, 329
Berkes, Johnny 240
Berle, Milton 61, 131, 274
Berlin, Irving 274, 320
Berlin, Mrs. Irving 274
Berlin Film Festival 228
Berman, Pandro S. 258
Bern Kunsthalle 33
Bernard, Herb 21
Bernard, Jan 185
Bernard, Joseph 306, 341
Bernardi, Herschel 298
Bernardi, Tom 220
Berne, Jack R. 152
Bernhardt, Eve 272
Berns, Irving 266
Bernstein, Aline 227
Bernstein, Elmer 166, 298, 312
Bernstein, Herman 75
Bernstein, Leonard 337
Bernstein-Cohen, Miriam 228
Berntzen, Rolf 293
Berthelot, Jean 212
Bertholon, George 147
Berti, Dehl 313
Besh-Fekete, Ladislas 247
Best, Edna 43, 103, 186, 198, 345
Best, Willie 52
The Best Little Whorehouse in Texas 228
The Best Man 32, 210

Best Plays of 1919–1920 232
Best Plays of 1921–1922 24, 96
Best Plays of 1924–1925 122
Best Plays of 1925–1926 30, 75, 203
Best Plays of 1926–1927 171
Best Plays of 1955–1956 216
The Best Years of Our Lives 38, 54, 137
Beth El Cemetery 15, 131
"The Betrothed" 43, 163, 311, 314
Bette: The Life of Bette Davis 178
Bettman Archive 190
Betty Boop 125
Between Two Worlds 115, 269
Betz, Matthew 242
Beuerman, Gus 116
Beulah 42
Beverly Hilton Hotel 190
Bewitched 221
Bezzerides, A. L. 62
Biberman, Abner 254
Bice, Robert 313
Bickenbach, Richard 154
Bicknell, Dorothy 122
The Bicycle Thief 97
The Big Apple 90, 268
The Big Broadcast 66, 321
The Big Carnival 344
The Big Cat 209
The Big Circus 273
Big City Blues 179
The Big Clock 117, 185, 202, 321
The Big Country 245
The Big Easy 186
The Big Heat 53, 129, 169, 182, 234, 280, 344
Big Jack 277
The Big Knife 24, 199, 298, 300
Big Leaguer 11, 24, 37, 43, 44, 45, 49, 71, 87, 90, 118, 121, 132, 135, 150, 167, 196, 199, 210, 235, 251, 269, 299, 330
The Big Payoff 223
The Big Pond 72
The Big Shot 150
The Big Sky 95
The Big Sleep 37, 54, 70, 86, 144, 320, 334, 339
Big Town 8, 27, 44, 52, 61, 69, 71, 112, 116, 134, 172, 196, 222, 227, 230, 235, 244, 251, 262, 270, 321
The Big Trail 334
The Big Trees 61
Big Valley 197, 298
The Biggest Bundle of them All 13, 23, 45, 46, 47, 66, 67, 80, 82, 90, 97, 106, 121, 128, 133, 134, 139, 223, 235, 251, 268, 320, 334, 338
Bikel, Theodore 13, 46, 70, 71, 298, 340
Bill, Tony 229
A Bill of Divorcement 42, 148, 149, 300

Bill of Rights 273
Billboard 106
Billy the Kid 172
Billy Wilder 108
Billy Wilder in Hollywood 107
Bindi, Clara 46
Bing, Herman 40, 287
Binns, Edward 47, 331
Binyon, Claude 247
Biography with Peter Graves 189; see also A&E Biography
Bird, H. L. 55
Birdman of Alcatraz 141, 182, 208, 270, 277, 339
The Birds 309
Biroc, Joseph 66, 233, 331
The Birth of a Nation 53, 89, 208, 334
Bischoff, Robert 306
Bischoff, Samuel 62, 69, 177, 290
Bishop, Joey 246
The Bishop's Wife 234
Bissell, Whit 49, 295, 311
The Bitch 277
Bitter Sweet 283
The Bitter Tea of General Yen 298
Bjornsterne, Bjorson 283, 293
Black, Arthur S. 152
Black, Martin 308
Black, Maurice 49, 50, 191, 291
Black Bart 169
Black Beauty 97
The Black Cat 68, 171
The Black Clock 8, 34
Black, Frank & Orchestra 72
Black Girl 326
Black Fury 88
Black Jack 235
Black Legion 155, 197
Black Narcissus 66
Black Tuesday 1, 11, 37, 50, 51, 53, 66, 67, 80, 86, 94, 121, 130, 132, 133, 134, 135, 140, 169, 172, 186, 235, 244, 256, 267, 284, 300, 301, 327
Black Widow 265, 273
Blackboard Jungle 129, 276
Blacklisting: Movies 118
Blackmail 8, 36, 51, 52, 55, 71, 75, 80, 87, 89, 90, 119, 120, 121, 128, 135, 135, 141, 150, 155, 159, 168, 172, 186, 196, 197, 199, 211, 217, 222, 235, 249, 250, 251, 255, 256, 336, 344, 345, 348
Blackman, Don 51
Blackmer, Sidney 34, 52, 184, 191
Blackwood, George 91, 163
Blair, Barbara 205
Blair, Janet 331
Blake, George 118, 177
Blake, Gladys 231
Blake, Jonathan 288
Blake, Robert (Bobby) 49, 52, 75, 76, 148, 345
Blakeley, James 42

Blakelock, Ralph 33
Blanc, Annie Marie 247
Blanc, Mel 159, 167, 262
Blanchard, Marie 173
Blane, Sally 52, 62, 348
Blangsted, Folmar 147
Blanke, Henry 103, 163, 259, 282
Blankfort, Henry 306
Blau, Bela 137
Bleich, Julius 163
Blees, Robert 135
Bletcher, Billy 98
Blind Alley 52, 88, 134, 141, 166, 180, 251, 263, 264
"Blind Alley" (radio) 52
The Blind Cattle King 276
Bliss, Lela 144, 248
Blithe Spirit 89
The Blob 210
Block, Haskell M. 232, 245
Block, Ralph 91, 200
Blocker, Dan 49
Une Blonde de Pekin 26, 52, 247
The Blonde from Peking 52, 247
Blonde Venus 100
Blondell, Joan 7, 13, 14, 53, 63, 64, 77, 78, 91, 166, 186, 197, 209, 222, 226, 244, 268
Blondie 159
Blood Alley 180
Blood and Sand 225
Blood on the Sun 196
Bloodline 301
Bloom, Claire 13, 53, 241, 298
Blossoms in the Dust 135, 135, 159
Blotz, Raymond, Jr. 331
Blue, Monte 53, 173
"The Blue Albatross" 53, 80, 141, 265
The Blue Angel 99
The Blue Bird 142
The Blue Dahlia 70, 93, 118, 180, 256
"The Blue Danube" 224
Blue Denim 159
The Blue Veil 53, 320, 348
Bluebeard 68, 244
The Blues Brothers 66
Blum, Gustav 147
Blume, Robert R. 206
Blumenstock, Morton 153
Blunt, John 200
Blystone, Jasper 308
Blystone, Stanley 314
Boardman, Truman 117
Bob & Carol & Ted & Alice 300
The Bob Cummings Show 89
Boccianti, Alberto 139
Bodalo, Jose 202
Bodner, Sadie 237
Body and Soul 99
The Body Snatchers 171
Boehm, Sydney 53, 131, 146, 284
Bogart 174, 175, 249
Bogart, Humphrey 3, 7, 8, 10, 20,

Index

27, 28, 37, 47, 53, 54, 58, 59, 63, 64, 81, 89, 112, 113, 118, 119, 148, 154, 173, 174, 175, 177, 222, 223, 249, 254, 255, 265, 268, 270, 274, 280, 329
Bogdanovich, Peter 303
Bohem, Endre 50, 52, 231
La Boheme 246
Bohemian Girl 136
Bohnen, Roman 54, 231
Bois, Curt 27, 54, 98
Bolero 97, 265
Bolger, Ray 237
Bolsheviks 83
Bolster, Anita 126, 277
Bolton, Arthur 170
Bolton, Guy 254
Bombois, Camille 279
Bonamano, Aldo 139
Bonanova, Fortunio 54, 108, 183
Bonanza 140
Bond, Peter 200
Bond, Ward 27, 54, 84, 85, 206, 207, 222
Bonerz, Peter 326
The Bonhomme Richard 97, 98
Bonn, Walter 25
Bonnard, Pierre 8, 33
Bonnie and Clyde 141, 309
The Bonnie Parker Story 260
Bono, Sonny 19
Bookbinder, Robert 27, 64, 174
Boom Town 54, 221
Boomerang 179
Boon, John A. 327
Boon, Robert 204
Boone, F. E. 199
Boone, Pat 148
Boone, Richard 12, 270
Booth, Frank M. 113
Booth, John Wilkes 334
Borboni, Paolo 46
Borden, Eugene 284
Bordertown 169
Bordman, Gerald 215, 227, 232, 252
Boren, Charles A. 19
Boretz, Alvin 298
Borg, Sven-Hugo 258
Borg, Veda Ann 177
Borge, Victor 146, 331
Borgnine, Ernest 217
Born Yesterday 88
Boros, Ferike 54, 191
Borzage, Dan 74
Bosley, Tom 12, 54, 270
"The Boss" 54, 134, 199, 263
Boss Lady 40
Boston American 145
Bosworth, Hallem 116
Bosworth, Hobart 116, 268, 281
Boteler, Wade 27, 52, 55, 184, 205, 287, 290
Bouchet, Barbara 138

Bouchey, Willis 29, 55, 74, 147, 332
Boudin, Eugebne 33
Boulle, Pierre 252
Boultin, Roy 55
Boulting, John 55, 169
Boulton, Davis 293
Bourbon Street Beat 197
Bourne, Peter 258
Bowen, Harry 341
Bowen, Sid 157
Bowerman, Frank A. 295
Bowers, William 318
Box Office 234
Boxhorn, Jerry 71
Boy, Did I Get a Wrong Number 197
Boy in the Plastic Bubble 160
Boy Meets Girl 143
Boy Slaves 209
A Boy Ten Feet Tall 12, 13, 27, 30, 47, 55, 56, 76, 80, 89, 121, 145, 157, 165, 168, 200, 202, 203, 210, 234, 235, 244, 276
Boyd, Rex 176
Boyd, William 155
Boyer, Charles 20, 56, 106, 126, 154, 259, 274, 306
Boyle, Edward 233
Boyle, Lyle 187
Boyle, Peter 19
Boyle, Robert 126
Boyne, Sunny 103
The Boys from Brazil 245
The Boys from Syracuse 265
Boys Town 118, 336
Bracey, Sidney 27, 194, 242
Bracken's World 14, 56, 160, 167, 208, 209, 230, 243, 244, 272, 310, 311, 314
Brackett, Charles 344
Bradford, Richard 56, 325
Bradley, Frank 74
Bradley, Harry 161, 194
Bradley, Jan 296
Bradley, Lee 74
Bradley, Paul 346
Bradley, Truman 225
Bradshaw, Charles 306
Brady, Ed 52
Brady, Harry 341
Brady, Scott 243
Brailowsky, Alexander 70
The Bramble Bush 275
Branagh, Kenneth 188
Branch, Houston 316, 317
Brand, Neville 67
Brando, Marlon 18, 19, 67, 99, 337
Brandon, Carolyn 189
Brandon, Cliff 238
Brandon, Henry 312
Brandon, Phil 238
Brandt, Joe 80
Brandt, Martin 258

Braque, Georges 33
Brave New World 298
The Brave One 321
Braverman Productions 295
Bray, Billy 316
Brayton, Margaret 88, 331
Breakfast at Tiffany's 22
Brecher, Egon 56, 85, 103, 105, 207
Breck Golden Showcase 56, 99, 310
Breen, Richard 18
Breese, Edmund 56, 57, 144
Bremen, Lennie 331
Brendel, Ed 301
Brennan, Walter 39, 40, 57, 83, 336
Brenner, Maurice 92
Brennon, Juliet 163
Brent, George 254, 267
Brent, Linda 272
Brent, Lynton 341
Brent, Romney 30, 57, 75, 246
Breon, Edmond 57, 345
Bretton, Ralph 271
Brewster, Carol 167
Brewster, Jimmy 184
Brewster, Katherine 195
Brewster McCloud 142
Brewster's Millions 142, 199
Brialy, Jean Claude 57, 238
The Bribe 150
Brice, Lew 322
The Bride of Frankenstein 68
Bride of the Storm 298, 300
Bridge, Alan 290
The Bridge of San Luis Rey 40, 65, 135, 187
The Bridge on the River Kwai 298
A Bridge Too Far 35
Bridges, Beau 57
Bridges, Jeff 57
Bridges, Lloyd 49, 57, 84, 98
Brierre, Maurice 341
Bright, John 222, 292
Bright Eyes 334
The Bright Shawl 5, 19, 23, 32, 35, 41, 47, 57, 58, 72, 87, 120, 123, 135, 159, 182, 198, 203, 251, 255, 271, 287, 292, 334, 335, 345
Bring, Lou & Orchestra 180
Bringing Up Baby 69, 122, 144, 148, 159, 172
Brion, Francoise 247
Brisbane, Arthur 49
Briskin, Sam 315
Brisson, Frederick 131
Bristol, Howard 21
British Lion/Bryanston–Seven Arts 55
Britton, Barbara 288
Britton, Ethel 215
Broad, Bertha 246
Broadway 167
Broadway Bill 332

Broadway Magic 253
The Broadway Melody 197
Brocco, Peter 21
Brock, J. K. 181
Brodel, Mary 162
Broderick, Johnny 48, 58, 62, 63, 150
Broderick, Robert 32
Brodie, Buster 306
Brodie, Don 58, 126, 177, 306, 341, 346
Brodkin, Herbert 285
Brodsky, Nicholas 65
Broekman, David & Orchestra 72, 242, 320
Brogan, Dorothy 148
Broken Arrow 243, 288
Broken Blossoms 41
Broken Glass 217
Broken Lance 217, 268, 334
Brolin, James 252
Bronson, Charles 268, 281
Brook, Claudio 246
Brook, Peter 33
Brooke, Clifford 218
Brooklyn Dodgers 44
Brooks, Alan 153
Brooks, Jan 138
Brooks, Jean 85
Brooks, Joe 272
Brooks, Martin E. 236
Brooks, Richard 173, 174
Brophy, Ed(ward) S. 58, 81, 97, 183, 184, 223, 249, 256, 290, 341
Brosnan, John 296
Brother Orchid 31, 34, 37, 42, 53, 58, 59, 60, 61, 67, 71, 80, 81, 88, 89, 95, 118, 120, 125, 127, 128, 133, 134, 156, 168, 172, 182, 186, 198, 200, 210, 218, 230, 235, 249, 259, 260, 267, 268, 289, 294, 329, 334, 335, 338
Brotherhood Week 28
The Brothers Karamazov 6, 23, 60, 68, 79, 101, 113, 117, 128, 165, 167, 182, 187, 196, 199, 220, 251, 253, 279, 285, 294, 314
Brotherton, Robert 33
Brown, Arthur, Jr. 187
Brown, Barry 154
Brown, Bernard B. 126, 277
Brown, Charles D. 59, 61, 97, 307
Brown, Clarence 222
Brown, Esther 313
Brown, Everett 52
Brown, Gene 23
Brown, Helen 25, 45, 51, 61, 70, 71, 308
Brown, Hillyard 25
Brown, Himan 259, 298
Brown, Hiram 321
Brown, Joe E. 91, 159, 160, 254, 301, 329, 335
Brown, John 337

Brown, Johnny 185
Brown, Johnny Mack 91
Brown, Molly 270
Brown, Pepe 236
Brown, Ray 63
Brown, Roy 63
Brown, Tom 63
The Brown Derby 57
Browning, Lynn 195
Browning, Tod 6, 61, 242
Brownlow, Kevin 32, 287
Bruce, Barbara 227
Bruce, David 95, 103, 282
Bruce, Marie 276
Bruce, Nigel 7, 61, 103, 316
Bruce, Virginia 61, 197, 198, 231
Brun, Alexander 189
Brunetti, Argentina 158
Bruning, Albert 137, 171, 185
Brunner, Robert F. 229
Bruno, Chick 63
Bruno, Frank 162
Brute Force 95
Bryan, Arthur Q. 183, 207
Bryan, Jane 61, 76, 89, 177, 198, 290
Bryan, William Jennings 270, 287
Bryant, Bill 62
Bryant, Nana 61, 122
Bryant, Paul 195
Bryant, William 138
Bryar, Claudia 209
Bryar, Paul 126, 331
Brynner, Yul 11, 61, 186, 226, 249, 312, 347
The Buccaneer 61, 88, 260
Buccella, Maria Grazia 202
Buchanan, Alice 333
Buchanan, Edgar 61, 97
Buck Benny Rides Again 29
Buck Rogers in the 25th Century 235
Buena Sera, Mrs. Campbell 300
Buena Vista 121, 229
Buffalo Bill 61
Bufman, Zeev 312
Bugs Bunny 197, 339
The Buick-Berle Show 61, 265, 274
A Bullet for Joey 11, 26, 31, 37, 47, 53, 61, 62, 83, 98, 101, 121, 133, 134, 141, 143, 164, 235, 251, 265, 268, 269, 320, 327, 330, 335, 348
Bullets or Ballots 7, 18, 35, 42, 48, 52, 53, 54, 58, 62, 63, 64, 71, 79, 88, 94, 98, 115, 118, 120, 127, 129, 132, 134, 141, 149, 150, 175, 179, 186, 195, 197, 201, 210, 217, 219, 221, 235, 237, 244, 251, 269, 301, 335
"Bullets or Ballots" (radio) 64, 154, 180, 199, 263
Bullitt 330
Bunce, Alan 270
Buono, Victor 64, 272

Bupp, Tommy 86, 290
Burch, Lou 339
Burden, Michael 313
Burgher, Fairfax 218
Burke, Billie 247
Burke, Charles E. 148
Burke, Frank 242
Burke, Johnny 30
Burks, Robert 59, 104, 173
Burlesque 156
Burne, Carol 19
Burnett, Edith 22
Burnett, W(illiam) R. 7, 64, 91, 132, 165, 190, 191, 192, 193, 194
Burns, Bob 113, 336
Burns, George 24, 64, 131, 148, 154, 209, 266, 292, 319
Burns, Lillian 286, 344
Burnside, John 248
Burnside, Norman 17, 104
Burr, Aaron 206
Burroughs, Clark 291
Burrows, Abe 154
Burt, Billy 231
Burt, Nellie 215
Burtis, James 125
Burton, Frederick 64, 65, 85, 161, 184, 287, 322
Burton, Richard 20, 220, 323
Burza, Norman 295
Bus Stop 12, 79, 118, 196, 272, 298
Busch, Niven 205
Busch, Paul 258
Bush, A. M. 163
Bush, Florence 111
Bush, James 161
Bushell, Anthony 125
Bushelman, Jeff 220
The Busy Body 168
But Not for Me 137
Butch Cassidy and the Sundance Kid 147, 230
Butler, David 167
Butler, Ed 63
Butler, John K. 187
Butler, Larry 200
Butterfield, Herb 175, 204, 283
Butterfield, Walton 147
Butterfield 8 209
Butterflies Are Free 19
Butterworth, Charles 301
Buttram, Pat 209
Buzzanca, Lando 166, 238
Buzzi, Ruth 185
By Love Possessed 142, 349
By Myself 175
"By-Products of the Atom" 65, 129, 168, 264
Bye Bye Birdie 31, 187, 304, 329
Byner, John 288
Byrd, Ralph 308
Byrne, Dolly 115
Byrne, Dorothy 330
Byrne, Francis 38
Byrne, Nancy 316

Byrnes, Harold 302
Byron, Arthur 65, 205, 341
Byron, Carol 258
Byron, Kate 218

Cabaret 19, 217
Cabin in the Cotton 41, 217, 223
Cabin in the Sky 217, 336
Caboblanco 166
Cabot, Bruce 254
Cabot, Sebastian 65, 284
Cadis, Dusty 42
Caedmon Records 206, 256
Café des Artistes 255
Caffrey Frank 312
Cage, Ruth 215
Caged 115, 221, 244
Cagney, James 3, 7, 19, 20, 21, 65, 79, 81, 116, 118, 132, 141, 223, 254, 255, 274, 286, 291, 292, 329, 339, 348
Cagney, Tim 313
Cagney by Cagney 291
Cagney, the Actor as Auteur 292
Cahn, Sammy 17, 18, 65, 152, 167, 223, 247, 271, 304, 330
Caillou, Alan 284
Cain, James M. 107, 108
Caine, Georgia 27
Caine, Michael 19
The Caine Mutiny 29, 49, 54, 118, 202, 244
Cairn, Bill 231, 280, 283
Caites, Joe 59, 60, 195, 290
Calamity Jane 94, 338
Calderon, Shmuel 228
Caldwell, Orville 30
Caldwell, Robert 44
Calhern, Louis 65, 104, 205, 223
Calhoun, Rory 65, 266
California Lutheran University 276
California Mail 175
California Melodies 65, 263
Calisti, Calisto 46
"Call Me Irresponsible" 65, 330
Call Me Madam 147, 243, 244, 294, 330, 338
Call Northside 777 54, 86, 144, 299
Call of the Wild 86, 319, 348
Call of the Yukon 217
Callahan, Mushy 118, 158
Callahan, Pepe 201
Callan, Michael 90, 247
Calleia, Joseph 52
Callender, Romaine 27, 66, 262
Calley, John 77
Calling Dr. Gillespie 61
Calloway, Cab 13, 66, 78
Calthrop, Donald 313
Calvert, E. H. 343
Calvert, Louis 22
Cambridge, Godfrey 46, 66
Camelot 196

Camel's Screen Guild Players 26, 66, 264
Cameron, Carol 75, 345
Cameron, Donald 54
Camille 87, 273, 309
Caminito 139
Camlin, Peter 138, 284
Campana, Nina 40
Campanis, Al 44, 298
Campbell, Alan 306
Campbell, Clay 137, 332
Campbell, Glen 19
Campbell, Howard 52
Campbell, William 44, 66
Campo, Pupi 152
"Camptown Races" 224
Can-Can 72
Canal Zone 244
Canaway, W. H. 210
"Cancer, Cause for Hope" 66, 129, 264
"Cancer in Men" 42, 66, 129, 264
"Cancer in Women" 66, 129, 264
Candida 142, 209, 285
Cannan, Denis 45
Cannes Film Festival 10, 18, 36, 66, 67, 157
Cannon, Dyan 19
Cannon, J. D. 325
The Cannonball Run 114
The Canterville Ghost 234
Cantinflas 12, 67, 90, 146, 223, 247
Cantor, Eddie 28, 113, 154, 331
Cantrell, Earl 219
Cantro, Bob 158
Cantway, Maxine 195
Cantzen, Conrad 333
Canudas, Federici 139
Canutt, Joe 295
Canutt, Yakima 293
Cape Fear 210
Caplan, Harry 224
Capone, Al 6, 7, 13, 48, 67, 68, 150, 185, 190, 193, 232, 261
Capps, McClure 266
Capra, Frank 12, 15, 48, 49, 68, 80, 94, 100, 101, 133, 150, 151, 154, 169, 259, 286, 308, 315, 327
Capra, Frank, Jr. 315
Capra, Lucille (Mrs. Frank) 315
Capra, Lulu and Tom 315
Capriccoli, Massimilliano 202
Captain Applejack 226
Captain Blood 90, 300, 334
Captain Eddie 40, 86, 285
Captain Horatio Horn 38
Captain Hurricane 271
Captain January 175
Captain Video 243
Captains Courageous 68, 90, 179, 210, 275, 320
Captains of the Clouds 172, 254
The Captain's Paradise 95

The Captive 211
Carden, Charles 60
Cardiff, Jack 66, 224
The Cardinal 160, 279
Career 169
Carew, James 316
Carew, Regina 177
Carey, Harry 39, 40, 68, 83, 177, 178, 274
Carey, Harry, Jr. 68, 73
Carey, Leonard 194
Carey, Leslie I. 25, 135
Carey, Macdonald 19
Carey, Tristram 54
Carfagno, Edward C. 78, 240, 295
Carillo, Leo 6, 68, 252, 301
Carl, Harry 176
Carle, Richard 181
Carleton, Claire 345
Carleton, Torey 167, 208
Carlisle, James 346
Carlon, Fran 45
Carlson, Richard 101
Carlsson, Carl 258
Carlyle Hotel 190
Carmel, Roger C. 42
Carmen 300
Carnal Knowledge 31
Carnegie Hall 106
Carnegie Lyceum Theatre 251
Carney, Art 12, 68, 155, 188, 270, 273
Carnovsky, Morris 5, 60, 68, 84, 122, 170, 227, 240, 252, 270, 314
Carothers, A. J. 229
Carousel 169, 196, 315
Carpenter, Claude 69
Carpenter, Ken 180, 204, 277, 332
Carpenter, Marion 187
The Carpetbaggers 180
Carr, Dan 74
Carr, Marian 233
Carr, Nat 207
Carr, Norman 154
Carradine, David 68
Carradine, John 11, 68, 73, 184, 312, 313
Carradine, Keith 68
Carradine, Robert 68
Carricart, Robert 272
Carrie 221, 237
Carrier, Albert 258, 324
Carroll, Albert 246
Carroll, Dihann 19
Carroll, Leo G. 13, 68, 258
Carroll, Lucia 207
Carroll, Toni 21
Carroll, Vance 341
Carruth, Milton 233, 242
Carruthers, Steve 248
Carry On Admiral 90, 319
Carson, Jack 9, 68, 69, 81, 165, 167, 183, 223, 237, 331

Index

Carson, Jill 258
Carson, Johnny 319
Carson, Robert 21, 184, 313
Carson Productions Group 190
Carter, Kay 240
Carter, Mrs. Leslie 5, 69, 186, 252, 300
Carter, Mel 325
Carter, Milton 97
Carter, Monte 341
Cartwright, Veronica 76, 340
Cartwright, William 29
Caruso, Anthony 147, 229
Carver, Tina 62, 147
Carvill, Henry 204
Casablanca 54, 90, 260, 294, 334, 339
Casanova, Eve 246
Casbah 95
Cascio, Michael 189
Case, Nelson 347
"A Case for the F.B.I." 69, 112, 263
"The Case of Kenny Jason" 11, 31, 66, 69, 87, 98, 234, 310
"A Case of Nerves" 69, 264, 305
The Case of the Black Cat 86
"The Case of the Missing Milk" 45, 263
Casey, Pat 301
Casey, Sue 167
Casino Royale 165
Cassavetes, John 28, 274
Casselberry, George 163
Cassell, Anne Frances 117
Cassell, Charles 117
Cassell, Clement 117
Cassell, Clement Comley 117, 195
Cassell, Frances 117
Cassell, Lloyd 117
Cassell, Seymour 42
Cassidy, Ted 200
Cassini, Oleg 306
Castle, Irene 32, 69
Castle, Vernon 69
Castrilli, Suni 206
Castro, Fidel 57
Caswell, Nancy 341
The Cat and the Canary 42, 234, 271
Cat on a Hot Tin Roof 90, 217, 230, 320
Cates, Joe 288
Cathcart, Daniel 184
Catlett, Walter 69, 207
Cattani, Rico 42
Catto, Max 284
Caughman, Sgt. John 163, 224, 328
Cavalcade 211
Cavalcade of America 69
Cavan, Allen 341
Cavanaugh, Hobart 91, 176
Cavanaugh, Jimmy 248
Cavender, Glen 86

C.B.C./Film Sales Company 80
CBS 11, 28, 45, 52, 54, 64, 65, 69, 80, 88, 96, 98, 111, 113, 115, 116, 127, 140, 145, 148, 155, 175, 178, 184, 199, 204, 225, 228, 237, 239, 262, 267, 270, 274, 285, 288, 305, 307, 325, 336, 339, 343, 347, 348
CBS Shakespeare Theatre 263, 307
CBS World Premiere Movie 325
Cecil, Nora 194
Ceiling Unlimited 69, 338
Celano, Guido 247
Celi, Adolpho 70, 139, 202
Cellini, Benvenuto 122, 150, 209
Centennial 228
Central Intelligence Agency (C.I.A.) 246
Century Lighting, Inc. 215
Century Theatre 206
Ceplair, Larry 158
Cerf, Bennett 274, 339
Cervantes, the Proud Rebel 329
Cesarbea, Juan 202
Cezanne, Paul 8, 33, 34, 315
Chagall, Marc 33
Chained 180
Challee, William 78
Challenor, Bromley 170
Chalmers, Helen 45
Chalmers, Thomas 241
Chamberlain, George Agnew 266
Chamberlain, Richard 35
Chambers, Joan 215
Chambers, Shirley 184
The Champ 58
Champion 110, 273, 301
Champion, Ken 262
Chandler, Eddie (Eddy) 52, 63, 98, 177, 183, 207, 341, 346
Chandler, George 91
Chandler, Jeff 26
Chandler, Lane 126, 162, 177
Chandler, Raymond 9, 17, 70, 107, 108, 344
Chaney, Lon 61, 242, 267
Chaney, Norman 301
Chang, Anna 144
Channing, Carol 24
Chanukah Festivals for Israel 42, 46, 49, 70, 71, 99, 179, 202, 211, 225, 246, 249, 252, 253, 256, 259, 260, 276, 287, 294, 299, 300, 304, 334
Chaplin, Charles 37, 53, 137, 254, 327
Chaplin, Saul 306
Chapman, Freddie 346
Chapman, Helen 231
Chapman, John 216
Chapman, Marguerite 7, 76, 97, 98
Charge of the Light Brigade 143
Charisse, Cyd 12, 72, 324
Charles, Marion 195, 296

Charles, Ray 78
Charley 53, 330
Charley's Aunt 130
Charlie Chan 40, 319
Charlie Chan at the Wax Museum 71
Charlie Chan in Panama 171
Charlie's Angels 129
Chase, Borden 97
Chase, James Hadley 246
The Chase 56, 160
Chase a Crooked Shadow 42
Chasen, Myra 206
Chauvenet, Virginia 275
Chauvin, Lilyan 324
Chayefsky, Paddy 11, 31, 48, 72, 77, 101, 196, 213, 214, 215, 216, 253
Cheaney (Cheeney), Lois 27, 290
"The Checker Player" 35, 72, 263, 321
Checkmate 65
Checkmate for MacDowell 72, 201
Chefe, Jack 306
Cheney Brothers 287
Cher 19
The Cherry Orchard 43
Chesterfield Tobacco 301
Chevalier, Maurice 72, 90, 146, 220, 223, 247, 248
Chevalier, Mike 220
Chevalier de la Legion d'Honneur 36
The Chevrolet Program 43, 72, 263
Cheyenne Autumn 13, 18, 27, 31, 38, 47, 49, 54, 66, 68, 73, 74, 76, 80, 87, 95, 121, 123, 128, 129, 132, 141, 143, 150, 169, 171, 188, 189, 198, 209, 210, 218, 220, 248, 251, 255, 256, 260, 273, 277, 279, 292, 300, 320, 335, 337, 339, 343, 348
The Cheyenne Social Club 221
Chiang Kai-shek 328
Chiang Kai-shek, Madame 328
"Chicago" 251
Chicago Art Institute 33
Chicago Herald Tribune 145, 160
Chicago Rabbinical Council 160
Chicago Stadium 145, 160
Chicago Sun Times 296
Chico and the Man 179
Chief Sitting Bull 225
The Chief Thing 6, 57, 75, 79, 82, 140, 220, 234, 253, 304, 314, 320, 339, 347
La Chienne 27, 253, 277, 278
A Child of the Century 337
Children of Darkness 209
Children's Crusade for Children 42, 76, 263
The Children's Hour 201
Childs, Monroe 333
Chilton, Frederick 30
The Chimes at Midnight 338

Index

Chin, Gum 181
China Clipper 221, 301
China Sky 335
The China Syndrome 188
Chinatown After Dark 172
Chiniquy, Gerry 262
Chiron, Andre 177
Chisholm, Frances Lundie 12, 76, 117, 272
Chitty, Erik 293
Chitty, Susan Richards 293
Chitty Chitty Bang Bang 330
Chon, Sydney 326
A Chorus Line 35
Christiani, Rita 306
Christians, Mady 25, 26, 76, 186, 198, 345
Christie, Agatha 344
Christine, Virginia 76, 186, 198, 233, 234, 236, 258, 345
A Christmas Carol 196, 206
Christmas in Connecticut 221
Christy, Ivan 341
Christy, Ken 51, 313
Chulay, John C. 229
Chung, Wong 40
Church Federation of Greater Chicago 160
Churchill, Berton 194, 322
Churchill, Sir Winston 12, 145, 292
Ciannelli, Eduardo 14, 199, 200, 339
Cichy, Martin 308
Cimarron 80
The Cincinnati Kid 13, 18, 31, 47, 53, 66, 76, 77, 78, 80, 84, 121, 128, 130, 132, 134, 154, 169, 184, 198, 199, 203, 210, 226, 235, 249, 251, 255, 260, 283, 292, 294, 298, 304, 309, 320, 338, 339
Cinema 181
The Cinema of Edward G. Robinson 44, 48, 146, 164, 236, 278
Cinema, the Magic Vehicle: A Guide to Its Achievement 85, 109, 174
CinemaScope 54, 135, 147, 152, 284, 322, 324, 332
Cinerama 121, 310
Cinerama Releasing Company (Cinerama Leasing Corp.) 293
The Circle 69, 283
Ciro's 155
The Cisco Kid 68
Citadel (Publishers) 48
Citizen Kane 54, 87, 145, 175, 190, 221, 261, 285, 301, 335, 338
Citizens Stamp Advisory Committee 255
The City 226
City Beneath the Sea 272
City Knickerbocker 215
City of Hope 208, 243, 336
Claire, Susan 293

Claire's Knee 57
Claman, Julian 137
Clampett, Robert 254, 339
Clancy, Howard 72
Clarence 198, 308, 325
Clarens, Carlos 28, 84, 292
Clark, Al 17, 247
Clark, Carroll 229, 331
Clark, Cliff 105, 207, 282
Clark, Davison 163
Clark, Ernest 293
Clark, Harvey 161
Clark, Marilyn 215
Clark, Robert 312
Clark, Roger 98
Clark, Steve 341
Clark, Wallis 163
Clark, Willis 64, 218
Clarke, Charles 308
Clarke, Gage 79, 233
Clarke, Mae 79, 205, 223
The Clash of the Titans 237
Classics of the Gangster Film 27, 64, 174
Claudia 299, 348
Claudia and David 88
Cleary, Leo 98, 203
Cleon Throckmorton, Inc. 227
Cleopatra 22, 80, 97, 150, 182, 206, 323, 343
Clesi Cinematografica 246
Cleveland, Grover 270
Cliff, John 61, 165, 229
Cliffe, Alice Belmore 30, 75
Cliffe, H. Cooper 32
Clifford, Dr. Hubert 238
Clifford, Jack 262
Climax! 11, 115, 182, 310, 329
Cline, Edward 343
Cline, Wilfred M. 167, 187
Clive of India 68, 115, 135, 196, 273
Close Encounters of the Third Kind 298
Clothier, William 18, 66, 74
Clovelly, Cecil 232
Clurman, Harold 5, 75, 79, 96, 136, 170, 252, 304, 314
Clute, Chester 64, 79, 178, 183, 207
CMG Worldwide 190
Coakley, Marion 263
Cobb, Edmund 98, 108, 332
Cobb, Irvin S. 4, 79, 84, 253, 287, 326
Cobb, Lee J. 14, 79, 106, 200, 201, 268
Coburn, Charles 247
The Cobweb 210, 343, 348
Coby, Fred 165, 313
Cocchi, John 193
Cochran, Dorcas 78
The Cocoanuts 130, 276
Cody, Harry 290
Cody, William F. (Buffalo Bill) 65

Coe, Billy 177
Coe, Fred 285
Coe, Peter 258, 313
Coffin, Haskell 347
Coffin, Tristram 98, 138
Cogley, John 118
Cohan, George M. 5, 79, 129, 143, 195, 252
Cohen, Albert J. 135
Cohen, Eli 228
Cohen, Jean 174
Cohen, Omna 228
Cohn, Harry 80
Cohn, J. J. 184
Cohn, Jack 80
Cohn, Phil 45
Cohon, Baruch J. 149
Colbert, Claudette 6, 23, 80, 153, 154, 186, 209, 256, 274, 301, 331
Cole, Dennis 243
Cole, George 170, 298
Cole, Gordon 312
Coleman, C. C. 108
Coleman, Charles 60, 80, 163, 194, 287
Coleman, Irene 177
Coleman, Robert 217
Coleman, William 231
Colgate Theatre of Romance 80, 264, 347
Colleano, Con 126
The Collected Works of Harold Clurman 79
Collectors Book Store 190
College of the City of New York 4, 20, 36, 114, 190, 344
Collier, Constance 7, 80, 316
Collier, William, Jr. 80, 191
Collier's 129
Collings, Pierre 153
Collins, Anthony 97
Collins, Chick 162
Collins, Frank J. 165
Collins, G. Pat 60, 262
Collins, Joan 12, 80, 89, 282, 284, 305
Collins, Ray 129
Collins, Tom 204
Collyer, Bud 69
Colman, Ronald 38, 180, 196, 228
Colombo, Alberto 44
Colombo, Harry 139
Colonna, Jerry 82, 237, 331
The Color of Money 229
Colton, Scott 161
Columbia Pictures 8, 38, 52, 80, 98, 120, 121, 129, 138, 162, 201, 219, 238, 280, 285, 304, 315, 316, 318, 332, 341
Columbia University 123, 143
Columbia Workshop 267
Columbia's Shakespeare 80, 81, 263, 285
Columbo 116, 248

Index

Comans, Edward 324
Combat Squad 209
Come and Get It 57, 209, 226
Come Back Charleston Blue 66
Come Back Little Sheba 52, 182, 315
Come Blow Your Horn 79, 275
Come to the Stable 155, 348
The Comedy of Terrors 171
Comegys, Kathleen 123
Comer, Sam M. 17, 231, 312
Command Decision 29, 107, 332
Command Performance 41, 82, 89, 264
Commandos Strike at Dawn 202
Committee for the First Amendment 82, 148, 153, 254
"Committee of 56" 253, 254
The Commonweal 174, 193, 201, 217, 218, 231, 233, 241, 285
Communion 26, 82, 83, 84
Communism 1, 10, 54, 61, 62, 83, 92, 93, 101, 132, 136, 145, 158, 159, 200, 213, 222, 244, 248, 253, 254, 257, 261, 266, 271, 311
Communist Manifesto 82
Como, Perry 243
Como, Rossella 202
The Complete Films of Edward G. Robinson 48
Complete Shorter Fiction of Oscar Wilde 127
Compson, Betty 290
Compson, Joyce 177, 207
Compton, Christine 185
Compulsion 47, 86
Comstock, Ned 189
Condylis, Paul 229
Confessions of a Hollywood Columnist 200
Confessions of a Nazi Spy 8, 9, 18, 27, 29, 48, 51, 53, 54, 56, 65, 84, 85, 86, 87, 88, 89, 98, 119, 120, 131, 134, 141, 142, 150, 171, 179, 187, 195, 197, 198, 222, 226, 227, 230, 235, 237, 251, 254, 259, 275, 277, 299, 320, 321, 333, 335, 339
Conforti, Gino 220
Conforti, Marylou 206
Conforti, Tony 206
Congress of the United States 73, 74, 184, 244, 261
Conklin, Heini 40
Conklin, Rus 312
Connard, Phyllis 60, 270
A Connecticut Yankee in King Arthur's Court 143
Connell, Richard 59
Connelly, Marc 274
Connolly, Walter 286
Connors, Chuck 295
Connors, Joe 63
Connors, Michael 49, 138, 312

Conquest 55
Conover 76
Conover, Teresa 287
Conrad, William 204
Conried, Hans 129, 130, 272, 326
Conroy, Frank 25, 26, 86, 184, 257, 285
Conroy, Thom 271
Conroy & Meltzer 116
Considine, John, Jr. 52
Constable, Jeanie L. 189
Considine, Shaun 213, 214, 215
The Constant Wife 292
Constantine Films 139
Constantine I 30, 65
Conte, Elaine 117, 272
Conte, John 53, 86
Conte, Richard 10, 41, 76, 86, 123, 130, 154, 157, 158, 186, 247, 256
Contini, Alfio 238
Contract on Cherry Street 283
Conway, Curt 214, 215
Conway, Morgan 59
Conway, Peggy 75
Conway, Russ 111, 331
The Coo Coo Nut Grove 69, 86
Coogan's Bluff 184
Cook, Clyde 40
Cook, Elisha, Jr. 6, 86, 147, 252
Cook, Jerry 312
Cook, Robert O. 229
Cook, Tommy 219, 237, 283, 331
Cook, Walter 231
Cook, Willis 200
Cooke, Joe 152
Cooke, Ray 205
Cooke, Thomas Coffin 218
Cooksey, Curtis 195
Cool Hand Luke 230
Cooley, Stanley 108
Coolidge, Phillip 86, 229
Coop, Denys 238
Cooper, Edna Mae 312
Cooper, Gary 39, 82, 167, 180, 222, 301, 348
Cooper, Gladys 211
Cooper, Irving 231
Cooper, Jackie 179
Cooper, Melville 115
Copeau, Jacques 60
Copeland, Alan 143
Copeland, Nick 184, 341
Copernic Films 246
Copland, Aaron 189, 328
Copper Sky 267
Copperfield 209
Cops and Robbers 12, 49, 86, 112, 134, 310
Coquette 42
Cora, Alfred 54
Coral Productions 139
Coran, Allan 343
Corbett, Harry H. 55
Corbett, Lois 237
Corby, Ellen 36, 86, 165

Corday, Denise 275
Cordell, Richie 46
Corden, Henry 312
Corey, George 219
Corey, Jeff 78
Corito, Carlos Luiz 139
Cormack, Bartlett 6, 86, 133, 252, 252, 261, 262, 327
Corman, Roger 29, 256
The Corn Is Green 41, 93, 167, 254, 339, 344
Cornell, Duffy 327
The Cornell Woolrich: First You Dream You Die 231
Cornwall, Ann 343
Corot, Jean Baptiste Camille 8, 33, 315
Corrado, Gino 327
Corrado, Gus 306
Correll, Boyd 187
Correll, Charles 29
Corrigan, Emmett 287
Corsaro, Franco 324
Corsaut, Aneta 138
The Corsican Brothers 265
Cort Theatre 333
Cortez, Ricardo 86, 205
Cortez, Stanley 50, 66, 86, 126
Corvette K-225 134, 301
Corwin, Norman 106, 107, 154, 336, 337
Cos, Vicki 76, 138
Coscia, Marcello 139
Cosgrove, Douglas 205
Cosma, Vladimir 228
Cosmopolitan 224
Cossart, Ernest 75
Costa, George and Michael 228
Costello, Don 327
Coster, Gordon 293
Cota, David 308
Cotler, Terry 316
Cotten, Joseph 14, 87, 154, 274, 295, 297, 338
Cotton Comes to Harlem 66
Couglin, Mildred 176
Counsellor-at-Law 90, 269
The Count of Monte Cristo 107, 348
Count Your Blessings 143
Counter-Attack 71, 244
The Country Girl 172
The Counts 46
Counts, Eleanor 98
County Fair 222
Courage of Lassie 93, 221
Courbet, Gustave 33
Court and Society Review 127
The Court Jester 171
The Court Martial of Billy Mitchell 140
Courtenay, Joan 324
Courtenay, William 87, 326, 333
Courtland, Charlyne 147
Courtneidge, Charles 60

Covarrubias, Manuel 30, 203
Cover Girl 32, 40
Cowan, Bob 302
Cowan, Jean 282
Cowan, Jerome 88, 198, 231
Cowan, Lester 341
Cowan, Paul 293
Cowie, Peter 50
Cowles, Jules 40, 341
Cox, Betsy 295
Cox Theatre 93
The Cradle Buster 321
The Cradle Snatchers 57, 129
Craig, Alec 85, 88, 103, 345
Craig, Hal 63, 346
Craig, James 88, 240
Cramer, Duncan 345
Cramer, Richard 278
Crandall, Bill 44
Crandall, Cecil A. 229
Crane, Helen 153
Crane, James L. 245
Cranston, Joe 204
Craven, Frank 40, 88, 159, 222, 230, 252, 326
Craven, James 126
Craven, Ruby 22
Crawford, Broderick 9, 52, 88, 183, 268
Crawford, Cheryl 75, 88, 171, 304
Crawford, Joan 106, 167, 254, 301
Crawford, John 21
Crazy Horse and Custer — The Untold Story 90
Creamer, Harry 327
The Creature from the Black Lagoon 97
Creed, Roger 272
Cregar, Laird 203
Crehan, Joseph 52, 59, 63, 88, 126, 177, 183, 205, 207
Crenna, Richard 268
The Creole (yacht) 230
Crescenzi, Marcello 246
The Crew Chiefs 283
Crewes, Laura Hope 5, 49, 252, 270, 314
Crime and Punishment U.S.A. 142, 210
Crime Doctor 189, 271
Crime Movies, an Illustrated History... 28, 84, 193, 292
Crime School 168, 172, 243
Crimes and Misdemeanors 119, 182
The Criminal Code 88, 89, 134, 217, 263
"The Criminal Code" (radio) 89, 179, 199, 217, 263
Cripps, Kernan 108, 191, 341
Crisp, Donald 8, 27, 58, 59, 89, 104, 254, 286
Criss Cross 95, 197
Crist, Judith 56, 140
Criswell, Floyd 341
Critic's Choice 88

Croccolo, Carlo 46
Crockett, Lute 173
Cromer, Dean 318
Cromwell, John 263
Cronyn, Hume 28
Crosby, Bing 13, 18, 89, 90, 223, 247, 248, 271, 272, 305, 331, 339
Crosby, Harry 326
Crosby, Phil 272
Cross, Charles 341
Crossfire 348
Crossroads 348
Crouch, John 315
Croue, Jean 60
Crouse, Russell 274
The Crowd Roars 210
Crowley, Jane 231
Crowther, Bosley 193
The Crucible 172
The Crusades 50, 97, 343
Crutcher, Norvell 148, 170
Cruz, Maria 19
Cry Freedom 35
Cry Havoc 53, 159, 294
Cry of the City 180, 243
Crystal, Billy 314
Cucciolla, Ricardo 139
Cue 314
Cuff, Bob 200
Cugat, Francis 332
Cukor, George 300
Cumberland, John 147
Cummings, Constance 89
Cummings, Hugh 59, 183, 207
Cummings, Irving 204
Cummings, Robert 89, 126, 224
Cummings, Robert, Sr. 89, 161
Cummins, Peggy 10, 76, 89, 90, 218, 238
Cunningham, Joe 177, 178, 213
Curley, Leo 344
Curran, Florence 195
Curran, Homer 293
Curran Theatre (San Francisco) 215
Currie, Finlay 238
Curse of the Cat People 94
Curtis, Billy 272
Curtis, Dick 278
Curtis, Donald 312
Curtis, Jamie Lee 187
Curtis, Jed 238
Curtis, Joseph 215
Curtis, Ken 74
Curtis, Sonny 220
Curtis, Tony 185, 187, 247, 326
Curtiss, Ray 40, 191, 194
Curtiz, Michael 8, 61, 89, 90, 101, 167, 177, 178, 281, 282
Cushing, Dr. Harvey 204
Custodio, Ana Maria 202
Cutner, Sidney 167, 302
Cutter, Murray 147, 165, 173
Cyrano de Bergerac 68, 118, 244

D.O.A. 168, 209
Dabney, Virginia 63, 177
Daddy Long Legs 270
Dae, Frank 306
Dahl, Alice 341
Dailey, Dan 90, 223, 247
Daily Variety 26, 54
Daisy Kenyon 211, 335
D'Albrook, Sidney 40, 341
Dale, Bobbie 341
Dale, Esther 52, 90
Dale, Margaret 205
Dale, Teresa 218
Daley, Cass 113
Daley, George 191
Dalgleish, Mac 21
Dalio, Marcel 126, 327
Dallas, Gertrude 245
Dalton, Cal 154
Dalton, Charles 179
Daly, Arnold 171
Daly, James 14, 325
Daly, John 339
Daly, Pat 290
Daly, Tom 278
Dalya, Jacqueline 126
Dalzell, Arch R. 236
Dames 41
Damn Yankees 32, 179, 334
Dana, Bill 300
Dana, Kenneth 122
Dancing in the Dark 267
Dandridge, Ruby 152
D'Angelo, William P. 42
Dangerous 93, 140
The Dangerous Years of Kiowa Jones 178
Daniels, Bebe 90, 160, 186, 287, 301, 335, 345
Daniels, William H. 66, 90, 151, 152, 184, 258, 271
Dann, Sam 70
The Danny Kaye Show 171
Danon, Raymond 246
Dansk Films 330
Dante, Joe 324
Dante, Michael 90, 284
D'Antonio, Carmen 74
Danzig, Gadi 228
D'Arbray, Anne 272
Darc, Mireille 90, 246
Dare, Adrienne 322
Darien, Frank 90, 125, 205, 306
Darin, Bobby 247
The Dark Angel 38
Dark Hazard 7, 31, 37, 41, 53, 64, 71, 91, 112, 117, 120, 123, 131, 132, 134, 140, 142, 162, 175, 186, 198, 210, 235, 254, 259, 268, 271, 298, 319, 335, 345
Dark Horses 123
Dark Mirror 137
Dark Passage 93
The Dark Tower 27, 92, 204, 205, 253

Index

Dark Victory 51, 93, 142, 249, 265
Darkness at Noon 10, 21, 83, 86, 92, 93, 101, 179, 182, 186, 213, 228, 229, 234, 252, 252
Darling, Jane 293
Darmour, Roy 344
Darnell, Linda 274, 347
Darrell, Steve 313
Darren, James 18, 220
Darro, Frankie 312
Dart, Justin 61
DaSilva, Howard 13, 84, 93, 241, 282
Dassin, Jules 49
Daugherty, Harry 270
Daugherty, Herschel 167, 270
Daughters of the American Revolution 193
Daumier, Honore 33, 315
Dauro, Gianna 46
Davenport, Harry 93, 104, 183, 306
Daves, Delmer 93, 226
Daviau, Allen 220
David, Hal 224
David and Lisa 93
David Golder 113, 238
Davidovich, Basil 159
Davidson, Bill 275
Davidson, Charlotte 117
Davidson, John 326
Davidson, William 183
Davies, James 231
Davies, Marion 145
Davis, Ann B. 186, 247
Davis, Bette 8, 14, 89, 93, 94, 100, 176, 177, 178, 198, 222, 223, 226, 249, 250, 254, 268, 329, 331
Davis, Bryan 344
Davis, Edward 341
Davis, Elias 288
Davis, George W. 78, 157, 181, 241, 258, 324, 325
Davis, Jerry 76, 272
Davis, Lew 341
Davis, Luther 236
Davis, Dr. Moshe 321
Davis, Robert 29, 85
Davis, Sammy, Jr. 13, 18, 90, 93, 223, 243, 247, 248, 272
Davis, Sylvia 215
Davrath, Natania 70, 71
Davy 283
Dawe, Ray 27
Dawn, Jack 240
The Dawn Patrol 41, 57, 116
Dawson, Billy 75, 103
Dawson, Frances 312, 245
Dawson, Frank 327
Dawson, Hal K. 52
Dawson, Ralph 25, 183, 207
Dawson, Richard 185
Day, Dennis 199
Day, Doris 9, 81, 94, 167, 223

Day, Francisco 312
Day, Lambert 219, 318, 332
Day, Laraine 9, 94, 186, 197, 327
Day, Richard 40, 74, 306
A Day at Santa Anita 93, 94, 286
A Day at the Races 112
Day of the Locust 211
The Day the Earth Stood Still 140, 298
The Days of Wine and Roses 187
Dayton, Ron 272
Dazians 92
Deacon, Don 200
Dead End 137, 138, 159, 179, 287, 320
Dead End Kids 138, 169
Dead Man's Eyes 244
Dead Pigeon 253, 318
Dead Reckoning 68
Dead Ringer 186
The Dead Tree (L'Arbre Mort) 33
Deadlier Than the Male 113
Deadline U.S.A. 88, 300, 348
Deadly Blessing 228
Dean, James 2, 255
Dean, Julia 94, 253
Dean, Priscilla 184
Deane, LeRoy 271
Dear Heart 129
Dear Me, the Sky Is Falling 299
Dear Ruth 33, 130
Dear World 209
Dearing, Edgar 27, 94, 278
Dearth, Earl 148
Death of a Salesman 79, 210, 217
Death of a Scoundrel 95
"Death Rides the Highway" 45, 263
Death Takes a Holiday 33
Deathtrap 130
deBecker, Ernestine 307
DeBecker, Harold 126
DeBeranger, Andre 57
DeBevoise, Charles 147
Deborba, Dorothy 301
DeBurgh, Shirley 248
Decameron Nights 130
DeCamp, Rosemary 211
DeCarlo, Yvonne 95, 248, 312
Decker, John 33, 278, 279
DeConcini, Ennio 202, 238
DeCorsia, Ted 45, 53
DeCuir, John 284
Dee, Vincent 111
Deering, John 85
Deering, Olive 312
The Deerslayer 244
Dees, Mary 184
DeFelice, Ermelinda 46
The Defiant Ones 46, 103
DeFore, Don 177
Degas, Edgar 8
Deghy, Guy 55
DeGraffenried, Tom 318
DeGray, Sidney 341

DeHart, Gail 147
DeHaven, Carter, III 111
DeHavilland, Olivia 94, 154, 222
Deighton, Marga Ann 284
DeKay, Drake 275
Dekker, Albert 34, 95, 164, 165
DeKova, Frank 95, 312
De la Brousse, Marcel 284
Delacroix, Eugene 33
De La Fouchardiere, Georges 278
De La Loma, Antonio 139
DeLand, Kenneth 312
De Lavallade, Carmen 70, 71
Delbo, Jean Jacques 247
Del Campo, Michael 170
Del Castillo, Miguel 139
Delevanti, Cyril 103, 294, 296
Delgado, John 272
del Junco, Dr. Tirso 255
Dell, Claudia 301
Delle Porte, Antonelle 238
Delmont, Betty 173
Delos Records, Inc. 333
Del Rey, Pilar 243
Del Rio, Dolores 13, 73, 74, 95
Del Ruth, Roy 194
The Deluge 5, 79, 95, 96, 103, 114, 156, 182, 197, 210, 253, 337
DeLugg, Milton 339
DeLuxe 42, 152, 293
Del Val, Jean 60, 308
del Valle, Jaime 117
DeMain, Gordon 341
Demara, Ferdinand Waldo, Jr. 49
DeMarch, Aime 247
Demarest, William 96, 141, 147, 231
DeMarney, Terernce 316
Demetrius and the Gladiators 243
DeMille, Cecil B. 1, 11, 17, 28, 49, 64, 83, 88, 96, 98, 101, 137, 146, 148, 149, 178, 203, 208, 213, 259, 267, 299, 311, 312, 313, 314, 339, 343, 347
Deming, Norman 219
Democratic National Committee Radio 97
Democratic National Convention 288
Dempsey, Jack 178
Denbeigh, Stephen 326
DeNiro, Robert 67
Denker, Henry 70, 71
Denning, Richard 97, 135
Dennis, John 229, 296
Dennis the Menace 247
dePackh, Maurice 157
Depp, Harry 40
The Depression 7, 329
Der, Ricky 160
Derain, Andre 33
DeRavenne, Charles 60
Derek, Bo 97
Derek, John 97, 248, 312
DeRolf, Paul 313

Index

DeRoubaix, Francois 246
Derrick, Allan 92
DeSantis, Joe 187
DeSapio, Carmine 243
The Desert Battalion 97, 196
The Desert Fox 23, 202, 235
Desert Fury 26, 321
The Desert Song 54, 95
DeSica, Vittorio 14, 46, 97
Design for Living 128
DeSimone, Roberto 46
Desire 209
Desire Under the Elms 160
The Desk Set 53, 148
DeSoto, Henry 278
The Desperate Hours 54, 142, 172
Desperate Journey 142
Deste, Luli 166, 186, 197, 316, 345
DeStepan, Joe 162
Destination Tokyo 49, 93, 334
Destiny 95
Destroyer 9, 49, 53, 54, 57, 58, 71, 76, 80, 87, 89, 97, 98, 107, 120, 129, 138, 149, 169, 188, 199, 227, 230, 235, 239, 251, 269, 320, 335
"Destroyer" (radio) 98, 199, 263
Destry Rides Again 51, 100, 107, 150, 168, 301, 314
DeSylva, Buddy 107, 108
Detective Story 29, 42, 110, 179, 201
Deutsch, Adolph 183, 207
"The Devil and Daniel Webster" 12, 38, 56, 99, 130, 189, 203, 234, 251, 253, 280, 310, 329, 336, 337
The Devil and the Deep 135, 254
The Devil at 4 O'Clock 280
The Devil Doll 61, 140
Devil Goddess 140
The Devil's Disciple 87
The Devil's Holiday 186
DeVinna, Clyde 52
DeVito, Danny 28
Devlin, Joe 99, 183, 207, 345
DeVol, Frank 138
DeVolterra, Daniel 289
Devotion 199
Dew, Eddie 98
Dewey, John 274
Dewey, Thomas E. 198
DeWilde, Brandon 18
DeWit, Jacqueline 167
DeWitt, George 152
DeWolfe, Stanley 171
Dexter, Von 237, 315
Diage, Louis 318, 332
Dial M for Murder 89, 115
Diamond, David 62
Diamond, Don 175
Diamond, I.A.L. 167, 344
Diamond Jim 33, 179, 273
Diana Productions 259, 277
Diary of a Chambermaid 187

The Diary of Anne Frank 37, 279
Diaz, Porfirio 6, 49, 72, 99, 150, 170, 171
Diaz, Rudy 200
Dibbs, Kem 98, 313
Dick, Bernard F. 108
Dick, Stuart 170
Dick, William 96
Dick Tracy 188
The Dick Van Dyke Show 330
Dickens, C. Stafford 75
Dickerson, Dudley 167
Dickinson, Angie 18
Dieterle, William 8, 99, 101, 103, 104, 254, 328
Dietrich, Marlene 9, 56, 70, 99, 102, 118, 128, 166, 186, 198, 207, 208, 223, 268, 331, 345
Dietz, Howard 173
Digges, Dudley 5, 22, 60, 101, 144, 170, 226, 246, 252, 314
Dillard, Mimi 78
Dillaway, Donald 194
Diller, Phyllis 220, 288
Dillinger 133, 272
Dillinger, John 13, 134
Dillon, Irving 22
Dillon, Tom 278, 346
Dills, Sen. Ralph C. 209
Dime, Jimmie 40
Dinehart, Alan 232
Dingle, Charles 327
Dinner at Eight 41, 142, 143, 219
Dinner at the Ritz 57, 305
Dino 218
Dino—Living High in the Dirty Business of Dreams 243
Dirigible 305
Dirigo, Carmen 25, 278
Dirty Dancing 339
Dirty Dingus Magee 167, 228
The Dirty Dozen 277
Disney, Walt 14, 84, 86, 133, 186, 228, 275, 319, 333, 348
Disneyland 153
Dispatch from Reuter's A 8, 24, 26, 31, 37, 41, 43, 48, 56, 61, 72, 75, 87, 88, 99, 102, 103, 115, 120, 141, 143, 155, 159, 168, 178, 180, 186, 188, 196, 197, 198, 203, 210, 226, 230, 235, 251, 256, 259, 268, 269, 299, 300, 333, 334, 335, 345
Disraeli 179, 335
Disraeli, Benjamin 32, 102
A Distant Trumpet 169
Les Distractions 90
Divine, Earl 27
Divine, Jerry 220
Divine, Lynn 220
Divine, Michael 220
Divine Lady 283
The Divine Woman 283
Dix, Lillian 195
Dix, Richard 5, 123, 232, 252, 301

Dixey, Henry E. 96, 103
Dobie Gillis 117
Dobkin, Lawrence 103, 165, 204, 312
Dr. Cook's Garden 20
Dr. Cyclops 95
Dr. Dolittle 35, 125
Dr. Ehrlich's Magic Bullet 8, 17, 18, 20, 31, 37, 48, 56, 58, 65, 72, 75, 87, 89, 93, 94, 99, 102, 103, 104, 105, 106, 114, 120, 128, 139, 142, 143, 155, 156, 159, 160, 161, 171, 180, 186, 197, 198, 203, 211, 224, 226, 230, 235, 237, 239, 241, 243, 249, 251, 259, 260, 261, 267, 268, 275, 291, 298, 301, 329, 333, 334, 335, 339, 345, 347
Dr. Jekyll and Mr. Hyde 271, 298, 345
Dr. Kildare 41, 94, 112, 150
Dr. Mabuse 182
Dr. Socrates 186
Dr. Strangelove, or How I Stopped Worrying and Loved the Bomb 250, 348
Dr. Who 298
"The Doctor with Hope in His Hands" 69, 105, 112, 264
Dr. Zhivago 179, 269, 285
Document A777 56, 79, 88, 106, 107, 115, 118, 146, 159, 179, 185, 234, 236, 256, 264, 276, 337, 348
Dodd, Rev. Neal 278
Dodge City 53, 142, 169, 254, 336
Dodsworth 137, 160, 199, 241
Dog Day Afternoon 283
Dolan, Carolanne 189
Dolenz, George 31, 62, 107, 320
Dolenz, Mickey 107
A Doll's House 53, 138, 163
Domenici, Franco 202
Dominguez, Joe 52
Dominick, Rex 229
The Dominoes 209
Don Giovanni 249
Don Juan 197
Donahue, Patricia 55
Donaldson, Ted 75, 219
Donath, Ludwig 308
Donfeld 78, 241, 272
Donlan, James 81, 91, 125, 163, 341
Donlevy, Brian 40, 107
Donlin, Mike 343
Donlin, Rita 341
Donnell, Jeff 209, 219
Donnelly, Ruth 81, 107, 186, 198, 249, 290, 345
Donovan, Margaret 42
Donovan, Tom 99
"Don't Blame Me" 326
Don't Go Near the Water 57, 269, 285

DoQui, Robert 78
Doran, Ann 69, 283, 345
Doran, Mary 177
Dorian, Charles 52
Dorman, Jan 293
Doro, Mino 324
Dorothy Chandler Pavilion 19
Dorr, Lester 98, 107, 194, 231, 327
Dors, Diana 267
Dorsay, Fifi 301
Dorsey, Maggie 306
Dos Passos, John 14, 326
Dostoevsky, Feodore 6, 60
Double Indemnity 9, 17, 18, 20, 36, 40, 47, 54, 65, 66, 67, 70, 71, 95, 98, 102, 107, 108, 109, 110, 119, 123, 125, 128, 130, 131, 141, 149, 150, 155, 198, 201, 202, 210, 222, 223, 224, 234, 235, 249, 251, 255, 257, 265, 268, 283, 286, 291, 298, 299, 304, 309, 320, 332, 344, 345
A Double Life 49, 138, 277
Doubravsky, Kurt 46
Douglas, Anne 199
Douglas, Carol 248
Douglas, Diana 110, 111, 158
Douglas, Don 306
Douglas, Freddie 200
Douglas, Gordon 271
Douglas, Kirk 12, 28, 72, 110, 111, 199, 217, 224, 323, 324, 325
Douglas, Melvyn 154, 228, 254, 273
Douglas, Michael 111
Douglas, Paul 72, 320
Dowdy, Andrew 62
Dowling, Eddie 274
Down Argentine Way 159
Downen, Don 177
Downes, Olin 274
Downing, Joseph 111, 161, 183, 290, 327
Doyle, Charles H. 218
Doyle, David 270
Doyle, James H. 195
Dozier, William 42
Dracula 61
Dracula — Dead and Loving It 230
Drafted 5, 111, 197, 253
Dragnet 221
Dragon, Carmen 163, 219, 224, 328
Dragon Seed 201
Dragonwyck 206, 221, 329
Drake, Allyn 341
Drake, Charles 111, 183
Drake, Jack 238
Drake, Geoffrey 200
Drake, Pauline 165
Drake, Tom 344
Drango 301
Drasnin, Robert 208, 236
Drayton, Noel 258
Dream Girl 269

Dreier, Hans 108, 231
Dreigroshenoper 126
Dresser, E. H. 326
Drew, Lowell 341
Drew, Roland 111, 183, 207, 316
Dreyfus, Captain Alfred 279
Drinkwater, Ros 293
Drisse, Gus 316
"The Drop-Out" 12, 38, 76, 111, 134, 140, 209, 220, 234, 235, 265, 310, 345
Dru, Joanne 112, 147, 223
Drum, Jim 231
Drums Along the Mohawk 68
The Dry and Lawless Years 190
Dryden, Robert 45
Dryer, Bernard 204
DuBarry 69
DuBarry Was a Lady 38, 69, 80
Dubbins, Don 258
Dubosc, Charles 246
Dubov, Paul 136, 175
Duck Soup 217
Duel in the Sun 52, 160, 245
Duell, Charles H. 57
Duff, Howard 25, 45, 112, 116, 199
Duffield, Brainerd 347
Duffy's Tavern 43, 159
DuFrane, Frank 184
Dufresne, Charles 33
Dufty, William 47
Dufy, Raoul 33
Dugan, Tom 69, 167
Duke, Patty 18
Dulcy 128, 325
Dulo, Jane 296
Dumb and Dumber 277
Dumbo 58
Dumbrille, Douglass 112, 163, 312
Dumont, Margaret 95
Duncan, Malcolm 245
Dune 298
Dundee, Jimmie 231
Dunhill, Ford 340
Duning, George 318
Dunkinson, Harry 341
Dunlap, Paul 51
Dunlap, Richard 18
Dunn, Emma 91, 112
Dunn, J. Malcolm 38
Dunn, Ralph 63, 177, 207, 278, 290, 346
Dunn, Thomas P. 346
Dunn-Leonard, Barbara 315
Dunne, Irene 277, 280, 301
Dunne, Phillip 254
Dunning, Decla 302
Dunphy, Jerry 258
DuPar, Edwin B. 59, 177
DuPont, Paul 70
DuPont Cavalcade of America 69, 204, 250, 263, 333
Dupont Show of the Week 86, 112, 310
Duran, Tommy 313

Durand, David 75, 287
Durand-Ruel Galleries 33
Durante, Jimmy 35, 112, 146, 154, 199, 247, 283, 331
Duryea, Dan 9, 10, 67, 95, 112, 141, 198, 223, 249, 257, 277, 278, 279, 280, 282, 345, 347
Duvall, Robert 19
Duvivier, Julien 9, 101, 107, 113, 125, 126, 306, 307
Dwyer, John M. 212
Dye, Diana 243
Dyer, William 346
Dynasty 80, 129
Dyrenforth, Dr. Harold 258

E.T., the Extraterrestrial 292, 298
Each Dawn I Die 111, 149, 265, 274
Eagle, S. P. 302, 306; *see also* Spiegel, Sam
Eagles, James 204
Eames, Clare 5, 28, 30, 60, 113, 159, 170, 203, 226, 252, 314
Earle, Edward 231, 313
Earp, Wyatt 73
Earthquake 140
The Easiest Way 112, 299, 334
East Is West 6, 34, 36, 47, 95, 113, 120, 132, 134, 179, 182, 190, 203, 217, 235, 239, 251, 253, 255, 267, 327, 330
East Lynne 172
East of Eden 95, 209
Eastman Color 55, 138, 228, 238, 247
Easton, Ruth 165
Eastwood, Clint 19, 149
Easy to Love 319
Eaton, Charles 275
Eaton, Jay 341
Eaton, Pearl 341
Eaton, Walter Prichard 243
Eaves Costumes, Inc. 92, 227
Ebi, Earl 203
Eckhardt, William 157
Eckhardt, Oliver 162
Eckman, Britton 258
The Ed Sullivan Show 35, 37, 49, 54, 113, 114, 118, 148, 160, 197, 245, 256, 274, 310, 321, 338
Ed Wood 182
The Eddie Cantor Story 140
Eddie Cantor's March of Dimes Special 113, 114, 199, 263
Eddinger, Lawrence 326
Edelman, Louis F. 63, 97
Edens, Roger 247
The Edge of Night 249
Edison the Man 130
Edmonds, Louis
Edouart, Farciot 108, 200, 231, 312
Edward, King of England 225

Index

Edward G. Robinson, a Pyramid Illustrated History of the Movies 24, 39, 48, 51, 63, 74, 103, 110, 124, 146, 152, 174, 176, 178, 181, 184, 192, 239, 241, 281, 303, 313, 343
The Edward G. Robinson Collection 33
"Edward G. Robinson's Blend" 292
Edward G. Robinson's World of Art 14, 33, 47, 114, 151, 152, 286, 319
Edward My Son 221
Edward Scissorhands 256
Edwards, Gary 315
Edwards, Jack 26
Edwards, Martha 176
Edwards, Ralph 185, 315
Edwards, Sam 258
Edwards, Vincent 199
Edwards, Virginia 287
Edwards, Waldo 147
Eejima, Susie 296
Effron, Howard 206
The Egg and I 80, 90, 115, 157, 197, 201
Eggar, Samantha 268
Ehrlich, Hedi (Mrs. Paul) 20, 104, 105, 138
Ehrlich, Max S. 135
Ehrlich, Dr. Paul 20, 48, 103, 104, 105, 114, 150, 227, 267
Eichelberger, Clark M. 254
Eight Is Enough 160, 330
Ein, Donald, Ellie and Felda 258
Ekberg, Carl 308
Elam, Jack 114, 229
El Boughdadly, Abbas 313
Eldredge, Florence 154
Eldredge, George 331
Eldredge, John 205
Eleanor Roosevelt Cancer Fund 35
Eleanor Roosevelt Humanitarian Award 36
Electrocution 4, 67, 114, 253
Elena 92
Elephant Walk 99, 267
11 Harrowhouse 336
Eliscu, Edward 114, 262
Elitch's Gardens 5, 114, 115, 211, 321, 330
Elizabeth the Queen 128, 220, 314
Elizabethan Society 4, 114
Ellenstein, Robert 165
Ellery Queen 189, 348
Ellington, Duke 330
Elliott, Bill 236
Elliott, Bob 143
Elliott, Dick 207
Elliott, Gordon (Bill) 63, 194
Elliott, Jack 208
Elliott, John 343
Elliott, Larry 320
Elliott, Maxine 65

Elliott, Robert 125
Elliott, Verne 207
Elliott, Yves 247
Ellis, Charles 96
Ellis, Herb 204
Ellis, Patricia 91
Ellsler, Effie 341
Elman, Mischa 35
Elmer Gantry 29, 169, 172, 182, 208, 247
Elson, Donald 78
Elston, Logan 212
Emergency 196
Emerson, Charles 88
Emerson, Ed 98, 347
Emerson, Faye 76, 207
Emerson, Hope 114, 115, 158
Emerson, Lillian 54
Emery, Calvin 346
Emery, Gilbert 63, 103, 115
Emhardt, Robert 325
Emma 172
Emmet, Katherine 153
Emmy Awards 236, 340
The Emperor Jones 271
The Emperor Waltz 94
The Enchanted Cottage 271
Enchantment 267
Enemies of the Law 272
An Enemy of the People 210
Engel, Lehman 215
Engel, Leonard A. 42
Engel, Roy 62
English, Harry 262
English, Lucy 163
Englund, Steven 158
Engstrom, Brigitta 258
Enright, Kevin 318
Enter Arsene Lupin 107
Enter Laughing 118, 330
Enter Madame 5, 114, 115, 211, 234, 253
The Entertainer 236
Entertainment Weekly 3, 298
Entratter, Corinne 157, 286, 344
Entratter, Jack 247
"Epitaph for a Spy" 11, 71, 115, 182, 197, 234, 310, 321, 329
Epper, Jean and Stephanie 74
Epstein, Pierre 206
Equini, Arrigo 46
Erdman, Richard 220
Eric, Elspeth 291
Erickson, C. O. 340
Erickson, Carl 287
Erlanger, Abe 252
Erlanger Productions 218
Erskine, Chester 24, 25, 115
Erway, Ben 308
Erwin, Stuart 301
Escape to Danger 22
Eshkol, Levi Premier 49, 71
Esmond, Annie 316
Esquire 76
Essler, Fred 278

Essman, Manuel 339
Essner, Rebecca (Rea) 117
Esther and the King 80, 166
Esway, Alexander 316
The Eternal Light 115, 116, 264, 265, 321, 338
Ethan Frome 197, 209
Etterre, Estelle 327
Eusebius 312
Eustrel, Anthony 313
Evangeline 103, 111
Evans, Bob 113, 177
Evans, Charles 165, 322
Evans, Dale 160
Evans, Doug 21
Evans, Edith Dame 18
Evans, Helena Phillips 322
Evans, Maurice 14, 76, 106, 115, 149, 252, 325
Evans, Michael 325
Evans, Nancy 219
Evanson, Edith 258
Everett, Chad 325
Everson, William K. 62, 342
"Every Eighteen Hours" 45, 112, 116, 263
Everybody Does It 140
Evreinoff, Nicholas 75
Ewing, Eleanor 122
Executive Suite 128
Exodus 79, 97, 186, 218, 265, 321
Eye of the Cat 244
Eye of the Stranger 182
Eye on Art 116, 310
Eyvind of the Hills 5, 42, 116, 150, 253, 348

The F.B.I. 69, 349
F.I.S.T. 344
Fabares, Shelley 325
Fabray, Nanette 209, 255
A Face in the Crowd 320
Face of Fire 167
"Face to Face with Gabriel" 115, 116, 265
The Facts of Life 156, 160
Fadden, Tom 176
Fail Safe 47
Fairbanks, Douglas, Jr. 7, 90, 116, 166, 169, 191, 192, 193, 268, 273, 301, 327
Fairchild, Cookie & Orchestra 114
The Falcon 58, 134, 267
Falcon Crest 348
Falk, Peter 13, 116, 188, 272
Falkenberg, Jinx 228
A Family Affair 65, 172
Family Theatre 117, 264
Famous Players 244
Famous Players–Lasky 244
Fancareggi, Ugo 238
Fancy Pants 156
Fanite, Richard 219
Fanning, Frank 27
Fanny 56, 72

Index

Fanny and Alexander 166
Fantasy Island 220
Fantoni, Sergio 166, 258
The Far Country 273
Faragoh, Francis Edward 17, 191
Faralla, William Dalio 148
"The Faraway Part of Town" 17, 223
Fareleigh, Margaret 163
Farentino, James 326
Farewell My Lovely 70, 143, 220
A Farewell to Arms 97, 115
Farley, Morgan 296
Farley, Patricia 40
Farmer, Gene 185
The Farmer Takes a Wife 128
The Farmer's Daughter 142, 255, 256, 265, 344, 348
Farnsworth, Richard 313
Farnum, Franklin 313
Farrar, Stanley 208, 347
Farrell, Glenda 7, 90, 91, 117, 186, 191, 335
Farrington, Betty 108
Farrow, John 117
Farrow, Mia 117
Farthingale, Hermione 293
Fast Times at Ridgemont High 334
Fatal Attraction 228
Fate Is the Hunter 129, 180, 309
Fates, Gil 339
Father Knows Best 111, 140, 348
Father of the Bride 43, 217, 237
Father's Day 234
Faulkner, William 27
Faust 245
Faversham, Phillip 91
Fay, Frank 299, 301
Faye, Alice 254, 273
Faye, Julia 231, 312
Faylen, Frank 60, 63, 117, 118, 177, 327
Fazan, Adrienne 258, 324
Fazenda, Louise 301
Fealy, Maude 313
Fear in the Night 172, 233, 234, 268
Fear Strikes Out 344
Feature Play Company 244
Federal Bureau of Investigation 349
Federation of Jewish Philanthropies 321
Feet First 172
Fegte, Ernst 21
Fehr, Rudi 173, 174
Fein, Bernard 272
Feindt, Cilly 324
Feldman, Milton 318
Feliciano, Jose 200, 223
Fell, Norman 215
Fellini, Federico 18
Fellowes, Rockcliffe 242
Feltenstein, George 189
Felton, Verna 204, 255, 277, 345

Fennelly, Parker 285
Fenton, Leslie 118, 144, 223
Ferber, Edna 274
Ferguson, Frank 44, 118, 332
Ferguson, Otis 105
Ferguson, Perry 300, 302
Ferrer, Jose 54, 84, 106, 113, 118
Ferri, Rafael 202
Festival Harmonic Orchestra 70, 71
Fetherstone, Ed 161, 177, 207, 341
Feuer, Cy 347
Feydeau, Georges 201
Fiddler on the Roof 46, 169
Der Fidele Bauer 54
Field, Betty 28, 118, 126, 269
Field, Margaret 231
Field, Mary 27
Field, Norman 98, 203, 237, 347
Field of Dreams 182
Fielder, Pat 331
Fielding, Edward 126, 137
Fields, Al 25
Fields, Stanley 118, 191, 268
Fields, W. C. 95, 306
Fields of Glory 5, 135, 137, 259, 287, 328, 329
The Fiercest Heart 43
Fiesta 72
Fifty Million Frenchmen 179
Fighting Father Dunne 140
The Fighting Gentleman 80
The Fighting 69th 221
Filauri, Antonio 231
The File on Thelma Jordan 40
Fillmore, Clyde 327
Fillmore, Henry 163, 224, 328
Film Comment 108, 152, 322
Film Culture 324
Film Daily 176
The Film Encyclopedia 66, 118, 125
Film Facts 139, 296
Film Guide 46, 50, 51, 135, 164, 185, 219, 229, 234, 239, 247, 257, 266, 294, 303, 319, 333
Film Guild Corporation 188, 266
Film Noir 9, 109, 110, 118, 119, 174, 233, 302
Film Society 228
The Filmgoer's Companion 306
Films in Review 43, 152, 290, 347
The Films of Claudette Colbert 153, 154
The Films of Frank Capra 94, 150
The Films of Fritz Lang 279
The Films of Rita Hayworth 305
Films of the Fifties 62
Films of the Forties 281
Films of the Thirties 287, 305
Filmways/Solar 77
Findley, Sylvia 51
Fine, Bud 341
Fine Feathers 334
Finian's Rainbow 336
Finkle David 288

Finn, Elfin 116
Finn, Mickey 272
Finn, Sammy 40, 184
Finney, Jack 138
Fiorello! 54
The Firebrand 61, 82, 87, 122, 123, 146, 150, 169, 182, 209, 221, 234, 251, 253
Firecreek 114
Fireman Save My Child 179
First Is Last 5, 43, 70, 82, 123, 130, 234, 253, 301
First Monday in October 332
First National 57, 63, 71, 91, 120, 123, 125, 144, 163, 177, 191, 195, 205, 287, 304, 317, 322, 335, 343
The First Nighter 294
The First Year 88, 211
Firstenberg, Jean 255
Fischer, Robert 326
Fishbein Gowns, Inc. 122
Fisher, Eddie 61, 237
Fisher, Larry 40, 341
Fisher, Lola 38
Fisher, Shug 74
Fiske, Dwight 129
Fiske, Harrison Grey 252
Fiske, Klaw & Erlanger 179
Fiske, Mrs. 65
Fittipaldi, Emerson 49
Fitzcarraldo 179
Fitzgerald, Barry 8, 18, 30, 95, 123, 282
Fitzgerald, Jerry 170
Fitzgerald, Wayne 212
Fitzmaurice, George 4, 32
Fitzroy, Emily 205
Fitzsimmons, Charles B. 42
Five Card Stud 144
Five Fingers 206
Five Graves to Cairo 42, 54, 283, 286
Five Star Final 7, 17, 32, 70, 90, 91, 120, 123, 124, 125, 141, 171, 186, 188, 195, 196, 197, 201, 208, 222, 230, 234, 235, 249, 250, 253, 254, 259, 268, 299, 301, 304, 309, 334, 335
Fix, Paul 241, 283, 339
Fiz, Robert 202
Fjeldstad, Oivin 293
Flaherty, Pat 25, 125, 167, 173, 266
Flamingo Road 340
Flanagan, Michael 262
Flaubert, Gustave 49
Flash Gordon 217, 298
Flaster, James Z. 138, 247
Flavin, James 60, 74, 88, 125, 161, 183, 207, 219
Die Fledermaus 300
Flege, Edmond 218
Fleischer, Max 125
Fleischer, Richard 125, 295, 296

Index

Fleischer, Stanley 165, 167
Fleischmann, Harry 52
Fleming, Victor 222
Flesh and Fantasy 9, 31, 43, 49, 56, 58, 66, 86, 89, 95, 98, 113, 118, 120, 125, 127, 143, 186, 187, 196, 197, 218, 220, 223, 235, 249, 251, 256, 259, 280, 292, 299, 328, 340
"Flesh and Fantasy" (radio) 127, 180, 264
Fletcher, Dorothy 60, 270
Fletcher, Moshe 228
Fleurs de Tahiti 8
Flick, W. D. 157, 306
The Flight of the Phoenix 24, 112
Flint, Sam 219, 341
Flippen, J(ay) C. 220, 236
Flirtation Walk 334, 335, 344
Florey, Robert 153
Flowers, Bess 108, 127, 138, 162, 177, 341, 346
The Fly 130, 298
Flying Down to Rio 95, 114, 254, 273
The Flying Irishman 202
Flynn, Charles J. 158
Flynn, Errol 141, 142, 167
Foch, Nina 11, 28, 87, 128, 164, 165, 186, 197, 198, 312
Fodor, Ladislas 306, 307
Fog Over Frisco 65
Fog Over London 27
Fogelson, Col. E. E. (Buddy) 247
Folger's Coffee 76
Follow Me Boys 202
Follow the Fleet 149
Folsey, George 57, 153
Folsom Prison 67, 257
Fonda, Henry 24, 29, 128, 131, 188, 209, 254, 268, 272, 306, 328
Fondato, Mrcello 139
Fontaine, Joan 70, 154
Fontana, Martin, Jr. 215
Fontanne, Lynn 5, 60, 128, 136, 199, 252, 314
Footlight Parade 65, 107, 254
Footloose 261
For a Few Dollars More 179, 329
"For He's a Jolly Good Fellow" 224, 271
For Our Vines Have Tender Grapes 27, 132, 240
For the Defense 11, 98, 115, 310
For the First Time 69, 209
For the Living 42, 65, 66, 129, 130, 168, 255, 264, 265, 284, 337, 339, 343
For Whom the Bell Tolls 292
Forain, Jean Louis 33
Forbes, Mary 113, 126
Forbidden Planet 298, 300
Forbstein, Leo F. 59, 85, 91, 103, 104, 124, 144, 163, 177, 191, 194, 205, 207, 282, 290, 317, 322, 343
Ford, David 215
Ford, Francis 341
Ford, Glenn 9, 11, 97, 122, 129, 332
Ford, Henry 230
Ford, John 7, 13, 73, 74, 79, 101, 129, 169, 254, 341, 342
Ford, Paul 12, 270
Ford, Wallace 81, 341
Ford Theatre 11, 29, 55, 111, 129, 133, 134, 264, 283, 310, 347
A Foreign Affair 100, 199, 211, 321, 344
Foreign Correspondent 43, 93, 141, 179, 210, 277
Foreman, Carl 200
Forever Amber 57, 140
Formica, Fern 126
Forrest, David 167
Forrest, George 293
Forrest, Sam 101, 129, 195, 252, 336
Forrest, William 138, 219
Forrester, Ross 64, 88, 178
Forsyth, Charlie 64, 88, 98, 175, 178, 203, 204, 208, 237, 347
Forsythe, John 11, 129, 135, 198
Fort, Garrett 242
Fort Apache 54, 118
Fort Apache the Bronx 35
Fortune, Wallace 122
The Fortune Cookie 344
Forty Naughty Girls 197
Forty Paintings from the Edward G. Robinson and Gladys Lloyd Robinson Collection 33
42nd Street 90, 168, 175, 211, 273
Foss, Bjorn 258
Foss, Wenke 293
Fosse, Bob 19
Foster, Bill 288
Foster, Dianne 76, 130, 332
Foster, Eddie 130, 177, 183, 184
Foster, Frohman 164
Foster, Mary 341
Foster, Norman 262
Foster, Phoebe 130, 326
Foster Preston 19, 322
Foster, Warren 154, 254
Foucher, Rosita 341
Foulger, Byron 99, 130, 161, 278
Foulk, Robert 199, 272
The Fountainhead 209
Four Daughters 90, 334
Four Feathers 292, 348
Four for Texas 64, 269
The Four Horsemen of the Apocalypse 107
The Four Hundred Blows 57
Four Jills in a Jeep 130, 168, 265
Four Just Men 107
Four Men and a Prayer 140
The Four Seasons 339
Four-Star Productions 148, 187
The Fourposter 267
The Fourteen Hours 144, 243
Fowler, Bruce 187
Fowler, Gene, Jr. 345
Fox, Allen 162, 184
Fox, Frederick 92
Fox, J. J. 213
Fox, William 322
Fox Film Corporation 321
Foy, Mary 344
Francen, Victor 306
Frances 299
Francis, Arlene 25, 130, 339
Francis, Connie 35, 49
Francis, Kay 7, 130, 162, 163, 186, 223, 329
Francis, Noel 291
Francis, Olin 40
Francisco, Betty 343
Frank, Christopher (Christian) J. 184, 341
Frank, Fredric M. 312
Frank, Otto 279
Frankenstein 7, 79, 171, 190, 298
Franklin, Clyde 54
Franklin, Miriam 108, 109
Franklin, William 246
Franz, Eduard 312
Franz, Joe 88, 178
Fraser, Elisabeth 25
"Frauds and Superstitions" 129, 130, 264
Frazee, H. H. 333
Frazer, Robert 307
Frazier, Harry 42
Freaks 61, 314
Freddy's Dead: The Final Nightmare 180
Frederici, Blanche 144
Frederick, John 62
Frederick's of Hollywood 220
A Free Soul 43, 136
Freebairn-Smith, Thomas 45, 347
Freeborn, Kay 293
Freed, Arthur 18, 273
Freed, Bert 199
Freed, Fred 270
Freedland, Michael 151
Freedman, Leo 215
Freeman, Everett 183
Freeman, Howard 89, 219
Freeman, Kathleen 130, 136
Freeman, Mona 109, 130, 186, 215, 252
Frees, Paul 204, 231, 272, 283
Fregonese, Hugo 50, 130
Freleng, Friz 86, 262
French Impressionism 114
French Research Foundation 56
Freres, Revellion 262
Freud 244
Freud, Sigmund 192

Freulich, Henry 161
Freund, Karl 173
Frey, Arno 307
Frey, Fran 45
Frezie, Benito 324
Friberg, Arnold 17, 312
Friday, Pat 82
Fried, Gerald 295
Fried, Walter 214, 215
Friede, Al 187
Friedhofer, Hugo 17, 104, 177, 282, 306
Friedland, Dalia 228
Friedman, Prof. Arthur B. 190
Friedman, Seymour 137
Friend, Budd S. 148
Friendly Persuasion 69
Fritch, Robert 307
Fritzell, James 138
Froehlich, William 92
The Frogmen 300
Frohoff, Louis 262
From Here to Eternity 141, 182, 285
Frome, Milton 340
Fromek, Joe 189
The Front 146 270
The Front Page 50, 79, 200, 234, 294
Frontier Gal 180
Frontiere, Dominic 284
Frost, Alice 178, 258
Frost, Terry 219
The Frozen Ghost 179
Frye, Derek 200
Frye, Dwight 75, 137
Fryer, Elmer 255
The Fugitive 51
Fulci, Lucio 238
The Full Monty 130
Fuller, Lance 136
Fulton, John P. 17, 278, 298, 312
Fung, Willie 144
Funny Face 195
Funny Girl 285, 304
Funny Lady 159
The Furies 149
Furman, Norman 176
Furness, George and Marion 224
Furusho, S. 245
Fury 90, 140, 182
Future Tense, the Cinema of Science Fiction 296
Fux, Herbert 238

G Men 33, 171, 201, 202, 244
Gabel, Martin 28, 270
Gable, Clark 21, 97, 190, 254
Gabor Zsa Zsa 211, 220, 247
Gabriel, Col. Arnold D. 163, 189, 224, 328
Gage, Jack 108
Gahagan, Herbert 215
Gaines, Richard 108, 131, 219
Gair, Barbara 321
Galerie Bernheim-Jeune 33

Galerie Bing 33
The Galerie Charpentier 33
Galerie Georges Petitot 33
Galia 90
Gallagher, Desmond 341
Gallagher, Skeets 301
Gallo, Lew 148
Gallois-Montbrun, R. 238
Galt, Galan 64, 178
The Gambler 68, 98, 253
The Gamblers 4, 131
Gamby-Hall Dancers 90, 153
Gamet, Kenneth 307
Gandhi 35
The Gangster 295, 300
Gansberg, Alan 48
Garbicz, Adam 85, 109, 174
Garbo, Greta 36, 90
Garde, James 324
Garden of Allah 325
The Garden of the Finzi-Continis 97
Garden of the Moon 189, 234, 329
Gardner, Arthur 187, 331
Gardner, Ava 154
Gardner, Ed 332
Gardner, Jack 63, 126, 134, 346
Gardner, Reginald 106
Garfield, John 8, 21, 84, 95, 118, 134, 154, 272, 281, 282, 337
Garfield, John, Jr. 134, 201
Gargan, Edward 27, 40, 134
Gargan, Jack 25, 346
Gargan, William 134, 280
Gariss, Jack 312
Garland, Beverly 136
Garland, Judy 154, 217, 223, 247, 254, 274
Garland, Tommy 158
Garmes, Lee 21
Garner, James 172
Garralaga, Martin 307
Garretson, Oliver S. 63, 282
Garrett, Betty 277
Garrett, Robert 258
Garrick Gaities 315
Garrick Theatre 5, 204, 254
Garrison, Harold 108
Garson, Greer 19, 35, 134, 247, 332
Gart, John 45
Garver, Annette 116
Garver, Felix 116
Garver, Florence 116
Garver, Irving 116
Garver, Kathy 313
Garvin, Gene 231, 312
Gary, Alberta 306
Gaslight 56, 57, 87, 135, 340
Gateson, Marjorie 287
The Gathering 35
The Gaucho 330
Gaudio, Tony 27, 59, 66, 134, 177, 183, 191, 205, 317
Gauguin, Paul 8, 33, 34, 164, 315

Gaul, George 60, 137
Gausman, Russell A. 25, 126, 135, 278
Gauthier, Jean-Michel 246
Gavin, John 19
The Gay Desperado 68
The Gay Divorcee 273
Gaye, Gregory 258
Gazzara, Ben 20, 31, 67
Geary, Bud 98, 177
Gehman, Richard 288
Geiger, Jason 117
Geiger, Martha 14, 117
Geiger, Milton 13, 134, 155, 163, 224, 231, 256, 280, 283, 315, 328
Geiger, Ronald 117
Geiger, Warren 117
Geist, Kenneth L. 157
Geller, Harry 208
Gelman, Jacques 247
Gemeentemuseum 33
The Gene Krupa Story 218
General Della Rovere 97
The General Died at Dawn 101
General Electric Theatre 12, 112, 134, 209, 265, 310
General Hospital 43
Genest, Emile 78
Gentleman Jim 125, 142, 149
Gentleman's Agreement 144, 155, 245, 349
The Gentlemen from Krakow 70, 134
Gentlemen Prefer Blondes 144, 283, 304, 336, 340
George, Anthony 313
George, John 242, 291
George M! 80
The George Raft Story 196
George S. Kaufman and His Friends 205
George Sidney: A Bio-Bibliography 340
George Spelvin Award 209, 261
George Washington Slept Here 101, 143, 334
Gerard, Hal 331
Geray, Steven 62, 340
Gericault, Jean-Louis 34, 315
Gering, Marion 135, 315
Gerlini, Piero 46
Germain, Stuart 99
German-American Bund 84, 85
Geronimo 217
Gerry, Alex 224
Gerry, Toni 62
Gershenson, Joseph 135
Gershon, Marjorie 228
Gershwin, George 255
Gershwin, Ira 254
Gerstand, Merritt B. 181
Gerstle, Frank 318
Gertsman, Maury 135
Gervaise 279

Index

Gessner, Nicolas 246
Get Smart 252
Getty, Estelle 314
The Ghost and Mrs. Muir 43, 187, 206
Ghost Goes West 244
The Ghost Steps Out 40
Ghost Story 116
Ghosts 163
Giant 218
Gianviti, Roberto 238
Giaume, Joseph 246
Gibbon, James 290
Gibbons, Cedric 44, 52, 135, 181, 184, 240, 254, 327, 328
Gibbons, James 177
Gibbs, Carmelita 62
Gibson, Judith 108
Gibson, Mimi 313
Gibson, Wynne 301
Gidget 261
Gielgud, John 65
Gifford, Frances 135, 240
Gigi 261
Gilbert, Eddie 288
Gilbert, Edwin 183
Gilbert, Henry 293
Gilbert, Herschel Burke 187, 233, 331
Gilbert, Jody 21
Gilbert, John 61
Gilda 80, 129, 145, 202, 223, 277
The Gilded Lily 202
Gilks, Al 316
Gill, Beverly 296
Gill, Brendan 77
Gill, Geula 70
Giller, James 195
Giller, Thomas 195
Gillespie, A. Arnold 240, 258
Gilligan's Island 142, 169
Gillingwater, Claude 163
Gillmore, Margalo 170, 227, 314
Giovannini, Giorgio 238
Girardot, Etienne 81, 135, 249, 341, 342
The Girl Can't Help It 208
A Girl in Every Port 115, 304
Girl in Room 17 26
The Girl in the Red Velvet Swing 80, 125
Girl with the Red Plume 7
Gish, Dorothy 5, 57, 135, 268, 280, 287, 328, 329
Gish, Lillian 135
Gitlis, Ivry 70, 71
Gittens, George 233
Gittleson, June 323
"Give My Regards to Broadway" 80, 90
Gladys Lloyd Robinson and Edward G. Robinson Collection 33
Glasgow Herald 107
Glasmon, Kubec 292
Glass, Ned 229

Glass, Paul 212
The Glass Key 107, 180, 237
The Glass Menagerie 197, 217, 348
The Glass Web 11, 37, 76, 94, 97, 121, 129, 130, 135, 136, 159, 172, 198, 210, 223, 248, 275, 310, 328
Glassmire, Gus 278
Glazer, Bert 62
Gleason, Jack 21
Gleason, Jackie 68, 136, 155, 183, 243
Gleason, James 136, 154, 202, 274, 306
Gleason, Keogh 324
Gleason, Lucille 202
Gleason, Pat 60, 315
Gleeson, Sgt. Harry H. 163, 224
Glengarry Glen Ross 188
The Glenn Miller Story 111, 201, 221, 275, 301
Glennon, Bert 266
Glicksman, Frank 325
Gloria 274
Glouner, Don 200
The Gnome-Mobile 130, 182
Go Ask Alice 185
The Goat Song 5, 43, 79, 128, 136, 137, 169, 171, 182, 196, 199, 203, 253, 267, 277, 314, 338, 339, 347
Goddard, John 62
Goddard, Mark 187
Goddard, Paulette 23, 137, 154, 186, 274, 331
The Goddess 72
Godey, John 229
The Godfather 18, 86, 99, 193, 329
The Godfather, Part II 304
The Godfather, Part III 142, 334
Godfrey, Ruth 312
Godfrey, Samuel T. 163, 176
Godowsky 35
Godzilla 298
Goebbels, Joseph 179
Goethe 245
Goff, Norris 114
Goin' South 56
Going in Style 64, 304
Going My Way 18, 54, 123, 196, 210, 300, 330
Going Wild 222
Gold, Donald 137
Gold, Zicha 228
Gold Rooster Plays 32
Goldberg, Isaac 163
Goldberg, William 117
Golden, John 336
Golden, Robert 51
Golden Boy 68, 79
Golden Earrings 100, 321
The Golden Girls 314
Goldenberg, Jack 116, 117
Goldenberg, Max 117
Goldenberg, Morris 3, 4, 60, 116, 117, 164

Goldenberg, Oscar 116, 117
Goldenberg, Zach 116
Goldfish, Samuel 259; *see also* Goldwyn, Samuel
Goldman, Laurence 69
Goldman, William 20
Goldsmith, Brian 149
Goldsmith, Jerry 111, 252, 258
Goldstein, Leonard 50
Goldstein, Robert 50, 335
Goldwyn, Samuel 38, 39, 40, 135, 137, 156, 259, 287, 327, 328, 329
Goldwyn Company 5
Goldwyn Studios 150, 259
Golitzen, Alexander 278
Golm, Lisa 85
Gomberg, Sy 212
Gomer Pyle, USMC 305
Gomez, Felipa 173
Gomez, Thomas 137, 173, 249
Gomphert, Frank 64
Gone with the Wind 29, 37, 51, 54, 84, 93, 149, 159, 169, 172, 220, 221, 222, 237, 311, 336
The Good Earth 222, 314
Good Gracious Annabelle 156
Good Housekeeping 145
"A Good Name" 12, 137, 138, 234, 250, 294, 310, 348
Good Neighbor Sam 13, 23, 29, 31, 38, 47, 76, 80, 82, 87, 95, 111, 121, 128, 137, 138, 141, 142, 182, 187, 203, 235, 251, 260, 279, 292, 298, 345
Good News 167, 186, 197
Good Sam 273
The Good, the Bad and the Ugly 329
Goodbye, Mr. Chips 57, 84, 134
Goode, Richard 344
Goodman, Benny & Orchestra 321, 331
Goodman, Frank 215
Goodman, John B. 126, 278
Goodrich, Jack 63
Goodson, Mark 339
Goodstein, Robert 312
Goodwin, Bill 155, 167
Goodwin, Harold 343
Goodyear Theatre 12, 137, 138, 148, 310
The Goose and the Gander 319
Goosson, Stephen 161
Gorcey, Leo 97, 138
Gordon, Gale 45, 199
Gordon, Leo 92
Gordon, Marianne 325
Gordon, Mary 60, 341
Gordon, Maude Turner 205
Gordon, Ruth 8, 28, 104, 105, 138, 139, 186, 198, 243, 249, 307, 345
The Gorgeous Hussy 86, 88, 271, 319

Index

Gorky, Maxim 5, 232, 253
Gorman, Tom 270
Gorme, Eydie 24
Gorog, Laszlo 306
Gorshin, Frank 185
Gorss, Saul 63
Gosden, Freeman 29
Gosnell, Ray 220
Gottlieb, Alex 167
Gottlieb, Richard 315
Gottlieb, Theodore 302
Goudal, Jetta 5, 57, 287
Gough, Lloyd 25, 84
Gould, Jack 106, 155
Gould, Morton 321, 328
Gould, Pauline 178
Gould, Sandra 167
Gould, William 86, 282
Goulding, Edmund 57
Goulding, Ray 143
Goulet, Violet 231
Gow, Gordon 125, 231
Grace, Henry 78, 241, 258
The Gracie Allen Murder Case 140
Graf, Bill 292
Graf, Louis 53
Graffman, Gary 70
Graham, Rev. Billy 347
Graham, Bob 206
Graham, Eddie 177
Graham, Fred 346
Graham, Jo 282
Graham, Sheila 200
Grand Hotel 43, 86, 88, 123, 211
Grand Prix 70, 220
Grand Slam 14, 22, 23, 47, 66, 67, 70, 71, 80, 106, 119, 121, 133, 139, 140, 141, 164, 168, 179, 187, 235, 244, 251, 268, 269, 304, 305
Granger, Bertram 108
Granger, Gerri 288
Granstedt, Greta 240
Grant, Cary 23, 280, 332
Grant, Gale 92
Grant, Kathryn 49, 89, 318
Grant, Lawrence 103
Grant, Ulysses S. 287
Granville, Bonita 75, 76
Granville, Charlotte 38, 287
The Grapes of Wrath 37, 54, 61, 68, 91, 125, 128, 129, 134, 219, 260, 277, 349
Grau, Gilbert C. 272
Grauman, Sid 306
Grauman, Walter 38, 236
Grauman's Chinese Theatre 306
Grauman's Egyptian Theatre 255
Graves, Peter 11, 48, 50, 51, 140, 189
Graves, Robert 341
Gray, Billy 12, 76, 111, 140, 325
Gray, Charles 306
Gray, Eden 122
Gray, Jack 341

Gray, Joe 272
Gray, Judd 108, 150
Gray, Lois 200
Gray, Marilyn 231
Gray, Maurine 341
Gray, Roger 40, 222, 341
Graziano, Rocky 208
Grease 32, 53
The Great Bank Robbery 86
The Great Dictator 112, 137
The Great Escape 210
Great Films: 50 Golden Years of Motion Pictures 193
The Great Gambini 319
The Great Gangster Pictures 271
The Great Garrick 95
The Great Gatsby 93, 142
The Great Imposter 234, 244
The Great Lie 35, 88, 149, 210
"The Great Man Votes" 140, 210, 264
Great Man's Lady 300
The Great McGinty 107, 142, 169
Great Movie Directors 110
The Great Movie Stars 57, 74
Great One: The Life and Legend of Jackie Gleason 155
The Great Race 116, 188, 202, 260
Great Radio Heroes 44
The Great St. Louis Bank Robbery 210
The Great Sebastians 128
The Great Waltz 54, 113, 275
The Great White Hope 43, 270
The Great Ziegfeld 61, 221, 255
The Greatest Show on Earth 96, 149, 175, 344
The Greatest Story Ever Told 95, 169, 218, 309
Greaza, Walter 44
Greco, El 34
Greeber, Rowby 185
The Greek Tycoon 165
Green, Alfred E. 91, 101, 140, 163, 219, 287, 291
Green, Bonnie 248
Green, Charlene 189
Green, Gov. Dwight R. 160
Green, Harry 32, 176
Green, Johnny 17, 18, 247, 340
Green, Mitzi 301
The Green Goddess 32, 140
Green Grow the Lilacs 294
The Green Pastures 29
Greenbaum, Everett 138
Greenberg, Joel 109, 126, 281
Greenberg, Stanley R. 295
Greene, Graham 289
Greene, Harrison 63
Greene, Jeanne 40, 176, 186
Greene, Lorne 11, 87, 140, 160, 299, 318
Greene, W. Howard 332
Greenleaf, Raymond 332
Greenstreet, Sydney 113, 167

Greenway, Tom 136, 318
Greenway Productions 42
Greenwich Village Theatre 116, 276
Gregg, Everley 316
Gregg, Virginia 237, 347
Gregory, James 324
Gregory, Wallace 63
Grenzbach, Charles 224
Grenzbach, Hugo 231
Grey, Joel 19
Grey, Shirley 194
Greystoke 269
Gribble, Henry 300
Gribboek, Robert 159
Grieg, Edvard 14, 49, 140, 166, 224, 245, 246, 293, 294
Grieg, Mrs. Edvard 150, 293
Grieg, Robert 306
Griffin, Carlton 341
Griffin, Robert 204
Griffith, D. W. 53, 68, 80, 89, 135, 327, 334
Griffith, E. H. 208
Griffith, Ray 194, 317
Griffith, Richard 193
Griffith, William W. 22, 30, 75, 140, 246
Griggs, Loyal 17, 66, 312
Grobel, Lawrence 104
Groman, Arthur 131
Gropper, Milton Hubert 336
Grossman, Samuel S. 276
Grot, Anton 32, 103, 141, 144, 191, 281, 282, 287, 322, 343
The Group Theatre 68, 75, 79, 304
Grubman, Anton 164
Gruenberg, Alex 315
Grumpy Old Men 31
Guadalcanal Diary 86, 167
Guard, Kit 40, 177, 341
The Guardsman 128, 199, 315
Guess Who's Coming to Dinner 76, 148, 172
Guest Star 53, 141, 265
Guffey, Burnett 66, 138, 141, 318
The Guild Theatre 75, 137, 171, 270
Guilden, Ira 70
Guilfoyle, Paul 21, 59, 88
Guillaroff, Sydney 78, 258
Guinness Book of World Records 54
Guion, Raymond 116
Gulf Screen Guild Theatre 28, 52, 141, 263
Gulf's We the People 141
Gump, Diane 313
Gun Crazy 188
Gunfight at the O. K. Corral 110, 114, 172
Gunga Din 51, 116, 146, 168, 197, 210, 267
Gunn, T. P. 326
The Guns of Navarone 38, 245, 260

Index

The Guns of the Magnificent Seven 269
Gunsmoke 172
Gunther, John 274
Guskin, Lud 69, 155, 347
Guskin, Paul 206
Guttman, Anna 116
Guttman, Henry 231
Guy, Ralph 92
A Guy Named Joe 54, 136, 237, 269, 321
Guys, Constantin 49, 151
Guys and Dolls 137, 206, 217, 271, 275, 305, 320
Gwenn, Edmund 140
Gwillim, Jack 55
Gypsy 144, 188, 203, 217, 285, 304

H. M. Pulham, Esq. 347, 348
Haade, William 27, 141, 173, 177, 231
Haas, Robert 91, 142, 163, 194, 291
Hackett, Joan 326
Hackett, John 148
Hackett, Walter 316
Hackman, Gene 19
Haden, Sara 240
Hagedon, Charles K. 324
Hagen, Erica 296
Hagney, Frank 62, 147, 313
Hail the Conquering Hero 144
Hailey, Oliver 243
Haines, Connie 237
Haines, Larry 45, 291
Haines, Robert T. 276
Haines, William 301
Hainey, Betty Jean 237, 347
Haire, Edward 111
The Hairy Ape 56, 156, 345
Hale, Alan 142, 207
Hale, Alan, Jr. 142
Hale, Bobby 103
Hale, Creighton 60, 86, 183
Hale, Edward Everett 205, 206, 256
Hale, Jonathan 165
Hale, Louise Closser 142, 153, 246, 314
Hale, Nancy 313
Hale, Richard 138
Hale, Wanda 157
Haley, Jack 113, 237
Halili, Genevieve 189
Hall, Alexander 161
Hall, Arsenio 313
Hall, Arthur Stuart 341
Hall, Ben 40
Hall, Betty 274
Hall, Charles 306
Hall, Claude 78
Hall, Danny 240
Hall, Diane 312
Hall, Donna 74
Hall, Evelyn 125
Hall, Porter 108, 142, 246, 314, 331

Hall, Sherry 278, 341
Hall, Thurston 27, 142
Hall, Willard 177
The Hall Johnson Choir 306
Haller, Ernest 207
Halligan, William 278, 306
Halliwell, Leslie 46, 51, 74, 135, 164, 185, 219, 229, 239, 257, 266, 294, 303, 306, 314, 319, 331, 333
Hallman, William E. 232
Halo, Grace 314
Halperin, Marty 190
Halsey, Brett 136
Halsey, Peter 293
Halsey, Adm. William F. 331
Halton, Charles 104, 126, 161, 162, 246, 314, 327
Hamilton, Chuck 74, 278
Hamilton, Daniel 22
Hamilton, Donald 332
Hamilton, George 12, 142, 324
Hamilton, John 85, 104, 142
Hamilton, Joseph 318
Hamilton, Kim 220
Hamilton, Margaret 81, 142, 290
Hamilton, Neil 42, 138, 142, 343
Hamilton, Scott 220
Hamilton, William 57
Hamlet 65, 76, 81, 115, 188, 236, 260
Hammer, Armand 15, 33, 142, 143, 344
Hammerstein, Oscar 57, 166, 169
Hammerstein Victoria Theatre 114
Hammett, Dashiell 203
Hammond, Charles 176
Hammond, Kay 313
Hammond, Virginia 333
Haney, Carol 201
The Hanging Tree 93, 279
Hankinson, Hank 118, 177
Hanlon, Bert 27, 143, 290
Hanlon, Tom 346
Hanna, Betty 218
Hannon, Betty 231
Hans Christian Andersen 171
Hans Eckelkamp Films 246
Hansen, Chuck 63, 173
Hanson, Peter 143, 147, 313, 332
Happy Days 54, 143, 311
The Happy Thieves 269
The Happy Time 56, 159, 234
Harbach, Otto 166
Harbaugh, Carl 32, 207
Harburg, E. Y. 274
Hard to Handle 201
The Hard Way 142, 199, 220, 221
The Harder They Fall 29, 141, 300
Harding, John 220
Hardwicke, Sir Cedric 11, 27, 143, 249, 312, 313, 293
Hardy, Michele 293
Hardy, Oliver 86, 301
Hare, Lumsden 32, 103, 143

Hari, Wilfred 104
Hariman, Averell 274
Harlan, Kenneth 177
Harlan, Richard 345
Harlow 90, 143
Harmon, Jim 81
Harmon, John 44, 290
Harness Bull 331
Harold and Maude 347
Harolde, Ralf 143, 282, 291
Harper 230, 334
Harper & Row 114
Harper's Bazaar 145, 279
Harper's Weekly 279
Harriet Craig 347
Harris, Arthur 71
Harris, Bill 189
Harris, Edna Mae 63
Harris, Howard 283
Harris, Jack 55
Harris, Julie 299
Harris, Ken 159
Harris, Major Sam 74, 231
Harris, Marcia 22
Harris, Phil 199
Harris, Robert B. 148, 187
Harris, Sam 5, 143, 195, 252
Harris, William, Jr. 38, 123, 232, 252
Harris, Winifred 27
Harris Theatre 326
Harrison, Doane 108
Harrison, Geneva 218
Harrison, Harry 295, 296
Harrison, James H. 346
Harrison, Linda 252
Harrison, Rex 170, 220, 298
Harrison, Robert 276
Harrison, Virginia 78
Harrison, William Henry 338
Harron, John 27, 86, 177, 290
Harry and Tonto 68
Hart, Ed 341
Hart, George Drury 122
Hart, John 167, 313
Hart, Moss 337
Hart to Hart 299, 334
Harte, Sam 206
Hartigan, Pat 341
Hartley, Neil 215
Hartzell, Harold 195
Harum, Avind 293
Harvey 61, 111, 172, 301
Harvey, Don C. 332
Harvey, H. M. 326
Harvey, Harry 25, 177
Harvey, John 215
Harvey, Laurence 13, 19, 143, 241
Harvey, Lew 52, 195
Harvey, Paul 81, 104, 290, 313, 341, 342
The Harvey Girls 31, 286
Haskell, Peter 209, 243
Haskin, Byron 17, 59, 103, 207, 282, 298

Hastings, Donald "Chippie" 44
Hatari 143
Hatch, William Riley 96
The Hatchet Man 7, 10, 27, 37, 56, 87, 101, 118, 120, 123, 132, 134, 141, 143, 144, 149, 154, 182, 186, 196, 197, 198, 202, 203, 217, 223, 225, 235, 239, 252, 252, 259, 334, 335, 338, 345, 348
Hatfield, Jack 177
A Hatful of Rain 31
Hathaway, Henry 12, 101, 144, 284, 285
Hauch, Edward 215
Haun, Harry 25
The Haunting 53
Hausman, Ernst 102, 103, 105
Hausner, Jerry 25, 45, 204, 220
Havemeyer, William Albert 293
Havlick, Gene 97
Havoc, June 144, 154, 158
Hawaii 261
Hawaii Five-O 97, 200
Hawkes, Kirby 204
Hawkins, David 46
Hawkins, William 216
Hawks, Howard 7, 39, 40, 83, 89, 101, 178, 316, 317
Hawley, H. Dudley 218
Haworth, Ted 17, 247, 340
Hawthorn Books 15, 26
Hayakawa, Ichiro 224
Hayden, Harry 144, 183, 306, 345
Hayes, Bernardine 219, 341
Hayes, George "Gabby" 301
Hayes, Helen 20, 200
Hayes, Herbert 219
Hayes, Jack 200
Hayes, Johnson 92
Hayes, Paul 22
Haygood, Amelia S. 333
Haymes, Bob 219
Haymes, Dick 112
Hayne, Donald 313
Haynes, Loren 206
Haynes, Marie 122, 195
Haynes, T. S. London 238
Hays, Arthur Gardner 154
Hays, Will 193
Hayter, James 293
Hayton, Lennie 327
Hayward, Chuck 74
Hayward, Louis 199
Hayward, Susan 10, 27, 40, 49, 144, 145, 157, 186, 274
Haywood, George 60
Haywood, Hilda 88
Hayworth, Rita 18, 145, 154, 228, 274, 280, 305, 306
"He Lied and I Listened" 207, 223, 268
He Ran All the Way 134
He Who Gets Slapped 283
Head, Edith 17, 18, 108, 126, 152, 224, 231, 247, 312, 315, 340

Hearn, Edward 109, 291, 341
Hearst, William Randolph 4, 145, 254, 256
The Heart of Show Business 89, 97, 145, 146, 156, 182, 286
Heartbreak House 285, 315
Heartbreak Kid 24
Hearts Aflame 172
Heath, John 220
Heather, Jean 108
Heaven Knows Mr. Allison 160, 220
Heaven with a Barbed Wire Fence 129
Hecht, Ben 7, 21, 38, 39, 40, 75, 83, 100, 122, 146, 200, 254, 259, 306, 327, 337
Hecht, Jenny 21
Heckart, Eileen 19
Hedda Gabler 65, 113, 163
Heflin, Van 106, 146, 154
Hefti, Neal 42
Heglin, Wally 327
Heidi 159, 226, 275
Heifetz, Jascha 35
Heindorf, Ray 59, 167, 282
The Heiress 156, 269
The Helburnesa 60
The Helen Morgan Story 252
Hell Divers 300
Hell on Frisco Bay 22, 37, 47, 49, 50, 53, 55, 71, 75, 83, 84, 96, 112, 118, 121, 131, 133, 143, 146, 147, 180, 182, 208, 223, 243, 249, 251, 256, 267, 283, 284, 301, 309, 321, 332, 335, 345, 348
Heller, Franklin 339
Heller in Pink Tights 234
Hellinger, Mark 59, 207, 347
Hello, Frisco, Hello 11, 91
"Hello My Baby" 224
Hell's Angels 134
Hellwig, Ed 277
Helm, Fay 206
Helm, Frances 206
Helmers, Peter 308
Helton, Percy 147, 331
Heman, Roger 157, 233, 306
Heming, Violet 326
Hemingway, Ernest 55, 202
Hendel, Hildegard 333
Henderson, Cracker 178
Henderson, Ed 345
Henderson, Florence 14, 90, 135, 223, 255, 293
Henderson, Jeanne 200
Henderson, Marcia 135
Henderson, Skitch 300
Hendrian, Dutch 183, 282, 341
Hendricks, Ben 63, 290
Hendricks, Ben, Jr. 177, 191
Hendrix, Wanda 280
Hendry, Len 231
Hendry, Marsh 229

Hengge, Paul 238
Hennessy, Dale 138
Henreid, Paul 84, 101, 154, 208, 280
Henrick, John 104
Henry, Bill 62, 74, 155
Henry, Buzz 200
Henry, Hank 247, 272
Henry, Mike 295
Henry, O. 24
Henry, Thomas Browne 158, 332, 344
Henry, Will 200
Henry, Behave 6, 82, 86, 147, 148, 149, 195, 234, 251, 252, 301, 332
Henry IV, Part I 81
Henry V 236
Hepburn, Katharine 28, 84, 86, 113, 148, 280, 320
Herald, Heinz 17, 104
Herbert, Galwey 30
Herbert, Henry 116
Herbert, Tim 209, 296
Herbert, Wilms 283
Here Come the Stars 43, 64, 148, 168, 310
Here Comes Mr. Jordan 217, 275
Hereford, Kathryn 258
Here's Hollywood 148, 310
Hergesheimer, Joseph 57
"Heritage" 12, 52, 71, 76, 102, 148, 182, 203, 235, 251, 310, 339, 348
Herman, Al 207, 290
Heron, Julia 345
Herrmann, Bernard 336
Herrmann, Edward 273
Hersh, Ben 21
Hersholt, Allan 209
Hersholt, Jean 6, 95, 106, 113, 155, 180, 190, 254, 267, 280
Hertz, David 52
Herzbrun, Bernard 25, 135
Herzog, Werner 179
Heston, Charlton 11, 14, 19, 24, 35, 48, 119, 128, 130, 148, 149, 186, 189, 248, 252, 255, 280, 294, 295, 296, 297, 312, 321, 347
Heston, Fraser 313
Heustis, Russell 162
Heydt, Louis Jean 104, 149, 161, 240
Heyes, Herbert 69
Heywood, Herbert 278
Hickey, Ralph B. 42
Hickman, Charles 341
Hickman, Cordell 306
Hickman, Howard 163, 205
Hickox, Sid 66, 144, 149, 194, 290
Hicks, Chuck 272
Hicks, Edward 326
Hicks, Russell 149, 278
Hiestand, John 136, 290

Index

High, Pauline 341
The High and the Mighty 52, 66, 94, 260, 321, 338
High Anxiety 330
The High Holy Days 149
"High Hopes" 17, 65, 152, 223, 330
High Noon 57, 180, 210, 220, 221, 329
High Sierra 64, 88, 172, 302, 320, 329
High Society 52, 65, 155, 199
High Wall 53
High Wide and Handsome 156
High Wind in Jamaica 200
Higham, Charles 84, 104, 109, 124, 126, 176, 177, 178, 207, 281
Highway Patrol 88
Highwood Productions 200
Higley, Hall 38
Hildebrand, Rodney 242, 341
Hill, Al 63, 98, 149, 150, 177, 184, 191, 195, 290, 327, 341, 343
Hill, Caryl Lee 272
Hill, George Roy 156
Hill, Gladys 302
Hill, Jack 301
Hill, Ramsay 204, 313
Hill, Sammie 204
Hill, Violet 147
Hillaire, Marcel 284
Hillcrest Country Club 43, 64
Hillebrand, Fred 158
Hilliard, Ernest 219
Hillier, Erwin 55
The Hi-Lo's 138, 298
Hilton, Arthur 126, 278, 316
The Hindenberg 221
Hindermann, Mario 247
Hinds, Samuel S. 150, 278
Hines, Harry 78
Hinton, Ed 313, 318
Hirsch, Foster 1, 24, 39, 48, 51, 63, 74, 110, 124, 152, 174, 176, 178, 181, 184, 192, 239, 241, 248, 281, 303, 313, 343
Hirschberg, Scott 122
Hirschfeld, Al 69
Hirshbein, Peretz 163
Hirshfeld, Zalmen 228
Hirshman, Herbert 285
Hirson, Roger O. 111
His Girl Friday 144, 260, 320
History Is Made at Night 68
Hitchcock, Alfred 2, 32, 68, 255, 257
Hitler 85, 179
Hitler, Adolf 84, 85, 104, 225, 227
Hitler—Dead or Alive 294
The Hitler Gang 54, 179, 321
Hitler's Madman 68
Hoag, Robert R. 241, 258, 295, 324
Hobbie, Duke 201

Hobbs, Peter 138
Hoch, Emil 253
Hodges, Eddie 75, 76, 152, 223, 315, 330
Hodgson, Leland 126
Hoff, Carl 208
Hoffenberg, Karl 208
Hoffenstein, Samuel 126, 306
Hoffman, Charles 42
Hoffman, David 126
Hoffman, Joseph 29
Hoffman, Max, Jr. 86, 177
Hoffman, Otto 40, 322
Hoffman, Robert 139
Hogarth, Lionel 163
Hoge, Ralph 21
Hogsett, Albert 308
Hohl, Arthur 52, 81, 150, 240, 341
Hoke, Travis "Weather" 176
Hold 'em Navy 97
Holden, James 167
Holden, William 154, 237
A Hole in the Head 12, 17, 18, 31, 41, 47, 49, 65, 68, 76, 81, 89, 90, 94, 100, 121, 128, 131, 150, 151, 152, 153, 154, 156, 169, 179, 186, 198, 223, 235, 244, 249, 251, 253, 259, 270, 275, 277, 288, 305, 308, 309, 315, 327, 328, 330, 336, 345, 348
The Hole in the Wall 6, 19, 43, 47, 75, 87, 89, 120, 132, 142, 153, 154, 186, 211, 235, 244, 251, 253, 256, 280, 320
Holiday 29, 156, 179
Holland, Bert 220
Holland, Betty Lou 99
Holland, Dick 184
Holland, Erik 258
Holland, John 258
Holland, Tom 98
Hollander, Frederick 207
Holley, Gibson 187
Holley, Ted 219
Holliday, Fred 207
Holliday, Hildegarde 75
Holliday, Judy 54
Holliday, Margaret 158
Hollister, Len 165
Holloway, Carol 341
Hollywood Bowl 128, 160, 224, 254, 328
Hollywood Canine Canteen 69, 154
Hollywood Cavalcade 338
Hollywood Citizen News 319
Hollywood Fights Back 37, 38, 42, 54, 56, 137, 144, 146, 154, 159, 160, 171, 182, 197, 256, 264, 276, 348
Hollywood Friars Honor George Jessel 168
The Hollywood Greats: Edward G. Robinson 15, 48, 154, 160, 168, 256, 265, 273, 277, 299, 311, 334

Hollywood Hotel 8, 64, 154, 155, 178, 263, 343
Hollywood in the Forties 109, 126, 281
Hollywood in the Thirties 40, 178, 323
Hollywood Independent Citizens of the Arts, Sciences and Professions 154
Hollywood on Hollywood 325
Hollywood Palace 13, 155, 256, 310, 315
Hollywood Palladium 280
Hollywood Reporter 82, 236, 318
Hollywood Showcase 155, 263
Hollywood Steps Out 69, 155
The Hollywood Studios 28, 110
Hollywood Talks Turkey 21
Hollywood Television Theatre 155, 311, 326
The Hollywood Ten 82, 83, 84, 158, 184, 321
Hollywood War Savings 155, 263
Holm, Celeste 12, 155, 270
Holman, Harry 40, 155, 207
Holmes, Brown 91
Holmes, Madeleine Taylor 201
Holmes, Stuart 103, 105, 155, 177, 231
Holmes, Wendell 291
Holmes, William 205, 346
The Holocaust 9, 100, 202, 227, 252, 337
Holohan, James B. 88
Holt, Jack 254
Homans, Robert 27, 40, 52, 155, 327, 341, 343
Hombre 270
Home from the Hill 197, 244
Home of the Brave 57
"Home on the Range" 223
Homel, Bob 229
Homes, Geoffrey 62
Homicidal 339
Homo Eroticus 166
Homolka, Oscar 293, 294
Hondo 117
The Honeymooners 68, 136, 155, 185, 197, 310
Honky Tonk 95
The Honorable Mr. Wong 27, 144, 155, 253
The Hoodlum 270
Hoover, Herbert 256
Hoover, J. Edgar 69, 84
Hope, Bob 35, 146, 155, 156, 237, 277, 280, 331, 347
Hope Floats 274
Hopkins, Arthur 5, 79, 96, 101, 156, 163, 164, 185, 231, 232, 252, 259, 275, 276
Hopkins, Bob 318
Hopkins, Miriam 39, 40, 47, 83, 95, 100, 156, 186, 195, 198, 248, 254

Index

Hopkins, Neil 320
Hopper, DeWolff 60, 156, 183, 207
Hopper, Edward 34
Hopper, Hedda 82, 156, 222, 247, 301
Hopper, William 156
Hopton, Russell 156, 194
The Horn Blows at Midnight 149, 169, 334
Hornbeck, William 152
Horne, Lena 35, 106, 146, 332
Horine, Agnew T. 176
Horowitz, Vladimir 35
Horse Feathers 305
Horsley, David S. 25, 135
Horta, Sam 42
Horton, Louisa 25, 156
Horvath, Charles 324
Horwitt, Arthur 236
Horwitz, Howie 42
Hosea, Robert 34
Hoskins, Alan 301
Hosley, Pat 291
The Hospital 72
Hot Millions 272
Hotchkiss, Preston 331
Houck, Doris 233
Hough, Horace 240
House, Billy 157, 291, 303
House Committee on Internal Security 159
House of Bamboo 172
House of Dark Shadows 43
House of Dracula 68
House of Rothschild 32
House of Seven Gables 189, 256
House of Strangers 10, 23, 27, 34, 36, 41, 66, 76, 86, 87, 94, 102, 111, 115, 118, 119, 120, 125, 128, 131, 144, 158, 168, 180, 182, 186, 198, 202, 203, 206, 217, 219, 221, 224, 235, 243, 249, 251, 255, 256, 268, 280, 299, 322, 328, 332, 345, 349
"House of Strangers" (radio) 158, 265, 280
House of Wax 169, 229, 256
House on 92nd Street 144, 196
House Un-American Activities Committee 10, 21, 26, 34, 47, 48, 54, 62, 82, 83, 86, 92, 96, 106, 118, 119, 145, 146, 148, 154, 158, 159, 184, 187, 200, 217, 244, 254, 261, 266, 299, 309, 311, 321, 330
Houseboat 189
Houseman, John 12, 154, 159, 169, 259, 317, 318, 323
Houston, Grace 25
Houtchens, Pat 296
Hovey, Ann 195
How Green Was My Valley 89, 129, 187, 344, 349
How I Play Golf— Trouble Shots 159, 286

How the Grinch Stole Christmas 171
How the West Was Won 12, 18, 90, 180, 203
How to Marry a Millionaire 37, 65, 255
How to Murder Your Wife 314, 321
How to Sleep 43
Howard, Arthur 184
Howard, Breena 78
Howard, Dorcy 266
Howard, Esther 306
Howard, Fredreick 322
Howard, Henry 176
Howard, Leslie 53, 81, 249, 329
Howard, Ron 82
Howard, Sidney 6, 113, 159, 180, 181, 227, 228, 253
Howard, Virginia 92
The Howards of Virginia 131
Howat, Clark 136, 165
Howdy Doody 185
Howe, James Wong 66, 102, 103, 104, 159, 241
Howe, Walter 275
Howell, Cheri 296
Howell, John 170
Howland, Jobyna 287
Howlett, Stanley 164, 246
Hoyt, John 69, 99
Hseuh, Nancy 74
Hubbard, Gordon 229
Hubbard, Lucien 17, 291
Hubbard, Mary 185
Hubbell, Carl 44, 298
Huber, Harold 81, 290
The Hucksters 131
Hud 159, 230, 270
Hudson, Barry 165
Hudson, Hal 148
Hudson, Robert 218
Hudson, Rock 18, 19, 35
Hudson Theatre 96, 326
Hueston, Fred 345
Hughes, Chris 272
Hughes, Everett 272
Hughes, Howard 23, 130, 261
Hughes, Kathleen 159, 223, 255
Hughes, John 183, 205
Hugo, Mauritz 258
Hull, Cordell 84
Hull, Henry 320
The Human Comedy 88, 130, 168, 221, 225
Human Wreckage 348
Humbert, George 57, 159, 177
Humoresque 131, 225
The Hunchback of Notre Dame 51, 93, 99, 143, 185
Hunt, Bowden 189
Hunt, Elizabeth 163
Hunt, Helen 137, 318, 332
Hunt, Hugh 78, 240
Hunt, Marsha 11, 21, 28, 76, 106, 154, 159, 223, 248, 255, 268, 327

Hunt, Phoebe 232
Hunter, C. Roy 113, 233, 242
Hunter, Kenneth 103
Hunter, Kim 252
Huntington Hartford 76
Hurley, Arthur 122, 253
Hurlie, Philip 306
The Hurricane 35, 68, 88, 137, 220
Hurricane Smith 88, 292
Hurst, Fannie 274
Husbands 116
Hush Hush Sweet Charlotte 24, 35, 64, 66, 87, 118, 147, 172, 221
Hush My Mouse 69, 159
Hussey, Ruth 52, 159, 160, 186, 197, 304, 345
The Hustler 136, 230
Huston, John 8, 10, 15, 17, 27, 41, 48, 49, 84, 101, 104, 113, 154, 160, 173, 174, 198, 203, 254, 302, 304, 338
Huston, Walter 81, 89, 113, 154, 160, 188, 254, 273, 274, 328, 336
The Hustons 104
Hutcheson, David 238
Hutchins, Bobby 301
Hutchinson, U. P. 238
Hutton, Bill 184
Hutton, Marion & the Modernaires 202
Hyams, Joe 247
Hyams, John 195
Hyatt, Don 86
Hyde, Mary Anne 126
Hyer, Martha 131
Hyland, Diana 14, 76, 160, 186, 208
Hymer, John B. 113
Hytton, Olaf 126

I Accuse 118
I Am a Fugitive from a Chain Gang 32, 52, 76, 100, 130, 182, 188, 222, 254, 332, 334
I Am an American 140, 160, 163, 224, 328
"I Am an American Day" 145, 160
I Am the Law 8, 30, 42, 65, 71, 87, 90, 98, 111, 118, 119, 120, 125, 128, 130, 132, 134, 141, 142, 149, 160, 161, 162, 171, 180, 186, 196, 201, 210, 235, 237, 244, 250, 268, 292, 305, 329, 334, 335, 347
I Can Get It for You Wholesale 182
I Cover the Waterfront 50
I Know My Love 199
I Love Lucy 38
I Love Trouble 117
I Loved a Woman 7, 27, 32, 41, 48, 71, 91, 111, 120, 123, 128, 130, 140, 142, 156, 162, 163, 179, 186, 197, 198, 200, 203, 210, 222,

223, 224, 235, 237, 251, 254, 259, 274, 319, 334, 335, 345
I Married a Witch 43, 172
I Never Sang for My Father 329
I Remember Mama 76, 86, 143, 237, 330
I Take This Woman 200
I Walk Alone 269
I Want to Live! 79, 86, 145
I Wanted Wings 281
I Will Not Go Back 134, 163, 224, 311, 315, 328
Ibsen, Henrik 4, 140, 163, 189, 245, 251, 252, 294
Ibsen, Lillebil 246
Ice Capades 112, 280
Ice Palace 169
The Iceman Cometh 101, 276, 315
Icons: Intimate Portraits 241, 257
An Ideal Husband 80
Idiot's Delight 128, 211, 288, 315
The Idle Inn 5, 43, 114, 156, 163, 164, 168, 171, 182, 253, 272, 345
If a Man Answers 256
If I Had a Million 300
If I Were King 210, 319
I'll Cry Tomorrow 86, 145, 210
I'll Never Go There Again 27, 157
Illegal 11, 23, 26, 27, 34, 36, 37, 47, 64, 66, 67, 71, 86, 87, 94, 95, 98, 103, 111, 120, 128, 133, 134, 141, 156, 164, 165, 172, 186, 197, 198, 208, 209, 210, 211, 223, 234, 252, 253, 267, 268, 269, 309, 332, 335
Illing, Peter 238
I'm All Right, Jack 55, 314
"I'm Dancing with Tears in My Eyes" 223
Imazu, Eddie 44, 152
Imbro, Gaetano 202
Imitation of Life 157, 179, 223, 234, 236
Immaculate Heart College 277
Imperial Studios 215
Impossible on Saturday 34
In a Lonely Place 197
In and Out 269
In Cold Blood 52, 129, 301
In Enemy Country 283
In Name Only 130, 332
In Old Arizona 169
In Old Chicago 52, 55, 76, 336
In Old Kentucky 135
In the Arena 149, 297, 313
In the Doghouse 90
In the Heat of the Night 169, 300
In the Wings 111
In Which We Serve 97
Ince, John 40, 341
Ince, Ralph 144, 191, 268, 281
Incident at Vichy 79, 217
Incident in San Francisco 235
The Incredible Hulk 298

The Incredible Shrinking Man 298
Independence Day 298
Independent Releasing Company 302
Indianapolis Star 195
Indrisano, John 324
Inescourt, Frieda 186, 307, 345
The Informer 129, 130, 141, 172, 210, 261, 277
Ingersoll, William 137
Inglis, Elizabeth 316
Ingraham, Rev. J. H. 312
Ingraham, Lloyd 181
Ingraham, Mitchell 184, 314
Ingraham, Sunny 341
Ingram, Rex 274
Inherit the Wind 31, 42, 86, 100, 221, 222, 320
The Ink Spots 274
Inkjinoff, Valery 247
Inn, Frank 220
"The Inner Voice" 165, 263
"Innocent Friends" 165, 263
The Inquisition in Hollywood 158
Inside Daisy Clover 138
The Insider 320
Inspiration Pictures 57, 120
Intermezzo 43, 265
International House 66
International Writers Guild 228
Interrupted Melody 244
An Intimate Dinner in Celebration of Warner Bros. Silver Jubilee 53, 116, 166, 211, 286, 348
Intimate Strangers 308
Intolerance 53, 197, 208
The Invasion of the Body Snatchers 210, 298
Invasion U.S.A. 272
The Invisible Man 320
Ireland, John 112
Irene 240, 306
Irish, William 233, 347
Irish National Players 101
Irma La Douce 201
The Iron Man 61
Irving, Ellis 103
Irving, Paul 103
Irving, Richard 111
Irving Thalberg Award 188
Irwin, Boyd 109, 278
Irwin, John 341
Is Zat So? 136
"Island in the Wilderness" 115, 166, 264
Island of Lost Souls 32, 58, 150
Islands in the Stream 272
Ismay, Joseph B. 49
Israel, Robert 189
Israel: Its Ancient Glories and Its Wonders of Today 166, 286
Istomin, Eugene 70
It All Came True 332
It Came from Outer Space 159, 169
It Had to Be You 223

It Happened One Night 37, 54, 61, 68, 155
It Pays to Advertise 211
It Takes a Thief 334
"It Isn't Peanuts" 166, 256, 263, 321
It's a Great Feeling 10, 17, 20, 21, 37, 47, 65, 81, 88, 90, 94, 119, 120, 133, 134, 141, 166, 167, 171, 198, 220, 221, 223, 234, 244, 251, 265, 292, 294, 304, 332, 334, 348
It's a Mad, Mad, Mad, Mad World 29, 112, 125, 160, 314
It's a Wonderful Life 41, 54, 68, 86, 118, 150, 155, 182, 200, 220, 301, 305, 320, 334
It's Always Fair Weather 72
It's Your Move 26, 29, 70, 167, 202, 314
Iturbi, Jose 35, 332
Ivan, Rosalind 32, 60, 167, 232, 278, 345
Ivanhoe 309
Ivano, Paul 126
Ivarsen, Ike 258
I've Got a Secret 225
Ives, Burl 20
Ivins, Perry 171

J. B. 209
J. Weiss & Sons, Inc. 92, 215
Jaap, Nelan 176
The Jack Benny Show 43
The Jack Rider 344
The Jackie Robinson Story 140
Jackman, Fred, Jr. 63, 137, 153, 205
Jackson, Andrew 256
Jackson, Anne 11, 76, 167, 215, 252, 334
Jackson, Cornwall 277
Jackson, Fred 153
Jackson, Joey 272
Jackson, Joseph 17, 291
Jackson, May Ann 301
Jackson, Michael 19, 256
Jackson, Selmer 85, 194
Jackson, Thomas E. 27, 167, 191, 278, 345
Jacob, Gordon 170
Jacobovitch, Alain 228
Jacobowsky and the Colonel 338
Jacobs, Marilyn 300
Jacques Seligman & Company 33
Jacquin, Maurice 246
Jaeckel, Richard 44, 167, 332
Jaeger, Frederick 163, 293
Jaffe, Bettye Ackerman 48, 167, 168, 189, 190, 209, 220
Jaffe, Sam 5, 14, 15, 34, 48, 54, 65, 131, 154, 163, 167, 168, 209, 220, 236, 252, 276, 290, 299, 319
Jaguar Productions 147

Index

Jailhouse Rock 285
James, Dennis 339
James Gladden 341
James, Henry 4, 231
James, Horace 195
James, Jeri Lou 76, 136
James, Jerry 231
James Cagney, a Celebration 291
Jameson, House Baker 75, 137
Jameson, Joyce 138
Jamison, Bud 161, 341
Jane Eyre 61, 208, 221, 234
Janney, Leon 70
Janney, William 322
Jans, Alice 195
Jaquet, Frank 103, 158, 168, 306
Jaws 328
Jay, John 49
Jay-Thorpe 262
The Jazz Singer 96, 125, 168, 335
Jeakins, Dorothy 17, 312
Jean Hersholt Humanitarian Award 19, 265
Jean-Louis 318, 332
Jeanne Eagles 131
Jefferson, Thomas 239, 256
Jeffrey, William 341
Jehlinger, Charles 111
Jenkins, Allen 27, 58, 59, 81, 168, 249, 272, 290, 301
Jenkins, Ed 219
Jenkins, Jackie "Butch" 41, 75, 168, 240
Jenkins, Joseph Wilcox 163, 233, 242
Jennings, DeWitt 168, 233, 242
Jenny, Rev. Ray Freeman 160
Jensen, Eulalie 291
Jensen, John 17, 312
Jensen, Karen 243
Jenson, Anne Frances 117
Jenson, Hortense 117
Jenson, Jack 117
Jenson, Roy 295
Jerome, Jerry 173, 184
Jerome, M. K. 177, 290
Jerusalem Is Her Name 168, 222, 252, 265
Jessel, George 148, 154, 168, 209, 274, 280, 319, 337
Jessup, Richard 13, 77
The Jest 156, 345
Jester, Ralph 17, 312
Jesus Christ Superstar 169
The Jetsons 298
Jett, Sheldon 345
Jewell, Austin 78
Jewell, Isabel 52
Jewell, Jack E. 316
Jewish Federation 259, 299, 344
Jewish Foundation Council 24, 149
Jewish Theological Seminary 321
Jewison, Norman 13, 76, 77, 101, 169

Jezebel 93, 142, 334
JFK 35, 129
Jiminez, Soledad 169, 177
Jimmy the Gent 340
Joan of Arc 41, 118
Joan of Lorraine 288
Joanna 95
Jobe, Bill 212
Jocelyn, June 313
"Joe Doakes and the White Star" 169, 263, 321
Johann, Zita 136, 169, 186, 198, 252, 314, 317, 318, 345
Johansen, Virgil 308
John, Alice 38
John Brown's Body 209
John Ford 73
John Golden Theatre 227
John Paul Jones 117
John Robert Powers 76
John W. Blake 326
Johnny Allegro 265
Johnny Apollo 33, 144
Johnny Belinda 36, 53, 142, 220, 221, 348
Johnny Eager 146, 172, 243
Johnny Got His Gun 159, 321
Johnny Guitar 118
Johns, Arthur 302
Johnson, Ben 73, 74, 169
Johnson, Bill 331
Johnson, Eleanor 116
Johnson, Hall 306
Johnson, J. Andrew 246
Johnson, J. McMillan 241, 258
Johnson, John Lester 63
Johnson, Lyndon B. 49, 71, 256
Johnson, Marjorie 345
Johnson, Nunnally 345, 346, 347
Johnson, Russell 51, 169
Johnson, Van 28
Johnston, J. W. 346
Johnstone, Babs 161
Johnstone, William 25, 175, 204
The Joker Is Wild 330
Jolley, Stan 177
Jolly Films 139
Jolson, Al 189, 224, 244, 277
Jolson Sings Again 244
The Jolson Story 140, 244
Jones, Bob 200
Jones, Bobby 159
Jones, Carolyn 12, 94, 151, 152, 169, 315
Jones, Chuck 159
Jones, Dean 185
Jones, Harmon 157
Jones, Jack 288
Jones, Jennifer 29
Jones, Pardner 341
Jones, Peter 189
Jones, Quincy 200
Jones, Robert Edmund 163
Jones, Roy 293
Jones, Shirley 18, 90, 223, 247

Jones, Stanley 165, 290
Jones, Teddy 275
Jones, Victor V. 21
Jones, Virginia 200
Jones, Wesley 157
Jordan, Bobby 75, 81, 89, 98, 169, 290
Jordan, Charles 327
Jordan, Geraldine 158
Jory, Victor 74, 169, 201, 339, 340
Josephine, Empress of France 226, 329
Josephus 312
Joslyn, Allyn 122, 169, 252
Jostyn, Jay 220
The Journey 167, 195, 240
Journey for Margaret 94, 234
Journey into Fear 87, 95, 221, 335
Journey to the Center of the Earth 37
Journey Together 9, 22, 23, 35, 47, 55, 87, 120, 165, 169, 170, 197, 198, 227, 234, 251, 298, 309, 319, 336, 345
Jowett, Corson 25, 302
Joy, Leatrice 52
Joy, Nicholas 115
Joyner, Harry 218
Juarez 53, 56, 180, 273
Juarez and Maximilan 6, 49, 68, 79, 99, 101, 150, 170, 171, 182, 184, 187, 196, 199, 210, 220, 234, 251, 253, 277, 314, 338
Judaism 227
Judge Priest 79, 182
Judgment at Nuremberg 27, 76, 100, 182, 285, 320, 338
Judgment in the Sun 27
Judy, Scott 189
The Juggler 23, 182
Jul, Leif 293
Julia Misbehaves 273
Julian, Paul 262
Julius Caesar 20, 65, 81, 114, 130, 134, 135, 149, 206, 256
Jumbo 112, 265
June, Ray 17, 40, 66
June Bride 88
The Jungle Book 65
Jungle Girl 135, 180
The Jungle Queen 273
Jungle Woman 196
Junior Bonner 199
Junior Miss 130
Juno and the Paycock 123
Jupiter Darling 168
Jurassic Park 35, 298
Jurgens, Curt 49
Jurist, Ed 288
Jussara 139
Just Tell Me When to Cry 125
Justice, James Robertson 238
Justin, John 170
Justman, Robert 21, 233

Index

KABC 188
KaDell, Carlton 45, 283
Kael, Pauline 293
Kagno, Marcia 75, 153
Kai-Shek, Chiang 239, 254
Kai-Shek, Madame Chiang 254
Kaliz, Armand 60, 191
Kalloch 161
Kamus, Natalie 167
Kamp, Kenner C. 248
Kandel, Aben 316
Kane, Bob 42
Kane, Byron 53, 331
Kane, Eddie 126, 177, 291, 301
Kane, Whitford 163
Kaneoko, Kazue 224
Kanin, Fay 241
Kanin, Garson 138
Kanin, Michael 184, 241
Kansas City Bomber 210
Kansas City Confidential 130
Kantor, Lenard 318
Kaper, Bronislau 240, 302
Kaplan, Sol 71, 306
Karath, Kym 76, 138
Karloff, Boris 7, 31, 89, 125, 171, 190, 291
Karlson, Phil 318
Karnes, Robert 331
Karp, Jack 131
Karsner, David 32, 48, 162, 163
Karr, Michael 228
Kasarda, John 206
Kate Smith's A & P Bandwagon 171, 263
Katima, Milton 321
Katz, Allan 185
Katz, Ephraim 66, 118, 125
Katz, Harry 224
Katzman, Jacob 176
Kaufman, George S. 204, 205
Kaufman, Hunter 176
Kaufman, Murray 243
Kaufman, Willy 85
Kaufmann, Stanley 74
Kay, Mary Ellen 313, 331
Kayden, William 237
Kaye, Danny 46, 131, 154, 167, 171, 237, 254, 274, 321, 332
Kaye, Davy 46
Keane, Edward 85, 161, 171, 278, 341
Keane, Richard 313
Keane, Robert Emmett 85
Kearney, James 123
Kearns, Joseph 204, 225
Keating, Monica 340
Keating, Peter 189
Keaton, Buster 301, 332
Keats, Norman 92, 318
Keefe, Cornelius 341
Keehne, Chuck 229
Keeler, O. B. 159
Keeler, Ruby 335
Keenan, Frank 5, 172, 245, 348

Keep Your Powder Dry 40
Keeper of the Flame 88
Kehner, Jim 184
Keighley, William 63, 101, 175, 319
Keightley, Cyril 275
Keith, Brian 11, 172, 198, 318, 332
Keith, Byron 302
Keith, Ian 312
Keith, Robert 172
Kellaway, Cecil 59, 172
Keller, Walter 69
Kelley, Alice 136
Kelley, Barry 172, 272, 331
Kelley, DeForrest 165, 172
Kelley, John 117
Kellogg, John 158
Kellogg, Phil 151
Kellogg, Ray 74
Kelly, Annette 215
Kelly, Gene 72, 154, 254, 274, 277
Kelly, Jack 51, 136, 172, 332
Kelly, John 184, 194, 207, 306, 322
Kelly, Kitty 183
Kelly, Maisie 238
Kelly, Mal 262
Kelly, Paula 295
Kelly, Wallace 312
Kelsey, Fred 183
Kemp, Hugh 347
Kemper, Charles 278
Ken Darby Chorus 331
Kendall, Cy 45, 52, 172, 178, 184, 278
The Kenell Murder Case 332
Kennealy, Hon. Martin 160
Kennedy, Arthur 73, 74, 172
Kennedy, Bryce 333
Kennedy, Charles 232
Kennedy, Edward M. "Ted" 49
Kennedy, Evelyn 229
Kennedy, Harold J. 206
Kennedy, John F. 100, 160, 254, 256, 270, 288
Kennedy, John Milton 98, 175, 203, 237, 347
Kennedy, Mary 204
Kenney, General 160
Kenney, Jack 183
Kenney, Kay 64
Kenny, Joseph E. 135
Kent, Barbara 172, 233
Kent, Ted J. 135
The Kentuckian 68, 130
Kentucky 57, 140, 149, 271
Kenyon, Charles 163
Kerman, David 88, 178
Kern, Jerome 154, 166
Kern, Robert J. 324
Kerr, Donald 136, 177, 346
Kerr, Joseph 25
Kerr, Walter 37
Kerrigan, J. M. 40, 172
Kesson, Frank 159
Ketchum, Dave 138
Kevin, Anne 92

Kevin, Sandy 78
Key, Alice 21
Key Largo 10, 17, 18, 37, 41, 47, 48, 50, 53, 67, 71, 83, 94, 101, 111, 112, 119, 120, 125, 129, 131, 133, 134, 135, 137, 141, 150, 156, 160, 172, 173, 174, 175, 182, 186, 188, 198, 218, 221, 223, 230, 234, 249, 251, 253, 267, 288, 292, 321, 323, 334, 335, 336, 337
"Key Largo" (radio) 175, 199, 264
Keyes, Evelyn 154, 274
Keyes, Paul W. 185
Keymas, George 21
Keys, Basil 46
Keys of the Kingdom 166, 245
Keystone Kops 229, 301
Khartoum 179
Kiam, Omar 40
Kibbee, Guy 91, 175, 322
Kibbee, Milton 63, 175, 177, 205, 278, 327
The Kibitzer 6, 82, 132, 140, 142, 171, 175, 176, 186, 235, 251, 252, 253, 305, 347
Kid Galahad 8, 18, 26, 43, 53, 58, 61, 68, 71, 79, 87, 88, 89, 90, 93, 95, 100, 112, 118, 120, 130, 131, 134, 149, 156, 159, 169, 175, 176, 177, 178, 182, 186, 198, 201, 217, 221, 222, 223, 230, 234, 251, 259, 268, 299, 304, 320, 321, 333, 334, 335, 338, 339
"Kid Galahad" (radio) 154, 172, 178, 199, 263
Kid Millions 118
Kidd, Jonathan 284
Kidnapped 61
Kieling, Wolfgang 238
Kiernan, William 17, 247
Kiesler, Alice 163
Kikuchi, Makoto 224
Kilbore, Sen. Harry 154
Kilgallen, Dorothy 243, 339
Kilian, Victor 52
Kill the Umpire 269
The Killers 61, 76, 95, 144, 181, 182, 199
Killifer, Jack 63, 291
Kilpatrick, Lincoln 295
Kilpatrick, Thomas 176
Kim 199, 321
Kim, Meayon Yon 204
Kim, William 204
Kind Lady 115
Kinesis Films/Miniter/Tecisa 202
King, Andrea 244
King, Charles 341
King, Jean 231
King, Jennifer 296
King, Joseph 63
King, Muriel 345
King, Sonny 272
King, Walter Woolf 313
King, Zalman 76, 178, 228

Index

The King and Four Queens 244
The King and I 61, 217, 226
King Creole 169
King Kong 33, 125, 267, 348
King Lear 65, 68, 81, 157, 319
King of Hearts 57, 256
King of Kings 97, 279, 335
King of the Lumberjacks 268
King of the Royal Mounted 301, 302
King of the Underworld 268
King Rat 141
King Sisters 332
King's Row 89, 118, 159, 241, 265, 334
Kingsberry, Jacob 163, 276
Kingsbury, Lillian 122, 232
Kingsford, Guy 63
Kingsford, Walter 88, 103, 178, 179, 226, 326, 327
Kingsley, Dorothy 83, 208, 243, 247
Kingsley, Sidney 10, 92, 101, 179, 229, 253
Kinnell, Murray 163
Kinney-Wolf 293
Kinoy, Ernest 285
Kinsella, Walter 54
Kinski, Klaus 139, 179
Kinski, Natassja 179
Kipling, Rudyard 14, 163, 315
Kippen, Manart 179, 218, 253, 276
Kirk, J. Francis 54
Kirkham, J. Ellis 122
Kirshner, May 92
Kismet 4, 65, 88, 179, 253
The Kiss 36
A Kiss in the Dark 241
Kiss Me, Kate 286, 348
Kiss of Death 144, 343
Kiss Them for Me 208
Kissel, William 147
Kisselgoff, Anna 71
The Kissing Bandit 220, 348
Kitson, Barbara 246
Kitt, Eartha 24, 70, 179, 321
Kittelson, Theodore 185, 293
Kittleson, John 185
Kitty Foyle 88, 179, 273, 300, 321
Klauber, Adolph 326
Klavin, Walter 270
Klaw, Marc 252
Klaw Theatre 30, 203
Klega, Danny 258
Klein, Charles 131
Klein, Earl 159
Kleiner, Harry 332
Kleinsinger, George 270
Kline, Brady 341
Kline, Richard H. 111, 295
Kling, Saxon 185
Klinowski, Jacek 85, 109, 174
Klipstein, Abner D. 215
Knapp, Evelyn 179, 291

Knickerbocker Holiday 160
Knight, Shirley 326
Knoblauch, Edward 179, 253
Knock on Any Door 40, 97, 270
Knoedler & Company 33, 141
Knopf, Christopher 148
Knotts, Don 300
Knowles, Pamela 189
Knox, Alexander 8, 84, 179, 249, 280, 282
Knox, Mickey 46
Knute Rockne — All American 37, 235, 243, 265
Kobal Collection 190
Kobayashi, Ikuo 224
Kobe, Gail 312
Koch, Ed 49
Koch, Howar 19, 271
Koch, Norma 200
Koch Institute 284
Koch, Dr. Robert 41, 104, 105
Koehler, Ted 205
Koenekamp, H. F. 167, 207, 282
Koestler, Arthur 83, 92, 179
Kohler, Fred, Jr. 219, 312
Kohlmar, Lee 287
Kojak 277
Kolker, Henry 63, 163
Komack, James 76, 152, 179
Komai, Tetsu 113
Komisarjevsky, Theodore 246, 253
Kopell, Bernie 138
Korngold, Erich Wolfgang 281, 282
Kosleck, Martin 85, 179
Kostolefsky, Joseph 152
Kotto, Yaphet 180, 212
Koussevitzky, Serge 35
Kovacs, Ernie 141, 247, 292
Kovaleske, Mitchell 167
Kovitz, Arthur 243
Kraft Music Hall 180, 224, 264
Kramer, Dr. Will 149
Kramer vs. Kramer 112
Kranz, Jack 118, 177
Krasna, Norman 224
Krasner, Milton 66, 157, 180, 278, 324, 345
Krembs, Felix 326
Krents, Milton E. 321
Kress, Harold F. 327
Krieg, Frank 25
Krims, Milton 84, 85, 103, 131
Kroeger, Berry 180, 284
Kroman, Carla 117
Kroman, Jeanne (Westervelt) 75, 117, 255
Kroman, Lisa (Zaslove) 117
Kroman, Manuel 254
Kronenberger, Louis 216
Kronman, Henry 254, 328
Krueger, Larraine 327
Kruger, Otto 8, 64, 102, 103, 104, 161, 180
Kruger, Paul 308

Krugman, Lou 175
Kuder, Edward 250
Kuehl, William L. 147
Kuhl, Calvin 344
Kulky, Henry 165
Kuller, Sid 21
Kullers, John "Red" 158
Kummer, Claire 38
Kummer, Frederic Arnold 333
Kuni, Satoko 224
Kunioshi, Yasuo 34
Kuri, Emile 229
Kurosawa, Akiro 13, 241
Kurrle, Robert 291
Kuter, Leo K. 173
Kuzman, Serge 42
Kyokawa, Tamae 224
Kyser, Kay 82, 331

LaBey, Louis 176
LaCava, Louis 340
Lachman, Mort 18
Lackteen, Frank 105, 180, 282, 313
LaCossitt, Henry 233
Ladd, Alan 11, 53, 107, 118, 146, 147, 180, 256, 277
Ladies' Man 211
Lady Be Good 195, 276, 294
Lady Caroline Lamb 269
Lady Esther's Screen Guild Players 127, 180
Lady Esther's Screen Guild Theatre 28, 52, 180, 263, 264
The Lady Eve 42, 96, 128, 299
Lady for a Day 68, 175, 244
Lady from Louisiana 222
The Lady from Shanghai 145, 338
Lady in the Dark 58, 143, 272, 276
Lady of the Pavements 330
A Lady to Love 6, 19, 29, 38, 47, 71, 102, 120, 135, 159, 165, 180, 181, 186, 188, 197, 198, 199, 203, 234, 250, 251, 253, 267, 279, 283
The Lady Vanishes 199, 340
The Ladykillers 200
Laemmle, Carl, Jr. 113, 233, 242, 328
Laemmle, Nina 148
LaGuardia, Fiorello 54
Laidlaw, Ethan 181, 191, 282, 313, 332
Laine, Frankie 288
Laird, Jack 212
Lake, Janet 324
Lally, Lorraine 147
Lally, Mike 27, 177
LaMal, Isabel 290
LaMar, Margaret 195
Lamarr, Hedy 280
LaMarr, Richard 25, 181

Lamb, Gil 138
Lambert, Tom 51
The Lambs 181, 182, 211
"Lambs' Gambols" 182
Lamour, Dorothy 156, 283
Lancaster, Burt 10, 24, 25, 26, 35, 76, 146, 154, 182, 254, 257
Lanchester, Elsa 306
Land, Barbara 207
Landau, Arthur 69
Landau, David 182, 205
Landau, Martin 182, 214, 215, 252
Landers, Scott 158
Landfield, David 248
Landi, Aldo Bufi 46
Landi, Elissa 81
Landis, Carole 290
Landsburg, Alan 29
Lane, Allen 291
Lane, Ben 138, 247
Lane, Charles 138, 182, 203, 291
Lane, Harry 225
Lane, Priscilla 254
Lane, Richard 59, 182
Lang, Charles B. 147, 177, 308
Lang, Fritz 9, 10, 119, 182, 259, 277, 278, 279, 342, 346, 347
Lang, Harry 225
Lang, June 126
Lang, Michel 246
Lang, Sven 276
Langdon, Dory 17, 247
Lange, Arthur 17, 342
Lange, Helmut 247
Langford, Frances 331
Langner, Lawrence 147
Langner, Ruth 136
Langsner, Clara 336
Langton, Paul 44
Lansbury, Angela 19
Lansing, Jeanne 152
Lansing, Joi 152
Lantz, Walter 299
Lapis, Joe 126
Lara, Augustine & Maria Teresa 247
Larceny, Inc. 9, 20, 27, 37, 54, 58, 68, 79, 81, 87, 88, 93, 111, 120, 125, 128, 130, 134, 136, 144, 156, 172, 183, 184, 219, 220, 222, 223, 235, 244, 248, 253, 256, 259, 260, 268, 299, 304, 334, 335, 348
Larch, John 165, 318
Lardner, Ring, Jr. 78, 84, 184
Larimore, Earle 5, 170, 184, 227, 252, 314
Larimore, Stella 276
The Lark 31
Larkin, Eddie 161
Larkin, John 291
Larned, Ellen 163, 246
Larner, Elizabeth 293
Larsen, Tambi 241
LaRue, Jack 272

LaRue, Roy 116
Lash, Harry 184
Lashelle, Joseph 325
Lashley, Ella Mae 306
Lasky, Jesse L. 95, 137, 154, 244, 312, 313
Lassie Come Home 340
Last Angry Man 23, 66, 159, 221, 222, 336
"Last Call" 131, 271
The Last Bridge 279
The Last Gangster 8, 37, 42, 52, 55, 58, 64, 65, 67, 71, 75, 86, 87, 90, 94, 119, 120, 130, 132, 133, 134, 135, 149, 166, 172, 184, 185, 186, 188, 198, 199, 201, 219, 226, 230, 235, 237, 244, 249, 251, 256, 271, 290, 299, 300, 304, 320, 335, 337, 338
The Last Hurrah 55, 58, 69, 86, 130, 136, 210, 235, 304, 348
"The Last I Ever Saw of My Man" 223
The Last Mile 130, 150, 190, 217, 301, 339
Last of the Mohicans 344
The Last Picture Show 169
The Last Starfighter 236
The Last Sunset 344
Last Time I Saw Paris 107
Lastfogel, Abe 214
The Late Christopher Bean 159, 197
The Late George Apley 42, 43, 89, 90
The Late Show 68, 112
Latell, Lyle 231
Latham, Stuart 170
Lathrop, Philip H. 78
Lathrop, Lawrence 346
Latimer, Jonathan 231
Latour, Donna 158
Lau, Fred 152
Lauck, Chester 114
Laugh-In 14, 185, 217, 311
Laughton, Charles 106, 155, 180, 185, 224, 267, 272, 275, 306
Launzi 5, 71, 156, 185, 186, 187
Laura 112, 184, 219, 256
Laurel, Stan 86, 301, 333
Lauren Bacall By Myself 37, 175
Laven, Arnold 187, 331
LaVerne, Lucille 186, 191
Lavi, Dahlia 166, 324
The Law of the Tropics 167
Lawford, Peter 49, 126, 186, 247
Lawler, Anderson 181
Lawman 244
Lawrence, Bill 155
Lawrence, Carl 278
Lawrence, Marc 84, 161, 173, 186, 308
Lawrence, Viola 17, 161, 247, 318, 341
Lawrence, W. E. 341
Lawrence of Arabia 118, 285, 298

Lawson, Kate 75, 227
Lawson, Priscilla 184
Lawton, Donald 284
Lax, Eric 148, 184, 175, 249
Layson, Lorena 163
Layton, Turner 327
Lazarus, Milton 293
Leach, Viola 195
Leachman, Cloris 19, 29
Leader, Anton M. 321, 348
League of Nations Association 254
Leakey, Phil 55
Lear, Norman 208
Leather, Derrick 228
The Leathernecks 286
Leave Her to Heaven 196, 269, 298
Leavitt, Sam 284
LeBaron, Eddie 284
Lecomte, Claude 246
Lederer, Francis 85, 187, 226, 299
Lee, Anna 126, 186, 187, 197, 258
Lee, Billy 76
Lee, Bruce 42
Lee, Carolyn 195
Lee, Dorothy 301
Lee, Gypsy Rose 13, 144, 340
Lee, Johnny 306
Lee, Leonard 135
Lee, Linda 112
Lee, Michele 288, 326
Lee, Morris 204
Lee, Phoebe 92
Lee, Robert E. 104
Lee, Robert N. 17, 191
Lee, Wendy 167
Leeds, Andrea 178
Leeds, Peter 318
Leetch, Tom 229
LeFranco, Tony 117
The Left-Handed Gun 243
LeGalliene, Eva 43
"The Legend of Jim Riva" 12, 43, 71, 76, 133, 134, 187, 234, 250, 251, 256, 270, 300, 305, 309, 310, 345
The Legend of Lylah Clare 283
"Legends of Hollywood" 3, 149, 255
LeGrand Sounds for Sight 228
Lehman, Ernest 25;7, 258
Leiber, Fritz 278
Leigh, Janet 14, 139, 140, 187, 247, 304
Leigh, Nelson 219
Leigh, Phillip 30, 60, 171, 187, 227, 246, 270
LeMaire, Charles 157
LeMaire, William 287
Lemmon, Jack 13, 18, 19, 23, 82, 87, 95, 138, 187, 188, 247, 248
Lemon, Warren 262
The Lemon Drop Kid 338
Lenin, Vladimir 83
Lenny, Bill 200
Lensky, Andre 163

Leon, Connie 306
Leon, Peggy 341
Leonard, David 163
Leonard, Gus 291
Leonard, Harry M. 284
Leonard, Queenie 258
Leonard, Robert 55
Leong, James 144, 242
Lepke 199
LeRoy, Mervyn 7, 9, 49, 101, 124, 131, 188, 190, 191, 193, 209, 222, 315, 322, 323, 327, 335
Lerpae, Paul 312
LeSaint, Edward 162
LeSeuer, Robert 262
Lesser, Sol 188, 259, 266, 327, 331
Lester, Bruce 126
Lester, Ellliott 322, 323
Letondal, Henri 62
Let's Make Love 220
The Letter 93, 134, 197, 300, 334
Letter from an Unknown Woman 76
Letter from Birmingham Jail 188, 251, 265
Letter to Three Wives 206
The Lettermen 208, 243
Levant, Oscar 180
Leve, Sam 70, 71
Leven, Boris 306
Levi, Gidi 228
Levien, Sonya 247
Levine, Emil 315
Levine, Maurice 70, 71
Levinson, Nathan 17, 298
Levitas, Willard 339
Levitt, Ruby R. 135
Levka, Uta 238
Levy, Albert E. 52
Levy, Benn W. 89, 204, 253
Levy, Herbert 91, 163
Levy, Jules V. 187, 331
Levy, Shmuel 228
Levy, Weaver 231
Levy, William Turner 94, 151
Lewis, Alfred 171
Lewis, Ben 44, 184
Lewis, Elliott 225, 336
Lewis, Fred Irving 262
Lewis, George 126
Lewis, George J. 147
Lewis, Harold 224
Lewis, Harry 173, 175, 188
Lewis, Jerry 208
Lewis, Meade "Lux" 233
Lewis, Mitchell 52
Lewis, Ralph 347
Lewis, Robert Q. 138
Lewis, Vera 27, 183
Lewisohn, Ludwig 22
Leyden, Norman 288
Libby, Fred 62
Liberace 155
Liberty 9, 107, 161
Library of Moving Images 190

Life 56, 73, 77, 101, 118, 206, 207, 216, 266, 271, 340
Life and Assassination of the Kingfish 35
Life Begins 239
The Life of Emile Zola 41, 65, 68, 93, 99, 100, 141, 197, 219, 222, 237, 279
The Life of Riley 244
A Life on Film 35, 194
Life with Father 53, 65, 90, 112, 142, 237, 255
Lifeboat 305
The Light in the Forest 112
The Light That Failed 199, 201, 292
Lightner, Winnie 301
Liliom 288, 315, 344
Liljevachs Konstalle 33
Lilson, John 327
Limelight 53, 61
Lincoln, Abraham 73, 74, 87, 103, 188, 189, 226, 255, 256, 269, 270, 274, 279
Lincoln Memorial 328
"A Lincoln Portrait" 189
Lindau, Rudolph A. 308
Lindbergh, Charles A. 330
Linder, Alfred 318
Lindgren, Harry 312, 331
Lindon, Lionel 212
Lindsay, Howard 275, 290
Lindsay, Julie 154
Lindsay, Margaret 189, 268, 278
Lindtner, Eli 293
The Line-Up 29
Link, John, Jr. 200
Linkletter, Art 146
The Lion in Winter 148
Lions at the Kill 27, 284
Lippman & Croneworth 318
Lipton, Lynne 220, 288
The Liquidator 319
Lisanby, Charles 288
Lisbon 187
Liszt, Franz 294
Liszt, Margie 324
Litel, John 189, 290
Literary Digest 342
Little, Alfred 30
Little, James 158
Little, Rich 255
Little, Thomas 157, 306, 308
"Little Annie Rooney" 224
The Little Betty Midget 301
"Little Big Man" 15, 17, 48, 140, 159, 167, 189, 190, 272, 273, 274, 277, 311, 321, 344
Little Billy 301
Little Caesar 6, 7, 17, 18, 34, 35, 39, 46, 47, 48, 49, 52, 54, 64, 67, 80, 81, 87, 90, 91, 92, 94, 103, 105, 111, 116, 117, 118, 120, 123, 128, 131, 132, 134, 135, 141, 146, 149, 150, 154, 155, 164, 167,

168, 172, 174, 178, 181, 185, 186, 188, 190, 191, 192, 193, 195, 202, 218, 224, 235, 249, 251, 256, 260, 268, 272, 288, 289, 298, 300, 314, 329, 332, 345
Little Caesar: A Biography of Edward G. Robinson 48
The Little Foxes 93, 112, 137
The Little Giant 7, 23, 31, 34, 35, 53, 58, 71, 76, 80, 81, 87, 107, 111, 123, 133, 134, 142, 149, 156, 186, 193, 194, 195, 197, 198, 201, 218, 224, 235, 249, 251, 256, 260, 268, 272, 289, 299, 314, 329, 332, 345
Little Lord Fauntleroy 140
The Little Minister 42, 143
Little Miss Broadway 277
Little Miss Marker 172
Little Miss Vitaphone 166
Little Old New York 200, 319
Little Romance 88
The Little Teacher 5, 80, 82, 129, 143, 182, 195, 253, 276, 292
Little Theatre 218
Little Women 35, 43, 135, 148, 187, 199, 244, 292, 300
Littlefield, Lucien 161, 183
Littlefield, Ralph 167, 278
The Littlest Rebel 344
Litvak, Anatole 8, 85, 101, 195
Livadary, John 318, 332
Live and Let Die 180
Liveright, Horace 122
Lives of a Bengal Lancer 143, 267
Livingstone, Margaret 291
Livingstone, Mary 72
Lloyd, Al 27
Lloyd, Alma 63
Lloyd, Dora & Ralph 293
Lloyd, Doris 126
Lloyd, Eugenia 117
Lloyd, George 40, 63, 195, 240, 278, 290
Lloyd, Gladys 6, 7, 8, 10, 11, 14, 23, 28, 33, 37, 43, 75, 88, 97, 117, 125, 143, 144, 147, 157, 171, 189, 191, 195, 196, 218, 226, 230, 238, 286, 291, 322, 344, 345, 347
Lloyd, Harold 172, 333
Lloyd, Norman 48, 159, 189, 255
Lloyd, Rollo 40
Lloyd, Suzanne 247
Lloyds of London 197
Lobert, John B. "Hans" 44, 49, 150, 196, 299
The Locket 86, 94, 300
Lockhart, Gene 8, 52, 103, 196, 222, 249, 282, 343
Lockheed's Ceiling Unlimited 196, 263, 347
The Lodger 143
Loeb, Philip 60, 137, 171, 196, 227, 270

Index

Loebel, Eric 255
Loesser, Frank 180, 207
Loew's Circuit 4, 43
Loft, Arthur 126, 161, 196, 223, 278, 345
Logan, Joshua 11, 48, 72, 101, 196, 213, 214, 215, 216, 252, 253
Logan, Mrs. Joshua 214
Loggia, Marjorie 79
Logue, Charles 233
Lohman, A. J. 295
Lom, Herbert 205
Lomas, Jack 136
Lombard, Carole 180, 267, 280
Lombardo, Guy 293
London, Jack 8, 189, 280, 281, 282
London, Julie 196, 266
London, Marc 185
London, Tom 40, 124, 341
London Evening Express 107
London Symphony Orchestra 238, 293
London Times 197
The Lone Ranger 288
Lonergan, Arthur 224
Lonergan, Lester 96
Lonesome 172
Long, Richard 197, 300, 302
Long, Walter 287, 341
Long Day's Journey Into Night 148, 269
The Long Flight 74
The Long Hot Summer 130, 270
The Long Voyage Home 123, 172, 260
Longenecker, Bob 117
The Longest Day 218, 349
Look Back in Anger 53
Look for the Silver Lining 69
Looking for Mr. Goodbar 228
Looney Tunes 69, 254, 262
Loos, Ann 219, 346
Lopez, Perry 147, 223
Lorch, Theodore 40
Lord, Fred 219
Lord, Jack 18
Lord, Marjorie 115, 126, 197
Lord, Pauline 5, 96, 111, 185, 197, 232, 252, 276, 333
Lord, Philip 333
Lord, Robert 27, 85, 124, 191, 194, 197, 205, 259
Lord Arthur Savile's Crime 125, 126, 127
Lord Jim 166, 199
Lorentz, Pare 105
Lorentz on Film: Movies 1927 to 1941 105
Loring, Eugene 247
Lorre, Peter 113, 154, 155, 197, 262
Los Angeles County Museum of Modern Art 33, 189
Los Angeles Express 323
Los Angeles Master Chorale Men's Chorus 305

Los Angeles Philharmonic Orchestra 254, 305, 328
Los Angeles Times 296
The Lost Flight 27
The Lost Horizon 168, 220, 335
The Lost Patrol 210
The Lost Squadron 33
The Lost Weekend 38, 66, 93, 283, 344, 348
Lotito, Louis A. 215
Lou Grant 34
Louise, Marie (Mrs. Napoleon) 226
Love, Andrew C. 321
Love, Bessie 170, 197, 198, 345
Love, Montagu 102, 103, 104, 197
The Love Bug 172, 319
Love Has Many Faces 273
Love Letters 99
Love Me or Leave Me 94
Love Me Tender 94, 243
Love Me Tonight 72, 292
Love Parade 61, 72
Love with the Proper Stranger 54, 180
The Loved One 221
The Loves of Carmen 95
The Loves of Isadora 197
Lovell, Dudley 46
Lovering, Otho 74
Lovett, Beresford 147, 175
Lovett, Dorothy 175
Lovsky, Celia 295
Low, Warren 27, 103, 104
Lowe, Edmund 301
Lowe, Edward T., Jr. 233
The Lower Depths 5, 198, 232, 252
Lowery, Patricia 331
Lowry, Judith 137, 314
Loy, Myrna 301, 154, 254, 330
"Loyalty" 148; *see also* "Heritage"
Lubin, A. Ronald 241
Lubin, Lou 27
Lucas, Brenda 293
Lucas (Lukas), Wilfred 59, 167, 198, 282, 287
Lucia de Lammermoor 249
Luciano, Lucky 150, 173, 198, 199
Luck of the Irish 172
Lucky Jordan 159
Lucky Lady 217
Lucky Luciano 48
Lucky Strike Program Starring Jack Benny 199, 264
"Lucy Goes to a Hollywood Premiere" 199, 310
The Lucy Show 38, 110, 112, 199, 234, 310
Ludwig, Edward 184
Ludwig, Otto 21
Ludwig, William 19, 52
Luecke, Gunter 247
Lueker, Art 173
Lugosi, Bela 182
Luick, Earl 124, 144, 163, 291

Luka, Jetta 228
Lukas, Paul 85, 199, 226
Lukas, Wilfred *see* Lucas, Wilfred
Lunatics and Lovers 179
Lund, Anna Lena & Margareta 258
Lund, Art 331
Lund, John 199, 231
Lundegard, Gerald 22
Lundigan, William 115
Lunt, Alfred 5, 38, 57, 60, 79, 82, 128, 136, 170, 199, 227, 252, 314
Lupino, Ida 8, 112, 113, 199, 237, 281, 282
Lupone, Robert 293
Lust for Life 110, 217, 260
The Lusty Men 334
Luthardt, Robert 340
Lux Radio Theatre 8, 54, 64, 71, 79, 88, 99, 112, 175, 178, 188, 199, 203, 204, 208, 237, 263, 264, 265, 347, 348
Lux Video Theatre 199, 310, 344
Luxury Liner 169, 211, 239, 340
Lycett, Eustace 229
Lyle, John Judge 190
Lynch, Ken 229
Lynch, Warren E 63
Lyndon, Alice 63
Lyndon, Barre 27, 231
Lynn, Barbara 127, 306
Lynn, Emmett 313
Lynn, Leni 76, 313
Lyon, Ben 90, 160, 205, 301
The Lyonsese 25
Lys, Lya 85
Lytell, Marjorie 91
Lytton, Herbert C. 126, 313

M 182, 197
Ma and Pa Kettle 90
Mabry, Moss 147, 165
MacArthur 40, 210, 236, 245
MacArthur, Charles 7, 38, 39, 83, 100, 146, 199, 200
MacArthur, James 200
Macasoli, Antonio 66, 139, 202
Macauley, Richard 59, 84, 200, 207, 308
Macbeth 113, 115, 156, 211, 234, 235, 325
Macchi, Valentino 139
MacCloy, June 327
MacDonald, Donald 45
MacDonald, Edmund 155
MacDonald, Eva 163, 232
MacDonald, J. Farrell 163, 200, 301, 341
MacDonald, Joseph 66, 200, 247, 340
MacDonald, Kenneth 98, 312
MacDonald, Robert 46
MacDonald, Wallace 291
MacDonnell, Norman 69
MacDougal, Ranald 209

Index

Macek, Carl 302
MacHarrie, Lindsay 64
Machiavelli 139
Machinal 156
Mack, Stanley 341
Mackay, Elsie 253
MacKaye, Fred 98, 117, 175, 203, 237, 347
Mackendrick, Alexander 55, 56, 200
Mackenna's Gold 14, 31, 47, 52, 66, 79, 80, 87, 94, 102, 121, 166, 169, 198, 201, 203, 209, 211, 223, 235, 245, 248, 251, 252, 260, 277, 285, 334, 339, 348
MacKenzie, Aeneas 312
Mackey, John 200
Mackintosh, Louis 194, 200
MacLaine, Shirley 12, 18, 81, 84, 201, 224, 239, 248, 259, 292
MacLane, Barton 63, 201, 207, 268
MacLean, Donald 312
MacLean, Fred 152, 173
MacLeish, Archibald 329, 336
MacMahon, Aline 125, 186, 201, 249, 254, 287, 345
MacMahon, Horace 177, 184, 201
MacMahon, J. E. 162
MacMurray, Fred 9, 18, 36, 67, 107, 108, 109, 110, 125, 155, 201, 202, 249, 257, 265, 292
Macollum, Barry 153, 313
The Macomber Affair 43
MacQuarrie, George 153, 326
Macready, George 202, 324
Mad as Hell: The Life and Works of Paddy Chayefsky 213, 214, 215
Mad Checkmate 14, 29, 47, 66, 67, 71, 72, 80, 82, 121, 133, 134, 165, 202, 235, 269, 314, 328
The Mad Doctor 219
Madama Butterfly 119, 135, 224, 225, 239, 248
Madame Curie 41, 134, 340
Madame X 42, 142, 220
Madden, Jerry 63
Made in Hollywood 50
Madigan 300, 343
Madison, Mae 291
Madison, Noel 88, 144, 191, 202
Madison Square Garden 46, 49, 70, 71, 99, 168, 179, 202, 249, 252, 256, 259, 276, 288, 294, 299, 334, 337
Maesso, Jose G. 202
Maggio, Dante 238
The Magic Christian 143
The Magic of Orson Welles 303
Magic Town 38, 91, 94, 211
Maginnis, Molly 206
The Magnificent Ambersons 42, 87, 221, 338
The Magnificent Dope 40

Magnificent Obsession 61, 307, 309, 334, 348
The Magnificent Seven 61, 210, 292, 330, 334
The Magnificent Yankee 65, 156
Magnum (Photographers) 295
Magrill, George 109, 202, 282
Maharan, Inc. 215
Maher, Frank 40
Maher, Joseph 215
Maher, Wally 64, 204, 225
Mahin, John Lee 184
Maid of Salem 292
Mail Call 202, 264
Main, Marjorie 336
The Main Event 107
Maisie 58, 294
Maitland, Marnie 55
The Majestic 182
The Major and the Minor 43, 273
Major Barbara 101, 221
A Majority of One 299
Make Room for Daddy 197
Make Room, Make Room 27, 296
Make Way for Tomorrow 54, 149, 268
Maki, Tsugundo 224
Making a Monster 55
"The Making and Remaking of *Double Indemnity*" 108
The Makropolous Secret 211
Malbin, Elaine 70
Malcolm, Robert 278
Malden, Karl 13, 31, 73, 74, 78, 131, 203, 255, 280, 319
The Male Animal 128, 234
Maley, Alan 229
Malleson, Miles 62, 170
Mallinson, Rory 62
Malotte, Stan 62
Maltese, Michael 262
The Maltese Falcon 35, 54, 86, 88, 134, 142, 160, 197, 263, 265, 234
"The Maltese Falcon" (radio) 199, 203
Maltin, Leonard 85, 140, 231, 247
Maltz, Albert 222
Malyon, Eily 85
Mamakos, Peter 62, 313
Mame 38
Mamorsky, Morris 321
The Man 275
Man and Superman 285
A Man for All Seasons 338
The Man from Dakota 118
The Man from U.N.C.L.E. 68, 330
Man Hunt 43, 68, 182, 277
The Man I Married 187, 208
"The Man in Black" 225
The Man in the Glass Booth 23, 180
The Man in the Iron Mask 43
Man in the Wilderness 344
The Man of a Thousand Faces 65

The Man of Destiny 5, 20, 71, 82, 113, 150, 182, 189, 203, 220, 226, 234, 253, 255, 285, 314
Man on a String 280
"Man on a Tightrope" 103, 199, 203, 204, 265
Man Who Came Back 226
The Man Who Came to Dinner 40, 79, 111, 112, 142, 143
The Man Who Dared 169
The Man Who Knew Too Much 43, 197
The Man Who Played God 32
The Man Who Saw Tomorrow 329
The Man Who Shot Liberty Valance 155, 187, 234, 260, 320
The Man Who Talked Too Much 164, 267
"The Man Who Thought He Was Edward G. Robinson" 112, 134, 204, 264, 305, 345
The Man Who Thought He Was Sherlock Holmes 275
"The Man Who Wanted to Be Edward G. Robinson" 112, 134, 204, 264, 305
The Man Who Would Be King 160
"The Man with Hope in His Hands" 69, 105, 112, 204, 264, 294
A Man with Red Hair 6, 79, 89, 153, 203, 204, 253
The Man with the Golden Arm 186, 301
The Man with Two Faces 7, 20, 27, 35, 55, 65, 79, 86, 88, 91, 92, 102, 112, 120, 123, 134, 141, 157, 175, 182, 186, 197, 198, 203, 204, 205, 223, 234, 235, 237, 251, 253, 309, 335
The Man Without a Country 198, 205, 206, 256
The Manchurian Candidate 49, 143, 172, 187
Mandalay 86
Mandel, Frank 122
Manet, Jeanne 248
Manhattan 283
Manhattan Melodrama 202
Mank, Gregory W. 317, 325
Mankiewicz, Don M. 340
Mankiewicz, Joseph L. 10, 101, 157, 166, 206
Manley, Nellie 312
Mann, Billy 327
Mann, Gertrude 163
Mann, Hank 40, 183
Mann, Helen 194
Mann, Larry 272
Mann, Ned 316
Manning, Knox 254
Manny 15, 48, 136, 206, 283
Manpower 8, 20, 32, 54, 61, 69, 79, 88, 94, 99, 101, 106, 111, 112, 118, 120, 125, 129, 142, 154, 155,

156, 172, 186, 198, 200, 201, 206, 207, 208, 210, 223, 235, 249, 251, 259, 263, 265, 268, 301, 304, 316, 334, 335, 337, 338, 345
"Manpower" (radio) 199, 208
Mansbridge, John B. 229
Mansfield, Jayne 11, 49, 117, 147, 164, 165, 208, 223
Manson, Maurice 272, 284
Mantell, Ethel 307
Mantle, Burns 24, 30, 122, 232, 262
Mapes, Ted 74
Marandel, Patrice 189
Marathon Man 236, 283
Marcellino, Mickey 167
March, Fredric 72, 101, 154, 214
March, Lori 99
"March of Time" 85, 119
Marchetti, Giulio 46
Marco Millions 288, 315
Marcus, Gerald 225
The Marcus Nelson Murders 277
Marcus Welby, M.D. 348
The Marcuse 78
Maren, Jerry 126
Margaret, Princess 55
Margie 40
Margo 24
Mariani, Fiorela 293
Marianne Productions 238
Marie, Rose 220
Marill, Alvin H. 1, 48, 146, 236, 278, 325
The Marilyn Encyclopedia 272
Marion, Paul 62
Maris, Mona 308
Mark Goodson–Bill Todman Productions 339
Mark of the Vampire 61
Mark of Zorro 42
Marked Woman 37, 199
Marker, Harry 113
Markey, Gene 43
Markle, Fletcher 29, 170, 347
Marks, George 194, 287
Marks, Herman 63
Marks, Owen 85, 144
Marlborough Galleries 33
Marley, J. Peverell 66, 165, 312
Marlowe, Frank 63, 341
Marlowe, Hugh 198, 208, 300
Marlowe, Kathy 165
Marlowe, Lucy 318
Marquis, Rosalind 63
Marr, Edward 64, 98, 175, 184, 203, 204, 237, 347
The Marriage Circle 53
Marriage Italian Style 97
The Married Priest 166
Mars Attacks 287, 300
Marsac, Maurice 115
Marsh, Mae 147, 208, 306
Marsh, Marian 124, 208

Marshall, Armina 246, 270, 314, 345
Marshall, E. G. 214
Marshall, George 159
Marshall, Herbert 332
Marshall, John 318
Marshall, Mort 270
Marshall, Peter 112
Marshall, Tully 144
Marshall, William 325
Marshek, Archie 224
Marson, Truda 237, 347
Marston, John 194, 287
Martel, Greg 78
Martell, Alphonse 284
The Martha Raye Show 208, 310
The Martian Chronicles 298
Martin, Chris-Pin 308
Martin, Dean 13, 90, 208, 220, 223, 243, 247, 248, 272, 284, 305, 326
Martin, Dick 185, 220
Martin, George Victor 240
Martin, Irene 21, 313
Martin, Leonardo 202
Martin, Lewis 331
Martin, Margaret 308
Martin, Marian 306
Martin, Nanomba "Moonbeam" 74
Martin, Nora 113
Martin, Ross 131
Martin, Tony 131, 254, 321, 324
Martins, Orlando 55
Martinson, Leslie 331
Marty 72, 217, 244, 305
Marum, Gene 295
Marx, Groucho 131, 254, 273, 274, 292
Marx, Harpo 86
Marx, Karl 82, 302, 309
Marx, Samuel 327
Marxism 83
Mary of Scotland 41, 198, 211, 315
Mary Poppins 319, 330
Mary Stuart 113
"The Mary Tree" 14, 56, 76, 160, 186, 208, 209, 230, 235, 243, 251, 311, 315
Marymount 273
*M*A*S*H* 167, 184, 221, 347
Maslow, Sophie 70, 71
Mason, Florence 122
Mason, Hal 55
Mason, Louis 282
Mason, Reginald 270
The Masquers 36, 209, 211, 261
Massaro, Francesco 238
Massey, Raymond 9, 14, 81, 131, 188, 200, 201, 209, 268, 345
Masters, Ruth 215
Masters of Modern Drama 232, 245, 251
Masterson, Jerry 185
Mastroianni, Marcello 67

Mata, Luis, Jr. 76, 284
Mata Hari 57
The Matchmaker 138
Mate, Rudolph 66, 209, 332
Matheron, Laure 229
Matheson, Muir 55, 316
Mathews, Allen 184
Mathews, Beverly 313
Mathews, Carmen 111, 209, 345
Mathews, Dorothy 343
Mathews, Lester 347
Mathieson, Juliann 242
Mathis, Johnny 46, 160, 223
The Mating Game 269
The Mating Season 270
Matisse, Henri 25, 34
Mattey, Robert A. 229
Matthews, Charles 18, 107, 172, 173
Mattox, Matt 90, 247, 293
Mature, Victor 158
Maurstad, Toralv 14, 166, 293
Maurstad, Tordis 293
Maverick 172
Mawson, Edward 326
Max, Edwin 178, 204, 208
Max Headroom 298
Maxey, Paul 51
Maximilian, Emperor 99, 170
Maxine Elliott's Theatre 123
Maxwell, Edwin 163, 317
Maxwell, Marilyn 160, 332
Maxwell House Coffee 23, 209, 299, 310
May, Billy & Orchestra 233, 288
May-Bar, Naomi & Ovadia 228
Mayberry, Dick 59
Mayer, Arthur 193
Mayer, Edwin Justus 122, 209
Mayer, Kenneth N. 318
Mayer, Louis B. 199
Mayhew, Kate 195
Maymor, Dorothy 274
Mayo, Archie 205
Mayo, Frank 85, 86, 177, 183
Mayo, Walter 40
Mayor of Hell 41
Maytime 254
Mazanovich, Maxine 195
Mazurki, Mike 73, 74
Mazzola, Eugene 313
Mazzone-Abbott Dancers 90, 167
Mazzuca, Joseph 158
MCA Television 190
MCAA 139
McAvoy, Charles 341
McBain, Diane 42
McCabe, Norman 254
McCaffrie, Pat 78
McCallion, James 165, 209
McCallister, Lon 86, 222, 266
McCann, Chuck 143
McCarter Theatre 92
McCarthy, Charles 122
McCarthy, Sen. Joseph 62, 159

Index

McCarthy, Kevin 11, 13, 14, 209, 210, 233, 234, 325
McCarthy, Valerie Crane 189
McCarty, John 189
McCauley, Daniel J. 241, 312
McClain, John 216
McCleary, Urie 258, 324, 327
McClelland, Charles 158
McClelland, Doug 21
McClelland, Fergus 55, 76, 210
McClory, Sean 74
McClure, Frank 346
McClure, William J. 186
The McConnell Story 180
McConnor, Vincent 347
McCoy, Frank 173, 312
McCoy, Harry 262
McCoy, Malachy 77
McCrea, Joel 39, 40, 83, 156, 198, 210
McCullough, Frank 54
McCullough, Philo 74
McCullough, Ralph 184
McDaniel, Ed 45
McDaniel, Hattie 210
McDaniel, Sam 91, 108, 210
McDonald, Adams 92
McDonald, Ed 45
McDonald, Francis 210, 282, 312
McDonald, Grace 126
McDonald, Joseph 17, 126
McDonald, Kathleen 96
McDonough, Joseph A. 126
McDowall, Roddy 252
McFadden, William 92
McFarland, Spanky 75, 345
McGann, William 167, 173, 301
McGaugh, Wilbur 341
McGavin, Darren 220
McGeehan, Patrick 347
McGill, Jerry 45
McGill, Wilbur 45
McGilligan, Patrick 292
McGinnis, Joel 346
McGivern, William 147
McGrane, Ione 245
McGrath, Larry 291
McGraw, Charles 98
McGuire, Tom 177, 191
McHugh, Frank 91, 140, 207, 210, 343
McHugh, Jack 205
McHugh, Matt 40, 322
McIntire, John 98, 225, 234
McIntyre, Paddy 293
McKaig, Alexander 262
McKay, Donald 148
McKay, Margaret 178
McKee, John 44, 74, 165, 210
McKelvey, Frank R. 229
McKenna, Harry 22
McKimson, Bob 86, 154, 339
McKinley, William 256, 273
McKinney, Florine 327

McLaglen, Victor 210, 223, 301, 308
McLean, Lorna 137
McMillan, Gloria 45
McMurphy, Charles 341
McNally, Ed "Skipper" 318
McNear, Howard 175, 204, 208, 225, 237
McNeile, Michael 170
McNulty, John 44, 346
McNutt, Patterson 176
McPhail, Douglas 184
McQuarrie, Benedict 186
McQueen, Steve 13, 18, 31, 76, 131, 210, 304, 338
McRae, Maurice 171, 209, 227, 270
McVeagh, Eve 136, 210, 318
McVey, Tyler 98, 229
McWade, Edward 59, 102, 210, 322
McWade, Robert 96, 163, 210, 211
McWade, Robert, Jr. 211
McWhorter, Frank 266
McWhorter, Julie 143
McWhorter, Richard 21
Meader, George 287
Meadows, Audrey 155
Meakin, Charles 346
Meany, George 237
A Medal for Benny 225
Medal of Freedom 100
Medea 29
Medical Center 14, 56, 320
Medill, Joseph 270
Meegan, Thomas 60, 275
Meehan, John 111
Meek, Donald 40, 81, 104, 153, 211, 222, 341, 342
Meeker, George 91, 183
Meersman, Peter 167
Meet Boston Blackie 182, 202
Meet John Doe 33, 57, 125, 136, 155, 196, 292, 299, 320
Meet Me in St. Louis 35, 93, 143, 208, 217, 234
Megrue, Roi Cooper 11, 79, 211, 253, 326
Mehta, Zubin 305
Mei-Chen 247
Meiser, Edith 75
Meisner, Sanford 5, 170, 252, 314
"Melancholy Baby" 223
Melchior, Lauritz 228
Melford, George 109, 313
Mell, Joe 21
Melle, Gil 212
Mellinger, Frederic 103
Mellor, William 44
Melody and Romance 276
Melton, James 64, 72
Melzer, Lewis 97
The Member of the Wedding 79, 336
Men in Black 320

Men in Exile 117
Men in White 68, 179
Men of the Night 286
Menczer, Erico 238
Mendelssohn, Felix 140
Mendes, Lothar 211, 308
Mendez, Alan 21
Menendez, Moises 202
Menjou, Adolphe 222
Menken, Helen 5, 49, 54, 114, 115, 211
Menken, Shepard 53, 204
The Mephisto Waltz 180
Mercer, Beryl 166, 211, 270, 314
Mercer, Johnny 332
Mercer, Joy 46
The Merchant of Venice 68
Mercier, Louis 284
Mercury Theatre 87, 159, 221, 301, 335, 338
Meredith, Burgess 14, 70, 71, 81, 137, 200, 201, 211, 254, 332
Meredith, Charles 165, 211
Meredith, Scott 205
Meredith, Iris 161
Merenda, Victor 46
Merivale, Philip 211, 300, 302
Merlin, Jan 165
Merlin, Joanna 312
Merlin, Sam 337
Merriam, Charlotte 291
Merrick, John 62, 313
Merrie Melodies 86, 154, 155, 339
Merrill, Lou 45, 64, 88, 178, 283
Merrill, Robert 299
Merrit, Abe 176
The Merry Widow 135, 314
Merton, John 313
Merton of the Movies 61, 91, 325
Mesenkop, Louis H. 312
Message in a Bottle 230
"The Messiah on Mott Street" 14, 31, 76, 128, 171, 180, 188, 211, 212, 213, 230, 234, 251, 271, 273, 311
Mestel, Stan 293
Methot, Mayo 54
MetroColor 46, 78, 258, 296, 324
Metropolis 182, 298
Metropolitan Opera 300
Metty, Russell 25, 66, 300, 302
Mexican Spitfire 330
Meyer, Torben 104
Meyer, William R. 85, 102
MGM 6, 8, 9, 14, 44, 46, 47, 52, 72, 78, 120, 121, 135, 137, 180, 181, 184, 199, 217, 239, 240, 241, 257, 259, 273, 283, 296, 297, 304, 314, 323, 324, 330
Michaelangelo 14, 34, 36, 82, 237, 238, 267
Michaels, Marilyn 288
Micheline & Jacqueline 138
Middle of the Night 11, 12, 28, 31, 32, 36, 37, 38, 48, 72, 76, 95,

100, 101, 113, 117, 130, 137, 150, 167, 171, 182, 186, 196, 197, 198, 213, 214, 215, 216, 217, 234, 236, 250, 251, 252, 253, 259, 274, 286, 304, 337, 345
Middlemass, Robert 52
Middleton, Charles 52, 113, 144, 217, 240, 287
Middleton, George 254
Midnight 187, 334
Midnight Lace 79
The Midrash 312
A Midsummer Night's Dream 99, 169, 210, 272
Midsummer Night's Sex Comedy 118
Mielziner, Jo 215, 217
Mighty Joe Young 33, 210, 243
Mignon 300
Mike Curb Congregation 19
Milagro Beanfield War 56
Milan, Lita 332
Mildred Pierce 32, 69, 88, 90, 179, 334
Miles, Art 40, 52
Milhollin, James 229
Miljan, John 312
Milland, Ray 66
Millay, Edna St. Vincent 185
Miller, A. C. 32
Miller, Ann 202
Miller, Arthur 10, 24, 25, 26, 83, 115, 217, 229, 250, 329
Miller, David H. 74
Miller, Ivan 52, 184, 217
Miller, Jack 315
Miller, Marilyn 166
Miller, Marvin 138
Miller, Mitch 321
Miller, Ron 229
Miller, Seton I. 63, 177, 217
Miller, Sidney 204
Miller, Walter 184
Millican, James 162
"The Million-Dollar Dog Stealing Racket" 45, 263
Million Dollar Mermaid 118
Mills, Frank 346
Millward, Charles 186
Milstein, Nathan 70
Milton, Franklin 78, 258, 324, 346
Milton, John 54, 281, 333
Milton, Robert 38
Minciotti, Esther 158, 198, 217, 345
Minciotti, Sylvio 158, 217
Minelli, Liza 19, 163, 185, 217, 315
Minelli, Vincente 12, 101, 217, 218, 322, 324, 325
Mineo, Sal 13, 73, 74, 218
Ministry of Fear 182, 217
Minjer, Harold 346
Mintz, Robert 42
Miracle in the Ra 146
Miracle of Morgan's Creek 107, 244

Miracle of the Bells 118, 211
Miracle on 34th Street 88, 147, 196, 270
Miracle Woman 299
Miracles for Sale 61
Mirage 37, 210
Miranda, Carmen 332, 339
Mirantz, Oscar 176
The Mirror Has Two Faces 37
Mirror Magazine 285
Les Miserables 42, 68, 185
The Misfits 210, 270, 334
Miss America 225
Miss Annie Rooney 94
Mission Impossible 140, 182
Mission to Moscow 54, 88, 179, 321, 338, 339
The Mississippi Gambler 217
Mr. and Mrs. North 97, 210
Mr. Blandings Builds His Dream House 42, 244, 255, 285
Mr. Broadway 274
Mr. Deeds Goes to Town 34, 68, 69, 107, 112, 182, 219, 299
Mr. Hobbs Takes a Vacation 334
Mr. Lucky 94, 255, 300
Mr. Moto 197
Mr. Pim Passes By 315
Mister Roberts 54, 65, 125, 128, 129, 187, 196, 217, 255, 314, 336
Mr. Samuel 6, 82, 171, 179, 190, 195, 218, 234, 253
Mr. Skeffington 249
Mr. Smith Goes to Washington 33, 51, 68, 84, 96, 142, 175, 219, 220, 292, 301, 348
Mr. Winkle Goes to War 9, 27, 32, 33, 38, 49, 66, 72, 75, 80, 87, 120, 125, 134, 140, 156, 182, 186, 188, 198, 218, 219, 223, 224, 227, 235, 239, 305, 332, 335, 345
Mitchell, Belle 296
Mitchell, Bruce 27
Mitchell, Carlyle 62
Mitchell, Carlyle, Jr. 63
Mitchell, Esther 75
Mitchell, Frank 126
Mitchell, Frank Billy 108
Mitchell, Fred M. 176
Mitchell, Grant 183, 184, 219
Mitchell, Howard 63, 158, 219, 278
Mitchell, Lisa 312
Mitchell, Shirley 331
Mitchell, Thomas 9, 12, 20, 81, 126, 220, 223, 249, 252, 270, 306, 326, 329
Mitchum, Robert 49, 219, 220
Miyaki, C. 245
Mizner, Wilson 194
"Moanin' Low" 173, 223
Mobsters 199
Modern Times 137, 198
The Modernaires 202

Modigliani, Amadeo 34
Moeller, Philip 22, 30, 60, 75, 101, 170, 203, 220, 227, 253, 270
Mohamed, Amena 313
Mohr, Gerald 66, 129, 130, 255
Mohr, Hal 63
Mohyeddin, Zia 55
Molinari (Musician) 35
Molinari, Ann 324
Moll, Giorgia 247
Molly 196
"Molly Malone" 175
Molnar, Ferenc 185, 253, 306
Momose, Maymi 224
Monarch Films 228
Mondder, Eric 340
Monet, Claude 8, 28, 34
Mong, William V. 91, 163
The Monkees 107
Monkey Business 144, 208, 223
Monkey Planet 252
Monogram Pictures 61
Monroe, Marilyn 3, 12, 155, 272
Monroe, Paul 339
Monsieur Beaucair 308
Monsieur Verdoux 265
Monson, Lex 46
Montague, John 92
Montague, Monte 40
Montalban, Carlos 247
Montalban, Ricardo 13, 73, 74, 220, 288
Montaldo Giuliano 139
Montana, Louise 74
Montand, Yves 12, 220, 224
Montgomery, Garth 29
Montgomery, George 219, 280
Montgomery, Ray 111, 167, 183, 220
Montgomery, Robert 332
Monthly Film Bulletin 44, 46, 50, 164, 225, 228, 229, 297, 331
Montoya, Ed 52
Mooch 14, 20, 167, 220, 256, 273, 286, 336
Mooch Goes to Hollywood 220
Moon and Sixpence 41, 277
The Moon Is Blue 54
The Moon Is Down 38, 330
"The Moon Is in Tears Tonight" 177, 268
Mooney, Martin 63
Moonjean, Hank 258
Moonstruck 169
Moore, Carlyle J. 177
Moore, Dennis 98
Moore, Dickie 75, 103
Moore, Dudley 338
Moore, Fay 233
Moore, Garry 270
Moore, George 315
Moore, Joanna 198, 220, 221, 229, 345
Moore, Michael 312

Index

Moore, Owen 221, 242
Moore, Richard 200
Moore, Roger 19
Moore, Terry 204, 237
Moorehead, Agnes 9, 10, 28, 186, 198, 221, 239, 240, 303, 338, 345
Moorhouse, Bert 184, 205
Moran, Frank 195
Moran, Polly 301
Moraweck, Lucien 69
Mordden, Ethan 28, 110
More American Graffiti 56
The More the Merrier 34, 131
Moreland, Beatrice 116
Moreno, Antonio 308
Morgan, Boyd "Red" 272
Morgan, Brewster 307
Morgan, Byron 124
Morgan, Dennis 166, 167, 221
Morgan, Frank 5, 122, 221, 252, 329
Morgan, Harry 25, 221
Morgan, Henry 154
Morgan, Jane 199
Morgan, Paula 313
Morgan, Sandra 126
Morgan, Will 162
Morheim, Louis 44
Mori, Toshia 144
Moriarty, David H. 212
Morin, Alberto 158, 173, 221, 324
Morin, Carolyn 272
Morison, Patricia 160
Morisot, Berthe 7, 34, 315
Morita, Mike 145
Moritz, Louisa 288
Morley, Robert 221, 294
Morning Glory 116, 148
Morny, John 92
Morocco 100
Morosco Theatre 122
Morra, Irene 167
Morra, Mario 202
Morricone, Ennio 139
Morris, Adrian 195
Morris, Dorothy 240
Morris, Frances 63, 221, 231, 346
Morris, McKay 75, 326
Morris, Nina 195
Morris, Philip 52, 341
Morris, Wayne 177, 178, 198, 221
Morrison, Adrienne 186
Morrison, Ann 158, 327
Morrison, Carl 340
Morrison, Shelley 201
Morros, Boris 306
Morse, Carlton E. 331
Morse, Ray 170
Morse, Terrill 322
Morse, Sen. Wayne 154
The Mortal Storm 90
Mortimer, Ed 27, 177
Mortimer, Henry 218, 333
Mortimer, Lee 285

Morton, Arthur 152
Morton, James C. 52
Moscovitch, Maurice 202
Moscow Art Theatre 231, 241, 265, 293
Moscow Strikes Back 17, 83, 221, 222, 286
Mosel, Tad 240
Moss, Jack 219
Moss Rose 90
The Most Happy Fella 180
Mostel, Zero 131
Mostoller 70, 71
Motel Hell 65
Mother 269
Mother Is a Freshman 159
Mother Wore Tights 90
Motion Picture Alliance for the Preservation of American Ideals 222
Motion Picture Committee for Hollywood War Saving 155
Motion Picture Guide 237
Motion Picture Relief Fund 344
Motion Picture World 32
Motion Pictures International 121, 228
Motley 215
Moulin Rouge 118, 160
Mount, Harry 341
Mount Sinai Hospital 130
Mourning Becomes Electra 184, 220, 315
The Mouthpiece 27, 76, 164, 165, 201, 234, 253, 267, 348
Mouzey-Eon 278
The Movie Crazy Years 14, 92, 188, 222, 225, 234, 311, 334, 338
Movie Maker 240
Movie Movie 68, 334
Movie Stars, Real People, and Me 213
Movieline 313
The Movies 193, 214
Movies Made for Television 325
Movietime, Inc. 190
Mower, Jack 86, 177, 222, 290, 341
Moyer, Ray 17, 138, 183, 231, 312
Moyles, Jack 204
MPI/Mordechai Slonim Films 228
Mrs. Bumpstead Leigh 103, 293
Mrs. Leffingwell's Boots 87
Mrs. Miniver 88, 134, 340, 344
Mrs. Parkington 134, 221
Much Ado About Nothing 81
Mudie, Leonard 60, 103
Mueller, Richard 312
Muir, Esther 184
Mule, Francesco 46, 268
Mule Train 277
Muleson, Many 74
Mullally, Don 69
Mullendore, Josep 331
Mulligan, Jim 185

Mulqueen, Kathleen 21
The Mummy 65, 169, 171
Muni, Paul 6, 8, 9, 20, 31, 67, 100, 102, 168, 169, 214, 222, 254, 274, 335, 336, 337
Munier, Ferdinand 126, 237, 341
Munro, Nan 293
Munsell, Warren P. 92
Munshin, Jules 277
Munson, Ona 8, 44, 45, 116, 125, 222, 266
Munster Go Home 95
The Munsters 95
Muramatsu, Nariko 224
Murder He Says 201
Murder, Inc. 116
Murder My Sweet 180, 321
Murder on the Orient Express 37, 343
Murderer's Row 166
Murphy, Al 25
Murphy, Audie 154
Murphy, George 280
Murphy, Horace 278
Murray, Bill 54
Murray, Charlie 301
Murray, Forbes 167, 219, 306
Murray, Isobel 127
Murray, John Fenton 277
Murray, Ken 335
Murray, Lyn & Orchestra 66, 106, 129
Murray, Zon 74
Musco, Nino 46
Muse, Clarence 109, 126, 223, 274, 278, 306
Musee de Batavia 33
Museum of Modern Art 33
Museum of Stockholm 33
Music Center Pavilion 305
"The Music Goes Round and Round" 223
The Music Man 169
"Musical Americana" 160, 163, 224, 328
"Musical Tour of the U.S.A." 328
Mustin, Burt 78
Mutchnik, Chaim 228
Mutiny on the Bounty 88, 101, 118, 168, 185, 300, 314
Mutual Network 106, 114, 117, 146, 199, 328, 336
My Brother Talks to Horses 168
My Cousin Rachel 107
My Daughter Joy 26, 89, 224, 238
My Dear Secretary 94
My Fair Lady 46, 285, 335
My Father and I 233
My Father—My Son 1, 12, 47, 75, 272
My Favorite Blonde 179
My Favorite Martian 334
My Favorite Spy 79
My Foolish Heart 145
My Friend Irma 80

My Geisha 12, 18, 47, 66, 80, 81, 84, 89, 119, 121, 156, 201, 220, 224, 225, 235, 239, 244, 248, 251, 259, 308, 309, 322
"My Kind of Town" 18, 65, 223, 251, 330
My Little Chickadee 55, 107, 142, 211, 269
My Man Godfrey 255
My Name Is Julia Ross 128
My Sister Eileen 144, 169, 187, 201, 221
My Six Convicts 130
My Son John 221
My Three Sons 96, 201
"My Wife Geraldine" 225, 234, 263, 305, 345
Myers, Alonzo 274
Myers, Henry 176
Myerson, Bess 70, 71, 225
Mylonas, Alan 246
Myra Breckenridge 119, 338
Myrow, Fred 295
Myrow, Jeff 29
Mystery of the Wax Museum 90, 168, 171, 348
Mystery Ship 244

N.A.A.C.P. Legal Defense and Education Fund 344
Nablo, James Benson 62
Nace, Anthony 161
Nadel, Arthur 331
Nadel, J. H. 306
Nagel, Anne 63
Naglis, Peter 170
Naish, J. Carroll 23, 144, 223, 225, 306, 317, 322
Nakao, Shunichiro 224
The Naked City 86, 90, 112, 123, 130, 201, 329
The Naked Gun 230, 244
The Naked Jungle 267
The Name Above the Title 150, 151
Napier, Alan 42
Napoleon I 5, 49, 178, 188, 203, 226, 255, 299, 329
Napoleon III 103, 178, 226, 269
Narciso, Grazia 258
Nardelli, George 284
Naremore, James 108, 303
Nash, George 326
Nash, Mary 32, 226
Nash, Ogden 248
Natheaux, Louis 177, 191
The Nation 22, 30, 75, 105, 109, 136, 176, 195, 204, 228, 232, 326
National Board of Review 18, 36, 53, 84, 226
National Gallery of Art 33
National Gallery of Ottawa 33
National Gallery of Scotland 33
National Parent-Teacher 164

National Repertory Theatre 347
National Screen Service 301
National Variety Artists 301
National Velvet 130, 168
Navy Blues 71
Nazarro, Cliff 274
The Nazi Spy Conspiracy in America 27, 48, 85, 321
Nazism 62, 82, 84, 85, 119, 132, 136, 158, 179, 199, 221, 222, 226, 227, 230, 250, 253, 260, 261, 275, 277, 285, 300, 302, 335, 338
Nazzari, Amadeo 313
NBC 19, 26, 28, 29, 61, 69, 72, 86, 116, 137, 141, 148, 149, 155, 165, 166, 180, 187, 190, 199, 204, 209, 212, 213, 222, 231, 237, 243, 250, 283, 286, 291, 300, 315, 319, 321, 331, 333, 336, 347, 348
NBC Star Playhouse (also *NBC Star Theatre*, *NBC Playhouse*) 225, 264, 265, 291
NBC Symphony Orchestra 336
Nea: A New Woman 256
Neal, Lloyd 116
Neal, Patricia 167
Neal, Tom 327
Ned McCobb's Daughter 6, 68, 101, 113, 159, 184, 187, 196, 199, 210, 220, 227, 228, 234, 251, 253, 314
Nedd, Stewart 165
Neff, Bill 62
Negri, Pola 180, 267
Nehan, Dod 238
Neither by Day Nor by Night 14, 34, 47, 48, 76, 80, 121, 156, 165, 178, 228, 251, 253
Nelson, Bob 136
Nelson, Charles 138
Nelson Frank 64, 88, 178
Nelson, Margie 248
Nelson, Miriam 138
Nelson, Sam 332
Nemirowsky, Irene 238
Nervig, Conrad 181
Ness, Ed 272
Nestell, Bob 118, 177
NET Playhouse on the Thirties 222, 225, 311
Nettleton, Lois 92, 186, 228, 252
Network 72, 301
Network of the Americas 145, 228, 263
Neuman, Emil 308
Neumann, Dorothy 313
Neumann, Harry 62
Neumann, Kurt 78
Neumann Mastering 333
Nevada Smith 182
Never a Dull Moment 14, 34, 47, 67, 71, 82, 86, 114, 121, 127, 138, 133, 134, 198, 220, 228, 229, 235, 244, 250, 251, 255, 260, 285, 292, 330, 345
Never So Few 107
Never Steal Anything Small 169
Neville, Francis M. 189
Nevins, Francis M., Jr. 231
New Brooms 300
The New Deal 173
New Faces 179
New Orleans 197
The New Republic 60, 96, 105, 136, 157, 171, 195, 232, 270
New York American 39, 64, 145, 162, 177, 205, 288, 342
New York Confidential 86
New York Daily Mirror 190
New York Daily News 25, 39, 99, 103, 103, 139, 157, 216, 217, 221, 229, 241, 258, 296
New York Drama Critics Circle Award 178, 217, 229
New York Evening Post 279
New York Giants 44, 49, 150, 196, 299
New York Herald-Tribune 26, 28, 39, 50, 51, 55, 59, 62, 64, 73, 77, 85, 91, 97, 102, 105, 110, 126, 135, 146, 152, 157, 161, 162, 164, 174, 178, 183, 185, 192, 195, 203, 205, 208, 216, 217, 219, 224, 231, 232, 234, 238, 241, 242, 247, 257, 262, 266, 271, 279, 281, 285, 288, 290, 303, 307, 308, 315, 324, 325, 331, 333, 342, 343, 346
New York Journal American 85, 178, 216, 305
New York Morning Telegraph 307
New York, New York 217, 299
New York Philharmonic Orchestra 70
New York Post 6, 40, 46, 73, 103, 146, 216
New York State Department of Education, Motion Picture Division 278
New York Sun 39, 63, 91, 97, 124, 204, 342
New York Times 11, 21, 22, 26, 28, 30, 38, 40, 45, 50, 51, 56, 58, 59, 60, 62, 64, 71, 73, 75, 77, 87, 91, 97, 99, 102, 105, 106, 110, 113, 122, 123, 124, 125, 135, 136, 138, 139, 143, 144, 146, 147, 152, 153, 155, 157, 160, 162, 164, 167, 170, 171, 173, 176, 178, 181, 183, 185, 192, 195, 196, 200, 201, 203, 204, 205, 206, 213, 216, 218, 221, 225, 227, 228, 229, 230, 232, 233, 234, 238, 239, 241, 245, 247, 253, 257, 262, 266, 269, 271, 275, 276, 279, 281, 285, 288, 289, 293, 297, 302, 303, 307, 308, 313, 315,

Index

317, 318, 323, 324, 327, 330, 332, 337, 340, 343, 345
New York World 181, 262, 275
New York World Telegram 64, 124, 195, 205, 216, 317, 323
New York World Telegram and Sun 99
The New Yorker 77, 96, 110, 138, 152, 173, 193, 217, 228, 239, 279, 293, 296
Newcombe, James 147
Newcombe, Mary 123
Newel Art Galleries 92
Newell, Norman 46
Newell, David 153
Newhoff, Irving 341
Newman, Alfred 40
Newman, Bernard 306
Newman, Eve 228
Newman, Lionel 42, 208
Newman, Paul 13, 35, 36, 67, 81, 82, 87, 229, 230, 241, 249, 257, 258, 292, 293, 309, 321
Newmar, Julie 200
Newquist, Roy 257
Newsies 186
Newsweek 73, 105, 152, 161, 164, 166, 174, 257, 271, 285, 297, 318, 324
Newton, Theodore 91
Niagara 144
Niarchos, Stavros 11, 22, 196, 230
Niblette, Philip 122
Nibley, Aaron 97
Niblo, Fred, Jr. 84, 308
Nicander, Edwin 232
Nichol, Hamish 170
Nicholas and Alexander 179, 298
Nicholas II Czar 143
Nichols, Dudley 278, 279
Nichols, Guy 96
Nichols, Lonnie 306
Nichols, Richard 75, 103
Nichols, Robert 318
Nicholson, James H. 29
Nicholson, Meredith P. 42
Nicolai, Bruno 139
Nicolaysen, Ann 220
Nielsen, Leslie, 14, 209, 230
Nielsen, Ray 39
Nielson, James 69
Nietzsche, Friedrich 281
The Night Angel 130
A Night at the Opera 275, 314
The Night Before Christmas 27, 183, 230, 248, 253
Night Has a Thousand Eyes 10, 24, 54, 61, 71, 87, 88, 94, 96, 107, 117, 119, 121, 125, 134, 141, 143, 155, 197, 198, 199, 221, 230, 231, 235, 244, 251, 268, 269, 272, 276, 280, 283, 304, 320, 321, 347
"Night Has a Thousand Eyes" (radio) 231, 264, 280

The Night Lodging 5, 38, 111, 156, 167, 182, 197, 198, 231, 232, 251, 252, 253, 330
Night Must Fall 211, 340
Night of the Hunter 185, 220
The Night Ride 6, 47, 71, 120, 132, 134, 168, 172, 232, 235, 271, 279, 328
A Night to Remember 131, 319, 348
Night Walker 40
Nightingale, Florence 130
Nightmare 11, 37, 47, 53, 66, 76, 79, 119, 121, 128, 156, 172, 186, 198, 210, 218, 223, 233, 234, 250, 251, 268, 276, 280, 327, 337, 344, 345
Nightmare Alley 195
Nigrin, Daniel 70
Niles, Ken 45
Nillson, Alice Babs 330
Nims, Ernest 302
1984 298
1937 Shakespeare Festival 263
Ninotchka 51, 84, 275, 344
Nitke, Maurice 122
Niven, David 40, 49, 234
Nixon, Leslie 170
Nixon, Richard 270
Nizzari, Joyce 152
No Highway in the Sky 100
No More Ladies 239
No Room for the Groom 38
No Time for Sergeants 309
Nobel Prize 8, 13, 48, 81, 103, 114, 257, 258, 274, 321, 322
Nobody's Fool 230
Nodell, Bella 163
Noerdlinger, Henry 312
Nokes, George 231
Nolan, Jeanette 225, 234, 345
Nolan, Lloyd 28
Nolan, Mary 234, 242
Nolan Bros. 92
None but the Lonelyheart 41, 54, 167, 286
The Noose 41
Nora Bayes Theatre 148
Norin, Gus 21, 331
Norma (costumer) 331
Norma Rae 270
Norman, Barry 154
Norris, Edward 104
Norris, Karen 325
North, Alex 74, 241
North, Clyde 96, 232
North, Jay 76, 141, 247
North, Mrs. Wilfred 205
North by Northwest 43, 47, 68, 86, 103, 182, 209, 252, 257, 294, 344
The North Star 159
Norton, Arthur J. 318
Norton, Edgar 60, 113
Norton, Ned 341
Norwegian Fairy Tales 245

Norwegian Victory Chorus 331
Norwood, Ralph 346
Nosferatu the Vampyre 179
Nothing Sacred 184, 338
Notorious 61, 65, 146, 237, 321
Nourse, Allen 318
Novak, Kim 247
Novello, Jay 175, 327
Now Voyager 93, 268
Nowell, Wedgewood 346
Nozaki, Albert 17, 312
Nugent, Elliott 234, 254, 316
Number 37 4, 234, 253, 279
The Nun's Story 237, 301
Nunzio Productions 206
Nurse Edith Cavell 115
Nussbaum, Dr. Max 130
Nuts 334
The Nutty Professor 130
Nye, Ben 42, 157, 252, 284
Nye, Louis 138, 143
Nye, Richard 30
Nyman, Ronald 258, 313

O Mistress Mine 199
Oakie, Jack 254, 301
Oakland, Simon 340
Oaks, Larry 293
O'Bannion, Dion 131
Oberon, Merle 19, 345
Oberst, Walter 108
Objective Burma 334
Oboler, Arch 331
O'Brien, David 115
O'Brien, Denise 293
O'Brien, Edmond 175
O'Brien, George 73, 74
O'Brien, Margaret 9, 31, 41, 75, 81, 89, 186, 234, 239, 240
O'Brien, Pat 6, 28, 82, 117, 147, 222, 234, 235, 237, 252, 254, 268, 273, 286
O'Brien, William 344
O'Brien-Moore, Erin 29
Occidental Petroleum Company 33, 143
Ocean's 11 86
Ocko, Daniel 308
O'Connell, Arthur 211
O'Connell, David J. 211
O'Connell, Helen 148
O'Connell, Hugh 262
O'Connor, Charles 262
O'Connor, Frank 341
O'Connor, John 293
O'Connor, Robert Emett 96, 341
O'Connor, Tim 99, 235
O'Day, Michael 45
The Odd Couple 68, 188
Odell, Cary 97, 200
O'Dell, Doye 318
O'Donnell, J. P. 29
Of Human Bondage 93
Of Mice and Men 51, 54, 88, 118, 143, 211

Index

Of Pups and Puzzles 286
Of Thee I Sing 143, 217
O'Farrell, Broderick 184
Offerman, George 86
Office of War Information 260, 286, 334
Officer de l'Instruction Publique 36
O'Gatty, Jimmy 183
Ogden, John 293
Ogden Family 195
O'Grady, Tom 306
"Oh Genevieve" 224
Oh God! 42, 64, 277
"Oh Susannah!" 224
Oh! What a Lovely War! 35
O'Hana Gallery 33
O'Hara, Barry 78
O'Hara, James 42, 74
O'Hara, Quinn 138
O'Herlihy, Dan 21, 235, 236
Ohman, Janice 183
O'Keefe, Dennis 98, 254
O'Keefe, Winston 29, 137
O'Kelley, Tim 324
Okey, Jack 62, 124, 317
Oklahoma! 93, 155, 169, 300, 315
The Oklahoma Kid 37, 55
Oland, Warner 113, 267, 319
Olcott, Helen 116
Old Acquaintance 100, 156
The Old Dark House 171, 185, 209
Old English 32
The Old Maid 100, 156, 211, 300
The Old Man and the Sea 159, 320
Old Man Rhythm 172
The Old Man Who Cried Wolf 14, 17, 34, 37, 38, 76, 94, 168, 171, 235, 236, 249, 251, 273, 300, 311
Old Testament 150
Old Towne Music Hall 189
"Old Turkey Buzzard" 200, 223
The Old Vic 53, 260
O'Leary, William 109
Oliver! 283
Oliver, Edna Mae 254
Oliver, Ted 52, 341
Olivier, Sir Laurence 19, 106, 236, 237, 260
Olonova, Olga 276
Olsen, Moroni 184, 237
O'Madigan, Isabel 302
O'Malley, Charles 291
O'Malley, Pat 98, 103, 183, 341
Omar Khayyam 99
The Omega Man 149
On a Clear Day You Can See Forever 220
On a Note of Triumph: Norman Corwin and the Great Years of Radio 106, 334
On Borrowed Time 101, 143, 196, 336
On Eagle's Wings 312
On Golden Pond 128, 148

On the Double 29
"On the Spot" 322
On the Town 330
On the Waterfront 38, 79, 142, 203, 298, 300, 339
Onassis, Aristotle 230
Once Around 274
Once Off Guard 27, 345
Once Upon a Honeymoon 285, 294
Once Upon a Time in America 338
Once Upon a Time in the West 114, 128
One Foot in Heaven 334
One Hour with You 72
"100 Greatest Movies of All Time" 3, 297, 298
"100 Years, 100 Stars" 3, 292
One Man's Way 160
One Million Years B. C. 338
One Touch of Nature 234, 237, 252, 253
One Touch of Venus 248
One, Two, Three 65, 130
One Way Passage 197
O'Neal, Ann 290, 346
O'Neal, Kevin 74
O'Neal, Ryan 220
O'Neal, Tatum 220
O'Neil, Barbara 30, 161, 186, 197, 237
O'Neill, Barry 204
O'Neill, Eugene 42
O'Neill, Henry 27, 63, 85, 104, 163, 205, 237
O'Neill, Howard 52
Only Angels Have Wings 34, 41, 125, 144, 145, 169
Only Victims 92, 330
"Only Yesterday" 199, 237, 264, 348
An Open Book (Gordon) 104, 139
An Open Book (Huston) 173
Opening Night 53
Operation Bikini 90
Operation Entertainment 68, 156, 171, 234, 237, 265, 269, 310, 320, 348
Operation Heartbeat 325
Operation San Pietro 14, 26, 34, 36, 47, 57, 67, 71, 80, 82, 121, 133, 134, 165, 166, 235, 237, 238, 244, 246, 251, 267, 275, 292
Operation X 10, 21, 22, 26, 71, 76, 80, 89, 90, 102, 121, 140, 198, 203, 218, 224, 235, 238, 239, 265, 305, 345
Operazione St. Peter's 238
Orbom, Eric 135
Orchestra Wives 40
The Oregon Trail 202
Orenbach, Al 308
Orlando, Don 324
O'Rourke, Tom 327
Orphans of the Storm 186, 345
Orpheum Players 4, 24

Orr, William T. 327
Orry-Kelly 91, 177, 194, 287
Orson Welles 303
Orth, Frank 306, 327
Ortolani, Riz 46
Osborne, John 18
Osborne, Robert 255
Osborne, Vivienne 111, 186, 239, 322
The Oscar A to Z (Mathews) 18, 107, 173, 281
The Oscar from A to Z (Pickard) 281
Oscar, Julius 274
O'Shea, Michael 66
O'Steen, Sam 272
Osterloh, Robert 69
O'Sullivan, Maureen 117
O'Sullivan, Robert 117
Othello 211, 236, 271
Other People's Money 245
Ott, Frederick W. 279
Ottoson, Robert 279
Oumansky, Alexander 163
Our American Scriptures 239, 263
Our Gang 52, 345
Our Betters 130
Our Hearts Were Young and Gay 26, 276
"Our Love Is Here to Stay" 255
Our Man in Havana 269
Our Man Flint 344
Our Miss Brooks 32
Our Town 88, 175, 188, 220, 294
Our Vines Have Tender Grapes 9, 27, 31, 41, 68, 75, 81, 83, 87, 88, 89, 102, 120, 123, 128, 131, 135, 149, 150, 168, 182, 186, 195, 198, 199, 203, 217, 221, 227, 234, 235, 239, 240, 249, 251, 267, 298, 309, 321, 335, 337, 345
Oury, Gerard 240, 241, 258
Ouspenskaya, Maria 104, 241
Out of the Fog 155
Out of the Past 110, 220, 329
The Outlaw 220, 278
Outrage (Lupino) 199
The Outrage 13, 27, 37, 47, 53, 80, 87, 88, 89, 93, 102, 121, 125, 143, 159, 168, 199, 229, 241, 242, 249, 251, 252, 267, 268, 285, 320, 337, 339
Outside the Law 6, 42, 47, 61, 75, 94, 120, 132, 134, 168, 221, 234, 235, 239, 242, 267, 328
Outward Bound 199, 211
"Over There" 80
Overbaugh, Roy 242
Overbey, D. 62, 347
Ovey, George 233, 327
Owen, Garry 63
Owen, Reginald 329
Owens, Gary 185
The Ox-Bow Incident 86, 93, 128, 186, 195, 221

The Oxford Companion to American Theatre 22, 24, 88, 122, 215, 217, 227, 252, 315
Oxford Companion to Film 110, 192
Oxford University 53

P. Lorillard Comedy Theatre 242, 263, 291
Paar, Jack 35
Pa-amoni, Zeev 228
Pabst, G. W. 126
Pabst Blue Ribbon Beer 23
Pacific Title 220
Pack, Charles Lloyd 293
Packer, Peter 29
Paddock, Robert Rowe 339
Padilla, Manuel 76, 272
Page, Gale 27, 104, 243
Page, Geraldine 320
Paget, Debra 34, 114, 127, 158, 243
Paid in Full 4, 94, 131, 243, 252, 253, 334
Paige, Erik 318
Paiva, Nestor 147, 243, 308
The Pajama Game 94, 201
Pal Joey 145, 286
Palace of the Legion of Honor 33
The Paleface 156
Paley, William S. 228
Palfi, Lotte 85
Pallach, Andrew 42
Pallette, Eugene 301, 306
The Palm Beach Story 80, 210
Palma, Joe 138
Palmer, Gregg 258
Palmer, Karen 308
Palmer, Tom 324
Panaieff, Michael 258
Panama Hattie 294
Panavision 46, 74, 152, 201, 258, 296
"Panic" 56, 230, 234, 243, 244, 310
Panos, John 206
Panzer, Paul 177
Papa's Delicate Condition 330
Pape, Lionel 307
The Paper Chase 159, 329
Papi, George 139
Papillon 169, 210
Papp, Frank 321
Parade 182
Parade of Stars 243, 336
The Paradine Case 68
Paradise Lost 282
Paramount on Parade 211
Paramount Pictures 9, 10, 55, 107, 108, 120, 121, 139, 153, 224, 231, 238, 244, 247, 301, 304, 313, 329
Pardon My Past 71, 118
Pardon My Sarong 61
Pardon Us 198
Pardy, Edmond J. 116

The Parent Trap 172, 309
Parikian, Manoug 293
Paris, Jerry 229, 244
Paris Blues 270
Paris Underground 269
Parish, James Robert 1, 21, 22, 39, 44, 48, 146, 174, 177, 185, 219, 236, 240, 258, 271, 278, 289, 290, 303, 313, 315, 325
Parish, Roger A. 212
Park Theatre 253
Parker, Dolores 158
Parker, Dorothy 274, 306
Parker, Eddie 136, 184
Parker, Eleanor 12, 152, 167, 243, 244
Parker, Franklin (Franklyn) 125, 322, 347
Parker, Jean 51, 186, 244
Parker, Marion 117, 255
Parker, Max 59, 207, 290
Parker, Sheldon 117
Parker, Steve 224, 259
Parker, Willard 244, 290
Parks, Larry 84, 98, 244
Parnell, Emory 152, 161, 183, 244, 327
Parrish, David 185
Parrish, Helene 152
Parrish, John 313
Parrish, Robert 51
Parsons, George 333
Pasadena Playhouse 275
Pascal, Ernest 126
Pascale, Jim 189
Pascin, Jules 34
Pasetta, Marty 19
Paskin, Barbara 154
The Passerby 4
La Passione 329
The Passover Plot 178
Passport to Fame 341
Pasteur, Louis 102
"The Pastorale" 224
Pat and Mike 79, 138, 148
Patent Leather Kid 41
Pathé color 138
Pathé Exchange, Inc. 32
Pathé–Gold Rooster Plays 120
Paths of Glory 221
Patrick, Butch 76, 187
Patrick, Gail 203, 306
Patrick, Gil 126
Patrick, Kevin 270
The Patriots 179
Patterman, David 321
Patterns 146, 301
Patterson, Floyd 243
Patterson, Rae 231
Patterson, Neil 203
Patterson, Shirley 98
Patton 47, 103, 203
Patton, George S. 196
Paul, Edward 306
Paul, Olga 92

Paul Rosenberg Galleries 33
Pawley, Edward 44, 184, 244
Pawley, William 63
The Pawn 5, 172, 182, 239, 245, 253
The Pawnbroker 300
Payment Deferred 211
Payne, John 268
Payne, Louis 346
Payton, Claude 40
PBS 14, 222, 326
Peabody, Dick 107, 200
Peabody Awards 106
Pearce, George C. 162
Pearce, Guy 306
Pearson, Billy 113, 289
Pearson, H. C. 238
Peary, Gerald 190
Peary, Harold 331
Peck, Ann B. 74
Peck, Charles 284
Peck, Gregory 14, 18, 113, 131, 154, 200, 245
Peck, Joseph 206
Peckinpah, Sam 76, 77, 169
Peck's Bad Boy 300
Pedrini, John 158, 272
Peer Gynt 5, 41, 57, 87, 140, 142, 163, 182, 189, 245, 246, 251, 253, 279, 288, 294, 314, 339, 347
Peerce, Jan 70, 246, 321
Pefferie, Dick 258
Peking Blonde 13, 47, 52, 80, 90, 98, 121, 132, 134, 165, 168, 235, 237, 239, 244, 246, 247, 251
Pemberton, H. W. 326
Pembroke, George 178
Pendleton, Gaylord (Steve) 86, 161, 341
Penn, Leonard 204
Penney, Edmund 313
Pennick, Jack 40
Pennies from Heaven 329
Pennington, Ann 327
Penny, Frank 208
Penny Serenade 292, 305
People Against O'Hara 66
People Are Like That 247, 264
People Will Talk 157
The People's Choice 179
Pepe 12, 17, 18, 20, 31, 47, 66, 72, 76, 80, 81, 86, 89, 90, 93, 96, 112, 119, 121, 132, 134, 141, 144, 156, 169, 186, 187, 198, 223, 235, 247, 248, 251, 253, 259, 268, 269, 273, 286, 288, 298, 323, 336, 345
Pepe le Moko 113
Pepper, Barbara 207
Pepper, Sen. Claude 154
Pepper, David 346
Percey, Gladys 312
Percival, Walter 291
Pereira, Hal 17, 224, 312

Perell, Sid 187
Perelman, S. J. and Laura 183, 248
Perez, Manny 262
The Perils of Pauline 179, 181
Perinal, Georges 238
Period of Adjustment 228
Perkins, Gil 52, 340
Perkins, Leslie 272
Perkins, Red 324
Perlman, Itzhak 70, 71, 249
Peromski, Z. 170
Perret, Gene 185
Perrin, Victor 51, 69
Perry, Albert 227
Perry, Bob 194
Perry, Frederick 96
Perry, Joyce 78
Perry, Kenneth R. 333
Perry, Paul 98
Perry Mason 156
Persoff, Nehemiah 131
Persson, Edvard 330
Pete and Gladys 221
Pete Kelly's Blues 208
Pete 'n' Tillie 270
Pete the Pup 301
Peter Gunn 115
Peter Ibbetson 209
Peter Jones Productions, Inc. 189
Peter Pan 34, 304
Peters, Brock 295
Peters, Don 98
Peters, Jon 313
Peters, Roberta 70, 71, 249
Peterson, Clarence 340
Peterson, Dorothy 198, 249, 345
Peterson, Pam 258
Peterson, Robert 137
Peterson, Sven 258
Petitot, Georges 246
Petrie, George 45
The Petrified Forest 24, 53, 249, 254, 277, 294, 319, 329
Petterson, Sigrid 258
Petticoat Junction 61
Pettyjohn, Angelique 42
Peyser, Arnold and Lois 35
Peyton, Charles 262
Peyton, Fr. Patrick 117
Peyton Place 140, 250, 334
The Phantom 99
Phantom Lady 86
Phelps, Donald 322
Phelps, Lee 52, 60, 126, 184, 207, 249, 278, 327, 331
Philadelphia Bulletin 26
The Philadelphia Story 146, 160, 206, 226, 301, 315
"The Philippines Never Surrendered" 69, 112, 249, 250, 264
Philips, Lee 137, 214, 215, 250
Philliber, John 108
Phillipe, Andre 284
Phillips, Howard 54
Phillips, Jimmy 341

Phillips, John 173
Phillips, Mary 54
Phillips, Paul 59
Phillips, Robert 200
Phillips, William 183
Philo 312
Phinney, William J. 96, 195
Phipps, Bill 332
Phone Call from a Stranger 167, 301
Photoplay 58, 153, 221
Picasso, Pablo 8, 34
Picerni, Paul 236
Picistrelli, Umberto 139
Pickard, R. A. E. 281
Pickard, Roy 66
Pickens, Slim 229, 250
Picker, David V. 18
Pickford, Mary 280, 327
Pickup on South Street 270
Picnic 159, 196, 299
Pictures Will Talk: The Life and Films of Joseph L. Mankiewicz 156
Pidgeon, Walter 29
Piel, Edward, Sr. 40, 144
Pierce, Jack 126, 278
Pierce, Todd 159
Pierce, Waldo 274
Piers, Gwendolyn 116
Pierlot, Francis 240
Piestrup, Don 220
The Pietà 14, 34, 36, 237, 238, 267
Piggott, Tempe 86
Pike, Kelvin 293
"Pilgrim's Chorus" 224
Pillar of Fire 312
Pillars of Society 4, 163, 250, 251, 253, 334
Pillow Talk 94, 168, 270
Pine, Howard 233
Pine, Philipi 51
Pine, Virginia 341
Pine/Thomas/Shane Productions 233
The Pink Panther 234, 334
Pinky 336
Pinocchio 275
Pippin, Horace 34
Pirandello, Luigi 6, 189, 253, 270
Piranha 210
The Pirate 199
Pisari, Mario 46
Pissarro, Camille 8, 33
Pitoeff, Sacha 258
Pitts, Michael 325
Pitts, ZaSu 45, 155
Pittsburgh 137, 141, 196
The Pittsburgh Kid 172
Pivar, Maurice 113, 242
The Plainsman 34, 142, 210
Planer, Franz F 97
Planet of the Apes 30, 115, 149, 251, 252, 298, 329
Platinum Blonde 57, 142, 305

Platt, Edward 165, 252
Platt, Livingston 262
Play It Again, Sam 270
Playboy 139, 201, 285
Playhouse 90 86, 165, 182, 252, 285, 301, 310, 334
Playhouse Theatre 195
Plaza Theatre 43
Please Don't Eat the Daisies 189, 339
Pleasence, Donald 20
Plough and the Stars 237, 325
Plummer, Rose 242
Plunkett, Walter 324
Plymouth Theatre 96, 164, 186, 232, 275
A Pocketful of Miracles 86, 88, 116, 189
Poe, Aileen 275
Poe, Edgar Allan 256
Pohl, Frederik & Frederik IV 295
Poitier, Sidney 18, 299
Pokras, Dan & Dmitri 92
Poldekin 5, 32, 83, 94, 182, 253, 308, 319, 325
Polianov, Alexis M. 176, 218, 232, 276
Police Academy 244
Polinoff, Xenia 186
Polis, Daniel 92
Polito, Sol 66, 85, 91, 254, 281, 282, 343
Pollard, Alex 306, 346
Pollet, Albert 231
Pollock, David 288
Pollock, Nancy R. 215
Pollumbaum, Phillip 176
Polly of the Circus 186
Polly with a Past 5, 253, 254
Polo with the Stars 254, 286
Polonsky, Abraham 329
Poltergeist 301
Ponedel, Bernard 152
Ponstance, William 54
The Poor Nut 234
Popeye 125
Porat, Orna 70
Porcasi, Paul 60, 163, 254, 291
Poretta, Frank 293
Porfirio, Robert 233
Porgy 315
Porgy and Bess 93, 137, 223, 315
Porky Pig 254
Porky's Double Trouble 69
Porky's Tire Trouble 69, 254
Porro, Franco 202
Port of Wickedness 26
Portalupi, Piero 46
Porter, Arthur Gould 278
Porter, J. Robert 201
Porter, Michael 176
Portrait in Black 334
The Poseidon Adventure 230
Posen, Alvah T. 176
Possessed 88

Index

Post, Ted 243
The Postman Always Rings Twice 172, 320
Poston, Tom 300
Potel, Victor 40
Potter, H. C. 52, 255
Poulton, Raymond 200, 238
Powell, Dick 53, 113, 148, 202, 228, 254
Powell, Edwin B. 284
Powell, Homer 42
Powell, James 331
Powell, Lee 184
Powell, Richard 341
Powell, Ricky 76, 212, 213
Powell, Russ 40
Powell, William 28, 30, 57, 255, 284, 287, 332
The Power 142
Power, Tyrone 237
The Power of Silence 276
"The Power of the X-Ray" 129, 255, 264
Powers, Eugene 176
Powers, John 45
Powers, Tom 5, 30, 108, 203, 226, 252, 255, 256, 314
Pradd, Theodore 219
Pratt, Hawley 262
Pratt, Judson 74, 243
Pratt, Purnell 125
Pratt, Thomas 317
Preim, Elizabeth Ottilie 206
Prendergast, Maurice 34
Prescription: Murder 330
The President's Analyst 66, 159
Presle, Micheline 256, 258
Presley, Elvis 26, 90, 178, 268
Presnell, Harve 18, 288
Press, Jacques 71
Prettyman, John 173
Previn, Andre 17, 247
Previn, Charles 126
Pretty Woman 42
The Price 172, 217, 329
Price, Edward 177
Price, Georgie 114
Price, Hal 233, 341
Price, Stanley 313
Price, Victoria 256, 289
Price, Vincent 11, 15, 34, 48, 106, 113, 127, 154, 166, 220, 256, 289, 312
Pride and Prejudice 134, 135, 159, 237
The Pride and the Passion 134, 135, 159, 237
The Pride of St. Louis 90
Pride of the Marines 334
Pride of the Yankees 137, 209, 269, 305
Prince, Adelaide 218
The Prince and the Pauper 197, 201
Prince of Egypt 312
Prince of Players 209

The Princess Bride 116
Princess Elizabeth Hospital 145
Princess O'Hara 268
The Princess O'Rourke 134
Pringle, Norman 74, 233
Prinz, Leroy 90, 167, 312
Prisoner of Shark Island 68, 196, 210, 336, 347
The Prisoner of Zenda 116, 155, 209
Pritchard, Robert 135
Prival, Lucien 86
A Private Affair 220
Private Files of J. Edgar Hoover 88
Private Life of Henry VIII 185
Private Lives 237
The Private Lives of Elizabeth and Essex 51, 141, 254
Private Secretary 294
Private War of Major Benson 61
Private Worlds 152
The Prize 13, 20, 29, 36, 37, 47, 68, 76, 80, 81, 87, 94, 102, 106, 112, 121, 125, 133, 134, 156, 166, 182, 187, 198, 199, 210, 229, 235, 236, 241, 249, 250, 251, 256, 257, 258, 259, 260, 292, 298, 309, 310, 321, 322, 335, 338
Prizzi's Honor 283
Procter & Gambles This Is Hollywood 259, 264, 304
The Professionals 42, 210, 276
Prohibition 67, 111, 133, 250, 256, 260, 271, 290
Project 20 12, 86, 134
Projection of America 286
Prokofiev, Serge 35
Protocol 261
The Proud Rebel 180
Prouty, Olive Higgins 300
Provine, Dorothy 13, 14, 34, 138, 229, 260
Pryor, Roger 52
Psycho 38, 187, 247, 266
The Public Enemy 7, 53, 65, 79, 118, 132, 211, 291, 338
Publisher's Weekly 26
Puccini, Giacomo 224
Puglia, Frank 327
Pulitzer Prize 24, 83, 92, 179
Pully, B. S. 152
Purcell, Gertrude 63, 300
Purchese, John 293
Purdy, Constance 108, 278
The Pursuit of Peace 106
Putterman, W. Zev 215
Pygmalion 128, 211, 285
Pyle, Denver 74

Quabius, Faith 296
Quadrille 199
Qualen, John 60, 74, 183, 258, 260
Quartet 336
Quayle, Anthony 14, 200, 201, 260

The Queen Bee 88, 294, 348
Queen of the Mob 219
Quick Millions 348
Quicker 'n' a Wink 286
The Quiet American 308
The Quiet Man 54, 123, 129, 210
Quigg, John 92
Quigley, Jack 160
Quine, Don 325
Quinn, Aidan 24
Quinn, Anthony 9, 70, 183, 260
Quinn, Edward 122
Quinn, James 341
Quinn, Phil 165, 167
Quirk, Lawrence J. 153, 154
Quitzau, Margery 92
Quo, Beulah 324
Quo Vadis 188, 305, 309

R. U. R. 288
Raab, Leonid 224
Rabar, Vernon 313
Rabbit Run 209
Rachel and the Stranger 348
Rachel, Rachel 230
Rachmil, Lewis J. 261, 318, 332
The Racket 6, 66, 67, 71, 86, 94, 114, 133, 134, 145, 153, 190, 192, 252, 253, 261, 262, 271, 343
Racketeer Rabbit 69, 197, 262
Rackin, Martin 146, 147
Raddis, Leslie 204
Radio Newsreel of Hollywood 263, 265
Radio Readers Digest 263, 265
Radio Yesteryear 29, 69, 72, 199, 204, 225, 237, 274
"Radium Against Cancer" 129, 264, 265
RAF Film Unit 227, 319, 336
Raffles 115, 130
Raft, George 9, 11, 15, 48, 61, 62, 99, 101, 107, 118, 154, 156, 198, 206, 207, 265, 268, 268, 271, 274, 329
Rage in Heaven 211
The Ragman's Son 109, 323
Ragtime 65, 235
Rahn, Pete 236
Rain or Shine 136
Rainger, Ralph 173, 306
The Rainmaker 57, 148
Rains, Claude 10, 81, 92, 101, 179, 254, 329
The Rains Came 241
Raintree County 221, 309, 344
Raker, Lorin 194
Raksin, David 324
Rally 'Round the Flag Boys 80, 338
Rameo, Neva 229
Ramon, George 316
Rancho Notorious 100, 172, 182
Randall, Renee 231
Randall, Tony 272, 324
Randall, William J. 200

Randole, Leo 75
Randolf, Anders 57
Randolph, Charles 177
Randolph, Jane 207
Randolph, Joyce 155
Random Harvest 134, 188, 210
Ranieri, Katina 18
Ranken, Arthur 341
Ransohoff, Martin 76, 77
Rapee, Erno 191, 343
Rapf, Matthew 44
Rappaport, John 185
Rapper, Irving 104, 177, 178
Rapport, Fred 346
Rascal 167
Rashomon 13, 27, 53, 241, 253, 268
Raskin, Judith 70, 71
Rasputin and the Empress 41, 142, 244
The Rat Pack 13, 247, 254, 271
Ratcliffe, E. J. 163, 274
Rathbone, Basil 226, 333
Ratoff, Gregory 238, 259, 265
Rattigan, Terence 170
Ravel, Frances 284
The Raven 197
Ravid, Rachel 228
Ravish, Tony 44, 298
Ravold, John 96
Rawlinson, Herbert 63, 129, 347
Ray, Harry 138
Ray, Joey 231
Rayan, Amy 163
Raye, Martha 208, 265
Raymond, Cyril 316
Raymond, Sid 102, 258
Raynold, Jack 184
Ray's Way 39
Raz, Avraham 228
Raz, Rivka 70
The Razor's Edge 42, 223, 349
Reagan, Maureen 167
Reagan, Ronald 27, 48, 49, 84, 112, 167, 237, 256, 265, 348
The Real Glory 209
The Real McCoys 57
Reap the Wild Wind 137
Rear Window 301, 347
Rebecca 29, 61, 143, 236, 277, 292
Rebecca of Sunnybrook Farm 96
Rebel Without a Cause 218, 252
Rebound 29
Red Channels 82, 266
The Red Cross at War 64, 266, 286
Red Dawn 169
The Red House 10, 29, 65, 80, 87, 93, 94, 102, 121, 125, 128, 141, 175, 186, 188, 196, 209, 222, 223, 235, 259, 266, 270, 285, 298, 304, 327
Red Light 169
Red Meat 27, 32, 48, 162
The Red Pony 134
Red River 57, 68, 112, 144

Redding, Harry 218
Redemption 38
Redfield, William 291
Redford, Robert 28
Redgrave, Michael 31, 67
The Redhead and the Cowboy 118
Redman, Anthony 212
Redon, Odilon 34
Redwing, Rodd (Rodric) 173, 267, 313
Reed, Alan 21
Reed, Donna 18, 247
Reed, George 306
Reed, Phillip 91
Reed, Tom 113, 205, 233
Reed, Walter 74
Reed and LeFevre Gallery 7
Reese, Della 148
Reese, Edward 30, 203
Reeve, Christopher 281
Reeve, Winifred Eaton 113
Reeves, Bob 27
Reference Guide to the American Film Noir: 1940–1958 279
Reflections in a Golden Eye 172
Regan, Barry 62
Regan, Phil 160
Regent, Robert 331
Reguerro, Francisco 248
Reh, Philo 183
Reicher, Frank 104, 137, 181, 267
Reichow, Otto 258, 308
Reifsnider, Lyle B. 167
Reilly, Charles Nelson 288
Reilly, Jean Burt 272
Reilly, Thomas 165
Reinhardt, Stephen 293
Reinhardt, Wolfgang 104
Reis, Irving 25, 267
Reisman, Del 208, 243
Reisman, Phil, Jr. 86, 99
Reisner, Alan 115
Reiss, Stuart A. 284
Remarque, Erich Maria 137
Remley, Ralph M. 63, 268, 344
Renavent, Georges 60, 167
Renay, Paul 306
Renison, Cyril 293
Rennie, James 268, 306
Reno, A. W. 276
Renoir, Auguste 315
Renoir, Jean 277
Renshaw, Elaine 105
Reo, Don 185
Repp, Stafford 42
Requiem for a Heavyweight 22, 260, 348
Resnick, Regina 71
"A Retrieved Reformation" 24
Return of the Cisco Kid 112
Reunion in France 41
Reunion in Vienna 199
Reuter, Julius Paul Baron von 8, 31, 43, 48, 87, 102, 103, 150, 269

Reuters 48, 49, 188, 230, 269
Reveille with Beverly 244
Revellion Freres 262
Revere, Anne 265
Revolutionary War 98
Rexall Drugs 61
Reynolds, Adeline DeWalt 306, 313
Reynolds, Alan 318
Reynolds, Burt 19
Reynolds, Debbie 18, 90, 175, 237, 247, 269, 286, 319
Reynolds, Gene 76
Reynolds, Helene 306
Reynolds, Quentin 274
Reynolds, Scott 189
Rhapsody in Blue 118, 254, 292, 334
Rhinoceros 334
Rhodes, Leah 173
Rhue, Madlyn 131
Rhythm on the Range 265
Ricciardi, William 317
Rice, Charles J. 17, 138, 247
Rice, Elmer 5, 22, 118, 253, 269, 274
Rice, Frank 40
Rice, Sam 322
Rich, Allen 92
Rich, David Lowell 148
Rich, Dick 51
Rich, Robert 321; *see also* Trumbo, Dalton
Rich Man, Poor Man 35
Richard, Dawn 313
Richard, Pat 312
The Richard Boone Show 300
Richard II 115
Richard III 53, 143, 156, 236, 269
Richards, Addison 63, 98, 165, 269, 312
Richards, Frank 62, 175
Richards, Jeff 44, 269
Richards, Keith 313
Richards, Paul 340
Richardson, Duncan 76, 136
Richardson, Jack 177, 341
Richardson, Sir Ralph 7, 269, 316
Richelieu, Cardinal 102
Richman, Peter Mark 255
Richmond, Bill 185, 288
Richmond, Hal 316
Richmond, June 274
Richmond, Kane 161
Rickert, Shirley Jean 301
"Rico Rising: Little Caesar Takes Over the Screen" 190
Riddle, Nelson 18, 42, 152, 271
Ride a Pink Horse 137
Ride Beyond Vengeance 335
Ride the High Country 210
Rider, Sid 170
Riders of the Purple Sage 107, 277
Ridgely, John 59, 86, 177
Ridges, Stanley 282

Ridgeway, Gen. Matthew B. 237
Riding High 112, 309
Riedel, Richard 126
Rieger, Daisy 163
Rietty, Robert 293
Rififi 285
Rigaud, George 139, 202, 269
Rigby, Cathy 49
Rigg, Carl 293
Riggs, C. A. 27, 59, 85, 103
Riggs, L. A. "Speed" 199
The Right Man 12, 24, 49, 54, 68, 150, 155, 188, 220, 256, 270, 273, 274, 310
The Right Stuff 299
Right You Are If You Think You Are 6, 68, 182, 187, 189, 196, 210, 211, 220, 251, 253, 270, 314, 320, 339, 345
Rigoletto 246
Rilla, Walter 238
Rin Tin Tin 277, 348
Ring, Cyril 162, 184
Les Ringards 90
Ringgold, Gene 306
Rio 103, 210
Rio Bravo 54, 57, 144
Rio Grande 169
Rio Lobo 113
Rio Rita 90
Rios, Lalo 44
Riot in Cell Block 11 49, 118
Risdon, Elisabeth 5, 270, 314
The Rise and Fall of Legs Diamond 95
Risen, Max 206
Riskin, Everett 161
Riskin, Robert 341
Riss, Dan 331
Ritchie, Charles 218
Ritt, Martin 13, 101, 241, 270
The Ritterma 12, 45, 151, 152, 186, 198, 249, 270, 345
The Ritz 339
Ritz Theatre 38
The Rivals 41
Rivas, Carlos 247, 313
Rivat Choir of Israel 70
River of No Return 65
Rivera, Carlos 62
Rivera, Diego 34
Rizzo, Carlo 46
RKO Pictures 120, 121, 125, 170, 261, 302, 346
Roach, Bert 290
Roach, Hal 89
Roach, James E. 187
The Road to Glory 265
Road to Morocco 156, 336
Road to Rio 243
Road to Utopia 41, 43, 112
The Roaring Twenties (film) 65, 143, 200
The Roaring Twenties (tv) 260
Robards, Jason, Jr. 28, 37, 67

Robb, Donald 312
Robbie, Seymour 288
Robbin, Gregory 164
The Robe 147, 167
Roberson, Chuck 74
Robert, Hans 232
Robert Taylor's Detectives 12, 133, 134, 141, 187, 270, 300, 305, 309, 310
Robert W. Bergman Studios 122
Roberta 23, 156
Roberts, Al 176, 266
Roberts, Allene 223, 270
Roberts, Beatrice 278
Roberts, Beverly 88
Roberts, Don 184
Roberts, Fred 248
Roberts, Pascale 246, 247
Roberts, Roy 308
Roberts, Stanley 18
Roberts, Tony 212, 270, 271
Roberts, Tracey 21
Robertson, Cliff 288
Robertson, John S. 5, 57, 101, 233, 271, 287
Roberson, Ric 189
Robertson, Willard 91, 184, 262, 271, 287
Robeson, Paul 95, 271, 306
Robin, Leo 306
Robin and the 7 Hoods 13, 18, 34, 47, 64, 65, 67, 71, 76, 80, 87, 89, 90, 93, 94, 111, 116, 121, 131, 132, 134, 168, 172, 188, 203, 223, 224, 234, 235, 251, 255, 260, 268, 271, 272, 275, 288, 305, 326, 330, 335
Robin Hood 140
Robin Hood of El Dorado 169
Robinson, Beulah 48, 117, 189, 255
Robinson, Dewey 194, 272, 278, 306
Robinson, E. R. 126
Robinson, Earl 274
Robinson, Edward G., Jr. (Manny) 1, 7, 10, 12, 15, 37, 47, 75, 117, 128, 129, 130, 148, 196, 206, 209, 236, 272, 273, 277, 340, 344
Robinson, Eleanor 117
Robinson, Frances 41, 175
Robinson, Jane 131
Robinson, Jenny 117
Robinson, June 117
Robinson, Kyle 27
Robinson, Dr. Marvin 117
Robinson, Peter 117
Robocop 236, 298
Robson, Mark 258
Robson, William N. 45, 154
Rocco, Alex 42
Rock-a-Bye Baby 115
Rockefeller, Nelson 228
Rocky 211

Rocky Horror Picture Show 298
Rod Serling's Night Gallery 14, 31, 180, 211, 212, 213, 230, 271, 273, 311
Rod Serling's Night Gallery: An After Hours Tour 211, 212
Rodgers, Richard 29, 166, 169
Rodney, John 112, 173, 223
Rodrigues, Percy 236
Roemheld, Heinz 59, 63, 113, 177
Roger Wagner Chorale 29
Rogers, Barbara 91, 195
Rogers, Bill 288
Rogers, Charles "Buddy" 242, 254, 301
Rogers, Ginger 11, 36, 69, 87, 129, 210, 257, 261, 273, 306, 318, 319
Rogers, Rod 167
Rogers, Roy 277
Rogers, Walter 287
Rogers, Will 344
Rogne, Mandine 187
Rogue Cop 283
Rogue River 65
Rohtla, Toomas 206
Roland, Gilbert 13, 73, 74, 273
Roli, Mino 139
"Roller Coaster" 339
Roman, Lawrence 331
Roman, Rick 21, 313
Roman, Ruth 14, 231, 236, 273
Roman Holiday 24, 245
Romance of Rosy Ridge 187
Romance on the High Seas 94
Romano, Tony 237, 331
Romanoff, Constantine 40, 308
Romantini, Joe 284
Romay, Lina 332
Romeo and Juliet 65, 156, 179, 209, 283, 292, 314
Romero, Alex 247
Romero, Carlos 296
Romero, Cesar 131, 295
La Ronde 57
Ronly-Riklis, Shalom 70
Room at the Top 143
Room Service 196
Rooney, Mickey 220
Roos, Joanna 163, 273, 324
Roosevelt, Buddy 177
Roosevelt, Franklin D. 42, 68, 84, 222, 237, 253, 254, 256, 270, 273, 274, 336
Roosevelt, Theodore 12, 24, 49, 72, 150, 162, 163, 220, 256, 270, 273, 274, 288
The Roosevelt Special 38, 43, 54, 56, 61, 80, 87, 97, 136, 137, 145, 160, 168, 171, 222, 223, 263, 265, 269, 273, 274, 337, 348
Root, Elizabeth 21
Root, Wells 316, 317
Roots 35
Rope 80

Roquemore, Henry 103
Rose, Billy 337
Rose, David 208
Rose, Jack 167
Rose, William 238
The Rose Tattoo 155, 159, 334
Rosebud: The Story of Orson Welles 302
Rosemary's Baby 38, 42, 52, 115, 139
Rosemond, Clinton 126, 291
Rosen, Sam 21
Rosen, Shoshana 228
Rosenbaum, Robert R. 138
Rosenberg, Edgar 340
Rosenberg, Frank P. 165
Rosenbloom, Maxie 27, 274
Rosener, George 86
Der Rosenkavelier 300
Rosing, Bodil 86
Ross, A. 233
Ross, Arthur S. 176
Ross, Barney 274
Ross, Bertram 70
Ross, Bill 148, 187
Ross, Earle 64, 88
Ross, George 165
Ross, Katharine 19
Ross, Virgil 262
Rossen, Arthur 312
Rossen, Robert 84, 282
Rossetti, Christina 340
Rosso, Nick 215
Rosson, Richard 317
Rosten, Norman 320
Roth, Gene 258
Rouault, Georges 8
Roubert, Matty 195
Rough Company 26
"The Rough Riders" 273
Rousseau, Henry 279
Rowan, Dan 59, 185
Rowland, Glenn, Sr. 220
Rowland, Henry 165
Rowland, Roy 240
Rowlands, Gena 11, 28, 48, 101, 113, 137, 186, 189, 190, 213, 214, 215, 252, 274, 275, 304, 345
Roxbury Productions 258
Roxie Hart 31, 61, 273, 338
Roy, Sue 55
Roy Scott Quintet 155
Royal Academy of Dramatic Arts 260
Royal Air Force 9, 120, 170
Royal Canadian Air Force 170
A Royal Fandango 5, 41, 82, 156, 235, 253, 274, 275, 320
Royal Film Performance 55
Royale Theatre 176
Royce, Lionel 86
Royce, Riza 138
Royle, Selena 246
Royle, William 207
Rozsa, Miklos 17, 108, 109, 266, 316

Rub, Christian 275, 287, 306
Ruberg, Clifford 343
Rubin, Benny 136, 152, 275
Rubin, Saul 24
Rubin, Stanley 111, 159, 243, 255
Rubinstein, Artur 92, 154
Rubio, Susan 189
Rudin, Milton 272
Ruddy, Albert 19
Rudolph, Louis 24
Rudolph, Oscar 42, 341
Ruhl, William 25
Ruhmann, Heinz 238, 275
Ruick, Melville 88, 178
Rumann, Sig 85, 104, 272, 275
The Running Man 54
Runthrough 317, 318
Runyon, Damon 81, 275, 290, 292
Rush, Barbara 13, 272, 275, 305
Rush, Celeste 178
Rush, Don 187
Rush, Dick 108, 341
Ruskin, Joseph 213, 272
Russell, Bing 44, 74
Russell, Elizabeth 240
Russell, Connie 223, 233, 234, 276, 327
Russell, Gail 10, 231, 276, 320
Russell, Helene 116
Russell, Henry & Orchestra 231, 280, 283
Russell, Jackie 229
Russell, Janet 347
Russell, Lillian 339
Russell, Lloyd 176
Russell, Mary 205
Russell, Rosalind 19, 20, 28, 81, 131, 254, 273, 280
The Russians Are Coming, the Russians Are Coming 46, 169, 172
Russo–Japanese War 274
Ruysdael, Basil 276, 332
Ryan, Mary 95, 276
Ryan, Robert 70, 106, 154, 276
Ryan, Tim 59
Ryan's Daughter 220
Ryder, Alfred 325
Ryder, Loren 17, 108
Rydin, Carl 258
Rynne, John 171

S. M. Stainach Stock Company 4, 131, 243
S. S. *Normandie* 156, 265
Sabato, Steve 206
The Saboteur 89, 180
Sabrina 54, 245, 344
Sachiko Productions 224
Sackheim, William 137
Sacripanti, Maruo 139
Saeger, Ray 346
Saenz, Eddie 158
Sagal, Boris 325

Sahara 112, 225
Saigon 118
Saint, Eva Marie 214
St. John, Howard 165
St. John, Jill 185, 220
St. Joseph, Ellis 126
St. Louis Blues 179
St. Louis Globe–Democrat 236
St. Louis Post Dispatch 19, 209, 216, 241, 294, 297, 319, 325, 331
St. Oegger, Joan 135
The Saint Strikes Back 156
Saint Subber, Arnold 20
St. Valentine's Day Massacre 67
Saito, Tatsuo 224
The Salad Days 192
Salamon, Amnon 228
Salamunovich, Mike 187
Sale, Virginia 98, 205
Salisbury, Leah 179
Salkowitz, Sy 46
Sally of the Scandals 197
Salmi, Albert 241
Salmon, Peter 293
Salt, Waldo 219
Salter, Hans J. 278, 279
Salter, W. 238
"Salute to Israel" 299
The Salvation Army 144
Salven, David 200, 312
Salven, Edward 271
Sammy Going South 27, 55, 210, 276
Samson and Delilah (film) 97, 149, 210, 237, 267
Samson and Delilah (stage) 4, 43, 116, 156, 168, 179, 197, 235, 253, 276
Samuel French Basic Catalogue of Plays and Musical 326
Samuel Goldwyn Company, Inc. 5, 259
Samuel Goldwyn Productions 137
Samuels, Joan 313
Samuels, Lesser 327
Samuels, Maurice 158
San Francisco 320
San Francisco Chronicle 296
San Quentin 27, 150
San Quentin (Prison) 88
Sanchez, Adam Edward 15, 75, 117, 255, 276, 277
Sanchez, Francesca Robinson 12, 14, 15, 48, 75, 76, 117, 131, 154, 189, 190, 196, 255, 276, 277, 340, 344
Sanchez, Ricardo Adan (Richard) 15, 117, 276, 277
The Sand Pebbles 35, 210
Sande, Walter 266, 327
Sanders, George 85, 277, 306
Sanders, Hugh 136
Sanders, Neara 126
Sanders, Sandy 62

Index

Sandoz, Mari 73, 74
Sandrich, Mark 208
Sanford, Donald S. 115
Sanford, Erskine 5, 136, 137, 170, 252, 277, 302, 314
Sanford, Gerald 212
Sanson, Yvonne 46
Santa Fe 270
Santa Monica Civic Auditorium 18
Santillo, Frank 241, 340
Santoro, Jack 341
Sanville, Richard 117
Saper, Jack 183
Sarchielli, Massimo 46
Sardo, Cosmo 167
Sargent, William 187
Sariego, Ralph 212
Sarnoff, Max 205
Sarris, Andrew 316, 317
Sasanoff, Michael 339
The Satan Bug 305
Satenstein, Frank 339
Saturday Evening Post 280
The Saturday Review 77, 152, 214, 325
Saum, Cliff 183
Saunders, Audrey 231
Saunders, Raymond 231
Saunders, Russell 74, 207, 231
Sauter, Eddie 212
Savage, Archie 306, 313
Savage, Bernard 60
Savage, Nellie 153
The Savage Innocents 308
Savalas, George 138
Savalas, Telly 14, 200, 277
Save the Tiger 187
Savings Bond Orchestra 53
Savings Bond Show 41, 156, 277, 288
Savoir, Alfred 38
Sawtell, Paul 219
Sawyer, Connie 152, 277
Sawyer, Geneva 308
Sawyer, Joe 85, 277, 341
Sayer, Stanley 224
Saylor, Sid 74, 277, 278
Sayonara 196, 220
Sayre, Jeffrey 207, 284
Scandal Sheet 222
Scandanato, Itala 46
Scannell, Frank 272
Scarface 64, 132, 144, 171, 217, 222, 314
Scarlet Letter 155, 283
Scarlet Pimpernel 209
Scarlet Street 10, 18, 27, 34, 40, 43, 58, 67, 80, 87, 89, 94, 95, 99, 111, 112, 119, 120, 128, 130, 141, 145, 149, 150, 167, 168, 171, 175, 180, 181, 189, 195, 198, 219, 223, 224, 235, 249, 251, 253, 255, 257, 259, 268, 269, 277, 278, 279, 292, 304, 320, 328, 333, 338, 345

Scarpaci, John 189
Scatchard, Michelle (Parker) 117
Scatchard, Willary 117, 255
Scatchard, Joseph 117
Scenes from the Yiddish Theatre 49, 294
Schaefer, George 326
Schafner and Sweet 176
Schallert, William 51
Scharff, Lester 327
Schary, Dory 272
Schaumer, Al 284
Scheiwiller, Fred 258
Schell, Maria 13, 179, 340
Schenk, Joseph 322
Scherle, Victor 94, 151
Scherman, Philip 163
Schiaffino, Rossanna 90, 324
Schickel, Richard 271, 291, 314
Schiffer, Robert J. 148
Schifrin, Lalo 78
Schik, Aniko 228
Schildkraut, Joseph 5, 6, 28, 29, 41, 122, 180, 181, 232, 233, 234, 245, 246, 252, 279, 314
Schildkraut, Rudolph 4, 252, 279
Schiller, Frederick 55
Schlamme, Martha 70
Schlatter, George 185
Schlickenmeyer, Dutch 63
Schmitt, William R. 242
Schnabel (music) 35
Schnabel, Stefan 324
Schnee, Charles 324
Schneider, Alan 49
Schneider, Howard 277
Schneider, Richard 35
Schneider, Romy 13, 138, 279
Schoenberg, Arnold 305
Scholl, Jack 177, 290
Schollin, Christina 166, 293
Schrager, Rudy 204
Schrank, Joseph 290
Schroeder, Edward 343
Schroeder, Maria 258
Schubert, Franz 224
Schukin, William 163
Schulman, Arnold 150, 152
Schultz, Ted 173
Schumann, Robert 140
Schumann-Heink, Ferdinand 177
Schumm, Hans 86
Schurz, Carl 13, 49, 72, 73, 74, 150, 188, 189, 255, 256, 279, 280
Schwab, Laurence 122
Schwartz, David R. 271
Schwartz, Ed 206
Schwartz, Sol 130
Schwerin, George 104
Schwerin, Mrs. 104
Schwier, Werner 247
Science Fiction: Studies in Film 295
Sciorra, Annabelle 28
Scott, Douglass 75, 184

Scott, George C. 20
Scott, Jacqueline 137
Scott, Janet 237
Scott, Martha 312
Scott, Simon 51
Scott, Steven 55
Scott, Wallace 183
Scott, Walter F. 176
Scott, Walter M. 42, 157, 284
Scott, Wally 278
Scotti, Vito 324
The Scoundrel 146
Scourby, Alexander 280, 284
Scratch 99, 329
Scratuglia, Giovanni Ivan 238
Screaming Eagles 272
Screen Actors Guild 20, 36, 50, 209, 211, 280
Screen Director's Playhouse 26, 134, 144, 158, 231, 264, 265, 280, 282
Screen Guild Players 140
Screen Snapshots 54, 112, 280, 281, 286
Screen Stories 164
The Sea Hawk 88, 90, 141, 142, 254
Sea Hunt 57
Sea of Grass 33, 41, 61, 149
The Sea Tiger 339
The Sea Wolf 8, 17, 30, 52, 53, 72, 90, 93, 94, 95, 101, 118, 120, 122, 132, 134, 141, 143, 179, 180, 181, 189, 196, 198, 199, 202, 203, 210, 222, 224, 227, 235, 249, 251, 254, 259, 268, 269, 280, 281, 282, 283, 298, 304, 334, 335, 336
"The Sea Wolf" (radio) 264, 280, 282
The Sea-Wolf (novel) 280
The Seagull 43, 199
Sealtest Variety Theatre 134, 264, 283, 289
Séance on a Wet Afternoon 35, 299
The Searchers 54
Sears, Allan 341
The Season 20
Seastrom, Victor 180, 181, 283
Seaton, George 209
Seaton, Scott 346
Secombe, Harry 223, 283, 294
Second Chorus 137
The Second Man 199
The Second Mrs. Tanqueray 41
Seconds 159
Secret Agent 65, 348
The Secret Beyond the Door 237
The Secret Garden 234
The Secret Hour 180, 267
The Secret Life of Walter Mitty 171, 286
Secret of Purple Reef 269
Secret Storm 249
Sedan, Rolfe 194

Seddon, Margaret 57, 198, 345
See Here, Private Hargrove 348
Seel, Charles 74, 98, 203, 208, 237, 347
Seff, Richard 92
Die Sehnsucht Jeder Frau 181, 279, 283
Seibu 224
Seid, Art 236
Seidel, Tom 327
Seidemann, Conrad 181
Seidenberg, Leon 163
Seigal, Robert E. 321
Seiter, William A. 97
Seitz, John F. 17, 66, 108, 109, 147, 231, 283
Selander, Lesley 241
Selbie, Evelyn 144
Seldes, Gilbert 307
Self, Clarence E. 111
Self, William 42
Selinsky, Vladimir 344
Sellers, Peter 299
Sellon, Charles A. 245
Selman, Joseph 245
Seltzer, Walter 295, 297
Selwart, Tonio 308
Selwyn & Company 259, 283, 300, 326
Selwyn, Arch & Edgar 252, 259, 283
Selzer, Milton 78, 283
Selznick, David O. 28, 254, 328
Semels, Harry 40, 291
Semple, Lorenzo, Jr. 42
Send Me No Flowers 29, 169
Sennett, Ted 110
Senz, Eddie 92
Separate Tables 145, 234
Sergeant Rutledge 208
Sergeant York 54, 57, 93, 125, 160, 254, 277, 321, 334, 347, 348
Serling, Rod 211, 213, 252
Seroff, Muni 308
Serpico 271
Serra, Raymond 15, 48, 206, 283
Sersen, Fred 157, 308
"A Set of Values" 11, 111, 129, 133, 134, 234, 283, 310, 345
The Set-Up 147, 276, 320
Seurat, Pierre 34
Seven Angry Men 209, 243
Seven Brides for Seven Brothers 269
Seven Chances 211
Seven Days in May 49, 110, 202, 208
Seven Keys to Baldpate 55, 112, 129, 237
Seven Sinners 89
"The Seven Symptoms" 129, 264, 265, 283
Seven Thieves 12, 17, 27, 36, 43, 47, 48, 50, 53, 65, 67, 76, 80, 87, 89, 90, 94, 106, 121, 128, 132, 133, 134, 135, 144, 180, 234, 235, 249, 251, 268, 280, 285, 300, 305, 322, 334, 336
The Seven-Year Itch 71, 274
Seventeen 308
1776 93, 217
The Seventh Cross 338
Seventh Heaven 76, 211, 265
Seventy Years of Cinema 50, 110
77 Sunset Strip 349
Sex and the Single Girl 180
Seymour, Anne 138
Seymour, Dan 173, 175
Seymour, Harry 207, 290
Shack Out on 101 40
Shackelford, Floyd 108
Shadduck, Jayne 195
Shadow of a Doubt 37, 87, 320
"Shadows Tremble" 86, 165, 171, 182, 251, 252, 285, 301, 310, 334
Shaffner, Franklin 252
Shaftel, Josef 46
Shaftel–Stewart Productions 46
The Shaggy D. A. 330, 332, 348
The Shaggy Dog 339
Shakespeare, William 4, 11, 21, 43, 68, 130, 149, 189, 248, 281, 307
The Shakespeare Cycle 80, 285
Shakespeare Festival 285
The Shakiest Gun in the West 298
Shalako 267
Shamroy, Leon 252
Shane 34, 61, 86, 146, 180
Shane, Maxwell 233
Shanghai Express 100
The Shanghai Gesture 222
Shanghai Lady 234
Shannon, Harry 266, 285, 332
Shapiro, Harry 92
Shapley, Dr. Harlow 154
Sharif, Omar 44, 200, 285
Sharma, Barbara 185
Sharp, Henry 164
Sharpe, Don 280, 283
Sharpe, Lester 86
Shatner, William 13, 241, 267, 285
Shaughnessy, Mickey 229, 285
Shavelson, Mel 18, 167
Shaw, Artie 154
Shaw, Brinsley 218
Shaw, Frank 25
Shaw, George Bernard 4, 5, 30, 87, 115, 189, 203, 253, 255, 315
Shaw, Hal R. 205
Shaw, Irwin 12, 323, 324
Shaw, Naomi 313
Shaw, Mary 163
Shaw, Reta 199
Shaw, Roland 293
Shaw, Sebastian 170
Shaw, Tom 200
Shayne, Konstantin 249, 250, 302
She Demons 29
She Done Him Wrong 221, 273
She Married an Artist 166
She Stoops to Conquer 325
She Wore a Yellow Ribbon 112, 169, 210
Shear, Joe 238
Shearer, Douglas 44, 52, 181, 240, 327
Shearer, Norma 301, 314
Shedd, Robert G. 232, 245
Sheehan, John 177, 231
Sheehan, Vincent 274
Sheiner, David 92
Sheldon, Edward 54
Sheldon, Ralph 46
Shelton, John 177
Shelton, Turner 315
Shenandoah 301
Shepherd of the Hills 68, 144
Sheridan, Ann 254, 268
Sheridan, Frank 341
Sheridan, Helen 246
Sheridan, Malise 326
Sherlock, Charles 86, 207
Sherman, Dick 233
Sherman, Lowell 301
Sherwood, Mark 76
Sherwood, Robert 148, 204, 249, 315, 316, 329
Sherwood, Roberta 148
Shevelove, Burt 270
Shields, Robert 318
Shields, Wilbert 122
Shigeta, James 325
Shimada, Teru 258
Shimomura, Akemi 224
Shine On Harvest Moon 168
"Shine On Harvest Moon" 223
Shining Victory 300
Shinn, Everett 57
Ship Ahoy 276
Ship Forever Sailing 28, 33, 41, 65, 68, 89, 234, 263, 285
Ship of Fools 43, 118, 275
Shipman, David 74
Shipman, Samuel 113, 123
Shirley, Irene 186
Shirley, Peg 215
Shock Treatment 53
Shoemaker, Ann 219
The Shoes of the Fisherman 97
Shoeshine 97
Shokus Videos 190
The Shootist 68, 221
The Shop Around the Corner 221
The Shopworn Angel 255
Shore, Dinah 35, 169, 237, 331, 332
Shore, Lillian 331
Short, Hassard 123
A Shot in the Dark 292
Shoup, Howard 104, 290
Show Boat 41, 118, 171, 217, 221, 223, 271, 286, 320, 329
Showcase 257
Shubert, Eddie 63
Shubert, The Messrs. 245, 252

Index

Shubert Theatre (New Haven) 215
Shuken, Leo 167, 200
Shumway, Lee 109, 161, 162, 286, 343
Shyer, Melville 278
Shyre, Paul 326
Sibelius, Celia 85
Sickert, Walter 34
Sid Kuller Productions 21
Sidman, Sid 44
Sidney, George 12, 13, 15, 18, 101, 117, 157, 247, 259, 287, 329, 340, 344
Sidney, George (actor) 301
Sidney, Jane Robinson 12, 14, 15, 19, 33, 47, 48, 114, 117, 130, 151, 152, 154, 157, 171, 182, 189, 199, 206, 29, 247, 261, 286, 294, 319, 344, 345
Sidney, Sylvia 23, 70, 268, 287, 337
Siegel, Al 327
Siegel, Bugsy 23
Siegel, Don 59
Siegel, Max 336
Siegel, Sol C. 157
Sign of the Cross 68
Sign of the Ram 179, 270
Signoret, Simone 220
Sigurjonsson, Johann 116
Silberstein, Mona 228
Le Silence Est d'Or 72
The Silence of the Lambs 37
The Silencers 166, 208
Siletti, Mario 44, 158
Silke, Jim 77
Sills, Milton 268, 281
Silva, Henry 229
Silva, Kathy 296
Silvani, Al 272
Silver, Charles H. 70
Silver, David 247
Silver, Johnny 229
The Silver Cord 159, 183, 215
Silver Dollar 7, 48, 55, 63, 75, 80, 87, 90, 94, 101, 111, 120, 123, 131, 140, 141, 142, 145, 150, 155, 162, 168, 186, 197, 198, 201, 203, 217, 224, 235, 249, 251, 256, 275, 287, 305, 334, 339, 345
Silvera, Daryl 74
Silverbush, Sam 218
Silverheels, Jay 173, 288
Silvers, Louis 88, 98, 175, 178, 203, 208, 237, 347
Silverstein, Eliot 137
Simmons, Dick 280, 283
Simmons, Ed 208
Simmons, Richard 272
Simmons, Richard Alan 137
Simms, Ginny 113, 114, 332
Simms, Hal 339
Simms, Larry 75, 183
Simon, Robert F. 115

Simone, Dario 238
Simone, Ralph 92
Simons, Henry 163
Simonson, Lee 22, 170, 288
Simple Souls 211
Simpson, Alan 130
Simpson, George 40
Simpson, Gloria Ann 318
Simpson, Reginald 162, 341
Simpson, Russell 287
The Sin of Madelon Claudet 283
Sinatra, Frank 12, 13, 18, 19, 20, 49, 68, 81, 87, 89, 90, 100, 130, 131, 151, 152, 154, 156, 165, 188, 223, 247, 248, 254, 259, 271, 272, 274, 277, 283, 288, 305, 327, 330, 331, 332, 337
Sinatra and His Rat Pack 288
Sinbad the Sailor 116
SinCap Productions 152
Since You Went Away 18, 80, 273
Sinclair, Andrew 73
Sinclair, Maud 163
Sing-Sing 256, 279
Singer, Isaac Bashevis 70
Singer, Stuffy 112
The Singers 288, 311
Singin' in the Rain 72, 79, 269
Singing Sergeants 163, 189, 224, 328
Singleton, Doris 204, 237, 347
Sinner's Holiday 179, 202
Sirasky, Fredric 206
Sisk, Robert 240
Sisley, Alfred 34
Sister Kenny 179, 249
The Sisters 93
Sistine Chapel 289
Sistrom, Joseph 17, 108
Sitgreaves, Beverly 275
Sitting Pretty 277
Six Characters in Search of an Author 348
Six Cylinder Love 129
Six Million Dollar Man 298
$64,000 Challenge 11, 34, 131, 234, 256, 288, 289, 310
$64,000 Question 288
Sjostrom, Victor *see* Seastrom, Victor
Skag 203
Skala, Lilia 340
Skelton, Red 277
Skelton, Scott 211, 212
Sketchley, Les 219
The Ski Bum 178
Ski Patrol 166
Skinner, Otis 166
Skippy 206, 271
Skyjacked 326
Slater, Christian 199
Slattery's Hurricane 343
Slaven, Buster 327
Slaytor, Joseph 326, 327
The Sleeping Car Murders 220

"Sleight of Hand" 134, 264, 283, 289
The Slender Thread 35, 277
Sleuth 206, 236
A Slight Case of Murder 8, 23, 37, 55, 58, 59, 61, 67, 75, 76, 81, 87, 107, 111, 112, 120, 128, 133, 134, 142, 143, 149, 154, 156, 168, 169, 183, 186, 189, 195, 198, 222, 223, 244, 249, 250, 251, 253, 260, 268, 275, 290, 291, 301, 314, 329, 334, 335, 345
"A Slight Case of Murder" (radio) 225, 242, 263, 290
Slim 268
Slimon, Scott 55
The Slippery Pearls 72, 156, 168, 286, 291, 301; see also *The Stolen Jools*
Sloane, Allan 70
Slocum, George 25
Slonim, Gisela & Mordechai 228
Smadar, David 228
Smalley, Phillips 162, 341
Smart, Jack 45, 307
Smart Money 7, 17, 18, 19, 50, 65, 71, 81, 87, 118, 120, 123, 131, 132, 134, 140, 141, 142, 143, 154, 156, 157, 171, 179, 182, 195, 223, 254, 291, 292, 305, 320, 335
Smash-Up, Story of a Woman 145, 159
Smiley, Ralph 62
Smilin' Through 283
The Smiling Lieutenant 302
Smith, Al 270
Smith, Alfred E. 288
Smith, Art 219
Smith, Benjamin B. 21
Smith, Bernard 74
Smith, Billy 183
Smith, Buffalo Bob 185
Smith, Sir C. Aubrey 126, 223, 291
Smith, C. E. 262
Smith, Charles B. 327
Smith, Dean 74
Smith, Dick 157, 203
Smith, F. Y. 159
Smith, George 285
Smith, Gerald L. K. 82
Smith, Gerald Oliver 326
Smith, Lt. Cdr. H. D., USN 97
Smith, Harry James 195, 292
Smith, J. B. 46
Smith, Jack Martin 42
Smith, Joe P. 173
Smith, Joel 62
Smith, Oscar 108
Smith, Loring 270
Smith, Roger 31
Smith, Wingate 74
Smoky Valley 332
Snader, Edward L. 195
The Snake Pit 107, 155

Snell, David 52, 327
Snow White 186
Snowball Express 330
Snowden, Eric 307
Snyder, Albert 108
Snyder, Billy 248
Snyder, John 277
Snyder, Ruth 107, 108
Snyder, William 229
So Big 175
Soble, Ron 78
Society Girl 143
Soderling, Walter 25, 161, 292
Sokoloff, Vladimir 27, 278, 292
Solari, Rudi 76, 187
Soler, Juan Albert 139
Solomon, Jack 74, 233
Solomon, Louis 219
Some Came Running 201, 218
Some Like It Hot 12, 187, 235, 247, 265, 271, 272, 301, 344
Somebody Up There Likes Me 135, 230
Something Big 208
Sometimes a Great Notion 167
Sommer, Elke 13, 19, 36, 101, 258, 292
Sommerfield, Lisa 206
Somper, Frank 224
Son of Flubber 221
Son of Kong 33
Son of Lassie 61
Son of Paleface 112
The Son of the Shiek 38, 197
Sondergaard, Gale 254, 274
Sondergaard, Quentin 148
A Song Is Born 137
Song of Bernadette 54, 61, 179, 243, 267, 338
Song of Love 54, 286
Song of Norway 14, 22, 47, 90, 121, 140, 141, 150, 163, 165, 182, 198, 221, 223, 224, 235, 248, 251, 253, 283, 293, 294
Song of Scherehazade 95
"The Song of Solomon" 346
A Song to Remember 134, 202, 222
Sonntag, Jack 42, 148
Sons and Lovers 334
The Sons of Katie Elder 208
Sophie Maslow Dance Company 49, 70, 71, 252, 294
Sorel, George 25, 60, 204, 294, 308
Sorrowful Jones 333
Sorry Wrong Number 221, 254, 299
Sosnick, Harry 53
Sosso, Pietro 302
Sothern, Ann 8, 42, 58, 59, 81, 186, 198, 268, 294
Sothern, Hugh 103
Soudiekinem, Sergei 75
Soule, Olan 78, 137, 167, 294

The Sound and the Fury 42, 270
The Sound of Music 46, 187, 244, 293, 294
Sound Associates, Inc. 92, 215
Sounder 209, 270
Sousa, John Philip 328
South of Suez 300
South Pacific 196, 217, 334
South to Karanga 166
Southern, Terry 77, 78, 84
Southon, Rev. G. E. 312
Soutine, Chaim 34
Sovey, Raymond 60, 294
Soylent Green 14, 15, 19, 27, 35, 47, 48, 49, 80, 87, 89, 94, 99, 119, 121, 125, 127, 140, 141, 148, 171, 199, 203, 224, 235, 249, 267, 280, 289, 294, 295, 296, 297, 298, 304, 311, 330
Space, Arthur 240, 266, 298, 345
Spanish-American War 7, 32, 127, 162, 274, 334
Spartacus 110, 128, 185, 237, 321
Sparv, Camilla 166, 200
Spaulding, George 158
Spears, Stephen 185
Speicher, Eugene 34
Speight, Rosalind 293
Spellbound 68, 146, 245, 269, 320
Spelling, Aaron 236
Spelvin, George, Jr. 176
Spelvin, George, Sr. 176
Spencer, Al(fred) E. 51, 200
Spencer, Dorothy 284
Spencer, Douglas 109, 231
Spencer, James P. 327
Spencer Tracy, Tragic Idol 275
Spencer's Mountain 93
Sperber, A. M. 148, 174, 175, 249
Spiegel, Sam 18, 298, 302
Spier, William 69, 204, 225
Spigelgass, Leonard 15, 19, 26, 47, 114, 213, 247, 298, 299
Spinetti, Victor 46
The Spiral Staircase 86, 344
The Spirit of St. Louis 298, 301
Splendor 156
Splendor in the Grass 156, 273
The Spoilers 41, 68, 107
The Sportsmen 199
Spottswood, James 96
Springfield Revival 19
Springfield Rifle 40
Sprotte, Bert 40
The Spy Who Came In from the Cold 270, 330
The Squaw Man 97, 137, 325, 330
Squire, Ronald 170
Staffansson, Vihjalmur 274
Stafford, Grace 85, 103, 183, 299
Stafford, Hanley 45
Stafford, Jo 277
Stage Door 32, 69, 80, 143, 267, 273
Stage Door Canteen 188, 209

Stage Fright 100
Stagecoach 51, 68, 76, 84, 129, 211, 220, 321
Stahl, Francis E. 74
Stahl, Walter O. 103
Stalag 17 140, 275, 344
Stalin, Josef 179
Stalling, Carl W. 86, 154, 155, 159, 254, 262, 339
Stalmaster-Lister Casting 187
The Standard Brands Hour 165, 263
Stander, Lionel 84, 184, 299
Standing, Wyndham 346
Stanhope, Ted 165, 306
Stanhope Hotel 213
Stanislavsky, Konstantin 232
Stanley, Ed 63, 86, 163
Stanley, Eric 27, 290
Stanley, Kim 14, 299, 325
Stanley, Marcoreta 313
Stanley, Robert 341
Stanton, Paul 219
Stanwyck, Barbara 9, 11, 23, 107, 108, 109, 110, 122, 126, 197, 198, 209, 226, 249, 280, 299, 301, 309, 329, 332, 345, 347
Stapp, Marjorie 165
The Star Chamber 180
A Star Is Born 37, 40, 69, 184, 221, 299, 338, 344
Star-Spangled Girl 244, 271
Star Trek 172, 285, 298
Star Trek: The Wrath of Khan 220
Star Wars 298
Star Witness 299
Stardust 155
Stark, Mike 158
Starmaker 63, 84, 104, 123, 124, 162, 176, 177, 190, 207
Starnes, Darrel 147
Starr, Frances 124, 299
Starr, Irving 29, 283
Stars and Stripes Forever 160, 243, 328, 334
Stars Salute '64 46, 259, 299, 310
Stassen, Harold 328
Stassino, Paul 55
State Fair 36
State of Israel Bonds Organization 36, 168, 299
State of Siege 220
State of the Union 42, 142
Statham, Jack 278
Station Six Sahara 330
Statler, Mary 74
Staub, Ralph 145, 146
Steamboat Round the Bend 79
Stedelijk Van Abbe Museum 33
Stedman, Myrtle 290
Steel 339
Steel Magnolias 201
Steers, Larry 27, 191, 300, 346
Stefani, Joseph 103
Stehli, Edgar 186

Index

Stehli, George 22
Steiger, Rod 22, 53, 67, 76, 89, 241, 267, 284, 285, 300, 305
Stein, Gary 206
Stein, Max 236
Steinback, Rudolph 86
Steiner, Max 27, 104, 147, 165, 173, 177, 332
Stella Dallas 5, 69, 94, 137, 142, 186, 209, 237, 253, 259, 283, 294, 300
Sten, Anna 39
Stengel, Anton 205
Stephens, Laraine 243
Stephenson, Bob 231
Stephenson, Henry 300, 326
Stephenson, James 85, 103, 300
The Sterile Cuckoo 217
Sterler, Hermine 104
Stern, Isaac 70
Stern, Steven Hilliard 228
Sternad, Rudolph 219
The Steve Allen Show 300, 310
Steve McQueen 77
Stevens, Connie 19
Stevens, George 19, 208, 300
Stevens, K. T. 300, 331
Stevens, Landers 191, 300
Stevens, Leith 25, 45
Stevens, Marvin 327
Stevens, Naomi 187, 236, 300, 345
Stevens (Stevenson), Onslow 231, 312
Stevens, Rise 70, 300
Stevens, Warren 51, 300
Stevenson, Bob 40
Stevenson, John 228
Stevenson, Robert 28
Stewart, Dick 136
Stewart, Donald Ogden 306
Stewart, French 28
Stewart, James 8, 13, 18, 29, 73, 74, 97, 146, 184, 188, 198, 209, 280, 300, 336, 347
Stewart, Paul 147, 223, 301
Stewart, Polly 75, 105
Stewart, Sy 46
The Stewartese 22
Stillman, Robert 266, 306
The Sting 156, 230, 334
Stokowski, Leopold 336
The Stolen Jools 32, 80, 88, 90, 116, 168, 200, 210, 286, 291, 299, 301, 348
The Stolen Lady 6, 68, 82, 253, 301
Stoloff, Morris W. 97, 161, 219, 318, 332
Stoltz, Myrl 233, 284
Stone, Andrew L. 14, 166, 259, 293, 294
Stone, George E. 63, 125, 191, 290, 301
Stone, James 136

Stone, Leonard 295
Stone, Milburn 51, 301
Stone, Sandra 62
Stone, Virginia 293
Stoney, Jack 184
Stop, You're Killing Me 88, 268
Storey, Ralph 289
Storm Over America 84
Storm Warning 94
"Stormy Weather" 66, 205, 223
Storrich, Dudley 316
The Story of Alexander Graham Bell 52, 149, 268
The Story of G. I. Joe 211, 220, 338
The Story of Louis Pasteur 8, 99, 100, 105, 134, 142, 222, 237, 292
The Story of Ruth 276
The Story of Temple Drake 156
The Story of Vernon and Irene Castle 69
Stothart, Herbert 254, 328
La Strada 260
Stradner, Rose 166, 184, 186, 198
Straight, Beatrice 285, 301
Strain, Vincent 176
Strait-Jacket 37
Strand, Paul 274
Strang, Harry 52, 207
Strange, Robert 38, 105, 123, 207, 301, 302
Strange Interlude 184, 197, 217, 220, 315
The Strange Love of Martha Ivers 146, 299
The Stranger 10, 17, 20, 34, 66, 71, 89, 95, 98, 119, 121, 128, 132, 141, 157, 160, 196, 211, 221, 227, 235, 249, 250, 251, 261, 269, 277, 286, 292, 298, 303, 309, 335, 338, 348
"The Stranger" (radio) 259, 264, 304
Stranger on the Run 178
Strangers on a Train 70, 273
Strangers When We Meet 61
Strangis, Sam 42
The Strangler 64
Strasberg, Lee 5, 75, 252, 304, 314
Strategic Air Command 160
Stratford Pens 23
Stravinsky, Igor 35
The Strawberry Blonde 69, 145
Streamlined Shakespeare 81
Street Scene 80, 118, 137, 156, 217, 260, 269
A Streetcar Named Desire 203, 217
Streeter, Reggie 184
The Streets of San Francisco 203
Streisand, Barbra 299
Strictly Dishonorable 217
Strictly Dynamite 330
Striepeke, Dan 252
Strike Up the Band 175, 283

Strindberg, August 245
Stritch, Rev. Samuel 160
Strode, Woody 112, 312
Struzan, Drew 255
Stuart, Nick 170
Stubbs, Harry 126, 233
Stumpf, Milton 137
Studer, Karl 247
Stupin, Paul 219
Sturgis, Eddie 242
Styne, Jule 17, 65, 167, 304
Sudden Fear 88
Suddenly 26, 55, 136
Suddenly Last Summer 95, 148, 298
Sudrow, Lyle 258
Sues, Allan 185
Sues, Leonard 331
Suez 61, 300
Sugar 304
"A Suite of Old American Dances" 328
Sukman, Harry 62
Sullavan, Margaret 154
Sullivan, Barry 268, 281
Sullivan, Charles 177, 183, 282, 304, 341
Sullivan, Ed 70, 113
Sullivan, Elliott 177, 290, 327
Sullivan, Jack 27, 177
Sullivan, Margareto 258
The Sullivans 220, 285
Sullivan's Travels 130, 210
Summer and Smoke 137
Summer Holiday 168
Summer Wishes, Winter Dreams 287
Summerfield, Marvin 325
Summertime 148
Sunday Bloody Sunday 197
Sunday in New York 309
Sunde, Mary 177
The Sundowners 220
Sunrise at Campobello 42, 134, 273, 315
Sunset Boulevard 283, 344
Sunshine Boys 64
Super-Panavision 201, 293
Superman 44, 129, 142, 279, 298
Support Your Local Gunfighter 130
Support Your Local Sheriff 55, 225
Surtees, Robert 240
Survivor from Warsaw 305
Susan and God 160
Susan Slept Here 201, 332
Suspense 69, 204, 225, 263, 264, 305, 348
Suspense in the Cinema 125, 231
Suspicion 61, 68, 261, 340
Susskind, David 99
Sutherland, Sidney 163
Sutton, Frank 187, 305
Sutton, Paul 184
Svengali 54, 141, 208, 283
Swamp Water 344

The Swan 211
Swanson, Gloria 226, 329, 347
Swashbuckler 156
Sweet Bird of Youth 42, 320
Sweet Charity 93, 220
Sweet Smell of Success 23, 103, 159, 200
Sweetland, Lee 331
Swenson, Karl 78, 258
Swerling, Jo 6, 7, 161, 175, 176, 252, 253, 305, 341
Swift, David 138, 259, 298
Swinburne, Nora 198, 305, 345
Swing Low, Sweet Chariot 50
Swing Time 94, 300
Swinging on a Star 330
Swingle, Ward 238
Swirsky, Dr. Shimaryahu T. 160
Swiss Family Robinson 43
Swiss Miss 294
Switch 334
Switzer, Carl "Alfalfa" 49, 312
Swoger, Harry 272
The Sword and the Rose 240, 241
Sydmeth, Louise 22
Sylos, Frank 236
Sylos, Paul 233
Symphony of the Air 70
Syndafloden 96

Tabor, Augusta 287
Tabor, Horace A.W. 7, 48, 150, 162, 288, 305
Tagewell, Charles 246
Taggart, Ben 78, 194, 219, 291, 305, 341
Taggart, Hal 138
Tahitian Flowers 164
A Tailor Made Man 292
Taiz, Lillian 168
Take Me Out to the Ballgame 182
Take One (LeRoy) 191
Take One (Overbey) 61, 346, 347
Takemi, K. 245
Takeuchi, Kyoko 224
Taking of Pelham 1–2–3 271
Talbot, Jill 154
Talbot, Nita 167
A Tale of Two Cities 43, 186
Tales of Manhattan 9, 23, 29, 31, 36, 47, 56, 58, 66, 87, 88, 91, 93, 95, 111, 113, 119, 120, 128, 136, 144, 145, 146, 157, 168, 172, 185, 188, 198, 208, 220, 223, 224, 225, 226, 235, 249, 251, 268, 269, 271, 272, 273, 275, 277, 298, 305, 306, 307, 322, 336
Tales of Terror 243
Tales of the Texas Rangers 244
The Talk of the Town 117
The Talker 197
The Tall Blond Man with One Black Shoe 90
The Tall Men 277, 285, 334

Tall Story 167
Tallman, Robert 225
Talmadge, Constance 113
Talmadge, Norma 58
"The Taming of the Shrew" 31, 81, 186, 189, 199, 251, 263, 285, 307, 345
Tamkin, David 25
Tammy and the Bachelor 57, 230, 269, 348
Tampico, 38, 40, 53, 61, 71, 87, 120, 1329, 134, 141, 186, 188, 198, 200, 210, 211, 223, 227, 235, 243, 249, 250, 251, 268, 307, 335, 336, 345
"Tangerine" 109, 223
Tani, Yoko 338, 339
Tank Battalion 272
Tannen, Charles 306, 331
Tannenbaum, Martin 243
Tannhauser 224
Tansman, Alexander 126
Tap 93
"Taps" 131, 271
Taradash, Daniel 19
Taras Bulba 61
Targets 171
Tarkington, Booth 5, 253, 308, 309
Tarzan, the Ape Man 96, 188
Tate, Sharon 76
Tate Gallery 33
Tatsuno, G. 245
Taurog, Norman 222
Taustine, Manny 206
Tayback, Vic 199
Taylor, Al 55
Taylor, Anne 213
Taylor, Deems 22, 154
Taylor, Dierdre 206
Taylor, Don 101, 211
Taylor, Dub 78, 152, 308, 309, 315
Taylor, Elizabeth 323
Taylor, Gilbert 170
Taylor, Sen. Glen 154
Taylor, Glenhall 283
Taylor, Glenn 137
Taylor, Jeffrey 293
Taylor, Lark 186
Taylor, Libby 27
Taylor, Renee 28
Taylor, Robert 84, 187, 222, 299, 309
Taylor, Robert Neil 184
Taylor, Rod 147, 309
Taylor-Morris, Maxine 206
Taylor-Young, Leigh 295
Tchaikovsky, Peter I. 222
Tea and Sympathy 29
Tead, Phil 163
The Teahouse of the August Moon 129, 336
Teal, Ray 327
Tearle, Conway 307

Tebeau, Marguerite 116
TechniColor 11, 139, 167, 201, 229, 312, 313, 332
Technirama 225
TechniScope 139
Tedrow, Irene 26, 78, 309, 313
Teitelbaum, Al 331
Tell Them Willie Boy Is Here 52
Telsun Foundation 340
Temple, Shirley 29
Temple Israel 15, 130
"Temptation" 223
Ten Cents a Dance 150
The Ten Commandments 1, 11, 17, 23, 29, 31, 34, 42, 47, 49, 53, 61, 66, 68, 80, 83, 84, 87, 90, 93, 94, 95, 96, 97, 103, 112, 121, 127, 128, 143, 148, 150, 164, 166, 171, 180, 181, 186, 198, 202, 203, 210, 213, 226, 234, 235, 243, 244, 248, 249, 251, 256, 267, 269, 297, 298, 309, 311, 313, 314, 335, 336, 337, 343
The Ten Commandments (1923) 96
Tenbrook, Harry 40, 194, 290, 314, 341
The Tender Trap 269
Tenoever, Ellen 206
Tenth Avenue Girl 112
Terms of Endearment 201
Terror Is a Man 187
Terry, Phillip 184, 307
Terry, Sheila 91
Terry-Thomas 202, 314
Tess of the Storm Country 250, 271
Test Pilot 320
Tester, Edward 55
Tetrick, Harry W. 295
Tetrick, Paul 340
Thacher, Russell 295, 297
Thalasso, Arthur 341
Thalberg, Irving 6, 181, 198, 314
Thalia Productions 266
Thank Your Lucky Stars 221
Tharp, Norman 326
That Certain Woman 244
That Hamilton Woman 23, 115
That Man from Rio 70
That Man Reuter 26
That Touch of Mink 94
Thatcher, Heather 126
Theatre Arts Monthly 170, 176, 303
The Theatre Guild 5, 6, 22, 30, 43, 57, 60, 68, 75, 79, 94, 99, 100, 101, 113, 117, 128, 136, 137, 140, 141, 147, 150, 163, 167, 169, 170, 184, 187, 189, 196, 203, 220, 227, 245, 252, 259, 270, 277, 285, 288, 300, 304, 314, 315, 320, 333, 336, 338, 339
Theatre Magazine 262
Theatre of Blood 221
Them! 149, 298
Theodora Goes Wild 61
Theodore, Lee 292

Index

Theodore, Paul 330
There Shall Be No Night 128
There's a Girl in My Soup 55
There's No Business Like Show Business 90, 210
These Three 156, 210
Thew, Harvey 287, 322
They Died with Their Boots On 189
They Drive by Night 265
They Got Me Covered 99
They Knew What They Wanted 6, 159, 180, 181, 185, 197, 220, 253, 267, 315
They Made Me a Criminal 338
They Only Kill Their Masters 186
They Shall Not Die 339
They Won't Forget 169, 180, 195, 210
Thief of Baghdad 334
The Thin Man 30, 159, 161, 255
The Thing 298
Things to Come 209, 298
The Third Man 87
The Third Man on the Mountain 305
The Third Voice 94, 196
13 Rue Madeleine 144
Thirty Seconds Over Tokyo 149, 188
36 Hours 43, 179
This Above All 211
This Gun for Hire 180, 321
This Is America 125
"This Is It" 13, 134, 256, 310, 315
This Is My Affair 347
This Is My Love 276
This Is Tom Jones 14, 43, 134, 163, 208, 217, 311, 315
This Is Your Life 49, 169, 310, 315
This Land Is Mine 211
This Reckless Age 299
Thoeren, Robert 238
Thomajan, Dale 322
Thomas, Sen. Albert D. 154
Thomas, Bill 17, 135, 229, 258, 284
Thomas, Danny 35, 131, 197, 237
Thomas, Dean 229
Thomas, Dolph 167, 173, 183, 207
Thomas, Marie 231
Thomas, Patti 237
Thomas, Richard H. 154
Thomas, Tony 281, 333
Thomas, William 233
The Thomas Crown Affair 169, 180
Thompson, Duane 202, 208, 347
Thompson, Harry 92
Thompson, J. Lee 200, 201
Thompson, Larry 219
Thompson, Natalie 327
Thompson, Ron 224
Thompson, W. H. 232
Thompson, Woodman 122
Thoms, Jerome 332
Thomsen, Hans 84
Thomson, David 302
Thomson, Kenneth 194

Thone, William L. 341
Thorn: 2022 27
The Thorn Birds 299
Thornberger, Maiken 258
Thornton, Cyril 40
Thoroughly Modern Millie 79, 275
Thorpe, Jim 40
Thos. Agnew & Sons 33
Those Redheads from Seattle 244
A Thousand Clowns 38
Thousands Cheer 234
Three Coins in the Fountain 180, 304
"Three Coins in the Fountain"(song) 65
3-D 11, 135
Three Days and a Child 34
Three Faces East 29, 129
The Three Faces of Eve 79, 336
Three Godfathers 169, 206
The 300 Spartans 209
Three Little Words 330
The Three Musketeers 221, 237, 286
Three Secrets 273
The Three Sisters 299
The 3:10 to Yuma 93, 129, 146
Three Violent People 143
Three Wise Fools 211
The Threepenny Opera 93
A Thrill a Minute with Jack Albany 229
The Thrill of It All 130
Thriller 256
Thugs with Dirty Mugs 69, 315
Thunder Alley 22
Thunder in the City 7, 23, 61, 71, 80, 111, 120, 135, 164, 166, 186, 197, 198, 224, 234, 235, 251, 269, 315, 316, 329, 337, 345
"Thunder in the City" 263, 316
Thunderball 70
Thurber, James 234
Tibbett, Lawrence 158, 224
Tiger at the Gates 31
Tiger Rose 330
Tiger Shark 7, 9, 20, 27, 30, 32, 39, 40, 53, 94, 102, 120, 123, 134, 144, 159, 169, 186, 198, 203, 208, 225, 235, 251, 268, 316, 317, 318, 335, 336, 345
Tight Spot 11, 36, 27, 47, 49, 80, 87, 89, 98, 121, 129, 131, 133, 134, 140, 141, 172, 210, 235, 251, 253, 257, 261, 273, 310, 311, 319, 319
Tighe, Janet 315
Tilford, Park C. 92
Till the Clouds Roll By 226
Till We Meet Again 209, 235, 286
Tilles, Andrew 189
Tillotson, David Lee 184
Time 56, 77, 109, 147, 157, 160, 166, 217, 291, 293, 297
"Time" (song) 228

Time Limit 203, 343
The Time Machine 65, 309
Time of the Cuckoo 79
The Time of Your Life 221, 243, 255, 272, 315
Time Out for Romance 140
Time-Warner, Inc. 335
Tinker, Tailor, Soldier, Spy 179
Tiomkin, Dmitri 200, 222
Titanic (1953) 169
To Be or Not to Be 209, 267
To Each His Own 199
To Have and Have Not 37, 54, 57, 144, 149, 294
To Kill a Mockingbird 245
To the Shores of Tripoli 221, 274
Tobacco Road 37, 348
Tobias, Willard 75
Tobin, Ann 203, 204, 208, 347
Tobin, Genevieve 7, 91, 162, 163, 186, 224, 319, 345
Todd, Ann 75, 105
Todd, Mabel 169
Todd, Mike 53
Todman, Bill 329
Toffel, Paul 62
Tol'able David 41, 68
Toler, Sidney 91, 253, 319
Tolnay, Akos 316
Tolstoy, Leo 221
Tom, Anna 231
Tom Jones 12, 18, 319
Tomack, Sid 158
The Tomb of Ligeia 22
Tombes, Andrew 183
Tomlin, Lily 185
Tomlinson, David 170, 319
Tomlinson, Tommy 170
Tommy 31
Tone, Franchot 274
The Tonight Show with Johnny Carson 64, 203, 310, 319
Too Hot to Handle 68
Too Long, America 263, 320
"Too Marvelous for Words" 208
Toohey, John Peter 262
Toomey, Regis 86, 97, 320
Tooth Gallery 33
Top Hat 211, 273
Topaz 129
Topkapi 221
Topper 68, 130, 142, 200, 334
Tor, Siegfried 258
Torchy Blane 117
Torme, Mel 288
Torn, Rip 13, 76, 78, 309, 320
Torrence, David 125
Torrid Zone 200, 22, 322
Tortilla Flat 221, 298
Toscanini, Arturo 35
Tosches, Nick 243
Totter, Audrey 62, 237, 320, 325
Touch of Evil 100, 149, 187, 221, 338
A Touch of the Poet 87, 299

Tough Guys (film) 110, 182, 334
The Tough Guys 22, 39, 44, 48, 124, 135, 144, 152, 177, 185, 219, 240, 258, 288, 290, 303, 313, 315
Toulouse-Lautrec, Henri de 34
Tovarich 54, 80, 195
The Tower of Lies 283
Tower of London 171, 237
The Towering Inferno 294
Town Without Pity 305
Towne, Aline 293
Townshend Harris Hall 36, 114
Tozere, Fred 86
Tracy, Spencer 5, 13, 20, 21, 28, 41, 73, 76, 82, 148, 214, 252, 254, 275, 320, 328
Trade Winds 249
Trader Horn 261
Trading Places 42
Trail of the Lonesome Pine 144, 334
Transcope 247
The Trap 140
Trapeze 182
Travers, Henry 5, 6, 30, 75, 252, 270, 314, 320
La Traviata 246
Travis, Michael 185
Treasure Island 180
Treasure of the Sierra Madre 52, 54, 160, 201
Treasury Star Parade 72, 166, 169, 263, 320
Tree, Dolly 52, 306
Tree, Dorothy 84, 85, 205
A Tree Grows in Brooklyn 24, 53, 136, 200, 208
Trevor, Claire 8, 10, 12, 17, 27, 28, 37, 44, 45, 48, 111, 113, 173, 186, 189, 218, 222, 249, 268, 321, 323, 324, 325, 345
Tri-Arts, Inc. 333
The Trial 338
"Trial and Error" 115, 265, 321, 338
The Trial of Mary Dugan 300
Triangle Studios 92
Trickett, Vicki 247
Triesault, Ivan 115, 258, 321
Trimachi, Sal 46
Trintignant, Jean Louis 67
The Trip to Bountiful 56
Trivas, Victor 17, 302
Trocolor, Bob 44, 298
Trog 883
Tromm, Ilse-Nore 29, 293
Trotti, Lamar 306
Trouble in Paradise 130
The Trouble with Angels 199
The Trouble with Harry 129, 166, 201
Trovaioli, Armando 238
Trowbridge, Charles 85, 321
True, Mary 75
True Colors 343
True Grit 277
True Lies 149
Truman, Harry S 256, 277

Trumbo, Dalton 83, 84, 240, 321
Tservantser, Nachman 228
Tsuda, Akiko 228
Tsur, Eitan 228
Tucker, Harland 177, 231, 321, 326
Tucker, Richard 70
Tucker, Sophie 146
Tully, Phil 158
Tuna 27, 316, 317
Tunney, Gene 178
Turner, George 162
Turner, John 55
Turner, Lana 23, 274
Turner, Leslie 344
Turner, Martin 184
Turner Entertainment Company 189
The Turning Point 201
Turrou, Leon G. 48, 84, 147, 321
Tuska, Jon 74
Tuttle, Frank 83, 84, 147, 321
Tuttle, Lurene 66, 129, 237, 283, 337
Tuttle, William 78, 97, 241, 258, 324
TV Guide 140, 165, 193, 215
TV Key Movie Guide 239, 240, 319
TV Movies 140, 231, 247
TV Radio Mirror 26
Twachtman, John Henry 34
Twardowsky, Hans von 86
Twelve Angry Men 38, 47, 79, 128
Twelve O'Clock High 103, 245
Twelve Star Salute 38, 171, 179, 246, 259, 310, 321
Twentieth Century 125, 144, 200
Twentieth Century (film company) 322
20th Century–Fox 9, 120, 121, 158, 284, 304, 306, 308, 321, 322, 349
20,000 Leagues Under the Sea 110, 125, 199
20,000 Years in Sing Sing 90, 197
23 Paces to Baker Street 144
The Twilight Zone 298
Twitchell, Archie 165
Two Against the World 268, 332
The Two Mrs. Carrolls 61
The Two of Us 72, 324
The Two Orphans 225
Two Seconds 7, 20, 64, 65, 71, 76, 87, 90, 94, 106, 120, 123, 125, 130, 141, 172, 186, 188, 196, 210, 225, 226, 234, 235, 239, 253, 254, 256, 259, 260, 268, 322, 323, 334, 335, 345
2001: A Space Odyssey 298
Two Weeks in Another Town 12, 18, 47, 72, 80, 87, 90, 95, 106, 111, 119, 121, 128, 141, 145, 154, 156, 159, 166, 180, 198, 202, 217, 218, 221, 224, 234, 235, 251, 259, 268, 273, 321, 323, 324, 325, 345
Two Weeks to Live 179

Two Women 97
Twombley, Roland 171
Twyfford, Curly 306
Tyke, John 341
Tyler, George C. 218, 252, 253, 325
Tyler, Harry O. 136, 205
Tyler, John 338
Tyler, Tom 59
Tyler, Walter H. 17, 312
The Typists and the Tiger 167, 334

"U. S. A." 14, 155, 311, 325
U.S.O. 97
Uberti, Anny Degli 139
Uedo, Kichijiro 268
Uemura, Shu 224
Uggams, Leslie 324, 326
The Ugly Dachshund 69, 338
The Ugly Duckling 69
Uhl, Richard 45
Ulbright, John 34
Ullman, Liv 19
Ultra Films 238
"U. M. C." 14, 56, 115, 140, 141, 145, 156, 198, 210, 235, 251, 299, 311, 320, 325, 347
Una Voce Poca Fa 28
Uncle Tom's Cabin 95
Uncle Vanya 237
Unconquered 237
Under Cover 87, 211, 283, 326
Under Fire 4, 32, 87, 88, 130, 182, 211, 234, 252, 253, 259, 283, 300, 326, 334
Under Sentence 4, 42, 79, 87, 177, 211, 220, 234, 245, 253, 256, 259, 283, 287, 326, 327
Under the Gaslight 103
The Undercover Man 217
Undercurrent 339
Underworld 146
An Uneasy Enemy 135
The Unfinished Dance 72
"The Unfinished Symphony" 224
Unholy Night 209
Unholy Partners 9, 21, 23, 33, 86, 94, 107, 111, 118, 120, 132, 134, 135, 141, 149, 155, 159, 179, 186, 188, 197, 199, 223, 230, 235, 244, 249, 250, 268, 276, 304, 327, 334
The Unholy Three 61, 242
The Unholy Wife 267
The Uninvited 26, 160, 276
Union Pacific 97, 107, 141, 179, 182, 244, 320
Union Station 270
United Artists 7, 21, 38, 40, 51, 62, 120, 121, 152, 192, 233, 266, 304
United China Relief Fund 128, 160, 239, 254, 320, 328
United Jewish Appeal 24, 339
United Jewish Welfare Fund 24, 286
United Nations 146, 263, 273, 328, 337

United Nations Commission on Human Righs 106
United Nations Radio 106
United Press International (UPI) 269
United States Air Force 23, 87, 125, 188, 328
United States Air Force Band 134, 163, 189, 224, 328
United States Army 74, 170, 274
United States Congress 73, 74, 261, 305, 337
Unites States Constitution 239
United States Military Academy, West Point 196
United States Navy 254, 274, 334
U. S. Olympic Committee Telethon 89, 155, 156, 310, 326
United States Post Office 3, 149, 203, 255
U. S. Rubber Hour 239, 263
United States Savings Bonds 264
United States Treasury Department 53
Universal Declaration of Human Rights 106
Universal-International 25, 12, 136, 328
Universal Pictures 113, 120, 233, 242, 278, 304, 314, 328
Universal Title 212
University of California, Los Angeles (UCLA) 33, 255, 273, 277
University of Chicago 86
University of North Carolina 76
University of Southern California (USC) 15, 190, 344
University Settlement House 237, 252
Uno Scacco Tutto Matto 26, 29, 202, 328
Unoste, Frank, Jr. 340
The Unseen 70
The Unsinkable Molly Brown 187, 269
The Unsuspected 61, 188
Untermeyer, Louis 274
The Untouchables 56
Up the River 201
Urecal, Minerva 231
Uris, Leon 166
Usher, Guy 194, 205
Ustinov, Peter 18
Utrillo, Maurice 8, 34

V 298
V. I. P.'s 309
Vadnay, Laslo 126, 306
Vague, Vera 183
Vail Construction Company 122
Valenti, Jack 19
Valentine, Paul 76, 158, 329
Valentino 26, 244
Valentino, Rudolph 38
The Valiant 222

Vallee, Rudy 336
Valley Forge 195
The Valley of Decision 134
The Valley of the Dolls 111, 300
Vallon, Nanette 59
Valmy, Ruth 346
Van, Bobby 288
Van Cleef, Lee 329, 331
Van Dyke, Dick 14, 29, 82, 128, 229, 244, 329, 330
Van Enger, Willard 59
Van Eyck (art) 289
Van Eyck, Peter 62, 330
Van Gogh, Vincent 34
Van Grove, Isaac 337
Van Haden, Anders 40
Van Heusen, James 17, 18, 65, 152, 223, 271, 330
Van Horne, Harriet 106, 107
Van Patten, Dick 255, 296, 330
Van Rooten, Luis 231, 270
Van Sickle, Dale 98
Van Sloan, Edward 171
Van Trees, James 66, 69, 163, 287
Van Unge, Karen 258
Van Zandt, Philip 231
Vanda, Charles 155
Vandergrift, Monte 27
Vanderveen, Joyce 312
Vanity Fair 172
Vanni, Renata 147, 345
Varden, Norma 115
Varesi, Elena 330
Varesi, Gilda 115, 232, 330
Variety 26, 32, 44, 46, 50, 55, 63, 74, 77, 91, 99, 103, 105, 106, 110, 113, 115, 167, 204, 205, 206, 233, 239, 241, 242, 246, 252, 271, 279, 294, 296, 303, 314, 318, 325, 327, 343, 346
Variety Clubs International 145
Varro, Juan 308
Vasile, Turo 238
The Vatican 36, 82, 237, 238
Vaughan, Dorothy 207
Vaughn, Hilda 106
Vaughn, Kerry 278
Vaughn, Laura 306
Vaughn, Lloyd 159
Vaughn, Robert 49, 92, 313, 330
Vaughn, William 86
Veiller, Anthony 300, 302
Velez, Lupe 113, 330
Venice Film Festival 279
The Venetian Affair 35
Venus de Milo 34, 194
Venuta, Benay 274
Vera Cruz 209, 272
Vera-Ellen 11, 44, 90, 330
Verdensberomtheder I Kobenhaven 286, 309, 330
The Verdict 230
Vermilyea, Harold 204, 287
Vermilyea, Jerry 305
Verne, Kaaren 62

Vernell, Carl 126
Vernon, Glenn 69
Vernon, Richard 293, 316
Vernon, Vinton 272
Verros, John 69, 136, 331
Vertigo 86, 286
"The Very Thought of You" 223
Vice Squad 11, 23, 26, 36, 37, 47, 66, 94, 98, 121, 133, 134, 135, 137, 141, 147, 172, 186, 188, 235, 249, 251, 269, 300, 311, 327, 329, 330, 331, 344
The Victor Borge Show 264, 331
Victor, Henry 86
The Victors 279, 292
Victory at Sea 280
The Victory Chest Program 41, 156, 264, 288, 331, 338
"Victory Extra" 41, 82, 89, 171, 264, 288, 331, 332, 338
Victory War Chest Orchestra 331
Vidar, Raanheld 258
Vidor, King 167, 222
Viet Nam Conflict 265
A View from the Bridge 68, 146, 217
Vigran, Herb 25, 147, 158, 164, 332
The Vikings 125
Vilfrid, Jacque 246
Villa, Roberto 238
Village of the Damned 277
Vincent Price: A Daughter's Biography 256, 289
Vincent Price Unmasked 289
Vines, Lee 339
Vinson, Helen 81, 186, 194, 197, 332, 335
Vinton, Victoria 63
The Violent Men 26, 29, 31, 37, 47, 55, 66, 71, 76, 80, 87, 95, 102, 118, 121, 122, 130, 133, 134, 141, 143, 167, 172, 181, 198, 203, 209, 235, 251, 261, 276, 285, 299, 332, 333, 338, 339, 345
Violent Saturday 11, 53
Violin of M'Sieur 135
The Virgin Queen 57, 80
Virginia City 149, 344
The Virginian 181, 210
The Virtuous Wives 187
The Visit 128, 199
VistaVision 313
Vitagraph Studios 134, 335
Vitale, Claude 246
Vitale, Joseph 62
Vitaphone 120, 124, 144, 163, 191, 335
Viva Villa! 68, 95, 146
Viva Zapata 260
Vlaminck, Maurice 34
Vogan, Emmett 85, 177, 219, 278, 333, 341
Vogeding, Frederick 40, 85

Index

Vogel, Joseph 231, 323
Voglin, Jack 302
Vohs, Joan 167, 331
The Voice 5, 87, 253, 333
Voice of America 264, 333
Voice of the Turtle 32, 221, 244, 254, 265
"The Voice on the Stairs" 69, 160, 263
Voices from the Hollywood Past 333
Voigt, Jon 85, 102, 103, 105, 333
Volare, Lorna 275
Voltaire 102
Volterra, Daniel de 289
Von Atta, Don 185
Von Brinken, William 164
Von der Heyde, Barbara 293
Von Eltz, Theodore 102, 103, 104, 161, 334
Von Morhart, Hans 308
Von Ryan's Express 166
Von Stroheim, Erich, Jr. 324
Von Twardowsky, Hans 86
Von Zell, Harry 113, 332
Voorhees, Donald 69
Vorkapich, Slavko 184, 222
Votrian, Peter 75, 147
Vuillard, Jean Edouard 8, 34
Vukotic, Milena 46
Vuolo, Tito 158

W. C. Fields and Me 301
WABD-TV 243
The Wackiest Ship in the Army 199
Waco 244
Waddington, Patrick 170
Wagenheim, Charles 78
The Wages of Fear 220, 330
Wagner, Richard 131, 224
Wagner, Charles L. 204
Wagner, Max 63, 165
Wagner, Robert 13, 19, 304, 334
Wagner, Roger 46, 305
Wagon Train 54
The Wagons Roll at Night 268
Wagschall, Bennie 163
Wait Until Dark 339, 349
Wake Island 117
The Wake of the Red Witch 276
Wakefield, Hugh 170
Wakeling, Gwen 306
Walburn, Fred 183
Wald, Jerry 173, 183, 207, 334
Waldorf Astoria Hotel 157
Waldridge, Harold 125
Waldron, Philip 177
Wales, Ethel 40
Walk East on Beacon 156
Walk on the Wild Side 299
Walk the Proud Land 288
Walker, Betty 215
Walker, Bill 152
Walker, Clint 49, 312
Walker, Dan 171
Walker, David 293

Walker, Henry 163
Walker, Joseph 66, 219, 306, 315
Walker, June 215
Walker, Nella 207
Walker, Ray 248
Walker, Sandy 86
Walker, Vernon 345
Walker, Walter 163
Walker, Zena 55
Wallace, Francis 177
Wallace, George 148
Wallace, Helen 136, 318
Wallace, Henry 228
Wallace, Irving 257, 258
Wallace, Mike 70
Wallace, Morgan 163, 291
Wallace, Regina 231, 237
Wallace, William 165
Wallach, Eli 12, 14, 70, 71, 167, 200, 201, 249, 284, 285, 334
Wallach, Fred S. 46
Waller, Eddy 98
Wallington, Jerry 283
Wallington, Jimmy 26, 280
Wallis, Hal B. 15, 17, 48, 59, 63, 64, 84, 93, 103, 104, 123, 124, 131, 144, 154, 162, 176, 177, 183, 190, 191, 201, 207, 222, 259, 282, 290, 322, 334
Wallis, J. H. 345
The Walls Came Tumbling Down 211
Walpole, Hugh 6, 204
Walsh, Mary 147
Walsh, Raoul 9, 19, 167, 207, 208, 334
Walsh, Richard 19
Walston, Ray 285, 334
Walt Disney Productions 228, 229, 304, 319, 348
Walter, Eugene 4, 243, 334
Walters, Hon. Francis 206
Walters, James M. 111
Walters, Luana 322
Walters, Polly 125, 291
Walthall, Henry B. 91
Walton, Jennie 293
The Waltons 86
Waltz, Patrick 138
Wanger, Walter 43, 153, 154, 259, 277
Wanted: Dead or Alive 210
War of the Worlds 298, 301, 338
The War, the West, and the Wilderness 32, 287
Ward, A. C. 325
Ward, Allan 30
Ward, Burt 42
Ward, Edward 52, 184
Ward, Janet 215
Ward, John 339
Ward, Ronald 238
Ward, Samuel Augustus 328
Warde, Harlan 167, 331
Wardley, Jeanne 218
Ware, Frank 124

Ware, Midge 78
Warfield, Joe 247
Waring, Fred 277
Warner, Albert 335
Warner, H. B. 123, 312, 335
Warner, Harry 49, 335
Warner, Jack L. 8, 84, 104, 131, 190, 191, 209, 243, 259, 282, 335
Warner, Sam 335
Warner, Sandra 187
Warner Bros. 6, 7, 9, 10, 11, 13, 14, 27, 28, 32, 38, 53, 58, 60, 63, 74, 81, 90, 91, 102, 103, 105, 107, 120, 121, 123, 124, 133, 147, 149, 150, 165, 166, 167, 173, 176, 177, 183, 189, 190, 193, 194, 197, 201, 205, 207, 222, 226, 227, 249, 259, 263, 272, 274, 281, 282, 288, 290, 291, 298, 304, 315, 322, 323, 326, 332, 334, 335, 343, 348, 349
Warner Bros. Radio Broadcast 37, 188, 335
Warner Brothers Directors 85, 102
WarnerColor 147
WarnerScope 166
Warner-Seven Arts 335
Warren, E. Allyn 113, 144, 184
Warren, Gov. Earl 331
Warren, Eda 231
Warren, Harry 332
Warren, John 312
Warren, Katharine 332
Warren, Mark 185
Warren, Phil 126
Warrick, Ruth 186, 198, 219, 335, 345
Warwick, Dionne 49
Warwick, Norman 55
Warwick, Robert 103, 287
Washam, Ben 159
Washington, Blue 306, 335, 336, 341
Washington, George 188, 194
Washington: Behind Closed Doors 228
Washington Post 129, 297
Washington Times 145
Wasiolek, Edward 60
Wassell, Dr. Corydon M. 254, 328
Watch on the Rhine 199, 223, 334
Waterloo Bridge 241, 309
Watermelon Man 66
Watergate Hotel 328
Waters, Bunny 247
Waters, Ethel 95, 243, 306, 336
Waters, Jim 248
Watkin, Pierre 98, 184, 333
Watkins, A. W. 316
Watkins, Linda 138
Watling, Jack 170, 336
Watson, Bobs 52, 75, 89, 197, 336
Watson, Coy, Jr. 190

Index

Watson, Delmar 75, 242
Watson, Harry 63
Watson, Henry 63
Watson, James A. 76, 236
Watson, Lane 346
Watts, Richard 216
Waxman, Franz 224
Waxmann, Harry 170
Way Down East 41
Way Down South 52
Waycoff, Leon 287; *see also* Ames, Leon
The Wayfarers 329
Wayne, Billy 27
Wayne, David 12, 99, 336
Wayne, John 20, 222
Wayne, Justina 88, 147
Wayne, Patrick 73, 74
The Wayward Bus 208
A Wayward Quest 60
WB Hollywood Novelty Series 254
We Americans 6, 88, 100, 129, 171, 222, 253, 301, 336
We Hold These Truths 33, 41, 57, 160, 263, 273, 301, 336, 337, 338
We Will Never Die 9, 23, 42, 43, 100, 146, 168, 202, 222, 227, 252, 252, 287, 288, 337
Wead, Frank 97
"The Weapon of Surgery" 129, 265, 337
Weatherwax, Paul 345
Webb, Amanda 313
Webb, George 177
Webb, Ira 69
Webb, Jack 196
Webb, James R. 18, 74, 165
Webb, Richard 231
Webb, Seward 126
Webber, Robert 268, 285
Webster, Clarence 306
Webster, Daniel 99, 150, 189, 235, 336, 337, 338
Webster, Harold 275
Webster, Paul Francis 306
Wedder, Noel 160
A Wedding 112
The Wedding Night 332
Wedlock, Hugh 277
Weeden, Bill 288
Weekend 90
Weekend at the Waldorf 338
Weidler, Virginia 76
Weidman, Jerome 70, 157
Weigel, Paul 103
Weill, Kurt 337
Weiner, Boris 164
Weinstein, Milton 344
Weisman, Ned 189
Weist, Dwight 45
Weitzenkorn, Louis 123, 124
Weizmann, Chaim 72, 338
Welch, Niles 287
Welch, Raquel 13, 19, 46, 90, 338
Welch, Robert 237

Welcome Danger 172
Weld, Tuesday 13, 76, 78, 309, 338
Welden, Ben 177, 184, 207, 338
Weller, Carrie 147
Welles, Alan 62
Welles, Orson 10, 69, 87, 101, 113, 119, 145, 154, 159, 190, 221, 227, 277, 301, 302, 303, 331, 332, 335, 336, 338
Welles, Ralph 233
Wellman, Harold 200
Wellman, William A. 144, 184, 222, 338
Wells, George 64, 88, 178, 203, 208, 237
Wendell, Howard 78, 112
Wengraf, John 258, 338
Wengren, Dave 40, 86
Wentworth, Martha 89, 302
We're No Angels 43
Werfel, Franz 6, 136, 170, 253, 338
Werle, Sgt. Floyd E. 163, 224, 328
Wertz, Clarence 40
Wessel, Dick 59, 207, 278, 338
Wessel, Jack 326
West, Adam 42, 187
West, Billy 341
West, Charles 40
West, Christopher 325
West, Vera 126
West End Theatre 234
West of Zanzibar 234
Westcott, Gordon 91
Westerfield, James 332, 338, 339
The Westerner 57, 305
Westervelt, Ralph 117
Westlein, Josephine Rosa 189
Westlein, Richard 189
Westley, Helen 5, 22, 75, 136, 246, 252, 270, 314, 339
Westmore, Bud 295
Westmore, Frank 312
Westmore, Perc 59, 104
Westmore, Wally 108, 135, 167, 173, 205, 207, 224, 231, 282, 291, 312
Weston, Jack 13, 78, 339
Weston, Ruth 178
Westworld 61, 330
Wetherfield, Alice 287
Wetter, Ottie 163
Wetzel, Edwin 126
Wever, Ned 258
Wexley, John 27, 85, 339
Weyl, Carl Jules 27, 63, 85, 104, 177, 339
The Whales of August 256, 294
"What Are We Fighting" 42, 129, 265, 339
What Did You Do in the War, Daddy? 166
What Price Glory? 156, 345
Whatever Happened to Baby Jane? 24, 64, 88, 93, 187, 313
What's Cookin' Doc? 69, 339

What's My Line? 130, 310, 339
What's New Pussycat? 279
"What's Your Sad Story?" 223
Wheaton, Glenn 237
Wheeler, Bert 301
Wheeler, John 54
Wheeler, Lyle 157, 284
When Do I Start? 78
When Harry Met Sally 277
When the Daltons Rode 61
When Tomorrow Comes 61
When Worlds Collide 143, 209, 283
When Women Had Tails 166
Where Do You Get Off? 286, 339
Which Way to the Front? 179
While the City Sleeps 88, 112, 182, 277
Whipple, Waldo 194
Whirlpool 80
Whiskey Galore 200
Whistling in Dixie 333
White, Alice 248, 339, 340, 343
White, Dan M. 74
White, George 69
White, Huey 177, 184
White, Lee 271
White, Leslie T. 331
White, Merrill 266
White, Pearl 181
White, Will J. 318
White Angel 130
White Banners 244
White Cliffs of Dover 143
White Christmas 90, 330
White Heat 65, 130, 149, 334, 348
White House Conference on National Beauty 328
The White Rose 208
Whiteford, Blackie 40, 52
Whitehead, Augustine 340
Whitehead, Joe 52
Whiteside, Walker 5, 245
Whitlock, Lloyd 162, 341
Whitman, Gayne 204, 250
Whitmore, James 24
Whitney, Eve 167
Whitney, Mildred 186
Whitney, Renee 194
Whitney, Steven 289
Whittaker, James 176
Whittington, Dick 243
Whitty, Dame May 126, 127, 223, 340
Who Has Seen the Wind? 13, 38, 46, 53, 76, 169, 198, 235, 251, 259, 279, 286, 310, 340
"Who Has Seen the Wind?" (song) 340
Who Is Killing the Great Chefs of Europe? 221
Who Is the Savage? 276
Who Was That Lady? 208
The Whole Town's Talking 7, 18, 31, 34, 35, 36, 38, 41, 49, 58, 64,

Index

65, 80, 81, 94, 95, 102, 111, 112, 120, 128, 129, 133, 134, 135, 143, 149, 150, 155, 181, 183, 186, 197, 198, 200, 203, 211, 218, 222, 223, 235, 248, 249, 250, 251, 256, 257, 263, 268, 277, 286, 289, 292, 298, 300, 304, 305, 322, 329, 333, 335, 340, 341, 342, 345, 348
"The Whole Town's Talking" (radio) 154, 342, 343
Whoopee! 114, 208
Whorf, David 42
Whorf, Richard 274
Who's Been Sleeping in My Bed? 130, 308
Why Marry? 283
"The Why of Cancer" 129, 265, 343
The Wicked Dreams of Paula Schultz 293
Wickenden, Dan 329
Widmark, Richard 13, 73, 74, 209, 343
The Widow from Chicago 6, 47, 120, 123, 132, 134, 141, 142, 149, 155, 190, 210, 235, 250, 251, 254, 286, 320, 335, 339, 343
Wilber, Robert 341
Wilborn, Charles M. 295
Wilbur, Bob 40
Wilbur, Crane 45, 94
Wilcox, Frank 312
Wilcox, Harlow 29, 69, 348
Wilcoxon, Henry 312, 343, 344
The Wild Bunch 95, 169
Wild in the Country 338
Wild Is the Wind 260
The Wild Party 179
Wild Strawberries 283
Wilde, Cornel 154, 347
Wilde, Oscar 125, 126, 127
Wilde, Percival 123
Wildenstein & Company (gallery) 7, 8, 33
Wilder, Billy 9, 17, 48, 67, 70, 95, 101, 107, 108, 109, 110, 119, 189, 201, 254, 344
Wilder, Leslie F. 181
Wildfire 57
Wildiss, William 277
Wiley, Howard 231, 331
Wilhelm, Wolfgang 103
Wilke, Hubert 253
Wilkerson, Martha 332
Wilkinson, Barrie 293
Wilkinson Sword Blades 23
Will Penny 149
Will Rogers Memorial Hospital for Respiratory Diseases 301
Will Success Spoil Rock Hunter? 208
Willa, Susanne 32
Willard 90
Willes, Jean 136
William, Warren 91, 267
William Morris Agency 151

Williams, Adam 331, 344
Williams, Andy 18
Williams, Billy Dee 19
Williams, Blaine 344
Williams, C. J. 176
Williams, Charles 306
Williams, Corinne 341
Williams, Don 154
Williams, Emlyn 106
Williams, Esther 277
Williams, Guinn "Big Boy" 52, 344
Williams, Jack 74
Williams, John 19
Williams, John D. 204
Williams, Joyce 27, 296
Williams, Maston 341
Williams, Noelle 312
Williams, Rhoda 158, 240
Williams, Rhys 233, 344
Williams, Robert B. 152
Williams, Valentine 103
Williams, Van 42
Williams, William 88, 341
Williamson, Mel 117
Willis, Edwin B. 44, 184, 240, 327
Willis, Leo 40
Willis, Matt 278
Willis, Norman 63
Willis, Tom 63
Willkie, Wendell 24, 270
Willson, Meredith 331
Wilson 179, 268, 298
Wilson, Charles C. 278
Wilson, Clarence Hummel 341
Wilson, Don 199, 202, 331
Wilson, Dorothy Clarke 312
Wilson, Georgiana 22
Wilson, Harry 272, 341
Wilson, Michael 252
Wilson, Nancy 340
Wilson, Sherry 295
Wilson, Stanley 111
Wilson, Stewart 178
Wilson, Woodrow 245, 256
Wilton, Eric 306
Winant, Ethel 323
Wincelberg, Simon 299
Winchell, Walter 104, 346
Winchester 73 112, 301
The Wind 283
Wind and the Lion 172
Wind in the Willows 325
Windom, William 14
The Window 300
The Winds of War 220
Windust, Bretaigne 115
Wine, Women and Horses 268
Winfield, Joan 207
Wing, Pat 194
Wing, Toby 194
Wingreen, Jason 236, 325
Wings 32
Wings of Desire 54
Wings of Eagles 237
Winkler, Bobbie 45

Winkler, Henry 82
The Winning of Barbara Worth 38
Winninger, Charles 126
Winslow, Dick 205, 229
The Winslow Boy 336
Winslowe, Paula 45, 203
Winsten, Archer 103
Winter, Ethel 70
Winters, Jonathan 288
Winters, Ralph E. 240
Winters, Roland 122
Winters, Shelley 70, 299
Winterset 68, 217, 271
Winwood Estelle 75
Wise, Jack 125
Wiser, Bud 162
Wishengrad, Morton 321
With a Song in My Heart 65, 145, 270
Withers, Isabel 207
Without Warning 344
Witko, Leo 163
"Witness for the Prosecution" (TV) 199, 310, 344
Witness for the Prosecution (film) 100, 185; (play) 294
Wittstatt, Hans 247
Wives Never Know 239
The Wizard of Oz 51, 84, 142, 188, 221
Wohl, Jack 185
Wolbert, Dorothea 322
Wolf Larsen 268, 281
The Wolf Man 42, 241
Wolfe, David 158
Wolfe, Ian 126, 204
Wolfen 283
Wolff, Paul 233
Wolfson, Martin 137
Wolheim, Louis 67, 163, 345
Wolny, Kerry 255
The Woman in the Window 9, 10, 17, 18, 20, 27, 34, 36, 43, 49, 52, 57, 58, 75, 88, 94, 98, 99, 106, 112, 119, 120, 128, 129, 141, 144, 160, 167, 168, 180, 182, 186, 196, 198, 203, 209, 218, 221, 223, 235, 249, 255, 261, 269, 277, 298, 300, 304, 309, 320, 329, 337, 345, 346, 347
"The Woman in the Window" (radio) 80, 199, 264, 347
"Woman of Sin" 21
Woman of the Year 184, 206
A Woman Under the Influence 115, 274
A Woman's Devotion 147
A Woman's Face 179
The Women 51, 88, 137
Women in Horror Films, 1930s 317
Wonder Man 330
The Wonderful Country 95
Wong, Atarne 231
Wong, Beal 207
Wong, Jean 231

Index

Wontner, Arthur 316
Wood, Douglas 104, 161, 347
Wood, Ernest 184
Wood, Forrest 296
Wood, Grant 34
Wood, Jean 313
Wood, Laurence 122
Wood, Marjorie 245
Wood, Natalie 19, 334
Wood, Sam 222, 300
Wood, Stanley G. 75, 137, 176, 246, 314
Woodbury, Frances 54
Woodbury, Joan 312
Woodhull, Victoria C. 170
Woodruff, Frank 64, 88, 178
Woods, Craig 97, 98
Woods, Donald 339
Woods, Harry 322
Woodward, Frances 45
Woodward, Joanne 35
Woody, Jack 162
Woody Woodpecker 298
Wooley, Harold 42
Woollcott, Alexander 204, 205, 232, 245
Woolley, Monte 18, 113, 274
Woolrich, Cornell 119, 231, 233, 347
Woolsey, Robert 301
Words and Music 330
Wordsworth, Richard 293
The World According to Garp 156
The World of Henry Orient 54
The World of Howard Hawks 316, 317
"World of Tomorrow" 69, 196, 263, 347
World Premiere Movie 311, 347
World War I 162, 182, 230, 254, 273, 327, 334, 335
World War II 9, 25, 32, 36, 97, 107, 113, 117, 119, 158, 162, 167, 219, 221, 230, 239, 265, 273, 281, 302, 334, 335
World Zionist Organization 338
The World's Greatest Showman 49, 61, 97, 137, 146, 156, 265, 299, 301, 310, 347, 348
Worrell, Denise 241, 257
Worth, Eric 170
Worthington, William 27, 163, 194
Woulfe, Michael 302
Wouters, Francine 246
Wragge, Eddie 218
Wray, Fay 146, 147, 249, 274, 301, 348
Wray, John 52, 341, 348
The Wreck of the Mary Deare 179
Wright, Ben 258
Wright, George, Jr. 326
Wright, Howard 136
Wright, Robert 293
Wright, Tom 212
Wright, Will 278, 306

The Wrong Man 217, 260
Wurtzel, Sam 51
Wuthering Heights 51, 84, 137, 146, 172, 200, 234, 236
Wyatt, Al 272
Wycherly, Margaret 5, 21, 28, 116, 252, 314, 348
Wyckhoff, Alvin 233
Wyler, William 39, 154, 209, 254
Wylie, Howard 280, 283
Wylie, I. A. R. 29
Wyman, Jane 9, 68, 167, 183, 273, 274, 348
Wynn, Ed 348
Wynn, Keenan 12, 14, 152, 154, 200, 201, 237, 274, 348
Wynn, May 332
Wynn, Phyllis 215

The X-Files 298
X Marks the Spot 234
Xerox Special 13, 310, 240

Yaeger, Edith 186
Yamada, Junjiro 224
Yamaoka, Otto 144
A Yank at Oxford 309
Yankee Doodle Dandy 65, 79, 90, 111, 159, 160, 209, 334, 335
"Yankee Doodle Dandy" (song) 80
Yapp, Cecil 232
Yarnell, Sally 158
Yarus, Buddy 219
The Yearling 135, 150, 245, 348
The Yellow Rolls Royce 68
Yellow Sky 288
Yes, Giorgio 329
Yes or No 58
Yesterday, Today and Tomorrow 97
Yiddish Players 265
Yisacher, Loui 228
Yordan, Philip 157
York, Duke 290
York, Jeff 177
Yoshkin, Nicolai 86
Yost, Dorothy 52
Yost, Herbert 137
You Can't Cheat an Honest Man 58
"You Can't Die Twice" 264, 305, 348
You Can't Get Away with Murder 111
You Can't Take It with You 33, 34, 68, 143, 150, 275, 301, 308
You Know I Can't Hear You When the Water's Running 38
You Only Live Once 182
You Only Live Twice 179
"You'll Never Know" 223
Young, Bob 98
Young, Carleton 74, 137, 348
Young, Dave 117
Young, Ernest F. 341
Young, Gig 40, 178, 268
Young, Glenn 79
Young, Irene 147

Young, Loretta 7, 10, 37, 52, 89, 143, 144, 166, 186, 196, 197, 302, 345, 348
Young, Robert 106, 154, 237, 348
Young, Roland 306
Young, Stephen 295
Young, Tammany 194
Young, Tiny 247
Young, Victor 65, 231
Young at Heart 94
Young Cassidy 309
Young Dillinger 64
The Young Doctors 201
Young Frankenstein 43
The Young in Heart 79
Young Jesse James 244
The Young Lions 275
Young Man with a Horn 110, 243
Young Mr. Lincoln 51, 54, 128, 301
The Young Philadelphians 275
The Young Savages 283
Young Tom Edison 320
Yuricich, Matthew 295
Yurka, Blanche 136
Yuro, Robert 236

Z 220
Zachry, Elizabeth 246
Zane Grey Theatre 12, 52, 148, 182, 272, 310, 339, 348
Zaner, Jimmy 184
Zanouba 138
Zanuck, Darryl F. 191, 259, 322, 348, 349
Zanzibar 88
Zaremba, John 318
Zarzo, Manuel 202
Zaslove, Lisa 117
Zaslove, Dr. Marshall 117
Zaslove, Natasha 117
Zaza 69, 186, 339
Zebba, Sam 166
Zeller, Robert 70
Zeppelin 22
Zerbe, Lawson 45
Ziegfeld, Florenz 137, 234
Ziegfeld Girl 90
Ziegman, Jerry 208
Zilzer, Wolfgang 85, 333; *see also* Voight, Jon
Zimbalist, Efrem, Jr. 76, 158, 349
Zimbalist, Stephanie 349
Zimmer, Jessie 92
Zimmerman, Victo 25
Zola, Emile 102
Zollinger, Jacob 147
Zolotow, Maurice 107
Zombies on Broadway 156
Zorba the Greek 260
Zorro, the Gay Blade 142
Zuckerman, Pinchas 338
Zuckert, Bill 78, 272
Zukor, Adolph 244
Zulu 38